THE OXFORD ENCYCLOPEDIA OF
BUDDHISM

THE OXFORD ENCYCLOPEDIA OF
BUDDHISM

Richard K. Payne
Georgios T. Halkias
EDITORS IN CHIEF

VOLUME 3
Q–Z

OXFORD
UNIVERSITY PRESS

OXFORD
UNIVERSITY PRESS

Oxford University Press is a department of the University of Oxford. It furthers the University's objective of excellence in research, scholarship, and education by publishing worldwide. Oxford is a registered trade mark of Oxford University Press in the UK and in certain other countries.

Published in the United States of America by Oxford University Press
198 Madison Avenue, New York, NY 10016, United States of America.

Library of Congress Cataloging-in-Publication Data

Names: Payne, Richard K., editor. | Halkias, Georgios, 1967– editor.
Title: The Oxford encyclopedia of Buddhism / Richard K. Payne, Georgios T. Halkias, Editors in Chief.
Description: New York : Oxford University Press, 2023. |
Includes bibliographical references and index. | Contents: Vol 1 — Vol 2 — Vol 3
Identifiers: LCCN 2023019480 (print) | LCCN 2023019481 (ebook) |
ISBN 9780190256890 (set) | ISBN 9780190605995 (vol. 1 ; hardback) |
ISBN 9780190606008 (vol. 2 ; hardback) | ISBN 9780197746073 (vol. 3 ; hardback) |
ISBN 9780190668433 (ebk)
Subjects: LCSH: Buddhism—Encyclopedias.
Classification: LCC BQ128 .O94 2023 (print) | LCC BQ128 (ebook) |
DDC 294.303—dc23/eng/20230509
LC record available at https://lccn.loc.gov/2023019480
LC ebook record available at https://lccn.loc.gov/2023019481

MIX
Paper from responsible sources
FSC® C008955

Sheridan Books, Inc., United States of America

About the *Oxford Research Encyclopedia of Religion*

The Oxford Encyclopedia of Buddhism is published as part of the *Oxford Research Encyclopedia of Religion*, a dynamic and scholarly digital resource. This online collection of overview articles provides in-depth, foundational essays on both core and emerging topics in religion. All articles are commissioned under the editorial leadership of international experts of the highest caliber and are vetted through rigorous peer review. A living reference work, the online publication is updatable and enriched with crosslinking and multimedia features. The essays are intended for scholars, practitioners, and university-level readers, including advanced undergraduates, graduate students, and researchers.

Oxford Research Encyclopedia of Religion
Editor in Chief: John Barton, University of Oxford

Selected print titles from the *Oxford Encyclopedia of Religion* series:

The Oxford Encyclopedia of Martin Luther
Edited by Derek R. Nelson and Paul R. Hinlicky

The Oxford Encyclopedia of Religion in America
Edited by John Corrigan

Contents

List of Articles ix

Thematic and Geographical Outlines xiii

Preface (vol. 1) xxi

Introduction (vol. 1) xxiii

Acknowledgments (vol. 1) xxix

THE OXFORD ENCYCLOPEDIA OF BUDDHISM

Directory of Contributors 2757

Index 2765

List of Articles

A

Abhidharmakośabhāṣya (Treasury of Metaphysics with Self-Commentary)
Abhisamayālaṃkāra (Ornament for Clear Realization)
American Buddhism during World War II Imprisonment
Amoghavajra
Art, Architecture, and National Memory-Making
Avalokiteśvara: The Bodhisattva of Compassion

B

Bodhisattvabhūmi (The Bodhisattva Stages)
The Body of the Buddha
The Bön Tradition of Dzogchen
Buddhaghosa
Buddhism and Bioethics
Buddhism and Biography
Buddhism and Globalization
Buddhism and Healing in China
Buddhism and Media
Buddhism and Medicine in India
Buddhism and Medicine in Japan
Buddhism and Medicine in Premodern Japan
Buddhism and Print Culture in China
Buddhism and Shinto
Buddhism and the Environment
Buddhism in Colonial Contexts
Buddhism in Film
Buddhisms in Diaspora: The Canadian Context of Chinese Buddhism
Buddhist Art and Architecture in Tibet
Buddhist Chaplaincy

Buddhist Cosmology
Buddhist Geography and Regionalism
Buddhist Meditation and Contemplation
Buddhist Philosophy as Philosophy
Buddhist Wall Paintings
Buddhist Wizards (*Vidhyadhāra/Weizzā/Weikza*): Contemporary Burma/Myanmar
Buddhist Wizards (*Vidhyadhāra/Weizzā/Weikza*): Origins and History

C

Candrakīrti's Middle Way Philosophy
Canon and Commentary in the Earliest Buddhist Manuscripts
Chan Literature
Chöd: A Tibetan Buddhist Practice

D

D. T. Suzuki: A Biography
D. T. Suzuki: Ideas and Influences
Debate in the Tibetan Tradition
Debate Traditions in Premodern Japan
Domestic Dharma in Japan
Dunhuang Art
Dunhuang Texts
Dzogchen

E

Early History of the Drukpa Kagyü School
Early Modern European Encounters with Buddhism
The Economics of Buddhism
Engaged Buddhism
Epigraphy and the Study of Buddhism: South Asia's Northern Corridor
Esoteric Buddhism in Southeast Asia
Ethics and Buddhism

F

Filial Piety in Chinese Buddhism
Fo Guang Shan
Four Noble Truths
From Manuscript to Print in South and Southeast Asia

G

Gelukpa
Global Buddhism
Global Theravada Buddhism: Asian Foundations
Global Theravada: Transmission beyond Asia
Globalizing Tantric Buddhism
Guardian/Protector Deities in Tibetan Buddhism

H

History of Buddhisms in China: The Nanbeicho Period (Late 4th Century to the Sui Dynasty)
Homa: Tantric Fire Ritual
Hsing Yun
Huineng
Humanistic Buddhism (Rensheng Fojiao 人生佛教 / Renjian Fojiao 人間佛教)

I

Imaging the Buddha in South Asia
The Imamura Families and the Making of American Buddhism
Intention in the Pali Suttas and Abhidharma

J

Japanese Buddhisms in Diaspora
Jātaka
Jebtsundamba Khutugtus of Mongolia

K

The Kadampa: A Formative Movement of Tibetan Buddhism
Kālacakra-Maṇḍala: Symbolism and Construction

L

Longchenpa

M

Madhyamaka
Mahāmudrā in India and Tibet
Mañjuśrī
Maritime Buddhism
Marpa Lotsawa Chökyi Lodrö
Mipam
Monastic Education in Contemporary Asia
Mongolian Buddhism in the Democratic Period
Mongolian Buddhism in the Early 20th Century
Mongolian Buddhism in the Yuan Period
Muslim–Buddhist Relations and Buddhism in Muslim Sources until the Mongol Period

N

Nāgārjuna
Naikan: A Meditation Method and Psychotherapy
Narratives of Buddhist Relics and Images
Nechung: A Tibetan Buddhist Oracle
Nichiren

P

Patronage of Buddhist Monasteries in Eastern India, 600–1300 CE
Perfections (Six and Ten) of Bodhisattvas in Buddhist Literature
The Philosophical Works and Influence of Dignāga and Dharmakīrti
Pilgrimage in Buddhist Tibet
Pilgrimage in China
Practices of Protection in the Pali World
Prajñāpāramitā and Khmer Esoteric Buddhism in the 10th to 13th centuries
Psychological Interpreters of Buddhism
Pure Land Buddhism in Tibetan Contexts

Q

Queering Buddhist Traditions

R

The Reincarnation System in Central Asian Buddhism
Rennyo
Ryōgen

S

The Sangha as an Institution
Śāntideva's Introduction to the Practices of Awakening (*Bodhicaryāvatāra*)
Sarvāstivāda Abhidharma
Secular Buddhism
Sheng Yen
Shingon
The Six Nara Schools
Sōka Gakkai
Southeast Asian Refugees in North America
Sri Lanka's Sinhala Buddhist Guardian Deities: Satara Varan Devi
The Study of Visual Culture in South and Southeast Asian Buddhism

T

Taixu
Tantra and the Tantric Traditions of Hinduism and Buddhism
Tantric Buddhism in Japan: Kukai and Saicho

Tantric Buddhism in Japan: Shingon, Tendai, and the Esotericization of Japanese Buddhisms
Tantric Revival in China
Theravāda Buddhism
Thích Nhất Hạnh in the Context of the Modern Development of Vietnamese Buddhism
Three Turnings of the Wheel of Doctrine (Dharma-Cakra)
Tibetan Book of the Dead (*Bardo Thödol*)
Tibetan Buddhism and the Gesar Epic
Tibetan Buddhist Power Objects
Tibetan Medicine and Its Buddhist Contexts
Tibetan Visionary Buddhism
Transmission of Buddhist Media and Texts
Tri Songdetsen
Tsangpa Gyare (1161–1211), Founder of the Drukpa Kagyü School
Tzu Chi

V

The Vajrakīla Tantras
Vinaya Rules for Monks and Nuns
Visualization/Contemplation Sutras (Guan Jing)

W

Western Buddhism and Race

X

Xuyun

Z

Zhentong (Other-Emptiness)

Thematic and Geographical Outlines

Over its two-and-a-half-millennia-long history Buddhism has developed a profusion of literary sources in several languages, reflecting an astounding variety of lineages, institutions, doctrines, practices, and teachers. As an academic field of study, it is changing and expanding in ways that make the image of a closed and comprehensive encyclopedia a mirage—an ever-enticing, ever-receding goal. Being aware of this, *The Oxford Encyclopedia of Buddhism* seeks to address the current needs of students, researchers, and scholars of Buddhism by surveying the richness of the tradition and the different fields of expertise that have emerged in the 21st century. The volume shows what a research encyclopedia of Buddhism is today: an ongoing organic development of nodes and networks of knowledge; an open-ended project accelerated by technological advancements in the fields of digital information. It inaugurates a promising beginning without a defining end.

The following thematic clusters are intended to facilitate use of this network, giving the user access to entries that may otherwise be difficult to locate in the alphabetic organization of the body of the work itself. As such, it includes well-established categories that the user may be expecting, and ones that are less familiar. As mentioned above, the field is continuously developing, and therefore it does not sort neatly into exclusive categories. Consequently, we have created two outlines—one thematic and one geographic. Additionally, while there are a total of 139 articles constituting this print version, several entries appear under more than one heading. This reflects the overall goal of this research encyclopedia. Rather than presuming to impose some conceptual framework onto the field, our goal has been to represent currently developing topics to facilitate the growth of Buddhist studies.

THEMATIC OUTLINE

ART, ARCHITECTURE, AND SYMBOLIC MOTIFS

Art, Architecture, and National Memory-Making
Buddhist Art and Architecture in Tibet
Buddhism in Film
Buddhist Wall Paintings
Dunhuang Art
Epigraphy and the Study of Buddhism: South Asia's Northern Corridor
From Manuscript to Print in South and Southeast Asia
Imaging the Buddha in South Asia
Kālacakra-Maṇḍala: Symbolism and Construction
Patronage of Buddhist Monasteries in Eastern India, 600–1300 CE
Prajñāpāramitā and Khmer Esoteric Buddhism in the 10th to 13th centuries
The Study of Visual Culture in South and Southeast Asian Buddhism

BUDDHAS, BODHISATTVAS, GUARDIANS, AND DEITIES

Avalokiteśvara: The Bodhisattva of Compassion
The Body of the Buddha
Buddhist Wizards (*Vidhyadhāra/Weizzā/Weikza*): Contemporary Burma/Myanmar
Buddhist Wizards (*Vidhyadhāra/Weizzā/Weikza*): Origins and History
Guardian/Protector Deities in Tibetan Buddhism
Mañjuśrī
Prajñāpāramitā and Khmer Esoteric Buddhism in the 10th to 13th centuries
Sri Lanka's Sinhala Buddhist Guardian Deities: Satara Varan Devi

HISTORICAL AND HISTORIOGRAPHIC STUDIES

Buddhism and Shinto
Buddhism in Colonial Contexts
Buddhisms in Diaspora: The Canadian Context of Chinese Buddhism
Buddhist Geography and Regionalism
Early Modern European Encounters with Buddhism
Global Buddhism
Globalizing Tantric Buddhism
History of Buddhisms in China: The Nanbeicho Period (Late 4th Century to the Sui Dynasty)
Japanese Buddhisms in Diaspora
Maritime Buddhism
Mongolian Buddhism in the Early 20th Century
Mongolian Buddhism in the Democratic Period
Mongolian Buddhism in the Yuan Period
Three Turnings of the Wheel of Doctrine (Dharma-Cakra)

PHILOSOPHICAL AND DOCTRINAL STUDIES

Buddhist Cosmology
Buddhist Philosophy as Philosophy
Dzogchen
Four Noble Truths
Intention in the Pali Suttas and Abhidharma
Madhyamaka
Mahāmudrā in India and Tibet
Perfections (Six and Ten) of Bodhisattvas in Buddhist Literature
The Philosophical Works and Influence of Dignāga and Dharmakīrti
The Reincarnation System in Central Asian Buddhism
Sarvāstivāda Abhidharma
Theravada Buddhism

Three Turnings of the Wheel of Doctrine (Dharma-Cakra)
Vinaya Rules for Monks and Nuns
Zhentong (Other-Emptiness)

RITUALS, CONTEMPLATIVE PRACTICES, AND APPLICATIONS

The Bön Tradition of Dzogchen
Buddhist Chaplaincy
Buddhist Meditation and Contemplation
Chöd: A Tibetan Buddhist Practice
Debate in the Tibetan Tradition
Debate Traditions in Premodern Japan
Dzogchen
Filial Piety in Chinese Buddhism
Homa: Tantric Fire Ritual
Kālacakra-Maṇḍala: Symbolism and Construction
Mahāmudrā in India and Tibet
Naikan: A Meditation Method and Psychotherapy
Nechung: A Tibetan Buddhist Oracle
Pilgrimage in Buddhist Tibet
Pilgrimage in China
Practices of Protection in the Pali World
Śāntideva's Introduction to the Practices of Awakening (*Bodhicaryāvatāra*)
Tibetan Buddhist Power Objects
Tibetan Visionary Buddhism

SCHOOLS, TRADITIONS, AND LINEAGES

The Bön Tradition of Dzogchen
Chan Literature
Chöd: A Tibetan Buddhist Practice
Dzogchen
Early History of the Drukpa Kagyü School
Esoteric Buddhism in Southeast Asia
Fo Guang Shan
Gelukpa
Global Theravada Buddhism: Asian Foundations
Global Theravada: Transmission beyond Asia
Globalizing Tantric Buddhism
Humanistic Buddhism (Rensheng Fojiao 人生佛教 / Renjian Fojiao 人間佛教)
Japanese Buddhisms in Diaspora
Jebtsundamba Khutugtus of Mongolia
The Kadampa: A Formative Movement of Tibetan Buddhism
Mongolian Buddhism in the Democratic Period
Pure Land Buddhism in Tibetan Contexts
Sarvāstivāda Abhidharma
Secular Buddhism
Shingon
The Six Nara Schools
Soka Gakkai
Tantra and the Tantric Traditions of Hinduism and Buddhism
Tantric Buddhism in Japan: Kukai and Saicho
Tantric Buddhism in Japan: Shingon, Tendai, and the Esotericization of Japanese Buddhisms
Tantric Revival in China
Theravada Buddhism
Tibetan Visionary Buddhism
Zhentong (Other-Emptiness)

SOCIAL, CULTURAL, AND INTELLECTUAL ISSUES

American Buddhism during World War II Imprisonment
Art, Architecture, and National Memory-Making
Buddhism and Bioethics
Buddhism and Biography
Buddhism and Globalization
Buddhism and Healing in China
Buddhism and Media

Buddhism and Print Culture in China
Buddhism and the Environment
Buddhism and Medicine in India
Buddhism and Medicine in Japan
Buddhism and Medicine in Premodern Japan
Buddhism in Colonial Contexts
Buddhism in Film
Buddhist Chaplaincy
Buddhist Geography and Regionalism
Muslim–Buddhist Relations and Buddhism in Muslim Sources until the Mongol Period
Domestic Dharma in Japan
The Economics of Buddhism
Engaged Buddhism
Ethics and Buddhism
Monastic Education in Contemporary Asia
Narratives of Buddhist Relics and Images
Patronage of Buddhist Monasteries in Eastern India, 600–1300 CE
Psychological Interpreters of Buddhism
Queering Buddhist Traditions
The Sangha as an Institution
Secular Buddhism
Southeast Asian Refugees in North America
The Study of Visual Culture in South and Southeast Asian Buddhism
Tibetan Medicine and Its Buddhist Contexts
Transmission of Buddhist Media and Texts
Western Buddhism and Race

TEACHERS AND HISTORICAL FIGURES

Amoghavajra
Buddhaghosa
Buddhist Wizards (*Vidhyadhāra/Weizzā/Weikza*): Origins and History
Buddhist Wizards (*Vidhyadhāra/Weizzā/Weikza*): Contemporary Burma/Myanmar
Candrakīrti's Middle Way Philosophy
D. T. Suzuki: A Biography
D. T. Suzuki: Ideas and Influences
Hsing Yun
Huineng
Jebtsundamba Khutugtus of Mongolia
Longchenpa
Marpa Lotsawa Chökyi Lodrö
Mipam
Nāgārjuna
Nichiren
Rennyo
Ryōgen
Taixu
Tantric Buddhism in Japan: Kukai and Saicho
The Body of the Buddha
The Philosophical Works and Influence of Dignāga and Dharmakīrti
The Imamura Families and the Making of American Buddhism
Thích Nhất Hạnh in the Context of the Modern Development of Vietnamese Buddhism
Tri Songdetsen
Tsangpa Gyare (1161–1211), Founder of the Drukpa Kagyü School
Tzu Chi
Xuyun

TEXTS AND PHILOLOGICAL STUDIES

Abhidharmakośabhāṣya (Treasury of Metaphysics with Self-Commentary)
Abhisamayālaṃkāra (Ornament for Clear Realization)
Bodhisattvabhūmi (The Bodhisattva Stages)
Canon and Commentary in the Earliest Buddhist Manuscripts
Chan Literature
Dunhuang Texts
Epigraphy and the Study of Buddhism: South Asia's Northern Corridor
From Manuscript to Print in South and Southeast Asia
Jātaka
The Vajrakīla Tantras
Tibetan Book of the Dead (*Bardo Thödol*)

Tibetan Buddhism and the Gesar Epic
Visualization/Contemplation Sutras (Guan Jing)

GEOGRAPHICAL OUTLINE

EAST ASIA

Amoghavajra
Buddhism and Healing in China
Buddhism and Medicine in Japan
Buddhism and Medicine in Premodern Japan
Buddhism and Print Culture in China
Buddhism and Shinto
Candrakīrti's Middle Way Philosophy
Chan Literature
D. T. Suzuki: A Biography
D. T. Suzuki: Ideas and Influences
Debate Traditions in Premodern Japan
Domestic Dharma in Japan
Filial Piety in Chinese Buddhism
Fo Guang Shan
History of Buddhisms in China: The Nanbeicho Period (Late 4th Century to the Sui Dynasty)
Hsing Yun
Huineng
Humanistic Buddhism (Rensheng Fojiao 人生佛教 / Renjian Fojiao 人間佛教)
Monastic Education in Contemporary Asia
Naikan: A Meditation Method and Psychotherapy
Nichiren
Pilgrimage in China
Rennyo
Ryōgen
Shingon
The Six Nara Schools
Sōka Gakkai
Taixu
Tantric Buddhism in Japan: Kukai and Saicho
Tantric Buddhism in Japan: Shingon, Tendai, and the Esotericization of Japanese Buddhisms
Tantric Revival in China
Thích Nhất Hạnh in the Context of the Modern Development of Vietnamese Buddhism
Tzu Chi
Visualization/Contemplation Sutras (Guan Jing)
Xuyun

EUROPE AND THE AMERICAS

American Buddhism during World War II Imprisonment
Buddhisms in Diaspora: The Canadian Context of Chinese Buddhism
Early Modern European Encounters with Buddhism
Southeast Asian Refugees in North America
The Imamura Families and the Making of American Buddhism
Western Buddhism and Race

INNER ASIA

Abhidharmakośabhāṣya (Treasury of Metaphysics with Self-Commentary)
Abhisamayālaṃkāra (Ornament for Clear Realization)
Bodhisattvabhūmi (The Bodhisattva Stages)
The Bön Tradition of Dzogchen
Buddhist Art and Architecture in Tibet
Buddhist Wall Paintings
Chöd: A Tibetan Buddhist Practice
Debate in the Tibetan Tradition
Dunhuang Art
Dunhuang Texts
Dzogchen
Early History of the Drukpa Kagyü School
Gelukpa
Guardian/Protector Deities in Tibetan Buddhism

Jebtsundamba Khutugtus of Mongolia
Kālacakra-Maṇḍala: Symbolism and Construction
Longchenpa
Mahāmudrā in India and Tibet
Mipam
Monastic Education in Contemporary Asia
Mongolian Buddhism in the Democratic Period
Mongolian Buddhism in the Early 20th Century
Mongolian Buddhism in the Yuan Period
Nechung: A Tibetan Buddhist Oracle
Pilgrimage in Buddhist Tibet
Pure Land Buddhism in Tibetan Contexts
The Sangha as an Institution
Soka Gakkai
The Kadampa: A Formative Movement of Tibetan Buddhism
Marpa Lotsawa Chökyi Lodrö
The Vajrakīla Tantras
Tibetan Book of the Dead (*Bardo Thödol*)
Tibetan Buddhism and the Gesar Epic
Tibetan Buddhist Power Objects
Tibetan Medicine and Its Buddhist Contexts
Tibetan Visionary Buddhism
Tri Songdetsen
Tsangpa Gyare (1161–1211), Founder of the Drukpa Kagyü School
Zhentong (Other-Emptiness)

SOUTH ASIA

Abhidharmakośabhāṣya (Treasury of Metaphysics with Self-Commentary)
Abhisamayālaṃkāra (Ornament for Clear Realization)
Bodhisattvabhūmi (The Bodhisattva Stages)
Buddhaghosa
Buddhism and Medicine in India
Muslim–Buddhist Relations and Buddhism in Muslim Sources until the Mongol Period
Epigraphy and the Study of Buddhism: South Asia's Northern Corridor
Esoteric Buddhism in Southeast Asia
Prajñāpāramitā and Khmer Esoteric Buddhism in the 10th to 13th centuries
From Manuscript to Print in South and Southeast Asia
Imaging the Buddha in South Asia
Jātaka
Kālacakra-Maṇḍala: Symbolism and Construction
Mahāmudrā in India and Tibet
Monastic Education in Contemporary Asia
Nāgārjuna
Patronage of Buddhist Monasteries in Eastern India, 600–1300 CE
Practices of Protection in the Pali World
Sarvāstivāda Abhidharma
Sri Lanka's Sinhala Buddhist Guardian Deities: Satara Varan Devi

SOUTHEAST ASIA

Buddhist Wizards (*Vidhyadhāra/Weizzā/Weikza*): Contemporary Burma/Myanmar
Buddhist Wizards (*Vidhyadhāra/Weizzā/Weikza*): Origins and History
Esoteric Buddhism in Southeast Asia
Prajñāpāramitā and Khmer Esoteric Buddhism in the 10th to 13th centuries
Practices of Protection in the Pali World
The Study of Visual Culture in South and Southeast Asian Buddhism

TRANS-REGIONAL

Art, Architecture, and National Memory-Making
Avalokiteśvara: The Bodhisattva of Compassion
The Body of the Buddha
Buddhism and Bioethics
Buddhism and Biography
Buddhism and Globalization
Buddhism and Media
Buddhism and the Environment

Buddhist Cosmology
Buddhist Geography and Regionalism
Buddhism in Colonial Contexts
Buddhism in Film
Buddhist Chaplaincy
Buddhist Meditation and Contemplation
Buddhist Philosophy as Philosophy
Canon and Commentary in the Earliest Buddhist Manuscripts
The Economics of Buddhism
Engaged Buddhism
Ethics and Buddhism
Four Noble Truths
Global Buddhism
Global Theravada Buddhism: Asian Foundations
Global Theravada: Transmission beyond Asia
Globalizing Tantric Buddhism
Homa: Tantric Fire Ritual
Intention in the Pali Suttas and Abhidharma
Japanese Buddhisms in Diaspora
Madhyamaka
Mañjuśrī
Maritime Buddhism
Nāgārjuna
Narratives of Buddhist Relics and Images
Perfections (Six and Ten) of Bodhisattvas in Buddhist Literature
The Philosophical Works and Influence of Dignāga and Dharmakīrti
Psychological Interpreters of Buddhism
Queering Buddhist Traditions
The Reincarnation System in Central Asian Buddhism
Secular Buddhism
Tantra and the Tantric Traditions of Hinduism and Buddhism
Theravada Buddhism
Three Turnings of the Wheel of Doctrine (Dharma-Cakra)
Transmission of Buddhist Media and Texts
Vinaya Rules for Monks and Nuns

Q

QUEERING BUDDHIST TRADITIONS

INTRODUCTION: QT MEETS BUDDHISM

Developed in the 1990s by foundational thinkers such as Eve Kosofsky Sedgwick, Judith Butler, and David Halperin, queer theory (QT) is rooted in multiple strands of feminist thought and critical theory (CT) and CT's developments in, among others, Derridean deconstruction, Foucauldian poststructuralism, and various postmodern schools of thinking.[1]

The "queer" ' in QT points to the subversive and dissident challenge that queer subjectivities pose to hegemonic and normative systems of sex/gender and sexual belonging and governance. Reappropriating a pejorative term for homosexuals, "queer," as a noun (broadly conceived) points to (the counterhegemonic aspects of) LGBTIQ+ subjectivities (lesbian, gay, bisexual, trans*, intersex, queer/querying, and more) and is used as such, stressing the interconnected mesh of both gender and sexual subjectivities and belongings; some scholars, however, prefer to differentiate trans* theory (gender) from QT (sexualities). QT's "queers" are not simply LGBTI people but are and aim to be *Querschläger*—societal ricochets exploding compulsory identitarian essentialism and exclusive dualisms/binarisms.[2]

As a verb, "queer(ing)" covers the semantic field of critiquing, challenging, subverting, resisting, undoing, and exploding oppressive and monolithic societal scripts of sex, gender, and sexualities.[3] Queering can be regarded as a trans- and interdisciplinary function of undoing: both epistemic and practical, theoretic and applied, permeable and focused, open and concrete. Organically the queering impulse resonates, intersects, overlaps, and synergizes with "cripping," decolonizing, and other modes of undoing that take various forms of marginalization as critical starting points, yet counterflow to and disrupt the oppressive societal scripts and centers that create the margins.[4] Hence, QT is both an engine for, and a beneficiary of, "intersectional theory"—which includes critical race theory, postcolonial theory, and critical disability studies, among others.[5]

It follows that the academic study of queer(ing) Buddhism(s), while partially overlapping, differs substantially in method and scope from investigations into Buddhism(s) & gender and Buddhism(s) & sexuality/-ies while exploring diachronically through the ages, and synchronically across different cultures and geographies, how the various Buddhist traditions have manifested a multitude of complex and divergent philosophical and ethical perspectives and regulations around sexualities and diverse sex/gender subjectivities.[6]

The academic study of Buddhist traditions remains dominated by "phallogocentric" (Derrida) modes of inquiry: textual-philological, historical, and (traditional-)philosophical inquiry with some space for "acceptable" anthropological and sociological research. Buddhist studies as a field has been slow to adapt critical modern and postmodern theoretical impulses which include scholars-cum-practitioners as Buddhist constructive-critical thinkers (academic "dharmologists" or "Buddhist theologians"); some professional bodies such as the American Academy of Religion (AAR) have taken steps to address the pertinent issues of the hegemonic politics of scholarship and have opened up to dharmological, intersectional, queer, and trans* perspectives.[7]

Prominently, the work of the late Rita Gross opened Buddhist studies to second-wave, "white" feminist thinking, which, in turn, has been powerfully critiqued by persons of color (POC) Buddhist feminist perspectives.[8] Notably, Gross's student Hsiao-Lan Hu extended Buddhist feminist thinking to third-wave feminism.[9] However, queer-intersectional strands of feminist inquiry are not yet sufficiently systematically explored in Buddhist studies.

Among the pioneer adapters of critical cultural theory and philosophy is the scholar of East Asian Buddhism Bernard Faure, who in 1991 named Michel Foucault and Jacques Derrida among his "cardinal and tutelar deities."[10] Faure continued his fruitful reception of Foucault in his trailblazing monograph on Buddhism and sexuality, *The Red Thread*.[11] Since then, Buddhist studies has explored the influence of Foucault and of "postmodern" philosophers such as Levinas and Deleuze, as well as some more detailed work on Buddhism and Derrida.[12] However, a systematic Buddhist appraisal of contemporary cultural/social theories and postmodern philosophies remains still embryonic, although important inroads have been made by, among others, Simon Gareth Smith, Carl Olson, Jin Y. Park, and Edwin Ng.[13]

In the case of QT and of foundational queer theorists, any comprehensive Buddhist appraisal is lacking. At the same time, there is a nascent reception of the queering impulses within global Buddhist traditions (see the section entitled "Queerness in Contemporary Global Buddhist Traditions"), but there is a lack of systematic attempts of queer Buddhist constructive-critical reflection or dharmology.[14]

BUDDHIST VIEWS ON SEXUALITY/-IES AND SEX/GENDER DIVERSITY

Research into the complex and interpellated fields of sexuality/-ies and sex/gender diversity in Buddhist traditions has often been marred by the traps of historicism and conceptual conflation.[15] This article treats the fields as separate for pragmatical reasons but acknowledges the multiple blurred lines and overlapping queer subjectivities and (un)belongings.

Buddhist Views on Sexuality/-ies. In philosophical terms, sensuality (Pāli *rāga*) and sensual passion (*kāma*) are regarded in Early Buddhism as manifestations of clinging/attachment (*upādāna*). *Kāmupādāna* ("sensual grasping") counts among the four major categories of *upādāna* in Early Buddhist scholasticism.[16] Sexual activity is therefore usually an enactment of desire/craving (*taṇhā*), Sanskrit (Skt.) *tṛṣṇā, lobha*—one of the three core (*mūla*) afflicting emotions ("defilements" *kilesa/kleśa*) that cease with enlightenment. This perspective means that all sexual activities can potentially be viewed as a "problem," but it does not automatically render Buddhist traditions "sex-negative."[17] Rather, sexuality features simply among bodily expressions and functions: "sex is just something that people do"[18] and, as such, connected with attachment; hence, sexuality is a training field for the cultivation of ethics (*sīla/śīla*) and right conduct (*sammā-kammanta/samyak-karmānta*). Non-(cis-)males, however, are persistently characterized as possessing untamed, predatory, and aggressive sexuality and are regarded as a threat to (male) monastic purity.[19] In consequence, female monastics are subjected to additional restrictive rules (including the eight "reverence rules": *garudhammas/gurudharmas*) and the ordination of anyone outside the normative male/female gender spectrum is prohibited (see the section "Buddhist Views on Sex/Gender Diversity").

In practical and in sociolegal terms, Early Buddhist texts discuss sexuality (and sex/gender diversity) within the context of monasticism. The monastic code (*vinaya*) regulates in detailed form the social life and the social interactions of monks and nuns including their sexuality. The monastic vow of celibacy (*brahmacariya/brahmacārya*/Chinese 梵行 fàn xíng, Tibetan [Tib.] tshangs par spyod pa) features prominently and the different Early Buddhist *vinayas* casuistically detail prohibited sexual acts and the scale of monastic punishments up to expulsion for each specific breach of celibacy. The extensive monastic rules and their legalistic etiology (origin cases) in sexual matters underline the foundational importance of monastic vows in a rhetoric trope of polarization that is arguably at times humorous.[20] In the context of breach of celibacy, the *vinayas* simply acknowledge that monastics can experience polymorph sexual desires and attractions, including same-sex desire. Among the breaches of celibacy, nonheteronormative desires and sexuality are not particularly singled out and are not more stigmatized than heterosexual acts.[21]

Sexual ethics for laypeople is only sparsely circumscribed in the vague formula of avoidance of "sexual misconduct" (*kāmesu micchācāra*). Sexual harming is primarily conceptualized as "sleeping with another's wife" (*Kesaputtiya-sutta* AN 3, 65 [2, 2, 5] i 189 PTS) and/or status/dependency violation (such as guardian status, existing marriage or engagement, *Cunda-sutta* AN 10, 176 [4, 2, 10] v 264). The texts consistently assume a patriarchal and heteronormative default perspective of men who desire women (or other nonnormative sex/genders, see the section "Buddhist Views on Sex/Gender Diversity"). The socioreligious stigmatization of intragender desire as such appears to surface in South Asian history only during the Kuṣāṇa period (in the first four centuries CE).[22] During this period, the influential Buddhist compendia such as the *Yogācārabhumiśāstra* and the *Abhidharmakośa* and their respective commentarial traditions attest to a shift in the production of sexual values. During this shift, intragender desire and sexual activity becomes condemned explicitly and in generalized terms; sexuality is being regulated in terms of time, location, and context to procreative penetrative acts of married male–female couples. The emerging monastic/scholastic view on lay sexual practices prominently emphasized the prohibition of "unnatural" (*anaṅga*) oral and anal sex and both male–male and male–third gender (see the section on "Buddhist Views on Sex/Gender Diversity") sexual acts become explicitly prohibited.[23] In the same period, Mahāyāna scriptures such as the *(Saddharma-) Smṛtyupasthāna-Sūtra* emerge, detailing hell punishments for various sexual crimes and actors, including men who have sex with men.[24] This social attitude has taken hold and prevails in most subsequent Buddhist civilizations—for example, in Tibet through influential religious compendia such as Gampopa's *Jewel Ornament of Liberation* (12th century CE) and, meeting (Neo-) Confucian family values, in Chinese and Korean Buddhism.[25] In Japan, conflicting attitudes toward same-sex relations arose within the medieval Buddhist traditions, most notably Shingon (真言), prominently including the praise of sexual relationships and mentorship between senior monks and novices.[26]

Buddhist Views on Sex/Gender Diversity. The conceptual differentiation between "sex" in terms of biology and "gender" in terms of culture is a product of modernity; premodern South Asia conceptualizes sex/gender not in neatly separated biological essentialized or culturally constructed terms but in terms of "faculties" (*indriya*) that express themselves in a hegemonic male and female binarism despite the early development of theoretical three- and fourfold sex/gender systems.[27] Already in Vedic times, an abject "third" sex/gender is acknowledged;[28] classical Buddhist and medical scholars developed a fourfold sex/gender system analogous to the fourfold system of Indian logic (tetralemma, Skt. *catuṣkoṭi*).[29] The philosophical "male–female" binary was completed with the third "neither . . . nor" and the fourth "both . . . and" categories.

The "both . . . and" sex/gender is termed *ubhatobyañjanaka* (二根 èr gēn), which roughly translates into "both-sexed." The term points to the occurrence of varieties in human sexual biology and development that are contemporarily subsumed under the larger umbrella of intersex; however, some intersex variants appear to be included in the third category as congenital third sex/gender person (*jāti-/napuṃsaka paṇḍaka* 扇搋 shàn chuāi);[30] East Asian Buddhist traditions sometimes collapse the third and fourth categories.[31] The term "hermaphrodite" that is used commonly as a translation of *ubhatobyañjanaka* is overwhelmingly regarded as offensive in contemporary intersex communities; hence, "both-sexed" appears to be the most neutral translation. Early sources do not provide much detail about *ubhatobyañjanakas*.[32] Yet it is evident that they were socially stigmatized and not admitted to ordination in the Buddhist sangha.

The term most commonly used in Buddhist texts for the third sex/gender category is the Vedic term *paṇḍaka*, meaning "(a person) without testes."[33] The etymology of *paṇḍaka* points to their lack of maleness (one early Chinese translation is literally "non-male": 不男, bù nán), that is, lack of normative sex/gender faculties as seen in comparison to the default male position.[34] The male (cis/hetero-) patriarchal lens on the third sex/gender is made clear by the fact that using a female starting point of comparison for *paṇḍaka* necessitates explicit qualification of the term as "female *paṇḍaka*" in Early Buddhist literature.[35] The Early Buddhist treatise *Milindapañhā* (*Questions of Milinda*, Miln. 93) notes the female sex/gender's intrinsic inferiority (*ittaratā*) and the intrinsic ambiguity (*anekaṃsikatā*) of the third sex/gender: *paṇḍakas* cannot be identified as either male or female ("neither . . . nor").

How, then, to conceptualize and to translate the *paṇḍaka*? Early Pāli Buddhist sources such as the late-canonical *Kathāvatthu* (Kv II, 1=167 PTS) point at (male) infertility and at impotence (*vossa* DN-a i 97 at DN 1, 12).[36] Only the commentarial scholasticism of the 4th and 5th centuries CE provides five descriptive *paṇḍaka* subcategories covering a variety of biological-procreative and psychosexual/gender-normative impotencies: infertilities and sexual behavior that contravenes nucleolar default-gender norms.

1. *jāti-/napuṃsaka-paṇḍaka* congenital impotence, which might include some intersex varieties of sex indeterminable at birth.
2. *pakkha-paṇḍaka* fortnightly cyclical impotence.
3. *opakkāmika-paṇḍaka* impotence inflicted as punishment.
4. *īrṣya-p./usūya—paṇḍaka* "jealousy" psycho/sociosexual impotence expressing itself in voyeurist behavior.
5. *āsitta—paṇḍaka* "sprinkled" psycho/sociosexual penetrative impotence assuming a passive sexual role of fellator (oral).

While infertile or, as a punishment, castrated males hence feature within the *paṇḍaka* category, the translation of the term as "eunuch," common in older literature, is misleading and, at least partially, anachronistic. Similarly, Leonard Zwilling's early article on homosexuality in Indic Buddhism overemphasizes sexual acts as described in the *paṇḍaka* subcategories 4 and 5; his still oft-quoted definition of *paṇḍakas* as "a socially stigmatized class of passive, probably transvestite, homosexuals" [37] is an example of the "doing the history of homosexuality" (hotly debated in early QT) as historicism, that is, by (anachronistic) readings of contemporary Global Northern "queer" subjectivities and belongings into pre- and early modern, and various Global Southern contexts.[38] John Powers in his study of masculinity in Early Buddhism uses the term "sexual deviants";[39] in doing so, he misses the crucial sex/gender element. While it is clear that *paṇḍaka* subcategories are connotated in classical South Asian Buddhist texts with nonnormative sexual practices, it remains important to stress that the term *paṇḍaka* does not primarily denote a sexual orientation, sexual nonnormativity, or "queerness;" *paṇḍaka* denotes, if one so wishes, a "genderqueerness": a queerness of sex/gender faculty (*indriya*). José Ignacio Cabezón in his foundational study on sexuality in classical Indian Buddhism uses the broad term "queer" for *paṇḍaka* with the explicit Wittgensteinian *caveat* of context.[40] Cabezón is perfectly explicit about *paṇḍaka* as a (sex/) gender signifier. Unfortunately, and perhaps unavoidably, at times, in the subsequent employment of the "queer" in Cabezón's translations and conceptual evaluations various Indic and Tibetan concepts beyond *paṇḍaka* (Tib. ma ning) collapse; additionally, the term "queer" transports contemporary and QT usages, which makes it as a translation for *paṇḍaka* into a somewhat infelicitous shortcut that problematically thrusts and collapses complex contemporary connotations onto the premodern term. Hence, the term *paṇḍaka* should remain untranslated or, if necessary, be described with the unsexy, yet more accurate term "gender-deficient."

In terms of sex/gender change, Buddhist texts are embedded in the wider premodern South Asian tradition whose literature abounds in narratives of sex/gender changes as either (a) unexpected and unwelcome (usually male to female, MtF, e.g., due to a curse); (b) unexpected and welcome (e.g., female to male, FtM); or (c) expected and welcome (e.g., by propitiating a supernatural being or deliberate magic).[41] Buddhist sex/gender change narratives reflect these patterns; commentators tend to emphasize the agency of karma, the ripening of wholesome causes for FtM and of unwholesome for MtF.[42] Importantly, the occurrence of sex/gender change is simply accepted as a regular phenomenon (Miln. 267, *Dilemmas* 7.4). In the *vinaya,* the buddha laconically and pragmatically accepts the change of sex/gender of monastics and confirms them in their changed sex/gender community.[43] While premodern Buddhist understandings of sex-change differ from modern and contemporary sexological views on trans* people and transgenderism, the clear precedents in the Early Buddhist foundational texts should be basis enough to safeguard against transphobia and trans* discrimination (although not necessarily for nonbinary and genderfluid individuals); unfortunately, transphobia is prevalent throughout traditional Buddhisms, due to the conflation of trans* with the third (and, to a lesser extent, the fourth) sex/gender categories and the general cultural mechanics of cis-hetero-patriarchal "aphallophobia" (which includes sexism, homo-, lesbo-, bi-, queer- and transphobia).[44]

QUEERNESS IN CONTEMPORARY GLOBAL BUDDHIST TRADITIONS

The spectrum of contemporary Buddhist attitudes to queerness ranges from total rejection to wholehearted embrace and, thus, reflects the polyphone and, at times, conflicting complexity of *global–glocal–local* and context-specific Buddhist traditions in their diachronic and synchronic messiness. Examples of queerphobic hate speech from Buddhist leaders do not help the attempts to queer Buddhist dialogues and the emerging of integrated intersectional subjectivities. The 2019 recording of a senior Burmese Buddhist monk mocking the suicide of a gay librarian, before whipping up a lynch mob against all homosexuals, is a chilling reminder of the plight of LGBTIQ+ Buddhists in many traditionally majority Buddhist countries and some of their transnational satellites in global Buddhist contexts.[45]

Theravāda. Within contemporary Theravāda traditions, anti-LGBTIQ+ sentiments and proof-texting regularly occur. For example, the influential modernist Vipassanā teacher Satya Narayan Goenka (1924–2013) viewed homosexuality as dangerous.[46] Within conservative Thai Buddhist discourses, both the Western category "gay" (คนผิดเพศ *khon lakphet,* lit. "unnatural person") and the indigenous Thai trans* category "*kathoei*" กะเทย (also often written as *kathoey* and frequently translated as "lady-boy") are regularly conflated and identified with the (abject) *paṇḍaka*—the third sex/gender category in premodern South Asia as mentioned in Buddhist scripture.[47] In the cases *kathoei* are ordained, the prerequisites are intact male genitals; ordination at a minor temple far away from the public eye; and the compassionate discretion of the preceptor.[48] However, in most cases, *kathoeis* and *khun laphet* continue to be excluded from ordination.[49] Prominently, in the early 2000s, Phra Phayom Konyano พระพยอม กลฺยาโณ called for a purge of gay monks from the sangha.[50] In March 2014, the popular *Woody Talk Show* featured a *kathoei* who became a monk; one year later, the military government moved to explicitly outlaw the ordination of "homosexuals" and provided prison sentences for homosexual monks.[51] Monasteries such as Wat Krueng Tai วัดครึ่งใต้ in the northern Thai town Chiang Khong เชียงของ even function as a Buddhist equivalents to Christian "pray-the-gay-away" anti-LGBTIQ+ "conversion therapy" or "re-education" camps.[52] The existence of such practices also within Buddhist contexts appears to have eluded the signatories of the European Buddhist Union who called for an end of (Christian) conversion therapy in a declaration of March 1, 2018.[53] At the progressive spectrum within Thai Buddhist discourses, Ven. Wontham (Waradhammo) พระวรธรรม is an outspoken proponent for queer rights;[54] he is calling for the ordination of anyone regardless of sexual orientation and gender identity.[55] Transnational Thai Theravāda traditions also include prominent inclusive voices such as the British Ajahn Brahm and the Australian Ajahn Sujato.[56] Sujato's compatriot Akāliko Bhikkhu describes himself as "an out and proud queer Buddhist monk." He founded the interdenominational Rainbodhi Sangha in 2019.[57]

East Asian Mahāyāna. Following the genealogy of Buddhist sexual ethics in East Asia, contemporary Sinitic Mahāyāna includes examples of the "hell and brimstone" end of the spectrum such as the influential Chan (禪 chán) master and globalizer Hsuan Hua 宣化 (1918–1995), who founded the Dharma Realm Buddhist Association. He condemns homosexuality with strong apocalyptic tropes of hell and of the doom of humanity.[58] In contrast, contemporary Sinophone Buddhist leaders such as the Humanistic Buddhist Master Hsing Yun of Fo Guang Shan stress acceptance and tolerance "as a form of generosity and a form of wisdom."[59]

The most vocal pro-LGBTIQ+ voice among contemporary Sinitic Buddhist leaders is the scholar-nun Ven. Chao-Hwei (昭慧, Zhāo Huì) of the intermonastic Hong Shi Buddhist College 佛教弘誓學院 (Taiwan).[60] Ven. Chao-Hwei has published widely on matters of Buddhist ethics and conducted the first Buddhist same-sex marriage ceremony in Taiwan in 2014.[61]

Vietnamese Chan (Thiền) is the main source of the socially engaged transnational mindfulness Community of Interbeing, founded by Thich Nhat Hanh (Thích Nhất Hạnh), with its seat in Plum Village, France. This community provides queer-inclusive and affirmative spaces since the 1990s.[62]

Japanese derived transnational Buddhist movements feature among the most LBGTIQ+ inclusive forms of contemporary Buddhism: the Buddhist Churches of America (BCA, 米国仏教団) is the long-established US branch of the Nishi Hongan-ji 西本願寺 Jōdo Shinshū 浄土真宗 (True Pure Land School) and has evolved to become a vocal advocate of inclusivity. BCA Revd. Koshin Ogui conducted the first same-sex marriage in the early 1970s in San Francisco.[63] In 2000, the Nishi Hongan-ji, the head temple in Kyoto for ten thousand plus affiliated Shin temples, issued a statement by the highest doctrinal expert that there were no objections to marriages involving same-sex couples and/or "transsexuals"; the liturgical text was changed from reading "husband" and "wife" to "spouse."[64] Still, some tensions remain with gender essentializing doctrines.[65] Gender-queer visibility in Japanese Buddhism has been heightened by the activities of the Jōdo Shū (浄土宗) priest Revd. Kōdō Nishimura 西村 宏堂 (b. 1989), who is gathering transnational fame as a makeup artist.[66]

SG-I (Sōka Gakkai 創価学会-International), a highly active *Lotus-Sutra* Buddhist and Nichiren-derived global NRM (new religious movement), gradually developed to be explicitly queer-affirming.[67] Some parts of the movement have welcomed LGB[TIQ] people since the 1980s and LGBT groups were established since the early 1990s; since 2015, such groups use the new umbrella "Courageous Freedom." In 1995, SG-I official policy changed to allow same-sex commitment ceremonies.[68]

Tibetan Buddhism. In line with the developments in Buddhist sexual ethics in the Tibetan cultural sphere, 20th- and 21st-century Tibetan Buddhist voices often inhabit a conflicted mid-spectrum; among others, the Fourteenth Dalai Lama has been, since 1997, on an evolving learning curve after causing consternation (and hurt) with traditionally Tibetan prohibitive views on masturbation, oral and anal sex, and homophobic remarks.[69] The Tibetan Buddhist struggle in exile and (post)modernity to reconcile traditionally Tibetan queerphobic attitudes with transnational (post)modernist values can also be exemplified at the position of the late Fourteenth Shamarpa (zhwa dmar pa), Mipham Chokyi Lodro (mi pham chos kyi blo gros, 1952–2014), the second most senior leader of the Karma Kagyu (karma bka' brgyud) school. For Shamarpa, LGBTIQ+ is a private matter which should not interfere with "civilized society" (read: the nucleolar heteronorm).[70]

While these high Tibetan Buddhist masters apparently maintain in public traditional heteronormative mindsets, transnationally and on a personal level, diversity of sexual orientation and gender identity appear to be nonissues for most Tibetan masters. For example, senior leaders of the Nyingma tradition such as the late Dudjom (bdud 'joms) Rinpoche (1904–1987) appear to have never problematized homosexuality.[71]

One of the most influential "crazy yogi" globalizers of Tibetan Buddhism, Chogyam Trungpa (chos rgyam drung pa, 1939–1987), was overtly sex-positive and LGB inclusive.[72] Trungpa's organization Vajradhatu/Shambhala attracted a significant number of gay and bisexual disciples: "In the Vajradhatu of Trungpa's day, gays as singles or couples were open and common, as was bisexual experimentation. The anecdotes are endless and outrageous."[73] Contemporary Shambhala has an active LGBTQ Network.[74] However, sexual scandals appear to weave like a red thread through Trungpa's controversial Buddhist (and post-Buddhist) legacy, from alleged coercion (in 1975) by Trungpa (the Merwin scandal), irresponsible transmission of HIV by Trungpa's bisexual dharma heir, up to the abuse scandal (starting in 2018) around the Sakyong Mipham, Trungpa's son and heir to Shambhala International.[75]

Among the younger generation of transnational senior Tibetan Buddhist leaders, His Holiness Ogyen Tinley Dorje (o rgyan 'phrin las rdo rje, 1985–) has been publicly supportive of the LGBTIQ+ community, as have the 12th Gyalwang Drukpa (rgyal dbang 'brug pa), Jigme Pema Wangchen ('jigs med padma dbang chen), and the prolific Tibetan Buddhist modernist Bhutanese master Dzongsar Jamyang Khyentse Rinpoche (dzong gsar 'jam dbyangs mkhyen brtse rin po che, 1961–), among many others.[76]

In Tibetan communities in exile, monastic-normative views on sexual ethics continue to be influential, while the reality of prohibited (both monastic and lay) sexual practices is widely acknowledge in Tibetan medical literature.[77] Contemporary Tibetan lay tantric and medicine masters such as Dr. Nida Chenagtsang do not regard queerness and queer sexuality as deviance and simply advocate for safe sex.[78]

The Tibetan category of the *ma ning* (as translation of *paṇḍaka*) is historically polysemous and in tantric and medical contexts sometimes highly positively connotated.[79] The category is, however, regularly mapped onto contemporary Tibetan (and Mongolian) queer and trans* subjectivities in a pejorative sense and conflated with other Tibetan derogative terms such as *polo molo/poli moli*.[80] Tibetan LGBT people appear to prefer to identify with English categories or neutral Tibetan descriptors.[81] Some attempts have been made in Global Northern convert Tibetan Buddhism to adopt the protector deity Maning Mahākala for queer tantric dharmology.[82] Since 2016, Tibetan trans* visibility has increased through the publication on social media of an interview (in Tibetan language) given by ex-monk and trans woman, Tenzin Mariko (bstan 'dzin ma ri ko).[83]

Within contemporary Tibetan Buddhism, this range of responses is consistent with the complexity of the globalization of the tradition while navigating premodern, modern, and postmodern modes of praxis (g)locally and transnationally.[84]

"Western" Buddhism. Queer Buddhists in the Global North are navigating the minefield of traditional prejudices with increasing confidence.[85] The San Francisco Bay Area saw the early gay-friendly activities of the Jōdo Shinshū BCA in the 1970s and one pioneering and still active network was established there in the 1980s in the form of the Gay Buddhist Group, later called the Gay Buddhist Fellowship.[86] The Gay Buddhist Group also spawned the Hartford Street Zen Center whose abbot Roshi Issan Dorsey (1933–1990) was a former drag queen and dharma heir of Zentatsu Baker-Roshi; Dorsey established a hospice for people dying of AIDS in the 1980s early epidemic.[87] Trungpa's transnational Tibetan Neo- and Post-Buddhism also provided queer spaces. LGBT (later LGBTIQ+) retreats were also held in America since the 1990s by Eric Kolveig and lesbian teacher Arinna Weisman.[88] Thich Nhat Hanh's transnational Plum Village community established a dedicated gay and lesbian network in 1992.[89]

In the context of the Western Neo-Buddhism, Triratna (formally known as the Friends of the Western Buddhist Order, FWBO) has developed into a queer-embracing space.[90] The movement was founded by Dennis Lingwood (Sangharakshita, 1925–2018) whose homosexual orientation was an open secret; that did not prevent Lingwood from acting in distinctively transphobic ways toward transman Michael Dillon/Lobzang Jivaka.[91] However, the order has ordained trans* members who are recognized in their affirmed gender as indicated by 2016 ordination and retreat events.[92] Similarly to the Tibetan (Post)Buddhist Shambhala movement (see subsection "Tibetan Buddhism"), FWBO/Triratna has been marred by sexual scandals; these include allegations against Lingwood and other senior male leaders relating to sexual misconduct and abusive sexual coercion of other junior male (mostly heterosexual) members.[93] Lingwood issued a statement of deep regret about his behavior on December 30, 2016, but the order continues to face criticism about its handling of the abuse also from a progressive group of ordained members who call themselves Interkula.[94]

(POST)MODERN QUEER BUDDHISTS AND DHARMOLOGY

Queer-feminist Buddhism can be regarded as a third wave of LGB(TIQ+) liberation within Buddhist culture. In Global "Buddhism beyond Modernity"[95] intersectional, inclusive practices and voices are increasingly appearing and produce nascent forms of queer dharmologies.

Queer Buddhists beyond Modernity. LGBTIQ+ subjectivities still face similar challenges in Buddhist contexts as in most traditional environments of vestigial governmentalities (such as "religions").[96] Queer and trans* make uneasy bedfellows, also because any intersection of "queer/religion" can become contentious from both sides. Queer people might feel that they are asked to exchange their identitarian agency for the belonging and soteriology a religion offers and which comes interpellated with biopolitical regulation; hence the second-wave global LGBT liberation (the "Gay International") often and dogmatically construes the ill-defined yet efficacious Western category of "religion" as hostile to queers/queering: this "homosecularism" sees queerness and religiosity as mutually exclusive.[97]

In Asian Buddhist contexts, queer and queer-inclusive Buddhist voices become more prominent. For example, in Thailand, Phra Wontham (Waradhammo) พระวรธรรม connects queer Buddhist practitioners through his *Neo-Buddhism* blogspot.[98] Vernacular Thai Buddhism also features strongly in Thai queer cinema enriching the societal discourse and queer cultural production.[99] In addition to the already mentioned Revd. Kōdō Nishimura's activities to increase genderqueer visibility in Japan (subsection "East Asian Mahāyāna"), in 2019 the *Sangha Japan* magazine featured the first Japanese-language article on Buddhist LGBT issues.[100] In the east Asia-Pacific, some trans* networks are consciously adapting as their icon the bodhisattva of compassion Guanyin (Guān [shì] yīn 觀[世]音).[101] Guanyin is ambigender in East Asian Buddhism traditions since the Tang (Táng 唐) dynasty, yet remains male-only in the Indo-Tibetan Buddhist traditions (Skt. Avalokiteśvara, Tib. sPyan ras gzigs "Chenrezig").[102]

In the Global North, the generally positive (orientalized and romanticized) image of the (post)modernist brand of "Buddhism" is often conducive to the search for a spiritual and/or religious home that some LGBTIQ+ people undergo within a tension between traditional religious rejection and "homosecularism." Queer and trans* people increasingly embrace various (post)modernist global and transnational forms of Buddhism and/or secularized Buddhism-derived meditation practices. In doing so, some have found their new Buddhist practice a catalyst of de-emphasizing or de-queering their queer subjectivities;[103] some are giving in to strong hetero-/and homonormative pressures.[104] Other LGBTIQ+ Buddhists have "expressed that their queer identities functioned as a profound 'doorway into dharma'" and "felt that there was a special compatibility between foundational Buddhist teachings and queer identities."[105]

Long after the trans* pioneer monastic Michael Dillon/Lobzang Jivaka (see "'Western' Buddhism"), multiple global (post)modernist traditions feature increasing visibility of queer and trans* ordained and authorized lay teachers, such as Catriona Reed who transitioned in 1996, four years after her authorization by Thich Nhat Hanh; [106] and the Sōtō 曹洞 Zen 禅 teacher Fugan 普願 Eugene Bush (authorized in 2010 by Katherine Thanas). A Vipassanā teacher from the Philippines, La Sarmiento, came out as gender nonconforming in 2012.[107]

Equally, postmodern modes of Buddhism feature intersectional voices such as Larry Yang of the Spirit Rock Meditation Center.[108] The African American Zen master Earthlyn Manuel has been arguing powerfully for an intersectional Buddhist approach to ending discrimination.[109] Lama Rod Owens, angel Kyodo Williams, and Jasmine Syedullah have developed a "Radical Dharma" approach which spawned camps and groups for queer and POC practitioners.[110]

Popular nondenominational English language magazines aimed at Global Northern Buddhists such as *Lion's Roar* and *Tricycle* have featured popular queer/trans* Buddhist articles and reflections, as have some organization-specific publications.[111]

Trans* Buddhist practitioners initiated an online virtual sangha in 2014, in order "to address systemic exclusion of transgender and gender-nonconforming people from Buddhist spaces."[112] Sakyadhita—International Association of Buddhist Women has hosted LGBT dharma workshops during the biennial conferences since 2010.[113] The European Buddhist Union established a "Rainbow Sangha" queer Buddhist network.[114] In Australia, the Rainbodhi Sangha was founded in 2019 as a "a community group for LGBTQIA+ Buddhists and friends."[115] In March 2018, Thich Nhat Hanh's European Institute of Applied Buddhism organized an LGBTIQ* retreat in Germany.[116]

Queer Dharmology. So, where from here for queer(ed) Buddhism and queer Buddhist "liberation theology"?[117] Five key queer-affirmative parameters can be suggested for the emerging queer and trans* Buddhist liberation dharmology:

1. *Reflexivity*: Self-reflective clarity and awareness of the cultural-specific (post)modernist positionalities that queer, trans, secular, POC, dis/abled, etc., Buddhist thinkers inhabit.
2. *Hermeneutics*: Liberatory hermeneutical strategies that challenge, defy, and subvert persistent anti-LGBTIQ+ proof-texting of premodern scriptures and traditional practices.[118]
3. *Conceptualization*: The development, in dialogue with QT, of constructive-critical queer readings of Buddhist tenets (such as karma, No-Self, emptiness).
4. *Signification*: The excavation and (re)signification of queer/trans-affirmative paradigms, symbolism, and role models.
5. *Application:* The adaptation of queer/trans* affirmative spaces and technologies of the (No-)Self in Buddhist practice including meditation.[119]

Carefully positioned (parameter 1) Buddhist liberation hermeneutics (parameter 2) can hence complicate and counter, for example, the conflation of Buddhist scriptural sex/gender/sexual behavior categories (see "Buddhist Views on Sexuality/-ies and Sex/Gender Diversity") with contemporary Global Northern LGBTIQ+ subjectivities. Such hermeneutics can demonstrate the power and governmental agenda behind any questionable "*dharma*-splaining" of "aphallophobia," including homo-, bi-, and transphobia.[120]

A philosophical queering (parameter 3)of Buddhist thought refers to the de- and reconstructive examination and the complicating of Buddhist core tenets such as karma and No-Self.

Mythopoetic-narrative excavation and resignification of queer/trans-affirmative icons (parameter 4) can focus on Avalokiteśvara—Guanyin 觀音 or tantric deities, working with tantric dharmologies around the ultimate identity of conceptual thought and orgasmic bliss.[121]

Also, the development of LGBTIQ+ specific and/or affirmative spaces for Buddhist practice (parameter 5) is documented in the subsection "Queer Buddhists beyond Modernity." Generally no prominently queer(ing) modification to any practice is being deemed necessary; Jeffrey Hopkins has proposed a detailed gay adaptation to Buddhist tantric sexual yoga.[122] However, it is implicit that any advanced practitioner of sexual yoga adapts the practices from the inherent andro- and heterocentric paradigms to their own situation.[123] It remains to be seen if and/or how queer(ed) radical Buddhist practices in terms of dehegemonizing and decentering power, authority, and privileged bodies will emerge.

The concluding discussion focuses on the opportunities for queer readings of Buddhist concepts; tenets such as "No-Self" and "emptiness" have been frequently mentioned as productive reference points for individual practitioners.[124] However, queer-inclusive scholar-practitioner voices such as Ven. Chao-Hwei have suggested that, when addressing systemic Buddhist discrimination of LGBTIQ+ people, it is urgent to, first, challenge simplistic understandings of *karma* 業 yè ("action," causality) and to stress the sociostructural dimensions of suffering and the karmatic responsibility of a society.[125] Similarly, the queer-inclusive Thai Buddhist monk Shine [Chai] Wontham (Waradhammo) stresses that individuals are LGBT not due to "bad" *karma*; rather, society incurs unwholesome karma by discrimination and hate speech and, specifically, Thai society by means of its patriarchal-oppressive structures.[126]

By deconstructing popular reductionist karma theories espoused in homiletic and didactic contexts, queering karma can then reject any essentializing and, judgmentally, individualizing understanding of rebirth and personhood as inherently contradictory to the philosophy of No-Self (Skt. *anātman* 無我 wúwǒ) and emptiness (Skt. *śūnyatā* 空 kōng) of the intrinsic existence of all phenomena and (empirical) persons (*pudgala-dharma-nairātmya* 人法無我 rénfǎ wúwǒ).[127] Instead, a more sophisticated view on karma and LGBTIQ+ subjectivities reaffirms that all re-becoming in Buddhism is without sameness, *continuity without identity* wherein empirical subjectivities express karmic continuations of past possibilities; the actualization of a human subject is accompanied by a subject-contextual merit potential; while limited by various societal blueprints and scripts (such as compulsory able-bodiedness,[128] heterosexuality, and gender binarism), those scripts are in themselves impermanent, changing, and in flux; Buddhist traditions are not the dharma but are ever-changing contexts and accessories of the dharma. Where they contribute to or produce systemic suffering, changing the scripts is the meritorious activity of Buddhist compassion. In this context, a misplaced discourse of No-Self might brush over the embodied identitarian facets that are subject to systemic suffering, such as gender, gender identity, and sexual orientation, race, able-bodiedness, among others. Hence, ill-placed discourses of No-Self and emptiness will de-emphasize social justice action.[129] Such dogmatic, mystic, or normative utilizations of No-Self and emptiness as Buddhist wisdom (*prajñā*) erases the complex and embodied experiences of the oppressed and marginalized and constitutes the *spiritual bypassing* of suffering in the conditioned world (samsara).[130]

QT (as introduced in the section "Introduction: QT Meets Buddhism") is a tool for resisting harmful societal scripts and can aid the compassion (*karuṇā*)-centered, "this-worldly" (socio-samsaric) focus in Buddhist thought and practice, as exemplified in various contemporary forms of socially engaged Buddhism and "Humanistic" Buddhism (人間佛教, rén jiān fó jiào), QT, and Buddhist philosophies that oppose essentialism with regard to human identity. Judith Butler has put forward her foundational notion of *performativity*;[131] this concept organically resonates with the Buddhist philosophy of No-Self and the Buddhist notion of *pratītyasamutpāda*, the nexus of inter- and codependently arising of all conditioned reality . Similarly, as Hsiao-Lan Hu has demonstrated, Butler's concept of *sedimentation* can be made fruitful for Buddhist approaches to karma.[132] Hence both Buddhist philosophies and QT focus on the specific, "messy," complex, contextual, ever-changing, and conditioned human experiences, and interactional negotiations, or *be(com)ing and interbe(com)ing.*[133]

But QT's deconstruction and antisocial turn/nihilism as seen in the important thought of Leo Bersani and Lee Edelman can also meaningfully be transformed by the neither...nor of the Buddhist middle way and emptiness; as can QT utopianism (proposed by Michael Snediker and José Esteban Muñoz) and *disidentification* find a meaningful grounding and reconnection in Buddhist altruistic virtue ethics.[134]

REVIEW OF LITERATURE

The section "Introduction: QT Meets Buddhism" introduces QT with literature and discusses the partially overlapping fields of Buddhisms & gender and Buddhisms & sexuality, Buddhist feminism, Buddhist studies' reception of critical cultural theory (including Foucault, Derrida, Levinas, and Deleuze), and the sparse amount of Buddhist studies literature engaging with QT literature.

Previous scholarship on Buddhism and LGBT(IQ+) subjectivities include early 1990s work by José Ignacio Cabezón and Leonard Zwilling who, together with Michael Sweet, trailblazed research in Early Buddhist and Indian medical taxonomy of sexual and gender diversity.[135] However, the pioneering "doing the history of queerness in the Buddhist traditions" entailed the danger of anachronisms (as discussed in the subsection "Buddhist Views on Sex/Gender Diversity") in the case of the third sex/gender category *paṇḍaka*. Hence, literature on the *paṇḍaka* is more fully reviewed in that section.

In 1990, John Stevens authored a slim volume on Buddhism and sex aimed at a general audience.[136] L. P. N. Perera's 1993 PhD thesis on sexuality in the Pāli *vinaya* contains a chapter on "Hetero- and Homosexual Deviations and Intersexualities" and gives "a useful review of evidence on sexual practices" mixed at times with "inappropriate opinions."[137]

Bernard Faure's *The Red Thread* constitutes the first substantial scholarly monograph on Buddhism and sexuality, with a wealth of material with emphasis on East Asian (in particular, Japanese) Buddhism.[138]

Peter Harvey deals with sexuality and gender diversity in his *Introduction to Buddhist Ethics* in the chapter "Homosexuality and Other Forms of 'Queerness.'"[139] Harvey combines historical-textual sources with the discussion of contemporary practices. His analysis is limited due to a lack of detailed familiarity with non-Indic material.

Janet Gyatso's 2003 article "One Plus One Makes Three" advances scholarship into gender diversity by the careful examination of Indic and Tibetan traditions; John Powers' 2009 monograph *A Bull of a Man* revisits the Indic material for male sexualities.[140] Bee Scherer's 2016 article "Variant Dharma" addresses some of the gaps in previous literature while combining textual studies with anthropology and dharmology.[141]

The new benchmark in the field is without a doubt José Ignacio Cabezón's magnum opus of 2017, *Sexuality in Classical South Asian Buddhism*.[142]

While the study of queerness in contemporary Thai Buddhism had already been pioneered by Peter A. Jackson in the 1990s, hybrid and/or anthropological studies on queerness within global (Northern) Buddhist contexts are rare before the 2010s, but emerge then steadily.[143]

Queer academic dharmology was pioneered by Roger Corless and includes the voices of José Ignacio Cabezón, Jeffrey Hopkins, Hsiao-Lan Hu, Bee Scherer, and Robert Shore-Goss.[144] Practitioner voices are increasingly represented since the pioneering publication of the two edited volumes of *Queer Dharma*.[145] In 2019, Trans Buddhist Voices were gathered in a dedicated anthology.[146] The section "(Post)Modern Queer Buddhists and Dharmology" provides ample literature.

PRIMARY SOURCES

Relevant primary sources are mentioned in the main body of this article. They include the vast amount of (para)canonical and commentarial texts pertaining to aspects of sex/gender and sexuality/celibacy. Such sources have been thoroughly considered, for example, in the benchmark works by José Ignacio Cabezón (*Sexuality in Classical South Asian Buddhism*, for classical South Asian and Tibetan sources) and Bernard Faure (*The Red Thread*, for East Asian sources).

For example, the *vinaya* (monastic discipline) of the different Early Buddhist traditions is of particular interest. The Pāli (Sthavira-/Theravāda) *vinaya* is easily accessible in Isaline B. Horner's classic translation.[147] However, as Shayne Clarke has pointed out, the study Early Buddhist monasticism calls for a closer attention to the other five *vinayas* in Sanskrit (Mūlasarvāstivāda, fragments only), Tibetan (Toh. 1–7, Mūlasarvāstivāda), and Chinese (T. 1421–1464), such as T. 1421 (Mahīśāsaka), T. 1425 (Mahāṃghika), T. 1428 (Dharmaguptaka), T.1435 (Sarvāstivāda), and T. 1441 (Mūlasarvāstivāda).[148]

Import sources for East Asian *Mahāyāna* precepts include the precept manual section of the Chinese *Brahmajāla Sūtra* T. 1484 and its **Mahāyāna-pratimokṣa*.[149]

Among the ethical-doctrinal compendia of particular interest are the *Abhidharmakośa (-bhāṣyam)* by Vasubandhu and the relevant passages of the vast *Yogācārabhūmi-śāstra* (T. 1579), attributed to Asaṅga.[150] Relevant Tibetan Buddhist ethical literature include the *Jewel Ornament of Liberation* by Gampopa (sGam po pa).[151]

FURTHER READING

Anderson, Carol S. "Gender in Pāli Buddhist Traditions." In *The Bloomsbury Research Handbook of Indian Philosophy and Gender*. Edited by Veena R. Howard, 197–215. London: Bloomsbury, 2020.

Cabezón, José Ignacio *Sexuality in Classical South Asian Buddhism*. Somerville, MA: Wisdom, 2017.

Corless, Robert. "Towards a Queer Dharmology of Sex." *Culture and Religion* 5, no. 2 (2004): 229–243.

Faure, Bernard. *The Red Thread: Buddhist Approaches to Sexuality*. Princeton, NJ: Princeton University Press, 1998.

Gleig, Ann. "Dharma Diversity and Deep Inclusivity at the East Bay Meditation Center: From Buddhist Modernism to Buddhist Postmodernism?" *Contemporary Buddhism* 15, no. 2 (2014): 312–331.

Gyatso, Janet. "One Plus One Makes Three: Buddhist Gender, Monasticism, and the Law of the Non-Excluded Middle." *History of Religions* 43, no. 2 (2003): 89–115.

Hu, Hsiao-Lan. "Buddhism and Sexual Orientation." In *The Oxford Handbook of Contemporary Buddhism*. Edited by Michael Jerryson, 662–677. Oxford: Oxford University Press, 2017.

Jackson, Peter A. "Male Homosexuality and Transgenderism in the Thai Buddhist Tradition." In *Queer Dharma: Voices of Gay Buddhists*. Edited by Winston Leyland, 55–89. San Francisco: Gay Sunshine Press, 1998.

Kemp, Jonathan. "Queer Past, Queer Present, Queer Future." *Graduate Journal of Social Science* 6, no. 1 (2009): 3–21. http://www.gjss.org/sites/default/files/issues/chapters/papers/Journal-06-01--01-Kemp.pdf.

Langenberg, Amy Paris. "Sex and Sexuality in Buddhism: A Tetralemma." *Religion Compass* 9, no. 9 (2015): 277–286.

Leyland, Winston, ed. *Queer Dharma: Voices of Gay Buddhists*. San Francisco: Gay Sunshine Press, 1998.

Powers, John. "Chapter 3: Sex and the Single Monk." In *A Bull of a Man: Images of Masculinity, Sex and the Body in Indian Buddhism*, edited by John Powers, 67–111. Cambridge, MA: Harvard University Press, 2009.

Scherer, Bee. "Variant Dharma: Buddhist Queers, Queering Buddhisms." In *Queering Paradigms VI: Interventions, Ethics and Glocalities*. Edited by Bee Scherer, 253–273. Oxford: Peter Lang, 2016.

Williams, angel Kyodo, Rod Owens, and Jasmine Syedullah. *Radical Dharma: Talking Race, Love, and Liberation*. Berkeley, CA: North Atlantic Books, 2016.

NOTES

1. For an accessible introduction into QT, see Jonathan Kemp, "Queer Past, Queer Present, Queer Future," *Graduate Journal of Social Science* 6, no. 1 (2009): 3–21; Eve Kosofsky Sedgwick, *Epistemology of the Closet* (Berkeley: University of California Press, 1990); Judith Butler, *Bodies That Matter: On the Discursive Limits of "Sex"* (New York and London: Routledge, 1993); and David Halperin, *Saint Foucault: Toward a Gay Hagiography* (New York: Oxford University Press, 1995).
2. B[ee] Scherer, "Introduction: Queering Paradigms," in *Queering Paradigms*, ed. B[ee] Scherer (Oxford: Peter Lang, 2010), 1–6; 1–2.
3. See Eve Kosofsky Sedgwick, "Queer and Now," in *Tendencies*, ed. Eve Kosofsky Sedgwick (New York and London: Routledge, 2004), 8.
4. See Robert McRuer, *Crip Theory: Cultural Signs of Queerness and Disability* (New York: New York University Press, 2006).
5. Bee Scherer, "*Queer*Thinking Religion: Queering Religious Paradigms," *Scholar & Feminist Online* 14, no. 2 (2017).
6. For initial overviews of these fields, see, e.g., Amy Paris Langenberg, "Buddhism and Sexuality," in *The Oxford Handbook of Buddhist Ethics*, ed. Daniel Cozort and James Mark Shields (New York: Oxford University Press, 2017), 567–591; and Liz Wilson, "Buddhism and Gender," in *Buddhism in the Modern World*, ed. David L. McMahan (New York: Routledge, 2012), 257–272. See also "Review of Literature" section.
7. This is largely due to the presence of the Buddhist Constructive-Critical Reflection Unit in the AAR; in contrast, the *International Association of the History of Religion* and many national bodies continue to explicitly reject theological modes of inquiry.
8. See Rita Gross, *Buddhism after Patriarchy: A Feminist History, Analysis, and Reconstruction of Buddhism* (Albany: State University of New York Press, 1993); and Hsiao-Lan Hu, "The White Feminism in Rita Gross's Critique of Gender Identities and Reconstruction of Buddhism," in *Buddhism and Whiteness: Critical Reflections*, ed. George Yancy and Emily McRae (Lanham, MD: Lexington Books, 2019), 293–308. For the study of Buddhist nuns, the theoretical frameworks of "liberal feminism" have been critiqued and complicated by Nirmala S. Salgado in her *Buddhist Nuns and Gendered Practices: In Search of the Female Renunciant* (New York and Oxford: Oxford University Press, 2013), see, in particular, the first three chapters.
9. Hsiao-Lan Hu, *This Worldly* Nibbāna*: A Buddhist-Feminist Social Ethic for Peacemaking in the Global Community* (Albany, NY: SUNY Press, 2011).
10. Bernard Faure, *The Rhetoric of Immediacy: A Cultural Critique of Chan/Zen Buddhism* (Princeton, NJ: Princeton University Press, 1991), xi.
11. Bernard Faure, *The Red Thread: Buddhist Approaches to Sexuality* (Princeton, NJ: Princeton University Press, 1998). Faure continues this line of inquiry in *The Power of Denial: Buddhism, Gender and Purity* (Princeton, NJ: Princeton University Press, 2003).
12. For example, Adrian Konik, *Buddhism and Transgression: The Appropriation of Buddhism in the Contemporary West* (Leiden, The Netherlands: Brill, 2009); and Malcom Voyce, *Foucault, Buddhism, and Disciplinary Rules* (Oxford and New York: Routledge, 2017); Jae-seong Lee, *Postmodern Ethics, Emptiness, and Literature: Encounters between East and West* (Lanham, MD: Lexington Books, 2015); Tony See and Joff Bradley, eds., *Deleuze and Buddhism* (London: Palgrave Macmillan, 2016); Simon

Sullivan, "A Life between the Finite and Infinite: Remarks on Deleuze, Badiou and Western Buddhism," *Deleuze Studies* 8, no. 2 (2014): 256–279; Youxuan Wang, *Buddhism and Deconstruction: Towards a Comparative Semiotics* (Richmond: Curzon Press, 2001); and Jin Y. Park, ed., *Buddhism and Deconstructions* (Lanham, MD: Rowan & Littlefield, 2006).

13. Simon Gareth Smith, *Buddhism and the Postmodern: The Nature of Identity and Tradition in Contemporary Society* (PhD diss., University of Leeds, 1997); Carl Olson, *Zen and the Art of Postmodern Philosophy: Two Paths of Liberation from the Representational Mode of Thinking* (Albany: State University of New York Press, 2000); Jin Y. Park, *Buddhism and Postmodernity: Zen, Huayan, and the Possibility of Buddhist Postmodern Ethics* (Lanham, MD: Lexington Books, 2008); and Edwin Ng, *Buddhism and Cultural Studies: A Profession of Faith* (London: Palgrave Macmillan, 2016).
14. See "Review of Literature" section.
15. See "Review of Literature" section.
16. See *Saṅgīti-Sutta* DN 33 iii 230 PTS; *Sammādiṭṭhi-Sutta* MN 9 i 51; *Visudhimagga* xvii, 240–569 PTS; 三聚經 (sān jù jīng, *Discourse on the Three Groups*) DĀ (Chin) 12 (T12 [1] 229b6–7); the other three *upādānas* are clinging to views (*diṭṭhi-*), to rules & rituals (*sīlabatta-*), and to the belief in an essential Self (*attāvāda-*).
17. See Paul David Numrich, "The Problem with Sex According to Buddhism," *Dialog: A Journal of Theology* 48, no. 1 (2009): 62–73; see also Amy Paris Langenberg, "Sex and Sexuality in Buddhism: A Tetralemma," *Religion Compass* 9, no. 9 (2015): 277–286.
18. Janet Gyatso, *Being Human in a Buddhist World: An Intellectual History of Medicine in Early Modern Tibet* (New York: Columbia University Press, 2015), 34.
19. Bee Scherer, "Variant Dharma: Buddhist Queers, Queering Buddhisms," in *Queering Paradigms VI: Interventions, Ethics and Glocalities*, ed. Bee Scherer (Oxford: Peter Lang, 2016), 253–273; 259; and Alan Sponberg, "Attitudes toward Women and the Feminine in Early Buddhism," in *Buddhism, Sexuality, and Gender*, ed. José Ignacio Cabezón (Albany, NY: SUNY Press, 1992), 3–36; 20.
20. Faure, *The Red Thread*, 79; Gregory Schopen, "The Learned Monk as a Comic Figure: On Reading a Buddhist Vinaya as Indian literature," *Journal of Indian Philosophy* 35, no. 3 (2007): 201–226; and Shayne Clarke, "Locating Humour in Indian Buddhist Monastic Law Codes: A Comparative Approach," *Journal of Indian Philosophy* 37, no. 4 (2009): 311–330.
21. For an overview, see Scherer, "Variant Dharma," 262–263; for a focus on female monastics, see Carol S. Anderson, "The Agency Buddhist of Buddhist Nuns," *Buddhist Studies Review* 27, no. 1 (2010): 41–60; for fuller discussions, see John Powers, *A Bull of a Man: Images of Masculinity, Sex and the Body in Indian Buddhism* (Cambridge, MA: Harvard University Press, 2009), Ch. 3 ("Sex and the Single Monk," 67–111); and José Ignacio Cabezón, *Sexuality in Classical South Asian Buddhism* (Somerville, MA: Wisdom, 2017), Ch. 3 ("Monasticism: Just Saying No to Sex," 173–219).
22. Scherer, "Variant Dharma," 263–266.
23. On the prohibition of oral and anal sex see Vasubandhu, *Abhidharmakośabhāṣya* at 4, 74a–b (p. 244 Pradhan); on wider prohibitions of sexual acts see the discussion in Scherer, "Variant Dharma," 263–265; and *Viniścaya-saṃgrahanī* of the *Yogācārabhūmi-śāstra* T. 1579 (30) 631b14–15 (Chinese), bsTan 'gyur D4038 132b (Tibetan).
24. Cabezón, *Sexuality in Classical South Asian Buddhism*, 45–65. Interestingly, the Old Uyghur (Silk Road) Buddhist hell traditions lack detailed interest in punishments for sexual wrongdoing and appear to reflect the vaguer and more general Early Buddhist attitude to lay sexual ethics (see Scherer, "Variant Dharma," 265).
25. sGam po pa, *Thar rgyan*, p. 74, ed. Sonam Gyatso; B[ee] Scherer, "Macho Buddhism: Gender and Sexuality in the Diamond Way," *Religion and Gender* 1 (2011): 99; Taehyeon (Daehyeon) 太賢 (大賢), *Beommanggyeong gojeokgi* 梵網經古迹記 T. 1815 on the **Mahāyānapratimokṣa* of the *Brahmajāla*

Sūtra (8th CE); A. Charles Muller, *Exposition of the Sutra of Brahma's Net* (Seoul, Korea: Jogye Order of Korean Buddhism, 2012), p. 281; see Scherer, "Variant Dharma," 264.

26. Paul G. Schalow, "Kūkai and the Tradition of Male Love in Japanese Buddhism," in Cabezón, *Buddhism, Sexuality, and Gender*, 215–230; and Faure, *The Red Thread*, 233–240.
27. See Carol S. Anderson, "Gender in Pāli Buddhist Traditions," in *The Bloomsbury Research Handbook of Indian Philosophy and Gender*, ed. Veena R. Howard (London: Bloomsbury, 2020), 207–212.
28. See Michael J. Sweet and Leonard Zwilling, "The Evolution of Third-Sex Constructs in Ancient India: A Study of Ambiguity," in *Invented Identities: The Interplay of Gender, Religion and Politics in India*, ed. Julia Leslie and Mary McGee (Oxford: Oxford University Press, 2000), 99–132, 100–107.
29. See B[ee] Scherer, "Gender Transformed and Meta-gendered Enlightenment: Reading Buddhist Narratives as Paradigms of Inclusiveness," REVER 6, no. 3 (2006): 65–76; 68–69; and Scherer, "Variant Dharma," 259.
30. Janet Gyatso, "One Plus One Makes Three: Buddhist Gender, Monasticism, and the Law of the Non-Excluded Middle," *History of Religions* 43, no. 2 (2003): 89–115; 96n16.
31. See the discussion of Saṅghabhadra's *Shanjian lu piposha* 善見律毘婆沙, T. 1462, 722b10–11 in Scherer, "Variant Dharma," 258.
32. See Anderson, "Gender in Pāli Buddhist Traditions," 203–205.
33. On *paṇḍakas*, see Albrecht Welzer, "Sanskrit paṇḍá- / páṇḍaka-*," *Zeitschrift der Deutschen Morgenländischen Gesellschaft* 148 (1998): 261–276; Powers, *A Bull of a Man*, 82–85; Scherer, "Variant Dharma," 254–260; Cabezón, *Sexuality in Classical South Asian Buddhism*, 407–410; and Anderson, "Gender in Pāli Buddhist Traditions," 205–207.
34. The most common term in Chinese Buddhist texts is 黃門 huáng mén ("yellow door," after the later Han court harem area, see A. Charles Muller, "黃門," *Digital Dictionary of Buddhism* (n.d.), accessed January 18, 2020 (login as "guest," password "guest").
35. On the female *paṇḍaka* in the Pāli tradition, see Carol S. Anderson, "Defining Women's Bodies in Indian Buddhist Monastic Literature," in *Refiguring the Body: Embodiment in South Asian Religions*, ed. Karen Pechelis and Barbara Holdredge (Albany, NY: SUNY Press, 2016), 255–284; 263–265; for the Mūlasarvāstivāda tradition, see Cabezón, *Sexuality in Classical South Asian Buddhism*, 433–441.
36. Scherer, "Variant Dharma," 257.
37. Leonard Zwilling, "Homosexuality as Seen in Indian Buddhist Texts," in Cabezón, *Buddhism, Sexuality, and Gender*, 209; see the critique in Scherer, "Variant Dharma," 257–258.
38. This debate in early QT was initiated by Eve Kosofsky Sedgwick in her *Epistemology of the Closet*, in which she criticized Michel Foucault and David Halperin's views on the conceptual genealogy of "the homosexual" in the 19th century. Halperin's decisive response against historizing gender and sexualities was his *How to Do the History of Homosexuality* (Chicago: Chicago University Press, 2002).
39. Powers, *A Bull of a Man*, 82–85.
40. Cabezón, *Sexuality in Classical South Asian Buddhism*, 13.
41. See William Norman Brown, "Change of Sex as a Hindu Story Motif," *Journal of the American Oriental Society* 47 (1927): 3–24; for a short survey, see Scherer, "Gender Transformed," 70–71.
42. See Scherer, "Gender Transformed"; this in line with the orthodox Theravāda and Mahāyāna view that any woman needs to be reborn as a man first before realizing enlightenment.
43. See Scherer, "Gender Transformed"; Carol S. Anderson, "Changing Sex in Pāli Buddhist Monastic Literature," in Scherer, *Queering Paradigms VI*, 231–251; Carol S. Anderson, "Changing Sex or Changing Gender in Pāli Buddhist Literature," *Scholar & Feminist Online* 14, no. 2 (2017); and Petra Kieffer-Pülz, "Sex-Change in Buddhist Legal Literature with a Focus on the Theravāda Tradition," *ARIRIAB—Annual Report of the International Research Institute for Advanced Buddhology at Soka University* 21 (2018): 27–62.

44. Bee Scherer, "Atypical Bodies: Queer-Feminist and Buddhist Perspectives," in *Cultural History of Disability in the Modern Age*, ed. David T. Mitchell and Sharon L. Snyder (London: Bloomsbury, 2020), 19–28.
45. "Buddhist Monk Plays Suicide of LGBTQ Librarian for Laughs," *Equality Myanmar*, July 4, 2019.
46. Roger Corless, "Coming Out in the Sangha: Queer Community in American Buddhism," in *The Faces of Buddhism in America*, ed. Charles S. Prebish and Kenneth T. Tanaka (Berkeley: University of California Press, 1998), 253–263; 255.
47. See Peter A. Jackson, "Male Homosexuality and Transgenderism in the Thai Buddhist Tradition," in *Queer Dharma: Voices of Gay Buddhists*, ed. Winston Leyland (San Francisco: Gay Sunshine Press, 1998), 55–89; 65–69; Paisarn Likhitpreechakul, "Semen, Viagra and Paṇḍaka: Ancient Endocrinology and Modern Day Discrimination," *Journal of the Oxford Centre for Buddhist Studies* 3 (2012): 91–127; on the complexity of premodern and modern *kathoey* identities, see Peter A. Jackson, "Performative Genders, Perverse Desires: A Bio-History of Thailand's Same-Sex and Transgender Cultures," *Intersections: Gender, History and Culture in the Asian Context* 9 (2003); see also Megan J. Sinnott, *Toms and Dees: Transgender Identity and Female Same-Sex Relationships in Thailand* (Honolulu: University of Hawai'i Press, 2004).
48. Phra Wontham (Waradhammo) พระวรธรรม, "'ชายข้ามเพศ' บวชพระได้หรือไม่?" ["Should 'Transmen' Be Ordained or Not?"], Teenpath.net (December 13, 2016).
49. This appears to be the standard interpretation of the 1944 *Monastic Ordination (Preceptor) Code*, section 14, see, e.g., พระอธิการรัตน รตโน (บัวทอง) Phra A-thikanratana Ratano (Buathong), "การ บริหาร จัดการ การ อบรม ผู้บวช ระยะสั้น ของ คณะสงฆ์ จังหวัด อ่าง ทอง Training Management for Short-Term Ordained Monks of Sangha in Ang Thong," [in Thai] (MA diss., Mahachulalongkorn University, Bangkok, 2018), 16–17. One example is the widely publicized case of the former "Miss Tiffany Universe" winner in 2009; see Cabezón, *Sexuality in Classical South Asian Buddhism*, 532–533.
50. Phra Phayom is also known under his honorific name Phra Pisan Thamphati พระ พิศาล ธรรมพาที (see "ประวัติ พระพยอม," [*Prawat Phra Phayom*, "The History (Biography) of Phra Phayom," *Kanlayano.org*], accessed January 13, 2020); on see incident see Peter Hacker, "Buddhism Grapples with Homosexuality," 365Gay.com (July 4, 2003); see also Damien Keown, *Buddhist Ethics: A Very Short Introduction* (Oxford: Oxford University Press, 2005), 62.
51. Andrew Potts, "Thai TV Discusses Cross-Dressing Gay Buddhist Monks for First Time," *Gay Star News*, April 28, 2014; and Kongpob Areerat, "Junta to Pass Law Banning Homosexuals from Monkhood," *Prachatai*, March 10, 2015.
52. Ian MacKinnon, "Buddhist Temple Encouraging Ladyboys to Be Masculine," *The Telegraph*, July 19, 2011; Dominique Mosbergen, "Two-Faced Thailand: The Ugly Side of 'Asia's Gay Capital,'" *Huffington Post*, October 20, 2015; and Chanatip Tatiyakaroonwong, "There Is No Heaven for LGBTI Here: Torture of LGBTI in Thai Society and in the World Context," *Prachatai*, June 27, 2019.
53. See "European Buddhists Call for a Ban on 'Conversion Therapy,'" *European Buddhist Union*, February 28, 2018.
54. See, e.g., Chaiyot Yongcharoenchai, "Young Monks Struggle with Gender Issues," *Bangkok Post*, May 26, 2013; Gaspar Ruiz-Canela, "The Rebel Buddhist Monk Who Supports Abortion and LGBT Rights," *EFE* English edition, January 16, 2020.
55. See Phra Wontham, "'ชายข้ามเพศ' บวชพระได้หรือไม่?"
56. Ajahn Brahm, "Gay Marriage, Why Not?," YouTube video, March 21, 2012; the British Theravāda monk Ajahn Brahm (b. 1951) is abbot of a Ajahn Chah อาจารย์ ชา (Achan Cha, *Bodhiñāṇa Thera* / Phothiyan Then โพธิญาณ เถร) Thai Forest Sangha lineage monastery in Western Australia; in 2009, he presided over the ordination of four bhikkhunīs (full nuns) and was consequently excommunicated from this sangha lineage (with headquarters in Wat Nong Paphong วัดหนองป่าพง, Ubon Ratchathani); and Ajahn Sujato, "Why Buddhists Should Support Marriage Equality," *Sujato's Blog*, March 21, 2012.

57. "About Us," *Rainbodhi*, accessed January 15, 2020.
58. Hsuan Hua 宣化, "Avoid Defying Natural Creation" (n.d., according to web.archive.org, first web-archived on July 1, 2011); see also Corless, "Coming Out in the Sangha," 255.
59. See Richard Madsen, "East Asian Buddhist Ethics," in *The Oxford Handbook of Buddhist Ethics*, ed. Daniel Cozort and James Mark Shields (New York: Oxford University Press, 2017), 279–291; 287–288.
60. See Hsiao-Lan Hu, "Buddhism and Sexual Orientation," in *The Oxford Handbook of Contemporary Buddhism*, ed. Michael Jerryson (Oxford: Oxford University Press, 2017), 662–677; Hu's important essay develops largely in dialogue with Chao-Hwei's thought.
61. See Hu, "Buddhism and Sexual Orientation," 664 and 676 (references); on conducting same-sex marriage see p. 663. One of Chao-Hwei's books is available in English: Zhao Hui, *Buddhist Normative Ethics* (Taoyuan, Taiwan: Dharma-Dhatu Publication, 2014).
62. See the testimonial by Laurie Arron, "On Love and Being Gay," *Mindfulness Bell* 48 (Summer 2008), 32–33.
63. See Jeff Wilson, "'All Beings Are Equally Embraced by Amida Buddha': Jodo Shinshu Buddhism and Same-Sex Marriage in the United States," *Journal of Global Buddhism* 13 (2012): 31–59; 37.
64. Wilson, "All Beings," 39.
65. See Thea Rae Maggard, "Queering Trans(theo)phobia: A Comparative Analysis between Jōdo Shinshū Buddhism and Roman Catholicism on Transgender Issues," *Religión e Incidencia Pública: Revista de Investigación de GEMRIP* 2 (2014): 109–136.
66. See, e.g., Helen Nianias, "Heard the One About Miss Universe and the Buddhist Monk?," *The Times*, February 2, 2017; Revd. Nishimura featured also in the popular *Queer Eye* TV franchise, in *Queer Eye: We're in Japan*, "Ep. 2: Crazy in Love" (Netflix, US release: November 1, 2019).
67. Corless, "Coming Out in the Sangha," 256; see also, e.g., Sharon E. Smith and Sally R. Munt, "The Dragon King's Daughter: Gender and Sexuality in Western Buddhist New Religious Movements," *Theology & Sexuality* 16, no. 3 (2010), 229–260.
68. "Courageous Freedom: SGI-USA's LGBTQ Community," *Soka-Gakkai International—USA*, May 19, 2016.
69. A video of the Dalai Lama's 1997 remarks was released in 2018, see Ben P. Joffe, "White Robes, Matted Hair: Tibetan Tantric Householders, Moral Sexuality, and the Ambiguities of Esoteric Buddhist Expertise in Exile" (PhD diss., University of Colorado, 2019), 319–324; see also the autoethnographic vignette in Cabezón, *Sexuality in Classical South Asian Buddhism*, 1–5; see further, Dennis Conkin, "The Dalai Lama and Gay Love," in Leyland, *Queer Dharma*, 351–356; Peter Harvey, *An Introduction to Buddhist Ethics: Foundations, Values and Issues* (Cambridge, UK: Cambridge University Press, 2000), 411–434; and James William Coleman, *The New Buddhism: The Western Transformation of an Ancient Tradition* (Oxford: Oxford University Press 2001), 164–165.
70. Shamar Rinpoche, *Creating a Transparent Democracy: A New Model* (New Delhi: New Age Books, 2007), 23.
71. See Coleman, *The New Buddhism*, 165.
72. See Scherer, "Macho Buddhism," 96 and 99–100; and B[ee] Scherer, "Globalizing Tibetan Buddhism: Modernism and Neo-Orthodoxy in Contemporary Karma bKa' brgyud Organizations," *Contemporary Buddhism* 13, no. 1 (2012): 125–137; 126–128.
73. Michael C. Hyman, "Practicing Together as a Gay Couple," in Leyland, *Queer Dharma*, 127–147; 136.
74. "Queer Dharma," *Shambhala Times*, accessed January 13, 2020.
75. Georg Feuerstein, *Holy Madness: Spirituality, Crazy-Wise Teachers, and Enlightenment*, rev. and exp. ed. (Prescott, AZ: Hohm Press, [1990] 2006), 95–96; Sandra Bell, "Scandals in Emerging Western Buddhism," in *Westward Dharma: Buddhism beyond Asia*, ed. Charles S. Prebish and Martin Baumann (Berkeley: University of California Press, 2002), 232–235; and "Report to the Community on the

Wickwire Holm Claims Investigation into Allegations of Sexual Misconduct," Shambhala Interim Board, February 3, 2019. However, in December 2019, the board already cleared the path back to power for the Sakyong, deeply disappointing the victims of sexual abuse; in consequence, the bestselling author and nun Pema Chödrön resigned from Shambhala as an "Acharya" (senior teacher) of Shambhala (Ani Pema aka Pema Chödrön, "Letter to the Acharyas and Shambhala Board Members," January 14, 2020).

76. Karmapa Ogyen Tinley is one of the two Seventeenth Karmapa hierarchs/claimants of the Karma Kagyu branch of Tibetan Buddhism. Ogyen Tinley was recognized by Karma Kagyu regent Tai Situpa and gained the backing of the Fourteenth Dalai Lama; the other Seventeenth Karmapa, Trinley Thaye Dorje (phrin las mtha' yas rdo rje, 1983–) was recognized by the senior regent, the Fourteenth Shamarpa. In October 2018, the two Karmapas met in mutual respect and embarked on the path to healing the divided Karma Kagyu school, see Gabriel Lefferts, "Karmapas Unite," *Tricycle*, October 11, 2018; see also, e.g., "The 17th Gyalwang Karmapa Expresses Support for LGBTQ Relationships," *Tibetan Equality Project*, November 1, 2017; on the 12th Gyalwang Drukpa see Ross Murray, "Spiritual Leader Visits GLAAD, Shares 'Live to Love' Philosophy," *GLAAD blog*, June 25, 2014; and on Dzongsar Khyentse see "Dzongsar Khyentse Rinpoche Urges Respect for LGBTQ People," *Lion's Roar*, February 6, 2015.
77. See Joffe, "White Robes, Matted Hair," 335–337; and Gyatso, *Being Human*, 33–34.
78. See Joffe, "White Robes, Matted Hair," 346 and 519 (note 230).
79. Gyatso, "One Plus One Makes Three," 100–101; and the more detailed discussion in Gyatso, *Being Human*, 321–341.
80. On the term, see Cabezón, *Sexuality in Classical South Asian Buddhism*, 531 (note 1342).
81. See Joffe, "White Robes, Matted Hair," 519 (note 229); see also Joffe's field notes on contemporary gay sexual culture, 315–317.
82. Dallas J. Baker, "Return of the Eunuch: Gender Disobedience as a Path to Awakening in Buddhist Tantra," *Postcripts* 4, no. 3 (2008), 339–366.
83. See Joffe, "White Robes, Matted Hair," 519 (note 229); the interview can be found on Facebook.
84. See Scherer, "Macho Buddhism"; and Bee Scherer, "Trans-European Adaptations in the Diamond Way: Negotiating Public Opinions on Homosexuality in Russia and in the U.K.," *ONLINE—Journal of Religions on the Internet* (December 6, 2014): 103–125.
85. See "Review of Literature" section.
86. Wendy Cadge, "Lesbian, Gay, and Bisexual Buddhist Practitioners," in *Gay Religion*, ed. Scott Thumma and Edward R. Gray (Walnut Creek, CA: Altamira Press, 2005), 139–151; 143–144; Roger Corless, "Gay Buddhist Fellowship," in *Engaged Buddhism in the West*, ed. Christopher S. Queen (Boston: Wisdom, 2000), 269–279; and "About," Gay Buddhist Fellowship, accessed January 13, 2020.
87. Roshi Dorsey himself died of AIDS-related complications; see Cadge, "Lesbian, Gay, and Bisexual Buddhist Practitioners," 144–145.
88. Justin Whitaker, "Intersections of Gender, Identity, and Buddhism: An Interview with LGBTIQ Meditation Teacher La Sarmiento," *Patheos*, February 23, 2015.
89. GLOBAL (Gay and Lesbian Organization of Buddhist Activists for Liberation) Sangha; see "Announcements," *Mindfulness Bell* 7 (1992), accessed January 15, 2020.
90. See Andrew Kam-Tuck Yip and Sharon Smith, "Queerness and Sangha: Exploring Buddhist Lives," in *Queer Spiritual Spaces: Sexuality and Sacred Places*, ed. Kath Browne et al. (Aldershot, UK: Ashgate, 2010), 111–138; 127–131.
91. See Pagan Kennedy, *The First Man-Made Man: The Story of Two Sex Changes, One Love Affair, and a Twentieth-Century Medical Revolution* (New York: Bloomsbury, 2008), 155; and Cabezón, *Sexuality in Classical South Asian Buddhism*, 535–536.

92. Michael Vermeulen, "The Rise of Rainbow Dharma: Buddhism on Sexual Diversity and Same-Sex Marriage," in *Compilation of Articles on Freedom of Religion or Belief and Sexuality*, ed. UN Special Rapporteur on Freedom of Religion or Belief (Geneva: UN OHCHR, 2017), 27–41; 38.
93. See Coleman, *The New Buddhism*, 171; and Robert Bluck, *British Buddhism: Teachings, Practice and Development* (London: Routledge, 2006), 155–156.
94. "A Statement by Urgyen Sangharakshita," *Triratna News*, January 4, 2017; "Triratna: How Are We Doing Now? A Triratna Interkula Survey to Assess How the Triratna Community Feels Now About Allegations of Past Misconduct—Survey Results and Report," *Interkula*, October 30, 2018; and Jamie Doward, "Buddhist, Teacher, Predator: Dark Secrets of the Triratna Guru," *The Guardian*, July 21, 2019.
95. See, for example, Ann Gleig, *American Dharma: Buddhism beyond Modernity* (New Haven, CT: Yale University Press, 2019).
96. Naomi R. Goldenberg, "The Category of Religion in the Technology of Governance: An Argument for Understanding Religions as Vestigial States," in *Religion as a Category of Governance and Sovereignty*, ed. Trevor Stack, Naomi Goldenberg, and Timothy Fitzgerald (Leiden: Brill, 2015), 280–292.
97. Scherer, "*Queer*Thinking Religion."
98. Phra Wontham (Waradhammo) พระวรธรรม, *Neo-Buddhism* blogspot (in Thai), accessed March 23, 2020; see Waradhammo's "blogger profile and statement" (in Thai), accessed March 23, 2020.
99. See Arnika Fuhrmann, *Ghostly Desires: Queer Sexuality and Vernacular Buddhism in Contemporary Thai Cinema* (Durham, NC: Duke University Press, 2016).
100. Bee Scherer, "流転輪廻という混沌を体現する—クィア仏教的「解放の神学」を目指して" (Embodying the Messiness of Saṃsāra: Towards Queer Buddhist "Liberation Theology"). Translated into Japanese with an introduction and notes by Kanae Kawamoto, "川本佳苗," サンガジャパン 32 (2019): 211–234.
101. See Cathryn Bailey, "Embracing the Icon: The Feminist Potential of the Trans Bodhisattva, Kuan Yin," *Hypatia* 24, no. 3 (2009): 178–196.
102. Independently, Taiwanese American LGBTIQ Buddhist scholar Hsiao-Lan Hu has developed an outline of Avalokiteśvara-based queer-intersectional Engaged Buddhism, see Hu, "Buddhism and Sexual Orientation," 669–673.
103. See Yip and Smith, "Queerness and Sangha," 137.
104. See B[ee] Scherer, "Queer as Kagyu: Negotiating Dissident Identities in Neo-Orthodox Buddhist Spaces," in *Queering Paradigms, Vol. 3: Bio-Politics, Place, and Representations*, ed. Kathleen O'Mara and Liz Morrish (Oxford: Peter Lang, 2013), 145–155.
105. See Ann Gleig, "Dharma Diversity and Deep Inclusivity at the East Bay Meditation Center: From Buddhist Modernism to Buddhist Postmodernism?," *Contemporary Buddhism* 15, no. 2 (2014): 312–3312; 318; see also the testimony of a young transgender SG-I member ("Courageous Freedom," *Soka-Gakkai International—USA*).
106. See Catriona Reed, "Coming Out Whole," *Tricycle*, June 19, 2019; and Emily DeMaioNewton, "A Transgender Buddhist Trailblazer 20+ Years Later: Interview with Caitriona Reed," *Tricycle*, June 19, 2019.
107. Whitaker, "Intersections of Gender, Identity, and Buddhism"; see also Hu, "Buddhism and Sexual Orientation," 663 and 673.
108. See, e.g., Larry Yang, "Toward Freedom and Enlightenment Queerly: LGBTQ and Dharma," *Huffington Post*, January 8, 2012. Yang focuses on training spiritual leadership within communities of color and LGBTQI communities. In 2016, Young was San Francisco Pride Parade's Community Grand Marshall (see Larry Yang, "Awakening Together: About Larry," accessed January 13, 2020).
109. See Zenju Earthlyn Manuel, *The Way of Tenderness: Awakening through Race, Sexuality, and Gender* (Boston: Wisdom, 2015); see the discussion in Hu, "Buddhism and Sexual Orientation," 665, 669, 673.

110. See angel Kyodo Williams, Rod Owens, and Jasmine Syedullah, *Radical Dharma: Talking Race, Love, and Liberation* (Berkeley, CA: North Atlantic Books, 2016); and *Radical Dharma*, accessed January 13, 2020.
111. See the collection of articles with links in Haleigh Atwood, "LGBTQ Buddhists: Teachings, Profiles, and Conversations," *Lions Roar*, June 13, 2019; see also, "Category: LGBT," *Tricycle*, January 13, 2020; and *Mindfulness Bell* (*Community of Interbeing*, Thich Nhat Hanh); and posts tagged "Queer Dharma," *Shambhala Times* (accessed January 13, 2020).
112. "Mission Statement," *Transbuddhists*, accessed January 13, 2020.
113. The first LGBT workshop Sakyadhita hosted took place at the conference from December 28, 2009 to January 2, 2010, in Vietnam. The pioneer of these workshops was the German lesbian/genderqueer Tibetan Buddhist (and dharma rapper) Rotraut Jampa Wurst; see also her testimonial: Rotraut Jampa Wurst, "Negotiating Spiritual Violence in the LGBT Community," in *Negotiating Spiritual Violence in the Queer Community*, ed. Jeff Sapp and Paul Chamness Iida (Charlotte, NC: Information Age, 2019), 146.
114. "Ranbow Sangha," EBU, accessed January 13, 2020. The network is facilitated by Michael Vermeulen, who also reported on sexual minorities in Buddhist cultures at a UN conference in Geneva, June 2016; see "Sexual Minorities and the Buddhist Spiritual Path," EBU, United Nations, Geneva, June 2016; and Vermeulen, "The Rise of Rainbow Dharma."
115. "About Us," Rainbodhi, accessed January 15, 2020.
116. "Coming Out, Coming Home—Coming Together—LGBTIQ," EIAB, accessed January 13, 2020.
117. See Scherer, "Variant Dharma," 267–270.
118. On "Liberation Hermeneutics," see Bee Scherer, "Translating the Lotus Sūtra into Social Action: Hermeneutics and Public Dharmology," *Buddhist–Christian Studies* 39 (2019): 147–168 and particularly 149–152. The circular argumentation regarding sexual ethical conduct is discussed in Cabezón, *Sexuality in Classical South Asian Buddhism*, 525–526.
119. Michel Foucault denotes processes that change the relation to one's own subjectivity as "technologies of the self" (see Michel Foucault, "Technologies of the Self," in *Technologies of the Self*, ed. Luther Martin, Huck Butman, and Patrick Hutton (Amherst: University of Massachusetts Press, 1988), 16–49.
120. Scherer, "Atypical Bodies."
121. On Guanyin see Bailey, "Embracing the Icon"; Hu, "Buddhism and Sexual Orientation," 669–673; on tantra see also queer practitioner perspectives such as Baker, "Return of the Eunuch"; Nick Dickinson, "The Path of Freedom: Gender in the Tantric Tradition of Arya Tara," in Sapp and Iida, *Negotiating Spiritual Violence*, 73–78; see also Jeffrey Hopkins, "The Compatibility of Reason and Orgasm in Tibetan Buddhism: Reflections on Sexual Violence and Homophobia," in Leyland, *Queer Dharma*, 335–347; 346–347; and Scherer, "Macho Buddhism," 103.
122. Jeffrey Hopkins, *Sex, Orgasm, and the Mind of Clear Light: The Sixty-Four Arts of Gay Male Love* (Berkeley, CA: North Atlantic Books, 1998).
123. See Joffe, "White Robes, Matted Hair," 352 and 520 (note 238).
124. Looking at No-Self and emptiness is a main feature in Global Northern queer dharmology, relevant to Buddhist practitioners (see Gleig, "Dharma Diversity," 316 and 318), and in the thought of Roger Corless, José Ignacio Cabezón, and Jeffrey Hopkins (see the overview in Langenberg, "Buddhism and Sexuality," 588); see also Scherer, "Atypical Bodies," 27–28.
125. Ven. Chao-Hwei, "「同志」豈必承負罪軛?" Tóngzhì'qǐ bì chéng fù zuì è? [Why must LGBT people be stigmatized?] *Hóngshì shuāngyuèkān* 弘誓雙月刊 83 (October 2006), accessed January 15, 2020; see the discussion in Hu, "Buddhism and Sexual Orientation," 665. Independently, Bee Scherer has made similar arguments as a Buddhist scholar-teacher, e.g., in a lecture in Patan (Nepal), January 2, 2013, documented in Scherer, "Variant Dharma," 268; see also Scherer, "Atypical Bodies," 28.

126. Phra Wontham (Waradhammo) พระวรธรรม, "เกย์ – เลสเบี้ยน วิบากกรรมของใคร" ["Gays and Lesbians—Who Has the Bad Karma?"], สะดือไกวัลย์: คนนอก (Navel[gazing] *Solely* [=*Skt.* kevala]—Outsider] *Blog* (December 20, 2006), accessed March 21, 2020.
127. This terminology has developed in the tradition of the *Laṇkāvatārasūtra* (T. 670 & 672) and in the *Saṃdhinirmocanasūtra* (T. 677).
128. McRuer, *Crip Theory* (see "Introduction," 1–32).
129. See the arguments put forward by Larry Yang (Gleig, "Dharma Diversity," 324); Zenju Manuel (Hu, "Buddhism and Sexual Orientation," 673); and Scherer, "Variant Dharma," 268.
130. See Robert Augustus Masters, *Spiritual Bypassing: When Spirituality Disconnects Us from What Really Matters* (Berkeley, CA: North Atlantic Books, 2010). Examples of spiritual bypassing in Buddhist Feminism can be found Rita Gross's work; see also, Hu, "The White Feminism," 297–298.
131. Butler, *Bodies That Matter.*
132. Hu, *This Worldly* Nibbāna, Ch. 4 ("Person-in-*Kammic*-Network," 91–125).
133. "Interbeing" is the term used by Thich Nhat Hanh for his mindfulness and socially engaged take on the *pratītyasamutpāda*; see Thich Nhat Hanh, *Interbeing: Fourteen Guidelines for Engaged Buddhism*, 3rd ed. (Berkeley, CA: Parallax, 1998).
134. Leo Bersani, *Homos* (Cambridge, MA: Harvard University Press, 2006); Lee Edelman, *No Future: Queer Theory and the Death Drive* (Durham, NC: Duke University Press, 2004); J[ack] Halberstam, "The Anti-Social Turn in Queer Studies," *Graduate Journal of Social Science* 5, no. 2 (2008): 140–156; Michael Snediker, *Queer Optimism: Lyric Personhood and Other Felicitous Persuasions* (Minneapolis: University of Minnesota Press, 2009); José Esteban Muñoz, *Cruising Utopia: The Then and There of Queer Futurity* (New York: New York University Press, 2009); José Esteban Muñoz, *Disidentifications Queers of Color and the Performance of Politics* (Minneapolis: University of Minnesota Press, 2015); Scherer, "Variant Dharma," 269–270; and Scherer, "Atypical Bodies," 28.
135. José Ignacio Cabezón, "Homosexuality and Buddhism," in *Homosexuality and World Religions*, ed. Arlene Swidler (Valley Forge, PA: Trinity Press International, 1993), 81–101; Zwilling, "Homosexuality as Seen in Indian Buddhist Texts"; Michael J. Sweet and Leonard Zwilling, "The First Medicalization: The Taxonomy and Etiology of Queerness in Classical Indian Medicine," *Journal of the History of Sexuality* 3, no. 4 (1993): 590–607; and Sweet and Zwilling, "The Evolution of Third-Sex Constructs."
136. John Stevens, *Lust for Enlightenment: Buddhism and Sex* (Boston: Shambhala, 1990).
137. L. P. N. Perera, *Sexuality in Ancient India: A Study Based on the Pali Vinayapitaka* (Kelaniya, Sri Lanka: Postgraduate Institute of Pali and Buddhist Studies, 1993), Ch. VII, 110–163; and Harvey, *An Introduction to Buddhist Ethics*, 72 (note 5).
138. Faure, *The Red Thread*, see chapters entitled "Buddhist Homosexualities" (Ch. 5, 207–240) and "Boys to Men" (Ch. 6, 241–278).
139. Harvey, *An Introduction to Buddhist Ethics*, 411–433.
140. Powers, *A Bull of a Man.*
141. Scherer, "Variant Dharma."
142. The responses to this monumental work include a *Review Symposium*, ed. Carol S. Anderson, *Religion* 49, no. 4 (2019): 717–751, with contributions by Carol S. Anderson, Sarah Jacoby, Amy Paris Langenberg, and a response by José Ignacio Cabezón. A more in-depth treatment of specifically female sexualities in South Asian Buddhism (and beyond) remains a desideratum; see Amy Paris Langenberg, "Reading against the Grain: Female Sexuality in Classical South Asian Buddhism," *Religion* 49, no. 4 (2019): 728–734.
143. Jackson, "Male Homosexuality"; see also Peter A. Jackson, *Dear Uncle Go: Male Homosexuality in Thailand* (San Francisco: Bua Luang Books, 1995); Peter A. Jackson and Gerard Sullivan, eds., *Lady Boys, Tom Boys, Rent Boys: Male and Female Homosexualities in Contemporary Thailand* (New York:

Haworth, 1999); Jackson, "Performative Genders, Perverse Desires"; Cadge, "Lesbian, Gay, and Bisexual Buddhist Practitioners"; Corless, "Coming Out in the Sangha"; Roger Corless, "Hermeneutics and Dharmology: Finding an American Buddhist Voice," in *Buddhist Theology: Critical Reflections by Contemporary Buddhist Scholars*, ed. Roger Jackson and John Makransky (London: Curzon, 2000), 95–107; Corless, "Gay Buddhist Fellowship"; Ann Gleig, "Queering Buddhism or Buddhist De-Queering? Reflecting on Differences amongst Western LGBTQI Buddhists and the Limits of Liberal Convert Buddhism," *Theology & Sexuality* 18, no. 3 (2012): 198–214; Gleig, "Dharma Diversity"; Scherer, "Macho Buddhism"; Scherer, "Queer as Kagyu"; Scherer, "Trans-European Adaptations"; Smith and Munt, "The Dragon King's Daughter"; and Yip and Smith, "Queerness and Sangha."

144. Robert Corless, "Towards a Queer Dharmology of Sex," *Culture and Religion* 5, no. 2 (2004): 229–243; see also Roger Corless, "Analogue Consciousness Isn't Just for Faeries: Healing the Disjunction between Theory and Practice," in *American Buddhism as a Way of Life*, ed. Garry Storhoff and John Whalen-Bridge (Albany, NY: SUNY Press, 2010), 183–194; José Ignacio Cabezón, "Thinking through Texts: Toward a Critical Buddhist Theology of Sexuality," Frederic P. Lenz Distinguished Lecture, Naropa University, Boulder, Colorado, September 23, 2008. See also the relevant sections in José Ignacio Cabezón, *Sexuality in Classical South Asian Buddhism*; Hopkins, "The Compatibility of Reason"; Hopkins, *Sex, Orgasm, and the Mind of Clear Light*; Hu, "Buddhism and Sexual Orientation"; Scherer, "Gender Transformed"; Scherer, "Variant Dharma"; Scherer, "Atypical Bodies"; and Robert Shore-Goss, "Queer Buddhists: Re-visiting Sexual Gender Fluidity," in *Queer Religion, Vol. 1: Homosexuality in Modern Religious History*, ed. Donald L. Boisvert and Jay Emerson Johnson (Santa Barbara, CA: Praeger ABC-Clio, 2012), 25–49.

145. Leyland, *Queer Dharma* and Winston Leyland, *Queer Dharma: Voices of Gay Buddhists. Vol. 2* (San Francisco: Gay Sunshine Press, 2000).

146. Kevin Manders and Elizabeth Marston, eds., *Transcending: Trans Buddhist Voices* (Berkeley, CA: North Atlantic Books, 2019).

147. Hermann Oldenberg, ed., *The Vinaya Piṭakaṃ: One of the Principal Buddhist Holy Scriptures in the Pāli Language*, 5 vols. (London: The Pali Text Society, 1879–1883); and I. B. Horner, trans., *The Book of the Discipline*, 6 vols. (London: The Pali Text Society, 1938–1966). Complementary translations of passages have been added by Petra Kieffer-Pülz, "Pārājika 1 and Saṅghādisesa 1: Hitherto Untranslated Passages from the Vinayapiṭaka of the Theravādins," *Traditional South Asian Medicine* 6 (2001): 62–84.

148. Shayne Clarke, "Monks Who Have Sex: *Pārājika* Penance in Indian Buddhist Monasticisms," *Journal of Indian Philosophy* 37, no. 1 (2009): 31–39. For an overview about the Sanskrit fragments, see Jin-il Chung, "Sanskrit-Fragmente des sogenannten Daśādhyāya-vinaya aus Zentralasien: eine vorläufige Auflistung," in *Sanskrit-Texte aus dem buddhistischen Kanon: Neuentdeckungen und Neueditionen IV* (SWBTTF 9), ed. Jin-il Chung, Claus Vogel, and Klaus Wille (Göttingen, Germany: Vandenhoeck & Ruprecht, 2002), 77–104; and Damchö Diana Finnegan, "'For the Sake of Women, Too': Ethics and Gender in the Narratives of the Mūlasarvāstivāda Vinaya" (PhD diss., University of Wisconsin, Madison, 2009), 27–28.

"Toh." refers to the number in the *Tōhoku* catalog based on the Derge (sde dge) edition of the Tibetan Buddhist canon (Kanjur, bka' 'gyur): Hakuju Ui, Munetada Suzuki, Yenshō Kanakura, and Tōkan Tada, eds., *A Complete Catalogue of the Tibetan Buddhist Canons: (Bkah-hgyur and Bstan-Hgyur)* (Sendai, Japan: Tōhoku Imperial University, 1934).

"T." refers to the text number in the *Taishō* edition of the Chinese canon: Junjirō Takakusu and Kaikyoku Watanabe, eds., *Taishō Shinshū Daizōkyō*, 100 vols. (Tōkyō: Daizō Shuppan Company, 1924–1934).

149. Translation with the authoritative commentary *Beommanggyeong gojeokgi* 梵網經古迹記 T. 1815 by the eighth-century Korean scholar Taehyeon (Daehyeon) 太賢 (大賢): A. Charles Muller, *Exposition of the Sutra of Brahma's Net* (Seoul, Korea: Jogye Order of Korean Buddhism, 2012).

150. The Sanskrit was edited by Prahlad Pradhan (Patna: K. P. Jayaswal Research Institute, 1967); the Tibetan translation can be found in the Kanjur, Toh. 4090. Translation by Louis de La Vallée (in French); English translation of de La Vallée's French by Leo M. Pruden, Vasubandhu, *Abhidharmakośabhāṣyam*, 4 vols. (Berkeley, CA: Asian Humanities Press, 1991); and *Yogācārabhūmi-śāstra* 瑜伽師地論 (*Yú qié shī dì lùn* T. 1579, translated into Chinese by Xuanzang 玄奘 from 646–648 CE; Tibetan translation Toh. 4035–4041.
151. Edition: Gampopa Sonam Rinchen, *The Jewel Ornament of Liberation* (dam chos yid bzhin gyi nor bu thar pa rin po che'i rgyan), ed. Khenpo Sonam Gyatso (Benares: Central Institute for Higher Tibetan Studies, 1999). Translation: Gampopa, *Jewel Ornament of Liberation: The Wish-Fulfilling Gem of the Noble Teachings*, trans. Khenpo Konchog Gyaltsen Rinpoche (Ithaca, NY: Snow Lion, 1998).

Bee Scherer

R

THE REINCARNATION SYSTEM IN CENTRAL ASIAN BUDDHISM

SEVEN CENTURIES OF REINCARNATION TRADITIONS AND INSTITUTIONS

In 1289, the renowned *tantrika* Orgyenpa Rinchen Pel (O rgyan pa rin chen dpal, 1229–1309) was sitting in his meditation room, recalling a vivid dream of his deceased teacher, Karma Pakshi (Karma Pak shi, 1204–1283), when a monk entered and told him a potter, his wife, and their son had arrived.[1] "They think their boy is the Karmapa (Karma pa)," he said, "and [want to ask you] if this is true."[2] Orgyenpa developed a plan to test the boy. He gathered his entire religious community and told them to "make a high throne [at the front of the assembly]. For if it is the Karmapa, he will not fear to sit on it."

When the five-year-old boy arrived, he purposefully strolled down the aisle and went to climb onto the throne, but his small body made its steps difficult to ascend. To reach the throne, he had to hook his long sleeve to it and pull himself up. The audience giggled. The boy regained his composure and announced to all, "I am the one renowned as the Karmapa." Then to Orgyenpa, "I taught you the dharma; now you need to teach me." He then stopped for a second, remembering something. Karma Pakshi and the first Karmapa, Düsum Khyenpa (Dus gsum mkhyen pa, 1110–1193), had both been known as "the black hat" gurus. The young boy Orgyenpa was enthroning, Rangjung Dorjé (Rang byung rdo rje, 1284–1339), would become "the third to wear the black hat crown."[3] He needed the hat, so he addressed Orgyenpa again, "Oh, and in my past life, didn't I give you some things? Didn't I give you my hat?" When he received the hat, he placed it on his head, only to have his small body confuse him again. The hat slipped over his small head and covered half his face. The audience could no longer hold in their laughter and dissolved into fits of giggles.

Rangjung Dorjé was the first child enthroned as a reincarnate, and the Karmapas ("those from Karma Monastery") became the first and longest-lived lineage of rebirths. Building on his predecessors' work and reputations, he developed a model of reincarnation that was copied across the Tibetan Plateau, the Himalaya, and the Eurasian steppe. A few centuries later, another lineage of reincarnates, the Dalai Lamas—the Karmapas' competitors—came to rule Tibet and exercise influence across the Himalaya and Central Asia. Their grip on power was always tenuous, however, and they lost most of it in 1959, when the Fourteenth Dalai Lama, Tenzin Gyatso (Bstan 'dzin rgya mtsho, 1935–), along with the Sixteenth Karmapa, Rangjung Rigpé Dorjé (Rang byung rigs pa'i rdo rje, 1924–1981), fled into exile after the Chinese communist invasion of their homeland. By this stage, Tibetan, Himalayan, and Central Asian religion and politics had been thoroughly entwined with the reincarnation body rosaries. After the Dalai Lama's exile, he and other reincarnates developed a large international following.

While Rangjung Dorjé's enthronement story gives us insight into the reincarnation tradition's beginnings, an early-21st-century controversy about several comments by the Fourteenth Dalai Lama provides insights into the reincarnation lineage's trajectory. The controversy began in 2007 when the Dalai Lama half-joked that his next reincarnation could be "a female, a foreigner, or even a bee." He later added that if it were a woman, "she must be more attractive (than a man)."[4] Western media and the Chinese government both criticized him. Western media interpreted his response as sexist rather than reading it—as it was most probably intended—as a commentary on the global objectification of women. The Chinese government was enraged. Their spokesperson, Zhu Qeiqun, claimed the Dalai Lama had been "irresponsible and disrespectful" about the tradition, and only the Chinese Communist Party—which denounces rebirth as superstition—could choose the next Dalai Lama or any reincarnate.[5]

This article will outline the reincarnation tradition's journey from southern Tibet in 1289 to 21st-century social media and geopolitics. It describes the precedents its early advocates used and how they blended two distinct phenomena—rebirths and deity emanations—to create reincarnation lineages. It explains how the tradition's religious, cultural, and social projects developed first, and how their political influence built on these. It then outlines this political influence by tracing the stories of the Karmapas and the Dalai Lamas. It concludes by examining the role that recognized reincarnates play today, the reverence in which many across the region still hold them, and the social, legal, and political problems these embodied lineages face.

PRECEDENTS

Precedents in India. Reincarnation institutions may have been a singular Tibetan innovation, but they were built on many precedents. Tibetan Buddhist culture frowned on noniterative innovation; to call something "invented" or "self-made" (Tib. *rang bso*) was an insult, so those promoting the reincarnation traditions leaned heavily on earlier Buddhist ideas and practices from India and Tibet.[6]

The idea of rebirth predated Buddhism in ancient India.[7] By the historical buddha's time, around the 5th century BCE, it was, for many, a social fact, linked with *karma-phala,* cause and result, and *samsara,* wandering through existence. In this worldview, a being's positive or negative actions (*karma*) of mind, speech, and body resulted (*phala*) in good and bad rebirths (*samsara*). The buddha's innovation was to insist there was no ultimate, singular, independent self (*ātman*) that propelled this wandering, but rather a constructed person that arose in dependence on an ever-changing collection of five karma-created aggregates (Skt. *pañca skandhāḥ*): form, feelings, perceptions, volitions, and consciousness. The buddha explained that deluded beings experienced suffering because they mistook these aggregates for a self. If they realized no-self, they could attain *nirvana,* or cessation, and become arhats.[8]

Early Buddhist traditions included discourses on rebirth and the storytelling tradition of the buddha's past lives. These stories were included within two genres, *jātaka* and *avadāna.* These morality tales focused on the exploits of the buddha-to-be on the path to awakening and became one of the traditions' most popular elements.[9] Later, Buddhist philosophers developed more complex ideas about the mechanisms that led to rebirth. In the *Abhidharmakośabhāṣya,* Vasubandhu enumerated a categorical description of this process. The five aggregates dissolved at death, were reborn in an intermediate state as scent-eating spirits, known as *gandharva,* and were then propelled by their karma and aggregates to take on a new body.[10]

Mahāyāna Buddhism also provided several concepts that were fundamental to the reincarnation tradition. Mahāyāna Buddhism's central protagonists are the bodhisattva (Tib. *byang chub sems dpa'*), who put aside their *nirvana* to aid beings, and thus create the karma to realize the union of form and emptiness, becoming a fully awakened buddha rather than an arhat.[11] On this path, bodhisattvas develop the ability to control future rebirths and create multiple, benevolent emanations.[12] Buddhist philosophers described these manifestations as *nirmāṇa* ("created things") and *vikurvita* ("assumed shapes").[13] High-level bodhisattvas and buddhas manifested in a celestial form, and even created entire realms, pure lands in which they guided beings. Practitioners developed strong bonds with these deities and prayed to be reborn in their realms.[14]

Another element of the Mahāyāna tradition that played a crucial role in Tibet's reincarnation tradition was the idea of the buddhas' "three bodies" (Skt. *trikāya*; Tib. *sku gsum*), which developed in the 4th century. The three bodies are (a) *dharmakāya* (Tib. *chos sku*), the "dharma body," buddhas' reality; (b) *sambhogakāya* (Tib. *long sku*), the "enjoyment body," buddhas' subtlest forms; and (c) *nirmāṇakāya* (Tib. *sprul sku*), "creation body," buddhas' ordinary forms.[15] Bodhisattvas strove to realize the *dharmakāya* for all beings. The power of this wish created the subtle, celestial *sambhogakāya* and the less-subtle, earthy *nirmāṇakāya.*

Vajrayāna Buddhism, which developed between the 5th and 11th centuries CE (in India), added further conceptual strata to rebirth and emanations. In Vajrayāna, each practitioner was empowered by their guru to first visualize in *sambhogakāya* form, and eventually through habituation with this image, see this form as their most subtle form. Through this seeing, they loosen their sense of self and realize the *dharmakāya* in one lifetime. To hasten realization, they trained in guru yoga, which meant seeing their guru as the *dharmakāya* in essence, the non-dual *sambhogakāya* in meditation, and the *nirmāṇakāya* in postmeditation states.[16] The bond between gurus and students passed from life to life. In Tibet, as many lineage gurus were also recognized as the reincarnation of tantric gurus, these tantric lineages became entwined with the reincarnation lineage.

Precedents in Tibet. Tibetan Buddhists venerated their Indic forebears but adapted their teachings to Tibetan cultures, traditions, and environments. They aligned tantric lineages with already existing patrilineal genealogies or "bone lineages" (Tib. *rus rgyus*) and used the same words—*trülwa* (*sprul ba*) and *trül* (*'phrul*)—to describe both bodhisattvas and kingly magical power, translating *nirmāṇakāya* as *trülku* (*sprul sku*).[17]

As a new group of Vajrayāna teachings was introduced to Tibet from India from the 10th century onward, tantric yogis began referring to their gurus as *trülku* or *nirmāṇakāya*. Several yogis also claimed the ability to manifest (*trül, sprul*) or emanate (*namtrül, rnam 'phrul*).[18] And the practice of *powa* (Skt. *saṃkrānti*; Tib. *'pho ba*) or the transference of consciousness, which was primarily associated with the Kagyü (Bka' rgyud) school, became closely associated with a yogin's ability to direct their consciousness at the moment of death. The biography of one of the Kagyü founders, Marpa Lotsawa(Mar pa lo tswa ba, 1012–1097), includes the story of his son Darma Dodé (Dar ma mdo sde), who when he died transferred his consciousness into a pigeon and then flew to India, where he re-transferred himself into a young Brahman boy's corpse and grew up to be tantric adept Tiphupa.[19]

While new tantra yogis developed these practices, those who maintained traditions from Tibet's imperial period (ca. 618–842), the Nyingmapa (Rnying ma pa, "old ones"), reformed their tradition through discovering previously concealed texts—physical and visionary—said to have been left for the rebirths of the students of the 8th-century *tantrika* Padmasambhava. These treasure texts recast Padmasambhava as the central figure in Tibet's taming (rather than conversion to Buddhism), as only he could subdue its unruly gods, spirits, and humans.[20] What is more, some of these found texts included stories about the special relationship between the bodhisattva of compassion, Avalokiteśvara (Tib. Spyan ras gsigs), and Tibet. Avalokiteśvara, the texts explained, had promised to help Tibet, and therefore continually manifested there, including as its first emperor, Songtsen Gampo (Srong btsan sgam po, 569–ca. 649).[21]

EVOLUTION

Emanations and Rebirths. Rebirth and emanations had become prominent themes in Tibetan religious life, but they were approached in various ways. The Kadampas formed a school founded by students of the Indian guru Atiśa (982–1054), who lived in Tibet for several years at the end of his life. They were a monastic school that focused on the gradual path, and one of their primary texts was Āryaśura's *Garland of Jātaka* (*Jātakamālā*). They did not merely study the stories of the buddha's life, however: They expanded on them by telling the past-life stories (Tib. *skye rim*, pronounced *kyérim*) of their founder, Atiśa's primary student, Dromtön Gyelwa Jungné ('Brom ston rgyal ba 'byung gnas, 1004–1064).[22] The first recorded recognition of a rebirth occurred in the same tradition around the same time. Jayülpa (Bya yul pa, 1075–1138), a Kadam teacher, recognized Gyergom Tsultrim Senggé (Gyer sgom tshul khrims senge, 1090–1171) as his teacher's rebirth, using the term *yangsi* (Tib. *yang srid*, "became again") to describe him. As in Rangjung Dorjé's recognition, Jayülpa returned the predecessor's hat to the young reincarnate.[23]

In the next century, the Kadampas began to combine these rebirth stories with emanation stories. They were keen Avalokiteśvara practitioners and began to claim that Dromtön had been the emanation of the bodhisattva of compassion. They were not the only lineage to claim emanation status for their hierarchs around the same time. The Sakya lineage, which descended through the family of the *tantrika* Sachen Künga Nyingpo (Sa chen kun dga' snying po, 1092–1158), claimed he was Avalokiteśvara's emanation, and the Sakya began to associate their abbots with the celestial bodhisattva of wisdom, Mañjuśrī.[24] And while the new schools promoted their gurus as emanations of celestial bodhisattvas, within the Nyingma's treasure tradition, the visionary Nyangrel Nyima Özer (1124–1194) filled the narrative gap between his 8th-century life as Guru Rinpoche's student and his 12th-century existence by listing a series of concatenating past lives. This was the first time a body rosary—albeit a chronologically difficult one—had been created.[25]

The Early Karmapas. After the well-known teacher Gampopa Sönam Rinchen (sgam po pa bsod nams rin chen, 1079–1153) combined Kagyü and Kadam practices into one lineage, his students further developed the rebirth and reincarnation themes in their writing. Two of these students, Düsum Khyenpa Pakmodrupa (Dus gsum mkhyen pa phag mo gru pa, 1110–1170) and the monk who would become known as the first Karmapa, Düsum Khyenpa (Dus gsum mkhyen pa 1110–1193), wrote so extensively about their past, present, and future lives that they were given the title "Düsum khyenpa" (Tib. *dus gsum mkhyen pa*), "knower of the three times." Like the Kadam, they called their collections of past-life stories *kyérim* (*skye rim*), and their stories' cosmographical spread rivaled that of the buddha's *jātaka*. Their past lives had been lived across the Buddhist cosmos, through eons, in various bodies. They also recorded their multiple current lives and plans for future emanations.[26]

Several years after Düsum Khyenpa's death, his grand-student, Pomdrakpa (Spom brag pa, 1170–1249), recognized a young aristocrat that lived near one of Düsum Khyenpa's three monasteries, Karma Monastery, as his rebirth. The young boy became known as Karmapa, the person from Karma, and, later in life, as Karma Pakshi. "Pakshi" was the Tibetan transliteration of the Mongolian word *bagshi*, meaning respected teacher, and Karma Pakshi received this name after he became guru to two Mongolian emperors, Kübilai Khan (1215–1294), when he was still a prince, and his older brother Möngké Khan (1209–1259).[27]

Karma Pakshi repaired and renovated Düsum Khyenpa's three monasteries: Karma, Kampo Nénang in southern Kham, and Tsurpu near Lhasa. He used the wealth he acquired from the Mongol courts to build large statues that made Tsurpu a pilgrimage site.[28] He wore a black hat that connected him with Düsum Khyenpa. He wrote a multilife autobiography—a "liberation story" or *namthar* (Tib. *rnam thar*) rather than a *kyerim*—combining his past and present life stories. Within this somewhat convoluted text, he includes memories of past lives as an Indian king, an anti-Mongol general, Indian *mahāsiddas*, Padmasambhava's student Nup Sanggyé (Gnubs sangs rgyas ye shes, 9th century), Marpa's grand-student Réchungpa Dorjé Drak (Ras chung rdo rje grags pa, 1085–1161), and Düsum Khyenpa.[29] Like Düsum Khyenpa, he claimed to emanate and wrote of his present and future manifestations. His decision to gift

Orgyenpa his black hat was also pivotal to the Karmapa body rosary's development. By this time, Orgyenpa had already recognized the rebirths of his teacher Götsangpa (Rgod tshang pa, 1189–1258) and Götsangpa's consort, Drowa Zangmo's ('Gro ba bzang po, 12th century) rebirth.[30]

Rangjung Dorjé, as the third Karmapa, developed multiple strategies to solidify the Karmapa reincarnation lineage. Unlike the second Karmapa, he was born poor, and his recognition was his only social standing. He wrote liberation stories of both previous Karmapas and weaved their life stories into a more extensive collection of Kagyü lineage biographies.[31] This collection was built on the already-popular genre of lineage prayers and was an early example of the new "golden rosaries" (Tib. *gser phreng*) biographical collection.[32] To establish the Karmapa rebirths as powerful and consistent, he blended the two ideas of manifestation and rebirth into one narrative. He portrayed the Karmapa consciousness as emanations of both Avalokiteśvara and the sixth, future buddha, Siṁha, but also stressed that they would take one primary rebirth at a time in Tibet. This central rebirth could become the mainstay of a tantric lineage and the basis for a reincarnation institution.[33]

He gave a detailed description of his consciousness's journey between Karma Pakshi's death and his birth.[34] This journey included a detour into a child's corpse, which had to be aborted when the child's parents thought he had become a zombie (Tib. *ro lang*).[35] He also wrote an extensive autobiography, edited and expanded the Tibetan version of the buddha's *jātaka tales,* and studied Buddhist traditions of fetal development.[36] Along with his literary output, he added to Tsurpu's and Karma's treasures, even though Karma Pakshi's family still controlled them.[37] He created a series of retreat centers in southern Tibet in sites associated with the lives of Padmasambhava and the Kagyü hero Milarepa, thus interlinking the Karmapas' stories with his heroes' lives, and through these adventures created the impression that he, like his heroes, could control the "forces that were active within human life."[38] He used the name "Karmapa" and wore the black hat. He was the first Karmapa to have the name "Dorjé," and all since him have carried it.

But along with this institution-building, Rangjung Dorjé's poetry also spoke frankly about the downside of life as a reincarnate. As a child, he wrote of his intense loneliness when he moved from Orgyenpa's monastery to Tsurpu.[39] Later, he wrote of his disgust for politics and explained his attempts to escape from the Mongol Yuan dynasty's two capital cities, Dadu (Beijing) and Shangdu (Xanadu).[40] He would not be the last reincarnate to find himself lonely and trapped.

Proliferation of Reincarnation Lineages. After Rangjung Dorjé's death, the Karma Kagyü lineage established several more reincarnation lineages. Khachö Wangpo (Mkha' spyod dbang po, 1350–1405) was recognized as the rebirth of the Karmapa's primary student, Dragpa Sengge (Grags pa seng ge 1284–1349), and his reincarnation lineage became the Sharmapas, wearers of the red hats.[41] For centuries, the Sharmapas and Karmapas acted as each other's teachers. Later, they created the Tai Situ lineage. The first of this line was Chökyi Gyeltsen (Chos kyi rgyal mtshan, 1377–1448), a member of Karma Pakshi's family. Until that point, Tsurpu and Karma Monasteries had been run by Karma Pakshi's family rather than the Karmapas or other reincarnates.[42] From Chökyi Gyeltsen's time onward, reincarnates—mostly from prestigious families—ran the monasteries.[43]

The charisma associated with the reincarnates, their ability to attract offerings, and their links to powerful families made this new tradition popular. It spread from the Karma Kagyü to the other Kagyü, Kadam, and Nyingma lineages. Each reincarnation institution adapted the Karmapas' model. The Karmapas were said to recognize themselves in that each Karmapa gave instructions for his next rebirth before he died. But the Karmapas recognized other Karma Kagyü reincarnates.[44] Other teachers left instructions for their next rebirth or faced a certain way when they died. Following Rangjung Dorjé's writing on fetal development, trained search parties would usually begin the search a year after a teacher died. They examined dreams, consulted oracles and astrologers, and tested the children with past-life memory tests when they met them.

Over time, the reincarnate lineages developed their estates, called *labrang* (Tib. *bla rang*), that managed their wealth. The *labrangs* were associated with monasteries but operated separately from them. The influence of the *labrang* depended on the inherited power and charisma of the reincarnates, and as reincarnation lineages proliferated, this varied.[45] The oldest lineages were the most prestigious, but those with powerful backers or a particularly charismatic member could become famous quickly.[46]

Although the reincarnation lineages proliferated quickly, there was little development in the tradition's doctrinal basis after Rangjung Dorjé. But as an increasing number of them were Vajrayāna teachers whose students called them *trülku*, this descriptor began to stick.[47]

STATES AND REINCARNATES

Reincarnates Take Their Place in Tibetan Society and Politics. Although the reincarnation tradition and its institutions started as a sociocultural phenomenon, its protagonists quickly influenced politics. After the Tibetan Empire's demise, influential families and associate monasteries organized Tibetan politics. During Karma Pakshi's life, the Mongols incorporated Tibet into their empire by creating allegiances with these family-monasteries' hierarchs. The Mongol rulers developed a special relationship with Sakya Monastery, and its leaders played a crucial role in Tibet's administration. Chögyal Pakpa (Chos rgyal 'phags pa, 1235–1280), recognized as an emanation of Mañjuśrī, was the most influential Sakya leader. He became Kübilai Khan's guru when Karma Pakshi left for Mongké Khan's court, and rose with his student; when Kübilai became Great Khan after Mongké, Pakpa became his state preceptor and the head of Tibet's administration.[48]

However, the Sakyapas were not the only Tibetan lineage to enjoy the patronage of Mongol Khans and princes. As the Karmapas' star rose, so did the Mongols' interest in them. Karma Pakshi played a dangerous game in moving from Kübilai's court to Mongké's capital, but managed to survive.[49] Rangjung Dorjé was summoned to the Mongol capitals later in life. The court may have invited him because they saw him as an alternative ruler to the strife-ridden Sakyapas, but this was not their only reason for summoning him.[50] The court summoned holders of esoteric knowledge from across the empire so that they could use this knowledge to predict and deflect hazards, such as earthquakes, floods, and military defeats, and procure sacred substances for them.[51] In Rangjung Dorjé's case, they were particularly interested in his ability to produce "long-life water" (Tib. *tshe chu*). After Rangjung Dorjé's death, his rebirth, Rölpé Dorjé (Rol pa'i rdo rje, 1340–1383), was invited to court specifically because he was

Rangjung Dorjé's rebirth. This was the court's first official recognition of the Karmapas' body rosary.[52]

The reincarnates' perceived other-worldly power meant they had a complex relationship with polities, from local governments to empires. In the reincarnates' worldview, a view that permeates their biographies and poetry, they had access to realms and powers the state could not influence and were, therefore, at least the rulers' equals. This complex relationship is evident in records of the visit by the Fifth Karmapa, Dézhin Shekpa (De bzhin gshegs pa, 1384–1415), to the newly established Ming dynasty court in 1407. Emperor Yongle (1360–1424) invited him to conduct a ritual for his deceased father, the Ming dynasty's founder, Hongwu (1328–1398). During the visit, Yongle reportedly offered to invade Tibet, set Dézhin Shekpa up as its king, and destroy Tibet's other lineages. Dézhin Shekpa rejected this offer, stating that it meant Yongle had misunderstood his teachings, but he left Nanjing with a trove of personal wealth and possibly a new black hat.[53]

After this, the Ming dynasty retreated from Tibetan politics, but the reincarnates' political roles increased. In theory, reincarnates could be recognized from any strata of society. Rangjung Dorjé, for example, was a child of landless potters. But during the 15th and 16th centuries, reincarnates were increasingly recognized among aristocratic families from central Tibet. This fed into the growing tensions between central Tibet's two largest provinces, Ü and Tsang, tensions that were exacerbated by sectarianism. Tsang remained a Karma Kagyü stronghold, and the Karmapas and Sharmapas advised its rulers. But a reformist Kadam group, the Geluk, founded by Tsongkhapa Lozang Drakpa (Tsong kha pa blo bzang grags pa, 1357–1419), was gaining influence around Lhasa, where they had established three monasteries: Ganden, Sera, and Drepung. Despite receiving ordination from the fourth Karmapa, Tsongkhapa was critical of the reincarnate model and refused to have his rebirth recognized, but he was recognized as an emanation of Mañjuśrī.[54] His reticence slowed rather than stopped the Geluk's establishment of reincarnate institutions. The first lineage they established was the Dalai Lamas.

The Dalai Lamas. Like the Karmapas, the Dalai Lama lineage is a lineage of rebirths and a series of Avalokiteśvara's emanations. The first of the line was Tsongkhapa's student, Gendün Drup (Dge 'dun grub pa, 1391–1474), who founded Tashilhunpo Monastery near Shigatse in 1447. Gendün Drup was not considered the lineage's originator until his rebirth, Gendün Gyatso (Dge 'dun rgya mtsho, 1476–1542), was recognized and enthroned at Tashilhunpo in 1487. Early in Gendün Gyatso's life, the Gelukpas' future was uncertain as to the Tsang kings, Karma Kagyü supporters were ascendant. But later in his life, thanks to the patronage of the Pakmodru ruler, Ngawang Trashi Drakpa (Ngag dbang bkra shis grags pa, r. 1499–1564), the Gelukpas' situation improved, and Gendün Gyatso became the abbot of Drepung Monastery. Ngawang Trashi Drakpa gifted Gendün Gyatso his residence at Drepung, and Gendün Gyatso renamed it the Ganden Podrang, "Tuṣita Palace."[55] The Dalai Lamas' government would be named after this residence.

Gendün Gyatso's rebirth, Sönam Gyatso (Bsod nams rgya mtsho, 1543–1588), was born into a family with strong ties to the Pakmodru. He was ordained as abbot of Drepung as a three-year-old and as an abbot of nearby Sera at fifteen. But his most significant contribution to the Dalai Lama reincarnation lineage and the Geluk was his successful conversion of several

Mongol rulers, including the Tümed Mongol leader, Altan Khan (1507–1582). At their first meeting, Altan Khan gave Sönam Gyatso the Mongolian title *ghaikhamsigh vcir-a dar-a say-in cogh-tu buyan-tu dalai*, which means "wonderful vajra holder, good, brilliant, commendable ocean." It was shortened to Dalai Lama. When they met, Sönam Gyatso evoked the precedent of Chögyal Pakpa and Kübilai Khan's relationship. Altan Khan then allowed the Geluk to proselytize successfully among his community.[56]

The Tümed–Geluk relationship was strengthened when Altan Khan's grandnephew, Yönten Gyatso (Yon tan rgya mtsho, 1589–1616), was recognized as Sönam Gyatso's rebirth. This recognition led to an increase in the number of pilgrims to Lhasa, a transfer of Mongol wealth to the Dalai Lama *labrang*, and the further spread of the Geluk tradition in Mongol domains.[57] The Geluk's success among the Mongols came at the expense of the other Tibetan schools, including the Kagyü and Sakya, and this influenced Tibetan politics. In reaction to the growing threat of a Geluk–Tümed alliance, the king of Tsang, Karma Tseten (Karma tshe brtan, d.1599), delayed the search for the Fifth Dalai Lama, relenting only after pressure from the Pakmodru rulers.[58]

When he was finally granted permission, the Fourth Dalai Lama's tutor, Lobzang Chokyi Gyeltsen (Chos skyid rgyal mtshan, 1570–1662), tasked with finding the new Dalai Lama, faced another dilemma: there were several candidates for the rebirth. To fix the stalemate, he and other senior monks traveled to the Kadampas' spiritual home, Reting Monastery. In front of its Jowo Jampel Dorjé (Jo bo 'jam dpal rdo rje) statue, they wrote the candidates' names on pieces of paper, placed them in dough balls, and drew lots.[59] The child whose name was picked came from an aristocratic family that claimed descent from the Tibetan emperors, were Nyingma practitioners, and lived in a fortress, Tagtse, in the Yarlung valley. They were also opponents of the Tsang king. Despite this, he was enthroned and named Ngawang Lozang Gyatso (Ngag dbang blo bzang rgya mtsho, 1617–1682).

The Great Fifth. At Drepung, Ngawang Lozang Gyatso maintained his familial commitment to the Nyingma school and led the Geluk. Some Geluk monks were unhappy with this, and another of the candidates for Dalai Lama, Dragpa Gyaltsen (Grags pa rgyal mtshan, 1619–1655), came to rival him for influence. After Dragpa Gyaltsen died in mysterious circumstances, his remains were said to make noise within his reliquary and had to be consigned to the river. Some of his followers blamed Ngawang Lozang Gyatso. Many would come to believe that his ghost was mistaken for the sectarian deity Dorjé Shugden (Rdo rje shugs ldan), whose propitiation is still controversial today.[60]

After this challenging start, Ngawang Lobsang Gyatso became history's most influential Dalai Lama, the "Great Fifth." Following the established script for Dalai Lamas, he took novice ordination young, studied throughout his teens, and received full ordination in 1638.[61] Just before he received this ordination, Gushri Khan (1582–1655), a Khoshot Mongol leader, arrived near Lhasa with around eight hundred soldiers. In the tradition of Altan and Kubilai Khan, Gushri Khan became Ngawang Lobsang Gyatso's patron.[62] He then demonstrated this patronage by invading the Beri Kingdom in nearby Kham, which Ngawang Lobsang Gyatso described as Bönpo or non-Buddhist, then moved on to Tsang. Ngawang Lobsang Gyatso declared horror at this invasion, but as it led to the Tsang king's demise and the exiling of the tenth Karmapa, Choying Dorjé (Chos dbying rdo rje, 1604–1674), he benefited from it immensely. Gushri Khan declared himself "King of Tibet" after this win, but he appointed the Dalai Lama as head of its religious affairs and the Dalai Lama's regent or *desi* (Tib. *sde srid*), Sönam Chöpel (Bsod nams chos dpal, 17th century), as head of secular affairs.[63] With this governmental structure, the regent could take responsibility for state actions, such as war, that the Dalai Lamas' monastic vows prevented them from performing.

Following the war, Ngawang Lobsang Gyatso spent decades consolidating the Dalai Lama institution and its rule of central Tibet. He recognized his tutor, Lobzang Chokyi Gyeltsen (Blo bzang chos skyid rgyal mtshan, 1570–1662), as the Fourth Paṇchen Lama, a lineage he traced to Tsongkhapa's primary student Khedrup Jé (Mkhas grub rje, 1385–1438), and declared him an emanation of the celestial Buddha Amitabha. The Paṇchen Lamas then took over the running of Tashilhunpo Monastery in Tsang.[64] Ngawang Lobsang Gyatso claimed the Dalai Lamas were emanations of Avalokiteśvara and created a list of their previous lives that included Songtsen Gampo, Dromtön, the Sakya hierarch Sachen Künga Nyingpo, and Tai Situ Jangchup Gyeltsen (Tai Situ Byang chub rgyal mtshan, 1302–1364), who ruled central Tibet after the Mongol Empire collapsed.[65] It did not include the Karmapas or other Kagyü lineages that claimed an association with the celestial bodhisattva. In the *Song of the Queen of Spring*, he rewrote Tibetan history to appear guided by the Dalai Lamas' previous emanations and to create precedents for his ascension.[66] He also composed an extensive autobiography.[67] Along with his literary outputs, he refurbished Lhasa's Jokhang Temple and began constructing a large building on nearby Marpori Hill, among the ruins of Songtsen Gampo's palace. He called this building the Potala, after Avalokiteśvara's Pure Land.[68]

To further strengthen his political position, he made allegiances with other Central Asian polities, including its rising power, the Manchu, who had established the Qing dynasty and extended their rule into China. In 1653, he visited Emperor Shunzi (r. 1643–1661) in Beijing and recognized him as an emanation of Mañjuśrī.[69] According to his biography, his meeting with the emperor established another guru–patron relationship (Tib. *chos yon*) between himself and a Central Asian ruler.[70]

On the Tibetan Plateau, he practiced uneven benevolence toward other lineages. His armies unsuccessfully invaded the recently established Drukpa Kagyü Kingdom of Bhutan several times.[71] He outlawed the Jonang tradition, converted their monasteries to Geluk, and prohibited the teaching of their signature doctrine on "other emptiness" (Tib. *gzhan stong*).[72] But he showed benevolence toward the Karma Kagyü, allowing the tenth Karmapa to return from exile and the Karmapas to re-establish themselves at Tsurpu and Karma.[73] Despite pressure from some Gelukpas, he continued to practice the Nyingma tradition, even revealing his own treasure text, and established Nyingma practices at his private monastery, Namgyel.[74]

By the time of his death in 1682, he had wrested political power from Gushri Khan's son, Tenzin Dalai Khan (Bstan 'dzin dalai khan, r. 1671–1696 or 1703), and appointed a young regent, Sangyé Gyatso (Sang rgyas rgya mtsho, 1653–1705), to do his bidding. His political philosophy began as "the union of religion and politics" (Tib. *chos srid zung 'brel*), in which the two systems would inform each other, and he worked to export this principle, along with the guru–patron relationship, into Central Asia.[75] By the end of his life, however, he described the Dalai Lama's role as "the holder of religion and politics" (*chos srid lugs gnyis ldan*) and assumed what Schwieger calls "a kind of sacred kingship."[76] As Schwieger also notes and events were to prove, it is uncertain whether his patrons, the Mongols and Manchus, understood his role in the same way.

The Dalai Lamas and the Qing Empire. Sangyé Gyatso kept the Fifth Dalai Lama's death a secret for almost fifteen years, ostensibly to finish the Potala's construction. During this time, he had the Dalai Lama's body mummified and placed in an elaborate stupa. He then followed established protocols to find the next Dalai Lama, asking for predictions from gurus and oracles, and sending a visionary to examine Lhamö Latso Lake in southern Tibet. According to these prognostications, the next Dalai Lama was born in Mönyul, near Bhutan on Tibet's southern borderlands. He was named Tsangyang Gyatso (Tshangs dbyangs rgya mtsho, 1683–1706) and kept under house arrest in south Tibet until the Fifth Dalai Lama's death was revealed in 1697.[77]

Tsangyang Gyatso found Lhasa in political turmoil. Gushri Khan's grandson, Lhazang Khan (Lha bzang Khan, 1677–1717), and the new Manchu Qing emperor Kangxi (r. 1661–1722) were vying for power, and Sangyé Gyatso had been struggling to remain in control. Tsangyang Gyatso did not make Sangyé Gyatso's task easier. He was very different from his predecessor. He returned his novice vows, liked wine, women, and song, and showed no interest in politics.[78] Neither the Geluk establishment nor his Mongol and Manchu patrons were impressed, but the public loved him. In 1705, Lhazang Khan had Sangyé Gyasto killed and took control of Lhasa. A year later, he arrested Tsangyang Gyatso, installed another boy, Ngawang Yeshe Gyatso, as the Sixth Dalai Lama, and sent Tsangyang Gyatso to Beijing. Tsangyang Gyatso died on the way, probably through foul play.[79] These actions made Lhazang Khan deeply unpopular and turned Tsangyang Gyatso into a legend. A story that he escaped his Mongol escort and roamed the countryside persisted. Poems attributed to him were collected into two texts still sung across Tibet and translated into multiple languages.[80]

Unrest continued in Lhasa. The Dzungar Mongols, the Khoshots' rivals, arrived in 1717, killed Lhazang Khan, and established a new government with Geluk support. Then the Qing dislodged the Dzungar on their second attempt and made Tibet a Qing protectorate. They also delivered the Dalai Lama, Kalzang Gyatso (Skal bzang rgya mtsho, 1709–1757), and set up a new Tibetan government in which he would be advised by a governing council, the Kashag (*bka' shag*).[81] Still, the unrest continued. In 1727, the Dzungar returned to defend Kalzang Gyatso in a civil war against the Qing-backed prime minister Polhané (Pho lha nas, 1689–1747). The emperor sent an army that overpowered the Dzungar and sent Kalzang Gyatso into exile in Kham. He was in 1735 allowed to return to Lhasa, but not to power.[82] A few decades later, the tables turned again. Polhané's son Gyurmé Namgyel (Gyur med rnam rgyal, d. 1750) invited the Dzungar back to fight the Qing without Kalzang Gyatso's support. When the Qing regained control, they returned Kalzang Gyatso to power. He died seven years later. By then, the Qing had helped establish a series of high-ranked, *khutuγtu* reincarnate lineages that could act as the Dalai and Paṇchen Lama's regents in their interregnums. They also began sending Manchu high officials, ambans, to represent them in Lhasa.[83]

The Eighth Dalai Lama, Jampel Gyatso ('Jam dpal rgya mtsho, 1758–1804), was a student of the charismatic Sixth Paṇchen Lama, Lobzang Pelden Yeshe (Blo bzang dpal ldan ye shes, 1737–1780), and uninterested in politics. After decades of resisting pressure to rule Tibet, he ruled for a short period in the 1770s, before Tibet experienced yet another crisis and he deemed himself unable to negotiate it. This was a crisis of state and the reincarnate systems' authority. It began when the Sixth Paṇchen Lama died from smallpox in Beijing, and his half-brother, the Tenth Sharmarpa, Chödrub Gyatso (Chos grub rgya mtsho, 1741/1742–1792), was angry that he did not receive an inheritance from his half-brother's *labrang*. The Sharmapa went on pilgrimage to Nepal, where he was accused of encouraging the newly formed Gurkha Kingdom to invade Tibet. The Gurkhas invaded twice, in 1788 and 1791. After the first invasion, they extracted a large indemnity from the Tibetans. During the second, they sacked Tashilhunpo and angered the Qing emperor, who sent a large force that defeated them. After peace talks, the Gurkhas blamed the entire incident on the Tenth Sharmarpa, who died in mysterious circumstances.[84]

The Qianlong emperor blamed the whole event on the concentration of reincarnates within aristocratic families, and he blamed this on the corruption of the oracles who guided their searches.[85] In 1792, he produced a *Discourse on Lamas* (Ch. *Lama Shuo*), in which he ruled that senior reincarnates within the Geluk should not come from aristocratic families, and they should be chosen by drawing lots from a Golden Urn (Ch. *jinping*; Tib. *gser 'bum*), which he placed in the Jokhang Temple in Lhasa. There were precedents for the Golden Urn in the reincarnate tradition; the Fifth Dalai Lama, for example, had been chosen by drawing lots. But the reaction to the Golden Urn among the Geluk and Tibetan elites was mixed. As Oidtmann has shown, although there was some resistance, many Gelukpas also embraced it.[86] Perhaps part of the reason for Geluk's support was Qianlong's partiality toward them. Another reason the Geluk hierarchs may have adopted the Golden Urn is because it gave them a new technology with which to increase their reincarnate numbers. Oidtmann says that between 1792 and 1911 approximately eighty reincarnations in Tibet and Mongolia were identified using the Golden Urn ritual. Among them, twenty-six were only reborn once, an increase of 23 percent.[87] The emperor's and the Geluk's influence in other spheres is less evident.[88] Even though they confiscated Sharmapa's monastery, Yangpachen, and banned him from reincarnating, the Karma Kagyü kept secretly finding his reincarnations.[89]

Qing influence and interest in Tibet ebbed and flowed over the next century. The Dalai Lama's influence also declined. The Ninth, Tenth, Eleventh, and Twelfth Dalai Lamas died young, and there were rumors they had been poisoned to maintain their regents' rule.[90] Despite adopting the Golden Urn's usage to install other reincarnates in line with Qing orders, there was a resistance to use them for the Dalai Lamas' recognition, and their search parties continued to rely on signs, visions, and oracles to find the rebirths.

By the 19th century, reincarnation lineages had developed a loose hierarchy. Like the Dalai Lamas and Karmapas, some were considered fully awakened buddhas or high-level bodhisattvas. Other lineages were considered merely able to guide their consciousness between lives.[91] But the boundaries between these categories were blurry. Charismatic rebirths could transform a common lineage's reputation, and highly influential lineages could lose their shine over several low-key rebirths.

Other Polities, Other Lineages. Although most scholarship of reincarnation politics has concentrated—for understandable reasons—on the relationship between the Dalai Lamas, the Mongols, and the Manchus, these were not the only state-sponsored or politically and socially influential reincarnate lineages. The Geluk reincarnates' political influence had spread geographically, beyond Tibet, other schools were influential in the Himalaya, and one female line challenged the otherwise overwhelmingly male and patriarchal culture of the reincarnate institutions.

As in Tibet, most Mongol reincarnates were found within aristocratic families, many of which relied on their descent from Chinggis Khan.[92] The Mongol Jebtsundamba Khutuγtu, also known as Bogd Gegeen, was the third most influential reincarnate after the Dalai and Paṇchen Lamas. The first of this lineage, Zanabazar (1635–1723), was the son of the Tüshit Khan, Gombodorj (1698–1701), and was identified as the Tibetan Jonangpa scholar Tāranātha's reincarnation.[93] After an anti-Qing rebellion in the mid-18th century, Qianlong declared that—as with the Dalai and Paṇchen Lamas—future Jebtsundampa Khutuγtu could not be aristocrats.[94]

The rise of reincarnates also profoundly affected the region between Outer Mongolia and central Tibet, Inner Mongolia and Amdo. As Inner Mongolia was close to Beijing, the powerful Geluk Changkya Khutuγtu reincarnation lineage, advisers to the Qing emperors in Beijing, established its summer residence there.[95] Amdo also became a Geluk stronghold, and after reincarnation institutions were established there in the 17th century, its monasteries and reincarnation lineages proliferated.[96] Geluk influence in the region also strengthened the Dalai Lamas' power there, bringing it closer into the Tibetan sphere.[97]

The Samding Dorjé Pakmo lineage, Tibet's most influential female reincarnation lineage, also played an important role. Tibet's history is replete with influential women practitioners and aristocrats, but most of them were not recognized as reincarnates, and this system was and is intensely patriarchal. No other female lineages possessed anything like the power of the Samding Dorjé Pakmo. This lineage began in the 15th century when a princess of Gungthang, a small southern Tibetan kingdom, became a renunciant and developed a reputation as an emanation of the deity Dorjé Pagmo (Skt. Vajravārāhī). This deity continued to emanate female beings, and the Samding Dorjé Pakmo lineage acquired a symbolic role in central Tibetan politics. Its reincarnates acted as advisors and allies first to the Karmapas and later to the Dalai and Paṇchen Lamas.[98]

The southern and eastern boundaries of the Vajrayāna Buddhist world also stood apart from the Geluk–Qing power matrix. In these regions, the Geluk was one among several schools, and there was a collage of independent and semi-independent kingdoms. The most prominent of these was Bhutan, founded in 1625 by Ngawang Namgyel (Ngag dbang rnam rgyal, 1594–1651), who had been one of two rival candidates for the rebirth of the Fourth Drukchen Rinpoche, Pema Karpo (Padma dkar po, 1527–1592), another lineage associated with Avalokiteśvara.[99] Ngawang Namgyel was widely respected, but the Tsang king refused to endorse him, so he migrated to the southern Himalaya. In the Kingdom of Bhutan, his lineage was known as Shabdrung (*zhabs drung*), and they headed a government with two deputies: a regent, Druk Desi, and a monastic leader, Jé Khenpo. After Ngawang Namgyel's passing, the two deputies' power increased. To further reduce the Shabdrung's power, they began finding his multiple emanations, representing his body, speech, and mind. This meant no one reincarnate held all his power. In 1907, one of Bhutan's ministers, Urgyen Wangchuk (O rgyan dbang phyug, 1862–1926), established a Bhutanese monarchy and exiled the Shabdrung reincarnates.[100] But the Je Khenpo remains Bhutan's highest religious authority and is always a reincarnate.

Other Vajyayāna Buddhist schools continued to support reincarnation lineages in their strongholds. The Sakya considered all members of the Khön family, based at their monastery in Tsang, to be emanations of Mañjuśrī.[101] The Karma Kagyü were powerful in Nangchen and Derge in Kham, the Naxi Kingdom, where the Tenth Karmapa sought refuge from Gushri Khan and Sikkim. The Nyingma lineages were influential across Tibet and the Himalaya, including the Kingdom of Sikkim, and northern Nepal.[102] Nyingma reincarnation lineages proliferated as they found up to five reincarnations of some lineages, representing the gurus' mind, speech, body, qualities, and activities. In the 19th century, reincarnates from the Sakya, Kagyü and Nyingma schools had leading roles in the *rimé* or "non-partisan" movement, based in Dergé. It was headed by two reincarnates, Jamyang Khyentsé Wangpo ('Jam dbyangs mkhyen brtse' dbang po, 1820–1892) and Jamgön Kongtrül ('Jam mgon kong sprul, 1813–1899), and it resisted Geluk sectarianism.[103] Both these reincarnates gave rise to multiple lineages.

REINCARNATIONS AND COLONIALISM

The Great Thirteenth and Fourteenth Dalai Lamas. The Thirteenth Dalai Lama, Thubten Gyatso (Thub bstan rgya mtsho, 1876–1933), survived a smallpox epidemic as a child to become the most politically influential Dalai Lama since the Great Fifth. In 1899, he became the first Dalai Lama to earn the Geshe Larampa degree, the highest degree in the Geluk system. In the same year, he headed off an attempt by Sichuan-based Chinese officials to take control of Nyarong by appealing directly to the Guangxu emperor (r.1875–1908). As he was concerned about both British and Chinese imperial intentions toward Tibet, he approached the Russian Czar for help through his debate partner, the Russian citizen Agvan Dorjiev (1854–1938). But as this request came during the "Great Game" between Britain and Russia in Central Asia, this overture only further antagonized the British, who used Dorjiev's presence as an excuse to invade Tibet and open it for trade. Over a thousand Tibetans died in this one-sided fight, and the Dalai Lama fled to Mongolia, where the Eighth Jebtsundamba Khutuγtu (1869–1924) hosted him.[104]

In Mongolia, the Dalai Lama failed to get protection from the Russians before falling out with the Jebtsundamba and leaving for Beijing. In Beijing, he met several foreign ambassadors, Emperor Xuantong (r.1908–1911), and the powerful Dowager Empress Cixi (1835–1908). Although the Qing court may have seen it differently, he described this meeting as a reaffirmation of the guru–patron relationship.[105] He returned to Lhasa in 1909.

Soon after returning home, he had to flee again to British India, as Qing troops invaded in 1910. These troops were led by Zhao Erfeng (1845–1911), a governor in Sichuan who had been appointed governor of Tibet. His colonial approach to Tibet drew from the European playbook and caused many deaths.[106] Thubten Gyatso avoided this chaos by staying in Sikkim, a British protectorate. After he received word that the Qing Empire had fallen, he returned to Tibet, declared it an independent country, and attempted to modernize it.[107] In the religious sphere, he took the side of the nonsectarian movement against the Geluk's most influential teacher, Pabongkha Dechen Nyingpo (Pha bong kha bde chen snying po 1878–1941), who advocated the propitiation of the sectarian deity Dorjé Shugden.[108] He also fell out with the Ninth Paṇchen Lama, Thubten Chokyi Nyima (Thub bstan chos kyi nyi ma, 1883–1937), who fled to Chinese Republican territory in Amdo after a tax dispute with the Ganden Podrang.[109]

After Thubten Gyatso died in 1933, his reforms faltered, and the regents sunk into infighting.[110] Luckily for them, the Chinese Republican government was also weak, and its attempts to control Tibet failed. Like the Qing, the new government tried to insist on the use of the Golden Urn, but it was not used to recognize either the Fourteenth Dalai Lama, Tenzin Gyatso (Bstan 'dzin rgya mtsho, 1935–), or the Tenth Paṇchen Lama, Chökyi Gyaltsen (Chos skyid rgyal mtshan, 1938–1989).[111]

The communist revolutionaries in Mongolia and China exercised much greater control over reincarnates. At first, in both countries, they negotiated with local elites, almost all of whom were reincarnates. They established a constitutional monarchy in Mongolia with the Eighth Jebtsundamba Khutuγtu as the head. But after his death in 1924, they did not replace him and, in 1928, they outlawed reincarnation.[112] His rebirth was found secretly in Tibet in 1936.

In eastern and central Tibet, reincarnates were co-opted into communist government positions before their power was eroded. The Dalai and Paṇchen Lamas were appointed members of the Standing Committee of the National People's Congress in 1954.[113] But after an uprising in Lhasa in 1959, the Dalai Lama and many other reincarnates, including the Karmapa, Sharmapa, and secretly recognized Jebtsundamba, fled to India. In the Great Leap Forward (1595–1962), the *labrang* system was dismantled and criminalized.[114] The Paṇchen Lama and other reincarnates who stayed in Tibet, including the Twelfth Samding Dorjé Pakmo, continued to play senior roles within the government in Tibet.[115] The Paṇchen Lama eventually broke with the government, in 1962 writing a petition against their policies that led to his imprisonment for nearly twenty years.[116]

Exiles and Green Shoots. The 1960s to 1980s were difficult times for exiled Tibetans. Many were destitute and looked to the reincarnates for support. But most reincarnates were desperate, too, living in refugee camps and surviving on charity. The young Dalai Lama was placed under enormous social and political pressure to provision his people and looked for support from Indian and Western sponsors.[117] The Sikkimese royal family supported the Sixteenth Karmapa, Rangjung Rigpé Dorjé (Rang byung rigs pa'i rdo rje, 1924–1981), allowing him to rebuild his monastery in Sikkim.[118] During the same period, a small group of charismatic reincarnates traveled internationally. The most influential among this group was Chögyam Trungpa (Chos rgyam drung pa, 1939–1987), who lived first in Scotland and later the United States, where he attracted many students, including celebrities, and a reputation for outlandish behavior.[119] Later, some reincarnates would be born in Western Buddhist families.[120]

Those who stayed in Tibet and Mongolia suffered greatly. They all lost their status, and only those who worked for the government were saved from imprisonment, torture, and even death. The Tibetans' plight began to change when China opened in the 1980s. Reincarnates returned from overseas with funds to rebuild monasteries.[121] The Chinese state established an official register of reincarnated "soul boys" (*Zhuanshi lingtong*). And in 1992, the government and the Dalai Lama both recognized the same child, Orgyen Trinlé Dorjé (O rgyan phrin las rdo rje, 1985–), as the Seventeenth Karmapa.

Mongolia's politics changed profoundly in the 1990s after the Soviet Union fell and it achieved independence. As Buddhism re-emerged, India sent Bakula Rinpoche (1918–2003), a scion of the Ladakhi royal family and well-regarded reincarnate, as its ambassador to Mongolia. The Ninth Jebtsundamba Khutuɣtu (1933–2012) came out of hiding and began visiting. He received Mongolian citizenship in 2010 and died there in 2012. When the Dalai Lama visited Mongolia in 2016, he announced he had found the Jebtsundamba's rebirth.[122]

Modern Lamas. As the millennium turned, reincarnation institutions grappled with old problems and new paradigms. Along with calls to curb reincarnates' power and reform their systems, these institutions were being remade by Western and Chinese hegemonies, which legally problematized, politically marginalized, culturally exoticized, and commodified them.[123]

One of the first pangs of modernization was a schism within the Geluk. In 1976, the Dalai Lama denounced a publication called *The Yellow Book* that listed the times Dorjé Shugden had harmed those who combined Nyingma and Geluk practices. After Pabongkha promoted this practice in the 1930s, it rose in popularity. But the Dalai Lama renounced it and refused to connect with its followers. Some responded that he was a fake Dalai Lama.[124] In 1997, a group of the deity-ghost's supporters murdered a senior teacher and his two attendants near the Dalai Lama's residence in Dharamshala.[125]

Another modernization pang occurred when the Karma Kagyü attempted to resolve a succession candidacy that stretched beyond legal boundaries. After the Sixteenth Karmapa died in the United States in 1981, his four regents took a decade to search for his reincarnation. As the search finally began, one of them, the third Jamgon Kongtrul, Karma Lodrö Chökyi Senge (Karma Blo gros chos kyi senge, 1954–1992), died, and the other three could not agree on a candidate. Two of the regents, namely, the Twelfth Tai Situpa, Pema Tönyö Nyinje (Padma don yod nyin byed, 1954–), and the Twelfth Gyaltsab Rinpoche, Dragpa Tenpa Yarpel (Grags pa bstan pa yar 'phel, 1954–), chose Orgyen Trinlé Dorjé. This choice made history by receiving endorsements from the Dalai Lama and the Chinese government. The other regent, the Fourteenth Sharmarpa, Mipam Chökyi Lodrö (Mi pham chos skyid blo gros, 1254–2014), disagreed and found another candidate, Trinlé Thayé Dorjé (Phrin las mtha' yas rdo rje, 1983–). Orgyen Trinlé was enthroned at Tsurpu, and Thayé Dorjé was enthroned in the Sixteenth Karmapa's compound outside Delhi. Their fight split the lineage and led to numerous court cases across India, New Zealand, and Europe. In the first months of 2000, Orgyen Trinlé fled Tibet for India, where despite being a minor he was kept under effective house arrest for over ten years before moving to the West. While living in India, he became an international celebrity, with large followings in Taiwan and Hong Kong.[126] Both he and Thayé Dorjé have struggled in their roles and, following the Sharmapa's death, are attempting to reconcile.

Along with these historical issues, abuse allegations have plagued reincarnate lineages since the 1980s. The novelist John Steinbeck and his wife Nancy Steinbeck detailed abuse they witnessed at Chögyam Trungpa's retreats.[127] When further accusations emerged, many of Trungpa's students defended him as a "Crazy Wisdom" yogi with unconventional behavior. But Chögyam Trungpa's choice of Ösel Tendzin (b. Thomas Frederick Rich, 1943–1990) as his heir was questioned more widely. Tendzin contracted HIV in the late 1980s but continued to have unprotected sex with some of his students. He died of AIDS in 1990, and a student who contracted HIV from him died shortly after.[128]

The allegations against Trungpa were the first of many. Allegations have ranged from decades-long, institutional sexual and physical abuse to imbalanced guru–student relationships that negate consent. Some of these cases are now before the courts in Western countries.[129] Reincarnates have also accused their guardians of abuse. These accusations have ranged from reports of commonplace physical abuse—sometimes framed as "training"—to detailed descriptions of horrific emotional, physical, and sexual assault.[130] None of these has been brought to court. Many abuse sufferers have called on the Dalai Lama to reform the institution, but given the reincarnation institutions' independent standing, he claims he can do little.[131] Rather than the Dalai Lama acting unilaterally, for this situation to change, each reincarnation institution needs to respond to these accusations with compassion and wisdom.

Along with abuse allegations, the reincarnation system is regularly criticized for its corruption in its dealings with Western and Chinese sponsors. Many reincarnates' activities within these two cultures are large, money-making enterprises.[132] Not all these interactions are corrupt. The reincarnates support large organizations, and there is tremendous pressure on them to raise funds. But there is no formal response to their commodification in these cultures and little religious instruction on it. There are no instructions, for example, on how young reincarnates brought up "imprisoned in a golden cage" should use the smartphones they are gifted.[133] The buddha did not proscribe Instagram scrolling or sexting, and the lineages are yet to develop moral frameworks for their usage.

These multiple issues have led many younger Tibetans, especially in Tibet, to doubt reincarnates.[134] There are also critics within the system. The Dalai Lama has repeatedly called for the system's reform.[135] Dzongsar Khyentse (Rdzong gsar mkhyen brtse, 1961–), a reincarnate from one of Jamyang Khyentse Wangpo's multiple rebirth lineages, has written coherent critiques of it, and somewhat paradoxically criticized the way some students responded to allegations of abuse against Sögyal Rinpoche (Bsod rgyal Rin po che, 1947–2019).[136]

Another issue for the reincarnation system, and possible space for reform, is the inclusion of more females in the lineages, which is happening slowly.[137] Almost all participants agree that further reforms like this will also be necessary, but these will be difficult given the tradition's nebulous, idiosyncratic systems. And, as it reforms internally, the reincarnation system must contend with a significant external political obstacle, the Chinese party-state.

FUTURE REINCARNATIONS?

After first working with, then banning, and then regulating reincarnates, the People's Republic of China (PRC) is now attempting to control Tibetan religious life by choosing its reincarnates, particularly its Dalai Lamas. It has been planning to recognize the next Dalai Lama since the death of the Tenth Paṇchen Lama in 1989. At that time, they ruled out the Dalai Lama's involvement in the recognition process and reacted angrily when he recognized a six-year-old child, Gendun Chokyi Nyima (Dge 'dun chos kyi nyi ma), as the next Paṇchen Lama.[138] After taking this child into custody, they recognized a party official's son, Gyaltsen Norbu (Rgyal mtshan nor bu, 1990–), as the Eleventh Paṇchen Lama by using the Qing Empire's Golden Urn in the Jokhang Temple.[139] Since then, they have recognized several *khutuγtu* reincarnates who would traditionally have found the next Dalai Lama. Furthermore, they have amended the law, creating the State Religious Affairs Bureau Order Number Five, which declares all reincarnations must be chosen by the PRC using the Golden Urn.[140] The Dalai Lama has refuted these attempts and insists the next Dalai Lama will be reborn outside Chinese-held territory.[141]

Despite possessing the political power to control a reincarnation process that they also deny exists, it is unclear whether the PRC has the cultural authority to implement its reincarnation policy. Given the problems the reincarnation traditions have experienced in recent years, it is also unclear whether future Dalai Lamas will have the social power to reinvigorate the reincarnation system. The Dalai Lama remains the reincarnation system's best advertisement, and as others have noted, if his body rosary falters, the whole system is at risk.[142] The multiple reincarnation systems have undergone many transformations in their seven-hundred-year history, but the next interregnum between Dalai Lamas may be their most difficult challenge yet.

REVIEW OF LITERATURE

Researchers have written about reincarnation from the perspectives of multiple disciplines and subdisciplines and, given its long history, have tended to focus on single historical periods. Studies of the early reincarnation systems and their precedents have tended to view them as religious, cultural, and social phenomena, using the participants' biographies, autobiographies, poetry, and traditional histories as sources. Studies of the 16th to the early 20th century have tended to focus on their politics and privilege via available archival documents. Those writing about the modern era have more access to documents and have approached it from a social science perspective.

Roger Jackson's book on rebirth throughout Buddhism and Naomi Appleton's book on the *jātaka* tradition are both helpful to understand reincarnation's Indian precedents.[143] Ronald Davidson's *Tibetan Renaissance* and Leonard van der Kuijp's several articles on the early emanations are beneficial to understand its Tibetan precedents.[144]

A series of religious and cultural history studies of the lineages' development were conducted in the 2010s. Daniel Hirshberg's study of Nyangrel Nyima Özer (1124–1194) traced his construction of concatenating previous lives; Charles Manson has written several articles and has a forthcoming book on the second Karmapa, Karma Pakshi; and I have written two books on the third Karmapa, Rangjung Dorjé.[145] Manson's work on Karma Pakshi is especially helpful as Karma Pakshi's literary style is famously dense. Frances Garrett's study of human embryos in Tibetan thought of this period approaches the subject differently but in its exploration of reincarnates' gestation process is extremely interesting.[146]

There is less political history written about this period, but Turrell Wylie wrote a formative article arguing that the Karmapa lineage survived because of the Mongol court's support, and one of Luciano Petch's comprehensive political histories of Tibetan politics focuses on the Central Tibet–Mongol relationship.[147]

Although there are excellent translations of the Fifth Dalai Lama's autobiography and history of Tibet, most writing on the Ganden Podrang period of Tibetan history focuses on the political relationship between Tibetan hierarchs and their Mongol and Manchu patrons.[148] Petech wrote several monographs on this subject, as did Elliot Sperling.[149] Peter Schwieger has written two books on the Dalai Lamas' rule: one, on their relationship with the Qing emperors, draws primarily from archival documents, and the other is a theoretical analysis of conflict among similar source materials.[150] Max Oidtman's monograph on the use of the Golden Urn in central Tibet, Amdo, and Mongolia covers similar ground but relies primarily on unstudied Manchu-language archives.[151]

Gray Tuttle has written several works that highlight the role of reincarnates in Amdo and China during the period leading up to communist rule, and Lobsang Yongdan wrote a fascinating study of an army general's recognition as a reincarnate during the same era.[152] Several extensive histories of Bhutan by Michael Aris and Karma Phuntso contain much information about that country's reincarnates, and Mervyn Goldstein's series of political histories perform the same function for modern Tibet.[153] And special mention should be made of Hildegard Diemberger's study of the Samding Dorjé Pakmo lineage.[154]

Donald Lopez wrote the field-transforming *Prisoners of Shangri La* in part about the relationship between Westerners and Tibetan reincarnates in the modern period. Martin Mills conducted an in-depth study of reincarnates within a monastic system in Ladakh, and Nicole Willock has looked at how reincarnate lineages re-established themselves after the Cultural Revolution.[155] Tanya Zivkovic's research into Tibetan death processes and Elijah Ary's searing depiction of life as a Western child recognized as a *trülku* are compelling.[156]

The reincarnations of the Dalai and Panchen Lamas and the Jebtsundamba Khutuγtu remain a topic of geopolitical interest, and there have been several informative works on it.[157] More generally, there have been multiple edited volumes of high-quality research articles on either the members of a particular lineage or several aspects of the reincarnation phenomenon.[158]

PRIMARY SOURCES

Primary sources for the historical study of reincarnation traditions can be found within several Tibetan-language genres: individual biographies of prominent reincarnates, "golden rosary" (Tib. *gser phreng*) biographical collections, and other works that address specific aspects of the reincarnation process.

The earliest text to discuss concatenate reincarnations was the biography of Nyangrel Nyima Özer (1124–1194), the *Chronicles of the Copper Palace*. This work has been studied by Daniel Hirshberg (see "Further Reading").[159]

As the Karmapas were the first to establish a reincarnation institution, the second, third, and fourth Karmapas' works offer many insights into the reincarnation system's development. A collection of works by the Second Karmapa, Karma Pakshi, may be of interest.[160] Charles Manson studied this work in his recent book on Karma Pakshi (see "Further Reading").[161] Karma Pakshi's biography by his successor, Rangjung Dorjé, may also be of interest.[162]

Within the works of the Third Karmapa, Rangjung Dorjé, several texts may be of interest. I used these works in my two studies of the Third Karmapa. These include his autobiography collection, *Glorious Rangjung Dorjé's Liberation Story*.[163] His autobiographical songs may also be of interest.[164]

The autobiography of the Fifth Dalai Lama, Ngawang Gyatso, also provides many insights into the development of the Dalai Lama institution. Most of this work has been translated by Samten Gyaltsen Karmay.[165]

Perhaps the most useful example of the "golden rosaries" genre is the previously mentioned extensive collection of biographies compiled by Situ Paṇchen (1700–1774) and his attendant Belo Tseden Kunkyab ('Be lo tshe dban kun khyab, 18th century). This large work includes biographies of most Karma Kagyü reincarnation traditions. This includes the biography and songs of the First and Fourth Karmapas, whose life stories are yet to be the subject of an in-depth study.[166]

One of the most well-known histories of Tibetan Buddhism, the Gö Lotsawa's (1392–1481) *Blue Annals*, also provides overviews of many early reincarnation lineages.[167] It was translated into English by George Roerich and Gendün Chöpel.[168]

Several other works that deal with aspects of the reincarnation tradition may be of interest as well. *Profound Inner Meaning* and its *Auto-commentary*, the influential work of the Third Karmapa, Rangjung Dorjé examine the process of gestation, and his study of this process informed his articulation of the reincarnation tradition. Francis Garret refers to these texts in her study (see "Review of Literature").[169]

Rangjung Dorjé's *Collected Works* also show his interest in the *jātaka* tradition. See, for example, his edition of the Buddha's *jataka* tales.[170]

DIGITAL RESOURCES

Most reincarnation and emanation lineages have websites that provide a history of lineage members and an overview of their institutions. See, for example:

His Holiness the 14th Dalai Lama of Tibet. http://dalailama.com/.
His Holiness the Sakya Trichen. http://www.hhthesakyatrizin.org/.
Sakya Tsechen Shedrub Dargä. http://www.sakyaling.de/.
The Karmapa (Örgyen Trinlé Dorjé). https://kagyuoffice.org/.
Thayé Dorjé, His Holiness the 17th Gyalwa Karmapa:). https://www.karmapa.org/.

The *Treasury of Lives* website hosts an impressive array of biographies of reincarnates and others, along with images:

Many of the primary-source texts that discuss the reincarnation lineages can be found at the Buddhist Digital Resource Centre:

FURTHER READING

Appleton, Naomi. *Narrating Karma and Rebirth: Buddhist and Jain Multi-Life Stories*. Cambridge, UK: Cambridge University Press, 2014.

Ary, Elijah. "The Westernisation of Tulkus." In *Little Buddhas: Children and Childhoods in Buddhist Texts and Traditions*. Edited by Vanessa R. Sasson, 398–426. New York: Oxford University Press, 2012.

Brauen, Martin, ed. *The Dalai Lamas: A Visual History*. London: Serindia, 2005.

Debreczeny, Karl, ed. *The Black Hat Eccentric: Artistic Visions of the Tenth Karmapa*. New York: Rubin Museum of Art, 2012.

Gamble, Ruth. *Reincarnation in Tibetan Buddhism: The Third Karmapa and the Invention of a Tradition*. Oxford: Oxford University Press, 2018.

Hirshberg, Daniel. *Remembering the Lotus Born: Padmasambhava in the History of Tibet's Golden Age*. Boston: Wisdom Publications, 2016.

Hirshberg, Daniel A., Derek F. Maher, and Tsering Wangchuk. "The Tulku (*sprul sku*) Institution in Tibetan Buddhism." In "The Tulku (sprul sku) Institution in Tibetan Buddhism." Edited by Daniel A. Hirshberg, Derek F. Maher, and Tsering Wangchuk. Special issue, *Revue d'Etudes Tibétaines* 3 (2017): i–iii.

Jamgon Kongtrul Lodro Taye. *Enthronement: The Recognition of the Reincarnate Masters of Tibet and the Himalayas*. Translated by Ngawang Zangpo. Boston: Snow Lion Publications, 1997.

Lopez, Donald. *Prisoners of Shangri-la: Tibetan Buddhism and the West.* Chicago: University of Chicago Press, 1998.

Manson, Charles. *The Second Karmapa Karma Pakshi: Tibetan Mahāsidda.* Boulder, CO: Shambhala Publications, 2022.

Mills, Martin. *Identity, Ritual and State in Tibetan Buddhism: The Foundations of Authority in Gelukpa Monasticism.* London: Routledge, 2010.

Ngag dbang blo bzang rgya mtsho. *A History of Tibet.* Translated by Zahiruddin Ahmad. Bloomington, IN: Research Institute for Asian Studies, 1995.

Ngag dbang blo bzang rgya mtsho. *The Illusive Play: The Autobiography of the Fifth Dalai Lama.* Translated by Samten G. Karmay. Chicago: Serindia, 2014.

Oidtmann, Max. *Forging the Golden Urn: The Qing Empire and the Politics of Reincarnation in Tibet.* New York: Columbia University Press, 2018.

Ortner, Sherry B. *High Religion: A Cultural and Political History of Sherpa Buddhism.* Princeton, NJ: Princeton University Press, 1990.

Petech, Luciano. *Central Tibet and the Mongols: The Yüan-Sa-skya Period of Tibetan History.* Rome: Istituto Italiano per il Medio ed Estremo Oriente, 1990.

Powers, John. *The Buddha Party: How the People's Republic of China Works to Define and Control Tibetan Buddhism.* New York: Oxford University Press, 2017.

Schwieger, Peter. *The Dalai Lama and the Emperor of China: A Political History of the Tibetan Institution of Reincarnation.* New York: Columbia University Press, 2015.

Shakabpa, Tsepon Wangchuk Deden. *Bod kyi srid don rgyal rabs.* 2 vols. Kalimpong, India: T. Tsepal Taikhang, 1976.

Shakya, Tsering. *The Dragon in the Land of Snows: A History of Modern Tibet since 1947.* London: Penguin, 1999.

Thondup, Tulku. *Incarnation: The History and Mysticism of the Tulku Tradition of Tibet* Boston: Shambala, 2011.

Tuttle, Gray, *Tibetan Buddhists in the Making of Modern China.* New York: Columbia University Press, 2005.

Willock, Nicole. *Lineages of the Literary: Tibetan Buddhist Polymaths of Socialist China.* New York: Columbia University Press, 2021.

Wylie, Turrell. "The First Mongol Conquest of Tibet Reinterpreted." *Harvard Journal of Asiatic Studies* 37, no. 1 (1977): 103–133.

Zivkovic, Tanya. *Death and Reincarnation in Tibetan Buddhism: In-between Bodies.* London: Routledge, 2013.

NOTES

1. Most Tibetan names are transcribed according to the THL Simplified Tibetan Phonemic Transcription, except for well-known names with a widely used alternate spelling. For the Tibetan spelling of these names, please see TreasuryOfLives.org. Names in notes are written in Tibetan transcription.
2. O rgyan pa's biography was written by his student Bsod nams 'od zer (14th century), *Grub chen o rgyan pa'i rnam par thar pa byin brlabs kyi chu rgyun* (Gangtok, India: Sherab gyaltsen lama, 1976), 248–249. For a study of O rgyan pa's biographies, see Brenda Li, "A Critical Study of the Life of the 13th-Century Tibetan Monk U rgyan pa Rin chen dpal Based on His Biographies," (DPhil diss., University of Oxford, 2011).
3. Rang byung rdo rje, "Rnam thar tshigs bcad ma," in *Rang byung rdo rje'i gsung 'bum*, vol. nga (Mthsur phu [Tsurpu], Tibet: Mkhan po lo yag bkra shis, 2006), 377.
4. Sugam Pokharel and Harmeet Kaur, "Dalai Lama Apologizes for 'Attractive' Female Successor Remark," *CNN*, July 3, 2019.
5. State Council, The People's Republic of China, "Dalai Lama Criticised for Reincarnation Remarks," Dalai Lama's Office, "Clarification and Context of Remarks Made by His Holiness the Dalai Lama in a Recent BBC Interview," *DalaiLama.com*, July 2, 2019. Concerning these comments, it should be noted that several graduated path texts state that gurus of both sexes are said to need "attractiveness" to encourage

students, primarily using kind speech, but also by manifesting in a healthy body. See Tsongkhapa, *The Great Treatise on the Stages of the Path to Enlightenment, Lam Rim Chen Mo*, trans. Joshua Cutler, Vol 2. (Boston: Snow Lion Publications, 2004), 225–232. This attractiveness is not necessarily physical and relies on a pleasant demeanor. It is something like charisma that permeates inside and out. His comment that a woman would need more of this "attractiveness" to defeat her objectification makes sense from this perspective. But it was not received that way. It must be challenging for an elderly monk to navigate today's media environment in his second language. But he is also the head of a patriarchal institution, and feminist reactions to this institution probably influenced the response to his comments.

6. Ruth Gamble, *Reincarnation in Tibetan Buddhism: The Third Karmapa and the Invention of a Tradition* (New York: Oxford University Press, 2018), 50.
7. Wendy Doniger O'Flaherty, *Karma and Rebirth in Classical Indian Traditions* (Berkeley: University of California Press, 1980), 3; and Florin Deleanu, "Research Notes on Rebirth in Mainstream Buddhism: Beliefs, Models, and Proofs," *Bulletin of the International Institute for Buddhist Studies* 3 (2020): 3.
8. Roger Jackson, *Rebirth: A Guide to Mind, Karma, and Cosmos in the Buddhist World* (Boulder, CO: Shambhala, 2022), 27–47.
9. Naomi Appleton, *Narrating Karma and Rebirth: Buddhist and Jain Multi-Life Stories* (Cambridge, UK: Cambridge University Press, 2014).
10. Vasubandhu, *Abhidharmakośabhāṣya* Chapter III, verses 4–19.
11. This union of form and emptiness is described differently in the various Indian and Tibetan schools of Buddhism. For a concise overview see Matthew Kapstein, *Tibetan Buddhism: A Very Short Introduction* (New York: Oxford University Press, 2013), 69–72.
12. Gamble, *Reincarnation in Tibetan Buddhism*, 30.
13. Gamble, *Reincarnation in Tibetan Buddhism*, 70.
14. Georgios T. Halkias, *Luminous Bliss: A Religious History of Pure Land Literature in Tibet* (Honolulu: University of Hawaii Press, 2012).
15. Guang Xing, *The Concept of the Buddha: Its Evolution from Early Buddhism to the Trikāya Theory* (London: Routledge, 2004), 132–136, 163–168.
16. Peter Schwieger, *The Dalai Lama and the Emperor of China: A Political History of the Tibetan Institution of Reincarnation* (New York: Columbia University Press, 2015), 19.
17. R. A. Stein showed that these terms were used to indicate the possession of magical, supernatural, or transformative powers. R. A. Stein, "Un ensemble sémantique tibétain: Créer et procréer, étre et devenir, vivre, nourrir, et guérir," *Bulletin of the School of Oriental and African Studies* 36, no. 2 (1973): 412–423. Gamble, *Reincarnation in Tibetan Buddhism*, 49–75.
18. Gamble, *Reincarnation in Tibetan Buddhism*, 68–71.
19. Gamble, *Reincarnation in Tibetan Buddhism*, 139–41. This well-known story was included in Gtsang smyon Heruka's famous version of Mi la ras pa's liberation story, *Rnal 'byor gyi dbang phyug chen po Mi la ras pa'i rnam mgur* (Delhi: Sherig Parkhang, 1990), 222–225. But Peter Roberts explained that the link between Dar ma mdo sde and Tipupa is not found in early versions of Marpa's story; see Peter Alan Roberts, *The Biographies of Réchungpa* (London: Routledge, 2007), 125–126. There were also stories of consciousness transferal in the canons of other new tantra lineages. Schwieger refers to one story of a king's transference of consciousness into an elephant cadaver: Schwieger, *The Dalai Lama and the Emperor of China*, 17.
20. Lewis Doney, "Early Bodhisattva-kingship in Tibet: The Case of Tri Songdétsen," *Cahiers d'Extrême-Asie* 24 (2015): 29–48.
21. These stories were later collated into the *Maṇi Bka' 'bum*. See Matthew Kapstein, "Remarks on the Maṇi Bka'- 'bum and the Cult of Avalokiteśvara in Tibet," in *Tibetan Buddhism: Reason and Revelation*, ed. Stephen Goodman and Ronald Davidson (Albany: State University of New York Press, 1992), 79–93; and Gamble, *Reincarnation in Tibetan Buddhism*, 64–66.

22. Franz-Karl Ehrhard, "The Transmission of the Thig-le bcu-drug and the bKa' gdams glegs bam," in *The Many Canons of Tibetan Buddhism*, ed. Helmut Eimer and David Germano (Leiden, The Netherlands: Brill, 2002), 31–33.
23. Las chen kun dga' rgyal mtshan, *Bka'gdams chos 'byung gsal ba'i sgron me* (Lhasa, China: Bod ljongs mi dmangs dpe skrun khang, 2003), 247. Daniel Berounský, "Entering Dead Bodies and the Miraculous Power of the Kings: The Landmark of Karma Pakshi's Reincarnation in Tibet, Part 1," *Mongolo-Tibetica Pragensia 10: Linguistics, Ethnolinguistics, Religion, and Culture* 3, no. 2 (2010): 17.
24. Leonard W. J. van der Kuijp, "The Dalai Lamas and the Origin of Reincarnate Lamas," in *The Dalai Lamas: A Visual History*, ed. Martin Brauen (Chicago: Serindia, 2005), 14–31.
25. Daniel Hirshberg, *Remembering the Lotus Born: Padmasambhava in the History of Tibet's Golden Age* (Somerville, MA: Wisdom Publications, 2016).
26. Rdo rje rgyal po, " 'Gro mgon phag mo gru pa'i skyes rabs kyi skor la chos tshan lnga," in *Rdo rje'i rgyal po gsung 'bum* (Kathmandu, Nepal: Khanpo Shedrup Tenzin and Lama Thinley Namgyal, 2003), 247–280; and Gamble, *Reincarnation in Tibetan Buddhism*, 36–38.
27. Leonard van der Kuijp, " 'Baγši' and 'Baγši-s' in Tibetan Historical, Biographical and Lexicographical Texts," *Central Asiatic Journal* 39, no. 2 (1995): 275–302.
28. Gamble, *Reincarnation in Tibetan Buddhism*, 84.
29. Charles Manson, "Introduction to the Life of Karma Pakshi (1204/6-1283)," *Bulletin of Tibetology* 45, no. 1 (2009): 25–52.
30. Bsod nams 'od zer, *Grub chen O rgyan pa'i rnam thar*, 202–203.
31. Rang byung rdo rje, "Bka' brgyud gyi gser phreng," in *Rang byung rdo rje'i gsung 'bum* (Tsurpu, Tibet: Mkhan po lo yag bkra shis, 2006), vol. nga: 1–352.
32. Ellis Gene Smith, "Golden Rosaries of the Bka' brgyud Schools," in *Among Tibetan Texts: History and Literature of the Himalayan Plateau*, ed. Kurtis Schaeffer (Boston: Wisdom Publications, 2001), 39–51.
33. Gamble, *Reincarnation in Tibetan Buddhism*, 78.
34. This was one of only a few times that a reincarnate describes this journey. Rang byung rdo rje, "Bar de'i [sic] rnam par thar pa," in *Rang byung rdo rje'i gsung 'bum* (Tsurpu, Tibet: Mkhan po lo yag bkra shis, 2006), vol. nga: 358–374; and Gamble, *Reincarnation in Tibetan Buddhism*, 136–151.
35. Rang byung rdo rje, "Rang byung rdo rje'i tshigs bcad ma," 377; and Gamble, *Reincarnation in Tibetan Buddhism*, 140.
36. Rang byung rdo rje, "Rnam thar tshigs bcad ma," 377–414; Rang byung rdo rje, "Ston pa'i skyes rabs," in *Rang byung rdo rje'i gsung 'bum* (Tsurpu, Tibet: Mkhan po lo yag bkra shis, 2006), vol. kha: 1–666; Rang byung rdo rje, "Zab mo nang don gyi gzhung," in *Rang byung rdo rje'i gsung 'bum* (Tsurpu, Tibet: Mkhan po lo yag bkra shis, 2006), vol. ja: 308–360; and Frances Garrett, *Religion, Medicine, and the Human Embryo in Tibet* (London and New York: Routledge, 2008), 112–117.
37. Gamble, *Reincarnation in Tibetan Buddhism*, 53–54.
38. Gamble, *Reincarnation in Tibetan Buddhism*, 199–227; Andrew Quintman, "Toward a Geographic Biography: Milarepa's Life in the Tibetan Landscape," *Numen* 55, no. 4 (2008): 363–410; and Geoffrey Samuel, *Civilized Shamans: Buddhism in Tibetan Societies* (Washington, DC: Smithsonian Institution, 1993), 282.
39. Rang byung rdo rje, "Rang byung rdo rje'i mgur rnam," in *Rang byung rdo rje'i gsung 'bum* (Tsurpu, Tibet: Mkhan po lo yag bkra shis, 2006), vol. nga: 292.5–6; and Gamble, *Reincarnation in Tibetan Buddhism*, 167–168.
40. Rang byung rdo rje, "Rang byung rdo rje'i tshigs bcad ma," 407–413; Rang byung rdo rje, "Rang byung rdo rje'i mgur rnam," 205.1–6; and Gamble, *Reincarnation in Tibetan Buddhism*, 251–256.
41. Schwieger, *The Dalai Lama and the Emperor of China*, 25.
42. Gamble, *Reincarnation in Tibetan Buddhism*, 263–272.
43. Schwieger, *The Dalai Lama and the Emperor of China*, 26.

44. Kong sprul Blo gros mtha' yas, *Enthronement: The Recognition of the Reincarnate Masters of Tibet and the Himalayas*, trans. Ngawang Zangpo (Boston: Shambhala Publications, 1997), 17–19, 63–68.
45. Melvyn C. Goldstein, *A History of Modern Tibet, 1913–1951: The Demise of the Lamaist State* (Berkeley: University of California Press, 1991), 35.
46. Kong sprul Blo gros mtha' yas, *Enthronement*, 121, 160.
47. Schwieger, *The Dalai Lama and the Emperor of China*, 16. Gamble, *Reincarnation in Tibetan Buddhism*, 1–23.
48. Tenzin Choephak Ringpapontsang, "Conquering the Conqueror: Reassessing the Relationship between Qubilai Khan and 'Phags pa Lama," (PhD diss., Australian National University, 2016).
49. Charles Manson, *The Second Karmapa, Karma Pakshi: Tibetan Mahāsidda* (Boulder, CO: Shambhala Publications, 2022), ch. 2.
50. This primarily political causation was argued in Turrell Wylie, "The First Mongol Conquest of Tibet Reinterpreted," *Harvard Journal of Asiatic Studies* 37, no. 1 (1977): 103–133.
51. Leonard W. J. van der Kuijp, "The Kalacakra and the Patronage of Tibetan Buddhism by the Mongol Imperial Family," in *The Central Eurasian Studies Lectures, Lecture 4*, ed. Federica Venturi (Bloomington: Department of Central Eurasian Studies, Indiana University, 2004); and Gamble, *Reincarnation in Tibetan Buddhism*, 242–262.
52. Si tu paṇ chen chos kyi byung gnas and 'Be lo tshe dban kun khyab, *Bka' brgyud gser 'phreng rnam thar zla ba chu shel gyi 'phreng ba*, vol. 1 (Varanasi, India: Vajra Vidya, 2004), 324–329.
53. Si tu paṇ chen, *Zla ba chu shel gyi 'phreng ba*, vol. 1, 396–342. Hugh Edward Richardson, "The Karma-pa Sect: A Historical Note," *Journal of the Royal Asiatic Society* 90, no. 3–4 (July 1958): 139–164; Management committee of cultural relics of the Tibetan Autonomous Region, *Xizang wenwu jingcui* (A selection of Tibetan cultural relics) (Beijing: Forbidden City Publishing House of the Palace Museum, 1992), 52–53, pl. 26. Patricia Berger, "Miracles in Nanjing: An Imperial Record of the Fifth Karmapa's Visit to the Chinese Capital," in *Cultural Intersections in Later Chinese Buddhsim*, ed. Marsha Weidner (Honolulu: University of Hawai'i Press, 2001), 145–168.
54. Ngag dbang byams pa, " 'Jam dpal dbyangs kyis rje bla ma la dngos su gnang ba'i gdams pa mdor bsdus," in *Gsung 'bum/ngag dbang byams pa*, vol. 1, (New Delhi: Ngawang Sopa, 1973–1974), 241–258.
55. Schwieger, *The Dalai Lama and the Emperor of China*, 28.
56. Max Oidtmann, *Forging the Golden Urn: The Qing Empire and the Politics of Reincarnation in Tibet* (New York: Columbia University Press, 2018), 31.
57. Sam van Schaik, *Tibet: A history* (New Haven, CT: Yale University Press, 2011), 116; and Schwieger, *The Dalai Lama and the Emperor of China*, 34–38.
58. Van Schaik, *Tibet: A history*, 118.
59. Ngag dbang blo bzang rgya mtsho, *Za hor gyi ban de ngag dbang blo bzang rgya mtsho'i 'di snang 'khrul ba'i rol rtsed rtogs brjod kyi tshul du bkod pa du kū la'i gos pa*, 3 vols (Lhasa, China: Bod ljongs mi dmangs dpe skrun khang, Xizang Zangwen guji chubanshe, 1989), 1:52; and Schwieger, *The Dalai Lama and the Emperor of China*, 41.
60. Georges Dreyfus, "The Shuk-Den Affair: Origins of a Controversy," *Journal of the International Association of Buddhist Studies* 21, no. 2 (1999): 227–270; Schwieger, *The Dalai Lama and the Emperor of China*, 41; and Frédéric Richard, "Shugs ldan and the Dalai Lama: A Conflict of Political Legitimation Processes?" *Revue d'Etudes Tibétaines* 55 (2020), 440–461.
61. Kurtis Schaeffer, "The Fifth Dalai Lama, Ngawang Lobzang Gyatso," in Brauen, ed. *The Dalai Lamas*, 65–91.
62. Darig Thokmay, "Game Changers of the Tibetan Buddhist Political Order in Central Asia in the Early Eighteenth Century," *Revue d'Etudes Tibétaines* 61 (2021), 300–322.
63. Zuiho Yamaguchi, "The Emergence of the Regent Sangs-rgyas-rgya-mtsho and the Denouement of the Dalai Lama's First Administration," *Memoirs of the Research Department of the Toyo Bunko* 57 (1999): 113–136.

64. Bya bral lha dbang rgya mtsho, "Pan chen bsod nams grags pa'i rnam par thar pa dad pa'i rol rtsed," in *Tshad ma rnam 'grel gyi dka' 'grel dgongs pa rab gsal* (Beijing: Krung go'i bod kyi shes rig dpe skrun khang, 1998), 1–24.
65. Nancy G. Lin, "Recounting the Fifth Dalai Lama's Rebirth Lineage," *Revue d'etudes tibétaines* 38 (2017): 65–83; and Ruth Gamble and Yangmotso, "Servant- Like Lords and Heavenly Kings: Jangchub Gyeltsen and the 5th Dalai Lama on Governance and Kingship," *Cahiers d'Extême-Asie* 24 (2016): 145–167.
66. Ngag dbang blo bzang rgya mtsho, *Gangs can yul gyi sa la spyod pa'i mtho ris kyi rgyal blon gtso bor brjod pa'i deb ther rdzogs ldan gzhon nu'i dga' ston dpyid kyi rgyal mo'i glu dbyangs* (Beijing: Mi rigs dpe skrun gangs gis bskrun pa, 1980).
67. Ngag dbang blo bzang rgya mtsho, *Rgya mtsho'i rnam thar*.
68. Schwieger, *The Dalai Lama and the Emperor of China*, 53.
69. Elliot Sperling, "Tibet's Foreign Relations during the Epoch of the Fifth Dalai Lama," in *Lhasa in the Seventeenth Century: The Capital of the Dalai Lamas*, ed. Françoise Pommaret (Leiden, The Netherlands: Brill, 2003), 123; and Oidtmann, *Forging the Golden Urn*, 35.
70. Ngag dbang blo bzang rgya mtsho, *Rgya mtsho'i rnam thar*, vol. 2, 391–416.
71. Michael Aris, *Bhutan: The Early History of a Himalayan Kingdom* (Delhi: Vikas Publishing House, 1980), 224, 227.
72. David Templeman, "Becoming Indian: A Study of the Life of the 16th–17th Century Tibetan Lama Tāranātha" (PhD diss., Monash University, 2008); and Cyrus Stearns, *The Buddha from Dolpo: A Study of the Life and Thought of the Tibetan Master Dolpopa Sherab Gyaltsen* (Ithaca, NY: Snow Lion, 2010).
73. Irmgard Mengele, "The Artist's Life," in *The Black Hat Eccentric: Artistic Visions of the Tenth Karmapa*, ed. Karl Debreczeny (New York: Rubin Museum of Art, 2012), 47.
74. Schwieger, *The Dalai Lama and the Emperor of China*, 61; and Dudjom Rinpoché, *The Nyingma School of Tibetan Buddhism: Its Fundamentals and History*, 2 vols., trans. and ed. Gyurme Dorjé with the collaboration of Matthew Kapstein (Boston: Wisdom, 1991), 1:821–824.
75. Schwieger, *The Dalai Lama and the Emperor of China*, 192.
76. Schwieger, *The Dalai Lama and the Emperor of China*, 51–57.
77. Tsepon Wangchuck Deden Shakabpa, *One Hundred Thousand Moons: An Advanced Political History of Tibet* (Leiden, The Netherlands: Brill, 2010, 1:391–408.
78. Erberto Lo Bue, "The Sixth Dalai Lama, Tsangyang Gyatso," in *The Dalai Lamas: A Visual History*, ed. Martin Brauen (London: Serindia, 2005), 93–101.
79. Simon Wickham-Smith, *The Hidden Life of the Sixth Dalai Lama* (Lanham, MD: Lexington Books, 2011); van Schaik, *Tibet: A history*, 136; and Oidtmann, *Forging the Golden Urn*, 37.
80. Sangs rgyas rgya mtsho, *Rgyal ba sku lnga pa drug par 'phos pa'i skor gyi gtam rna ba'i gcud len* (Lhasa, China: Block Print, n.d.).
81. Oidtmann, *Forging the Golden Urn*, 37.
82. Oidtmann, *Forging the Golden Urn*, 12.
83. Luciano Petech, *China and Tibet in the Early 18th Century: History of the Establishment of Chinese Protectorate in Tibet* (Leiden, The Netherlands: Brill, 1972), 223, 229–232; Schwieger, *The Dalai Lama and the Emperor of China*, 157–158; and Oidtmann, *Forging the Golden Urn*, 24.
84. Franz-Karl Ehrhard, "The Biography of sMan-bsgom Chos-rje Kun-dga' dpal-ldan (1735–1804) as a Source for the Sino-Nepalese War," in *Pramāṇakīrtiḥ: Papers Dedicated to Ernst Steinkellner on the Occasion of His 70th Birthday*, ed. Birgit Kellner, Helmut Krasser, Horst Lasic, Michael Torsten Much, and Helmut Tauscher (Vienna: Vienna Series for Tibetan and Buddhist Studies, 2007), 115–133.
85. Schwieger, *The Dalai Lama and the Emperor of China*, 175–184.
86. Oidtmann, *Forging the Golden Urn*, 95–155.
87. Oidtmann, *Forging the Golden Urn*, 5.

88. Both Oidtmann and Elliot Sperling suggest that the Fourteenth was chosen by the Golden Urn, but his lineage biographies do not mention this, and instead describe his previous life prophecies, and the endorsement of the Eighth 'Brug chen, Kung zig chos snang (1768–1822). Oidtmann, *Forging the Golden Urn*, 232; Elliot Sperling, "Reincarnation and the Golden Urn in the 19th Century: The Recognition of the 8th Panchen Lama," in *Studies on the History and Literature of Tibet and the Himalaya*, ed. Roberto Vitali (Kathmandu, Nepal: Vajra Publications, 2012), 97–107; and Mkhen po she rab phun tshog, *Bka' brgyud gser phreng rnam thar zla ba chu shel gyi phreng ba, smad cha kha* (Varanasi, India: Vajra Vidya Institute Library, 2014), 107–110.
89. Schwieger, *The Dalai Lama and the Emperor of China*, 186–192. Hunang Kim, "Reincarnation at Work: A Case of the Incarnation Lineage of Sumpa mkhan po," *Revue d'Etudes Tibétaines* 38 (2017), 246; and Oidtmann, *Forging the Golden Urn*, 239–243.
90. Charles Bell, *Tibet, Past and Present*, new ed. (New Delhi: Motilal Banarsidass, 2000), 124.
91. Oidtmann, *Forging the Golden Urn*, 24.
92. Schwieger, *The Dalai Lama and the Emperor of China*, 31. Jim Rheingans, "A Propos the Historical Study of Reincarnate Lamas in Tibetan Societies: *The Dalai Lama and the Emperor of China* by P. Schwieger," *Journal of Religious History*, 45, no. 4 (2021), 665.
93. Matthew W. King, "Mongolian Buddhism in the Early 20th Century," *Oxford Research Encyclopedia of Religion*, June 25, 2018.
94. Gray Tuttle, *Tibetan Buddhists in the Making of Modern China* (New York: Columbia University Press, 2005), 71–77; Agata Bareja-Starzyńska, "Jebtsundamba Khutugtus of Mongolia," *Oxford Research Encyclopedia of Religion*, March 28, 2018.
95. Marina Illich, "Imperial Stooge or Emissary to the Dge lugs Throne? Rethinking the Biographies of Chankya Rolpé Dorjé," in *Proceedings of the Tenth Seminar of the IATS*, ed. Bryan J. Cuevas and Kurtis R. Schaeffer (Leiden, The Netherlands: Brill, 2003), 3:17–31.
96. Gray Tuttle, "The Role of Mongol Elite and Educational Degrees in the Advent of Reincarnation Lineages in Seventeenth-Century Amdo," in *The Tenth Karmapa and Tibet's Turbulent Seventeenth Century*, ed. Karl Debreczeny and Gray Tuttle (New York: Rubin Museum of Art, 2016), 235–262.
97. Gray Tuttle, "Pattern Recognition: Tracking the Spread of the Incarnation Institution through Time and across Tibetan Territory," *Revue d'Etudes Tibétaines* 38 (2017): 29–63; and Oidtmann, *Forging the Golden Urn*, 204.
98. Hildegard Diemberger, *When a Woman Becomes a Religious Dynasty: The Samding Dorje Phagmo of Tibet* (New York: Columbia University Press, 2007).
99. John Ardussi, "Formation of the State of Bhutan ('Brug gzhung) in the 17th Century and Its Tibetan Antecedents," *Journal of Bhutan Studies* 11 (2004): 10–32.
100. Samdrup Rigyal and Alyson Prude, "Buddhism in Contemporary Bhutan," in *The Oxford Handbook of Contemporary Buddhism*, ed. Michael K. Jerryson (New York: Oxford University Press, 2017), 61–64.
101. Ronald M. Davidson, *Tibetan Renaissance: Tantric Buddhism in the Rebirth of Tibetan Culture* (New York: Columbia University Press, 2005), 345.
102. Sherry B. Ortner, *High Religion: A Cultural and Political History of Sherpa Buddhism* (Princeton, NJ: Princeton University Press, 1990).
103. Dudjom Rinpoche, *The Nyingma School of Tibetan Buddhism*, trans. Gyurme Dorje and Matthew Kapstein (Boston: Wisdom, 2002), 849–858; and van Schaik, *Tibet: A History*, 165–169.
104. Tsering Shakya, "The Thirteenth Dalai Lama, Thubten Gyatso," in Brauen, ed., *The Dalai Lamas*, 143–144.
105. Shakya, "The Thirteenth Dalai Lama, Thubten Gyatso," 145.
106. Scott Relyea, "Settling Authority: Sichuanese Farmers in Early Twentieth-Century Eastern Tibet," in *Frontier Tibet: Patterns of Change in Sino-Tibetan Borderlands*, ed. Stéphane Gros (Amsterdam: Amsterdam University Press, 2019), 179–216.

107. Shakya, "The Thirteenth Dalai Lama, Thubten Gyatso," 146.
108. Tsepon Wangchuk Deden Shakabpa, *Bod kyi srid don rgyal rabs* (Kalimpong, India: T. Tsepal Taikhang, 1976), 2:219–223.
109. Oidtmann, *Forging the Golden Urn*, 217.
110. Melvyn C. Goldstein, *A History of Modern Tibet, 1913–1951: The Demise of the Lamaist State* (Berkeley: University of California Press, 1992), 820.
111. Alexander Norman, "The Fourteenth Dalai Lama, Tenzin Gyatso 1876–1933," in Brauen, ed., *The Dalai Lamas*, 162–171.
112. Irina Y. Morozova, *Socialist Revolutions in Asia: The social History of Mongolia in the 20th Century* (London: Routledge, 2009), 70.
113. Amy Kellam, "How to Reincarnate Lawfully: The Rebirth of a Tibetan Religious Tradition with Socialist Characteristics," *The Journal of Comparative Law* 10, no. 2 (2016), 391.
114. Kellam, "How to Reincarnate Lawfully," 391.
115. Diemberger, *When a Woman Becomes a Religious Dynasty*, 288–314.
116. Losang Trinle Lhündrüp Chögigyeltsen, *A Poisoned Arrow: The Secret Report of the 10th Panchen Lama* (London: Tibet Information Network. 2011).
117. Norman, "The Fourteenth Dalai Lama, Tenzin Gyatso 1876–1933," 165.
118. Alexander Gardner, "The Sixteenth Karmapa, Rangjung Rigpai Dorje," *Treasury of Lives*, March 5, 2022.
119. Alexander Gardner, "The Eleventh Trungpa, Chogyam Trungpa," *Treasury of Lives*, March 5, 2022.
120. Jessica Marie Falcone, "A Transnational Tulku: The Multiple Lives of FPMT's Spanish-Born Lama Ösel," *Revue d'Etudes Tibétaines* 38 (2017), 220–240; and Elijah Ary, "The Westernisation of Tulkus," in *Little Buddhas: Children and Childhoods in Buddhist Texts and Traditions* ed., Vanessa R. Sasson (New York: Oxford University Press, 2012), 398–426.
121. Nicole Willock, "The Revival of the Tulku Institution in Modern China: Narratives and Practices," *Revue d'Etudes Tibétaines* 38 (2017), 183–201.
122. M. A. Aldrich, "The Dalai Lama in Mongolia: 'Tournament of Shadows' Reborn: Buddhism in Mongolia Has Always Had a Strong Connection to Geopolitics," *The Diplomat*, December 3, 2016.
123. John Osburg, "Consuming Belief: Luxury, Authenticity and Chinese Patronage of Tibetan Buddhism in Contemporary China," *Hau: Journal of Ethnographic Theory* 10, no. 1 (2020): 69–84.
124. Donald Lopez, *Prisoners of Shangri-la: Tibetan Buddhism and the West* (Chicago: Chicago University Press, 1998), 191.
125. Lopez, *Prisoners of Shangri-la*, 195–196; Richard, "Shugs ldan and the Dalai Lama," 440–461.
126. For overviews of both sides of this controversy see Lea Terhune, *Karmapa: The Politics of Reincarnation* (Boston: Wisdom Publications, 2004), and Tomek Lehnert, *Rogues in Robes: An Inside Chronicle of a Recent Chinese–Tibetan Intrigue in the Karma Kagyu Lineage of Diamond Way Buddhism* (Berlin: Blue Dolphin Publications, 2014).
127. John Steinbeck IV and Nancy Steinbeck, *The Other Side of Eden: Life with John Steinbeck* (New York: Prometheus Books, 2001), 279, 311.
128. Sandra Bell, "'Crazy Wisdom,' Charisma, and the Transmission of Buddhism in the United States," *Nova Religio* 2, no. 1 (1998): 55–75.
129. A detailed description of all of them would require another article. But there is an overview of some cases in Anna Sawerthal, "Abuse and Buddhism: Behind the Smiling Façade," in *Tibetan Buddhism in the West, Problems of Adoption and Cross-Cultural Confusion* (February 2, 2022).
130. Perhaps the most direct of these confessions was Yangsi Kalu Rinpoche's "Confession." "Confessions of Kalu Rinpoche," SpiceYourDay, November 28, 2011, YouTube video, 09:45. See also Ary, "The Westernisation of Tulkus."
131. Sawerthal, "Abuse and Buddhism."

132. Osburg, "Consuming Belief," 69–84.
133. Dzongsar Jamyang Khyentse Rinpoche, "Time for Radical Change in How We Raise our Tulkus," *Tricycle: The Buddhist Review*, August 22, 2016.
134. Françoise Ribin, "Souls Gone in the Wing? Suspending Belief About Rebirth in Contemporary Artistic Works in the Tibetan World," *Himalaya* 36, no. 1 (2016), 116–129.
135. Evan Osnos, "The Next Incarnation: As the Dalai Lama Turns Seventy-five, What Is Tibet's Future?" *The New Yorker*, September 27, 2010.
136. Dzongsar Jamyang Khyentse Rinpoche, "Time for Radical Change."; Richard Sandomir, "Sogyal Rinpoche Dies; Tibetan Buddhist Lama Felled by Abuse Accusations," *The New York Times*, September 1, 2019.
137. Lyudmila Klasanova, "Khandro Tashi Chotso Enthroned as Tulku in India," *Buddhist Door Global*, January 22, 2020.
138. Tsering Shakya, "Self-immolation, the Changing Language of Protest in Tibet," *Revue d'études tibétaines* 25, no. 2012 (2012): 28–29.
139. Fiona McConnell, "The Geopolitics of Buddhist Reincarnation: Contested Futures of Tibetan Leadership," *Area* 45, no. 2 (2012), 166; and Tsering Shakya, *The Dragon in the Land of Snows: A History of Modern Tibet since 1947* (London: Penguin, 1999), 444.
140. Xinhua, "Dalai Lama Critized for Reincarnation Remarks," March 11, 2015; Sergius L. Kuzmin, "Management as a Tool of Destruction: Reincarnation of 'Living Buddhas' in Modern Chinese Legislation," *The Tibet Journal* 42, no. 1 (2017): 37.
141. Ben Westcott, "When the Dalai Lama Dies, His Reincarnation Will Be a Religious Crisis. Here's What Could Happen," *CNN*, February 16, 2021.
142. Rustam Sabirov, "The Tulku Institution and Future of Buddhism in Mongolia," *Acta Mongolica* 18, no. 532 (2019), 119–129.
143. Jackson, *Rebirth: A Guide to Mind, Karma, and Cosmos in the Buddhist World*; Appleton, *Narrating Karma and Rebirth*; and Davidson, *Tibetan Renaissance.*
144. Van der Kuijp, "The Dalai Lamas and the Origin of Reincarnate Lamas"; Van der Kuijp, "'Baγši' and 'Baγši-s' in Tibetan Historical, Biographical and Lexicographical Texts"; and van der Kuijp, "The Kalacakra and the Patronage of Tibetan Buddhism by the Mongol Imperial Family."
145. Hirshberg, *Remembering the Lotus Born*; Manson, *The Second Karmapa, Karma Pakshi*; Manson, "Introduction to the Life of Karma Pakshi (1204/6-1283)"; Gamble, *Reincarnation in Tibetan Buddhism*; and Ruth Gamble, *The Third Karmapa Rangjung Dorje, Master of Mahamudra* (Boulder, CO: Shambhala Publications, 2020).
146. Garrett, *Religion, Medicine, and the Human Embryo in Tibet.*
147. Wylie, "The First Mongol Conquest of Tibet Reinterpreted"; and Luciano Petech, *Central Tibet and the Mongols: The Yüan-Sa-skya Period of Tibetan History* (Rome: Istituto Italiano per il Medio ed Estremo Oriente, 1990).
148. Ngag dbang blo bzang rgya mtsho, *The Illusive Play*. Ngag dbang blo bzang rgya mtsho, *A History of Tibet.*
149. Petech, *China and Tibet in the Early 18th Century*; Luciano Petech, "The Dalai-Lamas and Regents of Tibet: A Chronological Study," *T'oung Pao* 47, no. 3/5 (1959): 368–394; Elliot Sperling, "The 5th Karma-pa and Some Aspects of the Relationship between Tibet and the Early Ming," in *Tibetan Studies in Honour of Hugh Richardson: Proceedings of the International Seminar on Tibetan Studies*, ed. Michael Aris and Aung San Suu Kyi (Warminster, UK: Aris and Phillips, 1979): 280–289. Elliot Sperling, "Early Ming Policy toward Tibet: An Examination of the Proposition That the Early Ming Emperors Adopted a 'Divide and Rule' Policy toward Tibet (China)" (PhD diss., Indiana University, 1983); Elliot Sperling, "Karma Rol-pa'i rdo-rje and the Re-Establishment of Karma-pa Political Influence in

the 14th Century," in *The Relationship between Religion and State (chos srid zung 'brel) in Traditional Tibet*, ed. Christoph Cüppers (Lumbini, Nepal: Lumbini International Research Institute, 2004), 229; Sperling, "Reincarnation and the Golden Urn in the 19th Century," 97–107; and Elliot Sperling, "Pho-lha-nas, Khang-chen-nas, and the Last Era of Mongol Domination in Tibet," *Rocznik Orientalistyczny* 65, no. 1 (2012): 195–211.

150. Schwieger, *The Dalai Lama and the Emperor of China*; Peter Schwieger, *Conflict in a Buddhist Society: Tibet under the Dalai Lamas* (Honolulu: University of Hawai'i Press, 2021). Jim Rheingans also published a thoughtful review of this work. Rheingans, "A Propos the Historical Study of Reincarnate Lamas in Tibetan Societies." *Journal of Religious History* 45, no. 4 (2021): 659–667.
151. Oidtmann, *Forging the Golden Urn.*
152. Melvyn C. Goldstein, *A History of Modern Tibet, Volume 1: 1913–1951: The Demise of the Lamaist State* (Berkeley: University of California Press, 1989); Melvyn C. Goldstein, *A History of Modern Tibet, Volume 2: The Calm before the Storm: 1951–1955* (Berkeley: University of California Press, 2007). Melvyn C. Goldstein, *A History of Modern Tibet, Volume 3: The Storm Clouds Descend: 1955–1957* (Berkeley: University of California Press, 2013); and Melvyn C. Goldstein, *A History of Modern Tibet, Volume 4: In the Eye of the Storm, 1957–1959* (Berkeley: University of California Press, 2019).
153. Karma Phuntho, *The History of Bhutan* (London: Random House, 2013); and Michael Aris, *The Raven Crown: The Origins of Buddhist Monarchy in Bhutan* (Chicago: Serindia Publications, 2005).
154. Diemberger, *When a Woman Becomes a Religious Dynasty.*
155. Willock, "The Revival of the Tulku Institution in Modern China."
156. Tanya Zivkovic, *Death and Reincarnation in Tibetan Buddhism: In-between Bodies* (London: Routledge, 2013); and Ary, "The Westernisation of Tulkus."
157. Kellam, "How to Reincarnate Lawfully," 384–405; John Powers, *The Buddha Party: How the People's Republic of China Works to Define and Control Tibetan Buddhism* (New York: Oxford University Press, 2017), 92–129; and Sabirov, "The Tulku Institution and Future of Buddhism in Mongolia," 119–129.
158. Brauen, ed., *The Dalai Lamas*; Debreczeny, ed., *The Black Hat Eccentric*; and Daniel A. Hirshberg, Derek F. Maher, and Tsering Wangchuk, "The Tulku (*sprul sku*) Institution in Tibetan Buddhism," in "The Tulku (sprul sku) Institution in Tibetan Buddhism," ed. Daniel A. Hirshberg, Derek F. Maher, and Tsering Wangchuk, special issue, *Revue d'Etudes Tibétaines* 3 (2017).
159. Nyang rel Nyi ma 'od zer, *Bka' thang zangs gling ma* (Chengdu, China: Si khron mi rigs dpe skrun khang, 1989).
160. Karma Pak shi, *Grub chen karma pakshi'i bka' 'bum* (Gangtok, India: Gonpo Tseten, 1978).
161. Manson, *The Second Karmapa, Karma Pakshi.*
162. Rang byung rdo rje, "Bla ma rin po che'i rnam par thar pa'o: Karma pa'i rnam thar," in *Rang byung rdo rje'i gsung 'bum* vol. ca (Tsurpu, Tibet: Mkhan po lo yag bkra shis, 2006), 256–287.
163. Rang byung rdo rje, "Dpal chen Rang byung rdo rje'i rnam thar," in *Rang byung rdo rje'i gsung 'bum* (Tsurpu, Tibet: Mkhan po lo yag bkra shis, 2006), vol. ca, 353–376.
164. Rang byung rdo rje, "Rang byung rdo rje'I gsung 'gur [sic] thor bu," in *Rang byung rdo rje'i gsung 'bu* (Tsurpu, Tibet: Mkhan po lo yag bkra shis, 2006), vol. ca, 359–416.
165. Ngag dbang blo bzang rgya mtsho, *Za hor gyi ban de ngag dbang blo bzang rgya mtsho'i 'di snang 'khrul ba'i rol rtsed rtogs brjod kyi tshul du bkod pa du kū la'i gos pa.*
166. Si tu paṇ chen chos kyi byung gnas and 'Be lo tshe dban kun khyab, *Bka' brgyud gser 'phreng rnam thar zla ba chu shel gyi 'phreng ba*, 2 vols.
167. 'Gos Lo tsā ba gzhon nu dpal, *Deb ther sngon po*, ed. Lokesh Chandra (New Delhi: International Academy of Indian Culture, 1974).
168. This is published as: Ga Lotsawa, *The Blue Annals*, trans. George Roerich and Gendün Chöpel (New Delhi: Motilal Banarsidass, 1988).

169. Rang byung rdo rje, "Zab mo nang don," in *Rang byung rdo rje'i gsung 'bum* (Tsurpu, Tibet: Mkhan po lo yag bkra shis, 2006), vol. ja, 308–360; and Rang byung rdo rje, "Zab mo nang don gyi 'grel,", vol. ja, 361–634.
170. Rang byung rdo rje, "Ston pa'i skyes rabs," in *Rang byung rdo rje'i gsung 'bum* (Tsurpu, Tibet: Mkhan po lo yag bkra shis, 2006), vol. kha, 1–666.

Ruth Gamble

RENNYO

RENNYO 蓮如, 1415–1499

Rennyo was a Japanese pure land Buddhist priest of the Jōdo Shinshū 浄土真宗 tradition during the Muromachi 室町 period (1392–1573), the eighth head priest of Honganji 本願寺, the sect's head temple, which was created around the mausoleum of Shinran (1173–1262), the founder of Jōdo Shinshū, by Kakunyo 覚如 (1270–1351), Shinran's great-grandson, in 1321. Rennyo was the ninth-generation descendant of Shinran and is recognized as the eighth chief abbot by both the Jōdo Shinshū Hongwanji-ha 浄土真宗本願寺派 and the Shinshū Ōtani-ha 真宗大谷派, which together comprise the largest Pure Land Buddhist denomination in Japan.

Rennyo's priestly name given at the time of his ordination was Kenju 兼壽. He also received the cloistered title Shinshōin 信証院. In 1882, Emperor Meiji (1852–1912) awarded him the title of Great Master Etō (Etō Daishi 慧燈大師). Within the Jōdo Shinshū tradition, Rennyo is known as the second founder (*chūkō no so* 中興の祖), or the restorer of the tradition (*gosaikō no shōnin* 御再興の上人), who successfully popularized Jōdo Shinshū by rekindling the spirit of Shinran's promotion of the pure land Buddhist faith (*shinjin* 信心).

EARLY YEARS

Birth and Ordination. Rennyo was born in 1415 (Ōei 応永 22, 25th day of the second month) at Honganji in the Higashiyama Ōtani area of Kyoto, as the first son of Zonnyo 存如 (1396–1457), the seventh head priest of Honganji. The name of Rennyo's mother is not known. No historical records concerning his mother exist, suggesting that her background was humble. She may have been a servant for Zonnyo at Honganji. However, one biographical record, the *Rennyo Shōnin itokuki* 蓮如上人遺徳記, mentions that when Rennyo was six years old, his mother left Honganji.[1] Although there is no explanation of her departure, it is surmised that she left Honganji because of Zonnyo's official marriage to Nyoenni 如円尼 (d. 1460) in 1420. Nyoenni's father was the lord of the Ebina clan who was close to the Shōgun, Ashikaga Yoshimitsu 足利義満 (1358–1408). Although the Buddhist precepts prohibit ordained clerics from having a family, Jōdo Shinshū priests chose to follow the tradition of the founder Shinran who openly married and had children.

In 1431, Rennyo was ordained as a Buddhist priest at the age of 17. Following the tradition of his family, his ordination was held at Shōrenin 青蓮院, one of the major *monzeki* 門跡

(noble cloister) temples of the Tendai 天台 school.[2] Since Shinran was ordained at Shōrenin as an adopted son of his uncle Hino Noritsuna 日野範綱, Rennyo also received his ordination as a temporarily adopted son (*yūshi* 猶子) of Hirohashi Kanenobu 広橋兼郷 (1401–1446), of the aristocratic Hino family. Rennyo received the monastic name Kenju 兼壽, and was given his dharma name (*hōmyō* 法名), Rennyo.

This rather complicated arrangement for Rennyo's ordination was necessary because an aristocratic family connection, even nominally, was requisite for receiving ordination at prestigious *monzeki* temples. It should be remembered, too, that when Kakunyo established Honganji as a temple in Kyoto, Jōdo Shinshū was not fully recognized as an independent religious order; thus official recognition of the temple's status and priestly ordinations required affiliation with one of the established monastic Buddhist orders. In order to enshrine Shinran's mausoleum properly within a Buddhist temple, Kakunyo had to receive authorization from the Tendai school regardless of Tendai's past hostilities to the propagation of the exclusive nenbutsu practice (*senju nenbutsu* 専修念仏) by Hōnen 法然 (1133–1212) and his disciples, including Shinran.

Clerical Training. Although Rennyo received his initial ordination (*tokudo* 得度) at a Tendai temple, he did not receive further monastic training at Tendai monasteries. Instead, he received clerical training as a disciple of the monk Kyōgaku 経覚 (1395–1473), the abbot of Daijō-in (大乗院門跡 Daijōin monzeki) at Kōfukuji 興福寺, the famous Hossō 法相 school establishment in Nara. This arrangement was possible because of family connections with Kyōgaku, whose mother Shōrin 正林 (d. 1442) was a member of Rennyo's family, and Zonnyo and Kyōgaku were cousins.

As a Jōdo Shinshū priest, Rennyo received transmission of Shinran's teaching at Honganji from his father Zonnyo. Rennyo then served under Zonnyo, assisting with his father's missionary work for more than 20 years. Rennyo was known for his mastery in producing precise copies of the manuscripts of Shinshū scriptures, including a set of Shinran's main work *Kyōgyoshinshō* 教行信証 (On Teaching, Practice, Faith, and Realization, 1450) and its *nobegaki* 延書 (Japanese transliteration of *kanbun*, 1454). Among numerous works transcribed by Rennyo, the most famous is his copy of the *Tannishō* 歎異抄 (A Record in Lament of Divergences) preserved at Nishi Honganji, which is the oldest extant manuscript of the text. These precise reproductions of doctrinal manuscripts were crucial not only for the propagation of Jōdo Shinshū teaching but also for the survival of the Honganji tradition and its institutional authority.

As assistant to Zonnyo, Rennyo traveled to the eastern and northern regions of Japan. Zonnyo, during his tenure as the head priest of Honganji (1436–1457), took Rennyo first to the eastern regions (1447) and two years later to the northern regions (1449) to help with missionary work and to make direct connections with influential followers of Shinran's teaching, whose communities remained more or less independent at this time. Rennyo helped to unify these disparate communities under the Honganji umbrella.

Marriage and Family Life. Following the tradition of Shinran, Rennyo also married. In fact, he would marry five times. His first wife was Nyoryō 如了 (d. 1455), a daughter of Taira Sadafusa 平貞房 of the Ise 伊勢 Clan. The date of their marriage is not recorded, but their first son Junnyo 順如 was born in 1442 when Rennyo was 28 years old. They had four sons and three daughters. After Nyōryō's death in 1455, Rennyo married successively four more times (Renyū 蓮祐, d. 1470; Nyoshō 如勝, d. 1478; Shūnyo 宗如, d. 1486; and Rennō 蓮能, d. 1518). With these five wives, he fathered a total of 13 sons and 14 daughters.[3] When Honganji expanded its reach to the provincial areas in Rennyo's later life, he effectively used his large family by placing his male descendants in major temples to consolidate the institutional power of Honganji—a system known as the *ikkeshū* 一家衆 (family council).

During this period, however, Honganji was institutionally and financially in difficult straits despite its prestigious position within the Jōdo Shinshū tradition. Among the various factions of Jōdo Shinshū, the Bukkōji 佛光寺 branch boasted the most success in Kyoto. A record in the *Honpukuji yuraiki* 本福寺由来記 notes, for example, that Bukkōji was packed with pilgrims while Honganji was deserted.[4] Legends say that Rennyo's family was so poor that he had to read scriptures by moonlight because he could not afford to buy lamp oil.

TRANSFORMATION OF HONGANJI UNDER RENNYO

Appointment as the Eighth Head Priest of Honganji. In 1457, Zonnyo, the seventh head priest of Honganji, passed away. The succession of the lineage of Honganji was all but decided to go to Ōgen 応玄 (1433–1503), Zonnyo's first son with his official wife Nyoen. However, Ōgen's appointment was blocked by the sole opposition of Zonnyo's youngest son Nyojō 如乗 (1412–1460), who argued that Rennyo was the most qualified. At that time, Nyojō was the most influential Jōdo Shinshū priest in the Hokuriku region as the founder of Honsenji 本泉寺 in Kaga 加賀 Province and head priest of Zuisenji 瑞泉寺 in Etchū 越中 Province. In the end, Nyojō's opposition prevailed, and Rennyo, at age 43, was appointed as the eighth head priest of Honganji. Nyojō's support would also aid Rennyo in developing strong ties with the congregations in the Hokuriku provinces.

Institutional Reformation of Honganji. When Rennyo took up the position of head priest, Honganji's institutional foundation was in decline and its financial situation precarious. Although the temple housed Shinran's mausoleum and was recognized as the sect's spiritual center by its followers, as an institution Honganji was considered simply a minor branch temple of the Tendai school. In order to emphasize the temple's distinct doctrinal foundations, Rennyo removed Tendai-style practices from Honganji's liturgy, such as decommissioning the six ritual priests who came from the Tendai school to performed daily religious services at Honganji.[5]

Another of Rennyo's innovative reforms was to remove the upper seating level for the head priest of Honganji and place all seats in the temple at the common level (*hiraza* 平座). According to the *Honganji sahō no shidai* 本願寺作法次第 (An Outline of the Rituals and Practices of Honganji), Rennyo ordered the removal of the upper seating, which symbolized the aristocratic heritage of Shinran's family, since he believed that, if you act like a superior person (*jōrō* 上臈), the propagation of Shinran's teaching equally to everyone is not possible.[6]

During this period, Rennyo also began developing unique methods of propagation. He distributed handwritten six-character *myōgo* scrolls (*rokuji myōgo* 六字名号) of Amida

Buddha's name (*na-mu a-mi-da-butsu* 南無阿弥陀仏) to his followers to use as the main object of worship in their community services. Use of *myōgō* scrolls standardized the object of worship and allowed followers to hold congregational gatherings at any household simply by hanging the scroll as the object of worship. Additionally, in order to disseminate his message effectively, Rennyo began writing instructional letters in which he explained Shinran's teaching in colloquial Japanese, adopting the medieval literary style of *kana hōgo* 仮名法語 (Dharma message in *kana* script). His letters were usually written on one sheet of paper and were meant to be read frequently at congregational gatherings. These instructional notes were later collectively termed the *ofumi* 御文, or *gobunshō* 御文章 (both terms meaning "letters").

He also promoted recitation of Shinran's *Shōshinge* 正信偈 (The Hymns of True Faith) as an everyday practice for followers. *Shōshinge* is a lengthy hymn composed in Chinese by Shinran and found in the Chapter on Practice in his major work, the *Kyōgyōshinshō* 教行信証. Prior to Rennyo's time, daily rituals at Honganji were conducted six times a day following the ritual protocol of the *Rokuji raisan* 六時礼讃 (Liturgy at Six Times) based on Shandao's *Ōjōraisan* 往生礼讃 (Hymns of Birth in the Pure Land). This tradition had been created by Hōnen more than 250 years earlier. By introducing this new ritual, Rennyo highlighted the identity of the followers of Shinran's tradition as distinct from Hōnen's. For Rennyo, the *Shōshinge* seems to have represented the core of Shinran's thought, and in 1460 he composed the *Shōshinge-tai'i* 正信偈大意 (Outline of Shōshinge; written at the request of Dōsai 道西 of Kanegamori), the only commentary he ever wrote.

Destruction of Ōtani Honganji by the Tendai Militia-Priests. Under Rennyo's leadership, Honganji began expanding its institutional reach beyond Kyoto. Rennyo first recruited Honganji membership in Ōmi 近江 Province (Shiga Prefecture), especially in the areas of Katada 堅田, Akanoi 赤野井, and Kanegamori 金森, which controlled the shipping traffic on Lake Biwa. These areas had been a stronghold of the Tendai school. By converting them and bringing them into the institutional framework of Honganji, Rennyo was able to call on their support for shoring up the headquarter's finances. The support of the Ōmi merchants in fact enabled Rennyo to conduct one of the most important events in the history of the institution, the 200th memorial service of the founder Shinran.

However, the rapid growth of Honganji in this area, strategically significant for its commercial traffic connecting the eastern regions of Japan to Kyoto, raised concerns particularly for the Enryakuji, the Tendai headquarters located between Ōmi and Kyoto. In Kanshō 寛正 6 (1465), the Tendai militia-priests at Enryakuji attacked and completely destroyed Honganji (their second attempt), an event known as the Kanshō persecution *(Kanshō no hōnan* 寛正の法難). Rennyo retreated to Ōmi province, but the army of Tendai priests followed and attacked the strongholds of Rennyo's followers in Kenegamori and Akanoi.

In Ōnin 応仁 1 (1467) the authorities of Enryakuji pardoned Honganji after a deal was struck requiring Honganji to pay annual dues to Enryakuji as a branch temple of the Saitō-in. However, Rennyo did not return to Kyoto. Turmoil in the city at the onset of the Ōnin War (1467–1477) made it impossible to rebuild Honganji at its original site. Instead, in 1468, he decided to travel, making a tour of the eastern regions, and visiting Mount Kōya 高野山 and the Yoshino 吉野 region in Kii 紀伊 Province (Wakayama and Nara Prefectures).

Development of Yoshizaki as a Religious Township. Despite the agreement with Enryakuji, Honganji's troubles with the Tendai headquarters continued. As a result, in 1469 Rennyo entrusted the statue of Shinran to Miidera 三井寺, which was the only counterforce against Enryakuji, and in 1471 moved to Yoshizaki on the border of Echizen and Kaga Provinces (Fukui and Ishikawa Prefectures). It is not clear why Rennyo chose Yoshizaki, but it is likely that the area contained an estate owned by Kyōgaku, Rennyo's mentor in his early years.

At Yoshizaki, Rennyo not only built a temple to replace the original Honganji (known as the Ōtani Honganji); he also developed the surrounding areas into a religious township with residences for both priests and lay followers and that provided lodgings for travelers and other services. As a result, Yoshizaki as a religious township rapidly attracted large numbers of pilgrims mainly from northern provinces as far as Dewa and Ōshu.

In order to propagate the teaching effectively to Jōdo Shinshū communities scattered throughout Japan, Rennyo restarted his missionary work by writing more of his instructional letters. While based at Yoshizaki, Rennyo wrote 78 letters, which comprise approximately one-third of his currently extant letters. He also continued distributing the six-character *myōgo* scrolls as the main object of worship. He formulated new ways to popularize the *Shōshinge*, in 1473 creating for the first time a printed edition of the text and Shinran's *Wasan* 和讃 (Japanese Hymns) to promote the recitation of these two hymns as a standard religious service. By combining all of these elements—the instructional letters, six-character *myōgō* scroll, and recitation of *Shōshinge*—Rennyo's followers were able to conduct religious services at virtually any place they gathered. Such congregational gatherings were called *kō* 講 (meetings) or simply *yoriai* 寄合 (gatherings).

These religious meetings, however, gradually developed into semiautonomous religio-political fraternities that sought to resist the secular authorities in the Hokuriku regions. Rennyo tried to curb the use of force by his followers by instructing them not to cause disturbances and to "take the laws of the state as authoritative" (*ōbō ihon* 王法為本).[7] Despite his repeated admonitions, by 1474 skirmishes with local authorities had developed into full-scale peasant uprisings (*ikkō ikki*) led by Rennyo's followers in Kaga Province. (The revolts in Kaga continued for more than 100 years until the peasants were finally disarmed by the warlord Oda Nobunaga 織田信長 in 1580.) In order to avoid these continuing conflicts, Rennyo moved out of Yoshizaki in 1475.

RESTORATION OF HONGANJI IN YAMASHINA

Construction of Yamashina Honganji. After Rennyo left Yoshizaki in 1475, he temporarily moved to Kawachi Deguchi 河内出口 (Osaka Prefecture). It seems that he was considering several possible sites for rebuilding Honganji such as Sakai 堺 and Tonda 富田, both in Settsu 摂津 Province (Osaka Prefecture). But with the end of Ōnin War in 1477, he resolved to re-establish Honganji in Kyoto and reclaimed the statue of Shinran entrusted to Miidera since 1469. After exploring various locations in the Kyoto area, in 1478 he chose to build in Yamashina 山科, the eastern outskirt of Kyoto, instead of moving back to Higashiyama Ōtani.

Construction of the Yamashina Honganji started in 1478 and took five years to complete. The memorial hall for Shinran (Goeidō, or Mieidō 御影堂) was completed in 1480. The statue of Shinran was returned from Miidera and enshrined at Yamashina in the same year.

Construction of the Amida Hall (Amidadō 阿弥陀堂) was completed in 1483. With these two massive buildings standing side by side and surrounded by protective walls and trenches, Yamashina Honganji appeared rather like a castle built in an open field. As at Yoshizaki, but on a much larger scale, Rennyo developed the nearby area into a *jinaichō* 寺内町 (temple-city) providing services to pilgrims. Rennyo was 69 when the project to restore Honganji was finally complete.

Retirement and Last Years. While Rennyo and his group were settling in peacefully at Yamashina, the uprisings in Kaga Province intensified. In 1487, the local peasants ousted the lord of Kaga, Togashi Masachika 富樫正親 (1455–1488), and the battles of the *ikkō ikki* revolt ended two years later with the victory of Rennyo's followers. Kaga Province became an autonomous region governed collectively by these Honganji followers (*monto no mochitaru kuni* 門徒の持ちたる国) for the next 90 years until its resistance was crushed by Nobunaga's army in 1580.

At the same time as this victory in Kaga, in 1489 Rennyo at the age of 75 ceded his position as the head priest of Honganji to his fifth son Jitsunyo 実如 (1458–1525) and retired to the Southern Residence Hall (Minamidono 南殿) built adjacent to Yamashina Honganji. His reason for retiring is not known, but his intention to do so was already evident by his use of his *ingō* 院号 (cloistered title), Shinshōin 信証院, in an instructional letter written in 1477.[8]

Rennyo's retirement seemed to be merely nominal, and he actively continued to write his instructional letters. His last large-scale institutional development project was the Ishiyama Gobō 石山御坊 in Settsu, Ōsaka. Construction of the temple in Ōsaka-Ishiyama began in 1496 and was completed in 1497, with the temple situated on the banks of the Yodo River overlooking the river traffic. It is clear that Rennyo's construction of the Ishiyama Gobō sought to establish an outpost for further institutional expansion to the west. Ishiyama Gobō became Ishiyama Honganji 石山本願寺 after the destruction of Yamashina Honganji in 1532 during the Sengoku period.

One year after the completion of Ishiyama Gobō, Rennyo began to feel ill and returned to Yamashina. He died in early 1499 at Yamashina Honganji. He was 85. He was cremated and buried near Yamashina Honganji, and his tomb was eventually enlarged as a mausoleum. In 1882, Emperor Meiji (1852–1912) awarded him the title of Great Master Etō (Etō Daishi 慧燈大師).

FURTHER DEVELOPMENT OF HONGANJI AND LASTING LEGACY

Linking Congregations with the Family Council. Rennyo employed two rather contradictory systems to strengthen Honganji at the institutional level. First, he adopted the *kō* 講 (congregation) system to connect his followers to Honganji. The system of *kō* existed prior to Rennyo's time as cooperative devotional organizations created by lay followers in rural areas for worshipping a particular buddha, bodhisattva, or kami, often at a distant temple or shrine. Rennyo converted the village *kō* groups to direct devotion to Amida Buddha as well as to honor the Jōdo Shinshū founder Shinran, and offered them a direct affiliation with Honganji. Prior to Rennyo's efforts, the majority of Shinshū followers were not affiliated with temples, instead congregating at private practice halls called *dōjō* 道場. Rennyo's use of *kō* linked the independent *dōjōs* into a system managed by Honganji that benefited the followers by offering them direct access to the religion's spiritual authority and benefited the head temple financially through dues.

The second system Rennyo devised was the use of the hierarchical family lineage to incorporate and control congregations of Shinshū followers scattered in rural areas. Rennyo created a governing system based on his family's blood linage called *ichimon ikkeshū* 一門一家衆. The governing system consisted of a two-tiered structure, *ichimonshū* 一門衆 (the lineage of the eldest son) and *ikkeshū* 一家衆 (the lineage of branch families). The *ichimonshū* were direct members of the Honganji's head priest's family. The *ikkeshū* included the members of the families of the brothers of the head priest. There were already 35 *ikkeshū* at the time of Rennyo's death. During the time of Jitsunyo, the number of *ichimon ikkeshū* multiplied and expanded to further secure the family's grip on institutional authority. The combination of the *kō* system with the *ichimon ikkeshū* system resulted in an extremely powerful organization. Although the *kō* were relatively small, once they were united under the hierarchical authority secured by the blood lineage of *ichimon ikkeshū*, they were able to pool their interests and resources to form an extended religio-political unit powerful enough, for example, to take over the entire province of Kaga.

Compilation and Distribution of Rennyo's Letters. Rennyo's father Zonnyo had relied heavily on the distribution of copies of the Jōdo Shinshū scriptures, and Rennyo had worked as his father's scribe. He was thus highly familiar with the contents of the scriptures. However, instead of continuing to copy scriptures, Rennyo sought a more direct approach to preaching. He wrote instructional letters that were read aloud at religious meetings, through which his understanding of Shinran's teaching could be transmitted directly to his followers in his own words. The total number of letters that can be definitively attributed to Rennyo amount to more than 260.

Rennyo wrote his instructional letters in simple colloquial Japanese in order to transmit Shinran's teaching effectively. Rennyo seems to have taken particular care to keep his expressions as simple as possible to make his doctrinal instructions easy to understand. For example, in trying to convey the main purport of Shinran's interpretation of salvation by Amida Buddha's Other Power (*tariki* 他力), he consistently used simple phrases like *anjin* 安心 (settled mind), or the common verb *tanomu* たのむ (entrusting), instead of relying on the erudite Buddhist terminology used in classical Chinese texts.

After Rennyo's death, his son Jitsunyo, the ninth head priest of Honganji, selected 80 significant letters and compiled them in five volumes, later known as the *Gojō ofumi* 五帖御文 (Collected Letters of Rennyo in Five Volumes). The publication of the *Letters* was supervised by Shōnyo 証如 (1516–1554), the tenth head priest of Honganji. Since then, copies of Rennyo's *Letters* have been distributed not only to Shinshū priests but also widely circulated among lay followers.

REVIEW OF LITERATURE

Rennyo's life and thought are popular subjects in a wide range of academic studies in Japan, beginning with Buddhist studies and history, but also including other related fields from political science to women's studies.[9] However Western scholarship on Rennyo is still limited and generally focuses on the historical and institutional development of the Jōdo Shinshū tradition under Rennyo and Rennyo's influence on the development of premodern Japanese spirituality.[10] The significance of his life and work are also often discussed in historical studies on Muromachi Japan, especially the period from the Ōnin War through the end of the Sengoku period.[11] A complete translation of the collection of Rennyo's *Letters* in five volumes is available in a book by Minor L. Rogers and Ann T. Rogers, *Rennyo: The Second Founder of Shin Buddhism*.[12] Translations of various Japanese studies on Rennyo, including perspectives from folklore studies and comparative religion, can be found in *Rennyo and the Roots of Modern Japanese Buddhism*, edited by Mark L. Blum and Shin'ya Yasutomi.[13] This book has substantially broadened the scope of Western academic studies on Rennyo.

PRIMARY SOURCES

CONTEMPORARY CRITICAL EDITIONS OF RENNYO'S WRITINGS AND COLLECTIONS OF HIS SAYINGS

Jōdo Shinshū seiten zensho, vol. 5, Sōdenhen, ge. Kyoto: Jōdo Shinshū Hongwanji-ha, 2014.

Shinshū Shiryō Kankōkai, ed. *Rennyo ofumi, Taikei Shinshū shiryō, Bunsho kirokuhen*, vol. 6. Kyoto: Hōzōkan, 2008.

Shinshū Shiryō Kankōkai, ed. *Rennyo hōgo, Taikei Shinshū shiryō, Bunsho kirokuhen*, vol. 7. Kyoto: Hōzōkan, 2012.

Ōtani Chōjun, ed. *Rennyo shōnin zenshū*. 5 vols. Tokyo: Kawade Shobō Shinsha, 1989.

Shinshū shōgyō zensho, vol. 3, Rekidaibu. Kyoto: Ōyagi Kōbundō, 1970.

Inaba, Masumaru, ed. *Rennyo shōnin ibun*. Kyoto: Hōzōkan, 1937.

COLLECTIONS OF RENNYO'S BIOGRAPHIES AND OTHER HISTORICAL DOCUMENTS RELATED TO RENNYO

Shinshū Shiryō Kankōkai, ed. *Rennyoden, Taikei Shinshū shiryō, Denkihen*, vol. 5. Kyoto: Hōzōkan, 2009.

Shinshū Shiryō Kankōkai, ed. *Rennyoeden to engi, Taikei Shinshū shiryō, Denkihen*, vol. 6. Kyoto: Hōzōkan, 2007.

Shinshū Ōtaniha Kyōgaku Kenkyūsho, ed. *Rennyo shōnin gyōjitsu*. Kyoto: Shinshū Ōtaniha Shūmusho Shuppanbu, 1994.

Shinshū shiryō shūsei, vol. 10. *Rennyo to sono kyōdan*. Edited by Katada Osamu. Kyoto: Dōbōsha, 1978.

FURTHER READING

Blum, Mark L., and Shin'ya Yasutomi, eds. *Rennyo and the Roots of Modern Japanese Buddhism*. Oxford: Oxford University Press, 2006.

Dobbins, James C. *Jōdo Shinshū: Shin Buddhism in Medieval Japan*. Bloomington: Indiana University Press, 1989.

Nagao, Gadzin et al. *Letters of Rennyo: A Translation of Rennyo's* Gobunshō. Kyoto: Hongwanji International Center, 2000.

Rogers, Minor L. "Rennyo's Ofumi and Shinshu in Pure Land Tradition." In *Pure Land Tradition: History and Development*. Edited by James Foard, Michael Solomon, and Richard Payne. Berkeley, CA: Berkeley Buddhist Studies Series, 1996.

Rogers, Minor L., and Ann T. Rogers. *Rennyo: The Second Founder of Shin Buddhism*. Berkeley, CA: Asian Humanities Press, 1991.

Solomon, Michael. "Kinship and the Transmission of Religious Charisma: The Case of Honganji." *Journal of Asian Studies* 33, no. 3 (1974): 403–413.

Solomon, Michael. "The Dilemma of Religious Power: Honganji and Hosokawa Masamoto." *Monumenta Nipponica* 33 (1978): 51–65.

Solomon, Michael. "Honganji under Rennyo: The Development of Shinshū in Medieval Japan." In *Pure Land Tradition: History and Development*. Edited by James Foard, Michael Solomon, and Richard Payne. Berkeley, CA: Berkeley Buddhist Studies Series, 1996.

Tsang, Carol Richmond. *War and Faith: Ikko Ikki in Late Muromachi Japan*. Cambridge, MA: Harvard East Asian Monographs 288, 2007.

Weinstein, Stanley. "Rennyo and the Shinshu Revival." In *Japan in the Muromachi Age*. Edited by John Whitney Hall and Toyoda Takeshi. Berkeley: University of California Press, 1977.

NOTES

1. *Rennyo Shōnin itokuki*, in *Shinshū shōgyō zensho* (Kyoto: Ōyagi Kōbundō, 1970), 3:870; and *Jōdo Shinshū seiten zensho* (Kyoto: Jōdo Shinshū Hongwanji-ha, 2014), 5:1280.
2. Eisho Nasu, "Ordination Ceremony of the Honganji Priests in Premodern Japanese Society," in *Engaged Pure Land Buddhism: Challenges Facing Jōdo Shinshū in the Contemporary World*, ed. Kenneth K. Tanaka and Eisho Nasu (Berkeley, CA: Wisdom Ocean Publications, 1998), 201–220.
3. "Rennyo's Wives and Children," in *Rennyo: The Second Founder of Shin Buddhism*, ed. Minor L. Rogers and Ann T. Rogers (Berkeley, CA: Asian Humanity Press, 1991), 380.
4. *Honpukuji yuraiki*, in *Shinshū shiryō shūsei* (Kyoto: Dōbōsha, 1978), 10:661.
5. *Honganji sahō no shidai* 1, in *Jōdo Shinshū seiten zensho*, 5:970.
6. *Honganji sahō no shidai* 43, in *Jōdo Shinshū seiten zensho*, 5:979.
7. See letters 3–12 and 3–13 in Rogers and Rogers, *Rennyo: The Second Founder of Shin Buddhism*, 214–216; *Gobunshō* 3–12 and 3–13, in *Jōdo Shinshū seiten zensho*, 5:145–148.
8. See letter 4–2 in Rogers and Rogers, *Rennyo: The Second Founder of Shin Buddhism*, 220; *Gobunshō* 4–2, in *Jōdo Shinshū seiten zensho*, 5:152.
9. For those interested in reading contemporary academic studies on Rennyo in Japanese, a five-volume collection by leading Japanese scholars on Rennyo covering both historical and doctrinal studies is published in *Rennyo taikei* 蓮如大系, ed. Kakehashi Jitsuen, Nabata Takashi, and Minegishi Sumio (Kyoto: Hōzōkan, 1996). Critical editions of the primary sources on Rennyo are listed in the "Primary Souces" section in this article.
10. On the development of the Jōdo Shinshū tradition under Rennyo, see Michael Solomon, "Kinship and the Transmission of Religious Charisma: The Case of Honganji," *Journal of Asian Studies* 33, no. 3 (1974): 403–404; Stanley Weinstein, "Rennyo and the Shinshu Revival," in *Japan in the Muromachi Age*, ed. John Whitney Hall and Toyoda Takeshi (Berkeley: University of California Press, 1977), 331–358; and Michael Solomon, "Honganji under Rennyo: The Development of Shinshū in Medieval Japan," in *Pure Land Tradition: History and Development*, ed. James Foared, Michael Solomon, and Richard Payne (Berkeley, CA: Berkeley Buddhist Studies Series, 1996), 399–428; on Rennyo's influence on the development of premodern Japanese spirituality, see Minor L. Rogers, "Rennyo's *Ofumi* and Shinshu in Pure Land Tradition," in *Pure Land Tradition: History and Development*, 429–462.
11. Michael Solomon, "The Dilemma of Religious Power: Honganji and Hosokawa Masamoto," *Monumenta Nipponica* 33 (1978): 51–65; and Carol Richmond Tsang, *War and Faith: Ikko Ikki in Late Muromachi Japan* (Cambridge, MA: Harvard East Asian Monographs 288, 2007).

12. Minor L. Rogers and Ann T. Rogers, *Rennyo: The Second Founder of Shin Buddhism* (Berkeley, CA: Asian Humanities Press, 1991).
13. *Rennyo and the Roots of Modern Japanese Buddhism*, ed. Mark L. Blum and Shin'ya Yasutomi (Oxford: Oxford University Press, 2006).

Eisho Nasu

RYŌGEN

RYŌGEN, 912–985

Ryōgen, a Japanese Tendai 天台 Buddhist monk, lived during the mid-Heian 平安 period (794–1185) and was the eighteenth abbot (*zasu* 座主) of Enryakuji 延暦寺, the head temple of the Japanese Tendai school established by Saichō 最澄 (767–822) on Mount Hiei 比叡山 in the northeastern corner of Kyoto.[1] Ryōgen was a scholar monk of the lineage of Ennin 円仁 (794–864), the third abbot of Enryakuji. In 951 Ryōgen received the title of *ajari* 阿闍梨, the highest rank of an esoteric master. He became the eighteenth abbot of Enryakuji in 966 and was appointed great archbishop (*daisōjō* 大僧正), the highest monastic rank, in 981. He died on January 3, 985, and therefore is popularly called Ganzan-daishi 元三大師 (*ganzan*, the third day of the first month). He also received the posthumous name "Jie" 慈恵 in 987 and is known as the Great Master Jie (Jie Daishi 慈恵大師). Within the Tendai tradition, Ryōgen is considered the second founder (*chūkō no so* 中興の祖) of Enryakuji, having successfully restored and reformed the school's clerical order during his tenure as abbot.

EARLY YEARS

Becoming a Tendai Priest. According to early biographies, Ryōgen was born in the northern part of Ōmi 近江 Province (Shiga Prefecture).[2] His father belonged to the Kozu 木津 clan and his mother to the Mononobe 物部 clan. While both clans had distinguished historical origins, Ryōgen's parents seem to have belonged to relatively insignificant sub-branches. The biographies record neither the names of Ryōgen's parents nor his family's occupation. As for Ryōgen's birthplace, all biographical sources agree that Ryōgen was born in Azai-gun 浅井郡, but the exact village is uncertain. Currently in the area there is a temple, Gyokusenji 玉泉寺, which claims to be built at Ryōgen's birthplace.

Ryōgen's extraordinary gifts were first recognized by the eminent Tendai priest Kakue 覚恵 (871–954) when the boy was taken by his mother to visit the priest's residence at Bonshakuji 梵釈寺, one of the largest state temples in Ōmi Province. With a recommendation from Kakue, Ryōgen was admitted to Enryakuji on Mount Hiei as a student-servant (*dōji* 童子) in 923 at the age of twelve. He entered the Hōdōin 法燈院 of Saitō 西塔 under the supervision of Risen 理仙 (d. 928).

As a lay student-servant, Ryōgen received basic training to prepare for the Tendai priesthood. After five years of training with his master Risen, Ryōgen was ready for priestly ordination, but the process was thrown into disorder because of Risen's unexpected death. Risen's supervisor, Nittō 日燈, enlisted the aid of Funaki Yoshimi 船木良見 (dates uncertain), a provincial supervisor in Ise 伊勢 Province (Mie Prefecture), who found the priest Onkun 恩訓 (858–948), a Hossō scholar of Yakushiji 薬師寺, to act as sponsor for the ordination in place of Risen. After ordination, Ryōgen then received the precepts confirmation ceremony in the fourth month of 928 from the thirteenth Tendai abbot, Son'i 尊意 (865–940), and was given the priestly name Ryōgen. As an expression of gratitude to Funaki, one character, *ryō* 良 (also read as *yoshi*), of Ryōgen's name was taken from the name of Funaki Yoshimi.

Fame as a Debate Master. After his ordination Ryōgen continued to study at Saitō. Although Ryōgen did not have a strong supporter within the Tendai school, he excelled in doctrinal debates on Mount Hiei. Ryōgen's name gradually became publicly known beyond the Buddhist clerical community. In 937, his talent as a debate master came to the attention of the upper echelons of the aristocratic families when he visited Nara as an attendant of Kizō 基増, who was the lecturer (*kōshi* 講師) at the annual Yuima-e 維摩会 (assembly of the *Yuima-gyō* 維摩経), one of the most prestigious Buddhist ritual assemblies annually held at Kōfukuji 興福寺.[3] During the event, Ryōgen was invited to participate in a private doctrinal debate with students of the Six Nara schools. This debate was held at the request of Fujiwara Arihira 藤原在衡 (892–970), who was the representative of the emperor (*chokushi* 勅使).

At the debate Ryōgen demonstrated his skill by refuting the Hossō scholar Gishō 義昭 (920–969) of Gangōji 元興寺. Arihira was so impressed by Ryōgen's performance that he told Fujiwara Tadahira 藤原忠平 (880–949), the regent for the emperor, about the young Tendai scholar. Later, Tadahira, the leader (*chōja* 長者) of the Fujiwara family and the most powerful political figure in the imperial court, became one of Ryōgen's most generous sponsors.

Ryōgen's skills in doctrinal debate helped him to become acquainted with court nobles. But skill in doctrinal debate was not enough to gain patronage at the imperial court. He also needed to be able to perform esoteric rituals as a prayer-offering priest (*kitōsō* 祈祷僧) for his patrons. During the era of Tengyō 天慶 (938–947), Ryōgen studied Tendai esotericism with Kakue, the same priest who had recommended him to the Tendai priesthood. Under Kakue's tutelage, Ryōgen learned the three great esoteric practices (*sanbu-daihō* 三部大法) of the Japanese Tendai school and mastered the esoteric fire ritual (*goma* 護摩).[4] Toward the end of the Tengyō period, Ryōgen accompanied Kakue to a religious service held at Tadahira's residence. After the completion of the service, Tadahira, who remembered Ryōgen from his debate with Gishō in 937, asked Ryōgen to become his spiritual guide. Ryōgen's career seems to have brightened considerably, and his priestly rank rose to great dharma-master (*daihosshi* 大法師), the highest rank given to an ordinary priest (*bonsō* 凡僧), who had yet to have a position in the office of superintending clergy (*sōgō* 僧綱).[5]

RISE TO PROMINENCE AND POWER

Administrating Yokawa. A great turning point in Ryōgen's career came in 949 when his primary patron Tadahira died at the age of seventy. While the memorial services for Tadahira were in progress, Ryōgen suddenly withdrew to Yokawa 横川, the most remote place on Mount Hiei, to perform esoteric fire rituals for the repose of Tadahira's spirit at Ryōgon'in

楞厳院. Ryōgen first settled in a residence hall in Minamidani 南谷 at Yokawa. He later built his own residential quarters called Jōshinbō 定心房 here.

The origin of the Yokawa area dates back to 831, when the priest Ennin built a small retreat at the northernmost sector of Mount Hiei. During the time of Ennin and his successor Anne 安慧 (794–868, fourth abbot of Enryakuji), Yokawa was considered the most prestigious section on the mountain. After the death of Anne in 868, however, the prestige of Ennin's lineage was eclipsed by the rising power of the lineage of Enchin 円珍 (814–891, fifth abbot of Enryakuji). Yokawa gradually declined, and when Ryōgen chose Yokawa as his retreat it was largely abandoned except for a few priests.

Ryōgen's sudden retreat into Yokawa was not motivated merely by concern for his late patron. It seems that Fujiwara Morosuke 藤原師輔 (908–960), one of Tadahira's sons, secretly requested Ryōgen to perform esoteric rituals to ensure that his daughter Anshi 安子 (927–964), a consort to Emperor Murakami 村上天皇 (927–967, r. 946–967), would bear the crown prince. In 950, Anshi gave birth to a son, prince Norihira 憲平, and in the same year the emperor named Norihira crown prince. Norihira later became Emperor Reizei 冷泉天皇 (950–1011, r. 967–969).

As the grandfather of the next emperor, Morosuke had thus secured his position in the imperial court. To reward Ryōgen's performance as his prayer-offering priest, he sponsored the promotion of Ryōgen in the imperial court and within the Tendai school. At the strong recommendation of Morosuke, in 950 Ryōgen was appointed guardian priest for the crown prince (*tōgū gojisō* 東宮護持僧). In 951 Ryōgen received the title of *ajari*, the highest rank of an esoteric master. Ryōgen's swift promotion to these significant positions was unprecedented. He was forty years old and he was still an ordinary priest who did not have a position in the office of superintending clergy.

Morosuke also assisted Ryōgen in redeveloping Yokawa into the power center of Mount Hiei. With Morosuke's generous financial support, in 954 the Hokke-zanmaidō 法華三昧堂 was opened, marking the beginning of the revival of the traditional exoteric Tendai practices on Mount Hiei. There Ryōgen recruited and trained students to be the future leaders of the Japanese Tendai school. He enthusiastically sponsored sutra lectures and doctrinal debates at Yokawa. Genshin 源信 (942–1017), who was to become a leading Tendai scholar, was ordained and joined Yokawa around 956.

Morosuke's support, however, was not without conditions. Ryōgen pledged to Morosuke that his disciples would continuously perform rites for his and his family's prosperity even after his death. Morosuke, in return, pledged that his family, from generation to generation, would support Yokawa. In order to ensure that this would happen, Morosuke made one of his sons, Jinzen 尋禅 (943–990), a disciple of Ryōgen in 958. Ryōgen's ambitious plans for Yokawa were temporarily suspended by the sudden death of Morosuke in 960.

The Ōwa Debate. Morosuke's patronage of Ryōgen was well known, and, in order to avoid political intrigue after Morosuke's death in 960, Ryōgen withdrew from public activities for nearly four years. In 963, Ryōgen came into public view again when Emperor Murakami invited twenty priests—ten scholars from the Tendai school and ten from the Six Nara schools—to the imperial palace for a five-day doctrinal debate (*rongi* 論議) during the lecture meeting (*kōe* 講会) on the *Lotus Sutra*. The meeting was held at the Seiryōden 清涼殿, the emperor's private residence within the imperial palace. During the debate, later named the Ōwa debate (*Ōwa no shūron* 応和の宗論), Ryōgen led a relatively young and inexperienced team of Tendai scholars and wielded his considerable talent to challenge the doctrinal authority of the scholars of the Nara Buddhist schools.[6]

The five-day lecture meeting started on the twenty-first day of the eighth month of the third year of the Ōwa era (963). The doctrinal debate was coordinated with a series of formal lectures on the *Lotus Sutra*, with each lecture followed by questions to the lecturer. The series began with a lecture on the *Muryōgi-kyō* 無量義経 followed by eight lectures on each of the *Lotus Sutra*'s Lotus Sutra's eight fascicles. It concluded with a lecture on the *Kanfugen-gyō* 観普賢経. Lectures were delivered twice a day, once in the morning and once in the evening. The lecture format consisted of two priests: a leader (*dōshi* 導師) who delivered the lecture, and a respondent (*monja* 問者) who asked the questions.

The lectures progressed smoothly until the evening lecture of the second day. A heated debate erupted between Hōzō 法蔵 (905–969) of the Hossō school and Kakukei 覚慶 (927–1014) of the Tendai school over the interpretation of the ideas of one vehicle and buddha-nature expounded in the *Lotus Sutra*. According to the *sutra*, all the various Buddhist teachings and views, including non-Mahāyāna ones, can be subsumed under the Mahāyāna doctrine of one vehicle (*ichijō* 一乗) through which all sentient beings are able to attain buddhahood. The Tendai scholars supported their view of the one vehicle in the *Lotus Sutra* by citing the idea of the universal presence of buddha-nature (*shitsuu busshō* 悉有仏性) in all beings (existence) expounded in the *Nirvana Sutra*, which they considered as having scriptural authority equal to the *Lotus Sutra*. The Hossō scholars interpreted the same statements in the *Lotus Sutra* metaphorically. According to the Hossō theory, only sentient beings innately endowed with the ability to become a bodhisattva are able to attain buddhahood, that is, the theory of distinction of five human natures (*goshō kakubetsu* 五性各別). All other sentient beings, who are predetermined to follow non-Mahāyāna Buddhist paths or who do not have the potentiality to follow any of the Buddhist paths, are unable to realize buddhahood.

Kakukei, the respondent, challenged the Hossō school's theories of one vehicle and buddha-nature which contradicted the Tendai's interpretations of these ideas. Kakukei, however, still young and inexperienced in public debate, was no match against Hōzō, a renowned and experienced scholar. Seeing that Kakukei was being overwhelmed, Ryōgen replaced Kakukei and countered Hōzō's argument with the Tendai position that all sentient beings have the possibility of attaining buddhahood. A heated debate between Ryōgen and Hōzō went late into the evening without resolution and continued into the third day. Ryōgen's arguments for the Tendai views of one vehicle and buddha-nature overwhelmed Hōzō, who fell silent and then praised Ryōgen's eloquence as equal to that of Pūrṇa (Furuna 富楼那), one of the ten great disciples of the buddha.

After the argument between Ryōgen and Hōzō subsided, the lecture sessions continued according to schedule until the morning of the fifth day, when Chūzan 仲算 (927–969), a Hossō scholar of Kōfukuji 興福寺, resumed arguing against the Tendai interpretation of the *Lotus Sutra* presented by Ryōgen two days earlier. The emperor, impressed by Chūzan's performance against the Tendai priest Juchō 寿肇 (dates uncertain), requested that he continue to serve as a respondent for that evening's session against the Tendai priest Shōku 聖救 (909–998).

Although the opponent of the evening session of the last day was Shōku, Chūzan persisted in revisiting the exchange between Ryōgen and Hōzō in order to refute the Tendai interpretation of the one vehicle and buddha-nature. Chūzan's eloquence impressed the emperor and the attending courtiers. During these sessions, however, Ryōgen remained puzzlingly silent, even though Chūzan's counterarguments bore on his interpretations. Because Ryōgen refrained from further comment, Chūzan's counterargument prevailed. At the end of the debate, the emperor presented Chūzan with lavish praise and a silver grail.

The victory of the Hossō scholar Chūzan, however, did not hurt Ryōgen's reputation as a Tendai scholar in the imperial court. Although the Tendai school did not win the overall debate, Ryōgen demonstrated his sharp mind. His silence was perhaps a calculated move. Ryōgen understood that what the audience expected was sophisticated intellectual entertainment. He was astute enough to know that he should not overly humiliate the Hossō scholars from Kōfukuji, the family temple of the Fujiwara clan, if he wanted to maintain his popularity among the courtiers.

Although the Tendai team did not win, the Ōwa debate was a great success for Ryōgen, who immediately received wide public recognition. The next year (964), Emperor Murakami appointed him as one of the ten guardian priests (*naigubu jūzenjii* 内供奉十禅師) who protect the spiritual welfare of the emperor. Emperor Murakami, it seems, was satisfied with Ryōgen's performance at the Ōwa debate. At fifty-three Ryōgen could claim one of the most significant achievements of the priesthood: directly attending the emperor.

Becoming Abbot of Enryakuji. After the Ōwa debate, the imperial court quickly promoted Ryōgen. In 965 Ryōgen joined the ranks of priestly officers at the office of superintending clergy as a superintendent of the lower rank (*gonrisshi* 権律師). At fifty-five, he was the youngest member. Appointment to the office of superintending clergy was usually granted to priests as a reward for their years of public service and was typically determined by seniority within the priestly hierarchy. Ryōgen's promotion to this rank was thus highly unusual since he had no major public service experience other than the Ōwa debate and had served as the emperor's guardian priest for only one year. But from this eminent position, Ryōgen soon ascended to the pinnacle of the Tendai institution. In 966, the seventeenth abbot of Enryakuji, Kikyō 喜慶, died, and Emperor Murakami nominated Ryōgen to be the eighteenth abbot. Ryōgen was fifty-five years old, the youngest nominee since the fifth abbot, Enchin.

Emperor Murakami's appointment of Ryōgen to the highest administrative position of the Tendai school was extraordinary. The emperor promoted Ryōgen over at least two senior career priests, Bōsan 房算 (898–967) and Gajō 賀静. Bōsan was sixty-eight years old and a career member of the office of superintending clergy. He held the rank of minor bishop of the lower rank (*gonshōsōzu* 権少僧都), several ranks higher than Ryōgen, who was merely a superintendent of the lower rank. He was also the head priest of Onjōji 園城寺 and leader of Enchin's lineage. Gajō, eighty years old, was appointed to be a member of the office of superintending clergy at the same time as Ryōgen and was one of the most senior priests of Ennin's lineage.

Given that the imperial court passed over these two senior priests, the appointment of Ryōgen could hardly have been unanimously welcomed on Mount Hiei. Bōsan and Gajō seemed very disappointed with the emperor's decision. The next year, in 967, Bōsan resigned his position at the office of superintending clergy and retired to his retreat on Mount Hiei, where he died that same year. Gajō's disappointment was even greater. Gajō was shocked by the appointment of Ryōgen, who was a younger and less experienced priest from within the same lineage. Early the next year, Gajō also died, having remained indignant with the imperial court to the end. Ryōgen's power, however, was secure. He was not perturbed by these disaffections, and the senior priests on Mount Hiei were not able to interfere or overturn the decision of the imperial court.

REFORMATION OF JAPANESE TENDAI SCHOOL

Reconstruction of Enryakuji. A few months after Ryōgen took the abbot's office, he faced an unexpected disaster on Mount Hiei. A fire broke out at the Tōdō 東塔, the central complex at Enryakuji, and more than thirty buildings including the Kōdō 講堂, the Sōjiin 総持院, Jōgyōdō 常行堂, and Hokkedō 法華堂 were destroyed. These were some of the most significant structures of the monastery. The Kōdō, the main assembly hall at Tōdō, was the main building for the lecture meetings on the *Lotus Sutra*. The Jōgyōdō and Hokkedō were meditation halls for the four *samādhi* practices that were essential for traditional Tendai training. The destruction of the Sōjiin was also a great loss for Ryōgen and Ennin's lineage. The Sōjiin was founded by Ennin in 859 to serve as the initiation hall of the dharma-transmission *abhiṣeka* ceremony (*denbōkanjō* 伝法灌頂) of Tendai esotericism.

Ryōgen immediately undertook an aggressive reconstruction project. In 967, less than a year after the fire, the reconstruction of the essential practice halls, the Hokkedō and Jōgyōdō, was already completed. The Sōjiin, the symbolic center of Ennin's lineage, was completed in 971. Early in 972 the reconstruction of the Kōdō was finished. When the entire project was completed six years after the fire, the Mount Hiei complex emerged larger and more prosperous than ever.

Reinvigorating Doctrinal Debate. As Ryōgen labored over the reconstruction of Tōdō's buildings, he also introduced straightforward policies to revitalize the institutional foundations of the Tendai school. First, he promoted the traditional study of Tendai doctrine, which had been overshadowed by esoteric practices. In order to promote the study of doctrine, Ryōgen initiated an annual doctrinal debate, called the *kōgaku ryūgi* 広学竪義 (doctrinal discussion meeting of learned scholars), at the *Hokke'e* 法華会 (assembly of the *Lotus Sutra*) in 966.

The debates were held during the *minazuki'e* 六月会 (the assembly of the sixth month), a memorial ceremony for the founder, Saichō. *Kōgaku ryūgi* literally means "establishing a [doctrinal] principle (*ryūgi* 竪義) through [the debate between the learned scholars with] extensive knowledge [of scriptures] (*kōgaku* 広学)." *Kōgaku ryūgi* involved a formal discussion among questioners (*monja* 問者), critics (*nanja* 難者), and respondents (*rissha* 竪者) on various doctrinal issues of the Tendai school. During the debate a priest was selected to preside as a judge (*tandai* 探題). The judge chose topics for doctrinal discussion. A *rissha* responded orally to give his interpretation of the topics. A debate followed the formal response.

While developing the *kōgaku ryūgi*, Ryōgen successfully petitioned the imperial court for the right to have a Tendai judge for this doctrinal debate. Priests from the Six Nara schools had long monopolized the judgeship of all debates. For the *kōgaku ryūgi*, the imperial court for the first time granted the Tendai school the exclusive right to officiate a debate under the sole authority of the Enryakuji. With the right to judge, Tendai doctrine became as authoritative as the teachings of the Six Nara schools, and Tendai scholars no longer had to consult with scholars of other Buddhist schools to present their own views on the scriptures.

Concurrent with the promotion of Tendai studies, Ryōgen renewed the identity of the Tendai clerical community by creating strict rules of conduct for priests, who were often criticized for laxity in regulating themselves. In order to restore order on Mount Hiei, he issued *Tendai zasu Ryōgen kishō* 天台座主良源起請, a tract of twenty-six articles, in the seventh month of 970.[7] The twenty-six articles clearly reflect Ryōgen's concerns for the revitalization of the traditional communal services and doctrinal lectures and debates related to Tendai studies. In the articles Ryōgen required Enryakuji priests to diligently participate in lecture meetings, doctrinal debates, and communal religious services held at Enryakuji. He also prohibited unnecessarily elaborate receptions following the services. Those who failed to attend lectures and services were subject to disciplinary measures, including expulsion from the order.

Establishing the Three-Pagoda System (*santōsei* 三塔制). During this time, Ryōgen further expanded Yokawa. In 968 Emperor Reizei donated monies to build a Jōgyō-zanmaidō at Ryōgon'in, one of the Yokawa-area temples. The emperor provided funds to maintain fourteen resident priests to practice *jōgyō-zanmai* 常行三昧 (constant practice [of *nembutsu*] *samādhi*) and for six additional resident priests at the Hokke-zanmaidō in Yokawa. Emperor Reizei further granted the positions of *jūzenji* 十禅師 (ten meditation masters) and three annual ordinands to Ryōgon'in in response to the late Emperor Murakami's wishes.

Ryōgen had a clear objective in the development of Yokawa—the revival of Tendai studies—and he focused on training his disciples to be able to participate in the *kōgaku ryūgi*. In 967 Ryōgen introduced the seasonal lectures (*shikikō* 四季講) at his own residence hall Jōshinbō as soon as the official debate, *kōgaku ryūgi*, was approved by the imperial court. Ryōgen also started the semiannual doctrinal debate (*niki no ryūgi* 二季の竪義) in the spring and summer at Jōshinbō to prepare his students for the annual official debate at the *Hokke'e*.

In order to be eligible as a *rissha* (respondent) in the semiannual debates at Jōshinbō, Ryōgen required that his students successfully complete the seasonal lectures. In addition, he required the students to have several years of further training. The compilation of manuals for doctrinal debates perhaps started during this period under Ryōgen's guidance. As a result of their preparations, Ryōgen's disciples dominated the doctrinal lectures and debates as well as the *kōgaku ryūgi*, and Ryōgen, as the chief administrator of Mount Hiei, was able to promote his disciples over priests from the factions of Enchin's lineage. Ryōgen essentially turned Yokawa into a preparatory school for the future administrators who would determine the course of Japanese Tendai. Among Ryōgen's direct disciples, five priests were appointed Tendai abbots: Jinzen (nineteenth), Senga 暹賀 (twenty-second), Kakukei 覚慶 (twenty-third), Myōgu 明救 (twenty-fifth), and Ingen 院源 (twenty-sixth). His disciples also included such renowned Tendai scholars as Kakuun 覚運 (d. 1007), Kakuchō 覚超 (d. 1034), and Genshin 源信 (942–1017).

With Ryōgen's development of Yokawa, the number of resident priests sharply increased. By 972, the community had grown to more than two hundred, and senior administrators petitioned to have their own registry of priests (*kichō* 季帳). The advantage of having an independent registration was economic. Yokawa would be able to receive state stipends directly for its two hundred registered priests and for the maintenance of buildings, rather than these funds going to the Tōdō or Saitō, which at that time handled the Yokawa registration. Precedent for this move lay in Saitō, which had obtained administrative independence from Tōdō. Ryōgen, in obvious collaboration with the Yokawa administration, signed the petition without hesitation. Since then, Enryakuji has officially been split into three independent administrative entities, Tōdō, Saitō, and Yokawa, known as the three-pagoda system (*santōsei*). The independence of Yokawa was a major victory for Ryōgen, as he and his disciples thereafter monopolized the funds applied to the area.

FURTHER DEVELOPMENT OF ENRYAKUJI AND CONTROVERSY

Ryōgen's Dying Instructions. Shortly after the reconstruction of the fire-damaged buildings was completed in 972, Ryōgen fell seriously ill. Preparing for the worst, he wrote his dying instructions (later called the *Tendai zasu Ryōgen yuigō* 天台座主良源遺告) outlining how the temple and his estates should be managed after his death. The instructions included arrangements for his estate, belongings, funeral, and memorial services. He was particularly concerned about the treatment of his disciple Jinzen, who had inherited considerable property from Fujiwara Morosuke's family, making him the largest estate holder on Mount Hiei. Ryōgen entrusted his residence and most of his belongings to Jinzen and assured Morosuke's family that administrative power at Yokawa would be transferred to Jinzen.

However, Ryōgen survived his illness. Returning to office, he managed Mount Hiei as abbot for another thirteen years and continued to receive promotions within the clerical hierarchy. In 974 he became great bishop of the lower rank (*gondaisōzu* 権大僧都); in 975, great bishop (*daisōzu* 大僧都); in 977, archbishop of the lower rank (*gonsōjō* 権僧正); and in 979, archbishop (*sōjō* 僧正). In 981 Ryōgen was granted the title of great archbishop (*daisōjōi* 大僧正), the highest rank of the office of the superintending clergy. He was only the second priest to ascend to this title, the first being Gyōki 行基 (668–749) in 745.

As Ryōgen's rank rose and his administrative powers expanded, his influence began to reach beyond the borders of Mount Hiei and his own individual interests. In 974 he maneuvered to annex the Gion 祇園 shrine in Kyoto, taking it from the Hossō school.[8] Moreover, with his political connections, Ryōgen had virtually a free hand in assigning his disciples to higher administrative positions at Enryakuji and seeing to their promotion within the office of superintending clergy. Jinzen is a case in point. In 972 Jinzen was granted the special title of *isshin ajari* 一身阿闍梨 (one-life *ajari*) of Ryōgon'in, the head temple of Yokawa. The position was so named because it was granted to an individual priest for life (*isshin* 一身) and was not transferable to another priest. This was a new title created by Ryōgen specifically for the advancement of Jinzen. In 974, Jinzen was appointed to become a member of the office of superintending clergy with the title of minor bishop of the lower rank (*gonshōsōzu*). This promotion was extraordinary, because Jinzen was only thirty-one years old and was allowed to skip the rank of *risshi* to enter the office of superintending clergy. Jinzen was granted the title of great bishop (*daisōzu*) in 979 and became an archbishop of the lower rank (*gonsōjō*) in 981. Among Tendai priests, Jinzen held the highest rank in the office of the superintending clergy second only to Ryōgen, thus becoming a legitimate candidate for nineteenth abbot of Enryakuji at the age of thirty-nine.

Confrontation with Enchin's Lineage. For fifteen years as abbot of Enryakuji, Ryōgen promoted priests who pledged loyalty to his administration. This strategy, however, was based on ignoring members of Enchin's lineage, who often challenged Ryōgen's policies.[9] Thus excluded from the power structure, priests from Enchin's lineage became frustrated and resentful toward Ryōgen and his faction. Yokei 余慶 (919–991)—appointed head priest of Onjōji, the headquarters of Enchin's lineage, in 979—challenged Ryōgen's authority and tried to recover his lineage's status.

In a shocking development, in 981 Yokei was nominated abbot of Hosshōji 法性寺 with the political backing of Emperor En'yū 円融 (959–991, r. 969–984). Hosshōji had been administrated exclusively by the priests of Ennin's lineage since it was found by Fujiwara Tadahira in 925. When Yokei's nomination was announced, priests of Ennin's lineage immediately appealed to the imperial court. The court, however, rejected the appeal of the priests of Ennin's lineage and sustained Yokei's nomination. The Ennin faction protested the court's decision and picketed at Hosshōji to prevent Yokei from entering the temple for the inauguration ceremony. As a result, Yokei was forced to resign the abbacy without occupying the temple for even a single day.

After this incident, tensions between the two factions were heightened. Yokei, together with several hundred of his disciples and allies, temporally evacuated their residences on Mount Hiei. Confrontation between the factions continued over the next year. A rumor spread that Ryōgen had dispatched assassins to dispose of Yokei and the other leaders of Enchin's lineage and to destroy the temples in which they had sought refuge. Concerned, the imperial court dispatched the emperor's envoy (*chokushi* 勅使) to the abbot's office at Enryakuji in the first month of 982. The envoy ordered Ryōgen to secure the peace on Mount Hiei, and Ryōgen promised to restore order. But he categorically denied the rumor and defended his disciples from allegations of wrongdoing over the incident at Hosshōji. He excused the conduct of the priests who had blocked Yokei from entering Hosshōji by suggesting that they had only tried to maintain the dignity of Ennin's lineage in accordance with the temple's tradition. The confrontation ended with a victory for Ryōgen. In 982 the imperial court appointed Shōsan 正算, a disciple of Ryōgen, as abbot of Hosshōji.

Ryōgen's Death and the Sanmon–Jimon Schism. Toward the end of 984 Ryōgen's physical health declined and he was unable to remain at his residence on Mount Hiei. The rigors of living in the mountains were apparently too harsh for his weakened condition. He left for Sakamoto Guhōji 坂本求法寺, located at the foot of the mountain. On the third day of the first month in 985, Ryōgen passed away while reciting the name of Amida. He was seventy-four. Ryōgen's body was buried at a site deep in the mountains at Yokawa, north of his residence at Jōshin'in, in accordance with his will.

The following month, the imperial court appointed Jinzen the nineteenth abbot of Enryakuji. Fujiwara Kaneie sponsored Ryōgen's memorial services. As requested in his dying instructions of 972, the lecture meetings on the *Lotus Sutra* were held at his memorial service. This *sutra* lecture continued to be held annually on Ryōgen's memorial day with the support of the Fujiwara family. It was later called the *ganzan'e* 元三会, the assembly on the third day of the new year. In 987, Emperor Ichijō (980–1011, r. 986–1011) granted Ryōgen the posthumous name Jie 慈慧 ("compassion and wisdom") at the request of Jinzen.

Under Ryōgen's administration, Ennin's lineage had become tightly united, but this solidarity eventually resulted in a hardened resistance to Enchin's lineage. Within a few years after Ryōgen's death, a power struggle flared up again, and in 989 Ennin's faction even refused the order of the imperial court appointing Yokei as the twentieth abbot of Enryakuji. In 993 another major conflict between the two factions occurred when the priests of Enchin's lineage were overwhelmed by the power of Ennin's lineage and were unable to maintain their position on Mount Hiei. They all abandoned their residences and regrouped at Onjōji at the foot of the mountain. This incident split the Japanese Tendai school into two branches, the *sanmon-ha* 山門派 (mountain-gate branch), Ennin's lineage headquartered at Enryakuji on Mount Hiei, and the *jimon-ha* 寺門派 (temple-gate branch), Enchin's lineage centered at Onjōji at the foot of Mount Hiei.[10] After Yokei, the imperial court attempted to nominate other priests from Enchin's lineage as abbot of Enryakuji—nominating eight altogether—but their appointments were blocked by the *sanmon-ha* priests and none actually assumed any responsibility. They all resigned from the position in less than a week. Violent confrontations between the two factions continued throughout the Heian period.

LEGACY

Ryōgen's Successors. After the secession of the priests of Enchin's lineage, the fundamental institutional structure of Enryakuji on Mount Hiei established by Ryōgen remained under the control of his disciples. These disciples provided academic and administrative leadership. For example, five of his direct disciples, Jinzen (nineteenth), Senga (twenty-second), Kakukei (twenty-third), Myōgu (twenty-fifth), and Inge (twenty-sixth), became abbots of Enryakuji. Other disciples such as Myōgō, Kakuun, Shōkyū 聖救, Jitsuin 実因, Gonkyū 厳久, Genshin, and Kakuchō, became members of the office of superintending clergy. Although they left Yokawa, Shōkū 性空 of Shoshazan 書写山 and Zōga 増賀 of Tōnomine 多武峰 were also Ryōgen's direct disciples. During the 11th century the power and prestige of Enryakuji reached its zenith.

The popularity of Tendai doctrinal studies continued to thrive after Ryōgen. During the late 11th century, the Tendai school began administering three major official lecture meetings in Kyoto: the *hokke'e* 法華会 (from 1072) and *saishōe* 最勝会 (from 1082) at Enshūji 円宗寺, and *daijōe* 大乗会 at Hosshōji 法勝寺 (from 1078). These "Three Great Lecture Meetings of the Northern Capital" (*hokkyō sandaie* 北京三大会) came to be considered as prestigious as the three Great Lecture Meetings sponsored by the Six Nara schools. The lecturers appointed to these events automatically received a rank within the office of superintending clergy. The appointment of Tendai clerics further expanded the school's power. Additionally, lecture meetings on the *Lotus Sutra*, as part of private and public memorial services originally promoted by Ryōgen, became popular among courtiers in the capital, and their popularity gradually spread to the provinces in the 11th century.[11]

Ryōgen and his disciples also left their imprint on the doctrinal lectures and debating traditions of Enryakuji. Ryōgen himself authored manuals on debating techniques and strategies, as well as notes for *sutra* lectures, such as the *Kuhon ōjōgi* 九品往生義, as did many of his disciples including Genshin, Kakuun, Kakuchō, and Zōga.[12] While some of the manuals have been lost, and the authorship of the extant works is not clear, these texts compiled throughout the Heian period represent a significant source for understanding monastic debating. The manuals were not written for reading but primarily for memorizing and performing. They also contain personal notes from the debates or lectures of famous masters. The increase in production of these works after Ryōgen's tenure reflects the rise of interest in Tendai doctrinal study due to his influence.

Ryōgen's institutional reformation combined with the promotion of doctrinal studies ensured the continuation and success of the Tendai school throughout the Heian period. His efforts established the foundation for the doctrinal and institutional traditions that emerged during the Kamakura 鎌倉 period (1185–1333). Founders of the Kamakura Buddhist movements, such as Hōnen 法然 (1133–1212), Dōgen 道元 (1200–1253), Shinran 親鸞 (1173–1262), and Nichiren 日蓮 (1222–1282), all emerged from the Tendai school reformed by Ryōgen.

Posthumous Expansion of Ryōgen's Image and Power. As the power of Ennin's lineage at Enryakuji expanded, the image of Ryōgen as a symbol of power and unifier of Ennin's lineage also grew. At a private memorial service for Ryōgen held in 1030, forty-five years after his death, Keimyō 慶命 (965–1038), the twenty-seventh abbot of Enryakuji, lauded Ryōgen as an incarnation of Śākyamuni and Ennin. In his praise, Keimei also called Ryōgen Jie Daishi 慈恵大師 (Great Master Jie), although the imperial court had not officially granted him the title of *daishi*. By the end of the Heian period, people commonly referred to him as Jie Daishi or Ganzan Daishi 元三大師.

In later years, Ryōgen's image became associated with more infamous figures and episodes. Ryōgen's detractors, especially priests at Onjōji, believed him to be demonic, an incarnation of the chieftain of the realm of devils (*makai no tōryō* 魔界の棟梁), or a great king of devils (*daimaō* 大魔王). The *Heike monogatari* 平家物語 identified Ryōgen with Taira no Kiyomori 平清盛 (1118–1181), the leader of the Taira clan, who ousted the Fujiwaras from power. Ryōgen was also blamed for organizing priest-warriors (*sōhei* 僧兵) at Enryakuji and for fortifying Mount Hiei so as to expand his influence over the imperial court. The earliest documents to identify Ryōgen as the initiator of priest-warriors date to the Muromachi period (1334–1560), and allegations that Ryōgen organized a cadre of armed priest-warriors were advanced by historians of the Mito school of Neo-Confucian studies (Mitogaku 水戸学) in the *Dai Nihon shi* 大日本史 edited during the Edo period (1603–1867).[13]

Toward the end of the 12th century, the authority of the imperial court declined and political power passed from the aristocracy to the warrior class. Enryakuji, however, survived this political turbulence and remained the most influential Buddhist institution of the Kamakura period. Ryōgen was transformed into a divine figure who protected Mount Hiei. Priests on Mount Hiei came to believe that Ryōgen's spirit remained on the mountain, protecting the heritage of Ennin's lineage. They carved statues or drew pictures of him and enshrined them at the major buildings of Enryakuji as a guardian. For example, when strife between *gakushō* 学生 (scholar priests) and *dōshū* 堂衆 (practitioner priests) erupted on Mount Hiei in 1204, three wooden figures of Ryōgen were carved and enshrined in the three pagodas on Mount Hiei in the belief that they would quell the riot. In 1211, ten thousand copies of Ryōgen's image were printed and posted all over Mount Hiei to protect *gakushō* from the violent *dōshū*. They believed Ryōgen to be a manifestation of the bodhisattva Kannon or an incarnation of the divine guardian of Buddhism, Fudō 不動 (Acalanātha).[14]

Ryōgen's image as a powerful leader had a great impact, eventually leading to the popular worship of Ryōgen as a miracle-worker. Those who worshipped his image, whether printed or sculpted, believed that they would be protected from enemies and natural disasters or cured of disease. Woodcut prints of Ryōgen's image began circulating as popular talismans as early as the Kamakura period. Two types of images, *mamedaishi* 豆大師 (thirty-three small figures of Ryōgen with long left eyebrow printed on one sheet of paper) and the *tsunodaishi* 角大師 (a stylized Ryōgen with two horns on his head), became popular. These woodcut prints would be posted at the entrance gate or the door of a house to ward off evil spirits. They are popularly used as talismans and are the subject of miraculous stories of the faithful. In the Edo period, people attributed to Ryōgen the invention of *omikuji* お御籤 (fortunes printed on slips of paper), which actually originated in China.[15]

REVIEW OF LITERATURE

Despite his outstanding career as an eminent scholar and powerful administrator on Mount Hiei, study of Ryōgen's life and works in Western scholarship is still very limited. Currently the most comprehensive study on Ryōgen is by Paul Groner, *Ryōgen and Mount Hiei: Japanese Tendai in the Tenth Century* (2002).[16] Groner's work not only covers Ryōgen's historical role as an institutional reformer of Japanese Tendai tradition in the 10th century, but also carefully places him in the context of the doctrinal and cultural background of Japanese Buddhism in the Heian period.[17] Prior to Groner's book, there were only a few essays on Ryōgen by Neil McMullin primarily focusing on Tendai's religio-institutional engagement with mid-Heian politics under Ryōgen's administration.[18] Groner's earlier work, *Saichō: The Establishment of the Japanese Tendai School* (reprint 2000), originally published in 1984, provides the background for understanding the significance of Ryōgen's reformation of the Tendai tradition. For those who are not familiar with the history of Japanese Buddhism in the Heian period, Richard Bowring's *The Religious Traditions of Japan: 500–1600*, especially Part II, "From Saichō to the Destruction of Tōdaiji (800–1180)" (107–237), provides the broader historical and cultural context in which Ryōgen's reformation of the Tendai tradition emerged. For those interested in the posthumous expansion of the image of Ryōgen, Haruko Wakabayashi's *Seven Tengu Scrolls: Evil and the Rhetoric of Legitimacy in Medieval Japanese Buddhism*, and Michel Strickmann's *Chinese Poetry and Prophecy: Written Oracle in East Asia*, provide useful information for understanding the status of Ryōgen's figure in Japanese Buddhist folklore.

PRIMARY SOURCES

Ryōgen's Biographies and Other Historical Documents Related to Ryōgen

Jie daisōjō den 慈慧大僧正傳. In *Zoku Tendaishū zensho*, Shiden, vol. 2, Nihon Tendai sōdenrui, vol. 1. Tokyo: Shunjūsha, 1988, 191–201.

Jie daisōjō shūi den 慈恵大僧正拾遺傳. In *Zoku Tendaishū zensho*, Shiden, vol. 2, Nihon Tendai sōdenrui, vol. 1. Tokyo: Shunjūsha, 1988, 202–215.
Jie daishi den 慈慧大師傳. In *Zoku Tendaishū zensho*, Shiden, vol. 2, Nihon Tendai sōdenrui, vol. 1. Tokyo: Shunjūsha, 1988, 216–225.
Ōwa shūron nikki (應和宗論日記). In *Dainihon Bukkyō zensho*, vol. 61, 1. Tokyo: Suzuki Gakujutsu Zaidan, 1972.
Tendai zasu Ryōgen kishō 天台座主良源起請. In *Heian ibun*, vol. 2. Edited by Takeuchi Rizō, 431–440. Tokyo: Tōkyōdō shuppan, 1974.
Tendai zasu Ryōgen yuigō 天台座主良源遺告. In *Heian ibun*, vol. 2. Edited by Takeuchi Rizō, 441–448. Tokyo: Tōkyōdō shuppan, 1974. A photo reproduction of this text is available in *Heian: Jie Daishi Jihitsu yuigō* 平安・慈恵大師自筆遺告, Nihon meiseki sōkan, vol. 13. Edited by Shigemi Komatsu and Hirabayashi Moritoku. Tokyo: Nigensha, 1977.

Major Japanese Studies Related to Ryōgen's Life and His Restoration of Enryakuji

Eizan gakuin, ed. *Ganzan Jie Daishi no kenkyū*. Kyoto: Dōbōsha, 1984.
Hirabayashi, Moritoku. *Ryōgen*. Tokyo: Yoshikawa Kōbunkan, 1976.
Kageyama, Haruki. *Hieisanji: Sono kōsei to shomondai*. Kyoto: Dōbōsha, 1978.
Murakami, Shūichi. *Hieizan shi: Tatakai to inorino seiiki*. Tokyo: Tokyo Bijutsu, 1994.
Ozaki, Kōjin. *Nihon Tendai rongishi no kenkyū*. Ōtsu, Shiga-ken: Hokke daie jimukyoku, 1971.
Yamada, Etai. *Ganzan daishi*. Tokyo: Daiichi shobō, 1959.

FURTHER READING

Adolphson, Michael, Edward Kamens, and Stacie Matsumoto, eds. *Heian Japan: Centers and Peripheries*. Honolulu: University of Hawaii Press, 2007.
Bauer, Mikaël. "The Yuima-e as Theater of the State." *Japanese Journal of Religious Studies* 38 (2011): 161–179.
Bowring, Richard. *The Religious Traditions of Japan: 500–1600*. Cambridge, UK: Cambridge University Press, 2005.
Groner, Paul. *Saichō: The Establishment of the Japanese Tendai School*. Berkeley, CA: Berkeley Buddhist Study Series, 1984.
Groner, Paul. *Ryōgen and Mount Hiei: Japanese Tendai in the Tenth Century*. Kuroda Institute Studies in East Asian Buddhism Series, vol. 15. Honolulu: University of Hawaii Press, 2002.
Groner, Paul. "Training Through Debates in Medieval Tendai and Seizan-ha Temples." *Japanese Journal of Religious Studies* 38 (2011): 233–261.
Henning, Hans Martin. "Der Enryakuji-Abt Ryôgen (912–985 u. Z.) und das Tengensannen-chûdô-kuyô-ganmon." *Zeitschrift der Deutschen Morgenländischen Gesellschaft* 153 (2003): 379–393.
McMullin, Neil. "The Sanmon–Jimon Schism in the Tendai School of Buddhism: A Preliminary Analysis." *Journal of the International Association of Buddhist Studies* 7 (1984): 83–105.
McMullin, Neil. "The Enryakuji and the Gion Shrine–Temple Complex in the Mid-Heian Period." *Japanese Journal of Religious Studies* 14 (1987): 161–184.
McMullin, Neil. "The *Lotus Sutra* and Politics in the Mid-Heian Period." In *The Lotus Sutra in Japanese Culture*, 119–141. Edited by George Tanabe and Willa Tanabe. Honolulu: University of Hawaii Press, 1989.
Minowa, Kenryō, and Paul Groner. "The Tendai Debates of 1131 at Hosshōji." *Japanese Journal of Religious Studies* 41 (2014): 133–151.
Nakamura, Kyoko Motomochi. *Miraculous Stories from the Japanese Buddhist Tradition*. Cambridge, MA: Harvard University Press, 1973.
Nasu, Eisho. *Doctrine and Institution in Japanese Tendai Buddhism: A Study of Jie Daishi Ryōgen (912–985)*. PhD diss., Graduate Theological Union, 1996.

Rhodes, Robert. *Genshin's* Ōjōyōshū *and the Construction of Pure Land Discourse in Heian Japan*. University of Hawaii Press, 2017.

Strickmann, Michel. *Chinese Poetry and Prophecy: Written Oracle in East Asia*. Stanford, CA: Stanford University Press, 2005.

Swanson, Paul. "T'ien-t'ai Studies in Japan." *Cahiers d'Extrême-Asie* 2 (1986): 219–232.

Tanabe, Willa Jane. "The Lotus Lectures: *Hokke Hakko* in the Heian Period." *Monumenta Nipponica* 39 (1984): 393–407.

Wakabayashi, Haruko. "From Conqueror to Devil King: Ryōgen and Notions of *Ma* in Medieval Japanese Buddhism." *Monumenta Nipponica* 54 (1999): 481–507.

Wakabayashi, Haruko. *Seven Tengu Scrolls: Evil and the Rhetoric of Legitimacy in Medieval Japanese Buddhism*. Honolulu: University of Hawaii Press, 2012.

NOTES

1. This biographical overview of Ryōgen is based in part on my dissertation, *Doctrine and Institution in Japanese Tendai Buddhism: A Study of Jie Daishi Ryōgen (912–985)*, Graduate Theological Union, 1996. Paul Groner's *Saichō: The Establishment of the Japanese Tendai School*, focusing on the introduction and early development of Japanese Tendai in the early 9th century, provides essential information for understanding the significance of Ryōgen's redevelopment of the Tendai tradition in Japan.
2. The first official biography of Ryōgen, *Jie daisōjō den* 慈慧大僧正伝, was written in 1031, forty-six years after Ryōgen's death. A supplement to this official biography, *Jie daisōjō shūi den* 慈恵大僧正拾遺伝, was written by Bonshō 梵照 (962–1032), one of Ryōgen's disciples, in 1032. There is yet another biography of Ryōgen, *Jie daishi den* 慈慧大師伝, but it was composed in 1396 by Ranpa Keishi 蘭坡景茝 (*c.* 14th century) during the Muromachi 室町 period (1334–1560), almost four hundred years after Ryōgen died. These three texts are available in *Zoku Tendaishū zensho*, Shiden, vol. 2, Nihon Tendai sōdenrui, vol. 1 (Tokyo: Shunjūsha, 1988), 191–225.
3. For the history and development of the Yuima-e service, see Paul Groner, *Ryōgen and Mount Hiei: Japanese Tendai in the Tenth Century* (Honolulu: University of Hawaii Press, 2002), 129–135, and Mikaël Bauer, "The Yuima-e as Theater of the State," *Japanese Journal of Religious Studies* 38 (2011): 161–179.
4. These are esoteric ritual practices of the Taizōkai 胎蔵界 (womb-realm), Kongōkai 金剛界 (diamond-realm), and Soshitsuji 蘇悉地 (Susiddhi).
5. Since Buddhism was officially introduced to Japan in the mid-6th century, the imperial court allowed the clerical community to autonomously administer its internal affairs. During the Nara 奈良 period (710–794) the legal foundation of the Japanese Buddhist clerical community rested on the members of the office of superintending clergy (*sōgō*) that had been put into place during the pre-Nara period. The superintending clerics, selected from within the clerical community, maintained the register of the priests and made regular reports to the state according to the ordinances for monks and nuns (*sōniryō* 僧尼令). For the development and outline of the ordinances for monks and nuns and *sōgō* system, see Kyoko Motomochi Nakamura, *Miraculous Stories from the Japanese Buddhist Tradition* (Cambridge, MA: Harvard University Press, 1973), 20–25; and Richard Bowring, *The Religious Traditions of Japan: 500–1600* (Cambridge, UK: Cambridge University Press, 2005), 54–64.
6. An English translation of the record of the Ōwa debate, the *Ōwa shūron nikki* 応和宗論日記, is available in Groner, *Ryōgen and Mount Hiei*, 331–343. Original Japanese text is in *Dainihon Bukkyō zensho* (Tokyo: Suzuki Gakujutsu Zaidan, 1971), 61:1.
7. An English translation of the text, "Invocation of Tendai Abbot Ryōgen," is available in Groner, *Ryōgen and Mount Hiei*, 345–366. Original Japanese text is found in *Heian ibun* (Tokyo: Tōkyōdō shuppan, 1974), 2:431–440.

8. For Enryakuji's annexation of the Gion shrine, see Neil McMullin, "The Enryakuji and the Gion Shrine–Temple Complex in the Mid-Heian Period," *Japanese Journal of Religious Studies* 14 (1987): 161–184.
9. Regarding this problem, see Paul Groner, "The Early History of Factionalism within the Tendai School," in *Ryōgen and Mount Hiei*, 15–44.
10. For the rise of factionalism under Ryōgen's administration and eventual development of the Sanmon–Jimon schism, see Neil McMullin, "The Sanmon–Jimon Schism in the Tendai School of Buddhism: A Preliminary Analysis," *Journal of the International Association of Buddhist Studies* 7 (1984): 83–105; and Paul Groner, "Factionalism and Ryōgen's Efforts to Control the Order," in *Ryōgen and Mount Hiei*, 218–244.
11. For a comprehensive study of the development of doctrinal debates in the Japanese Tendai school, see Ozaki Kōjin, *Nihon Tendai rongishi no kenkyū* (Ōtsu, Shiga-ken: Hokke daie jimukyoku, 1971).
12. The full title is *Gokuraku jōdo kuhon ōjōgi* 極楽浄土九品往生義. *Kuhon ōjōgi* is a commentary on the section of the nine grades of birth in Amida's Pure Land in the *Guanwuliangshoujing* 観無量寿経. Japanese text is found in *Dainihon Bukkyō zensho* (Tokyo: Suzuki Gakujutsu Zaidan, 1971), 41:89–104. Scholars generally agree that this text was most likely written under the direction of Ryōgen at the request of his major aristocratic patron, Fujiwara Morosuke. See Groner, *Ryōgen and Mount Hiei*, 68–69.
13. See Groner, *Ryōgen and Mount Hiei*, 293–295. For the record identifying Ryōgen as the originator of priest-warriors, see *Dainihonshi* vol. 366, Shi 志 123, Butsuji 仏事 3, Kazantei, Kanwa 1 華山帝, 寛和元年.
14. Wakabayashi Haruko, "From Conqueror to Devil King: Ryōgen and Notions of *Ma* in Medieval Japanese Buddhism," *Monumenta Nipponica* 54 (1999): 481–507. See also Groner, *Ryōgen and Mount Hiei*, 295–301.
15. For a study of Ryōgen and *omikuji*, and some sample images of *mamedaishi* and *tsunodaishi*, see Michel Strickmann, *Chinese Poetry and Prophecy: Written Oracle in East Asia* (Stanford, CA: Stanford University Press, 2005), 7–33.
16. Groner's work includes translations of three documents, "Record of Ōwa Debate," "Invocation of Tendai Abbot Ryōgen," and "Dying Instructions of the Great Archbishop Jie," which are crucial to understanding Ryōgen's restoration of the Japanese Tendai tradition. As Groner notes in his preface, these translations are adopted from the PhD dissertation by Eisho Nasu, *Doctrine and Institution in Japanese Tendai Buddhism: A Study of Jie Daishi Ryōgen (912–985)*, Graduate Theological Union, 1996.
17. It is also noteworthy that Groner includes a chapter on the role of nuns in Japanese Buddhism. See Paul Groner, "Ryōgen and the Role of Nuns in Ninth- and Tenth-Century Japan," in *Ryōgen and Mount Hiei*, 245–288.
18. In addition to McMullin's articles, "The Sanmon–Jimon Schism" and "The Enryakuji and the Gion Shrine-Temple Complex" cited previously, see also his "The *Lotus Sutra* and Politics in the Mid-Heian Period," in *The Lotus Sutra in Japanese Culture*, ed. George Tanabe and Willa Tanabe (Honolulu: University of Hawaii Press, 1989), 119–141.

Eisho Nasu

S

THE SANGHA AS AN INSTITUTION

The sangha (Sanskrit, *saṃgha*; Pali, *saṅgha*; Tibetan, *dge 'dun*; Japanese, *sōgya*; Chinese *sengjia* 僧伽) is the third of the three jewels, or three refuges, of the Buddhist world. Sangha is a term which originally meant "multitude, assemblage"[1] and has been used more broadly to refer to guilds, religious schools, and political groups. In terms of Buddhism, it refers to the group of people responsible for learning, protecting, and maintaining access to the teachings of the buddha over the course of time. This can be articulated in two different ways. Most often, in both historical and contemporary usage, it refers to the monastic community, as in a definition from the *Thai-English Dictionary* by Domnern Garden and Sathienpong Wannapok:[2] "Buddhist monastic order; clergy, Buddhist monk, chapter of (not less than four) Buddhist monks." (Although there are currently no legally recognized orders of nuns that have undergone ordination in Thailand, this definition could be extended to include female as well as male clergy.) This is not simply a contemporary usage, since within Pali texts at least, the term refers primarily to the "community of the ordained" or "the community of the noble ones."[3] Although scholars have argued that sangha should be only used in the strict sense—to refer to the ordained—it can also refer to the Buddhist community as a whole, the "four-fold community" of monks (*bhikkhu*), nuns (*bhikkhunī*), laymen (*upāsaka*), and laywomen (*upāsikā*).[4] In other words, where the first two jewels are very specific (even as there is great diversity across time and space over what these might have meant), the sangha can refer more broadly to those that have been part of the Buddhist community. Emblematic of this, in some introductory textbooks like Donald W. Mitchell's *Buddhism: Introducing the Buddhist Experience*, there is a chapter on the buddha and a chapter on the teachings of the buddha but no chapter on the sangha. In a sense, the rest of the book is the chapter on the sangha.[5]

There is a challenge, in thinking about the sangha, between the universal and the specific. The nature of the sangha has varied across Buddhist schools, as well as across time and space, and it is impossible to provide a coherent account of all aspects of the sangha. At the same time, it is important to acknowledge this diversity, lest one privilege a specific school in a particular time and place as the paradigmatic example of the sangha. For example, there is a tendency within encyclopedias when considering the term "sangha" to begin with the earliest Buddhist communities, because they provide a relatively coherent phenomenon to discuss. While in some ways we can understand the sangha as constituted through its relation to the teachings of the buddha (which are themselves quite diverse), and in particular through the *vinaya*, if we think about the sangha more broadly as the Buddhist community, then the diversity contained within the concept of the sangha—from forest renunciates to the marriage of politics and religious institutions in pre-1959 Tibet to the married priests of Japan—becomes more of a challenge to define. Yet it is a necessary one, lest the mythical origins of the religion be reified as historical reality. In order to avoid this problem, it is salutary to highlight the underlying structures that have constituted sanghas—Buddhist communities—in various times and places, while at the same time using examples from across the Buddhist world to highlight some of the different ways that Buddhists have organized their communities.

DEFINING THE SANGHA

If the sangha is to be defined as the Buddhist community, it is necessary to determine who is Buddhist. Some aspects of this determination are straightforward, others less so. The Buddhist status of monks, nuns, and novices is marked on their bodies by their shaved heads and the robes they wear, as well as by the fact that they tend to live in distinct places and keep a specific number of precepts. However, the Buddhist status of laymen and laywomen is much less obvious. In some parts of contemporary Asia, such as the countries of mainland Southeast Asia or the Himalayan kingdom of Bhutan, the percentage of the population that is identified (or identifies itself) as Buddhist is quite high—over 90 percent in the case of Thailand and Cambodia. In these cases, there is a close correlation between being Buddhist and being a citizen of a particular nation-state. Being Buddhist is as much a part of being Thai as it is about any kind of considered choice, and in this sense Buddhist identity can be viewed as an aspect of nationalist and statist projects.[6] In other societies, there is a much higher degree of religious pluralism. In China, for example, approximately 18 percent of the population has been identified as Buddhist in recent surveys—the same as the percentage of those who follow "folk religion"—while in Japan and Singapore, approximately one-third of the population is identified as Buddhist, with other religions (or non-affiliation) comprising the remainder of the populations.[7] In these cases, being Buddhist often entails a more conscious choice to be a part of a Buddhist community, or to engage in Buddhist activities, such as taking the three refuges. Perhaps unsurprisingly given the difference between these varying locations, there are different meanings attributed to engaging in specifically Buddhist activities by region. For example, in the Theravāda communities of Southeast Asia, taking the three refuges is an act that is done regularly, whenever one participates in a Buddhist ceremony, whereas in Chinese Buddhist contexts taking the three refuges entails a much higher level of commitment, linking oneself to a specific Buddhist teacher. Moreover, it is sometimes more appropriate to suggest that people engage in Buddhist activities rather than having an explicitly Buddhist identity. In contemporary Japan the majority of funerals are Buddhist, performed by Buddhist priests, and link families to a specific Buddhist sect or temple, a legacy of the mandatory parishioner (*danka*) system from the Tokugawa era (1600–1868). These funerals may be the only formal interactions that the family has with the temple, and so it both is and is not appropriate to think about these individuals as Buddhist, and thus part of the sangha.[8]

In a broader sense, the sangha is made up of four parts: nuns and monks, laywomen and laymen. One way to define these different parts of the sangha is in relation to the precepts. Monks and nuns (and, in a few cases to be discussed below, laypeople) undergo an ordination ritual in which they agree to learn and follow a certain number of precepts (though they do not usually learn these precepts during the ritual itself). The number of precepts varies according to the Buddhist tradition, with each of the major streams of Buddhism (Theravāda, Mahāyāna, and Vajrayāna) following a different disciplinary code. For example, in the Pali Vinaya followed by Theravāda monastics, monks who have taken the higher ordination (Pali, *upasamadā*) are ultimately responsible for following 227 different precepts of varying degrees of importance, while nuns are responsible for 311 precepts. Those males who take the novice ordination (Pali, *pabbajjā*) in Southeast Asia are responsible for only ten different precepts, while laypeople usually attend to only five precepts (Pali, *pañcasīlāni*): to refrain from killing, stealing, committing sexual impropriety, taking intoxicants, and lying. The degree to which lay Buddhists take precepts formally varies, and so too does the degree to which these individuals should be considered part of the sangha. In China, men and women who take the five precepts can go through a type of ordination; in Southeast Asia, repeating the five precepts is more common and therefore not as much of a marker of Buddhist identity. Mahāyāna and Vajrayāna Buddhists attend to other *vinaya* codes. Monastics of China, Korea, Taiwan, and Vietnam have generally followed the rules of the Dharmaguptaka Vinaya, and Vajrayāna monks of Central Asia have generally followed the Mūlasarvāstivāda Vinayas (all three of the complete extant *vinaya* collections have different numbers of rules). Moreover, even when a monastic community formally follows a *vinaya* code, the way the community follows the code can change over time. While the Tendai monks of the late Heian and early Kamakura periods followed the Dharmaguptaka Vinaya, they increasingly considered it to be more important to follow the forty-eight bodhisattva vows. In the late 19th century, it became far more common for Japanese Buddhists to be priests who conducted rituals than to be monks following the *vinaya*. Similarly, tantric adepts in the Vajrayāna world are understood to be able to break *vinaya* rules in order to foster wisdom or power.

If we think about the sangha in less strict terms, it becomes clear that throughout history defining the Buddhist community has been a more complex endeavor than allowed for by the straightforward division of the ordained and lay supporters. These other figures have had different kinds of relationships to the precepts. Among the most common types of figures throughout Buddhist history have been wizards, yogis, and other practitioners of magic. These figures, such as the mahāsiddhas (Tibetan, *druptop chenpo*; one who attains great powers or siddhas) of Vajrayāna Buddhism or the *weikzas* ("wizards" who engage in esoteric practices; the word is a Burmese form of the Pali term *vijjadhāra*) of modern Myanmar, have not always been formally ordained; at times, their engagement with yogic or tantric practice moved them away from mainstream parts of the sangha or even society at large. However, their marginal status and their ability to perform magic (often in service of protecting Buddhism in some capacity) also makes them a part of the sangha. A second category within the sangha comprises kings and other high politicians. While these figures may be seen in some ways simply as part of the laity, kings often had a specific role as both protector par excellence of the dharma and also as sponsor and/or patron of the monastic community. This notion of the particular role of kings goes back to the tradition of the *cakravartin*, the "wheel-turning monarch," which was part of the prophecy surrounding Siddhartha's birth, as well as to Ashoka (*c.* 268–232 BCE), remembered as a paradigmatic king who both supported and purified the sangha. The king or emperor's special status within the sangha has taken a variety of forms, from periods in which the Chinese emperor was also seen as a bodhisattva; to the unique figure of the Dalai Lama, incorporating political responsibilities into his office; to the *dhamma- rāja / deva- rāja* combination of the kings of the Chakri dynasty in Siam and Thailand who have fostered ideologies of being both a god-king (*deva-rāja*) and a *dhamma*-king (*dhamma-rāja*). A third type includes social roles that complicate the idea of a clear distinction between lay and ordained. For example, in very different ways, ritual specialists among Newar Buddhists and Japanese priests exhibit aspects of both lay and ordained life.[9] This is even more the case for the temple wives of Shin Buddhist priests in Japan (*bōmori*), who were historically responsible for maintaining the religious life of Shin temples but had little formal status, making them "neither nun nor laywoman."[10] Former monks might also be considered to be part of sanghas that are not easily encapsulated in the four-fold typology. Common within parts of the Buddhist world where there is temporary ordination, former monks (*khanan*) have had important roles in some Theravāda societies as meditation teachers or medical practitioners whose authority comes in part from previously having been monks. While unique in some ways to Southeast Asia, these figures, like the practitioners of magic and kings, point to the idea that sanghas have often not been limited to the four-fold group of monks, nuns, laymen, and laywomen.

The relationship between the different parts of the sangha has been defined by a complicated mix of hierarchy and institutional relations. At the most basic level, monastics and non-monastics have maintained a symbiotic, hierarchical relationship (though the hierarchical relationships have played out differently in the case of political authorities, whether state or king). Monastics, whose "burden" (*dhura*) it is to either study the teachings of the buddha or to practice it through meditation (or both), have a responsibility to both preserve and protect the teachings of the buddha and to propagate it to the laity. This propagation has taken a variety of forms over the millennia, such as delivering sermons, writing philosophical tracts and popular narratives, and sponsoring or participating in the construction of monastic complexes, including images, murals, and other forms of material culture. Laywomen and laymen, on the other hand, are responsible for supporting monastics. They generally do this by providing material support, whether alimentary or financial, as well as human power. Monastics are generally constrained by both the *vinaya* and social custom from fully engaging in economic activities and so have relied upon the laity to fulfill those roles for them. The constraints, and therefore the needs of monastics for lay interventions, have varied significantly. Monasteries in China were significant landowners prior to land reform during the 1950s under the Communists, and so many of these monasteries were maintained through the rents they earned or the labor of their serfs. At the same time, there is a strong ideological basis within Chan/Zen forms of Buddhism for monks to perform some degree of labor (agricultural or otherwise) to maintain themselves and their temples. In Theravāda communities, on the other hand, monks have generally been prevented by the *vinaya* from doing certain types of labor, such as farming, and so have relied much more directly on the merit-making activities of the communities of which they are a part.

These different roles have played a factor in the complexities of hierarchies between monastics and lay folk. In many, if not most, Buddhist societies, monastics—and particularly monks—are seen as being above the laity, structurally and ideally if not always in practice. Monks and nuns often receive material support from lay Buddhists; in doing so, monastics provide laywomen and laymen the opportunity to make merit, acting as "fields of merit." (While the dynamics of merit mean that, ideally, donations from lay to ordained Buddhists preclude gifts from binding monastics into networks of reciprocity,[11] in practical terms, monks and nuns have understood that the donations of lay supporters make them responsible to their patrons.) The worthiness of monastics to receive the donations of the laity is a function of several different factors: their having made a sacrifice to "leave society," their adherence to the *vinaya*, and the time that they have spent acquiring wisdom or knowledge, through meditation, study, or both. These also serve to imbue monastics with a quality of sacredness, in terms of being set apart. Being set apart means that monastics have been, and often are, constrained in their participation in various spheres of society (such as politics or commerce), but it also places them above the laity. Often, this social hierarchy is visible in the ways that laywomen and laymen interact with monastics. The laity pay obeisance to monastics; they are often seated below them and may very well keep their head, if not their whole body, below the ordained during interpersonal interactions. The patterns of the relationship between monastics and laypeople described here should be understood in ideal terms rather than as representing hard and fast rules for their interactions. While monastics have often been perceived as having higher status, countervailing discourses such as the Vimalakīrti Sutra seemingly criticize the superiority of monks and nuns. Greedy or corrupt Buddhist monks were sometimes depicted as comic figures in classical Chinese and Japanese literature.

The hierarchical relationship between lay and ordained Buddhists has been varied, and while monastics have often wielded influence in a variety of Buddhist societies, they have normally not held offices in which they wielded formal political authority. This has generally been because monastics are thought to have exited the formal strictures of society. They have been more likely to serve in advisory roles than in secular governing ones. In Theravāda societies, scholars have conceptualized this in terms of a symbiotic relationship between monastic and political authorities. In exchange for material support, monastic institutions would legitimize the political authority of kings (or states). In other contexts, such as Tokugawa Japan, monastic authorities have been wholly under the authority of the government, serving as agents of the state, even if indirectly. Sometimes Buddhist authority has been appropriated by governing structures, such as in late imperial China, when the Son of Heaven was also conceptualized as being a bodhisattva, or in the millenarian movements of Southeast Asia, when kings (or rebelling would-be kings) would claim to be the coming of Maitreya, the future buddha. Only rarely have monastics wielded direct political authority, with the most famous exception being that of the office of the Dalai Lama, the formal head of state in Tibet from the 15th century to the mid-20th. There are two conclusions to be drawn about relationships between monastics and laypeople: first, that idealized notions of the sangha do not always map directly onto the actual experiences of monastics; second, that there are a number of possible visions for what constitutes the proper political role of the sangha within society.[12]

It is also important to highlight that hierarchies are not limited to the relationship between monastics and laity: intra-sangha relationships are also marked by significant stratification. In the contemporary world, this can be seen in the interactions between senior monks and novices, who often bend low when approaching their superiors. (Given that novices are not infrequently taller than elderly monks, this can lead to some significant contortions.) There are a number of different vectors along which these internal hierarchies have been determined. The most common has to do with time in robes. The date of a monastic's ordination is assiduously marked, as it affects his or her status in ways both small (where one sits in an assembly of monastics) and large (eligibility for titles and offices, such as the former rules for deciding who should be the supreme monk [*sangha-rāja*] in Thailand by seniority within the Supreme Sangha Council). While seniority is a central factor for status throughout Buddhist communities, there are others, such as educational attainment or charisma. The first is more easily measurable through degrees (whether traditional ones like the *geshe* degree in Tibetan Buddhism or *vinaya dhara* [monks trained to have *vinaya* expertise] in Burma, or modern ones like the PhD). Charismatic attainments, the result of prowess in meditation or preaching, for example, are more ambiguous. In northern Thailand, such monks are sometimes given the informal but prestigious title of *khrūbā* (venerable teacher). In other places, the authority given to a monk is less obvious.

Gender is another extremely important vector of hierarchy within the sangha. This is seen perhaps most clearly in a classical sense by the narrative of the Buddha's reluctance to establish an order of nuns (ultimately requiring the intervention of his disciple Ananda). However, it is also clear and evident from the fact that seniority of ordained women is subordinated to that of ordained men such that, infamously, even the most junior male novice has seniority over the most senior nun. Buddhist ideologies are not solely misogynistic, and sometimes express the capability of women to attain wisdom, but they also interact with other types of gendered hierarchies, such as those of Confucianism. Because donations to monastics from lay supporters often work according to the logic of maximizing merit, this has meant that in many contexts nuns have received less material support from lay communities and have been more likely to be impoverished.[13]

CONSTITUTING SANGHAS

One can make a useful distinction between the sangha, the third jewel, and sanghas, specific collections of Buddhists, especially the ordained. The sangha is an ideal vision of the community, presumably without internal boundaries between different kinds of Buddhists, as in the concept of the "sangha of the four quarters" (*cāturdiśa-saṅgha*).[14] Sanghas, on the other hand, are groups of monastics linked or constituted by their ability to perform community rituals (*sangha-kamma*) together. Among the important *sangha-kamma* are the fortnightly recitation of the disciplinary codes (Pali, *pāṭimokkha*; Sanskrit, *prātimokṣa*) and ordination. At the most basic level, following the same *vinaya* determines belonging in a sangha. While monastics from one group might productively interact with those of another group (for example, at international conferences or on study missions), the various *vinayas* preclude monastics from participating in the foundational actions of different groups. Indeed, in some ways, it could be said that a sangha is constituted by its very adherence to a specific *vinaya*.

This implies a legalistic dynamic to the constitution of a sangha. One aspect of this dynamic that has been important in some parts of the Buddhist world is a careful attention to proper locations for the ecclesiastical acts of a sangha. For example, in Pali forms of Buddhism, the formal acts of the community must take place inside a specifically demarcated space (*sīmā*). Literally a boundary, this is a space "in which all members of a single local community have to assemble as a complete saṅgha (*samagga saṅgha*) at a place appointed for ecclesiastical acts." According to Kieffer-Pülz, failure to complete these acts within a properly established *sīmā* renders invalid the *sangha kamma*. As such, an elaborate set of rules for the establishment of *sīmās* is laid out in the *vinaya*.[15] Questions around validity of the *sīmā* seem to hold greater significance within sanghas following the Pali *vinaya*, but the space within which ecclesiastical acts take place has been of importance within other Buddhist communities as well.[16] For example, in early 9th century Japan the monk Saichō spent many years lobbying the state to allow him to build an ordination platform, which would allow him to conduct ordinations using the "bodhisattva vows." (That these efforts on Saichō's part were also a bid for independence from the restrictions on the number of ordinands assigned to Tendai as a result of the platform controlled by the Ritsu [Vinaya] sect reminds us that religious and political motivations are often deeply entangled.)

Ordination is the process by which someone enters into a sangha. Ordination rituals vary significantly, ranging from highly elaborate celebrations which reaffirm the wider Buddhist community as well as bring the young man or woman into the community, to simple ceremonies with just a group of fully ordained monks and the candidate(s). At their core, however, these rituals constitute formal requests to be accepted into the sangha. More broadly, ordination formally incorporates Buddhists (usually, but not always, monastics) into the sangha community by giving them a place within the institutional structure and tying them into lineages of teachers and thinkers. Newly ordained monks and nuns, for example, have preceptors (*upajjhāya*) who are responsible for making sure that they are trained, that they learn the precepts, and that they know to act properly as *bhikkhunī, bhikkhu, sāmaṇerī*, or *sāmaṇera* (nun, monk, novice nun, novice monk, respectively). The scope of this training varies widely depending on the age of the monastic. In parts of the Buddhist world where the ordination of minors is common, preceptors for novices, especially those under the age of fifteen, may not only be responsible for the instruction of the novices in religious training but also required to act *in loco parentis*.[17] While the preceptor's formal responsibility to train a newly ordained monk lasts at least five years, even after the formal training is over the relationship often remains central, particularly for the junior member of the pair. The late king of Thailand Bhumipol Adulyadej (Rāma IX) was ordained as a young man in the 1950s; his preceptor was the abbot of Wat Bowonniwet Vihāra. While the former was only a monk for a few weeks, the two formed a lifelong friendship, and when it came time to appoint a new supreme monk (*sangha-rāja*), Rāma IX chose his former preceptor. While ordinations are most commonly for monks, nuns, or novices, in Mahāyāna East Asia, laymen and laywomen have sometimes gone through a type of ordination where they take the three refuges or the five precepts, an act which usually ties them semiformally into a teacher's lineage.[18] In some sects in contemporary Japan, the wives of priests undergo an ordination in order to enter more fully into the structure of the institution.[19]

All Buddhist communities have at least two different ordination rituals for monastics: the novice ordination (*pabbajjā*) and the higher ordination (*upasampadā*). Ordaining as a novice entails taking on the ten novice precepts, while the higher ordination makes the new monk or nun responsible for the full range of precepts listed in each respective *vinaya* (though it takes several years to learn the full list). Because of this, religiously (and in terms of cultivation), the higher ordination is more important. However, it is sometimes the case that the ordination of novices holds a more significant place in the life of the community. For example, in much of Southeast Asia, Theravāda Buddhism has historically been closely tied to village life, and the ordination of boys is often a time of great communal celebration. The boys are brought to the village temple dressed as Prince Siddhartha, and over the course of the ritual ceremony they are transformed into novices. The higher ordination, where a young man takes on the full responsibilities and precepts of a monk, is often a quieter affair. There needs to be a quorum of five monks to make the ordination legitimate, and the public parts of the event will usually be attended by lay sponsors (family or neighbors), but much of the formal ordination takes place outside of the view of the public. There is significant variety within Buddhist traditions about requirements for the higher ordination. In the Theravāda world, there is often a long period of time between the novice and higher ordination. The Pali Vinaya requires that a young man be at least twenty before taking the higher ordination (a rule that is normally honored), but novices need merely be old enough "to scare away the crows," often between ten and fifteen. Entry into the *bhikkhunī* sangha required a two-year probationary period as a female novice trainee (*sikkhamāna*) before taking the higher ordination,[20] and in Japan Saichō is said to have required twelve years of training before allowing his students to take the higher ordination.[21] At the same time, however, the two ordinations have sometimes been combined into a single event, though of extended duration. In China in the first half of the 20th century, candidates for ordination would come to a temple, study for a period of time to prepare to undergo the novice ordination, and then remain to study at the temple for several more weeks before also undergoing the higher ordination. While separated by several weeks, during which novices learned the disciplinary rules for the higher ordination, these were part of the same extended ritual process.[22]

The legitimacy of the higher ordination, often determined through a combination of Buddhist traditions and local governmental rules, is a central concern. For example, the higher ordination requires a quorum of monastics to be present. In the Pali tradition, ten monks were required in what is now India, but five were sufficient in outer regions (as long as one was a *vinaya* expert). There was a higher bar stipulated for nuns, requiring a group containing fully ordained monks as well as nuns. Establishing a quorum of monks or nuns has at times been impossible and has required the reestablishment of the higher ordination through either visiting or immigrating monastics. This process occurred quite frequently in the history of Southeast Asia, with Lankan monks traveling to what are now Thailand and Burma to reestablish the higher ordination, and vice versa. It is the inability to develop a quorum of fully ordained nuns under the Pali Vinaya that is given as the official reason by many Theravāda monks for their unwillingness to recognize a reestablished order of fully ordained nuns. In addition to questions of a quorum, many states have asserted their right to certify the legitimacy of the higher ordination. This has been done in a variety of ways: requiring monks to register with the state or placing restrictions on the locations and circumstances under which the higher ordination may be conducted. The desire on the part of states (both Buddhist and not) to limit the numbers of monks who have undertaken an officially recognized ordination has often been caused by anxiety that the sangha, as a well-organized institution, could be a potential rival to a state. This is not a fear limited to the modern era; the government of 9th-century Japan was reluctant to grant Tendai monks under Saichō the right to establish a higher ordination platform in large part because it would free the sect from limits placed on the number of monks who could undertake the higher ordination. States have also had material interests in this limitation: tax and corvée labor exemptions meant it was in the interest of the state to control the number of monastics it recognized as legitimate.

Ordination, while important, is only one of the first moments in the life of a monastic. Since one of the central responsibilities of the sangha is the maintenance and propagation of the teachings of the buddha, it is not surprising that the training of monks and nuns has included significant investment into education. Educational frameworks and institutions have varied significantly across time and space in the Buddhist world, ranging from apprenticeships between a monk and a preceptor to universities with formal curricula and modern facilities. The curricula of formal monastic pedagogical institutions have usually begun with Buddhist philosophical frameworks (Mahāyāna, Theravāda, or both), but have also included other subjects which may or may not be seen as specifically Buddhist. For example, in Nālandā, Xuanzang reported that he studied not just Yogācāra and other forms of Buddhist philosophy but also the Vedas and Sanskrit grammar. In contemporary institutions, such as those in China or Thailand, monks, nuns, or novices are likely to study history, mathematics, law, and temple management.[23] Whether in premodern or modern educational contexts, the pedagogical framework is a reflection of the roles that monks might be expected to take within the sangha. This can perhaps be seen most clearly in the case of the efforts of the 20th-century Chinese monk Taixu to shift the training of monks from a series of years-long tutorials to a "modern" school that sought to enable monks to help modernize China.[24]

There are multiple motivations for ordination, and these can affect communal decisions for how to train monastics. While on the surface it might seem obvious that people become ordained in order to pursue a religious calling and the salvific ends therein, it is likely that in many, if not most, cases ordination is impacted by instrumental as well as salvific concerns. In much of mainland Southeast Asia, it has been common for several hundred years for men to ordain for a short period of time in order to receive training on how to be a proper man within a given society. Disrobing in this context (as a life decision, rather than as the result of a *vinaya* infraction) is not seen as having any negative consequences (though it does change one's standing in the community). In Tibetan areas prior to 1949, monasteries served an overflow role when population numbers overwhelmed the capacity of families to feed their children,[25] which may have been a factor in the development of "mass monasticism" in the region (the idea that every third son ought to be given to a monastery). In Japan, where it became the norm by the early 20th century that the ordained would be married, becoming a priest has been a matter of family inheritance, and responsibility for temples has tended to pass from father to son. (It is not only in Japan that family ties and traditions affect decisions about ordination; Chinese monks and nuns in the contemporary period are likely to cite an aunt or an uncle who was Buddhist as a motivation for their initial attraction to the religion.) Moreover, in many different contexts throughout Buddhist history, down to and including contemporary Myanmar and Thailand, training as a Buddhist monk provided young men with an education which allowed them a greater degree of social mobility within society than would otherwise be possible. In all these cases, social ideals and practices have had an important impact on the contours of the sangha as an institution.

MANAGING SANGHAS

In addition to encompassing the Buddhist community (whether defined as only those who have been ordained or as the four-fold community), sanghas are also one of the institutional faces of Buddhism. As such, they require governance, both from the standpoint of external political authorities, both modern and premodern, and the internal running of the community. As is evident in the discussion of education under Constituting Sanghas, sanghas are managed by a variety of actors: ordained and lay Buddhists as well as states. In most cases, this management has been local or national in form. While lineages can have international branches, in general there have been very few truly transnational institutions within Buddhism. Those that have existed, such as the International Association of Buddhist Universities (IABU) or the World Fellowship of Buddhists, have tended to be alliances rather than governing institutions. Intra-sangha interactions—those between monks, nuns, and novices as well as between monastics and lay folk—are shaped in large measure by the rules of the *vinaya*. These rules do not delineate all possible interactions, but taken as a whole they provide a robust framework to guide and manage the interactions of Buddhists. For example, the *vinaya* not only forbids sexual interactions for monastics; it also outlines those with whom a monk or a nun can be in a room alone, or with whom it is appropriate to eat. (The rules of the *vinaya* are divided and grouped according to the severity of the action.) The various *vinayas* also stipulate some of the rules of inheritance of the possessions of monks and nuns. Centrally, the *vinaya* emphasizes the importance of the unity of the sangha, with actions which destroy the unity of the sangha (*sanghabheda*) being among the most serious.

Monasteries vary in size and complexity in their organization. Most monasteries have an abbot or abbess who is responsible for overall management, but depending on size and wealth there are a number of other responsibilities carried out by monastics. Many of these speak directly to the religious projects of the monastery, such as running educational programs or meditation centers, or of the particular responsibility of a specific monk or nun, such as being in charge of discipline. However, they also include far more prosaic responsibilities, such as the management of both financial and material resources (clothing, books, and so forth) of the monastery, organization and usage of the spaces of the monastery, organization of the labor of monastics, management of lands owned by the monastery, and management of the kitchen (indeed, in Chan/Zen monasteries in particular, the job of cook seems to have been particularly important).[26] In village monasteries of Southeast Asia or the private monasteries of

China, these jobs would have been done by one or two monastics, perhaps with the help of lay members of the community (especially in cases where there are jobs that are forbidden to monks). Larger monasteries, such as those of imperial China or the monastic universities around Lhasa, had much more elaborate organizational structures. In the latter cases, the *vinaya* only provided the outline of a management structure, and there are rules and systems particular to specific locations.

While in a specific monastic location, an abbot or abbess often has wide-ranging latitude in his or her ability to act, individual monasteries are often organized in relation to larger frameworks that may be organized by denomination or lineage, or by the secular government. This is particularly the case in the modern era, where the organizational structure of Buddhism relies in part on the way that a given government has chosen to organize and manage religious institutions, as well as the legal and constitutional status of religion in general and Buddhism specifically. Many modern governments declare that religions such as Buddhism are organized and managed by internal religious bureaucracies, but in many cases it is the secular governments that have required that bureaucratic structures be developed in the first place. The Buddhist Association in modern China, for example, is a quasi-governmental organization filled with ordained and lay Buddhists who are nominally responsible for managing relations between formal state institutions and Buddhist monasteries and convents. The Buddhist Association was developed by Buddhists in the 1950s, but it has taken its current form precisely because of the rules and laws stipulated by the party-state of the People's Republic of China.[27] This is not limited to China, of course; modern states are involved in certifying ordinations, and where sanghas run schools for minors governments are involved, even if only indirectly, in determining what the schools teach, at least for non-Buddhist subjects. Management of sanghas by the state is not limited to the modern era and in fact goes back at least to the legend of Ashoka, who is remembered as having purified the sangha of a large group of illegitimate monks. Moreover, the imperial government in China often regulated ordinations at Buddhist monasteries, in part because monks were exempted from corvée labor responsibilities.

In a general sense, the management of sanghas is in part about determining the proper role and activities of monastics within society. The degree of intervention by modern states into the management of Buddhism depends on both the imagined role that Buddhism takes in the national community and the formal constitutional structures that define it. This means that there is significant variety across the Buddhist nations of Asia, and debate about the proper intervention by states in managing sanghas is ongoing.[28] Just as sanghas vary in their definition and organization across the Buddhist world and Buddhist history, these roles are not easily generalizable. In some contexts, monastics have been deeply involved in political processes; in others they have been outside of these processes, sometimes by choice and sometimes by stipulation of the state. Indeed, in a broader sense, determining how a sangha is conceptualized within a particular Buddhist society requires understanding the interactions of local Buddhist traditions, *vinaya* structures, and rules and governing frameworks of the national government.

REVIEW OF LITERATURE

Summarizing scholarship on the sanghas within Buddhism presents several challenges. Because sangha refers to both the Buddhist community and the institutional aspects of

Buddhism, the concept of the sangha is present either implicitly or explicitly whenever Buddhists are under consideration. This means that a genealogy of "sangha" could conceivably contain most of the scholarship on Buddhism over the last two centuries. Despite this, much early European and American scholarship on Buddhism was only incidentally about sanghas, being more concerned with elucidating the variety of Buddhist teachings across the Buddhist world. Scholarship concerned with institutional aspects of sanghas, such as the work on Buddhist communities in French Indochina in the *Bulletin de l'École française d'Extrême-Orient*, tended to be more about the polities than about the religion. While often containing excellent scholarship, they have a relatively weak notion of the sangha as a whole. Sanghas have been a widespread subject largely since the end of the 1960s (not coincidentally, when the Cold War brought about an expansion of funds for academics, particularly from the American academic community, to travel to Asia).

One important early problem in the study of Buddhism was in thinking about how the teachings of the Buddha spread and multiplied, and this has been a major theme throughout the last century and a half of the study of Buddhism. Scholars such as Etienne Lamotte and Sukumar Dutt sought to understand how Buddhism developed in India.[29] While their work was often focused on the development of systems of thought, it also contained considerations of monastic communities. Similarly, scholars thinking about the spread of Buddhism into East Asia, such as Erik Zürcher, were concerned with both philosophical and institutional developments.[30] Starting in the 1980s, though, scholars became more concerned with the way that institutional developments, such as competition between different Chan schools in China, were hidden to a certain extent by philosophical arguments.[31] More recently, scholars have returned to thinking about the sociology of early Buddhist communities, reconstructed from canonical and epigraphical materials, but also using more recent sociological tools.[32]

A major development in the last decades of the 20th century and the first decades of the 21st is a turn to the *vinaya* as a source for thinking about the sociology of sanghas. Early scholars, such as I. B. Horner, spent most of their effort on translating the canonical forms of the *vinaya*. This yielded some valuable considerations of how the *vinaya* affected the sangha.[33] However, from the 1980s, scholars such as Gregory Schopen argued forcefully for the need to consider *vinaya* texts, as well as epigraphical materials, to begin to understand how members of the sangha represented themselves.[34] While this call has been widely influential, there are several different directions in which considerations of the *vinaya*—and discipline more broadly—have led scholars to understand sanghas explicitly. Scholars have begun to consider how the sangha is formed and perpetuated through processes of education.[35] At the same time, they have investigated the ways that sanghas remain deeply affected by family connections.[36]

Another important line of scholarship that considers sanghas has been explicit considerations of Buddhism, politics, and governance (i.e., the relationship of the sangha with particular states). This has been a particularly important issue within the study of Southeast Asian forms of Buddhism, starting with the work of Stanley Tambiah in the 1970s on Buddhism and politics in Theravāda civilizations and continuing down to more recent work, such as that on the sangha's role in political upheaval in Sri Lanka, and in defense of Buddhism in anti-colonial movements in Burma.[37] Yet work on the participation of Zen monks and priests in the war effort during World War II and Taiwanese Buddhist participation in politics in the 1990s shows that the dynamics of Buddhism and politics are not limited to Southeast Asia.[38]

The early 2000s have also seen scholars begin to think more explicitly about the intersections of secular law, *vinaya*, and sangha formation.[39]

There are two other trends within recent scholarship on sanghas that intersect with key directions in contemporary scholarship. The first is a consideration of the order of nuns, and in particular the effort to reestablish the higher ordination of nuns, within the Theravāda Buddhist communities.[40] The second is the problem (real or perceived) of modernity; that is, how does the modernization of Buddhist societies affect the formation of the sangha and the roles that monks and nuns play in modern society?[41]

FURTHER READING

Bunnag, Jane. *Buddhist Monk, Buddhist Layman: A Study of Urban Monastic Organization in Central Thailand*. Cambridge, UK: Cambridge University Press, 1973.

Clark, Shayne. *Family Matters in Indian Buddhist Monasticisms*. Honolulu: University of Hawai'i Press, 2014.

Dreyfus, Georges. *The Sound of Two Hands Clapping: The Education of a Tibetan Buddhist Monk*. Berkeley: University of California Press, 2003.

Gernet, Jacques. *Buddhism in Chinese Society: An Economic History from the Fifth to the Tenth Centuries*. Translated by Franciscus Verellen. New York: Columbia University Press, 1995.

Kieffer-Pülz, Petra. "Rules for the *Sīmā* Regulation in the *Vinaya* and Its Commentaries and Their Application in Thailand." *Journal of the International Association of Buddhist Studies* 20, no. 2 (1997): 141–153.

McDaniel, Justin Thomas. *Gathering Leaves and Lifting Words: Histories of Buddhist Monastic Education in Laos and Thailand*. Seattle: University of Washington Press, 2009.

Mrozik, Susanne. "A Robed Revolution: The Contemporary Buddhist Nun's (Bhikṣuṇī) Movement." *Religious Compass* 3, no. 3 (2009): 360–378.

Samuels, Jeffrey. *Attracting the Heart: Social Relations and the Aesthetics of Emotion in Sri Lankan Monastic Culture*. Honolulu: University of Hawai'i Press, 2009.

Schopen, Gregory. *Buddhist Monks and Other Business Matters: Still More Papers on Monastic Buddhism in India*. Honolulu: University of Hawai'i Press, 2004.

Silk, Jonathan A. *Managing Monks: Administrators and Administrative Roles in Indian Buddhist Monasticism*. New York: Oxford University Press, 2008.

Tambiah, Stanley J. *Buddhism and the Spirit Cults in North-east Thailand*. Cambridge, UK: Cambridge University Press, 1970.

Welch, Holes. *The Practice of Chinese Buddhism, 1900–1950*. Cambridge, MA: Harvard University Press, 1967.

NOTES

1. T. W. Rhys-Davids and William Stede, *Pali-English Dictionary* (London: Pali Text Society, 1921–1925), 667.
2. Domnern Garden and Sathienpong Wannapok, *Thai-English Dictionary*, 4th ed. (Bangkok: SE-Education Public Company Limited, 2009), 525.
3. "Sangha," *Access to Insight*.
4. Buddhist communities have used a variety of languages. In order to avoid establishing one language as the standard form or having to repeat all possible permutations of a term, I shall primarily use English (monk or nun) rather than terms in Pali, Sanskrit, Tibetan, Chinese, etc., though I also recognize that the terms in English are not always perfect reflections of emic categories.

5. Donald W. Mitchell, *Buddhism: Introducing the Buddhist Experience*, 2d ed. (Oxford: Oxford University Press, 2008).
6. Duncan McCargo, "Informal Citizens: Graduated Citizenship in Southern Thailand," *Ethnic and Racial Studies* 34, no. 5 (2011): 833–849.
7. Pew Research Center, "Global Religious Diversity: Half of the Most Religious Diverse Countries are in Asia-Pacific Region," http://www.pewforum.org/2014/04/04/global-religious-diversity/.
8. Ian Reader, *Religion in Contemporary Japan* (Honolulu: University of Hawai'i Press, 1991).
9. David Gellner, *Monk, Householder, Tantric Priest* (Cambridge, UK: Cambridge University Press, 1992), 141; and Stephen G. Covell, *Japanese Temple Buddhism: Worldliness in a Religion of Renunciation* (Honolulu: University of Hawai'i Press, 2005).
10. Jessica Starling, "Neither Nun nor Laywoman: The Good Wives and Wise Mothers of Jōdō Shinshū Temples," *Japanese Journal of Religious Studies* 40, no. 2 (2013): 277–301.
11. Nicolas Sihlé, "Towards a Comparative Anthropology of the Buddhist Gift (and Other Transfers)," *Religion Compass* 9, no. 11 (2015): 352–385.
12. Ian Harris, introduction to *Buddhism and the Political Process*, ed. Hiroko Kawanami (New York: Palgrave MacMillan, 2016), 1–10.
13. Charlene Makely, *The Violence of Liberation: Gender and Tibetan Buddhist Revival in Post-Mao China* (Berkeley: University of California Press, 2007).
14. Charles S. Prebish, "Varying the Vinaya: Creative Responses to Modernity," in *Buddhism in the Modern World: Adaptations of an Ancient Tradition*, eds. Steven Heine and Charles S. Prebish (New York: Oxford University Press, 2003), 46.
15. Petra Kieffer-Pülz, "Rules for the *Sīmā* Regulation in the *Vinaya* and Its Commentaries and Their Application in Thailand," *Journal of the International Association of Buddhist Studies* 20, no. 2 (1997): 141.
16. Ann Heirman, "Chinese Nuns and Their Ordination in Fifth Century China," *Journal of the International Association of Buddhist Studies* 24, no. 2 (2001): 294, fn. 85, 296.
17. Jeffrey Samuels, *Attracting the Heart: Social Relations and the Aesthetics of Emotion in Sri Lankan Monastic Culture* (Honolulu: University of Hawai'i Press, 2009).
18. Holmes Welch, *The Practice of Chinese Buddhism, 1900–1950* (Cambridge, MA: Harvard University Press, 1967), 361.
19. Covell, *Japanese Temple Buddhism*, 121.
20. Hiroko Kawanami, *Renunciation and Empowerment of Buddhist Nuns in Myanmar-Burma* (Leiden, The Netherlands: Brill, 2013), 81.
21. Paul Groner, *Saichō: The Establishment of the Japanese Tendai School* (Berkeley: University of California Press, 1984), cited in Covell, *Japanese Temple Buddhism*, 215.
22. Welch, *The Practice of Chinese Buddhism, 1900–1950*, 285–294.
23. Thomas Borchert, *Educating Monks: Minority Buddhism on China's Southwest Border* (Honolulu: University of Hawai'i Press, 2017).
24. Raul Birnbaum, "Buddhist China at Century's End," in *Religion in China Today*, ed. Daniel Overmyer (Cambridge, UK: Cambridge University Press, 2003).
25. Matthew Kapstein, *The Tibetans* (Oxford: Blackwell, 2006), 219.
26. Shohaku Okamura and Jisho Warner, eds., *Nothing is Hidden: Essays on Zen Master Dogen's Instructions for the Cook* (New York: Weatherhill, 2001).
27. Ji Zhe, "Secularization as Religious Restructuring: Statist Institutionalization of Buddhism and Its Paradoxes," in *Chinese Religiosities: Afflictions of Modernity and State Formation*, ed. Mayfair Yang (Berkeley: University of California Press, 2008), 233–260.

28. Benjamin Schonthal, *Buddhism Politics and the Limits of the Law: The Pyrrhic Constitutionalism of Sri Lanka* (New York: Cambridge University Press, 2016).
29. Etienne Lamotte, *Histoire du bouddhisme indien: des origines à l'ère Śaka* (Louvain, Belgium: Institute Orientaliste, 1958); and Sukumar Dutt, *Buddhist Monks and Monasteries of India: Their History and Contribution to Indian Culture* (London: George Allen and Unwin, 1962).
30. Erik Zürcher, *The Buddhist Conquest of China: The Spread and Adaptation of Buddhism in Early Medieval China* (Leiden, The Netherlands: Brill, 1972).
31. John R. McRae, *The Northern School and the Formation of Early Ch'an Buddhism* (Honolulu: University of Hawai'i Press, 1986); and Bernard Faure, *The Will to Orthodoxy: A Critical Genealogy of Northern Chan Buddhism* (Stanford, CA: Stanford University Press, 1997).
32. Torkel Brekke, "The Early *Saṃgha* and the Laity," *Journal of the International Association of Buddhist Studies* 20, no. 2 (1997): 7–32; and I. Mabbet, "The Early Buddhist *Saṃgha* in its Social Context," *Nagoya Studies in Indian Culture and Buddhism* 21 (2001): 101–129.
33. John Holt, *Discipline, the Canonical Buddhism of the Vinayapitaka* (Delhi: Motilal Banarsidass, 1981); and M. Wijayaratna, *Le moine bouddhiste selon des textes du Theravāda* (Paris: Cerf, 1983).
34. Gregory Schopen, *Bones, Stones, and Buddhist Monks: Collected Papers on the Archaeology, Epigraphy and Texts of Monastic Buddhism in India* (Honolulu: University of Hawai'i Press, 1997).
35. Anne M. Blackburn, "Looking for the Vinaya: Monastic Discipline in the Practical Canons of the Theravāda," *Journal of the International Association of Buddhist Studies* 22 (1998): 281–309; Anne M. Blackburn, *Buddhist Learning and Textual Practice in Eighteenth-Century Lankan Monastic Culture* (Princeton, NJ: Princeton University Press, 2001); Georges Dreyfus, *The Sound of Two Hands Clapping: The Education of a Tibetan Buddhist Monk* (Berkeley: University of California Press, 2003); and Justin McDaniel, *Gathering Leaves and Lifting Words: Histories of Buddhist Monastic Education in Laos and Thailand* (Seattle: University of Washington Press, 2008).
36. Shayne Neil Clarke, *Family Matters in Indian Buddhist Monasticisms* (Honolulu: University of Hawai'i Press, 2014); Liz Wilson, ed., *Family in Buddhism* (Albany: State University of New York Press, 2013); and Jeffrey Samuels, *Attracting the Heart: Social Relations and the Aesthetics of Emotion in Sri Lankan Monastic Culture* (Honolulu: University of Hawai'i Press, 2009).
37. Stanley J. Tambiah, *World Conqueror, World Renouncer: A Study of Buddhism and Polity in Thailand against an Historical Background* (Cambridge, UK: Cambridge University Press, 1976); Ananda Abeysekara, *Colors of the Robe: Religion, Identity and Difference* (Columbia: University of South Carolina Press, 2002); and Alicia Marie Turner, *Saving Buddhism: The Impermanence of Religion in Colonial Burma* (Honolulu: University of Hawai'i Press, 2014).
38. Brian Victoria, *Zen at War* (Lanham, MD: Rowman and Littlefield, 2006); and Richard Madsen, *Dharma's Democracy: Religious Renaissance and Political Development in Taiwan* (Berkeley: University of California Press, 2007).
39. Rebecca Redwood French and Mark A. Nathan, eds., *Buddhism and Law: An Introduction* (New York: Cambridge University Press, 2014).
40. Kawanami, *Renunciation and Empowerment of Buddhist Nuns in Myanmar-Burma*; and Susanne Mrozik, "A Robed Revolution: the Contemporary Buddhist Nun's (Bhikṣuṇī) Movement," *Religious Compass* 3, no. 3 (2009): 360–378.
41. Don A. Pittman, *Towards a Modern Chinese Buddhism: Taixu's Reforms* (Honolulu: University of Hawai'i Press, 2008); and Thomas Borchert, "Worry for the Dai Nation: Sipsongpanna, Chinese Modernity and the Problem of Buddhist Modernism," *Journal of Asian Studies* 67, no. 1 (2008): 107–142.

Thomas Borchert

ŚĀNTIDEVA'S INTRODUCTION TO THE PRACTICES OF AWAKENING (*BODHICARYĀVATĀRA*)

INTRODUCTION

The *Introduction to the Practices of Awakening* (*Bodhicaryāvatāra;* hereafter, BCA) is a short verse presentation of the training practices for developing the virtuous character of the bodhisattva, the Mahāyāna Buddhist exemplar who commits to remaining in samsara to save all beings from suffering. The text was written by the monk scholar Śāntideva, who resided in India at the monastic university of Nālandā *c.* 8th century CE. The text had significant influence in India and Tibet and continues to be an influential source for contemporary Buddhist practice. It interweaves ritual, meditation, and philosophical argumentation as mutually supportive aspects of bodhisattva practice.[1] As a result of its powerful depiction of the virtues of the bodhisattva and its employment of philosophical argument to establish normative conclusions, it has become an influential text in the developing academic field of Buddhist ethics.

THE AUTHOR, THE TEXT, AND ITS INFLUENCE

Very little is known about the life of Śāntideva. He is thought to have lived at the Buddhist university of Nālandā between the 7th and 8th centuries CE and to have been a proponent of the Mahāyāna Madhyamaka school of philosophy. In addition to the BCA, Śāntideva is also the author of the *Training Manual* (*Śikṣāsamuccaya*), a primarily prose work that also presents a summary of the bodhisattva path, composed mainly of extended quotations from Mahāyāna sutras. The intended audience for the BCA appears to be male monastics; this is suggested by its use of meditations on the repulsiveness of female bodies to eliminate male lust (BCA 8:41–8:63).

Two versions of the BCA are extant. The longer and more influential version contains 913 verses in ten chapters and exists in the original Sanskrit as well as premodern translations into Tibetan, Newari, Mongolian, and Chinese. It is the basis for almost all existing commentaries on the BCA and all contemporary translations. A Tibetan translation of a shorter version of the text was discovered in the caves of Dūnhuáng in China at the beginning of the 20th century. This shorter version, which Akira Saito has argued is the older one, is composed of 701 verses divided into nine chapters.[2]

There are several significant differences between the two versions. The shorter version is ascribed to Akṣayamati and gives the Sanskrit title as *Introduction to the Practices of the Bodhisattva* (*Bodhisattvacaryāvatāra*). The longer version is ascribed to Śāntideva and is titled *Introduction to the Practices of Awakening* (*Bodhicaryāvatāra*). Saito argues that the name Akṣayamati is probably an epithet applied to Śāntideva, perhaps due his practice of quoting from the *Akṣayamatinirdeśa Sūtra* in his other extant text, the *Training Manual.*[3] Saito also argues that the shorter version is the older one, and that the longer version was probably revised by later authors, who incorporated additional material, largely from the *Training Manual.*[4] However, this is disputed by Paul Harrison, who argues that the text may have been revised and expanded by Śāntideva himself.[5] Another difference is that the second chapter of the shorter version has been divided into two chapters in the longer version, resulting in ten chapters in total, in contrast to the shorter version's nine. Most of the other significant differences between the two versions occur in the eighth and ninth chapters (chapters 7 and 8 for the shorter work), both of which have been significantly expanded in the longer version. This article will focus only on this longer and more influential version.

PREMODERN INFLUENCE OF THE *BODHICARYĀVATĀRA*

Ten Indian commentaries on the BCA have been preserved in Tibetan translation, suggesting that the text had significant influence in India. The most influential of these and the only commentary surviving in Sanskrit is the 10th-century commentary, the *Bodhicaryāvatārapañjikā* by Prajñākaramati. Additional Sanskrit commentaries that are extant in Tibetan translation include the *Bodhisattvacaryāvatārasaṃskāra* by Kalyāṇadeva (11th century), the *Bodhisattvacaryāvatārapañjikā* of Vairocanarakṣita (11th century), and the *Bodhicaryāvatāratā tparyapañjikā* of Viśeṣadyotani (early 13th century).[6]

Many additional commentaries were composed in Tibet, where the text has been extremely influential. The shorter version of the BCA was translated into Tibetan in the 8th or 9th century, while the longer and more influential version was introduced in the 11th century.[7] Among the most important Tibetan commentators are Bsod nams rtse mo (1142–1182) and Rgyal tshab rje Dar ma rin chen (1364–1462).[8] An influential 19th-century commentary from the Tibetan tradition was composed by Kunzang Pelden.[9] Commentaries continued to be composed on the BCA by contemporary Tibetan Buddhist scholars and practitioners, including Tenzin Gyatso and Kelsang Gyatso.[10] The text's wide-ranging influence includes its use in Tibetan monastic university education and in ceremonies, such as receiving the bodhisattva vow.[11] It is also one of the primary source texts for the Tibetan tradition of mind transformation.[12]

The BCA was introduced to Nepal in 1040 by the great Indian scholar Atisha, who taught there for one year on his way to Tibet. Its longstanding influence in Nepal is attested to by the existence of numerous manuscripts dating from the 11th century on.[13] It continues to be an important text for Newar Buddhism, the form of Buddhism that developed in Nepal.[14] It was translated into Mongolian in 1305, where, due to the influence of Tibetan Buddhism and the close political ties between the countries, it became an important text.[15] It was also translated into Chinese in the 10th century during the Sòng dynasty; however, it seems to have had little influence there.[16]

INFLUENCE IN THE 20TH AND EARLY 21ST CENTURIES

The BCA continues to be an important source of spiritual inspiration for practitioners of Tibetan Buddhism; it is taught and studied at dharma centers around the world. The Fourteenth Dalai Lama, Tenzin Gyatso, has used it as the subject of many of his public lectures.[17] An influential commentary from a practitioner perspective was published by the American Tibetan Buddhist nun Pema Chödrön.[18]

The BCA has also been of increasing importance in the emerging academic field of Buddhist ethics; a growing body of scholarly work analyzes its structure and its potential cross-cultural significance. Charles Goodman, in a series of publications, has argued that Śāntideva is best understood as a consequentialist, whose deepest normative commitment is to the impersonal maximization of well-being. Part of Goodman's argumentative strategy is to cite passages that he takes to illustrate Śāntideva's consequentialist commitments, such as an impartial commitment to eliminating suffering.[19] Goodman also identifies structural similarities between Śāntideva's ethical commitments and those held by Western consequentialists. For instance, both are agent-neutral, in that they give the same underlying moral aim to all agents, the impartial promotion of well-being and removal of suffering.[20] Both also condone balancing, that is, permitting agents to cause small harms when these will bring about greater benefits.[21] Moreover, both are morally demanding in requiring great commitment and arguably sacrifice of their adherents.[22] Given these structural similarities, Goodman argues, we can best understand Śāntideva as ascribing to a consequentialist theory of right action.

It is uncontroversial that Śāntideva places enormous importance on eliminating the suffering of oneself and others; there is therefore a consequentialist element to his thinking. However, there has been disagreement among scholars as to how strong a case can be made that impersonal maximization of good outcomes is his deepest normative commitment. For instance, Gordon Davis has argued that there are also deontic elements to Śāntideva's thinking that cannot be understood as having merely instrumental value.[23] In addition, Śāntideva places great importance on other-regarding virtues, such as generosity and compassion, a central component of which is the aim to lessen the suffering of others. Arguably, therefore, Śāntideva's commitment to eliminating suffering could be understood as grounded by a commitment to developing one's own virtuous character, where other-regarding virtues are conceived of as character traits of central importance.[24] Finally, some scholars have argued that we misunderstand Śāntideva when we take him to be placing the same emphasis on theory of right action as 20th- and 21st-century Western ethical theory. Jay Garfield, for instance, has argued that we better understand Śāntideva's moral concerns when we characterize his thought as providing a moral phenomenology, in articulating and developing virtuous states of mind, resulting in a more accurate and compassionate perception of the world.[25]

Contemporary scholars have also begun to analyze Śāntideva's contributions in the philosophical area of well-being. One point of discussion is whether Śāntideva considers the apparently demanding bodhisattva path as conducive to the practitioner's own benefit. Edelglass has argued that the bodhisattva sacrifices his own well-being in developing painful compassion for others.[26] Harris and Jenkins, in partial contrast, have both argued that Śāntideva conceives of and develops the bodhisattva's virtues in such a way that even other-regarding virtues such as compassion benefit the bodhisattva herself.[27]

The BCA is also unusual among Indian Buddhist ethical texts in providing extended arguments for moral conclusions. Two of Śāntideva's arguments in particular have attracted significant contemporary interest. In chapter 6, he argues for the irrationality of anger by appealing to the dependently originated nature of all phenomena and the nonexistence of autonomous agency. Charles Goodman has argued that Śāntideva's connection of universal causation with the irrationality of blame suggests a commitment to hard determinism, the view that there is only one possible future and that therefore blame is irrational.[28] Other scholars have defended a compatibilist reading of Śāntideva's argument.[29] The second argument is presented in the eighth chapter, where Śāntideva argues that accepting the truth of not-self entails a rational obligation to impartial benevolence, an equal commitment to everyone's well-being. Several contemporary scholars have analyzed the cogency of Śāntideva's argument, as well as its importance in his moral thought.[30]

THE STRUCTURE OF THE TEXT

Śāntideva describes the BCA as a brief introduction (*avatāra*) to the training discipline (*saṁvara*) of the bodhisattva (1:1). The first four chapters are devoted to *bodhicitta*, the intention to attain full awakening for the sake of all sentient beings. The first chapter praises bodhicitta, and the second and third chapters present the Mahāyāna ritual of supreme practice (*anuttarapūja*), during which the bodhisattva vow is taken (3:22–3:23). The fourth chapter presents arguments and meditations that enable the bodhisattva to maintain and deepen bodhicitta and his commitment to the bodhisattva path. Chapters 5 through 9 provide meditations and arguments to develop the perfections (*pāramitās*), a scheme of six virtues central to many Mahāyāna presentations of the bodhisattva path. Four of these chapters focus on a single perfection each: patience (*kṣānti*: chapter 6), effort (*vīrya*: chapter 7), meditative concentration (*samadhi*: chap 8), and wisdom (*prajñā*: chapter 9). The fifth chapter is devoted to introspection (*saṃprajanya*) and mindfulness (*smṛti*), but some scholars believe that this chapter functions as Śāntideva's presentation of the perfection of ethical restraint (*śīla*).[31] Surprisingly, there is no chapter devoted to the perfection of generosity (*dāna*), although there are several verses on generosity scattered throughout the text (3:11, 5:9–5:10, 7:25–7:26).

A significant feature of the BCA is its incorporation of philosophical argumentation into contemplations designed to develop virtuous character. In the patience chapter, for instance, Śāntideva argues that anger is irrational since sentient beings do not possess sufficient control over their actions to deserve blame (6:22–6:33). Likewise, in the effort chapter, he argues that the fearful nature of samsara, which includes repeated death and rebirth, should motivate devotion to Buddhist practice (7:4–7:13). These passages function simultaneously as arguments meant to convince an interlocutor (or oneself) of their claims, as well as meditations to develop the virtue in question. This repeated use of reasoning as a means of developing virtue largely accounts for the text's philosophically important status.

BODHICITTA AND THE SUPREME RITUAL: *BODHICARYĀVATĀRA* CHAPTERS 1–4

The first four chapters of the BCA are dedicated to the development of bodhicitta, the wish to attain full awakening for the benefit of all sentient beings. The first chapter praises bodhicitta, emphasizing its karmic benefits for the practitioner, in terms of both developing positive karmic merit (1:17–1:19) and preventing past karmic seeds from ripening (1:11). Several verses in this chapter also employ perfectionist reasoning, arguing that the development of bodhicitta, and the bodhisattva's virtues, are the noblest and most excellent of human goals. For instance, bodhicitta is compared to a priceless jewel (1:24–1:25), which has been found to be valuable by the buddhas of the past (1:11), and Śāntideva claims that those who develop it should be honored above all others (1:23, 1:30).

In the first chapter, Śāntideva also distinguishes between two kinds of bodhicitta: aspiring bodhicitta (*bodhi-praṇidhicittam*) and the bodhicitta of setting out (*bodhi-prasthānam*) (1:15). A plausible explanation of this distinction is that aspiring bodhicitta refers to the mental intention to take up bodhisattva practice, and that the bodhicitta of setting out refers to actual progress in bodhisattva training. If this is correct, then the first three chapters are dedicated to aspiring bodhicitta, while the rest develop the bodhicitta of setting out.

The second and third chapters present a seven-part ritual, called the ritual of supreme worship (*anuttarapūja*), in which the bodhisattva prepares himself to take the bodhisattva vow. The ritual is comprised of seven parts: (a) praise, (b) worship, (c) confession of faults, (d) rejoicing in merit, (e) requesting the teaching, (f) supplication for the buddhas to remain, and (g) dedication of merit.[32] The vow itself is taken toward the end of the ritual, in verses 3:22–3:23.

> Just as the Sugatas of old adopted bodhicitta,
> and just as they properly conformed to the practice of the
> Bodhisattvas,
> So I myself shall generate the bodhicitta for the
> sake of the world; and so I myself shall properly engage in
> those practices. (3:22–3:23, translation altered)[33]

In chapter 4, the newly dedicated bodhisattva engages in a series of meditations designed to protect and deepen his commitment to the bodhisattva path. Early in the chapter, Śāntideva acknowledges that the commitment to liberate all sentient beings is unbelievably ambitious, and he contemplates the negative karmic consequences of abandoning it, such as future unfortunate rebirths (4:1–4:14). These passages are among many within the text in which Śāntideva contemplates death and the potential for negative rebirth as a source of motivational energy for progression on the bodhisattva path (see also 7:4–7:13). The chapter also considers an extended contemplation on the harmfulness of mental afflictions such as anger and craving, in causing the mind to lack control (4:26–4:27) and in bringing about negative karmic consequences (4:30–4:36).

The next five chapters present meditations and arguments to help the bodhisattva develop the perfections, or closely related virtues such as mindfulness, introspection, and compassion. The development of many of these virtues incorporates a self and other benefiting structure that is one of the key features of Śāntideva's presentation of the bodhisattva path.[34] Patience, for instance, benefits oneself by preventing loss of karmic merit and by calming the mind (6:1–6:5) while also eliminating the motivation to harm others (6:22–6:126). To better understand this feature of the text, it is important to understand how Śāntideva characterizes the mental afflictions and the perfections; the following section, therefore, provides a brief introduction to these concepts.

THE PERFECTIONS (*PĀRAMITĀS*) AND THE MENTAL AFFLICTIONS (*KLEŚAS*)

Like many Mahāyāna authors, Śāntideva holds that the central mental afflictions are delusion (*avidyā/moha*), craving (*rāga/lobha*), and anger (*krodha/dveṣa*). Delusion is the superimposition of permanence, unity, and intrinsic existence upon fragmental, impermanent, and empty phenomena. Craving and anger are affective responses to this basic error. Based upon falsely perceiving the objects of experience as unified, enduring, and possessed of intrinsic existence, one craves to possess them, becomes angry when one does not have them or when they are lost, and so on. Śāntideva also frequently refers to envy and pride in the BCA (8:12, 8:140), both of which arise as a result of falsely reifying elements of experience into enduring selves of which we can be overly proud, in the case of oneself, or of whose achievements and possessions we can be jealous, in the case of others.

Śāntideva holds that the mental afflictions are the ultimate sources of suffering. Although his treatment is not systematic, we can identify four reoccurring and overlapping ways in which the afflictions damage the well-being of their possessor. First and most basically, they destabilize the mind, leading to a lack of mental, verbal, and physical control (4:26–4:29). This results in harmful mental, physical, and verbal actions, resulting in the second source of disvalue caused by the mental afflictions: negative karmic effects, such as rebirth in hell (4:26, 4:30–4:32). A third source of disvalue is the psychological suffering that is either constituted by or results from the mental afflictions. Examples include the mentally painful feeling of a mind filled with anger (6:3) and the emotional disturbance of fear in relation to death and unfortunate rebirths (2:38–2:44, 7:3–7:13). Finally, the mental afflictions disrupt social relationships, a disadvantage that is caused in particular by anger (6:4–6:5) as well as envy and pride (8:9–8:25).

The perfections, and closely related bodhisattva virtues such as compassion, mindfulness, and introspection, are the qualities that comprise the character of the advanced bodhisattva. Ultimately, they will enable the bodhisattva to work tirelessly for sentient beings' welfare. They also function to eliminate the mental afflictions, and it is this feature that receives the most attention in the BCA. Each perfection acts as an antidote that dissolves one or more of the afflictions and in so doing lessens the suffering of the bodhisattva. Generosity, for instance, eliminates craving; patience eliminates anger; wisdom eliminates delusion. The relation between the perfections and the mental afflictions therefore accounts for the structure of benefiting self and other, which is a striking and repeating feature of the BCA. Eliminating the mental afflictions by developing the perfections and related virtues lessens the bodhisattva's own suffering while simultaneously preparing her to benefit others most effectively.[35]

GENEROSITY (*DĀNA*)

Since generosity is one of the perfections, the absence of a generosity chapter in the BCA is a surprising omission, for which there is no obvious explanation. There are, however, several passages scattered throughout the BCA that concisely articulate Śāntideva's account of generosity, the most significant of which comes in the fifth chapter.

> If the perfection of generosity makes the world free of
> poverty, how is it possible that the Protectors of the past
> acquired it, when the world is still impoverished today?
> The perfection of generosity is interpreted simply as a state
> of mind due to the intention of giving away everything,
> together with the fruits of that, to all people. (5:9–5:10)

In the passage, Śāntideva replies to a hypothetical opponent who argues that the fact that poverty has not been eradicated suggests that no bodhisattva or buddha has ever developed perfect generosity. In response Śāntideva defines the perfection of generosity as the mental state that intends to give all possessions to sentient beings. The verse illustrates a distinctive feature of Śāntideva's treatment of the perfections. Even those that seem to apply to physical actions, such as generosity and ethical restraint, are reinterpreted as mental states. The bodhisattva gives perfectly when he adjusts his attitude to be willing and eager to give anything in his possession whenever the possibility arises; the actual offering of items to those in need follows as a matter of course.

MINDFULNESS (*SMṚTI*), INTROSPECTION (*SAṂPRAJANYA*), AND ETHICAL DISCIPLINE (*ŚĪLA*): *BODHICARYĀVATĀRA* CHAPTER 5

The fifth chapter is named after the mental state of introspection (*saṃprajanya*) and includes an extended treatment of the closely related mental state of mindfulness (*smṛti*). However, several scholars have understood this chapter to act as Śāntideva's chapter on ethical discipline (*śīla*).[36] This is because a vigilant mind, possessing mindfulness and introspection, will eliminate all aggressive mental states that would motivate physical or verbal abuse against sentient beings. Here again we find Śāntideva's tendency to focus on the mental causes of physical and verbal action. Ethical discipline just *is* virtuous awareness of mind, as constituted by mindfulness and introspection, since these are the mental abilities that ensure the bodhisattva will not harm sentient beings.

Śāntideva does not define mindfulness, but his description of it as a rope that restrains the mind and keeps it focused on virtuous objects (5:2–5:3) suggests that it is a kind of morally efficacious focusing attention. *Smṛti*, the term translated as mindfulness, literally means memory, suggesting that it is not limited to presently experienced external objects of awareness but can also recall or bring to mind the bodhisattva's ethical commitments, such as his vow to help sentient beings.[37] When interacting with hostile sentient beings, therefore, the mindful bodhisattva will fulfill his commitment to benefit them. When lethargic in his practice, he will focus on the fact that human rebirth provides rare opportunities for spiritual practice (4:15–4:20). When encountering objects of potential craving, such as attractive companions, the mindful bodhisattva focuses on unpleasant bodily features through strategies such as imagining the bones beneath the skin (8:52) or contemplating excrement and digested food inside the body (8:58–8:62).

The role of introspection is to support the maintenance of mindful awareness by monitoring the quality of attention and alerting the bodhisattva when a mental affliction arises. Śāntideva defines it as "the repeated examination of the state of one's body and mind" (5:108). Introspection, therefore, is a kind of meta-awareness that tracks the quality of mindful attention and the overall condition of the bodhisattva's mind and body. When there is a lapse in virtuous physical or mental activity, through improper bodily etiquette (5:70–5:80, 5:91–5:96) or through the arising of a mental affliction (5:48–5:53), introspection alerts the bodhisattva to the arisen danger. Śāntideva repeatedly uses the image of imagining one's mind like a block of insentient wood as a way of enabling the bodhisattva to temporarily halt the progress of the mental affliction.

> When one sees one's own mind to be attached or repulsed,
> then one should neither act nor speak, but remain still like a
> piece of wood.
> When my mind is haughty, sarcastic, full of conceit and
> arrogance, ridiculing, evasive, and deceitful,
> When it is inclined to boast, or when it is contemptuous of
> others, abusive, and irritable, then I should remain still like a
> piece of wood. (5:48–5:50)

Each time one of these mental afflictions or other harmful intentions begins to form, disrupting mindfulness, the bodhisattva is alerted by introspection, freezes all mental and physical activity, and turns his attention to eliminating it. The final step of the procedure is made explicit in verse 5:54.

> Perceiving in this way that the mind is afflicted or engaged
> in fruitless activities, the hero should always firmly control it
> by means of an antidote to that. (5:54)

The bodhisattva, alerted by introspection to the presence of the mental affliction, applies the appropriate mental antidote to eliminate it. Frequently these antidotes are the virtuous mental states themselves: patience and compassion are antidotes to anger, generosity is the antidote to craving, and so on. The relevant psychological principle, shared widely in Buddhist psychology, is that certain mental states are incompatible and cannot coexist in the same mind. If one is angry and can generate patience, the anger will be eliminated, and so on. A primary role of each perfection therefore is to act as the antidote to the relevant mental affliction. In the sections to follow, we will see instances of this strategy at work in Śāntideva's development of patience, effort, compassion, and wisdom.

PATIENCE (*KṢĀNTI*): *BODHICARYĀVATĀRA* CHAPTER 6

Śāntideva depicts patience (*kṣānti*) as the antidote to harmful mental frustration in response to difficult circumstances. Most of chapter 6 develops patience to eliminate anger arising toward sentient beings who attempt to harm us (6:22–6:126), but Śāntideva also gives significant attention to preventing harmful aversion that arises in response to physical pain (6:12–6:21). Although the chapter presents numerous meditations to prevent and eliminate anger, they are all based upon the Buddhist tenet of dependent origination, which Śāntideva employs to analyze anger according to its causal factors.[38]

> Finding its fuel in mental pain originating
> from an undesired event and from an
> impediment to desired events, anger
> becomes inflamed and destroys me.
> Therefore, I shall remove the fuel of that
> enemy, for that foe has no function other than to harm me.
> Even if I fall into extreme adversity, I should not disrupt my
> happiness. When there is frustration, nothing is
> agreeable, and virtue is forsaken. (6:7–6:9, translation altered slightly)

Verse 6:7 identifies mental pain (*daurmanasya*) as a salient causal condition for anger. Verses 6:8 and 6:9 then introduce the general strategy for eliminating anger that is deployed throughout the chapter. Since mental pain is a causal condition for anger, if we eliminate mental pain by keeping the mind happy, anger will never arise.[39] The remainder of the chapter is primarily comprised of a series of overlapping arguments that what appears to be an unfortunate circumstance, the kind of event that would ordinarily cause mental pain, is actually neutral or even positive in relation to well-being or the bodhisattva's commitment to progressing on the bodhisattva path.

In verses 6:12–6:21, Śāntideva applies this strategy to physical pain. This section of the chapter presupposes a distinction made in Buddhist psychology between physical pain (*kāyika-duḥkha*) and mental pain (*caitasika-duḥkha=daurmanasya*).[40] Physical pain occurs as a result of the functioning of one of the five physical senses: painful tactile sensations, harsh sounds, bad smells, and so on. Mental pain is an adverse mental reaction to a difficult circumstance, such as verbal abuse, loss of reputation, and so on. For ordinary persons, physical pain causes mental pain, and Śāntideva's insight in these verses is that if we can break this link then we can prevent anger from arising by eliminating its causal condition. Therefore, he offers a series of arguments that physical pain is not actually bad, at least for the properly trained individual. For instance, verse 6:14 argues that we can become accustomed to enduring physically painful sensations without mental distress by repeated practice. Verse 6:21 draws attention to positive aspects of physical pain in relation to bodhisattva training, such as its propensity to increase our compassion and to motivate sincere Buddhist practice. The goal in each case is to eliminate any mentally adverse reaction to unavoidable physical pain. This should not be confused with a facile masochism, however; Śāntideva is explicit elsewhere that the body should be preserved to facilitate training on the bodhisattva path (5:70). Nevertheless, when physical pain cannot be avoided without violating one's bodhisattva commitments, the bodhisattva should not mentally recoil against it. If he is successful in this, he will not become angry.

Much of the rest of the chapter is composed of arguments that change the bodhisattva's attitude toward enemies who try to harm him. Again, the goal is to alter the bodhisattva's perspective on unpleasant situations, so that mentally adverse reactions, and thereby anger, are prevented.[41] For instance, Śāntideva argues that the bodhisattva should be glad when encountering enemies, since this is a condition for developing the perfection of patience (6:104–6:107). The most influential of these meditative arguments, however, is presented in a series of verses in which Śāntideva argues that accepting the Buddhist tenet of dependent origination suggests that it would be irrational to blame individuals for their actions.

> A person does not intentionally become angry, thinking, "I shall get angry," nor does anger originate, thinking, "I shall arise."
> All offenses and vices of various kinds arise under the influence of conditions, and they do not arise independently.
> An assemblage of conditions does not have the intention, "I shall produce," nor does that which is produced have the intention, "I shall be produced." (6:24–6:26)
> Thus, everything is dependent on something else, and even that on which something is dependent is not autonomous. Hence, why would one get angry at things that are inactive, like apparitions? (6:31)

In these verses, Śāntideva argues that anger arises based upon a deluded belief that individuals act independently as autonomous, intrinsically existing agents (6:31). Instead, harmful acts arise dependent on innumerous causal factors; completely absent is any autonomous mental factor of willing (6:24–6:26). Since our anger arises based upon a mistaken understanding of reality, it is irrational, and contemplating this fact will lessen and finally eliminate it.

The argument is a good example of a repeating feature of Śāntideva's text: his use of philosophical argumentation to dispel mental afflictions, in this case anger. This can be successful because the mental afflictions arise as a result of delusion, through the superimposition of independence, endurance, and unity on dependent, impermanent, and fragmentary experience. Śāntideva's arguments draw attention to the way phenomena actually exist—in these verses, as dependently arisen—and therefore eliminate our mistaken understanding of the world, and the resulting mental afflictions.[42]

EFFORT (*VĪRYA*): *BODHICARYĀVATĀRA* CHAPTER 7

The seventh chapter is devoted the development of effort (*vīrya*), a motivational factor that enables the bodhisattva to progress along the bodhisattva path. Śāntideva defines effort as "enthusiasm for virtue" (1:2). His presentation of it is divided into two parts. In the first part, Śāntideva introduces four negative mental qualities that effort eliminates: laziness, clinging to the reprehensible, apathy, and self-contempt (2:2). He then offers a series of meditations to develop effort and eliminate each of these mental states. For example, verses 7:4–7:14 are comprised of meditations to eliminate laziness, with most of these verses focused on the terrors of death.

> Seeing despondent relatives with their eyes swollen and red,
> with tears on their faces from the impact of their grief and
> the faces of the messengers of Yama,
> Tormented by the recollection of your own vices, hearing the
> sounds of hell, and befouling your body with excrement out
> of fear, what will you do when you are so terrified?
> Realizing "I am like a live fish," your fear is appropriate
> now. How much more when you have committed vices and
> face the intense suffering of hell? (7:9–7:11)

The second half of the chapter develops six "powers," mental states that are supportive of the development of effort. The powers, as presented in verse 7:32, are aspiration, self-confidence, delight, letting go, dedication, and determination.[43] An intriguing aspect of this section is Śāntideva's use of language ordinarily used to describe the mental afflictions to characterize virtuous mental states conducive of effort. For instance, he uses the term pride (*māna*) to refer both to an inflated sense of self-importance that causes suffering (7:56ab) and to the self-confidence necessary to progress on the path (7:56cd). Likewise, Śāntideva uses sexual imagery to describe the intensity of the delight the bodhisattva takes in his bodhisattva training and virtuous activities (7:62), while at the same time condemning ordinary sexual passion as impoverished and conducive to craving (7:64).

MEDITATION (*DHYĀNA*): *BODHICARYĀVATĀRA* CHAPTER 8

The organizational structure of the eighth chapter is challenging. The chapter's name, *dhyāna*, suggests that it should be devoted to developing the perfection of concentration, a mental state of single pointed focus on an object of meditation. Nevertheless, although there are occasional references to concentration meditation in the chapter (8:1–8:2, 8:4, 8:6, 8:89), Śāntideva does not present an extended explanation of how concentration is developed. The first half of the chapter is composed of overlapping but distinguishable sections in which samsaric social life is criticized (8:5–8:25), the wilderness is praised as a place of tranquility (8:15–8:16, 8:29), and a series of charnel ground meditations designed to eliminate lust are presented (8:30–8:71). Śāntideva's intention with these meditations seems to be to develop aversion to samsara and decrease lust, rather than to develop strong concentration. It may be that Śāntideva's focus on reducing craving in this chapter is partly explained by the need to calm the mind before initiating concentration meditation; nevertheless, it is surprising that instructions for developing concentration itself are not presented.

In the second half of the chapter, a series of meditations are presented on the disadvantages of self-cherishing (8:111–8:139) and the development of compassion (8:89–8:110, 8:140–8:154). Two of these sets of meditations have become particularly influential, both in the Tibetan Buddhist tradition and in contemporary academic scholarship. The first, called "equalizing self and others," presents a series of meditations designed to equalize concern for all persons (8:90–8:107). The meditation takes the form of an extended argument, which has garnered significant contemporary philosophical attention. It takes as one of its basic premises that all people are similar in wanting to avoid suffering and attain happiness.

> One should first earnestly meditate on the equality of oneself
> and others in this way: "All equally experience suffering and
> happiness, and I must protect them as I do myself." (8:90)

The specifics of how Śāntideva develops the argument that follows is a topic of dispute among both his traditional commenters and contemporary scholars.[44] One plausible way of understanding the argument is that Śāntideva is using a two-part strategy to support his conclusion that it is irrational to prioritize one's own well-being over that of others. In the just quoted verse, Śāntideva draws attention to the shared nature of suffering, and its intrinsic badness, as establishing a prima facie reason to eliminate it. For the remainder of the argument, he considers various responses by a hypothetical opponent that might justify a greater concern for one's own suffering. The most powerful of these justifications is that it is reasonable to give somewhat greater priority to removing one's own suffering, given that it is one's own. In response, Śāntideva invokes the basic Buddhist tenet of metaphysical selflessness (*anātman*) to show that this argument is based on the mistaken belief in an enduring unified self (*ātman*) (8:101–8:102). Since persons do not exist, except as conceptually designated bundles of impermanent aggregations, they cannot be appealed to in justifying the prioritization of one's own well-being. We are, however, committed to removing suffering, given its intrinsically negative feel (8:102) and the universal acceptance that it is bad (8:103). Therefore, we should commit to removing all of it impartially.

The equalizing self and other meditations are followed by a second set of influential meditations also designed to strengthen impartial compassion (8:140–8:154). In these meditations, called "exchanging self and others," the bodhisattva imaginatively exchanges his position respectively with persons in lower, equal, or higher social positions. From the other's vantage point, he contemplates the negative emotions they habitually feel toward him. For instance, he mentally examines the envy the person of low social standing experiences in relation to his higher social position (8:140–8:146), and the arrogant pride of the person of high social status who is contemptuous of him (8:151–154). Although Śāntideva is not explicit about what the meditation is meant to achieve, plausibly it is intended to stimulate equal compassion toward oneself and others by deepening the bodhisattva's understanding of the painfulness of experiencing mental afflictions such as envy and pride. The meditations may also be intended to provide antidotes to the bodhisattva's own mental afflictions. By contemplating how painful his ordinary behavior is to the person of low social standing, for instance, the bodhisattva diminishes his arrogant pride.[45] This set of meditations has exerted great influence on the Tibetan traditions, becoming one of the foundational sources for their practices of mind training (*Lojong*).[46]

WISDOM (*PRAJÑĀ*): *BODHICARYĀVATĀRA* CHAPTER 9

The wisdom chapter presents an extended defense of the Madhyamaka doctrine of emptiness (*śūnyatā*), the core Madhyamaka claim that no entity has intrinsic existence (*svabhāva*), but instead exists in dependence on causes and conditions and conceptual labeling. Early in the chapter, Śāntideva explicates the two truths, claiming that intellectual activity belongs to the realm of conventional truth (*saṃvṛtisat*), while the ultimate truth (*paramārthasat*) transcends conceptual thought (9:2). Although Śāntideva's explanation here is sparse, he is generally understood to be articulating the Madhyamaka position that conventional reality consists of a realm of commonsense objects dependent on conceptual imputation for their existence. Śāntideva goes on to distinguish levels of practitioners, relative to their understanding of Buddhist metaphysics. Ordinary Buddhists are superior to non-Buddhists, but there are qualitative differences in the understanding of Buddhist practitioners as well (9:3–9:4). Plausibly, Śāntideva's meaning is that his own Madhyamaka school's positions are superior to those of other Buddhists.

Most of the remainder of the chapter is devoted to defending the Madhyamaka position of emptiness against criticisms by Buddhist and non-Buddhist schools, as well as critiquing Śāntideva's opponents' metaphysical positions. Śāntideva's opponents include early (non-Mahāyāna) Buddhists (9:40–9:56), Yogācāra Buddhists (9:18–9:27), and the Sāṃkhya (9:60–9:67, 9:127–9:130) and Nyāya (9:68–9:69, 9:118–9:125) schools of Brahmanical philosophy. For instance, Śāntideva argues that the Yogācāra claim that consciousness is self-illuminating is incoherent, since it violates the principle that nothing can act on itself (9:17). Against the early Buddhists, Śāntideva argues that realizing the shared doctrine of the Four Noble Truths is not sufficient for liberation (9:40), since it will not wholly eliminate the mental afflictions and karma (9:45–9:47). Instead, contemplating the emptiness of phenomena is required for freedom from samsara (9:48). Śāntideva also argues that the Nyāya claim that an unchanging eternal god created the universe is incoherent, since creation itself requires a change in the creator's state (9:120), and that the Sāṃkhya claim that material objects are comprised of the three constituencies of *sattva, rajas,* and *tamas* is untenable, since a single object cannot have three natures (9:128). The chapter also includes a series of arguments for the selflessness of persons and the emptiness of various aspects of reality, including the emptiness of the body (9:79–9:84), atoms (9:86), hedonic feelings such as pain (9:89–9:98), and mental afflictions such as craving (9:98).

DEDICATION

The tenth chapter concludes the BCA with a fifty-eight-verse dedication in which the bodhisattva commits his karmic merit (*puṇya*) accumulated during bodhisattva practice to the welfare of all beings. Many of the verses are dedicated to removing the suffering of beings in particular realms of rebirth, such as those reborn in hells (10:6–10:17), as hungry ghosts (10:18), and humans suffering from various afflictions (10:19–10:41). This chapter also contains evocative reaffirmations of the bodhisattva's commitment to work for sentient beings' benefit, and striking characterizations of compassion, including the following verse in which the bodhisattva dedicates himself to remaining in samsara forever.

> For as long as space endures and for as long
> as the world lasts, may I live dispelling the
> miseries of the world. (10:55)

REVIEW OF LITERATURE

The first Sanskrit edition of the BCA was published by I. P. Minayeff in 1890.[47] La Vallée Poussin created a Sanskrit edition of the BCA and Prajñākaramati's commentary between 1902 and 1914 and translated the BCA into French in 1907.[48] P. L. Vaidya (1959) and Dwārikādās Śāstrī (2001) also published editions of the BCA.[49] The first English translation, which omits most of chapter 9, was published in 1909 by L.D. Barnett. Numerous translations have appeared in Western languages, including French (Finot, 1920), Italian (Pezzali, 1975), German (Steinkellner, 1981), and additional English translations from the Sanskrit (Śāntideva, 1970, 1997, 2008, 2016) and the Tibetan (Śāntideva, 1979, 2006).[50] Gomez provides a critique of several late 20th-century English-language translations.[51]

Studies of Śāntideva's ethical and mystical thought were published by Pezzi.[52] Har Dayal's influential study of the bodhisattva in Mahāyāna Buddhism takes the BCA as one of its primary sources.[53] Dissertations by Michael Sweet and Peter Oldmeadow provide studies of BCA chapter 9, focused on wisdom, with Oldmeadow also providing a translation of Prajñākaramati's commentary to this chapter.[54] Barbra Nelson's dissertation analyzes Śāntideva's account of patience and provides a translation of Prajñākaramati's commentary to BCA chapter 6.[55] Paul Williams published a collection of essays on various ethical, metaphysical, and epistemic topics of the BCA.[56] Paul Harrison analyzes the relation between the BCA and Śāntideva's other text, the *Training Manual*.[57] In a series of important publications, Akira Saito analyzes the relation between the two recensions of the BCA.[58]

In the late 20th and early 21st centuries, increasing academic attention has been paid to the BCA, with an increase in philosophically sensitive analysis of aspects of his moral thought. A number of articles have focused on Śāntideva's analysis of the relationship between metaphysics and ethics, such as his argument in the eighth chapter that rejecting the existence of an enduring unified self rationally entails a commitment to altruism, or his argument in the sixth chapter that, given the truth of dependent origination, anger is irrational.[59] Studies have also appeared analyzing the underlying structure of Śāntideva's thought. Charles Goodman has argued that Śāntideva is best understood as an ethical consequentialist.[60] Criticisms of

Goodman's position have been made by Barnhart and Harris.[61] Other scholars have argued that Śāntideva is best understood as a proponent of virtue ethics or a moral phenomenologist.[62] Recent studies have also analyzed Śāntideva's conception of well-being or drawn connections with Western philosophical work on moral demandingness.[63] Francis Brassard provides a book-length study of Śāntideva and bodhicitta.[64] Amod Lele's dissertation studies Śāntideva's ethical commitments in both of his texts.[65] Stephen Harris has made a study of Śāntideva's use of afflictive emotions in moral development.[66] A recent coauthored collection on Madhyamaka ethics includes a number of important studies of the BCA.[67] In addition, a collection edited by Jonathan Gold and Douglas Duckworth is focused entirely on the BCA, with studies of various features of the text including metaphysics, ethics, ritual aspects of the text, and its influence in Tibet.[68]

DIGITAL MATERIALS

James B. Apple. "Perfections (Six and Ten) of Bodhisattvas in Buddhist Literature." *Oxford Bibliographies.* https://www.oxfordbibliographies.com/display/document/obo-9780195393521/obo-9780195393521-0034.xml.

Paul B. Donnelly. "Madhyamaka." *Oxford Bibliographies.* https://www.oxfordbibliographies.com/view/document/obo-9780195393521/obo-9780195393521-0199.xml.

FURTHER READING

The Cowherds. *Moonpaths: Ethics and Emptiness.* New York: Oxford University Press, 2016.

Gold, Jonathan, and Douglas Duckworth, eds. *Readings of Śāntideva's Guide to Bodhisattva Practice.* New York: Columbia University Press, 2019.

Gómez, Luis O. "The Way of the Translators: Three Recent Translations of Śāntideva's Bodhicaryāvatāra." *Buddhist Literature* 1 (1999): 262–354.

Goodman, Charles. *Consequences of Compassion: An Interpretation and Defense of Buddhist Ethics.* Oxford: Oxford University Press, 2009.

Goodman, Charles. "Śāntideva." In *The Stanford Encyclopedia of Philosophy.* Fall 2016 edition. Edited by Edward N. Zalta. https://plato.stanford.edu/archives/fall2016/entries/shantideva/.

Lele, Amod. "Ethical Revaluation in the Thought of Śāntideva." PhD diss., Harvard University, 2007.

Pelden, Kunzang. *The Nectar of Manjushri's Speech.* Translated by the Padmakara Translation Group. Boston: Shambhala, 2010.

Saito, Akira. "Śāntideva." In *Brill's Encyclopedia of Buddhism,* Vol 2. Edited by Jonathan Silk, 391–397. Leiden, The Netherlands: Brill, 2019.

Williams, Paul. *Altruism and Reality: Studies in the Philosophy of the Bodhicaryāvatāra.* Richmond, UK: Curzon Press, 1998.

NOTES

1. See Jonathan Gold's "Introduction. Participatory Authorship and Communal Interpretation: The *Bodhicaryāvatāra* as a "World Classic," in *Readings of Śāntideva's Guide to Bodhisattva Practice,* ed. Jonathan Gold and Douglas Duckworth (New York: Columbia University Press, 2019), 1–26.

2. Akira Saito, *A Study of Akṣayamati (=Śāntideva)'s Bodhisattvacaryāvatāra as Found in the Tibetan Manuscripts From Tun-Huang* (Project number 02801005, Faculty of Humanities, Miye University, 1993).
3. Saito, *A Study of Akṣayamati*, 20.
4. Saito, *A Study of Akṣayamati*. See also Chiko Ishida, "Some New Remarks on the Bodhicaryavatra Chap. V," *Journal of Indian and Buddhist Studies* 37, no. 1 (1988), 476–479.
5. Paul Harrison, "Śāntideva: The Author and His Project," in *Readings of Śāntideva's Guide to Bodhisattva Practice*, ed. Jonathan Gold and Douglas Duckworth (New York: Columbia University Press, 2019), 27–44.
6. Paul Williams, *Altruism and Reality: Studies in the Philosophy of the Bodhicaryāvatāra* (Richmond, UK: Curzon Press, 1998), 3–4.
7. Saito, *A Study of Akṣayamati*.
8. For a more complete survey, see Williams, *Altruism and Reality*, 3–5.
9. Kunzang Pelden, *The Nectar of Manjushri's Speech*, trans. Padmakara Translation Group (Boston: Shambhala, 2010).
10. Geshe Kelsang Gyatso, *Guide to the Bodhisattva's Way of Life: How to Enjoy a Life of Great Meaning and Altruism* (Ulverston, UK: Tharpa, 2020); Tenzin Gyatso, *A Flash of Lightning in the Dark of Night: A Guide to the Bodhisattva's Way of Life* (Boston and London: Shambhala, 1994); and Tenzin Gyatso, *Healing Anger: The Power of Patience From a Buddhist Perspective* (Ithaca, NY: Snow Lion, 1997).
11. Fredrik Liland, "The Transmission of the Bodhicaryāvatāra: The History, Diffusion, and Influence of a Mahāyāna Buddhist Text" (M.A. thesis, University of Oslo, 2009), 33–34.
12. Thupten Jinpa, "Bodhicaryāvatāra and Tibetan Mind Training (Lojong)," in *Readings of Śāntideva's Guide to Bodhisattva Practice*, ed. Jonathan Gold and Douglas Duckworth (New York: Columbia University Press, 2019), 146–161.
13. Liland, "The Transmission of the Bodhicaryāvatāra," 22–23.
14. Liland, "The Transmission of the Bodhicaryāvatāra," 25–26.
15. Liland, "The Transmission of the Bodhicaryāvatāra," 45–49.
16. Liland, "The Transmission of the Bodhicaryāvatāra," 40–42.
17. Liland, "The Transmission of the Bodhicaryāvatāra," 59–60.
18. Pema Chödrön, *No Time to Lose: A Timely Guide to the Bodhisattva's Way of Life* (Boston: Shambhala, 2005).
19. Charles Goodman, *Consequences of Compassion: An Interpretation and Defense of Buddhist Ethics* (Oxford: Oxford University Press, 2009), 89–90.
20. Goodman, *Consequences of Compassion*, 75.
21. Goodman, *Consequences of Compassion*, 89–90.
22. Goodman, *Consequences of Compassion*, 90–92.
23. Gordon Davis, "Traces of Consequentialism and Non-Consequentialism in Bodhisattva Ethics," *Philosophy East and West* 64, no. 1 (2013): 275–305.
24. Stephen Harris, "Demandingness, Well-Being and the Bodhisattva Path," *Sophia* 54, no. 2 (2015): 201–216.
25. Jay L. Garfield, "What Is It Like to Be a Bodhisattva: Moral Phenomenology in Śāntideva's *Bodhicaryāvatāra*," *Journal of the International Association of Buddhist Studies* 33 (2010): 333–357; and Jay L. Garfield, "Seeing Sentient Beings: Śāntideva's Moral Phenomenology," in *Readings of Śāntideva's Guide to Bodhisattva Practice*, ed. Jonathan Gold and Douglas Duckworth (New York: Columbia University Press, 2019), 192–208.
26. William Edelglass, "Buddhism, Happiness, and the Science of Meditation," in *Meditation, Buddhism, and Science in Context*, ed. David L. McMahan and Erik Braun (Oxford: Oxford University Press, 2018), 62–83.

27. Stephen Jenkins, "Benefit of Self and Other: The Importance of Persons and Their Self-Interest in Buddhist Ethics," *Dharma Drum Journal of Buddhist Studies* 116 (2015): 141–169; and Harris, "Demandingness, Well-Being and the Bodhisattva Path."
28. Charles Goodman, "Resentment and Reality: Buddhism on Moral Responsibility," *American Philosophy Quarterly* 39, no. 4 (2002): 359–372.
29. Mark Siderits, "Paleo-Compatabalism and Buddhist Reductionism," *Sophia* 47 (2008): 29–42; Daniel Breyer, "Freedom With a Buddhist Face," *Sophia* 52, no. 2 (2013), 359–379; and Bobby Bingle, "Blaming the Buddha: Buddhism and Moral Responsibility," *Sophia* 57 (2017): 295–311.
30. Stephen Harris, "Does Anātman Rationally Entail Altruism? On Bodhicaryāvatāra 8:101–103," *Journal of Buddhist Ethics* 18 (2011): 92–123; Mark Siderits, "The Reality of Altruism: Reconstructing Śāntideva," *Philosophy East and West* 50, no. 3 (2000): 412–424; Jan Westerhoff, "The Connection Between Ontology and Ethics in Madhyamaka Thought," in *Moonpaths: Ethics and Emptiness*, ed. The Cowherds (New York: Oxford University Press, 2016), 203–220; and Williams, *Altruism and Reality*.
31. See "Translators' Introduction" by Kate Crosby and Andrew Skilton in Śāntideva, *The Bodhicaryāvatāra*, trans. Kate Crosby and Andrew Skilton (Oxford: Oxford University Press, 2008), xxvii–xlii.
32. Eric Huntington, "Ritual Structure and Material Culture in the Guide to Bodhisattva Practice," in *Readings of Śāntideva's Guide to Bodhisattva Practice*, ed. Jonathan Gold and Douglas Duckworth (New York: Columbia University Press, 2019), 132-145.
33. Translations are by Wallace and Wallace, unless otherwise indicated. Śāntideva, *A Guide to the Bodhisattva Way of Life (Bodhicaryāvatāra)*, trans. Vesna Wallace ad Allan Wallace (Ithaca, NY: Snow Lion, 1997).
34. See Jenkins, "Benefit of Self and Other." See also Harris, "Demandingness, Well-Being and the Bodhisattva Path."
35. For studies of the interrelation of altruism and self-interest in Buddhist ethics, see Stephen Jenkins, "The Circle of Compassion: An Interpretive Study of Karuna in Indian Buddhist Literature" (Ph.D. dissertation, Harvard University, 1999); and Jenkins, "Benefit of Self and Other."
36. See introductory notes by Crosby and Skilton in Śāntideva, *The Bodhicaryāvatāra*, 30–31.
37. For a discussion of the temporal aspects of *sati* (Pali) and *smṛti* (Sanskrit), see George Dreyfus, "Is Mindfulness Present-Centered and Non-Judgmental? A Discussion of the Cognitive Dimensions of Mindfulness," *Contemporary Buddhism* 12, no. 1 (2011): 41–54; and Bhikku Bodhi, "What Does Mindfulness Really Mean? A Canonical Perspective," *Contemporary Buddhism* 12, no. 1 (2011): 19–39.
38. Barbra Nelson, "Kṣānti in the Bodhisattva Path of Śāntideva" (Ph.D. dissertation, University of Sydney, 2003).
39. Nelson, "Kṣānti."
40. Harris, Stephen, "Suffering and the Shape of Well-Being in Buddhist Ethics," *Asian Philosophy* 24, no. 3 (2014): 242–259.
41. On the role of perspective in Buddhist accounts of patience, see Nicolas Bommarito, "Patience as Perspective," *Philosophy East and West* 64, no. 2 (2014): 269–286.
42. For an influential interpretation of these passages as presenting a hard determinist position, see Goodman, "Resentment."
43. I am following Crosby and Skilton's interpretation of these verses. See Śāntideva, *The Bodhicaryāvatāra*, 63–64.
44. For a summary of ways to understand the argument, see Jay Garfield, Stephen Jenkins, and Graham Priest, "The Śāntideva Passage," in *Moonpaths: Ethics and Emptiness*, ed. The Cowherds (New York: Oxford University Press, 2016), 55–76.
45. Pelden, *Nectar*, 298–307.
46. Jinpa, "*Bodhicaryāvatāra* and Tibetan Mind Training (*Lojong*)."
47. I. P. Minayev, "Bodhicaryāvatāra," *Zvoirao* 4 (1890): 153–228.

48. Śāntideva, *Bodhicaryāvatāra: introduction à la pratique des futurs Bouddhas: poème de Çāntideva*, trans. and annotated by Louis de La Vallée Poussin (Paris: Librairie Bloud, 1907); and Śāntideva, and Prajñākaramati, *Bodhicaryāvatāra: Together With Prajñākaramati's Bodhicaryāvatāra Pañjikā*, ed. Louis de La Vallée Poussin (Calcutta: Bibliotecha Indica, 1902–1914).
49. Śāntideva, *Bodhicaryāvatāra of Arya Śāntideva: With Commentary Pañjikā of Shri Prajñākaramati and Hindi Translation*, ed. and trans. Swami Dwarika Das Shastri. Bauddha Bharati series 21 (Varanasi, India: Bauddha Bharati, 1988); and Śāntideva, *Bodhicaryāvatāra of Śāntideva. With the Commentary Pañjika of Prajñākaramati*, ed. P. L. Vaidya. Buddhist Sanskrit Texts 12 (Darbhanga, India: Mithila Institute, 1960).
50. Translations include L. D. Barnette, *The Path of Light* (New York: E.P. Dutton, 1909); *La marche a la lumière, Bodhicaryavatara: poème Sanscrit de Śantideva*, trans. and with an introduction by Louis Finot. Les classiques der l'orient, Vol. 2 (Paris: Éditions Bossard, 1920); *Il Bodhicaryāvatāra di Śāntideva*, trans. Amalia Pezzali (Bologna, Italy: Egidi, 1975); and *Eintritt in das Leben zur Erleuchtung (Bodhicaryāvatāra): Lehrgedicht des Mahāyāna*, trans. Ernst Steinkellner (Düsseldorf, Germany: Eugen Diederichs, 1981). Additional English translations from Sanskrit include Śāntideva, *Entering the Path of ENLIGHTENMENT: The Bodhicaryāvatāra of the Buddhist Poet Śāntideva*, trans. Marion L. Matics (New York: Macmillan, 1970); *A Guide to the Bodhisattva Way of Life (Bodhicaryāvatāra)*, trans. Vesna Wallace and Alan Wallace (Ithaca, NY: Snow Lion, 1997); *The Bodhicaryāvatāra*, trans. Kate Crosby and Andrew Skilton (Oxford: Oxford University Press, 2008); and "Introduction to the Practice of the Bodhisattva Path," trans. Luis Gomez, in *The Norton Anthology of World Religion*, ed. Jack Miles (New York: Norton, 2016), 1077–1123. Additional English translations from Tibetan include *A Guide to the Bodhisattva's Way of Life*, trans. Stephen Batchelor (Dharmsala, India: Library of Tibetan Works & Archives, 1979); and *The Way of the Bodhisattva: A Translation of the Bodhicaryāvatāra*, trans. Padmakara Translation Group (Boston: Shambhala, 2006).
51. Luis Gómez, "The Way of the Translators: Three Recent Translations of Śāntideva's *Bodhicaryāvatāra*," *Buddhist Literature* 1 (1999): 262–354.
52. Amalia Pezzali, "Śāntideva, a Mystic of Buddhism," in *Proceedings of the 9th International Congress for the History of Religions*, ed. Congress Organising Committee (Tokyo: Maruzen, 1960), 398–402; and Amalia Pezzali, *Śāntideva: mystique bouddhiste des VIIe et VIIIesiècles* (Florence: Vallecchi Editore, 1968).
53. Har Dayal, *The Bodhisattva Doctrine in Buddhist Sanskrit Literature* (Delhi: Motilal Banarsidass, 1970).
54. Michael J. Sweet, "Śāntideva and the Mādhyamika: The Prajñāpāramitā-Pariccheda of the Bodhicaryāvatāra" (Ph.D. dissertation, University of Wisconsin-Madison, 1977); and Peter R. Oldmeadow, "A Study of the Wisdom Chapter of the Bodhicaryavatarapañjikā of Prajñākaramati" (Ph.D. dissertation, Australian National University, 1994).
55. Nelson, "Kṣānti."
56. Williams, *Altruism and Reality*.
57. Harrison "Śāntideva."
58. Saito, *A Study of Akṣayamati*; Akira Saito, "Śāntideva in the History of Mādhyamika Philosophy," in *Buddhism in India and Abroad: An Integrating Influence in Vedic and Post-Vedic Perspective* ed. Kalpakam Sankarnarayan, Motohiro Yoritomi and Shubhada A. Joshi (Mumbai: Somaiya, 1996), 257–263; and Akira Saito, *A Study of the Dūn-Huáng Recension of the Bodhisattvacaryāvatāra* (Project Number 09610021, Faculty of Humanities, Mie University, 2000).
59. Luis O. Gómez, "Emptiness and Moral Perfection," *Philosophy East and West* 23 (1973): 361–373; Raymond Martin, "Would It Matter All That Much if There Were No Selves?," in *Pointing at the Moon: Buddhism, Logic, Analytic Philosophy* ed. Jay Garfield, Tom Tillemans, and Mario D'Amato (Oxford: Oxford University Press, 2009), 115–134; John Pettit, "Review of Altruism and Reality: Studies in the Philosophy of the Bodhicharyavatara," *Journal of Buddhist Ethics* 6 (1999), 120–137; Williams, *Altruism*

and Reality; Siderits, "The Reality of Altruism"; Jon Wetlesen, "Did Śāntideva Destroy the Bodhisattva Path?," *Journal of Buddhist Ethics* 9 (2002): 34–88; Westerhoff, "The Connection Between Ontology and Ethics"; Harris, "Does Anātman Rationally Entail Altruism?"; Harris, Stephen, "Altruism in the Charnel Ground: Śāntideva and Parfit on *Anātman*, Reductionism and Benevolence," in *Ethics Without Self, Dharma Without Atman: Western and Buddhist Philosophical Traditions in Dialogue*, ed. Gordon Davis (New York: Springer, 2018), 219–234; Goodman, "Resentment"; Siderits, "Paleo-Compatabalism and Buddhist Reductionism"; Nicolas Bommarito, "Bile & Bodhisattvas: Śāntideva on Justified Anger," *Journal of Buddhist Ethics* 18 (2011): 356–381; Breyer, "Freedom With a Buddhist Face"; and Bingle, "Blaming the Buddha."

60. Goodman, *Consequences of Compassion*.
61. Michael Barnhart, "Theory and Compassion in the Discussion of Buddhist Ethics," *Philosophy East and West* 62, no. 1 (2012): 16–43; and Stephen Harris, "On the Classification of Śāntideva's Ethics in the *Bodhicaryāvatāra*," *Philosophy East and West* 65, no. 1 (2015): 249–275.
62. Paul Williams, "Is Buddhist Ethics Virtue Ethics," in *Destroying Mara Forever, Buddhist Ethics Essays in Honor of Damien Keown*, ed. John Powers and Charles Prebish (Ithaca, NY: Snow Lion, 2009), 113–140; Matthew MacKenzie, "Buddhism and the Virtues," in *The Oxford Handbook of Virtue*, ed. Nancy Snow (Oxford: Oxford University Press, 2018), 153–170; Barbra R. Clayton, *Moral Theory in Śāntideva's Śikṣāsamuccaya: Cultivating the Fruits of Virtue* (London and New York: Routledge, 2006); Garfield, "What Is It Like to Be a Bodhisattva"; and Garfield, "Seeing Sentient Beings."
63. Daniel Cozort, "Suffering Made Sufferable: Śāntideva, Dzongkaba, and Modern Therapeutic Approaches to Suffering's Silver Lining," *Journal of Buddhist Ethics* 20 (2013), 357–375; Edelglass, "Buddhism, Happiness, and the Science of Meditation"; Amod Lele, "The Compassionate Gift of Vice: Śāntideva on Gifts, Altruism and Poverty," *Journal of Buddhist Ethics* 20 (2013), 702–734; and Harris, "Demandingness, Well-Being and the Bodhisattva Path."
64. Francis Brassard, *The Concept of Bodhicitta in Śāntideva's Bodhicaryāvatāra* (Albany: State University of New York Press, 2000).
65. Amod Jayant Lele, "Ethical Revaluation in the Thought of Śāntideva" (Ph.D. dissertation, Harvard University, 2007).
66. Stephen Harris, "The Skillful Handling of Poison: *Bodhicitta* and the *Kleśas* in Śāntideva's *Bodhicaryāvatāra*," *Journal of Indian Philosophy* 45 (2017): 331–348.
67. Cowherds, *Moonpaths: Ethics and Emptiness* (New York: Oxford University Press, 2016).
68. Jonathan Gold and Douglas Duckworth, eds., *Readings of Śāntideva's Guide to Bodhisattva Practice* (New York: Columbia University Press, 2019).

Stephen E. Harris

SARVĀSTIVĀDA ABHIDHARMA

THE SARVĀSTIVĀDA SCHOOL AND ITS FUNDAMENTAL TREATISES

Sarvāstivāda (All-exist School) is an Abhidharma school of Buddhist thought whose adherents are generally known as the Sarvāstivādins. This school may have been effectively established by Kātyāyanīputra (*c.* 150 BCE) with his *Jñānaprasthāna* (Foundation of Knowledge).[1] Eventually the orthodox Sarvāstivādins based in Kaśmīra composed the *Abhidharma-mahāvibhāṣā* (*Mahāvibhāṣā śāstra*; hereafter MVŚ), a gigantic commentary on the *Jñānaprasthāna*, and came to be known as the Vaibhāṣikas (advocates of the [great] commentary) because they upheld the collectively sanctioned orthodox Sarvāstivāda views in this *Mahāvibhāṣā* (Great Commentary).

This school possesses a well-defined Abhidharma canon of seven texts: (1) *Dharma-skandha* ("doctrine-aggregate) by Śāriputra; (2) *Saṅgīti-paryāya* (Representation of Collectively Sanctioned Doctrines) by Mahākauṣṭhila;[2] (3) *Prajñapti-śāstra* (/*Prajñapti-bhāṣya*; Treatise of Conventional Designations) by Mahā-maudgalyāyana; (4) *Vijñāna-kāya* (Consciousness-collection) by Devaśarman; (5) *Prakaraṇa-pāda* (/*Prakaraṇa-grantha*; hereafter PrP; Treatise on the Topical Categories) by Vasumitra;[3] (6) *Jñāna-prasthāna* (hereafter JPŚ) by Kātyāyanīputra; and (7) *Dhātu-kāya* (Element-collection) by Pūrṇa. Of these, the first three belong to the earlier period; or, very probably, the first two may be considered to be the earliest. The rest may be grouped under the later period. Nearly all of them are preserved only in ancient Chinese translation, though the full version of the *Prajñapti-śāstra* is also extant in a Tibetan translation.

Some of the earlier texts must have originally existed as independent treatises, and came to be gradually "Sarvāstivādized," a process that probably took place sometime before the composition of JPŚ. But there are indications that subsequently they were influenced by the overwhelmingly authoritative JPŚ, incorporating some of its doctrines. Thus, the extant version of the *Dharma-skandha*, while generally still preserving throughout the very early format of commentarial elaboration of sutra passages, with little signs of systematization or development in respect to doctrinal presentation of argumentation, nevertheless has already incorporated the classification of the ninety-eight *anuśaya* ("proclivities") in its chapter on the *śrāmanya-phala*.[4] This ninety-eight-*anuśaya* taxonomy was a clear advancement on the basis of Sutra analysis of seven proclivities, and came to dominate the general Sarvāstivāda tradition.[5] Another example is the well-known innovation in PrP of the five-category taxonomy of all dharmas—matter (*rūpa*), thought (*citta*), thought-concomitants (*caitasika*), and the unconditioned (*asaṃskṛta*) dharmas—in place of the traditional *skandhas-dhatu-āyatana* taxonomy (see the section on "The Five-Category Subsumption of Seventy-Five Classes of Dharmas"). This was in fact a further systematization on the basis of the earlier attested, albeit as yet unsystematized or generalized, analysis in JPŚ in terms of these five categories of dharmas.[6]

Indeed, among the seven canonical texts, JPŚ contributed most significantly and definitively to the doctrinal articulation of Sarvāstivāda Abhidharma. As remarked by Yin Shun, in this regard, a distinctive feature of JPŚ is its ability to bring out the integrative and coordinating functions vis-à-vis the dharmas—avoiding the pitfall of mechanistic expositions of dharmas conceived of as abiding individually in their intrinsic natures.[7] Yin Shun illustrates this hermeneutical contribution with the innovative definition of the retribution-cause (*vipāka-hetu*), hitherto confined to volition (*cetanā*) or bodily and vocal karmas. JPŚ now extends the constituent scope of this cause to include all the five aggregates (*skandha*): "all the *citta-caitasika-dharmas*, . . . all the bodily and vocal karmas (*rūpa*), the *cittaviprayukta-saṃskāras*, serve as the retribution-cause of the [corresponding] retribution."[8] (See also the section "Doctrine of Causality.")

Most importantly, JPŚ consolidates and further clarifies the central thesis of *sarvāstitva* through its various topics of discussion from various doctrinal perspectives; particularly noteworthy is the perspective of acquisition (*prāpti*) or endowment (*samanvāgama*), a unique Sarvāstivāda doctrine often elaborately discussed in terms of the tritemporal existence of dharmas. MVŚ certainly highlights and elaborates on this intention and endeavor of JPŚ in numerous contexts. To conserve space, only one such context is cited below.[9] Here, JPŚ discusses the binding of a tritemporal defilement, and in the process also clearly affirms its tritemporal existence. The commentary, MVŚ, elaborates on it, analyzing further in terms of acquisition:

JPŚ (T26, 939c10-21):

> [i] Have all past *saṃyojanas* ("fetter"; a synonym for defilement) bound (已繫, **upanibaddha*; i.e., to the object)?
>
> Answer: All past *saṃyojanas* have bound. There are *saṃyojanas* which have bound [but] are not past; viz, future or present *samyojanas* that have bound.
>
> [ii] Will all future *saṃyojanas* bind in the future?
>
> Answer: There are four possible cases (*catuṣkoṭi*): . . .
>
> [iii] Are the present *saṃyojanas* now binding?
>
> Answer: The present *saṃyojanas* are now binding. There are *saṃyojanas* which are binding, [but] are not present; viz, past and future *samyojanas* that are now binding.

MVŚ (T27, 311c8-312b5):

> "[JPŚ:] Have the past *saṃyojanas* bound?"
>
> Question: What is the purpose of this discussion?
>
> Answer: The purpose is to refute the doctrinal positions of others and demonstrate the true principle: There are some who claim that the past and the future do not exist truly. . . . To refute them, it is demonstrated here that the past and future exist truly. [There are also other purposes] . . .
>
> A *saṃyojana* vis-à-vis its acquisition is of three types: (1) [the *saṃyojana*] is like a head bull (*vṛṣabha*), leading before the acquisition; (2) it is like a calf, following after its acquisition; (3) it is like a figure and its shadow, co-nascent with its acquisition.

In the first case, the *saṃyojana* precedes its acquisition; in the second, the *saṃyojana* succeeds its acquisition; in the third, the *saṃyojana* and its acquisition are co-nascent.[10]

> [i] The past *saṃyojanas* have bound: A *saṃyojana*, as well as its acquisition have existed in the past; it has already bound, hence said to have bound.
>
> There are *saṃyojanas* which have bound, [but] are not past: A future or present *saṃyojana* that has bound—a *saṃyojana* existing in the future or present; its acquisition has already bound in the past. This is the case of a *saṃyojana* that is like a calf, following after its acquisition. . . .
>
> [ii] There are four possible cases: (1) A future *saṃyojana* is not one that will bind—A future *saṃyojana* that has been abandoned (*prahīṇa*), . . . will definitely not retrogress: the future *saṃyojanas* . . . of a non-retrogressive (*aparihāṇa-dharman*) *arhat* will definitely not retrogress; . . . (2) There are *saṃyojanas* that will bind, [but] are not future—the past *saṃyojanas* which have been abandoned . . . of a retrogressive (*parihāṇa-dharman*) *arhat*, will definitely retrogress; . . . (3) There are future *saṃyojanas* that will

bind in the future ... (4) There are *saṃyojanas* which are neither future nor will bind in the future.

[iii] All present *saṃyojanas* are now binding: A present *saṃyojana* necessarily possesses a present acquisition; because the two are necessarily co-existent, like a shape and its shadow. There are *saṃyojamnas* that are now binding, [but] are not present: A past or future *saṃyojana* that is now binding; i.e., a past or future *saṃyojana* that possesses a present acquisition—a past *saṃyojana* that has preceded like a bull leader, or a future *saṃyojana* that comes along subsequently to its acquisition, like a calf following [the bull]; it is said to bind at the present because its acquisition is present.

The special position that the *Jñānaprasthāna* occupies is seen from the fact that it was generally regarded in the school as the "body," whereas the other six were called the "feet" (*pāda*).[11]

However, it would seem that the *Prakaraṇa* (*c.* 100 BCE) was likewise highly esteemed by the Sarvāstivādins, including the compilers of MVŚ, and especially by the so-called Western Masters (*pāścātya*) or Outside Masters (*bahirdeśaka*) based mainly in the Gandhāra region. This text is best known for its innovative systematization of the totality of dharmas into a five-category taxonomy (see the section "The Five-Category Subsumption of Seventy-Five Classes of Dharmas") in its first chapter, "The Analysis of the Five Categories" (辯五事品), which, before Xuanzang's translation, had been translated into Chinese (T no. 1557) by An Shigao around 148 CE and again by Facheng in the Tang Dynasty. Another important contribution of PrP is its distinctive tendency toward organization and succinctness—a tendency that had come to significantly influence the composition style of the post-MVŚ manuals starting with the **Amṛtarasa*.

The following discussion in MVŚ (231c3–12) on the "ordinary-worldling-nature" (*pṛthagjanatva*) shows that the authority of both JPŚ and PrP were highly respected by the Sarvāstivāda community in general. Moreover, in spite of the indication that PrP had been doctrinally influenced by JPŚ, the same discussion further suggests that even at the time of the compilation of MVŚ the relative chronology of JPŚ and PrP had not been fully agreed upon among the Sarvāstivādins:

Question: Why is it that this original treatise (JPŚ) speaks of the ordinary-worldling-nature, and not the ordinary-worldling-dharma, whereas PrP speaks of the ordinary-worldling-dharma and not the ordinary-worldling-nature?

Answer: The ordinary-worldling-nature excels, not the ordinary-worldling-dharma; this original treatise speaks in terms of that which excels. Since this original treatise has already spoken of the ordinary-worldling nature, PrP does not mention it again. Since this original treatise has not spoken of the ordinary-worldling dharma, PrP mentions the ordinary-worldling dharma. This shows that that [PrP] was composed later than this [JPŚ].

According to some: since that [*Prakaraṇa*] treatise has already spoken of the ordinary-worldling-dharma, this treatise (JPŚ) does not mention it again. Since that treatise has not spoken of the ordinary-worldling-nature, this treatise mentions it. This shows that that [PrP] was composed earlier than this [JPŚ].[12]

MVŚ, which establishes the doctrinal authority of the Sarvāstivāda, is encyclopedic in scope. It is now extant only in Chinese translations, of which Xuanzang's version (T no. 1545) comprises two hundred fascicles. It is undoubtedly an extremely important Abhidharma manual, providing a wealth of information on the various schools of thought known up to the time of its compilation. However, gigantic as it was, both its structure and doctrinal interpretations were dictated by those of JPŚ, of which it purported to be a commentary. Moreover, its discussions were often long-winded and lacked systematization. More importantly, its submission to the absolute authority of JPŚ had provoked reaction from certain sectors within the broad Sarvāstivāda communities.

This led to a line of development of Abhidharma manuals, beginning with the **Amṛtarasa* (Taste of Ambrosia) by a certain Ghoṣaka, preserved in a Chinese translation (T no. 1553) of sixteen short chapters in just two fascicles. Essentially, it is a succinct, systematic composition based on JPŚ, MVŚ, and PrP, with a clear emphasis on praxis and realization (as its title, *Amṛtarasa*, suggests), and an inclination toward the Gandhāra (Western) school of thought (more so than to the Kaśmīra orthodoxy). In short, it represented the beginning of a line of commentarial development that stresses systematization and an attitude of openness.

Vasubandhu's *Abhidharmakośabhāṣya* (hereafter AKB; *c.* 4th century CE), extant now in its Sanskrit original and in Chinese and Tibetan translations, may be regarded as the culmination along this line of development. Puguang's summarized description (T41, 1c10–2a19) of the structure and content of this text is in Table 1.[13]

Vasubandhu often favors the views of the Sautrāntikas, a group of masters emerging from around the late 2nd century CE, who were anti-Ābhidhārmikas, claiming to take the sutras rather than the Abhidharma treatises as authoritative.[14] But he does not affiliate himself with any particular school of thought. At the end of chapter 8 of AKB, he states:

> This Abhidharma proclaimed by us is for the most part established according to the principles of the Kaśmīrian Vaibhāṣikas (*kāśmīra-vaibhāṣikāṇāṃ nīti-siddhaḥ*). Whatever herein has been badly grasped by us is our fault. But then, with regard to the principle of the True Doctrine, the Buddha and the sons of the Buddha alone are the authority (*pramāṇa*).[15]

However, his brilliant exposition of the Abhidharma doctrines, often advocating the Sautrāntikas against the Vaibhāṣikas, led to strong reactions among the latter. Saṃghabhadra, an equally brilliant junior contemporary of Vasubandhu, eventually composed the **Nyāyānusāra* (Conformity to True Principles; hereafter Ny; T29, no. 1562) to defend the Vaibhāṣika orthodoxy against Vasubandhu's critique in AKB. This text is now preserved only in a Chinese translation by Xuanzang, comprising eighty fascicles (Xuanzang's translation of AKB comprises thirty fascicles). It is one of the most important Abhidharma texts representing the orthodox Sarvāstivādin views brilliantly expounded and articulated by Saṃghabhadra. Its importance also lies in its recording of a large amount of detailed expositions of the Dārṣṭāntika-Sautrāntika doctrines—mostly not available elsewhere—particularly those represented by the Śrīlāta, mostly just quoted as "the Sthavira" (the Elder). It is no exaggeration to state that this text is decidedly indispensable for a proper understanding of the Sarvāstivāda and Dārṣṭāntika-Sautrāntika doctrines.[16]

Table 1. Puguang's Summary of the Structure and Contents of AKB

	CHAPTER	ELUCIDATION		
Non-self *dharmas*	1. *Dhātu*	Essential nature of dharmas	With-outflow & outflow-free: general exposition	
	2. *Indriya*	Functions of dharmas		
	3. *Loka*	With-outflow fruits	With-outflow & outflow-free: separate expositions	Separate expositions on with-outflow
	4. Karma	Causes of retribution		
	5. *Anuśaya*	Conditions for the karmas		
	6. *Mārga-pudgala*	Outflow-free fruits		Separate expositions on outflow-free
	7. *Jñāna*	Causes for the realization of the fruits		
	8. *Samāpatti*	Conditions for the *jñānas*		
No-self doctrine	9. *Ātmavāda-pratiṣedha*	Principle of non-self-ness		

Partly as a reaction to the distractive disputations abounding in these Abhidharma polemical texts, Skandhila composed a succinct Abhidharma manual, entitled **Abhidharmāvatāra*, now extant only in Chinese (T no. 1554) and Tibetan (Tohoku no. 4098, Peking no. 5599). It expounds the totality of the Sarvāstivāda doctrines without sectarian polemics, in an eight-category (*padārtha*) scheme—five *skandhas* and three *asaṃskṛtas*. The Xuanzang tradition tells us that Skandhila was Saṃghabhadra's teacher. Judging from the scheme of presentation and the contents of this work, it may be inferred that he was an orthodox Vaibhāṣika who nevertheless displayed an open-minded attitude evident in his inclination to some doctrinal positions of the Western Masters.[17]

ORIGIN AND DEVELOPMENT OF THE SARVĀSTIVĀDA ABHIDHARMA

Very soon after the Buddha's demise, or possibly earlier, some monks began to specialize in either Sutra, or Vinaya, or in elaboration and exposition of the doctrines. In the Pali *suttas* (and generally also the corresponding Chinese *āgamas*), such specialization is reflected in such terms as *suttantika, vinaya-dhara, dhamma-dhara, dhamma-kathika* and *mātikā-dhara*. However, noticeably, they usually occur in a stock-phrase description of learned monks, and therefore could possibly be later insertions in the gradual process of the compilation of the canon. For instance, the Majjhima-nikāya teaches that a monk possessing eleven qualities is capable of growth in the Dhamma-vinaya. One is that he frequents and learns from the learned monks "who are 'experts in the *Dhamma*' (*dhamma-dhara*), who are 'experts in the Vinaya' (*vinaya-dhara*), and who are 'experts in content-summaries' (*mātikā-dhara*)."[18] On the other hand, in the Vinaya, we find not only the appellations of these specialist monks mentioned together in the same context, but also descriptions of their specific natures or roles. For instance, the *Mahāvagga* of the Vinaya-piṭaka records that on the *Pavaraṇā* day at the end of the rainy retreat, they gather in their respective groups to engage in mutual discussion and deliberation: the *suttantikas* rehearse the *suttas* together; the *vinaydharas* ascertain the Vinaya together; and the *dhammakathikas* discuss the *Dhamma* together.[19]

The Ābhidhammikas/Ābhidhārmikas, "Specialist in the Abhidhamma/Abhidharma," may be considered to have been in the main evolved from the *dhammadharas*/*dharmadharas* and the *mātikā-dharas*/*mātṛkā-dharas*. It may be said that "Sarvāstivādins" in a narrower sense refers to the Sarvāstivāda Ābhidhārmikas. However, while the Ābhidhārmikas constituted the mainstream of the schools, there were other Sarvāstivādins who were basically anti-Abhidharma. These were the early Dārṣṭāntikas (the Illustrators), who were mainly *sūtra*-centred, being evolved from the *suttantikas*/*sūtrānta-dharas*(/*sūtra-dharas*)—even though some masters from this subgroup also came to exhibit a certain amount of Abhidharmic tendencies in their doctrinal expositions or disputations with the Ābhidhārmikas properly so called. It is important to note that these early Dārṣṭāntikas figuring in MVŚ were still Sarvāstivādins, sharing the doctrine of the tritemporal existence of dharmas. They were generally well respected by the compilers of MVŚ, who nonetheless criticized and rejected their views. Two of the most prominent Dārṣṭāntika masters, Dharmatrāta and Buddhadeva, were spoken of by these compilers as among the "four great masters of the Sarvāstivāda" (see the section "Ascertainment of the Contents of the *Sūtras*"). In general, the Dārṣṭāntikas may be characterized as being primarily concerned with meditative praxis and popular preaching.[20] Subsequent to MVŚ, these masters, partly under the influence of the Mahāsāṃghikas and the Vibhajyavādins, evolved into the Sautrāntikas, totally rejecting the central Sarvāstivāda doctrine of the tritemporal existence of the dharmas. In the post-MVŚ texts, such as AKB, the *Abhidharmadīpa-Vibhāṣāprabhāvṛtti*, and Ny, the two appellations, "Dārṣṭāntika" and "Sautrāntika," are often interchangeable.

We also see a group of praxis-oriented meditators in MVŚ, known as the *yogācāra* masters. They are mentioned some 140 times in the text and appear to have been highly respected, even by the Ābhidhārmikas. Moreover, some of their doctrinal explanations based on meditative experiences must have significantly contributed to the body of Sarvāstivāda doctrines pertaining to meditative praxis and spiritual realization. These doctrines also probably contributed to those of the subsequent Dārṣṭāntika-Sautrāntikas and of the early Mahāyānist Yogācāras seen in the Basic Section (**Maulī Bhūmi*) of the *Yogācārabhūmi*.[21] An example is the epistemological doctrine in the Basic Section that a moment of mental consciousness necessarily follows immediately after a moment of sensory consciousness.[22] In MVŚ, this position is explicitly stated to be held by the *yogācāra* masters.[23]

Both the Theravāda and Sarvāstivāda Ābhidhammikas/Ābhidharmikas claim that Abhidhamma/Abhidharma is "Buddha's word" (*buddha-vacana*), that is, it is taught by the Buddha himself. However, in the case of Sarvāstivāda, it is acknowledged that the seven canonical texts were actually composed by the Buddhist masters on the basis of the scattered Abhidharma teachings in the Buddha's discourses and compiled them into structured texts. The following are the major doctrinal features in the sutras generally considered to have contributed to the development of the Abhidhamma/Abhidharma canon: (1) group discussion and analysis on the Buddha's discourses in the form of *abhidhamma-kathā/abhidharma-kathā* and *vibhaṅga*; (2) summary statements of doctrinal contents in the form of *mātikā/mātṛkā*, such as the list of the thirty-seven doctrinal topics known as the *bodhipakṣya-dharmas* (factors conducive to Enlightenment); (3) exposition of implicit and profound teachings in the form of *vedalla/vaidalya* (splitting open/unraveling [the profound or nonobvious]) and *upadeśa* (expository elaboration)—noteworthily, *vedalla* and *upadeśa* constitute, respectively, the last member of the Theravāda ninefold division (*navaṅga*) and the Sarvāstivāda twelvefold division (*dvādaśāṅga*) of the Buddha's teachings. And in either tradition, this last member is claimed to represent the Abhidhamma/Abhidharma.[24]

In Sarvāstivāda, the feature of *mātṛkā* came to be extended from the original signification of a doctrinal summary list. Saṃghabhadra mentions *mātṛkā* as being synonymous with *abhidharma* and *upadeśa*; and, quoting Mahākāśyapa, cites the early Sarvāstivāda canonical texts: the *Saṅgītiparyāya*, the *Dharma-skandha*, and the *Prajñapti-śāstra* as among examples of *mātṛkā*.[25] Similarly, in explaining the *Abhidharma-piṭaka*, the *Mūla-sarvāstivāda-vinaya-kṣudraka-vastu* also says, "the four *smṛtyupasthānas*, the four *samyak-prahāṇas* . . . the *Dharma-saṃgīti*, the *Dharma-skandha*—these are collectively known as *mātṛkās*."[26]

Saṃghabhadra further argues that in the twelvefold division of the *sūtra-piṭaka* (*sūtra, geya, vyākaraṇa*, etc.), *upadeśa*, the twelfth division, representing the Abhidharma, in fact serves as the very criterion or authority for nonerroneously unraveling and ascertaining the true meanings of all the other eleven divisions. Accordingly, he claims, Abhidharma is not only properly *buddha-vacana*, but indeed the *pramāna* of Sutra. In brief, for the Ābhidhārmikas, Abhidharma is the explicit (*nītārtha*) and definitive (*lākṣaṇika*) teachings of the Buddha, in contrast to the *sūtras*, which are generally, or at least in some cases, implicit (*neyārtha*) and intentional (*ābhiprāyika*).[27]

DEFINITION, NATURE, AND PURPOSE OF ABHIDHARMA

Sarvāstivāda Abhidharma minutely analyzes the complexity of the human experiences together with his environment and arrives at a definite list of fundamental factors of existence known as dharmas, each being a unique force contributing in a definite manner to the experiential complex. As articulately defined in AKB, "a dharma is so called because it sustains its specific characteristic (*svalakṣaṇadhāraṇād dharmaḥ*)." For instance, "matter" (*rūpa*) is a dharma because the characteristic specific to it—such as resistance (*sapratighatva*) or visibility (*sanidarśanatva*)—is always sustained (always remains unchanged). Likewise, "sensation" (*vedanā*) is another dharma, a mental force, whose specific characteristic is invariably "experience" (*anubhava*). "Understanding" (*prajñā*), another distinct dharma, also a mental force, whose specific characteristic is "discernment of dharmas" (*dharma-pravicaya*), contributes to the human faculty of understanding in any cognitive act.

The term, "*abhi-dharma*" (*abhi-* meaning "facing," "toward") is defined thus:

> This is called *abhidharma* since it is a dharma facing toward the dharma in the highest sense, nirvana, or dharma-characteristic. (AKB, 2)

This etymological definition underscores the soteriological—rather than "scholastic"—significance of Abhidharma: It is a direct realization, not a mere intellectual understanding of reality (nirvana), or of the true nature of the real existents (the specific characteristics of all the dharmas)—the conditioned (*saṃskṛta*) and the unconditioned (*asaṃskṛta*) ones, those with outflow (*sāsrava*, or impure) and those that are outflow-free (*anāsrava*, or pure). It is only through such a direct realization (*abhisamaya*) that liberation from the saṃsāric predicament, along with all the existential unsatisfactoriness (*duḥkha*) that it entails, comes to be possible. The following stanza from AKB on the purpose of the Buddha's teaching of the Abhidharma clarifies this soteriological nature:

> Since other than the discernment of dharmas there is no
> Excellent means for the appeasement of defilements,
> And on account of defilements that the world wanders in this existence-ocean
> —Thus, for this reason, it has been taught, they say (i.e., the Vaibhāṣikas), by the Teacher.

Abhidharma in the absolute (true) sense is declared to be the outflow-free *prajñā*. And *prajñā* is defined as the "discernment of dharmas" (*dharma-pravicaya*), which is absolutely indispensable for transcending saṃsāra.

In the conventional sense, however, "Abhidharma" includes all forms of understanding capable of conducing to this pure *prajñā*: all the with-outflow understandings that are derived from listening (*śruta-mayī*), from reflection (*cintā-mayī*), and from cultivation (*bhāvanā-mayī*); understanding that is innate (*upapatti-pratilambhika*), as well as the Abhidharma treatises which provide intellectual learning.[28]

THE FIVE-CATEGORY SUBSUMPTION OF SEVENTY-FIVE CLASSES OF DHARMAS

The process of *dharma-pravicaya* leads to the ascertainment of some seventy-five classes or types of dharmas, subsumable into five major classes. The five-category taxonomy is attributed to Vasumitra, author of the *Prakaraṇa-pāda*. It is a systematization developed on the basis of JPŚ (see the section "Sarvāstivāda School and Its Fundamental Treatises") and of the traditional taxonomy in the Sutra, of the Five Aggregates (*skandha*), Twelve Abodes/Entrances (*āyatana*), and Eighteen Elements (*dhātu*). The figure, "seventy-five," seems to have been eventually arrived at by a pupil of Xuanzang (*c.* 602–664 CE), Puguang, on the basis of his studies of AKB. The correlation of these taxonomies is represented in Table 2:[29]

Table 2. Correlation Between the 5 Categories, 5 Skandhas, 12 Āyatanas, and 18 Dhātus.

5 categories	5 skandha-s		12 āyatana-s	18 dhātu-s

rūpa (11) — rūpa-sk

5 faculties

5 sensory objects

avijñapti

caksur-āy	caksur-dh
śrotra-āy	śrotra-dh
ghrāna-āy	ghrāna-dh
jihvā-āy	jihvā-dh
kāya-āy	kāya-dh

citta (1) — mano-āy — mano-dh

caitta (46): vedanā-sk, samjñā-sk

rūpa-āy	rūpa-dh
śabda-āy	śabda-dh
gandha-āy	gandha-dh
rasa-āy	rasa-dh
sprastavya-āy	sprastavya-dh

viprayukta-samskāra (14) — samskāra-sk

sam prayukta = caitta (44) — dharma-āy — dharma-dh

viprayukta (14)

vijñāna-sk

caksur-vij	caksur-vij-dh
śrotra-vij	śrotra-vij-dh
ghrān-vij	ghrāna-vij-dh
jihvā-vij	jihvā-vij-dh
kāya-vij	kāya-vij-dh
mano-vij	mano-vij-dh

asamskrta (3)

pratisamkhyā-nirodha
apratisamkhyā-nirodha
ākāśa

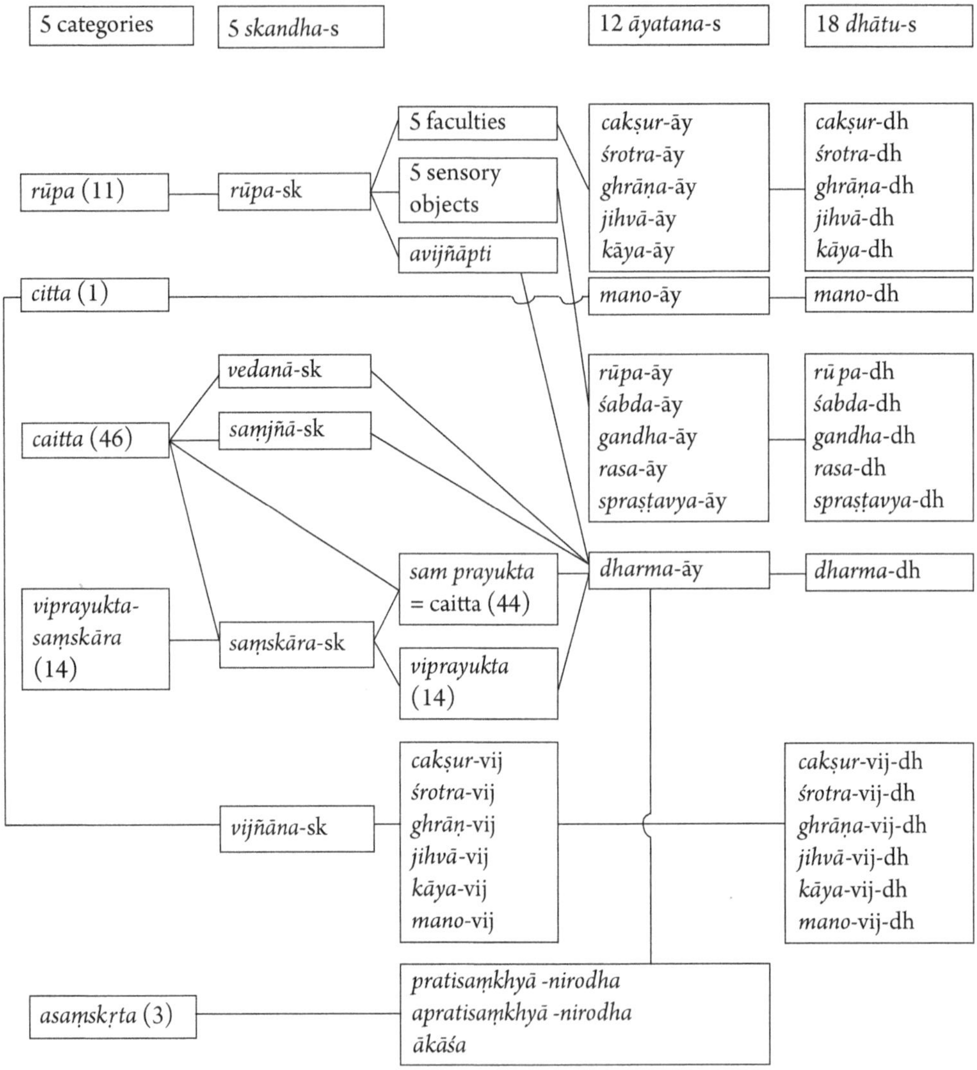

Diagram Text Abbreviations

sk = skandha	āy = āyatana	dh = dhātu
vij = vijñāna	vij-dh = vijñāna-dhātu	

Among the five basic categories, the first noteworthy feature is that, under *rūpa*, there is a dharma known as *avijñapti* (noninformation). In spite of being a type of material entity, it is invisible and nonresistant, existing as a serial continuity of karmic force. This is a special and controversial karma doctrine of the Sarvāstivāda, formulated to account for the preservation of karmic efficacy. Once projected by a physical or vocal karma—known in contrast as *vijñapti* (information/informative) karmas—it arises continuously in every moment, interacting with the person's mental series and modifying the resultant status of the karma until the time of retribution or the person's death. It additionally came to be further developed in connection with the conception of restraint (*saṃvara*), irrestraint, (*asaṃvara*), and neither-restraint-nor-irrestraint (*nava-saṃvara-nāsaṃvara*), with further stipulated conditions for its acquisition and relinquishment.

Its nature of being an invisible and nonresistant matter is highlighted in Saṃghabhadra's definition:

> That morally defined, non-resistant matter, which [continues to] exist in the thought at the time even subsequent to [the karmic action] having been done, and even when the thought and thought-concomitant is of a dissimilar moral species [from that when the action was done], and even in the thoughtless state—this is conceded as the non-informative [matter]. (*kṛte'pi visabhāge'pi citte cittātyaye ca yat | vyākṛtāpratighaṃ rūpaṃ sā hy avijñaptir iṣyate ||*)[30]

Another noteworthy category is the conditionings disjoined from thought (*cittaviprayukta-saṃskāra*). Unlike the Theravāda, which subsumes all dhammas under the dualistic scheme of *nāma* (the nonmaterial factors) and *rūpa*, the Sarvāstivāda recognizes a category of real entities under this appellation—real forces in the universe—that are neither material nor mental in nature. It may be considered an important doctrinal innovation of the Sarvāstivāda. An example of this category is a dharma called "acquisition" (*prāpti*; see also the JPŚ discussion on *saṃyojana* cited in the section "Sarvāstivāda School and Its Fundamental Treatises"). It is the sine qua non making possible the possession of a dharma by a sentient being. For instance, the phenomenon of a human possessing craving (*rāga*) is explained thus: craving—and, for that matter, any other negative or positive (such as faith) dharma—is an existent force in the universe. The person in which craving with regard to a cognitive object arises comes to be specifically linked with him necessarily through an "acquisition" of this instance of craving. Once so linked, the person continues to possess this craving, irrespective of whether he is conscious of it or not in the given moment—until the serial flow of this acquisition is interrupted by a sufficiently strong counteragent, a specific *prajñā*. At this juncture, another important *cittaviprayukta-saṃskāra dharma* of the opposite nature, a nonacquisition (*aprāpti*), conspires or coordinates to ensure the delinking (and no further arising) of this craving from the person.

Being a force that is neither material nor mental, such a dharma can act on other dharmas of both types, and, in the case of acquisition, even on an unconditioned dharma. When one attains nirvana as a result of spiritual striving, it is not the case that the path pertaining to the domain of the conditioned "produces" a fruit that is unconditioned. The path as the cause produces the acquisition (a conditioned dharma) of the nirvana, so that the latter comes to be linked with the person: It is this particular person that acquires the nirvana, not any other sentient being. As a matter of fact, the existence of acquisition as a real entity is emphatically argued for by the Sarvāstivādins for whom it is, specifically, the sine qua non for establishing the distinction between an ordinary worldling (*pṛthagjana*) and a noble one (*ārya*). Thus, the *Abhidharmāvatāra* argues:

> If acquisition were non-existent, when defilements like greed, etc., arise, the trainee (*śaikṣa*), being without an outflow-free thought, ought not to be an *ārya*. [Likewise,] an ordinary worldling gives rise to a skillful or non-defined thought, he ought to be at that moment regarded as one who is detached (*vītarāga*). Moreover, there being no acquisition of nirvana for the *ārya* and ordinary worldling, both of them would be similar to each other and, therefore, both ought to be called an ordinary worldling or *ārya*.[31]

The category of the unconditioned dharmas is likewise noteworthy. Unlike in the Theravāda Abhidhamma, the unconditioned in the Sarvāstivāda is not confined to nirvana. There are three types: cessation through deliberation (*pratisaṃkhyā-nirodha*), cessation without deliberation (*apratisaṃkhyā-nirodha*), and Space (*ākāśa*). Of these, the first two are pluralistic. In MVŚ, it can be observed that their ontological status is a contentious issue. The Dārṣṭāntika masters mostly deny the reality of all the three (MVŚ, 388c); some, like the Bhadanta (大德), deny Space (MVŚ, 388c24–28). In AKB, the Sautrāntikas explicitly state that "all the unconditioned is not real entity."[32] However, all the three *asaṃskṛtas* are attested in the earliest canonical Abhidharma texts of the Sarvāstivāda.[33] The *Jñānaprasthāna*, in an Abhidharmically more formal manner, enumerates *ākāśa* and *apratisaṃkhyā-nirodha* as the two types of dharmas that are "to be penetrated (*pratividhātavya*), to be fully known (*parijñātavya*), not to be abandoned (*aprahātavya*), not to be cultivated (*abhāvayitavya*), and not to be directly realized (*asākṣāt-kartavya*)"; whereas the *pratisaṃkhyā-nirodha* is "to be penetrated, to be fully known, not to be abandoned, not to be cultivated, and to be directly realized."[34]

The term "deliberation" (*pratisaṃkhyā*) refers to an outflow-free understanding (*prajñā*) strong enough to effectuate a disjunction (*visaṃyoga*)—and hence a liberation—from a given defilement. "There are in fact as many disjunction-entities as there are conjunction-entities (*saṃyoga-vastu*)."[35] As the following discussion in MVŚ shows, for the Sarvāstivāda, each abandonment of defilement is actually a nirvana; even though this designation is specifically reserved for an *arhat*'s perfect attainment:

> Question: The abandonment of any [defiled] dharma such as *satkāya-dṛṣṭi* is nirvana; why does it herein speak only of the absolute abandonment of greed (*rāga*) and so on up to the absolute abandonment of all defilements?
>
> Answer: Although the abandonment of each and every [defiled] dharma is nirvana, herein it speaks only of the "perfect nirvana." . . . Furthermore, the name nirvana is [reserved] exclusively for the stage of the non-trainee. The stage of the trainee being yet incomplete, it is not called nirvana.[36]

The "cessation without deliberation" is not a disjunction. It is likewise pluralistic.

> It is . . . not acquired through deliberative understanding. . . . It is . . . not acquired through deliberation by means of necessary effort, necessary preparation or necessary exertion. Furthermore

> ... It is [acquired] on account of the deficiency in conditions (*pratyaya-vaikalyāt*). Thus, when one is focused [on an object] in one direction, all the other objects—visible, sound, smell, taste and tangible—in the other directions cease. The thought and thought-concomitants that would have taken these objects do not arise absolutely (*atyantam*); they do not arise owing to the deficiency in conditions. On account of this non-arising, their cessations without deliberation are acquired.[37]

Saṃghabhadra vehemently argues for the reality of the *apratisaṃkhyā-nirodha* having this efficacy:

> Should it be claimed that a condition that is lacking is simply a condition that is non-existent (/the deficiency in conditions is simply the non-existence of conditions), it is also unreasonable. For, a non-existent cannot obstruct the arising of an existent. From this decisive principle, it is not the mere deficiency in conditions which is called the *apratisaṃkhyā-nirodha*. Rather, there exists a distinct *dharma* (*dharmāntara*) which is acquired (*prāpta*) owing to the deficiency in conditions. This [real entity] has the special efficacy capable of obstructing a dharma susceptible to arising, causing it never to arise—this is called the *apratisaṃkhyā-nirodha*. If it is the case that there was not a distinct *dharma* capable of obstructing, and the non-arising of the dharma was due simply to the deficiency in conditions; then when the required species of conditions happen to assemble subsequently, the previously non-arisen dharma ought to arise again.[38]

A spiritually significant example of *apratisaṃkhyā-nirodha* is that of existence in the unfortunate planes of existence (*durgati*), acquired by an *ārya* when he attains the spiritual fruition of stream-entry (*srotaāpatti*). A practitioner in fact can acquire such *apratisaṃkhyā-nirodhas* by practicing *dāna*, *śīla*, or penetration into a doctrinal teaching, and so on.[39]

The third type of the unconditioned, space, is the most controversial among the Abhidharma schools. MVŚ distinguishes the conditioned space-element (*ākāśa-dhātu*) and the unconditioned space (*ākāśa*):

> What is the difference between space and the space-element? Space is not matter; the space-element is matter. Space is invisible (*anidarśana*); the space-element is visible (*sanidarśana*). Space is non-resistant (*apratigha*); the space-element is resistant (*sapratigha*). Space is outflow-free; the space-element is with-outflow. Space is unconditioned; the space-element is conditioned.[40]

Saṃghabhadra further articulates the difference between the two—the unconditioned space is both nonobstructive and not obstructed by other things:

> the space-element is a fine *rūpa*; although not obstructing others, it is obstructed by others, and is so classifiable as impermanent and conditioned (*saṃskṛta*). Space has the characteristic of being neither obstructive to others nor being obstructible by others, at the time when material elements are being produced.[41]

DISCERNMENT OF DHARMAS (*DHARMAPRAVICAYA*): SCOPE, FUNDAMENTAL STANDPOINTS, AND METHODOLOGY

MVŚ defines the scope of the Ābhidhārmikas' "discernment of dharmas" as follows:

> The meanings of the *abhidharma-piṭaka* should be understood by means of fourteen things: (1–6) the six causes (*hetu*), (7–10) the four conditions (*pratyaya*), (11) subsumption/inclusion (*saṃgraha*), (12) conjunction (*saṃprayoga*), (13) endowment (*samanvāgama*), (14) non-endowment (*asamanvāgama*). Those who, by means of these fourteen things, understand the *abhidharma* unerringly, are called Ābhidhārmikas, not [those who] merely recite and memorize the words.
>
> Other masters say that the meanings of the *abhidharma-piṭaka* should be understood by means of seven things: (1) skillfulness with regard to causes (*hetu-kauśalya*), (2) skillfulness with regard to conditions (*pratyaya-kauśalya*), (3) skillfulness with regard to intrinsic characteristic (*svalakṣaṇa-kauśalya*), (4) skillfulness with regard to common characteristic (*sāmānyalakṣaṇa-kauśalya*), (5) skillfulness with regard to subsumption and non-subsumption (*saṃgraha-asaṃgraha-kauśalya*), (6) skillfulness with regard to conjunction and disjunction (*saṃprayoga-viprayoga-kauśalya*), (7) skillfulness with regard to endowment and non-endowment (*samanvāgama-asamanvāgama-kauśalya*). Those who, by means of these seven things understand the *abhidharma* unerringly, are called Ābhidhārmikas.[42]

The **Abhidharmāvatāra* too explains the thought-concomitant, *prajñā*, as "the examination (*upalakṣaṇa*), as the case may be, of the following eight kinds of dharma: subsumption, conjunction, endowment, cause, condition, fruit, intrinsic characteristic, common characteristic."[43] From the soteriological perspective of the Ābhidhārmikas, *prajñā* may be considered as the most important dharma in sentient existence—so much so that it is said to be the true intrinsic nature of *abhidharma* itself. This is in fact quite in keeping with the whole of Buddhism, which consistently underscores the indispensability of *prajñā*/*paññā* for the attainment of ultimate, absolute liberation. In this process, it is a specific and sufficiently strong mode of operation of *prajñā* that counteracts a defilement(s), resulting in a corresponding state of spiritual attainment. It is for this reason that in the above *Abhidharmāvatāra* definition of *prajñā*, we find the whole scope of Ābhidhārmika *dharma-pravicaya*. And within this scopic enumeration, it is the investigation into intrinsic characteristics, which is the same as that of intrinsic natures (*svabhāva*), that may be considered the most important.[44] Failure to truly ascertain the intrinsic natures of dharmas is tantamount to the ignorance of the true nature of reality—the essential cause of the inherent unsatisfactoriness (*duḥkha*) of saṃsāric existence.

INVESTIGATION IN TERMS OF DOCTRINAL PERSPECTIVES

Abhidharma also investigates the nature of dharmas from different doctrinal perspectives. In AKB, there are some twenty-two such perspectives in the first chapter: (1) visible (*sa-nidarśana*), invisible (*anidarśana*); (2) resistant (*sa-pratigha*), nonresistant (*apratigha*); (3) skillful (*kuśala*), unskillful (*akuśala*), nondefined (*avyākṛta*); (4) connected with/pertaining to (*pratisaṃyukta*) sensuality sphere, to fine-materiality sphere, to nonmateriality sphere; (5) with-outflow, outflow-free; (6) with-reasoning (*savitarka*), with-investigation (*savicāra*); (7) with cognitive object (*sa-ālambana*), without cognitive object (*anālambana*); (8) appropriated (*upātta*), nonappropriated (*anupātta*); (9) great elements (*bhūta*), derived from great elements (*bhautika*); (10) accumulated (*saṃcita*), nonaccumulated (*asaṃcita*); (11) that which cuts (*chinatti*), that which is cut (*chidyate*); (12) that which burns (*dāhaka*), that which is burnt (*dahyate*); (13) that which weighs (*tulayati*), that which can be weighed (*tulya*); (14) the five species: retribution-born (*vipākaja*), accumulative (*aupacayika*), emanational (*naiḥṣyandika*), yoked with a real entity (*dravya-yukta*), momentary (*kṣaṇika*); (15) acquisition (*prāpti/pratilambha*), endowment (*samanvāgama*); (16) external, internal; (17) participative/active (*sabhāga*), nonparticipative/facsimile (*tat-sabhāga*); (18) abandonable through seeing/vision (*darśana-heya*), abandonable through cultivation (*bhāvanā-heya*), not to be abandoned (*aheya*); (19) view (*dṛṣṭi*), not view; (20) consciousness (*vijñāna*), object of consciousness (the cognized; *vijñeya*—i.e., what elements are cognized by which consciousness); (21) permanent, impermanent; (22) faculties (*indriya*), nonfaculties.[45]

Thus, through such a process of perspectival analysis, the nature of an ultimate real factor in the universe can be articulately determined. For example, a given mental factor is invisible, nonresistant, skillful/unskillful/neutral, nonaccumulative, emanational, momentary, a consciousness or object of consciousness, and so on.

THE ASCERTAINMENT OF THE CONTENTS OF THE SUTRAS

An essential aspect of the "discernment of dharmas" is the discernment or ascertainment of the meanings of the sutras. The explicit Ābhidhārmika standpoint is that one must truly discern the meanings of the sutras, rather than blindly clinging to their literal expressions. JPŚ states:

> one should therefore discern the meanings of the sutras. As the Bhagavat has said: Animals have their final abode in the forest; birds have their final abode in the sky; the *ārya*s have their final abode in nirvana dharmas find their final abode in discernment.[46]

On this, the MVŚ explains:

> The wise ones should therefore skilfully discern the meanings of the sutras, and should not understand them [merely] at face value. If one does so, one will not only make the noble teachings appear contradictory, but also generate topsy turvy views in one's own mind. [47]

This Ābhidhārmika standpoint of the need to critically ascertain the sutras is also shared by other Sarvāstivāda masters, including some Dārṣṭāntikas. In this connection, we may note an interesting discussion in MVŚ on the wording of the *Dharmacakrapravartana-sūtra*. In this sutra, the Buddha says: (1) first he gained the pure spiritual insight that: "this is the truth of unsatisfactoriness (*duḥkhasatya*)"; (2) next, that this truth was to be fully known (*parijñeya*); (3) next, that it has been fully known (*parijñāta*).[48] The Venerable Dharmatrāta remarks that he is horrified by these sutra wordings, which contradict a noble one's sequence of spiritual realization—the initial insight that the truth will be known (i.e., [2]) cannot arise subsequent to his having fully gained the pure insight (i.e., [1]).[49] Nevertheless Dharmatrāta, considering that this first preaching had led to the spiritual realization of the five *bhikṣus* together with a host of divine beings, simply adjusts the sequence of the wording, without actually rejecting the sutra. He asserts:

This sutra should have said as follows:

> "This is the noble truth of unsatisfactoriness." With regard to [these dharmas] unheard before by me . . . Likewise for the truths of origination, cessation and the path.
> "This noble truth of unsatisfactoriness is to be fully known by understanding. This noble truth of origination is to be fully abandoned by understanding. This noble truth of cessation is to be directly realized by understanding. This noble truth of the path is to be cultivated by understanding. With regard to . . . unheard of before."

The Ābhidhārmikas here do not deny Dharmatrāta's criticism. But they assert that instead of adjusting the wording, one should search for the sutra's intention (**abhiprāya*): A preacher of the Dharma may either follow a sequence that accords with that of the preaching—as in the case of this sutra; or a sequence that accords with that of spiritual realization (*abhisamaya*)—as proposed by Dharmatrāta.[50]

This discussion reflects the attitude of ancient (at least by the time of MVŚ) critical scholarship, essentially matching modern Buddhist critical scholarship! Elsewhere, the MVŚ compilers differentiate Sutra and Vinaya from the Abhidharma thus:

> In the Abhidharma, one should seek the true nature and characteristics of dharmas, not sequential order [of exposition—as one should in the Sutra], or introductory account (*nidāna*)[—as one should in the Vinaya]: there is nothing wrong that [an exposition] is given earlier or later, or without an introductory account.[51]

The following articulate remarks by the later Ābhidhārmika, Saṃghabhadra (*c.* early 5th century CE), illustrates further their critical approach to the study of the sutras:

> Simply because one comes across a sutra incomplete in meanings, one must not [rush to] generate obstinate denial of other noble teachings. This is because, the noble teachings comprise a large variety; there is no single sutra wherein all meanings are to be found. The noble teachings are twofold: Some are explicit in meaning (*nītārtha*), others implicit (*neyārtha*); some are context-dependent, others are not; some expound the conventional, others the absolute truth (*parmārtha-satya*); some expound generically, others specifically; some expound from their own viewpoint, others from others' viewpoint; some pertain to the characteristics of *dharmas* (*dharma-lakṣaṇa*), others to religious instructions (**śāsana*)—there are such innumerable perspectives. Sometimes, even though the exposition of a certain doctrinal point is found in a sutra, its signification (*artha*) cannot be clarified (made manifest) unless it is considered together with other [related] expositions. Take for instance, the statement in a sutra that one must apply the mind (*manas-√kṛ*) to the *saṃskāras*. To begin with, it is first to be clarified what "*saṃskāras*" [here] refer to. There are many types of "*saṃskāra*" referred in the

sutras: The "*saṃskāras*" in the sutra reference "*avidyā pratyayāḥ saṃskārāḥ*"; the *kāya-saṃskāraḥ* in other sutras, referring to the in-breathing and out-breathing, *vitarka, vicāra, saṃjñā, cetanā*; . . . [the "*saṃskāra*"] in the sutra statement "all *saṃskāras* are impermanent." . . . One must investigate into all such [related notions and contexts].

Thus, there should be places in the noble teachings that fully elucidate the intrinsic natures, names, etc., of dharmas. This is because the Bhagavat, in order to benefit sentient beings to be guided (*vineya*), takes into consideration the particular contexts, occasions, and personality types, etc.—and then he expounds to them accordingly particular doctrinal perspectives (*dharma-paryāya*). Since there is no single sutra in which complete exposition [of a given doctrine] can be found, it is difficult to discern its [proper] signification in isolation from other expositions elsewhere.[52]

In the above-cited scope of Ābhidhārmika studies, subsumption stands out as a most important taxonomical device for *dharma-pravicaya*. To discern the reals (the dharmas), one must determine their intrinsic natures. And a rigorous methodology for this is subsumption. For instance, the sutras speak at different places of "understanding," "knowledge," "insight," "views" (proper and improper ones), "vision," defiled and nondefiled "nescience" (*akliṣṭa-ajñāna*), "wisdom," and so on.[53] Through the methodological device of subsumption, all these are ascertained as having the same intrinsic nature of *prajñā*: there are different modes of being of *prajñā*. As a matter of fact, it is this methodology that outstandingly contributed to determination of the Abhidharmic list of dharmas.

MVŚ further explains the soteriological function of the study of subsumption: Necessarily starting with the examination of the subsumption of dharmas in respect of intrinsic nature, one comes to eradicate the clinging to the ideation of the self (*ātman*) and a unity as an ontological existent. With this, progressively, one finally acquires the pure *prajñā* into reality, coming to be liberated:

> Subsumption in respect of intrinsic nature applies without being independent of occasion and causes. Independence of time—at no time(/on no occasion) is there no *saṃgraha* of a dharma in respect of its intrinsic nature. Independence of causes—without any cause, a dharma is subsumed [by itself] in respect of its intrinsic nature, since without dependent on causes and conditions it exists in itself ("it has its intrinsic nature").

One wishing to examine all dharmas should first examine their subsumption in respect of their intrinsic natures (examine how they are subsumed in terms of their intrinsic nature).

Question: what advantage is there, what merit, in examining the subsumption of dharmas in respect of intrinsic nature?

Answer: It removes the ideation of the self and the ideation of a unity [as a true entity in itself]], and one then readily perfects the cultivation of the ideation of dharmas and distinctness. [In this way one progressively realizes the impermanence of all material and non-material dharmas.]

In this way, one will come to acquire the seeds similar to the gateway of liberation of emptiness (*śūnyatā*). Examining that conditioned dharmas are empty and not self, one will come to be deeply averse to samsara, thus further acquiring the seeds similar to the gateway of liberation of the signless (*animitta*). Not delighting in samsara, one then comes to take deep delight in nirvana, thus further acquiring the seeds similar to the gateway of liberation of non-aspiring (*apraṇihita*).

With regard to these three *samādhis* [of liberation], one generates the medium with the support of the lower, and the higher with the support of the medium, bringing forth *prajñā*, becoming detached from the triple spheres, attaining perfect enlightenment and realizing absolute quiescence. Indeed, when one examines the subsumption of dharmas in respect of intrinsic nature, one comes to gain these advantages and merits.[54]

THE CENTRAL DOCTRINE OF *SARVĀSTIVĀDA* VERSUS *VIBHAJYAVĀDA*

The Sarvāstivāda's fundamental standpoint is that all the previously mentioned categories of dharmas—both the conditioned and the unconditioned—exist throughout time as unique, ultimate reals. This doctrine is expressed by the statement "all exists" (*sarvam asti*), hence the name of the school, Sarvāstivāda. This "all" therefore firstly indicates the reality of each and every ultimate factor that is truly a "dharma," that is, each exists uniquely in its intrinsic nature (*svabhāva*) and uniquely maintains its intrinsic characteristic (*svalakṣaṇa*). It further indicates that every conditioned dharma is existent throughout the three periods of time—future, present, and past—and this is expressed by stating that its intrinsic nature always exists (*sarvadā asti*).

The tritemporal existence of a dharma is articulated by Saṃghabhadra from the epistemological perspective:

> The characteristic of a real existent (*sal-lakṣaṇa*) is that it serves as an object-domain for generating cognition (覺, *buddhi*).

This is divisible into two: What exists truly (*dravyato'sti*) and what exists conceptually (*prajñaptito'sti*), the two being designated on the basis of conventional truth and absolute truth. If, with regard to a thing, a cognition (*buddhi*) is produced without depending on anything else, this thing exists truly—for example, *rūpa, vedanā*, etc. If it depends on other things to produce a cognition, then it exists conceptually/relatively—for example, a vase, army, etc.

Those that exist truly are further divisible into two: Those that have only their essential natures (*svabhāva/svarūpa*) and those that, [in addition,] have activities (*kāritra*). Those that have activities are again of two types: with or without function (*sāmarthya/vyāpara/śakti*) . . . Those that exist relatively are also of two types: having existence on the basis of something real or on something relative, like a vase and an army, respectively.[55]

Thus, the past and future dharmas are existent as much as the present ones, because they are equally efficacious in generating distinctive cognitions:

> [Dharmas pertaining to] the past and future times are not non-existent as [ontological] entities, since the cognitions taking them as cognitive objects (*ālambana*) are distinctive [in each case]—just as in the case of the present dharmas, visibles, sounds, etc. [On the

other hand,] since non-existent dharmas are not distinctive, no distinctive cognition can be generated therefrom.[56]

To summarize: any act of cognition at all—be it a true cognition (as that through spiritual insight), or an imagination, or an illusion, or even a cognition of "absence,"—necessarily presupposes an existent object. These existent objects, of course, may be either relative existents such as a "person," or absolute existents such as matter, sensation, and so on. This Sarvāstivāda doctrine that a notion or concept (*prajñapti*) is necessarily based ultimately on some absolute reals came to importantly influence the epistemological and ontological doctrines of the subsequent Buddhist schools, particularly the Yogācāra.

Within the broader lineage of Sarvāstivāda, all members—whether Ābhidhārmikas, Dārṣṭāntikas, *yogācāras*, or other individual masters—subscribe to this central doctrinal position of *sarvāstitva*, and are known as the *Sarvāstivādāḥ* or *Sarvāstivādinaḥ*. This position is diametrically opposed by those called the *Vibhajyavādāḥ*/*Vibhajyavādinaḥ* (Distinctionist), who include the Sautrāntikas, the Mahāsāṃghikas, the Mahīśāsakas, the Dharmaguptakas, the Kāśyapīyas, and others. Their contrasting position, known as Vibhajyavāda, is that only the present—or, for some, the present and those karmas that have not yet given fruits (*adattaphala*)—exists; the future and the past dharmas do not exist.

In AKB, Vasubandhu defines and contrasts the two doctrinal positions and their respective adherents as follows:

> Those who hold that "all exists"—the past, the present and the future—are the Sarvāstivādas. On the other hand, those who making a distinction (*vibhajya vadanti*), hold that some exist—viz, the present and the past karma that has not given fruit—and some do not exist—viz, what has given fruit and the future—are the Vibhajyavādins.[57]

In Saṃghabhadra's Ny, a post-AKB polemic in defense of the Vaibhāṣika orthodoxy, an additional requirement for the definition is noticeable:

> It is only those who believe in the real existence of the three periods of time, as discussed above, as well as of the three kinds of the unconditioned, who can be considered as belonging to the Sarvāstivāda.[58]

This same requirement is also found in the ADV: Sarvāstivāda is so called because it accepts [the reality of] the three periods of time, distinguished on account of activity, and the three reals [—the three unconditioned].[59] It seems possible that even as late as the time of the AKB and Ny, there were still some Buddhists, both within and without the broad Sarvāstivāda lineage—including some sections of the Sautrāntika-Dārṣṭāntikas—who would accept the doctrine in a revised or different version from that adopted by the orthodox Vaibhāṣikas. It is perhaps because of this that Saṃghabhadra felt it necessary to dissociate the Vaibhāṣikas distinctly from the others whom he could not accept as real Sarvāstivādins in any sense. In Ny, he names them as follows:

Pudgalavādins, called by him "the Superimposers or Additionists (Samāropavādin)" on account of their acceptance of the reality of the Person (*pudgala*) in addition to that of the tri-temporal dharmas;

Vibhajyavādins who accept the existence of only the present and the past karma that has not given fruit;

Kṣaṇikavādins (holders of the view that nothing exists for more than a moment, *kṣaṇa*) who accept only the reality of the 12 *āyatanas* of the present *kṣaṇa*;

Prajñaptivādins (holders of the view that all exists as mere concept, *prajñapti*) who deny the reality of even the dharmas of the present;

Vaināśikas ("Destructionists"/"Annihilationist") who hold that all dharmas are without *svabhāva*, like empty flowers.

The Sautrāntikas, here referred to as the Kṣaṇikavādins, are singled out by Saṃghabhadra who denies that they qualify as Sarvāstivādins, for their view "differs from the Vaināśikas by just a mere *kṣaṇa*!"[60]

But if a dharma's intrinsic nature remains the same throughout times, how can its tritemporality be accounted for? The following four major theories on this issue are given in MVŚ, attributed to the "Four Great Masters" of the Sarvāstivāda:

The Venerable Dharmatrāta says that there is change in mode of being (*bhāva-anyathātva*). The Venerable Ghoṣaka says that there is change in characteristic (*lakṣaṇa-anyathātva*). The Venerable Vasumitra says that there is change in state (*avasthā-anyathātva*). The Venerable Buddhadeva says that there is change in [temporal] relativity (*anyathā-anyathātva*).

[I] The advocate of "change in mode of being" asserts that when dharmas operate (*pra-√vṛt*) in time, they change on account of their modes of existence/being (*bhāva*); there is no change in substance. This is like the case of breaking up a golden vessel to produce another thing—there is just a change in shape, not in *varṇa-rūpa*. It is also like milk, etc., turning into curds, etc.—just the taste, digestibility, etc., are given up, not the *varṇa-rūpa*. Similarly, when dharmas enter into the present from the future, although they give up their future mode of existence and acquire their present mode of existence, they neither lose nor acquire their substantial essence (AKB: *dravya-bhāva*). Likewise, when they enter the past from the present, although they give up the present mode of existence and acquire the past mode of existence, they neither give up nor acquire their substantial nature.

[II] The advocate of "change in characteristic" asserts that when dharmas operate in time, they change on account of characteristic (*lakṣaṇa*); there is no change in substance. A dharma in each of the temporal periods has three temporal characteristics; when one [temporal] characteristic is conjoined, the other two are not severed. This is like the case of a man being attached to one particular woman—he is not said to be detached from other women. Similarly, when dharmas abide in the past, they are being conjoined with the past characteristic but are not said to be severed from the characteristics of the other two temporal characteristics. When they abide in the future, they are being conjoined with the future characteristic but are not said to be severed from the characteristics of the other two temporal characteristics. When they abide in the present, they are being conjoined with the present characteristic, but are not said to be severed from the characteristics of the other two temporal characteristics.

[III] The advocate of "change in state" asserts that when dharmas operate in time, they change on account of state (*avasthā*); there is no change in substance. This is like the case of moving a token [into different positions]. When placed in the position (*avasthā*) of ones, it is signified as one; placed in the position of tens, ten; placed in the position of hundreds, hundred. While there is change in the positions into which it is moved, there is no change in its substance. Similarly, when dharmas pass through the three temporal states, although they acquire three different names, they do not change in substance.

In the theory proposed by this master, there is no confusion as regards substance, for the three periods are differentiated on the basis of activity (*kāritra*).

[IV] The advocate of "change in [temporal] relativity" asserts that when dharmas operate in time, they are predicated differently [as future, present, or past], relative to that which precedes and that which follows (cf. AKB: *pūrvāparam apekṣyānyo'nya ucyate avasthāntarato na dravyāntarataḥ*); there is no change in substance. This is like the case of one and the same woman who is called "daughter" relative to her mother, and "mother" relative to her daughter. Similarly, dharmas are called "past" relative to the succeeding ones, "future" relative to the preceding ones, "present" relative to both.

The compilers of MVŚ fully endorse Vasumitra's theory, and criticize the other three. On Dharmatrāta's theory, they question:

> Apart from a dharma's *svabhāva*, what is it that is called its *bhāva*? When a conditioned dharma reaches the present from the future, its preceding mode of existence ought to cease. When it reaches the past from the present, its succeeding mode of existence ought to arise: How can it be logical that what is past can arise and what is future can cease?[61]

Vasubandhu's criticism in AKB is much more severe, branding it a Sāṃkhya doctrine of *pariṇāma*.

Saṃghabhadra, however, argues that Dharmatrāta's theory is in part similar to Vasumitra's theory.[62] In fact, Saṃghabhadra himself consistently employs the *bhāva-anyathātva* theory along with Vasumitra's *avasthā-anyathātva* theory in his exposition and defense of the thesis of *sarvāstitva*. In this way, Saṃghabhadra is able to argue more cogently that the tritemporal existence of a dharma implies neither its permanence (*nityatā*)[63]—since "all that is permanent does not traverse times"[64]; nor that its existence is identical in the three temporal periods—since "it is conceded that the past, the future and the present assume different modes of existence (*bhāva*)"[65]:

> The essential nature of a dharma remains always; its mode of existence (*bhāva*) changes: When a conditioned dharma traverses time, it gives rise to its activity (*kāritra*) in accordance with the causal conditions, without abandoning its *svabhāva*; immediately after this, the activity produced ceases. Hence it is said that the *svabhāva* exists always and yet it is not permanent, since its *bhāva* changes.[66]

This is part of Saṃghabhadra's response to Vasubandhu's critique of the Vaibhāṣika position—which is ridiculed as an act of the Almighty (*īśvara*)—that a dharma's *sva-bhāva* ("intrinsic nature") exists always and yet its *bhāva* ("nature," "mode of being") is not acknowledged to be permanent, nor is its *bhāva* acknowledged to be distinct from its *svabhāva*.[67] That is, notwithstanding the fundamental Sarvāstivāda position that a dharma's intrinsic *nature* always remains the same, the Vaibhāṣika has come to further hold that a dharma's mode of being (= *nature*) changes throughout times—an ostensibly contradictory position which is as arbitrary as an act of the almighty god who can simply say and do whatever He likes! This ridicule implies that between the completion of MVŚ and AKB, such a position must have become an integral part of the Sarvāstivāda-Vaibhāṣika exposition of *sarvāstitva*. From this perspective, Saṃghabhadra's advocation of Dharmatrāta's theory is not an innovation. Nevertheless, it was he who most articulately (at least in the extant Abhidharma texts) demonstrated its doctrinal significance for the thesis of *sarvāstitva*.

Another exposition of Saṃghabhadra follows, in which he brilliantly argues that a dharma with the same intrinsic nature can assume different modes of being, and thus a distinct mode of being implies a distinct existence of that dharma. Such a position, when successfully established, importantly supports the defense that the claim of the tritemporal existence of a dharma does not amount to a doctrine of its permanence.

> [Opponents:]—When a conditioned dharma is traversing the three periods of time, there being no variation in respect to its essential nature (體相; **svarūpa*, **svabhāva*), how can there be difference in respect to existence (有; *astitva*) and mode of existence (性 [類]; *bhāva*)?
>
> [Saṃghabhadra:]—Isn't it observed that there are dharmas co-existing simultaneously, whose essential natures do not vary, but whose existences and modes of being differ? For instance, the Earth Elements (*pṛthivī-dhātu*), etc., differ as being internal and external; sensations (*vedanā*), etc., differ as being [sensations] of oneself and [sensations] of others, and as being pleasurable, etc.
>
> [For a given entity], this mode of being and existence cannot be different. When its mode of being changes, it necessarily exists differently. It is on this account that Earth, etc., while identical in respect to essential nature, can be said to differ in respect to their modes of being—as internal and external. [Likewise], sensations, etc., while identical in respect to their essential nature of being experience (*anubhava*), can be said to be different modes of being, pleasure, etc. Again, it is like the eye, etc., within the same serial continuity (i.e., same sentient being), which, while identical in respect to their essential nature of being derived matter of tranquillity (*rūpa-prasāda*), differ among them as distinct species of existence—since their efficacies (*gong neng*; 功能) of seeing, hearing, etc., are distinct.[68] It is not the case that, therein, the efficacy differs from the existence, so that there can be the different efficacies, such as seeing, etc.[69] Rather, the efficacy of seeing, etc., is none other than the existence of the eye, etc. A distinct efficacy necessarily implies a distinct existence.
>
> Thus, we know that there are dharmas which, while existing simultaneously and not differing in respect to essential nature, [nonetheless] differ in respect to mode of being.

> Since it is seen that there are dharmas existing simultaneously, which while not varying in respect to their essential natures, differ in respect to their modes of being, we know that when a dharma is traversing the three periods of time, while not varying in respect to essential nature, it has different modes of being. In this way, the Abhidharma tenet comes to be well established.[70]

The Vaibhāṣikas further articulate on the difference between the "activity" of a dharma on the one hand and its efficacy or potency or capacity on the other. The latter notion generically characterizes an existent—an eye is observed to be existent because it has the efficacy for seeing a visible—and is represented by several Sanskrit terms, including *śakti* (power), *vyāpara*, *kriyā*, *sāmarthya*, and so on. A past dharma (a karma) is existent because it can exercise the efficacy of generating or "giving of fruit" (*phala-dāna*) at the present moment. By contrast, "activity," when used strictly or formally, is specifically represented by the Sanskrit *kāritra*, defined as a dharma's efficacy for inducing the next moment of its own existence in its serial continuity. It is its "efficacy for projecting its own fruit" (**svaphala-ākṣepa-sāmarthya*). This "activity" is also described as the grasping/seizing of fruit (*phala-grahaṇa* / *phala-pratigrahaṇa*): the determination of a present dharma's causal relation with its future fruit-to-be. Since, unlike such efficacy as an eye's seeing a visible, or a past karma's "giving of fruit," a dharma's activity exists necessarily and uniquely in every present dharma, it comes to be officially adopted by the Sarvāstivādins as the criterion for temporal distinction of conditioned dharmas.[71]

The long drawn out controversy on *sarvāstivāda* versus *vibhajyavāda* is an extremely important historical fact that must not be overlooked by any Buddhist historian for a proper perspective of the understanding of the development of Buddhist thought in which its reverberation is continuously seen in various forms throughout the centuries, both within and outside India.

DOCTRINE OF CAUSALITY

Given the Sarvāstivāda theory of distinctive tritemporal dharmas, which in their intrinsic nature are totally unrelated to one another and totally devoid of any activities, it is of fundamental importance that the school has an articulated causal doctrine capable of accounting for the arising of dharmas as phenomena and their dynamic interrelatedness in accordance with the Buddha's teaching of conditioned co-arising (*pratītya-samutpāda*).[72] Moreover, for the establishment of each of the dharmas as an ontological existent, a conditioning force (*saṃskāra*), its causal function in each case must be demonstrated. It is probably for this reason that the Sarvāstivāda was also known as *Hetuvāda (說因部)—a "School which expounds on causality."[73] Indeed, as discussed earlier, *hetu* or *hetu-kauśalya* and *pratyaya* or *pratyaya-kauśalya* top the lists of the fundamental topics of Ābhidhārmika investigation. The Sarvāstivādins eventually articulated a doctrine of four conditions, six causes, and five fruits.[74] Noticeably, significant portions of the Sarvāstivāda canonical *abhidharma* treatises are devoted specifically to these topics. Thus, the *Vijñāna-kāya-śāstra* discusses the four conditions (*pratyaya*) at length; JPŚ expounds on the six causes; and the chapter "On *saṃgraha*, etc." of the *Prakaraṇa-pāda-śāstra* contains a total of twenty doctrinal perspectives connected with *hetu-pratyaya*.[75]

It was Kātyāyanīputra who innovated a doctrine of the six causes in JPŚ. Prior to this, the Sarvāstivādins had been sharing with other Buddhists the doctrine of the four conditions: (1) condition qua cause (*hetu-pratyaya*), (2) equal-immediate condition (*samanantara-pratyaya*), (3) condition qua object (*ālambana-pratyaya*), and (4) condition of dominance (*adhipati-pratyaya*).

The six causes are:

(1) Efficient cause (*kāraṇa-hetu*). This is the most generic cause, either in the sense of a general causal contribution or simply of being nonobstructive: "A conditioned dharma has all dharmas, excepting itself, as its efficient cause, for, as regards its arising, [these dharmas] abide in the state of non-obstructiveness."[76]

(2) Homogeneous cause (*sabhāga-hetu*). This obtains in the case of a mental series and among physical matter. "The similar dharmas are the homogeneous causes of dharmas similar [to them], for example, the five *skandhas* which are skilful, are [the homogeneous causes] of the five skilful *skandhas*, among themselves. Likewise the defiled and the non-defined five *skandhas*, [in each case, among themselves]."[77]

(3) Universal cause (*sarvatraga hetu*). "The universal dharmas arisen previously and belonging to a given stage (*bhūmi*) are the universal causes of later defiled dharmas belonging to their own stage.... On account of their being a cause applicable to all defiled dharmas, they are established [as a cause] separate from the homogeneous causes and [also] because they are the cause of [defiled dharmas] belonging to other categories [of abandonability] (5 categories: (i)–(iv) defilements are abandonable either through insight into the four Truths, or (v) through the path of cultivation) as well, for, through their power, defilements belonging to categories different from theirs are produced."[78] The Vaibhāṣikas hold that three defilements are universal: doubt (*vicikitsā*), view (*dṛṣṭi*), and ignorance (*avidyā*), which are abandonable by insight into unsatisfactoriness, the cause of unsatisfactoriness, together with their conjoined and co-existent dharmas."[79]

(4) Coexistent cause (*sahabhū hetu*). "The co-existent [causes] are those that are reciprocally effects . . . For example: the four great elements are co-existent [causes] mutually among themselves; so also, thought and the dharmas that are thought-accompaniments (*cittānuvarttin*); . . . [The case of the co-existent cause] is like the staying in position of three sticks through their mutual strength/support—this establishes the causal relationship (*hetuphalabhāva*) of the co-existents."[80] Conascence is a necessary, but not sufficient, condition for two or more dharmas to be coexistent causes. Saṃghabhadra articulates that this causal category obtains in only three cases: "[i] among those that share the same effect; or [ii] that are reciprocally effects; or [iii] where by the force of this, that dharma can arise. Such co-nascent [dharmas] have a cause-effect relationship [i.e., are coexistent causes]."[81]

(5) Conjoined cause (*saṃprayuktaka-hetu*), a subset of the coexistent causes. As stated previously, thought and concomitants necessarily arise in conjunction. Mental factors, in their role of contributing to their mutual arising and operational coordination, are called "conjoined causes." Moreover, being so conjoined and coordinated, they accomplish the same activity in grasping the same object.

(6) Retribution (/maturation) cause (*vipāka-hetu*). This is the karmic cause, leading to a corresponding karmic fruit, that is, determining the specific type of rebirth that a sentient being will experience. The fruit is necessarily morally neutral (*avyākṛta*): If the retribution cause leads to a desirable (*iṣṭa*) fruit, it is "skilful" (*kuśala*); if it leads to an undesirable (*aniṣṭa*) fruit, it is "unskilful" (*akuśala*). Neutral and outflow-free dharmas do not yield any retribution fruit.

Since the time of the *Jñānaprasthāna*, the Sarvāstivādins have held that retribution causes and fruits comprise all the five *skandhas*: that is, not only thought and the thought-concomitants, but also the matter accompanying thought (*cittānuvṛttaka-rūpa*) and the conditionings disjoined from thought (see also the section "The Sarvāstivāda School and Its Fundamental Treatises")—the ideationless attainment (*asaṃjñī-samāpatti*), the cessation attainment (*nirodha-samāpatti*), all acquisitions that are unskilful and skilful but with-outflow (*sāsrava*), and the accompanying characteristics of the conditioned (*saṃskṛta-lakṣaṇa*)—can constitute retribution causes.[82]

Of these six causes, the truly innovative, and by far doctrinally most important, is the coexistent cause. For the Sarvāstivādins, the fact of direct perception (*pratyakṣa*) cannot be established without the type of simultaneous causality represented by this cause. This is because, given that a sensory faculty and its object last only one single moment—a doctrine commonly accepted by all Abhidharma schools with the exception of the Sāṃmitīya, etc—if the corresponding consciousness (*qua* effect) were to arise in the second moment (as claimed by the Sautrāntikas and others), it would not have an existent object. If direct perception cannot be established, then inferential knowledge too would be impossible—and this would result in the absolute impossibility of any knowledge of the external world!

Rejecting the *sahabhū* causality, the Dārṣṭāntika-Sautrāntikas have to admit that all perceptions are indirect (*apratyakṣa*) and representational.[83] In the first moment, the sensory faculty and object exist; the sensory consciousness then arises in the next moment: As the object arises only to cease, it leaves behind an imprint or exact resemblance (*ākāra*) of itself, which becomes the cognitive object (*ālambana*) that generates the corresponding knowledge of it in the next moment. Thus, external reality is never known directly. Its knowledge is necessarily derived from our mental content. This Sautrāntika theory came to be known as the "theory of the inferability of the external object" (*bāhyārtha-anumeyavāda*).[84]

More importantly, the coexistent cause serves as the only valid paradigm of causation. In general, if *X* causes *Y*, both *X* and *Y* must be existent at the same time (an utter void or a nonexistent cannot be causally efficacious)—although they may belong to different time periods with respect to their own temporal frame of reference; that is: *X* may be past or present or future, and *Y* may also be past or present or future, *but X and Y must coexist, although not necessarily be conascent*. To borrow Dharmatrāta's terminology, they are both existent but are not necessarily of the same mode of existence (*bhāva*). Where *X* and *Y* are necessarily conascent (i.e., both existing at the same *present* moment), the causality involved reduces to the category known as the coexistent cause. In fact, in the Sarvāstivāda conception, all dharmas in their intrinsic nature have always been existent; it is only a matter of inducing their arising through causes and conditions. This is the fundamental principle underlying the Sarvāstivāda doctrine of causality. Past and future dharmas are also endowed with efficacies including that of actually giving an effect, although it is only a present dharma that has "activity."

This Sarvāstivāda theory of simultaneous or coexistent causality has come to significantly impact the subsequent development of Buddhist thoughts. For the Mahāyāna Yogācāra school in particular, this theory is indispensable for the establishment of some of their most fundamental teachings, including the *ālayavijñāna* doctrine, with its explanations on seeds (*bīja*) and perfuming (*vāsanā*), and the doctrine of cognition-only (*vijñaptimātratā*).

ABBREVIATIONS

ADV	P. S. Jaini, ed. *Abhidharmadīpa with Vibhāṣāprabhāvṛtti*. Patna, 1959.
AKB	P. Pradhan, ed. *Abhidharmakośabhāṣyam of Vasubandhu*. Patna, 1975.
Entrance	K. L. Dhammajoti. *Entrance into the Supreme Doctrine*. 2nd rev. edn. Hong Kong, 2008.
JCBSSL	*Journal of the Centre for Buddhist Studies, Sri Lanka*.
JPŚ	*Jñānaprasthāna-śāstra* 阿毗達磨發智論 (T no. 1544).
MVŚ	*Abhidharma-mahā-vibhāṣā-śāstra* 阿毘達磨大毘婆沙論 (T no. 1545).
Ny	**Abhidharma-nyāyānusāra* 阿毘達磨順正理論 (T no. 1562).
PrP	*Abhidharmaprakaraṇa-śāstra* 阿毘達磨品類足論 (T no. 1542).
Sar Abhi	K. L. Dhammajoti. *Sarvāstivāda Abidharma*. 5th rev. ed. Hong Kong, 2015.
T	J. Takakusu, ed. *Taishō Shinshu Daizokyo* 大正大藏經. 1924–1932.

PRIMARY SOURCES

Abhidharmadīpa with Vibhāṣā-prabhāvṛtti. Edited by P. S. Jaini. Patna: K. P. Jayaswal Research Institute, 1959.

Abhidharmakośa-bhāṣya of Vasubandhu. Chapter I. Edited by Y. Ejima. Tokyo: Sankibo, 1989.

Abhidharmakośabhāṣya of Vasubandhu. Chapter IX: Ātmavādapratiṣedha. Edited by C. L. Lee. Tokyo: Sankibo, 2005.

Abhidharmakośabhāṣyam of Vasubandhu. Edited by P. Pradhan. Patna: K. P. Jayaswal Research Institute, 1975.

Abhidharmakośakārikā of Vasubandhu. Edited by V. V. Gokhale. "The Text of the Abhidharmakośakārikā of Vasubandhu." *Journal of the Bombay Branch, Royal Asiatic Society*. Vol. 22. Bombay: Royal Asiatic Society, 1946.

Kathāvatthu. Edited by A. C. Taylor. London: The Pali Text Society, 1894–1897.

Kathāvatthuppakaraṇa Aṭṭhakathā. Edited by J. Minayeff, 1–22. London: The Pali Text Society, 1889.

Prakaraṇābhidharmāvatāra (*rab tu byed pa chos mngon pa la 'jug pa zhes bya ba*). (Tohoku no. 4098, Peking no. 5599). Translated by Dānaśīla Jinamitra and Ye-shes-sde.

Sphuṭārthābhidharmakośavyākhyā of Yaśomitra. Edited by U. Wogihara. Anastatic reproduction. Tokyo: Sankibo, 1971.

FURTHER READING

Armelin, I. *Le Coeur de la Loi Suprême: Traité de Fa-cheng. Abhidharmahṛdayaśāstra de Dharmaśrī*. Paris: Paul Geuthner,1978.

Aung, Shwe Zan, and C. A. F. Rhys Davids. *Compendium of Philosophy (Abhidhammattha Saṅgaho)*. London: The Pali Text Society, 1910.

Aung, Shwe Zan, and C. A. F. Rhys Davids. *Points of Controversy or subjects of discourse: Being a translation of the Kathāvatthu from the Abhidhammapiṭaka*. London: The Pali Text Society, 1915.

Broeck, José van den. *La Saveur de l'immortel (A-pi-t'an Kan Lu Wei Lun)*. Louvain-la-Neuve: Institut Orientaliste, 1977.

Cox, Collett. "On the Possibility of a Non-existent Object of Consciousness: Sarvāstivādin and Dārṣṭāntika Theories." *Journal of the International Association of Buddhist Studies* 11, no. 1 (1988): 31–87.

Cox, Collett. *Disputed Dharmas. Early Buddhist Theories on Existence. An Annotated Translation of the Section on Factors Dissociated from Thought, from Saṅghabhadra's Nyāyānusāra*. Tokyo: The International Institute for Buddhist Studies, 1995.

Cox, Collett. "From Category to Ontology: The Changing Role of *Dharma* in Sarvāstivāda Abhidharma." *Journal of Indian Philosophy* 32 (2004): 543–597.

De La Vallée Poussin, Louis. *L'Abhidharmakośa de Vasubandhu*. 6 vols. Paris: Library Orientaliste Paul Geuthner, 1923–1931.

De La Vallée Poussin, Louis. "La controverse du temps et du *pudgala* dans le *Vijñānakāya*." *Études Asiatiques* 1 (1925): 343–376.

De La Vallée Poussin, Louis. "Cosmologie Bouddhique." *Études Asiatiques oubliées à l'occasionde 25e anniversaire de l'École Française d'Extrême-Orient* 1 (1925): 295–350.

De La Vallée Poussin, Louis. "Documents d'Abhidharma." *Mélanges Chinois et Bouddhiques* 1 (1931–1932): 65–121.

De La Vallée Poussin, Louis. "Documents d'Abhidharma: La Controverse du Temps; les deux, les quatre, les trois vérités." *Mélanges Chinois et Bouddhiques* 5 (1936–1937): 1–187.

De La Vallée Poussin, Louis. "Documents d'Abhidharma: Texts relatifs au nirvana et aux *asaṃskṛtas* en général I–II." *Bulletin de l'École Française d'Extrême-Orient* 30 (1930): 1–28, 247–298.

De La Vallée Poussin, Louis. "Notes bouddhiques II, Le Vijñānakāya et le Kathāvatthu." *Académie Royale de Belgique, Bulletin de la Classe des Lettres*, 5th series, 8, no.11 (1922): 516–520.

De La Vallée Poussin, Louis. *Vasubandhu et Yaçomitra, Troisième chapitre de l'Abhidharmakoça Kārikā, Bhāṣya et Vyākhyā, Avec une analyse de la Lokaprajñapti et de la Kāraṇaprajñapti de Maudgalyāyana*, 326–350. London: Kegan Paul, Trench, Trübner & Co., 1918.

Dessein, B., and W. Teng, eds. *Text, History and Philosophy: Abhidharma across Buddhist Scholastic Traditions*. Leiden: Brill, 2016.

Dhammajoti, K. L. "Abhidharma and *Upadeśa*." *JCBSSL* 3 (2005): 112–125.

Dhammajoti, K. L. "Abhidharma Debates on the Nature of the Objects of Sensory Perception." *JCBSSL* 10 (2012): 203–234.

Dhammajoti, K. L. *Abhidharma Doctrines and Controversies on Perception*. 4th rev. edn. Hong Kong: The Buddha-Dharma Centre of Hong Kong, 2018.

Dhammajoti, K. L. "*Ākāra* and Direct Perception: Vaibhāṣika versus Sautrāntika." *Bukkyō Kenkyū* (2007): 1–34.

Dhammajoti, K. L. "The *apramāṇa* Meditation in the Sarvāstivāda: With Special Reference to *Maitrībhāvanā*." *JCBSSL* 8 (2010): 165–186.

Dhammajoti, K. L. "The *aśubhā* Meditation in the Sarvāstivāda." *JCBSSL* 7 (2009): 248–295.

Dhammajoti, K. L. "The *Citta-caitta* Doctrine of Śrīlāta." *JCBSSL* 5 (2007): 217–241.

Dhammajoti, K. L. "The Defects in the *Arhat*'s Enlightenment: His *Akliṣṭa-ajñāna and Vāsanā*." *Bukkyō Kenkyū* 27 (1998): 65–98.

Dhammajoti, K. L. "The Doctrine of the Six-Stage Mindfulness of Breathing." *Buddhist and Pali Studies in Honour of Venerable Professor Kakkapalliye Anuruddha*, 639–650. Hong Kong: Centre of Buddhist Studies, The University of Hong Kong, 2009.

Dhammajoti, K. L. *Entrance into the Supreme Doctrine: Skandhila's Abhidharmāvatāra*. 2nd rev. edn. Hong Kong: Centre of Buddhist Studies, The University of Hong Kong, 2008.

Dhammajoti, K. L. "Exposition on the Elements (*Dhātunirdeśa*): Chapter 1 of the *Abhidharmakośabhāṣya*—Part I." *JCBSSL* 15 (2018): 135–171.

Dhammajoti, K. L. "From Abhidharma to Mahāyāna: Remarks on the Early Abhidharma Doctrine of the Three *yānas*." *JCBSSL* 9 (2011): 153–169.

Dhammajoti, K. L. "The Karmic Role of the *avijñapti* in Sarvāstivāda." *Bukkyō Kenkyū* 27 (2003): 69–90.

Dhammajoti, K. L. (2016). "*Kleśaprahāṇa, Pratyakṣa* and Discriminative Discernment: Sarvāstivāda Doctrines and Later Yogācāra Discussion." *JCBSSL* 13 (2016): 155–189.

Dhammajoti, K. L. "The *Nirvedhabhāgīyas* as Preparation for the Realization of Truth: The Abhidharma and Early Yogācāra Perspectives." *JCBSSL* 12 (2015): 299–317.

Dhammajoti, K. L. "*Prajñā-vimukta, Ubhayatobhāga-vimukta* and *Vimokṣāvaraṇa*: The Sarvāstivāda Perspective." *Buddhist Meditative Praxis: Traditional Teachings and Modern Application*, 25–49. Hong Kong: Centre of Buddhist Studies, The University of Hong Kong, 2015.

Dhammajoti, K. L. *Sarvāstivāda Abhidharma*. 5th edn. Hong Kong: The Buddha-Dharma Centre of Hong Kong, 2015.

Dhammajoti, K. L. "Sarvāstivādin conception of nirvana." *Buddhist and Indian Studies in Honour of Professor Sodo Mori*, 335–348. Tokyo: Kokusai Bukkyoto Kyokai, 2002.

Dhammajoti, K. L. "The Sarvāstivāda Doctrine of Simultaneous Causality." *JCBSSL* 1 (2003): 17–54.

Dhammajoti, K. L. "The Sixteen-Mode Mindfulness of Breathing." *JCBSSL* 6 (2008): 251–288.

Dhammajoti, K. L. "Summary and Discussion of the *Abhidharmakośa-bhāṣya*." *Abhidharmakośa-Bhāṣya of Vasubandhu: The Treasury of the Abhidharma and Its (Auto) Commentary*, 1–69. Delhi: Motilal Banarsidass, 2012.

Dhammajoti, K. L. "Yogācāra Refutation of Tri-temporal Existence." *JCBSSL* 14 (2017): 235–247.

Dietz, S. *Fragmente des Dharmaskandha: Ein Abhidharma text in Sanskrit aus Gilgit*. Göttingen: Vandenhoeck & Ruprecht, 1984.

Dietz, S. "A Brief Survey on the Sanskrit Fragments of the Lokaprajñaptiśāstra." *Annual Memoirs of the Otani University Shin Buddhist Comprehensive Research Institute* 7 (1989): 79–86.

Frauwallner, E. *Studies in Abhidharma Literature and the Origins of Buddhist Philosophical Systems*. Translated by Sophie Francis Kidd under the supervision of Ernst Steinkellner. Albany: State University of New York Press, 1995.

Imanishi, J. *Fragmente des Abhidharmaprakaraṇabhāṣya in Text und Übersetzung (Abhidharmatexte in Sanskrit aus den Turfanfunden II)*. Göttingen: Philosophisch-historische Klasse, no. 1, 1975.

Jaini, P. S. *Collected Papers on Buddhist Studies*. Delhi: Motilal Banarsidass, 1975.

Jong, J. W. de. "Les Sūtrapiṭaka des Sarvāstivādin et des Mūlasarvāstivādin." *Buddhist Studies*, ed. Gregory Schopen, 229–236. Berkeley: Asian Humanities Press, 1979.

Kajiyama, Y. "Controversy between the *sākāra-* and *nirākāra-vādins* of the Yogācāra School: Some materials." *Journal of Indian Buddhist Studies 14*, no. 1: 429–418.

Kajiyama, Y. "An Introduction to Buddhist Philosophy: An Annotated Translation of the *Tarkabhāṣā* of Mokṣākaragupta." *Memoirs of the Faculty of Letters, Kyoto University*, no. 10 (1966): 1–173.

Karunadasa, Y. *Buddhist Analysis of Matter*. Colombo: Department of Cultural Affairs of the Government of Sri Lanka, 1967.

Karundasa, Y. *The Dhamma Theory: Philosophical Cornerstone of the Abhidhamma. Wheel Publication*, no. 412/413. Kandy: Buddhist Publication Society, 1996.
Karundasa, Y. *The Theravāda Abhidhamma: Its Inquiry into the Nature of Conditioned Reality*. Hong Kong: Centre of Buddhist Studies, The University of Hong Kong, 2010.
Kato, J. *Kyōryōbu no Kenkyū [A Study of the Sautrāntika]*. Tokyo: Shunjū-sha, 1989.
Kritzer, R., N. Yamabe, T. Fukuda, B. Dessein, and Y. Honjō. "The Sautrāntikas." *Journal of the International Association of Buddhist Studies* 26, no. 2 (2003): 201–384.
Masuda, J. "Origin and Doctrines of Early Indian Buddhist Schools." *Asia Major* 2 (1925): 1–78.
Matsuda, K. *Newly Identified Sanskrit Fragments of the Dharmaskandha in the Gilgit Manuscripts*. Kyoto: Bun'eido, 1984.
Mitomo, K. *A Study of the Abhidharmadīpa*. Kyoto: Heirakuji Shoten, 2007.
Mookerjee, S. *The Buddhist Philosophy of Universal Flux*. Delhi: Motilal Banarsidass, 1935.
Nishi, G. *Studies in Abhidharma Buddhism* (Japanese). Tokyo: Kokushokankōkai, 1975.
Pruden, L. M. (trans.) *Abhidharmakośabhāṣyam by Louis De La Vallée Poussin*. 4 vols. Berkeley: Asian Humanities Press, 1988.
Pruden, L. M. (trans.) *KARMASIDDHIPRAKARAṆA: The Treatise on Action by Vasubandu by E. Lamotte*. Berkeley: Asian Humanities Press, 1988.
Przyluski, J. "Dārṣṭāntika, Sautrāntika and Sarvāstivādin." *Indian Historical Quarterly* 16, no. 2 (1940): 246–254.
Przyluski, J. "Sautrāntika et Dārṣṭāntika." *Rocznik Orjentalistyczny* 8 (1931): 14–24.
Sakurabe, H. "*Abhidharmāvatāra* by an Unidentified Author." *Nava Nālanda Mahāvihāra Research Publication*, vol. 2 (1960), 359–370.
Sakurabe, H. *A Study of the Abhidharmakośabhāṣya: Dhātunirdeśa and Indriyanirdeśa* (Japanese). Kyoto: Hōzōkan, 1969.
Sakurabe, H. "A Japanese Translation of the Tibetan Version of the *Abhidharmāvatāra*." Appendix in *A Study of Buddhist Terms*. Kyoto: Bun'eidō, 1975.
Samtani, N. H. (trans.). *Gathering the Meanings: The Arthaviniścaya Sutra and Its Commentary Nibandhana*. Berkeley: Dharma Publishing, 2002.
Sangpo, G. L. (trans.). *Abhidharmakośa-Bhāṣya of Vasubandhu*. Translated into French by Louis de La Vallée Poussin. 4 vols. Delhi: Motilal Banarsidass, 2012.
Stcherbatsky, T. *The Central Conception of Buddhism and the Meaning of the Word "Dharma."* Reprint. Delhi: Motilal Banarsidass, 1970.
Stcherbatsky, T. "*The Soul Theory of the* Buddhists." Reprint. Delhi: Bhāratīya Vidyā Prakāśana, 1976.
Tatia, N. "Sarvāstivāda." *Nava Nālandā Mahāvihāra Research Publication* 2 (1960): 75–138.
Van Velthem, M. *Le traité de la descente dans la profonde loi (Abhidharmāvatāraśāstra) de l'Arhat Skandhila*. Louvain-la-Neuve: Institut Orientaliste, 1977.
Willemen, C., *et al. Sarvāstivāda Buddhist Scholasticism*. Leiden: Brill, 1998.
Yin Shun. *An Investigation into the Source of the Vijñaptimātratā Philosophy*. Reprint (1st edn, 1944). Taipei: Zhengwen Publication Society, 1974.
Yin Shun. *A Study of the Śāstras and Ācāryas of the Sarvāstivāda and Other Schools*. Taipei: Zhengwen Publication Society, 1968.
Yin Shun. *History of Indian Buddhist Thoughts*. Taipei: Zhengwen Publication Society, 1988.

NOTES

1. MVŚ, 4c4–11, gives several explanations on this title: It is so named because: (i) all absolute knowledges have this as their initial foundation; (ii) all absolute knowledges are established with this as their basis;

(iii) this is the causal condition (*pratyaya*) for generating mighty knowledge; (iv) all knowledges rely on this to reach the other shore; (v) this excels all in unfolding the intrinsic characteristics (*svalakṣaṇa*) and common characteristics (*sāmānya-lakṣaṇa*) of all dharmas; (vi) this is the gateway for generating all mundane (*laukika*) and supramundane (*lokottara*) knowledges. Also, cf. MVŚ, 2b16–19: Kātyāyanīputra composed this for dispelling ignorance (*avidyā*) and bringing forth (發; *pra-√sthā*) wisdom, like a lamp dispelling darkness and bringing forth light.

2. Śāriputra, according the Xuanzang tradition. (For example, cf. Puguang's ascription of authourship of the canonical texts: T41, no. 1821, 8b26–c12).
3. In Yin Shun opines that this Vasumitra is none other than the Vasumitra (*c.* 100 bce) recognized in MVŚ as one of the "four great masters of the Sarvāstivāda." Yin Shun, *History of Indian Buddhist Thoughts* (Taipei, 1966), 148.
4. Cf. Yin Shun, *A Study of the Śāstras and cāryas of the Sarvāstivāda and Other Schools* (Taipei, 1964), 131.
5. For example, JPŚ at Dīgha-nikāya III, 254, 284; Saṃyutta-nikāya V, 60; and Aṅguttara-nikāya, IV, 9.
6. This has been pointed out by Yin Shun, *Study of the Śāstras*, 149, 154; *History of Indian Buddhist* Thoughts (Taipei, 1986), 68a; and, *Study of the Śāstras*. See JPŚ, 974c19–975a2, 929a11–13, 987b14–15, 1025c9–12 (here all the three types of unconcoditioned dharma are mentioned), etc.
7. Yin Shun, *Study of the Śāstras*, 188.
8. JPŚ, 920c27–921a4.
9. For the notion of *prāpti*, see JPŚ § IV; *samanvāgama* refers to the continuous *prāpti* of a dharma, without losing it. See Sar Abhi, §11.3.1.1.
10. See also, Sar Abhi, §11.3.1.2.
11. Cf. Puguang, *Commentary on the Abhidharmakośabhāṣya* 《俱舍論記》 T41, no. 1821, 8c9–11: "The preceding six treatises have less doctrinal topics; it is the *Jñānaprasthāna* that contains the most extensive doctrinal perspectives. Accordingly, the Abhidharma masters of later time spoke of the six as the feet, and of the *Jñānaprasthāna* as the body."
12. MVŚ, 231c3–12.
13. See a "Summary and Discussion of the *Abhidharmakośabhāṣya*," in Lodrö Sangpo (trans.), *Abhidharmakośabhāṣya of Vasubandhu: The Treasury of the Abhidharma and Its (Auto) commentary* (Delhi, 2012), 1:1–69.
14. Cf. U. Wogihāra (ed.), *Sphuṭārthā Abhidharmakośā-vyākhyā of Yaśomitra*, 11: *kaḥ sautrāntikārthaḥ | ye sūtraprāmāṇikā na śāstraprāmāṇikāḥ | te sautrāntikāḥ |* ("What is the meaning of "Sautrāntika"? Those who take the sutras, and not the treatises, as authority are the Sautrāntikas.").

    For a most insightful discussion of the Sautrāntikas, see Yin Shun, *Study of the Śāstras*, especially chapters 10–13; Yin Shun, Part II, chapters 1–3. J. Kato *Kyōryōbu no Kenkyū* [*A Study of the Sautrāntika*] (Tokyo, 1989) is a book-length study of the Sautrāntikas that contains useful material cited from the Sanskrit and Tibetan in addition to Chinese, though many of his major views and explanations have in fact already been made by Yin Shun (which Kato apparently fails to acknowledge). See also, K. L. Dhammajoti, especially chapters 2, 6–10.
15. AKB, 460.
16. For a discussion of Saṃghabhadra's doctrinal contribution, see K. L. Dhammajoti, "The Contribution of Saṃghabhadra to our Understanding of Abhidharma Doctrines," in *Text, History, and Philosophy: Abhidharma across Buddhist Scholastic Traditions*, ed. B. Dessein and W. Teng, 223–247. There is no modern translation of Ny. However, Louis De La Vallée Poussin has presented very helpful French translations of many of its passages in several works, especially "Documents d'Abhidharma" (see "Further Reading" for details) and the very rich annotations in his *L'Abhidharmakośa de Vasubandhu* (1923–1931). In English, K. L. Dhammajoti has also translated numerous passages from Ny (see "Further Reading" for details).

17. For an English translation and study of this work, see *Entrance*. For further discussion on the Sarvāstivāda Abhidharma literature, see Erich Frauwallner, *Studies in Abhidharma Literature and the Origins of Buddhist Philosophical Systems*, (trans. Sophie Francis Kidd); Sar Abhi, chapter 4; and C. Willemen, B. Dessein, and C. Cox, *Sarvāstivāda Buddhist Scholasticism* (Leiden, 1998), especially ch. 3 and 4.
18. Majjhima-nikāya I, Mahāyamakavagga, *Mahāgopālaka-sutta*, 223: *idha, bhikkhave, bhikkhu ye te bhikkhū bahussutā āgatāgamā dhammadharā vinayadharā mātikādharā te kālena kālaṃ upasaṅkamitvā paripucchati, paripañhati: "idaṃ, bhante, kathaṃ? imassa ko attho"ti? tassa te āyasmanto avivaṭañceva vivaranti, anuttānīkatañca uttānī karonti | anekavihitesu ca kaṅkhāṭhānīyesu dhammesu kaṅkhaṃ paṭivinodenti* | Same stock phrase in the Dīgha-nikāya, *Mahāparinibbāna-sutta*, and several *suttas* of the Aṅguttara-nikāya.
19. Vinaya, *pavāraṇākkhandhaka*: *idha pana, bhikkhave, aññatarasmiṃ āvāse tadahu pavāraṇāya bhikkhūhi dhammaṃ bhaṇantehi . . . pe . . . suttantikehi suttantaṃ saṅgāyantehi . . . vinayadharehi vinayaṃ vinicchinantehi . . . dhammakathikehi dhammaṃ sākacchantehi* |
20. Cf. Yin Shun (1968), 365–367; Sar Abhi, §3.6; Dhammajoti, KL (2018), § 2.2.
21. Cf. Dhammajoti, KL (2018), ch. 2, esp. §§2.3, 2.4; Yin Shun (1968), 615.
22. V. Bhattacharya, ed., *The Yogācārabhūmi of Ācārya Asaṅga*, 58: *na cāsti pañcānāṃ vijñānakāyānāṃ saha dvayoḥ kṣaṇayor utpattiḥ nāpy anyonyasamanantaram anyonyotpattiḥ* | *ekakṣaṇotpannānāṃ pañcānāṃ kāyavijñānānām anantaraṃ manovijñānam avaśyam utpadyate* |
23. MVŚ, 291b1–3.
24. Cf. K. L. Dhammajoti, "Abhidharma and *Upadeśa*," *JCBSSL* 3 (2005): 112–125.
25. T29, 330b6–19.
26. T24, no. 1451, p. 408b6–11; also quoting Mahākāśyapa. See also Sar Abhi, §1.1.2.
27. Cf. Sar Abhi, §2.2.
28. AKB, 2 f.
29. See Sar Abhi, §2.4.1, and chart on p. 39.
30. Cf. Ny, 335b29–c8. The Sanskrit is quoted in U. Wogihāra, *op.cit.*, 32. Vasubandhu's definition (AKB, 8) is as follows: *vikṣiptācittakasyāpi yo 'nubandhaḥ śubhāśubhaḥ* | *mahābhūtāny upādāya, sā hy avijñaptir ucyate* || Saṃghabhadra (*loc. cit.*) objects to it, and criticizes particularly its description of the *avijñapti* as a serial flow (*anubandha*).
31. See *Entrance*, 108.
32. AKB, 92: *sarvam evāsaṃskṛtam adravyam* |
33. For instance: the *Saṅgītiparyāya* (T26, no. 1536, 369c6–8) and the *Dharmaskandha* (T26, no. 1537, 505a5). Likewise in the more developed canonical texts, as PrP (T26, 692c9–10).
34. T26, no. 1544, 1025c9–12.
35. AKB, 4.
36. MVŚ, 147b2–5. Cf. Sarv Abhi, §16.2.
37. MVŚ, 164b13–21. Cf. AKB, 4. Also cf. Sarv Abhi, §16.3, and *Entrance*, 127.
38. Ny, 434b12–17. See also *Entrance*, 45; 207n374.
39. For example, cf. MVŚ, 164c30–165a15; etc.
40. 388b19–21.
41. Ny, 429c13–16.
42. MVŚ, 116b.
43. *Entrance*, § 4.5.8.
44. Cf. MVŚ, 179b4–5: "Its intrinsic being (自體; **svarūpa, *ātma-bhāva*) and intrinsic characteristic (自相; *svalakṣaṇa*) are none other than its intrinsic nature (自性; *svabhāva*). Thus, it is said, 'intrinsic natures of dharmas are their very intrinsic characteristics; their homogenous nature is their common characteristic (共相, *sāmānya-lakṣaṇa*).'" Also cf. U. Wogihāra, *op. cit.*, 889 f: "To be existent as an absolute entity is to be existent as an intrinsic characteristic" (*paramārthena sat svalakṣaṇena sad ity arthaḥ*).

45. Cf. Gelong Lodrö Sangpo (2012), 1:14.
46. JPŚ, 922c.
47. MVŚ, 145c.
48. Cf. Saṃyutta-nikāya, *Dhammacakkapavattana-sutta*: "*idaṃ dukkhaṃ ariyasaccan"ti me, bhikkhave, pubbe ananussutesu dhammesu cakkhuṃ udapādi, ñāṇaṃ udapādi, paññā udapādi, vijjā udapādi, āloko udapādi* | "*taṃ kho panidaṃ dukkhaṃ ariyasaccaṃ pariññeyyan"ti me, bhikkhave, pubbe . . . pe . . . udapādi* | "*taṃ kho panidaṃ dukkhaṃ ariyasaccaṃ pariññātan"ti me, bhikkhave, pubbe ananussutesu dhammesu cakkhuṃ udapādi, ñāṇaṃ udapādi, paññā udapādi, vijjā udapādi, āloko udapādi* |
49. This is actually stated in the specifically Abhidharmic terminology: the *ajñātam-ājñāsyāmi-indriya* must first arise; then the *ājñātendriya*; and finally the *ājñātāvindriya*. For the nature and functions of these three outflow-free *indriyas*, see AKB, 40, 49.
50. MVŚ, 410c10-411a10.
51. MVŚ, 1c18–25.
52. 708b26–c19. Saṃghabhadra's remarks here are made in the context of arguing for the Sarvāstivāda position that defilements can also be abandoned through the mundane paths (*laukika-mārga*).
53. For a detailed discussion, see K. L. Dhammajoti, "The Defects in the *Arhat*'s Enlightenment: His *Akliṣṭājñāna* and *Vāsanā*," *Bukkyō Kenkhū* 27 (1998): 65–98.
54. 307a9–307a28. Cf. also Ny, 342c8–19.
55. Ny, 621c20–622a2.
56. Ny, 640c4–6. See also, Ny, 622b19–27; and Sarv Abhi, §3.5.3.3.
57. AKB, 296: *ye hi sarvamastīti vadanti atītam anāgataṃ pratyutpannaṃ ca te sarvāstivādāḥ* | *ye tu kecid asti yat pratyutpannam adatta-phalaṃ cātītaṃ karma kiṃcin nāsti yad datta-phalam atītam anāgataṃ ceti vibhajya vadanti te vibhajyavādinaḥ* |
58. Ny, 630c.
59. ADV, 259: *icchaty adhva-trayaṃ yasmāt kṛtyataś ca dhruva-trayam* | *sarvāstivāda ity uktas tasmād . . .* ||
60. Ny, 630c–631a. A similar distinction between the Sarvāstivāda and other schools is also made in the ADV, 257 f.
61. MVŚ, 396b18–22.
62. Ny, 631, b9–10.
63. See also, Sarv Abhi, 122 *f*; and Ny, 633c, 136.
64. Ny, 630b3–4. See also, Sar Abh, § 3.5.3.2.
65. Ny, 630b4–5.
66. Ny, 633c24–26. Further examples: Ny, 628b26–27: 非去來有如現在, 以於一切同實有中, 許有種種有性別故. Also, establishing tri-temporality in terms of both Vasumitra's as well as Dharmatrāta's theories: Ny, 633b29–c11: 又略說者: 如諸有為, 實體雖同而功能別; 如是三世實體雖同, 於中非無作用差別, 以有性類有無量種 ... 是故現在過去未來三種有性, 條然差別. 寧如現在, 去來亦然? 依有, 可言有未生滅; 約所無故, 未生滅成. 謂: 於有中先闕作用, 彼未有故, 名未已生. 有法後時復闕作用, 彼已無故, 名為已滅. 故唯有中, 有未生滅. 由斯建立三世理成.
67. AKB, 298: *svabhāvaḥ sarvadā cāsti bhāvo nityaśca neṣyate* | *na ca svabhāvād bhāvo 'nyo vyaktam īśvaraceṣṭitam* |
68. 有性類別. In Xuanzang's translation of the *Abhidharmakośabhāṣya*, 有性 corresponds to both *astitva* and *bhāva*.
69. Considering the immediately following sentence, 見等功能, I believe that 性 in 性等功能差別 is a script error for 見.
70. Ny, 625, a19–b2: 諸有為法歷三世時, 體相無差, 有性寧別? 豈不現見, 有法同時, 體相無差, 而有性別? 如地界等, 內外性殊; 受等, 自他, 樂等, 性別. 此性與有, 理定無差. 性既有殊, 有必有別. 由是: 地等, 體相雖同, 而可說為內外性別; 受等, 領等體相雖同, 而可說為樂等性別.

又如眼等, 在一相續, 清淨所造色體相同, 而於其中, 有性類別; 以見聞等功能別故. 非於此中, 功能異有, 可有(見)等功能差別. 然見等功能, 即眼等有; 由功能別故, 有性定別. 故知諸法, 有同一時, 體相無差, 有性類別. 既現見有法體同時, 體相無差, 有性類別; 故知諸法歷三世時, 體相無差, 有性類別. 如是善立對法義宗.

71. Cf. Ny, 631c5-17; Sar Abhi, §5.5.
72. Cf. MVŚ, 105c, 108c, 283b, 396a, etc.
73. T 49, 15b.
74. See Sar Abhi, §§ 6 and 7.
75. Cf. Sar Abhi, §§ 4.1.2 ff.
76. AKB, 82.
77. AKB, 85.
78. AKB, 89.
79. MVŚ, 90c; Ny, 416c.
80. AKB, 83–85.
81. Ny, 419c.
82. Cf. MVŚ, 96a–c.
83. Cf. ADV, 47: *dārṣṭāntikasya hi sarvam apratyakṣam* |
84. Cf. K. L. Dhammajoti, *Abhidharma Doctrines and Controversies on Perception*, 4th rev. ed. (Hong Kong, 2018), ch. 8 and 9.

K. L. Dhammajoti

SECULAR BUDDHISM

INTRODUCTION

As a quasi-religious movement, Secular Buddhism builds on the secularizing trends within the Buddhist tradition in the modern era. While this article focuses specifically on the movement known as Secular Buddhism (sometimes called Secular Dharma), secularization and the creation of Buddhist modernism are important parts of the cultural context of Secular Buddhism and are introduced first as background.

Considered next is the history of Buddhism in the modern era (which we stipulate for our purposes here as beginning around the start of the 19th century through the first quarter of the 21st century). That history is marked by engagements between European and American societies on the one hand, and Buddhist societies on the other. Buddhist leaders actively responded to the social, economic, and political changes created by that engagement, and many of those responses can be interpreted retrospectively as contributing to a secularizing of Buddhism. Further contributing to these developments were the distinction between religion and non-religion that informed Victorian apologetics for Buddhism, Perennialist teachings regarding the mystical unity of all religions, and neoliberal structuring of the individual as an isolated agent in competition with others. Cumulatively, all of these were then constructed within the semiotic opposition of secular and religious.

As a distinct self-identified movement, Secular Buddhism began to be institutionalized at the end of the 20th century. Culturally, Secular Buddhism is an instance of Western Buddhism, but it does not fit neatly into the category systems that have been created to understand

Western Buddhism. Scholars have proposed a variety of frameworks for sorting the different forms of Buddhism in Westernized nations into meaningful categories.[1] In some cases the categories are formed on the basis of social groups that have distinct histories, such as immigrant, convert, and natal, or on the basis of the mode of transmission, such as import, export, and baggage.[2] In other instances, the process has been organized chronologically into several processive stages, such as contact, confrontation and conflict, ambiguity and adaptation, recoupment (or reorientation), and innovative self-development.[3] Secular Buddhism, however, does not fit well into any of these established academic categories. While most adherents self-identify as secular, identifying oneself as Buddhist appears to be optional. However, those who do self-identify as Buddhists are not converts in the sense of membership in any of the forms of culturally Asian Buddhism that have developed in the West over the last century and a half. Despite these ambivalences regarding the Buddhist tradition, some Buddhist scholars effectively locate Secular Buddhism within a broad conception of the tradition. Philippe Turenne, for example, sees Secular Buddhism as a source for critical reflection and greater responsiveness to the conditions of contemporary society while at the same time preserving important aspects of the tradition.[4]

HISTORICO-IDEOLOGICAL BACKGROUND

The context within which Secular Buddhism has been created is the modern history of religion in the cultural West. More specifically, it is located in the larger "spiritual but not religious" trends that have molded popular religious culture in the West from the mid-20th century onward. Robert C. Fuller uses the phrase "secular spirituality" and says that "eight central attributes of secular spirituality can be identified: eclecticism, self-growth, relevance to life, self-direction, openness to wonder, authenticity beyond churches, metaphysical explanations, and communal and ecological morality."[5] While Secular Buddhism employs Buddhist concepts, categories, and concerns, seeing it as located within secular spirituality provides a perspective that highlights other sources that contribute to Secular Buddhist discourse.

Viewing Secular Buddhism from "in front," it appears to have originated recently and to be a coherent system of thought and practice. If, however, we go around the back, we find that Secular Buddhism is a bricolage, a structure composed of preexisting elements, appropriated and pasted together, which is not to deny the creativity of the proponents of Secular Buddhism who have constructed it.[6] Those elements constitute the ideological "prehistory" of Secular Buddhism. Both perspectives—front and back—are needed for a full understanding of Secular Buddhism.

The historico-ideological background of Secular Buddhism is organized here under five rubrics: Asian movements to modernize Buddhism, liberal Protestant thought, Victorian apologetics of non-religion, Perennialism, and neoliberal ethics. Each of these has been extensively studied, and here we can only summarize key issues and reference relevant research.

Asian Movements to Modernize Buddhism. The modernization of Buddhism began in Asia in the mid-19th and early 20th centuries, motivated by resistance to European imperialism. "Resistance" is used here, rather than reaction, so as to emphasize the creative agency of those involved. In many cases Buddhist modernizers promoted changes that, looking back, can be described as secular. In some instances, for example, they sought to involve lay members in meditation practice, and some movements were either founded by lay adherents or with significant lay leadership.[7] Other aspects of the modernization include creating a modernized system of thought, that is, ideology, and reforms of the sangha.

An important instance of this modernization is Thailand, where the modernization of Buddhism began under the direction of King Mongkut (r. 1851–1868).[8] Mongkut not only mandated the modernization of monastic education, including training in Pali, and "restructuring the Buddhist order along national political lines," but also promoted a "demythologized and more rationalized Buddhist worldview, while at the same time standardizing Buddhist ritual observances."[9] Other examples include Anagārika Dharmapāla's innovations, such as founding the Mahabodhi Society, as well as Soka Gakkai in Japan, Ambedkar's Buddhist resistance to the Indian caste system, Taixu's creation of a "humanistic Buddhism," and Thailand's Young Buddhist Association.[10] Many of these were explicitly anticolonial in nature, such as the Burmese Vipassana movement largely established by Ledi Sayadaw, which identified being Burmese with being Buddhist in a rhetoric of resistance to British colonialism.[11]

In China, Taixu was a key figure in the modernization of Buddhism in the early 20th century.[12] Like many of the early contributors to the project of modernizing Buddhism, and like many Secular Buddhists today, he appropriated modern science. For example, Taixu suggested that the mythic realm of unlimited abundance, Uttarakuru, is a planet in our solar system. This no doubt seems quaint by the standards of the present, but this problem has always plagued the science and religion discourse. Claims of truth or authority, whether Buddhist or Christian, have sometimes been based on scientific theories, but those theories often then become outdated. The emphasis on the scientific in Secular Buddhist rhetoric is another instance of a strategy that stretches back over a century and a half.

There is no one model of secularization, and the processes involved continue into the present. The scholarship on what is referred to as "multiple secularities" is extensive.[13] Looking at Buddhist instances, we find work on Japan, Tibet, China, and other Asian countries as well.[14]

Liberal Protestant Thought. In the process of resisting the criticisms of Buddhism made by Christian missionaries, modernizing Asian Buddhists adopted many of the critics' conceptions about the nature of religion, which are based in the Liberal Protestant theology of the late 19th century. These conceptions include the ideas of a single historically existing founder with a unique religious revelation recorded in a holy text, who establishes a specific church, usually as a reformer acting in opposition to a corrupt religious tradition burdened by meaningless ritualism and clerical venality. This template for a religion and its religious historiography has its proximate origin in the rhetoric of the Reformation. It was, however, also adopted by Buddhist reformers, to such an extent that the movement was famously dubbed "Protestant Buddhism" by Richard Gombrich and Gananath Obeyesekere.[15] The same themes that pervade post-Reformation Protestant historiography are evident in this quote from the speech given by Anagārika Dharmapāla (1864–1933) at the Chicago Parliament of Religions:

> Twenty-five centuries ago India witnessed an intellectual and religious revolution which culminated in the overthrow of monotheism, priestly selfishness, and the establishment of a synthetic religion, a system of life and thought which was appropriately called

> Dhamma—Philosophical Religion. All that was good was collected from every source and embodied therein, and all that was bad was discarded. Speculation in the domain of false philosophy and theology ceased, and active altruism reigned supreme.[16]

Dharmapāla's tribute to Buddhism also includes the theme of the unity of Buddhism and science, such as claims that the Buddha knew what is only now coming to be understood in science and philosophy, such as evolution and monism.

Another important element in the formation of the ideology of Secular Buddhism is the emphasis on interiority and personal experience. As J. Brent Crosson indicates, "according to a resonant bias of both contemporary SBNR [spiritual but not religious] movements and Reformation polemics, the true core of religion is located in an individual disposition."[17] In the sociology of religion, the phrase "privatization of religion" has sometimes been used to mean the view that it is an individual rather than public matter. For example, José Casanova has referred to the "privatization thesis" as the idea that in secular societies "religious belief is reduced to a private matter, lacking the significance it had previously had in the lives of societies."[18] To clarify the rhetoric of Secular Buddhism, however, it is best to distinguish between this sociological conception of religion as an individual rather than a public matter, and the psychological significance of the idea that the (absolute) foundation of religious commitment is experiential and, as such, is private in the sense that the term private is used in philosophical discourse regarding "private language." For our purposes here, therefore, the privatization of religion refers to the conception that its most important aspect is experiential, that is, a private, transformative experience that individuals claim as a basis for belief and action, including social beliefs and actions. This idea regarding the private character of religion is widespread in Western popular religious culture. This idea of private religious experience also informs the concept of spirituality, and its history. As Ira Helderman has said, "if one looks for it, one can relatively easily detect the Protestant prototype that generates a spirituality of deinstitutionalized, internal religious experience."[19] This Protestant prototype also contributed to the conception of Buddhism in the Victorian era.

Victorian Apologetics: Buddhism as "Non-Religion." Lois Lee employs the category of "non-religion," which she distinguishes as more neutral than "areligious" and "secular."[20] She explains that the characteristics of non-religion are diverse, combining with "religious, spiritual, and secular characteristics in numerous configurations."[21] In particular she highlights an anticlerical attitude, atheistic and nontheistic worldviews, ambivalence about or rejection of religious ritual, and instances of non-religious identification. Jack L. Graham employs Lee's concept of "non-religion" in a study of the Secular Buddhist Association. As background he explores the Victorian rhetoric that created the characterization of religion as irrational and superstitious, and which then understood Buddhism to be rational and therefore non-religious.[22]

The ideological grounding inherited by Secular Buddhism includes the rhetorical claims of 19th-century Buddhist apologists, who promoted a representation of original, true, pure, authentic Buddhism as both essentially rational and actively opposed to the superstitions of Brahmanic ritualism and the caste system. The dichotomy of reason versus superstition is fundamental to the distinction of religion and non-religion, which served to reinforce apologetic descriptions of Buddhism, such as that given by Dharmapāla quoted in the preceding section. Such descriptions emphasized, for example, interpretations of Buddhist teachings as congruent with modern science, while science and religion were in a state of war with one another.[23] The interpretation of Buddhism as atheistic also contributed to its status as non-religion.[24] More important for understanding Secular Buddhism than the specific characteristics is that this Victorian rhetoric establishes a representation of Buddhism in contrast to, and in competition with, the religious studies representation of Buddhism as another instance of the overall category of world religions.[25] In this Victorian image, because Buddhism is rational and nontheistic, it is not a religion.

Perennialism. Buddhist modernism has become widely accepted by both convert and Westernized natal Buddhists as "what Buddhism really is."[26] Often a central component of that representation of Buddhism is the rhetorical distinction between some true, universal core and later culturally determined "religious" trappings. For many in the cultural West, the Buddhist modernist image of Buddhism is simply the true essence of Buddhism, and what doesn't fit into that representation is dismissed as *merely* cultural. This understanding draws on the rhetoric of Perennialism, which promotes an image of all religions as sharing a single universal and ineffable truth, directly revealed to mystical insight, and outside of any particular religious culture. Popularized by Aldous Huxley and propagated widely by Huston Smith, these conceptions of a higher mystical unity of all religions have effectively become a naturalized part of Buddhist modernism.[27] In the rhetoric of Perennialism, the differences between religions are explained by the linguistic and cultural limitations imposed when mystics attempt to convey their ineffable experience to others. The claim that the original, pure, authentic teachings of Śākyamuni Buddha are timeless and ultimately in agreement with all other "wisdom traditions" is directly informed by Perennialist conceptions.[28] Adopted into Secular Buddhism, the rhetoric of Buddhist modernism frequently includes the self-referential claim that it is the universal and unproblematic structure for understanding Buddhism and Buddhist movements.

An example of Perennialist influence is the grounding of the idea of karma in a modernist, psychologized perspective, such as the claim that "in a nutshell karma and rebirth is an explanation for human hurt, the existential problem at the heart of so much of religion, why do we suffer? It is the Buddhist response to the same question that we find in Christianity's original sin."[29] This interpretation of karma and rebirth is an instance of the Perennialist universalism that underlies much of Secular Buddhist rhetoric. Couched here in terms of the presumedly universal existential problem of suffering, the implicit rhetoric is that all religions are ultimately the same—or in this specific case, that Buddhist teachings of karma and rebirth and the Christian concept of original sin simply point to the same existential universal of human hurt. This kind of rhetoric evidences the grounding in Perennialism, which often argues that there is a view that transcends any particular religion but encompasses the wisdom of them all.

Neoliberalism. The context of the rise of Secular Buddhism in the West includes profound changes in Anglo-American society in the last part of the 20th century. These changes can be marked by the elections of Margaret Thatcher and Ronald Reagan in 1979 and 1980, respectively. The ideology that justified those changes is neoliberalism, which has become the unreflectively accepted, hegemonic ideology of the world's economically, militarily, and culturally dominant societies. By the beginning of the 21st century, it had become not simply an economic or social theory, but effectively a cosmology that views everything in terms of "individuals in competition."[30] Competition between individuals is not only seen in economic and social relations but is structured into the legal system and naturalized as explaining the natural world.

In neoliberal societies, individuals are not only seen as being in competition with one another but are isolated agents who primarily express their agency through consumption. This neoliberal subjectivity constructed the modern self-help and pop-psychology industries. These intertwined social institutions are based on the Western ethos of self-improvement and have become multimillion-dollar businesses. Teachings are marketed through books, workshops, training programs, and retreats of various kinds. In the 20th century, this system of marketing was adopted by a variety of Buddhist teachers.[31] The consumer model of the relation between a Buddhist teacher and their audience changes structures of authority—as, for example, away from monastic seniority to experiential accomplishments. Monastic relations of *dana* being given to the sangha have in large part been replaced by customers purchasing services.[32] There is a consequent inversion of power—the consumer holds economic power over which teachings are given value in a competitive marketplace, and therefore demand molds the nature of the teachings presented and the aspects emphasized.

Neoliberal subjectivity contributes not only to a sense of being an isolated individual, but also to splitting the self into a conscious agent, an "I," and the personal object of agency, "myself." The "I" as agent seeks to control the workings of a person's own mind. Self-improvement is embedded in the therapeutic culture that first makes the self into a problem to be solved and then offers solutions in the marketplace of spiritual self-help.[33] In this neoliberal framework, meditation becomes a technology of the mind that is context-free and value-neutral, one that can be excised from its culture of origin without damage to the technology and applied without constraint for the benefit of any and all peoples. As the frequently repeated trope has it, "one doesn't need to be a Buddhist to practice mindfulness."

The treatment of Buddhist practice as a context-free and value-neutral mental technology extends the discourse that treats religion as separable from culture and fails to recognize the cultural basis for this very view. Such a conception of the dharma as existing independently of any particular culture is itself a cultural artifact—a way of conceptually constructing a Buddhism that can then be appropriated and reinterpreted but freed from any entanglement with Asian culture.[34] Secular Buddhism has been criticized for this dynamic of extracting meditation from its cultural context of origin. Acknowledging the issue, the Secular Buddhist Association website published a rebuttal to the effect that this construct of a Buddhism denatured from Asian culture is not intended to denigrate Asian culture but is instead a means of avoiding the historical harm of imperialistic appropriation.[35] Although not made explicit, the implication would seem to be that those forms of Buddhism in the West that do not attempt to expunge Asian cultural aspects are themselves the ones guilty of imperialistic appropriation of a foreign culture.

The ideological prehistory of Secular Buddhism encompasses influences from the mid-19th century through the end of the 20th century. This period saw movements to modernize Asian societies, including their Buddhist cultures, the rise of liberal Protestant thought, an apologetics for Buddhism as an instance of non-religion, the Perennialist doctrine that all religions are ultimately the same, and neoliberal economic and social ideology emphasizing the isolated individual in a competitive world. All these influences were interpreted in the framework of a semiotic opposition of secular and religious.

SEMIOTICS: SECULAR AND RELIGIOUS AS AN OPPOSITIONAL PAIRING

The rhetoric of Secular Buddhism participates in the modern use of the term "secular" as the paired opposite to religious.[36] Helderman describes this pairing, saying "with the two terms placed side by side, the borderline between religion/secular made visible by a backslash or dash, the semiotics of such a construct are clear. The concept visually represents the religious and the not-religious as antonyms, but also as intimately connected."[37] This modern construct reflects the post-Enlightenment conceptions of society as the "neutral" container within which a variety of institutions, including a variety of religions, exist in a state of competition with one another.[38] The rhetorical grounding for some current understandings of the relation is what Helderman has called the "standard secularization narrative" in which "religious traditions, once so central to human society, will be proven false and made obsolete by scientific truths."[39] The idea that "Buddhism is a religion" is itself a modern construct formed out of 19th-century modernity's reconstruction of the social order in which religion is defined narrowly as individual, private, experiential, and morally uplifting but separate from the political and economic.[40] This conception has been exported globally as part of the social order of late modern, neoliberal capitalism, and as such it provides the conceptual basis for the spread of Secular Buddhism to societies participating in that social system. Most presentations of Secular Buddhism distinguish between secular and religious in the minimal oppositional relation: to be secular is to not be religious.[41]

This minimal approach (secular is not-religious) itself, however, requires further nuance. In addition to a transcendent divine, secularism may also reject the idea of the supernatural (forces and agencies not explainable by reference to natural law) and the extraordinary (capacities and powers that are beyond those of an ordinary human).[42] As a concept whose object is constituted by its usage as a social convention, the meaning of the term *secular* varies widely from one social location to another. As Mark Juergensmeyer has explained, "secular" is "a complicated notion, or set of notions that are seen differently in different cultures."[43] In addition to a negative conception, that is, rejecting a transcendent divine, supernatural agencies, and extraordinary humans, "secular" can also be used to identify a positive conception, "a worldview laden with value assumptions about the nature of the self and its relationship to society."[44] Sarah Shaw has provided an informative survey of changing meanings of the term and its derivatives—secular, secularization, secularism.[45] Most often the Secular Buddhist discourse simply presumes the dichotomous nature of secular and religious, which is only rarely explicitly theorized or nuanced.

Despite the rhetorical opposition between secular and religious in Secular Buddhist discourse, in many ways the movement constitutes its own religious tradition, including a set of faith commitments. One of the sharper critics of Secular Buddhism is Glenn Wallis, as found in several posts on his website "Speculative Non-Buddhism" and in his book *A Critique of Western Buddhism: Ruins of the Buddhist Real*.[46] One particular post, titled "On the Faith of

Secular Buddhists," was written as a critique of a presentation made by Stephen Batchelor, perhaps the single most visible proponent of Secular Buddhism.[47] Wallis groups his analysis under five articles of faith that are in his view axiomatic because "they go unchallenged, indeed unquestioned by Secular Buddhists of all stripes, including the secular–scientistic community around Jon Kabat-Zinn." In Wallis's critique these five articles of Secular Buddhist faith undermine any claim that Secular Buddhism constitutes a radical reinterpretation of Buddhism; instead it simply replicates the values and beliefs of the dominant Western religious culture. The first article of faith is that the dharma constitutes a timeless, transcendent truth, beyond conditioned reality. The second is that this timeless dharma was revealed by the human Śākyamuni Buddha, which instances a focus on the founder as the authoritative source of a tradition. Third is the idea that the teachings that can be identified as uniquely those of the founder constitute a pragmatically useful teaching for our time. The self-sufficiency of Buddhism is the notion that one need not look outside the system of Buddhist thought, or in other words, that philosophical and religious sources that pursue the same goals that Secular Buddhism does, but that are not "Buddhist," can be safely ignored. The last of the five articles of faith is that this is not a matter of faith at all, but rather that the Secular Buddhist view is simply "*natural, empirical, pragmatic,* and *in accord with science.* The teachings, as the ancient trope has it, are simply *how things are.* They are *phenomenologically* obvious."[48]

In contrast, Sarah Shaw argues that the developments of Buddhism in the contemporary world, such as secular mindfulness practice, are a continuation of the universalism that has been part of the Buddhist tradition from its earliest period. Citing the work of Peter Skilling, she explains that the universalism of Buddhism "is framed as the wish for ourselves and others to find happiness and freedom, and it informs the Buddhist approach to a sensibly balanced transmission in many languages, together with the promotion of tolerance, shared cultures, and new technologies."[49]

THE DISCOURSE OF SECULAR BUDDHISM: TWO COMPLEMENTARY ASPECTS

Secular Buddhism can be understood under two complementary, though not opposed, approaches: a positive understanding, that is, what its proponents desire to create, and a negative one, that is, being constituted by what it is not.

Creating a New Buddhism. Sometimes Secular Buddhism is represented as being a new form of Buddhism relevant to the modern world, while other representations claim that, being a return to the original teachings and practices of the Buddha Śākyamuni, it is a purification of the tradition. A pragmatic intent to understand the teachings and practices as useful in the present, however, unifies both approaches. Winton Higgins argues that contemporary secularity is "a complex and frequently misunderstood *religio-cultural development* in the West."[50] With this sense of secularism as a cultural development in mind, he asserts that "Secular Buddhism's specific reason for being is to participate in that cultural development in aid of the dharma practice of those embedded in it, while situating itself in the Buddha's living (as opposed to sedimented) tradition of practice and thought."[51]

One of the sources actively making Secular Buddhist views available is *Tricycle* magazine. *Tricycle: the Buddhist Review* was initiated in 1991 under the editorship of Helen Tworkov and presents itself as a nonsectarian medium for Western Buddhists. As of 2021, it has expanded as an online project including dharma talks, a film club, e-books, a podcast, and online courses, in addition to the magazine itself.[52] In an explanatory section of the Tricycle website, a series of articles titled "Buddhism for Beginners" present Secular Buddhism in a systematically codified fashion. Several of the ideas presented there can be traced to earlier arguments by specific figures, such as Stephen Batchelor and Winton Higgins, though without attribution. Included is a normative view, as, for example, in the claims that:

> While secular dharma practitioners have been connected with a range of Buddhist lineages, and none, secular dharma is a development out of certain modernizing trends within different schools of Buddhism. A secular space is open-minded and tolerant and does not discriminate on the basis of ethnicity, gender, ability, beliefs, or faith. Those who engage with a secular dharma community are not required to adopt metaphysical beliefs or become involved in activities generally associated with religion, Buddhist or otherwise, such as chanting or praying.[53]

The Secular Buddhist Network makes its own set of claims, saying that:

> While all secular Buddhists share a skeptical view of the supernatural deities and processes of traditional Buddhism (e.g., rebirth), there is a wide range of views among secular Buddhists concerning various beliefs, perspectives and practices.
>
> Even though there is no secular Buddhist orthodoxy, all secular Buddhists share a framework for a more mindful and compassionate life.
>
> Awakening in the context in which we find ourselves, this framework is in essence a pragmatic program for human flourishing that has no use for metaphysical beliefs and religious truth-claims. A secular dharma stands for a developmental direction that is typically Buddhist in its open-minded skepticism and its desire to let the dharma speak most effectively, that is in culturally available terms.[54]

While the assertion that "there is no secular Buddhist orthodoxy" is widely repeated, like the claim that Secular Buddhism does not include any social hierarchy, it is a rhetorical claim that plays a key role in the Secular Buddhist discourse.

The constructive motivation for Secular Buddhism is evidenced by "Ten Theses of Secular Dharma," which are abstracted from Stephen Batchelor's book *After Buddhism* and posted on the Secular Buddhist Association website.[55] These are:

1. A secular Buddhist is one who is committed to the practice of the dharma for the sake of this world alone.
2. The practice of the dharma consists of four tasks: to embrace suffering, to let go of reactivity, to behold the ceasing of reactivity, and to cultivate an integrated way of life.
3. All human beings, irrespective of gender, race, sexual orientation, disability, nationality, and religion, can practice these four tasks. Each person, in each moment, has the potential to be more awake, responsive, and free.
4. The practice of the dharma is as much concerned with how one speaks, acts, and works in the public realm as with how one performs spiritual exercises in private.

5. The dharma serves the needs of people at specific times and places. Each form the dharma assumes is a transient human creation, contingent upon the historical, cultural, social, and economic conditions that generated it.
6. The practitioner honors the dharma teaching[s] that have been passed down through different traditions while seeking to enact them creatively in ways appropriate to the world as it is now.
7. The community of practitioners is formed of autonomous persons who mutually support each other in the cultivation of their paths. In this network of like-minded individuals, members respect the equality of all members while honoring the specific knowledge and expertise each person brings.
8. A practitioner is committed to an ethics of care, founded on empathy, compassion, and love for all creatures who have evolved on this earth.
9. Practitioners seek to understand and diminish the structural violence of societies and institutions as well as the roots of violence that are present in themselves.
10. A practitioner of the dharma aspires to nurture a culture of awakening that finds its inspiration in Buddhist and non-Buddhist, religious and secular sources alike.[56]

While including a page devoted to Batchelor's ten theses, the Secular Buddhist Association offers its own definition.[57] That definition, however, is framed in terms of what Secular Buddhism is not, that is, critiquing the old Buddhism. The first of the two definitional claims relates to the often interconnected pair of doctrines, karma/kamma and rebirth.

Critiquing the Old Buddhism. The negative definition, "Secular Buddhism is a Buddhism that is not religious," locates Secular Buddhism in a semiotic opposition with religious Buddhism, both terms then being constructed dialectically by the oppositional relation between the two.[58] Dating from the second half of the 19th century, the modern concept of "religion" constructed "Buddhism" as it has come to be conceived in both popular and academic cultures since that time. It is this modern conception of Buddhism that Secular Buddhists often seem to mean by categories such as "religious Buddhism," "traditional Buddhism," or "ancestral Buddhism," and to which they define themselves in opposition. This oppositional relation takes place on multiple levels. Superficially there is the rejection of what are conventionally referred to as the "trappings" of religion. More deeply, Secular Buddhists question a wide variety of beliefs, values, and practices they associate with religious Buddhism.

The Secular Buddhist Association's self-definition begins negatively, by calling into question the common Buddhist teachings of karma and rebirth. Karma, translated literally as "action," is generally taken by both traditional sources and academic scholarship as central to Buddhist thought. It is frequently interpreted moralistically and has been linked to the idea of rebirth in one of the six realms of existence: humans, demi-gods, gods, hungry ghosts, animals, and hell-beings.[59] Most Secular Buddhist adherents simultaneously reject the teaching of rebirth and consider the Pali canon authoritative. As the Pali canon as a whole includes numerous references to rebirth, the consequence is a need for textual criticism, as a lay practice rather than an academic one.[60] The apparent contradiction is resolved by a kind of textual fundamentalism that selects only some texts from the Pali canon as authentic teachings of Śākyamuni. In some cases the process of selection simply reflects the preconceived ideas that the teachings are rational and eschew superstition, that is, the ones selected are those that reinforce the preconceived view.

Matching the ethical interpretation of rebirth is the moralistic interpretation of karma in which only actions with moral significance are considered to have an effect on one's status in one's next birth, and actions in that birth determine one's status in the following as well—the cycle of saṃsara from birth through sickness and old age to death. In many interpretations, the moral valence of karma is determined by one's intentions and is symbolically framed in terms of the "three poisons" (*triviṣa*). The Secular Buddhist Association's self-definition emphasizes an agnostic attitude toward the teaching of rebirth:

> 1. We allow questioning of a literal interpretation of rebirth.
>
> A minority of Secular Buddhists believe in literal rebirth. More believe in non-literal rebirth (i.e., that we are reborn from moment to moment). Many are "agnostic" on rebirth (i.e., that belief or non-belief in literal rebirth does affect the truth and power of the rest of Gautama Buddha's teachings as they have been transmitted—both belief and non-belief can be valid). By allowing such questioning and exploration without excluding questioners and explorers, we allow for more and ultimately deeper engagement with the Dhamma.[61]

Although given in this self-definition as a kind of agnosticism, much of Secular Buddhist rhetoric does tend to reject the idea of rebirth, particularly when rebirth is treated as central to the Buddha's teachings, and therefore a necessary marker of Buddhist identity.[62] Displacing rebirth from its historically central place in the tradition, Batchelor for example theorizes that it was merely part of the common worldview of Vedic India and was not necessarily supported by the Buddha himself. Any reference to rebirth in the Pali canon is then bracketed as an expression of the Buddha's cultural context, rather than central to his own teachings.[63]

Consequently, Secular Buddhists either reject the idea of karma along with rebirth or reinterpret it as well. One view

> reinterprets these [karma and rebirth] as processes which take place within a single lifetime i.e. given The Buddha's teaching on Dependent Origination, we are in a constant process of incarnation/reincarnation during our lifetimes. Karma is understood to mean that every thought or act will leave an impression on our mind or to some degree effect [*sic*] a previously made impression.[64]

Another line of reinterpretation is to replace "the ideas of karma and rebirth with more useful ideas on purpose and ethics."[65] By naturalizing karma and rebirth in this fashion, any reference to the "supernatural" is avoided.

In an interview appearing in *Tricycle* magazine, Batchelor also gives a negative definition of Secular Buddhism by contrasting it with other forms of Buddhism:

> So what sort of Buddhism does a self-declared secular Buddhist like myself advocate? For me, secular Buddhism is not just another modernist reconfiguration of a traditional form of Asian Buddhism. It is neither a reformed Theravāda Buddhism (like the

> Vipassana movement), a reformed Tibetan tradition (like Shambhala Buddhism), a reformed Nichiren school (like the Soka Gakkai), a reformed Zen lineage (like the Order of Interbeing) nor a reformed hybrid of some or all of the above (like the Triratna Order, formerly the Friends of the Western Buddhist Order). It is more radical than any of these: it seeks to return to the roots of the Buddhist tradition and rethink Buddhism from the ground up.[66]

Another approach to defining Secular Buddhism in terms of what is rejected is found on the website "Secular Buddhism. No Robes. No Ritual. No Religion."[67] The range of new social institutions supporting the movement (see the section "Institutionalizing Secular Buddhism") is evidenced by this site, which was created by Rick Bateman to serve a weekly Secular Buddhist meeting group.[68] The home page for the site gives a concise summary statement of the site creator's own conception of what Secular Buddhism is not:

> Secular Buddhism is a non-religious form of Buddhism unique to the West. Tradition, robes and ritual are absent as are non-English terms. It is devoid of authority through title or lineage. It is atheistic i.e. there is no consideration of the supernatural or reincarnation. Karma is considered only in the sense the word as commonly used in English of one's intentions, actions and their results in this life....
>
> It is not however simply a New Age mash-up of spirituality. It is still primarily focused on the study and practice of the Buddhism's core teachings of The Four Noble Truths and The EightFold Path. It is, if anything, an attempt to return to the original teachings of The Buddha.[69]

As with Batchelor's statement quoted earlier, notice here again the claim of returning to the original teachings of Śākyamuni.

For some Secular Buddhists there is also a rhetorical identification of religion with the corrupt exercise of power in an anticlerical stance congruent with Reformation-era attacks on the established Church. Implicitly, this entails an inverse claim that because Secular Buddhism is not religious, it does not have the kind of authoritarian power relations that facilitate sexual exploitation, financial manipulation, and other abuses of power.

For example, employing one of the most clichéd critiques leveled against "traditional" Buddhism—that it is not actually Buddhism in the sense of the essential teachings of the Buddha—Sam Harris, a popularizer of atheistic views who writes on Buddhism, has asserted that "the wisdom of the Buddha is currently trapped with the religion of Buddhism."[70] Harris goes on to employ the trope that "traditional" Buddhists are mistaken about what they are doing, saying that "most Buddhists worldwide" engage with Buddhism as a religion "in many of the naïve, petitionary, and superstitious ways in which all religions are practiced." Indeed, Harris argues that it is "morally and intellectually indefensible" for Buddhists to continue to identify with Buddhism as a religion as it "lends tacit support to the religious differences in our world." Harris represents "religion" as the source of conflict and as insistently dogmatic, for example when he says that "given the degree to which religion still inspires human conflict, and impedes genuine inquiry, I believe that merely being a self-described 'Buddhist' is to be complicit in the world's violence and ignorance to an unacceptable degree."

The desire to create a kind of Buddhism that meets the needs of modern people is the positive, constructive dimension of Secular Buddhism. Secular Buddhism is, therefore, a complex social phenomenon that can in part be understood as being modeled on other kinds of quasi-religious institutions found throughout Western popular religious culture, such as self-help and pop psychology. Those social institutions also provided vehicles for the promotion of Secular Buddhism. Despite drawing both form and content from self-help and pop psychology, Secular Buddhism is more complex than simply a version of either of those expressed in Buddhist language.

The negative understanding of Secular Buddhism does not provide the kinds of sharp delineations, either conceptual or sociological, that might be expected of a definition. Taken together with the positive understandings, the two do, however, serve as a way of identifying Secular Buddhism as a discourse, that is, a loosely interconnected and mutually supporting set of beliefs, claims, and assertions that offer a convincing view of the human, the social, the environmental, and the cosmological. Secular Buddhism not only functions as a discourse but has a variety of institutional forms.

INSTITUTIONALIZING SECULAR BUDDHISM

Secular Buddhism has moved beyond simply being a matter of personal beliefs and personal identity to the creation of Secular Buddhist institutions. Though there are claims of authority over the movement, as of 2020 it had no central authority, and the institutional forms of Secular Buddhism are varied.[71] These include websites oriented toward interested individuals, groups with formal membership, affiliated publishers, YouTube video series, books and online literature, and educational institutions. Institutionalization also necessarily involves strategies for claiming authority, which include personal experience, the rhetoric of original and authentic, a kind of selective textual fundamentalism focused on texts from the Pali canon, and claiming an identity between Buddhism and science.[72]

Communities: Into the Virtual. Superficially, Secular Buddhism may seem to be an international phenomenon. While proponents of Secular Buddhism can be found across the globe including in Asia, affiliated institutions and organizations are primarily located in the United Kingdom, Europe, and the United States, and additionally Australia and New Zealand.[73] A different perspective, however, reveals that it is largely located in countries where Protestant religious culture is dominant.[74] John Torpey makes a distinction between active and latent religiosity that is useful in understanding this fact.

Active religion is the sort of piety that one observes in houses of worship, at religious festivals and pilgrimages, and in the everyday religious practices of the faithful. Latent religion, by contrast, manifests itself more subtly, especially through the organization of public space and time, but also in terms of the sensibilities underlying particular regions and states.[75]

Protestant religious culture is the latent religiosity that conditions the reception of Secular Buddhism. Rather than being universal in its appeal, therefore, its own cultural accretions appear to somewhat limit its outreach beyond those societies whose religious culture has been formed by modern Protestant thought. This cultural location is not to be confused with racial location. While historically many of the media-familiar figures are white, the Secular Buddhist

Association highlights the importance of BIPOC (Black, Indigenous, People of Color) Buddhists among Secular Buddhist sanghas. In the FAQ section of the Secular Buddhist Association website, Jennifer Hawkins points out that the membership of Secular Buddhist sanghas is reflective of the communities in which they are located.[76] The Association also actively provides support for a variety of constituencies, including, for example, meetings in Spanish (eSangha eSpañol).

The advent of online communities has created different kinds of institutional structures, ones that are geographically diffuse and decentralized. Even before the move of so many Buddhist groups to the web in response to the COVID-19 pandemic, many Secular Buddhists actively engaged with digital media as a means of facilitating practice and community. Use of web-based platforms as well as their own websites has created the opportunity for previously local Secular Buddhist groups to establish an increasingly global presence. In 2017, for example, a New Zealand–based Secular Buddhist teacher, Ramsey Margolis, initiated an online group meditation using Zoom called "Online, Together, Meditating, Secular."[77] This was modeled on other Secular Buddhist Association events, known as "Practice Circles." According to the report on the Secular Buddhist Association website, those in attendance for the first session were evenly balanced by gender, located not only in New Zealand but also Australia, Austria, and the United States, and constituted an ethnically diverse group.

This trend toward online activities accelerated during the COVID-19 pandemic and continued into 2021. Events hosted online have facilitated much wider outreach. For example, the Secular Buddhist Network began hosting online meetings via Zoom, and the first of these in January 2021 included some forty-one participants from Costa Rica, Ireland, the United Kingdom, New Zealand, France, Australia, Germany, Canada, and the United States.[78] Whether this will continue after the pandemic fades is of course an open question. The range of Secular Buddhist institutions goes beyond meditation groups, either online or in person. The Secular Buddhist Association, for example, has a series of blog posts by Doug Smith, which are also available on his YouTube channel.[79]

Education: Academic and Informal. While some Secular Buddhists appear to hold a negative view of the academic study of Buddhism, Bodhi College (located in Totnes, between Exeter and Plymouth on the south coast of England) has embraced an academic model of instruction. Founded by Stephen and Martine Batchelor, Bodhi College is explicitly oriented toward a secularized understanding of Buddhism and offers an educational program that integrates both theory and practice in accord with the present-day model of contemplative education.[80] The curriculum is structured according to three categories: "Bodhi College courses encompass meditative learning *(suta)*, critical examination *(cintā)* and practical cultivation *(bhāvanā)* of the Dharma as found in the early strata of Buddhist texts."[81] This approach is presented as a middle-way approach that is, therefore, congruent with the teachings of Śākyamuni Buddha. In keeping with Secular Buddhist ideas more generally, the curriculum focuses on the sutta and vinaya sections of the Pali canon and excepts the abhidhamma.[82] This exclusive focus on the study of sutta and vinaya in Pali is augmented only by study of these sections in other canonic and paracanonic languages. The program description actively embraces the Secular Buddhist rhetoric of focusing on the "original" teachings of the Buddha, compared to which the rest of the Buddhist tradition is derivative: "The College's inspiration stems from the Dharma as found in the earliest Buddhist texts, which underlies many of the contemporary forms of meditation—such as mindfulness and vipassana."[83]

During 2020, Bodhi College rescheduled its courses and retreats into an online format, and this continued in 2021. While motivated by the COVID-19 pandemic then affecting both Britain and Europe, this shift to online instruction is congruent with a preexisting engagement with technology found throughout the Secular Buddhist community. In contrast to the long-standing Buddhist modernist trope that meditation is the only requirement for awakening, and that any pedagogy can be an impediment, Bodhi College emphasizes the value of "an in-depth exploration of these teachings [from the early Buddhist canon] that is not usually possible in a traditional silent retreat setting."[84]

Another kind of institution that is a vehicle for Secular Buddhism is online instruction programs now offered by some Buddhist publications. For example, although starting out as a glossy print magazine, *Tricycle: The Buddhist Review* has recreated itself as an online presence, including articles, e-books, podcasts, a film club, and online courses. One course offered through Tricycle by Stephen and Martine Batchelor employs the name "Secular Dharma." The course description highlights several Secular Buddhist themes:

> The Buddha's teachings—the dharma—arose in a very different world from the one we live in today. This pragmatic online course sets out an encompassing vision for understanding and practicing dharma in the contemporary world. At its heart is an easy acronym we can all learn to apply, ELSA: Embrace, Let go, See, and Act. Join Stephen and Martine Batchelor as they clarify the core elements of Buddhist thought and meditation practice for the way we live today.[85]

The goal of the course is described using the kind of rhetorical contrast that we have noted already: "human flourishing rather than the attainment of 'enlightenment'," with even the scare quotes around the term enlightenment indicating a pejorative view of the goal of Buddhism as traditionally understood.[86] Beyond the online resources already mentioned, other informal educational platforms include Noah Rasheta's (author of *No-Nonsense Buddhism for Beginners*) Secular Buddhism website and podcast and Bernat Font's Spanish-language site, budismosecular.org.[87] The creation of institutions separate from traditional ones simultaneously entails a need for creating alternative ways of claiming authority.

Claiming Authority. One of the noteworthy aspects of the development of Secular Buddhism is the strategic shifts in how claims to authority are made. The originally rather anarchic situation has already shifted, however, such that traditional sources of authority, for example monastic status, seniority, and academic training, have largely been displaced by claims based on meditative experience, a claim to represent the true original teachings of the Buddha, the authority of selected texts from the Pali canon, and identifying Secular Buddhism with science. One way to understand these changes is that they evidence the role of the marketplace in molding the presentation of Secular Buddhism in the mode of self-help programs. These shifts have not taken place without contestation, however, nor have the other types of claims to authority disappeared from the broader Buddhist world.

The Authority of Experience. For over two and a half millennia the transmission of authority within Buddhism has depended on the monastic institutions that originated with the community that formed around Śākyamuni Buddha. Sources in the Pali canon that describe the order include four basic groups of adherents: monks (*bhikkhus*), nuns (*bhikkhunīs*), male lay adherents, and female lay adherents.[88] Like much of modern Western popular religious culture following the Reformation, however, some Secular Buddhists reject or at least question the institutionalized authority of monastic lineages, holding a critical attitude toward monks that is reminiscent of Reformation-era anticlericalism.[89] Rather than seniority as an initiated member of the sangha, cumulative meditative experience and training is often treated as the primary measure of authority. While historically many of the proponents of Secular Buddhism had some monastic training, the rise of educational and training programs separate from monastic ones means that the next generation of leaders may not.

The emphasis on the authority of direct experience, a theme found throughout Western religious culture since the Enlightenment, provides a congenial context for a pragmatic understanding of the teachings, and more radically to a pragmatic conception of truth. Wiggins, for example, explains that in contrast to a correspondence theory of truth, "truth refers to ethical, practical outcomes. A *true statement* is one that points the way to human flourishing through skilful ethical practice."[90] Wiggins argues for seeing this claim as congruent with the anti-metaphysical stream of Western thought traceable to the work of Friedrich Nietzsche (1844–1900).

The Authority of the Original. Another strategy for claiming authority frequently employed by Secular Buddhists is the rhetorical conflation of original, pure, and authoritative. This is usually expressed in a form such as *the original teachings of the Buddha Śākyamuni are pure of any later corruptions, and therefore it is these teachings that are authoritative.* The website for Bodhi College, a Secular Buddhist educational institution discussed in the section "Education: Academic and Informal," asserts that "our courses draw on the early teachings of the Buddha before they became codified into the doctrines of the different Buddhist traditions."[91] One of the consistent post-Reformation themes reflected here is that it is later sectarianism that obscures or corrupts the original, pure, and authoritative teachings of the Buddha Śākyamuni. Indeed, the slogan of Bodhi College is "Early Buddhist Teaching for Today."[92]

The Authority of Textual Selectivity. A consistent theme throughout much of Secular Buddhist discourse is the identification of the Pali canon with the original teachings of the Buddha. Indeed, one at times encounters the idea that the Buddha spoke Pali.[93] While there are a variety of positions taken within the Secular Buddhist community regarding the status of specific texts and the canon generally, a consistent dynamic is selectivity, that is, selecting those parts of the Pali canon that are congruent with secular preconceptions, rather than accepting the whole of the canon as authoritative.

The Secular Buddhist movement is diverse, and even an exclusive commitment to the Pali canon is not universal among Secular Buddhists despite its dominance in the discourse. For example, the fifth definitional statement of the "Secular Buddhism: No Robes. No Ritual. No Religion" website is that "Secular Buddhism recognizes all Buddhist writings, from the Pali Cannon [*sic*] to contemporary works, save those based on concepts of theism and rebirth."[94] In other words, a determination is made in advance as to what the authoritative teachings are not—those with any kind of "theism," presumably characterizations of the Buddha as more than simply a human teacher, and rebirth. Selectively excluding those texts leaves a working corpus that reaffirms the preexisting judgments as to what Buddhism "really" is.

The Authority of Science. As Wakoh Shannon Hickey has noted, "modernist religious movements reinterpret and reform traditional religious doctrines and practices for modern circumstances, adapting them particularly to contemporary scientific understandings of the world."[95] Claiming congruence with science has in many cases manifested as asserting that the Buddha's teachings are identical with, anticipate, or are explained by modern science, and an emphasis on rationality as the standard for reinterpreting the dharma for a contemporary audience is central to Secular Buddhist discourse.[96] This interpretive strategy has a long history in the modern representations of Buddhism to Western audiences. Because both Buddhism and science are socially constructed categories, the relation between the two is malleable. Ira Helderman points out "that all these imagined relationships between religion and science show themselves to be intrinsically unstable."[97]

The claim to be scientific, rational, or empirical is frequently encountered in Secular Buddhist discourse. For example, according to one self-definition, Secular Buddhism "is scientific. It is based solely on the natural laws of cause and effect."[98] This is matched by an epistemological claim that Secular Buddhism "is empirical. Personal experience and direct validation are the only authority." Taken together, these statements indicate a pre-critical, Baconian conception of science. In this view, there is no consideration of the socially constructed nature of science, nor any explicit discrimination between science as method and as content. A more nuanced understanding is, however, offered by Higgins, along with a distinction between two different cultural styles within Secular Buddhism.

In Higgins's analysis, Secular Buddhism as found in the United States is a form of scientistic atheism, that is, a view in accord with Anglo-American or analytic philosophy with its emphasis on truth claims. Higgins contrasts this "scientistic" version of Secular Buddhism with a version he calls "interpretive" and that he sees as more aligned with Continental philosophy. "Brutally summarised, the first of these pursues *knowledge* in the form of truth-claims, and prioritises metaphysics and epistemology; whereas the second pursues *wisdom* and embraces such post-metaphysical schools as phenomenology, existentialism and pragmatism."[99] Higgins goes on to show how the relation between science and Buddhism has changed over time, and that the current commitment to cognitive science understood broadly is simply the latest manifestation.[100]

Buddhism's romance with Western natural science has waxed and waned since it first received the accolade of "scientific religion." But now it's waxing again around neuroscience, genetics and genomics, once more on the basis of a supposedly shared interest in the human mind. The findings of these now heavily commercialised branches of science are contested, but also hyped and oversold, often with Buddhists' help.[101]

In this way the Secular Buddhist claim to be scientific is not simply an epistemological position but simultaneously claims the authority that science holds in contemporary Euro-American society. The ability to produce quantifiable changes in brain activity correlated with positive emotions has been taken as proof of the utility of meditation.[102] Robert Wright's work *Why Buddhism Is True: The Science and Philosophy of Meditation and Enlightenment* also exemplifies this strategy.[103] Viewed critically, Wright's work may be seen as a circular argument (a *petitio principii* fallacy) on the grounds that he reinterprets Buddhism so as to accord with modern science, specifically evolutionary psychology, and then says that this Buddhism is true because it is supported by science. More generously, he may be seen as creating a convergence between two distinct fields by emphasizing the similarities of specific parts of each: a naturalistic interpretation of Buddhism, and evolutionary psychology.

SUMMARY: LATOUR'S FOUR TRACES

The work of Bruno Latour on group formation provides a framework within which we can summarize Secular Buddhism as it exists at the beginning of the third decade of the 21st century. Latour describes group formation as a process having four elements: "groups are made to talk; anti-groups are mapped; new resources are fetched so as to make their boundaries more durable; and professionals with their highly specialized paraphernalia are mobilized."[104] These four—spokespersons, defining anti-groups, defining groups, and second-order spokespersons—constitute the "traces left by the formation of groups."[105] All four of these "traces" reveal important aspects of the ongoing process of group formation in Secular Buddhism.

Several figures have been identified as spokespersons, figures who are either self-identified as Secular Buddhists or are identified as such by other proponents. Speaking on his own behalf, one individual proponent specifically described Secular Buddhism by identifying spokespersons, apparently presuming the reader is already familiar with the style of Buddhism each represents:

> Secular Buddhism is an informal term used to describe a style of Buddhism most similar to that practiced and advocated by modern American or European Buddhists such as Jack Kornfield, Stephen Hagen, Sharon Salzberg, Joeseph [*sic*] Goldstein, Joko Beck and Stephen Batchelor.[106]

In the first trace, the newly forming group is given voice. Latour explains that "first, to delineate a group, no matter if it has to be created from scratch or simply refreshed, you have to have spokespersons which 'speak for' the group existence—and sometimes are very talkative."[107]

Defining anti-groups is the second trace of the process of group formation. In the case of Secular Buddhism, displacing existing forms of authority, whether monastic, temple, or academic, necessitates defining them as the anti-group. While much Secular Buddhist rhetoric includes claims of opposing the authority of established Buddhism on the grounds that it is decadent, abusive, or oppressive, at the same time these claims comprise a strategy of claiming authority for oneself.

The anti-group for Secular Buddhism is variously identified, and Latour notes that actors "engage in criticizing other agencies accused of being fake, archaic, absurd, irrational, artificial or illusory. In the same way group performation maps out for the benefit of the enquirer the anti-groups making up their social world, accounts of agency will constantly add new entities while *withdrawing* others as illegitimate."[108]

The anti-group for Secular Buddhism has been named variously. Some authors use the phrase "traditional Buddhism" to signify both Asian antecedents and, in some usages, forms that, having originated in Asia, developed in Europe and the United States over the course of the 20th century. Another phrase employed in this oppositional rhetoric is "ancestral Buddhism," used for example by Higgins.[109] One of his assertions highlights the role of such categories as semiotic opposites, rather than as empirically descriptive. For example, Higgins asserts that "for most Asian Buddhists, both those who have stayed at home and those who have migrated to the West and joined ethnic diasporas, ancestral Buddhist life and observance persevere largely untouched by modern innovations."[110] This description is inaccurate for both groups—those who stayed home and those who migrated. The image serves, however, the longstanding colonialist rhetoric of opposition between the passive, unchanging, pastoral, feminine, and conservative East, and the active, progressive, industrial, masculine, and modernizing West. Such representations are not only inaccurate but can be considered self-serving, patronizing, and antagonistic. These categories, such as traditional or ancestral, constitute part of a pattern of rhetorical oppositions, ones used not as empirically informed sociological or historical descriptors, but instead creating the anti-group.

Deploying semiotically oppositional pairs in the construction of anti-groups is, of course, not limited to Secular Buddhists, as for example when Secular Buddhist rhetoric in turn molds responses in conformity with the oppositional relation. One instance of this reflexivity is Bhikkhu Bodhi's distinction between Secular Buddhism and what he calls "Classical Buddhism."[111] As characterized by Bodhi, Secular Buddhism is distinguished by its focus on the present "existential situation" of the human being, without recourse to "non-naturalistic assumptions." Thus, samsara is interpreted as our present suffering, rather than pointing to repeated rebirth as in Classical Buddhism. This interpretive strategy is then also extended to the concept of nirvana. In Bodhi's characterization, Secular Buddhists

> interpret the idea of samsara as a metaphor depicting our ordinary condition of bewilderment and addictive pursuits. The secular programme thus re-envisions the goal of Buddhist practice, rejecting the idea of irreversible liberation from the cycle of rebirths in favour of a tentative, ever-fragile freedom from distress in this present life.[112]

Bodhi's oppositional evaluation continues through additional topics central to Buddhist thought, which he identifies as "the Buddha, the Dharma, and the Sangha." The oppositional structuring initiated by Secular Buddhists rejecting what they describe as religious Buddhism also then structures responses to Secular Buddhism. This dynamic replicates the relation between the criticisms of Buddhism made by Christian missionaries in the 19th century and the construction of a response to that criticism by Buddhist apologists in the form of Buddhist modernism. Whatever it is called, the anti-group is often created by projection, that is, like Jung's concept of the Shadow, or Said's concept of the exotic Other, the negative qualities, characteristics, practices one wishes to assert are not one's own are then projected onto the other.

The third trace is the creation of new groups, and the boundaries of those groups made durable. The several Secular Buddhist institutions, such as the Secular Buddhist Association, serve to consolidate a group identity. The Secular Buddhist Network also actively works to create community and maintains a list of local communities, groups, and centers.[113] The website encourages viewers to add their own local group to the listings.

Professionals, or what Latour also calls "second-order spokespersons," reify the group, constituting the fourth trace. They first lend an aura of actuality. In this case, the aura of actuality is created by the repeated assertion, either explicit or implicit, that Secular Buddhism is an actual thing and not just a passing curiosity. Second, at the same time, these representations give Secular Buddhism legitimacy, the status of being a valid option. Latour specifically points to academics and journalists as second-order spokespersons. For him, "any study of any group by any social scientist is part and parcel of what makes the group exist, last, decay or disappear."[114] Thus, not only interviews appearing in popular Buddhist magazines, but also book reviews and essays in professional journals, book-length monographs, and entries in encyclopedias, such as this one, contribute to the aura of actuality and legitimacy.[115]

CONCLUSION

The negative formation of Secular Buddhism semiotically binds it not only to religious Buddhism but also to "religion" more generally, and therefore with two other concepts that constellate the meaning of Secular Buddhism, superstition and science.[116] Like the oppositional relation between secular and religious, there is an oppositional relation between science and superstition. This in turn creates a double semiotic pairing of secular with science, and religion with superstition. Thus, the rejection of aspects of the Buddhist tradition identified as superstition is an essential part of the negative definition of Secular Buddhism. In clearing away those parts of the Buddhist tradition understood as inhibiting its useful application in the present, this negative, or critical aspect of Secular Buddhist discourse is the inverse of the intent to create a new form of Buddhism that is useful of people in the present day.

Secular Buddhism is a rapidly changing and developing phenomenon. One of the more significant developments in contemporary Western Buddhism is what Ann Gleig has called postmodern forms of Buddhism. Her research points to recent developments within the groups that she refers to as "American Buddhist meditation-based convert lineages."[117] While there is some overlap with Secular Buddhism, these developments point to "an increasing interrogation of Buddhist modernism" as such, and a range of postmodern forms.[118] One possible future trajectory for Secular Buddhism would be a fuller integration with postmodern interpretations of Buddhist teachings and practices.

It should be noted that as of 2021 the Secular Buddhist movement is not formally institutionalized and continues to change and develop. This article is therefore simply a "snapshot" of its developmental trajectory.

REVIEW OF LITERATURE

The study of Secular Buddhism is a new field, but a collection of essays edited by Richard K. Payne, *Secularizing Buddhism: New Perspectives on a Dynamic Tradition*, provides an academic overview.[119] In addition to the introductory survey, the volume includes twelve essays by scholars and practitioners on the topic. Moreover, the *Journal of Global Buddhism* has published half a dozen essays on the topic; see in particular those by Winton Higgins, Jørn Borup, Stephen Batchelor, and David Bubna-Litic and Winton Higgins.[120] An important critique of Western Buddhism, including in its secularized forms, is by Glenn Wallis.[121]

Although the academic study of Secular Buddhism is not well advanced, each of the several themes discussed in this article does have its own literature, some of it quite extensive. Consequently we are here selective regarding which sources provide the most relevant orientation to the topic. The topics are secularity/secularization, including the modern conception of society as a neutral container of different religions, and the category of world religions; Protestant Buddhism and Buddhist modernism; the culture of self-help, including the secularized version of Buddhist meditation under the rubric of mindfulness; and the multiplicity of secularities.

The literature on secularism/secularity is expansive and continues to grow. A comprehensive treatment is provided by Phil Zuckerman and John R. Shook, *The Oxford Handbook of Secularism*.[122] Talal Asad, an anthropologist who has been influential for the study of religion, has produced a volume examining the relation between the concepts of the secular, secularism, and secularization, which provides detailed nuancing between the religious, social, political, and historical dimensions of these concepts.[123] The creation of the modern conception of society as a neutral container of different religious traditions has been examined by Timothy Fitzgerald.[124] Application of the religious-secular binary to Buddhism is based on the idea that Buddhism is a religion, a way of treating Buddhism that originated in the formation of the category of world religions.[125]

The phrase "Protestant Buddhism" was employed by Richard Gombrich and Gananath Obeyesekere to describe the kind of Buddhist modernism that was created in Sri Lanka from the latter part of the 19th century.[126] This classic continues to be of value for understanding the history of Buddhist modernism as the background to Secular Buddhism. Heinz Bechert established the category of Buddhist modernism in 1966.[127] More recently, David L. McMahan has produced both a monograph and a collection of essays devoted to the topic.[128] Most usages of the category in Buddhist studies literature now follow from McMahan's formulation.

The culture of self-help and pop psychology has been very formative for Secular Buddhism, and the best single study is by Eva Illouz, who explains the important role of psychology in Western popular culture.[129] The psychologization of popular religious culture, particularly in the form of self-help, is the context for Buddhism in the West. As a secularized version of Buddhist meditation, mindfulness has attracted a great deal of scholarly attention. Jeff Wilson provides the best overview of the topic, the thesis of which is that American religious culture and Buddhist meditation are dialectically changing one another.[130] The best study of the history of secularized mindfulness and its grounding in Western culture is by Wakoh Shannon Hickey.[131] Particularly valuable as an empirical study of how the borders between the concepts of the secular, religion, and Buddhism are negotiated by practicing psychotherapists is by Ira Helderman.[132] This work demonstrates how it is that the way that these concepts are structured has societal consequences.

Multiple secularities is the focus of a research group at the University of Leipzig. The project's website provides access to several publications relevant to the secularization of Buddhism.[133] The publications of the research group include both working papers and a "Companion to the Study of Secularity," which is envisioned as an ongoing online publication.

David McMahan's "Buddhism, Meditation, and Global Secularisms" is also relevant in this regard.[134]

FURTHER READING

Batchelor, Stephen. *Buddhism Without Beliefs: A Contemporary Guide to Awakening*. New York: Riverhead Books, 1997.

Batchelor, Stephen. "A Secular Buddhist." *Tricycle: The Buddhist Review* (Fall 2012). https://tricycle.org/magazine/secular-buddhist/.

Gleig, Ann. *American Dharma: Buddhism Beyond Modernity*. New Haven, CT: Yale University Press, 2019.

Gombrich, Richard, and Gananath Obeyesekere. *Buddhism Transformed: Religious Change in Sri Lanka*. Princeton, NJ: Princeton University Press, 1988.

Hickey, Wakoh Shannon. *Mind Cure: How Meditation Became Medicine*. Oxford: Oxford University Press, 2019.

Latour, Bruno. *Reassembling the Social: An Introduction to Actor-Network Theory*. Oxford: Oxford University Press, 2005.

Lopez, Donald S. *The Scientific Buddha: His Short and Happy Life*. New Haven, CT: Yale University Press, 2012.

Payne, Richard K., ed. *Secularizing Buddhism: New Perspectives on a Dynamic Tradition*. Boulder, CO: Shambhala, 2021.

Purser, Ron. *McMindfulness: How Mindfulness Became the New Capitalist Spirituality*. London: Repeater Books, 2019.

Swearer, Donald. "Lay Buddhism and the Buddhist Revival in Ceylon." *Journal of the American Academy of Religions* 38, no. 3 (1970): 255–275. https://doi.org/10.1093/jaarel/XXXVIII.3.255.

Swearer, Donald. "Bhikkhu Buddhadāsa's Interpretation of the Buddha." *Journal of the American Academy of Religion* 64, no. 2 (1996): 313–336. https://doi.org/10.1093/jaarel/LXIV.2.313.

Wallis, Glenn. *A Critique of Western Buddhism: Ruins of the Buddhist Real*. London: Bloomsbury, 2019.

NOTES

1. See Shannon Hickey, "Two Buddhisms, Three Buddhisms and Racism," *Journal of Global Buddhism* 11 (2010): 1–25.
2. Jan Nattier, "Who Is a Buddhist? Charting the Landscape of Buddhist America," in *The Faces of Buddhism in America*, ed. Charles S. Prebish and Kenneth K. Tanaka (Berkeley: University of California Press, 1998), 183–195, at 189.
3. Martin Baumann, "The Transplantation of Buddhism to Germany: Processive Modes and Strategies of Adaptation," *Method and Theory in the Study of Religion* 6, no. 1 (1994): 35–61. For an analysis of the orientalist dimensions of this process, see Ellen Goldberg, "The Re-Orientation of Buddhism in North America," *Method and Theory in the Study of Religion* 11, no. 4 (1999): 340–356.
4. Philippe Turenne, "Buddhism Without a View: A Friendly Conversation With Stephen Batchelor's Secular Buddhism," in *Secularizing Buddhism*, ed. Richard K. Payne (Boulder, CO: Shambhala, 2021), 185–205.
5. Robert C. Fuller, "Secular Spirituality," in *The Oxford Handbook of Secularism*, ed. Phil Zuckerman and John R. Shook (Oxford: Oxford University Press, 2017), 571–586.
6. Véronique Altglas, *From Yoga to Kabbalah: Religious Exoticism and the Logics of Bricolage* (Oxford: Oxford University Press, 2014), 2.

7. Donald Swearer, "Lay Buddhism and the Buddhist Revival in Ceylon," *Journal of the American Academy of Religions* 38, no. 3 (1970): 255–275.
8. See, for example, Ruth Streicher and Adrian Hermann, "'Religion' in Thailand in the 19th Century," in HCAS "Multiple Secularities—Beyond the West, Beyond Modernities," Leipzig University, 2019; and Monika Wohlrab-Sahr and Marian Burchardt, "Revisiting the Secular: Multiple Secularities and Pathways to Modernity," Working Papers Series of the HCAS "Multiple Secularities—Beyond the West, Beyond Modernities" 2, Leipzig, 2017. On King Mongkut, see Donald Swearer, "Bhikkhu Buddhadāsa's Interpretation of the Buddha," *Journal of the American Academy of Religion* 64, no. 2 (1996): 313–336, at 322.
9. Swearer, "Bhikkhu Buddhadāsa's Interpretation of the Buddha," 323.
10. Douglas Ober, "Buddhism in Colonial Contexts," in *Oxford Research Encyclopedias/Religion*, ed. John Barton (Oxford: Oxford University Press, 2019), n.p.; Brooke Schedneck, "International Buddhist Organizations," in *The Oxford Handbook of Contemporary Buddhism*, ed. Michael Jerryson (Oxford: Oxford University Press, 2017), 398–416, at 399; Richard Hughes Seager, *Encountering the Dharma: Daisaku Ikeda, Soka Gakkai, and the Globalization of Buddhist Humanism* (Berkeley: University of California Press, 2006); Vidhu Verma, "Reinterpreting Buddhism: Ambedkar on the Politics of Social Action," *Economic and Political Weekly* 45, no. 49 (December 4–10, 2010): 56–65; and Charles Jones, "Establishing the Pure Land in the Human Realm," in *Secularizing Buddhism: New Perspectives on a Dynamic Tradition*, ed. Richard K. Payne (Boulder, CO: Shambhala, 2021), 115–133.
11. Matthew J. Walton, "Burmese Buddhist Politics," in *Oxford Handbooks Online* (Oxford: Oxford University Press, 2015), n.p.; and Donald S. Lopez, *The Scientific Buddha: His Short and Happy Life* (New Haven, CT: Yale University Press, 2012), 98.
12. Jones, "Establishing the Pure Land in the Human Realm."
13. For one view of the issues, see Markus Dreßler, "Religionization and Secularity," in HCAS "Multiple Secularities—Beyond the West, Beyond Modernities," Leipzig University, 2019.
14. For Japan, see Aike P. Rots and Mark Teeuwen, "Formations of the Secular in Japan," *Japan Review* 30 (2017): 3–20; Erica Baffelli, "Contested Positioning: 'New Religions' and Secular Spheres," *Japan Review Japan Review* 30 (2017): 129–152; Christoph Kleine, "The Secular Ground Bass of Pre-modern Japan Reconsidered: Reflections upon the Buddhist Trajectories Towards Secularity," Working Papers Series of the HCAS "Multiple Secularities—Beyond the West, Beyond Modernities" 5, Leipzig, 2018. For Tibet, see Dagmar Schwerk, "Buddhism and Politics in the Tibetan Cultural Area," HCAS "Multiple Secularities—Beyond the West, Beyond Modernities," Leipzig University, 2019. For China, see André Laliberté, "Multiple Secularities in Culturally Chinese Societies," HCAS "Multiple Secularities—Beyond the West, Beyond Modernities," Leipzig University, 2020.
15. Richard Gombrich and Gananath Obeyesekere, *Buddhism Transformed: Religious Change in Sri Lanka* (Princeton, NJ: Princeton University Press, 1988).
16. Dharmapala, "The World's Debt to Buddha," in *The World's Parliament of Religions*, Vol. 2, ed. John Henry Barrows (Chicago: The Parliament Publishing Company, 1893); cited in Sarah LeVine and David N. Gellner, *Rebuilding Buddhism: The Theravāda Movement in Twentieth-Century Nepal* (Cambridge, MA: Harvard University Press, 2005), 3.
17. J. Brent Crosson, "The Politics of Spirituality and Secularization in Western Modernity," in *Oxford Research Encyclopedias, Religion*, ed. John Barton (Oxford and New York: Oxford University Press, 2019), n.p.
18. John Torpey, "Religion and Secularization in the United States and Western Europe," in *The Post-Secular in Question: Religion in Contemporary Society*, ed. Philip Gorski et al. (New York: NYU Press, 2012), 288–289.

19. Ira Helderman, *Prescribing the Dharma: Psychotherapists, Buddhist Traditions, and Defining Religion* (Chapel Hill: The University of North Carolina Press, 2019), 45.
20. Lois Lee, "Non-Religion," in *The Oxford Handbook of the Study of Religion*, ed. Michael Strausberg and Steven Engler (Oxford and New York: Oxford University Press, 2016), 84–94, at 84–85.
21. Lee, "Non-Religion," 85.
22. Jack L. Graham, "Nonreligious Buddhism: Understanding Secular Buddhism as the Result of a Dialogue Between Victorian Constructions of 'Buddhism' and the Discourse of Non-Religion," University of Oxford, 2018.
23. Graham, "Non-Religious Buddhism," 11.
24. Graham, "Non-Religious Buddhism," 14.
25. Tomoko Masuzawa, *The Invention of World Religions: Or, How European Universalism Was Preserved in the Language of Pluralism* (Chicago: University of Chicago Press, 2005), 121–146.
26. See, for example, Robert Wright, *Why Buddhism Is True: The Science and Philosophy of Meditation and Enlightenment* (New York: Simon and Schuster, 2017).
27. See Richard K. Payne, "How Not to Talk About Pure Land Buddhism: A Critique of Huston Smith's (Mis)Representations," in *Path of No Path: Contemporary Studies in Pure Land Buddhism Honoring Roger Corless*, ed. Richard K. Payne (Berkeley: Institute of Buddhist Studies and Numata Center for Buddhist Translation and Research, 2009), 147–172.
28. Richard K. Payne, "Traditionalist Representations of Buddhism," *Pacific World: Journal of the Institute of Buddhist Studies*, 3rd series, no. 10 (2008): 177–223.
29. James Ford, "The Problem of Our Suffering: A (Modernist) Zen Buddhist Meditation," see online, September 16, 2017.
30. Ron Purser, "Secular Buddhism in a Neoliberal Age," in *Secularizing Buddhism: New Perspectives on a Dynamic Tradition*, ed. Richard K. Payne (Boulder, CO: Shambhala, 2021), 207–219.
31. See Richard K. Payne, "Mindfulness and the Moral Imperative for the self to Improve the self," in *Handbook of Mindfulness: Culture, Context, and Social Engagement*, ed. Ronald E. Purser, David Forbes, and Adam Burke (Cham, Switzerland: Springer, 2018), 121–134.
32. Richard K. Payne, "Religion, Self-Help, Science: Three Economies of Western/ized Buddhism," *Journal of Global Buddhism* 20 (2019): 69–86, at 79.
33. Purser, "Secular Buddhism in a Neoliberal Age," 213–214. See also Payne, "Mindfulness and the Moral Imperative."
34. Regarding the problematic character of this kind of claim, see Funie Hsu, "American Cultural Baggage: The Racialized Secularization of Mindfulness in Schools," in *Secularizing Buddhism: New Perspectives on a Dynamic Tradition*, ed. Richard K. Payne (Boulder, CO: Shambhala, 2021), 79–93; and Funie Hsu, "What Is the Sound of One Invisible Hand Clapping? Neoliberalism, the Invisibility of Asian and Asian American Buddhists, and Secular Mindfulness in Education," in *Handbook of Mindfulness: Culture, Context, and Social Engagement*, ed. Ronald E. Purser, David Forbes, and Adam Burke (Cham, Switzerland: Springer, 2016), 369–381.
35. See online.
36. Akincano M. Weber, in his essay "Secular Buddhism: New Vision or Yet Another of the Myths It Claims to Cure?," *Insight Journal* (Aug. 2013), opens with a more nuanced discussion of the semiotics of "secular" that includes several additional connotations. The dialectic of secular and religious is acknowledged by Seth Zuihō Segall, "Why I Am Not a Secular Buddhist," Secular Buddhist Network.
37. Helderman, *Prescribing the Dharma*, 42.
38. Timothy Fitzgerald, *The Ideology of Religious Studies* (New York and Oxford: Oxford University Press, 2000).
39. Helderman, *Prescribing the Dharma*, 33.

40. Masuzawa, *The Invention of World Religions*.
41. Richard K. Payne, "Conscious and Unconscious Dynamics in the Secularizing Discourse," in *Secularizing Buddhism: New Perspectives on a Dynamic Tradition*, ed. Richard K. Payne (Boulder, CO: Shambhala, 2021), 285–314.
42. The historical background of this complex of supernatural and extraordinary as the "preternatural" is discused by Crosson, "The Politics of Spirituality and Secularization in Western Modernity."
43. Mark Juergensmeyer, "The Imagined War Between Secularism and Religion," in *The Oxford Handbook of Secularism*, ed. Phil Zuckerman and John R. Shook (Oxford: Oxford University Press, 2017), 71–84, at 74.
44. Juergensmeyer, "The Imagined War Between Secularism and Religion," 74.
45. Sarah Shaw, "Has Secularism Become a Religion? Some Observations of Pali Buddhism's Movement to the International Stage," in *Secularizing Buddhism: New Perspectives on a Dynamic Tradition*, ed. Richard K. Payne (Boulder, CO: Shambhala, 2021), 29–55, at 32.
46. Glenn Wallis, *A Critique of Western Buddhism: Ruins of the Buddhist Real* (London: Bloomsbury, 2019).
47. Glenn Wallis, "On the Faith of Secular Buddhists," Speculative Non-Buddhism, May 9, 2012.
48. Wallis, "On the Faith of Secular Buddhists," emphases in original.
49. Shaw, "Has Secularism Become a Religion?," 51.
50. Winton Higgins, "The Coming of Secular Buddhism: A Synoptic View," *Journal of Global Buddhism* 13 (2012): 109–126, at 123.
51. Higgins, "The Coming of Secular Buddhism," 123.
52. Tricycle.
53. Tricycle, "Buddhism for Beginners: Can Someone Be a Secular Buddhist? Why 'Secular'? Isn't Buddhism a Religion?."
54. Secular Buddhist Network, SBN Editor, "An Introduction to Secular Buddhism."
55. Mark Knickelbine, "Batchelor's Ten Theses of Secular Dharma," November 23, 2015.
56. Knickelbine, "Batchelor's Ten Theses of Secular Dharma."
57. See online.
58. David L. McMahan, "Buddhism and Secular Subjectivities: Individualism and Fragmentation in the Mirrors of Secularism," in *Secularizing Buddhism: New Perspectives on a Dynamic Tradition*, ed. Richard K. Payne (Boulder, CO: Shambhala, 2021), 57–78; and Payne, "Conscious and Unconscious Dynamics."
59. In some schemas there are five realms. These are the desire realms (*kāmadhātu*), which are the ones most commonly presented in popular teachings regarding rebirth. Other realms include the form (*rūpadhātu*) and formless realms (*ārūpyadhātu*) as well. The complex issue of Buddhist cosmology is discussed in Rupert Gethin, *Foundations of Buddhism* (Oxford: Oxford University Press, 1998), 112–132.
60. On rebirth in the Pali canon, see Bhikkhu Anālayo, *Rebirth in Early Buddhism and Current Research* (Boston: Wisdom Publications, 2018).
61. See online.
62. Roger R. Jackson, "Avoiding Rebirth: Modern Buddhist Views on Past and Future Lives," in *Secularizing Buddhism: New Perspectives on a Dynamic Tradition*, ed. Richard K. Payne (Boulder, CO: Shambhala, 2021), 239–263.
63. Stephen Batchelor, *After Buddhism* (New Haven and London: Yale University Press, 2015), p. 3.
64. See online, July 18, 2010.
65. See online.
66. Batchelor, "A Secular Buddhist," Tricycle, Fall 2012.
67. See online, July 4, 2010.

68. The site points toward the Secular Buddhist Association, but appears to have no formal relations with the SBA.
69. See online, posted July 18, 2010.
70. See online, accessed 11 December 2019; originally published on "Shambhala Sun," March 19, 2006.
71. This is already beginning to change, for example with claims found on the Secular Buddhist Association website that some people are not "genuine" Secular Buddhists, and the expressed intent to develop an authorized Secular Buddhist teacher training program. Jennifer Hawkins, "Frequently Asked Questions on Secular Buddhism," Secular Buddhist Association, 2020.
72. See Richard K. Payne, "Buddhism and the Sciences: Historical Background, Contemporary Developments," *Journal of Dharma Studies* 3 (2020): 219–243.
73. See online.
74. Bernat Font attempts to obscure this cultural locatedness of Secular Buddhism by claiming that it is part of "the great enterprise of rooting Buddhism not so much in the West but in contemporaneity." Bernat Font, "Secular Buddhism," Secular Buddhist Network.
75. Torpey, "Religion and Secularization," 290.
76. Hawkins, "Frequently Asked Questions."
77. Jennifer Hawkins, "Online, Together, Meditating, Secular: An Event Announcement from New Zealand!" Secular Buddhist Association, December 2, 2017.
78. See online.
79. See online and online.
80. "Contemplative educators have embraced practices that center on interiority as the critical source for personal and intellectual growth and the strengthening of exterior ways of understanding." Patricia Owen-Smith, *The Contemplative Mind in the Scholarship of Teaching and Learning* (Bloomington: Indiana University Press, 2018), 20.
81. See online, 2019.
82. For an instance of the attitude toward abhidhamma, see a post on the Bodhi College blog by Letizia Baglioni, "Why 'Early' Buddhism?, 2020.
83. See online, 2021; see also Baglioni, "Why 'Early' Buddhism?"
84. See online, 2020.
85. See online.
86. Another course representing a Secular Buddhist understanding, "The Four Noble Truths," is offered by four teachers at Bodhi College.
87. secularbuddhism.com.
88. Bhikkhu Anālayo, "The Four Assemblies and Theravāda Buddhism," *Insight Journal* (2015).
89. Stephen Batchelor, *Confession of a Buddhist Atheist* (New York: Spiegel and Grau, Random House, 2010), 6.
90. Winton Higgins, "Secular Buddhism and the Western Search for Meaning."
91. Bodhi College, 2020.
92. Bodhi College, 2020.
93. This has been given authoritative expression by Richard Gombrich, *Buddhism and Pali* (Oxford: Mud Pie Books, 2018), 69.
94. See online, 18 July 2010.
95. Wakoh Shannon Hickey, *Mind Cure: How Meditation Became Medicine* (Oxford: Oxford University Press, 2019), 11.
96. Donald S. Lopez, Jr., *Buddhism and Science: A Guide for the Perplexed* (Chicago: University of Chicago Press, 2008), 3. See also Lopez, *The Scientific Buddha*. Science is also seen as providing a tool that can correct Secular Buddhist practice. Dana Nourie, "Why Scientific Scrutiny Is Vital to Buddhist Practice," Secular Buddhist Association, September 3, 2011.

97. Helderman, *Prescribing the Dharma,* 37.
98. See online.
99. See online.
100. See also Ramsey Margolis, "Science, Meditation, Emotion, Creativity," Secular Buddhist Network, reposted from Creative Dharma: A Newsletter, December 2020.
101. See online.
102. Rachel Nuwer, "The World's Happiest Man Is a Tibetan Monk," *Smithsonian Magazine,* November 1, 2012.
103. For a succinct treatment, see "Is Buddhism True? An Interview with Robert Wright," Garrison Institute, November 30, 2017.
104. Bruno Latour, *Reassembling the Social: An Introduction to Actor-Network Theory* (Oxford: Oxford University Press, 2005), 30–34. My thanks to my friend Wendi Adamek for calling my attention back to Latour.
105. Latour, *Reassembling the Social,* 31.
106. See online, posted July 18, 2010.
107. Latour, *Reassembling the Social,* 31.
108. Latour, *Reassembling the Social,* 56.
109. Higgins, "The Coming of Secular Buddhism," 113.
110. Higgins, "The Coming of Secular Buddhism," 112.
111. Bhikkhu Bodhi, "Facing the Great Divide," *Inquiring Mind* 31, no. 2 (Spring 2015).
112. Bodhi, "Facing the Great Divide."
113. See online.
114. Latour, *Reassembling the Social,* 33.
115. For example, Roger Jackson, review of Stephen Batchelor, *Alone With Others: An Existential Approach to Buddhism, Journal of the International Association of Buddhist Studies* 7, no. 2 (1984): 208–216; Stephen Batchelor, "A Secular Buddhism," *Journal of Global Buddhism* 13 (2012): 87–107; Higgins, "The Coming of Secular Buddhism"; Winton Higgins, "The Flexible Appropriation of Tradition: Stephen Batchelor's Secular Buddhism," *Journal of Global Buddhism* 18 (2017): 51–67; and Richard K. Payne, ed., *Secularizing Buddhism: New Perspectives on a Dynamic Tradition* (Boulder, CO: Shambhala, 2021).
116. For a brief discussion of his ideas about the interconnections of the concept religion with several other discursive categories, see Timothy Fitzgerald, "Critical Religion: 'Religion' Is Not a Stand-Alone Category," in *Religion, Theory, Critique: Classic and Contemporary Approaches and Methodologies,* ed. Richard King (New York: Columbia University Press, 2017), 435–454.
117. Ann Gleig, *American Dharma: Buddhism Beyond Modernity* (New Haven, CT: Yale University Press, 2019), 5.
118. Gleig, *American Dharma,* 5.
119. Payne, *Secularizing Buddhism.*
120. *Journal of Global Buddhism.*
121. Wallis, *A Critique of Western Buddhism.*
122. Phil Zuckerman and John R. Shook, eds., *The Oxford Handbook of Secularism* (Oxford: Oxford University Press, 2017).
123. Talal Asad, *Formations of the Secular: Christianity, Islam, Modernity* (Stanford, CA: Stanford University Press, 2003).
124. Timothy Fitzgerald, *The Ideology of Religious Studies* (Oxford: Oxford University Press, 2000); and Timothy Fitzgerald, *Discourse on Civility and Barbarity: A Critical History of Religion and Related Categories* (Oxford: Oxford University Press, 2007).
125. Masuzawa, *The Invention of World Religions.*

126. Gombrich and Obeyesekere, *Buddhism Transformed.*
127. Heinz Bechert, Hellmuth Hecker, and Duy Tu Vu, *Buddhismus, Staat und Gesellschaft in den Ländern des Theravāda-Buddhismus*, Vol. 1 (Berlin: Alfred Metzner Verlag, 1966).
128. David L. McMahan, *The Making of Buddhist Modernism* (Oxford: Oxford University Press, 2008); and David L. McMahan, ed., *Buddhism in the Modern World* (London: Routledge, 2012).
129. Eva Illouz, *Saving the Modern Soul: Therapy, Emotions, and the Culture of Self-Help* (Berkeley: University of California Press, 2008).
130. Jeff Wilson, *Mindful America: The Mutual Transformation of Buddhist Meditation and American Culture* (Oxford: Oxford University Press, 2014).
131. Hickey, *Mind Cure.*
132. Helderman, *Prescribing the Dharma.*
133. Multiple Secularities, research group, University of Leipzig.
134. David McMahan, "Buddhism, Meditation, and Global Secularisms," *Journal of Global Buddhism* 18 (2017): 112–128.

Richard K. Payne and Casey Alexandra Kemp

SHENG YEN

EARLY YEARS (1931–1942)

A prominent theme that stands out in Sheng Yen's early years is hardship and trauma. In later parts of his life, this theme continued but was expressed as, in his own words, a "crisis mentality" (*weiji gan* 危機感) that was part of his own self-representation and how he viewed the sociopolitical world around him: the deplorable state of "Han" Chinese Buddhism he witnessed, the dissemination of non-Han Buddhist traditions in Taiwan, and the absence of vitality or presence of Chinese Buddhism as a whole in the West.[1] It was these perceptions that fueled his great resolve, resilience, and creativity.

Sheng Yen was born on January 22, 1931, to the Zhang 張 farming family as the youngest of six siblings—three older brothers and two older sisters—in the southeastern part of Nantong County (present-day Nantong City) in Jiangsu Province, China. He was feeble, nutritionally deficient, and physically underdeveloped as a premature infant. His mother did not formally name him but instead wished the young Sheng Yen health by nicknaming him Baokang 保康, meaning "to preserve [your] health." Not having a formal name didn't matter since owing to his poor physical condition he never left the house until he was six. In the very year that Sheng Yen was born, China witnessed a great calamity, which is far from the narratives of auspicious birth of great Buddhist luminaries. The disastrous floods of the Yangtze River caused his family to become destitute from the destruction of their family housing and farmland.[2] They were left with nothing and soon were forced to move to an area 20 *li* away with better agricultural prospects.[3]

In 1938, when he was seven, the family was confronted with another flood.[4] His father took him to assist distant relatives and other victims from the flood, which was created by the leadership of the China's Nationalist Army during the Second Sino-Japanese War (1937–1945) to slow the Imperial Japanese Army's trek toward Wuhan, China. It resulted in a 5,000-foot-wide breakout of flooding from bombing an extensive dike in the Yellow River in Henan Province.

The uncontrollable overflows of water spilled into northern Jiangsu Province via the Yangtze River, ruining agricultural plots, killing over 800,000 people, and creating nearly four million refugees. The aftermath was extensive: two million acres of agricultural farmland was out of production for nearly nine years. Sheng Yen recalls being horrified (*jingju buyi* 驚懼不已) as a child by the sight of corpses of men, women, and children floating down the Yangtze River in varying states of decomposition:

> The corpses of men, women, and children were floating down [the river]... all of them were already decomposing. Typically, the corpse(s) of men floated down the river face down with their backs bloated, arched, protruding out of the water. Perhaps due to their belly fat, the corpses of women always faced upward with their heads and legs sunken back into the water—this situation was the complete opposite to that of the men—with their hair spread out in the water, along with the corpses, drifting on the water slowly... as for children's corpses, the bellies were blown up like blowfish, just drifting. Once in a while you could see ducks that were hatched after the disaster, without any misgivings, feeding on the eyes of the corpses of children.... Under the scorching sun, the stench from these corpses permeated the area.[5]

According to him, the sight of the corpses was actually less frightening than the effects from the invasion of the Japanese military.[6] He recounted seeing massacres of children and men alike. The Japanese committed brutal and inhumane acts of rape against the women, regardless of age. Sheng Yen witnessed firsthand the effect of the terror upon women, as his family home was used as a hiding place to store women away from the danger of being brutally raped by the soldiers.[7]

The war lasted for eight years, deeply impacting Sheng Yen. In his memoirs, he vividly describes the traumatic events in the form of the deaths, the cruelty of war, and natural calamities. His life attained some stability later, at the age of nine, when he began learning with local village tutors. Because of schooling, Sheng Yen was given the name Zhang Zhide 張志德 by his family. He was not taught mathematics or any other subject besides reading and writing. One cannot help but think that his later success as a prolific writer came from the exclusivity of the teachings he received at a young age.

NOVICE YEARS (1943–1949)

In the summer of 1943, the abbot of the Guangjiao Monastery (Guangjiao si 廣教寺) in Nantong district (Nantong 南通) on Mount Lang (Langshan 狼 山) sought a new novice monk. Sheng Yen's horoscopic details (*shengchen bazi* 生辰八字), along with those of other young boys, were passed through networks of laypeople to Mr. Dai Hanqing 戴漢清.[8] The monastery placed the names to be divinely drawn before Mahāsthāmaprāpta Bodhisattva (Dashizhi pusa 大勢至菩薩), the patron bodhisattva of the monastery.[9] Three consecutive times, Sheng Yen's name came up.

When Mr. Dai went back to Sheng Yen's home to "collect" him to the monastery, his parents were reluctant to let the young Sheng Yen go. But he was eager to leave his family home to become a monk. Sheng Yen recalled his mother's unwillingness to let him go: "Son, you will soon go to become a monk. Aren't you sad? ... won't you miss me? Are you really willing to go? Sigh! Your mom can't see you go."[10] Sheng Yen cried, feeling that his excitement to leave had caused his mother sorrow. Yet his mother was most likely blaming herself, and his father, for the impoverished and helpless situation that caused him to leave. Knowing that their son was probably better off in the monastery, the parents allowed Sheng Yen to go with Mr. Dai to the monastery. Sheng Yen recounted, "Even though I wasn't able to return home again, and would be entering a completely unfamiliar environment, I was not afraid at all. I felt as if this trip was a trip to heaven."[11] The Buddhist monastery was certainly no heaven, but it was a powerful institution and at least he no longer had to worry about food or shelter.

At Guangjiao Monastery, Sheng Yen was considered slow-witted; as stated earlier, he was marked with obstacles of mental and physical underdevelopment in his early life and so was given the novice's name Changjin 常進 or "always diligent." The abbot advised him to prostrate diligently to Guanyin Bodhisattva (Guanyin pusa 觀音菩薩) to overcome his heavy "karmic obstructions" (*yezhang* 業障). Sheng Yen would prostrate five hundred or more times every morning and night. He did this for over three months. By his own account, during one particularly noteworthy morning, he had a vision of Guanyin Bodhisattva pouring liquid over his head. When he came out of this vision, he found that his memory had improved. Prior to this, he had difficulties reciting and memorizing the liturgy, but after this vision he gained the ability of an almost photographic memory; he could easily memorize whole scriptures and liturgy.[12]

JING'AN BUDDHIST SEMINARY IN SHANGHAI (1946–1949)

Sheng Yen's time in the Guangjiao Monastery was short-lived. The monastery was situated in an area where the Chinese Communist Party's (CCP's) New Fourth Army (Xinsi jun 新四軍) and the Guomindang (GMD) youth Nationalist Army (Guojun 國軍) were battling.[13] In 1946, Sheng Yen was sent to a branch monastery in Shanghai. Yet Sheng Yen's situation did not improve there. His main duty was to perform funerary rituals (*zuo jingcan* 做經懺) for the dead and this propelled him to secretly enroll in a Buddhist seminary.

When Sheng Yen first arrived, he did as he was told but doing so did not satisfy his yearning for studying and reading books. As he later recalled, he became frustrated, likening his performances of rituals to preserving the "empty shell" (*kong jiazi* 空架子) of Buddhism.[14] He rejected the commercialization of funerary practices (*shangye hua de foshi* 商業化的佛事) but acknowledged the need for them in people's lives. In later years, Sheng Yen would regard these rituals as a sign of Buddhism's deterioration (*liubi de xingcheng* 流弊之形成), from the mixing of medieval Daoist and funerary Buddhism.[15] In any case, Sheng Yen wanted a proper clerical education.

In 1948, at age 17, Sheng Yen secretly submitted an entrance exam essay to the Jing'an Buddhist Seminary and was accepted. Although this was in direct opposition to his superior's wish at Guangjiao Monastery, Sheng Yen was allowed to study there. There were two reasons for his admission. First, he convinced the abbot that the seminary should have a monastery representative, especially when the director of its educational administration (*jiaowu zhuren* 教務主任) was from their own monastery. Second, the abbot had acquired a new novice to relieve him of the funerary rituals. Thus, Sheng Yen was allowed to become a student of Jing'an Buddhist Seminary. This seminary was founded by the eminent monk-activist and writer

Taixu 太虛 (1890–1947). It was there that Sheng Yen first became aware of Taixu's thought. Taixu's ideologies were later the subject and inspiration for much of Sheng Yen's study and future pursuit of the modernization of Buddhist teachings. It was also at the seminary that Sheng Yen first met Dongchu Denglang 東初鐙朗 (1907–1977), a student of Taixu. In 1959, Dongchu would become Sheng Yen's root mentor.[16] However, by the time Sheng Yen had enrolled at the seminary, Taixu had passed the position of dean of the seminary to Master Chisong Milin 持松密林 (1894–1972), and Master Baisheng Dongfu 白聖東富 (1904–1989) served as the associate dean.[17]

Sheng Yen's time at a Buddhist seminary was short, but he greatly enjoyed his time there and soaked up all that he could of the Buddhist doctrine. According to him, his time at the seminary was life-changing. It was there that he realized the richness of the Buddhist teachings. This couldn't have been more jarring from the funerary rituals that he was forced to perform. Sheng Yen was an excellent student at Jing'an. His essays were always well received and, because he had a fabulous memory, he was able to remember various scriptures and doctrinal teachings—even though he didn't know the deeper significance of these teachings at the time.

Between the fall of the Qing dynasty in 1911 and 1949, when the CCP took over China, Sheng Yen had survived the Second Sino-Japanese War, a divided China with various political powers competing for control, and the defeat of the GMD army by the CCP.[18] No one at the seminary knew what might happen to them under the CCP regime, and when an opportunity arose for Sheng Yen and his classmates at the seminary to leave China, they took it. Since they could not afford to purchase a boat ride to Hong Kong or elsewhere, the only option for them was to join the GMD army.

ARMY YEARS (1949–1960)

Sheng Yen fled to Taiwan on May 15, 1949, through the harrowing escape from the CCP under gunfire:

> When our small boat arrived near the mouth of the Wusong [the port going out of Shanghai], we saw dense machine guns fire from both sides [GMD and CCP]. The CCP army seemed to have noticed our boat on the Huangpu River [leaving out of Shanghai]. They then targeted us. Bullets were flying over our heads, whistling in the air. An announcement over the loudspeaker ordered us to take shelter below the deck of the cabin. We stayed there until we arrived at the Yellow Sea. Only then were we allowed to catch a breath of fresh air on deck.[19]

With the CCP takeover of China, Sheng Yen felt that Buddhism was on the brink of extinction and his future was uncertain.

Owing to negative impressions of the military in his childhood, Sheng Yen's decision to join the army was difficult. He had resisted the idea of joining the army: "In our village, whenever soldiers would arrive our lives would always be disrupted. Yet now I'm willing to be one of them."[20] However, one of his teachers at the Jing'an Seminary, Lin Ziqing 林子青 (1910–2002), encouraged him to spread Buddhism in Taiwan.[21] His parting words to Sheng Yen were:

"In the furnace of this great era of [discord], may you smelt your [resolve] to become even stronger!" Sheng Yen felt very grateful, taking his words to heart.[22]

For purposes of registering a name when joining the army, Sheng Yen chose "Zhang Caiwei" 張採薇 as a reminder of his resolve. For him, "Caiwei" alluded to the loyalty and resolve of the two sons of the last Shang dynasty (ca. 1600–1046 BCE). The story goes that when these two sons of the Shang king were faced with the fall of their dynasty to the Zhou ruler, they refused to accept the food given by the Zhou. Instead, they starved themselves by "picking" (*cai* 采) and eating "ferns" (*wei* 薇) in hiding.[23] Sheng Yen saw himself in the same perilous political situation as the Communists took over China.

He spent ten years in the GMD army as a telegraph operator. Intending to keep his vow of deepening his understanding of both foundational and Mahāyāna forms of Buddhism, he used his spare time, which was usually in the middle of the night, hunched over a text with a handmade light from an ink jar ignited by peanut oil. Sheng Yen read any material he could obtain at that time in Taiwan. For the first couple of years, he couldn't get many Buddhist texts or scriptures at all. Finally, in 1952, he was able to read some general Buddhist works that were in circulation.[24] Soon after, he began to publish response essays to those works he read in Taiwanese Buddhist periodicals. His various essays had the same theme of challenging the mystical and superstitious elements found in Chinese Buddhist doctrine.[25] This was, after all, the form of Buddhism in Taiwan, characterized by funerary rituals as well, just as in the mainland. In his eyes, Buddhism in Taiwan was worse. Chinese monks in Taiwan were looked down upon; they were of low education and owing to the lack of resources did not engage in the study of Buddhism. This was also only a few years after the Japanese had left Taiwan after 50 years of colonialism.[26] Influenced by his seminary experience and the works of Taixu, Sheng Yen took it upon himself to redefine the richness of Chinese Buddhism as something useful in the world.

Life in the army, by modern standards, was extremely harsh and, to quote Sheng Yen, "semi-primitive" (*ban yuanshi hua* 半原始化).[27] The soldiers had no electricity or running water. For the latter, they had to use a local well, and the water there was basically muddy, so they always had to boil it. Still, water was very scarce, and the soldiers drank that water without complaint. They were issued one uniform, one hat, one towel, one pair of underwear, and one bowl for eating; they had to get their own chopsticks somehow. The situation improved only when the United States assisted Taiwan through the Mutual Security Act in 1951.[28]

Toward the end of his army years, the late nights spent reading and studying caused Sheng Yen to develop a severe case of insomnia. He became quite ill. He was diagnosed with the ailment of an "oversensitive nervous system" (*shenjing guomin zheng* 神經過敏症). He attempted to practice quiet meditation (*jingzuo* 靜坐) to remedy it. In the army, even among a squad made up of former monastics, it was unconventional to practice seated meditation. His fellow soldiers mocked him and even tried to disturb him while he practiced. At that time, Sheng Yen had not been formally taught meditation and thus had mostly drowsiness or scattered thoughts during his sessions.[29] He had no qualified teacher. Furthermore, the years of studying and writing about Buddhism led him to many unanswered questions. He later described his situation as developing a natural "doubt mass" (*yituan* 疑團), the great sense of wonderment and existential questioning as understood in Chan (Jp. Zen) Buddhism. He could not manage his own crisis mentality and had major concerns about the viability of the Buddhadharma itself:

Figure 1. Sheng Yen (first row, second from right) in the army with his telegraph squad in 1950.
Source: Photo courtesy of Dharma Drum Mountain.

> When I was in my early twenties, I practiced very hard in the army, and as a result had some experiences. In my mind I also made various plans, and had various anxieties and doubts, about how best to further my practice. The recurring thoughts were: "How should I further my practice?" and "What will happen in the future?" I was filled with questions.[30]

Sheng Yen's condition worsened. He struggled to perform his usual duties. In 1959, he received permission to take a six-month leave from the army. His first stop was in paying visits to various Buddhist monasteries in Taiwan. In Kaohsiung, at Master Yueji's 月基 (1914–1987) temple, Fojiao tang 佛教堂, he met Chan master Lingyuan Hongmiao 靈源宏妙 (1902–1988), who was passing through the area and was also staying overnight there.[31] Lingyuan was a dharma heir of the eminent Chan master Empty Cloud, or Xuyun 虛雲 (1839–1959).[32]

SPIRITUAL AWAKENING (1959)

Upon visiting Fojiao tang, he was placed in the same sleeping quarters as Master Lingyuan. Meeting him there was a critical moment in Sheng Yen's life. Upon seeing Lingyuan in seated meditation all night on the platform bed, Sheng Yen was inspired to seek some instruction from him, although he did not know who he was. The great "doubt mass" that arose from the years of unanswered questions and crisis from early experiences came pouring out. Every time Sheng Yen asked a question, Lingyuan would ask, "Anymore? Anymore?" (*haiyou ma*

還有嗎?), without truly answering any of them, fueling the fire of his doubt. As Sheng Yen continued to ask, his wonderment and existential crisis grew until Lingyuan suddenly pounded his hand on the platform bed and shouted: "Put them down!" (*Fangxia* 放下!). The platform shook from the force of his strike. Lingyuan then exclaimed: "*Who* has all these questions?!" (*Sheiyou namoduo wenti* 誰有那麼多問題?!). Suddenly, the great doubt mass that had built up in Sheng Yen's mind completely shattered.

Sheng Yen said that he had dropped everything and said, "I felt a great weight being suddenly lifted from me.... The whole world was fresh, as though I were seeing it for the first time."[33] Elsewhere he stated, "This experience released me, like jumping out of a metal cocoon constructed by myself," realizing that the world

> no longer belonged to himself, nor was there a need to say that his life was used to benefit the world or sentient beings. What remained was simply to do and learn what needed to be done in the Buddhadharma and for sentient beings.[34]

REORDINATION (1960)

After this encounter and with the help of Master Dongchu, Taixu's student whom he met when he was at Jing'an Seminary, and other networks, Sheng Yen was released from the army in January 1960 on the pretense of an "illness," so he was able to reordain as a monk. This time, Sheng Yen reordained with intense decisiveness; he had witnessed a war-torn China, the deterioration of funerary Buddhism, and the low education and social status of monks. This was juxtaposed with the richness of the Buddhist teachings and his personal experience of awakening promised in the scriptures. For him, what needed to be done was to revive Buddhist orthodoxy from the thick, encrusted layer of ritualism. He vowed to bring out the richness of Buddhist doctrine and efficacy of its methods of practice.

In September 1961, one year after harsh monastic training under Dongchu, Sheng Yen received the full *bhikṣu* ordination and the bodhisattva precepts.[35] He formed a close relationship with Dongchu, but Sheng Yen already had a vision of what he wanted to do with his life as a monk again. Just one month after the ordination, he left Dongchu for a six-year solitary retreat to Meinong 美濃 district in the small Chaoyuan temple 朝元寺 of the Kaohsiung mountains from November 1961 to February 1968.[36] Sheng Yen vowed to deepen his understanding and practice of Buddhism without depending on anyone or trying to be anyone. He was driven by his ambition. Even though Dongchu did not approve of his leaving, Sheng Yen left anyway. No one was going to stop him.

SOLITARY RETREAT AND PURSUIT OF A PHD (1961–1975)

Sheng Yen structured his retreat with a balance of studying and meditating. Within the first six months of his retreat, he systematically read through the *vinaya*, or Buddhist monastic codes and narratives, and studied the *Āgama* scriptures, which contain the early teachings of the Buddha. According to him, apparently he proceeded to read through the entire Mahāyāna Buddhist canon for the next few years. The entire Buddhist canon that he had read was a reprint of the Japanese Taisho canon, supplied by his teacher Dongchu. These readings, according to him, gave him a solid foundation in buddhadharma.[37] He also wrote several books from the many notes he accumulated as he was reading through and studying the canon.

Throughout the retreat, he also engaged in meditation practice from early evening into the night. He practiced all the major contemplative methods discussed in the scriptures in order to become familiar with their respective stages of practice, their strengths, and their pitfalls.[38]

Figure 2. Sheng Yen in solitary retreat. Photo taken in 1961.
Source: Photo courtesy of Dharma Drum Mountain.

He finally settled on a practice of "nonabiding" (*wuzhu* 無住) that he would later associate with Silent Illumination Chan (*mozhao chan* 默照禪).[39]

Toward the end of the retreat, Sheng Yen felt that having personal insight and practice was insufficient to revive Chinese Buddhism. Apparently, he did not want to make the same mistake as his predecessor, Taixu, whom he felt had lacked the administrative, practical, and institutional skills to realize his vision for Buddhist educational reform. He believed that in order to concretely reform Han Chinese Buddhism, he needed to go through a formal, modern educational training program in Buddhist studies so he could understand how Buddhist universities operated. His plan, at the time, was to model clerical education on the modern education system. Thus, at the end of his six-year retreat, he began to study the Japanese language so that he could pursue graduate work in Japan. It is uncertain whether he had planned this all along when he decided to reordain as a monk; after all, he was greatly influenced by Taixu's vision of Buddhist education. Perhaps he also had the ambition to distinguish himself from the rest of the Buddhist clerics in Chinese Buddhism at the time.

Against all odds and with little support from Dongchu and no support at all from his fellow Chinese clerics living in Taiwan, he was accepted by Risshō University into their graduate program on the basis of his Chinese Buddhist publications.[40] In Japan, he focused on modern academic approaches to the study of Buddhism and understanding how seminaries and Buddhist universities operated. He unexpectedly received more than just academic training.

During his breaks from graduate studies, Sheng Yen went to different Buddhist institutions and even non-Buddhist organizations to observe and participate in their practices. He did intensive retreats within various Buddhist schools. However, he was especially drawn to Zen. He joined three intensive retreats with Rōshi Ban Tetsugyu 伴鐵牛 (1910–1996) at Iwate Prefecture's Kannon-ji 観音寺.[41] As a student of the Zen master Harada (Daiun) Sogaku 原田 (大雲) 祖岳 (1871–1961), Ban Tetsugyu was associated with the newly formed Sanbōkyōdan lineage 三宝教団 of Zen, literally "Three Treasures Religious Organization." Harada's other student, Yasutani Haku'un 安谷白雲 (1885–1973), had founded the Sanbōkyōdan lineage in 1954 to combine the practice of Sōtō and Rinzai Zen. Eventually, Ban gave Sheng Yen the seal of approval (Ch. *Yinke*; Jp. 印可) for his Chan experience during the third intensive retreat, just after he had acquired his doctorate, and encouraged him to go to the United States and teach there.

At the time, Sheng Yen had no plans to go to the United States; he was planning to rebuild Buddhist monastic education in Taiwan. Yet, after returning to Taiwan, where the tension between China and Japan was still in the air, he discovered that no one really welcomed him and no one was interested in building Buddhist higher education programs. Sheng Yen was heartbroken by the resistance and inertia he met in Taiwan. At the same time, he received an invitation from Mr. C. T. Shen, the man who had secretly supported his academic studies in Japan, to serve as the abbot of the Temple of Enlightenment (Dajue si 大覺寺) in the Bronx, New York.[42]

A NEW CAREER AS A CHAN MASTER (1975–2009)

The decision to move to New York seemed obvious at the time and so on December 10, 1975, Sheng Yen arrived in America. Zen had entered the American consciousness a decade earlier, and there was a growing interest in practicing Zen meditation.[43] In fact, he was asked to teach meditation by several Americans. In the next phase of his life, Sheng Yen began a process of teaching Chan and learning what he needed to know about running a monastic institution and how to create an experience-oriented form of practical Buddhism for Americans. Although he was unable to use any of his academic training initially to reform monastic education as he had hoped, teaching Chan to Americans was precisely what Sheng Yen needed to do in order to gain traction as an international Chan master. After receiving international recognition, he returned to Taiwan to revive Buddhism there.

Sheng Yen led his first intensive Chan retreat at C. T. Shen's personal estate on Long Island in May 1977 after a year-long preparation meditation course teaching his handful of American students. They were serious about practice, and many had good insights from that retreat. But from his writings during this time, it is clear that he did not see himself as a typical "Chan master." Unlike teachers of the Zen that was being taught in America, he avoided aligning himself with any Chan lineage and was, in fact, critical of sectarian biases (*zongpai menhu* 宗派門戶).[44] Instead, he stressed the importance of transmitting orthodox Buddhadharma (*zhengxin de fojiao* 正信的佛教) and responding to the needs of the modern environment. He was still obviously in his mode of reviving Han transmission of Chinese Buddhism, even though his American students just wanted to learn about Chan.

The form of Chan he taught was his way of remedying the lack of doctrine in Japanese Zen. In other words, he reinserted foundational Buddhist teachings into his Chan for his Western students, who hitherto had been exposed only to Zen.[45] The Chan that he taught was neither separate from the world nor identical with ordinary popular meditation. He felt that the essence of practice was not to seek awakening but to be free from the bondage of vexations (*fannao* 煩惱). When vexations are absent, wisdom naturally manifests. In order to realize wisdom, Sheng Yen set up no fixed teachings or methods. However, he was keen to articulate concrete stages in the process of self-cultivation. This had been, after all, missing in his own training and absent in what he had observed in Japanese Zen.

In the late 1970s, the prevailing emphasis in America was on a kind of Zen that was iconoclastic, stageless, and centered on *kōan* practice. Sheng Yen countered this popular conception by looking outside of Chan at the wealth of resources available in the Buddhist teachings. He was critical of this popularly espoused form of Buddhism separated from Buddhadharma. During this early phase of his Chan teaching career, he experimented with many Buddhist methods on his American students, aiming to establish a strong foundation of Buddhadharma. Later, his Chan teachings would be defined by something similar to Sanbōkyōdan's combining of Caodong (Jp. Sōtō) and Linji (Jp. Rinzai) methods of self-cultivation, except through a doctrinally rich foundation of Buddhadharma.

In 1976, when Dongchu visited Sheng Yen in New York, he gave Sheng Yen the Chan lineage transmissions of both the Linji 臨濟 and the Caodong 曹洞 lines.[46] No ceremony was involved. It was a casual event. Apparently, this seems to be the norm as he later received the Linji transmission from Lingyuan in the same fashion. This strengthened Sheng Yen's resolve to transmit Chan in the West, beginning with his students in America. With Dongchu's passing in the following year and the obligation of taking care of his temple in Taiwan, Sheng Yen became forever tied to Taiwan. Instead of staying permanently in America to establish a strong foundation and community of Western practitioners, as many Japanese and Tibetan Buddhist teachers did, Sheng Yen had to travel back and forth every three months from America to Taiwan, dividing his energy and time.[47]

When Dongchu passed away in Taiwan in 1977, Sheng Yen stayed in Taiwan for a year to take care of Dongchu's temple. In 1978, he paid a visit to Chan master Lingyuan. Upon meeting him again, Lingyuan gave him dharma transmission (*chuanfa* 傳法), making Sheng Yen a 57th-generation lineage holder of the Linji Yixuan 臨濟義玄 (767–866) school of Chan Buddhism. This transmission was also done in a casual manner.[48]

These events gave Sheng Yen the responsibility to continue the Chan lineage in the West. For the next 30 years, he would travel tirelessly between Taiwan and the United States and Europe to lead intensive Chan retreats. But during this process, he was also able to realize his vision of establishing higher education training for monastics, create a seminar, and build an institutional presence of international Buddhist studies in Taiwan.

After inheriting Dongchu's Chung-Hwa Institution of Buddhist Culture, which was really a Buddhist temple, Sheng Yen renamed it the Chung-Hwa Institute of Buddhist Studies (CHIBS) in 1985 and turned it into an academic institution with Buddhist scholars, both Chinese and European, living and teaching there. With the goal of advocating for Buddhist educational

Figure 3. Sheng Yen at the old Nongchan Monastery in Taiwan.
Source: Photo taken in 1992. Photo courtesy of Dharma Drum Mountain.

reform via the academic study and research of Chinese Buddhism, the CHIBS in 2007 launched the Dharma Drum Buddhist College, which is the first private Buddhist college in Taiwan and is accredited by the Ministry of Education. He also created a cooperative publishing venture with Columbia University. Sheng Yen held academic Buddhist studies conferences to bring together academic research and interdisciplinary exchange. He convened the first Chung-Hwa International Conference on Buddhism Studies at the Taipei National Center Library in 1991. In 2004, he hosted a three-part conference for the World Youth Peace Summit.[49]

In 1998, on the occasion of his dialogue with H. H. the Fourteenth Dalai Lama in New York City, Sheng Yen formulated one of his most important and systematic doctrinal classification charts (*panjiao tu* 判教圖), linking Indian Buddhism to Chinese Tiantai and Huayan schools that culminated in what he perceived to be orthodox Chan Buddhism. Doctrinal classification has historically been a hermeneutical way for Chinese Buddhists to systematize and harmonize the various Buddhist teachings and scriptures.[50] This chart laid out the blueprint for this thought, subsequent teachings and publications, and his final establishment of the Dharma Drum Lineage of Chan. I have published a book monograph about the circumstances of the founding of this new Chan lineage, so I will not flesh out the significance of this here. Suffice it to say that Sheng Yen imagined Chan Buddhism to be the pinnacle of the Han transmission of Chinese Buddhism, the richness of which had influenced the whole of East Asia.

His notion of the Dharma Drum Lineage was not restricted to a sectarian understanding of "school" in the narrow sense of Chan Buddhism, so often characterized in modern academic studies as one faction engaging in power struggles with others. While it was conceived as a strict master–disciple "spiritual genealogy," it was not limited to the construction and perpetuation of a premodern form of Chan Buddhist history. He wanted this new lineage to preserve, reformulate, and institutionalize the most viable and positive aspects of Han Chinese Buddhism, which for him was the basis of the whole East Asia Buddhism.

Sheng Yen's creation of this lineage evolved out of the historical trajectory of his life experiences in China and the changing religious landscape of Taiwan and the West where he lived and taught. Central to these contributing circumstances was the crisis he perceived in the current state and future viability of the Han transmission of Chinese Buddhism, a unique and distinctive tradition of Buddhist teaching and practice that found its inspired origins and development in China, among Han Chinese peoples. Dharma Drum Lineage, in this sense, is an imagined tradition with an aim to change the course of Chinese Buddhism as a whole for posterity. In Sheng Yen's own words, he was "inheriting the past and inspiring the future" (*chengxian qihou* 承先啟後).

THE RISE OF DHARMA DRUM MOUNTAIN (2005–)

Dharma Drum Mountain was formally established in October 2005, even though the land was purchased in 1989. It was a long and arduous journey to make Dharma Drum a reality for Sheng Yen. His construction team experienced numerous setbacks, from required changes to the topology of the site to other governmental proscriptions. In order to gain the support of Buddhists and the government of Taiwan, Sheng Yen worked tirelessly to promote what he called a movement of "uplifting the character of humans; building a pure land in the human realm" (*tisheng rende pinzhi; renjian jingtu* 提昇人的品質, 建設人間淨土). Through his many social programs, Dharma Drum Mountain had become one of the largest and most influential Buddhist organizations in Taiwan and elsewhere in the Mandarin-speaking world.

Sheng Yen envisioned Dharma Drum Mountain as a utopia, a world or environment based on Buddhist values, a response to the uncertain sociopolitical situation in Taiwan that he had witnessed. It would also be the ideal place for him to fulfill his dream of unifying the study and practice of Chinese Buddhism. In the process of promoting his vision for Dharma Drum Mountain, Sheng Yen created a modern form of Buddhism that was devoid of "superstition," in opposition to the folk traditions of Chinese religion, and distinct from other non-Han Buddhist traditions that began to spread in Taiwan in the 1990s.

Since the ending of martial law (*jieyan ling* 戒嚴令) in Taiwan in 1987, local community-based cultic traditions and temple religions, which are broadly construed here as folk beliefs and practices, not only were able to exercise their religious freedom beyond state control, but also began to influence the larger society as well as politics at the national level. The ending of martial law in 1987 coincided with the rise of Taiwan's booming economy.[51] Many of these cultic or folkloric traditions promoted, in the eyes of Sheng Yen, ambivalent moral values based on a materialist and self-serving ethos (*gongli de* 功利的; *gongyong de* 功用的) that needed to be rectified and transformed (*jiucheng huadao* 糾正化導) as their impact became more prevalent in Taiwan.[52] His criticism also focused on their dependence on and yet contentious relationship with Buddhism.

As Buddhism in Taiwan began to flourish economically, developed modern forms of education, and exhibited increased social mobility and change, new forms of Buddhism also began to be widely disseminated. After World War II, very few representatives from the South Asian transmission of Buddhism (*nanchuan fojiao* 南傳佛教) came to Taiwan. However, during the 1990s, a veritable surge in publication of *vipassanā* literature, coupled with a lack of Taiwanese Buddhist innovations, led to a huge upsurge of readers and followers of *vipassanā* practitioners, which prepared the way for *vipassanā* teachers to visit Taiwan. The 1990s also witnessed a surge of Kagyu and Nyingma Tibetan Buddhist teachers who came to Taiwan to promote their Buddhism. After the Tibetan exile, global networks of Tibetan lamas devoted much energy to establishing centers around the world. In Taiwan, their efforts proved very fruitful since Taiwan's economic boom provided the conditions for particularly generous donations to Tibetans in Dharamshala. For the rising middle class, many of whom were not particularly religious, this Tibetan form of Buddhism was something at once familiar and exotic: familiar because it resembled the Daoist rituals; and exotic because it was colorful and ornamental and its empowerment ceremonies promised blessings and riches. These conditions made Taiwan a frequent destination for many Tibetan teachers. In 1997, with the visit of the Dalai Lama, who was perceived as a religious celebrity, Tibetan Buddhism became even more of an exotic spirituality.

Sheng Yen saw what was happening in Taiwan as a crisis in an already pluralistic society. It was in this context that Sheng Yen succeeded in shaping Dharma Drum Mountain as both a modern Chan Buddhist monastery for the laity and a Buddhist educational institution, both secular and religious, that aimed to help Taiwanese society. His brand of Buddhism was close enough to contemporary Chinese Buddhism in Taiwan to make it seem familiar to the Taiwanese, so that it was perceived as a continuation of Chinese Buddhism. However, his Dharma Drum Lineage adds a distinctly new flavor to Buddhism in many respects. It is an alternative option for many Taiwanese practitioners. Sheng Yen was the first to reintroduce intensive Chan meditation retreats in Taiwan when all other Buddhist institutions were engaging mostly in ritual practices. He was the first Chinese Buddhist cleric with a doctorate degree, and he was internationally known not only in the United States but in Europe. Thus, he was able to successfully draw from a younger demographic pool: college and graduate students as well as the educated elite and educated Buddhists in Taiwan. He had the greatest number of longtime Western students of any Buddhist organization in Taiwan. His character was such that he gave Dharma Drum a level of prestige and legitimization on a par with prominent cultural figures and intellectuals.

On an international stage, he became the keynote speaker at the Millennium World Peace Summit of Religious and Spiritual Leaders held at the United Nations (UN) in 2000. In 2001, he was invited to present the concluding address at the International Conference on Religious Cooperation held in Taipei. By 2003, Sheng Yen was acclimated and recognizable across academic and political circles. Former UN Secretary-General Kofi Annan extended an invitation to Sheng Yen to speak at a meeting for the "World Council of Religious Leaders" in 2003, and Sheng Yen was appointed as one of the chairs of that council as part of the official unit of the UN to aid the Secretary-General on religious matters.[53] In Taiwan, he was the meditation teacher of two Taiwanese presidents: former president Li Teng-hui 李登輝 (1923–2020), a Christian, and former president Ma Ying-jeou 馬英九 (1950–).[54]

Sheng Yen began life at the margins of society in abject poverty but later became one of the most influential Buddhist clerics of the 20th century. The chaos of the Communist takeover of China and the perils and challenges of joining the army for ten years after leaving monkhood eventually led him to a spiritual awakening and back to monasticism, the only station in life that he found meaningful and familiar. Realizing the frailty of the Han transmission of Chinese Buddhism, he pursued higher Buddhist education in Japan to prepare for his goal of reforming it, only to be temporarily sidetracked into becoming a Chan master in the States. Before he passed away in 2009, he was able to realize his goal. He had elevated the overall educational level of Chinese monastics by building a Buddhist college and a seminary and created the Dharma Drum Mountain in Taiwan for training leaders in transmitting orthodox Han Chinese Buddhism through the Dharma Drum Lineage of Chan.

PRIMARY SOURCES

I relied mostly on Sheng Yen's autobiographies to narrate his life and work. The two primary autobiographies are *Guicheng* 歸程 (*The Return Home*), first published in 1968, and *Shengyan fashi xuesi lichen* 聖嚴法師學思歷程 (*The Intellectual Development of Venerable Sheng Yen*), first published in 1993.[55] Separated by a period of 25 years, these two books have different authorial voices and provide a window into his self-image at two junctures of his life.

The Return Home is an impassioned account of Sheng Yen's early years living in poverty as a novice monk, experiencing the trauma of natural disasters, the tribulations of Japanese colonization, and the Communist rise in China. These events compelled him to escape mainland China by joining the move of the Nationalist Party (Guomindang 國民黨, GMD) army to Taiwan, and he includes his reflections on returning to monasticism. Sheng Yen wrote this memoir in the late 1960s, at the beginning of his six-year solitary retreat in the southern mountains of Taiwan. The book was his way of acknowledging his past and bidding farewell to the world he left behind. He wanted to express his gratitude toward the buddhadharma for giving him a second chance at life as a monk and express his love for his parents for showing him how two people of very humble backgrounds could exemplify such great love.[56] This book is a window into his memories and feelings.

The Intellectual Development of Venerable Sheng Yen, written in a literary style, details various life events that influenced and often inspired his own intellectual and religious development. Written when he was in his sixties, this book recounts many of the same events in his life from his early years onward but from the perspective of the formation of his thought, concerns, and life purpose. *The Return Home* stops at the time he returned to monasticism; this book includes his pursuit of higher education in Japan after he finished his solitary retreat. It details his life in Japan, observing the modern developments of Japanese Buddhism and how they influenced his view of the potential of Chinese Buddhism. He also recounts his life as a Chan teacher leading retreats and giving public university talks in the United States and England. Traveling the world had exposed him to new ideas, which in turn forced him to re-examine and reinterpret the buddhadharma to meet the demands of modern people. When he wrote this book, he was already quite accomplished; he had published dozens of works on Buddhism, including sutra commentaries, Chan practice instructions, academic papers, and even travelogues. The year the book was published, it won the Sun Yat Sen Academic and Cultural Foundation literary award in Taiwan.[57]

REVIEW OF SECONDARY LITERATURE

To date, there is curiously no sustained academic study of Sheng Yen's life and work in the Chinese secondary literature. There are, however, Chinese normative biographies of his life, many of which were written by his monastic or lay disciples.[58]

Two sources stand out in this category. Both were written by Sheng Yen's lay students but were quite useful in my research because they are distinguished by their thoroughness of research. The first is *A Chronological Biography of Master Sheng Yen* in four volumes by Lin Qixian. This monumental work took years to complete.[59] It surveys nearly all of Sheng Yen's writings published through different venues and places them in chronological order. Although this work does not provide any analysis of Sheng Yen's oeuvre, it does provide a chronology to analyze the various shifts in Sheng Yen's thought, which pointed me to examine the historical contexts in which he lived.

The second work that I consulted is a biography of Sheng Yen written for a general audience by Shi Shuqing.[60] Ms. Shi is an accomplished writer of literature, and the book was published by the China Times Cultural Corporation, one of the largest media and publishing houses in Taiwan. Ms. Shi interviewed Sheng Yen for a couple of years and participated in retreats in both Taiwan and New York. Sometimes she would travel with Sheng Yen, observing his daily experiences. Her book captures his life in an eloquent way but from a non-scholarly perspective with limited historicization.

Scholarship on Sheng Yen in English is scanty. There is a chapter devoted to Sheng Yen and his Dharma Drum Mountain by Richard Madsen in his 2007 book that explores the religious renaissance that has reformed, revitalized, and renewed the practices of Buddhism and Daoism in postwar Taiwan.[61] Other studies on contemporary Taiwanese Buddhist monasteries helped situate my study of Sheng Yen. The first is by Stuart Chandler, who historicized the Buddha Light International Organization of Fo Guang Shan by Xingyun, the Buddhist monk who helped to arrange for Sheng Yen's solitary retreat site in the 1960s.[62] The other is by Julia Huang, who studied the Ciji or Compassionate Relief Organization—arguably the largest Buddhist organization in Taiwan, headed by the nun, master Cheng Yen (1937–).[63] Although these monographs were not studies of Sheng Yen, they nonetheless provided a context for Taiwanese Buddhism, which helped my own academic monograph on Sheng Yen.[64] These sources took me across space, time, and areas of Sheng Yen's involvement both capriciously and predictably, showing how he conformed to certain constructed social norms while contesting others.

DIGITAL MATERIALS

Hsing Yun (Xingyun). WorldCat: https://search.worldcat.org/search?q=ti%3AHsing%20Yun%20%28Xingyun%29.

Fo Guang Shan. WorldCat: https://search.worldcat.org/search?q=ti%3AFo%20Guang%20Shan.

Buddhism and Globalization. WorldCat: https://search.worldcat.org/search?q=ti%3ABuddhism%20and%20Globalization.

Global Buddhism. WorldCat: https://search.worldcat.org/search?q=ti%3AGlobal%20Buddhism.

The Buddhist Tzu Chi (Ciji) Movement. WorldCat: https://search.worldcat.org/search?q=ti%3AThe%20Buddhist%20Tzu%20Chi%20%28Ciji%29%20Movement.

Taixu. WorldCat: https://search.worldcat.org/search?q=ti%3ATaixu.

Chan literature. WorldCat: https://search.worldcat.org/search?q=ti%3AChan%20literature.

FURTHER READING

Dharma Drum Corporation Editorial Committee. *Fagu shan de gushi* 法鼓山故事 [The Story of Dharma Drum Mountain]. Taipei: Dharma Drum Corporation, 2007.

Jones, Charles. *Buddhism in Taiwan: Religion and the State: 1660–1990*. Honolulu: University of Hawaii Press, 1999.

Katz, Paul R. "Religion and the State in Post-War Taiwan." *The China Quarterly* 174 (2003): 395–412.

Laliberté, André. *The Politics of Buddhist Organizations in Taiwan: 1989–2003: Safeguarding the Faith, Building a Pure Land, Helping the Poor*. London and New York: RoutledgeCurzon, 2004.

Lin, Qixian 林其賢. *Shengyan fashi nianpu* 聖嚴法師年譜 [A Chronological Biography of Master Sheng Yen]. 4 vols. Taipei: Dharma Drum Corporation, 2016.

Madsen, Richard. *Democracy's Dharma: Religious Renaissance and Political Development in Taiwan*. Berkeley: University of California Press, 2007.

McMahan, David L. *The Making of Buddhist Modernism*. Oxford: Oxford University Press, 2008.

Pittman, Don A. *Toward a Modern Chinese Buddhism: Taixu's Reforms*. Honolulu: University of Hawaii Press, 2001.

Sharf, Robert. "Sanbōkyōdan: Zen and the Way of New Religions." *Japanese Journal of Religious Studies* 22, nos. 3–4 (1995): 417–458.

Sheng Yen. *Guicheng* 歸程 [The Return Home]. Taipei: Dongchu chubanshe, 1968; reprint, Taipei: Dharma Drum Corporation, 1999.

Sheng Yen. *Hoofprint of the Ox*. New York: Oxford University Press, 2002.

Sheng Yen. *Sheng Yen fashi xuesi lichen* 聖嚴法師學思歷程 [The Intellectual History of Dharma Master Sheng Yen]. Taipei: Zhongzheng shuju, 1993.

Yu, Jimmy. *Reimagining Chan Buddhism: Sheng Yen and the Creation of the Dharma Drum Lineage of Chan.* New York: Routledge, 2022.

Yu, Jimmy. "Revisiting the Notion of *Zong*: Contextualizing the Dharma Drum Lineage of Modern Chan Buddhism." *Journal of Chinese Buddhist Studies* 26 (2013): 113–151.

NOTES

1. The word "Han" is an ethnocentric category that inherits a particular nationalist ideology that came into being as a political discourse against the Manchus and other nation-builders at the beginning of 20th-century China. Sheng Yen inherited this category of "Han transmission of Chinese Buddhism" from his Buddhist predecessors. "Non-Han" Buddhist traditions would refer to Tibetan Buddhism, South Asian Buddhism, and so on. For a thorough discussion of Sheng Yen's usage, see my *Reimagining Chan Buddhism: Sheng Yen and the Creation of the Dharma Drum Lineage of Chan* (New York and London: Routledge, 2022), 78–84.
2. See Chris Courtney, "Central China Flood, 1931"; Zhang Jiayan, *Coping with Calamity: Environmental Change and Peasant Response in Central China, 1736–1949* (Vancouver, Canada: University of British Columbia Press, 2014); David Pietz, *Engineering the State: The Huai River and Reconstruction in Nationalist China 1927–1937* (New York and London: Routledge, 2002), 61–70; and Charles H. Southwick, "China's Environmental Challenge," *Science* 222, no. 4624 (1983): 565.
3. One *li* is roughly one-third of a mile.
4. See Kathryn Edgerton-Tarpley, "Between War and Water: Farmer, City, and State in China's Yellow River Flood of 1938–1947," *Agricultural History* 90, no. 1 (Winter 2016): 94–116.
5. See Sheng Yen, *Guicheng* 歸程 [The Return Home] (Taipei, Taiwan: Fagu chubanshe, 1968; and reprint, Taipei: Dharma Drum Corporation, 1999), 16.
6. See Sheng Yen, *Guicheng*, 37.
7. Sheng Yen, *Guicheng*, 39.
8. See Alison R. Marshall, "Moving the Spirit on Taiwan: New Age Lingji Performance," *Journal of Chinese Religions* 31, no. 1 (2003): 81–99. Scholars have historicized the close relationship between Daoist masters and mediums in premodern and modern times; see Edward L. Davis, *Society and the Supernatural in Song China* (Honolulu: University of Hawaii Press, 2001); and Robert Hymes, *Way and Byway: Taoism, Local Religion, and Models of Divinity in Sung and Modern China* (Berkeley: University of California Press, 2002).
9. See Sheng Yen, *Xuefo chunyi* 學佛群疑 *[Common Questions in Learning about Buddhism]* (Taipei: Dharma Drum Publications, 1988), 117.
10. See Yen, *Guicheng*, 46. The traditional Chinese calculation of age is different. In this system, a child is one year old at birth, and another year is added (*xusui* 虛歲) when the beginning of the first solar term (*lichun* 立春) passes, even when the child's birthday has not arrived yet. Thus, Sheng Yen was technically 12 years old when he left for the monastery.
11. See Yen, *Guicheng*, 48.
12. See Sheng Yen, "Women de shiming 我們的使命," 58.
13. Traditionally, the acronym for the Nationalist Party has been KMT, from the Wade–Giles romanization *Kuomin tang*. I use GMD (Guomindang 國民黨) because the Pinyin system has become the international standard for spelling Chinese terms. China saw 50 years of concessions to various treaties with the British, the Americans, and the French. Meanwhile, it was experiencing civil war and wars with Japan. In 1912, it finally became the Republic of China, nominally headed by Sun Yatsen's 孫中山 (1866–1925) GMD.
14. See Yen, *Guicheng*, 99.

15. Yen, *Guicheng*, 103–104.
16. See Sheng Yen, "Shi'en nanbao" 師恩難報 [The Difficulty in Expressing Gratitude Toward My Teacher], in *Diaonian Youhua*, 13. This essay is a eulogy for Dongchu and also describes Sheng Yen's meeting and relationship with him; and see also Sheng Yen, *Jiaoyu, wenhua, wenxue* 教育·文化·文學 [Education, Culture, and Literary Studies] (Taipei: Fagu chubanshe, 2007), 152–153.
17. Master Chisong was one of the first Chinese monks to study Japanese Esoteric Buddhism in Japan. Originally, he studied Huayan Buddhism under Master Yuexia 月霞 (1858–1917). See Dongchu, *Zhongguo fojiao jindai shi*, vol. 2 中國佛教近代史, 下冊 [A History of Contemporary Chinese Buddhism, vol. 2] (Taipei, Taiwan: Dongchu Publications, 1974), 989; also *Zhonghua wenshi ziliao wenku* 中華文史資料文庫 [Storehouse of Materials on Chinese History] (Beijing: Zhonguo wenshi, 1996), 534–535. Information on Chisong can also be found on "Database of Modern Chinese Buddhism" (http://buddhistinformatics.ddbc.edu.tw/dmcb/Chisong_%E6%8C%81%E6%9D%BE) 近代中國佛教檢索. After 1949, Baisheng became a prominent monk who held control of the Buddhist Association of the Republic of China (BAROC) for almost three decades. See Charles B. Jones, *Buddhism in Taiwan: Religion and the State: 1660–1990* (Honolulu: University of Hawai'i Press, 1999), 132–133. See also Sheng Yen, *Diaonian Youhua 悼念·遊化* [Eulogies and Travelogues] (Taipei: Fagu chubanshe, 2005), 94.
18. For a brief political and intellectual history of the late Qing, see essays by Marius Jansen, Wellington Chan, and Michael Gasster in *The Cambridge History of China: Late Ch'ing, 1800–1911, Part 2*, ed. Denis Twitchett and John K. Fairbank (Cambridge, UK and New York: Cambridge University Press, 1980), 2:339–534; The collapse of the dynastic system ushered in the Republic of China (Zhonghua minguo 中華民國) with Sun Yatsen 孫中山 (1866–1925) as the first provisional president or founding father and later Yuan Shikai 袁世凱 (1859–1916) as the formal first president. The death of Yuan Shikai stimulated the turbulent "era of the warlords" with local power centers competing for dominance. The divided country was partly reunited under the army of Chiang Kai-shek 蔣介石 (1887–1975) and the Nationalist Party in 1928, only to be invaded by the Japanese in 1937, during the Second Sino-Japanese War. See Edward A. McCord, *The Power of the Gun: The Emergence of Modern Chinese Warlordism* (Berkeley: University of California Press, 1993), 161; Diana Lary, *The Chinese People at War: Human Suffering and Social Transformation, 1937–1945* (Cambridge, UK and New York: Cambridge University Press, 2010); and See Edmund S. Fung, *The Intellectual Foundations of Chinese Modernity: Cultural and Political Thought in Republican China* (Cambridge, UK: Cambridge University Press, 2010), 27–31.
19. See *Guicheng*, 153.
20. See *Guicheng*, 153.
21. Sheng Yen recounts meeting him again in 1988 when he visited mainland China, after some 40 years, in *Huozai qingliang* 火宅清涼 [Pure and Cool in a Burning House] (Taipei: Dharma Drum Corporation, 1991), 44. Lin Ziqing was an outstanding writer and an authority on the life and work of Master Hongyi's 弘一 (1880–1942). He had also researched many historical, theoretical, and literary aspects of Buddhism. See Lin Zhiming 林志明, *Lin Ziqing wenji* 林子青文集 [Complete Collection of Lin Ziqing], 4 vols. (Taipei: Dharma Drum Corporation, 2008).
22. Sheng Yen, *Shengyan fashi xuesi lichen*, 24.
23. See *Guicheng*, 148.
24. More research needs to be done on the availability of Buddhist texts, including scriptures and general writings, in Taiwan during the early to mid-20th century. Existing scholarship on religious printing during this period suggests that there were more popular religious texts in circulation in Taiwan than Buddhist texts when Sheng Yen arrived there; see Philip Clart and Gregory A. Scott, *Religious Publishing and Print Culture in Modern China, 1800–2012* (Berlin: De Gruyter, 2015), specifically the chapters by Rostislav Berezkin and Paul R. Katz.

25. His published essays in various Buddhist journals, from his twenties as a soldier to his late thirties before he went to Japan, focused on popular topics such as the mystical dimensions within Buddhism, which he clarified using Buddhist doctrine. For his early essays, see, for example, "Yinguo xianbao lu" 因果現報錄 [Record of Instant Karma] in *Ciming* 慈明 2 (October 1962): 19; "Guishen de zhonglei" 神鬼的種類 [Typology of Spirits and Gods] in *Ciming* 慈明 2 (date unknown): 16–17; and "Tan shentong" 談神通 [On Supernatural Abilities] in *Hongkong Buddhist Journal* 香港佛教 35 (April 1963): 2–7.
26. When mainland Buddhist monks reached Taiwan in 1949, the island had already experienced centuries of tumultuous history that molded the local Buddhist traditions in distinctive ways. For example, Taiwan has been on the periphery of traditional China since the 12th century, but after the Chinese defeat in the Sino-Japanese War of 1895, it was ceded to the Japanese colonial empire until its "retrocession" into the fold of the Republic of China in 1945. Buddhism in Taiwan during this colonial period was dominated by the married clergy system of Japanese Buddhism. Chinese monks were discriminated against. Until 1945, most Taiwanese Buddhists were cut off from the Buddhists from Zhejiang and Jiangsu provinces, the most dynamic centers of Buddhist activity in mainland China; and see André Laliberté, *The Politics of Buddhist Organizations in Taiwan: 1989–2003 Safeguarding the Faith, Building a Pure Land, Helping the Poor* (London and New York: Routledge, 2004), 34–35.
27. See Yen, *Guicheng*, 159–160.
28. For more information about US–Taiwan relations during this time, see Chiang, Min-hua, "The US Aid and Taiwan's Post-War Economic Development, 1951–1965," *African and Asian Studies* 13, nos. 1–2 (2014): 100–120.
29. See Yen, *Guicheng*, 202–203.
30. See Sheng Yen, *Sheng Yan fashi jiao mozhao chan* 聖嚴法師教默照禪 [Master Sheng Yen Teaches Silent Illumination] (Taipei: Fagu chubanshe, 2002), 99.
31. Master Lingyuan was tonsured by Xuyun on behalf of the latter's deceased disciple. Thus, even though Lingyuan was Xuyun's dharma heir, he was technically a grand disciple of Xuyun. For studies and biographies on Xuyun, see Daniela Campo, "Chan Master Xuyun: The Embodiment of an Ideal," in *The Transmission of a Model in Making Saints in Modern China*, ed. David Ownby, Vincent Goossaert, and Ji Zhe (New York: Oxford University Press, 2017), 99–136; Charles Luk, trans., *Empty Cloud: The Autobiography of the Chinese Zen Master Xu Yun* (Rochester, NY: Empty Cloud Press, 1974; rev. ed., Element Books Ltd., 1988); and for an updated English translation of Xuyun's collected writings, see Sheng Yen, *Attaining the Way: A Guide to the Practice of Chan Buddhism* (Boston: Shambhala, 2006), 87–118.
32. See Yen, *Sheng Yan fashi jiao mozhao chan* 聖嚴法師教默照禪, 99.
33. See Sheng Yen, *Getting the Buddha Mind*, 5.
34. See Yen, *Shengyan fashi xuesi lichen*, 51.
35. In this essay, Sheng Yen recounts the "harsh" way that Dongchu trained him, "The difficulty in expressing gratitude toward my teacher" (*Enshi nanbao* 師恩難報), in *Diaonian youhua*, 15–19; 23.
36. The location of his solitary retreat was arranged by two masters, Hsing Yun or Xingyun 星雲 (1927–), who later formed one of the largest Buddhist organizations in Taiwan, the Fo Guang Shan or Buddha Light International Organization, and Haolin 浩霖 (1927–2015), who remained a close friend of Sheng Yen. Technically, Sheng Yen's retreat was two intervals of three years. He came out of the retreat after three years to receive treatment for an eye cataract, after which he returned to retreat for another three years, against Dongchu's wishes.
37. See Yen, *Shengyan fashi xuesi lichen*, 169–170.
38. These details come from my conversations with Sheng Yen around 1996, when I was interviewing him for a biography in English. These interviews took place over a span of a month at the Chan Meditation Center in Queens, New York, but the book was never completed.

39. See Yen, *Guicheng*, 294.
40. Dongchu had always wanted Sheng Yen to stay by his side. After the first three years of his solitary retreat, Sheng Yen was asked by Dongchu to end his retreat. Sheng Yen resisted and after he completed his six years of retreat, Dongchu also wanted him to return to him. This time, the news of Sheng Yen wanting to go to Japan for advanced doctoral work shocked the Taiwanese community. It is uncertain why Sheng Yen received no support from his Taiwanese Buddhist community. Perhaps it was due to the ill will leftover from the Japanese colonization; most elder Taiwanese clerics were concerned with "de-Japanifying" Taiwanese Buddhism. Or perhaps many also held an inferiority complex vis-à-vis Japanese Buddhism with regard to modernization.
41. Ban Tetsugyu 伴鉄牛 was born in Hanamaki city (Iwate Prefecture) on June 4, 1910. He was ordained as a Sōtō Zen monk by Fuchizawa Chimyo 淵沢智明 Rōshi on July 9, 1917, and received dharma transmission (*inka*) from him. From 1931 to 1938, he practiced at Hosshin-ji 発心寺 Temple. He became a student at a Sōtō Zen university, Komazawa University, in 1938 and graduated in 1941. After the war, he became a *tanto* 単頭 or head monk at Hosshin-ji in 1947, and also a *tanto* at Hōon-ji 法恩寺 in Iwate Prefecture in 1948, and became a master of Tosho-ji 東照寺. He also received Dharma transmission from Harada Daiun Sogaku 原田大雲祖岳 (1871–1961). Ban Tetsugyu established two temples in Japan: Kannon-ji 観音寺 in Iwate in 1971 and Tetsugyu-ji 鉄牛寺 in Oita in 1985. On May 10, 1992, he retired from Tosho-ji, and he passed away on January 21, 1996. He was 86 years old. Ban Tetsugyu was known to be an extremely strict Zen teacher. For his teachings in Japanese, see Ban Tetsugyu 伴鉄牛, *Gendai mumonkan* 現代無門関 [A Modern *Gateless Gate*] (Fukuoka 福岡県, Japan: Nakagawa Tetsugen 中川鉄厳, 1980) and *Gendai hekigan roku* 現代碧巌録 [A Modern *Blue Cliff Record*] (Fukuoka 福岡県, Japan: Nakagawa Tetsugen 中川鉄厳, 1983). There is also a three-volume autobiography: Ban Tetsugyu 伴鉄牛, *Gutoku tetsugyu: Ban Tetsugyu jiden* 愚禿鉄牛: 伴鉄牛自伝 [Ignorant Bull: The Autobiography of Ban Tetsugyu] (Fukuoka 福岡県, Japan: Nakagawa Tetsugen 中川鉄厳, 1976–1981). Sheng Yen did three intensive retreats with him. In my interview with the current abbot of Tokyo's Tosho-ji 東照寺, Master Deguchi Tetsujyo 出口鐵城 (b. 1951), I learned that Sheng Yen must have done his retreats at Kannon-ji in Iwate Prefecture in 1975.
42. For a brief biography of C. T. Shen, see Sheng Yen, *Footprints in the Snow*, 146. Later Sheng Yen had learned that C. T. Shen supported his doctorate studies in Japan because the latter was an admirer of his Buddhist essays when he was writing and publishing in the army and his solitary retreat. C. T. Shen had been following Sheng Yen's career from a distance.
43. See Richard Hughes Seager, *Buddhism in America* (New York: Columbia University Press, 1999); and for American's earlier exposure to Buddhism, see Thomas Tweed, *The American Encounter with Buddhism, 1844–1912* (Chapel Hill and London: University of North Carolina Press, 1992).
44. In his books on Chan, he avoided sectarian views and in his works on other subjects, such as precepts, he avoided the common practice of Chinese clerics of aligning themselves with a particular school or precept lineage; see Sheng Yen, *Chanmen lishu ji* 禪門驪珠集 [Dragons and Pearls within the Chan Gate] (Taipei: Dongchu chubanshe, 1984; reprint, Taipei: Dharma Drum Corporation, 1999), 4; *Pusajie zhiyao* 菩薩戒指要 [Essence of the Bodhisattva Precepts] (Taipei: Dharma Drum Corporation, 1996), 13; and also his autobiography, *Shengyan fashi xuesi lichen*, 170–173.
45. For more on Sheng Yen's formulations of Buddhist orthodoxy and Chan Buddhism, see chapters 2 through 4 of my *Reimagining Chan Buddhism*, 58–181.
46. Technically Master Dongchu was only the 50th-generation lineage holder from Chan master Dongshan Liangjie 洞山良价 (807–869), in the Jiaoshan sublineage (*Jiaoshan xi* 焦山系) of the Caodong school. His Linji affiliation comes from the fact that he also trained at a Linji monastery, Tian'ning Monastery 天寧寺 in Changzhou City, Jiangsu Province, and was tonsured at Linji Monastery at Mount Putuo. I am unable to confirm whether he received a separate transmission in the Linji line from Dongchu; my

understanding that he received both lines from Dongchu comes from my own conversation with him. See Yen, *Shengyan fashi xuesi lichen*, 51. Dongchu had only one other disciple, master Shengkai 聖開 (1918–1996), who did not stay in touch with Dongchu after his tonsure in 1967.

47. See Yen, *Shengyan fashi xuesi lichen*, 137–138.
48. Sheng Yen had told me in a conversation that when he saw master Lingyuan, the later asked him what he had been doing for the past few years in America, and Sheng Yen replied that he had been "Deceiving Americans, teaching them Chan." Lingyuan proceeded to state that, "Well then, you'll need proper credentials to do that," and proceeded to ask his attendant to take out the Dharma transmission book and gave a new dharma name for Sheng Yen and simply asked him to make three prostrations to acknowledge the responsibility to continue the Linji lineage of Chan. My conversation with Sheng Yen occurred in the summer of 1995.
49. "Venerable Master Sheng Yen, University Founder: DDSU" (https://www.ddsu.org/english/%3Fpage_id=1056).
50. See my *Reimagining Chan Buddhism*, 100–110.
51. For the sociopolitical repercussions of the ending of the martial law, see James D. Seymour, "Taiwan in 1987: A Year of Political Bombshells," *Asian Survey* 28, no. 1 (January 1988): 71–77.
52. Sheng Yen explains the commonality among various folkloric beliefs (*mingjian xingyang* 民間信仰) as materialist (*gongli de* 功利的) and self-serving (*gongyong de* 功用的), which he observed as "unreasonable demands that come from selfish desires" (*sili er qiu buheli de liyi* 私利而求不合理的利益); and see Sheng Yen, "Taiwan de zongjiao wenti 台湾的宗教問題" [Religious Questions in Taiwan], in *Mingri de fojiao* 明日的佛教 (A Buddhism for Tomorrow) (Taipei: Dharma Drum Corporation, 2005), 191–192.
53. Master Sheng Yen (https://chancenter.org/cmc/bios-2/), Chan Meditation Center.
54. See my *Reimagining Chan Buddhism*, 14–17.
55. Yen's *Guicheng* 歸程 (The Return Home) was first published in 1968, and his *Shengyan fashi xuesi lichen* 聖嚴法師學思歷程 (The Intellectual Development of Venerable Sheng Yen) was first published in 1993. By analyzing his autobiographies, we gain access to Sheng Yen's own imagination of himself in history. By using other sources, I am able to place him in the circumstances of the times that might have influenced him. I try to maintain a balance between the authorial voice coming from these sources and my reconstruction of the historical contingencies that shaped Sheng Yen's life.
56. See *Guicheng* 歸程 [The Return Home] (Taipei: Fagu chubanshe, 1968; reprint, Taipei: Dharma Drum Corporation, 1999), 3.
57. See the Sun Yat Sen Academic and Cultural Foundation website (http://www.sysacf.org.tw/index.php%3Faction=grants_detail%26fid=39%26cid=121%26id=259).
58. There is a series of multivolume conference proceedings from Taiwan, the *Sheng Yen yanjiu* 聖嚴研究 (Studies of Sheng Yen), dating back to 2010. The volumes can be downloaded from the Sheng Yen Education Foundation website (http://www.shengyen.org.tw/ListOrdinary.aspx%3Fpid=252%26lang=cht%26type=L).
59. See Lin Qixian 林其賢, *Shengyan fashi nianpu* 聖嚴法師年譜 [A Chronological Biography of Master Sheng Yen], 4 vols. (Taipei: Dharma Drum Corporation, 2016). Mr. Lin also has an earlier version of this work, documenting Sheng Yen's literary production until age 70. I used both for this research.
60. See Shi Shuqing 施叔青, *Kumu kaihua: Shengyan fashi zhuan* 枯木開花: 聖嚴法師傳 [Blossoms from a Withered Tree] (Taipei: Shibao Publishing, 2000).
61. See Richard Madsen, *Democracy's Dharma: Religious Renaissance and Political Development in Taiwan* (Berkeley: University of California Press, 2007).
62. See Stuart Chandler, *Establishing a Pure Land on Earth: The Foguang Buddhist Perspective on Modernization and Globalization* (Honolulu: University of Hawaii Press, 2004).

63. See Julia Huang, *Charisma and Compassion: Cheng Yen and the Buddhist Tzu Chi Movement* (Cambridge, MA and London: Harvard University Press, 2009).
64. My own academic study of Sheng Yen is the only sustained study of Sheng Yen in any language; see Jimmy Yu, *Reimagining Chan Buddhism*.

Jimmy Yu

SHINGON

The word *Shingon* 真言 is the Japanese pronunciation of the Chinese term *zhenyan*, literally meaning "true words," and serves as the Sino-Japanese translation of the Sanskrit word *mantra*.

Shingon is often referred to as Shingon Esoteric Buddhism, "Secret Mantra Teachings of the Buddha," or simply as Esoteric Buddhism, and is often taken to be in some sense synonymous with tantric Buddhism, or Vajrayāna, depending on text and context. Modern scholars and premodern scholiasts have at times played into this ambiguity.[1] In the Japanese context, in addition to functioning as a broadly defined area of study or esoteric ritual culture within which many major state temples participated, Shingon also came to be the name of a particular sect or school, the Shingon-shū 真言宗 that looks to the monk Kūkai 空海 (774–835) as its founder, with antecedents in China and India.[2]

Mantras are generally understood to express supramundane power and invoke or manifest a deity or divine source of power and produce spiritual effects in this world or the next. Mantras are said not simply to represent that power but, rather, to be that power in a fundamental sense, collapsing the distinction between signifier and signified. Many mantras are written in some form of Sanskrit. In China, *hanzi* 漢字, or Chinese characters, were often used to transliterate these mantras, but in many cases in China, and especially in Japan, they are often written in the Siddhaṃ script, an early script for writing Sanskrit. Mantras often begin with the Sanskrit syllables "Oṃ" or "Namaḥ," and conclude with the phrase "*hūṃ*" or "*svāhā*," and so on, and may contain the name or esoteric appellation of a buddha, bodhisattva, or god, or some variation thereof. While mantras often function to invoke a particular deity, they are also said to distill the power of a deity or text. Mantras often function alongside *dhāraṇī*, which may be defined as invocations that are generally, but not always, longer than mantras, sometimes a paragraph or a page in length. *Dhāraṇī* and spells appear throughout Mahāyāna scriptural literature, and diverse genres of *dhāraṇī* texts have been very influential throughout Mahāyāna Buddhist history. Mantra, *dhāraṇī*, and spells are not always so clearly defined, and there is a high degree of fluidity between these three. Later Shingon mantra theory suggests that the physical world and spiritual world are woven together like the syllables of a mantra, fundamentally composed of the same basic elements that abide in a state of fundamental union (yoga), and in the same way, buddhas, bodhisattvas, and gods, and even ordinary beings, are ultimately contiguous or interconnected. The path to realizing one's participation in this ultimate reality is opened through esoteric initiation, or *abhiṣeka* 灌頂 (C. *guanding*, J. *kanjō*), into the ritual and doctrinal engagement with the tantras, of which mantra recitation forms an integral part.

How best to distinguish Shingon from tantric Buddhism, Vajrayāna, and Esoteric Buddhism is an ongoing area of scholarly dialogue. The term 'tantra' is defined variously in Anglophone popular and academic literature, but at its most basic, a tantra is a loosely defined genre of ritual manuals, among other similar genres, that may be found throughout South Asian religions, including Hinduism, Buddhism, Jainism, and so on. The tantras draw on South Asian spell craft and secrecy, or esotericism, and generally require initiation and are said to lead to rapid attainment of spiritual prowess. Buddhist tantras draw on and presuppose a high level of fluency in mainstream Buddhist doctrine and practice. Mahāyāna and Theravāda Buddhist cultures have their own unique tantric traditions, which commonly include such features as esoteric transmission, nonduality, sacred physiology, the magical power of language (especially Sanskrit), subversive sexual imagery, and militaristic imagery, as well as literal or metaphorical utilization of substances regarded as impure, such as meat, alcohol, blood, or semen, that are transformed into tools for awakening.

Indo-Tibetan tantric discourse often employs the term *Vajrayāna*, diamond or lightning bolt vehicle, to emphasize the diamond-like indestructibility of Buddha nature and/or the rapidity, or "lightning bolt" quality, of the tantric path. So central is Vajrayāna discourse and the practice of tantras within Tibetan Buddhism that the whole of the Tibetan tradition is sometimes mistakenly assumed to be synonymous with Vajrayāna, which is more correctly understood as a particular discourse about the tantras. Vajrayāna is often paired with or contrasted with the *pāramitā-yāna*, the vehicle of the perfections. While the *pāramitā-yāna* is exoteric, the Vajrayāna is esoteric, the *pāramitā-yāna* gradual, the Vajrayāna is rapid, and so on.[3]

In the East Asian context, the situation is a bit more complicated. Tantras were not necessarily seen as a fundamentally separate kind of text set apart from sutras. And South and Central Asian spell craft and cultural esotericism fit well with similar aspects of Chinese culture. For example, the *Mahāvairocana sūtra* 大日経 (T. 848; C. *Darijing*; J. *Dainichikyō*), is labeled as a tantra in Tibet but a sutra, or *jing* 経, in Chinese.[4] While the term *Vajrayāna* does appear in the East Asian context, the term *Mijiao* 密教 (J. *Mikkyō*) or "secret teachings," is somewhat more common, thus emphasizing the esoteric quality of tantric culture and ritual initiation and transmission. Therefore, it may be helpful to use the term *Vajrayāna* when referring to the Tibetan reception of the tantras and *Esoteric Buddhism* when referring to the East Asian reception of the tantras. Shingon has also at times functioned as a synonym for East Asian Esoteric Buddhism, as such scholars may at times think of Shingon, or Shingon Esoteric Buddhism, as a loosely constituted constellation of lineages, texts, and practices associated with the eastward flow of the tantras.

CHINESE DEVELOPMENTS

Early Mahāyāna Buddhist texts transmitted into China included spell texts and *dhāraṇī* texts alongside sutras and philosophical treatises. Some of the most important early genres of *dhāraṇī* texts were dedicated to esoteric emanations of Avalokiteśvara Bodhisattva. This likely reflects the proliferation of *dhāraṇī* texts and protection spells within Indian Buddhism. In the mid-6th century, Atikūṭa 阿地瞿多 (mid-6th century) translated the *Dhāraṇīsaṃgraha-sūtra* 陀羅尼集経 (T. 901), which sits stylistically somewhere between the more diffuse *dhāraṇī* texts and spell texts and the more integrated tantric systems of the Tang dynasty (618–906).[5] In this era, many of the elements so characteristic of Shingon Esoteric Buddhism begin to be systematically integrated, such as mantra, esoteric fire rituals known as *homa* 護摩 (C. *humo*, J. *goma*), *abhiṣekha*, and so on.

Shingon Esoteric Buddhism flourished at the very pinnacle of Chinese Buddhist culture during the Tang.[6] Śubhakarasiṃha 善無畏 (637–735), Yixing 一行 (683–727), Vajrabodhi 金剛智 (669–741), and Amoghavajra 不空金剛 (705–774), are generally regarded as the founders and early transmitters of Esoteric Buddhism to China. These figures, Amoghavajra in particular, promoted the esoteric transmission of the tantras, *abhiṣekha*, the attainment of buddhahood in this very body 即身成仏 (C. *jishen chengfo*; J. *sokushin jōbutsu*), and the construction and ritual consecration of mandalas. Two of the most important texts transmitted in this period include the *Mahāvairocana-sūtra* and the **Sarva-tathāgata-tattva-saṃgrahaṃ nāma mahāyāna-sūtram* 金剛頂瑜伽中略出念誦経 (T. 866), commonly referred to as the *Vajraśekhara-sūtra* cycle.

Shingon tradition suggests that East Asian Esoteric Buddhism begins with Śubhakarasiṃha, purportedly a central Indian prince who entered the sangha after taking up arms against his brothers in a succession dispute. More recent research, however, has suggested that while Śubhakarasiṃha certainly transmitted many of the elements now associated with Shingon Esoteric Buddhism, it is unlikely that he understood himself or was understood in China as transmitting a new kind of Buddhism. As a monk he studied under a master named Dharmagupta, learning *dhāraṇī*, and mastering the three mysteries. According to tradition, under Mt. Kukkuṭapāda he had mystical encounters with Avalokiteśvara and Mahākāśyapa. Later, a divine being implored him to travel to China to teach in the land guarded by Mañjuśrī, the bodhisattva of wisdom. Śubhakarasiṃha embarked on a journey to China, arriving in Chang'an in 716.

Śubhakarasiṃha was a prolific translator but is known in particular for the *Mahāvairocana-sūtra*, which he produced in collaboration with Yixing. The *Susiddhikara-sūtra* 蘇悉地羯羅経 (T. 893), also translated by Śubhākarasiṃha, became an important text in the Japanese Tendai Esoteric tradition. The *Mahāvairocana sūtra* presents a dialogue between Mahāvairocana and Vajrapāṇi Bodhisattva. The first chapter provides a more doctrinal exposition of the nature of mantra and mind, and the subsequent chapters lay out systematically mandalas, mudras, and mantras and thus generally fit within the genre of tantric ritual manual. This text generally corresponds to the Womb Realm Mandala 胎蔵界曼荼羅 (J. *Taizōkai mandara*), said to be an expression of ultimate reality in its quiescent and compassionate nature.

Śubhakarasiṃha's collaborator Yixing was a famous polymath with facility in Tiantai, Chan, Daoism, and astronomy, as well as other fields. He also wrote an extremely influential commentary on the *Mahāvairocana-sūtra*, the *Darijingshu* 大日経疏 (T. 1796), which is particularly focused on the concept of attaining buddhahood in this body.[7]

Doctrinal knowledge and initiation are only the initial stages along the Shingon path, which emphasizes the corporeality of awakening. The fundamental unity of ordinary beings and buddha reality is not limited to a doctrinal proposition but, rather, is said to be actualized within the ritual arena, which reveals the inherent wisdom and compassion woven into the very fabric of reality. This coordinated ritual invocation is referred to as the three mysteries 三密 (C. *sanmi*; J. *sanmitsu*). Ordinarily, it is understood that body, speech, and mind function as the three sites of karmic production. However, in the Shingon system, the body, speech, and mind of the practitioner is said to abide in a nondual union, or yoga, with the body, speech, and mind of Mahāvairocana, or ultimate reality. The mystery of body is realized through the performance of mudras, coded movements of the hands, fingers, and body imbued with esoteric meanings such as the elements, sacred Sanskrit syllables, buddhas, bodhisattvas, gods, and so on. The mystery of speech is realized through chanting mantras, sacred incantations performed in conjunction with these mudras, as with mudras the syllables of the mantra themselves may be encoded with special esoteric meanings. The mystery of mind is realized through visualization, contemplation, and devotional practices dedicated to mandalas or mandalic depictions of deities in palatial geometric structures pulling together the diverse elements and symbols of the esoteric tradition. Through initiation and empowerment, or *adhiṣṭhāna* 加持 (C. *jiachi*, J. *kaji*), of the three mysteries, the esoteric truth that all forms are aspects of Mahāvairocana, all sound and speech comprise the words of Mahāvairocana, and all mentation is the mind of Mahāvairocana; thus, one is awakened to the esoteric truth that one is always already a participant in dharmakāya, the "dharma body," or ultimate reality. Realizing one's nonduality with this awakened reality is referred to as the attainment of buddhahood in this very body. As a living buddha, the Shingon practitioner is said to be able to perform rituals that may bring rain, slay enemies on the battlefield, cure illnesses in the body, help one attain rebirth in a buddha or bodhisattva's pure land, and so on.[8]

Following Śubhakarasiṃha, Vajrabodhi arrived in 719 in Canton via the southern sea route. Supposedly, Vajrabodhi studied under a mysterious eight-hundred-year-old monk named Nāgabodhi, who is supposed to have studied under the 2nd-century Madhyamaka master Nāgārjuna. Vajrabodhi presented his teachings on the mantra path in terms of the distinction between exoteric and esoteric and performed *abhiṣekha* empowerments, and sometimes employed the term *Vajrayāna*. Purportedly from a Brahmin family in southern India, Vajrabodhi studied at the great monastery Nālandā. Vajrabodhi is said to have employed child mediums to communicate with King Yama, the lord of hell, when Emperor Xuanzang's daughter became ill. That his daughter returned from the land of the dead for a short period inspired Emperor Xuanzang to give him patronage. Vajrabodhi is credited with introducing the *Vajraśekhara-sūtra* cycle, which, alongside the *Mahāvairocana-sūtra*, respectively constitutes the ritual and doctrinal foundations for Shingon Esoteric Buddhism.[9]

This sutra also corresponds to the Vajra Realm Mandala 金剛界曼荼羅 (J. *Kongōkai mandara*), which is said to depict ultimate reality as dynamic wisdom. The Womb Realm Mandala and Vajra Realm Mandalas taken together constitute the dual-mandala system. The Vajra and Womb are ultimately nondual expressions of ultimate reality and serve as important repositories of esoteric art and ritual and serve as powerful objects of devotion in their own right.[10]

Vajrabodhi's student Amoghavajra is regarded by some as the true founder of what we now know as East Asian Esoteric Buddhism, as a particular approach and lineage consciousness rooted in the three mysteries, *abhiṣekha* initiation, and so on. Amoghavajra was of Indo-Sogdian descent and moved to China at a young age. Amoghavajra studied under Vajrabodhi's tutelage and later traveled to Sri Lanka and the Malay Peninsula and returned to Chang'an in 756, introducing a systematic approach to the tantras. During the An Lushan 安禄山 rebellion, Amoghavajra was asked by the emperor to use his spiritual prowess to fight against the Tibetan armies. Amoghavajra was an extremely prolific translator who, among other things, produced new versions of the *Renwang-jing* 仁王経 (T. 246) and a new translation of the

Vajraśekhara-sūtra, *Jingangding yiqie rulai zhenshi shedasheng xianzheng dajiaowang jing* 金剛頂一切如来真実摂大乗現証大教王経 (T. 874). A ritual dedicated to the Buddha Amitāyus, *Wuliangshou rulai xiu guanxing gongyang yigui* 無量壽如來修觀行供養儀軌 (T. 930, hereafter, *Wuliangshou yigui*), is a foundational text in Japanese Shingon Buddhist ritual training and helped inspire much of what has come to be known as Esoteric Pure Land Buddhism. Another important Shingon text translated by Amoghavajra is the *Adhyardhaśatikāprajñāpāramitā Sūtra* 大樂金剛不空眞實三摩耶經 般若波羅蜜多理趣経 (T. 243), commonly known by the abbreviated Japanese title, *Rishukyō* 理趣経. This text is chanted daily in contemporary Shingon temples.[11]

From the Song 宋 (960–1279) period, we see a decline in clearly defined Esoteric lineage consciousness and, at the same time, the broad diffusion of Esoteric thought and practices integrated into the previously established *dhāraṇī* and spell texts that flourished at the foundations of Chinese Buddhism. During the Mongol-led Yuan 元 dynasty (1271–1368), the Han Chinese–led Ming 明 dynasty (1368–1644), and the Manchurian-led Qing 清 dynasty (1644–1911), Tibetan Esoteric Buddhism, or Vajrayāna, flourished within the highest echelons of Chinese Buddhist culture, with emperors often pursuing a priest–patron relationship with Lamas from Tibet.[12]

SHINGON IN JAPAN

While Shingon is today regarded as a sect of Japanese Buddhism, when Shingon was first transmitted to Japan, it largely functioned as a body of ritual and doctrinal repertoires on which monastic and lay practitioners could draw. As in China, Shingon lineages flourished alongside and as a complement to other areas of doctrinal and ritual specialization and in close proximity to the imperial family, serving to legitimate the ruler's religio-political power and authority. As *dhāraṇī* texts and early esoteric systems flourished in China, these texts, images, and practices were transmitted to Japan. For example, various dhāraṇī texts and texts associated with Śubhakarasiṃha, Vajrabodhi, and Amoghavajra were in circulation in Japan before Kūkai's career.[13]

In addition to the official transmission and circulation of texts that would become associated with Esoteric Buddhism, Mahāyāna spell culture and esotericism circulated beyond so-called orthodox circles. For example, the ascetic En no Gyōja 役行者 (7th–8th century), who practiced in the Katsuragi mountains 葛木山, was both an object of fear and fascination. While many legends surround this figure, we may think of En no Gyōja as a symbol for the more widely diffused *sanrin gyōja* 山林行者, ascetic of the mountains and forests. This culture of unorthodox practitioners of the esoteric arts would later serve an important role in the establishment and broader diffusion of Shingon Esoteric Buddhism throughout Japan, eventually influencing such movements as Shugendō 修験道 and what came to be known as Shintō 神道.

KŪKAI AND SHINGON BUDDHISM

Kūkai is regarded as the de facto founder of Shingon in Japan. In Kūkai's career, we see the unification of official and unofficial monastic engagement with Esoteric Buddhism and the systematic integration of Tang Esoteric Buddhist ritual culture into the monastic curriculum. Thereafter Esoteric Buddhist theory and practice came to have a great influence on Japanese religion and culture. Kūkai was born Mao 真魚 of the Saeki 佐伯 family, a branch of the Ōmoto clan, purportedly on the island of Shikoku where the temple Zentsūji 善通寺 now stands. It seems that the fortunes of this aristocratic family were waning, and at the age of fifteen, Kūkai enrolled in the state academy, which was primarily based in the Confucian classics. However, it seems that the young Kūkai grew disillusioned with this life path and dropped out to pursue ascetic practice on the island of Shikoku. In Kūkai's *Sangō shiki* 三教指帰, written in 797, he explores the teachings of Buddhism, Daoism, and Confucianism, and argues for the superiority of Buddhism. Today a famous 88-temple pilgrimage route dedicated to Kūkai encircles Shikoku, where he pursued his austerities. At some point, Kūkai encountered a monk who may have inspired him to pursue the religious life and introduced him to the *Kokūzōbosatsu shomon shichibutsu daranikyō* 虚空蔵菩薩諸問七仏陀羅尼経 (T. 1333), from which is derived the *gumonjihō* 求聞持法, a ritual dedicated to Ākāśagarbha Bodhisattva. According to this text, if one recites the mantra of Ākāśagarbha one million times, the practitioner will acquire perfect memory and the ability to remember and understand all the Buddha Dharma. Through this mantra practice one night, he had a profound experience as he saw the rising morning star. When he sought counsel from leading authorities, he was advised to travel to China to study Esoteric Buddhism there. The *Mahāvairocana-sūtra* seems to have also inspired Kūkai as this sutra/tantra contains many mantras in the Siddhaṃ script, and there were purportedly no monks in Japan who could explain these mantras, so it was essential that Kūkai travel to China.

As luck would have it, Kūkai was ordained at Tōdaiji in 804, just in time for the emperor's special envoy to China. As part of this mission, Kūkai was able to learn the latest forms of Chinese Buddhism. There he studied in the capital in Chang'an 長安, a major hub of the Silk Road and was able to study under Huiguo 恵果 (746–805) at Qinglongsi 青龍寺, as well as an Indian master named Prajñā, from whom he learned Sanskrit. In 806, Kūkai returned to Japan, residing in Kyushu until he was invited to the capital three years later. At that time the emperor became aware of his high level of proficiency in Esoteric Buddhist rituals, and he was quickly given additional resources and responsibilities. From that time, he resided at Takaosanji 高雄山寺, now known as Jingoji 神護寺, where he performed an esoteric state protection ritual in 810. Takaosanji would become an important Shingon center. In 816, Emperor Saga 嵯峨天皇 (785–842, r. 809–823) gave Kūkai permission to establish a monastic training center dedicated to Shingon Esoteric Buddhism on Kōyasan, where his mausoleum would be established after he passed away on the mountain in 835. The importance of Kōyasan as a pilgrimage site is examined in more detail in a later section. In 822, Kūkai established the *abhiṣeka* hall at Tōdaiji in Nara, the central institution of the monastic administration bureau in the old capital. In 823, Kūkai was appointed abbot of Tōji (Eastern Temple), one of the two main temples near the front gates of the new capital in Kyoto.

Tōji, or the Eastern Temple, was established shortly after the capital was moved to Heian-kyō, and along with Saiji, the Western Temple, Toji was positioned near the gates of the new capital. After Kūkai took over the administration of Tōji, he established on the temple grounds an educational institute called Shugeishuchi-in 綜芸種智院 there, which is said to have been like a public school where commoners could be educated, the first of its kind. The main object of devotion at Tōji is the Medicine Buddha, and as it was located in the capital, various rituals connected to the court have been central to Tōji's ritual activity, including the Mishuhō.

Throughout its history, Tōji has been a major landholding institution, and given its connection to Kūkai's legacy, it has often served as a key center for Shingon scholarship and practice. Following Kūkai, his top disciple Jichie 実恵 (786–847) and Hossō scholar took charge of Tōji as *chōja* 長者. Beginning with Kangen 観賢 (853–925), the third Tōji *chōja*, Kongōbuji was placed under the charge of the Tōji *chōja*. In 921, Kangen procured for Kūkai the honorific title Kōbō Daishi 弘法大師, "the great master who spreads the dharma," by which Kūkai is commonly known today. Tōji apparently experienced a period of decline but was revived in the medieval period as popular devotion to Kūkai as a bodhisattva-like savior figure spread.

In 827, Kūkai was appointed to the top post within the monastic bureau and began performing important rituals for the imperial court. In 834, Kūkai established the *Mishuhō* 御修法, an important ritual in the court's calendar. Just before he retired to Kōyasan and passed away in 835, Kūkai established the Shingon-in 真言院 chapel inside the imperial palace, the first temple to be built inside the palace. Throughout his life, Kūkai was a prolific ritual master, scholar, and administrator working at the very pinnacle of Heian and Nara Buddhist institutional life. Through his efforts, Shingon Esoteric Buddhism was firmly established as an important area of study within Japanese Buddhism. While we may think of Shingon Buddhism as a particular school of Japanese Buddhism, during Kūkai's day, to be a practitioner or mantra, one simply had to receive *abhiṣeka* from a qualified teacher. In other words, the study and practice of Shingon Buddhism functioned within the broader network of traditions, empowering scholars of Madhyamaka, Yogācāra, Vinaya, or practitioners of Pure Land, Tendai, or Zen, to participate in this new ritual culture.[14]

KŪKAI'S SHINGON TEACHINGS

During Kūkai's lifetime, he was a prolific writer and ritual theorist. Emperor Junna 淳和天皇 (785–840; r. 810–823) asked Kūkai to summarize his teachings, which led to the composition of the *Himitsu mandara jūjushinron* 秘密曼荼羅十住心論 (T. 2425), wherein he delineates ten levels at which beings may comprehend the dharma:[15]

1. 異生羝羊心, mind like a sheep, consumed by desires
2. 愚童持斎心, mind like a foolish child (this seems to have referred to materialistic philosophies like Confucianism)
3. 嬰童無畏心, mind like a smart child (this includes religious philosophies like Daoism and Brahmanism, non-Buddhist traditions oriented toward the spiritual)
4. 唯蘊無我心, mind that comprehends the five aggregates and no-self (non-Mahāyāna Buddhism)
5. 抜業因種心, mind that is free from the laws of karma (non-Mahāyāna *pratyekabuddha*)
6. 他縁大乗心, mind that comprehends interconnectedness and compassion (Mahāyāna, Yogācāra)
7. 覚心不生心, mind that comprehends non-arising, śūnyatā, and wisdom (Mahāyāna, Madhyamaka)
8. 一道無為心, mind that comprehends the One Vehicle (Mahāyāna, Tiantai)

9. 極無自性心, mind that moves beyond the extremes of nothingness and self-nature (Mahāyāna, Huayan)
10. 秘密莊厳心, the mind of esoteric adornment (Mahāvairocana Buddha)

It is common to read this as a simple polemic wherein Kūkai is presenting his teachings as the ultimate, while everything else is provisional. However, there are vertical and horizontal readings of this list. On one hand, the Esoteric is the highest, or deepest, insight into the nature of reality as understood by a buddha; on the other hand, the Esoteric perspective is actually inherent in all the levels to varying degrees. From the Esoteric perspective, even the shallow may reveal the deep.

MAJOR WORKS

While Kūkai is best known today for his innovative teachings on the nature of ritual, his theory of mantra, and the exoteric and esoteric revelation of Buddhist teachings, during this lifetime he was best known as a ritual master working within the state monastic system. Important works attributed to Kūkai include the *Benkenmitsu nikyōron* 弁顕密二教論 (T. 2427), for example, which is generally taken to be Kūkai's profound statement on the major differences between the exoteric and esoteric. *Sokushin jōbutsugi* 即身成仏義 (T. 2428) provides the theoretical foundation for the three mysteries as the path to buddhahood in this body. According to Kūkai, the six elements that compose all things are the body of *dharmakāya*, and through the practice of the three mysteries, one is able to fully realize the fundamental nonduality of practitioner and buddha reality, attaining Buddhahood in this very body. *Shoji jissō gi* 声字実相義 (T. 2429) explores Kūkai's theory that reality is itself an expression of, or constituted by, the primordial mantra of *dharmakāya*. *Unjigi* 吽字義 (T. 2430) explores the deeper meanings of the seed syllable hūm: *h, a, ū, m*. In Esoteric Buddhism, mantras are saturated with deeper and deeper levels of meaning, with each syllable corresponding so such concepts as causation, emptiness, the bodies of the buddha, and so on. This text may in some sense be considered a template for deep engagement with other mantras and seed syllables.[16]

SHINGON LINEAGE

One of the interesting components of the Shingon tradition is its unique conception of lineage. While Chan Buddhism and various other lineages connect their transmission to Śākyamuni Buddha, Shingon lineage traces itself back to the cosmic buddha Mahāvairocana Tathāgata, an anthropomorphic depiction of the *dharmakāya*. Ultimately, Shingon lineage depicts Śākyamuni as an emanation of Mahāvairocana. It is from Mahāvairocana that the Esoteric teachings arise, while so-called Exoteric Buddhist teachings and texts arise through accommodated forms in response to the capacities of beings. Mainstream Mahāyāna Buddhist Buddhology presupposes a "three-body" theory, or *trikāya*. Śākyamuni Buddha, the historical founder and corporeal form, may be conceived of as a nirmāṇakāya, a form taken on by ultimate reality so as to meet beings where they are. Next, buddhas like the Medicine Buddha, Amitābha Buddha, or Akṣobhya Buddha may be thought of as *saṃbhogakāya* buddhas, or reward bodies that beings may encounter in a Pure Land or a deep state of meditation.

Nirmana-kaya and *saṃbhogakāya* buddhas participate in and are expressions of *dharmakaya*, the body of reality. In general, these diverse forms taken on by ultimate reality are active in teaching and guiding beings, while the *dharmakaya* is quiescent, fundamentally non-arising, and so on. Drawing on nondualistic Mahāyāna teachings, however, Shingon thinkers like Kūkai emphasized the idea that the *dharmakāya* itself teaches and that Shingon is precisely this teaching. In other words, Shingon is said to be a direct transmission of ultimate reality itself realized through the practice of the three mysteries. It is not exactly that Śākyamuni is not included but, rather, that the historical Buddha is seen as a participant, one who as well received this fundamental transmission.

SHINGON PRACTICES

Preliminary ritual training in Shingon begins with the *shido kegyō* 四度加行, a fourfold ritual regimen that allows a monk to take the *denbō kanjō* 伝法灌頂, signifying that the practitioner is able to train others. The four components of the *shido kegyō* include *jūhachi dōhō* 十八道法, a ritual template beginning with purifying incantations and numerous *mudrās* and mantras. This template expands to integrate diverse rituals, such as the following three: *Kongōkai hō* 金剛界法, or rituals for the Vajra Realm Mandala, then the *Taizōkai hō* 胎蔵界法, rituals for the Womb Realm Mandala, and then the *goma hō* 護摩法, or apotropaic fire ritual. Traditionally, the study of the *shido kegyō* was premised on the preliminary study of Yogācāra or Madhyamaka.[17]

In addition to the secret teachings for ordained monastics, there are also practices available for laypeople. For example, the *Kōmyō Shingon*, which was further popularized by the Kegon scholiast Myōe 明恵 (1173–1232), was an important mantra practice during the medieval period. This mantra is recited for Pure Land rebirth and may be used to empower sand, which is then sprinkled over the body of a deceased person to aside them in achieving an advantageous rebirth.[18] Other important practices include the *Ajikan* 阿字観, or contemplation of the letter *a*. In tantric texts, the Sanskrit language is considered holy and uncreated, the cosmic speech of ultimate reality. The letter *a* is the first letter of the Sanskrit alphabet and indicates a negation prefix. Therefore, this letter is considered the mother of all letters and signifies the uncreated, unborn, non-arising of dharmas, emptiness, and *dharmakāya*. Contemplation of this letter upon a moon disk sitting atop a lotus blossom is part of some elite monastic practices but, in recent years, has become a practice open to laity as well, a Shingon response to the popularity of Zen meditation.[19]

KŌYASAN

Kūkai established Kōyasan as a dedicated practice site, far from the capital so that his students could focus on their practice without the distractions of capital life. Supposedly, one reason for choosing this site is that the eight peaks around the high mountain plain were said to resemble the eight-petaled lotus 八葉蓮華 (J. *hachiyō renge*) of the Womb Realm Mandala. Kūkai was a very in-demand ritual master, performing ceremonies for the court and training students, but toward the end of his life was able to retire to Kōyasan where he passed away.

His disciple Shinzen 真然 (804–891) built Kongōbuji 金剛峰寺 on the mountain. In 883, Shinzen led Emperor Yōzei 陽成天皇 (869–948, r. 876–884) to Kōyasan to pray for rebirth in Tuṣita. It appears that some of Kūkai's disciples had come to believe Kūkai shared a special relationship with Maitreya Bodhisattva, and soon legends emerged that Kūkai had not died on the mountain but, rather, entered into a state of eternal meditation, awaiting the descent of Maitreya. Early medieval legends would elaborate on this theme, and Kōyasan became a highly sought-after pilgrimage destination among marginal ascetics, aristocrats, and emperors. After Jichie, the administration of Tōji passed to Shinzei 真濟 (800–860), who consolidated the annual ordinands 年分度者 (J. *nenbundosha*) for Tōji and Kōyasan as a way to promote the site as a powerful Shingon center. However, repeated fires, financial mismanagement, competition between Tōji- and Kōyasan-based factions, as well as Kōyasan's distance from the capital all contributed to the eventual marginalization of the site. In 900, Emperor Uda 宇多天皇 (867–931, r. 887–897) made a pilgrimage to Kōyasan, and in 1023, Fujiwara no Michinaga's 藤原道長 (966–1028) made a pilgrimage as well; however, between these two trips, very few high-profile pilgrimages were made to Kōyasan, and the mountain site languished in obscurity until the mid-11th century when monks in Nara and Heian contributed to a revival of Kōyasan and the study of Kūkai's ritual and doctrinal theory.[20]

TENDAI AS A SHINGON SCHOOL

While Kūkai is often regarded as the founder of a distinct sect or school of Japanese Buddhism, when we read him in the institutional and cultural context of the early 9th century, we see that Kūkai functioned within the established order of his day, helping to update and influence elite Japanese ritual culture in particular. Following Kūkai's career, training in Shingon Esoteric Buddhist ritual prospered at Tōdaiji and Kōfukuji in the old capital of Nara; Tōji, Takaosanji, Daigoji 醍醐寺, and Ninnaji 仁和寺 in the Heian capital; and Enryakuji 延暦寺 on Mount Hiei, and Onjōji 園城寺 at the base of Mount Hiei.

Enryakuji and Onjōji are associated with Tendai Buddhism, transmitted to Japan by Saichō 最澄 (767–822), a monk who was part of the same delegation to China as Kūkai. Saichō had been chosen by the emperor because he had a stellar reputation, and his practice site on Mount Hiei was in an auspicious position for a temple to protect the realm. Saichō was supposed to travel to Chang'an like Kūkai, but his ship was blown off course, and he ended up studying on Mount Tiantai, where he acquired training in Tiantai studies, Esoteric Buddhism, the precepts, and a Zen lineage as well. While the Tendai Buddhist tradition we now associate with Saichō is often thought of as a sect or school of Japanese Buddhism, in the Chinese and Japanese context, Tendai has rather functioned as a comprehensive Mahāyāna tradition, and competition, diversity, and debate within the Tendai tradition were at least as great within as without.

Beginning with Saichō, Mt. Hiei monks trained in a dual curriculum focused on the Tiantai teachings and Esoteric Buddhism. While Saichō returned to Japan before Kūkai and was actually the first to perform Esoteric rituals for the emperor and the court, once Kūkai returned to Japan and his considerable acumen came to light, Kūkai quickly overshadowed Saichō. At one point, Kūkai performed rituals for Saichō and his students. Later, Saichō wrote to Kūkai to receive texts for his own study, but Kūkai replied that Saichō would have to come study with him first. Either due to his own busy schedule or perhaps because he took this as a rebuke, relations between the two cooled shortly thereafter. However, later generations of Tendai monks would establish their lineages as major players in Japanese Buddhist history, especially when it comes to Shingon Esoteric Buddhism. For this reason, we may also in some sense think of Tendai as a Shingon school at this time. After Saichō, monks on Hieizan came to establish themselves as major figures in the development of Japanese Esoteric Buddhism. The Tendai stream is often referred to as Taimitsu 台密, while the stream said to come from Kūkai's teaching is labeled Tōmitsu 東密, in reference to Tōji.[21] However, the situation is more complicated, with the streams overlapping and influencing each other throughout history.

Saichō's student Ennin was one of the most important Esoteric Buddhist thinkers in Japan. In 835, Ennin traveled to China, where he studied Tiantai doctrine, Pure Land practice, and Esoteric Buddhism. In China, Ennin studied the *Susiddhikāra*, alongside the *Mahāvairocana* and *Vajraśekhara* systems, which came to be the third great Esoteric text that practitioners drew on in Japan. Ennin returned to Japan suddenly in 842 in response to Emperor Wuzong 武宗 (814–846; r. 840–846) persecution of Buddhism. In 849, he began performing *abhiṣekha* on Mount Hiei and became abbot of Enryakuji in 854. Ennin divided Mahāyāna Buddhism into exoteric doctrinal traditions and esoteric ritual traditions. The esoteric was further divided into *rimitsu* 理密 (esoteric in principle: *Lotus*, nirvana, and *Avataṃsaka*) and *jirigumitsu* 事理俱密 (esoteric in principle and practice: *Mahāvairocana* and *Vajraśekhara*). In other words, while some teachings may contain some of the insights associated with Esoteric Buddhism, they lack the ritual component that brings these insights to life. In addition to his expertise with Tendai thought and Esoteric ritual, Ennin was also influential in his promotion of Pure Land practices, especially the *jōgyō sanmai* 常行三昧 (constant practice samādhi) and the five-tone *nenbutsu*. While Enryakuji may have functioned as the orthodox center for these Esoteric Tendai Pure Land practices, unofficial mountain practitioners drew on these traditions, promoting what some scholars refer to as *yama nenbutsu* 山念仏, or "mountain *nenbutsu*." Kōya 空也 (aka, Kūya, 903–972) was in Ennin's lineage and is closely associated with these mountain-based *nenbutsu* lineages, which went on to impact practice centers throughout Japan.

Enchin, the fifth abbot of Enryakuji, is regarded as the next great Taimitsu thinker. In 828, Enchin studied under Gishin 義真 (781–833), and in 851, traveled to China and studied on Tiantaishan 天台山, and even received initiations at Qinglongsi, the temple where Kūkai had studied. Enchin is regarded as the founder of the Jimon lineage, in contrast to the Sanmon lineage associated with Ennin. The Jimon lineage is based in Miidera 三井寺 (or Onjōji), at the base of the mountain and near Lake Biwa. Onjōji would by the medieval era emerge as a major center for Esoteric Buddhism in the capital alongside Tōji and Enryakuji.

Annen 安然 (841–902?) is often regarded as the third great Taimitsu theorist. Unlike Ennin and Enchin, Annen did not go to China. Nevertheless, his impact on Shingon thought in Japan was rather profound. Drawing on Zhiyi, Annen established a fivefold doctrinal categorization system in the *Taizō kongo bodaishingi ryaku mondō shō* 胎蔵金剛菩提心義略問答抄 (T. 2397): three vehicle teachings 三乗 (J. *sanjō*): the Tripitaka (*zō* 蔵), teachings common to Mahāyāna and Hinayana (*tsū* 通), teachings unique to the Mahāyāna (*betsu* 別), and the one vehicle teachings (*ichijō* 一乗): Perfect (*en* 円, including Tendai and Kegon) and Esoteric (*mitsu* 密).[22] While Ennin and Saichō saw Tendai and Shingon as unified, Annen saw

Tendai Shingon as superior to Tendai alone, absent Esoteric ritual empowerment. Annen was critical of Kūkai's Ten Stages of Mind, which positioned Tendai below Kegon, arguing that from the ultimate perspective of Shingon Esoteric Buddhism, all these distinctions should be collapsed as there is no fundamental difference between the buddhas who preached the different teachings. In thinking about the fluidity of what it meant to be a Shingon monk at this time, in the *Shingonshū kyōjigi* 真言宗教時義 (T. 2396), Annen describes himself and his teachings as Shingon. It seems that at this time, Shingon was understood as a repertoire of ritual knowledge on which monks who were initiated could draw, regardless of what we might imagine as sectarian affiliation.[23]

Under the monk Ryōgen 良源 (912–985), Mount Hiei truly emerged as a dominant center in the Japanese Buddhist landscape. Ryōgen was a skilled ritual master and, in some sense, a politician who built important relationships with Fujiwara no Morosuke 藤原師輔 (908–960) and eventually conferred tonsure to Morosuke's son, Jinzen 尋禅 (943–990), who later became the abbot of Mount Hiei. This helped establish the precedent for the position of abbot being occupied by the sons on aristocratic families.[24]

KŪKAI STUDIES AND THE KŌYASAN REVIVAL

Kūkai studies emerged as an influential area of scholasticism, and eventually served as a foundation for a network of temples, including Nara- and Heian-based institutions, as well as Kōyasan to serve as a check on the rising power of Mount Hieizan as a center of Shingon scholarship and ritual practice. In particular, monks at Ninnaji like Shōshin 性信 (1005–1085) and his student Saisen 済暹 (1025–1115), followed by Kyōjin 教尋 (d. 1141), Jōson 定尊 (*c.* 1118), Jitsuhan 実範 (*c.* 1089–1144), and Kakuban 覚鑁 (1095–1144), were especially influential. Saisen received abhiṣekha from Shōshin in 1084 and is remembered as the editor of the *Zoku henjōhokki shōryōshū hoketsu shō* 続遍照発揮性霊集補闕鈔 (3 fasc.), a work that had previously been lost, and helped systematize and promote Kūkai's thought as a focal point for Shingon scholarship.[25]

Ninnaji was founded by Emperor Uda 宇多天皇 (867–931; r. 887–897). Ninnaji is associated with the Hirosawa-ryū 広沢流, a major Shingon lineage. The principal object of devotion at Ninnaji is Amitābha Buddha, and near the main hall is a hall dedicated to Kūkai. In the early medieval period, Shukaku Hōshinnō 守覚法親王 (1150–1202) of Ninnaji was a major figure in elite Buddhist circles. Shukaku also resided on Kōyasan in 1177.[26]

Daigoji is another important center for Shingon practice affiliated with the imperial family. Daigoji was founded by Shōbō 聖宝 (832–909) in 874 and received its name from Emperor Daigo 醍醐天皇 (885–930; r. 897–930), who was buried there in 930. Shōbō is regarded as the founder of the Ono-ryū 小野流 lineage of the Shingon tradition. Shōbō began his career in Nara, and Daigoji maintained a close institutional relationship with Tōdaiji. Shōbō studied the dual mandala system under Shinzen 真然 (804–891) and Amitābha-centered rituals under Shinga 真雅 (801–879), both disciples of Kūkai. Shōbo also practiced mountain austerities in Kinbusen 金峯山 in Yamato 大和 (Nara Prefecture) and was later regarded as a Shugendō master. As Daigoji is near Mount Kasatori 笠取山, it has also been associated with mountain ascetics. The archives of Daigoji remain a major resource that deserves more sustained attention.

Because Kūkai did not necessarily found a new school or promote a sectarian lineage consciousness, diverse factions were able to compete for mastery of Esoteric ritual culture through the early medieval period. However, the dedicated lineage-based study of Kūkai's doctrinal works and devotion to his mausoleum on Kōyasan seems to have entered a period of decline. However, by the end of the 11th century, as Kūkai studies began to emerge as a dynamic area of scholasticism, Heian- and Nara-based institutions began to work for the revitalization of Kōyasan. Maitreya devotee and Yogācāra scholar Jōyo 定誉 (958–1047) was an important missionary and fundraiser affiliated with Kōfukuji, who, inspired by a vision, worked to promote Kōyasan as a pilgrimage site. In addition to Jōyo, Ningai 仁海 (951–1045) was an ascetic and ritual master known for his proficiency with rain-making rituals who is credited with inspiring Fujiwara no Michinaga 藤原道長 (966–1028) to visit Kōyasan in 1023. In 1088, Emperor Shirakawa 白河天皇 (1053–1129; r. 1073–1087) began the work of rebuilding the Great *Stūpa* on Kōyasan.[27] Lineages of wandering ascetics continued propagation efforts. In 1073, Kyōkai 教懐 (1001–1093) established the Odawara 小田原 lineage. Kyōkai practiced the *Amida hō* 阿弥陀法, *Uṣṇīṣavijayā-dhāraṇī* 尊勝陀羅尼, the *Amida shingon* 阿弥陀真言, alongside the Womb and Vajra Mandalas, and had an important relationship with Emperor Shirakawa, who helped further expand Kōyasan's facilities.[28]

Kōyasan was popular as a pilgrimage destination and a place where people prayed for rebirth in the Tuṣita heaven of Maitreya, the Pure Land of Amitābha, and so on. Emperors Shirakawa and Toba 鳥羽天皇 (1103–1156), aristocrats like Fujiwara no Michinaga and Fujiwara Yorimichi 藤原頼通 (992–1074), warriors like Saitō Tokiyori 斎藤時頼 (dates unknown), Taira no Kiyomori 平清盛 (1118–1181), Kumagai Naozane 熊谷直実 (1141–1208), Ashikaga Yoshimitsu 足利義満 (1358–1408), and Ashikaga Takauji 足利尊氏 (1305–1358), the poet Saigyō 西行 (1118–1190), and monks like Myōhen 明遍 (1142–1224) and Chōgen 重源 (1121–1206) contributed to the growing popularity of Kōyasan as a devotional site and pilgrimage destination. The main lineage of Kōyasan is the Chūin-ryū 中院流, established by Meizan 明算 (1021–1106), and an important figure in the Kōyasan revival. The main object of devotion in the Chūin-ryū is Mahāvairocana, while other ritual lineages take other Buddhas or Bodhisattvas as their focus.

KAKUBAN

Kakuban is commonly regarded as the second founder of Shingon and an important systematizer of Esoteric Pure Land Buddhism. Kakuban studied at Ninnaji from 1107. Kakuban also studied at Tōdaiji and Kōfukuji and Kōyasan, as well as Daigoji and Onjōji. In this way, Kakuban's training reveals the interconnected nature of these different Shingon lineages and thus resists simplistic sectarian categorization. In 1115, he studied on Kōyasan, and in 1130, Emperor Toba helped him establish Daidenbō-in 大伝法院. In 1134, Kakuban was appointed to high administrative positions overseeing Kongōbuji and Daidenbō-in, but conservative reactions on the mountain forced him to step down in 1134. In 1140, this friction led to Kongōbuji monks attempting to assassinate Kakuban and burning his temple. Kakuban then moved down mountain with a large number of his followers and established Negoroji 根来寺.[29]

Kakuban is commonly regarded as promoter of the esoteric *nenbutsu* 秘密念仏 (J. *himitsu nenbutsu*), the recitation of the name of the Buddha Amitābha, "Namo Amida Butsu," as a mantra imbued with various levels of esoteric meaning and potency. For example, the *Gorin kujimyō himitsu shaku* 五輪九字明秘密釈 (T. 2514) examines the Amitābha mantra, and the *Amida hisshaku* 阿弥陀秘釈 (T. 2522) examines the *nenbutsu*. Often scholars suggest that Kakuban syncretized Esoteric Buddhism with Pure Land Buddhism, while others note that Shingon and tantric Buddhism, as expressions of Mahāyāna Buddhism, take for granted a Pure Land soteriological cosmology and have always had diverse perspectives on the Pure Land, Amitābha Buddha, and various practices said to lead to Pure Land rebirth. For Kakuban and some later interpreters, going for rebirth in the Pure Land and the attainment of Buddhahood in this very body are not necessarily two different things. Ninnaji, where Kakuban studied, has Amitābha as its main object of devotion, and Kōyasan was a hotbed of Pure Land activity.

LATER DEVELOPMENTS

One of the most important teachers on Kōyasan during the early medieval period was Kakkai 覚海 (1142–1223), who took the position of abbot of Kongōbuji in 1216. Kakkai is known for his immanentalist Pure Land thought, emphasizing the nonduality of this world and the Pure Land.[30] Kakkai and his prominent students were also known for *rokudai funimon shisō* 六大不二思想, or "six elements, nondualist thought," which built on Kūkai's thought in the *Sokushin jōbutsu gi*, which posits that the six fundamental elements (earth, water, fire, wind, space, consciousness) are nondual with the *dharmaḳaya*. Under Chōgaku 長覚 (1340–1416) of Muryōju-in 無量寿院 this became a dominant point of view in the in late medieval period.[31]

Kakkai's student Dōhan 道範 (1179–1252) was an extremely prolific and influential Kōyasan scholar-monk who drew on the works of his teachers and Kakuban and promoted devotion to Kūkai as a bodhisattva-like savior figure capable of aiding beings in the attainment of Pure Land rebirth and buddhahood in this body. Dōhan regarded these two goals as fundamentally unified and, in his *Himitsu nenbutsu shō* 秘密念仏抄, argues for a comprehensive view of the recitation of the name of Amitābha not simply as a practice meant for ordinary beings of lower capacities; rather, Dōhan also saw the *nenbutsu* as the compassionate activity of *dharmakāya* in the world as the life-breath of all beings.[32] Recitation of "Namu Daishi Henjō Kongō 南無大師遍照金剛," as a kind of Kūkai *nenbutsu*, is a common practice in some Shingon lineages today. Although many different versions proliferated in different lineages, the one currently in use first appears in Dōhan's *Himitsu nenbutsu shō*.[33]

Through the medieval period, Shingon lineages and temples formed a heterogeneous network of temples, interconnected with other institutions and areas of doctrinal and ritual studies. For example, Eizon 叡尊 (1201–1290), led a popular Vinaya-Shingon revival known as Shingon Risshu 眞言律宗 at Saidaiji 西大寺 in Nara.[34]

Raiyu 頼瑜 (1226–1304) is one of the most important medieval Shingon scholiasts and is regarded as the founder of the Shingi Shingon School 新義真言宗, which is distinguished from the Kogi Shingon School 古義真言宗. As seen in the lives of Kakuban and Dōhan, ongoing factionalism on Kōyasan led Raiyu to permanently move the Daidenbō-in to Mount Negoro, where it remains today.

Yūkai 宥快 (1345–1416) was another important and extremely prolific medieval scholiast who, along with Chōkaku, is regarded as having established the medieval Shingon orthodoxy, undermining unorthodox practitioners on Kōyasan, especially *nenbutsu hijiri*. In the 14th century, the central administration on Kōyasan imposed a hierarchy with scholar-monks 学侶 (J. *gakuryo*) on the top, ritual practitioners 行人 (J. *gyōnin*), and the miscellaneous *hijiri* last. Scholar-monks Yūkai and Chōkaku endeavored to enforce a Shingon orthodoxy at this time to reign in these purportedly disruptive *hijiri*. Officials on Kōyasan issues an edict in 1413 banning the more disruptive *hijiri* activities, such as ecstatic dancing, loud chanting, and so on. In 1606, the Tokugawa Shōgun declared that these unofficial *hijiri* groups must choose a sectarian affiliation.

SHINGON AND ZEN

As Zen was transmitted to Japan in the 12th and 13th centuries, the "special transmission outside the scriptures," functioned alongside, and was at times refracted through Esoteric Buddhism. Today some Shingon Buddhists practice Zen as part of the Shingon curriculum and even believe that Kūkai traveled to China in order to study Zen but ended up discovering Esoteric Buddhism. Figures like Enni Ben'en 円爾弁円 (1202–1280), Mujū Ichien 無住一円 (1226–1312), Shinchi Kakushin 心地覚心 (1207–1298), Keizan Jōkin 瑩山紹瑾 (1264–1325), and others were influenced by and drew on Esoteric Buddhism in their articulation of Zen. Gyōyū 行勇 (1163–1241) and Kakushin even studied on Kōyasan with Dōhan. In particular, proficiency in dhāraṇī was a shared area of concern among practitioners of Zen and Shingon. Zen temples at this time were sites for *homa* fire rituals, rituals for the promotion of this-worldly benefits, rituals for feeding hungry ghosts, and Zen masters produced charms, talismans, and so on, commonly associated with Estoeric Buddhism. The monk Eisai 栄西 (1141–1215), commonly regarded as the founder or transmitter of Rinzai Zen 臨済禅 (Linji Chan), was well known in his own day as an Esoteric Tendai practitioner. Gyōyū was an early disciple of Eisai and helped establish Kongōsanmai-in through the patronage of Hōjō Masako. Zen, Pure Land, and Shingon functioned together in various contexts, such as Kōyasan. Shinji Kakushin began his career at Tōdaiji in Nara, received the Bodhisattva precepts from Dōgen 道元 (1200–1253), studied on Kōyasan in 1225, and was connected with the *nenbutsu hijiri* Kayadō lineage at Mitsugon-in 密厳院,[35] and studied Shingon under Dōhan and Zen under Gyōyū at the Zenjō-in 禅定院 of Kongōsanmai-in 金剛三昧院.[36]

DISCUSSION OF THE LITERATURE

In 1571, the warlord Oda Nobunaga 織田信長 (1534–1582) burned down Mount Hiei, crippling the once powerful Mount Hiei–based monastic institutions. As a result, Shingon lineages that identify Kūkai as their founder were able to in some sense fill the void in Esoteric ritual knowledge. As Kōyasan was not burned down, many ritual lineages were preserved there. During the Tokugawa period (1600–1868), in response to the violence of the late medieval period, temple networks were required to establish main and branch temple relations and refrain from intersectarian debate. This led to a solidification of sectarian lines. In 1611, the Tokugawa bakufu declared Kōyasan, Ninnaji, Jingoji, Tōji, and Daigoji as Shingon-shū head temples.[37]

In thinking about the evolution of Shingon within the broader context of the eastward flow of Mahāyāna Buddhism, as well as the particular context of premodern Japanese Buddhism, we can see that Shingon as a discourse, and as a more or less clearly defined sectarian identity draws upon the esoteric lineage discourse found throughout Mahāyāna Buddhism, as well as the dhāraṇī and spell culture found throughout South and East Asia. Through the work of Kūkai, and later Japanese monastic scholiasts and ritual masters, Shingon evolves as a distinct area of praxis.

Katsumata Shungyō 勝又俊教, ed. *Kōbō Daishi Chosaku Zenshū* 弘法大師著作全集. Tokyo: Sankibō Busshorin, 1968.
Mikkyō Bunka Kenkyūjo 密教文化研究所, ed. *Kōbō Daishi zenshū* 弘法大師全集, 8 vols. Kōyasan, Wakayama, Japan: Mikkyō bunka kenkyūjo, 1965–1968.
Mikkyō Bunka Kenkyūjo 密教文化研究所, ed. *Kōbō Daishi zenshū* 弘法大師全集, 5 vols. Mount Kōya, Japan: Mikkyō bunka kenkyūjo, 1970–1977.
Yūshō Miyasaka, ed. *Kōbō Daishi Kūkai Zenshū* 弘法大師空海全集. Tokyo: Chikuma Shobō, 1983.

It is my understanding that the following resource, published somewhat more recently, is one of the most authoritative collections of Kūkai's works:

Mikkyō Bunka Kenkyūjo 密教文化研究所, ed. *Teihon Kōbōōbon KoZenshū*. 定本弘法大師全集 Kōbō Daishi zenshū 弘法大師全集, 10 vols. Kōyasan, Japan: Mikkyō bunka kenkyūjo, 1991–1997.

For the collected works of the Shingon tradition, including canonical works as well as commentaries and sub-commentaries, see the following resources:

Kōyasan Daigaku Mikkyō bunka kenkyūjo 高野山大学密教文化研究所, ed. *Shingonshū zensho* 眞言宗全書, 44 vols. Wakayama, Japan: Kōyasan Daigaku, 1977.
Zoku Shingonshū Zensho Kankōkai 續眞言宗全書刊行會, ed. *Zoku Shingonshū zensho* 續眞言宗全書, 42 vols. Wakayama, Japan: Zoku Shingonshū Zensho Kankōkai, 1975–1988.
One of the most useful reference works in the study of Esoteric Buddhism includes:
Mikkyō Jiten Hensankai 密教辞典編纂会, ed. *Mikkyō daijiten* 密教大辭典 (rev., expanded, small print edition 縮刷版, 改訂増補). Kyoto: Hōzōkan, 1983.

For a collection of textual resources from Daigoji, see:

Tōkyō daigaku shiryō hensanjo 東京大學史料編纂所, ed. *Daigoji monjo* 醍醐寺文書. Vol. 15, Tokyo: Tōkyō daigaku shiryō hensanjo, 1955.

One of the most useful primary resources for the study of Kōyasan:

Shinkō Kōya shunju hennen shūroku 新校高野春秋編年輯録. Ed. Hinonishi Shinjō 日野西眞定. Tokyo: Micho Shuppan, 1982; rev., and expanded 2nd ed., 1998. (Org. pub., DNBZ 131).

For texts related to Esoteric Pure Land Buddhism consult:

Hase Hōshū 長谷寶秀, ed. *Shingon shū anjin zensho* 真言宗安心全書, 2 vols. 1973; repr., Kyoto: Daigakudō shoten.

SELECTED SECONDARY SCHOLARSHIP

The following bibliography contains a list of works consulted as well as notable research on this topic. A few, however, stand out as especially important.
In English, the most important works on Kūkai's thought and Shingon Buddhism follow:
Abé, Ryūichi. *The Weaving of Mantra: Kūkai and the Construction of Esoteric Buddhist Discourse*. New York: Columbia University Press, 1999.
Hakeda, Yoshito S. *Kūkai: Major Works*. New York: Columbia University Press, 1976.
Kushida Ryōkō 櫛田良洪. *Shingon mikkyō seiritsu katei no kenkyū* 真言密教成立過程の研究. Tokyo: Sankibō busshorin, 1964. 558
Kushida Ryōkō 櫛田良洪. Zoku Shingon mikkyō seiritsu katei no kenkyū 続真言密教成立過程の研究. Tokyo: Sankibō busshorin, 1979.

Orzech, Charles D., Henrik H. Sørensen, and Richard K. Payne, eds. *Esoteric Buddhism and the Tantras in East Asia*. Leiden, The Netherlands: Brill, 2011.

Shingen Takagi, and Thomas Eijō Dreitlein, eds. *Kūkai and the Philosophy of Language*. Tokyo: Keio University, 2010.

The following works are important for the study of Tōji, one of the most important temples and centers for Shingon practice and the popularization of devotion to Kūkai:

Amino Yoshihiko 網野善彦. *Chūsei Tōji to Tōjiryō shōen* 中世東寺と東寺領荘園. Tokyo: Tokyo Daigaku Shuppankai, 1978.

Hashimoto Hatsuko 橋本初子. *Chūsei Tōji to Kōbōdaishi shinkō* 中世東寺と弘法大師信仰. Kyoto: Shibunkaku shigaku sōsho, 1990.

Satō, Ayumi 佐藤愛弓. *Chūsei Shingonsō no gensetsu to rekishi ninshiki* 中世真言僧の言説と歴史認識. Tōkyō: Bensei Shuppan, 2015.

For the study of Daigoji and Shingon temples in medieval Japan, see the following sources:

Fujii Masako 藤井雅子. *Chūse Daigoji to shingon mikkyō* 中世醍醐寺と真言密教. Tokyo: Bensei Shuppan, 2008.

Nishi Yayoi 西弥生. *Chūsei mikkyō jiin to shuhō* 中世密教寺院と修法. Tokyo: Bensei Shuppansha, 2008.

For the study of Ninnaji, see the following:

Abe Yasurō, and Yamasaki Makoto 山崎誠, eds. *Shukaku hosshinnō to Ninnaji goryū no bunkenteki kenkyū, ronbunhen* 守覚法親王と仁和寺御流の文献学的研究, 論文編. 2 vols. Tokyo: Benseisha, 1998.

Horiuchi Noriyuki 堀内規之. *Saisen kyōgaku no kenkyū-Insei ki Shingon mikkyō no sho mondai* 済暹教学の研究-院政期真言密教の諸問題. Tokyo: Nonburu, 2009.

On Kōyasan and Kūkai devotion, see the following:

Hyōtani Kazuko 俵谷和子. *Kōyasan shinkō to kenmon shinshi: Kōbō daishi nyūjō densetsu wo chūshin ni* 高野山信仰と権門貴紳: 弘法大師入定伝説を中心に. Tokyo: Iwata Shoin, 2010.

Murakami Hiroko 村上弘子. *Kōyasan shinkō no seiritsu to tenkai* 高野山信仰の成立と展開. Tokyo: Yūzankaku, 2009.

For the study of Esoteric Pure Land, see the following:

Tomabechi Seiichi 苫米地誠一. *Heianki shingonmikkyō no kenkyū: Heianki no shingonmikkyō to mikkyōjōdokyō* 平安期真言密教の研究: 平安期の真言教学と密教浄土教, vol. 2. Tokyo: Nonburu sha, 2008.

On Raiyu and Shingi Shingon scholasticism, see the following:

Sakaki Yoshitaka 榊義孝. *Shingi kyōgaku no sō—Raiyu sōjō nyūmon* 新義教學の祖ー頼瑜僧正入門. Tokyo: Nonburu, 2003.

On Tendai Esoteric Buddhism, see the following:

Tkubo Ryōshun 大久保良峻. *Taimitsu kyōgaku no kenkyū* 台密教学の研究. Kyoto: Hōzōkan, 2004.

For the study of Esoteric Buddhism in broader East Asian context, see the following:

Kamikawa Michio 上川通夫. Nihon chūsei Bukkyō to Higashi Ajia sekai 日本中世仏教と東ア ジア世界. Tokyo: Hanawa Shobō, 2012.

For the study of medieval Japanese Buddhism and politics, within which Shingon Esoteric Buddhism played an essential role, see the following:

Adolphson, Mikael S. *The Gates of Power: Monks, Courtiers, and Warriors in Premodern Japan*. Honolulu: University of Hawai'i Press, 2000.

Conlan, Thomas. *From Soverign to Symbol: An Age of Ritual Determinism in Fourteenth- Century Japan*. Oxford: Oxford University Press, 2011.

Dobbins, James C., ed. *Japanese Journal of Religious Studies*. Special Issue: Kuroda Toshio and his Scholarship 23, no. 3/4 (Fall 1996).

Kuroda Toshio 黒田俊雄. *Nihon chūsei no kokka to shūkyō* 日本中世の国家と宗教. Tokyo: Iwanami Shōten, 1975.

Ruppert, Brian. *Jewel in the Ashes: Buddha Relics and Power in Early Medieval Japan*. Cambridge, MA: Harvard University Press, 2000.

Sueki Fumihiko 末木文美士. *Kamakura Bukkyō keiseiron: shisōshi no tachiba kara* 鎌倉仏教形成論: 思想史の立場から. Tokyo: Hōzōkan, 1998. 593

Sueki Fumihiko 末木文美士. *Kamakura Bukkyō tenkairon* 鎌倉仏教展開論. Tokyo: Transview, 2008.

Taira Masayuki 平雅行. *Nihon chūsei no shakai to Bukkyō* 日本中世の社会と仏教. Tokyo: Hanawa Shobō, 1992.

Taira Masayuki 平雅行. "Kamakura chūki ni okeru Kamakura Shingon-ha no sōryo—Ryōyu, Kōhō, Jitsugen 鎌倉 中期における鎌倉真言派の僧侶--良瑜・光宝・実賢." *Machikaneyama ronsō* 待兼山 論叢 43 (2009): 1–27.

Uejima, Susumu上島享. *Nihon Chūsei Shakai No Keisei to Ōken* 日本中世社会の形成と王権. Nagoya, Japan: Nagoya Daigaku Shuppankai, 2010.

FURTHER READING

Abe Ryūichi, "From Kūkai to Kakuban: A Study of Shingon Buddhist Dharma Transmission." PhD diss., Columbia University, 1991.

Abé, Ryūichi. "Saichō and Kūkai: A Conflict of Interpretations." *Japanese Journal of Religious Studies* 22, no. 1–2 (1995): 103–137.

Abé, Ryūichi. *The Weaving of Mantra: Kūkai and the Construction of Esoteric Buddhist Discourse*. New York: Columbia University Press, 1999.

Abe Yasurō and Yamasaki Makoto 山崎誠, eds. *Shukaku hosshinnō to Ninnaji goryū no bunkenteki kenkyū, ronbunhen* 守覚法親王と仁和寺御流の文献学的研究, 論文編. 2 vols. Tokyo: Benseisha, 1998.

Adolphson, Mikael S. *The Gates of Power: Monks, Courtiers, and Warriors in Premodern Japan*. Honolulu: University of Hawai'i Press, 2000.

Beghi, Clemente. "The Dissemination of Esoteric Scriptures in Eighth Century Japan." In *Esoteric Buddhism and the Tantras in East Asia*. Edited by Charles Orzech, 661–682. Leiden, The Netherlands: Brill, 2011.

Bodiford, William M. "Zen and Esoteric Buddhism." In *Esoteric Buddhism and the Tantras in East Asia*. Edited by Charles D. Orzech, 924–935. Leiden, The Netherlands: Brill, 2011.

Chen, Jinhua. "The Formation of Early Tendai Esoteric Buddhism in Japan: A Study of Three Japanese Esoteric Apocrypha." PhD diss., McMaster University, 1997.

Chou, Yi-liang. "Tantrism in China." In *Tantric Buddhism in East Asia*. Edited by Richard K. Payne, 33–60. Boston: Wisdom Publications, 2006.

Conlan, Thomas. *From Soverign to Symbol: An Age of Ritual Determinism in Fourteenth-Century Japan*. Oxford: Oxford University Press, 2011.

Davidson, Ronald M. *Indian Esoteric Buddhism: A Social History of the Tantric Movement*. New York: Columbia University Press, 2002.

Davidson, Ronald M. "Some Observations on the Usṇīsa Abhiṣeka Rites in Atikūṭa's *Dhāraṇīsaṃgraha*." In *Transformations and Transfer of Tantra: Tantrism in Asia and Beyond*. Edited by István Keul, 77–98. Berlin and New York: Walter de Gruyter, 2012.

Dobbins, James C., ed. *Japanese Journal of Religious Studies*, Special Issue: Kuroda Toshio and his Scholarship 23, no. 3/4 (Fall 1996).

Dobbins, James C. "Envisioning Kamakura Buddhism." In *Re-Visioning Kamakura Buddhism*. Edited by Richard K. Payne, 24–42. Honolulu: University of Hawaii Press, 1998.

Dolce, Lucia. "Taimitsu: The Esoteric Buddhism of the Tendai School." In *Esoteric Buddhism and the Tantras in East Asia*. Edited by Charles Orzech, 744–767. Leiden, The Netherlands: Brill, 2011.

Dolce, Lucia, with Shinya Mano. "Godai'in Annen." In *Esoteric Buddhism and the Tantras in East Asia*. Edited by Charles Orzech, 768–775. Leiden, The Netherlands: Brill, 2011.

Ford, James. "Exploring the Esoteric in Nara Buddhism." In *Esoteric Buddhism and the Tantras in East Asia*. Edited by Charles Orzech, 776–792. Leiden, The Netherlands: Brill, 2011.

Fujii Jun 藤井淳. *Kūkai no shisōteki tenkai no kenkyū* 空海の思想的展開の研究. Tokyo: Transview, 2008.

Fujii Masako 藤井雅子. *Chūse Daigoji to shingon mikkyō* 中世醍醐寺と真言密教. Tokyo: Bensei Shuppan 勉誠出版, 2008.

Gardiner, David Lion. "Kūkai and the Beginnings of Shingon Buddhism in Japan." PhD diss., Stanford University, 1995.

Giebel, Rolf W., trans. *Two Esoteric Sutras: The Adamantine Pinnacle Sutra, The Susiddhikara Sutra*. Berkeley, CA: Numata Center for Buddhist Translation and Research, 2001.

Gieble, Rolf W., and Dale A. Todaro, trans. *Shingon Texts*. Berkeley: Numata Center for Buddhist Translation and Research, 2004.

Goble, Geoffrey C. *Chinese Esoteric Buddhism, Amoghavajra, the Ruling Elite, and the Emergence of a Tradition*. New York: Columbia University Press, 2019.

Gorai Shigeru 五来重. *Kōya hijiri* 高野聖. 2011; repr., Tokyo: Kadokawa bunko, 1975.

Groner, Paul. *Saichō: The Establishment of the Japanese Tendai School*. Honolulu: University of Hawai'i Press, 1984.

Groner, Paul. *Ryōgen and Mount Hiei: Japanese Tendai in the Tenth Century*. Honolulu: University of Hawai'i Press, 2002.

Hakeda, Yoshito S. *Kūkai: Major Works*. New York: Columbia University Press, 1972.

Hashimoto Hatsuko 橋本初子. *Chūsei Tōji to Kōbōdaishi shinkō* 中世東寺と弘法大師信仰. Kyoto: Shibunkaku shigaku sōsho 思文閣史学叢書, 1990.

Hodge, Stephen. *The Mahā-Vairocana-Abhisaṃbodhi Tantra, With Buddhaguhya's Commentary*. London and New York: Routledge, 2003.

Horiuchi Noriyuki 堀内規之. *Saisen kyōgaku no kenkyū-Insei ki Shingon mikkyō no sho mondai* 済暹教学の研究-院政期真言密教の諸問題. Tokyo: Nonburu, 2009.

Hyōtani Kazuko 俵谷和子. *Kōyasan shinkō to kenmon shinshi: Kōbō daishi nyūjō densetsu wo chūshin ni* 高野山信仰と權門貴紳: 弘法大師入定伝説を中心に. Tokyo: Iwata Shoin, 2010.

Kagiwada Seiko 鍵和田聖子. "Tōmitsu to Taimitsu no sōgo eikyō kara mita juyō to kensan no tenkai 東密と台密の相互影響から見た受容と研鑽の展開." PhD diss., Ryūkoku University, 2014.

Kamikawa Michio 上川通夫. Nihon chūsei Bukkyō to Higashi Ajia sekai 日本中世仏教と東アジア世界. Tokyo: Hanawa Shobō 塙書房, 2012.

Keyworth, George A. "The Esotericization of Chinese Buddhist Practice." In *Esoteric Buddhism and the Tantras in East Asia*. Edited by Charles D. Orzech, 516–519. Leiden, The Netherlands: Brill, 2011.

Kiyota, Minoru. *Shingon Buddhism: Theory and Practice*. Los Angeles: Buddhist Books International, 1978.

Kuroda Toshio 黒田俊雄. *Nihon chūsei no kokka to shūkyō* 日本中世の国家と宗教. Tokyo: Iwanami Shōten, 1975

Kushida Ryōkō 櫛田良洪. *Shingon mikkyō seiritsu katei no kenkyū* 真言密教成立過程の研究. Tokyo: Sankibō busshorin, 1964. 558

Kushida Ryōkō 櫛田良洪. Zoku Shingon mikkyō seiritsu katei no kenkyū 続 真言密教成立過程の研究. Tokyo: Sankibō busshorin, 1979.

Lindsay, Ethan. "Pilgrimage to the Sacred Traces of Kōyasan: Place and Devotion in Late Heian Japan." PhD diss., Princeton University, 2012.

Londo, William, trans., Hinonishi Shinjō, "The Appearance and Evolution of the Hōgō of Kōbō Daishi," *Japanese Religions* 27, no. 1 (2002) 1–18.

Londo, William. "The Other Mountain: The Mt. Kōya Temple Complex in the Heian Era." PhD diss., University of Michigan, 2004.

Lopez, Donald S. Jr., *Elaborations on Emptiness: Uses of the Heart Sutra*. Princeton, NJ: Princeton University Press, 1996.

Matsunaga Yūkei 松長有慶. *Mikkyō no rekishi* 密教の歴史 Kyoto: Heirakuji shoten, 1969.

McMullen, Matthew. "The Development of Esoteric Buddhist Scholasticism in Early Medieval Japan." PhD diss., University of California, 2016.

McMullin, Neil. "The Sanmon–Jimon Schism in the Tendai School of Buddhism: A Preliminary Analysis." *Journal of the International Association of Buddhist Studies* 7, no. 1 (1984): 83–105.

Morrell, Robert E. "Shingon's Kakukai on the Immanence of the Pure Land." *Japanese Journal of Religious Studies* 11, no. 2–3 (1984): 195–220.

Murakami Hiroko 村上弘子. *Kōyasan shinkō no seiritsu to tenkai* 高野山信仰の成立と展開. Tokyo: Yūzankaku, 2009.

Nakamura Honnen 中村本然. "Dōhan no Jōdo kan 道範の浄土観." *Kōyasan daigaku ronsō* 高野山大学論叢 29 (1994): 149–202.

Ninnaji Konbyōshi Kozōshi Kenkyūkai 仁和寺紺表紙小双紙研究会, ed. *Shukaku hosshinnō no girei sekai: Ninnajizō konbyōshi kozōshi no kenkyū* 守覚法親王の儀礼世界: 仁和寺蔵 紺表紙小双紙の研究, 2 vol. Tokyo: Bensei Shuppan 勉誠出版, 1995.

Nishi Yayoi 西弥生. *Chūsei mikkyō jiin to shuhō* 中世密教寺院と修法. Tokyo: Bensei Shuppansha 勉誠出版, 2008.

Tkubo Ryōshun 大久保良峻. *Taimitsu kyōgaku no kenkyū* 台密教学の研究. Kyoto: Hōzōkan, 2004.

Tmura Seigai 大村西崖. *Mikkyō hattatsushi* 密教発達志 Monograph on the Development of Esoteric Buddhism, 5 vols. Tokyo: Bussho Kankōkai Zuzōbu Kokusho Kankōkai, 1918.

Orzech, Charles D. "Seeing Chen-yen Buddhism: Traditional Scholarship and the Vajrayāna in China." *History of Religions* 29, no. 2 (1989): 87–114.

Orzech, Charles D. *Politics and Transcendent Wisdom: The Scripture for Humane Kings in the Creation of Chinese Buddhism*. University Park: Pennsylvania State University Press, 1998.

Orzech, Charles D. "Esoteric Buddhism in the Tang: From Atikūṭa to Amoghavajra (651–780)." In *Esoteric Buddhism and the Tantras in East Asia*. Edited by Charles D. Orzech, 263–285. Leiden, The Netherlands: Brill, 2011.

Orzech, Charles D. et al. "Introduction: Esoteric Buddhism and the *Tantras* in East Asia: Some Methodological Considerations." In *Esoteric Buddhism and the Tantras in East Asia*. Edited by Charles D. Orzech, 3–18. Leiden, The Netherlands: Brill, 2011.

Payne, Richard. *The Tantric Ritual of Japan: Feeding the Gods, The Shingon Fire Ritual*. Śata-Piṭaka Series, vol. 365. Delhi: International Academy of Indian Culture: Aditya Prakashan, 1991.

Payne, Richard K. "Ajikan: Ritual and Meditation in the Shingon Tradition." In *Re-visioning "Kamakura" Buddhism*. Edited by Richard K. Payne, 219–248. Honolulu: University of Hawaii Press, 1998.

Payne, Richard K. ed. *Tantric Buddhism in East Asia*. Boston: Wisdom Publications, 2006.

Proffitt, Aaron P. *Esoteric Pure Land Buddhism* (Honolulu: University of Hawaii Press, 2022).

Quinter, David. *From Outcasts to Emperors: Shingon Ritsu and the Mañjuśrī Cult in Medieval Japan*. Leiden, The Netherlands: Brill Academic Publishers, 2015.

Rambelli, Fabio. "True Words, Silence, and the Adamantine Dance: On Japanese Mikkyō and the Formation of the Shingon Discourse." *Japanese Journal of Religious Studies* 21, no. 4 (1994): 373–405.

Rambelli, Fabio. "In Search of the Buddha's Intention, Raiyu and the Worlds of Medieval Shingon Learned Monks." In *Shingi Shingon kyōgaku no kenkyū: Raiyu sōjō shichihyakunen goenki kinen ronshū* 新義真言教学の研究: 頼瑜僧正七百年御遠忌記念論集, Edited by Sanpa Gōdō Kinen Ronshū Henshū iinkai 三派合同記念論集編集委員会, 35–64. Tokyo: Daizō Shuppan, 2002.

Ruppert, Brian. *Jewel in the Ashes: Buddha Relics and Power in Early Medieval Japan*. Cambridge, MA: Harvard University Press, 2000.

Ruppert, Brian. "Dharma Prince Shukaku and the Esoteric Buddhist Culture of Sacred Works (Shōgyō) in Medieval Japan." In *Esoteric Buddhism and the Tantras in East Asia*. Edited by Charles D. Orzech, 794–800. Leiden, The Netherlands: Brill, 2011.

Sakaki Yoshitaka 榊義孝. *Shingi kyōgaku no sō—Raiyu sōjō nyūmon* 新義教學の祖一頼瑜僧正入門. Tokyo: Nonburu, 2003.

Sanford, James. "Wind, Waters, *Stūpas*, Mandalas: Fetal Buddhahood in Shingon." *Japanese Journal of Religious Studies* 24, no. 1–2 (1997): 1–38.

Sanford, James H. "Breath of Life: The Esoteric Nenbutsu." In *Tantric Buddhism in East Asia*, Edited by Richard K. Payne, 161–190. Boston: Wisdom Publications, 2006.

Satō Mona 佐藤もな. "Chūsei Shingonshū niokeru jōdo shisō kaishaku: Dōhan Himitsu nenbutsu shō wo megutte 中世真言宗における浄土思想解釈道範『秘密念仏抄』をめぐって." *Indo tetsugaku Bukkyōgaku kenkyū* インド哲学仏教学研究 9 (2002): 80–92.

Sharf, Robert H. "Visualization and Mandala in Shingon Buddhism." In *Living Images: Japanese Buddhist Icons in Context*. Edited by Robert H. Sharf and Elizabeth Horton Sharf, 151–197. Stanford, CA: Stanford University Press, 2001.

Sharf, Robert H. "On Esoteric Buddhism in China." In Appendix to *Coming to Terms with Chinese Buddhism: A Reading of the Treasure Store Treatise*, 263–278. Honolulu: University of Hawai'i Press, 2002.

Sharf, Robert H. "Thinking through Shingon Ritual." *Journal of the International Association of Buddhist Studies* 26, no. 1 (2003): 59–86.

Shingen Takagi and Thomas Eijō Dreitlein, eds. *Kūkai and the Philosophy of Language*. Tokyo: Keio University, 2010.

Shinohara, Koichi. *Spells, Images and Maṇḍalas: Tracing the Evolution of Esoteric Buddhist Rituals*. New York: Columbia University Press, 2014.

Snodgrass, Adrian. *The Matrix and Diamond World Mandalas in Shingon Buddhism*. 2 vols. New Delhi: Aditya Prakashan, 1988.

Stone, Jacqueline. *Original Enlightenment and the transformation of Medieval Japanese Buddhism*. Princeton, NJ: Princeton University Press, 1999.

Strickmann, Michel. *Mantras et mandarins: Le bouddhisme tantrique en Chine*. Paris: Éditions Gallimard, 1996.

Sueki Fumihiko 末木文美士. *Kamakura Bukkyō keiseiron: shisōshi no tachiba kara* 鎌倉仏教形成論: 思想史の立場から. Tokyo: Hōzōkan, 1998. 593

Sueki Fumihiko 末木文美士. *Kamakura Bukkyō tenkairon* 鎌倉仏教展開論. Tōkyō: Transview, 2008.

Tachikawa Musashi 立川武蔵, and Yoritomi Motohiro 頼富元宏. *Nihon no mikkyō* 日本密教. Tokyo: Shunjūsha, 2000.

Taira Masayuki 平雅行. *Nihon chūsei no shakai to Bukkyō* 日本中世の社会と仏教. Tokyo: Hanawa Shobō 塙書房, 1992.

Taira Masayuki 平雅行. "Kamakura chūki ni okeru Kamakura Shingon-ha no sōryo—Ryōyu, Kōhō, Jitsugen 鎌倉 中期における鎌倉真言派の僧侶--良瑜・光宝・実賢." *Machikaneyama ronsō* 待兼山 論叢 43 (2009): 1–27.

Ten Grotenhuis, Elizabeth. *Japanese Mandalas: Representations of Sacred Geography*. Honolulu: University of Hawaii Press, 1999.

Tinsley, Elizabeth. "Kūkai and the Development of Shingon Buddhism." In *Esoteric Buddhism and the Tantras in East Asia*. Edited by Charles D. Orzech, 691–708. Leiden, The Netherlands: Brill, 2011.

Togano'o Shōun 栂尾祥雲. *Himitsu bukkyōshi* 秘密仏教史. Koyasan, Japan: Koyasan University Press, 1959.

Tomabechi Seiichi 苫米地誠一. *Heianki shingonmikkyō no kenkyū: Heianki no shingonmikkyō to mikkyōjōdokyō* 平安期真言密教の研究: 平安期の真言教学と密教浄土教, vol. 2. Tokyo: Nonburu sha, 2008.

Unno, Mark. *Shingon Refractions: Myoe and the Mantra of Light.* Boston: Wisdom Publications, 2004.

Van der Veere, Hendrik. *A Study into the Thought of Kōgyōdaishi Kakuban with a Translation of His* Gorin kuji myō himitsushaku. Leiden, The Netherlands: Hotei Publishing, 2000.

Wada, Shūjō 和多秀乘, and Takagi Shingen 高木訷元, eds. *Kōbō Daishi to Shingonshū* 弘法大師と真言宗. Tōkyō: Yoshikawa Kōbunkan, 1984.

Wedemeyer, Christian. *Making Sense of Tantric Buddhism: History, Semiology, and Transgression in the Indian Traditions.* New York: Columbia University Press, 2012.

Yamasaki, Taiko. *Shingon: Japanese Esoteric Buddhism.* Boston: Shambhala, 1988.

Yan Yaozhong 严耀中. *Hanzhuan Mijiao* 汉传密教. Xuelin chubanshe 学林出版社, 2006.

Yoritomi, Motohiro 頼富本宏. "Chūgoku mikkyō no nagare 中国密教の流れ." In *Chūgoku mikkyō* 中国密教. Edited by Tachikawa Musashi 立川武蔵 and Yoritomi Motohiro 頼富本宏, 15–39. 2005; repr., Tokyo: Shunjūsha, 1999.

NOTES

1. For overviews of how modern scholars define Esoteric Buddhism and the tantras in East Asia, see: Richard K. Payne, ed., *Tantric Buddhism in East Asia* (Boston: Wisdom Publications, 2006); Christian Wedemeyer, *Making Sense of Tantric Buddhism: History, Semiology, and Transgression in the Indian Traditions* (New York: Columbia University Press, 2012); Yan Yaozhong 严耀中, *Hanzhuan Mijiao* 汉传密教 (Beijing: Xuelin chubanshe 学林出版社, 2006); Yoritomi Motohiro 頼富本宏, "Chūgoku mikkyō no nagare 中国密教の流れ," in *Chūgoku mikkyō* 中国密教, ed. Tachikawa Musashi 立川武蔵 and Yoritomi Motohiro 頼富本宏 (Tokyo: Shunjūsha, 1999, repr. 2005), 15–39; and Charles D. Orzech, Richard K. Payne, and Henrik H. Sørensen, "Introduction: Esoteric Buddhism and the *Tantras* in East Asia: Some Methodological Considerations," in *Esoteric Buddhism and the Tantras in East Asia*, ed. Charles D. Orzech, Henrik H. Sørensen, and Richard K. Payne (Leiden, The Netherlands: Brill, 2011), 3–18.
2. Regarding the trans-sectarian nature of Shingon in Japan, see Matthew McMullen, "The Development of Esoteric Buddhist Scholasticism in Early Medieval Japan" (PhD diss., University of California, Berkeley, 2016).
3. Donald S. Lopez Jr., *Elaborations on Emptiness: Uses of the Heart Sutra* (Princeton, NJ: Princeton University Press, 1996), 78–104.
4. Robert Sharf, *Coming to Terms with Chinese Buddhism: A Reading of the Treasure Store Treatise* (Honolulu: University of Hawai'i Press, 2002), 263–278.
5. Charles D. Orzech, "Esoteric Buddhism in the Tang: From Atikūṭa to Amoghavajra (651–780)," in *Esoteric Buddhism and the Tantras in East Asia*, ed. Charles D. Orzech, Henrik H. Sørensen, and Richard K. Payne (Leiden, The Netherlands: Brill, 2011), 263–285; Ronald M. Davidson, "Some Observations on the Usṇīsa Abhiṣeka Rites in Atikūṭa's *Dhāraṇīsaṃgraha*," in *Transformations and Transfer of Tantra: Tantrism in Asia and Beyond*, ed. István Keul (Berlin and New York: Walter de Gruyter, 2012), 77–98; and Koichi Shinohara, *Spells, Images and Maṇḍalas: Tracing the Evolution of Esoteric Buddhist Rituals* (New York: Columbia University Press, 2014).
6. Geoffrey C. Goble, *Chinese Esoteric Buddhism, Amoghavajra, the Ruling Elite, and the Emergence of a Tradition* (New York: Columbia University Press, 2019).
7. Much of the information on the Tang Esoteric masters can be found in the biographies translated in Yi-liang Chou, "Tantrism in China," *Harvard Journal of Asiatic Studies* 8 (1945): 241–332, repr. (without appendices) in Payne, *Tantric Buddhism in East Asia*, 33–60.
8. Shingen Takagi and Thomas Eijō Dreitlein, *Kūkai and the Philosophy of Language* (Tokyo: Keio University, 2010), 397–398.

9. See Chou, "Tantrism in China."
10. Robert H. Sharf, "Thinking through Shingon Ritual," *Journal of the International Association of Buddhist Studies* 26, no. 1 (2003): 59–86
11. See Goble, *Chinese Esoteric Buddhism.*
12. George A. Keyworth, "The Esotericization of Chinese Buddhist Practice," in *Esoteric Buddhism and the Tantras in East Asia,* ed. Charles D. Orzech, Henrik H. Sørensen, and Richard K. Payne (Leiden, The Netherlands: Brill, 2011), 516–519.
13. Ryūichi Abe, *The Weaving of Mantra: Kūkai and the Construction of Esoteric Buddhist Discourse* (New York: Columbia University Press, 1999). See also Clemente Beghi, "The Dissemination of Esoteric Scriptures in Eighth Century Japan," in *Esoteric Buddhism and the Tantras in East Asia,* ed. Charles D. Orzech, Henrik H. Sørensen, and Richard K. Payne (Leiden, The Netherlands: Brill, 2011), 675–681.
14. Overviews of Kūkai's life and teachings may be found in the following resources: Elizabeth Tinsley, "Kūkai and the Development of Shingon Buddhism," in *Esoteric Buddhism and the Tantras in East Asia,* ed. Charles D. Orzech, Henrik H. Sørensen, and Richard K. Payne (Leiden, The Netherlands: Brill, 2011), 691–708; and Yoshito S. Hakeda, *Kūkai: Major Works* (New York: Columbia University Press, 1972), 1–60.
15. The list may be found here: T. 245, 303c29–304a05. Following this, there is a lengthy explanation of all ten.
16. Hakeda, *Kūkai: Major Works*: For an overview of Kūkai's thought, see 76–100; and For translations of some of his major works, see 101–276.
17. Sharf, "Thinking through Shingon Ritual."
18. Mark Unno, *Shingon Refractions: Myōe and the Mantra of Light* (Somerville, MA: Wisdom Publications, 2004).
19. Richard K. Payne, "Ajikan: Ritual and Meditation in the Shingon Tradition," in *Re-visioning "Kamakura" Buddhism,* ed. Richard K. Payne (Honolulu: University of Hawaii Press, 1998), 219–248.
20. William Londo, "The Other Mountain: The Mt. Kōya Temple Complex in the Heian Era" (PhD diss., University of Michigan, 2004); and Ethan Lindsay, "Pilgrimage to the Sacred Traces of Kōyasan: Place and Devotion in Late Heian Japan" (PhD diss., Princeton University, 2012).
21. Lucia Dolce, "Taimitsu: The Esoteric Buddhism of the Tendai School," in *Esoteric Buddhism and the Tantras in East Asia,* ed. Charles D. Orzech, Henrik H. Sørensen, and Richard K. Payne (Leiden, The Netherlands: Brill, 2011), 744–767.
22. Toganoo Shōun 栂尾祥雲, *Himitsu bukkyōshi* 秘密仏教史 (Koyasan, Japan: Koyasan University Press, 1959), 228–230.
23. Lucia Dolce, with Shinya Mano, "Godai'in Annen," in *Esoteric Buddhism and the Tantras in East Asia,* ed. Charles Orzech (Leiden, The Netherlands: Brill, 2011), 744–767.
24. Paul Groner, *Ryōgen and Mount Hiei: Japanese Tendai in the Tenth Century* (Honolulu: University of Hawaii Press, 2002).
25. Londo, "The Other Mountain."
26. Brian Ruppert, "Dharma Prince Shukaku and the Esoteric Buddhist Culture of Sacred Works (Shōgyō) in Medieval Japan," in *Esoteric Buddhism and the Tantras in East Asia,* ed. Charles D. Orzech, Henrik H. Sørensen, and Richard K. Payne (Leiden, The Netherlands: Brill, 2011), 794–800.
27. Londo, "The Other Mountain."
28. Gorai Shigeru 五来重, *Kōya hijiri* 高野聖 (2011; repr., Tokyo: Kadokawa bunko 角川文庫, 1975).
29. Abe Ryūichi, "From Kūkai to Kakuban: A Study of Shingon Buddhist Dharma Transmission" (PhD diss., Columbia University, 1991); and Hendrick Van der Veere, *A Study into the Thought of Kōgyō Daishi Kakuban with a Translation of his* Gorin kuji myō himitsushaku (Leiden, The Netherlands: Hotei, 2000).

30. Robert Morrell, "Shingon's Kakukai on the Immanence of the Pure Land," *Japanese Journal of Religious Studies* 11, nos. 2–3 (1984): 195–220.
31. Thomas Conlan, *From Soverign to Symbol: An Age of Ritual Determinism in Fourteenth-Century Japan* (Oxford, UK: Oxford University Press, 2011).
32. Nakamura Honnen 中村本然, "Dōhan no Jōdo kan 道範の浄土観," *Kōyasan daigaku ronsō* 高野山大学論叢 29 (1994): 149–202; James H. Sanford, "Breath of Life: The Esoteric Nenbutsu," in *Tantric Buddhism in East Asia*, ed. Richard K. Payne (Boston: Wisdom Publications, 2006); Satō Mona 佐藤もな, "Chūsei Shingonshū niokeru jōdo shisō kaishaku: Dōhan Himitsu nenbutsu shō wo megutte 中世真言宗における浄土思想解釈道範『秘密念仏抄』をめぐって." *Indo tetsugaku Bukkyōgaku kenkyū* インド哲学仏教学研究 9 (2002): 80–92; and Aaron Proffitt, *Esoteric Pure Land Buddhism* (Honolulu: University of Hawaii Press, forthcoming).
33. William Londo, trans., Hinonishi Shinjō, "The Appearance and Evolution of the Hōgō of Kōbō Daishi," *Japanese Religions* 27, no. 1 (2002) 1–18.
34. David Quinter, *From Outcasts to Emperors: Shingon Ritsu and the Mañjuśrī Cult in Medieval Japan* (Leiden, The Netherlands: Brill Academic Publishers, 2015).
35. Gorai, *Kōya hijiri*, 282–299.
36. William M. Bodiford, "Zen and Esoteric Buddhism," in Orzech, et al., eds., *Esoteric Buddhism and the Tantras in East Asia*, ed. Charles D. Orzech, Henrik H. Sørensen, and Richard K. Payne (Leiden, The Netherlands: Brill, 2011), 924–935.
37. Abe, *Weaving of Mantra*, 409–416.

Aaron Proffitt

THE SIX NARA SCHOOLS

THE NARA PERIOD'S DYNAMIC RELIGIOUS HORIZON

During the Nara period (710–794), the Japanese religious landscape was a dynamic and eclectic whole, consisting of emerging Buddhist schools based on Chinese and Korean lineages, *kami* (神) worship, and several elements of "continental" thought and religiosity. Buddhism never arrived isolated from Chinese and Korean culture, and the Chinese classics and various Chinese histories had a profound impact on the course of the Nara period's history. Texts and rituals later named Confucian, or specific imagery that would become part of the Daoist tradition in China found their way to the early Japanese state along with the first Buddhist texts and commentaries.

The Buddhist tradition was introduced from the Korean kingdom of Paekche during the Asuka period (飛鳥; 6th–7th), and enigmatic figures such as the female sovereign Suiko (推古天皇; 554–628) or Emperor Tenji (天智天皇; 662–671) revealed strong involvement in the country's earliest Buddhist rites, policies, and patronage. Asuka Buddhism (*Asuka bukkyō* 飛鳥仏教) represents the earliest stage of the Japanese Buddhist tradition; temples such as Asukadera (飛鳥寺) and Hōryuji (法隆寺), built in 596 and 607 respectively, were examples of how certain aristocratic families (*ujizoku* 氏族) became the religion's first patrons. Hōryuji's Beetle Cabinet (*Tamamushi zushi* 玉虫厨子), constructed in the 640s and depicting scenes from the Golden Light Sutra and the Lotus Sutra, or the famous Bronze Medicine Buddha's head (*c.* 685), presently kept at Kōfukuji (興福寺), are remaining witnesses of this dynamic period.

The term *Hakuhō Buddhism* (*Hakuho bukkyō*; 白鳳仏教) is used to describe the developments following the Asuka period, which took place between the second half of the 7th century and the move to the new capital Heijōkyō (平城京) in 710. This was a period of immense growth, as exemplified by the over seven hundred archaeological sites that date from this period. *Nara Buddhism* (*Nara bukkyō* 奈良仏教) refers to the period between 710 and the relocation to Heiankyō (today's Kyōto) in 794. The Heian period (794–1185) was dominated politically by the Fujiwara regents (*sekkan* 摂関) and the Retired Emperors (*in* 院). The temples developed into powerful blocs in this period, often growing into complicated internal structures of which the *monzeki* (門跡), often rendered as "imperial cloisters," would represent the presence of the nobility and court factionalism within the temples. From the point of view of Buddhist thought, we see an increasing doctrinal, ritual, and genealogical entanglement between the *exoteric* (*kengyō* 顕教) Nara schools and the *esoteric* (*mikkyō* 密教) forms of Japanese Buddhism, Shingon (真言) and Tendai (天台), mainly introduced from the late 8th century.

The distinction between Nara Buddhism and Heian Buddhism goes however much further than merely the relocation of capitals; during these centuries, the Buddhist tradition operated in a rapidly changing political and institutional context in which the role and position of the temples, their community, and religious discourse changed significantly. One of the main theoretical questions related to Asuka-Nara Buddhism is the problematization of the term *state Buddhism* (*kokka bukkyō* 国家仏教), a concept that was widely accepted and uncritically applied until the 1970's, but has now been under scrutiny for several decades. Identification of classical Buddhism with state Buddhism is a tenacious one because the Buddhism of the Kamakura period (鎌倉仏教; 1185–1333) is usually presented as popular Buddhism (*minshū bukkyō* 民衆仏教), in contrast with the elitist Buddhism of the classical era, a distinction that has been criticized by many Western and Japanese scholars but still persists in many introductory works and in popular perception.

In the 13th year of Kimmei's rule (欽明天皇; ?–571), emissaries from the Korean kingdom of Paekche presented scriptures, temple banners, and a guild statue of Shaka Buddha (the historical Buddha) to the Yamato (大和; i.e., Japanese) court, accompanied by the first Buddhist (female) monastics. Initially, the introduction of this new religious system became part of violent factionalism at the emerging court; but soon after its acceptance, temple networks were built, rules and regulations for the monastic community were promulgated, and courtiers, men and women alike, became active patrons of the temples and their lineages. Yet, there was more to the emerging Japanese Buddhist world than the political and economic relation between the court and the temples. The ritual production of texts and their materiality, the devotion expressed on donated statues or sutras, official histories, and origin chronicles (*engi* 縁起) or clan histories (*kaden* 家伝), reveal an eclectic world replete with multiple layers of meaning. The hermeneutical framework of Nara Japan was also not just Buddhist: the relation between the buddha and the kami (*gods*) and their corresponding temples and shrines, the reception of Confucian texts and rituals such as the *sekiten* (釈奠) commemorative ritual or the development of the *onmyōdō* (陰陽道; yin-yang divination) tradition all interacted with the Buddhist schools of the Nara period. In addition, when dealing with Nara and early Heian period Buddhist texts we should realize that the former were produced in a predominantly Confucian and the latter in an increasingly Buddhist narrative framework.[1]

The production of Buddhist commentaries by Nara monastics reached its height by the late 8th and early 9th centuries, with few exegetic texts being written during the first decades of the Nara period.[2] The Buddhist schools were clearly part of a larger cultural, political, and religious shift that occurred around the early Heian period.

Introductions to pre-modern Japanese Buddhism usually describe its early stages during the classical period (*kōdai*; 古代) by referring to the Six Schools (*roku shū*; 六宗) of the Nara period and in extension, the *Eight schools* of the Heian era (794–1185). Indeed, in his *Essentials of the Eight Schools* (八宗綱要 *Hasshū kōyō*), the Kamakura (1185–1333) monk Gyōnen (凝然; 1240–1321) outlined the history and doctrine of these eight schools for the sovereign, demonstrating that there was indeed a perceived distinction and an identity assigned to these *schools* at the time this work was written. From 806, a new ordination system had been implemented in which each year a fixed number of ordinands were assigned to a specific school. This system of yearly ordinands started in 696, but the early 9th century adaption divided the number in schools, a rule that de facto created clear sectarian divisions. While an examination of Nara and Heian period primary sources clearly shows the existence of certain lineages, centered around the transmission of specific doctrines, the nature of these schools (*shū*; 宗) and their relation during the Nara period was a very eclectic one. In other words, dividing the Buddhist landscape according to these *Six Schools* does not further our understanding of the period's doctrinal and institutional developments.

Significant for our comprehension of these Six Schools and their place in premodern Japanese Buddhism are two factors that are, in fact, quite often overlooked. First, their shared doctrinal concerns and genealogical overlap should be acknowledged; temples and lineages that came to be identified with a specific school in reality housed monks who might have focused on one specific teaching, but by doing so studied at other institutions and actively borrowed key texts and concepts from different forms of Buddhist thought. This was especially the case for those monastics who belonged to Hossō, Sanron, and Kegon lineages. Second, the early Japanese community's strong relation with Korean Buddhism (more specifically Silla), and the influence of the continent on early Japanese doctrinal, institutional, and artistic developments should not be overlooked. In addition, these two matters should be situated within the larger institutional framework of the *ritsuryō* polity (*ritsuryōsei* 律令制), a set of laws and penal codes modeled after Chinese Sui and T'ang period precedents.

Nara period Buddhism has often been introduced with a focus on the Six Schools disconnected from the period's political and institutional history. To adequately address the Six Schools, an overview of the 8th century's political and institutional history is relevant for understanding the context in which Buddhism developed. A concise overview of the schools and their temples, situates doctrine, ritual, and lineage within their historical context.

Caution should be taken, however, not to limit the discussion of Nara-period Buddhism to these Six Schools and their relation to the court and the formulation of the ritsuryō codes. An inquiry into Buddhist practice, the production of texts, devotion, rituals, and patronage cuts across this limited framework and enables us to imagine a more complete picture of Nara Buddhism. In this context, it has to be noted that far too often the role of women in both politics and the early Buddhist community has been neglected. For example, to understand the spread of Buddhism in connection with state sponsorship, the role of court women must be taken into consideration. Traditionally, categories such as Court Buddhism (*kyūtei bukkyō*

宮廷仏教) or state Buddhism have been discussed from an institutional point of view without sufficiently taking into account women's role in the promotion of Buddhism.[3] The role of Fuhito's wife, Agata Inukai Tachibana no Michiyo (県犬養三千代; ?–733) and her daughter Imperial Consort Kōmyō (光明皇后; 701–760), Empress Kōken's (孝謙天皇; 718–770) conflict with Fujiwara no Nakamaro (藤原仲麻呂; 706–764), or the foundation of Hokkeji (法華寺), a convent for nuns, in 741 are but a few examples of the necessity to reconsider the importance of women in the development of Buddhism during the Nara period.

THE TUMULTUOUS 8TH CENTURY

According to a well-known account in the *Nihon Shoki* (日本書記), one of Japan's first official histories, Buddhism was officially introduced to Japan in 552. Discrepancy exists surrounding this date since another text, the *Gangōji garan engi narabi ni riku shizai chō* (元興寺伽藍縁起并流記資財帳) provides an earlier date, 538.[4] However, in reality, the transmission of the Buddhist teachings and its scriptures was a process that would last for centuries as part of the larger encounter between Japan and East Asia.

From its very outset, Buddhism was part of political discourse in Japan and by the late 6th century it had become a vital element in the building of a centralized court.[5] Some of the names connected with this early stage are the Soga (蘇我) family, Empress Suiko, and her regent Shōtoku Taishi (聖徳太子; 574–622). Especially the latter would become the focus of a cult that bombarded him as the patron saint of early Japanese Buddhism, a view that persists to present day.[6] The importance of Prince Shōtoku aside, the development of Japanese Buddhism in relation to the continent and the institutionalization of the connection between the Buddhist order and the court find their origins in this early stage.

Contrary to popular perception, 8th century Japan was, politically, not a peaceful period but an era of intense strife and violent factionalism. Indeed, the period from Emperor Tenji (626–671) over Empress Jitō (持統天皇; 690?–697), Monmu (文武天皇; 683–707), Genmei (元明天皇; 661–721), Gensho (元正天皇; 680–748), Shōmu (聖武天皇; 701–756), Junnin (淳仁天皇; 733–765), Kōken/Shōtoku (孝謙天皇;称徳天皇; 718–770), up to Kōnin (光仁天皇; 709–782) represents a particular turbulent phase within the imperial lineage often described as the opposition between the Tenji and Tenmu lineages. This rivalry started in 672 following Tenji's death, when Tenmu (then still called Prince Ōama) confronted Prince Ōtomo (大友皇子; 648–672) in the so-called Jinshin Rebellion, a disturbance over imperial succession. As a result of Tenmu's victory, succession shifted to his lineage, a situation that wouldn't change until Kōnin's (光仁天皇; 709–781) accession in 770.

In 645, a short but violent uprising at court had resulted in the so-called "Taika reforms." Several Nara-period sources such as the *Nihon Shoki* and the *Kamatari den* describe how Prince Naka no Ōe (中大兄皇子), the later sovereign Tenji (天智; 626–671), and Nakatomi no Kamatari stabbed and killed Soga no Iruka (蘇我入鹿; ?–645) in front of Empress Kōgyoku (皇極天皇; 594–661). Iruka, and the Soga in general, had amassed tremendous influence at court, to the extent that it eclipsed the authority of the sovereign. Naka no Ōe, Kōgyoku's eldest son, seems to have rebelled against this to take power back to his line. This event did not merely instigate the institutional reforms known as *Taika* (Great Change), but also seems to have "wrestled Buddhist power . . . from long-held Soga patronage."[7] Historical overviews of the period have often described the 645 uprising as the start of a Chinese *tennō*-centered (天皇) style of governance, but it might be better to view these events as part of a longer evolution of the import of Chinese models of rule.[8]

Despite the *Kamatari den*'s assertion that "the entire populace called it a period of great peace," the decades following the events of the mid-7th century were rife with political rivalry and bloodshed. Naka no Ōe was first practically in charge of court politics after 645 and after Saimei's (斉明天皇; 594–661) death became sovereign as Tenji, in 661. His son was set to be his heir, but instead his brother Tenmu (天武天皇; ?–686) became the monarch after the Jinshin rebellion of 672 and was in turn succeeded by his consort Jitō (持統天皇; 645–702), who held the position till her death in 702. This split has often been described as the start of a rivalry between the Tenji and Temmu lines, lasting several generations and ending with the enthronement of Kōnin.

In 710, Genmei started the construction of a new capital, Heijōkyo, in collaboration with the courtier Fujiwara no Fuhito (藤原不比等; 659–720), son of the illustrious Nakatomi no Kamatari (中臣鎌足; 614–669), the patriarch of the Fujiwara clan. Rule and Buddhism went hand in hand, and the capital was built in relation to the construction of several temples that, throughout the following centuries, would develop into large complexes. More specifically, the "Four Great Temples" (*shidaiji* 四大寺) located in the previous capital Fujiwarakyō (藤原京) were moved to the new city: Daianji (大安寺; originally *daikan daiji*), Yakushiji (薬師寺), Gangōji (元興寺; originally Asukadera), and finally Kōfukuji, the new head temple of the Fujiwara allegedly based on an earlier, smaller temple called Yamashinadera (山階寺). The number of these official temples grew to seven (*Nanto shichidaiji*; 南都七大寺) by the mid-8th century and consisted of the earlier Four Great temples and Tōdaiji (東大寺), Saidaiji (西大寺), and Hōryuji. What would institutionally define the contours of the Buddhist temples and their relation with the court, however, would be the promulgation of the *Rules and Regulations for Monks and Nuns* (*sōniryō* 僧尼令) as part of the *Taihō ritsuryō* (大宝律令) promulgated in 701, and the establishment of a state-regulated monastic network *kokubunji* (国分寺) in 741.

Especially the *sōniryō* is often taken as the start of the state's grip on the Buddhist establishment. Central to understanding the significance of this *sōniryō* and the state-regulated network is that these measures effectively turned the monastic community into a government bureaucracy. The establishment of a *Ministry of Monastic Affairs* (*sōgō* 僧綱) in 624 had already created an institutional space for Buddhism within the larger framework of the state, and it seems that these 8th-century developments concluded a long and gradual development in which the monastic community became a part of the state structure. The following 9th and 10th centuries clearly demonstrated that the Buddhist institutions were about to change significantly, and the Heian period saw the gradual formation of these temples as veritable Gates of Power (*kenmon* 権門) that have been described as examples of the shared sovereignty characteristic of the Heian era.[9] By that time, the *ritsuryō* order had effectively ceased to exist, but its temples and Buddhist lineages did not.

In institutional terms, the period from the 7th to the 8th century was one of great institutional innovation not limited to the relation between Buddhism and the state, as illustrated by the foundation of the Council for Affairs of the Deities of Heaven and Earth (*jingikan* 神祇官), a construct related to *kami* worship functioning alongside the Council of State (*daijōkan*

太政官). Of note is that, while the *ritsuryō* were in fact adaptations from Chinese examples, this *jingikan* was a specifically Japanese phenomenon. This Council of State conducted rites in accordance with a Code of Kami Law (*jingiryō*) and was part of the aforementioned *ritsuryō* system.[10] The growing influence and number of Buddhist monastics illustrates that shrines and temples were an integral part of the state and therefore were heavily involved in this era's tumultuous episodes. The Buddha and the kami would coexist throughout Japanese history, only to be separated by 19th-century Meiji laws, but it seems that the establishment of an official temple network and the completion of Tōdaiji under Shōmu's reign pushed Buddhism to the forefront during the Nara period.[11]

It is in the figure of Tenmu's great-grandson, Shōmu (聖武天皇; 701–756), that scholars have discerned the zenith of *ritsuryō* kingship, of which Buddhism had become an integral part.[12] Kōmyo, daughter of Shōmu's consort Fuhito, and Agata Inukai Michiyo, was equally responsible for the propagation of Buddhism around this period. She supervised the construction of temples, for example Sumidera (隅寺), sponsored the copying of Buddhist texts there in 737 and acted as patron for influential monks such as Genbō. Sumidera and her personal residence evolved into Hokkeji, a nunnery that headed a state network of nunneries called the Hokke metsuzai no tera (法華滅罪之寺) by 741, following a decree issued by Shōmu.[13] The most iconic temple of the era, however, was the monumental Tōdaiji, illustrative of the surge in Buddhist temples under Shōmu and Kōmyō.

Construction of Tōdaiji has to be seen as part of Shōmu's promulgation, in 741, to establish a statewide network of official temples. The pinnacle of this network was a grand state temple called *Konkōmyō shiten'ō gokokuji* (今光明四天王護国寺), or Tōdaiji. The temple's full name refers to the Sutra of Golden Light (*Konkōmyō kyō*; 金光明經) and reveals how Shōmu saw his role as sovereign as a true *cakravartin* or a universal Wheel Turning king (*tenrin'ō* 轉輪王). His instructions followed right after a period of intense domestic unrest: in 737 an epidemic had ravaged the Japanese islands, and in 740 Fujiwara no Hirotsugu (藤原広嗣; ?–740) had started a revolt directed toward the monk Genbō and the courtier Kibi no Makibi (吉備真備; 695–775), both supporters and advisors of Shōmu. In addition, only months before the 741 edict, Shōmu decided to move the capital to Kuni (恭仁), a plan that was soon abandoned. It seems that by ordering a wide network of state temples headed by the grand Tōdaiji, the sovereign established himself as a strong, universal ruler. In 743, Shōmu then ordered the construction of the temple's centerpiece, a statue that would, from then on, represent the splendor of Nara period Buddhism: Tōdaiji's Great Buddha or *Rushana Butsu* (盧遮那仏) presents a depiction of Vairocana Buddha, a central figure in the Flower Garland Sutra (Kegon kyō; 華厳経), a text strongly supported only decades before by Empress Wu (武則天; 625–705) in China, and also of great importance in Silla Buddhism. The casting of the monumental image was started in 747 and completed by 749. Three years later, in 752, the image was dedicated and an Opening of the Eyes Ceremony was carried out by the monk Bodhisena (菩提遷那; 704–760). The first monk to head the temple was the monk Ryōben, originally from Kōfukuji. From the outset, the temple functioned as a state temple and would receive its official ordination platform (*kaidan* 戒壇) in 754, led by the Chinese monk and Vinaya (*kairitsu* 戒律) or "precepts" master Ganjin (鑑眞; 688–763). In 759, he would start his own ordination platform at the newly constructed Tōshōdaiji (唐招提寺).

The construction of Tōdaiji and its Great Buddha and the consolidation of an official temple network under the supervision of the ritsuryō monarch have often given this period's Buddhism the reputation of "state religion." However, one should not lose sight of the overly Confucian bureaucratic system and discourse, of which Buddhism was still a subservient part. It is this tension, and possibly different views on Buddhism's role, that could have been the cause of the discord between Shōmu's daughter Kōken and the court's main figure, Fujiwara no Nakamaro (藤原仲麻呂; 706–764) and the violent suppression of the latter's revolt and decapitation in 764. Much debate exists regarding the nature of Nakamaro's disturbance and the deteriorating of his relationship with the Retired Sovereign Kōken, but research has suggested that Nakamaro's implementation of new Buddhist policies might have been the source of their discord.[14] It is likely that Kōken, who later would become sovereign again as *Shōtoku*, envisaged a Buddhist state, while Nakamaro was determined to render Buddhism subservient to the state. His creation of the position of abbot (*bettō* 別当) at Kōfukuji in 757 should be seen in this light: the function of abbot was created not to provide the temple with independence, but to control the monastic community through a cleric official appointed by the Fujiwara.[15] In other words: Buddhism and its institutions were an important factor in this century's political and military upheaval. Traditionally brought up in this context is Shōtoku's (Kōken) relation with the monk Dōkyō, whom she promoted to the unprecedented position of Hōō (法王; Dharma King) in 766, a position that put him de facto in charge of all matters Buddhist.[16] Often, this has been interpreted as Dōkyō's influence over the female sovereign and his attempts to usurp the throne. However, rather than just accepting this traditional narrative, one must consider the adversary situation and factional struggles Shōtoku had to confront and her negative portrayal in later sources such as the Nihon Ryōiki (日本霊異記), which elaborated on her alleged affair with Dōkyō.[17]

The smallpox epidemic of 737 had caused a major blow to the court's composition, killing among others the four main Fujiwara bureaucrats (the Fujiwara Four), including Nakamaro's father Fujiwara Muchimaro (藤原武智麻呂; 680–737). As a result, power relations in the court bureaucracy had changed, the consequences of which were still felt during Shōtoku's time. Right after the epidemic, it was Tachibana no Moroe (橘諸兄; 684–757) who became the most influential courtier at the Great Council of State. In time, he was heavily opposed by Nakamaro, who was able to become the court's most influential politician by the late 750's. While the latter favored a Chinese, Confucian style court and clearly saw Buddhism as an entity that had to be tamed by the state, Shōtoku might have seen this differently.

Japanese institutional developments in the 6th and 7th centuries are usually described in terms of the Ritsuryō state (*ritsuryō kokka* 律令国家), a concept referring to the adaption of a Chinese-style set of laws mentioned above. The first stage in the gradual development of this Japanese system was the promulgation of the *Ōmi-ryō* (近江令) in 668, under Tenji, followed by the *Asuka Kiyomihara-ryō* (飛鳥浄御原令) in 689.[18] However, a full-fledged legal code with both penal and administrative laws wasn't completed until 701 with the *Taihō ritsuryō* (大宝律令), a legal codex that effectively transformed Japan into a centralized bureaucratic state. Fujiwara no Fuhito, one of the architects of Heijōkyō, drafted a new set, the *Yōro ritsuryo* (養老律令) in 718 which was implemented, and adapted, by his grandson Nakamaro several decades later in 757. An important part of this legal corpus was the *Regulations for Monks and Nuns* (*Sōniryō* 僧尼律), a list of specific rules and restrictions for the monastic community.[19]

The main institution to control the application of this code was the Ministry of Monastic Affairs, but the main question that arises here is whether these codes and the Ministry restricted the monastic community or provided it special status.[20] In this context, the Confucian character of the Nara state's structure and discourse have to be noted, and that the monastic community was expected to keep the precepts and protect the state through correct services.[21] This Confucian basis is clearly evidenced by the creation of the state college (*daigaku*) or the provincial colleges (*kokugaku*), centers of learning for the bureaucracy in which a curriculum based on the Confucian classics and the Chinese histories was taught. In other words, the regulations for the Buddhist community were entrenched in a Confucian context. This meant that Buddhism was integrated into a Confucian system and that monastics, both male and female, received the status and duties of government officials, or rather *priest officials* (*sōkan* 僧官). In this context, ordination received an extra dimension: an ordained monastic became an official sanctioned by the state, providing the state the right to grant this privilege and outlaw extra-legal ordinations (*shido* 私度). However, despite the state's regulation, unofficial ordinations would become an important part of Nara Buddhism, as exemplified by the life of Gyōki (行基; 668–749), originally an unofficial monk looked upon with suspicion by the court, but who would become vital in raising donations for the state's main temple, Tōdaiji.[22] In the Buddhist world, the authority to apply the precepts and the organization of the Sangha fall under the responsibilities of the clergy themselves; but in a Japanese context, the state assumed this responsibility through the creation of the Ministry and the *Sōniryō*, a logic that extended to *kami* worship (Shintō) rites as well. In other words, Buddhism's role in "protecting the nation" is an important factor to understand the community's relation to the early state.

Alongside the *Sōniryō*, the creation and composition of the Ministry of Monastic Affairs revealed a constant tension between the state's effort to control Buddhism and the Buddhist community's growing strength to guard its own sphere.[23] The earliest usage of the word *Sōgō* dates back to 701, but the list of appointees goes back to 624. The number of priests in this Ministry increased throughout the Nara and Heian periods, but originally this government agency consisted of the high positions of *supreme priest* (sōjō 僧正), *senior priest general* (*daisōzu* 大僧都), *junior priest genera*l (*shōsōzu* 小僧都), and a master of precepts (*risshi* 律師). These were assisted by a number of lesser positions such as the *ritual master* (*igishi* 威儀師), who featured in important rituals such as the Yuima-e at Kōfukuji.[24] The Ministry's main functions consisted of the preparation of ordination certificates, overseeing the top positions (*sango* 三綱) at the official temples, the management of temples' possessions, and the appointment of provincial masters (*kokushi,* 国師).[25] As stipulated in the *Sōniryō*, the members of the Sōgō were appointed by the court upon recommendation by the Sangha. The *List of Appointments of the Ministry of Monastic Affairs* (*Sōgō bunin* 僧綱補任) shows that these positions were controlled by the Nara monasteries such as Kōfukuji and Tōdaiji.

While the construction of Japan's first permanent capital *Heijōkyō* (平城京) is seen as a watershed moment, it should not be forgotten that, over the course of the Nara period's eight decades, the sovereign quite often resided somewhere else, de facto changing the capital temporarily. The construction and rapid abandonment of a new capital, Nagaokakyō (長岡京), by Kanmu in 784 and the final relocation of the capital to Heiankyō by 794 show that this period was not as stable as usually portrayed. Quite often the attempt to move the capital to

Nagaoka has been described as a strategy by the sovereign to escape the influence of the Buddhist temples within the perimeter of *Heijōkyō*, but given the close presence of monasteries to the new capital or the connection between the Fujiwara family and the highest positions at the monastic centers, it is likely that the decision to move was inspired by multiple factors such as an attempt for a new dynastic beginning based on the Chinese concept of the Heavenly Mandate.[26] After less than ten years however, Nagaoka was abandoned, and it is Heiankyō that would become Japan's capital for the next millennium to come.

THE SIX SCHOOLS

The Six Nara schools consist of Sanron (三論), Jōjitsu (成実), Hossō (法相), Kusha (倶舎), Ritsu (律), and Kegon (華厳). However, it should be made clear from the beginning that the exact number of the Nara schools is rather misleading since both Jōjitsu and Kusha never developed into independent systems of thought. In addition, Sanron, Hossō, and Kegon all developed in time into shared lineages, merging with the later esoteric transmission (exoteric-esoteric Buddhism) from the early Heian period onwards, mainly Shingon.

Jōjitsu is in fact an Abhidharma development based on Harivarman's (dates unknown) *Satyasiddhi-śāstra*, transmitted to Japan by the Korean monk Hyegwan (Jap. Ekan; 慧灌; dates unknown). From early on, it was closely related to Sanron, and it seems it only enjoyed a certain degree of independence during the beginning of the 8th century, before becoming part of Sanron, as exemplified by its yearly ordinands being listed under Sanron by 806.

Ritsu (*Risshū*) focuses on the precepts or the *vinaya* (*kairitsu* 律宗), and its transmission is commonly attributed to the Chinese monk Jianzhen (Jpn. Ganjin), who was invited to Japan in 754, became a member of the Sōgō, and built his own ordination platform at Tōshōdaiji in 759.

Kusha was originally based on Vasubandhu's *Abhidharmakośa-bhāṣya*, a text belonging to the Sarvāstivāda that was translated into Chinese by Paramārtha and brought to Japan around the middle of the 8th century, perhaps as part of the corpus introduced by Dōshō, showing that, from early on, Kusha was brought to Japan as part of the Hossō transmission.[27] Although counted as a school, it never existed as a separate institution, and its questions and discussions might be best seen as part of Japan's Mind Only tradition.

The Hossō schools' transmission happened in several phases. It is the outgrowth of the Indian Yogācāra tradition, originating in the philosophy of Asanga (4th), Vasubandhu (5th), Sthiramati (7th), and Paramārtha (499–569). China received this tradition through three stages: Bodhiruci's translation in 513 of the *Daśabhūmikasūtra-śāstra* (*Jūji kyō ron*; 十地経論), Paramārta's arrival in China in 546, and Xuanzang's foundation, in 659 of the Faxiang (法相) school, Hossō's direct predecessor. The text at the basis of the Hossō school is the *Treatise on Consciousness Only*, composed by Xuanzang, based on ten Sanskrit commentaries on Vasubandu's *Thirty Verses* (*Triṃśikā vijñapti Kārikā*). This text focuses on the nature of consciousness that would form the focus of countless Japanese commentaries and ritual debates throughout the premodern period.[28]

The Japanese Hossō school was originally divided into two branches: a northern and southern faction, based at Kōfukuji and Gangōji. The latter was in fact mainly a center of Sanron and would later merge with the former that thus became Hossō's head temple. Before moving on to the establishment of these temples, a brief look at the introduction of Hossō to Japan is in order.

There were several transmissions to Japan. First, Dōshō (道昭; 629–700) left for Tang China in 653, followed by the monks Chitsū (智通; dates unknown) and Chidatsu (智達; dates unknown). The third phase consisted of Chiran (智鸞; dates unknown), Chiyū (智雄; dates unknown), and Chihō (智鳳; dates unknown) from Silla. The fourth, Genbō (玄昉; ?–746) brought back a vast corpus of texts that would end up at Kōfukuji. Dōshō is a good case to illustrate the relation between the different schools of Buddhism that were transmitted to Japan by the Nara period. Originally, he was mainly interested in Sanron but resided at Gangōji prior to his departure to Tang China.[29] Upon his return, he is said to have favored Hossō and brought the study of Mind Only Buddhism to Gangōji, known for its study of Sanron. It is clear that Hossō and Sanron were close in Japan from the very beginning: Dōshō was a Gangōji-Sanron monastic with a growing interest in Hossō. This mixture becomes even more poignant when taking into consideration that Gangōji became the center of Hossō's Southern branch. Genbō, a direct dharma descendant of Dōshō through Gien (義淵; ?–728), travelled to Tang China in 717, and returned almost two decades later, in 735. Several sources such as the *Sangoku buppō denzū engi* (三国仏法伝通縁起) and the *Genkō Shakushō* (元亨釈書) mention that he studied Mind Only in China under Zhizhou (智周; 668–723). Genbō brought to Japan around five thousand texts (both exoteric and esoteric), which were allocated to Kōfukuji, where he settled and Zenshu (善珠; 723–797) became his disciple.

Kōfukuji's founding history and connections with the nearby Kasuga shrine are a prime example of the Nara period's emerging temples complexes: large religious centers that would, in the following Heian period, develop into influential power blocs, the so-called *kenmon* (Gates of Power). In general, scholarship has assumed that Kōfukuji originated from Yamashina-dera (山階寺), a family temple founded by the wife of Fujiwara no Kamatari, Kagami no Ookimi (鏡女王; ?–683) in 669. The main primary source used to describe the origins of this temple and its main ritual, the Vimalakīrti Assembly or *Yuima-e* (維摩会) is, in fact, a later text, the 9th century *Origin Chronicle of Kōfukuji* (*Kōfukuji engi* 興福寺縁起) by Fujiwara no Yoshiyo (藤原良世; 823–900).[30] The story tells that after Kamatari fell ill, his wife built Yamashina-dera, and that later the temple was moved and renamed Umayasaka-dera (厩坂寺). It is claimed that this temple was, in its turn, rebuilt in the new Nara capital by Fuhito and supported by Kōmyō. Thus, just like Gangōji found its origins in Asuka-dera, founded in 596, it seems that Kōfukuji's history stretches back to long before 710, even predating the name *Fujiwara* itself. This is the officially accepted account and since the dawn of modern scholarship, Japanese and Western scholars alike have accepted this version. It is unclear, however, where Kōfukuji's predecessors were located, what their size was, and what artifacts they held. In fact, reasonable doubt has been cast upon their actual existence, based on the limited timeframe and the complete absence of archaeological data. Of more importance perhaps, is the early connection between the temple, its main ritual, and the Fujiwara, a connection that found its clear expression in the new city and center of the *ritsuryō* state, Heijōkyō. The temple was not an elaborate complex from the beginning, and it has to be stressed that the immense Heian-period Kōfukuji was the result of a long evolution of construction projects, elaborate patronage and political involvement by the court. For example, the temple's octagonal hall (*hokuen-dō* 北円堂) was constructed in 721, but destroyed in

1180, and restored in 1240. The original tōkon-dō (東金堂) dates from 726 and was reconstructed in 1425. In 730, a five-story pagoda (*gojū no tō*; 五重塔) was built, which was struck by lightning and destroyed by fire, but rebuilt in 1426.

Several documents suggest that, by the middle of the 8th century, Fujiwara no Nakamaro became heavily involved with the temple's internal organization, its main ritual, and its financial basis. In 758, Nakamaro reached the unprecedented position of Great Protector (*taihō* 大保) and was granted the honorary name *Emi no Oshikatsu* (恵美 押勝). It was during these years that he greatly influenced Kōfukuji's direction for centuries to come. First, in 757, he put into effect his grandfather's *Yōrō ritsu ryō*, created the position of Kōfukuji abbot, and appointed Jikun (691–777), a monk of common background, to be the first in that position. Second, in the same year, Nakamaro issued a memorial that granted land originally belonging to Kamatari to the Yuima-e, providing a different account of the ritual's history. In later accounts, such as the Origin Chronicle mentioned above, the origin of the Yuima-e is traced back to his great-grandfather Kamatari recovering from illness. However, this memorial precedes this account and thus provides insight into his personal involvement in the creation of this ritual.

It is unclear how Kōfukuji's Vimalakīrti Assembly looked like in the 8th century. The *Origin Chronicle of Kōfukuji* includes a story that usually has been interpreted as historical truth. The text states that, in 705, when Kamatari was ill, a Korean nun called Hōmyō (法明) recited one part of the Vimalakīrti Sutra, curing him. As a result, Kamatari ordered for a ritual to be held from that day on. However, after his death this early Yuima-e seems to have been discontinued, only to be revived by his son Fuhito, who also gave the ritual its seven-day format.[31] In its matured version, the ritual lasted seven days and centered around debates between monks of opposing schools. The main ritual position was that of the Lecturer, a high function that would evolve into a prerequisite to (in theory) proceed to the Ministry of Monastic Affairs. While Kōfukuji became the official site of the Yuima-e in 801, and was conducted yearly after the Nara period, the ritual was not yet held every year in its early stage and alternated between several temples. In addition, while there is very little detailed information regarding Heian period sessions, much less is known about the first decades of this grand ritual. What is clear, however, is that the debates included monks from the Hossō, Sanron, and Kegon schools, and that the topics of debate related to central passages and questions of the Mind Only School.

While Kōfukuji is still impressive today, Gangōji's pre-modern splendor no longer survives. Not too far from present-day Kōfukuji and the Kasuga Shrine, all that remains is a stone stele in the modern city of Nara. Constructed in Heijōkyō in 716, this temple found its origins in Asukadera (or "Hōkōji" 法興寺), often considered the first full-scale temple in Japan and connected with the names of Empress Suiko and Shōtoku Taishi. Several 8th-century sources, such as the *Nihon Shoki*, the *Shoku Nihongi*, and the *Gangōji garan engi narabi ruki shizaichō* (The origin chronicle of the Gangōji community and a list of its possessions) composed in 747, describe the temple's origins and accumulated wealth. While the official histories describe events from the point of view of the established imperial line, the Origin Chronicle or "engi" belongs to a different genre, that of Buddhist history writing, which describes the flourishing of the dharma (Buddhist teachings), temples, and famous monks or nuns in mythical terms.

The text reveals the factionalism at court before and around the time of the temple's creation and confirms the opposition between the supporters of Buddhism of the Soga clan, on the one hand, and those that opposed the new religion, the Nakatomi and Mononobe, on the other hand. The text reveals that the temple was built following a vow by Soga no Umako (蘇我馬子; ?–626) in 587 and completed by 596, confirming the importance of the Soga for Japan's earliest Buddhist beginnings.[32] It is important to keep in mind that this most certainly was not just a religious opposition, as often portrayed in past scholarship. The clash between the indigenous kami and buddha was also, if not foremost, an expression of political factionalism, in which certain lineages had become in charge of certain functions at the emerging court—the Nakatomi as those responsible for the correct execution of rituals. It is their descendants who, as Fujiwara, would become the founders and sponsors of Kōfukuji's Yuima-e, one of the main state rituals of the Heian period. In other words: their ritual function and institutional centrality at the court remained, but Buddhism would become a central component to their role.

Sanron, roughly corresponding to Indian Madhyamaka thought asserting that everything changes and lacks inherent existence, became one of the Nara and Heian period's main Buddhist teachings. Sanron literally means "Three Treatises," referring to Nāgārjuna's Madhyamaka-śāstra (*Chūron* 中論) and Dvādaśanikāya-śāstra (*Jūnimon ron* 十二門論), and Āryadeva's Śata-śāstra (*Hyakuron* 百論).[33] The Korean monk Hyegwan (Jpn. Ekan 慧灌; ?–?), student of Jizang, who arrived in Japan in 625 and settled at Gangōji, represents Sanron's first transmission. Some of the influential Sanron monks of the 8th century clearly show the overlap between the Hossō and the Sanron lineages. The earliest recorded, and perhaps the first, lecturer of the Hossō school's prime ritual, the Yuima-e, was in fact the Chinese Sanron monk Fuliang (福亮), who appears to have presided over the ritual in 658. In addition, his student Chikō (智光; 709–781) is a prime example of how Nara period monks were not confined to their own school. With 14 titles, he can be considered as on the most scholarly productive authors of the Nara period, and his works represent, on the one hand, the overlap between Sanron, Hossō, and Kegon within Japanese Buddhism, and on the other, the dialogue and conflict between Madhyāmika and Yogacāra teachings on an East Asian level. In his commentary on the Heart Sutra, the *Hannya Shingyō Jutsugi* (般若心経述義), Chinese Sanlun is directly connected with Japanese Sanron, demonstrating the continuity within the transmission of the school across East Asia. In this text, Chikō directly attacked the Hossō school's understanding of the Heart Sutra. In his argumentation, however, he uses insights accepted by other schools. For example, he considers the Hear Sutra as the distillation of the larger Perfection of Wisdom corpus, an idea he borrowed from Kegon's Fazang (法藏; 643–712), and Kuiji (窺基; 632–682), and Yuance (圓測; 613–696) of the Chinese Mind Only (Hossō) School.[34] To clarify the purpose of the Heart Sutra, he relies on specific Kegon categories such as the 52 progressive stages of bodhisattva practice. In addition to this, he also wrote an extensive commentary on the actual main source of inspiration of Kōfukuji's Yuima-e, the Vimalakīrti Sutra.

The Kegon (Ch. Huayan; 華厳) school represents one of East Asia's major Buddhist traditions and is based on both the *Avataṃsaka-sūtra* (Jpn. *Kegon-kyō* 華厳経) and an elaborate commentarial tradition on this text by Sung and Tang Chinese thinkers such as Dushun (杜順; 557–640), Zhiyan (智儼; 602–668), and Fazang. Once again illustrating the eclectic character of early Japanese developments, it was the Hossō monk Ryōben who brought this body of thought to Japan. It is not surprising that a Hossō priest would be interested in Kegon concepts given the school's borrowing of *Yuishiki* (唯識) or "Consciousness Only" elements and interest in the *Tathāgatagarbha* (*nyorai zō* 如來藏) discussions found in texts such as the *Awakening of Faith* (Jpn. *Daijō kishin ron* 大乘起信論).[35] After the construction of Tōdaiji, Ryōben established Kegon there, where in later centuries it would engage with esoteric Buddhism in the same way Hossō and Sanron would, also resulting in merged exoteric-esoteric lineages (*kenmitsu* 顕密) in the Heian period.

THE CONTINUITY OF THE NARA PERIOD'S TEMPLES AND THEIR TEACHINGS

The development of the *ritsuryō* codes and the gradual establishment of a Buddhist monastic network clearly transcend the conventional periodization that divides early Japanese history into convenient blocks. However, the compilation and application of these legal codes and the increasingly complex relation between the court and the temples were in fact the prelude of a specifically Japanese form of *shared sovereignty* that would emerge in the second half of the Heian period. The backbone of the Nara era, the *ritsuryō* codes, gradually became obsolete, and in the following centuries, the temples emerged as influential institutional, economic, and religious "Gates of Power" (*kenmon*); a phenomenon that challenged the authority of a single political Nara/ritsuryō-era center and resulted in a dynamic codependent relationship between the court and the periphery. The temples themselves underwent a similar internal process of decentralization: while quite inclusive during the 8th and 9th centuries, they developed toward exclusive institutions consisting of competing sub-temples who brought the factional strife of the court within the temple walls. What connects Nara and Heian period developments however, is the continuation of lineages (mainly Hossō, Sanron, and Kegon) *and* their gradual synthesis with esoteric Buddhism from the 9th century onwards. This exoteric-esoteric Buddhism revitalized the tradition and carried the Nara schools' temples, commentaries, and rituals into the early medieval period. To fully understand medieval Buddhism, it is therefore necessary to realize that Nara Buddhism did not disappear at the end of the 8th century: in conversation with the teachings of Kukai and Saicho, key concepts of the Nara schools survived for centuries to come.

REVIEW OF LITERATURE

In recent years scholars of premodern Japanese studies have produced in-depth studies of the Asuka (538–710), Nara, and Heian periods. Topics addressed range from the involvement of women in patronage, the presence and influence of East Asian systems of thought, the category of state Buddhism, and the import of esoteric Buddhism. What characterizes the state of the field of the past decade is most certainly an interdisciplinary approach that situates Buddhist doctrinal, ritual, and artistic developments in their larger social and historical context. One area that is most certainly still in need of being included more in the study of Japanese religiosity concerns the field of archaeology.

When Buddhism made its way into the Japanese landscape, it was part of a larger wave of East Asian thought. Along with texts that would later be identified with the Confucian and Daoist traditions, Buddhism was one aspect of *Chinese Learning* that fascinated the Japanese. Scholars have produced many studies on the presence of continental symbolism and the creation of a long-neglected system of divination called *onmyōdō*, a uniquely Japanese tradition sometimes erroneously identified as Daoism. Matthias Hayek, Hayashi Makoto, James Robson, and Bernard Faure, among many others, have discussed the tradition of divination and its institutional significance, though it remains difficult to pinpoint what this *onmyōdō* precisely was.[36] Herman Ooms, in dealing with imperial symbolism, also discussed the impact of continental imagery on the formation of sovereignty.[37]

The overall history of the 8th century suggests that the application of the term 'Six Nara Schools' might not be the most insightful way to address the complex web of doctrine, ritual, and institutional developments that ran throughout the Nara period. In her monumental edited volume *Engendering Faith*, Barbara Ruch has shown how female patronage was an integral part of Nara Buddhism. A similar approached is expressed in Brian Ruppert's *Jewel in the Ashes*. It would be a mistake, however, to assume that female involvement was limited to donating to the temples. As explored in detail by Bryan Lowe in *Ritualized Writing*, female members of the court were actively involved in the scriptural culture of the 8th century. Central to this culture of writing were the notions of devotion, faith, and ritual; and several scholars have explored the formation of Buddhist ritual and its significance for the court and the state. Mikael Bauer and Asuka Sango have explored the creation and role of important state rituals throughout the Nara and Heian periods.[38]

Although certain scholars of archaeology such as Gina Barnes, Edward Kidder, and David McCallum have connected the fields of archaeology and religious studies to interpret the construction and significance of tombs, tumuli and later temples, scholars of the Asuka and Nara period's history and religion should certainly devote more attention to archaeology. In addition, the recent surge in interdisciplinary approaches has certainly widened our understanding of Nara period Buddhism, but this has pushed the analysis of texts to the background. It is encouraging to see, however, that the most recent works seem to realize this and accord textual study the attention it warrants.[39]

FURTHER READING

Bowring, Richard. *The Religious Traditions of Japan 500–1600*. Cambridge, UK: Cambridge University Press, 2005.

Deal, William E., and Brian Ruppert, eds. *A Cultural History of Japanese Buddhism*. Malden, MA: Wiley Blackwell, 2015.

Lowe, Bryan. *Ritualized Writing: Buddhist Practice and Scriptural Cultures in Ancient Japan*. Kuroda Studies in East Asian Buddhism. Honolulu: University of Hawai'i Press, 2017.

Piggott, Joan R. *The Emergence of Japanese Kingship*. Stanford, CA: Stanford University Press, 1997.

Ruch, Barbara. *Engendering Faith: Women and Buddhism in Premodern Japan*. Center for Japanese Studies. Ann Arbor: University of Michigan Press, 2002.

NOTES

1. Ryuichi Abe, *The Weaving of Mantra: Kūkai and the Construction of Esoteric Buddhist Discourse* (New York: Columbia University Press, 2013), 179.
2. Abe, *The Weaving of Mantra*, 183; and Abe refers here to the work of Inoue Mitsusada.

3. Masatsugu Hongō, "State Buddhism and Court Buddhism: The Role of Court Women in the Development of Buddhism from the Seventh to the Ninth Centuries," in *Engendering Faith: Women and Buddhism in Pre-Modern Japan*, ed. Barbara Ruch (Ann Arbor: University of Michigan Press, 2002), 43.
4. For a comparison between the *Nihon Shoki* and the *Gangōji engi*, see Donald Fredrick McCallum, *The Four Great Temples: Buddhist Archaeology, Architecture, and Icons of Seventh-Century Japan* (Honolulu: University of Hawai'i Press, 2009), 1–11.
5. William E. Deal and Brian Ruppert, *A Cultural History of Japanese Buddhism* (Malden, MA: John Wiley & Sons, 2015), 24.
6. On the development of the Shōtoku Taishi cult, see Michael Como, *Shotoku: Ethnicity, Ritual, and Violence in the Japanese Buddhist Tradition* (New York: Oxford University Press, 2008).
7. Deal and Ruppert, *A Cultural History of Japanese Buddhism*, 46.
8. Joan R. Piggott, *The Emergence of Japanese Kingship* (Stanford, CA: Stanford University Press, 1997), 102.
9. Mikael Adolphson, *The Gates of Power* (Honolulu: University of Hawai'i Press, 2000), 354.
10. Helen Hardacre, *Shinto, A History* (New York, Oxford University Press, 2017), 17–18; 30–31.
11. Hardacre, *Shinto, A History*, 93.
12. Piggott, *The Emergence of Japanese Kingship*, 236.
13. Lori Meeks, *Hokkeji and the Reemergence of Female Monsatic Orders in Premodern Japan* (Honolulu: University of Hawai'i Press, 2010), 2; and Hongō, "State Buddhism and Court Buddhism," 47.
14. Shōmu's daughter was sovereign twice: as Kōken (749–758) and as Shōtoku (764–770). She was retired sovereign during Junnin's rule (758–764).
15. Bauer, "The Power of Ritual," 80.
16. Piggott, *The Emergence of Japanese Kingship*, 75.
17. Ross Bender, *Performative Loci of Shoki Nihongi Edicts* (Charleston, NC: CreateSpace Independent Publishing Platform, 2015), 5–6.
18. Jun'ichi Enomoto, "Japan's Ritsuryō System in the 'East Asian World,'" *Acta Asiatica* 99 (2010): 1–17; Abe, *The Weaving of Mantra*, 26; and Deal and Ruppert, *Cultural History of Japanese Buddhism*, 53.
19. Richard Bowring, *The Religious Traditions of Japan 500–1600* (Cambridge, UK: Cambridge University Press, 2005), 54–55.
20. Bowring, *Religious Traditions of Japan*, 58.
21. Abe, *The Weaving of Mantra*, 24.
22. Goodwin, 23; Bowring, *Religious Traditions of Japan*, 61; and Deal and Ruppert, *Cultural History of Japanese Buddhism*, 63–64.
23. Abe, *The Weaving of Mantra*, 32–33.
24. Bauer, "The Power of Ritual," 57.
25. Abe, *The Weaving of Mantra*, 30–31; and Bowring, *Religious Traditions of Japan*, 58.
26. Ellen Van Goethem, *Nagaoka, Japan's Forgotten Capital*, vol. 29 (Leiden, The Netherlands: Brill, 2008), 6.
27. Charles Muller, *Digital Dictionary of Buddhism*, http://www.buddhism-dict.net/ddb/.
28. Bauer, "The Power of Ritual."
29. Bowring, *Religious Traditions of Japan*, 59–60.
30. Bauer, "The Power of Ritual," 23; Allan G. Grappard, *The Protocol of the Gods: A Study of the Kasuga Cult in Japanese History* (Berkeley: University of California Press, 1993), 49; and Bowring, *Religious Traditions of Japan*, 77.
31. Bauer, "The Power of Ritual," 27.
32. McCallum, *The Four Great Temples*, 42.
33. See also Muller, *Digital Dictionary of Buddhism*, for a list of texts and commentaries regarding the Six Nara Schools.

34. Abe, *The Weaving of Mantra*, 187.
35. Muller, *Digital Dictionary of Buddhism*, http://www.buddhism-dict.net/ddb/.
36. Bernard Faure, "A Religion in Search of a Founder?" in *The Way of Yin and Yang: Divinatory Techniques and Religious Practices*, ed. Faure and Iyanaga Nobumi (Kyoto: École Française d'Extrême-Orient, 2012); Matthias Hayek and Makoto Hayashi, eds. "Onmyōdō in Japanese History," *Japanese Journal of Religious Studies* 40, no. 1 (2013); and James Robson, "Daoism," in *The Norton Anthology of World Religions*, ed. Jack Miles (New York: W. W. Norton, 2015), 1473–1496.
37. Ooms Herman, *Imperial Politics and Symbolics in Ancient Japan, the Tenmu Dynasty, 650–800* (Honolulu: University of Hawai'i Press, 2009).
38. Brian Ruppert, *Jewel in the Ashes: Buddha Relics and Power in Early Medieval Japan* (Cambridge, MA: Harvard University Press, 2000); Bryan Lowe, *Ritualized Writing: Buddhist Practice and Scriptural Cultures in Ancient Japan*, Kuroda Studies in East Asian Buddhism (Honolulu: University of Hawai'i Press, 2017); and Mikaël Bauer, "The Power of Ritual."
39. McCallum, *The Four Great Temples*.

Mikaël Bauer

SŌKA GAKKAI

HISTORICAL OVERVIEW

Founding and Early History. The founder of the Sōka Gakkai, Makiguchi Tsunesaburō, was born in 1871. Trained as an educator, he spent most of his adult life first as a teacher and then principal in Tokyo public elementary schools.

In 1928, through the mediation of a fellow school principal, Makiguchi converted to Nichiren Shōshū, one of the smaller sects of Nichiren Buddhism known for its doctrinal rigidity. On November 18, 1930, Makiguchi published, with the assistance of his disciple Toda Jōsei, the first volume of his magnum opus, *Sōka kyōikugaku taikei* (*The System of Value Creating Pedagogy*). This was the first occasion for the term "Sōka Kyōiku Gakkai" ("Value Creating Education Society") to appear in print, and it has come to be commemorated by the organization as the date of its founding.

Over the course of the 1930s, the organization and its activities took on an increasingly religious tone; from the middle years of the decade, Makiguchi began to express views increasingly at variance with the official dogma of the emperor's divinity, at the time enforced through an elevation of Shintō rites and practices to the status of a state-sanctioned religion. When, in the early 1940s, the military-dominated government mandated acceptance and enshrinement of the amulet of Amaterasu, the tutelary deity from whom the imperial line was said to be descended, Makiguchi, considering this incompatible with his religious convictions, refused and encouraged the members of the Sōka Kyōiku Gakkai to refuse also.

In June 1943, Makiguchi, Toda, and other leaders were summoned by the Nichiren Shōshū priesthood to the sect's head temple, where they were urged to accept the talisman, which Makiguchi again refused to do. In July 1943, Makiguchi, Toda, and other top leaders of the Sōka Kyōiku Gakkai were arrested on charges of *lèse-majesté* and violating the Peace Preservation Law, the principal legal device for the suppression of dissent. On November 18, 1944, Makiguchi died of malnutrition while still confined in the Tokyo Detention Center. The organization, which had counted some three thousand members prior to its suppression, had been effectively dismantled.

Toda Jōsei was released on July 3, 1945. During his detention, he dedicated himself to the study of the *Lotus Sutra* and the recitation of its *daimoku* or title, Namu-myōhō-renge-kyō in Nichiren's formulation. Through this, Toda experienced a religious awakening that would propel his efforts to rebuild the organization, which he renamed Sōka Gakkai, in the postwar era.

In August 1947, Toda met Ikeda Daisaku, who had been brought to a Sōka Gakkai discussion meeting by a friend. Ikeda soon after joined the organization, inspired by Toda and determined to make him his mentor in life. The two developed a relationship of mentoring and collaboration, and Ikeda would succeed Toda as leader of the movement after the latter's death in 1958.

On May 3, 1951, Toda, who had been general director of the organization under Makiguchi, became its second president, announcing his determination to achieve a membership of 750,000 households. "If this goal is not realized while I am alive," he declared, "do not hold a funeral for me. Simply dump my remains in the bay at Shinagawa."[1]

The prewar Sōka Kyōiku Gakkai had published a number of periodicals, and this was continued by Toda's Sōka Gakkai, which began publishing the monthly *Daibyaku renge* (*Great White Lotus*), in July 1949, and the newspaper-format *Seikyō shimbun* (*Sacred Teachings*), in April 1951. Initially published thrice monthly, it became a weekly in September 1953 and a daily in 1965. Hand-delivered by members, it now claims a daily circulation of approximately 5.5 million.[2]

Following Toda's inauguration as president, the organization set out on a "great march of propagation." Toda appears to have had considerable personal charisma and a capacity for inspiring people to great personal and organizational exertion. Against a backdrop of postwar deprivation and dislocation, the organization entered a period of dramatic growth.

In November 1951, *Shakubuku kyōten* (*Handbook of Propagation*) was published. This contained Toda's essay on the mystery and eternity of life in conjunction with the key teachings of the Nichiren tradition, as well as specific refutations of the belief systems of other religions, both traditional and new. In September 1952, Toda registered the Sōka Gakkai as an independent religious body under the 1951 Religious Corporations Act.

The holding of small group discussion meetings (*zadankai*), which had been promoted by founding president Makiguchi as a means of sharing faith testimonials, encouraging doctrinal study and propagation activities, became a core organizational activity under Toda. The simplicity of its message, the tight-knit, intergenerational support network provided by the multilayered organizational structure, and a focus on Buddhist practice as a vehicle for transforming real-life circumstances all contributed to the Sōka Gakkai's acceptance, particularly among the marginalized strata of Japanese society. The membership grew rapidly, with women's and youth cohorts taking an especially active role, from around five thousand households at the time of Toda's inauguration, to almost eight hundred thousand by the time of his death in April 1958.

Starting in 1954, Toda encouraged selected members to stand for political office and the membership at large to support them; a total of 53 Sōka Gakkai-sponsored candidates were elected to office in the local elections held in April 1955; three members gained seats in the July 1956 elections for the House of Councillors (the upper house of Japan's bicameral legislature).

In the early years of the Sōka Gakkai's involvement in politics, the objectives were often framed in overtly religious language, sparking public concern that the group would seek to impose its brand of Nichiren Buddhism if it gained political power.

Six months prior to his death, in September 1957, Toda spoke at a gathering of approximately fifty thousand youth members and urged them to take up the cause of abolishing nuclear weapons, stating that this was his prime injunction to them.

Ikeda's Presidency. Following Toda's death, Ikeda Daisaku was widely recognized as his heir apparent. Ikeda had worked under Toda's direct tutelage and had led highly successful propagation and election campaigns. Ikeda was formally inaugurated as the organization's third president in May 1960; he continued Toda's legacy of energetic proselytization, leading a growth in membership to 3 million households by 1962 and 7.5 million by 1970. The Sōka Gakkai in Japan currently claims some 8.27 million member families.[3]

The Kōmei (often translated as "Clean Government") Party was founded by Ikeda in 1964. In the January 1967 general election, for the first time, Sōka Gakkai-supported candidates ran for seats in the House of Representatives, gaining 25 (of a total of 486 seats for the body). In the December 1969 election, 47 Kōmei Party candidates were elected to the House of Representatives, and the party received just over 10 percent of the popular vote. It was now the third largest party in the Japanese Diet. The party took generally centrist positions and became known for its anti-corruption stance and success in introducing social welfare legislation.

During the 1960s and 1970s, Ikeda founded a number of educational and cultural institutions, starting with the Institute of Oriental Philosophy (1962); the Minshu Ongaku (democratic music) or Min-On Concert Association (1963); the Sōka Junior and Senior High Schools (1968); Sōka University in (1971); and the Fuji Art Museum (1973).

In September 1968, Ikeda addressed a gathering of Sōka Gakkai university students; in this speech he called for the normalization of relations with China, the recognition of the Beijing government and its seating at the United Nations in place of the Taipei government.

In May 1974, following the normalization of Sino-Japanese relations, Ikeda traveled to China for the first time. In September 1974, he traveled to the Soviet Union, meeting with Premier Aleksey Kosygin. In December 1974, he visited China a second time, meeting with Premier Zhou Enlai, hospitalized, at the time, for cancer treatment. In January 1975, Ikeda traveled to the United States, where he met with Secretary of State Henry Kissinger. Ikeda has described these meetings as a form of citizen diplomacy, in which he conveyed the concerns and intentions of the different parties in an effort to defuse tensions.

In 1970, in response to an incident in which Kōmei Party politicians had attempted to dissuade a publisher from releasing a book highly critical of the Sōka Gakkai, it was announced that clear institutional separation would be established between the religious and political bodies. The degree and nature of the Sōka Gakkai's influence on party policy has remained the subject of considerable speculation, but has not been adequately documented. The party's commitment to domestic programs of social welfare and environmental protection, as well as a foreign policy stance that stresses peaceful diplomacy, are seen as broadly compatible with the Sōka Gakkai's values; Sōka Gakkai members have remained the Kōmei Party's core source of electoral support.

From around this time, propagation efforts in Japan slowed, and membership stabilized at around 8 million member households. A period of institutional maturation and diversification began, symbolized by an emphasis on the secular values of "peace, culture, and education."

Internationalization. Immediately following his inauguration as third president, Ikeda initiated efforts to internationalize the movement, starting with travels to North and South America in October 1960. In 1961, he traveled to Hong Kong, Sri Lanka, India, Myanmar, Thailand, and Cambodia. In these and subsequent travels, he met with and encouraged fledgling Sōka Gakkai memberships. In the United States, many early members were Japanese "war brides" who had married American servicemen; elsewhere they were more typically employees of Japanese companies or (as in Brazil) people with roots in the Japanese immigrant community.

Where there was a sufficient core of members, Ikeda established districts and chapters, making the corresponding leadership appointments. The first organization to be incorporated outside Japan was in the United States, in 1963.

Although the pace at which each national organization has "localized"—with general membership and leadership responsibility shifting away from the original Japanese transplants—has differed, the demographics of established organizations typically present a cultural and economic profile reflective of the host society. In this sense, the Sōka Gakkai has achieved a degree of international reach and integration largely unseen in other Japanese Buddhist schools or new religions.[4]

In January 1975, representatives from fifty-one countries and territories met in Guam, where they created an umbrella organization for Sōka Gakkai Buddhists around the world. This became the Sōka Gakkai International (SGI), with Ikeda as its first president. Since as early as 1966, the Sōka Gakkai's stated policy has been that affiliated organizations outside Japan would never engage in political activities.[5] Thus far, this has proven to be the case: while individual SGI members have run for political office in a number of countries, they have done so without the organized support of fellow SGI members or the endorsement of the constituent national organization.

In April 1979, Ikeda resigned as president of the Sōka Gakkai, to be succeeded by Hōjō Hiroshi (1923–1981). Ikeda retained his position as SGI president.

Peace Activities. In its literature, the Sōka Gakkai traces the inspiration for its peace activities, in particular its advocacy for nuclear weapons abolition, to the speech made by Toda in September 1957.

In 1974, Sōka Gakkai youth members began collecting and editing testimonials of wartime experiences in what eventually became an eighty-volume series entitled "To the generations who do not know war." A similar series collected and edited by women members came to 20 volumes.

Sōka Gakkai youth members collected ten million signatures for the abolition of nuclear weapons. These were delivered by Ikeda to then UN Secretary General Kurt Waldheim in January 1975. Similar petition drives for nuclear abolition were held in 2000, 2010, and 2014.

Since 1983, Ikeda has issued annual "peace proposals" in which he presents philosophical perspectives on peace and conflict resolution as well as making specific proposals for, inter alia, structural reforms of the United Nations. Sōka Gakkai members and organizations worldwide look to these proposals as providing a theoretical basis as well as a general agenda for socially engaged activities.

The Sōka Gakkai (and/or SGI) has established consultative and collaborative relations with a number of United Nations agencies, including the UN Department of Public Information, the UN Department of Disarmament Affairs, the Office of the UN High Commissioner for Refugees, and the Office of the UN High Commissioner for Human Rights. These NGO activities have been focused primarily on education and public information outreach, rather than specific policy advocacy or lobbying. They have taken the form of international exhibitions on such themes as nuclear disarmament, human rights, and sustainable development. In recent years, SGI representatives have attended key international conferences and, in this capacity, have cooperated with other civil society representatives, including the representatives of other religions.

In addition to his proposals, Sōka Gakkai members look to Ikeda as an exemplar of dialogue across differences. Over the course of decades, Ikeda has met with a wide range of political, intellectual, and cultural figures including: Arnold Toynbee, André Malraux, Margaret Thatcher, Mikhail Gorbachev, Joseph Rotblat, Nelson Mandela, Rosa Parks, Pérez Esquivel, Linus Pauling, Wangari Maathai, Betty Williams, Abdurrahman Wahid, and Hu Jintao. Many of Ikeda's interlocutors, among them Toynbee, Gorbachev, Rotblat, and Pauling, have collaborated with him in published dialogues.

In July 1981, following Hōjō Hiroshi's death, Akiya Enosuke (1930–) became the fifth president of the Sōka Gakkai.

In the 1980s and 1990s, the Sōka Gakkai's program of institution building continued. Tokyo Fuji Art Museum was established in 1983, followed by Sōka Women's College (1985), the Boston Center for the 21st Century (established 1993; renamed Ikeda Center for Peace, Learning, and Dialogue in 2009), the Toda Institute for Global Peace and Policy Research (1996), and the Makiguchi Foundation for Education (1996). In 1987, Sōka University of America was established in Southern California, becoming a four-year liberal arts college in 2001.

Schism with Nichiren Shōshū. In the early 1990s, relations with the Nichiren Shōshū priesthood, which had been marked by tension and collaboration since the lay organization's founding, deteriorated decisively. In November 1990, Ikeda gave a speech that was interpreted within the priesthood as demeaning their status, in particular the role of the high priest. The conflict escalated quickly, culminating a year later in the priesthood's excommunication of the entire global membership of the Sōka Gakkai.

Following the schism, Sōka Gakkai members in Japan began conducting their own funerary services, breaking with a long-standing cultural tradition whereby the ceremonial intercession of Buddhist priests was seen as necessary to ensure the safe passage of the dead to their next existence. From 1993 onward, members worldwide were encouraged to return the Gohonzon scroll previously conferred by the priesthood, to be replaced by a new one issued by the Sōka Gakkai. In May 1998, the Nichiren Shōshū priesthood had the Shōhondō (Grand Main Temple), donated by the Sōka Gakkai in 1972, torn down.

In October 1999, the Kōmei Party formed a coalition with the Liberal Democratic Party (LDP), starting its first sustained experience of being a governing party since its formation.

The LDP–Kōmei coalition was voted out in 2009, but was returned to power in the December 2012 general election.

The Kōmei Party's participation in successive ruling coalitions has both symbolized and accelerated the process of mainstreaming the Sōka Gakkai's religio-political status within Japanese society. At the same time, it has raised questions regarding the compatibility of the religious organization's commitment to peace and the political party's pragmatic decision making, in particular regarding issues of national security and military realignment.

In November 2006, Harada Minoru (1941–) became the sixth president of the Sōka Gakkai.

In November 2013, the Sōka Gakkai opened the Daiseidō (Hall of the Great Vow) as part of its headquarters complex in central Tokyo, creating a focal point for the organization's religious functions.

Controversies. The Sōka Gakkai's conversion efforts were conducted under the banner of *shakubuku*—a two-character term (lit. "break and subdue") found in the *Lotus Sutra* to indicate propagation involving the direct refutation of erroneous beliefs as opposed to a more gradualist approach. These efforts were driven by the conviction that "false religions are the source of all misery,"[6] and taxonomies of the ills arising from different religions were a key feature of early conversion activities. Shakubuku thus involved a pointed critique of religious traditions that may have been practiced by families for generations, often playing a key role in funerary and other rituals associated with the veneration of ancestors.

The exclusive devotion demanded by Nichiren doctrine was seen as necessitating the elimination of all other objects of worship—from Shintō talismans to Buddhist altars—as a precondition for conversion. While Sōka Gakkai policy required that any such objects be disposed of by the inductee as an expression of their free choice,[7] this policy was not always followed, and the act itself was seen as violating traditional conceptions of loyalty to a family's sect or practice. Such activities gained the Sōka Gakkai a reputation as a violent religion (*bōryoku shūkyō*) in the press and were accompanied, in the late 1950s and early 1960s, by incidents of ostracization in rural communities sometimes resulting in denial of access to communally managed resources or to family graves on the grounds of the temples of other sects.

While much of the critical reaction to the Sōka Gakkai in the early 1950s was consistent with prevailing academic and media discourse surrounding popular or new religions—that they were irrational and appealed to the desire of the masses for "worldly benefits"—the organization's entry into politics in the mid-1950s attracted unprecedented levels of attention. Anxieties were intensified by the Sōka Gakkai's use of such terminology as "the fusion of the Buddhist and secular law" (*ōbutsu myōgō*), and references to a "state-established high sanctuary" (*kokuritsu kaidan*), which became the focus of concerns that the organization's ultimate objective was to use state power to impose its religious beliefs.

In 1970, as the political scientist Fujiwara Hirotatsu was preparing to publish a book highly critical of the Sōka Gakkai, it came to light that Kōmei Party officials had met with the author and publisher of the book and had urged them not to publish the book in its current form. The incident was brought up in the Diet as a potential infringement of constitutional guarantees of free speech, generating intense controversy. On May 3 of that year, Ikeda addressed a meeting of Sōka Gakkai members to which various cultural and literary figures, as well as print and broadcast media, were invited. While denying any intention to interfere with freedom of speech, Ikeda acknowledged that the politicians' actions had "caused those concerned to feel pressured and caused a great deal of concern in society as a whole"[8] and apologized for this. Together with the institutional separation of the religious organization and political party, it was announced that the religious terminology that had aroused public concern would no longer be used.

Along with the organization's evident wealth (it owns hundreds of meeting places and facilities throughout Japan), Ikeda's personality, leadership style, intentions, overseas travels, and meetings with prominent figures have continued to be the focus of intense speculation, derision, and criticism, most persistently from Japan's raucous tabloid press.

In 1976, the tabloid monthly *Gekkan pen* began publishing a series of articles accusing Ikeda of having inappropriate relations with a number of women. The Sōka Gakkai sued for libel, with the Tokyo District Court finding for the plaintiffs in 1983.

Ikeda's overseas activities and awards (he has received numerous honorary degrees, most prominently from universities in China) have been portrayed as a quest for a recognition that has eluded him domestically. For his part, Ikeda has described his motivation as the desire to promote understanding of the Sōka Gakkai's ideals and goals, in this way protecting fledgling Sōka Gakkai memberships in different national settings, while forging ties of trust and mutual understanding among cultures.

RELIGIOUS PRACTICES AND BELIEFS

The Nichiren Heritage. The Sōka Gakkai locates itself within the Mahāyāna Buddhist tradition, identifying its active proselytization and sociopolitical engagement as expressions of the bodhisattva ideal of compassionate action. In recent years, "engaged Buddhism" has been incorporated into its self-definitional discourse. Doctrinally, it asserts the full compatibility of its teachings and practices with those propounded by Nichiren, which, since the schism with the Nichiren Shōshū priesthood, it has referred to as "Nichiren Buddhism." Prior to the schism, it often positioned itself as an association of lay followers of the Nichiren Shōshū sect, but this was consistently paralleled with assertions of interpretive uniqueness and independence.

Nichiren asserted that the *Lotus Sutra* represented the culmination of the Buddha's teachings and encouraged exclusive devotion to this sutra. He based this on the view that the Lotus Sutra alone offered a path to enlightenment for all people—including those, such as women and people of the "two vehicles" (Śrāvakayāna and Pratyekabuddhayāna; practitioners advanced in their intellectual understanding but excessively attached to that understanding), to whom it was elsewhere closed.

The *Lotus Sutra's* message of universal enlightenment was elaborated into a philosophical system by the Chinese Buddhist teacher Zhiyi (538–597, founder of the T'ien T'ai school), from whom Nichiren drew his core theoretical framework, including such concepts as the mutual possession of the ten worlds (Jpn *jikkai gogu*) and three thousand realms in a single thought moment (*ichinen sanzen*). For Nichiren (and the Sōka Gakkai), the significance of these concepts is that they posit Buddhahood as an ever-present, immanent possibility in all people, regardless of differences of gender, educational background, capacity for intellectual understanding, etc.

Like other Japanese Buddhist schools that arose in the Kamakura Period (1185–1333), such as Pure Land and Zen, Nichiren's innovations centered on the simplification and concretization of the means of practice. To this end, he focused on the title of the Lotus Sutra in its translation into Chinese by Kumārajīva (343/344–413)—Chn *Miao-fa-lien-hua-ching*; Jpn *Myōhō-renge-kyō*—which, according to such T'ien T'ai teachers as Miao-lo (711–782), contained the very essence of the entire twenty-eight-chapter sutra. By appending *namu* (a transliteration of the Sanskrit *namas*, to offer obeisance), Nichiren derived Namu-myōhō-renge-kyō, which he said expressed the ultimate law by which all Buddhas throughout the universe had become enlightened.

Later in his career, Nichiren took the theoretical developments of Tiantai Buddhism and gave them visual expression as a calligraphic mandala, or *gohonzon*, in which exemplars of the various conditions of life, from hell to buddhahood, are represented by their names written in Sino-Japanese characters. As Nichiren described in a letter written to a female follower in 1277: "It is the object of devotion that depicts Shakyamuni Buddha, the World-Honored One, seated in the treasure tower of Many Treasures Buddha, and the Buddhas who were Śākyamuni's emanations as perfectly as a print matches its woodblock. Thus the five characters of the Lotus Sutra's title [*myō hō ren ge kyō*] are suspended in the center, while the four heavenly kings are seated at the four corners of the treasure tower. Śākyamuni, Many Treasures, and the four leaders of the Bodhisattvas of the Earth are side by side at the top." Nichiren then describes the representatives of other states of life, including deluded, destructive ones, represented in the *gohonzon* and states that, "Illuminated by the light of the five characters of the Mystic Law, they display the dignified attributes that they inherently possess."[9]

Nichiren asserted that the practice of chanting the *daimoku* or title of the *Lotus Sutra*, Namu-myōhō-renge-kyō, with faith in the Gohonzon enables all people to "display the dignified attributes that they inherently possess," that is, to manifest their Buddha nature and attain the state of ultimate enlightenment in their present form.

Sōka Gakkai members are encouraged to seek enlightenment through the daily chanting of *daimoku* and the recitation of key passages of the *Lotus Sutra*. Individual and group study of Nichiren's writings, as well as the guidance of the first three presidents, and regular participation in discussion meetings are all considered essential. Acceptance of a printed scroll *gohonzon* marks initiation and official membership.

In parallel with this individual soteriology, Nichiren also contended that a society's prevailing conditions can be explained by its collective relationship to the Buddhist dharma. Where the people and their leaders embrace the true dharma, there will be peace and flourishing; where they reject it and persecute those who follow the true teachings, disorder and decline will inevitably follow. As he wrote in a letter to a follower in 1280, "Buddhism is like the body, and society like the shadow. When the body bends, so does the shadow."[10]

Nichiren further asserted that persecutions incurred in the course of courageously refuting erroneous doctrines will enable believers to expunge their individual negative karma, opening the way to enlightenment as well as correcting society's underlying spiritual orientation. Nichiren's 1260 submission of his treatise *Risshō ankokuron* (*On Establishing the True Teachings for the Peace of the Land*) to the highest level of Shogunate authority was undertaken based on this logic.

In this treatise, Nichiren quoted the *Great Collection Sutra* as part of his practice of "remonstrating with the sovereign."

> Though for countless existences in the past the ruler of a state may have practiced the giving of alms, observed the precepts, and cultivated wisdom, if he sees that my teaching is in danger of perishing and stands idly by without doing anything to protect it, then all the inestimable roots of goodness that he has planted through the practices just mentioned will be entirely wiped out... Before long, the ruler will fall gravely ill, and after his life has come to an end, he will be reborn in the great hell.[11]

Nichiren interpreted the repeated exiles and attempts on his life, provoked by his outspoken criticism of established religious and secular authorities, as confirmation that he was indeed the "votary of the Lotus Sutra," bringing its message of universal salvation to the people of the corrupt Final Dharma age (*mappō*).

Interpreting for Modernity. At the start of the 20th century, Nichiren's ideas were the subject of renewed attention and interpretation. His this-worldly focus and direct engagement with social and political realities caused many Japanese thinkers, both within and outside traditional Nichiren schools, to see him as modeling a form of Buddhist practice relevant to the modern world. Interpretations ranged from the emperor-centered "Nichirenism" of Tanaka Chigaku (1861–1939) to the tender, cosmic lyricism of the poet Miyazaki Kenji (1896–1933) and the Nietzschean transcendence of Takayama Chogyū (1871–1902).

Makiguchi's 1928 reception of Nichiren Shōshū was mediated by Mitani Sokei (1878–1932), a fellow school principal and author of a detailed exegesis of Nichiren's *Risshō ankokuron*, and it is likely that this text played an important role in the conversion process.

Makiguchi's thinking at this point was already the product of his decades-long attempt to effect a synthesis between premodern Japanese sensibilities—such as an East Asian appreciation of the natural and social embeddedness of human existence—with Anglo-American pragmatism and continental idealism. These critiques coalesced as his theory of value, which prioritized the subjective experience of value over disembodied "truth." For Makiguchi, an enhanced capacity to "create value," the ability to generate the values of beauty, gain, and good for oneself and others, constituted the essence of human happiness. He saw this, in turn, as the purpose to which education and religious faith should be directed. Makiguchi's pragmatic approach to religion—his insistence that the validity of faith propositions could be subjected to empirical verification—established a template that has continued to characterize the Sōka Gakkai.

Makiguchi adopted Nichiren's teaching of persecution undergone for the sake of the dharma to frame the significance of the Sōka Kyōiku Gakkai's 1943 suppression by the authorities. This logic—sometimes psychologized in terms of people's deep resistance to authentic happiness—has likewise been employed by the Sōka Gakkai to explain negative reactions from potential converts as well as from society as a whole.

Toda Jōsei's Mass Appeal. Makiguchi's reception of Nichiren may be seen as representing an encounter between a Buddhist worldview and the values of scientific rationalism or secular humanism, something that contributed to its acceptance among the educators who made up the core of the Sōka Kyōiku Gakkai's initial membership. In contrast, Toda offered a more distinctly religious message that carried greater mass appeal.

During his imprisonment in the final years of World War II, Toda engaged in intense, prayerful recitation of the *daimoku* and experienced a religious awakening in which he saw that the term "Buddha" referred to "nothing other than life itself,"[12] and that it was his mission as one of the Bodhisattvas Emerging from the Earth (*jiyu no bosatsu*) described in the Lotus Sutra to share this truth with the people of Japan.

Within the Sōka Gakkai, Toda's awakening in prison is accorded great significance. In a published dialogue on the Lotus Sutra conducted with leaders of the Sōka Gakkai's Study Department responsible for doctrinal issues, Ikeda Daisaku stated: "Mr. Toda's enlightenment that the Buddha is life itself is a declaration that life is the absolute and supreme reality. It was his initial challenge to all warped and twisted points of view that would destroy the dignity of human life."[13]

Toda also had a talent for expressing Buddhist concepts in easily accessible formulations, referring, for example, to the Gohonzon as a "device for manufacturing happiness."[14] Toda's knack for recasting Buddhist concepts in accessible language extended even to the idea of enlightenment. In September 1947, the president of Tokyo University, Nambara Shigeru (1889–1974), delivered a speech to the university's graduating class in which he stated the greatest imperative for Japanese society in the wake of defeat in the war was not a political or economic revolution, but a "human revolution" (*ningen kakumei*). Toda seized upon this term, using it to express the fundamental change in life orientation that would be wrought by committed Buddhist practice (specifically, the chanting of the *daimoku* and proselytization activities). In Toda's recasting, the enlightenment of human revolution was not an ineffable inner realization, but a fully embodied experience of what he termed "absolute happiness." Thus, he spoke of and urged his followers to achieve health revolution, personal finance revolution, family revolution, etc.—to employ their Buddhist practice as a means of effecting concrete changes in the material conditions of life.

Like the vitalist aspects of Toda's approach, this stance was, in many senses, compatible with the approach attributed to the "new religions" that (re)emerged in the postwar era. At the same time, the ethos and praxis of the Sōka Gakkai—such as exclusive devotion to a single faith, energetic proselytization, engagement with political realities—were transgressive of a number of social and religious norms. These included the pervasive distaste among Japanese intellectuals for "irrational" popular religions, the long-standing privileging of educated religious hierarchies over lay believers in established sects, and the modern norm of confining religion to private, interior realms. The Sōka Gakkai's transgression of this last norm through direct electoral engagement was particularly salient in a postwar Japan struggling to define the contours of its renewed democratic dispensation and the roles to be played by civil society actors, including religious groups.

Ikeda's Recasting: Peace, Culture, Education. During the late 1950s, and in particular after the presidency was acceded to by a dynamic, youthful leader (Ikeda was thirty-two when he was inaugurated in 1960), the Sōka Gakkai exhibited considerable optimism as the rapid expansion of the organization's membership made the goal of converting the Japanese populace appear close at hand. Nichiren's vision of this was often cited:

> The time will come when all people will abandon the various kinds of vehicles and take up the single vehicle of Buddhahood, and the Mystic Law alone will flourish throughout the land. When the people all chant Nam-myoho-renge-kyo, the wind will no longer buffet the branches, and the rain will no longer break the clods of soil. The world will become as it was in the ages of Fu Hsi and Shen Nung [legendary Chinese sovereigns said to have presided over eras of peace and flourishing]. In their present existence the people will be freed from misfortune and disasters and learn the art of living long.[15]

At the same time, however, the Sōka Gakkai generally avoided describing *kōsen-rufu*, a phrase from the *Lotus Sutra* meaning to "declare and spread widely" the Buddha's teachings, in terms of millennialist inevitability. Rather, it was posited as the outcome of the cumulative effect of human revolution undertaken in the context of many individual lives.

In December 1964, Ikeda began writing a novelized account of Toda Jōsei's life and leadership during the early phase of the organization's reconstruction. According to Ikeda, the core theme of the novel, as well as its title, is *human revolution*, a process whose scope of influence he describes as follows: "A great human revolution in just a single individual will help achieve a change in the destiny of a nation, and, further, will enable a change in the destiny of all humankind."[16] The novel has taken on canonical status within the Sōka Gakkai, and this formulation is seen as the essential expression of the core dynamic of inner change and social engagement, one fully compatible with Nichiren's vision.

The new president also oversaw the development of a more expansive definition of the movement's objectives. As Ikeda put it in his May 1970 speech: "Kōsen-rufu, therefore, does not mean the end-point or terminus of a flow, but it is the flow itself, the very pulse of living Buddhism within society."[17] This statement was indicative of a gradual shift in focus away from numerical propagation goals, toward ensuring that Buddhist values played a shaping role in society as a whole. From around this time, there was also increasing stress on the themes of "peace, culture, and education." Today, kōsen-rufu is often linked to the idea of human dignity, or the inherent dignity of all life, and the ideal of a society in which such dignity is universally realized.

One thread linking Sōka Gakkai's success in postwar Japan and in a range of national settings can be seen in the movement's consistent engagement with key aspects of modernity. In the years following his conversion, Makiguchi sought to bring scientific modes of thinking into conversation with Nichiren Buddhism through a stress on universal causality and empirical verification. In the postwar era, Toda created rational bureaucratic organizational structures that facilitated conversion activities and ensured that new converts were provided with fine-grained pastoral attention. Toda's tutelage of Ikeda in the 1950s centered on inculcating familiarity with contemporary developments in a spectrum of modern disciplines, something Ikeda says was done with a future of global propagation in view. It is probably also significant that the movement was, from its inception and over the course of its development, based in the major urban centers of Tokyo and Osaka.

The idea of universal causality gives rise to a highly rational cosmology—one that is ultimately free of random or meaningless residue. In the Sōka Gakkai's interpretation, the past-oriented explanatory power of karma is counterbalanced with the possibility of creating positive causes—and thus value—through present exertions in faith. On an organizational level, collective support and a sense of shared purpose are set against a strong doctrine of individual responsibility—"Ultimately, you yourself are the protagonist of your human revolution."[18] These elements together have proven an effective and convincing formula for confronting the atomizing and disempowering forces of modernity, including in its contemporary manifestation in globalization.

Also important in the success of the Sōka Gakkai in gaining adherents internationally is that these core teachings have been expressed and implemented flexibly in different cultural settings. To this end, the organization has deployed the concept of *zuihō-bini*. This is translated in the Sōka Gakkai Dictionary of Buddhism as "the precept of adapting to local customs" and defined as follows: "in matters the Buddha did not expressly either permit or forbid, one may act in accordance with local custom so long as the fundamental principles of Buddhism are not violated."[19] The SGI Charter, adopted in October 1995, states that, "SGI shall, through its constituent organizations, encourage its members to contribute toward the prosperity of their respective societies as good citizens."[20]

Relations with Nichiren Shōshū. Because it provided the system of doctrine and terminology on which the Sōka Gakkai drew for much of its interpretative efforts—and housed the character mandala (*daigohonzon*, object of worship) that was seen as the source of religious power and legitimacy—Nichiren Shōshū has at times been described as the "parent sect" of the Sōka Gakkai. This characterization is not entirely accurate, however, as the Sōka Gakkai from the outset maintained its identity as an organization of lay believers, in which they exercised autonomy and leadership. Makiguchi, for example, encouraged his followers to learn to recite the liturgically significant portions of the *Lotus Sutra*, something typically reserved for Buddhist priests. To quote a passage from the official record of Makiguchi's interrogation following his arrest in 1943:

> I personally disliked the idea of formally becoming a priest. If I were to become ordained and have a temple, I would be confined in my actions to the teachings of Nichiren Shōshū. It would hardly be appropriate for me to promote my theory of value at a temple. I believe that my real purpose is fulfilled in remaining a lay believer and introducing my theory of value into the faith principles of Nichiren Shōshū. This is where the unique characteristics of the Sōka Kyōiku Gakkai are to be found.[21]

Confluence of interests, the shared experience of postwar devastation, and Toda's personally warm relations with some members of the Nichiren Shōshū priesthood made the first decades following the end of World War II a period of relatively successful collaboration between the Nichiren Shōshū priesthood and the Sōka Gakkai. Hori Nichikō (1867–1957), 59th high priest of the Nichiren Shōshū head temple Taiseki-ji, for example, was widely recognized for his scholarship and was personally close to Toda. Hori supported the Sōka Gakkai's efforts to produce, in 1952, a collection of the writings of Nichiren accessible to lay believers by guiding the rendering of treatises originally written in classical Chinese into Japanese. For the Sōka Gakkai, the priesthood offered a lineage connection to Nichiren and a historical pedigree that would distinguish it from the "new religions" of the era. For the Nichiren Shōshū priesthood, the large and growing Sōka Gakkai membership was a welcome source of financial and logistical support.

In the postwar period, the Sōka Gakkai donated more than 350 temples to Nichiren Shōshū, most prominent among them being the Shōhondō (Grand Main Temple), completed in 1972, to house the *daigohonzon* mandala considered to be fundamental to the sect. The structure was said to symbolize the wings of a crane opening in flight, with seating for 5,400 lay believers and 600 priests. It is said to have cost more than 35 billion yen.

Following the completion of this edifice, the number of monthly pilgrims to the Nichiren Shōshū head temple greatly increased. The significance of the Shōhondō relative to certain texts attributed to Nichiren—whether it represented the achievement of kōsen-rufu, and whether it could only be the fulfillment of such prophecy if officially sanctioned by "imperial edict and shogunal decree"[22]—became an object of controversy particularly among priests with a more fundamentalist-literalist orientation.

Sōka Gakkai criticism of the priesthood had always focused on the latter's passivity, its unwillingness to actively engage in conversion or pastoral activities. Such criticisms can be found in Sōka Gakkai publications, including those published under Makiguchi's prewar leadership. Related to this was the implicit criticism that the priesthood had become ossified and too comfortable in its traditional role and privileges, failing to make efforts to give expression to Buddhist ideas in forms accessible to modern society.

For its part, the priesthood found the Sōka Gakkai's assertiveness troubling and harbored suspicions that the Sōka Gakkai leadership's regular expressions of deference, although voiced in the most elevating registers of honorific language, were not in fact heartfelt. These suspicions were further heightened by a number of Ikeda's statements made in the period 1977–1978, in which, inter alia, he asserted that the Sōka Gakkai comprised both a lay and ordained aspect, and that its activity centers were the functional equivalent of temples. (Thus donations made by members to the Sōka Gakkai carried the same significance as a source of merit traditionally attributed to offerings made to priests and temples.) The priesthood demanded a public retraction of this position, with which the Sōka Gakkai complied. In April 1979, Ikeda still felt compelled to resign as president of the organization.

The conciliatory gesture of Ikeda's resignation could not permanently obscure, much less resolve, the structural contradictions between a dynamic lay movement with an increasingly international orientation and a priesthood whose attachment to strict dogmatic purity and limited number of adherents had kept it on the periphery of Japanese society—and thus largely insulated even from domestic pressures for adaptation and change.

Tensions resurfaced in the late 1980s and, on November 28, 1991, the priesthood excommunicated all Sōka Gakkai members worldwide who refused to pledge exclusive allegiance to Nichiren Shōshū. The great majority of Sōka Gakkai members globally chose to remain with the lay movement over an association with the priesthood, and today the Sōka Gakkai celebrates this event as a "Day of Spiritual Independence."

The Impact of the Schism. Since the schism, the Sōka Gakkai has deployed a number of interpretative strategies relative to what it now terms "Nichiren Buddhism." These strategies were shaped by the need to meet a range of disparate goals, including: maintaining consistency with earlier interpretations to a degree that would be comfortable for members long familiar with those interpretations; establishing the Sōka Gakkai's independent religious authority and autonomy; creating a heritage that would sustain the movement and serve as a referent for internal and societal legitimacy; satisfying the needs of a growing non-Japanese membership for whom the intra-Nichiren doctrinal debates that had distinguished Nichiren Shōshū were opaque or irrelevant; and creating greater compatibility with modern academic engagements with Buddhist texts.

Ikeda's dialogue on the Lotus Sutra with the leaders of the Sōka Gakkai Study Department, serialized in the monthly *Daibyaku renge* from 1995 to 1999, probably represents the most systematic effort to meet these diverse imperatives. Later published in six volumes, the dialogue provides a chapter-by-chapter exegesis of the Lotus Sutra. The subtitle of the work, "A discussion on religion in the twenty-first century," conveys the scope of its ambition.

While Ikeda and his interlocutors draw on the T'ien T'ai hermeneutics developed in China and Japan, as well as those of Nichikan (1665–1726), the 18th-century high priest regarded as the most significant systematizer and "restorer" of doctrinal clarity in the Nichiren Shōshū school, they do so with great freedom. For example, the T'ien T'ai classification and periodization of the sutras, according to which Shakyamuni preached the Lotus Sutra in the last eight years of his life, had long been treated within Nichiren Shōshū doctrine as historical fact. In contrast, in the dialogue there is a straightforward acknowledgement that contemporary research places the compilation of the major Mahāyāna texts, including the Lotus Sutra, in the first centuries of the Common Era. Where conflicts with long-standing interpretative texts are substantive, Ikeda and colleagues often drill down to the motivations underlying the text, which are typically ascribed to the Buddha's determination to share a message of salvation with all people, of all levels and styles of understanding.

The term "Buddhist humanism" has gained an important place in the Sōka Gakkai's self-definitional lexicon in the post-schism period. In Ikeda's dialogue on the Lotus Sutra and on numerous other occasions, he has frequently referenced Bodhisattva Never Disparaging (Jpn Fukyō Bosatsu)—a figure in the Lotus Sutra who endures harsh abuse and persecution in order to share a message of capacity for enlightenment—as embodying the ideal of Buddhist humanism. In this way, Bodhisattva Never Disparaging offers a paradigm of compassionate engagement with others.

The increased focus on Bodhisattva Never Disparaging has paralleled the Sōka Gakkai's use of the language of human dignity as a key self-definitional concept. In like manner, there has been an adoption of the secular terms and goals generated by UN-centered processes, such as sustainability, human development, and human security. There has also been a broadened referencing of Buddhist scriptures, with more regular attention to texts not particularly valued by Nichiren or the Nichiren Shōshū exegetical tradition.

The status of the *gohonzon* enshrined at the Nichiren Shōshū head temple Taiseki-ji has been another key focus of contention. From the postwar reconstruction period and, in particular, after the completion of the Grand Main Temple (Shōhondō) in 1972, the Great Gohonzon (*daigohonzon*) of the second year of Kōan (1279) was treated as the ultimate source of religious authority. In the post-schism period, the Sōka Gakkai has stressed the universal salvific commitment underlying Nichiren's inscription of the *gohonzon*, expressed in its dedicatory phrase, "Bestowed up all the living beings of Jambudvīpa [the entire world]"; in November 2014, it issued a statement explicitly rejecting the idea of a unique locus of religious authority—an act with potentially important decentering implications for the movement.

> The position that one special sanctuary exists in one particular place, and that the Gohonzon enshrined there is the fundamental Gohonzon, with all other Gohonzon only demonstrating any efficacy through a link to that Gohonzon—almost as if it were acting like a source of electricity that all others must be "plugged into" to function—is a view of the Gohonzon that can only hinder the substantive progress of our movement for worldwide kōsen-rufu in the present as well as in the future.[23]

One of the more visible changes in the religious modalities of the post-schism Sōka Gakkai has been an increase in interfaith activities. This was also codified in the 1995 Charter: "SGI shall, based on the Buddhist spirit of tolerance, respect other religions, engage in dialogue and work together with them toward the resolution of fundamental issues concerning humanity."[24] In Japan, the Sōka Gakkai's communication and collaboration with other religious bodies remain very limited, although Shintō shrine-centered festivals (*matsuri*) have been redefined as expressions of local culture and participation by members welcomed as forms of community outreach. In other national and multilateral settings, there have been a number of collaborative engagements with the representatives of other faith traditions, including participation in joint statements by faith communities on the humanitarian impact of nuclear weapons.

There have also been independent activities by national organizations designed to respond to the interests and needs of their respective societies. Such activities include a youth anti-violence movement in the United States, activities for nuclear abolition and the abolition of the death penalty (Italy), and for biodiversity and ecological integrity (Brazil).

Since the schism, the Sōka Gakkai has increasingly stressed the importance of the "mentor-disciple relationship." Over the history of the movement, the intense loyalty directed toward the successive presidents by the membership has sparked charges that the organization is little more than a cult of personality. Today, the first three presidents are referred to as the "Three Founding Presidents," with the implication that the example of their lives, as well as the written record of their ideas (Ikeda's complete works comprise 150 volumes in Japanese), contain the charismatic essence and interpretive guidelines that will be required by the movement going forward.

The three founding presidents are themselves seen as embodying an ideal of discipleship, seeking the truth of Buddhism through their respective mentors, and putting the mentor's teachings into practice. This relationship is presented as embodying and making possible the realization of universal human values, and Ikeda in particular has frequently cited examples of discipleship from outside Buddhist, or even religious contexts, such as the bonds between educators, researchers, and others. More than a competing form of lineage, the mentor-disciple bond is seen as the expression of a multigenerational commitment to a shared ideal—in this case that of "kōsen-rufu."

The movement toward greater accommodation with the social norms and sensitivities of Japanese society is one that has been ongoing for some decades, with the 1970 "freedom of speech incident" as one turning point. Evidence of this can be seen in the evolving style of faith testimonials carried in the organization's publications, where there has been a growing emphasis on psychological realizations and shifts in attitude over more dramatically visible outcomes. For example, where testimonials related to natural disasters in earlier generations were almost always focused on narratives of miraculous survival, this has been almost entirely absent with regard to the 1995 Kobe earthquake or the March 2011 Tōhoku compound disaster of earthquake, tsunami, and nuclear meltdown. Rather, faith experiences arising from these disasters have centered on often very frank accounts of coping with feelings of grief and despair, as well as on contributions by Sōka Gakkai members in support of recovery efforts in their communities.

While the increasing recognition and interaction with other faith traditions can be located on a trajectory of maturation, accommodation, and integration, so long as the Sōka Gakkai holds to an exclusive devotion to the practices prescribed by Nichiren, based on his interpretation of the Lotus Sutra, it will to some degree remain anomalous within the more syncretic religious landscape of Japan.

REVIEW OF LITERATURE: HISTORICAL SOURCES

The intensity of feelings generated by the organization's early phase of rapid expansion—the gulf between those who felt saved and those who felt harassed by the Sōka Gakkai—meant that there was, initially, only limited space for nuanced discussion regarding its nature and objectives. Supportive voices were loudly heralded in Sōka Gakkai publications, while a wide range of dark allegations, reflecting anxieties provoked, inter alia, by the organization's political involvement and the memories of Nichirenist support for wartime militarism, shaped public perception.

Fujiwara's *I Denounce Soka Gakkai* can be read as a compendium of early anxieties, expressed as comparisons to Communism, prewar Japanese fascism, and Nazism. More balanced academic accounts first emerged in the 1960s, from researchers using the methodologies of religious studies, anthropology, and the sociology of religion. Murakami's *Sōka Gakkai–Kōmeitō* was one of these, a carefully researched account of the historical process of the Sōka Gakkai's development, including the socioeconomic backdrop for the Sōka Gakkai's decision to enter politics, by one of Japan's leading religious scholars. *Japan's New Buddhism: An Objective Account of Soka Gakkai*, by the investigative journalist Murata Kiyoaki, reflected more than a decade of engagement with and writing about the organization.[25]

Cold War interest in Japan's role as a stable ally also shaped the research questions posed by U.S.-based researchers, which tended to be sociopolitical or sociological. Dator's *Builders of the Third Civilization* was developed through participant observation and has one of the earliest accounts of non-Japanese members and their motivations. White's *The Sokagakkai and Mass Society* was one of the earliest methodologically rigorous sociological studies of the Sōka Gakkai to be conducted and published in English.[26]

The 1980s saw the growth of empirical research into the history of the Sōka Gakkai. Saitō's *Wakaki Makiguchi Tsunesaburō* was the first biographical portrait to fully locate Makiguchi in the context of his times and the larger sweep of modern intellectual history. A special issue of the *Journal of Oriental Studies* edited by Miyata Kōichi brought together essays in English on different aspects of Makiguchi's thought and praxis, as did *Tsunesaburo Makiguchi (1871–1944): Educational Philosophy in Context*, a volume edited by Jason Goulah and Andrew Gebert that focused on Tsunesaburō's educational ideas. Machacek and Wilson's *Global Citizens* is a collection of articles by established researchers with in-depth knowledge of the Sōka Gakkai. Levi McLaughlin paints a portrait of the organization that draws on historical analysis and fieldwork.[27]

Since the 1990s, there has been a proliferation of monographs on the Sōka Gakkai's presence in different national and cultural settings. Among them are: Jane Hurst, *Nichiren Shoshu Buddhism and the Soka Gakkai in America* (1992, USA); Phillip Hammond and David Machacek, *Soka Gakkai in America: Accommodation and Conversion* (1999, USA); Maria Immacolata Macioti, *The Buddha within Ourselves: Blossoms of the Lotus Sutra* (2002, Italy); Ronan Alves Pereira, "The Transplantation of Soka Gakkai to Brazil: Building 'the Closest Organization to the Heart of Ikeda-Sensei,'" in *Japanese Journal of Religious Studies* (2008, Brazil); and Helen Waterhouse, "Praying for the Dead in Soka Gakkai International: UK," in *Annual Review of the Sociology of Religion* (2013, UK). Others, including Karel Dobbelaere, *Soka Gakkai: From Lay Movement to Religion* (2001); Richard Hughes Seager, *Encountering the Dharma: Daisaku Ikeda, Soka Gakkai, and the Globalization of Buddhist Humanism* (2006); Sor-Ching Low, "The Re-invention of Nichiren in an Era of Globalization: Remapping the Sacred," in *Journal of Global Buddhism* (2010); and Daniel A. Metraux, *How Soka Gakkai Became a Global Buddhist Movement* (2010), have sought to provide an overview of the internationalization process.[28]

Stone's *Original Enlightenment* places Nichiren in the context of Japanese Buddhism and the relationship between Nichiren's thought and a newly emerging "nonlinear" paradigm of liberation. Hurst, Metraux, and Bocking all offer analysis of the causes and significance of the schism with Nichiren Shōshū.[29]

Efforts to come to grips with the significance of the Kōmei Party's role in coalition politics since its 1999 entry into a ruling coalition include Anne Mette Fisker-Nielsen, *Religion and Politics in Contemporary Japan: Soka Gakkai Youth and Komeito* (2012) and George Ehrhardt et al., *Kōmeitō: Politics and Religion in Japan* (2014).[30]

PRIMARY SOURCES

Since its inception, the Sōka Gakkai has produced a variety of periodicals, as well as large numbers of books and, more recently, audiovisual and web-based materials. In addition to periodicals, such as the *Seikyō shimbun* and *Daibyaku renge*, that are under the direct publishing auspices of the organization, various affiliated publications with specific audience orientations have been developed. As the movement's internationalization has progressed, this culture has been mirrored in the efforts of national organizations to produce periodicals: currently more than fifty organizations produce their own publications, and many national and subnational organizations maintain a web presence.

The Japanese-language page for the Sōka Gakkai (http://www.sokanet.jp/info/gaiyo.html)[31] presents information about current activities, as well as a library of study materials, including online lectures on Nichiren's texts.

The Soka Gakkai International (http://www.sgi.org/general-info)[32] site, in English, Spanish, and Chinese, provides explanatory materials, member testimonials, highlights of activities of national organizations, as well as study resources. It also provides links to a number of related websites, including the SGI YouTube Channel (https://www.youtube.com/user/SGIVideosOnline), the Nichiren Buddhism Library (http://www.nichirenlibrary.org), the *SGI Quarterly* (http://www.sgi.org/resources/sgi-quarterly-magazine/), and the official sites, with biographical information and text archives, of the three founding presidents: Daisaku Ikeda (http://www.sgi.org/about-us/founding-presidents/daisaku-ikeda.html), Josei Toda (http://www.sgi.org/about-us/founding-presidents/josei-toda.html), and Tsunesaburo Makiguchi (http://www.sgi.org/about-us/founding-presidents/tsunesaburo-makiguchi.html). The People's Decade for Nuclear Abolition (http://www.peoplesdecade.org/) site provides information about the organization's activities in this field.

FURTHER READING

Bocking, Brian. "Of Priests, Protests, and Protestant Buddhists: The Case of Soka Gakkai International." In *Japanese New Religions in the West.* Edited by Peter B. Clarke and Jeffrey Somers, 117–131. New York: Routledge, 1994.

Chilson, Clark. "Cultivating Charisma: Ikeda Daisaku's self Presentations and Transformational Leadership." *Journal of Global Buddhism* 15 (2014): 65–78.

Dator, James. *Soka Gakkai, Builders of the Third Civilization: American and Japanese Members.* Seattle: University of Washington Press, 1969.

Dobbelaere, Karel. *Soka Gakkai: From Lay Movement to Religion.* Translated by Olivier Urbain. Salt Lake City, UT: Signature Books, 2001.

Ehrhardt, George, Axel Klein, Levi McLaughlin, and Steven R. Reed, eds. *Kōmeitō: Politics and Religion in Japan.* Japanese Research Monograph 18. Berkeley, CA: Institute of East Asian Studies, 2014.

Fisker-Nielsen, Anne Mette. *Religion and Politics in Contemporary Japan: Soka Gakkai Youth and Komeito.* New York: Routledge, 2012.

Fujiwara, Hirotatsu. *I Denounce Soka Gakkai.* Translated by Worth C. Grant. Tokyo: Nisshin Hodo, 1970.

Gosho Translation Committee, trans. and ed. *The Writings of Nichiren Daishonin.* 2 vols. Tokyo: Sōka Gakkai, 2003.

Goulah, Jason, and Andrew Gebert, eds. *Tsunesaburo Makiguchi (1871–1944): Educational Philosophy in Context.* New York: Routledge, 2014.

Hammond, Phillip, and David Machacek. *Soka Gakkai in America: Accommodation and Conversion.* New York, Oxford University Press, 1999.

Hardacre, Helen. "Constitutional Revision and Japanese Religions." *Japanese Studies* 25, no. 3 (2005): 235–247.

Hurst, Jane. *Nichiren Shoshu Buddhism and the Soka Gakkai in America.* Oxford: Oxford University Press, 1992.

Ikeda, Daisaku, Katsuji Saito, Takanori Endo, and Haruo Suda. *The Wisdom of the Lotus Sutra: A Discussion.* 6 vols. Santa Monica, CA: World Tribune Press, 2000–2003.

Ikeda, Daisaku, and Arnold Toynbee. *Choose Life: A Dialogue.* Translated and edited by Richard Gage. London: I. B. Tauris, 2007.

Kisala, Robert. "Soka Gakkai: Searching for the Mainstream." In *Controversial New Religions.* Edited by James R. Lewis and Jesper Aagaard Petersen, 139–152. Oxford: Oxford University Press, 2005.

Kodaira, Yoshihira, ed. *Shakubuku Kyōten.* Tokyo: Sōka Gakkai, 1958.

Low, Sor-Ching."The Re-invention of Nichiren in an Era of Globalization: Remapping the Sacred." *Journal of Global Buddhism* 11 (2010): 27–43.

Machacek, David, and Bryan Wilson, eds. *Global Citizens: The Soka Gakkai Buddhist Movement in the World.* London: Oxford University Press, 2000.

Macioti, Maria Immacolata. *The Buddha within Ourselves: Blossoms of the Lotus Sutra.* Translated by Richard M. Capozzi. Lanham, MD: University Press of America, 2002. The original was published in 1996, under the title *Il Buddha che è in noi* (Rome: Seam).

Makiguchi, Tsunesaburō. *Makiguchi Tsunesaburō zenshu.*10 vols. Tokyo: Daisan Bunmeisha, 1981–1988.

McLaughlin, Levi. "Sōka Gakkai in Japan." In *Handbook of Contemporary Japanese Religions.* Edited by Inken Prohl and John Nelson. Boston: Brill, 2012.

McLaughlin, Levi. "Did Aum Change Everything?" *Japanese Journal of Religious Studies* 39, no. 1 (2012): 51–75.

Metraux, Daniel. "The Dispute between the Sōka Gakkai and the Nichiren Shōshū Priesthood: A Lay Revolution against a Conservative Clergy." *Japanese Journal of Religious Studies* 19, no. 4 (1992): 325–336.

Metraux, Daniel A. *How Soka Gakkai Became a Global Buddhist Movement.* Lewiston, NY: Edwin Mellen Press, 2010.

Miyata, Koichi, ed. "Ideas and Influence of Tsunesaburo Makiguchi." Special Issue, *Journal of Oriental Studies* 10 (2000).

Murakami, Shigeyoshi. *Sōka Gakkai-Kōmeitō.* Tokyo: Aoki Shoten, 1967.

Murata, Kiyoaki. *Japan's New Buddhism: An Objective Account of Soka Gakkai.* New York: Weatherhill, 1969.

Pereira, Ronan Alves. "The Transplantation of Soka Gakkai to Brazil: Building 'the Closest Organization to the Heart of Ikeda Sensei.'" *Japanese Journal of Religious Studies* 35, no. 1 (2008): 95–113.

Saitō, Shōji. *Wakaki Makiguchi Tsunesaburō.* Tokyo: Daisan Bunmeisha, 1981.

Seager, Richard Hughes. *Encountering the Dharma: Daisaku Ikeda, Soka Gakkai, and the Globalization of Buddhist Humanism.* Berkeley: University of California Press, 2006.

Shimazono, Susumu. *From Salvation to Spirituality: Popular Religious Movements in Japan.* Melbourne, Australia: Trans Pacific Press, 2004.

Stone, Jacqueline. *Original Enlightenment and the Transformation of Medieval Japanese Buddhism.* Honolulu: University of Hawai'i Press, 1999.

Stone, Jacqueline. "By Imperial Edict and Shogunal Degree." In *Buddhism in the Modern World: Adaptations of an Ancient Tradition.* Edited by Steven Heine and Charles S. Prebish, 193–219. Oxford: Oxford University Press, 2003.

Toda, Jōsei. *Essays on Buddhism.* Translated by Takeo Kamio. Tokyo: Seikyō Press, 1961.

Toda, Jōsei. *Toda Jōsei zenshu.* 9 vols. Tokyo: Seikyō Shimbunsha, 1981–1988.

Urbain, Olivier, ed. *A Forum for Peace: Daisaku Ikeda's Proposals to the UN.* London: I. B. Tauris, 2014.

Waterhouse, Helen. 2013. "Praying for the Dead in Soka Gakkai International: UK." In *Annual Review of the Sociology of Religion, Vol. 4: Prayer in Religion and Spirituality.* Edited by Giuseppe Giordan and Linda Woodhead. Leiden, The Netherlands: Brill, 2013.

White, James W. *The Sokagakkai and Mass Society.* Stanford, CA: Stanford University Press, 1970.

Yampolsky, Philip, ed. *Selected Writings of Nichiren.* Translated by Burton Watson. New York: Columbia University Press, 1990.

NOTES

1. Jōsei Toda, *Toda Jōsei zenshu* (Complete works of Toda Jōsei), 9 vols. (Tokyo: Seikyō shimbunsha, 1983–1990), vol. 3, 431.
2. Seikyo Online.
3. Soka Gakkai International: SGI Membership.
4. Soka Gakkai International.
5. Sōka Gakkai Overseas Bureau, *The Nichiren Shōshū Sōkagakkai,* (Tokyo: Seikyō Press, 1966), 200.
6. Yoshihira Kodaira, ed., *Shakubuku kyōten* (Handbook of propagation), (Tokyo: Sōka Gakkai, 1958), 309.
7. Toda, Complete Works of Toda, vol. 4, 392.
8. Daisaku Ikeda, "*Shakai no sosei e daibunka undō*" (A great cultural movement to revive society), *Seikyō Shimbun,* May 4, 1970, 4.

9. Gosho Translation Committee, trans. and ed. *The Writings of Nichiren Daishonin*, 2 vols, (Tokyo: Sōka Gakkai, 1999–2006), vol. 1, 831–832.
10. Gosho Translation, *Writings of Nichiren*, vol. 1, 1039.
11. Gosho Translation, *Writings of Nichiren*, vol. 1, 25.
12. Toda, Complete Works of Toda, vol. 3, 501.
13. Daisaku Ikeda, Takanori Endo, and Katsuji Saito. *The Wisdom of the Lotus Sutra*, 6 vols, (Santa Monica, CA: World Tribune Press, 2000–2003), vol. 1, 37.
14. Toda, Complete Works of Toda, vol. 4, 144.
15. Gosho Translation, *Writings of Nichiren*, vol. 1, 392.
16. Daisaku Ikeda, *The Human Revolution*, 2 vols. (Santa Monica, CA: World Tribune Press, 2004), vol. 1, viii.
17. Daisaku Ikeda, "*Shakai no sosei*" (A great cultural movement) 4.
18. Daisaku Ikeda, *Kibō no asu e* (Toward a hopeful tomorrow). (Tokyo: Seikyō shimbunsha, 1995), 39.
19. Soka Gakkai Nichiren Buddhism Library.
20. Soka Gakkai International: SGI Charter.
21. Makiguchi Tsunesaburō. *Makiguchi Tsunesaburō zenshu* (Complete works of Makiguchi Tsunesaburō), 10 vols, (Tokyo: Daisan Bunmeisha, 1981–1988), vol. 10, 188.
22. Jacqueline Stone, "By Imperial Edict and Shogunal Degree," in *Buddhism in the Modern World: Adaptations of an Ancient Tradition*, ed. Steven Heine and Charles S. Prebish, (Oxford: Oxford University Press, 2003), 199–219.
23. Minoru Harada, "Reaffirming the Original Spirit of Nichiren Buddhism," *World Tribune*, (December 12, 2014), 2–3.
24. Soka Gakkai International: SGI Charter.
25. Hirotatsu Fujiwara, *I Denounce Soka Gakkai*, trans. Worth C. Grant (Tokyo: Nisshin Hodo, 1970); Shigeyoshi Murakami, *Sōka Gakkai–Kōmeitō* (Tokyo: Aoki Shoten, 1967); Kiyoaki Murata, *Japan's New Buddhism: An Objective Account of Soka Gakkai* (New York: Weatherhill, 1969).
26. James Dator, *Soka Gakkai, Builders of the Third Civilization: American and Japanese Members* (Seattle, WA: University of Washington Press, 1969); James W. White, *The Sokagakkai and Mass Society* (Stanford, CA: Stanford University Press, 1970).
27. Shōji Saitō, *Wakaki Makiguchi Tsunesaburō* (Tokyo: Daisan Bunmeisha, 1981); Koichi Miyata, ed., "Ideas and Influence of Tsunesaburo Makiguchi," Special Issue, *Journal of Oriental Studies* 10 (2000); Jason Goulah and Andrew Gebert, eds. *Tsunesaburo Makiguchi (1871–1944): Educational Philosophy in Context* (New York: Routledge, 2014); David Machacek and Bryan Wilson, eds. *Global Citizens: The Soka Gakkai Buddhist Movement in the World* (London: Oxford University Press, 2000); Levi McLaughlin, "Sōka Gakkai in Japan," in *Handbook of Contemporary Japanese Religions*, ed. Inken Prohl and John Nelson (Boston: Brill, 2012a).
28. Jane Hurst, *Nichiren Shoshu Buddhism and the Soka Gakkai in America* (Oxford: Oxford University Press, 1992); Phillip Hammond and David Machacek, *Soka Gakkai in America: Accommodation and Conversion* (New York: Oxford University Press, 1999); Maria Immacolata Macioti, *The Buddha within Ourselves: Blossoms of the Lotus Sutra*, trans. Richard M. Capozzi (Lanham, MD: University Press of America, 2002); Ronan Alves Pereira, "The Transplantation of Soka Gakkai to Brazil: Building 'the Closest Organization to the Heart of Ikeda-Sensei,"' *Japanese Journal of Religious Studies* 35, no. 1 (2008): 95–113; and Helen Waterhouse, "Praying for the Dead in Soka Gakkai International: UK," in *Annual Review of the Sociology of Religion, Vol. 4: Prayer in Religion and Spirituality*, eds. Giuseppe Giordan and Linda Woodhead (Leiden, The Netherlands: Brill, 2013); Others, including Karel Dobbelaere, *Soka Gakkai: From Lay Movement to Religion*, trans. Olivier Urbain (Salt Lake City, UT: Signature Books, 2001); Richard Hughes Seager. *Encountering the Dharma: Daisaku Ikeda, Soka Gakkai,*

and the Globalization of Buddhist Humanism (Berkeley: University of California Press, 2006); Sor-Ching Low, "The Re-invention of Nichiren in an Era of Globalization: Remapping the Sacred," *Journal of Global Buddhism* 11 (2010): 27–43; Daniel A. Metraux, *How Soka Gakkai Became a Global Buddhist Movement* (Lewiston, NY: Edwin Mellen Press, 2010).
29. Jacqueline Stone, *Original Enlightenment and the Transformation of Medieval Japanese Buddhism* (Honolulu: University of Hawai'i Press, 1999); Jane Hurst, *Nichiren Shoshu Buddhism;* Daniel Metraux, "The Dispute between the Sōka Gakkai and the Nichiren Shōshū Priesthood: A Lay Revolution against a Conservative Clergy," *Japanese Journal of Religious Studies* 19, no. 4 (1992): 325–336; Brian Bocking, "Of Priests, Protests, and Protestant Buddhists: The Case of Soka Gakkai International," in *Japanese New Religions in the West*, eds. Peter B. Clarke and Jeffrey Somers (New York: Routledge, 1994), 117–131.
30. Anne Mette Fisker-Nielsen, *Religion and Politics in Contemporary Japan: Soka Gakkai Youth and Komeito* (New York: Routledge, 2012); George Ehrhardt, et al., eds. *Kōmeitō: Politics and Religion in Japan* (Berkeley, CA: Institute of East Asian Studies, 2014).
31. SOKAnet.
32. Soka Gakkai International.

Andrew Gebert

SOUTHEAST ASIAN REFUGEES IN NORTH AMERICA

BACKGROUND: THE TWO MAIN SOUTHEAST ASIAN SCHOOLS OF BUDDHISM

The Buddhism of Southeast Asia is commonly identified as divided into two large sects or schools, Theravāda and Mahāyāna. Theravāda can be translated as "the way of the elders." Mahāyāna is Sanskrit for "the great vehicle," since its adherents regard it as offering a path to salvation for the largest number of people. One of the major distinctions between these two schools or sects has to do with the role of the bodhisattva (literally, "enlightened being"). To simplify a complex doctrinal issue, bodhisattvas, in Mahāyāna Buddhism, are individuals who have achieved enlightenment but delay passing over into nirvana in order to help with the salvation of others. The position of Theravāda Buddhism is that all must move toward enlightenment and salvation by their own efforts.

Theravāda Buddhism is the dominant approach in most of Southeast Asia, including Burma, Thailand, Laos, and Cambodia. Mahāyāna Buddhism established itself in China, Japan, and Korea. Mahāyāna Buddhism began to find adherents in Vietnam in the 2nd and 3rd centuries of the common era. By the 5th century, Chinese-style Mahāyāna Buddhism had become one of Vietnam's predominant religions. While there are some Theravāda Buddhists in Vietnam, the border that separates Vietnam from Cambodia and Laos can also be regarded as a religious boundary between the Theravāda and Mahāyāna schools.[1]

SOUTHEAST ASIAN BUDDHISM

Theravāda Buddhism put down roots in the Theravāda countries of Southeast Asia in two senses. It became an official religion in most of them with strong state support, at least until revolutionary governments took power in Cambodia and Laos in the mid-1970s (and, in the case of Laos, state connections to religion continued even under a government dedicated to socialism). In addition, Theravāda beliefs and practices adopted many local, preexisting religious elements, especially beliefs in spirits. In this way, the religion became highly localized over the centuries.

Official support for Buddhism and localization of tradition sometimes exerted different pressures. Some Buddhist leaders criticize the "folk Buddhism" of spirit cults as departing from orthodox Buddhist teachings. In all of the Theravāda Buddhist countries of Southeast Asia, animism and spirit cults, derived from pre-Buddhist beliefs, are heavily intertwined with Buddhist practices and influence those practices. The Lao, Cambodians, Burmese, and Thai generally believe that spirits inhabit specific locations, affect human life, and must be placated. Shamans and other specialists in dealing with the spirit world are everyday parts of life. These specialists are frequently current or former Buddhist monks.

The Buddhism of the Theravāda countries places a heavy emphasis on the role of monks. Rather than separate those in monasteries from laypeople, this emphasis on monasticism actually brings the monastic activities in temples closer to their lay supporters. While there are individuals who spend their lives in temples, a temporary period of ordination is the ideal for all men in the Theravāda countries of Southeast Asia, usually before marriage or late in life for widowers. In addition, boys considered too young for entering the monastic state often live at the temple and serve as novices. Thus, Buddhism is deeply interwoven into community life in Laos and Cambodia. The *CIA World Factbook* has estimated that 96.8 percent of the people in Laos were Buddhists in 2013 and that 96.9 percent of the people in Cambodia were Buddhists in 2008.[2]

One of the central religious concepts of Theravāda Buddhism that Cambodian and Lao refugees brought to North America was that of "making merit." The primary source of merit in a Theravāda Buddhist land is the temple. Throughout most of the Theravāda Buddhist countries, each village will have a temple at its geographic and cultural center. Villagers make merit by feeding monks, donating robes, and contributing labor.

Social life in Cambodia and Laos was ordered by rituals centered on the sangha. Temples are gathering places, and virtually all ceremonies, which are timed according to the agricultural cycle of seasons, take place at temples. Traditionally, in Cambodia the *Chol Chnam*, or New Year Festival, is held annually about the month of April. In the Spring, *Vissakh Bochea* marks the anniversary of the birth, death, and enlightenment of the Buddha. The following June or July, *Chol Vossa* is a ritual recognition of a season of penitence, during which monks must remain in the temple or on temple grounds. At the end of the *vossa* season, around September, Cambodian Buddhist communities have traditionally celebrated the *Kathen*. One of the signal activities of the *kathen* is the provision of offerings to the monks by the laity, with the offering of new robes playing a particularly important part.

Each of these occasions has its equivalent in Laos. The New Year festival, called *Songkan* or *Pimai* (literally, "New Year") in Lao, is a popular event because of the energetic splashing of water. The popularity and joyousness of these kinds of festivals frequently overshadows their essentially religious nature, though. The throwing of water is a purification rite, and monks conduct religious services in memory of the dead to begin the new lunar year. The Cambodian *Vissakh Bochea* is known in Laos as *Visakha Bucha,* when adherents listen to sermons by monks and in the evening walk in circles around major temples holding candles. The penitential season is known as *Phansa,* marked by the day of *Khao Phansa*. This is also followed by the

Kathin ceremony, in which adherents make offerings of robes and other useful gifts to monks. These holidays can be seen as bringing individuals in communities into a shared pattern of life by marking out cycles of time according to ritual recognitions of a normative order centered on the temples and the monks in the temples.

When Communist governments came to power in Vietnam, Cambodia, and Laos in 1975, officials in all three countries viewed religion with suspicion. However, the most intense opposition to religion came in Cambodia, where the brutal Khmer Rouge regime attempted to completely redesign Cambodian society, turning the entire country into a forced labor camp, in that everything inherited from the pre-revolutionary period would be extirpated. Perhaps as much as one-third of the population died, by execution, starvation, or illness. As part of its effort at revolutionary transformation, the Khmer Rouge undertook a campaign to completely obliterate the country's Buddhist institutions and traditions. The Khmer Rouge forced monks to abandon their monastic robes, destroyed temples, and murdered religious leaders. During the Khmer Rouge period, from 1975 to 1980, the number of monks in Cambodia dropped from between sixty-five and eighty thousand to about three thousand.[3]

Although the Communist government in Laos did not try to eradicate Buddhism, as the Khmer Rouge did, the new regime did attempt to coopt religious activities and to get religious officials to promote the official ideology. The government attempted to move education in the country away from religion and toward the support of secular goals. Buddhist monks who did not collaborate with the regime were frequently sent to re-education camps.

Although early Buddhism came to Vietnam from India, Vietnamese Buddhism has been influenced primarily by Chinese sources, distinguishing Vietnam in religion, as well as in culture, from its Theravādin neighbors in Cambodia and Laos. Two varieties or schools of Mahāyāna Buddhism predominate in Vietnam. One of these is Pure Land Buddhism (in Vietnamese *Tinh Đô Tông*, pronounced "tin doh tohng"), in which adherents recite prayers and chants to reach a state of enlightenment or to be reborn in the Pure Land. Vietnamese Buddhism is also heavily influenced by the tradition known in Vietnamese as *Tiền*, which is more commonly known in the West by its Japanese name, Zen. This latter school places a heavy emphasis on meditation as a route to enlightenment.

Quan Âm, the Bodhisattva of Compassion, is an especially important figure in Vietnamese Buddhism. Known in Chinese as Kuan Yin, Quan Am is a female, goddess-like figure whose statue may be found in Vietnamese Buddhist temples around the world. Quan Am offers protection, guidance, and fertility to followers. Among Pure Land Buddhists, Amitābha Buddha, known as *A Di Đa Phật* in Vietnamese and as *Amida Butsu* in Japanese, occupies a central place in belief and practice. Adherents of the Pure Land school believe that by living ethically and by chanting this Buddha's name daily, they will reborn in a pure land.

There are Theravāda Buddhist temples in Vietnam, mainly in the southern part of the country. These are most often associated with ethnic Cambodians (Khmer) in Vietnam. Vietnamese religions also include other faiths connected to Buddhism or influenced by it. Two of the most notable are *Hòa Hảo* ("hoh-uh how") and *Cao Đài* ("gow dye"). The first is based on Mahāyāna Buddhism but is recognized as a distinct religion. The second is a syncretistic religion, one that brings together elements of different belief systems. It includes influences from Buddhism, Confucianism, and Catholicism and recognizes individuals from both Asian and European history and traditions as saints.

The extent to which Buddhism continues to prevail in Vietnam is difficult to estimate, in part because Vietnamese Buddhism is so often mingled in common practice with Confucianism and folk religions, and in part because information on religion in Vietnam comes from the country's officially atheist government. The *CIA World Factbook* has cited 2009 estimates that 81.8 percent of people in Vietnam reported adhering to no religion, 7.9 percent were Buddhists, and 6.6 percent were Christians. These figures most likely drastically undercount religious adherents in Vietnam. In 1974, the CIA estimated that about one-third of the people in what was then South Vietnam were Buddhists, and about 11 percent were Christians. According to the Pew Center's 2012 report *Faith on the Move*, more Buddhists living outside their country of origin had come from Vietnam than from any other country of origin. Moreover, the same report showed 49 percent of Vietnamese who had migrated to another country identified as Buddhist and 20 percent identified as Christian.[4]

Although the constitution of the Socialist Republic of Vietnam guarantees religious freedom, the government sees independent religious organizations as threats to its monopoly of power. There is a state-run Vietnamese Buddhist Church, but the non-state Unified Buddhist Church of Vietnam (UBCV), which was banned by the Vietnamese government in the early 1980s, apparently has greater popular support. The Unified Buddhist Church is also linked to the Unified Buddhist Church of Vietnam in America, in the United States, and to the Unified Vietnamese Buddhist Congregation of Canada.

THE GROWTH OF THE SOUTHEAST ASIAN POPULATION IN NORTH AMERICA

Before the 1970s, Buddhism in North America was primarily limited to relatively small immigrant communities from mainland China, Taiwan, and Japan, and to some converts in the wider population. However, the arrival of refugee populations from Vietnam, Laos, and Cambodia after 1975 greatly increased the number of adherents to Mahāyāna and Theravāda Buddhism.

The movement of people from these countries to North America was a consequence of American involvement in the war in Vietnam, which spread to Laos and Cambodia. In 1975, as North Vietnamese forces took power in Saigon, the United States evacuated about 65,000 "high risk" individuals from Vietnam by air and sea. President Gerald Ford authorized the admission of 130,000 refugees from Indochina (Cambodia, Laos, and Vietnam) into the United States. Among them, 125,000 were Vietnamese. Catholics made up a disproportionately large minority of the refugees from Vietnam, but many were Buddhists.

The number of Southeast Asian refugees admitted to the United States dropped sharply after 1975. But the numbers began to increase again in 1978 as a result of an enlarged resettlement program developed in response to the lobbying of concerned American citizens and organizations. Reports of Vietnamese fleeing their country by sea in small and often unseaworthy vessels created the image of the "boat people" and stirred international sympathy. News of the often-hostile reception of the boat people in neighboring countries and their sufferings at the hands of pirates created pressure in the United States to expand the refugee program. The conflicts between Cambodia and Vietnam and Vietnam and China brought attention to the refugee situation in the Southeast Asian region.

The year 1980, as a result, saw another sharp spike in refugee arrivals from Vietnam in the United States, which then continued as a steady stream. The South East Asian refugee crisis also led the US Congress to pass the most comprehensive piece of refugee legislation in American history, the Refugee Act of 1980. In place of the "seventh preference category" established in 1965, which admitted refugees as part of the total number of immigrants allowed into the United States, the Refugee Act provided for an annual number of admissions for refugees. This number was to be independent of the number of immigrants permitted, and it was to be established each year by the president in consultation with Congress.

After the 1980 peak, the United States continued to admit over twenty thousand refugees from Vietnam per year throughout the 1980s and first half of the 1990s. After the United States and Vietnam reestablished formal diplomatic relations the refugee flow from Vietnam dropped sharply, and it mostly came to an end by the 21st century. Although the United States had been home to very few people of Vietnamese background in 1970, by 2015 there were nearly two million American citizens and residents of Vietnamese descent. This population was created, directly or indirectly, by refugee resettlement.

At the end of 1975, the United States Congress agreed to accept more people who had fled from Laos and were living in refugee camps in Thailand, and the United States brought in 10,200 refugees from Laos in 1976. More Lao refugees made the move in the following years, with 400 arriving in 1977; 8,000 in 1978; 30,200 in 1979; 55,500 in 1980; and 19,300 in 1981. Admissions from Laos diminished following the high point around 1980 but continued to trickle in over the course of the 20th century.

Refugees from Cambodia began to arrive in the United States in large numbers following the 1980 Refugee Act. In 1981 alone, 38,000 Cambodian refugees were admitted. This massive flow from Cambodia came to an end by the 1990s, but the Cambodian American population continued to increase.[5]

By 2016, according to US census estimates, the Southeast Asian–origin population of the United States included 1,719,000 Vietnamese, 260, 600 Cambodians, and 211,800 Lao. Although they were widespread around the country, they often settled in ethnic communities, inspired partly by the desire to be close to religious institutions. The greatest concentration of people of Southeast Asian origin was in Southern California. By 1990, the Vietnamese community in Orange County had become known as "Little Saigon," and about one-quarter of all Vietnamese Americans lived in the Los Angeles-Orange County area by 2000. Long Beach, in the Los Angeles area, held the greatest concentration of Cambodians, and the area along Tenth Street in Long Beach became known as the "New Phnom Penh." Lao were the least concentrated of the Southeast Asian groups, but they had formed small communities in various locations around the United States.[6]

Although Canada admitted smaller numbers of refugees than the United States, the northern country was active in refugee resettlement from the period immediately following the fall of South Vietnam. In 1975–1976, Canada took in approximately 6,500 Vietnamese. Following a United Nations High Commission for Refugees (UNHCR) meeting in Geneva in July 1979 to discuss the plight of refugees from Southeast Asia, Canadian Prime Minister Joe Clark announced that his country would take in 50,000 refugees from Vietnam, Cambodia, and Laos. In April 1980, the Canadian government increased this number to 60,000. By 1986, the Southeast Asian foreign-born population of Canada included 100,000 Vietnamese, 14,000

Cambodians, and 15,000 Lao. The arrival of people from Southeast Asia to Canada slowed during the 1990s, but the Southeast Asian population continued to grow.[7] The 2016 Canadian census recorded 240,615 people of Vietnamese origin, 38,490 people of Cambodian origin, and 24,590 people of Lao origin. Southeast Asians in Canada were a primarily urban population, with the greatest concentrations in Toronto, Montreal, and Vancouver.[8]

ORIGINS AND SPREAD OF SOUTHEAST-ASIAN-REFUGEE THERAVĀDA BUDDHISM IN NORTH AMERICA

The Buddhism of Southeast Asia began to arise in North America only in the late 20th century. We can divide its establishment to two historical trends in immigration that have been significant for the kinds of sacred order provided by Theravāda Buddhism. One trend was the appearance of Southeast Asian immigrants, most notably from Thailand and, to a much lesser extent, from Burma (later Myanmar) and Sri Lanka. Massive refugee movements from Laos and Cambodia from about 1980 onward made up the second trend. When Cambodian and Lao Buddhists reached North America, they drew on existing Theravāda Buddhism, mainly Thai, prior to establishing temples associated with their own national-origin groups, and close ties among Thai, Cambodian, and Lao Buddhists in North America have continued. Therefore, any consideration of the Buddhism of Cambodians and Lao in North America must also include references to the Buddhism of the Thai and the Sri Lankans.

Although Theravāda Buddhist influences reached America as early as the 19th century, frequently through the medium of theosophy, the establishment of Southeast Asian Buddhism really only dates from the late 20th century. The first signs of an interest by Thai authorities in bringing Theravāda Buddhism to the United States appeared in 1961, when the supreme patriarch of Thai Buddhism visited the United States and received a report of an available site for a temple on Staten Island. However, the Thais learned that the land was not available to them and they gave up plans to send two Buddhist monks.

In 1964 and 1965, monks from Sri Lanka arrived in the United States to set up a Buddhist cultural center in Washington, DC. Again, the Thai government played a part. The association that grew out of the efforts of the Sri Lankan monks founded the first permanent temple on land in Washington purchased from the Thai government. A few years later the first specifically Thai temple was founded in Los Angeles in the early 1970s, with close cooperation from the Religious Department in Thailand and the ceremonial participation of the Thai monarchy in the casting of a Buddha image for the temple.

People arriving in North America from Cambodia and Laos often attended Thai temples into the 1980s. When Cambodians and Laotians began building their own temples, these often drew on organizational support from Thai Americans and from Thailand. When Cambodians in New York created the first Cambodian temple there in the mid-1980s, a monk in Thailand provided the image of the Buddha. Across the Canadian border, the Cambodian temple in Ottawa was headed by a Khmer-speaking Thai monk.

By mid-1979, the Washington, DC-area Cambodian Buddhist Society had established Wat Buddhikarama, reportedly the first Cambodian Buddhist temple in the United States. Three years later, in 1982, the expanding Cambodian population of Long Beach, California led Cambodian refugees in Southern California to establish Wat Kemara Buddhikaram in Long

Beach. In mid-1985, the Khmer Buddhist Society opened the first Cambodian Buddhist temple in New York City in the Bedford Park section of the Bronx. Throughout the mid-to late 1980s, Cambodian Buddhist temples proliferated around the United States and southern Canada.[9]

Lao temples proliferated during the same period of time. Where Thai temples existed, the Lao were often included more readily than the Cambodians, because of the close similarity between Thai and Cambodian language and culture as well as between their religious practices. Nevertheless, as this article will discuss, the refugee situation of the Lao and the existence of identifiable Lao communities often led to the establishment of their own temples. Frequently, Thai religious establishments served as an initial base for creating separate Lao establishments.

In 1980, the first Lao Buddhist monk in the New York metropolitan area, Satu Khamphoui Sinnolai, found housing with four Thai monks in the Bronx. At that time, he was reportedly one of only five Lao Buddhist monks in the United States, with two others in Washington, DC, one in Oregon, and another in Illinois. This Lao Buddhist monk, initially aided by the Thai American religious establishment, became the core of a new Bronx Lao temple.[10]

Theravāda Buddhist temples became central features drawing Lao and Cambodian people in North America to specific locations. In 1989, the US Office of Refugee Services published a document entitled "Profiles of Some Good Places for Lao People to Live in the United States." The presence or accessibility of a Lao temple was one of the chief characteristics of a good place for Lao people to live.[11]

In the quarter of a century from the middle of the 1960s to the beginning of the 1990s, Theravāda Buddhism went from having almost no presence in North America to being an established religion in towns and cities around the nation. Although a small part of this growth had been due to the creation of meditation centers for convert Buddhists, most of it was the consequence of immigration. At the end of the 20th century, Paul Numrich, a scholar of Theravāda Buddhism in North America, estimated the total number of Asian or immigrant Theravāda Buddhist temples to be about 150, housing between 450 to 600 monks.[12] Similarly, Charles S. Prebish estimated that there were 146 Theravāda Buddhist temples in the United States in 1996, with all but the Washington temple built in the years following 1970.[13]

For the refugee groups, the temples became key sources of building social identity around a coherent temporal order.[14] One of the earliest group activities of Cambodian Buddhists in Washington in 1979 was a *kathen* ceremony for some of the first Cambodian monks.[15] Religious beliefs and rituals established normatively rich patterns that enabled adherents to comprehend themselves and their places in the world.[16] The Venerable Uang Mean explained to a reporter in 1979, "without Buddhism our people cannot live. Like without food, they cannot live. Buddhism is a part of life. It is an important part of life. For a Cambodian, even the sight of a monk is a remedy and they feel refreshed."[17]

Reestablishing Buddhism in North America was especially important for Cambodian refugees because of their traumatic experiences during the violent Khmer Rouge period. These experiences may also have made the challenge of organizing themselves and establishing temples especially challenging for refugees from Cambodia because they were coming from a recent history of extreme social disruption.[18]

When the first Lao monk arrived in the New York area in 1980, local Lao people greeted him with flowers, incense, candles, and fruit, and they immediately began the search for a place to use as a temple.[19] When the Lao community of Iberia, Louisiana set out to build an ethnically based neighborhood, the first step was to build a temple and to staff it with a monk.[20]

Over the course of the 1980s, the Lao American population both grew and spread out from its initial points of entry into North America. From 47,683 in 1980, numbers of Lao in the United States grew to 147,375 in 1990 and then to 167,792 in 2000. A little over one-third of Lao in the United States could be found in California in 2000, but they had become the most geographically distributed of the major groups within the Theravāda tradition. They often formed small communities in various parts of their new homeland. In Texas, for example, communities of 500 to 1,000 Lao could be found in Amarillo, Dallas, Euless, Houston, and Irving. To the north, an estimated 3,000 to 4,000 ethnic Lao lived in St. Paul and Minneapolis, along with the larger number of Hmong from the highlands of Laos. By the time of the 1991 Canadian census, Canada was home to about 14,500 Lao, with about half of them settled in either Toronto or Montreal.

As these smaller Lao communities formed, they were motivated to establish temples by the absence of existing Thai temples, as well as by their own specific group needs. Lao families in the New York area pledged to raise money to create the temple around Satu Khampoui Sinnolai. Near the city of New Iberia, Louisiana, Lao residents who had been drawn to the area by the availability of jobs in oil-related construction during the early 1980s began plans to create a temple with a surrounding residential neighborhood in 1986, completing the temple in 1987, according to one detailed study.[21] Other temples serving Lao communities were established during the 1980s in places as widespread as Tucson, Arizona; Denver, Colorado; St. Petersburg, Florida; Atlanta, Georgia; Salt Lake City, Utah; Rockford, Illinois; Des Moines, Iowa; Amarillo, Texas; Wichita, Kansas; Manassas, Virginia; St. Louis, Missouri; Lowell, Massachusetts; Rochester, New York; Oklahoma City, Oklahoma; Portland, Oregon; Murfreesboro, Tennessee; and Providence, Rhode Island.[22]

In the Lao and Cambodian Theravāda temples in North America, as in the home countries, the biggest event of the year is the "Water Festival," or Lunar New Year celebration. In addition to celebrants enthusiastically throwing water at each other, a practice that originated as a cleansing ritual, the festival also includes activities such as parades with young women performing traditional dances. Lao and Cambodian Buddhists typically welcome outsiders to the New Year celebration, which they see as an opportunity to familiarize other people in North America with their cultures.

The Theravāda Buddhism of the refugee populations has undergone some changes as it has adapted to life in North America.[23] The New Year Festival, which is held at the full moon of the fifth month in Laos and Cambodia, generally occurs around the time of Easter, and celebrations at temples in many Lao and Cambodian temples in America have been reset to Easter weekend, when people have time free from work. In Southeast Asia, monasticism is a permanent occupation only for a few monks. In general, all men have the goal of becoming monks, at least for short periods of time, before marriage or as widowers. Because it is difficult to take time out from work in America, though, monasticism has tended to become a profession, with monks brought in by the lay members of a temple.[24]

This last trend, the founding of temples by laypeople that bring in monks to serve in temples, has tended to shift power from monks to committees of laypeople. The rising role of laypeople in American Theravāda Buddhism has on occasions led to conflict within communities and between local communities and organizations formed on transnational bases. Oakland, California, for example, has seen a legal battle since 2005 between members of the Oakland Cambodian Buddhist Temple and the Massachusetts-based International Community of Buddhist Monks. The struggle began in 2004 when members of the Oakland Cambodian Buddhist Society Board of Directors transferred control of the Oakland temple to the International Community of Buddhist Monks. Many of the local Oakland Cambodians regarded this decision as illegal and as a disenfranchisement of the Oakland community.[25]

Another major change concerns the cultural role of temples. In Southeast Asia, Theravāda temples are often the center of life, especially in small villages. However, the temples are also part of the larger cultures. In North America, temples have the explicit purpose of cultural preservation within a larger culture that is non-Buddhist and in which the Lao and Cambodians are members of minority ethnic groups. Language classes, the teaching of traditional arts and crafts, instruction in traditional dances, and other efforts to maintain cultural practices frequently take place in the temples.

VIETNAMESE BUDDHISM IN NORTH AMERICA

The expansion of the Vietnamese-origin population throughout the United States and in the major urban centers in the southern part of Canada has produced an expansion and institutionalization of Vietnamese Buddhism in these countries. Every location that has a significant Vietnamese population has seen a growth in Mahāyāna Buddhism and the creation of Buddhist religious organizations.[26]

Vietnamese Buddhism arrived in North America even during American military involvement in that country. The Vietnamese meditation master Thích Nhất Hạnh visited the United States in 1961, introducing his approach to mindfulness meditation. The first Vietnamese Buddhist center opened in Los Angeles in 1970, before the refugee influx. In 1975, the first Vietnamese Buddhist temple was established in Los Angeles, serving the spiritual needs of the incoming refugees. The growth of the Vietnamese American population over the years resulted in a corresponding growth of Buddhist religious establishments. A Vietnamese temple was established in Phoenix, Arizona in 1983 and another in Sugar Land, Texas (in the Houston area) in 1990. By 2005, there were an estimated 376 Vietnamese Buddhist centers in the United States, with 114 Vietnamese Buddhist centers in California, 28 in Texas, and 12 in Florida.

One of the most significant events in the institutionalization of Vietnamese Buddhism in North America was the founding of the International Buddhist Monastic Institute at the University of Oriental Studies in Los Angeles in 1979. In June 1981, the Institute moved to the San Fernando Valley, just north of Los Angeles. In contrast to temples and other centers of religious activity, the function of the Institute is primarily educational. Its goals are to preserve Buddhist texts, train monks, and maintain traditional practices.

The year 1983 saw the first traditional ordination of overseas monks at the International Buddhist Monastic Institute, attended by Vietnamese monks from around the world in exile from their homeland. In 1992, Vietnamese Buddhists in the United States formed the Unified Buddhist Church of Vietnam in America, a wing of the Unified Buddhist Church in the home country. In addition to promoting the faith, this organization became involved in some wider civic and political activities. For example, when the United States decided to close the refugee camps in Southeast Asia, the Unified Buddhist Church lobbied the American government not to repatriate those in the camps, and it sponsored monks in the camps for resettlement.

On December 26, 2005, an estimated two thousand Vietnamese Buddhists and eighty North American monks and nuns gathered at the Diệu Pháp Pagoda in San Gabriel, California to celebrate the thirtieth anniversary of the United Buddhist Church of Vietnam's official movement for religious and political freedom. The centerpiece of the memorial was a sixty-foot-long altar, with twenty-two tablets inscribed with the names of twenty-two monks who had died for the cause of religious liberty. US President George W. Bush sent a letter praising the work of the organization, and the UBCV Patriarch Thích Huyền Quang and the UBCV deputy leader sent messages smuggled out from their house arrests in monasteries in Vietnam.[27]

In the area around Orange County's Little Saigon, in Southern California, site of one of the largest and most significant Vietnamese communities in North America, Vietnamese Buddhists opened numerous temples over the years, located mainly in Garden Grove and Santa Ana. Ironically, Little Saigon, in Westminster, with the nation's largest Vietnamese population, lacked a temple until 2008, when the Chùa Diệu Ngự temple opened in a warehouse on Chestnut Street. In 2014, the Vietnamese of Little Saigon began construction of an elaborate traditional temple next to the warehouse. Dedicated in 2016, the temple was an important community center and a location for celebrations such as the annual Lunar New Year festival.

San Jose, in Northern California, had a Vietnamese American population of over one hundred thousand people by 2016, and accordingly, many Vietnamese Buddhist temples were located there. These included the Từ Lâm Temple in the northern part of San Jose, the Pao Hoa Buddhist Temple in the northeast, and the Đức Viên Buddhist Pagoda in the southeast.

Because the area of Houston, Texas had such a large Vietnamese population, it was also home to several Vietnamese Buddhist establishments by the early 21st century. Among the most significant of these were the Vietnamese Buddhist Center in Sugar Land, on the western side of Houston, and the Phật Quang Vietnamese Buddhist Pagoda in South Houston. After Houston, metropolitan New Orleans held the largest Vietnamese population in the southern United States. The largest proportion of New Orleans Vietnamese were Catholic, but the New Orleans area held important Buddhist temples, including the Vạn Hạnh Buddhist Temple in New Orleans East, on Chef Menteur Highway, not far from a major Vietnamese Catholic church, and the Liên Hoa Temple in Terrytown, a suburb just outside the city of New Orleans on the west bank of the Mississippi. The Liên Hoa temple, built in 2014, is the largest Buddhist temple of the entire Gulf Coast region.

All of the locations in Canada with significant Vietnamese populations established temples and other Buddhist centers. In 1983, a Vietnamese monk founded the General Vietnamese Buddhist Association in Canada, which later became known as the Unified Vietnamese Buddhist Congregation of Canada and is also called the Union of Vietnamese Buddhist Churches in Canada. The stated goals of this organization have been to disseminate religious doctrine, advocate for persecuted Buddhists back in Vietnam, maintain the faith in temples in Canada, and train Canadian Vietnamese monks and nuns.[28]

The Vietnamese Buddhists of Toronto formed a number of religious communities, generally divided along dedication to the meditation (Zen) or Pure Land schools. In 2000, Toronto-area Vietnamese Buddhists announced the launching of a campaign to build the Pháp Vân Buddhist Cultural Centre in Mississauga, to include a temple as well as a cultural center. After it was completed, this became a focal point of religious life for many Vietnamese Buddhists in the Greater Toronto region. However, by the early 2000s, Vietnamese Buddhists in Toronto had established at least seven temples and a number of meditation groups.[29]

Montreal may have been the first place in Canada to see the establishment of Vietnamese Buddhism. During the summer of 1975, about a dozen Vietnamese refugees in the Montreal area gathered together to discuss creating a place to practice their religion. By the early fall of that year, they formed the Liên Hoa (or "Lotus Flower") Group of Buddhist Adepts. The group met first in a school and later in private homes but formed the Vietnamese Buddhist Association to raise funds to purchase land and build a permanent temple in the town of Brossard. The Liên Hoa temple funded the arrival of Vietnamese clergy, but disagreements over the extent to which clergy or laity should control the temple led to a split that resulted in the founding of the Community of Vietnamese Buddhists in Canada, and the establishment of the Tam Bảo (or "Three Jewels") temple in a former synagogue in the Montreal area in 1982. Other splits, as well as the growth of the Montreal Buddhist population, led to the creation of additional Vietnamese Buddhist temples in the region over the following years.[30]

The largest Vietnamese Buddhist temple in Vancouver is the Chân Quang (or "True Light") Temple, associated with the World Vietnamese Order. The Chân Quang Temple follows the Pure Land tradition. It has been active in serving the religious needs of Vancouver's Vietnamese community, holding numerous weekly services, with special activities at times such as the Lunar New Year. There are also several Vietnamese temples on Vancouver Island. In the suburb of Burnby, a Vietnamese Buddhist group founded a temple in 2002.[31]

Vietnamese Mahāyāna Buddhists, like the Buddhists of the Theravāda tradition, have had to make some accommodations to life in North America. Work schedules often make it difficult for laypeople to travel to temples on weekdays, so many activities at temples have been set for weekends. Moreover, like the Theravāda temples in America, Vietnamese Mahāyāna temples have taken on broad functions as cultural centers as well as places for religious practices. Because the entry of refugees from Vietnam largely ended by the 1990s, the vast majority of young people have either been born in the United States or Canada or have spent nearly all of their lives in these countries. By the 21st century, many of the young people not only were not born in Vietnam but had parents who were American-born. These younger Vietnamese have tenuous connections to the ancestral country and its customs. Often they have very limited Vietnamese language skills.

Buddhist temples, and also Vietnamese Catholic churches, have become locations for preserving and passing on culture. Vietnamese language classes and classes in Vietnamese cooking (notably vegetarian cooking among Buddhists) take place in the religious centers. The New Year festival (or Tét) in most communities is held at temples or churches. As in Vietnam, the New Year festival in North America is in late January or early February. Traditional families may hold a ceremony the afternoon before Tét during which deceased ancestors are invited to come back and spend the festival days with the living. As in Western New Year celebrations, fireworks may be set off at midnight to herald the coming year. Several young men dressed up as a dragon, the symbol of power and nobility, perform the dragon dance on the streets or other open spaces. The dragon dance also has become an important part of the cultural exhibitions in schools and other places. On the morning of Tết, families awaken early and dress in their best clothes. People offer each other New Year's wishes and give the children lucky red envelopes containing money. Tết is considered a time for visiting and entertaining guests, and non-Vietnamese are heartily welcomed to most of the celebrations and ceremonies.

Many Vietnamese Americans, especially Buddhists, also celebrate the traditional holiday of Trung Nguyên, or Wandering Souls Day, which falls in the middle of the seventh lunar month (usually around August). On this holiday tables filled with food are offered to the wandering souls of ancestors. In some cases money and clothes made of special paper may be burned at this time.

CONCLUSION

The Vietnamese, Lao, and Cambodian Buddhists in North America face many of the same challenges as earlier immigrants from other religious backgrounds, such as adaptation to an unfamiliar culture. However, Buddhism is less familiar to local people in the new homeland than the Catholicism, Protestantism, or Judaism of previous generations of immigrants. The Southeast Asians have also arrived in much larger numbers than earlier Buddhist immigrants. This has led to the establishment of Buddhist-based ethnic communities in many locations, and temples are both social centers of these communities and expressions of ethnic identities. Buddhist religious establishments have therefore become bridges between the immigrants' old and new worlds, but they have also given rise to some rivalries and even conflicts concerning institutional governance, precisely because religion is so fundamental to their social lives.

The North American environment is also reshaping Southeast Asian Buddhism to some extent. In the pluralistic religious setting of North America, Buddhist temples have often become one denomination among many. Temples not only carry on many traditions and folkways for their adherents, they also serve as means of presenting those traditions and folkways to outsiders. Laypeople have taken on greater roles in decision-making and organization than they would have in the lands of their ancestors.

The Southeast Asian Buddhist groups arrived in North America in waves of refugees. Although there is now some non-refugee immigration from their countries, this is limited. Young Vietnamese, Cambodian, and Lao Buddhists in the United States and Canada are growing up as members of religious minorities with relatively few new arrivals from their home countries. For these young people, successfully integrating into North American society depends on developing an understanding of the culture and institutions of the larger environment while also retaining the direction and support of ethnic communities. Religious organizations, as network centers, play a key part in accomplishing this twofold task.[32]

REVIEW OF LITERATURE

Much of the literature on the Buddhism of Southeast Asian refugees in North America has focused on how religions brought from the home country help new arrivals to adapt to life in a new land. The literature also tends to concentrate heavily on community studies, such as examinations of Vietnamese Buddhism in particular locations. One of the earliest works to treat the theme of Vietnamese Buddhism as a way of adapting to life in the New World was Paul Rutledge's *The Role of Religion in Ethnic Self-Identity: A Vietnamese Community*. Based on Rutledge's fieldwork as an anthropologist among the Vietnamese of Oklahoma City, the book examines how Vietnamese Buddhism and Catholicism became the bases of ethnic identification and group organization of newly resettled people in the late 1970s and early 1980s.[33]

In "Center for Vietnamese Buddhism: Recreating Home," Thuan Huynh describes how the Center for Vietnamese Buddhism in Houston, Texas has enabled local Vietnamese to recreate a little piece of Vietnam within their Texas surroundings.[34] Allison Truitt's article "Not a Day but a Vu Lan Festival: Celebrating Filial Piety in the Vietnamese Diaspora" examines the social functions of a Vietnamese festival at four Buddhist institutions along the US Gulf Coast, paying particular attention to how this festival promotes dedication to an ideal of motherhood and national identity.[35]

The best information available on Canadian Buddhism, including Vietnamese Buddhism in Canada, can be found in Bruce Matthews's book *Buddhism in Canada*. The book takes a geographic approach, with each of the chapters describing Buddhism in different Canadian regions.[36]

The best book on North American Theravāda Buddhism is Wendy Cadge's *Heartwood: The First Generation of Theravāda Buddhism in America*.[37] Cadge details the history of American Theravāda from its origins in the late 20th century among Thai and Sri Lankan immigrants and examines the connections of these origins to the religious lives of refugee groups from Laos and Cambodia. Carl L. Bankston III and Danielle Hidalgo provide a shorter general overview of contemporary Theravāda Buddhism in the United States and Canada in "Temple and Society in the New World: Theravāda Buddhism in North America."[38]

Carol A. Mortland's *Cambodian Buddhism in the United States* is an essential resource for anyone interested in the religious lives of Southeast Asians in diaspora. This anthropological study includes information on beliefs, rituals and practices, temples and temple personnel, congregations and lay activities, and the difficulties and challenges of Cambodian Buddhism in the new country.[39] The volume edited by Bruce Matthews on Canadian Buddhism provides portraits of Lao and Cambodian Buddhism in the regions of Canada. Marybeth White's chapter in this book, "Lao Buddhism in Toronto: A Case Study of Community Relations," is an especially useful examination of Buddhism in one of Canada's largest Lao settlements.[40]

FURTHER READING

Chan, Sucheng. *Survivors: Cambodian Refugees in the United States*. Urbana: University of Illinois Press, 2004.

Crosby, Kate. *Theravāda Buddhism: Continuity, Diversity, and Identity*. Chichester: Wiley Blackwell, 2014.

Fields, Rick. *Taking Refuge in L.A.: Life in a Vietnamese Buddhist Temple*. New York: Aperture Foundation, 1987.

Langford, Jean. *Consoling Ghosts: Stories of Medicine and Mourning from Southeast Asians in Exile*. Minneapolis: University of Minnesota Press, 2013.

Mitchell, Scott A. *Buddhism in America: Global Religion, Local Contexts*. New York: Bloomsbury Academic, 2016.

Mortland, Carol. *Grace after Genocide: Cambodians in the United States*. New York: Berghahn Books, 2017.

Rutledge, Paul J. *The Vietnamese Experience in America*. Bloomington: Indiana University Press, 1992.

Seager, Richard Hughes. *Buddhism in America.* New York: Columbia University Press, 2012.

Vanlandingham, Mark. *Weathering Katrina: Culture and Recovery among Vietnamese Americans.* New York: Russell Sage Foundation, 2017.

Zhou, Min, and Carl L. Bankston III. *Growing Up American: How Vietnamese Children Adapt to Life in the United States.* New York: Russell Sage Foundation, 1998.

NOTES

1. Carl L. Bankston III, "The Birth of Buddhism," in *Great Events from History: The Ancient World,* ed. Mark W. Chavalas (Pasadena: Salem Press, 2004), 376–378.
2. Central Intelligence Agency, *CIA World Factbook,* vol. 53 (Washington, DC: Central Intelligence Agency, 2016).
3. Ian Harris, "Sangha Groupings in Cambodia," *Buddhist Studies Review* 18 (2001): 65–72.
4. The Pew Forum on Religion and Public Life and Philip Connor, "Buddhist Migrants," in *Faith on the Move: The Religious Affiliation of International Migrants,* by The Pew Forum on Religion and Public Life and Philip Connor (Washington, DC: Pew Research Center, 2010), 39–42.
5. Readers can find a succinct general history of Southeast Asian refugee settlement in Carl L. Bankston III and Danielle Hidalgo, "The Waves of War: Immigrants, Refugees, and New Americans from Southeast Asia," in *Contemporary Asian America,* 3rd ed., ed. Min Zhou and Anthony C. Ocampo (Albany: New York University Press, 2007), 120–151.
6. US Census Department, "American Community Survey, 2016," Census.gov.
7. Canadian Encyclopedia, "Southeast Asian Refugees in Canada."
8. Statistics Canada (StatCan), "Data Tables, 2016, Immigration and Ethnocultural Diversity."
9. On Buddhism among Cambodians in Canada, see especially Janet McClellan, *Cambodian Refugees in Ontario: Resettlement, Religion, and Identity* (Toronto: University of Toronto Press, 2009).
10. Carl L. Bankston III and Danielle Hidalgo, "Temple and Society in the New World: Theravāda Buddhism and Social Order in North America," in *North American Buddhists in Social Context,* ed. Paul D. Numrich (Leiden, The Netherlands: Brill, 2008), 51–86.
11. David North and Noradeth Dithavong, *Profiles of Some Good Places for Lao People to Live in the United States* (Washington, DC: US Department of Health and Human Services, 1989).
12. Paul D. Numrich, "Theravāda Buddhism in America: Prospects for the Sangha," in *The Faces of Buddhism in America,* ed. Charles S. Prebish and Kenneth K. Tanaka (Berkeley: University of California Press, 1998), 147–162.
13. Charles S. Prebish, *Buddhism: The American Experience* (JBEOnline Books, 2004).
14. Edward R. Canda and Thitiya Phaobtong, "Buddhism as a Support System for Southeast Asian Refugees," *Social Work* 37 (1992): 61–67.
15. Lucy Starr Norman, "Cambodian Refugees Consider Temple a Tie with Lost Past," *Washington Post,* November 1, 1979, A4.
16. Nancy J. Smith-Hefner, *Khmer American: Identity and Moral Education in a Diasporic Community* (Berkeley: University of California Press, 1999).
17. Norman, "Cambodian Refugees," A4.
18. Inger Agger, "Calming the Mind: Healing after Mass Atrocity in Cambodia," *Transcultural Psychiatry* 52 (2015): 543–560.
19. Charlotte Evans, "Laotian Buddhist Monk Finds a 'Heaven' in Rye," *New York Times,* December 1, 1980, B2.
20. Carl L. Bankston III, "Bayou Lotus: Theravāda Buddhism in Southwestern Louisiana," *Sociological Spectrum* 17 (1997): 453–472.

21. Bankston, "Bayou Lotus," 453–472.
22. Bankston and Hidalgo, "Temple and Society," 51–86.
23. See, especially, Chean Rithy Men, "The Changing Religious Beliefs and Ritual Practices among Cambodians in Diaspora," *Journal of Refugee Studies* 15 (2002): 222–233.
24. Bankston, "Bayou Lotus," 453–472.
25. Min Zhou, Carl L. Bankston III, and Rebecca Kim, "Rebuilding Spiritual Lives in the New Land: Religion among Southeast Asian Refugees in the United States," in *Asian Immigration and Transplanting and Transforming Religions*, ed. Pyong Gap Min and Jung Ha Kim (Walnut Creek: Altamira Press, 2001), 37–70.
26. Louis-Jacques Dorals, "Faith, Hope, and Identity: Religion and the Vietnamese Refugees," *Refugee Survey Quarterly* 26 (2007): 57–68.
27. Quang Minh Thich, "Vietnamese Buddhism in America" (PhD diss., Florida State University, 2007).
28. Bruce Matthews, "Preface," in *Buddhism in Canada*, ed. Bruce Matthews (New York: Routledge, 2006), xvi–xxii.
29. Janet McClellan, "Buddhism in the Greater Toronto Area: The Politics of Recognition," in *Buddhism in Canada*, ed. Bruce Matthews (New York: Routledge, 2006), 105–119.
30. Louis-Jacques Dorais, "Buddhism in Québec," in *Buddhism in Canada*, ed. Bruce Matthews (New York: Routledge, 2006), 120–141.
31. James Placzek and Larry DeVries, "Buddhism in British Columbia," in *Buddhism in Canada*, ed. Bruce Matthews (New York: Routledge, 2006), 1–29.
32. Zhou, Bankston, and Kim, "Rebuilding Spiritual Lives."
33. Paul Rutledge, *The Role of Religion in Ethnic Self-Identity: A Vietnamese Community* (New York: Rowman & Littlefield, 1989).
34. Thuan Huynh, "Center for Vietnamese Buddhism: Recreating Home," in *Religion and the New Immigrants: Continuities and Adaptation in Immigrant Congregations*, ed. Helen Rose Ebaugh and Janet Chafez (Walnut Creek: Altamira Press, 2000), 45–66.
35. Allison Truitt, "Not a Day but a Vu Lan Festival: Celebrating Filial Piety in the Vietnamese Diaspora," *Journal of Asian American Studies* 18 (2015): 289–311.
36. Bruce Matthews, ed., *Buddhism in Canada* (New York: Routledge, 2006).
37. Wendy Cadge, *Heartwood: The First Generation of Theravāda Buddhism in America* (Chicago: University of Chicago Press, 2004).
38. Bankston and Hidalgo, "Temple and Society."
39. Carol A. Mortland, *Cambodian Buddhism in the United States* (Albany: SUNY Press, 2017).
40. Marybeth White, "Lao Buddhism in Toronto: A Case Study of Community Relations," in *Buddhism in Canada*, ed. Bruce Matthews (New York: Routledge, 2006), 105–119.

Carl L. Bankston III

SRI LANKA'S SINHALA BUDDHIST GUARDIAN DEITIES: SATARA VARAN DEVI

INTRODUCTION

The Sinhala phrase *satara* [*hatara*] *varan devi* is first deployed in a 15th-century inscription at Gadaladeniya Rajamahavihara (10 km west of Kandy in Uda Peradeniya) referring to Vishnu, Saman, Vibhīṣaṇa, and Skanda as divine protectors par excellence of Lanka during what is conventionally referred to as "the Gampola period" (mid-14th through early 15th centuries).[1] These four protectors, who are collectively labeled as the *satara varan devi* of Lanka in the Gadaladeniya inscription, are actually mentioned individually as part of a serial list of gods in an earlier 14th-century inscription found on a rock outcropping within the premises of the Buddhist *vihāra* of Lankatilaka, just a few kilometers south of Gadaladeniya. This earlier inscription, carved exquisitely in both the Sinhala and Tamil languages, refers to the sculpted images of Kihireli-Upulvan (later conflated with Vishnu; see fig. 1), Sumana (also known as Saman; see fig. 2), Vibhīṣaṇa-Ganapathi (probably an attempt to equate Vibhīṣaṇa with Ganesa; see fig. 3), and Kanda Kumara (also known as Kataragama Deviyo and Skanda; see fig. 4) along with their "spouses." All of these iconic figures were established in Lankatilaka's *devalaya* shrine that abuts and surrounds the *buduge* (buddha image house) at Lankatilaka.[2] This combination of *devalaya* and *viharaya* within the same building structure spatially represents two dimensions of Sinhala Buddhist religiosity: the *laukika* (immediate and this -worldly) and *lokottara* (eventual and otherworldly or soteriological end), respectively. Over time, these same deities came to be identified as *satara varan devi* in many literary and other inscriptional sources, and sometimes appeared in other various combinations to include Vishnu, Skanda, Saman, Vibhīṣaṇa, Natha, Pattini, Boksal, Aiyyanar, Pulleyar (Ganesa), and Mangara. By the mid-18th century, when the ritual proceedings of the *asala perahara*, the annual ten-night ritual processions of the *Dalada* (tooth relic of the Buddha) that became the preeminent public rite of the Kandyan kingdom, were fixed by King Kirti Sri Rajasimha (r. 1751–1782), Saman and Vibhīṣaṇa had been replaced by the goddess Pattini (the protagonist of the Tamil epic *Cilappatikaram*) and Natha (the devolved identity of the Mahāyāna bodhisattva Avalokiteśvara), the latter of which having been conflated with the "god of Senkadagala" (Kandy). In Kirti Sri's definitive identification of the *satara varan devi*, each of the major trajectories of religious traditions that had dominated South India in the previous millennium and a half (the Vaishnava, Shaiva, Shakta, and Mahāyāna Buddhist) were all represented as functional supporting castes to the Theravāda Buddha at the apex of a sociocosmic hierarchical conception. Before this 18th-century reification occurred, there were a number of apparent conflations among the deities who at times came to constitute the *satara varan devi* such as Upulvan with Rāma and Vishnu, Saman with Mahasena (a deified ancient king) and Lakṣmaṇa (from the *Ramayana*), Skanda (Siva's son in the *Puranas*) and Murugan (the South India mountain god who had become something of a Tamil national deity) with Kataragama Deviyo (a powerful local and regional deity in southeast Lanka), as well as elements of Vibhīṣaṇa's cult absorbed into Natha's. The history of religions from the 13th through the 18th century in Sri Lanka was a period of great flux and transformation, mirroring the continuously changing social and political history on the island.

Although the constellations of the *satara varan devi* specific to Sinhala Buddhist religious culture has its origins at least from the 14th century, the very concept of four protection deities derives its inspiration from many different preceding traditions in South Asian religious culture. While there exists extended scholarly explorations of the origins and evolution of Vishnu, Natha, and Pattini, antecedent traditions such as *caturmaharajika* (the four great cosmic kings) and *dikpāla* deities and their relation to Buddhist, Sanskrit Puranic, epic, South Indian, and literature relevant to local deities has not been examined in any great depth to date.[3]

The concept and significance of *caturmaharajika* and *dikpāla* deities likely owes its origins to the tradition of *lokapala* deities. Heinrich Zimmer located the origins of the *lokapāla* myth in "pre-Aryan" or "pre-Vedic cosmology." He notes especially a creation myth in the *Rigveda* imagining Mount Sumeru rising from the midpoint of the surface of the earth. At the vertical axis of the egg-shaped cosmos emerge four divine kings: Virūpākṣa in the west, Virudhaka in the south, Dhṛtarāshtra in the east, and Kubera-Vaiśravaṇa in the north, guarding each of the four quarters and ruling over *nagas*, gnomes, *gandharvas*, and *yakṣas*.[4] The summit, called Amarāvatī, is said to have been presided over by Indra, king of the gods.

It is probable that this concept of *lokapala* deities was filtered into the later *Rigveda* in an incipient form, in the same way as non-Sanskrit words from Dravidian and Mundarian sources were accommodated.[5] For example, a divinity in the *Rigveda* is described as guarding the regions through spreading out his arms in the form of Hiraṇyagarbha. One of the Rigvedic hymns identifies Hiraṇyagarbha as the ruler of the universe who controls it by enveloping or embodying.[6] Hiraṇyagarbha's protective aspect is also highlighted in this hymn qualifying him as the guardian deity of the whole world. The concept is elaborated in the *Viṣṇudharmottara Purāṇa*, composed between the 4th and 7th centuries CE, to show how Viṣṇu is the sole guardian of the universe.[7] In this context, Viṣṇu, who is understood as primordially formless, is also announced as possessing a form filling the entire universe with his eight arms, pointing to the "four quarters" and "intermediate directions."[8] In the next chapter of the same *purana*, the concept takes on yet another level of precision wherein the god is described as possessing five faces that represent the five basic elements (earth, water, heat, wind, and sky) and his ten arms represent the ten regions of the universe.[9] Here, numeric symbolism was deployed to articulate cosmological and ontological projections of substance and power.

The four different subjects or devotees of the *lokapala* deities (the *nagas*, spirits, *gandharvas*, and *yakṣas*) are also mentioned in various Vedic, Buddhist, Jain, and later Vedic sources variously reflecting imagined figures understood as ranging from pure evil to extremely pious forces. A general consensus among scholars is that these constructions could be indirect references to some of the non-Vedic tribes who came to interact with Vedic culture and were later embraced within it.[10] This interpretation, however, is decidedly uneven. Interaction was likely always a two-way process. From the beginning, Vedic culture in India was influenced by the mythologies and practices of non-Vedic tribes whose identities, in turn, were often collapsed by *brahmanas* into the residual categories of *yakṣas* or *rakṣasas*.[11] Here it is worth noting that Vibhīṣaṇa is identified in Valmiki's *Ramayana* as a *rākṣasa*, a category of nonhuman powers used in many sources as synonymous with *yakṣa*. Vibhīṣaṇa's wife, Saramā, is also mentioned as the daughter of a *gandharva* (divine musician) king, Sailusa, thereby reflecting how non-Vedic tribal names were often lumped together into the *yakṣa* classification.[12]

Although the notion of guarding various regions of the world continued to be part of Vedic and later Vedic understandings with different numbers of quarters (or regions) ranging from four to eight to ten within different schemes, they also came to be identified with specific *Rigvedic* deities such as Agni, Yama, Varuna, and Soma.[13] What this means is that in spite of the employment of the *lokapāla* concept, neither the non-Vedic *lokapālas* nor their subjects (*nagas*, spirits, *gandharvas*, *yakṣas*) per se were accepted wholesale as part of the Brahmanic divine world. In fact, early Vedic literature portrayed non-Vedic people and their deities as largely vulgar and deleterious forces. Later Vedic literature shows that there had been a gradual process of incorporation and transformation in which non-Vedic deities had earned a semidivine status before they were eventually recognized as fully divine.[14] Names and schemes varied from text to text. But one deity who became consistently established was Kubera.[15] This is significant, given Kubera's *yakṣa* status and his relation to his half-brother, Vibhīṣaṇa. The *Ramayana* mentions that Ravana expelled his older half-brother, Kubera, from his kingdom and took away his celestial chariot.[16] In the *Mahabharata*'s version, Ravana's younger brother, Vibhīṣaṇa, follows Kubera to his new kingdom whereupon Kubera appoints him as the head of the armies of *yakṣas* and *rakṣasas*.[17] This account portrays Vibhīṣaṇa not only as faithful to Kubera, but also how he won over his confidence and came to be regarded as the commander of the *rakṣasas* and *yakṣas*.

While Kubera was promoted as one of the *dikpālas* on par with other Vedic deities, the Vedic deities identified as *dikpālas* were being somewhat demoted in their status. This means guarding or protecting no longer was seen as a highest rank in the Brahmanic divine order. This shows further how later Brahmanic literature identified various non-Vedic guardian deities of villages and towns, deities who are ubiquitous throughout the Indian subcontinent, with their roots in the unknown past, as *kshetrapalas* ("lords of the fields") and placed them *outside* of the shrines to guard against deleterious characters and forces. Basically, the function of these *kshetrapalas* was not really to rule over subjects or respond to the plaints of devotees, but rather to keep the impurity of "evil" or disorder at bay.[18]

Unlike Brahmanic adaptations, the early Buddhists, as mentioned in the *Digha Nikaya*, incorporated the non-Vedic mythology of Sumeru (Mount Meru) and Amaravati into their own cosmological system.[19] Buddhists also retained the same non-Vedic *lokapalas*, often referring to them as *caturmaharajika devas* (four divine kings): Virupaksha (Virupakkha), Virudhaka (Virudaka), Dhṛtarāshtra (Dhatarattha), and Vaishravana (Vessavana/Kubera).[20] This generous incorporation occurred only on Buddhist terms, as these were labeled in their scriptures as a lower class of supernatural beings.[21] Their primary function in the Buddhist cosmos changed from guarding the regions of the world to protecting the Buddha per se. These gods appear in Buddhist art and sculpture as guarding the four cardinal points of Buddhist *stūpas* and attending on the Buddha during all major events of his life.[22]

The *Mahāmāyūrī* is a great example that shows how Buddhists incorporated hosts of non-Vedic and Vedic deities to fit into their scheme, with the Buddha as the warranting figure at the apex.[23] The text lists these deities in hierarchical order, *caturmaharajikas* (four world guardians) attending on the Buddha along with a list of the tutelary deities of 177 cities, twenty-eight *mahayakshas* (great *yakṣas*), and a multitude of female deities, all belonging to the *yakṣa* category. It is possible that the strategy in play here was this: by including these many deities worshiped by various different groups, Buddhist cosmology was to articulate a view that one and all are encompassed within this scheme. In any case, this exhaustive rendering contains not just Vibhīṣaṇa, Lankesvara ("lord of Lanka"), Ravana, and Vaishravana (Kubera), but also Indra, Vishnu, and Gopala (Krishna as a cowboy), all of whom are labeled as tutelary *yakṣas*! This must have been the Buddhist strategy of subsuming or subordinating non-Vedic, Vedic, and epic deities. The Buddhists did not deny their existence, but only put them in what they deemed a proper place. It could also have been a strategic ploy to enfold and subordinate Vaishnava traditions especially, including the deities of the great epics, by bringing deities such as Vishnu and Gopala down to the level of Ravana and other *rakṣasas*.

What is important for this discussion is the fact that deities like Vibhīṣaṇa are listed as guardian deities of a city, and so is Vishnu! What this indicates is that Vibhīṣaṇa, along with Vishnu, had established credentials as guardian deities of cities in mainland India before they were each included as one of the *satara varan devi* in Sri Lanka. On the one hand, while they demoted Vishnu, by this time so well-established in Puranic Brahmanism as a supreme deity, on the other hand, they elevated Vibhīṣaṇa, formerly only a *yakṣa* in Brahmanic literature.

Sinhala Buddhist culture was open to receiving not just the Buddhist *caturmaharajika* tradition, but also various schemes of Brahmanic *dikpāla* traditions as well. In doing so, the Sinhala Buddhists followed the path of early Buddhists in India (i.e., subsuming all of these supernatural figures into one category of deities). This is precisely what happened to *dikpāla* deities. The early evidence for the portrayals of *dikpāla* gods finds mention in the *Mahāvaṃsa* as four heavenly kings guarding a *stūpa* built by Duttagamani (101–77 BCE) in Anuradhapura following his defeat of Elara, the long-reigning and righteous Tamil king.[24]

While these guardian deity traditions can be understood as antecedent legacies for establishing a later formal tradition of *satara varan devi*, there was also another practice of precedence attributed to Sinhala rulers of the past: praying to spirits to protect the borders of their kingdoms. The *Mahāvaṃsa* mentions that Pandukabhaya (437–367 BCE), after establishing his kingdom in Anuradhapura, sets up shrines to various gods at the gates that faced four cardinal directions. In this context, of particular interest is a banyan tree shrine set up at the Western gate of Anuradhapura for Vessavana, or Kubera, along with a Palmyra-palm for the "Demon of Maladies."[25] Here again the appearance of Kubera as a *yakṣa* shows not only his non-Vedic roots but his prominence throughout the Indian subcontinent. This is an important detail, as his relation to Vibhīṣaṇa would be well-known, especially after Sri Lanka's identification with the *Rāmayān*'s Lanka. The practice of venerating deities as border guards remained alive and was part of the legacy for medieval Sri Lanka's *satara varan devi*.[26]

The intense interaction with South India and the influx of Indian mercenaries, traders, and others into the island brought several deities of Puranic, epic, and South Indian origins during the medieval period. For example, shrines were built to Pattini, the goddess of South India epic origins, Siva as Ishvara, Ganesha, Kandasamy (later identified with Kataragama Deviyo and Skanda), Aiyyanar, and Sudasun (Viṣṇu), along with local Lankan deities such as Mangara, Saman, Natha, and Upulvan.[27] By the 14th century, Sinhala Buddhist deity shrines not only included the gods from these different schemes (the *caturmaharajika, dikpāla* and *satara varan devi*), but also new deities such as Gaṇeśa, Suyama, and Santushita. While the Brahmanic religion subordinated village gods by making them guardian deities to guard temples from human thieves and evil spirits, medieval Sinhala Buddhists did the same thing functionally to Brahmanic deities by relegating their status to guard Buddhist shrines with the same intention.[28] Indeed, perhaps the best known eventual attribute of Vishnu is that he became known as the guardian of the *Buddhaśāsana* ("Buddhist tradition") per se.

For another example, in a 15th-century inscription at Gadaladeniya, Kanda Kumara was identified with the Vedic deity Skanda and then made into one of the guardian deities.[29] Or again, Boksal is associated with Alutnuwara, an important cultic site several kilometers to the west, associated with the popular deity Dadimunda. The reason Boksal is listed in the same category as the rest of the *satara varan devi* indicates that he was believed to be guarding one of the five regions identified as part of Kotte kingdom.[30] Later, in another context, Boksal was integrated with the South Indian deity Aiyyanar to become identified as one of the four guardian deities of Sinhala rulers.[31] In these instances, the choices of rulers and their religious advisors were probably guided either by their own or their subjects' preferences.

The function of Sinhala guardian deities seems to be symbolically reinforced in an inscription issued by the Alakeshvara rulers, who originally came from Kerala, and whose lineage ruled Kotte from the capital at Jayavardhanapura (1412–1597).[32] The inscription mentions that Alakeshvara protected his fort by building shrines to the *satara varan devi* (i.e., Kihirali [Upulvan], Saman, Vibhīṣaṇa, and Skanda Kumara at the four corners of the ramparts surrounding the palace).[33] This reference makes it clear that the main purpose of these *satara varan devi* was to protect Sinhala Buddhist rulers. This duty is in contrast to the task of *caturmaharajikas* and *dikpālas* who attend on the Buddha and whose function was clearly more cosmic than locally political.

In any case, the functioning concept of the *satara varan devi*, once it was politically instrumentalized, became a mainstay with successive rulers through the end of the Lankan monarchy and then through the colonial period into the present, thereby reflecting the religious sentiments of different groups who had come to form part of Sinhala Buddhist society and who, just like their Burmese and Thai counterparts, as noted by Hans-Dieter Evers, observed dual aspects (the cosmic and political) in their religious system, a development which was well-integrated into the symbolic articulations of complementary spaces of the "*viharaya* and *devalaya*."[34] While *viharaya* or *buduge* (image house) contains the image of the Buddha, *devalaya* hosts at least one, and in the case of Lankatilaka, all of the images of that version of the *satara varan devi*, thereby affording an opportunity for devotees to pay homage to the Buddha and gain merit before transferring the merit from their propitiations to a deity in the *devalaya* to help empower his progression as a bodhisattva through simultaneously helping his petitioning devotees in this world to lead safe and secure lives. Parenthetically, it is important to note that most contemporary devotees approach the various deities composing the collective *satara varan devi* for thoroughly *laukika* (immediately existential or mundane) reasons. Their hope for divine assistance is powered by the belief that the deity, warranted by the Buddha to act on his behalf, will exercise compassion and thereby further progress on the path to realize selflessness.

At Kelaniya Rajamahaviharaya, close to the modern capital of Colombo, Vibhīṣaṇa is the deity worshiped in his prominent *devalaya* as one of the *satara varan devi*. In the absence of royalty in the contemporary scene, the function of these *satara varan devi* has been understood in terms of hierarchical power and as constituting a "political geography." As Deborah Winslow noted succinctly:

> Varan (sanctioned authority) is delegated by higher beings to lower beings. The Buddha gave varan over all the Buddhist world to the highest god, Sakra, who in turn delegated varan for Sri Lanka to the Four Guardian Gods (*satara varan devi*). The Four Guardian Gods vary (by informant), but they are always drawn from among the gods just under Sakra, Natha, Vishnu, Skanda (also called Kataragama), Saman, Pattini, and Vibhīṣaṇa. In addition to being national guardians, these deities are also said to have delegated authority to provincial rulers, who in turn have delegated *varan* for local areas to lower local gods and goddesses.[35]

It was noted that Kanda Kumara, a local upcountry deity, became Skanda. In the same way Upulvan became Rāma and Vishnu, Saman merged with the Vedic deity Yama temporally and then with Lakshmana. That is, there occurred an uploading of the status of the deities once they figured in the constructions of *satara varan devi*. The sequencing of the process and the circumstances of these assimilations are further demonstrated in the wide variety of currents in play within the formulations of the *satara varan devi*, as illustrated in the following sections.

KANDA KUMARA-SKANDA

This is the only god with a residual Saivite identity among the four deities and, in many of the constructions of *satara varan devi*, who is not related somehow to *Ramayana* characters. He is first mentioned in the *Mahāvaṃsa* as being worshiped by a royal figure of the 7th century.[36] He absorbed the cult of Mahasena, one of the deified early Sinhala kings.[37] This fits into the profile of Skanda, who was worshiped as Mahasena (military commander of *devas*) by Kushana rulers in ancient India.[38] By the Fifteenth century, probably because Skanda, as the Puranic son of Śiva and Parvati, had become a popular Śaivite deity among South Indians who had emigrated to Lanka, Buddhist monks of renown *viharas*, as in the case of Vishnu, brought him into the Buddhist pantheon of deities by making him one of the guardian deities. This is clearly what happened at Lankatilaka. Considering his early Vedic status, this was comparatively a demotion. These Brahmanic high gods, such as Viṣṇu as well, were shorn of their soteriological significance and placed in functioning protective power. The local deity, Kataragama Deviyo, whose popularity is still known through many ceremonial songs handed down from generations past, was also blended into the identity of this god.[39] As shown in the Gadaladeniya inscription, Skanda was conflated with Kataragama Deviyo to constitute one of the *satara varan devi*. Thus, there are no less than three different strands of deities from Brahmanic and Buddhist contexts who were eventually enfolded into this one particular composite figure, which is no doubt one of the fundamental reasons that this deity remains one of the most popularly venerated gods in Sri Lanka.[40]

UPULVAN-RĀMA-VISHNU

The *Mahāvaṃsa* mentions that the god "in color like the lotus" (*uppalavannassa*), identified in Sinhala as Upulvan, was one of those to whom was entrusted the guardianship of Lanka by the Buddha on the advice of Sakka.[41] While this shows the continuation of the local tradition of venerating guardian deities, it also explains how the Buddhist layer was added on to bring the indigenous deity Upulvan into the Buddhist cosmos by assigning specific responsibilities. According to the *Cūḷavaṃsa*, royalty patronized Upulvan at least from the 9th century, with his popularity continuing into the 15th century in a temple dedicated to him at Devundara (now Devinuwara at the southern tip of the island).[42] Evidence shows that South Indian *brahmanas* who spoke Tamil served as priests in this temple and, as such, played a key role in the transformation of Upulvan into Rāma–Vishnu. The fact that Brahmin priests appointed in these temples spoke Tamil indicates that there was constant cultural flow between South India and Sri Lanka, an influence that led to the conflation of Upulvan, Dunu Deviyo (the "bow god"), and Rāma.[43] Rāma is often described in Sinhala *kavi* (poetry) as the carrier of the *randunu* (golden bow).[44] Rāma, along with his brother Lakṣmaṇa, were identified as two of the *satara varan devi*, fusing their identities with Upulvan and Saman, respectively.[45]

Rāma's merger with Upulvan is preserved in popular culture in the form of rituals performed to ward off impurities or evils.[46] One of the folk ballads, the *Sataran Waran Mal Yahana* ("Flower Altar of the Four Guardians") addresses the four guardian deities, acknowledging Vishnu as one of the four. The ballad describes Vishnu as holding Rāma's arrow in one hand and his golden bow in the other and being addressed as "bosat" (bodhisattva), revealing how Viṣṇu was understood by his Buddhist devotees as a buddha-in-the-making.[47] This new identity was actually a second demotion for Viṣṇu. As a supreme Vaiṣṇavaite deity in India, he was first understood to create and preserve the world in the Brahmanic scheme of cosmogony. When he was brought into the Sinhala Buddhist fold, his assignment changed to guarding the *Buddhaśāsana*, a first demotion. As is seen in places like Lankatilaka, bringing him in to be part of the *satara varan devi* was probably a master stroke strategically on the part of the Buddhist monk-scholars intent on subordinating the status of these gods, effectively making sure to slate them carefully within the hierarchy of Buddhist cosmology.[48]

Because Vishnu appeared in both schemes as one of the *dikpāla*s and later in the *satara varan devi*, some scholars have confused these schemes as one and the same.[49] Studying the paintings at Mahiyangana, William Ward used the word *lokapala*s (the Brahmanic scheme of *dikpāla*s) and *satara varan devi* as synonymous.[50] Ward identified one of the four deities as Viṣṇu. While it is true that Viṣṇu appears in the Brahmanic scheme of deities and then becomes part of the *satara varan devi*, it was only after his identity was conflated with the indigenous deity Upulvan that this occurred in Lanka. So, the function of this conflated Viṣṇu was not the same as the Vishnu in the Brahmanic scheme.

The discussion of Rāma (the preeminent of the ten *avatars* of Vishnu in Puranic literature) would not be complete without a note on what happened to the *Ramayana* in Sri Lanka during the colonial period. Colonial rule elicited many reactions from the Sinhala Buddhists, among them an explosion of literature with *Ramayana* themes.[51] This phenomenon was similar to what happened in India, as explained by Sheldon Pollock: "[T]he period of some two hundred years starting around the mid-twelfth century witnessed a coding of political reality via Ramayana themes such as did not exist—or at least not to anywhere near the same degree—in the previous era."[52] One of these adapted and short versions of the *Ramayana*, written in Pāli and belonging to either the late 18th or early 19th century, was the *Rāma Sandesa*. Here, a Buddhist monk composed this *sandesa* during the last years of the last Kandyan king, Sri Vikrama Rajasimha (r. 1798–1815). This text seeks blessings from Rāma to protect the ruler and the *Buddhaśāsana*, clearly identifying him with Vishnu–Upulvan in the temples located in Kandy and Hanguranketa.[53] Since it is composed in Pāli, the author's intention is not so much to make it accessible to the public. In John Holt's words about this text:

> It is a fitting summary of how Rāma was incorporated into the evolving portrayal of Visnu at the time of the Lankan kingship's disestablishment in the early nineteenth century. That the Upulvan/Rāma dimension of the "Buddhist Visnu" would fade in its importance in the nineteenth and twentieth century, and that the protector of the *Buddhaśāsana* motif would remain important, is indicative of the historical disappearance

of Lankan kingship, on the one hand, and the serious threat posed to the *Buddhaśāsana* by the intruding British and Christian presence, on the other.[54]

SAMAN-YAMA-LAKSHMANA

A third deity of the *satara varan devi* is Saman or Sumana, the god of Sumanakuta or Sri Pada.[55] Sumanakuta (Adam's Peak) is mentioned in the *Mahāvaṃsa* as one of the sites visited by the Buddha during one of his three visits to the island.[56] The mountain is also known in Sinhala as Samanola (the "abode of Saman").[57] Saman's main shrine is now in Ratnapura at the southern base of the mountain. First, Yama, the Vedic deity, who also appeared as one of the *dikpālas*, seems to have been identified with Saman. Probably because there was no ritual currency involving Yama, this identity also does not seem to have lasted very long. Saman, like Skanda and Vishnu, as noted, is portrayed as one of the *satara varan devi* at Lankatilaka. In an early 15th-century inscription in Saman's main shrine in Ratnapura, Saman came to be identified as Lakṣmaṇa, the stalwart brother of Rāma in the *Ramayana*. This identity has endured in popular forms of worship and ritual storytelling.[58] In addition in Saman's shrine in Ratnapura, some *yatikas* (prayers offered by *kapuralas*, deity shrine priests) directly identify Saman with Lakṣmaṇa.[59] How Lakshmana gained this identity can be deduced from the version of the *Ramayana* preserved in popular tales and rituals in which Lakṣmaṇa not only remains loyal to Rāma, but also, after the death of Rāvaṇa, on Rāma's bidding, goes into the city of Lankapura and oversees the coronation of Vibhīṣaṇa as Lanka's new king. As if to commemorate this key event, there are two images of this nature, the details of which are discussed here.

The first image portraying this scene comes from Kelaniya, the very cultic seat of Vibhīṣaṇa. At Kelaniya, unlike the rest of the guardian deities shown standing singularly, Vibhīṣaṇa appears seated on a throne along with his consort Sarama, on his left, and with Lakshmana, standing on his right, placing a garland around his neck. Both Vibhīṣaṇa and his consort raise their right hands in *abhaya mudra* (fearlessness or protection). The symbolism in this image is multivalent. It illustrates the key moment that is repeatedly told in poetry and legends that after Rāvaṇa was vanquished, Rāma entrusts Lakshmana to coronate Vibhīṣaṇa as the ruler of Lanka. As noted (see "Vibhīṣaṇa"), this is an important factor for Vibhīṣaṇa's cultic status. And this is also a critical moment for Lakṣmaṇa, as this helps him to acquire an elevated divine status. In the panel, Vibhīṣaṇa looks handsome by anthropomorphic standards except for the tusks that protrude on either side of his lips, the telltale signs of his *rakṣasa* past. His gesture of *abhaya* establishes his main function of protection of the people of Sri Lanka as a god-king (*devarāja*).

Although the focus in this image is Vibhīṣaṇa's coronation, Lakshmana's crucial role is also clear. Probably for this reason, Sinhala Buddhists hold special affection for Lakshmana as a guardian deity, since his conflation with the indigenous Saman is apparent.

VIBHĪṢAṆA

While the induction of Rāma is attributed to the apparent popularity of the *Ramayana*, Vibhīṣaṇa's gaining of the same status can be attributed to the belief that Sri Lanka is the Lanka of the *Ramayana*. His origins as a *yakṣa* and his relationship with Kubera might have also played a role in his veneration. Starting from the 14th century, he is singularly identified as one of the *satara varan devi* both in inscriptions and in *sandesa* literature. The *Uttamala Sandesa,* written in Pāli by the Buddhist monk Gathara, not only praises him as a great friend and protector of Lankadipa (Sri Lanka), its ruler Parakramabahu, and the *Buddhaśāsana*, but also as an enemy to those who deviate from *dhamma* (the Buddha's teaching).[60]

This is an elevated position for Vibhīṣaṇa, whose duty is now not just guarding the kingdom, but also the *Buddhaśāsana* per se, thereby qualifying him as a bodhisattva, an ideal in line with the aspiration of Sinhala Buddhist rulers.[61] The assumption here is that the island is Dhammadīpa (island of *Buddha dhamma*) and as such punishing those deviating from *dhamma* forms part of Vibhīṣaṇa's responsibility. *Yatikas* (priestly petitions) recited to Vibhīṣaṇa do describe his bearing of weapons depicting his warrior dimension.

Here is a succinct version of Vibhīṣaṇa's profile as known from the generic *yatika* recited by the contemporary *kapurala* in his Kelaniya *devalaya*:

> Going to the island of Sri Lanka—shining with bright splendor,
> Becoming a king at that time—he became famous as king Vasvis.
> Having this king as husband, the Queen named Naikasi
> Begot a prince and he became famous by the name Vibhīṣaṇa.
> Full of steady, deep virtues—endowed with a fierce radiance of glory,
> The prince named Vibhīṣaṇa glittered in the world like the Sun.
> His glorious brother was named Rāvaṇa, who defeated the three worlds.
> The Princess named Sītā, the Queen of Prince Rāma,
> [was] Kidnapped [by Ravana] and brought here. In the war that followed
> Vibhīṣaṇa crossed over to the side of Rāma leaving his brother Ravana.
> Prince Rāma defeated Rāvaṇa in the war and became victorious,
> Saved Princess Sītā in this lovely Lanka,
> Handed over Lanka to Vibhīṣaṇa for protecting its people.
> This is how Prince Rāma returned to Dambadiva [India].[62]

These verses, although surprisingly brief, agree in general with the outline of Valmiki's *Ramayana*. At the same time, using phrases such as "kidnapped and brought her here," "in this lovely Lanka," the prayer clearly identifies "Lanka" with Sri Lanka and Vibhīṣaṇa as native to the island. While it certainly praises Vibhīṣaṇa as the protagonist of the story, it does not miss the opportunity to take pride in Ravana's valor. There are no laudatory remarks for Rāma except for a simple statement that Rāma returned to India with Sita only after entrusting Lanka to Vibhīṣaṇa so that he would protect its people. Notice that not just Vibhīṣaṇa but Ravana also receives praise as a "glorious brother . . . who defeated the three worlds." The poem also succeeds in drawing a boundary line between outsiders and insiders: Rāma and Sītā belong to India while the brothers, Rāvaṇa and Vibhīṣaṇa belong to Sri Lanka. This is probably a reflection of how Rāma eventually disappeared into Vishnu who himself was downsized, while Vibhīṣaṇa, who started as a *yakṣa* with credentials as native to and ruler of the island, organically acquired the same stature as Vishnu in the Sinhala Buddhist cosmos. At least this is true in his *devalaya* at Kelaniya where multitudes of his devotees continue to throng to worship him.

NATHA

The origins and eventual incorporation of Natha into the *satara varan devi* cannot be attributed to a transformation of a deity of originally Brahmanical beginnings. However, there is an indigenous element present in his mature composite configuration. Natha's original identity was none other than Mahāyāna bodhisattva Avalokiteśvara, whose cult had thrived from the 8th through the 11th centuries, largely in the south and southeastern littorals of the island (based on an analysis of surviving sculpture [Holt, 1991, 72–90]).[63] In the Sinhala upcountry, he eventually came to be regarded as the indigenous "god of Senkadagala" (the oldest name for the city of Kandy, the late medieval upcountry royal capital of Lanka) and ultimately as the tutelary deity of the dynasty of Kandyan kings from the late 16th through the early 19th centuries. It is not until Kirti Sri's reorganization of the *asala perahara* in the 1750s that Natha seems to have been identified formally as one of the *satara varam devi* of the Kandyan kingdom (Holt, 1996).[64] His central *devalaya* (deity shrine), the oldest remaining architectural structure in the city of Kandy today, is located adjacent to the *Dalada Maligava* (Temple of the [Buddha's] Tooth-Relic) and the former royal palace. Natha's shrine became the ritual hub for annual rites celebrated throughout the kingdom. But of greater significance is the fact that Natha finally came to be identified as the deity who would eventually be reborn as Metteyya (Sanskrit: Maitreya; Sinhala: Maitri), the future buddha following Gotama's dispensation. Maitri will again make known the *dhamma* for the soteriological benefit of those reborn during his time (Holt, 1991, 214–215).[65] As such, Natha is regarded by many devotees as the highest and most virtuous of the Sinhala deities, ranking immediately below the Buddha Gotama at the apex of the divine hierarchy. Like the *devalayas* dedicated to other higher deities in the Sinhala pantheon, Natha's shrines also field *laukika* petitions from the faithful on *kemmura days* (Wednesdays and Saturday mornings), the most inauspicious times of the week when people are more likely to feel the greatest need for divine compassion (*karuṇā*). Compassion has remained the divine trait most commonly associated with him since his introduction to the island as Avalokiteshvara. The iconography of Natha images in his *devalayas* dating from the 14th to the 18th centuries remains consistent with Avalokiteshvara's insofar as he is always depicted with a buddha in his crown, indicating not only his near buddha status, but his unequivocal identification with the *lokottara* soteriological path. His epithet of Natha derives from Lokanatha ("lord of the world"), a name often given to Avalokiteshvara wherever his cult spread throughout South and Southeast Asia (Holt, 1991, 41).[66] Significant for the religion as a whole, relevant to the needs of local people where his shrines are located, Natha epitomizes the nature of Buddhist divinity insofar as he responds compassionately to the immediate existential needs of his petitioners while simultaneously embodying and symbolizing their future soteriological hopes. He is both *laukika* (present–this-worldly) and *lokottara* (future–otherworldly) significant. Indeed, the performance of meritorious acts of positive karmic efficacy by laity are often motivated by the desire to be reborn in Maitri's future time. Often, merit derived from these karmic actions is ritually transferred to deceased family members so that they might gain rebirth in Maitri's era too. This motivation for rebirth during Maitri's era is not limited to the Sinhala Buddhist context, but can be found in virtually all other Theravāda-oriented religious cultures as well (Holt, 1993).[67] Natha is therefore the one deity among the *satara varan devi* who bridged the orientations of *laukika* and *lokottara*, indicated at the outset of this article.

CONCLUSION

As laid out in this article through sketching the progression of the concept of guardian deities, religious leaders of Vedic, Buddhist, and Puranic religious orientations incorporated the concepts and cults of various tribes or emigrants into their respective religious practices as a way to accommodate them, yet subordinate them into their fold. The concept of guardian deities was first appropriated by Vedic priests who, for the most part, were reticent in accepting tribal cults as guardian deities, while the early Buddhists in India seemed to make quick progress in winning over different tribes by folding their cults into part of the popular Buddhist pantheon of deities. The Buddhists also included Vedic and Puranic deities in their scheme. These accommodations did not change Buddhist soteriology, as these deities were organized hierarchically and mobilized functionally to serve the purposes of the Buddha and his *sangha* and *sasana*. This strategy of accepting and subordinating an assortment of deities was later followed by Sinhala Buddhist monks and rulers in Sri Lanka, as illustrated at some length. Tracing the evolution of the *satara varan devi*, with a focus especially on, say, Vibhīṣaṇa, along with his companion guardian deities, demonstrates how these adaptations fit the religious sentiments of different groups and were somewhat tactical, political, and context oriented. This proved to be effective in maintaining Buddhism as the religion of the political hierarchy while also meeting the practical religious needs of plebian Buddhist practitioners. Moreover, as is the case of Natha, as well as with others, these deities also eventually were tied to the soteriological or *lokottara* orientation of the tradition by being identified as bodhisattvas, or "buddhas-in-the-making." While that is so, it is more likely the case that in places like Lankatilaka and Kelaniya, today devotees continue to approach the Buddha in the *buduge* to make merit first and then proceed to the *devalaya* to pray to their chosen deity, whether Vibhīṣaṇa, Vishnu, Skanda, or others, for help with their worldly worries and existential concerns, thereby addressing the "dual orientations" of the religion: the *lokottara* (ultimate) and *laukika* (immediate or practical).

REVIEW OF LITERATURE

Scholarly discussions of the *satara varan devi* per se are very limited and usually consist of passing references in most secondary sources of Sri Lankan cultural history or Buddhism. The references provided in "Further Reading" and in the text notes comprise an extensive guide to the topic of deities within the Buddhist religious culture of Sri Lanka.

One of the reasons that the study of deities in Theravāda Buddhism has been limited in the past, especially by Euro-American scholars, is due to the manner in which the Buddhist religion has been construed as an anthropocentric and rational spiritual path, beginning with 19th-century philologists and then influential social scientists such as Durkheim and Weber.[68] Moreover, other Westerners, such as the American reformer and theosophist Henry Steele Olcott and his protegee, the Anagarika Dharmapala, or Thomas William Rhys Davids, and Caroline A. F. Rhys Davids and I. B. Horner, who pioneered the translation efforts of the Pāli Text Society, all emphasized the nontheocentric nature of Buddhist soteriology.[69] The nature and function of deities in the lives of Buddhists was regarded as peripheral or nonessential.

Beginning in the last half of the 20th century, scholars such as S. J. Tambiah, Gananath Obeyesekere, and Richard Gombrich wrote influential books based on fieldwork that brought the significance of the supernatural within Theravāda Buddhist religious culture into sharp focus, in the process theorizing the importance of deities in the daily religious lives of most Buddhist people.[70] While S. Paranvitana had earlier published studies on Saman and Upulvan, which were based on the material residues of their cults, Tambiah, Obeyesekere, and Gombrich framed the significance of deity veneration within the context of cosmology, ritual, ethics, and soteriology.[71] Gombrich's study was especially lucid in relation to how the powers of various deities, including those of the *satara varan devi*, are understood as active forces in the lives of Buddhists in traditional highland Sri Lanka. Obeyesekere's study of Pattini was also a scholarly landmark in terms of the ritual and textual materials collected, but problematic insofar as his interpretations tended to force a psychoanalytic understanding on the cult, largely ignored the ethnotheological perspectives of Sinhala and Tamil adherents, and left the upcountry Kandyan region out of his considerations. Moreover, his general discussion of Sinhala deities mistakenly minimized the continuing importance of deities such as Natha and Vishnu, whose cults continue to thrive. Extensively researched interdisciplinary studies by John Holt on Natha and Vishnu, and Sree Padma's studies of Vibhīṣaṇa, are the most recent scholarly efforts aimed at providing a nuanced understanding of the importance of deities in the history, art history, ritual, and devotional expressions of Sri Lankan Buddhists who venerate *satara varan devi*.[72]

PRIMARY SOURCES

Primary sources and references to primary sources on the cults of deities comprising the *satara varan devi* may be found in Gombrich, Obeyeskere, and Holt.[73]

FURTHER READING

Duncan, James. *The City as Text: The Politics of Landscape Interpretation in the Kandyan Kingdom*. Cambridge, UK: Cambridge University Press, 1990.

Geiger, Wilhelm. *Culture of Ceylon in Mediaeval Times*. Wiesbaden, Germany: Otto Harrassowitz, 1960.

Gombrich, Richard. *Precept and Practice: Traditional Buddhism in the Rural Highlands of Ceylon*. Oxford: Clarendon Press, 1971.

Holt, John Clifford. *Buddha in the Crown: Avalokiteśvara in the Buddhist Traditions of Sri Lanka*. New York: Oxford University Press, 1991.

Holt, John Clifford, ed., and Meddegama, Udaya, trans. *The Anagatavamsa Desana: The Sermon of the Chronicle-to-be*. Delhi: Motilal Banarsidass, 1993.

Holt, John Clifford. *The Buddhist Visnu: Religious Transformation, Politics and Culture*. New York: Columbia University Press, 2004.

Holt, John Clifford. 1996. *The Religious World of Kirti Sri: Buddhism, Art And Politics in Late Medieval Sri Lanka*. New York: Oxford University Press.

Mirando, A. H. *Buddhism in Sri Lanka in the 17th and 18th Centuries*. Dehiwala, Sri Lanka: Tisara Prakasakayo, 1985.

Obeyeskere, Gananath. *The Cult of the Goddess Pattini*. Chicago: University of Chicago Press, 1983.

Padma, Sree. "Are *Satara Varan Devi* Sinhala Buddhist Deities? Vibhīṣaṇa, A Case Study." *Sagar* XXVI (2018): 92–119.

Padma, Sree. "Borders Crossed: Vibhīṣaṇa in the Ramayana and Beyond." *South Asia: Journal of South Asian Studies* 42, no. 3 (September 2019): 747–767.

Paranvitana, S. *The God of Adam's Peak*. Ascona, Switzerland: Artibus Asia, 1958.

Seneviratne, H. L. *Rituals of the Kandyan State*. Cambridge, UK: Cambridge University Press, 1978.

Winslow, Deborah. "A Political Geography of Deities." *Journal of Asian Studies* 43 (1984): 273–284.

NOTES

1. The authors acknowledge with gratitude the assistance of Tilak Jayatilleke, Konara Buddhika, and the *kapuralas* at the Vibhisana *devalaya* at Kelaniya and Visnu *devalaya* at Lankatilaka. Some of the content in this article was published earlier in Sree Padma, "Are Satara Varan Devi Sinhala Buddhist Deities? Vibhīṣaṇa, A Case Study," *Sagar* XXVI (2018): 92–119; and John Holt, *The Buddhist Visnu: Religious Transformation, Politics, and Culture* (New York: Columbia University Press, 2004).
2. S. Paranavitana, *The Shrine of Upulvan at Devundara. Memoirs of the Archaeological Survey of Ceylon*, vol. VI (Colombo: Archaeological Department, 1953), 21, note 2; Kingsley de Silva mentions the images of the same set of *satara varan devi* existing in Gadaladeniya; see K. M. De Silva, *A History of Sri Lanka* (New Delhi: Penguin Books, 2005), 51, 54, 92–93.
3. John Clifford Holt, *Buddha in the Crown: Avalokiteśvara in the Buddhist Traditions of Sri Lanka* (New York: Oxford University Press, 1991); John Holt, *The Buddhist Visnu: Religious Transformation, Politics and Culture* (New York: Columbia University Press, 2004); and Gananath Obeyesekere, *The Cult of Goddess Pattini* (Chicago: University of Chicago Press, 1984).
4. Heinrich Zimmer, *The Art of Indian Asia: Its Mythology and Transformations*, ed. Joseph Campbell, vol. 1 (Princeton, NJ: Princeton University Press, 1968), 47.
5. Asko Parpola, *Deciphering the Indus Script* (Cambridge, UK: Cambridge University Press, 1994), 133, 137, 140.
6. *The Hymns of the Rigveda*, trans. Ralph T. H. Griffith, 2nd ed. (Kotagiri, India: A. A. Macdonell, 1896), 487 [10–121].
7. Stella Kramrisch, *The Vishnudharmottara*, 2nd ed., part III, *A Treatise on Indian Painting and Image-Making* (Calcutta, India: Calcutta University Press, 1928), 5.
8. Kramrisch, *The Vishnudharmottara*, III, chap. 47, 70.
9. Kramrisch, *The Vishnudharmottara*, III, chap. 48, 71.
10. N. N. Bhattacharya, *Indian Demonology* (New Delhi: Manohar, 2000), 122–126; Gail Sutherland, *The Disguises of the Demon* (Albany: State University of New York Press, 1991), 66; and L. A. Waddell, "Evolution of the Buddhist Cult, Its Gods, Images and Art," *Imperial and Asiatic Quarterly* 66 (January 1912): 126.
11. To show the relation between *raksasas* and *yaksas*, it is said that they were born of the same mother, possessing red eyes and dark bodies; see Bhattacharya, *Indian Demonology*, 111. Later Vedic literature identifies *yaksa* "as a species of certain non-human beings, demons, ogres or spirits"; see O. H. de A. Wijesekera, "The Philosophical Import of Vedic Yaksa and Pāli Yakkha," *University of Ceylon Review* 3, no. 1 (April 1945): 73–95.
12. Ralph T. H. Griffith, trans., *Ramayana* (Benaras, India: Lazarus, 1915), 7, 11–12; and Bhattacharya, *Indian Demonology*, 138.
13. Sutherland, *Disguises of the Demon*, 65, 180; and J. N. Banerjea, *The Development of Hindu Iconography* (Calcutta, India: University of Calcutta, 1956), 519ff.
14. Bhattacharya, *Indian Demonology*, 41; and Ram Nath Misra, *Yaksa Cult and Iconography* (New Delhi: Munshiram Manoharlal, 1981), 59–70.

15. Sutherland, *Disguises of the Demon*, 65.
16. Bhattacharya, *Indian Demonology*, 112–114.
17. Sutherland, *Disguises of the Demon*, 63–64.
18. Sutherland, *Disguises of the Demon*, 80.
19. Prithvi Kumar Agrawala, "The Kumbhnada Figures in Sanchi Sculpture," *East and West* 37 (1987): 179–189; and Zimmer, *Art of Indian Asia*, 47.
20. E. Senarat, ed., *Mahavastu*, vol. III, 217, 309 (Paris: Impremerie Nationale 1882–1897); S. Lefmann, ed., *Lalitavistara* (Halle, Germany: Leben und Lehre, 1908), chap. XXIV; and E. B. Cowell and R. A. Neil, eds., *Divyavadana* (Cambridge, UK: Cambridge University Press, 1886), 147.
21. Robert Decaroli explains the ways in which what he calls the native South Asian cults of "spirit deities" have been inducted into Buddhism; refer to Robert Decaroli, *Haunting the Buddha: Indian Popular Religions and the Formation of Buddhism* (New York: Oxford University Press, 2004).
22. J. P. Vogel, *Indian Serpent-Lore* (London: A. Probsthain, 1926; repr. Varanasi, India: Indological Book House, 1972), 213; Aurel Stein, *Ancient Khotan* (Oxford: Clarendon Press, 1907), figs. 30–31, pl.11; Alfred Foucher, *The Beginnings of Buddhist Art*, trans. L. A. Thomas and F.W. Thomas (Paris: P. Geuthner, 1917), 171, pls. XXVI 2; XXVII; G. Yazdani, *Ajanta* (New Delhi: Gyan Books, 1930), pt. I, pt. II, 6–7, plate IX; James Burgess, *The Buddhist Stūpas of Amaravati and Jaggayyapeta in the Krishna District, Madras Presidency*, vol. 6 (London: Trubner, 1887), 45, pl. xvii, fig. 1, pl. xviii, fig. 1; and Robert Knox, *Amaravati: Buddhist Sculpture from the Great Stūpa* (London, British Museum Press, 1992), pl. 61.
23. V. S. Agrawala and Sylvan Levi, "Geographical Contents of Mahamayuri," *Journal of Uttara Pradesh Historical Society (JUPHS)* XV, no. II (1942): 24–52; and Moti Chandra, *Jain Miniature Paintings from Western India* (Ahmedabad, India: S. M. Nawab, 1949), 15.
24. W. Geiger Tr., *Mahāvaṃsa* (London: Pāli Text Society, 1934), XXX, 89.
25. *Mahāvaṃsa*, X, 89–90.
26. W. A. de Silva, "Ceremonial Songs of the Sinhalese Guardian Spirits (Deva)." *Journal of the Ceylon Branch of the Royal Asiatic Society of Great Britain &Ireland* 28, no. 73 (parts I–IV, 1920): 36.
27. Siri Sunandasabha Mahathera, ed., *Paravi Sandesa* (Matara, Sri Lanka: Mudrana Yantralaya, 1925), 140; Mudaliyar C. Rasanayagam, *Ancient Jaffna* (New Delhi: Asia Educational Services, 1984), 331ff; D. B. Jayatilaka, ed., *Tisara Sandesa* (Colombo, Sri Lanka: Lankabhinava Visruta Press, 1935), 83; to learn about Mangara's myth and ritual, see Gananath Obeyesekere, "The Vaddas: Representations of the Wild Man in Sri Lanka," in *Beyond Primitivism: Indigenous Religious Traditions and Modernity*, ed. Jacob K. Olupona (New York: Routledge, 2004), 272–294: David Scott, *Formations of Ritual: Colonial and Anthropological Discourses on the Sinhala Yaktovil* (Minneapolis: University of Minnesota Press, 1994), 103–104; *Culavamsa*, trans. Wilhelm Geiger (London: Humphrey Milford, 1929), XCVII, 46, XCIX, 42, C, 248.
28. C. J. Fuller, "The Hindu Pantheon and the Legitimation of Hierarchy," *Man*, n.s. 23 (1988): 20.
29. Senarath Paranavitana and Humphry William Codrington, eds., *Epigraphia Zeylanica (EZ)*, vol. IV (London: Oxford University Press, 1943), 21, 25, 26.
30. The names of these five regions differed in records issued under Kotte rulers at various times. "In modern times the 'Five Countries' were Denuvara (Udanuvara or Yatinuvara), Tumpane, Harispattuva, Dumbara, and Hevahate." See Paranavitana and Codrington, *EZ*, IV, 20.
31. Holt, *Buddha in the Crown*, 131, 133. According to H. Parker's version as guardian deity, Vibhisana gradually replaced Vishnu; see H. Parker, *Ancient Ceylon* (New Delhi: Asian Educational Services, 1981), 668.
32. Amaradasa Liyanagamage, "Keralas in Medieval Sri Lankan History: A Study of Two Contrasting Roles," *Kalyani: Journal of the Humanities and Social Sciences of the University of Kelaniya* 5, no. 6 (1986): 73.
33. G. P. V. Somaratne, "Jayawardhanapura: The Capital of the Kingdom of Sri Lanka c. 1400–1565," *Sri Lanka Archives* 2 (1984): 3.

34. Hans-Dieter Evers, "Buddha and the Seven Gods: The Dual Organization of a Temple in Central Ceylon," *Journal of Asian Studies* 27, no. 3 (May, 1968): 541–542.
35. Debora Winslow, "A Political Geography of Deities: Space and the Pantheon in Sinhalese Buddhism," *Journal of Asian Studies* 43, no. 2 (February, 1984): 275.
36. *The Mahāvaṃsa* mentions Kajaragama five times and Kataragama once, both of which are identified as the place for Skanda; see *Mahāvaṃsa*, XIX, 54, 62; XLV, 45; LVII, 2, 66; LVIII, 6. For details about the cult of Kataragama, see Sunil Goonasekera, *Walking to Kataragama* (Colombo, Sri Lanka: International Center for Ethnic Studies, 2007).
37. *Mayurasandesa* (*abinava*) refers to a temple in Dewundara as that of Mahasena or Skanda; see Hugh Nevill, "Sinhala Verse (Kavi)," *Ethnology*, ed. P. E. P. Deraniyagala, vol. 3 (Ceylon: Ceylon National Museums Manuscript Series, vol. VI, 1955), 130.
38. Richard D. Mann, "The Early Cult of Skanda in North India: From Demon to Divine Son" (PhD diss., McMaster University, 2003), 200–203.
39. de Silva, "Ceremonial Songs," 16–17.
40. See Gananath Obeyesekere, *Medusa's Hair* (Chicago: University of Chicago Press, 1984).
41. *Mahāvaṃsa*, VII, 2–9; and Nevill, "Sinhala Verse (Kavi)," 171–173, 183; vol. 2, 118.
42. *Culavamsa*, LXXXII, 49, LXXXV, 85–89, XC, 100–102; B. Gunasekera, *A Contribution to the History of Ceylon* (Colombo, Sri Lanka: Mudaliyar, 1815), 47; *Hamsa Sandesa*, ed. R. Dharmakirtti Sri Dharmarama (Colombo, Sri Lanka: Pradhana Nayaka Mahimi, 1926), 51; *EZ*, III, no. 36, 333ff.
43. Joseph Pearson, ed., *Memoirs of the Colombo Museum*, vol 6 (Colombo, Sri Lanka: Colombo Museum, 1914), 70–74; *EZ*, III, 331–337; and D. E. Hettiaratchi, "Civilization of the Period: Literature and Art," in *History of Ceylon*, ed. H. C. Ray, vol. I, part II (Colombo, Sri Lanka: Ceylon University Press, 1960), 770–778.
44. There are three poems, *Randun Pralaya, Randun Kavi*, and *Randun Upata*, that recite Rāma-Visnu-Nararayana as carrying the golden bow; see Nevill, "Sinhala Verse (Kavi)," vol. 3, 171–173.
45. S. Paranavitana, *The God of Adam's Peak* (Ascona, Switzerland: Artibus Asiae, 1958), 4–78.
46. C. E. Godakumbura, "The Ramayana: A Version of Rāma's Story from Ceylon," *Journal of the Royal Asiatic Society of Great Britain and Ireland* no. 1 (April, 1946): 14–22. Although the Kohomba Kankariya rite claims its origins to the 5th century BCE when it was supposed to have been performed for King Panduvasadeva, the earliest literary reference to the rite is made only in the 15th century; see also Holt, *The Buddhist Visnu*, 227.
47. Holt, *The Buddhist Visnu*, 145–146.
48. Much of *sandesa* literature was authored by the Buddhist monks. See M. H. F. Jayasooriya, ed., *Kokila Sandesa Warnana* (Sinhala) (Colombo, Sri Lanka: Mahabodhi Press, 1962); Rapiel Tennakoon, ed., *Sevul Sandesaya* (Colombo, Sri Lanka: M. D. Gunasena, 1968); Kumaratunga Munidasa, ed., *Gira Sandesa Viwaranaya* (Colombo, Sri Lanka: K. A. Ariyadasa, 1963); Kumaratunga Munidasa, ed., *Mayura Sandesaya* (Colombo, Sri Lanka: M. D. Gunasena, 1963); A. V. Suraweera, ed., *Tisara Sandesaya* (Colombo, Sri Lanka: S. Godage Brothers, 2006); Rev. Kitalagama Devamitta, *Kirala Sandeshaya ha Mayura sandeshaya* (Colombo, Sri Lanka: M. D. Gunasena, 1961); Punnada, *Wattaka Sandesaya* (Ambalangoda, Sri Lanka: Vidyaprakasa Press, 1900); and D. J. B. Wijesekara, *Wana Sevul* (Colombo, Sri Lanka: Lankabhinawa Press, 1916).
49. For example, in Lankatilaka, Visnu is seen in the *viharaya* within the *torana* of the buddha image as part of the *devamandala* serving the buddha while also portrayed as one of the *satara varan devi* in his *devalaya*. His appearance in *deva mandala* has been consistent from this period onward, although Asoka de Zoysa reports that the tradition started a little later. See Asoka de Zoysa, *Madawala Viharaya Revisited* (Colombo, Sri Lanka: S. Godage and Brothers, 2014), 211.
50. William Ward, "Recently Discovered Mahiyangana Paintings," *Artibus Asiae* 15 (1952): 108–113.

51. James Alwis, *Ravana Hella*; K. R. Perera, *Ravana Yuddhaya*; Hugh Nevill, *Janakavi Sangrahaya*. The titles of Palm leaf manuscripts in the British Museum: *Ran Dun Deviya, Yatu Kumara Kavi, Hakgedi Santhiya, Randun Alngiya, Randun Mangalya,* and *Randunu Parale.*
52. Sheldon Pollock, "Ramayana and Political Imagination in India," *Journal of Asian Studies* 52, no. 2 (May 1993): 273.
53. Holt, *The Buddhist Visnu*, 142–145.
54. Holt, *The Buddhist Visnu*, 146.
55. In Sinhala Kavi, "mountain" is referred to as "samanala"; see Nevill, "Sinhala Verse (Kavi)," vol. 3, 183.
56. *Mahāvaṃsa*, I, 33: "Mahasumana of the Sumanakuta mountain" is said to have received a handful of hairs from the buddha in a golden urn and heaped them with gems etc., at the place where the buddha sat and that's where later a *stūpa* was built; *Culavamsa*, XCVII, 30–32, LXXXVI, 19–29: "magnificent image of Sumanadeva (taken) to the Sumantakuta . . . and set up in the courtyard of the cetiya of the sacred footprint" (for veneration); I, 77: "the Master . . . left the traces of his footsteps plain to sight on Sumanakuta"; VII, 67; XV, 96–97; XXXII, 49–50.
57. *EZ*, vol. II, 217.
58. Nevill, "Sinhala Verse (Kavi)," 3 (1955), 183: "Saman Deviyo is the deified spirit of the brother of Rāma who vanquished Ravana"; see also de Silva, "Ceremonial Songs," 17.
59. Anuradha Seneviratne, "Rāma and Ravana: History, Legend and Belief in Sri Lanka," *Ancient Ceylon: Journal of the Archeological Survey Department of Sri Lanka* 5 (1984): 234.
60. Harishchandra Abeyaratne, *Historical Information from Uttamala Sandesa (Medieval Sri Lankan History)* (Colombo, Sri Lanka: S. Godage, 2003), 84–85.
61. Decaroli, *Haunting the Buddha*, 9.
62. *Yatika* recorded when the *kapurala* recited his praise to Vibhisana in his shrine at Kelaniya (Udaya Meddegama, trans.).
63. Holt, Buddha in the Crown, 72–90.
64. John Clifford Holt, *The Religious World of Kirti Sri: Buddhism, Art And Politics in Late Medieval Sri Lanka.* (New York: Oxford University Press).
65. Holt, *Buddha in the Crown*, 214–215.
66. Holt, *Buddha in the Crown*, 41.
67. John Clifford Holt, and Udaya Meddegama, trans., *The Anagatavamsa Desana: The Sermon of the Chronicle-to-be* (Delhi: Motilal Banarsidass, 1993).
68. See the introduction to Emile Durkheim, *The Elementary Forms of Religious Life* (New York: Free Press, 1995), and the opening chapter focused on Buddhism in Max Weber, *The Religions of India* (New York: Free Press, 1958).
69. See Olcott's "Diary Leaves," in *The Sri Lanka Reader: History, Politics and Culture*, ed. John Clifford Holt (Durham, NC: Duke University Press, 2011), 335–349.
70. S. J. Tambiah, *Buddhism and the Spirit Cults of North-East Thailand* (Cambridge, UK: Cambridge University Press, 1970); Gananath Obeyesekere, *The Cult of the Goddess Pattini* (Chicago: University of Chicago Press, 1983); and Richard Gombrich, *Precept and Practice* (Oxford, UK: Clarendon Press, 1967).
71. S. Paranvitana, *The God of Adam's Peak; and The Shrine of Upulvan at Devundara. Memoirs of the Archæological Survey of Ceylon.*
72. Holt, *Buddha in the Crown*; *The Buddhist Visnu*; Padma, "Are *Satara Varan Devi* Sinhala Buddhist Deities?"; "Borders Crossed: Vibhīṣaṇa in the Ramayana and Beyond," *South Asia: Journal of South Asian Studies* 42, no. 3 (September 2019): 747–767.
73. Gombrich, *Precept and Practice*; Obeyesekere, *The Cult of the Goddess Pattini*; Holt, *Buddha in the Crown*; *The Buddhist Visnu*; see also Goonasekera, *Walking to Kataragama.*

Sree Padma and John Holt

THE STUDY OF VISUAL CULTURE IN SOUTH AND SOUTHEAST ASIAN BUDDHISM

Doctrinal studies, assuming a perpetuating hierarchy of textual supremacy over visual material, often define the field of Buddhist studies to this day. Even though the role of Buddhist imagery and visual culture in the study of Buddhism has been given more credence in recent decades, it still suffers from two major problems that will be addressed throughout this article. Firstly, greater attention should be paid to "emic" understandings, that is, understandings drawn from the perspective of those who participate—or once participated—in the Buddhist visual culture being studied. Secondly, the study of visual culture should be more closely integrated with other methods generally used in the study of Buddhism, namely, philology, epigraphy, and anthropology.

With these two points in mind, we now turn to a historical overview of the study of Buddhist art and the visual culture of South and Southeast Asia, in an attempt to clear away the inherited undergrowth that blocks us from seeing it historically. Only by enlarging the scope of how visual material is studied can we understand how it can be more meaningfully used to illuminate the world of Buddhist practice.

EARLY BUDDHIST VISUAL CULTURE

Buddhist visual culture originated on the Indian subcontinent following the historical life of Siddhārtha Gautama, approximately in the 5th to 4th century BCE, and thereafter evolved through contact with other cultures as it spread throughout South and Southeast Asia and beyond. For approximately five hundred years after the historical Buddha departed, the Lord was never portrayed anthropomorphically in South Asian Buddhist art, even though perfectly realized images of Yakṣas, Nāgas, Apsarās, and others had already come into execution.[1]

This early phase is generally called "aniconic" in Buddhist art historical literature, a term that became popular with pioneer scholars in the field like Alfred Foucher (1865–1952) and Ananda K. Coomaraswamy (1877–1947), who were the first to publish research on the subject in the early 20th century.[2] Foucher suggested that the initial nonappearance of the Buddha in Indian or Gandhāran art was not due to a lack of technical skill, but simply to the absence of the idea of representing an anthropomorphic Buddha. Furthermore, he related that Buddhist texts, "from an iconographical point of view," were blank, "as sterile as the researches on the spot."[3] He thus argued implicitly for what Tryggve Mettinger, in his study of Jewish art, later described as "*de facto* aniconism,"[4] that is, a nonprescriptive absence of an anthropomorphic deity. From that point on, the accepted wisdom in Buddhist art was that visual signs or symbols such as a wheel, a tree, a seat, or footprints represented actual scenes from the life of the Buddha, or even, perhaps, represented the Master himself without depicting him physically.[5]

A Buddha footprint (*buddhapāda*), a bodhi tree, or a *stūpa* can indeed serve as a focal point for worship and commemoration. Hence each of these could function as an "icon" or image on its own (*mūrti*, *pratimā*, or *rūpa* in Sanskrit). The issue at stake then becomes that the Buddha was initially represented symbolically through what Gilles Béguin calls "non-manifested images" (*avyaktamūrti*), perhaps echoing ancient Vedic traditions of not representing gods anthropomorphically.[6] Bodhi trees, *stūpas*, and Buddha footprints as cult objects are widespread in Buddhist Asia. Hence, it may be unsuitable to speak of an "aniconic" phase that would have preceded an "iconic" period. Indeed, such representations could often be used side by side. In other words, Buddha images did not suddenly replace *stūpas* and other indexical symbols of the Buddha—rather they coexisted over a long period of time up until this day.

This traditional theory of "aniconism," however, has come under heavy criticism by Susan Huntington, who focuses attention on the presumed absence of a Buddha figure in early Buddhist visual culture.[7] Her most effective strategy involves reading early narrative panels as devotional processions, reenactments, and even "portraits" of the famous sites of Indian Buddhism after the lifetime of the Buddha, rather than as representing the original events. Instead of straightforward depictions of episodes in the Buddha's life, she interprets the majority of early Indian reliefs as representing the activities of *darśana* (literally "looking at," "seeing," or "viewing"). This includes ritually paying respect or homage to a sacred image or devotional object, depicting the associated events contemporary to the sculptor, and portraying important pilgrimage sites (*tīrtha*s). If Huntington is correct, these reliefs would be a record of secondary celebrations and lay devotional practices of the primary events of the Buddha's lifetime.[8] Accordingly, the platforms or seats (*āsanas*), often placed in front of bodhi trees, or the wheel-pillars depicted in reliefs from Bhārhut, Sāñcī, Amarāvatī, and other locations would represent actual relic-thrones at the major Buddhist pilgrimage sites as well as the sacred nuclei of worship.

Thus, according to Huntington, the vacant or empty throne would not so much show the presence of the Buddha per se, but rather remind us of his sitting place and leave us with his physical absence after he had already departed. One could object, however, that at times the invisible presence of the sitting and missing Buddha was precisely implied artistically through the scene of worship focused on a sacred empty throne. Therefore, we believe that the depiction of the throne in early Buddhist visual culture should not be seen purely as a symbol or "aniconic substitute" for the physical form of the Buddha. On the contrary, it was rather an artistic means to indicate his invisible and ineffable presence at sacred sites going back to his lifetime.

In sum, while a large number of reliefs adorning the railings and drums of early Buddhist *stūpas* in India can be understood as generic scenes of worship, they are sometimes supplemented by other inscriptions and iconographic devices that help associate them more firmly and ritually with the life of the Buddha. Naturally, the ravages of time have taken their toll on the Buddhist art and architecture that we find and deal with in modern times. We do not see much of the color painted on sculptures. Nor do we find paper or highly mobile and fragile cloth art items, although these must have been circulating in south Asia very early. Buddhist devotees in India and beyond thus developed their own myths and legends over the centuries concerning the first portrait of the Buddha on cloth paintings (*paṭa*).[9] Keeping this in mind, we could suggest that early textual and oral Buddhist narratives, along with the related reliefs found chiseled in stone, were paralleled by narrative cloth scrolls that brought those folk stories, worship scenes, and ritual processions down to the level of living people.[10]

IMAGES AND TEXTS

What is the relationship between the various Buddhist scriptures and early Buddhist visual culture? Can Buddha images or Buddhist symbols be "read" and interpreted in the light of such texts? Should Buddhist iconography be studied and understood solely in the context of early Buddhist narratives? Or can it be better understood through the examination of later iconographic treatises, or even ritual manuals? How shall we explain the occasional discrepancies between the known texts and extant imagery? Do we still have sufficient preserved texts and images to even ask these questions?

As we endeavor to answer these questions, an important factor to consider is the possible impact of art on narrative texts concerned with the life of the Buddha. Indeed, some of the earliest Buddhist narratives in India are not literary texts but sculpted low reliefs from Bhārhut and Sāñcī (*c.* 2nd–1st centuries BCE). It is clear that these works of art chiseled in stone could have easily influenced the biographical and oral tradition dealing with the Buddha's life. For example, one of the pillars at Sāñcī *stūpa* no. 1 has a representation of a monkey making an offering of a bowl of honey to the Buddha, whose presence is suggested by a tree and an empty throne.[11] This brings to mind the miraculous episode that supposedly took place at Vaiśālī, commonly found in the early Buddhist art of India, but not in the literary texts until centuries later. Similarly, Buddhologist Étienne Lamotte has pointed out that artists often drew their inspiration from texts, but that texts were sometimes, in turn, influenced by the works created by the sculptors in ancient India.[12]

Another way that artworks may have influenced texts relates to the peculiar "characteristics of the Great Man" (*mahāpuruṣalakṣaṇa*), that is, of the Buddha. Several of these distinctive marks, such as the cranial protuberance said to be like a turban (*uṣṇīṣa*) or the tuft of hair between the eyebrows (*ūrṇā*), have elicited speculation among scholars. Another physical sign, explained in many texts, is that the Buddha had webbed fingers (and toes) like the feet of a swan. This is probably the result of some confusion caused by the technical exigencies of the sculptural medium, which must leave a "web" of stone between the unfolded fingers of the Buddha image to avoid breakage. It thus appears obvious that many Buddhist texts may have been regularly revisited and interpreted in light of these artistic practices.

STYLE AND ICONOGRAPHY

In the study of Buddhist art and architecture, a crucial distinction between style and iconography is often made. Buddhist iconography is generally defined as prescriptive and regulated by texts, and so it does not easily change from one region to another except when certain iconographic innovations are introduced. Conversely, style reflects the diversity of regional aesthetics and visual cultures, as well as historical developments. Style is quite fluid, depending on the date and the geographical origin of the material object or structure, although some Indian artistic schools, such as the Gupta or Pāla styles, did enjoy transregional fame.

The architectural structure of the *stūpa*, for example, has spread widely across Buddhist Asia, taking on many diverse forms and names as region-specific details were incorporated into the design. Yet the *stūpa*'s overall function and symbolism remain the same: a monumental structure where sacred relics can be kept safe and venerated.[13] In the same vein, buddha or bodhisattva images, irrespective of where or when they were created, are normally clearly identifiable by informed Buddhists, thanks to iconographic devices or specific attributes known to them. According to tradition, the representation of the Buddha, for instance, should convey the ideals of the thirty-two major characteristics of the Great Man, although some of these distinctive marks are not publicly visible and, at any rate, many others are rarely depicted in images or sculptures of the Buddha. By definition, all buddhas are alike, and the biography and iconography of Śākyamuni (the historical Buddha Gautama) conditioned those of past, future, and other transcendental buddhas. Thus, at times, positive identification of buddha images remains problematic for art historians. Sometimes epigraphical or textual evidence adds data to our inferences, but each case also depends on its specific cultural, ritual, and archeology/archeological context.[14]

Similarly, the origins and identifications of the Bodhisattva Avalokiteśvara in early Buddhist art have long been controversial. There is no firm evidence of when worship and artistic production of Avalokiteśvara began in south Asia.[15] Many believe that the concept originated in Gandhāra or Mathurā in the early centuries CE, which saw the gradual rise of the Mahāyāna movement, but there are no decisive arguments and attempts to locate a cult of Avalokiteśvara (and Amitābha) in Gandhāran art have been bitterly disputed in recent decades.[16] In general, discrepancies between art, inscriptions, and texts are widespread. For this reason, the interpretations of art historians, who chiefly study the style and iconography of buddha and bodhisattva images, often diverge from those of Buddhist textual scholars, who are generally more well-versed in philological and epigraphical studies. Rarely do these two categories of scholars agree on a single interpretation. Sadly, collaborative efforts and research between philologists, epigraphists, and art historians remain the exception.[17]

Even among art historians, disputes arise as to the identification of the Bodhisattva Avalokiteśvara.[18] While some scholars suggest that early Avalokiteśvara images already have a number of distinctive iconographic features that clearly separate him from Prince Siddhārtha, the future Buddha Maitreya, or other celestial bodhisattvas, others argue that these features cannot conclusively identify Avalokiteśvara, since they can be found at times in other bodhisattva images as well.[19] For example, the lotus flower held in one hand and the small buddha effigy presumably found in Avalokiteśvara's headdress may both appear in other images as well, making a positive identification of bodhisattvas problematic. However, the iconographic ambiguity we find in early cult images of Avalokiteśvara is due to a lack of context; it may not have posed the same problems in the past for local contemporary Buddhists in India. With the sudden emergence of Indian esoteric Buddhism in the material, epigraphical, and textual records from approximately the 7th century onward, a new class of devotees, donors, and patrons frequently inscribed ritual images with significant mantras and specific *dhāraṇīs* often linked to certain Buddhist deities.[20]

TERMINOLOGY IN ART HISTORY

Generally speaking, Sanskrit terminology is quite prevalent among art historians' descriptions of Buddhist art and architecture. Such technical vocabulary, however, can be quite perplexing and bring confusion when repeated without questions. Thus, a deeper knowledge of Buddhist texts, practices, and rituals altogether would be helpful for art historians in the study of Buddhist iconography.

It is indeed useful to make clear distinctions, for nonspecialists, between certain terms that are often used uncritically such as *stūpas* and *caityas*—the latter name gave rise to the words *chedi* in Thailand and *zedi* in Myanmar. Often these terms are considered synonyms in English, but they are not. For instance, on one hand, a *caitya* or "object of veneration" is not necessarily a *stūpa*, although all *stūpas* are regarded as *caityas*. Strictly speaking, a buddha image or a bodhi tree can also be regarded as a *caitya*. On the other hand, the cognate word "pagoda," seems to have a different etymology from *dhātugarbha* or *dägaba* in Sinhalese, later transliterated as "pagoda" by Westerners in the colonial era. In the narrow sense, as a depository location for a relic (*dhātu*), "pagoda" is equivalent to an Indian *stūpa*, but stylized as a tiered tower with multiple eaves as commonly seen in Nepal, China, Vietnam, Korea, and Japan. It is uncommon in Myanmar, Thailand, Cambodia, and other parts of South or Southeast Asia except, of course, in modern Chinese temples as a product of the Chinese diaspora. The generic term often refers in English to religious complexes in a broader sense although "pagoda" would not be an accurate word to describe an Indian Buddhist temple (*vihāra*). Nor would it be accurate for describing a Southeast Asian monastery compound, known as *kyaung* in Myanmar or *wat* in modern Thailand, Laos, and Cambodia.

Conversely, there are inappropriate cases where English religious terms predominate in the description of certain Buddhist artifacts. For example, the term "votive," which is used extensively in the English- and French-language literature (as in "votive tablets or *stūpas*"), seems equally improper. In fact, these Buddhist tablets bear little similarity to other objects for which the term is commonly used in Western art, such as the medieval Christian plaques (*ex voto*) expressing gratitude to a saint that crowd the walls of European churches. This terminology, which still dominates art historical literature, is most likely influenced, consciously or not, by the pioneering work on Buddhist art by the French art historian Alfred Foucher, whose views were profoundly embedded in the Catholic practices and popular traditions of his day. One such view is that these artifacts were possibly manufactured at the great holy Indian sites as souvenirs (*memento*) for pilgrims, as with those acquired at Lourdes in France. As Peter Skilling has stressed, however, this interpretation has no basis in Buddhist texts, rituals, or in the archeology/archeological record.[21] Although it is impossible to know what they were originally labeled in India, clay-molded miniature Buddhist images are called *tsha tsha* in Tibetan, possibly deriving from the Sanskrit word *sañcaka*. In Thailand today, the images are simply named "holy sealings" or "imprints" (*phra phim*). In Cambodia, they are similarly qualified as "sacred images" (*braḥ patimā*), while in Myanmar they are called "sacred terracotta" (*mye-bon-hpaya*). Other terms, such as "clay sealings," "stamped" or "molded images," and so on, have been scarcely used. Employing different terms may also encourage scholars to reflect upon, and question, the ritual functions of these artifacts.

RITUAL POSES (*ĀSANAS*) AND GESTURES (*MUDRĀS*)

The importance of *āsanas* (sitting postures) and *mudrās* (ritual hand gestures) in understanding Buddhist visual culture and iconography has often been stressed by art historians. Yet, the extant textual tradition, composed or compiled mainly during the late Indian medieval period, cannot always explain the use of such terms. These expressions have become standardized today and are widely used by scholars with little question of their appropriateness.[22] Such jargon, however, is rooted in some inherent misconceptions. We should be aware that these terms are neither indigenous nor known to have been used in East and Southeast Asia. Most likely, the terminology was initially limited to certain times and places in South Asia, in very specific ritual contexts. It is not known to have been used early, broadly, or even consistently in a Buddhist environment, at least probably not before the early second millennium CE.

The traditional Sanskrit term for "hands," used in drama treatises such as the *Nāṭyaśāstra*, is *hasta*. Conversely, the term *mudrā* literally means "seal" or "signet ring," and becomes a polyvalent term in tantric praxis, referring to a variety of different things, including a female tantric consort. As *mahāmudrā*, or the "great seal," it refers to a body of tantric teachings. The term was never used in iconographic texts to describe the hands of the deities—let alone those of the Buddha—represented in art. Its usage should be limited to "hand gestures" used in later tantric texts or in a ritual context where *mudrās* are performed by the worshipper, the priest, or the visualized deity.

Similarly, *āsana*, or its equivalent term *pīṭha*, literally means "a sitting place," "a seat," or "a stool," and it is only by extension that it came to designate a particular "sitting posture" in Sanskrit. In Pali sources, however, *āsana* never means "posture" per se, for which there is a completely different term. In Theravāda Buddhist countries such as Thailand, buddha images are thus found in four natural postures or attitudes (*iriyāpatha*): standing, sitting, lying down, and walking (a Thai artistic innovation from Sukhothai in the 13th–15th centuries CE).

To give a more specific example, the Sanskrit term *bhadrāsana* was initially conceived as an object, a good, worthy, or auspicious seat (typically elevated or raised) that is equivalent to the *bhadrapīṭha* of Indian lore. The "auspicious throne," or *bhadrāsana*, thus originally signaled the glorious and royal—even cosmic—status of its occupant (whether that was a buddha or a bodhisattva). Similarly, the sitting posture with legs pendant, also called *bhadrāsana* (previously, and wrongly, dubbed "European posture" in the literature) owes its origin to the same royal and "auspicious" throne-seat.[23] But it is only from the Pāla period onward (*c.* 8th–12th centuries CE), that the term also has a demonstrable textual basis as a sitting pose in south Asia. During this period, it occurs in at least one iconographic treatise and several late tantric Buddhist ritual texts, also composed in Sanskrit. The earliest known extant example of the term *bhadrāsana* being used to signify "sitting posture" comes from the *Citrakarmaśāstra*, a *śilpaśāstra* possibly composed in southern India or Sri Lanka in the late first or early second millennium CE.[24]

LIVING TRADITIONS AND LIVING ICONS

While Buddhism is often considered a single living tradition in many parts of South and Southeast Asia, it follows several parallel paths as it continues to evolve and be produced, both religiously and artistically, in varying forms and in various times over the globe. Indeed, it might be best to reconsider the idea of a "single" religious institution and see Buddhism participating in several traditions as it engages with the lives and customs of the people who practice it. While most scholars understandably focus on antiquities that have achieved international fame, and thus led to inappropriate standardizations of what "Buddhist art" is, much modern Buddhist visual culture remains unstudied, because scholars are not sufficiently attuned to the many contemporary expressions of Buddhism taking place throughout the world today.[25] Many of these are already or have the potential of producing their own artistic language. Here we can think, for example, about the long, painted Prince Vessantara scrolls of northeast Thailand, as well as other art being created outside of urban centers that receives little attention from art historians.[26] Any art historian and anthropologist of Buddhism ought to draw attention to this constantly emerging work. Otherwise, people will always think that Buddhist art is only located in the past.

Moreover, for Buddhists across all traditions, an image of the Buddha is more than just a picture, a souvenir, or a piece of art; it is a surrogate for the Buddha, imbued with all his qualities. In China and Japan, this is nicely recounted by narrative means through the legend of King Udayana who, in the absence of the Lord, is said to have ordered the carving of the first sandalwood image of the Buddha in his own likeness.[27] This legend is also known in Sri Lanka and mainland southeast Asia, although the frame story differs in many respects and is always associated there with King Pasenadi the Kosalan.[28] This alone explains how and why these Buddha icons are still treated by Buddhist devotees with utmost reverence as living beings and are worshiped with offerings of flowers, incense, candles, and sometimes clothes, food, and water. In their natural settings of monastery, temple, or altar in the home, these Buddha images are placed above the heads of worshipers on a special pedestal.

Consecration ceremonies govern the making of all Buddha images, regardless of their size or the substance from which they are made.[29] This is done prominently by celebrating the "opening of the divinity's eyes."[30] The same holds true for all Buddhist artifacts or other indexical (non-figural) signs of the Buddha, such as *stūpas* (and the relics enshrined therein), bodhi trees, footprints, and so on. That is to say that for Buddhist devotees, any consecrated Buddhist icon should not be kept outside places of worship. Naturally, for the enjoyment of Western tourists or amateurs, and also for security reasons, foreign museums, and art galleries worldwide usually forbid the in situ worship or even physical "viewing" or auspicious contact with these displayed icons, thus participating in what has been called the "secularization of Buddhism" through their "aesthetic objectification."[31] While these objects are often presented only to please the eyes or for scholarly reasons, museums increasingly understand that traditions evolve, and that public interaction is integral to appreciation. Thus, Buddhist art as a sacred and devotional tradition can and should be presented and understood in emic terms in a museum setting. While, as Skilling has written, "Buddhist art was not made to be viewed in a museum,"[32] Western galleries are beginning to show that they might not be antithetical to a dynamic view of Buddhist art and practice.[33]

WORK OF ART AND WORK OF MERIT

How, then, is Buddhist visual culture in South and Southeast Asia to be perceived from an emic perspective? Looking at the insider's core values, one must ask why so much effort was made in the past in producing Buddhist art, even though it was, at times, seldom physically seen. For example, the magnificent reliefs carved on gateways and railings at Sāñcī and many other Buddhist monuments in India and southeast Asia are placed too high to be viewed. Is the emic value of a Buddhist icon or relief always dependent on its visibility?

Small Buddhist images or ornamented tablets are often deposited or enshrined within *stūpas* and within larger Buddhist icons. Unseen, they nevertheless emanate potency. In Japan, there is also the concept of "hidden" or "secret buddhas" (*hibutsu*). These are famous statues which are concealed from general public view and are more or less permanently unavailable for worship, although they can be brought out for specific religious ceremonies on rare occasions.[34] The concealment of such powerful icons is again intended to emphasize their power and transcendence, as in the case of the Emerald Buddha or Phra Kaeo Morakot, the most famous Buddha icon in Thailand.[35] It may also serve to protect them from ritual pollution by the impure influences of the mundane world, or to preserve the personal privacy of these living embodiments of the Buddha.

In Buddhist art, the beneficial action of making merit (*puṇya*) for patrons and donors, along with their family members and ancestors, was and still is crucial. This concept also mattered to the artists and craftsmen who were paid or commissioned to produce artworks. Thus, in its original, emic context, the value of Buddhist art may lie primarily in its production for the sake of making merit, i.e., good deeds, often driven by an ideology of reward.[36] The prototypical understanding of Western art, in contrast, assumes that art is produced primarily for the viewer's aesthetic gaze and to communicate the essence of an idea. These ideas are central to the Western approach to art interpretation.

Ideally, a new and innovative approach to studying Buddhist visual culture in the West would seek to bridge the artificial gaps between the various disciplines (textual, art, and anthropological studies), as it challenges similarly synthetic Buddhist categories, such as "Theravāda" or "Mahāyāna." Scholars are becoming cautious about imposing clean models based on their own backgrounds which push them into thinking that things conform to their constrained expectations. Removing the artificial framework these terms convey thus paves the way to studying Buddhist art more within its original and diverse Asian context.[37]

This new approach can only be taken through the comprehensive study of sites and objects, taking into account their various historical, local, and cultural contexts. The rich legacy of Buddhist art and architecture produced in South and Southeast Asia is inspired by the veneration of relics and icons, and the rituals associated with them. But art and rituals are often temporally and culturally specific. While the material record is generally the product of ideologies for which the analysis of liturgies, inscriptions, and literary narratives is helpful, the material object or work of art in front of us must be allowed to convey its multitude of meanings and values. Additionally, the contemporaneous exploration of ongoing Buddhist artistic, ritual, and textual practices will more adequately inform us of how older objects were active. In other words, much more remains to be studied.

REVIEW OF LITERATURE

The last few decades of the 20th century and the early years of the 21st century have been stimulating for the field of visual culture studies in South and Southeast Asian Buddhism. New archeology/archeological discoveries; a new awareness of the dynamic nature of Buddhist practice today; and important publications that have shed new light on several historical periods, geographical areas, and iconological subjects have all substantially broadened the field. Monographs on specific aspects of Buddhist art history and iconography published during this period appeal to a wide range of audiences. There are highly specialized books, written by art historians like Claudine Bautze-Picron,[38] Pia Brancaccio,[39] or Robert L. Brown.[40] There are also less technical manuals or textbooks intended for general readers and students, but still written or edited by specialists, including Gilles Béguin,[41] Kurt Behrendt,[42] and Pratapaditya Pal.[43] Finally, there are more focused catalogues of exhibitions (organized by curators like Pierre Baptiste and Thierry Zéphir,[44] Forrest McGill,[45] and John Guy[46]), aimed at museum goers, art lovers, and collectors of Indian and southeast Asian antiquities.

Meanwhile, a new approach focusing more on praxis has also emerged in South and Southeast Asian Buddhist studies. This approach has been pioneered in the works of textual scholars, epigraphists, and anthropologists such as Gregory Schopen,[47] Yael Bentor,[48] Peter Skilling,[49] Justin McDaniel,[50] John S. Strong,[51] Donald K. Swearer,[52] and Leedom Lefferts.[53] These authors have published several new interpretations and translations of Buddhist texts or inscriptions, and have often studied Buddhist ritual practices in relation to texts and objects.

This in turn raises the question as to whether artwork is a "text" that can be easily "read." The problem of linking text to images, and vice versa, has been frequently acknowledged but seldom studied by textual specialists. Hopefully, Buddhist studies scholars, philologists, epigraphists, and anthropologists will gradually incorporate more aspects of Buddhist visual culture and the study of art into their examination of texts, practices, and rituals. Bernard Faure, an expert on Japanese religions, once affirmed that "Buddhist art, if there is such a thing, is perhaps too important to be left to art historians alone."[54] His main point is that we must see Buddhist artifacts in interaction with, and activated by, human behavior. Thus, the study of art, material, and visual cultures is becoming a more integral part of religious and Buddhist studies.[55] Further cooperative work across disciplinary lines is needed for the in-depth study of Buddhism in South and Southeast Asia.

FURTHER READING

Appleton, Naomi, Sarah Shaw, and Toshiya Unebe. *Illuminating the Life of the Buddha: An Illustrated Chanting Book from Eighteenth-Century Siam*. Oxford: Bodleian Library, 2013.

Brancaccio, Pia, and Kurt Behrendt, eds. *Gandhāran Buddhism: Archaeology, Art, Texts*. Vancouver, Canada: University of British Columbia Press, 2006.

Chirapravati, Pattaratorn. "Buddhism and Thai Art." *Religion Compass* nos. 3–4 (2009): 566–579.

Eck, Diana. *Darśan: Seeing the Divine Image in India*. Chambersburg, PA: Anima Books, 1985.

Fraser-Lu, Sylvia, and Donald M. Stadtner, eds. *Buddhist Art of Myanmar*. New York: Asia Society, 2015.

Gifford, Julie A. *Buddhist Practice and Visual Culture: The Visual Rhetoric of Borobudur*. London: Routledge, 2011.

Green, Alexandra. *Buddhist Visual Cultures, Rhetoric, and Narrative in Late Burmese Wall Paintings*. Hong Kong: Hong Kong University Press, 2018.

Huntington, Susan L. *The Art of Ancient India*. With contributions by John C. Huntington. New York: Weatherhill, 1985.

Kim, Jinah. *Receptacle of the Sacred: Illustrated Manuscripts and the Buddhist Book Cult in South Asia*. Berkeley, CA: University of California Press, 2013.

Leoskho, Janice. *Sacred Traces: British Explorations of Buddhism in South Asia*. Aldershot, UK: Ashgate, 2003.

McDaniel, Justin. "The Bird in the Corner of the Painting: Some Problems with the Use of Buddhist Texts to Study Buddhist Ornamental Art in Thailand." *Moussons* no. 23 (2014): 21–53.

Park, David, Kuenga Wangmo, and Sharon Cather, eds. *Art of Merit: Studies in Buddhist Art and its Conservation; Proceedings of the Buddhist Art Forum 2012*. London: Archetype, 2013.

Revire, Nicolas. " 'The Birth of the Buddha' at Angkor." *Journal of the Siam Society* 107, no. 2 (2019): 63–90.

Revire, Nicolas. "Glimpses of Buddhist Practices and Rituals in Dvāravatī and Its Neighbouring Cultures." In *Before Siam: Essays in Art and Archaeology*, edited by Nicolas Revire and Stephen A. Murphy, 240–271. Bangkok: River Books, 2014.

Revire, Nicolas. "'Kinsman of the Sun': An Early Buddha Image in the Asian Art Museum, Berlin, and Solar Symbolism." *Indo-Asiatische Zeitschrift* nos. 20–21 (2017): 3–14.

Revire, Nicolas. "Solar Symbolism in Early Buddhist Literature." *Berliner Indologische Studien/Berlin Indological Studies*, no. 23 (2017): 143–156.

San San May, and Jana Igunma. *Buddhism Illuminated: Manuscript Art from Southeast Asia*. Seattle: University of Washington Press, 2018.

Tan, Heidi, ed. *The Many Streams of Buddhist Art in Thailand*. Singapore: Asian Civilisations Museum, 2012.

Zwalf, Wladimir, ed. *Buddhism: Art and Faith*. London: British Museum Press, 1985.

NOTES

1. For a detailed overview of this vast subject, see Yuvraj Krishan, *The Buddha Image: Its Origin and Development* (New Delhi: Munshiram Manoharlal, 1996); Klemens Karlsson, "The Formation of Early Buddhist Visual Culture," *Material Religion: The Journal of Objects, Art and Belief* 2, no. 1 (2006): 68–95; and Robert DeCaroli, *Image Problems: The Origin and Development of the Buddha's Image in Early South Asia* (Seattle: University of Washington Press, 2015).
2. Alfred Foucher, *The Beginnings of Buddhist Art and Other Essays in Indian and Central-Asian Archaeology* (Paris: Paul Geuthner, 1917); Ananda K. Coomaraswamy, "The Origin of the Buddha Image," *Art Bulletin* 9, no. 4 (1927): 287–329; and Juhyung Rhi, "Reading Coomaraswamy on the Origin of the Buddha Image," *Artibus Asiae* 70, no. 1 (2010): 151–172.
3. Foucher, *Beginnings of Buddhist Art*, 8–9.
4. Tryggve N. D. Mettinger, *No Graven Image? Israelite Aniconism in Its Ancient Near Eastern Context* (Stockholm: Almqvist & Wiksell, 1995).
5. See Susan L. Huntington, "Early Buddhist Art and the Theory of Aniconism," *Art Journal* 39, no. 4 (1990): 401–408; and Huntingon, "Aniconism and the Multivalence of Emblems: Another Look," *Ars Orientalis* 22 (1992): 111–156. *Contra* Huntington, see Vidya Dehejia, "Aniconism and the Multivalence of Emblems," *Ars Orientalis* 21, no. 1 (1991): 45–66; Rob Linrothe, "Inquiries into the Origin of the Buddha Image: A Review," *East and West* 43, no. 1–4 (1993): 241–256; and Ashley Thompson, "In the Absence of the Buddha: 'Aniconism' and the Contentions of Buddhist Art History," in *A Companion to Asian Art and Architecture*, ed. Rebecca M. Brown and Deborah S. Hutton (Oxford: Blackwell, 2011), 398–420.
6. Gilles Béguin, *Buddhist Art: An Historical and Cultural Journey* (Bangkok: River Books, 2009), 39–40.
7. See Susan L. Huntington, *Lay Ritual in the Early Buddhist Art of India: More Evidence Against the Aniconic Theory* (Amsterdam: Royal Netherlands Academy of Arts and Sciences, 2012); Huntington, "Buddhist Art Through a Modern Lens: A Case of a Mistaken Scholarly Trajectory," in *In the Shadow of the Golden Age: Art and Identity in Asia from Gandhara to the Modern Age*, ed. Julia A. B. Hegewald (Berlin: EB-Verlag, 2014), 79–112; and "Shifting the Paradigm: The Aniconic Theory and Its Terminology," *South Asian Studies* 31, no. 2 (2015): 163–186.
8. For different interpretations on how to "read" these early visual narratives, see Vidya Dehejia, *Discourse in Early Buddhist Art: Visual Narratives of India* (New Delhi: Munshiram Manoharlal, 1997). See also Robert Brown, "Narrative as Icon: The Jataka Stories in Ancient Indian and Southeast Asian Architecture," in *Sacred Biography in the Buddhist Traditions of South and Southeast Asia*, ed. Juliane Schober (Honolulu: University of Hawai'i Press, 1997), 64–112.

9. Peter Skilling, "Paṭa (Phra Bot): Buddhist Cloth Painting of Thailand," in *Buddhist Legacies in Mainland Southeast Asia: Mentalities, Interpretations and Practices*, ed. François Lagirarde and Chalermpow P. Koanantakool (Bangkok: Princess Maha Chakri Sirindhorn Anthropology Centre, 2006), 227–233.
10. For picture-scroll traditions in modern India, see Thomas Kaiser, Joan Clough, and Karina Moschke, eds., *Painted Songs: Continuity and Change in an Indian Folk Art* (Stuttgart: Arnoldsche Art Publishers, 2012).
11. Béguin, *Buddhist Art*, 71, fig. 22.
12. Étienne Lamotte, *Histoire du bouddhisme indien. Des origines à l'ère śaka* (Louvain-la-Neuve, Belgium: Université de Louvain, 1976), 738.
13. Adrian Snodgrass, *The Symbolism of the Stūpa* (Ithaca, NY: Cornell University Press, 1985); and John S. Strong, *Relics of the Buddha* (Princeton, NJ: Princeton University Press, 2004).
14. For two case studies, see Nicolas Revire, "Iconographical Issues in the Archeology of Wat Phra Men, Nakhon Pathom," *Journal of the Siam Society* 98 (2010): 75–115; and Arlo Griffiths, Nicolas Revire, and Rajat Sanyal, "An Inscribed Bronze Sculpture of a Buddha in *Bhadrāsana* at Museum Ranggawarsita in Semarang (Central Java, Indonesia)," *Arts Asiatiques* 68 (2013): 3–26.
15. On the relative lateness of epigraphical references to Avalokiteśvara in India, that is, in the 5th to 6th century CE, see Gregory Schopen, "The Inscription on the Kuṣān Image of Amitābha and the Character of the Early Mahāyāna in India," *Journal of the International Association of Buddhist Studies* 10 (1987): 99–134.
16. See John C. Huntington, "Avalokiteśvara and the Namaskāramudrā in Gandhara," *Studies in Indo-Asian Art and Culture* 1 (1972): 91–100; John Brough, "Amitābha and Avalokiteśvara in an Inscribed Gandhāran Sculpture," *Indologica Taurinensia* 10 (1982): 65–70; and Gérard Fussman and Anna Maria Quagliotti, *The Early Iconography of Avalokiteśvara/L'iconographie ancienne d'Avalokiteśvara* (Paris: De Boccard, 2012). *Contra*, see Richard Salomon and Gregory Schopen, "On an Alleged Reference to Amitābha in a Kharoṣṭhī Inscription on a Gandhārian Relief," *Journal of the International Association of Buddhist Studies* 25, no. 1–2 (2002): 3–31; and Daniel Boucher, "Is There an Early Gandhāran Source for the Cult of Avalokiteśvara?" *Journal Asiatique* 296, no. 2 (2008): 297–330.
17. For one exception, see Paul Harrison and Christian Luczanits, "New Light on (and from) the Muhammad Nari Stele," in *Nendo daiikkai kokusai shinpojiumu puroshīdingusu: Jōdokyō ni kansuru tokubetsu kokusai shinpojiumu* 年度第1回国際シンポジウムプロシーディングス浄土教に関する特別国際シンポジウム [*Special International Symposium on Pure Land Buddhism*] (Kyoto: Ryukoku University Research Center for Buddhist Cultures in Asia, 2011), 69–127, figs. 197–207.
18. Naturally, the same holds true for the problematic identification of the Bodhisattvas Maitreya and Mañjuśrī in early Buddhist art, on which see Anna Maria Quagliotti, "Mañjuśrī in Gandharan Art: A New Interpretation of a Relief in the Victoria and Albert Museum," *East and West* 40, no. 1–4 (1990): 99–113; John C. Huntington, "A Re-examination of a Kaniṣka Period Tetradrachm Coin Type with an Image of Mētrago/Maitreya on the Reverse (Göbl 793.1) and a Brief Notice on the Importance of the Inscription Relative to Bactro-Gandhāran Buddhist Iconography of the Period," *Journal of the International Association of Buddhist Studies* 16, no. 2 (1993): 79–88; and Inchang Kim, *The Future Buddha Maitreya: An Iconological Study* (New Delhi: DK Printworld, 1997).
19. See Claudine Bautze-Picron, "The Universal Compassionate Bodhisattva: Miscellaneous Aspects of Avalokitasvara/Avalokiteśvara in India," *Silk Road Art and Archaeology* 10 (2004): 225–290; and Akira Miyaji, "Iconography of the Two Flanking Bodhisattvas in the Buddhist Triads from Gandhāra: Bodhisattvas Siddhārtha, Maitreya and Avalokiteśvara," *East and West* 58, no. 1–4 (2008): 123–156. *Contra*, see Juhyung Rhi, "Early Mahāyāna and Gandhāran Buddhism: An Assessment of the Visual Evidence," *The Eastern Buddhist*, New Series, 35, no. 1–2 (2003): 152–202; and Christian Luczanits,

"The Bodhisattva with the Flask in Gandharan Narrative Scenes," *East and West* 55, nos. 1–4 (2005): 163–188.

20. Along these lines, see Nicolas Revire, Rajat Sanyal, and Rolf Giebel, "Avalokiteśvara of the 'Three and a Half Syllables': A Note on the Heart-Mantra *Ārolik* in India," *Arts Asiatiques* 76 (2021).
21. Peter Skilling, "Buddhist Sealings: Reflections on Terminology, Motivation, Donors' Status, School-Affiliation, and Print-Technology," in *South Asian Archaeology 2001*, ed. Catherine Jarrige and Vincent Lefèvre, vol. 2, *Historical Archaeology and Art History* (Paris: Éditions recherches sur les civilisations, 2005), 677–685.
22. Richard Smith, "Questions Regarding the Word Mudra: A Preliminary Survey of Gestures on Indian Icons and their Designation," *Asianart.com*, September 09, 2015.
23. Nicolas Revire, "The Enthroned Buddha in Majesty: An Iconological Study" (PhD diss, Université de la Sorbonne Nouvelle, 2016).
24. Walter E. Marasinghe, ed. and trans., *Citrakarmaśāstra Ascribed to Mañjuśrī, Being Volume II of Vāstuvidyāśāstra* (Delhi: Sri Satguru Publications, 1991), 112–113.
25. See Jonathan S. Walters, *Finding Buddhists in Global History* (Washington DC: American Historical Association, 1998). For the case of northeast Thailand, see Leedom Lefferts, "Northeast Thai-Lao Theravāda Buddhism: Peripheral, Central, or Varietal?" *Journal of Global South Studies* 34, no. 2 (2017): 225–248.
26. See Leedom Lefferts and Sandra Cate, *Buddhist Storytelling in Thailand and Laos: The Vessantara Jataka Scroll at the Asian Civilisations Museum* (Singapore: Asian Civilisations Museum, 2012); and Thomas Kaiser, Leedom Lefferts, and Martina Wernsdörfer, *Devotion: Image, Recitation, and Celebration of the Vessantara Epic in Northeast Thailand* (Stuttgart: Arnoldsche Art Publishers, 2017).
27. Martha L. Carter, *The Mystery of the Udayana Buddha* (Naples, Italy: Istituto Universitario Orientale, 1990).
28. Richard F. Gombrich, "Kosala-Bimba-Vaṇṇanā," in *Buddhism in Ceylon and Studies on Religious Syncretism in Buddhist Countries*, ed. Heinz Bechert (Göttingen: Vandenhoek & Ruprecht, 1978), 281–303; Nicolas Revire, "'Please Be Seated (還坐)'—Faxian's Account and Related Legends Concerning the First Buddha Image," in *From Xiangyuan to Ceylon: The Life and Legacy of the Chinese Buddhist Monk Faxian (337–422)*, ed. Jinhua Chen and Kuan Guang (Singapore: World Scholastic Publishers, 2020), 351–373.
29. The same is naturally true with Hindu deities and embodied gods. For a modern example from Tamil Nadu in southern India, see Soumhya Venkatesan, "Object, Subject, Thing: Tamil Hindu Priests' Material Practices and Practical Theories of Animation and Accommodation," *American Ethnologist* 47, no. 4 (2021): 447–460.
30. In Indo-Tibetan context, see Yael Bentor, *Consecration of Images and Stūpas in Indo-Tibetan Tantric Buddhism* (Leiden, The Netherlands: Brill, 1996). For a Thai example, see Donald K. Swearer, *Becoming the Buddha: The Ritual of Image Consecration in Thailand* (Princeton: Princeton University Press, 2004).
31. Pamela Winfield, "Curating Culture: The Secularization of Buddhism through Museum Display," in *Secularizing Buddhism: New Perspectives on a Dynamic Tradition*, ed. Richard K. Payne (Boulder, CO: Shambhala, 2021), 95–114.
32. Peter Skilling, "The Aesthetics of Devotion: Buddhist Arts of Thailand," in *The Many Streams of Buddhist Art in Thailand*, ed. Heidi Tan (Singapore: Asian Civilisations Museum, 2012), 31.
33. One example is the Smithsonian Institution's exhibition *Encountering the Buddha: Art and Practice Across Asia*, on display October 14, 2017–January 17, 2022 at the Freer Gallery of Art & Arthur M. Sackler Gallery, Washington DC in the United States of America. See also, Louise Tythacott, "Curating the Sacred: Exhibiting Buddhism at the World Museum Liverpool," *Buddhist Studies Review* 34, no. 1 (2017): 115–133.

34. Fabio Rambelli, "Secret Buddhas: The Limits of Buddhist Representation," *Monumenta Nipponica* 57, no. 3 (2002): 271–307; and Michitaka Suzuki, "Invisible Hibutsu (Hidden Buddha) and Visible Icon," in *Spacial Icons: Performativity in Byzantium and Medieval Russia*, ed. Alexei Lidov (Moscow: Indrik, 2011), 663–693.
35. Robert L. Brown, "The Miraculous Buddha Image: Portrait, God, or Object?" in *Images, Miracles, and Authority in Asian Religious Traditions*, ed. Richard H. Davis (Boulder, CO: Westview Press, 1998), 37–54.
36. Peter Skilling, "Rhetoric of Reward, Ideologies of Inducement: Why Produce Buddhist 'Art'?" in *Art of Merit: Studies in Buddhist Art and its Conservation; Proceedings of the Buddhist Art Forum 2012*, eds. David Park, Kuenga Wangmo, and Sharon Cather (London: Archetype, 2013), 27–37. See also Jinah Kim and Todd Lewis, eds., *Dharma and Puṇya: Buddhist Ritual Art of Nepal* (Leiden, The Netherlands: Hotei, 2019).
37. For a full critique of this kind, see Nicolas Revire, "Review Article: *The Roots of Thai Art*, by Piriya Krairiksh (English translation by Narisa Chakrabongse), Bangkok, River Books, 2012," *Journal of the Siam Society* 101 (2013): 233–242.
38. Claudine Bautze-Picron, *The Buddhist Murals of Pagan: Timeless Vistas of the Cosmos* (Bangkok: Orchid Press, 2003); Bautze-Picron, *The Bejewelled Buddha from India to Burma: New Considerations* (New Delhi: Sanctum Books, 2010); and Bautze-Picron, *The Forgotten Place: Stone Images from Kurkihar, Bihar* (New Delhi: Archaeological Survey of India, 2014).
39. Pia Brancaccio, *The Buddhist Caves at Aurangabad: Transformation in Art and Religion* (Leiden, The Netherlands: Brill, 2010).
40. Robert L. Brown, *The Dvāravatī Wheels of the Law and the Indianization of South East Asia* (Leiden, The Netherlands: Brill, 1996).
41. Béguin, *Buddhist Art*. See also Nicolas Revire, "Book Review of Gilles Béguin (English translation by Narisa Chakrabongse), *Buddhist Art: An Historical and Cultural Journey*, Bangkok, River Books, 2009," *Journal of the Oxford Centre for Buddhist Studies* 14 (2018): 156–164.
42. Kurt Behrendt, *How to Read Buddhist Art* (New York: Metropolitan Museum of Art, 2019).
43. Pratapaditya Pal, ed., *Buddhist Art: Form and Meaning* (Mumbai: Marg Publications, 2007).
44. Thierry Zéphir, ed., *L'âge d'or de l'Inde classique: l'empire des Gupta* (Paris: Réunion des Musées Nationaux, 2007); and Pierre Baptiste and Thierry Zéphir, eds., *Dvāravatī: aux sources du bouddhisme en Thaïlande* (Paris: Réunion des Musées Nationaux, 2009).
45. Forrest McGill, ed., *The Kingdom of Siam: The Art of Central Thailand, 1350–1800* (San Francisco: Asian Art Museum, 2005).
46. John Guy, ed., *Lost Kingdoms: Hindu-Buddhist Sculpture of Early Southeast Asia* (New York: Metropolitan Museum of Art, 2014).
47. See Gregory Schopen, *Bones, Stones, and Buddhist Monks: Collected Papers on the Archaeology, Epigraphy, and Texts of Monastic Buddhism in India* (Honolulu: University of Hawai'i Press, 1997); and Schopen, *Figments and Fragments of Mahāyāna Buddhism in India: More Collected Papers* (Honolulu: Hawai'i University Press, 2005).
48. Bentor, *Consecration of Images and Stūpas*.
49. See Peter Skilling, ed., *Past Lives of the Buddha: Wat Si Chum—Art, Architecture and Inscriptions* (Bangkok: River Books, 2007); and Peter Skilling et al., eds., *How Theravāda is Theravāda? Exploring Buddhist Identities* (Chiang Mai, Thailand: Silkworm Books, 2012).
50. See, for example, Justin McDaniel, *The Lovelorn Ghost and the Magical Monk. Practicing Buddhism in Modern Thailand* (New York: Columbia University Press, 2014).
51. See, for instance, John S. Strong, *The Legend and Cult of Upagupta: Sanskrit Buddhism in North India and Southeast Asia* (Princeton, NJ: Princeton University Press, 1992); and Strong, *Relics of the Buddha*.

52. Swearer, *Becoming the Buddha.*
53. Lefferts and Cate, *Buddhist Storytelling.* See also Kaiser et al., *Devotion.*
54. Bernard Faure, "The Buddhist Icon and the Modern Gaze," *Critical Inquiry* 24, no. 3 (1998): 768.
55. Toward this endeavor, see for example David L. McMahan, *Empty Vision: Metaphor and Visionary Imagery in Mahāyāna Buddhism* (London: Routledge, 2002), which argues that vision and visuality is increasingly important in the texts themselves.

Nicolas Revire

T

TAIXU

METHODOLOGY

Taixu 太虛 (1890–1947) wrote and spoke for a broader audience than any of his monastic Buddhist contemporaries. His collected works contain 1,447 titles in thirty-two volumes. He gave hundreds of talks to religious and secular audiences at monasteries; Buddhist academies; lay Buddhist organizations; twenty-seven universities in China, Japan, France, Germany, the United States, and Burma; six prisons; and a radio address in London. Many of his talks and writings were motivated by contemporary events or topics in public discourse.

In addition to being a gifted speaker and writer, Taixu also dedicated much of his life to Buddhist reform. His life's work involved a dynamic between propagation and reform. This dynamic originated with his first exposure to political reform thought in 1908. He realized that Buddhism also needed to change and further became inspired to use Buddhism to benefit society.

Taixu's interest in propagation, which represented his missionary side, is evident in his talks and writings. His many essays on current affairs generally demonstrated a good understanding of the matter at hand and presented a Buddhist perspective. He also had high expectations for the missionary potential of his trip to Europe and North America in 1928–1929, but he later remarked that they had been unrealistic. He envisioned China as a Buddhist country similar to Thailand and Sri Lanka. His project of creating a pure land on Earth and his Humanistic Buddhism both represent his conviction that Buddhism's resources could benefit the world in new ways. His missionary impulse also appeared in his reform projects, such as monastic education, his work to make monasticism more relevant to China's new society, and his effort to establish the Maitreya school as the faith of modern propagators.

Taixu's interest in reform was most evident in his numerous proposals for monastic restructuring. Similarly, he sought leadership of the Buddhist Association as a means to implementing his intended reforms. His Buddhist academies and the changes he implemented as abbot of several monasteries involved monastic reform. He was politically active in support of monasticism and sought to reform lay Buddhist organizations. Taixu held the conviction that lay Buddhists were able to do more than make offerings and make merit. His Maitreya school aimed to meet the religious needs of clergy and lay Buddhists. His reform work not only served to make monasticism more relevant to society, but also sought to maintain opportunities for the elite monastic training that he himself had received.

Both reform and propagation are guided by the principle of progress on the bodhisattva path. This involves various Mahāyāna elements such as the ten virtues, bodhisattva precepts, the aspiration for enlightenment, the innate potential for enlightenment, great vows, dedication of merit, and particularly the world as a sacralized buddha land or Pure Land.

TAIXU'S EARLY LIFE AND FORMATIVE EXPERIENCES

Taixu was born on January 8, 1890, during the reign of Guangxu in the Qing dynasty. Because he was born in the twelfth lunar month, his mathematical age is generally two years less than his age calculated by the Chinese method of reckoning one *sui* for every year in which a person lives. His given name was Gansen and later his uncle gave him the name Peilin to use as a student. His surname was originally Zhang because his father married into his mother's family so that they could have a male heir. Despite this, he later used his father's surname, Lü. He had a difficult childhood, suffering the death of his father at a young age and moving in with his maternal grandmother when his mother remarried.[1] His uncle, a schoolteacher, taught him for three years. He later attempted to raise funds from his father's family to continue his education with the goal of taking the imperial exam and becoming an official. That did not work out, and he instead became an apprentice in a general store.

The years Taixu spent with his grandmother as a young boy enriched his life in various ways. She took him on pilgrimages to Buddhist and Daoist sites in the Zhejiang and Jiangsu area and tried to prepare him for life. During their travels, he heard tales of bodhisattvas and Daoist immortals, enriching his inner world with popular religious mythology. This fascination grew in him until one day in 1904 when he quietly walked away from his job as a shop apprentice to join a monastery. It was not until his second year as a monk that Taixu began to understand that Buddhism was different from Taoism. As a result, he shifted his efforts from seeking magical powers to seeking enlightenment through Chan practice. From a Mahāyāna Buddhist perspective, this was his aspiration for enlightenment (*bodhicitta*). He memorized the *Lotus Sutra*, attended lectures on the *Lengyan jing* (**Śuraṅgama sutra*) and Tiantai texts, and read other works including Chan discourse records, biographies of eminent monks, apologetical works, and Confucian classics. He received Chan training from his preceptor Jichan, one of the most important Chan masters of the period.

In 1907, Taixu spent the fall and winter in a retreat reading sutras and doing meditation. The religious experiences he had during this retreat gave him new insight into the sutras, doctrinal texts, and Chan discourse records that he had been studying. His biographer Yinshun characterized this experience as insight into the Chan and perfection of wisdom traditions.[2]

If Taixu had followed the normal pattern, he would have continued his cultivation over the next ten or twenty years, received an administrative position in an important monastery, and eventually become an abbot. As abbot, he would oversee the training of his monks, deliver sutra lectures, meet with important visitors, and promote his style of Buddhist practice from his monastery. However, Taixu did not follow this pattern.

In the spring of 1908, a reform-minded monk named Huashan visited Taixu's monastery. At the time, Taixu's world was so deeply Buddhist he dismissed Huashan's support of the movement for political reform in China led by Kang Youwei and others and his argument that Buddhism must also reform. Nonetheless Taixu's curiosity led him to read the books Huashan had brought with him, and they debated for over ten days. This culminated in a moment that inspired Taixu to change his life's direction. According to Taixu's autobiography, Tan Sitong's *Exposition of Benevolence* in particular triggered a deep commitment to go out into the world and use Buddhism to its benefit.[3] Taixu referred to this as a "great vow" (*hongyuan* 弘願), another important step on the Mahāyāna path.[4]

As Taixu read and thought about the writings calling for political reform, he would have been struck by their occasional use of Buddhist concepts and terms. Works by Kang Youwei, Liang Qichao, Tan Sitong, and Zhang Taiyan made reference to Buddhist concepts such as bodhisattva, Pure Land, ultimate bliss, universal buddhahood, and the elimination of suffering. For example, Tan Sitong's *Exposition of Benevolence* mentions a future utopia (*Datong* 大同) free from social divisions, where everyone has attained buddhahood and Maitreya Buddha has appeared. Kang Youwei portrays a utopian state free from social and political distinctions. He preferred to "evolve" the entire world toward a pure land (a synonym he used for the Confucian *Datong* utopia) rather than leaving it for one. These reformers variously argued that Buddhism could be an antidote to Confucian autocracy, was sophisticated enough to respond to Western science and philosophy, and could become a religion for all countries.[5] They used Buddhist concepts in the service of political reform and were therefore not religiously systematic. Nonetheless, these thinkers served to expand Taixu's horizons beyond monastic Buddhism, leading him and many other monks to political activism. Most important however, they presented Taixu with the idea that Buddhism could help solve the problems of China and even the world.

Taixu's shift was not instantaneous. During the months that followed, he continued to learn Buddhist teachings. He also began to act in ways that defied his superiors. He disobeyed his Chan teacher and preceptor Jichan, and then defied the wishes of his master Zangnian, who asked Taixu to join the famously strict meditation program at Jinshan Monastery.[6] Instead, Taixu enrolled at Jetavana Hermitage in the spring of 1909, an innovative nonsectarian Buddhist school established by Yang Renhui after his contact with the Mahabodhi Society. Taixu remarked that he decided to enroll when he heard that it was "an organization participating in *a world Buddhist movement*."[7] Taixu was deeply influenced by the vision of Buddhism as an international and even pan-national phenomenon.

FROM RADICAL BUDDHIST TO BUDDHIST RADICAL

Between 1908 and 1913, Taixu's political involvement became increasingly radical. After spending one semester at Jetavana Hermitage, he embarked on his first activist project: working with the Sangha Education Association to prevent government appropriation of monastic property for schools. Through the monk Qiyun, Taixu moved beyond reform thought to the "stronger brew" of revolutionary groups, which involved secret meetings and subversive agendas.[8] By around 1910, Taixu had connected with the small but growing anarchist circles in China. His religious experience of 1907 and its relativizing of worldly matters may have predisposed him to interest in anarchist thought.[9] Anarchist ideas were coincidentally arriving in China around this time and would continue to animate elite intellectual life through the New Culture period.[10] Anarchism's emphasis on personal virtue and responsibility rather than power relationships appealed to intellectual elites who sought an alternative to the coercive power of the Qing.

By 1912, Taixu had entered China's political history as one of two leading figures in a faction that had split from the more institutionally oriented Chinese Socialist Party.[11] His "pure" or "new" socialists advocated a stance of no religion, no government, and no family. Taixu explained that in the future, when everyone had attained buddhahood, there would be no need for religion,[12] an idea that Taixu had previously encountered in Tan's *Exposition of Benevolence*. Taixu's Buddhist-influenced socialism thus became part of the history of anarchism's reception in China.[13]

Taixu's political and religious worlds collided in 1912 with the "invasion," "conflict," or "uproar" of Jinshan. After the Republic of China was founded on January 1, 1912, Taixu sought to create and lead a Buddhist Association that would be recognized by the government and allow him to carry out reforms. At this time, his ideas for Buddhist reform were derived from his socialist platform. Through his political connections he visited the president's office and was encouraged to proceed and was presumably asked to gain the support of other Buddhist leaders. With the monk Renshan, he arranged a meeting with various abbots at the prestigious Jinshan Monastery to present his charter for their approval. As the meeting proceeded, Renshan proposed that the monastery be turned into a Buddhist school. Because Taixu had brought hundreds of socialists to the meeting, they passed Renshan's proposal and nominated Renshan to be in charge of the new school. The other Buddhist monks could not abide the loss of their monastery. Several days later, violence ensued against Renshan, who filed a lawsuit against the monastery. These incidents had negative consequences for Taixu: public opinion favored Jinshan Monastery; Taixu gained notoriety in Buddhist circles; and his Buddhist Association was now an impossibility.

Taixu's political activism would continue until 1914.[14] The experience and knowledge that he gained during this time would later be put to use for the benefit of his Buddhist projects. For example, Taixu's conviction that Buddhism could make great contributions to society, which marked the beginning of this period, served as an important factor in his political activism. Later, the same conviction animated his projects, particularly Humanistic Buddhism and the ideal of creating a Pure Land on Earth.

Also through his political activities, Taixu met leaders, became conversant with the structure of government, and learned methods for accomplishing political aims. This knowledge and these connections would later assist his efforts as a religious figure defending Buddhism against state efforts toward secularization.[15] For example, when monks were required to serve in the army in 1936, Taixu wrote to officials in several ministries asking for noncombatant participation for clergy, which was granted. In 1943 he mobilized the Buddhist Association against a 50 percent tax on higher-income monasteries. When the Ministry of the Interior did not grant the petition, Taixu wrote a letter of protest to Chiang Kai-shek and the tax was canceled.[16]

Taixu was also a student of the methodology of political movements. He created national and international networks, such as the Greater East Asian Buddhist Conference of 1925 in Tokyo, which was "perhaps the first international Buddhist conference of modern times."[17] He emphasized that participation in Buddhist organizations should be voluntary. He also wrote and spoke to audiences outside of the monastery and worked to reform Buddhist education. His magazine *Haichaoyin* 海潮音 ("voice of the tide") was widely circulated and genuinely welcomed readers' contributions and involvement. His writings often have clear statements about what should be done in light of the current situation. He later referred to his lifetime efforts as a Buddhist reform movement (*yundong* 運動), or a Buddhist movement to "save the world" (a common expression at the time referring to social and political reform).[18]

Taixu's interest in utopianism also dates to this period. At this time in China, the utopian concept of *Datong* (grand unity) was widely discussed in writings on political reform. The concept of a future *Datong* appeared in late Qing reform works, reemerged in the radical socialisms of the Republican period, and held a prominent place in Sun Yat-sen's "Three Principles of the People," the Nationalist ideology. In Taixu's political writings, *Datong* became an important theme used to express his conceptions of anarcho-socialism.[19] After his political period, utopian themes continued to appear in his Buddhist writings. His text on creating a Pure Land on Earth is consciously utopian with its discussion of utopian ideas in world history. At the same time, it places the concept of utopia (and people's efforts to bring it about) into a Buddhist framework, calling it a pure land on Earth.

Because of his well-known history of radicalism, subsequent generations of radically inclined monks were drawn to Taixu. Paradoxically, he served as a moderating force. His experiences as a radical, combined with his subsequent rededication to Buddhism, gave him the perspective to critique them and redirect their energies. A letter published in 1939 was emblematic of his attitude. In it, Taixu reprimanded a radical monk who sought to follow modern trends but did not sufficiently understand Buddhism.[20] Humanistic Buddhism would challenge younger monks to learn more about Buddhist teachings as they engaged with the world. Taixu's Maitreya School also gave religious structure to the lives of radically inclined student monks who attended his Buddhist academies.

Taixu's shift back to Buddhism was evident in a 1920 discussion comparing anarchism with Buddhism. Explaining that both identify family and property as bonds of suffering, he described a systemic problem with anarchism; that is, it lacks a proper method for realizing its goal of ending bondage and instead relies on people's envy, greed, hatred, rebelliousness, viciousness, and destructiveness to carry out its goals. This in turn produces more suffering. Buddhism, by contrast, has methods of cultivation that break attachments, create individual virtue, and allow people to live together harmoniously.[21]

TAIXU'S SEALED RETREAT

In October 1914, Taixu consciously stopped his political involvements and began a three-year retreat in a two-room facility on the island of Putuoshan.[22] Taixu's disillusionment with political activism was due to multiple factors, including Yuan Shikai's repression and assassination of socialist party leaders and the outbreak of the First World War, which caused a deep uncertainty in Taixu about Western political theories.[23]

Disillusioned with political activism, Taixu reflected on his Buddhist identity. He remarked,

> I realized that I was unable to settle into an ordinary worldly life. . . . I could no longer bear to spend my time exclusively on worldly matters. Therefore, that autumn I entered into a sealed retreat at Putuo[shan].[24]

He later reflected that he began the retreat to work on the cultivation of precepts and concentration, as well as arrogance and laziness.[25] Finally, he expressed dissatisfaction with his own skills of propagation and conversion, which in context could mean the failure of his politics to generate interest in Buddhism. "Upon reflection I realized that I had not mastered the Buddha's system of converting [people] to the Dharma."[26]

Once the retreat began, he settled into a daily routine:

> I got up early to do meditation and prostrations, and read scriptures until noon. In the afternoon, I did some writing and read books and newspapers, including both new and old works. In the evening after doing prostrations, I did some meditation before retiring.[27]

During his retreat, he read Indian and Chinese works on monastic discipline, as well as works on the Yogācāra and Pure Land traditions. He also continued to keep up with current events and theories.

During this retreat, two religious experiences deepened his understanding of Buddhism. According to his own description, the first of these gave him insight into the *Awakening of Faith* and the *Lengyan jing* (**Śuraṅgama sutra*). These two texts took on a central role in Taixu's understanding of Buddhism.[28]

The second experience occurred when Taixu was contemplating a passage in a Yogācāra text. He saw the diversity of dependently arisen phenomena, each with its individual qualities, and also saw the deeper order that connected them. As a result, his thinking and writing became profoundly and tightly organized. He described this as insight into "truth as not abandoning the conventional, and the conventional as penetrating the truth."[29] This deeper perspective on the diversity of phenomena and the importance of conventional truth informed his subsequent projects. He continued reading Yogācāra texts during the retreat, which facilitated his subsequent use of Yogācāra as a basic Buddhist framework for interpreting worldly ideas in biology, psychology, social evolution, physics, and philosophy.[30]

One of the first things he wrote during his retreat was an extensive work entitled *A Proposal for Institutional Reform in the Sangha*. Rather than negating institutions as he had in the socialist party, Taixu set about designing a perfect system. He proposed scholastic and regional divisions rather than networks based on dharma transmission, loosely based on the Japanese model.

These monasteries, however, would be unified under a single Vatican-like central monastery, the "Buddhadharma Saṅghārāma."[31] These reforms were never implemented, although Taixu published new proposals every few years based on sociopolitical changes.

MONASTIC EDUCATION

Prior to the Republican period, monastic education included training in monastic discipline, cultivation (such as Chan, Pure Land, or Tiantai), liturgy, and exegetical learning. The latter centered on sutra lectures. A senior monk would expound on a sutra of his specialization in a lecture series. Monks from other monasteries were welcome to attend. As a specialist, the lecturer would incorporate existing commentaries into his own exegesis. The lecturer would have to accommodate a wide range of students. This type of education aimed to help monks understand the content of sutras, especially in regard to individual cultivation. It also aimed to provide a background useful for preaching. In this manner, monks who were so inclined could gradually obtain a Buddhist education from a number of different teachers, focusing on one text at a time.[32] Taixu's own education began with the traditional sutra-lecture model and then shifted to the newer model when he attended Jetavana Hermitage.

Between 1909 and 1920, several new Buddhist schools were founded on the model of secular schools, with multiple classes taught concurrently each semester: Yang Wenhui's Jetavana Hermitage, Yuexia's Avataṃsaka University, and Dixian's Guanzong Study Society. Buddhist cultivation was generally required, but these programs differed from the sutra-lecture model by having set curricula and a set duration.

In 1922, Taixu founded the Wuchang Buddhist Academy, which was the first nonsectarian Buddhist school founded by a monk. It was not located in or affiliated with any monastery and was funded by lay sponsors who served on its board of directors. Liang Qichao served as the board's honorary chairman.[33] Taixu designed it with reference to Yang Wenhui's Jetavana Hermitage, Japanese Buddhist schools, and the traditional public monastery (*conglin*). The school enrolled lay and monastic students in the fall of 1922, and the first class graduated in 1924. The school represents a foundational moment in the history of Buddhist academies.

In 1927, Taixu was appointed as director of the Minnan Buddhist Academy and abbot of the host monastery, Nanputuo si in Xiamen. In 1932, he founded the Sino-Tibetan Doctrinal Institute in Sichuan, and stayed there during the Japanese occupation. Following a 1929 conversation in Paris with the president of the Asiatic Society, Sylvain Lévi, Taixu began working to integrate his schools and other institutions into a World Buddhist Institute network, a plan that was never fully realized.[34]

By the 1940s, students and teachers from Taixu's Buddhist academies came to hold important positions in over fifty Buddhist academies in China.[35] Students from his academies also went on to become abbots or important Buddhist leaders overseas. Prominent students included Fafang, Fazun, Daxing, Zhifeng, Huijue, Fushan, and Mingshan from Wuchang and Yinshun, Dongchu, Zhumo, Hongchuan, Yanpei, and Cihang from Minnan.[36]

Taixu's Wuchang Academy served as a starting point for a new phenomenon. A discursive space emerged as student monks and their teachers published articles in Buddhist magazines. Taixu's own magazine, *Haichaoyin*, founded in 1920, took a leading role in publishing not only articles on Buddhism, but also information useful for activism. Particularly after 1928, as the government followed a secular modernist path, uncertainty arose about Buddhism's status in the new China. Student monks and their teachers, through the academy networks and magazines, came to form a discursive community that used activism, appeals to the Constitution, and arguments about Buddhism's contributions to society when Buddhism was threatened. Beyond this activism, they also formulated and expressed a new Buddhist identity for clergy under the Republic: the student-monk.[37]

Buddhist academies were also religious organizations. As Wuchang was not connected with a monastery, Taixu effectively put the monastery back into the academy through his emphasis on the traditional monastic (*conglin*) lifestyle. Wuchang and Minnan academies were liturgically structured around the Maitreya Pure Land tradition, with annual Maitreya Pure Land retreats. With Taixu's own innovative model of the Maitreya School, students chanted the relevant texts in the daily liturgy and gained experience in practicing Yogācāra meditation, the bodhisattva precepts, and Maitreya Pure Land practices.

Despite the success of his academies, the relatively short duration of the Buddhist academy program (two to four years) meant that Taixu could not implement the twelve-year monastic training program that he wrote about elsewhere. Nonetheless, Taixu's academies, their students, networks, and collective activities represent actual implementations of Taixu's reform vision.

MAITREYA PURE LAND

The Maitreya devotional tradition, which originated in India, has existed in China since at least the time of Daoan in the 4th century. Major historical figures include Xuanzang and Kuiji. Over the centuries Buddhist monks have debated the relative merits of Maitreya's Tuṣita heaven versus Amitābha's Sukhāvatī, with the latter gaining the majority of followers. In the early modern period, Maitreya practitioner Hongzan (1612–1686) compiled a three-fascicle work collecting information about people, events, texts, and mantras of that tradition. Taixu mentions this text in 1919, one of the few clues about his early interest in the tradition.[38]

The Maitreya tradition resembles other Pure Land practices, but with the goal of attaining rebirth in Tuṣita Heaven, where the bodhisattva Maitreya resides. According to its main text, the *Sutra of Maitreya's Ascent*,[39] Maitreya and those reborn in his land will leave Tuṣita in the distant future and be reborn on Earth. Maitreya will then attain buddhahood, and his devotees will receive predictions of their future enlightenment. To attain rebirth in Tuṣita, one should observe the five precepts and ten virtues, contemplate the ten virtues, dedicate one's merit to one's future rebirth, invoke the name of Maitreya, and have devotion toward Maitreya. One of the benefits of rebirth is "non-retrogression," a state from which it is impossible to lose ground in one's cultivation.

In 1924, while running the Wuchang Buddhist Academy, Taixu published a work outlining an innovative interpretation of the Maitreya tradition, the *Three Essentials of the Maitreya School*.[40] By calling it a school (*zong* 宗), Taixu indicated that he wished to elevate it beyond its traditional status as a "dharma gate" (*famen* 法門), or cultivational approach. He did so by bringing in other texts and practices, although he did not introduce the concept of a transmission lineage. This system was taught to students at Taixu's Buddhist academies, and later, in its second stage, it was also taught to dedicated lay Buddhists. Taixu published several articles but generally did not mention the Maitreya school in other works or talks, which is why this aspect of his life is less well known. This interpretation appears to have been intended for his Buddhist academy students and committed lay Buddhists, although he never specifically placed any limits on it.

The "three essentials" are three texts related to Maitreya. The first two are found in the *Yogācārabhūmi śāstra*, a long treatise traditionally said to be taught by Maitreya. The third text, the *Sutra of Maitreya's Ascent*, comes directly from the Maitreya devotional tradition. Taixu explained their roles in the preface to his *Three Essentials of the Maitreya School*. The first essential, the conceptual foundation or "object of cognition," is the *Yogācārabhūmi's* chapter "On Knowing Reality."[41] Taixu remarked that this also includes Chan meditation and set out four ways that human beings perceive reality. The first essential includes practices such as the contemplation of emptiness of dharmas, the four all-embracing virtues, and the six perfections. The second essential, identified as the "practice," is the text on bodhisattva precepts from the same treatise. The *Sutra of Maitreya's Ascent* is the third "essential," which Taixu identified as the result or "fruit" of adopting the ideas and practices of this school.

In this way, Taixu set forth a system with meditation, precept practice, and a devotional component. At Taixu's academies, these texts were incorporated into the lives of students through a daily schedule of cultivation and recitation and annual retreats. They were also studied in classes as part of the curriculum. One may presume that Taixu saw the Maitreya school as containing powerful concepts and practices suitable for future Buddhist leaders.

In its first stage, from 1922 to 1928, Taixu emphasized the Yogācāra contemplative aspect in the first essential. The second stage began when Taixu lectured on the *Sutra of Maitreya's Ascent* to a Buddhist group in Paris in 1929.[42] During this stage, rebirth in Maitreya's Inner Court received extra emphasis, although it had always been present in the system of "three essentials." Taixu also broadened the Maitreya school in several ways. He explicitly stated that it encompassed all three tiers of his doctrinal classification scheme (see section on "Taixu's Doctrinal Classification"), indicating that it embraces but goes beyond the scope of Humanistic Buddhism. He also added a catalog of texts for a Maitreya canon. Taixu identified Maitreya as receiving the inheritance of all Śākyamuni Buddha's sutras and methods of cultivation. Finally, he remarked that Maitreya cultivation would bring about security and happiness in the world, which would hasten Maitreya's arrival and create a Pure Land on Earth, a concept he had introduced in 1926.

Taixu himself became dedicated to Maitreya Pure Land practice around 1924, according to a work written in 1935.[43] Unfortunately, Taixu did not write much about this, but his close disciples testified to his devotion. Taixu also appeared in a photograph emulating the popular image of Maitreya as a corpulent joyful monk.[44] Finally, following his final stroke in 1947, his disciples recited the name of Maitreya Buddha as he passed away. His last words were "Sukhāvatī is so clear and cool; Tuṣita is so delightful."[45]

ESTABLISHING A PURE LAND ON EARTH

In 1926, two years after publicizing works on the Maitreya school, Taixu published "On the Establishment of a Pure Land in the Human Realm," the first of two essays on constructing a Pure Land on Earth.[46] The title is striking for its departure from the normal understanding of pure lands. In the Indian Mahāyāna Pure Land tradition, the suffering and defilement of this world are the very reasons one seeks rebirth in the pure land of Buddha Amitābha. After rebirth, one can receive teachings from that buddha and progress on the path to buddhahood in the pure land.

By contrast, Taixu's model emphasizes improving our world or constructing a pure land on Earth. He justifies this with the claim that the suffering of this world can also lead to a different response: "second, one imagines how this human realm can become a perfectly regulated environment, implemented by measures of reform."[47] This reference to reform-based political policies also ties in with the Chinese interest in utopian thought.

Taixu structured his essay around two human needs: the need for physical security of person and possessions, and the need for "immortality and bliss." The best way to attain the first is with "Uttarakuru," while the second need is best met in the pure land of Buddha Amitābha. At the opening of the text, we can see a dual-track model based on the varying needs of human beings.

According to descriptions in early Indian Buddhist sutras, Uttarakuru is a paradisiacal land located in the north. Its physical environment is pleasing to the senses, and the basic needs for food, shelter, and intimacy are provided for automatically and without difficulty. It is part of the human realm in Buddhist cosmology, and the lifespan for people born there is set at one thousand years. One can be reborn there after death by observing the ten virtues.

Uttarakuru is held up as a reference point for building a Pure Land on Earth. This involves not only high moral virtue but also advanced technology. For example, when Uttarakuru is said to have huskless white rice that cooks easily over gemstones, Taixu remarks, "these are clearly modern electric, coal, or gas stoves."[48] The implication is that we are already on the way. As everyone works for their own betterment and the common good, this world will gradually become an earthly Pure Land.

The theme of utopias runs throughout Taixu's proposal. He was influenced by a book on world utopias by Liu Renhang, a Buddhist, for which Taixu wrote a preface.[49] Repeating content from that book, Taixu lists several examples: Uttarakuru, Confucian *Datong*, Christian utopias of St. Peter and Tolstoy, political utopias of Socrates and Plato, as well as contemporary Western utopian novels by Edward Bellamy and H. G. Wells.[50] Taixu refers to all of these as "pure lands in the human realm," refiguring them into his Buddhist framework.

This is particularly relevant for *Datong*, a utopian ideal explicitly used to guide Sun Yat-sen's ideology of the Three Principles of the People. Taixu is effectively saying that Buddhism shares in the goals of creating security, improving society, and carrying out reconstruction. These ambitions dominated public discourse following China's 1911 revolution. For example, Sun Yat-sen's writings from 1919 and 1924 used the term "reconstruction" (*jianshe* 建設) in their titles, the same word Taixu uses for "establishing" a Pure Land. Taixu recognizes these goals but shifts the focus to a Buddhist framework that also has a nonpolitical method for attaining security of life and property—the ten virtues. He also includes refuge into rational principles underlying the buddha, dharma, and sangha.[51]

In this proposal, the creation of a Pure Land on Earth relies on the Buddhist doctrine of karma. The creation of good karma by virtuous action on a large scale leads to good karmic results on a large scale: an improved society. The efforts of an individual therefore contribute to the communal creation of an earthly Pure Land.

This foundation brings Taixu's readers closer to attaining "immortality and bliss." To get there, Taixu remarks that all one has to do is add the practices of invocation (*nianfo*) and transfer of merit. One will then be equipped for rebirth in Amitābha's Sukhāvatī or Maitreya's Tuṣita Heaven.[52]

From here, Taixu identifies a final goal. Whether one is working to create a Pure Land on Earth or attain rebirth in a Pure Land, one is removing various obstructions that prevent the pure mind of awakening from manifesting. When it manifests, one attains buddhahood, and the "pure land of the ocean of awakening" is attained. Following this, Taixu returns to the topic of creating a Pure Land on Earth, and remarks that pure lands are always established through making vows. For this, Taixu holds up the model of Dharmākara, the bodhisattva who made forty-eight vows. He carried out difficult Mahāyāna practices and was willing to give up his life and property. When he attained buddhahood, he became Amitābha Buddha and his vows were actualized, which created his own pure land. Finally, he gained true life (*dharmakāya*) and true property (a pure land).[53]

Thus, three levels may be identified in Taixu's proposal: the creation of a pure land on Earth, rebirth in a traditional Buddhist pure land, and creation of a pure land by attaining buddhahood.

Taixu's model of using communal ethical action ("shared karma," *gongye* 共業) to create a Pure Land on Earth is not found in the sutras. In this connection, Taixu remarks that the sutras contain very few descriptions of how people could participate in the creation of pure lands, aside from buddhas and advanced bodhisattvas. He therefore sought a way for communal salvation (*gong du* 共度) in addition to the existing methods of saving oneself or saving others.[54] The method that he describes contains several identifiable components: widespread interest in bottom-up mobilization;[55] the ideal of egalitarian religious participation; Buddhist ideas of morality and the ten virtues; the canonical association of the ten virtues with Uttarakuru and Maitreya's Tuṣita Heaven; the Mahāyāna concept of buddha lands, which requires not only an advanced bodhisattva but also that bodhisattva's actual influence in helping others progress on the path; and statements in the sutras that the world is created through karma.[56] Taixu would later associate the concept of creating a pure land on Earth with the Maitreya Pure Land tradition and Humanistic Buddhism.

The creation of a Pure Land on Earth was adopted in various ways by Buddhist leaders, including Yinshun, Hsing Yun, and particularly Sheng Yen.[57]

HUMANISTIC BUDDHISM

The English term "Humanistic Buddhism" is used to translate two different Chinese terms: *rensheng* Buddhism and *renjian* Buddhism. *Rensheng* 人生 is a non-Buddhist term that means "the lives of humans" or "humanistic." The term *renjian* 人間 is a Buddhist term that refers to the human realm, one of the six realms of samsara (the others are the realms of hell-beings, hungry ghosts, animals, asuras, and devas). Taixu used both terms, but in different ways.

Renjian Buddhism originated with a 1934 issue of *Haichaoyin* dedicated to this theme, with one article by Taixu and the rest by his disciples. References to *renjian* Buddhism are often preceded by the verbs *create* or *establish*. It resembles Taixu's project of creating a Pure Land in the human realm with its participatory aspect, in that individuals share the work of creating a

Buddhist world according to their interest and ability. *Renjian* Buddhism is open-ended in another way: it does not include the systematic treatises in Taixu's *rensheng* Buddhism and is therefore a work in progress. The term *renjian* Buddhism is used by later figures who each interpret it differently. Taixu's relative emphasis on *rensheng* Buddhism, however, is clear, and so this article does not further discuss *renjian* Buddhism.

For Taixu, *rensheng* Buddhism contains three interrelated components: a shift in the role of the clergy to spend more time teaching and engaging with lay Buddhists; a greater emphasis for lay Buddhists to focus on the intellectual understanding of Buddhism and ethical development; and a systematic treatise on Buddhist doctrines useful to both types of Buddhists. Taixu published works on *rensheng* Buddhism in 1928 and again in 1938–1946.

Taixu's Creation of Humanistic Buddhism in Context. Historical events helped shaped Taixu's thinking about Buddhism. The fall of the Qing dynasty in 1911 and the fall of Confucian ideology around the same time meant that Buddhism's role in society was no longer defined by Confucian politics. Buddhism therefore had new opportunities to expand into the public realm. At the same time, Buddhism's discourse of being above worldly affairs was increasingly challenged. This was most evident in the ongoing political trend of confiscating monastic property for use as schools, which began before the revolution and lasted for many decades. The national goals of universal education and transition to vernacular written language represented a cultural shift away from the elite. Taixu believed that these changes required a readjustment of Buddhism's relationship with the state and role in society.[58] In Humanistic Buddhism, we can also see a move to participate in China's reconstruction on Buddhist terms, a shift toward the religious needs of the growing class of nonelite, educated citizens, and a discourse of participation and engagement as prerequisites for transcendence. In its fullest implementation, Humanistic Buddhism was intended for everyone with a goal of creating a Buddhist China.

Although Taixu did not formally introduce the term "Humanistic Buddhism" until 1928, its beginnings are evident in a number of activities and innovations. Whenever public intellectuals made negative remarks about Buddhism, Taixu published refutations, usually in Buddhist magazines. For example, when Chen Duxiu argued that China should follow science rather than superstitious religion, Taixu replied that Yogācāra treatises were scientific and even surpassed the empiricism of science. When the Confucian revivalist Liang Shuming argued that what China truly needed was Confucianism, Taixu argued that Buddhism was actually well-suited to the new China. It could resolve problems arising from the material focus of science, resolve problems that remained in Confucianism, and provide guiding principles for culture and society. Taixu agreed with Liang that security and happiness should be the first priority in society. But, whereas Liang called for the promotion of Confucian culture to achieve this, Taixu called for the promotion of Buddhism. Buddhism could benefit society at three levels. At the most basic level, it could promote happiness and security by improving people's morality; this in turn creates good karma for humanity which results in a better future. At a higher level, Buddhism can help people become liberated from ignorance and suffering. At the highest level are the benefits brought by Mahāyāna enlightenment.[59] Taixu's response, which represents an important defense against the argument that Buddhism is an elitist tradition, would become an integral part of Humanistic Buddhism.

Taixu also spent considerable energy working out a new lay Buddhist religiosity. This model would not require elite, reclusive practice, but instead included concepts and practices that would bring genuine results on the Buddhist path, so that Buddhists would have something other than the frustration of not attaining enlightenment. It also moved beyond the apotropaic needs of the "faithful masses" for protection and worldly benefits, to include a sophisticated doctrinal system. This involved a system of Buddhist learning and a requirement for ethical action based on the ten virtues.[60] Taixu also incorporated the idea that a spiritual calling should exist within one's everyday life and should not require seclusion away from society. This created a foundation establishing practitioners on the bodhisattva path, preparing them for further progress.

In 1928, Taixu formally introduced Humanistic Buddhism with the publication of three components: a guide to Humanistic Buddhism for lay Buddhists, instructions to his monastic disciples, and a systematic theoretical work on Buddhist doctrine.

Taixu's guide for lay Buddhists outlined a suitable approach for learning Buddhism.[61] His readers were reminded that Humanistic Buddhism is not only relevant to the times, but also adheres to Buddhism's core truths. Taixu identified three themes in Humanistic Buddhism: it is oriented to the betterment of humanity, founded upon universal wisdom and compassion for all beings, and is gradual rather than sudden. The lay Buddhist begins with a proper understanding of Buddhism and cultivation of their character. The next step is the aspiration for enlightenment (*bodhicitta*). With this foundation, one can go from the ten faiths to the ten abidings in the fifty-two-stage path to buddhahood.

In the instructions for clergy, Humanistic Buddhism serves four purposes.[62] First, it is an exegetical approach for clergy in learning Buddhism and teaching it to all levels of society. Second, it serves as the guiding mindset for reforming monasteries. Taixu specifically mentions that monasteries should move away from "serving ghosts and gods" to "serving human society." Here, service to ghosts and gods refers to funerary rites and other rituals performed for the deceased. Taixu also worked to create simplified life-cycle rituals, particularly with his short-lived "Dharma Center" (Fayuan), which was the venue for the first Buddhist wedding in Chinese history. Third, Humanistic Buddhism benefits monasticism by preventing it from becoming irrelevant and from blindly seeking to adapt to society. Taixu saw these two tendencies as problems with conservative and radical clergy, respectively. Fourth, to carry out these goals, clergy were called upon to understand and be able to teach a wide range of Buddhist doctrines. This involves what Taixu called the "theoretical" component of Humanistic Buddhism, which he had published separately.

The Theoretical Component of Humanistic Buddhism. In 1928, Taixu began publishing *True Realism* (*Zhen xianshi lun* 真現實論), a series of texts that he identified as the theoretical foundations for Humanistic Buddhism. Although the title *True Realism* is not obviously Buddhist, the content has a Buddhist orientation. According to Taixu, this theory of realism describes the person and the world and identifies their real nature. Taixu called it "true" realism because at the highest level of perception, one perceives what in Buddhist doctrine is *dharmatā* (*faer* 法爾), or reality as it is.

Taixu's writings on true realism occupy six of the thirty-two volumes in his *Collected Works* and represent an important part of Taixu's vision for continuity of the Buddhist tradition into the present. *True Realism* is composed of three different textual components. The first component, the *Zongyi lun* 宗依論, was published serially beginning in 1928 and takes up more than six hundred pages. The first and second components are long treatises resembling systematic theology in the Christian tradition. The *Zongyi lun* lays out early Buddhist and Mahāyāna concepts of the self and world. It also discusses contemporary issues in science, philosophy, and religion that relate to Buddhist teachings, such as freedom and evolution. As a more detailed example, Taixu identified Buddhist causation as the basis for ethics. He refutes other types of causation, including theistic fall–based models and materialist progress–based models.[63] Overall, the first component presents a basic understanding of Buddhist teachings.

The second component, the *Zongti lun* 宗體論, is more than 250 pages and was published serially beginning in 1938. Whereas the first component aims to be explanatory, this component sets forth a five-part proposition for the reader: (1) reality is characterized by constant change; (2) change has a true nature, which is emptiness, not a supreme deity or evolution; (3) this nature can be awakened to or realized by the sudden method of the Chan school or graduated learning of Humanistic Buddhism and the bodhisattva path; (4) once this nature is awakened to, certain changes occur, such as reversal of the twelve links of dependent origination; (5) these four parts have certain relationships with each other. This proposition is not controversial from a Buddhist perspective. But if it is looked at as a philosophical treatise, then the proposition that it makes and leaves up to the reader is religious: if one accepts it, then one may begin to do Buddhist practices on the basis of faith in its doctrines.

The first and second components are theoretical in nature and do not recommend any specific practice. They are characterized by an emphasis on the direct cognition of reality, frequent explanation of Yogācāra doctrines (while also including content from Abhidharma and early Buddhism), and the interpretation of secular ideas from within this Buddhist framework. The Yogācāra text "On Knowing Reality," which was one of the "three essentials" of Taixu's Maitreya School, also plays a prominent role in his True Realism texts.

The third "applied" component of True Realism was compiled by the editors of Taixu's collected works in accordance with his wishes. This component consists of 139 shorter works in twelve subcategories: culture, religion, the Confucian tradition (*guoxue* 國學), philosophy, morality, psychology, science, life philosophy, society, education, public health, and literary arts. These works demonstrate Taixu's intent to bring Buddhism into all of these arenas and ideally make China a Buddhist nation.

Chan in Humanistic Buddhism. As Taixu conceived it, Humanistic Buddhism is a system of gradual learning and realization. In this regard, it is not compatible with Chan's "sudden" methodology. At the same time, it did rely on the Chan tradition in certain ways. A 1938 *True Realism* work describes a rural monastery dedicated to cultivation, including Chan, where monks would train for up to twelve years, at which point they would become qualified to guide Humanistic Buddhism.[64] In 1944, Taixu published a work entitled *Chinese Buddhist Learning*, in which he argued that "chan" 禪 (a term that includes meditation and Chan) was the core feature of Chinese Buddhist history. He further argues that literati, or scholar-officials, shaped the Chan tradition's emergence and development. For serious intellectuals interested in Buddhism, this work recommends figuring out and editing Chan encounter dialogues, following the model of lay Buddhist Qu Ruji (1548–1610), who compiled the influential *Records of Pointing at the Moon* (*Zhiyue lu* 指月錄).[65]

The Legacy of Taixu's Humanistic Buddhism. Taixu did not call Humanistic Buddhism a "school," nor did he identify a lineage of patriarchs. Humanistic Buddhism is part of a new exegetical scheme that incorporates existing traditions without radically reinterpreting them. The lack of dharma transmission or sectarian identity made it possible for subsequent figures to be innovative in their own approaches within this framework. Later Buddhist figures who put forth their own versions of Humanistic Buddhism include Yinshun, Cihang, Sheng Yen (Dharma Drum Mountain), Hsing Yun (Buddha's Light), Cheng Yen (Tzu Chi), and Zhao Puchu, who incorporated his version into the Buddhist Association of China.[66] Thich Nhat Hanh also associates his Engaged Buddhism with Taixu's Humanistic Buddhism.[67]

TAIXU'S DOCTRINAL CLASSIFICATION

Taixu formulated a system of doctrinal classification that was closely related to his reform agenda and his vision for spreading Buddhism throughout the world. In the 1920s, he formulated a system that he used for the rest of his life.[68] This system contains three tiers, with Mahāyāna at the top.

Below the Mahāyāna, the next tiers center on the *śrāvaka* (voice-hearer) and human vehicles respectively. "Vehicle" refers to a given spiritual path to enlightenment, such as the "great vehicle" (Mahāyāna). Taixu uses innovative terminology for the first two tiers. He calls the first tier "the dharmas common to the five vehicles." For Taixu, the five vehicles are the human, deva, *śrāvaka*, *pratyekabuddha* (solitary buddha), and buddha or bodhisattva vehicles. This scheme of five vehicles existed previously in Chinese Buddhism, notably with Zongmi (780–841). The "dharmas," or teachings and practices, that are shared by all five vehicles are actually just the human-vehicle practices of moral virtue. Taixu's choice of phrasing represents his doctrinal position in two ways. First, the fact that these practices are found in all vehicles means that they are not optional expedients. Second, and more important, this places human vehicle practices firmly on the path to buddhahood, making it a genuine option for Buddhist practice.

The second tier, "the dharmas common to the three vehicles," refers to teachings and practices shared by the *śrāvaka*, *pratyekabuddha*, and Mahāyāna traditions. This includes the traditional Buddhist teachings about the four noble truths, eightfold noble path, five aggregates, twelve links of dependent origination, and liberation from samsara, which are common to all three vehicles. Taixu remarks that although most people in the present are suited to human-vehicle practices, deva- and *śrāvaka*-vehicle practices will continue to be done by a minority. Taixu supports these practices for dedicated practitioners and monastics and did not adopt an "anti Hīnayāna" stance.

Taixu argues that different teachings ("vehicles") were most effective at different times in history. At the earliest stage, voice-hearer teachings served to bring the greatest number of people to enlightenment. After that, Mahāyāna teachings became the most effective. In the next period, deva-vehicle teachings served the same purpose. For Taixu, deva-vehicle practices include those of the Pure Land and Tantric traditions. Tantra is included because it employs cultivation of a subtle deva-body. The Pure Land tradition is included because its goal was rebirth in a heavenly realm: Maitreya's Tuṣita heaven is located in a deva realm and, for ordinary people,

Amitābha's Pure Land is like a heavenly paradise. Taixu argues that in the present era, which he identifies with the "final stage of the Dharma," the best way to bring people to the buddha vehicle is through human vehicle practices. Taixu remarks that this is the goal of Humanistic Buddhism, involving a direct connection between the human vehicle and the buddha vehicle.

The highest tier is termed "the dharmas unique to the Great Vehicle (Mahayana)." These teachings and practices, found only in the Mahāyāna tradition, include great compassion, aspiration for enlightenment (*bodhicitta*), *prajñā*-wisdom of the emptiness of dharmas, universal learning of all methods of cultivation, universal salvation of all beings, purifying countless pure lands, and striving for peerless buddhahood. It relies on the Indian Mahāyāna sequence of the arising of *bodhicitta*, making vows, and attaining enlightenment, which in turn generates a buddha field (or Pure Land) that is determined by one's previous vows. This tier is higher than the two preceding tiers, and it serves to orient them to Mahāyāna ideals. Taixu interchangeably calls it the buddha vehicle, bodhisattva vehicle, and great vehicle, and argues that since the bodhisattva has no set form, the bodhisattva is superior to both lay and monastic identities.

This three-tiered system has several features. First, it does not favor one single practice or school, unlike most systems of doctrinal classification. The Mahāyāna tradition, which is highest, contains three equal subtraditions: Yogācāra, Madhyamika, and Tathāgatagarbha. This exemplifies Taixu's typically liberal stance regarding one's choice of Buddhist practice.

Second, this system downplays the deva and *śrāvaka* vehicles. Taixu remarked that deva-vehicle practices were seen as superstitious and *śrāvaka*-vehicle practices were seen as escapist; as a result, if one promotes these ideas they will become obstructions. During his later years, Taixu broadened his stance, saying that deva-vehicle practices are "supplemental" to the first-tier practices, which reflected consistent lay interest in Pure Land and Esoteric or Tantric Buddhism.

Third, this system demonstrates connections with Taixu's reforms for Buddhism. The vastly expanded first tier corresponds with Taixu's efforts to make Buddhism more accessible. The first tier focuses on the ten faiths in the highly influential fifty-two-stage path to buddhahood in Chinese Buddhism.[69] When one progresses to the next stage (the ten abidings), one undertakes practices due to faith in the Buddhist fruits of those practices. For Taixu, it was important that faith be voluntary, a conviction based on understanding.

The system also reflects Taixu's intended reforms for clergy. They would be responsible for mastering an intellectual understanding of Buddhism and teaching it to others. They would also engage in Buddhist cultivation and teach it to interested practitioners.

Finally, Taixu's doctrinal classification describes the underlying framework connecting his separate projects, such as Maitreya School, Pure Land on Earth, and Humanistic Buddhism.

Taixu's three-tiered model of doctrinal classification was used by the editors of his collected works, who employed the three tiers and three Mahayana schools as six of its twenty divisions. Taixu's three-tiered system of doctrinal classification has been adopted by several Buddhist figures, including Yinshun, Sheng Yen, and Hsing Yun.[70]

TAIXU'S FINAL TEN YEARS

During the years of the Sino-Japanese war (1937–1945), Taixu lived at his Sino-Tibetan Doctrinal Institute in Chongqing, in the same city as the Nationalist government. During this period, he wrote many works including an autobiography, his Chan-centric history of Chinese

Buddhism, and the final works of his Humanistic Buddhism project. He also made a trip to Southeast Asia to meet with Buddhists of those countries. This trip was also a diplomatic mission to rally support against Japan, sponsored in part by the Republican government. In addition to carrying out his political role, Taixu saw firsthand the Buddhism of countries like Burma and Sri Lanka. Impressed by Buddhism's pervasiveness, he remarked that although those countries had "Hīnayāna" teachings, Buddhism was so deeply ingrained in society that it would be more correct to call it Mahayana practice. In India he visited Buddhist pilgrimage sites and met with Gandhi, Nehru, Tagore, and the German monk Lama Govinda Anagarika, whose questions led Taixu to give a talk that was later called "My Religious Experiences."

The war with Japan raised three issues for Buddhist monks: whether they would be willing to participate in war, whether they would accept the role of killing, and whether it is right for nations to fight one another. For the first question, Taixu advocated clerical responsibility to contributing to the nation's welfare. He explained, "Nothing has a definitive nature and everything has the possibility to change. It is the same with a society or nation. Individuals can change society through their efforts." Further, this must be done with compassion. With regard to the question of whether Buddhist monks may kill in a war, which would go against Buddhist precepts, Taixu remained silent. With regard to the question of one nation fighting with another, Taixu responded with a threefold model. The first priority is the welfare of the world and humankind. Following this is the welfare of one's nation. Third is the welfare of the individual and family. During wartime, however, the second item must temporarily take priority.[71]

While living in Chongqing, he began working on his final reform project, the Bodhisattva Learning Center. He presented the finished proposal at a monastery in 1947 during the last public talk of his life.[72] Whereas Taixu's earlier proposals had been systematic visions for specific changes encompassing all monasteries, this proposal describes only a single facility, the Bodhisattva Learning Center. It would be more like a dharma center found in the West than a traditional monastery. This proposal, like his earlier plans, was never realized.

The name "Bodhisattva Learning Center" (*Pusa xuechu* 菩薩學處) can be understood in two ways in Chinese. The obvious reading is a "bodhisattva learning (*xue*) place (*chu*)." But the term *xuechu* is also a Tang dynasty translation of the Sanskrit *śikṣāpada*, a technical term for "precept." In this light, the name could also be understood as simply "bodhisattva precepts," reflecting Taixu's high valuation of those precepts for both lay and clergy. According to its draft charter, it would be a place for clergy to reside and teach newly ordained monks. It would also welcome lay "bodhisattvas," and they would work together for education, charity, and production. It could house selected visitors and would be run by a board of directors (much as Taixu's Wuchang Academy) comprising well-known lay Buddhists and monastic figures. It would send people to provide instruction at other locations wishing to create a similar institution, thus operating on a type of franchise model. It would promote the practice of lay, monastic, and bodhisattva precepts, as well as cultivation of the bodhisattva path, particularly the six perfections and the four all-embracing virtues. When people at all levels of society cultivate these practices according to their abilities, then Humanistic Buddhism will be implemented and a "paradisiacal land of peace and happiness will be created."[73] This simple model links Taixu's various projects together, representing one possible way forward in the difficult times to come.

TAIXU, TRADITION, AND MODERNITY

As a modernizer, Taixu was a transitional figure. In his early years, during the Qing dynasty, he was trained by elite establishment monks. Later, he came to be one of the most informed Buddhist monks with regard to the new political, social, and philosophical ideas circulating in China before and after the 1911 revolution. It seems there was no modern idea or institution that he did not write about. Over time, he engaged with ideas that were structurally important to China, such as *Datong*, reconstruction, science, rational knowledge, freedom, social duty, citizenship, evolution, cosmology, and popular sovereignty. Taixu was drawn to these ideas, took them seriously, thought about them deeply, found value in them, and worked to integrate them into his thinking. As Justin Ritzinger has argued, Taixu holds modern values in constellation with Buddhist values. Even Taixu's seemingly traditional Maitreya School shows surprising parallels with elements of political thought, such as utopianism, rational knowledge, and individual ethical excellence.[74]

If Taixu's Maitreya School is traditional with modern elements, then his Humanistic Buddhism is modern with traditional elements. It explicitly identifies itself with rational knowledge and ethical behavior. Yet there are also statements about going beyond rational knowledge to a higher knowledge of reality, particularly in his *True Realism*. Further, Taixu understands rational knowledge to correspond to the ten stages of faith. Once one accepts Buddhism rationally, it becomes possible to have the aspiration for enlightenment. From there, one can begin carrying out cultivation based on faith in Buddhism's claims about the fruits of practice. At this point, the reader is returned to the Buddhist cosmology: this cultivation will take countless eons.[75] Progress is no longer toward a better society but toward the reduction of ignorance and afflictions. Freedom becomes buddhahood,[76] and the nation becomes a buddha land. The underlying structure is Buddhist.

His proposal for creating a Pure Land on Earth contains a similar dynamic. The main theme is the construction of a Pure Land on Earth: improving the world through moral action and creating security of life and property. At the end of that proposal, the reader is presented with (but not obligated to follow) the model of Dharmākara. As a bodhisattva, he was willing to give up his life, property, and nation—the very foundations of the Pure Land on Earth. After accumulating wisdom and merit over countless eons, Dharmākara attained buddhahood. Here, the limitations of normal time, progress, and social perfection become evident. Taixu remarks, "without abandoning what is limited, everything becomes unlimited."[77]

What then is the exact relationship between modern worldly virtue and the traditional Buddhist ideal of transcendence? From a modern secular perspective, the two remain ever-present, mutually irreducible, and bound in an uneasy tension. From a Buddhist perspective, however, the relationship is clear. Taixu used modern secular ideas as a means or vehicle for propagating Buddhism. The fact that those ideas are modern and often Western in origin is less important than their role in structuring China's politics, society, economics, and culture—in other words, ordinary reality. The moral practice of improving the real world likewise becomes a means of exploring Buddhist principles.

REVIEW OF LITERATURE

In 1968, Holmes Welch introduced Taixu to the West in a chapter from his *Buddhist Revival in China*, a book implicitly linked with Heinz Bechert's thesis of a 20th-century revival of

Buddhism. Welch documents Taixu's activities as part of the revival of Chinese Buddhism, but he sees Taixu as a superficial self-promoter with uncritical followers. Further, his final chapter asks whether the revival in Chinese Buddhism was actually meaningful. Despite Welch's personal doubts about Taixu, his research on this period is authoritative.[78] Don Pittman's 2001 monograph on Taixu, *Toward a Modern Chinese Buddhism: Taixu's Reforms*,[79] argues that Taixu relied on Mahayana Buddhism as a universal tradition central to his modernizing effort. As a case study of the methods of proselytization used by a modern religious figure in China, the book focuses on the value of Taixu's vision, in contrast with Welch's chapter, which focuses on Taixu's failures. Gotelind Müller-Saini's 1993 study looks at the Buddhist component of modernization in China.[80] She examines the approaches of Taixu and Ouyang Jingwu by comparing the manner in which they situated Buddhism in response to Western ideas. Whereas Ouyang attempted to situate Buddhism in a position superior to Western philosophy, Taixu strove to locate Buddhism on the map of Western philosophical discourse. Eric Goodell's work identifies the origins and features of Taixu's Humanistic Buddhism and places it in a broader Buddhist context.[81] Justin Ritzinger's *Anarchy in the Pure Land* sheds new light on the depth of Taixu's involvement with radical politics following the revolution and pieces together his personal involvement with the Maitreya Pure Land tradition, both of which are often overlooked.[82] Ritzinger argues that political ideas from Taixu's radical period influenced the construction of his Maitreya School. In 2021, Charles Jones published an analysis and translation of one of Taixu's most important works, "On the Establishment of a Pure Land in the Human Realm."[83] For Jones, Taixu's interest in the Pure Land tradition is essentially religious. Lai Rongdao has demonstrated that Taixu's Buddhist academies and their networks of students utilized Buddhist magazines as a discursive space to discuss ways of protecting Buddhism and create a modern clerical identity.[84] Taixu's works play a prominent role in Erik Hammerstrom's studies of early 20th-century Buddhist attitudes on science.[85] Luo Tongbing's article on Taixu's changing attitudes to tantric or esoteric Buddhism also includes the interesting period in 1934–1937 when Taixu took initiations under the sixth Panchen Lama to learn more about Tantric Buddhism.[86] Yushuang Yao and Richard Gombrich outline Christian influences on Taixu.[87] Yang Huinan argues that the worldly emphasis in Taixu's Humanistic Buddhism represents the incorporation of Confucian elements.[88]

PRIMARY SOURCES

Taixu. *Taixu dashi quanshu* 太虛大師全書. Edited by Yinshun 印順. 32 vols. Taipei: Shandao si, 1980.

Taixu's collected works were compiled in China shortly after his death and first published as a complete set in Taipei in 1955. Early editions were sixty-four volumes while later editions published the same content in thirty-two volumes. The content of all editions is divided into twenty thematic sections. A reliable digital edition based on the 1980 edition cited above was published as a CD-ROM in 2005.[89] See Digital Materials for a current online version. In the electronic versions, Taixu's many charts and tables are recreated with text and lines rather than photographic facsimiles. The prefaces include detailed accounts of the collection's compilation and publication.

Yinshun 印順, ed. *Taixu dashi nianpu* 太虛大師年言普 (Chronological biography of Taixu), revised edition. Taipei: Zhengwen 正聞, 1992.

While editing Taixu's collected works, Yinshun also compiled a biography of Taixu's life, chronicling events by month and sometimes by day. Almost every entry provides citations to primary sources. It also describes Taixu's early life, lists most of his pseudonyms, and identifies his first- and second-generation disciples. This work is indispensable for research on Taixu.

Huang Xianian 黃夏年, ed. *Minguo fojiao qikan wenxian jicheng* 民國佛教期刊文獻集成. 209 vols. Beijing: Quanguo tushuguan wenxian suowei fuzhi zhongxin, 2006. Hereafter cited as MFQ.

Huang Xianian 黃夏年, ed. *Minguo Fojiao qikan wenxian jicheng bubian* 民國佛教期刊文獻集成補編. 86 vols. Beijing: Quanguo tushuguan wenxian suowei fuzhi zhongxin 全國圖書館文獻縮微復制中心, 2008. Hereafter cited as MFQB.

These two collections contain black and white facsimile reproductions of the many Buddhist magazines that were published during the early Republican period in China, including Taixu's magazine, *Haichaoyin* 海潮音. Some of Taixu's writings not included in TDQ may be found here. See Digital Resources for an online search interface.

Huang Xianian 黃夏年 ed., *Xijian minguo fojiao wenxian huibian (baozhi)* 稀見民國佛教文獻彙編(報紙). 12 vols. Beijing: Zhongguo shudian, 2008.

This contains facsimile reproductions of Buddhist newspapers from the early Republican period.

DIGITAL MATERIALS

For a fuller bibliographical study, see Charles B. Jones's entry for "Taixu" in Oxford Bibliographies Online (https://www.oxfordbibliographies.com/view/document/obo-9780195393521/obo-9780195393521-0260.xml?rskey=YEGTni&result=1&q=taixu#firstMatch).

Taixu's collected works and Yinshun's chronological biography in Chinese are available on the Yinshun Foundation (https://www.yinshun.org.tw/) website.

The "Database of Modern Chinese Buddhism (http://buddhistinformatics.dila.edu.tw/dmcb/Main_Page)," edited by Erik Hammerstrom and Gregory Adam Scott, is hosted by the Dharma Drum Institute of Liberal Arts (DILA). This database is a good starting point for Republican period Buddhism in China and includes categories such as biographies and institutions.

The DILA hosts a digital search tool for the *Minguo fojiao qikan wenxian jicheng and Minguo fojiao qikan wenxian jicheng bubian* (http://buddhistinformatics.dila.edu.tw/minguofojiaoqikan/search.php) collections of Buddhist periodicals from the Republican period. The collections themselves have not been digitized.

Gregory Scott's *Digital Catalogue of Chinese Buddhism* (https://bib.buddhiststudies.net/search.php) provides a searchable database of Chinese-language Buddhist publications from 1860 to 1949, incorporating information from *Minguo fojiao qikan wenxian jicheng*, *Minguo fojiao qikan wenxian jicheng bubian*, and several other bibliographic sources.

FURTHER READING

Chan, Wing-tsit. *Religious Trends in Modern China*. New York: Octagon Press, 1978.

DeVido, Elise A. "The Influence of Chinese Master Taixu on Buddhism in Vietnam." *Journal of Global Buddhism* 10 (2009): 413–458.

Goodell, Eric. "Taixu's Youth and Years of Romantic Idealism, 1890–1914." *Chung-Hwa Buddhist Journal* 21 (2008): 77–121.

Hammerstrom, Erik J. "Yogācāra and Science in the 1920s: The Wuchang School's Approach to Modern Mind Science." In *Transforming Consciousness: Yogācāra Thought in Modern China*. Edited by John Makeham, 170–197. New York: Oxford University Press, 2014.

Jones, Charles B. *Taixu's "On the Establishment of the Pure Land in the Human Realm": A Translation and Study*. London: Bloomsbury Publishing, 2021.

Lai, Rongdao. "The Wuchang Ideal: Buddhist Education and Identity Production in Republican China." *Studies in Chinese Religions* 3, no. 1 (2017): 55–70.

Luo, Tongbing. "The Reformist Monk Taixu and the Controversy about Exoteric and Esoteric Buddhism." In *Images of Tibet in the 19th and 20th Centuries*. Edited by Monica Esposito, 433–471. Paris: EFEO, 2008.

Müller-Saini, Gotelind. "Buddhism and Historicity in Early 20th Century China: Ouyang Jingwu, Taixu and the Problem of Modernity." *Orientierungen* 2 (2007): 28–51.

Pacey, Scott. "Taixu, Yogācāra, and the Buddhist Approach to Modernity." In *Transforming Consciousness: Yogacara Thought in Modern China*. Edited by John Makeham, 149–169. New York: Oxford University Press, 2014.

Pittman, Don Alvin. *Toward a Modern Chinese Buddhism: Taixu's Reforms*. Honolulu: University of Hawai'i Press, 2001.

Ritzinger, Justin R. *Anarchy in the Pure Land: Reinventing the Cult of Maitreya in Republican China*. New York: Oxford University Press, 2017.

Sueki, Fumihiko. "Chinese Buddhism and the Anti-Japan War." *Japanese Journal of Religious Studies* 37, no. 1 (2010): 9–20.

Welch, Holmes. *The Buddhist Revival in China*. Cambridge, MA: Harvard University Press, 1968.

Welch, Holmes. *The Practice of Chinese Buddhism, 1900–1950*. Cambridge, MA: Harvard University Press, 1973. Originally published in 1967.

NOTES

1. For a fuller account of Taixu's early years, see Eric Goodell, "Taixu's Youth and Years of Romantic Idealism, 1890–1914," *Chung-Hwa Buddhist Journal* 21 (2008): 77–121.
2. Yinshun, "Geming shidai de Taixu fashi" 革命時代的太虛大師 [Master Taixu of revolutionary times], in *Huayu xiangyun* 華雨香雲 (Taipei: Zhengwen, 2000), 292.
3. Tan Sitong 譚嗣同, *Renxue* 仁學 [Exposition of Benevolence] (Beijing: Huaxia, 2002).
4. Taixu, "Zizhuan" 自傳 [Autobiography], in *Taixu dashi quanshu* 太虛大師全書 [Collected works of Master Taixu], ed. Yinshun (Taipei: Shandao si, 1980), 29:191 (hereafter cited as TDQ).
5. Sin-wai Chan, *Buddhism in late Ch'ing Political Thought* (Hong Kong: Chinese University Press, 1985), 37–46, 141, 148; see also Kang Youwei, *Datong shu* 大同書, (Shanghai: Zhonghua shuju, 1935), 346–352.
6. Taixu, "Zizhuan," TDQ, 29:196.
7. Taixu, "Wo de fojiao gaijin yundong lüeshi" 我的佛教改進運動略史 [A brief history of my movement to reform Buddhism], TDQ, 29:72–73 (emphasis added).

8. Holmes Welch, *The Buddhist Revival in China* (Cambridge, MA: Harvard University Press, 1968), 16.
9. Taixu's biographer Yinshun links Taixu's state of mind to Chan realizations that "rendered all things relative," translated in Justin R. Ritzinger, *Anarchy in the Pure Land: Reinventing the Cult of Maitreya in Modern Chinese Buddhism* (New York: Oxford University Press, 2017), 73; see also Peter Berger, *Sacred Canopy: Elements of a Sociological Theory of Religion* (Garden City, NY: Doubleday, 1967), 98: "To the mystic this world and all its works . . . are relativized. In extreme cases this relativization may lead to a religiously legitimated anarchism."
10. Peter Zarrow, *Anarchism and Chinese Culture* (New York: Columbia University Press, 1990), 3.
11. Ritzinger, *Anarchy in the Pure Land*, 52.
12. Taixu, "Wushen lun" 無神論 [On atheism], TDQ, 21:284–295.
13. Cao Shixuan 曹世鉉, *Qingmo minchu wuzhengfupai de wenhua sixiang* 清末民初無政府派的文化思想 (Beijing: Shehui kexue wenxian chubanshe, 2003), 201.
14. See Ritzinger, *Anarchy in the Pure Land*, 27–101, for an account of Taixu's political period.
15. On the government's secularizing agenda, see Rebecca Nedostup, *Superstitious Regimes: Religion and the Politics of Chinese Modernity* (Cambridge, MA: Harvard University Press, 2009).
16. Rongdao Lai, "Praying for the Republic: Buddhist Education, Student-Monks, and Citizenship in Modern China (1911–1949)" (PhD diss., McGill University, 2013), 242; and Yinshun, ed., *Taixu dashi nianpu* 太虛大師年言普 [Chronological biography of Taixu], rev. ed. (Taipei: Zhengwen, 1992), 410, 505–507.
17. Welch, *Buddhist Revival*, 166.
18. Taixu, "Lüeshi" of 1940, TDQ, 29:67, and "Gao tuzhong shu" 告徒眾書 [A letter to my disciples and supporters] of 1928, TDQ, 17:585 respectively.
19. Ritzinger, *Anarchy in the Pure Land*, 74.
20. Da moushi shu 答某師書 [A letter to a certain monk], TDQ, 26:85–87.
21. Taixu, "Tangdai Chanzong yu xiandai sichao" 唐代禪宗與現代思潮 [Tang dynasty Chan and modern intellectual trends], TDQ, 20:226.
22. Ritzinger, *Anarchy in the Pure Land*, 60. He ended the retreat after twenty-seven months.
23. Ritzinger, *Anarchy in the Pure Land*, 60.
24. Taixu, "Zizhuan," TDQ 29:208.
25. Taixu, "Chan lü mi jing sixing lun" 律禪密淨四行論 [On four types of practice: Vinaya, Chan, Esoteric, and Pure Land], TDQ, 1:365.
26. Taixu, "Gao tushong shu" [A letter to my disciples and supporters], TDQ, 17:584. I have not followed the translation in Ritzinger, *Anarchy in the Pure Land*, 60.
27. Taixu, "Zizhuan," TDQ, 29:210. See also Reichelt's description quoted in Don Pittman, *Toward a Modern Chinese Buddhism: Taixu's Reforms* (Honolulu: University of Hawai'i Press, 2001), 82.
28. Sheng Yen, "Four Great Thinkers in the History of Modern Chinese Buddhism," in *Buddhist Ethics and Modern Society: An International Symposium*, ed. Charles Wei-hsun and Sandra A. Wawrytko (Westport, CT: Greenwood Press, 1991), 285. For a study of the *Awakening of Faith* in modern times, see Francesca Tarocco, "Lost in Translation? The *Treatise on the Mahāyāna Awakening of Faith* (*Dasheng Qixin Lun*) and Its Modern Readings," *Bulletin of SOAS* 71, no. 2 (2008): 323–343.
29. Taixu, "Wo de zongjiao jingyan" 我的宗教經驗 [My religious experiences], TDQ, 21:349; and "Zizhuan," TDQ, 29:216.
30. Scott Pacey, "Taixu, Yogācāra, and the Buddhist Approach to Modernity," in *Transforming Consciousness: Yogacara Thought in Modern China*, ed. John Makeham (New York: Oxford University Press, 2014), 149–169.
31. Taixu, *Zhengli sengqie zhidu lun* 整理僧伽制度論 [A proposal for institutional reform in the Sangha], TDQ, 17:153.

32. Welch, *Buddhist Revival*, 103–107; and Holmes Welch, *The Practice of Chinese Buddhism, 1900–1950* (Cambridge, MA: Harvard University Press, 1973), 310–314.
33. Yinshun, *Taixu dashi nianpu*, 141.
34. Taixu, "Gao guonei foxue tongzhi shu" 告國內佛學同志書, TDQ, 26:219; and Welch, *Buddhist Revival*, 262.
35. Rongdao Lai, "The Wuchang Ideal: Buddhist Education and Identity Production in Republican China," *Studies in Chinese Religions* 3, no. 1 (2017): 56.
36. For a brief biography of Cihang, see Charles Jones, *Buddhism in Taiwan: Religion and the State, 1660–1990* (Honolulu: University of Hawai'i Press, 1999), 102–105. Stefania Travagnin has published multiple works on Yinshun, including "What Is Behind Yinshun's Re-statement of the Nature of the Mūlamadhyamakakārikā? Debates on the Creation of a New Mahāyāna in Twentieth-century China," *Buddhist Studies Review* 29, no. 2 (2012): 251–272. On Zhumo (Chuk Mor) and Yanpei, see Jack Meng-Tat Chia, *Monks in Motion: Buddhism and Modernity across the South China Sea* (New York: Oxford University Press, 2020). On Fazun, see Gray Tuttle, *Tibetan Buddhists in the Making of Modern China* (New York: Columbia University Press, 2007).
37. Lai, "Wuchang Ideal."
38. Taixu, "Fu Wang Rongzi jushi shu" 復王容子居士書, TDQ, 26:110; Hongzan, *Doushuai guijing ji* 兜率龜鏡集, CBETA 2020 version of *Shinsan Dainihon zokuzōkyō* 新纂大日本續藏經, edited by Kawamura Kōshō et al., (Tokyo: 1975–1989), #1643. On other sources for Taixu's early interest in Maitreya, see Ritzinger, *Anarchy in the Pure Land*, 110–112.
39. *Mile shangsheng jing* 彌勒上生經 [Sutra of Maitreya's ascent], CBETA 2020 edition of the *Taishō shinshū dai zōkyō* 大正新脩大藏經, edited by Takakusu Junjirō and Watanabe Kaikyoku et al. (Tokyo: Taishō Issaikyō Kankōkai, 1924–1934; hereafter cited as T), #452, 14:418b1–420c22.
40. For a study of Taixu's involvement with the Maitreya tradition, see Ritzinger, *Anarchy in the Pure Land*, 105–209.
41. For a translation from the Sanskrit version of this chapter (which is slightly different from the Chinese version), see Janice Dean Willis, *On Knowing Reality: The Tattvārtha Chapter of Asaṅga's Bodhisattvabhūmi* (New York: Columbia University Press, 1979), 147–175.
42. Ritzinger, *Anarchy in the Pure Land*, 122.
43. Taixu, "Chan lü mi jing sixing lun," TDQ, 1:365.
44. Reproduced in Ritzinger, *Anarchy in the Pure Land*, 114.
45. Ritzinger, *Anarchy in the Pure Land*, 114, 218.
46. The second was published 1931, and both are translated in Charles Jones, *Taixu's "On the Establishment of the Pure Land in the Human Realm": A Translation and Study* (London: Bloomsbury Publishing, 2021).
47. Jones, *Taixu's On the Establishment of the Pure Land*, 87, 93. My translation.
48. Jones, *Taixu's On the Establishment of the Pure Land*, 61. These remarks about technology originally come from Liu Renhang, *Dongfang datong xuean* 東方大同學案 (Shanghai: Shanghai shudian, 1991), fasc. 6.
49. Liu Renhang, *Dongfang datong xuean*. For the influence of Tang Dayuan and the context of the "New Village" movement, see Jakub Zamorski, "An Old Savior in a New Paradise: Buddha Amitābha in Tang Dayuan's 'New Pure Land,'" *Journal of Chinese Buddhist Studies* 32 (2019): 97–125.
50. Jones, *Taixu's On the Establishment of the Pure Land*, 93–94.
51. Jones, *Taixu's On the Establishment of the Pure Land*, 95–96.
52. Jones, *Taixu's On the Establishment of the Pure Land*, 102.
53. Jones, *Taixu's On the Establishment of the Pure Land*, 111.
54. Taixu, *Weimojie suoshuo bukesiyi jietuo jing shi hui jiwen shang* 維摩詰所說不可思議解脫經釋會紀聞上 [Commentary and notes on the *Vimalakīrti-nirdeśa sutra*], for example TDQ, 11:711–722, 758.
55. Ritzinger, *Anarchy in the Pure Land*, 226–227.

56. For example, "All worlds come into being on the basis of the power of karma," *Qishi jing*, T#24, 1:310b24, a sutra quoted by Taixu in his discussion of Uttarakuru in *On the Establishment of the Pure Land*, Jones, *Taixu's On the Establishment of the Pure Land*, 58.
57. Jones, *Taixu's On the Establishment of the Pure Land*, 129–139.
58. Eric Goodell, "Conservative and Progressive Models for Buddhism under the Republic of China," in *Religion, Culture, and the Public Sphere in China and Japan*, ed. Albert Welter and Jeffrey Newmark (Singapore: Springer, 2017), 43–68.
59. Taixu, "Lun Liang Shuming Dong Xi wenhua jiqi zhexue" 論梁漱溟東西文化及其哲學 [On Liang Shuming's *Eastern and Western Cultures and their Philosophies*], TDQ, 25:304–305.
60. Taixu specifically emphasizes Humanistic Buddhism's rational and ethical components in "Rensheng de fojiao" 人生的佛教 [Buddhism for peoples' lives], TDQ, 3:238–242.
61. Taixu, "Rensheng foxue de shuoming" 人生佛學的說明 [An explanation of Humanistic Buddhist learning], TDQ, 3:206–216.
62. Taixu, "Duiyu zhongguo fojiao geming seng de xunci" 對於中國佛教革命僧的訓詞 [Instructions for Chinese Buddhist revolutionary clergy], TDQ, 17:596–604.
63. Taixu, Zongyi lun, TDQ, 19:454, 458.
64. Taixu, "Jiren chengfo de zhen xianshi lun" 即人成佛的真現實論 [The attainment of buddhahood by this very person with True Realism], TDQ, 24:463.
65. Eric Goodell, "Taixu's History of the Chan Tradition," in *Approaches to Chan, Sŏn, and Zen Studies: Chinese Chan Buddhism and Its Spread throughout East Asia*, ed. Albert Welter, Steven Heine, and Jin Y. Park (Albany: State University of New York Press, forthcoming).
66. On Yinshun and Zhao Puchu, respectively, see Marcus Bingenheimer, "Some Remarks on the Usage of Renjian Fojiao and the Contribution of Venerable Yinshun to Chinese Buddhist Modernism," in *Development and Practice of Humanitarian Buddhism: Interdisciplinary Perspectives*, ed. Mutsu Hsu, Jinhua Chen, and Lori Meeks (Hua-lien, Taiwan: Tzuchi University Press, 2007), 141–161; and Ji Zhe, "Zhao Puchu and His Renjian Buddhism," *Eastern Buddhist* 44, no. 2 (2013): 35–58.
67. Elise A. DeVido, "The Influence of Chinese Master Taixu on Buddhism in Vietnam," *Journal of Global Buddhism* 10 (2009): 436.
68. This discussion is based on Taixu's explanation in Taixu, "Wo zenyang panshe yiqie fofa" 我怎樣判攝一切佛法 [How I classify all Buddhist teachings], TDQ, 1:509–529.
69. For an introduction to the fifty-two-stage path, see Tōru Funayama, "Buddhist Theories of Bodhisattva Practice as Adopted by Daoists," *Cahiers d'Extrême-Asie* 20 (2011): 15–24.
70. Yin-shun, *The Way to Buddhahood* (Boston: Wisdom Publications, 1998); Sheng Yen, *Orthodox Chinese Buddhism: A Contemporary Chan Master's Answers to Common Questions* (Elmhurst, NY: Dharma Drum Publications, 2007), 145–147.
71. Sueki Fumihiko 末木文美士, "Chinese Buddhism and the Anti-Japan War," *Japanese Journal of Religious Studies* 37, no. 1 (2010): 9–20.
72. Taixu, "Pusa xuechu" 菩薩學處 (1940), TDQ, 17:530–531; "Pusa xuechu jiangyao" 菩薩學處講要 (1947), TDQ, 17:281–327.
73. Pittman, *Toward a Modern Chinese Buddhism*, 221.
74. Ritzinger, *Anarchy in the Pure Land*.
75. Taixu, "Rensheng foxue de shuoming" [An explanation of humanistic Buddhist learning], TDQ, 3:209.
76. Taixu, "Fotuo xuegang" 佛陀學綱, TDQ, 1:255.
77. Taixu, "Chuangzao renjian jingtu" 刱造人間淨土 [Creating the Pure Land in the Human Realm], TDQ, 24:430. I have not followed the translation in Jones, *Taixu's On the Establishment of the Pure Land*, 125.
78. Welch, *Buddhist Revival*, 51–71.
79. Pittman, *Toward a Modern Chinese Buddhism*.

80. Gotelind Müller (now Müller-Saini), *Buddhismus und Moderne: Ouyang Jingwu, Taixu und das Ringen um ein zeitgemasses Selbstverstandnis im chinesischen Buddhismus des frühen 20 Jahrhunderts* [Buddhism and modernity: Ouyang Jingwu, Taixu and the quest for a timely self-definition of Chinese Buddhism in the early twentieth century] (Stuttgart: Franz Steiner Verlag, 1993); and Müller, "Buddhism and Historicity in Early 20th Century China: Ouyang Jingwu, Taixu and the Problem of Modernity," *Orientierungen* 2 (2007): 28–51.
81. Eric Goodell, "Taixu's (1890–1947) Creation of Humanistic Buddhism" (PhD diss., University of Virginia, 2012); Goodell, "Conservative and Progressive Models for Buddhism Under the Republic of China," in *Religion, Culture, and the Public Sphere in China and Japan*, ed. Albert Welter and Jeffrey Newmark (Singapore: Springer, 2017), 43–68; and Goodell, "Taixu's History of the Chan Tradition," forthcoming.
82. Ritzinger, *Anarchy in the Pure Land.*
83. Jones, *Taixu's On the Establishment of a Pure Land in the Human Realm.*
84. Lai, "The Wuchang Ideal."
85. Erik J. Hammerstrom, *The Science of Chinese Buddhism: Early Twentieth-Century Engagements* (New York: Columbia University Press, 2015).
86. Luo Tongbing 羅同兵, "The Reformist Monk Taixu and the Controversy about Exoteric and Esoteric Buddhism," in *Images of Tibet in the 19th and 20th Centuries*, ed. Monica Esposito (Paris: EFEO, 2008), 433–471.
87. Yu-shuang Yao and Richard Gombrich, "Christianity as Model and Analogue in the Formation of the 'Humanistic' Buddhism of Tai Xu and Hsing Yun," *Buddhist Studies Review* 34, no. 2 (2017): 205–212.
88. Yang Huinan 楊惠南, "Renjian fojiao de jingdian quanshi: shi yuan ru ru fo huoshi huigui yindu" 人間佛教的經典詮釋—是援儒入佛或是回歸印度? [Scriptural interpretation of "Buddhism for this World": Is it "Applying Confucianism into Buddhism" or returning to Indian Buddhism?], *Chung-Hwa Buddhist Journal* 13 (May 2000): 482–511.
89. *Taixu dashi quanshu* 太虛大師全書 (Taipei: Yinshun wenjiao jijinhui, Taipei, 2005), CD-ROM.

Eric Goodell

TANTRA AND THE TANTRIC TRADITIONS OF HINDUISM AND BUDDHISM

"Tantrism," or the tantric traditions, originated as a development within Hinduism during the first millennium CE. Over the course of this millennium Hinduism went through a remarkable series of transformations, transitioning from the ancient Vedic tradition into the classical traditions of Hinduism. This period saw the rise of both the tantric and the Bhakti devotional movements. While the latter drew from the tendency toward monotheism seen in late Vedic literature, tantrism developed from Vedic ritual traditions as well as from the yogic and meditative traditions that developed both within ancient Hinduism as well as in rival Buddhist and Jain traditions. Hinduism as currently practiced is a product of the intermixture of tantric and devotional approaches to practice that developed during the first millennium CE.

The connection of contemporary Hindu practices, such as daily worship ceremonies (*pūjā*, *nityapūjā*) conducted by many Hindus in private shrines or public temples, to tantric traditions is not well understood by most Hindus or even by scholars, as the rich liturgical literature produced by Hindu traditions has, until relatively recently, been largely ignored.[1] While most

Hindu traditions have received some influence from the tantric traditions, the focus here will be the Hindu traditions that clearly and unambiguously identify as tantric. But tantrism, while originating in a Hindu context, is not limited to Hinduism. Early Hindu tantric traditions had a striking impact on South Asian Mahāyāna Buddhist traditions, leading to the development of distinctly Buddhist tantric traditions. They also had a less striking but still real impact on Jainism and several other religious traditions. Buddhist tantric traditions, which emerged during the 7th century CE, were rapidly transmitted to Southeast, East, and Central Asia, leading to the establishment of several distinct East Asian and Tibetan traditions. These, in turn, had an impact on the development of Daoism and Shintoism in East Asia, as well as the Bön tradition in Tibet.

The tantric traditions of Hinduism and Buddhism have been simultaneously infamous as well as poorly understood. Due to the strong association of tantric traditions with magical practices, and of the so-called "left-handed" (*vāmācāra*) tantric traditions with sexuality and violent ritual practices, the tantric traditions have, over the past few centuries at least, been associated with black magic in India. Tantric traditions have had a tremendous impact on the practice of Hinduism that is now poorly appreciated by most Hindus; the term *tantra* is now best known in South Asia in the compound *tantramantra*, which is the equivalent in modern languages such as Hindi to "abracadabra" or "hocus-pocus" in English, terms that originated in Western magical practices that now designate "mumbo-jumbo, nonsense, gibberish"[2] and "magic, trickery, or sleight of hand,"[3] respectively. The title *Tantra Mantra* was given to a recent Hindi horror film featuring black magic.[4] The term *tantra* in modern Indian languages "is frequently used to conjure notions of effective black magic, illicit sexuality, and immoral behavior."[5] Western scholars of Indian culture and history often treated tantric traditions with disdain, using its alleged degeneracy as an excuse to ignore this important aspect of Asian religious history.[6]

DEFINING TANTRA/TANTRIC TRADITIONS

Tantric traditions are manifold, spanning several religious traditions and cultural worlds. As a result they are also diverse, which makes it a significant challenge to come up with an adequate definition, one that is broad enough to be applicable to all of the tantric traditions, but not too broad, including traditions that would not identify themselves as tantric, and thus should be excluded from this rubric.

The tantric traditions have been given several labels, but there is no single label that is accepted by all of these traditions. The adjective *tantric*, an English word derived from the Sanskrit term *tāntrika*, means simply that which relates to the *tantras*, the genre of scripture that serves as the canonical basis for the various tantric traditions. Tantras are works that primarily focus on ritual and meditative practices, so the term *tantric* also envelops the practices associated with these scriptures, which were traditionally disseminated by the *tāntrikas* (the Sanskrit term also designates tantric practitioners), along with the texts.[7] So "tantric traditions" are the communities of practitioners who practice, preserve, and transmit through both time and space both the texts and the practices traditionally associated with them.

It is important to note the use of this term in a plural form. Tantric traditions are multiple and also originated as multiple, distinct traditions of both text and practice. One of the most important tropes in the history of the dissemination of tantric traditions is that of lineage, the transmission of teachings along an uninterrupted lineage, from master to disciple, the so-called *guruparaṃparā*. This focus on lineage is found throughout the tantric world; originating in India, this emphasis was transmitted to Tibet and East Asia and remains an important concern of contemporary tantric communities.

In the West the tantric traditions have often been labeled "Tantrism," a neologism coined by Western scholars that does not reflect the self-understanding of any particular tantric tradition. As André Padoux noted,

> The word "Tantrism" is assuredly a Western creation. India traditionally knows only texts called Tantras. These texts, moreover, fall far short of covering the entire Tantric literature; nor are only Tantric texts called Tantras. India also knows the word *tantraśāstra*, "the teaching of the Tantras," as well as the adjective *tāntrika*, "Tantric," which is opposed to *vaidika*, "Vedic," thereby placing a new form of revelation and rites against Vedic tradition and rites.[8]

The concept is based upon the *tantras*, key scriptures in many tantric traditions, but as Padoux notes, not all tantric traditions use the term *tantra* for their scripture, and the term is also used for nontantric works. We might also add that tantric traditions also use other terms for their scriptures; Hindu tantric traditions also use the terms *āgama, jñāna, saṃhitā, siddhānta, vidyā*, and *upaniṣad* to designate scriptures,[9] while Buddhist traditions also used the terms *sūtra* and *kalpa* for some of their scriptures. So the presence or absence of tantras cannot be taken as a defining characteristic of these traditions. Likewise, while the East Asian tantric Buddhist traditions preserve Chinese translations of many of the tantras, the term *tantra* itself is not well known by these traditions, nor do they identify themselves as "tantric."[10] But the very term *tantra* points to an important feature of even these traditions. The scriptures known as *tantras*, which were transmitted to East Asia, tend to be heavily focused on the description of ritual, meditative, and yogic practices. These traditions tend to be heavily practice-oriented, with the goals of this practice ranging from worldly success to ultimate liberation, however defined.

Obviously it would be ideal to define *tantra* in terms of a single defining characteristic. Were there a single feature that all tantric traditions shared, this would naturally make it far easier to delineate exactly what the term designates. Such attempts include the Tibetan scholar Tsongkhapa's (1357–1419 CE) argument that deity yoga, the visualization of oneself as a deity, is the defining characteristic of tantric practice, an argument that was problematized by his contemporary Ngorchen Kunga Sangpo (1389–1456 CE), who noted that not all esoteric works classified as tantras feature this practice.[11] While the visualization of oneself as a deity is an important aspect of many tantric traditions, it is not found in all. It is also a somewhat arbitrary definition, as there are also many other elements of tantric practice that are found in most, if not all, tantric traditions.

One solution to this problem is to delineate a range of features that tend to characterize tantric traditions. This was done by Teun Goudriaan, who first attempted to define "Tantrism" in terms of union with divinity, much like Tsongkhapa. He defined it as "the systematic quest for salvation or for spiritual excellence by realizing and fostering the bipolar, bisexual divinity within one's own body."[12] He then went on to list a number of "tantric elements" that characterize this path to practice, including distinct paths of practice (*sādhana*), the use of mantras and mandalas, visualization and worship of the deities, distinct initiation ceremonies, and yogic practices involving the subtle body.

This definition is quite useful as it indicates the range of ritual and contemplative techniques employed by tantric practitioners in order to achieve magical powers (*siddhi*) as well as liberation. Liberation in the Hindu theistic traditions is generally defined as the attainment of union with or proximity to the supreme deity, while it is defined as the achievement of the awakening of a buddha by Buddhists. For both traditions liberation is characterized by both knowledge and freedom.

While we might debate which elements of tantric practice might be included in a definition or taxonomy of yantrism, it should be noted that tantric traditions of all sectarian affiliations, be they Buddhist or Hindu, are characterized by a strong focus on ritual and meditative practice. From a certain perspective, yantrism is, as Jean Filliozat stated, "merely the ritual and technical aspect of Hinduism."[13] This makes sense when one considers that tantric ritual largely supplanted the older Vedic ritual system in Hinduism. Likewise, in Buddhism, tantrism originated simply as the ritual facet of Mahāyāna Buddhism as it came to be practiced in India around the mid-first millennium CE, and it emerged as an independent tradition only when its practitioners developed a self-conscious sense of distinction vis-à-vis mainstream "exoteric" Mahāyāna Buddhist traditions. Hence, as André Padoux argued, "Tantrism" per se is simply an academic category, abstracted from

> the various forms taken over the course of time by large sections of Hinduism and Buddhism. Depending upon the background, the origins, and the local influences, the evolution was more or less marked by a rejection of orthodox Vedic rules and notions; it included more or less local autochthonous cults and beliefs, local religious behaviors, and magical and/or other practices.[14]

As there was, however, considerable borrowing among these traditions, there are commonalities that can be found among these traditions, although they are diverse enough to resist reduction to a single defining quality shared by all of them.

THE ORIGINS OF TANTRIC TRADITIONS

The origins of the tantric traditions is an enigma, largely due to the paucity of historical evidence in India from the period when it seems that they first emerged, during the Gupta dynasty (320–550 CE). This paucity of evidence has led to a great deal of unbridled speculation regarding the origin of these traditions. There is no hard evidence for the existence of tantric traditions prior to the mid-first millennium CE. While it is clear that some aspects of the tantric traditions, such as characteristic practices or iconography, considerably predate the historical formation of these traditions, the various attempts to date Tantrism prior to the first millennium CE are based on very flimsy evidence.[15]

The tantras themselves, as well as associated scriptures (*āgama*, *saṃhitā*, etc.), are understood by their respective traditions to be revealed works, initially taught by deities. In the Śaiva tradition, scriptures are believed to have originated in teachings given by Śiva to his wife, Devī;

these teachings were then later conveyed to human sages such as Matsendranāth.[16] The Śākta and Vaiṣṇava tantric traditions, on the other hand, hold the Goddess and Viṣṇu, respectively, to be the original divine teachers. Some Buddhist tantric traditions claim that their scriptures were taught by timeless cosmic buddhas and then revealed to adepts.[17] These myths, while claiming that scriptures originate in a timeless divine expression, nonetheless point to their revelation as being meditated by great realized adepts (*mahāsiddhas*) who lived during the early medieval period, around the 7th through 13th centuries, more or less when most tantric scriptures actually came to light.

To the extent that tantric scriptures discuss their origins, these disclosures tend to be mythical rather than historical. Treating these myths as history is naturally methodologically unsound. For example, a number of Buddhist tantras, following the textual model of the Buddhist sutra genre, begin with an opening passage (*nidāna*) that indicates the circumstances in which the scripture was taught. A number of tantras claim that they were, like the sutras, initially taught by Śākyamuni Buddha. Despite these origin claims, however, there is absolutely no evidence that any of the Buddhist tantras originated when the Buddha lived, around the 5th century BCE.[18] These passages represent attempts to legitimate these works as awakened speech (*buddhavacana*) and cannot be taken as historical evidence.

While attempts to root aspects of tantric traditions in the distant past are speculative at best, there is no doubt that these traditions, as they emerged, were heavily dependent on earlier Indian traditions of thought and practice. One of the biggest influences on tantric traditions was the far older Vedic tradition of Hinduism. Vedic Hinduism featured the priestly class, Brahmins, who had the sacred duty to memorize the oral sacred literature of the tradition, the *Veda*s, and also learn the complex ritual practices the tradition advocated. These rituals focused on offerings to the gods made into a sacred fire, which ranged from largely vegetarian offerings made into small domestic (*gṛhya*) fires that householders were to maintain, to the larger "solemn" (*śrauta*) rites that required animal sacrifice. This tradition developed circa 1500–500 BCE, reaching its peak right around 500 BCE, just prior to rise of the renunciant traditions that would challenge it. Although there was tension between advocates of the Vedic tradition and advocates of *some* of the tantric traditions, the tantric traditions drew heavily from Vedic ritual practice traditions nonetheless.[19]

This borrowing includes wholesale adaptation of the key Vedic rite of fire sacrifice, *homa*,[20] and the transformation of the Vedic rite of royal consecration, *rājyasūya*, into the tantric rite of initiation qua "consecration," *abhiṣeka*.[21] Even the distinctly tantric practice of visualizing oneself as a deity had Vedic precursors; some Vedic rites required ritual identification with the deity, via both inner visualization and outer ritual actions.[22] This was a natural outcome of the decline of the Vedic *śrauta* sacrificial system around the 5th through 13th centuries.[23] And its decline was accompanied by the parallel rise of the tantric traditions, which developed new ritual systems that borrowed heavily from Vedic precursors.

One of the key factors leading to the emergence of the tantric traditions was the rise of the world-renouncing *śramaṇa* movement a thousand years earlier, around the mid-first millennium BCE. This movement, which started within Hinduism but led to the development of rival traditions, namely Buddhism and Jainism, was characterized by its highlighting of the goal of liberation (*mokṣa*) from cyclic existence (*saṃsāra*) as the key religious goal, as well as the articulation of distinct paths of practice for reaching this goal. These include, most notably, renunciation and asceticism as a key requisite for liberation. Buddhist and Hindu *śramaṇa* traditions held that liberation resulted from a process of "awakening" (*bodhi*) in which the practitioner achieves a special knowledge or gnosis (*jñāna*) that liberates one from the cycle of awakening. The practice of meditation and yoga were seen as key practices to develop this realization. Tantric traditions inherited this assumption, and many of the contemplative practices, from earlier renunciant traditions.

Buddhist tantric traditions, naturally, accepted the cosmological and philosophical frameworks developed by earlier Buddhist traditions, as well as many of their contemplative practices. Hindu tantric traditions, in turn, accepted and further developed the sophisticated cosmological and psychological doctrines developed by the Sāṃkhya school, as well as the contemplative practices developed by its sister Yoga school.[24] Both of these traditions facilitated the transmission of ideas and practices developed by Hindu *śramaṇa* groups.

The early first millennium CE also saw another important development in Hinduism, namely, the rise of the Bhakti devotional movement. This development occurred around the same time as the rise of the tantric traditions. It was characterized by tendency toward monotheism, in that devotion to a single supreme creator god was seen as the key to salvation. This tendency is ancient in Hinduism and is very clear in some of the later *Upaniṣads* dating to the second half of the first millennium BCE.[25] Relatively early works such as the *Bhagavad Gīta*, estimated to date circa 100 CE,[26] call for devotion to God as the supreme path to liberation.

The popularity and explosive growth of devotional Hinduism had a significant effect on the tantric traditions. Devotion to God is a central feature of most Hindu tantric traditions,[27] and the Vaiṣṇava Pāñcarātra tradition in particular fused both Bhakti and tantric modes of practice.[28] Given Buddhism's rejection of the notion of a supreme Creator God, one would expect that the Bhakti influence would be less apparent in Buddhist tantric traditions. This may be the case, but while the influence was less, it was not nonexistent. In the Buddhist context devotion is typically limited to the guru, but this is seen as an essential requisite for tantric practice. The necessity of devotion to the guru is strongly emphasized in later works such as *The Fifty Stanzas on the Guru* (*Gurupañcāśikā*).[29]

The exact time in which tantric traditions emerged in India remains an enigma due to a dearth of historical evidence in South Asia from the first half of the first millennium CE. However, as we will see in the next section below, the available evidence suggests that the 5th century CE was the most likely period in which the first tantric traditions emerged, and they likely emerged first in the context of the Śaiva tradition of Hinduism.

HINDU TANTRIC TRADITIONS

The Śaiva Traditions. While the origins of tantric traditions are unclear, available evidence indicates that distinctly tantric forms of Hinduism emerged first among unorthodox Śaiva Hindu traditions around the fifth century CE. Thence it spread to other Hindu traditions, as well as to Buddhism; distinctly tantric forms of Buddhism emerged during the 7th century. It is impossible to precisely date the emergence of tantric Hindu traditions due to the poor state of textual preservation in these traditions; no Hindu tantric manuscripts from earlier than the 9th century have been preserved.

Nonetheless, the available evidence points to the 5th century as the most likely time when Śaiva Hindu tantric traditions first emerged. One of the earliest references to tantric texts and/or practices is found in a 423 CE Gaṅgdhār stone tablet inscription. The inscription includes the following reference to a temple to the Mothers (*mātṛ*):

> Also for the sake of religious merit, the king's minister caused to be built . . . this most terrible of abode, strewn with a multitude of [images of] Ḍākinīs [i.e.,] of the Mothers, that drove of joyous over-the-top gong-bangers who are pumped up to the rain clouds [on] the powerful winds raised by the Tantras.[30]

This is the earliest datable reference both to the term *tantra* qua ritual manual, as well as to the ḍākinīs, a class of goddesses who are closely linked to the tantric traditions. While we do not know exactly what texts or ritual traditions were being deployed in early 5th century Gaṅgdhār, it was almost certainly Śaiva. This is because the Śaiva tantric tradition is the only tradition for which there is evidence to date to the 5th century.

Śaiva literature is traditionally divided into three "paths": the "supreme path" (*atimārga*), the "path of mantra" (*mantramārga*), and the "path of the clans" (*kulamantra*). The Atimārga was produced by three distinct groups: the Pāñcārthika Pāśupatas, the Lākulas or Kālamukhas, and the Kāpālikas or Mahāvratins. These were ascetic groups who sought liberation and were also reputed to possess magical powers, and they likely constituted the context in which many practices that later came to characterize the tantric traditions first developed. The earliest of these groups, the Pāśupatas, likely formed no later than the 2nd century CE.[31] The Kāpālikas, on the other hand, who apparently date to about the 5th century, were a major influence on the development of later Hindu and Buddhist tantric traditions due to the antinomian and violent nature of their observances.[32]

The earliest tantric tradition to emerge was likely the Śaiva Mantramārga tradition of the 5th century. It was subdivided into the Śaiva Siddhānta tradition, which was widespread throughout India during the second half of the first millennium CE, but later was restricted to South India. It was characterized by public rituals performed by priests. The Mantramārga also included non-Siddhānta traditions that generally focused on private worship. The latter was subdivided into works of two genres: the Mantrapīṭha, focusing on the deity Bhairava, and the goddess-centered Vidyāpīṭha.[33] The earliest Mantramārga works appear to date to the 5th century, around the same time as the Gaṅgdhār inscription. According to Alexis Sanderson,

> the earliest text corpus of this tradition, the *Niśvāsatattvasaṃhitā*, which has come down to us in a Nepalese palm-leaf manuscript of the ninth century, was composed at a time from the fifth to seventh centuries and that the *Mūlasūtra* (/*Niśvāsamūla*), which is certainly the earliest work within that corpus, was composed at a time between *c.* 450 and 550 AD.[34]

The Vidyāpīṭha tantras are notable for their antinomian nature. They borrow from the older Kāpālika tradition the focus on the charnel ground as the ideal site of practice and are characterized by practices connected with female divinities known as Yoginīs or Ḍākinīs. Both violent and sexual practices are common in these works. The Vidyāpīṭha tantras are poorly preserved, but they appear to have been popular around the 6th and 7th centuries.[35] While we have no definitive evidence proving the existence of Vidyāpīṭha texts around this time, there is circumstantial evidence. This evidence includes references to non-Buddhist *ḍākinītantras* and *bhaginītantras* that prescribe violent and sexual practices by the Buddhist philosopher Dharmakīrti in his auto-commentary on his *Pramāṇavārtika*, which was composed around the late 6th to early 7th century.[36]

The erotic and transgressive practices and the focus on female deities that characterized the Vidyāpīṭha tantras were further developed in a final "path" of Śaiva tantric practice, the Kulamārga or "Path of the Clans," the clans here referring to the clans of yoginīs into which the initiated male adept or "hero" (*vīra*) sought entry. This tradition of practice was widely known as the Kaula tradition. According to Alexis Sanderson this tradition shared five features with the earlier Kāpālika and Vidyāpīṭha traditions that set them apart from other Śaiva traditions:

1. Erotic ritual with a female companion;
2. Sanguinary practices for the propitiation of the fierce gods Mahābhairava/Bhairava and Cāmuṇḍā;
3. The notion that supernatural powers may be attained through the extraction by yogic means of the vital essences of living beings;
4. Initiation through the consumption of consecrated liquor; and
5. The centrality of states of possession.[37]

The Kaula tradition was clearly established by the 9th century and may have originated a century or so earlier. It also was the matrix from which the closely related Śākta tradition developed. It developed four well-known subtraditions. The Eastern transmission focused on Śiva and the goddess as Kuleśvara and Kuleśvarī. From it developed the Trika tradition that focused on a trio of goddesses: Parā, Parāparā, and Aparā. The Northern transmission featured the fierce goddess Guhyakālī; from it developed the Krama tradition, focusing on the goddess Kālī. The Western transmission took the hunchbacked goddess Kubjikā as its central deity, while the Southern transmission focuses on the beautiful goddess Kāmeśvarī or Tripurasundarī.[38] These traditions were well established in Kashmir by the 9th century. Particularly important were the nondual Trika and Krama traditions that see no ultimate distinction between the deity and practitioner.[39]

During the 10th century a new school of Śaivism developed, the Nondual School of Kashmir Śaivism. Alexis Sanderson argues that it was the product of the confrontation of the more conservative Śaiva Siddhānta tradition and the transgressive Kaula tradition. He describes this as follows:

> By the tenth century the Śaiva scene was dominated by the confrontation of two radically opposed schools: on the one hand, a group of nondualistic traditions, principally the Trika and the Krama, and on the other, the dualistic Śaiva Siddhānta. The nondualists, upholding the doctrine that the world and persons are no more than the play of the power of a universal consciousness-self, operated from within transgressive cults "tainted" by the Kāpālika culture of the cremation grounds and the erotico-mystical soteriology of the Kaulas.[40]

The Nondual School of Kashmir Śaivism integrated elements of both the transgressive nondualistic traditions and the more orthodox dualistic Śaiva Siddhānta. The end result was a nondualistic system in which the transgressive elements were internalized and hence rendered less offensive to the orthodox.

One of the best known Kashmir Śaiva theologians was Abhinavagupta (*c.* 975–1025 CE). He was a prolific author who wrote a number of commentaries on major works from the Trika and Krama traditions, as well as works in philosophy and aesthetics. According to David White, he bridged the divide between the conservative and transgressive schools operating at the time by transforming the way the "hard-core" Kaula practices were understood. In his exegesis of Kaula works he "sublimates, cosmeticizes, and semanticizes many of its practices into a type of meditative asceticism whose aim is to realize a transcendent subjectivity."[41] He thus played the role of domesticating the "hard-core" practices, creating in their place "soft-core" contemplative exercises. This is apparently the origin of the distinction in the tantric traditions between "left-handed" or unorthodox practice (*vāmācāra*) and "right-handed" or orthodox practice (*dakṣiṇācāra*). A similar development also occurred in Buddhist traditions; a tendency to neutralize the more transgressive elements of tantric practice, often by transforming the practice from external rituals to completely internalized visualizations.[42]

The last of the major Śaiva tantric traditions to develop is the Nāth or "Split-Ear" Kānphaṭa tradition. It is a medieval tradition that grew out of the heterodox Śaiva renunciant orders, namely the Pāśupatas and Kāpālikas.[43] While primarily Śaiva in orientation, some Nāths have also assumed Vaiṣṇava and Buddhist identities, and some also drew elements from Sikhism and Islam.[44] It emerged around the 12th or 13th century and quickly rose to prominence, "so much so that by the nineteenth century, the term 'yogi' was often construed, by India's British colonizers, to refer to a member of one of the Nāth Yogī orders."[45] This sect produced the tantric texts of the Haṭhayoga tradition that are believed to have been revealed by the great adept Gorakṣa or Gorakhnāth. They produced several tantric scriptures, such as the *Gorakṣasaṃhitā*, the *Khercarīvidyā*, and the *Haṭhayogapradīpikā*, which were composed around the 14th and 15th centuries.[46] While a relatively late tradition, they have been a significant influence on the contemporary practice of yoga. They practice a distinct form of tantric yoga involving breath control (*prāṇāyāma*) and the retention and transformation of sexual fluids via complex yogic exercises.[47]

The Śākta Traditions. The Hindu Śākta traditions are traditions focusing on the Goddess (*devī*) in one of her many manifestations, as the supreme deity. The Śākta traditions involve both devotional strands and tantric strands, with popular Śākta practice being largely devotional in practice. Nonetheless, the Śākta traditions have maintained strong tantric tendencies, having preserved ritual and contemplative practices originating in Hindu tantric circles.[48]

The Śākta tradition is closely related to the Śaiva tradition, and the textual basis of many Śākta traditions are rooted in the goddess-oriented Vidyāpīṭha and Kaula traditions. The Kaula tradition, being almost entirely goddess oriented, is as much a Śākta tradition as it is Śaiva. This is because these are clearly overlapping categories. The nondual Śaiva and Śākta traditions both focus on the "bipolar, bisexual divinity within one's own body," as Goodriaan described it.[49] This divinity is typically conceived as a male deity (Śiva or Viṣṇu) in union with his wife, Śakti. The distinction between Śaiva and Śākta in the Kaula tradition is largely one of emphasis, the deity upon which one primarily focuses.

However, the Śākta tradition was not exclusively tied to the Śaiva tradition. The worship of goddesses was a venerable practice widespread throughout South Asia. While goddesses are relatively few in the ancient Vedic pantheon, there was tremendous growth in goddess worship during the first millennium CE, as indicated by the *Purāṇa* literature composed during this era.[50] One of the great works of the early Śākta tradition, the *Devī-Māhātmya*, extols the goddess, in her numerous manifestations, as the supreme creator deity. This work was composed around the 6th century, around the same time as the goddess-oriented Vidyāpīṭha tantras were initially circulating.[51]

The Kaula tantras provide the early scriptural basis for the Śākta tradition. Of particular historical importance is the Kaula Southern transmission, which constitutes the tantras of the clan of the goddess Śrī (*śrīkula*), and the Northern and Eastern transmission, which gave rise to the tantras of the clan of the goddess Kālī (*kālīkula*).[52] These became by far the most popular Śākta tantric traditions. The former, focusing on beautiful and erotic goddess Śrī, gave rise to the Śrī Vidyā tradition, which is an orthodox, "right handed" tradition that became particularly popular in South India.[53] It is also the tradition that gave rise to the Śrī Yantra, a mystical diagram formed by nine interlocking triangles that is probably one of the most widespread and best known tantric images.

The Kālīkula tradition, focusing on the fierce goddess Kālī, gave rise to the traditions of practice focusing on Kālī, which are particularly important in East and South India. Kālī remains one of the best known and beloved of Hindu goddesses, despite her ferocious appearance.[54] She is also the focus of a considerable devotional tradition.[55] Kālī is also included in the ten Mahāvidyās, a group of ten goddesses whose worship remains very popular in Bengal.[56] Two of the goddesses included in this group, Tārā and Chinnamastā, originated as Buddhist goddesses who were later absorbed into this Hindu tantric pantheon.[57]

Śākta communities in northeastern India produced a number of tantras, such as the *Cīnācāra Tantra* and *Bṛhannīla Tantra* during the late medieval period, around the 15th and 16th centuries. These scriptures focus on the worship of goddesses and drew from both older Hindu as well as Buddhist works.[58]

Other Hindu Tantric Traditions. The Vaiṣṇava tradition of Hinduism has tended to be far more engaged with the Bhakti devotional mode of Hindu practice and correspondingly less engaged with the tantric mode of practice. However, the Pāñcarātra sect, which dates back to the 5th or 6th century and focused on Viṣṇu qua Nārāyaṇa, produced a number of tantric works, although this sect no longer identifies as tantric.

The Pañcarātra tradition claims to have had a canon of 108 texts, revealed by Viṣṇu in His form of Vāsudeva or Nārāyaṇa, most of which are apparently lost.[59] While some scholars have argued that the oldest Pāñcarātra texts may date to the 5th century CE,[60] Pāñcarātra scriptures are notoriously difficult to date due to a dearth of dateable early commentaries and manuscripts preserved by this tradition. One of the oldest works of this tradition, the *Ahirbudhnyasaṃhitā*, likely dates to the 8th century.[61] There is indication of early influence from Kashmir Śaivism on Pāñcarātra scriptures. But as these works were later preserved by the Śrīvaiṣṇava tradition in South India, there is also evidence of later Pāñcarātra influence on the South Indian Śaiva Siddhānta tradition.[62]

During the medieval period another tantric Vaiṣṇava tradition emerged in Bengal. Known as the Sahajiyā tradition, it flourished in Bengal around the 16th through 19th centuries. It taught that each individual is a divinity, embodying the divine couple Kṛṣṇa and his consort Rādhā. This tradition integrated earlier Hindu and Buddhist tantric practices within a Vaiṣṇava theological framework.[63]

A few minor Hindu tantric traditions also deserve a brief mention. The Saura tradition of Hinduism, which focuses on the Sun god Sūrya, produced several tantras, most notably the *Saurasaṃhitā* that was also known as the *Sauratantra*. This tradition went into decline during the medieval period and is now almost extinct, and very few copies of this work have survived. The South Indian Vīraśaiva tradition, generally not considered to be a tantric tradition, did in fact produce one tantra that has survived, the *Pārameśvaratantra*.[64]

Hindu Tantra in Global Contexts. Hinduism, unlike Buddhism, has traditionally been primarily located in South Asia and has not fostered a great deal of missionary activity. However, Hindu traditions were disseminated to Southeast Asia along with Buddhism around the 5th through 11th centuries, and during this time Śaiva tantric traditions were established in the kingdoms of the Khmers and Chams, in contemporary Cambodia and Vietnam, and in Java, in contemporary Indonesia.[65] Tantric forms of Hinduism continue to be practiced in the Hindu enclaves in Indonesia, most notably on the island of Bali, the majority of the residents of which are practicing Hindus.[66]

Tantric Hinduism, in its Śaiva and Śākta forms, has also been disseminated around the world, most notably to Europe and America, by Hindu gurus during the 20th and 21st centuries. This was motivated both by the growing South Asian diaspora communities in the West as well as by growing interest in Asian religious traditions among non-Indian Westerners from the 1960s onward. Many of these gurus have been successful in establishing religious communities abroad, serving both diaspora Indian communities as well as converts to Hinduism.[67]

BUDDHIST TANTRIC TRADITIONS

The early history of Buddhist tantric traditions is far clearer than that of Hindu traditions. This is due to the international Buddhist network that led to the rapid dissemination of new Buddhist works. Many works of Buddhist tantric literature were rapidly translated into Tibetan and Chinese, and the date when a translation was made provides us with *terminus ad quem* for the respective work. While there are still many lacunae in our understanding of the early history of tantric Buddhist traditions, available evidence points to the mid-7th century as the most likely point at which historically datable traditions began to take shape. The earliest known dateable tantric text is the *Awakening of Mahāvairocana Tantra* (*mahāvairocanābhisaṃbodhi-tantra*), which was composed around the mid-7th century and was reportedly be one of the texts collected by the Chinese pilgrim Wu-xing (無行) *c.* 680 CE.[68] The Chinese pilgrim Wu-xing also commented on the emergence of a new "teaching about mantra" (真言教法), which was very popular during his time in India.[69]

The emergence of tantric Buddhist traditions at this times appears to have been the result of a slow process of development of magical literature in Mahāyāna Buddhist traditions over the course of several centuries. For at least two centuries, around the 5th century CE, Buddhists produced a growing number of works focusing on magical formulas known as *dhāraṇī* and ritual practices that employ them. These gradually became more sophisticated, leading ultimately to the composition of the "esoteric sutras" and tantras.[70] Many of the early Buddhist tantric scriptures, which later were labeled "ritual tantras" (*kriyātantra*), are basically grimoires, compilations of magical rituals which were purported to achieve various worldly ends. Interestingly, the same is true of the early Śaiva tantric scriptures that were composed around the same time, around the 7th century.[71] More sophisticated tantric traditions developed during the 8th century and onward. These new traditions featured practices advocating union with a deity, and they typically claim to promote a secret method for the rapid achievement of buddhahood. These traditions focused upon scriptures that were later classified as Yoga, Mahāyoga, and Yoginī tantras.[72] There was considerable Śaiva influence on the developing Buddhist traditions. The Buddhist Yoginītantras in particular, which focus on female goddesses known as Yoginīs or Ḍākinīs and feature antinomian practices, and which were composed around the 8th century onward, drew heavily from Śaiva Vidyāpīṭha scriptures.[73]

There was rapid growth and dissemination of the newly emerging tantric Buddhist traditions. Within a few decades after their initial composition, early tantric traditions of text and practice were disseminated to East and Southeast Asia. This was facilitated by the active trade and diplomatic exchanges between India and China during the 7th and early 8th centuries, via overland trade routes via Central Asia and also maritime trade routes via South East Asia. The Sarvadurgatipariśodhana and Trilokavijaya mandalas, and, presumably, their associated practice and textual traditions, were introduced to Java *c.* 700 CE.[74] Moreover, the Central Asian monk Amoghavajra, who journeyed from China to India and back via the maritime route during the mid-8th century, reported that there was a new canon of eighteen tantras, which he attempted to convey back to China and partially translated into Chinese.[75] This suggests that there was a very rapid production of new tantric texts and practice traditions around the mid-7th through mid-8th centuries.

Tantric traditions were established in China during the Tang dynasty, and thence disseminated to Korea[76] and Japan.[77] While the institutionalized esoteric Buddhist school did not survive the Wuzong emperor's (武宗, 814–846; r. 840–846) infamous persecution of Buddhism in the mid-9th century, esoteric Buddhist traditions survived in peripheral areas in China.

It appears that tantric Buddhist texts and practices were first disseminated to Tibet during the 8th century, shortly after their initial dissemination to East and Southeast Asia. Buddhist traditions view the 7th century as the time when Buddhism first reached Tibet, although there might have been gradual dissemination of Buddhism into the region earlier. The translation of Buddhist scriptures began, apparently, during the late 7th century and continued with imperial support during the 8th and 9th centuries, with most of the "early" translations made between 779 and 838 CE.[78] As evidenced by imperial catalogs compiled during this period,[79] as well as tantric manuscripts preserved at Dunhuang, which were assembled around the mid-10th through early 11th centuries,[80] a significant number of tantric scriptures and ritual texts were translated into Tibetan during the imperial period. The Nyingma tradition of Tibetan Buddhism is based upon teachings transmitted to Tibet during the imperial period by renowned masters such as the great adept (*mahāsiddha*) Padmasambhava.[81]

With the collapse of the Tibetan empire in 841 CE and the consequent loss of imperial patronage, the transmission and translation of tantric works to Tibet appears to have slowed but did not cease altogether.[82] Official patronage of translation activity resumed in the late 10th century, when King Lha bla ma Ye shes 'od is reported to have sent twenty-one novice monks to Kashmir to receive further training. One of them, Rin chen bzang po (958–1055 CE), became a renowned translator, thus initiating the second or "Later Transmission" (*phyi dar*) of Buddhism to Tibet.[83]

The Later Transmission period focused on the transmission and translation of "new" tantras and their associated ritual literature. They were considered to be "unexcelled *tantras*" (*bla na med pa'i rgyud*), the highest category of Buddhist teaching. Their high status was due to the fact that many of the them (all of them, if creative commentarial strategies are employed) teach "perfection-stage" (Skt. *niṣpannakrama*; Tib. *rdzogs rim*) yogic practices involving manipulation of the "channels, winds, and drops" (Skt. *nāḍi*, *prāṇa*, and *bindhu*; Tib. *rtsa*, *rlung*, and *thig le*), the network of subtle channels and the energy centers (Skt. *cakra*; Tib. *'khor lo*) that house the "wind" or vital energy and "drops" of subtle consciousness. Collectively these constitute what was known as the "subtle body" (Skt. *sūkṣmadeha*; Tib. *lus phra ba*). Advocates of the new Tibetan traditions based on these scriptures claimed that yogic practices involving the manipulation of the subtle body were requisites to complete awakening.

The "new" schools that developed in Tibet beginning in the 11th century were largely based on these "unexcelled *tantra*" scriptures, also known as *mahāyogatantra*s and *yoginītantra*s, and the exegetical and ritual literature associated with them. They include the Kadam (Bka' gdams), Kagyü (Bka' brgyud), Sakya (Sa skya), Jonang (Jo nang), and Geluk (Dge lugs) traditions, which were established between the 11th and 15th centuries. Tibetan Buddhists would later play important roles in the dissemination of Buddhism (and associated tantric traditions) to China and Mongolia, and eventually throughout the world, with the diaspora of Tibetan lamas in the 20th century following the Chinese invasion and occupation of Tibet in 1950.

INFLUENCE ON OTHER RELIGIOUS TRADITIONS

Tantric Hindu and Buddhist traditions influenced a number of other religious traditions, both within South Asia as well as in other areas of the world. Because tantric traditions first emerged in South Asia, their impact there is naturally the most significant. The South Asian traditions that were influenced by the tantric traditions to some degree include Jainism, Islam, and Sikhism. Daoism and the Shinto tradition in East Asia were influenced by East Asian tantric Buddhist traditions, and the Bön tradition of Tibet was thoroughly transformed by its encounter with tantric Buddhism. Lastly, the "New Age" spiritual movement that developed in the West during the latter half of the 20th century was also strongly influenced by Hindu and Buddhist tantric traditions.

While Jainism did not preserve any self-consciously "tantric" traditions, various Jain authors described a variety of tantric meditations and rituals, beginning circa 800 CE. Generally speaking, many Jains were interested in tantric practices, although given the Jain focus on nonviolence as well as strict celibacy for monks and nuns, Jain tantric texts did not advocate any of the transgressive ritual practices involving sex or violence.[84] Jains did produce several tantric texts, such as the 11th-century *Bhairavapadmāvatīkalpa*, which, as the name suggests, evinces influence from Hindu Śaiva-Śākta traditions.[85] Jains borrowed goddesses from the Śaiva Mantramārga tradition, some of which served as lineage goddesses for prominent Jain families. The worship of these goddesses, however, was changed to suit Jain moral teachings. Jains, who worshipped their tantric goddesses with vegetarian offerings only, did not perform animal sacrifices.[86]

Probably the best known mode of tantric practice during the medieval period is the tantric form of yoga focusing on the subtle body and the movement of vital energy within it. Sufi Muslims in Bengal also developed a form of tantric yoga under the influence of the Nātha and Sahajiyā Vaiṣṇava traditions. The Sufi tantric yoga tradition borrowed the concept of the subtle body and Islamicized it, translating it into Islamic categories. This development occurred rather late; none of the extant texts of this tradition predate the 16th century.[87]

Tantric yogic practice was also adopted by some Sikhs. One of the best known advocates of this practice was Harbhajan Singh Khalsa (1929–2004), better known as Yogi Bhajan, who widely taught Kundalini yoga in America and Europe. Yogi Bhajan claimed to be part of a practice lineage going back to Guru Nanak, the founder of Sikhism. While there is no evidence supporting this claim, it appears that, as Michael Stoeber suggests, "some form of Kundalini Yoga was practiced historically by some Sikhs, albeit perhaps secretly and in very small numbers."[88]

When tantric Buddhist traditions reached China at the beginning of the 8th century, there was already a long history of borrowing between Buddhist and Daoist communities. Many elements of tantric Buddhist practice were taken up by Daoist traditions. But tantric Buddhists, in turn, also borrowed the Daoist practice of venerating the Big Dipper constellation and developed distinctly tantric modes worshipping this divinity.[89] The Shinto tradition of Japan also borrowed elements of tantric Buddhist practice, most notably the *goma* (Skt. *homa*) rite of makings offerings into a sanctified fire.[90]

The Bön tradition of Tibet, the indigenous Tibetan religious tradition, was transformed by its encounter with tantric Buddhist traditions, so much so that it should also be considered a tantric tradition. Tibetan Buddhist traditions borrowed significantly from the Bön tradition, but the Bön tradition was likewise deeply influenced by Buddhism.[91] The Bön tradition developed a scriptural canon on Buddhist models and borrowed not only the genre of the tantras but also a number of tantric practices.[92] Bön practitioners, for example, developed their own Mahāyoga and Yoginī or "Mother" tantras, based upon the Indian Buddhist models.[93]

Lastly, the growth of interest in tantric practice in the West has led to the development of a number of new spiritual traditions deeply influenced by Hindu and Buddhist tantric traditions founded by Westerners, which Hugh Urban has labeled "New Age Tantra." These include Pierre Bernard's Tantrik Order, Aleister Crowley's Ordo Templi Orientis, and Nik Douglas's New Tantric Order in America.[94] These traditions have adapted venerable tantric ideas and practices to meet the needs of spiritual seeker in new and contemporary contexts.

REVIEW OF LITERATURE

There are three primary approaches to the study of the history of tantric traditions: textual, archeological, and ethnographic. The first two are most important for the study of history of tantric traditions in general and indispensable for those traditions that are now defunct, which persist only in the textual and archeological record. But as numerous tantric traditions have survived in South, East, and Central Asia, ethnographic studies in these communities are an important additional source of information concerning them.

As all of the known tantric traditions have been the products of literate communities, the study of the voluminous texts composed and preserved by these traditions has been one of our largest sources of information concerning them. Many thousands of texts have been composed and preserved by tantric communities, the majority of which have not been edited, studied, or translated. This literature was often ignored by past generations of scholars, some of whom deemed tantric literature as unworthy of study. Moriz Winternitz's extensive *Geschichte der indischen Literatur,* for example, devoted only two pages to a very brief discussion of tantric literature.[95]

Thousands of works of tantric literature have been preserved in South Asia, and several thousand, many for which the Sanskrit original is now lost, were also translated into Tibetan and Chinese and preserved by East and Central Asian communities. Tibetan, Mongolian, Chinese, and Japanese authors have also composed many thousands of original tantric works, such as commentaries and ritual and meditative manuals. Only a small fraction of these works have been critically edited, studied, or translated into Western languages. The study of these texts is an ongoing effort, which, as it proceeds, should deepen our understanding of the history of tantric traditions.

However, textual study alone is insufficient. This is partly because exclusive focus on written records leads to a distorted understanding of the traditions that gave rise to them, since these records, arguably, reflect an elite perspective.[96] In addition to textual evidence it is important to take into consideration as well archaeological and art historical evidence. This includes epigraphic and numismatic inscriptions as well as the wide range of different types of religious art. Inscriptions indicating the donors who contributed to the construction or fabrication of a temple, monument, or work of art can provide important information regarding the communities who supported tantric institutions. Moreover, some facets of tantric history are only known via archeological evidence. An example of this are the so-called Cauṃsāṭha Yoginī temples, built during the 9th to 13th centuries throughout India, but particularly across the middle of the country. They feature depictions of the female divinities known as yoginīs, many of which are notable for their ferocious and/or erotic appearance. Various attempts have been made to connect these temples to the surviving scriptures, such as Śaiva/Śākta Kaula tantras,[97] but no convincing link has been established between these temples and surviving texts. They represent an important aspect of South Asian history that can only be understood via archeological and art historical approaches, although continued research into the large amounts of unstudied or poorly studied texts may also shed light on these temples.[98]

Ethnographic study of contemporary tantric communities is an additional important source of information. From such study we can gain more information about the texts and practices preserved by the communities. These include questions such as which texts and practices are actually employed by these communities and how the practices as described in the texts compare to those undertaken by contemporary communities. These are important questions, as the study of ritual and contemplative practices via texts alone is problematic at best, if not completely impossible.

It is possible that the study of texts alone can lead to an incomplete or distorted understanding of history, and sometimes observing living communities can serve as a corrective to these problems. For example, a number of tantric texts call upon male practitioners to seek out low-caste or outcaste women to serve as partners in courses of practice (*sādhana*) involving sexual activity. Some of these texts appear to valorize these female partners; Miranda Shaw used this evidence to argue that Indian tantric communities often empowered women to serve as gurus or spiritual leaders.[99] It is of course possible that women were able to serve as gurus in early medieval India. However, ethnographic studies of low-caste women who serve as sexual partners for male tantric practitioners have painted a much darker picture of what life is like for such women,[100] suggesting that the textual passages that valorize these women should not be uncritically accepted at face value.

It goes without saying that our study of tantric traditions should take into consideration all available evidence. While this interdisciplinary approach is beyond the capacity of any individual scholar, the collective works of various scholars employing different methodologies will over time deepen our understanding of these traditions.

PRIMARY SOURCES

There are an unknown number of tantric manuscripts, written not only in Sanskrit but also medieval dialects, the so-called Prakrit and Apabraṃśa dialects, as well as modern languages such as Hindi, Bengali, Tamil, and Newari. Many have survived in India despite a climate that is generally not conducive to manuscript preservation. However, the vast majority of surviving tantric works have been preserved by the Newar community of the Kathmandu valley, who have preserved a wide range of tantric Hindu and Buddhist texts and traditions and have been aided by a climate that is far more amenable to text preservation.

Many of these surviving texts were originally preserved in monastery and temple libraries as well as private text collections. There are also several collections in Kathmandu that are open to the public, most notably the National Archives of Nepal, the Kaiser Library, and the Asha Archives. Over 18,000 rare manuscripts, many of which are of Hindu and Buddhist tantric texts, were microfilmed by the Nepal-German Manuscript Preservation Project, and these titles are now being cataloged by the successor project, the Nepalese-German Manuscript Cataloguing Project. It is possible to request microfilm or digital scans of these manuscripts through this very important project. A smaller collection of scanned Sanskrit Buddhist manuscripts is freely available online via the Digital Sanskrit Buddhist Canon, a project sponsored by the University of the West in Los Angeles. A number of tantric works are included in the works available on their website.

Many tantric manuscripts from Nepal and India are also owned by university libraries and archives around the world. Lists of library collections containing these manuscripts have been prepared by Dominik Wujastyk and Audrey Truschke. In addition to the resources listed on these websites, the University of Tokyo also has a large collection of tantric Buddhist Sanskrit manuscripts, which are scanned and available on the library's website.

There are a number of resources for those interested in studying the tantric Buddhist literature translated into or composed in the Tibet language. For those interested in studying Tibetan primary texts, one of the best resources is the Tibetan Buddhist Resource Center. Like the Nepal-German Manuscript Preservation Project, the Tibetan Buddhist Resource

Center has sponsored the scanning of many thousands of Tibetan manuscripts, some of which are quite rare. Their collection includes scans of the entire Tibetan canon of translated works from India, the Kanjur (*bka' 'gyur*), Tenjur (*bstan 'gyur*), and the Nyingma tantric canon (*rnying ma rgyud 'bum*), as well as numerous works by Tibetan masters.

Several organizations are working to translate Tibetan Buddhist works to make them accessible to those who do not read Tibetan or Sanskrit. The organization 84000: Translating the Words of the Buddha is sponsoring the English translation of the entire Tibetan Kanjur as well as the Nyingma tantric canon, including translations of all of the canonical Buddhist tantras. These translations, as they are completed, are published as digital texts freely available on their web site. The Tsadra Foundation is also sponsoring the translation of Tibetan works. They are producing digital publications as well apps for accessing these on various devices.

A number of tantric works were also translated into Chinese, and these are included in one of the best known and most widely accessible canonical collections of Chinese Buddhist scriptures, the Taishō Tripiṭaka (Ch. 大正新脩大藏經; Jp. Taishō Shinshū Daizōkyō). Much (but not all) of this canon has been digitally published by the organization CBETA, and the tantric translations are included among the texts freely available on their website.

DIGITAL MATERIALS

- **Himalayan Art Resources:** One of the best resources for tantric art from South and Central Asia is Himalayan Art Resources, a web resource made possible by the Rubin Foundation. It contains high-quality digital images, freely available for download, of religious art from the Himalayan region. It features Tibetan Buddhist art but also contains images from the Bön and Hindu traditions as well. It features the artwork from the collection of the Rubin Museum of Art in New York as well as art from the collections from several other museums with excellent Himalayan art collections, namely the Los Angeles County Museum, the Asian Art Museum in San Francisco, the Guimet Musee National in Paris, the Museum of Culture in Basel, Switzerland, the Tibet House Museum in New Delhi, and the Zanabazar Museum in Ulaanbaatar Mongolia.
- **The Smithsonian Institution:** The Arthur M. Sackler Gallery and Freer Gallery of Art at the Smithsonian Institution in Washington, DC also has a great deal of tantric art in their collections, much of which is viewable and downloadable from their website. Some of the images from their recent exhibition on yoga are available as well. The catalog for this exhibit, *Yoga: The Art of Transformation*, edited by Debra Diamond,[101] contains numerous high-quality reproductions of stunning works of art, many of which originated in the South Asian tantric traditions.
- **84000: Translating the Words of the Buddha:** Provides free access to translations of Tibetan Buddhist canonical texts, including many tantras.
- **CBETA**: Provides free access to digital versions of canonical Buddhist texts in Chinese translation from the Taishō Tripiṭaka. This includes a good number of tantric works.
- **The Nepalese-German Manuscript Cataloguing Project:** Provides access to images of rare manuscripts from Nepal, including many tantric Hindu and Buddhist texts.
- **The Tibetan Buddhist Resource Center:** Provides access to a wide range of scanned Tibetan texts, including many works on tantric subjects.

FURTHER READING

GENERAL INTRODUCTIONS TO HINDU TANTRA

Several works provide good introductions to tantric traditions. For Hindu traditions, one of the best overall introductions to tantric Hindu traditions for nonspecialists is Gavin Flood's *The Tantric Body*. For specialists, on the other hand, Alexis Sanderson's monograph-length article, "The Śaiva Age: The Rise and Dominance of Śaivism during the Early Medieval Period" provides a very rich introduction to the Śaiva tantric traditions and their influence on other Hindu and Buddhist traditions. David White provides in-depth introductions to the Hindu tantric traditions of alchemy and yoga, on the one hand, and "tantric sex" on the other, in his works *The Alchemical Body: Siddha Traditions in Medieval India* and *Kiss of the Yoginī: "Tantric Sex" in Its South Asian Contexts*. Hugh Urban's *Tantra: Sex, Secrecy, Politics, and Power in the Study of Religion* is one of the best introductions to the Western reception of tantric traditions.

Flood, Gavin. *The Tantric Body: The Secret Tradition of Hindu Religion*. London: I. B. Taurus, 2006.

Sanderson, Alexis. "The Śaiva Age: The Rise and Dominance of Śaivism During the Early Medieval Period." In *Genesis and Development of Tantrism*, edited by Shingo EINOO, 17–349. Tokyo: Institute of Oriental Culture, University of Tokyo, 2009.

Urban, Hugh B. *Tantra: Sex, Secrecy, Politics, and Power in the Study of Religion*. Berkeley: University of California Press, 2003.

White, David Gordon. *The Alchemical Body: Siddha Traditions in Medieval India*. Chicago: University of Chicago Press, 1996.

White, David Gordon. *Kiss of the Yoginī: "Tantric Sex" in its South Asian Contexts*. Chicago: University of Chicago Press, 2003.

GENERAL INTRODUCTIONS TO BUDDHIST TANTRA

Ronald Davidson's works *Indian Esoteric Buddhism: A Social History of the Tantric Movement* and *Tibetan Renaissance: Tantric Buddhism in the Rebirth of Tibetan Culture* provide excellent introductions to the rise of Indian Buddhist tantric traditions and their dissemination to Tibet, respectively. David Snellgrove's *Indo-Tibetan Buddhism* provides slightly outdated but still useful introductions to both Indian and Tibetan Buddhist traditions. The best introductions to East Asian tantric traditions include the volume *Esoteric Buddhism and the Tantras in East Asia*, edited by Charles Orzech, Henrik Sørensen, and Richard Payne, and Ryūichi Abé's monumental study on Kūkai and his role in the dissemination of tantric Buddhism to Japan.

Abé, Ryūichi. *The Weaving of Mantra: Kūkai and the Construction of Esoteric Buddhist Discourse*. New York: Columbia University Press, 1999.

Davidson, Ronald M. *Indian Esoteric Buddhism: A Social History of the Tantric Movement*. New York: Columbia University Press, 2002.

Davidson, Ronald M. *Tibetan Renaissance: Tantric Buddhism in the Rebirth of Tibetan Culture*. New York: Columbia University Press, 2005.

Orzech, Charles D., Henrik H. Sørensen, and Richard K. Payne, eds. *Esoteric Buddhism and the Tantras in East Asia*. Leiden, Netherlands: Brill, 2011.

Snellgrove, David L. *Indo-Tibetan Buddhism*. London: Serindia, 1987; reprint, Boston: Shambhala, 2002.

TRANSLATIONS AND TEXTUAL STUDIES: HINDU

Teun Goudriaan and Sanjukta Gupta's *Hindu Tantric and Śākta Literature* remains one of the best introductions to classical and contemporary Hindu tantric literature. Dominic Goodall has edited a collaborative translation and edition of one the oldest surviving tantras in his *The Niśvāsatattvasaṃhitā: The Earliest Surviving Śaiva Tantra*. James Mallison, on the other hand, has edited and translated a much later but very influential text on *haṭhayoga*, *The Khecarīvidyā of Adīnātha*. Loriliai Biernacki's *Renowned Goddess of Desire: Women, Sex, and Speech in Tantra* is a textual study based on later Śākta literature, with particular focus on the light they shed on the role of women in Śākta Hindu traditions.

Biernacki, Loriliai. *Renowned Goddess of Desire: Women, Sex, and Speech in Tantra*. Oxford: Oxford University Press, 2007.

Goodall, Dominic, ed. *The Niśvāsatattvasaṃhitā: The Earliest Surviving Śaiva Tantra*, Vol. 1. Pondicherry: Institute Français de Pondichéry, 2015.

Goudriaan, Teun, and Sanjukta Gupta. *Hindu Tantric and Śākta Literature*. Wiesbaden, Germany: Harrassowitz, 1981.

Mallinson, James. *The Khecarīvidyā of Ādinātha: A Critical Edition and Annotated Translation of an Early Text of Haṭhayoga*. London: Routledge, 2007.

TRANSLATIONS AND TEXTUAL STUDIES: BUDDHIST

Stephen Hodge's *The Mahā-Vairocana-Abhisaṃbodhi Tantra with Buddhaguhya's Commentary* is a translation of what appears to be the earliest Buddhist tantra, along with an influential commentary composed by the 8th-century master Buddhaguhya. Rolf Giebel's "The Chin-kang-ting ching yü-ch'ieh shih-pa-hui chih-kuei: An Annotated Translation" is a study and translation of an important 8th-century text that sheds considerable light on the history of Buddhist tantric literature. David Gray's *The Cakrasaṃvara Tantra* and David Snellgrove's *The Hevajra Tantra* are studies and translations of two important later Buddhist tantric works. Koichi Shinohara's *Spells, Images, and Mandalas: Tracing the Evolution of Esoteric Buddhist Rituals* is study of the early development of tantric Buddhist rituals and the scriptures that describe them. Christian Wedemeyer's *Making Sense of Tantric Buddhism* attempts to explain the significance of transgressive textual passages in the Buddhist tantras. Sarah Jacoby's *Love and Liberation: Autobiographical Writings of the Tibetan Buddhist Visionary Sera Khandro* is a study of a major Tibetan female spiritual leader, based both on her autobiographical writings as well as the author's fieldwork in northeastern Tibet.

Giebel, Rolf. "The Chin-kang-ting ching yü-ch'ieh shih-pa-hui chih-kuei: An Annotated Translation." *Journal of Naritasan Institute for Buddhist Studies* 18 (1995): 107–201.

Gray, David. *The Cakrasamvara Tantra: A Study and Annotated Translation*. New York: American Institute of Buddhist Studies, 2007.

Hodge, Stephen. *The Mahā-Vairocana-Abhisaṃbodhi Tantra with Buddhaguhya's Commentary*. London: RoutledgeCurzon, 2003.

Jacoby, Sarah. *Love and Liberation: Autobiographical Writings of the Tibetan Buddhist Visionary Sera Khandro*. New York: Columbia University Press, 2014.

Shinohara, Koichi. *Spells, Images, and Mandalas: Tracing the Evolution of Esoteric Buddhist Rituals*. New York: Columbia University Press, 2014).

Snellgrove, David. *The Hevajra Tantra: A Critical Study*. 2d ed. Bangkok: Orchid, 2010.

Wedemeyer, Christian K. *Making Sense of Tantric Buddhism: History, Semiology, & Transgression in the Indian Traditions*. New York: Columbia University Press, 2013.

ETHNOGRAPHIC STUDIES

Ethnographic studies of tantric communities are relatively uncommon, given the secrecy that usually shrouds these traditions. But several studies have been published on Hindu and Buddhist communities that deserve serious attention. June McDaniel's *The Madness of the Saints* and *Offering Flowers, Feeding Skulls* are studies of popular traditions of worship in Bengal that include the Śākta tradition. She provides accessible perspectives on Śākta worship as undertaken in contemporary India. Toni Huber's *The Cult of Pure Crystal Mountain* is a study of an important Tibetan pilgrimage site connected with the Yoginī tantras. Richard Kohn's *The Lord of the Dance: The Mani Rimdu Festival in Tibet and Nepal* is a detailed study of a rNyingma tantric Buddhist festival among the Sherpas in Nepal.

Huber, Toni. *The Cult of Pure Crystal Mountain: Popular Pilgrimage and Visionary Landscape in Southeast Tibet*. New York: Oxford University Press, 1999.

Kohn, Richard J. *Lord of the Dance: The Mani Rimdu Festival in Tibet and Nepal*. Albany: State University of New York Press, 2001.

McDaniel, June. *The Madness of the Saints: Ecstatic Religion in Bengal*. Chicago: University of Chicago Press, 1989.

McDaniel, June. *Offering Flowers, Feeding Skulls: Popular Goddess Worship in West Bengal*. Oxford: Oxford University Press, 2004.

NOTES

1. Richard Davis, *Ritual in an Oscillating Universe: Worshipping Śiva in Medieval India* (Princeton, NJ: Princeton University Press, 1991), 3–10.
2. "abracadabra, n. and int." OED Online. March 2015. Oxford University Press.
3. "hocus-pocus, n., adj., and adv." OED Online. March 2015. Oxford University Press.
4. This film, given the title *Tantra Mantra* in English and *Tantraṃ Mantraṃ* in Hindi, was released in 2009 by Ambika films.
5. Douglas Brooks, *The Secret of the Three Cities: An Introduction to Hindu Śākta Tantrism* (Chicago: University of Chicago Press, 1990), 5.
6. See Hugh B. Urban, *Tantra: Sex, Secrecy, Politics, and Power in the Study of Religion* (Berkeley: University of California Press, 2003), 15.
7. See André Padoux, "What Do We Mean by Tantrism," in *The Roots of Tantra*, edited by Katherine Ann Harper and Robert L. Brown (Albany: State University of New York Press, 2002), 17–24.
8. André Padoux, "A Survey of Tantric Hinduism for the Historian of Religions," *History of Religions* 20.4 (1981), 345–360.
9. See Alexis Sanderson, "The Doctrine of the Mālinīvijayottaratantra," in *Ritual and Speculation in Early Tantrism. Studies in Honour of André Padoux*, edited by T. Goudriaan (Albany: State University of New York Press, 1992), 281 (281–312), and Dominic Goodall, *Bhaṭṭa Rāmakaṇṭha's Commentary on the Kiraṇatantra, Volume 1: Chapters 1–6* (Pondicherry: Institut Français de Pondichéry, 1998), xxxvi.
10. Charles D. Orzech, Henrik H. Sørensen, and Richard K. Payne, *Esoteric Buddhism and the Tantras in East Asia* (Leiden, The Netherlands: Brill, 2011), 8–10.
11. Ronald M. Davidson, *Indian Esoteric Buddhism: A Social History* (New York: Columbia University Press, 2002), 119.

12. Teun Goudriaan, "Hindu Tantric Literature in Sanskrit," in *Hindu Tantric and Śākta Literature*, edited by Teun Goudriaan and Sanjukta Gupta (Wiesbaden, Germany: Harrassowitz, 1981), 1–172.
13. This point was made in a review published in *Journal Asiatique* 256 (1968): 267; quoted in Padoux, "What Do We Mean by Tantrism?," 19.
14. Padoux, "What Do We Mean by Tantrism?," 23.
15. See, for example, Thomas McEvilley's "The Spinal Serpent," in *The Roots of Tantra*, ed. Katherine A. Harper and Robert L. Brown (Albany: State University of New York Press, 2002), 93–113. In this essay he argued that tantric yoga practices involving manipulation of energy in the central channel of the subtle body, such as Kuṇḍalinī yoga, originated in the Indus Valley Civilization (3300–1300 bce) if not earlier.
16. Goudriaan, "Hindu Tantric Literature in Sanskrit," 4–5.
17. For a discussion of the revelatory nature of the Buddhist tantras, see David Gray, "On the Very Idea of a Tantric Canon: Myth, Politics, and the Formation of the Bka' 'gyur," *Journal of the International Association of Tibetan Studies*, no. 5 (December 2009): 1–37.
18. Alex Wayman reported the Buddhist claim that the tantras were disseminated secretly for centuries before being revealed and tentatively suggests that this occurred around the 5th century CE. There is, however, no evidence that any of the Buddhist tantras were composed by this early date. See his *Yoga of the Guhyasamājatantra: The Arcane Lore of the Forty Verses* (Delhi: Motilal Banarsidass, 1977), 97.
19. For a discussion of critiques of the validity of tantric revelation by advocates of the Vedas and the defense of tantric revelation by advocates of tantric traditions, see Gavin Flood, *The Tantric Body: The Secret Tradition of Hindu Religion* (London: I. B. Tauris, 2006), 48–60.
20. Regarding this see Richard K. Payne, *The Tantric Ritual of Japan, Feeding the Gods: The Shingon Fire Ritual* (New Delhi: Aditya Prakashan, 1991); Richard K. Payne and Charles D. Orzech, "Homa," in Orzech, et al., *Esoteric Buddhism and the Tantras in East Asia*, 133–140.
21. Davidson, *Indian Esoteric Buddhism*, 124; Alexis Sanderson, "Religion and the State: Śaiva Officiants in the Territory of the Brahmanical Royal Chaplain," *Indo-Iranian Journal* 47 (2004): 229–300.
22. See Vrajavallabha Dviveda, "Having Become a God, He Should Sacrifice to the Gods," in *Ritual and Speculation in Early Tantrism: Studies in Honor of André Padoux*, ed. Teun Goudriaan (Albany: State University of New York Press, 1992).
23. Alexis Sanderson, "The Śaiva Age: The Rise and Dominance of Śaivism During the Early Medieval Period," in *Genesis and Development of Tantrism*, ed. Shingo Einoo (Tokyo: Institute of Oriental Culture, University of Tokyo, 2009), 41–43 (41–350).
24. Flood, *The Tantric Body*, 69, 103–105.
25. Gavin Flood, *An Introduction to Hinduism* (Cambridge: Cambridge University Press, 1996), 153.
26. Barbara Stoller Miller, *The Bhagavad-Gita: Krishna's Council in Time of War* (New York: Bantam, 1986), 3.
27. Padoux, "What Do We Mean by Tantrism?," 20.
28. See Flood, *The Tantric Body*, 101, and Gerhard Oberhammer, "Beobachtungen zur 'Offenbarungsgeschichte' der Paramasaṃhitā," in *Studies in Hinduism II: Miscellanea to the Phenomenon of Tantras*, ed. G. Oberhammer (Vienna: Verlag der Osterreichischen Akademie der Wissenschaften, 1998), 21–41.
29. For a translation and study of this work see Gareth Sparham, *The Fulfillment of All Hopes: Guru Devotion in Tibetan Buddhism* (Boston: Wisdom, 1999).
30. Translated in David Gordon White, *Kiss of the Yoginī: "Tantric Sex" in its South Asian Contexts* (Chicago: University of Chicago Press, 2003), 207. See as well D. C. Sircar, *Select Inscriptions Bearing on Indian History and Civilization*, Vol. 1. 2d ed. (Kolkata: University of Calcutta, 1965), 399–405.
31. Alexis Sanderson, "The Impact of Inscriptions on the Interpretation of Early Śaiva Literature," *Indo-Iranian Journal* 56 (2013): 211–244.
32. For more information on the Kāpālikas see David N. Lorenzen, *The Kāpālikas and the Kālāmukhas: Two Lost Śaivite Sects*. (1972; 2d rev. ed., Delhi: Motilal Banarsidass, 1991).

33. Alexis Sanderson, "Śaiva Texts," in *Brill's Encyclopedia of Hinduism*, Vol. 6, edited by Knut A. Jacobsen (Leiden and Boston: Brill, 2015), 10–42.
34. Sanderson, "The Impact of Inscriptions on the Interpretation of Early Śaiva Literature," 234. It should be noted that Dominic Goodall and his collaborators in the editing and translating the *Niśvāsatattvasaṃhitā* argue that the work as a whole was completed by the 7th century, while the "early kernel," the *Mūlasūtra*, was likely composed a century earlier. See Dominic Goodall, ed. *The Niśvāsatattvasaṃhitā: The Earliest Surviving Śaiva Tantra, Volume 1*. (Pondicherry: Institute Français de Pondichéry, 2015), 72–73.
35. Sanderson, "Śaiva Texts," 21–22.
36. See David Gray, "Eating the Heart of the Brahmin: Representations of Alterity and the Formation of Identity in Tantric Buddhist Discourse," *History of Religions* 45, no. 1 (2005): 45–69; Alexis Sanderson, "History Through Textual Criticism in the Study of Śaivism, the Pañcarātra and the Buddhist Yoginītantras," in *Les Sources et le temps. Sources and Time: A Colloquium, Pondicherry, 11–13 January 1997*, edited by François Grimal (Pondicherry: Institut Français de Pondichéry/École Française d'Extrême-Orient, 2001), 11–12, no.10 (1–47).
37. Sanderson, "Śaiva Texts," 28.
38. Flood, *An Introduction to Hinduism*, 166.
39. Alexis Sanderson, "Śaivism and the Tantric Traditions," in *The World's Religions*, edited by S. Sutherland, L. Houlden, P. Clarke, and F. Hardy (London: Routledge and Kegan Paul, 1988), 681–683 (660–704).
40. Alexis Sanderson, "Śaivism: Śaivism in Kashmir," in *Encyclopedia of Religion*, Vol. 12, 2d ed., edited by Lindsay Jones (Detroit: Macmillan Reference, 2005), 8047–8048.
41. White, *Kiss of the Yoginī*, 16.
42. Regarding this see David Gray, "Disclosing the Empty Secret: Textuality and Embodiment in the *Cakrasamvara Tantra*," *Numen* 52, no. 4 (2005): 417–444.
43. David White, *The Alchemical Body: Siddha Traditions in Medieval India* (Chicago: University of Chicago Press, 1996), 7.
44. See David Lorenzen and Adrián Muñoz, eds., *Yogi Heroes and Poets: Histories and Legends of the Nāths* (Albany: State University of New York Press, 2011), x. For a discussion of a Buddhist Nāth yogī see David Templeman, "Buddhaguptanātha: A Late Indian *Siddha* in Tibet," in *Tibetan Studies: Proceedings of the Seventh Seminar of the International Association for Tibetan Studies, Graz 1995*, Vol. 2, edited by Ernst Steinkellner (Vienna: Verlag der Österreichischen Akademieder Wissenschaften, 1997), 955–965.
45. David White, *Sinister Yogis* (Chicago: University of Chicago Press, 2009), 14.
46. James Mallinson, *The Khercarīvidyā of Ādinātha: A Critical Edition and Annotated Translation of an Early Text of Haṭhayoga* (London: Routledge, 2007), 4–5.
47. For a detailed discussion of this tradition of yoga see David White, *The Alchemical Body*.
48. See June McDaniel, *Offering Flowers, Feeding Skulls: Popular Goddess Worship in West Bengal* (Oxford: Oxford University Press, 2004), 6–13.
49. Goudriaan, "Hindu Tantric Literature in Sanskrit," 1.
50. For a survey of this evidence see Tracy Pintchman, *The Rise of the Goddess in the Hindu Tradition* (Albany: State University of New York Press, 1994).
51. Pintchman, *The Rise of the Goddess in the Hindu Tradition*, 119.
52. Flood, *An Introduction to Hinduism*, 184–185.
53. See Brooks, *The Secret of the Three Cities*.
54. See Rachel Fell McDermott and Jeffrey J. Kripal, eds., *Encountering Kali: In the Margins, at the Center, in the West* (Berkeley: University of California Press, 2003).
55. McDaniel, *Offering Flowers, Feeding Skulls*, 145–208, 235–254.
56. See David Kinsley, *Tantric Visions of the Divine Feminine: The Ten Mahāvidyās* (Berkeley: University of California Press, 1997).
57. See Sanderson, *The Śaiva Age*, 240–243.
58. Loriliai Biernacki, *Renowned Goddess of Desire: Women, Sex, and Speech in Tantra* (Oxford: Oxford University Press, 2007), 150–159.

59. Flood, *The Tantric Body*, 54.
60. See H. Daniel Smith, "The Three Gems of the Pāñcarātra Canon: A Critical Appraisal," *Studies in the History of Religions*, supplement to *Numen* 22 (1972), 43, no. 2 (41–49).
61. Sanderson, "History Through Textual Criticism," 35.
62. Sanderson, "History Through Textual Criticism," 37–39.
63. See Edward C. Dimock Jr., *The Place of the Hidden Moon: Erotic Mysticism in the Vaiṣṇava-Sahajiyā Cult of Bengal* (1989; reprint, Delhi: Motilal Banarsidass, 1991), 35–40.
64. Goudriaan, "Hindu Tantric Literature in Sanskrit," 110–111.
65. Sanderson, "The Śaiva Age," 117–123.
66. See Martin Ramstedt, ed., *Hinduism in Modern Indonesia* (London: Routledge, 2003).
67. For profiles of a number of these gurus and the communities they have established in the West, see Ann Gleig and Lola Williamson, ed., *Homegrown Gurus: From Hinduism in America to American Hinduism* (Albany: State University of New York Press, 2014).
68. Stephen Hodge, *The Mahā-vairocana-abhisaṃbodhi Tantra, with Buddhaguhya's Commentary* (London: RoutledgeCurzon, 2003), 14–15.
69. Davidson, *Indian Esoteric Buddhism*, 118.
70. For a fascinating analysis of the development of this literature see Koichi Shinohara, *Spells, Images, and Mandalas: Tracing the Evolution of Esoteric Buddhist Rituals* (New York: Columbia University Press, 2014).
71. Goodall, *The Niśvāsatattvasaṃhitā*, 78–84.
72. For a discussion of the different classes of Buddhist tantras, see Jacob Dalton, "A Crisis of Doxography: How Tibetans Organized Tantra During the 8th-12th Centuries," *Journal of the International Association of Buddhist Studies* 28.1 (2005): 115–181.
73. See Sanderson, *The Śaiva Age*, 124–240.
74. Max Nihom, "The Mandala of Caṇḍi Gumpung (Sumatra) and the Indo-Tibetan Vajraśekharatantra," *Indo-Iranian Journal* 41.2 (1998): 251 (245–254).
75. Regarding Amoghavajra and his attempt at transmitting this canon of tantric literature, see Rolf Giebel, "The Chin-kang-ting ching yü-ch'ieh shih-pa-hui chih-kuei: An Annotated Translation," *Journal of Naritasan Institute for Buddhist Studies* 18 (1995): 107–201; David Gray, "On the Very Idea of a Tantric Canon: Myth, Politics, and the Formation of the Bka' 'gyur," *Journal of the International Association of Tibetan Studies*, no. 5 (2009): 12–13 (1–37).
76. See Henrik Sørensen, "Early Esoteric Buddhism in Korea: Three Kingdoms and Unified Silla (ca. 600–918)," in Orzech, Sørensen, and Payne, *Esoteric Buddhism and the Tantras in East Asia*, 575–596.
77. Regarding the establishment of the Shingon school of esoteric Buddhism Japan during the 9th century, see Ryūichi Abé, *The Weaving of Mantra: Kukai and the Construction of Esoteric Buddhist Discourse* (New York: Columbia University Press, 1999).
78. Adelheid Herrmann-Pfandt, "The Lhan Kar Ma as a Source for the History of Tantric Buddhism," in *The Many Canons of Tibetan Buddhism*, edited by Helmut Eimer and David Germano (Leiden, Netherlands: Brill, 2002), 132 (129–149).
79. According to Tibetan historical sources, three catalogs of translated texts were made during the Tibetan imperial period. These include the *Lhan/lDan kar ma*, which has been dated to 812 CE (Herrmann-Pfandt, "The Lhan Kar Ma as a Source for the History of Tantric Buddhism," 129), and the *'Phang-thang-ma*, which has been dated to 842 ce (Brandon Dotson, " 'Emperor' Mu rug btsan and the 'Phang thang ma Catalogue," *Journal of the International Association of Tibetan Studies*, no. 3 (December 2007): 4 [1–25]). The third catalog, the *mchims phu ma*, is apparently lost.
80. Jacob Dalton and Sam van Schaik, *Tibetan Tantric Manuscripts from Dunhang: A Descriptive Catalogue of the Stein Collection at the British Library* (Leiden, Netherlands: Brill, 2006), xxi.
81. For an introduction to the rNying ma school and its tantric teachings, see Khetsun Sangpo, *Tantric Practice in Nying-ma* (Ithaca, NY: Snow Lion, 1996); Dudjom Rinpoche, *The Nyingma School of Tibetan Buddhism, Its Fundamentals and History* (Boston: Wisdom, 1991).

82. Cathy Cantwell and Robert Mayer, *A Noble Noose of Methods: The Lotus Garland Synopsis: A Mahāyoga Tantra and Its Commentary* (Vienna: Österreichische Akademie der Wissenschaften, 2012), 6–9.
83. See Ronald Davidson's study of this era of Tibetan religious history, his book *Tibetan Renaissance: Tantric Buddhism in the Rebirth of Tibetan Culture* (New York: Columbia University Press, 2005).
84. Mircea Eliade, *Yoga: Immortality and Freedom* (Bollingen Series 56), (Princeton, NJ: Princeton University Press, 1970), 210.
85. Goudriaan, "Hindu Tantric Literature in Sanskrit," 111.
86. Sanderson, *The Śaiva Age*, 243–245.
87. Shaman Hatley, "Mapping the Esoteric Body in the Islamic Yoga of Bengal," *History of Religions* 46.4 (2007): 351–353 (351–368).
88. Regarding this practice see Michael Stoeber, "3HO Kundalini Yoga and Sikh Dharma," *Sikh Formations* 8.3 (2012): 358 (351–368).
89. See Christine Mollier, *Buddhism and Daoism Face to Face: Scripture, Ritual, and Iconographic Exchange in Medieval China* (Honolulu: University of Hawai'i Press, 2008), 141–146.
90. Regarding this see Richard Payne, "The Homa of the Northern Dipper," in *Tantric Traditions on the Move: Their Development Through Time, and Transmission Through Cultural Space*, ed. David Gray and Ryan Overbey (Oxford and New York: Oxford University Press, 2016), 292–293.
91. See David Snellgrove, *Indo-Tibetan Buddhism: Indian Buddhists and Their Tibetan Successors* (Boston: Shambhala, 2002), 403–404.
92. For a translation of a Bön tantra, see Michael Walter, "The Tantra a Vessel of bdud rtsi: A Bon Text," *Journal of the Tibet Society* 8 (1987): 25–72.
93. See Andrea Loseries-Leick, "Symbolism in Bon Mother Tantra," in *Tibetan Studies: Proceedings of the 6th Seminar of the International Association for Tibetan Studies, Fagernes 1992, Volume 1*, ed. Per Kvaerne (Oslo: Institute for Comparative Research in Human Culture, 1994), 501–506.
94. Urban, *Tantra*, 207–230.
95. Goudriaan, "Hindu Tantric Literature in Sanskrit," 2.
96. Davidson, *Indian Esoteric Buddhism*, 8–9.
97. Peter Bisschop, "The Abode of the Pañcamudrās: A Yoginī Temple in Early Medieval Vārāṇasī," in *"Yoginī" in South Asia: Interdisciplinary Approaches*, ed. István Keul (London: Routledge, 2013), 47–60.
98. Bisschop's article, "The abode of the Pañcamudrās," provides an example of this; it concerns early medieval textual accounts of a Cauṃsāṭha Yoginī temple in Vārāṇasī which has not survived to the present day.
99. See Miranda Shaw, *Passionate Enlightenment: Women in Tantric Buddhism* (Princeton, NJ: Princeton University Press, 1994).
100. See Bholanath Bhattacharya, "Some Aspects of the Esoteric Cults of Consort Worship in Bengal: A Field Survey Report," *Folklore* (Calcutta) 18, no. 10 (October 1977): 310–324; 18, no. 11 (November 1977): 359–365; 18, no. 12 (December 1977): 385–397.
101. Debra Diamond, ed., *Yoga: The Art of Transformation* (Washington, DC: Smithsonian Institution, 2013).

David B. Gray

TANTRIC BUDDHISM IN JAPAN: KUKAI AND SAICHO

SAICHŌ AND EARLY HEIAN BUDDHISM

The Heian period (794–1185) began with the movement of the capital from Nara to Kyoto (called Heian-kyō 平安京 at the time). The move had clear political motives related to competition between imperial lines and a desire to reform the Buddhist church. Established leaders in Nara were opposed to the move, and none of the major Buddhist temples were transplanted into Kyoto, unlike during the previous move of the capital from Asuka to Nara in 710. The move was made by Emperor Kanmu 桓武 (r. 781–806), though without the wholesale enmity toward Nara Buddhism that an earlier generation of scholarship tended to suggest. Rather, Kanmu's concerns seem to have lain more in purifying monastic practice and in redressing the imbalance marked by the dominance of the Hossō (法相) school over the Sanron (三論) school in terms of numbers of monks ordained in each. Displeasure with the political dominance of members of the Fujiwara family, whose tutelary temple was the Hossō temple Kōfuku-ji (興福寺), may also have been a factor.

Saichō played a significant role in the emergence of nascent political and religious forces in the new capital. The Tendai school he established also had a profound and lasting impact; several of the medieval Buddhist leaders—such as Shinran, Dōgen, and Nichiren—were ordained as Tendai monks and trained at the monastic center of Enryaku-ji (延暦寺) on Mt. Hiei (比叡山). Saichō's unfolding relationship with emperor Kanmu brought him into central circles of influence. While the two of them shared an interest in developing new forms of Buddhism, Saichō was more purely religious in his aims; Kanmu was focused on consolidating the power of his regime. Their separate passions dovetailed neatly.

Saichō was ordained in Nara and in 788 built a small hut on Mt. Hiei, which was just northeast of what was to become the new capital but at the time was remote. A votive text he wrote expressing his intentions for solitary retreat in the mountains reveals a sincere bodhisattva spirit dedicated to working to free all beings from suffering.[1] In addition to studying Buddhist texts about "consciousness only" (*yuishiki* 唯識) theories, Saichō apparently read widely in the Chinese Huayan (華厳) tradition, including Fazang's 法蔵 commentaries on *The Awakening of Faith in the Mahāyāna* (大乗起信論). One of his key mentors in Nara was the Hossō monk Gyōhō 行表(722–797). It seems that he learned about the Tiantai tradition (from which came the Japanese name Tendai) from Fazang's works and that he was able to study at temple libraries texts by the Tiantai founder Zhiyi 智顗 (538–597). Groups of other monks in Nara also studied Tiantai texts. The "one vehicle" (*ichijō* 一乗) teaching of the *Lotus Sutra*, from which scripture Zhiyi took much of his exegetical inspiration, became a central theme in Saichō's thought. The hut he built on Mt. Hiei was named the "temple for meditation on the One-vehicle" (*ichijō shikan'in* 一乗止観院). Saichō was committed to purifying elements of Japanese Buddhism by creating a model of a bodhisattva practitioner dedicated to textual study and meditation in an isolated location where concentration was enhanced. There were many Buddhist monks in Nara with similar inclinations, known as disciples of "mountain practice" *sanrin shugyō* 山林修行, but it seems they were a minority.[2]

Saichō was familiar with at least one of the texts that was to become central to the Japanese tradition, since he had copied Yixing 一行 and Śubhakarasiṃha's (Chinese name Shanwuwei 善無畏) commentary on the *Darijing* (J. *Dainichi-kyō* 大日経) (Takagi 1991: 117). Yixing's utilization of Tiantai doctrine to explain the *Darijing* contributed to the emergence of interpretations that the one vehicle teaching of the *Lotus Sutra* and the Tantric teaching of the *Darijing* were consistent with one another.[3] This view became a backbone of Saichō's approach toward tantric texts and a bone of contention between him and Kūkai. While Saichō was initiated into some tantric practices during his trip to China in 804, and brought back tantric texts, it is clear that his primary motivation was to return to Japan as a legitimate transmitter of

Tiantai teachings. Once he returned, however, Emperor Kanmu was more interested in Saichō's exposure to esoteric Buddhism than to Tiantai, and soon requested that Saichō perform a *kanjō* initiation ceremony for the emperor and a few others. The emperor probably hoped that this ritual would help him to heal from illness. Saichō obliged and gained much recognition from doing so. Yet his chief interest remained in strengthening the foundation for Tiantai study and practice in Japan, for which project he was well equipped. To serve as well Kanmu's interest in promoting tantric practice, however, Saichō sought the assistance of Kūkai once the latter returned from China.

In 798 Saichō began giving public talks on the *Lotus Sutra*, first in Nara and later a series at Takaosan-ji (高雄山寺) (also known as Jingo-ji 神護寺), on the western edge of what became the new capital. His chief sponsor for the Takao lectures was Wake no Hiroyo (和気広世), a prominent court aristocrat and devout Buddhist who was also an advisor to Emperor Kanmu. This series seems to have placed Saichō on the emperor's radar as someone who could capably represent a new approach to Buddhist studies that might help cool the flames of Hossō-Sanron disputes in Nara. The following year Wake Hiroyo's petition for Saichō to go to China on a government mission was granted. The stated aim was to gather new texts and to receive personal transmission from a Tiantai master. He left from the port in western Japan near Dazaifu in 803 but was turned back due to bad weather and remained in Dazaifu for another year. There is some speculation but no evidence that he might have first met Kūkai there before the two of them left together for China, in separate boats, on a mission in 804. It is unclear how or why Kūkai was able to join the mission, but he stayed in China about a year longer than did Saichō. Kūkai sailed on the first ship with the official envoy Fujiwara Kadonomaro, while Saichō was on the second ship. Perhaps it was Kūkai's superb skills in classical Chinese that earned him this role, since he ended up drafting some important documents in China for the envoy.

Saichō and Kūkai took separate paths in China and it appears they did not meet there. According to some of Saichō's biographies, he received a transmission on Mt. Tiantai from Wei Xiang of Guojing-si 国清寺, where he stayed over a month, that included a Daibutsuchō-hō (大仏頂法) ceremony.[4] Subsequently, with his translator Gishin 義真 and a large group of Chinese monks, he took bodhisattva vows from Daosui 道邃. Later in his career in Japan, Saichō wanted to replace the standard Shiburitsu (四分律) vows (that all monks were required to take during ordination) with the bodhisattva vows from the *Brahma's Net Sutra* (梵網經 Ch. *Fanwang jing*, J. *Bonmōkyō*,) for all Tendai monks. There was no precedent for this in China, where monks who took bodhisattva vows did so in addition to the Shiburitsu ones. When he traveled back to Mingzhou (明州) in order to return to Japan, he learned that he needed to wait six weeks because the ship had arrived at different port. He decided to visit Yuezhou (越州), where he and Gishin received a tantric transmission from Shunxiao 順暁. The precise nature of this transmission is unclear and has long been debated in Japan.[5] While Saichō's tantric initiation came during an unplanned trip to Yuezhou, his earlier exposure to tantric texts in Japan coupled with his apparent fondness of Yixing's approach in his commentary on the *Darijing* that laid the ground for asserting that the Lotus and tantric teachings were in accord (what later Tendai exegetes called *enmitsu itchi* 円密一致) supports the view that Saichō's receiving of an esoteric transmission was not something alien to his interests. Saichō was able to return with copies of as many as 120 texts in a total of 345 fascicles, twelve of which were tantric in nature. Nevertheless, according to Groner, "despite the importance which Saichō placed on his transmissions from China, the content of most of Saichō's teachings came from his studies in Japan before and after his stay in China."[6]

Upon his return in 805, Saichō submitted his report to the court, which then ordered a set of all his imported texts to be copied for each of the seven major Nara temples. Emperor Kanmu was gravely ill and requested Wake no Hiroyo to spare no expense to arrange an elaborate *kanjō* ceremony at Takaosan-ji on his behalf. This was Japan's first such ceremony, complete with a new mandala Saichō had brought from China. Kanmu demonstrated more interest in tantric than in Tiantai teachings, apparently believing that tantric rites were effective both at healing illness and in appeasing angry spirits of deceased relatives.[7]

In 805 Saichō proposed a revision to the state ordination system that would give three ordinands each to the Hossō and Sanron schools and two to Tendai as well as to the Kegon and Ritsu schools. The proposal was approved; however, the Tendai ordinands were divided into two tracks: one for *Shikan* (止観) (centered on Tiantai study) and one for *Shanagō* (遮那業) (centered on tantra). This result surely surprised Saichō, who was not adequately prepared to develop a full-fledged tantric training program. The court requirement clearly balanced Saichō's interests with those of the emperor. But then in early 806 Emperor Kanmu died and was succeeded by his brother. The new Emperor Heizei 平城 showed little support for Buddhism or for Saichō, nor did his reign last long. Heizei abdicated due to illness and passed the throne to another brother, the Emperor Saga 嵯峨. Under the fourteen years of Saga's reign there was tremendous growth in Buddhism and support for both Saichō and Kūkai, who emerged on the scene in the capital in 809.

Kūkai returned to Japan in 806 after two years of study in China but did not enter the capital until 809. His return was a great surprise to some in Japan since he had been given a stipend for twenty years of study. There has been speculation that his three-year wait in Dazaifu might have been court imposed as some sort of reprimand for his early return, but it seems more likely that permission for him to enter the capital was delayed due to political disquiet related to the two proximate changes in leadership. Kūkai did submit a report from his travels, along with the texts and other materials he had acquired, immediately upon settling in Dazaifu. It is also known that Saichō made a copy of this report (extant in his handwriting), the *Goshōrai mokuroku* (御将来目録). More so than anyone in Japan, Saichō would have realized that what Kūkai reported to have studied in China, and the texts and other religious objects he brought back, represented a tremendously valuable resource for the nation. Saichō also surely recognized that Kūkai could be immensely helpful to him in the task of training monks in the new *Shanagō* curriculum. It was inevitable that the two would soon meet. It appears that in 809 first Kūkai visited Saichō on Mt. Hiei and soon afterward Saichō requested to borrow texts from Kūkai to copy. For three or four years the two communicated, and in some ways collaborated to incubate new forms of Buddhism, as can be seen in the various letters between them that have been preserved.[8]

In attempting to evaluate their relationship, it is important to understand that not only was Saichō seven years Kūkai's senior, but he was also well known among prominent Buddhists in Nara and, at the time of Kūkai's return, had maintained a close relationship with Emperor Kanmu and one of his close advisors for several years. Kūkai had no such recognition; he was younger and a complete outsider to the circles Saichō frequented. Yet his report evidenced unparalleled exposure to esoteric Buddhist traditions on the continent and a fervent desire to promote them. In seeking Kūkai's assistance, Saichō demonstrated both humility and prudence. And, as it turned out, he introduced Kūkai to powerful people who became significant to the latter's own rise to prominence.

KŪKAI'S PATH TO PROMINENCE

A text Kūkai wrote in 797 on the occasion of his leaving the government college, where he was studying Chinese classics, describes his upbringing and his reasons for dropping out. This was the *Rōko shiiki* (聾瞽指歸), *Indicating the Aim for the Deaf and Blind* (revised in 804 as *Sangō shiiki* (三教指歸), *Indicating the Aims of the Three Teachings*).[9] He wrote that he had studied Confucian and Daoist texts extensively but found Buddhism more compelling. He noted that upon meeting an unnamed monk, he learned a particular meditation of mantra recitation (the *Kokūzō gumonji hō* (虛空藏求聞持法), "Ākāśagarbha's Method for Seeking, Hearing and Retaining") and that its practice transformed him. From the time he left the college to the time he got ordained, just prior to departing to China in 804, there are no extant documents to trace his movements. It is suspected that his ordination was hurriedly performed, more or less at the last minute, in order that he could accompany the official Japanese envoy on the mission trip to China. It is probable that Kūkai was selected because his facility in Chinese, both written and spoken, was highly regarded. It is also likely that before the China trip, he was a lay Buddhist practitioner (or "privately ordained monk" *shidosō* 私度僧) who frequented Nara temple libraries as well as places for solitary retreat in the mountains. It is abundantly clear that not only was he widely read in Buddhist texts before he traveled to China, but that he was also intimately familiar with the contents of temple library collections. His *Indications of the Aims of the Three Teachings*, written before he left, contains extensive citations from Buddhist scripture. And his detailed knowledge of what was available in Japan is evident in the fact that only a very small portion of the hundreds of texts he brought back from China already existed in Japan.

He was sent to the Tang capital as a government student who would benefit his homeland by studying things Chinese, and he had a stipend for a twenty years' stay. A later text of questionable authenticity (the *Goyuigo* 御遺告) says that he wanted to go to China to better understand a tantric text he had found in Nara but could not understand, the *Dainichi-kyō*.[10] This account fits a traditional narrative that places his interest in things tantric quite early. It is also possible, however, that his encounters with experienced teachers and esoteric Buddhist texts while in China were more fortuitous. We simply do not know. What we do know is that he had close encounters in China with knowledgeable esoteric Buddhist teachers and that he returned to Japan energized to transmit something he thought was needed and was powerful.

In early 805 he got permission to reside at the Ximingsi temple (西明寺) in the capital city of Chang'an (長安). Ximingsi was an important center for translation and study where Kūkai learned Sanskrit from the Central Asian monk Prajnā. A few months later he met the monk Huiguo 惠果 (746–805) at the Qinglongsi temple (青龍寺), who had studied under Amoghavajra 不空 (J. Fukū; Ch. Bukong, 705–774), a crucial figure in the promulgation of tantric ritual at the Tang imperial court. Kūkai relied heavily on many of the esoteric Buddhist texts that Amoghavajra had translated into Chinese and garnered much prestige from being his second-generation student. He also seems to have modeled his own later ambitions to be a tantric master whose rituals could protect the emperor and strengthen the state on Amoghavajra's accomplishments. Regarding Huiguo's historical status, while Shingon tradition portrays him as the leading disciple of Amoghavajra, in fact he was one of several, none of whom left writings.

Kūkai's dramatic accounts of his meeting with and studies under Huiguo depict the mentorship as a karmically charged moment destined to bring great benefit to Japan. Huiguo is reported to have anticipated Kūkai's arrival and to have set aside other duties to concentrate solely and hurriedly on transmitting all his knowledge to this young Japanese monk. Kūkai's training was intensive enough to permit Huiguo to purportedly claim, on his deathbed after just six months of teaching, that he had conveyed all there was to convey. Shortly after Huiguo's death, Kūkai decided to return to Japan.

According to his official report, the *Goshōrai mokuroku* (御請來目録), Kūkai brought back with him 142 sutras, 42 Sanskrit texts, 32 commentaries, 5 mandala, and several paintings and ritual implements. His report also refers his bringing a new esoteric teaching to Japan and uses the term "diamond vehicle" (J. *kongōjō* 金剛乗; Skt. *vajrayāna*) to describe it. The text has a tone that balances excitement with the requisite humility of someone reporting to the court after returning exceedingly early from an assigned mission. His zeal appears in passages like this one: "Former transmitters of the Dharma [merely] tugged at leaves and swam in tributaries. What I now transmit unearths the very root itself and fully exposes the wellspring."[11] A version of the *Goshōrai mokuroku* exists in Saichō's hand. He must have copied it shortly after Kūkai submitted it to the court, and he later made his requests to borrow texts from Kūkai based on its content. As noted at the end of the section "Saichō and Early Heian Buddhism," athough Kūkai was virtually unknown in the new capital, Saichō surely recognized immediately that this young monk with many new texts and an account of having trained with a disciple of Amoghavajra in Chang'an represented a precious resource for the imperial reign. When Kūkai entered the capital in 809, after three years in Dazaifu and once the new Emperor Saga had been enthroned, Saichō took little time in pressing his connections to get Kūkai settled.

SAICHŌ AND KŪKAI'S RELATIONSHIP

The best documents for studying their relationship are the letters they wrote one another. We have mostly ones from Saichō and only a few from Kūkai. One collection of Saichō's letters was compiled by the Shingon monk Dokai 退快 in 1391.[12] Some scholars think the letters might have been edited to depict Saichō as being more dependent on Kūkai. Most of the existing letters show Saichō's chief interest to be borrowing texts to copy. Letters to Kūkai and others during a period in 809 indicate Saichō retreated from outside activities to remain on Mt. Hiei. Most scholars assume this was to copy texts from Kūkai. His borrowing of texts—both tantric ones and Huayan and Tiantai texts new to Japan, over thirty in all—appears to have continued for at least three years. The two men seem to have been working together to create novel models for study and practice in the new capital and beyond. As it turned out, however, their cooperation lasted only a few years since they eventually developed very different agendas.

In the tenth month of 812, Saichō asked Kūkai to offer a *kanjō* initiation at Takaosan-ji. Only four people attended, including two Wake brothers. Two months later Kūkai offered another *kanjō* there, though this time over 140 people participated. A record of these two events is extant in Kūkai's hand and it lists Saichō first, suggesting that they were performed on his behalf to help him consolidate the knowledge needed to build his *Shana* course in tantric study on Mt. Hiei. In 813 Saichō sent some of his closest disciples to study with Kūkai at Takaosanji: Enchō 円澄, Kōjō 光定, and Taihan 泰範. With these two ceremonies, Kūkai entered central stage in the new world of Heian Buddhism. The second *kanjō* was attended by many of the most respected elder monks from Nara. It must have been abundantly clear to them that Kūkai more so than Saichō was the resident master of the newly imported esoteric Buddhist practices.

It was likely in 813 that changes emerged in Saichō and Kūkai's relationship. Letters from Saichō up to this time convey his view that the Tendai one vehicle teaching was completely harmonious with tantric teachings. By all accounts, the two of them held different views of the tantric teachings (and practices), and it appears Saichō was neither capable of comprehending why Kūkai thought them to be so unique and superior nor willing to prioritize them over other teachings, as was Kūkai's clear intention. Saichō's priority lay in establishing the Tendai school; his work in the tantric materials was secondary, mainly in order to accord with the court's expressed will. Kūkai, on the other hand, was firmly determined to promote his beloved tantric teachings above all else. Nonetheless, he stressed in many of his writings that there was no contradiction between the "exoteric" (nontantric) teachings of the Nara schools and Tendai and his "esoteric" Shingon ones. He simply believed the Shingon practices had more transformative power. In any case, each was single-minded in his vision; they simply were not aiming in exactly the same direction.

It was also likely in 813 that Kūkai penned a letter in response to Saichō's request to borrow a commentary on a *Perfection of Wisdom* text (*Hannya-haramita-rishūkyō* 般若波羅蜜理趣経), a letter that has received much attention over the centuries. While some scholars doubt the letter's authenticity, others think it was addressed to Saichō's disciple Enchō instead (the salutation says only, "to master Chō").[13] Of central interest is the letter's apparent refusal to loan the requested text, coupled with its critique of the requester's inadequate appreciation of the need for studying profound esoteric Buddhist teachings in person, master-to-student, not just by reading texts. Some scholars consider this letter inauthentic because the language is too directly harsh for Kūkai to have written to Saichō (other letters from Kūkai are cordial). Others counter that, considering the different views on tantric teachings they had shared with one another, coupled with Saichō's frequent requests to copy and his resistance to take more time to study with Kūkai as he had his disciples do, such an admonition from Kūkai was appropriate. Takagi—focusing on the meaning of a key term "*rishū*" (理趣) (meaning the deeper "purport" or "principle" of the teachings)—suggests that the letter might not be a refusal to loan a text, but rather could be a clarification of Kūkai's views on the proper way to approach Tantric study.[14] However one sees the letter, there ought to be no surprise that Saichō wanted to copy all the new texts (Kūkai himself exhausted a government stipend copying texts in China), nor that he was too busy getting his own Tendai programs in place on Mt. Hiei to be able to dedicate much time to study at Takaosan-ji. Regardless to whom this letter was written, it is a clear mark of the emergence of Kūkai's confidence in his role as the new Japanese master of tantric studies, and its timing corresponds with the end of their correspondence.

Another incident often considered a catalyst to the decline in their relationship was the moment (also thought to be in 813) when Saichō's disciple Taihan, who had been sent to study with Kūkai, wrote a letter to Saichō refusing to return to Mt. Hiei. Extant letters show Saichō was distraught over the prospect of losing his trusted student; they implore Taihan to recognize the equivalence of the Lotus and the tantric teachings. Taihan's response mirrors Kūkai's view of the unique features of tantric practice, thereby revealing an irreconcilable split with Saichō. In response to those claiming Taihan "defected" to Kūkai in a manner that would have pressed a wedge between the two masters, it is important to note that in 812, when Saichō had written to Taihan and other disciples to ask them to handle administrative matters on Mt. Hiei because he was ill, Taihan wrote back to decline, claiming that he was having difficulty with others in the Mt. Hiei community that made him feel he was possibly violating his precepts. It is unclear what Taihan meant, but we do know that other students of Saichō were leaving Mt. Hiei to reside instead at Nara temples, indicating that Saichō was experiencing trouble maintaining his community.[15] One reason might have been the requirement Saichō imposed that Tendai monks be dedicated to twelve years of secluded practice on Mt. Hiei.

Also in 813 Kūkai wrote a document, *Kōnin ikai* (弘仁遺誡) ("Admonitions of the Kōnin [era]"), that was directed to those who had received one of three *kanjō* he had administered. It comprised a list of general guidelines, including exhortations to hold firmly both to the exoteric and esoteric precepts, and it explained the unique power of tantric teachings. It was a clear statement of what he believed the proper behavior and attitude ought to be for recipients of an esoteric Buddhist *kanjō*. Considering that several of Saichō best disciples were recipients, the text might also be seen as a recommendation for what ought to be the focus the Tendai *Shanagō*.[16]

Soon after Kūkai wrote the *Kōnin ikai*, Saichō wrote *Ehyō Tendai-shū* (依憑天台集) ("Collection of sources [demonstrating] reliance upon Tiantai"), in which he outlined in detail how the major schools of Chinese Buddhism to which Japan was heir depended upon doctrines from the Tiantai school.[17] He was taking a new direction, away from a concern to learn from Kūkai to bolster his *Shana* program and toward a focus on persuading people in Nara that Tendai was the most important school of Buddhist thought. A new preface he wrote for this work in 816 pointedly criticized the "new Shingon school" for disregarding the value of textual transmission. From 816 Saichō made promoting Tendai his priority, both by traveling to eastern Japan to lecture and build stupas and by composing texts that championed Tendai views and critiqued other views, in particular some of the doctrines supported within the Hossō school. His famous written debates with the Hossō scholar Tokuitsu 徳一 are an example.[18] Around the same time, in 817 Kūkai began construction of a new monastic center in the mountains far south of the capital, at Mt. Kōya, and also wrote *Kan'ensho* (勧縁疏) ("Letter of entreaty to those with a connection [to the Buddhadharma]"), which he sent (along with a collection of scriptures) to multiple acquaintances throughout Japan to request help in copying and disseminating tantric texts. Many consider this letter a short trial version of his longer *Benkenmitsu nikyōron* (辨顕密二教論) ("Treatise distinguishing the two teachings, exoteric and esoteric"), in which we can also detect an emphasis on differences with Tendai.[19] Both these texts clearly articulate Kūkai's vision of the unique and superior lineage, textual corpus, doctrine, and practice of his Shingon school. Two letters between them exist from 814 to 816, but no correspondences after 816.[20] Thus, it appears that by 816 the two men were no longer cooperating and may even have been competing in carving out separate visions for their respective schools. It is also from 816 that Saichō's writing becomes most productive and that Kūkai concentrates much of his energy on gathering resources to build a monastic complex on distant Mt. Kōya.[21]

THE JAPANESE TANTRIC PARADIGM

While Kūkai has been seen by some as more of a systematizer than an original thinker, this characterization is hard to evaluate fully because we do not have access to any writings from his Chinese teacher Huiguo. It is possible that the idea of using the two mandalas as a pair was Kūkai's, as maybe was his theory of the "preaching of the Dharmakāya" (*hosshin seppō* 法身説法). The same goes for his theory of "attaining enlightenment in this very body" (*sokushin jōbutsu* 即身成仏), especially in terms of the integration of the six elements, four mandalas, and three secrets as representing essence (*tai* 体), attributes (*sō* 相) and function (*yū* 用) of the Dharmakāya. And while his development of a ten-stage hierarchy of spiritual states was dependent in part on terminology from the *Dainichikyō*, the layering of both exoteric and esoteric interpretations onto each level was likely Kūkai's original idea, one that Sueki praises as brilliant and sophisticated, reminiscent of Hegel.[22] However, it was probably Kūkai's ritual innovations that got more traction in his day, and subsequently, than his doctrinal ones. It is reasonable to think that the Nara schools did not even consider Shingon as a new "school" in the traditional sense of having an identifiable doctrinal interest. His new theories received little apparent pushback, aside from the constructively engaging critique by Tokuitsu in his "Undetermined matters of Shingon" (*Shingon miketsu bun* 真言未決文).[23] At the same time, it appears that none of the texts written by scholars of the six Buddhist schools, by request of Emperor Saga in 830, acknowledged the presence of esoteric elements in Tendai.[24] In the Tendai school's early years, practitioners learned about esoteric Buddhism mostly from Kūkai.

The model of Buddhist practice employed by much of Japanese esoteric Buddhism was derived from Indian Tantric thought that was itself grounded in core ideas about the world from the Māhayāna schools of Madhyamaka and Yogacāra. The first clear articulation of this model in Japan is commonly attributed to Kūkai. It appears in his *Benkenmitsu nikyōron* (辨顕密二教論) ("Treatise distinguishing the two teachings, exoteric and esoteric"), *Sokushin jōbutsu-gi* (即身成仏義) ("The meaning of becoming a Buddha in this very body"), *Shōji jisshō-gi* (聲字実相義) ("The meaning of sound, word and reality"), and other less systematic texts.[25] While Saichō wrote almost nothing on the topic, his disciples, and in particular the later Tendai scholar Annen, were prolific, and they developed the earlier ideas in some innovative ways, while relying on the basics of the model expressed by Kūkai.[26] A summary of some key elements of the early model follows.

Veering away from a standard Māhayāna understanding of "three bodies" of the buddha, Kūkai's writings assert that the highest teachings that express the deepest truths of awakening came not from the flesh-and-blood historical Buddha Śākyamuni (Skt. *nirmāṇakāya*, Jpn. *ōgejin* 應化身), whose language conveyed the truth only indirectly, or from the more subtle *saṃbhogakāya* (Jpn. *hōjin* 報身) that manifests in visions, but rather directly from the *dharmakāya* (Jpn. *hosshin* 法身), or the very root source of awakening. Further, he writes that it is only by mastering the ritual process of contemplation that employs the "three secrets" (*sanmitsu* 三密) that one can attain awakening. Three-secret practice is a method of engaging body, speech, and mind in a manner that unites the practitioner directly with the *dharmakāya* via *mudrā* (bodily gestures), *mantra* (condensed utterances), and *mandala* (envisioning the world as a manifestation of awakened awareness). The standard Māhayāna understanding of the *dharmakāya* holds it to exist beyond thought and language and thus to be incapable of communicating with sentient beings. It is entirely transcendent. Kūkai understood language more broadly to include all three secrets; he thought that consecrated practice of *mudrā*, *mantra*, and *mandala* permitted the practitioner to open his entire being to the deepest level of ultimate reality. This level is not beyond language but rather inside it; the entire universe including the vibrations of speech and the gyrations of consciousness is none other than the cosmic body of the *dharmakāya*. Tantric practice gives one the key to unlock the secret treasury that is right before our eyes.[27]

Kūkai presented this model as being entirely consistent with the non-esoteric teachings yet as offering an extra step that engages all dimensions of a practitioner's being to "unearth the very root itself and fully expose the wellspring." He characterized Shingon practice as complementing other Buddhist practices by adding what amounts to a sort of turbo-charged process fueled by the three-secrets ritual. The practice was widely accepted in the Nara temples even during his lifetime and became a mainstay of monastic Japanese Buddhist culture. There was a significant contrast between his collaborative manner of introducing the new tantric teachings and Saichō's antagonistic approach, couched in reproach, toward what he saw as a conservative Nara establishment not adequately committed to Māhayāna bodhisattva practice.

The esoteric Buddhist rituals promoted by Kūkai as well as by later practitioners of both the Shingon and Tendai schools brought this model to bear directly onto matters social as well as political. Aristocrats and members of the court sought esoteric rites to ensure safe childbirth and to overcome illness, among other aims.[28] The tantric paradigm was very conducive to imagining the interconnection of domains visible and invisible, mundane and spiritual. Experts trained at exploiting such connections were in demand. There is no reason to suspect that Saichō would have been any less interested than Kūkai in employing them widely.

On matters of doctrine, Saichō stayed within the parameters of Tendai exoteric thought, and his championing of certain interpretations of the teachings of the Lotus Sutra received more criticism than did Kūkai's writings.[29] It was only after his death that his disciples, having studied with Kūkai and more importantly traveled to China to bring back new texts and initiations, developed unique approaches to tantric practice that had major impact.[30] Annen (安然; 841–889?), for example, is considered by some scholars to be one of the most significant innovators of the Heian period. After Kūkai's death it was the Tendai school that witnessed vibrant doctrinal growth, not Shingon. It is commonly understood that Kūkai's compelling articulation of the foundations needed little elaboration. Or it might have been that doctrine was less relevant to the practice than was proper ritual procedure and paraphernalia. On the other hand, Saichō's silence on tantric doctrinal matters may have been a catalyst for Tendai writers to develop new forms of practice, ones that soon competed effectively with Shingon.

PERSPECTIVES ON THEIR RELATIONSHIP

As Akamatsu has noted, the closeness of Saichō and Kūkai's relationship is made evident in three documents extant in their handwriting: *Shōrai mokuroku*, *Kanjōrekimyō* (灌頂歴名) and *Fūshinchō* (風信帖).[31] The first was Kūkai's report to the court upon returning from

China, a copy of which exists in Saichō's hand. The second, listing the names of people who attended Kūkai's 812 *kanjō* at Takaosan-ji, with Saichō's name listed first, is in Kūkai's writing. The third is a letter Kūkai wrote to Saichō, probably in 812 from Takaosan-ji. It is a response to a communication from Saichō that included a copy of Tiantai Zhiyi's "Great Calming and Contemplation" (*Mohe zhiguan* 魔訶止観) that he was loaning to Kūkai and Saichō's request that Kūkai visit Mt. Hiei. The letter says:

> I received your letter. Upon reading it, I felt as if you were here. I also received the *Mohe zhiguan* text you sent and am beside myself with delight. It has become cold and I hope that you are well. I am fine and would like to follow your suggestion to come to Mt. Hiei. However, at present I am occupied with matters of small personal interest [religious practice?] from which I am unable to take leave. I have been thinking, though, that you and I and *Murōsan* ought to meet in order to discuss important matters regarding the furthering of the Buddha-dharma.[32] Together we can raise high the banner of the Dharma and repay the kindness of the Buddha. I would like it if you could come stay at my residence for a while. Please do not be concerned about troubling me. Such is my wish.
>
> Inexcusably, I have written poorly and in haste.
> Sent by the monk Kūkai
> *11*th day of the 9th month
> To my friend on the eastern peak, from your respectful student.[33]

Based on its first two words of salutation, *fūshin* (風信), the letter is commonly referred to as *Fūshinchō*.[34] The letter testifies to many things. First, it shows Kūkai's gratitude and deference to the elder monk. Second, it shows that the borrowing of texts between them went in both directions. Finally, it demonstrates Kūkai's interest in teaming up with Saichō to promote the Dharma. This cooperative spirit lasted only another two years or so, but at one point it seems to have been strong.

Abe Ryūichi's article on their relationship focuses on conflicts of interpretation and "unbridgeable differences" between the two in order to highlight "the intrinsic connection between subsequent historical development and the religious philosophies advanced by Saichō and Kūkai."[35] Thus, he links later sectarian tensions between the Tendai and Shingon schools to differences of view that appeared during the founders' lifetimes. He rightly points to irreconcilable positions among their doctrinal priorities, especially regarding esoteric Buddhism. His focus on early ruptures helps provide an interpretative frame for the later disputes. Another approach would be to investigate their relationship by looking at how historical sectarian discord creates bias by coloring visions of the past. Some modern scholars representing both schools have taken this latter approach. The Shingon scholar Ōyama Kōjun wrote: "There have been many disputes . . . regarding the relationship between Dengyō Daishi and Kōbō Daishi. However, most of these ought to be understood as biased viewpoints that are not derived from a proper understanding of actual historical events."[36] The Tendai scholar Kiuchi Gyōō wrote that interpretations "of the relationship between Saichō and Kūkai are made from a self-serving perspective" that "result[s] in the elevation of one's own founder" and gives "rise to distorted evaluations."[37] Each of these criticisms is aimed at scholarship in both schools. Naturally, however, what counts as "distorted" and as "actual" is often debated. Nonetheless, it seems that Japanese scholarship has become increasingly aware of the problems of sectarian bias.

Parts of Gardiner's doctoral dissertation (1994, revised: 2024) focus, unlike Abe's study, on the importance of seeing how and why the two men cooperated rather than on aspects of their split. This perspective aims to counter sectarian tendencies by revealing how much each benefited from the other's presence, in spite of their differences.[38] Saichō's *Shana* program could not have gotten off the ground without Kūkai's assistance, and Kūkai's entrance onto the central stage of early Heian Buddhism seems inconceivable without Saichō's support. The significant contributions each of them made to the successful development of the other's school is noteworthy.

Many earlier mentions of the two, perhaps following the account of Tsuji Zen'nosuke, portray Saichō as a humble and sincere practitioner while depicting Kūkai as a savvy political operator who skillfully manipulated circumstances to his advantage.[39] Other accounts reject Tsuji's interpretation by tending to see Saichō as sincere yet rather bullish in determination and argumentative, while viewing Kūkai as more cooperative.[40] In terms of their relations with established Buddhism in Nara, this latter portrayal captures the flavor of some of their writings, as Saichō showed antagonism toward the Sōgō (僧綱) (council of monastic affairs), toward Hossō doctrine and toward the standard ordination precepts.[41] On the other hand, Kūkai kept good relations with many key monks in Nara, established an esoteric Buddhist initiation hall at the important Tōdaiji (東大寺) temple, fashioned a rhetorical posture that expressed the value of non-esoteric teachings and introduced tantric practices broadly. His collaborative approach prefigured the blending of esoteric and exoteric practice well into the Kamakura period. At the same time, Saichō's administrative innovations for Tendai (part inspired by Amoghavajra) secured not only the long-term success of the school but were borrowed by other schools, including Shingon.[42] There is no doubt that the strong foundation Saichō established for Tendai allowed it to flourish into the Kamakura period to become the birthing ground of some of the most influential figures in Japanese Buddhist history: Honen, Shinran, Dōgen and Nichiren were all Tendai monks who studied on Mt. Hiei. Still, the impact of tantrism in Tendai was strong, and it is difficult to imagine the burgeoning of Tendai had it not developed a viable *Shana* program.

Sueki considers the early Heian period that is marked by the unique yet different contributions of Saichō and Kūkai to be one of the most productive periods of Japanese Buddhist history.[43] Much scholarship has noted the power of the tantric paradigm on all Japanese Buddhism, even in the so-called "reform" schools of the Kamakura period. Kuroda's articulation of how the "exoteric-esoteric system" (*kenmitsu seidō* 顕密制度) prevailed throughout all medieval Japanese Buddhism acknowledges this in political as well as in religious circles.[44] Sueki Fumihiro argues that the Kamakura thinkers were mostly reforming aspects of doctrine and practice established in the Heian period. The contributions of Saichō and Kūkai to subsequent centuries of Japanese Buddhism are indelible. Important differences aside, they both shared an emphasis on the centrality of meditation to the study of Buddhism, and they embodied this priority by aiming to establish substantial monastic centers for practice in the mountains. Compared to the urban temple concentration in Nara, this was a major shift in paradigm.

REVIEW OF LITERATURE

English sources are quite limited but Japanese ones abound. With Kūkai's status as a cultural hero in Japan, there is more on him in Japanese than on Saichō, but a large portion is also popular writing directed to a mass audience, in part stemming from what the Japanese called a "mikkyō boom" in the 1980s and 1990s. The esoteric Buddhist concept of the mandala was marketed as an indigenous creation embodying the value of diversity within an ethos of universal sacrality. Kūkai entered the public imagination like never before.

In English, Hakeda's seminal but somewhat dated *Kūkai: Major Works* is still a helpful overview and it touches on connections with Saichō. Bowring's *Religious Traditions of Japan* has solid chapters on each figure and their achievements in ushering in what he calls "the beginnings of a 'Japanese' Buddhism." Perhaps the best general English source on their relationship remains Groner's *Saichō*, which has a substantial and balanced chapter on his relations with Kūkai. Next is Abe's "Saichō and Kūkai," an essay that offers solid detail on the sources for documenting their relationship while arguing that an analysis of their different views on esoteric Buddhism illuminates the nature of later sectarian disputes. His *The Weaving of Mantra* is comprehensive on Kūkai and with references to Saichō in places. Gardiner's dissertation, "Kūkai and the Beginings of Shingon Buddhism" has a chapter on the two that focuses on how much they benefited from one another. One of his aims is to counter a traditional Shingon perspective that tends to portray Saichō as subordinate to Kūkai. Dolce's (2006) very thorough essay on Tendai esoteric Buddhism goes well beyond Saichō's contributions and offers good insight. Gardiner's "Transmission Problems?: Kūkai and the Early Dissemination of Esoteric Buddhist Texts" focuses on the topic of writing and copying, and serves as a corrective to the view that takes Saichō's extensive copying of the esoteric texts Kūkai brought back from China as problematic by demonstrating as well Kūkai's intensive efforts to copy and promulgate such texts.

Japanese sources have been abundant for ages, and many since the 1980s avoid the stark sectarianism that commonly characterized prewar scholarship. Sueki's 1996 volume offers an excellent summary of the two men's contributions (chapter 4). Other reliable modern sources include: Katsuno's book on early relations between monks on Mt. Hiei and Mt. Kōya; Kushida's volume on the foundations of the Shingon school; and Kiuchi, Misaki, and Shimizutani on the development of the Tendai esoteric tradition. Sonoda's fine non-sectarian historical work on Saichō and early Tendai is rich. More recently, Ōkubo's Taimitsu scholarship is extensive and draws on generations of his predecessors. Takagi's two volumes on the written exchanges of Saichō and Kūkai are also rich in detail and insight.

From a broader perspective, Sueki's work often combines textual particularity with astute general comments aiming to revise entrenched historical narratives. His monumental study of the Tendai scholar Annen (1995) is exemplary in this regard. In this and other writings, Sueki pushes against the long-standing bias that portrays Heian Buddhism as elitist and sees the Kamakura "reformation" as more populist.[45] He encourages redressing the scholarly imbalance that has long concentrated on Buddhist schools emerging from the Kamakura founders (Hōnen, Shinran, Dōgen, Nichiren) at the expense of neglecting earlier foundations, and argues that Kamakura period developments hold more continuity with the past than rupture. In this light, Saichō and Kūkai appear as seminal figures for all later history, as two men who paved the way for Buddhism to become significantly Japanese.

FURTHER READING

Abe, Ryūichi. "Saichō and Kūkai: A Conflict of Interpretations." *Japanese Journal of Religious Studies* 22, nos. 1–2 (1995): 103–137.

Abe, Ryūichi. *The Weaving of Mantra*. New York: Columbia University Press, 1999.

Bowring, Richard. *Religious Traditions of Japan: 500–1600*. Cambridge, UK: Cambridge University Press, 2005.

Akamatsu Toshihide 赤松俊秀. "Kukai to Saichō no kōsai ni tsuite" (最澄と空海の交際について). In *Kūkai* 空海 (*Nihon meisō ronshū* 日本名僧論集 3). Edited by Wada Shujō 和多修秀 and Takagi Shingen 高木訷元, 134–143. Tokyo: Yoshikawa kobunkan, 1982.

Chen, Jinhua. "The Formation of Early Esoteric Buddhism in Japan: A Study of the Three Esoteric Japanese Apochrypha." PhD diss., McMaster University, Toronto, 1997.

Dolce, Lucia. "Reconsidering the Taxonomy of the 'Esoteric': Taimitsu Hermeneutical and Ritual Practices." In *The Culture of Secrecy in Japanese Buddhism*. Edited by Mark Teeuwen and Bernard Scheid, 130–171. London: Routledge, 2006.

Dolce, Lucia. "Taimitsu: The Esoteric Buddhism of the Tendai School." In *Esoteric Buddhism and the Tantras in East Asia*. Edited by Charles Orzech, 744–767. Leiden, The Netherlands: Brill, 2011.

Fukunaga Mitsuji 福永光司. *Saichō, Kūkai* (最澄—空海) (*Nihon no meicho* (日本の名著) 3). Tokyo: Chuokoronsha, 1973.

Gardiner, David. "Kūkai and the Beginnings of Shingon Buddhism in Japan." PhD diss., Stanford University, Berkeley, CA, 1994. Revised as *Kūkai: Japan's First Vajrayāna Visionary*. Berkeley: Institute of Buddhist Studies and BDK/America, 2024.

Gardiner, David. "Buddhist Spirituality in the Heian and Kamakura Periods." In *Buddhist Spirituality II: Later China, Korea, Japan and the Modern World*. Edited by Yoshinori Takeuchi, 186–200. Crossroads Press, 1999.

Gardiner, David. "Transmission Problems?: Kūkai and the Early Dissemination of Esoteric Buddhist Texts." *Japanese Religions* 28, no. 1 (2003): 5–68.

Gardiner, David. "Selected translations from Kūkai's *Benkenmitsu nikyōron, Sokushin jōbutsugi, Jūjūshinron* and *Shōji jissōgi*." In *Sourcebook in Japanese Philosophy*. Edited by Thomas Kasulis and James Heisig, 149–175. Honolulu: University of Hawaii Press, 2011.

Groner, Paul. *Saichō: The Establishment of the Japanese Tendai School*. Honolulu: University of Hawaii Press, 1984.

Hakeda, Yoshito. *Kūkai: Major Works*. New York: Columbia University Press, 1972.

Hayami Tasuku 速水侑. *Nihon bukkyōshi: kōdai* (日本仏教史：古代). Tokyo: Yoshikawa kōbunkan, 1986.

Hayami Tasuku 速水侑. *Heian kizoku shakai to bukkyō* (平安貴族社会と仏教). Tokyo: Yoshikawa kōbunkan, 1975.

Katsumata Shunkyō 勝又俊教. *Mikkyō no nihonteki tenkai* (密教の日本的展開). Tokyo: Shunjūsha, 1981.

Katsunō Ryūshin 勝能隆信. *Hieizan to Kōyasan* (比叡山と高野山). Tokyo: Shibundo, 1959.

Kiuchi, Gyōō 木内尭央. *Tendai mikkyō no keisei* (天台密教の形成). Tokyo: Keisuisha, 1984.

Kushida Ryōkō 櫛田良浜. *Shingon mikkyō seiritsu katei no kenkyū* (真言密教成立過程の研究). Tokyo: Sankibō Busshorin, 1964.

Matsunaga Yūkei 松長有慶. *Mikkyō no rekishi* (密教の歴史). Kyoto: Heirakuji shoten, 1969.

Matsunaga Yūkei 松長有慶. *Shingonshū: Nihon no bukkyō: hito to oshie* (真言宗：日本の仏教、人と教え). Tokyo: Shōgakkan, 1986.

McMullen, Matthew Don. "The Development of Esoteric Buddhist Scholasticism in Early Medieval Japan." PhD diss., University of California, Berkeley, 2016.

Misaki Ryōshū 三崎良周. *Taimitsu no kenkyū* (台密の研究). Tokyo: Sobunsha, 1988.

Ōkubo Ryōshun 大久保良峻. *Taimitsu kyōgaku no kenkyū* (台密教学の研究). Tokyo: Hozokan, 2004.

Ōkubo Ryōshun 大久保良峻. *Saichō to Kūkai no kaikaku* (最澄空海の改革). In *Nihon bukkyō no ishizue* 日本仏教の礎. Tokyo: Kosei shuppansha, 2010, 138–196.

Ōkubo Ryōshun 大久保良峻. "The Identity between the Purport of the Perfect and Esoteric Teachings." *Japanese Journal of Religious Studies* 41, no. 1 (2014): 83–102.
Ōkubo Ryōshun 大久保良峻. *Saichō no shisō to Tendai mikkyō* (最澄の思想と天台密教). Kyoto: Hōzōkan, 2015.
Shimizutani Kyōjun 清水谷恭順. *Taimitsu kyōgaku no kenkyū* (台密教学の研究). Kyoto: Hōzōkan. 2004.
Sonoda Kōyū 薗田香融. *Tendai-shū: Nihon no bukkyō, hito to oshie* (天台宗：日本の仏教、人と教え). Tokyo: Shogakkan, 1986.
Sueki, Fumihiko 末木文美士. *Heian shoki bukkyō shisōshi no kenkyū* (平安初期仏教思想史の研究). Tokyo: Shunjusha, 1995 (2nd printing, 2006).
Sueki, Fumihiko 末木文美士. *Nihon bukkyōshi: shisō toshite no apurōchi* (日本仏教史:思想としてのアプローチ). Tokyo: Shinchosha, 1996.
Takagi Shingen 髙木訷元. *Kūkai no shokan* (弘法大師の書簡). Kyoto: Hozokan, 1981.
Takagi Shingen 髙木訷元. *Kūkai shisō no shoshiteki kenkyū* (空海思想の書誌的研究). Kyoto: Hozokan, 1991.
Takagi Shingen 髙木訷元. *Kūkai to Saichō no tegami* (空海と最澄の手紙). Kyoto: Hozokan, 1999.
Wada Shujō 和多修秀 and Takagi Shingen 髙木訷元, eds. *Kūkai* (空海) (*Nihon meisō ronshū* (日本名僧論集) 3). Tokyo: Yoshikawa kobunkan, 1982.
Tachikawa Musashi 立川武蔵 and Yoritomi Motohiro 頼富元宏, eds. *Nihon mikkyō* (日本密). Tokyo: Shunjūsha, 2005.
Takeuchi Kōzen 武内孝善. *Kōbōdaishi Kūkai no kenkyū* (弘法大師空海の研究). Tokyo: Yoshikawa kobunkan, 2006.
Takeuchi Kōzen 武内孝善. *Kūkai no kenkyū* (空海伝の研究). Tokyo: Yoshikawa kobunkan, 2015.

NOTES

1. See Paul Groner, *Saichō: The Establishment of the Japanese Tendai School* (Honolulu: University of Hawaii Press, 1984), 28.
2. Sonoda Kōyū 田香融, "Kodai bukkyō ni okeru sanrin shugyō to sono igi: toku ni jinenchishū o megutte" ((古代仏教における山林修行とその意義：特に自然智宗をめぐって), 1957). Repr., *Heian bukkyō no kenkyū*, 27–52, Kyoto: Hozokan, 1981.
3. See Lucia Dolce, "Reconsidering the Taxonomy of the 'Esoteric': Taimitsu Hermeneutical and Ritual Practices," in *The Culture of Secrecy in Japanese Buddhism*, edited by Mark Teeuwen and Bernard Scheid, 145–149 (London: Routledge, 2006).
4. Groner, *Saichō*, 6. Groner explains the claim is spurious and that it was made by Saicho's disciples to strengthen the appearance of his esoteric lineage.
5. Groner, *Saichō*, 53–61.
6. Groner, *Saichō*, 64.
7. Groner, *Saichō*, 66–67.
8. See Groner, *Saichō*, 79; Ryūichi Abe "Saichō and Kūkai: A Conflict of Interpretations," *Japanese Journal of Religious Studies* 22, nos. 1–2 (1995): 103–137; David Gardiner "Kūkai and the Beginnings of Shingon Buddhism in Japan" (PhD diss., Stanford University, Berkeley, CA, 1994); David Gardiner, "Transmission Problems?: Kūkai and the Early Dissemination of Esoteric Buddhist Texts," *Japanese Religions* 28, no. 1 (2003): 5–68; Takagi Shingen, 髙木訷元. *Kūkai shisō no shoshiteki kenkyū* (空海思想の書誌的研究) (Kyoto: Hozokan, 1991); and Takagi Shingen, 髙木訷元. *Kūkai to Saichō no tegami* (空海と最澄の手紙) (Kyoto: Hozokan, 1999).
9. See a translation of the *Sangō shiiki* in Yoshito Hakeda, *Kūkai: Major Works* (New York: Columbia University Press, 1972), 101–139.

10. See Katsunō Ryūshin, 勝能隆信 *Hieizan to Kōyasan* (比叡山と高野山) (Tokyo: Shibundo, 1959), 116.
11. Adapted from Hakeda, *Kūkai,* 143. See also Hakeda's translation at 143.
12. Groner, *Saichō,* 77–79.
13. Groner, *Saichō,* 84–87.
14. Takagi Shingen 髙木訷元, "Rishūshaku-kyō no shōshaku denshō o meguru jakkan no mondai" (理趣釈経の諸借伝承をめぐる若干の問題), in *Kōbōdaishi to shingon shū* (弘法大師と真言宗) (*Nihon bukkyō shūshi ronshū* (日本仏教宗史論集) 4), edited by Wada Shujō 和多修秀 and Takagi Shingen 髙木訷元, 92–120 (Tokyo: Yoshikawa Kobunkan).
15. Groner, *Saichō,* 87.
16. Takagi Shingen, *Kūkai shisō no shoshiteki kenkyū,* 128–129.
17. Groner, *Saichō,* 88.
18. Groner, *Saichō,* 90–95.
19. Gardiner, *Kūkai and the Beginnings of Shingon Buddhism,* 217–218; Gardiner, "Transmission Problems?"
20. Groner, *Saichō,* 85.
21. Groner, *Saichō,* 90.
22. See Hakeda's translation of Kūkai's abridged version of his "Treatise on the ten stages of mind of the secret mandala" (秘密曼荼羅十住心論 *Himitsu mandara jūjūshinron*), the "Precious key to the secret treasury" (秘蔵宝鑰 *Hizōhōyaku*), *Kūkai,* 157–224. Sueki Fumihiko 末木文美士, *Nihon bukkyōshi: shisō toshite no apurōchi* (日本仏教史:思想としてのアプローチ) (Tokyo: Shinchosha, 1996), 86–87.
23. Ryūichi Abe, *The Weaving of Mantra* (New York: Columbia University Press, 1999), 204–235.
24. Groner, *Saichō,* 287.
25. See Hakeda, *Kūkai,* for partial translations of each of these. The latter two have been more recently translated, with detailed annotation, by Takagi Shingen and Thomas Dreitlein, in *Kūkai and the Philosophy of Language* (Tokyo: Keio University Press, 2010). The received tradition that Kūkai wrote the *Benkenmitsu nikyōron* and that it was the first articulation of core esoteric ideas in Japan has recently been challenged. See Matthew Don McMullen, "The Development of Esoteric Buddhist Scholasticism in Early Medieval Japan" (PhD diss., University of California, Berkeley, 2016).
26. Dolce, "Reconsidering the Taxonomy of the 'Esoteric'"; Sueki Fumihiko, 末木文美士, *Heian shoki bukkyō shisōshi no kenkyū* (平安初期仏教思想史の研究) (Tokyo: Shunjusha, 1995).
27. For more on Kūkai's theory of language, see also Thomas Kasulis, "Truth Words: The Basis of Kūkai's Theory of Interpretation," in *Buddhist Hermeneutics,* edited by Donald Lopez (Honolulu: University of Hawaii Press, 1998), 257–272; and Abe, *Weaving of Mantra*), 275–304.
28. See Hayami Tasuku, 速水侑, *Heian kizoku shakai to bukkyō* (平安貴族社会と仏教) (Tokyo: Yoshikawa kōbunkan, 1975).
29. Groner, *Saichō,* 282, 287.
30. Dolce, "Reconsidering the Taxonomy of the 'Esoteric.'"
31. Akamatsu Toshihide 赤松俊秀, "Kukai to Saichō no kōsai ni tsuite" (最澄と空海の交際について), in *Kūkai* (空海) (*Nihon meisō ronshū* (日本名僧論集) 3), edited by Wada Shujō 和多修秀 and Takagi Shingen 髙木訷元, 134 (Tokyo: Yoshikawa kobunkan, 1982).
32. Likely a reference either to Shūen or Ken'ne, two of Saicho's students originally from Murō-ji (室生寺) temple.
33. Gardiner, *Kūkai and the Beginnings of Shingon Buddhism,* 258.
34. A Japanese Wikipedia page contains an image of the original text: https://ja.wikipedia.org/wiki/風信帖.
35. Abe, "Saichō and Kūkai," 103–104.

36. Ōyama Kōjun 大山公淳, "Dengyō Daishi no mikkyō ni tsuite" (伝教大師の密教について), in *Dengyō Daishi kenkyū* (伝教大師研究), 184 (Tokyo: Waseda Daigaku, 1973).
37. Gyōō Kiuchi, 木内堯央, *Tendai mikkyō no keisei* (天台密教の形成) (Tokyo: Keisuisha, 1984), 180.
38. Gardiner, *Kūkai and the Beginnings of Shingon Buddhism*, 194–224.
39. Abe, "Saichō and Kūkai," 134–135.
40. Sueki, *Nihon bukkyōshi*, 93–94.
41. Groner, *Saichō*, 88–95.
42. Groner, *Saichō*, 60.
43. Sueki Fumihiko, *Nihon bukkyōshi*, 118.
44. On Kuroda's term, see James C. Dobbins, "Exoteric-Esoteric (Kenmitsu) Buddhism in Japan," in *Encyclopedia of Buddhism*, Vol. 1, edited by Robert E. Buswell Jr., 271–275 (New York: Macmillan Reference USA, 2004). Note that Kuroda's term refers not only to a style of combined religious practice but beyond that to the entire system—ideological and institutional—of medieval Japanese Buddhism. For articles on Kuroda and his theory, which has its critics, see the "The Legacy of Kuroda Toshio" (Special issue), *Japanese Journal of Religious Studies* 23, no. 3–4 (Fall 1996).
45. For example, see Sueki Fumihiko, *Nihon bukkyō shisō shi ronkō* (日本仏教思想史論考), 191–194 (Tokyo: Daizō Shuppan, 1993) (rev. ed. 1996),; and Sueki Fumihiko, *Nihon bukkyōshi*, 86–87.

David L. Gardiner

TANTRIC BUDDHISM IN JAPAN: SHINGON, TENDAI, AND THE ESOTERICIZATION OF JAPANESE BUDDHISMS

The two established traditions of Japanese esoteric Buddhism (*mikkyō* 密教) of Taimitsu 台密 and Tōmitsu 東密 represent developments within the Tendai 天台 and Shingon 真言 schools, respectively. The name "esoteric Buddhism" indicates that both the Taimitsu and Tōmitsu traditions emerged within monastic communities dedicated to Buddhist practice that identified particular elements of their doctrine "esoteric." What was identified as esoteric, however, varied from case to case. Definitions of the term became vital hermeneutical tools as well as sources of contention. This was the case in the Tendai school in particular, which sought to distinguish itself from Shingon's early domination of the field of discourse on esotericism. From a broad pan-Asian perspective, the term "tantrism" applies to the various manifestations of both Taimitsu and Tōmitsu traditions because they share characteristics in common with forms of Indian religion known as tantra and, most significantly, with the Buddhist forms of tantra developed in India known as Vajrayāna (Jpn. *kongōjō* 金剛乗), meaning "vehicle of the thunderbolt/diamond." Thus, Taimitsu and Tōmitsu are referred to variously as Japanese esoteric Buddhism, Japanese Vajrayāna, Japanese tantric Buddhism, or Japanese tantrism. This last term is suggestive of the syncretic nature of many of the practices, which incorporated elements of Shintō and Daoism (i.e., not only Buddhism), as well as of the fact that tantric forms of practice in Japan preexisted the Tendai and Shingon schools but were often not considered as esoteric by later traditions because of the exclusive nature of the taxonomies these traditions proffered.

The origins of the Taimitsu and Tōmitsu traditions can be traced to the founders of the Tendai and Shingon schools, Saichō 最澄 (767–822) and Kūkai 空海 (774–835), respectively. From the

9th until the 19th century cross-fertilization of doctrines and practices across lineages from both schools was common in spite of various rhetorical strategies that promoted sectarian competition rather than cooperation. The unique features that distinguished Japanese esoteric Buddhism were the "three secret practices" (Jpn. *sanmitsugyō* 三密行) of employing ritual hand gestures (Skt. *mudrā*), recitation of sacred formulas (Skt. *mantra*), and visualization of various deities (and sometimes oneself as deity) as part of an envisioned "perfected world" (Skt. mandala). These three secret practices were used in ritual contexts to unify the practitioner with a deity (whether envisioned as external, internal, or both) in order to imbue the practitioner with extraordinary powers that could accomplish a variety of proximate ends, including healing illness, bringing rain, and vanquishing enemies, as well as the ultimate goal of Buddhist enlightenment. Japanese esoteric Buddhism thus had broad application in contexts that were always "religious" insofar as Buddhist monks were involved, but that extended easily into the quotidian political concerns of the royal court and eventually to private sponsors, primarily aristocrats.

The teachings and practices of Japanese esoteric Buddhism thus had a huge impact not only on Japanese religion, but also on many aspects of Japanese culture. Its influence left indelible marks on almost every form of religious practice, Buddhist or not, that later developed in Japanese history, including forms of Pure Land and Zen Buddhism. In PureLand teachings, we can detect likely esoteric influence in the emphasis that, with proper perspective, our ordinary world can be seen as a Pure Land, and in Zen, in master Dōgen's 道元 (1200–1253) teaching that meditation is best understood not as a means to enlightenment, but rather as an expression of one's inherent awakening. Carl Bielefeldt has noted the thread of continuity between the Buddhism of the Heian (794–1185) and Kamakura (1185–1336) periods by suggesting how *mikkyō* influenced the famous Kamakura founders Shinran, Nichiren, and Dōgen:

> [T]he ideologies of all three of these famous religious thinkers can be seen as an attempt to define the true practice of the Tendai Buddha vehicle: a sudden practice to be based solely on the absolute truth of Buddhahood itself, not on the *upāya* of the relative teachings and gradual practices. Already during the Heian period the notion had grown up within Tendai itself that the theory of the perfect teaching could best be put into practice through the three mysteries (*sanmitsu*) of *mikkyō*, in which the physical, verbal, and mental acts of the practitioner were identified with the body, speech, and mind of the Buddha and that the traditional methods of the *bodhisattva-marga* [path] could be superseded by the esoteric techniques of the Vajrayāna, handed down in the lineage of the tantric masters. Such techniques were sudden both in theory and in fact: they were based throughout on the principle of the identity of man and Buddha, and they were intended to bring about the full realization of the identity in this very existence. In this sense *mikkyō*, which itself of course originated as a Mahāyāna reform movement, had strong affinities with Zen and the other Kamakura schools; and it is not surprising that elements of it played a significant role in their development.[1]

This quotation expresses an important theme regarding the role of the basic esoteric Buddhist religious paradigm as a steady undercurrent throughout Japanese Buddhist history.

The remaining sections provide an introduction to the early centuries of Tendai and Shingon esoteric Buddhism.

TAIMITSU

Origins. If one were to follow the narrative arc of much of the Japanese scholarship on esoteric Buddhism (and much of the Western -language scholarship that mirrors it), an instinctive place to start a discussion would be with Kūkai's travels to China and his subsequent importation, formulation, and successful promotion of *mikkyō*. After all, it was Kūkai's careful designation of the category of "esoteric teachings" as opposed to "exoteric ones" (*kengyō* 顕教), and his skillful grafting of core esoteric practices onto the body of existing Buddhist ritual in Japan, that drew Saichō and his disciples to study with Kūkai. Subsequently, Saichō's Tendai school incorporated *mikkyō* elements into its theory and practice. Yet while it has become *de rigueur* to construct a trajectory of events that positions Kūkai as the sole founder of esoteric Buddhism in Japan, the actual circumstances are more complex. First, Saichō and Kūkai went to China on the same mission (on different boats) and it was Saichō who returned a year earlier than Kūkai and quickly won the favor of Emperor Kanmu, who was interested first and foremost in new esoteric practices. Saichō soon received permission from the government for his Tendai school to train four annual ordinands (Jpn. *nenbundosha* 年分度者), and to his likely surprise, they were equally distributed: two for esoteric study (Jpn. *shanagyō* 遮那業) and two for study of traditional Tendai practice (Jpn. *shikangyō* 止観業). Tendai thus established at the Enryakuji 延暦寺 temple near the capital city the first official training system for *mikkyō*, with the full support of the emperor. Furthermore, at the emperor's behest, Saichō also performed the first tantric initiation (Skt. *abhisekha;* Jpn. *kanjō* 灌頂) in Japan, at the Takaōsanji 高尾山寺 temple, also near Kyoto. There is thus no question that the new practices of esoteric Buddhism first emerged, and with force, in Saichō's Tendai school. Kūkai did not enter the capital to share what he had learned in China until about three years after Saichō did.

The narrative that presents Kūkai as the progenitor of Japanese esoteric Buddhism is not, however, entirely without merit. After all, it was Kūkai's definition of what properly constituted esoteric as opposed to exoteric Buddhism that was the starting point for later theories emerging within both Tendai and Shingon schools. Even though many Tendai monastic scholars defined "esoteric" in ways that contrasted with Kūkai's terms, it was the force of Kūkai's theories and of his eventual success on various fronts in the capital and beyond that forced Tendai monks to develop creative ways to construct a model of esoteric theory and practice that could effectively compete with Kūkai's. Unless it could develop a model of its own, Tendai *mikkyō* ran the real risk of getting swallowed up by the juggernaut of Kūkai's Shingon creations.

Regardless of the various definitions of esoteric put forth by both Tendai and Shingon exegetes, the interpretive frameworks placed around the textual and ritual transmissions Saichō and Kūkai brought back from China paved the way for building the identity of a new tradition in Japan. The chief texts of early Tendai and Shingon *mikkyō*—the *Mahāvairocana-sūtra* (Jpn. *Dainichikyō* 大日経) and *Vajraśekhāra-sūtra* (Jpn. *Kongōchōkyō* 金剛頂経)—had already been studied in Japan for decades in Nara (the capital before Kyoto and location of the major monastic centers), and ritual practices with many of the deities that became central to the later unfolding of "mainstream" *mikkyō* were also well established, together with the material presence of icons for these practices.[2] Although it is clear that Kūkai was the first to place a rhetorical wedge between his lineage and the existing traditions by carefully defining the features of true esoteric teachings, the overlaps remained robust. Kūkai's taxonomy distinguished esoteric and exoteric teachings based on (1) which "body" of the buddha was understood to have taught a particular scripture and (2) the presence or absence of a "three mysteries" (Jpn. *sanmitsu* 三密) ritual practice. However, limiting our investigation by accepting the hermeneutical distinctions advocated by Kūkai blinds us to vital historical continuities that these very taxonomies—whose function lies primarily in establishing boundaries between a putative "pure" and "less pure"—manage to plainly obscure. It is plausible to understand the origins of esoteric Buddhism in Japan as simply comprising the various forms of tantrism developed in the 8th century that became systematized into sectarian lineages (of Tendai and Shingon) in the 9th. One advantage of this model is that it permits, and even encourages, the recognition that central to all forms of esoteric Buddhism of the Nara period and beyond was the employment of a ritual model by trained specialists that invoked (or "channeled") the power of deities in the service of material and spiritual ends in contexts that were public (for the imperial house and the state) as well as private (on the one hand, for aristocratic wielders of power and, on the other, for the specialists themselves, mainly monastics who were seeking Buddhist enlightenment, among other ends). Thus, even though the classical models of Tendai and Shingon esoteric Buddhism identify boundary lines between this broader tradition and their more rarified forms, elements related to this more catholic model of Japanese Tantrism have held sway in various aspects of Japanese religious life and, arguably, in other forms of cultural transmission as well.

Early Years. This section presents an outline of the contributions of some of the accomplished monk-scholars of the early Tendai tradition, up until the late Heian period (10th century). It also comments on some broad religious and political topics germane to the study of the history of religion in Japan.

Although a virtual garden of what might be called esoteric Buddhist practices predated him, Saichō was responsible for introducing those seeds that would grow into the later Taimitsu tradition. His accomplishments in this area cannot be adequately addressed, however, without reference to the emperor's strong support and to Saichō's relationship with Kūkai.

As a young monk ordained at Tōdaiji 東大寺 temple in Nara in 785, Saichō became frustrated with the lack of serious religious practice and so, in 788, he moved to a hermitage on Hiei-zan (Mount Hiei 比叡山) outside what later became the capital of Kyoto. After the capital was moved to Kyoto in 794, Saichō's dedication to Buddhist practice came to the attention of the new Emperor Kanmu 桓武, who sought assistance in legitimizing his new regime, distancing it from court intrigues in Nara (some of which involved clergy), and in securing a skilled monk to perform religious services. Clearly, he hoped that Saichō would fit the bill, and fit it he did.

One of Saichō's chief interests was in enhancing studies of the Chinese Tiantai 天台 tradition in Japan. Through extended exposure to this school's preferred scripture, the *Lotus Sutra* (Jpn. *myōhō rengekyō* 妙法蓮華経), and to commentaries by the putative Tiantai founder Zhiyi 智顗 (538–597), Saichō was determined to bolster the quality of Mahāyāna Buddhist practice in Japan—in terms of ethics, textual study, and meditation—by further promulgating Tiantai. Since his vision dovetailed with that of the new emperor, Saichō was sent as part of an official government mission to China. Upon his return, Emperor Kanmu appeared less interested in Saichō's Tendai studies (and related materials he had brought back) than he was in Saichō's knowledge (which was relatively minimal) of the newly emerging esoteric practices and in their potential for their immediate applicability for his person, office, and country.

Soon Saichō was asked by Kanmu to perform two esoteric initiations (Jpn. *kanjō* 灌頂) at Takaōsanji in 805, the first two ever performed in Japan based on the newly imported texts and mandalas. The emperor ordered that no expense be spared and had new buddha images commissioned and other accouterment prepared for a lavish ceremony.[3] Various accounts suggest that the emperor was concerned for his health and that it improved soon afterward. Saichō's first esoteric Buddhist performances, which contained new and exotic ritual paraphernalia and gestures, propelled him to fame in the royal court and among leading Buddhist clerics. His second initiation was attended by many of the leading monks in Nara along with top court administrators. The newly imported *mikkyō* had established a footing in Japan.

While Saichō's public practice of esoteric Buddhism got off to a stellar start, his single-minded focus on developing a rigorous training center for Tendai monks, based on a combination of traditional Tiantai meditation and *mikkyō* ritual, still required his full attention. Considering the complex nature of his ambitions and his very brief training in esoteric thought and ritual in China, he possessed neither the time nor the knowledge to fully train his students in the new forms of *mikkyō* that had drawn such great attention. Having studied at length in Nara, he already had a grasp of how various "quasi-esoteric" rituals were performed; he had read a commentary on the *Dainichi-kyō*, was aware of what texts existed in Japan, and made some efforts to supplement them while in China by making copies of new texts.[4] However, once he met the recently returned Kūkai and recognized the superior knowledge this junior monk possessed, his strategy for building a strong esoteric program in Mount Hiei was to send his best students to study with Kūkai. Before addressing his relationship with Kūkai, a brief word is needed on his encounters with esoteric traditions in China.

With the goal of gathering Tiantai texts, Saichō left for China in the same mission fleet as Kūkai did in 804.[5] In China, he managed to receive transmission of the *Daibutsuchōhō* 大佛頂法 rite (based on a Chinese translation of the *Uṣṇīṣa-vijaya dhāraṇī sūtra*) from the monk Weixiang 惟象 at Guoqingsi 国清寺, a temple where many Tendai monks later went to study. He returned with related texts and a painted mandala. This ritual was in vogue in the Tang dynasty and was subsequently practiced often in Tendai lineages. Esoteric practices were present at the time in Chinese Tiantai, including the use of *dhāraṇī* for such purposes as curing disease and prolonging life, and the Tiantai monk Yixing 一行 (683–727) wrote an authoritative commentary on the Chinese version of the *Mahāvairocana-sūtra*. Saichō also received an initiation, with his disciple Gishin, from Shunxiao 順暁 in Yuezhou 越州. He later wrote that this was a "two-mandala" initiation, but some modern scholars dispute the claim, and Saichō's disciples themselves were unclear about the nature of the initiation. Paul Groner concludes that there is no good evidence to support Saichō's claim and that he likely made it after having met Kūkai and learned of his comprehensive two-mandala system. Saichō's early description of the initiation did not convey it as involving both mandalas, but his later exposition of his practice lineage in his *Kenkairon* 顕戒論 and *Naishō buppō sōjū kechimyakufu* 内証佛法相承血脈譜 asserted so. Groner supposes that the hurried nature of the initiation, and the fact that Saichō's disciple, Gishin, orally translated it for Saichō and might not have known the terminology well himself, could have been reasons for Saichō's ambiguity about what had transpired, though new clarity seemed to have emerged once he began to compete with Kūkai for patronage.[6]

Some modern scholarship suggests that Saichō's encounters with esoteric Buddhism in China were accidental and his interest in it not genuine. It is true that his encounters were not all planned. His stay in Yuezhou came about due to a travel delay for six weeks, allowing him to take an unplanned trip. His interest in esoteric Buddhism, however, predated the China trip and was neither new nor forced. What was forced was Emperor Kanmu's demand upon Saichō's return that the new Tendai school include a strong component of esoteric study and practice. His compliance with this requirement probably reflected more of an extrinsic rather than intrinsic interest for Saichō. Keeping in good graces with the emperor was important to him. Since Saichō had no capacity of his own to substantially integrate esoteric practices into a Tendai program of study, he sought help from Kūkai to train his disciples so that they could train others.

Early Taimitsu and Kūkai. When Saichō first received initiations for both mandalas from Kūkai in late 812 (first the Diamond Realm, with only the influential aristocratic Wake 和家 brothers, and later the Womb Realm with Saichō's disciples Kōjō 光定, Enchō 円澄, and Taihan 泰範, along with 141 others, including major players in the royal court and high-ranking monks from Nara), Kūkai was not yet well known in Japan and had yet to write any of the doctrinal treatises that later made clear his views on *mikkyō*. These initiations at Takaōsanji were at once a powerful jumpstart for the esoteric wing of Tendai and a launching pad for Kūkai's nascent public career. Within a few months, Saichō sent his disciples Kōjō, Enchō, and Taihan to study with Kūkai at Takaōsanji, and it is possible that Kōjō and Enchō went again after Saichō's death.[7] Correspondence between Kūkai and Saichō reveals that the latter also borrowed many of the new esoteric texts Kūkai had brought back from China, though at one point it appears Kūkai may have written a curt response that cut Saichō off from any further "transmission by writing" and urged him to come study full time under Kūkai if he was serious about learning *mikkyō*.[8] At some point during the next two years, their relationship came to an end. One factor might have been Saichō's disciple Taihan, who refused Saichō's request for him to return from studying with Kūkai to Mount Hiei. It was out of this early matrix of relationships—and from the subsequent studies of *mikkyō* that Saichō's disciples performed first under Kūkai and later on their own journeys to China—that the seeds of what became Taimitsu were planted. For the next ten years, Saichō spent most of his time developing the institutional foundations of the Tendai school, including the creation of documents outlining its distinct lineage (the *Naishō buppō sōjō kechimyakufu* 内証仏法相承血脈譜, and *Kenkairon engi* 顕戒論縁起), advocacy for a new precepts ceremony exclusive to Mahāyāna, and arguing against the Hossō school's doctrines about buddha-nature and for the prominence of the *Lotus Sutra* in the teachings of buddha.[9] He authored no texts dedicated to clarifying the role of the esoteric teachings within Tendai. The development of Tendai esoteric Buddhism was thus primarily left to his disciples.

Ennin. Ennin 円仁 (794–864, posthumously Jikaku Daishi 慈覺大師) and Enchin 円珍 (814–891, posthumously Chishō Daishi 智証大師) both traveled to China to study esoteric Buddhism. Ennin had been on Mount Hiei for twelve years when Saichō died in 823. In addition to having studied closely with Kūkai, he traveled to eastern Japan with Saichō in 817 to promote Tendai and to construct stupas. He spent nine years in China (838–847) and became head abbot (after Saichō and Gishin) on Mount Hiei in 854. In China, he studied in Chang'an with several esoteric Buddhist masters who were disciples of Kūkai's teacher Huiguo 慧果.[10]

In Ennin's writing we see the first systematic expression of Saichō's view that the "perfect teaching" (*enkyō* 円教) of the Chinese Tiantai school is as complete an expression of Buddhist truth as any "esoteric teaching" (*mikkyō* 密教). This is a position Saichō stated in various writings, including in his letters to Kūkai to protest the latter's claims that *mikkyō* was superior, but he did not develop his argument fully in writing. The relationship between these teachings became a central focus for Taimitsu exegetes. The Chinese Tiantai founder Zhiyi 智顗 (538–597), who had no exposure to the esoteric traditions, classified Buddhist doctrines into four categories, with the teachings of the *Lotus Sutra* and *Flower Garland Sūtra* alone qualifying as perfect teachings. Zhiyi was concerned primarily with how a particular teaching expresses the nature of ultimate reality. While not disagreeing with Zhiyi, Saichō instead emphasized that the superiority of the bodhisattva path expressed in the one vehicle teaching (as opposed to the teachings of the two "Hīnayāna" vehicles of *śrāvaka* and *pratyekabuddha*) was what made the *Lotus Sutra* a "perfect" teaching.[11]

Zhiyi's writings on the two truths were thorough and creative. His endeavors to carve out a creative rendering of the Indian Madhyamaka school's presentation of the ontological and epistemological relationship between "emptiness" (ultimate truth) and "appearances" (conventional truth) was richly sophisticated. It manifested a unique Chinese version of the "middle way" that proposed a third truth that unites the original two. This third truth purported to represent the acquired vision, or experiential domain, of a buddha. Because Zhiyi was not familiar with the kinds of esoteric texts and practices that Saichō, and in particular Kūkai, encountered more than two centuries after his death, his classifications did not touch such topics. But it was imperative for the growth of Tendai that Saichō's disciples fashion hermeneutical strategies to bring together the perfect and the esoteric teachings. Much of the development of Taimitsu doctrine lay in articulating the relationship between the understood messages of the *Lotus Sutra*, in particular Zhiyi's interpretations of its core teaching, and the central themes of the esoteric scriptures. Due to the two conditions that (1) the initial comprehension that Tendai scholars had of esoteric texts derived from Kūkai's interpretations, and (2) Kūkai and Saichō disagreed about the relative profundity or finality of these respective teachings, Tendai exegetes were forced to engage in a delicate balancing act to demonstrate "the unified aim of the perfect and the esoteric" (Jpn. *enmitsu itchi* 円密一致). Saichō left neither writings on esoteric Buddhism nor a strategy for unifying it with the perfect teaching. Thus, the task of establishing a foundation for Taimitsu fell first to Ennin and Enchin, both of whom drew widely from their initiations in China and the many texts they brought back, and later to Annen, who, while never traveling to China, nonetheless made immense contributions to Taimitsu doctrine. All three of these men were also responding to Kūkai, who was the first in Japan to articulate a clear theory about the place of esoteric teachings in the larger Buddhist tradition.

Ennin's response to "unifying the aims of the perfect and the esoteric" was to assert that the Lotus teachings were a perfect expression of "principle" (Jpn. *ri* 理), or the theoretical aspect of the esoteric, while the rituals of *mikkyō* with its two mandalas—the Womb World

(Jpn. *taizōkai* 胎蔵界) and Diamond World (Jpn. *kongōkai* 金剛界)—completed the "phenomenal" (Jpn. *ji* 事), or practical, dimension. He thus saw the three mysteries practice as the "esoteric combination of principle and phenomena" (Jpn. *riji gumitsu* 理事具密).[12] This formula used two potent Chinese terms that roughly correspond to the classical Buddhist concepts of ultimate and conventional truth, with the twist that "principle" also references Zhiyi's portrayal of the final state of the nonduality of the two truths. One of Ennin's shifts from Saichō's positions toward a more *mikkyō*-centered hermeneutic was to consider the *Lotus Sutra* teachings in the light of esoteric ones rather than to measure all teachings by *Lotus* standards. For example, he interpreted the "eternal" (Jpn. *kuon* 久遠) buddha of the *Lotus Sutra* to be Dainichi 大日, the purported dharma-body preacher of the esoteric scriptures.[13] In interpreting esoteric (Jpn. *himitsu* 秘密) to mean not only Vajrayāna teachings but also the most advanced understanding of reality, he followed Chinese exegetes such as Yixing 一行 (683–727). Ennin's commentaries—the first to be written in Japan—on the *Vajraśekhara-sūtra* (*Kongōchōkyō* 金剛頂経) and *Sussidhikara-sūtra* (Jpn. *Soshitsuji-kyō* 蘇悉地経), plus the text of a *Mahāvairocana-sūtra* commentary he brought from China, became major treatises in the later Taimitsu tradition.[14] His contributions to Tendai esoteric doctrine were seminal and his later connections with the imperial court were significant. He was frequently invited to the palace, beginning in 850, and from 860 to 864 he bestowed esoteric initiations and bodhisattva vows on the emperor and members of the court, all the while working to train disciples. His accomplishments may have successfully allowed Taimitsu rituals to supersede Shingon ones at the court.[15] Hayami Tasuku refers to Ennin's contributions to Taimitsu practice as "epoch making."[16]

Ennin wrote a commentary on the *Soshitsuji-kyō* and, like Saichō and Kūkai, placed it in the category of *Vinaya* (texts on monastic discipline). He explained that the text reveals how the two mandalas can be seen as united, since the text demonstrates the higher essence that underlies both worlds. Because the idea of these three parts (as opposed to just two) was difficult to explain clearly, it underwent many changes throughout Taimitsu history. Esoteric practice evolved such that some Taimitsu monks attempted combinatory initiations using both mandalas at the same time, but debates continued about exactly how this related to the *Soshitsuji-kyō*.[17]

Enchin. Enchin was ordained as a *shikan-gyō* 止観業 monk (to train in non-Tantric Tendai), though some think he favored the *shana* 遮那 (esoteric) practice.[18] He placed *mikkyō* in the highest position in the traditional Tendai doctrinal classification scheme. He also gave initiations in 862 into the practice of both of the mandalas to Shūei 修睿, a Shingon monk at Onjōji 園城寺 (also known as Miidera 三井寺).[19] This is just one instance of a cross-fertilization of esoteric teachings that occurred in both directions between Tendai and Shingon after Kūkai's death. Enchin's positions on most doctrinal issues are hard to determine, since many of his writing have been lost and extant ones differ in content. He did present critiques of Kūkai's ten-stage scheme in his *Dainichikyōshiki* 大日経指帰.[20] This was naturally a long-time target of Tendai scholars because Kūkai had placed Tendai at stage eight, beneath Kegon 華厳 (Ch. Huayan) at stage nine and Shingon at stage ten. One of the challenges facing Taimitsu exegetes was articulating the differences between their view on the esoteric teachings and that of Kūkai. This challenge was further complicated by the tension between Saichō's claim that the teachings of the *Lotus Sutra* and the *mikkyō* texts were equal and later Taimitsu authors' proposition that what was esoteric about each was different.

Enchin's five years in China (853–858), studying both in the capital of Chang'an and at Mount Tiantai, was very productive.[21] He brought back more new texts than had Kūkai and later wrote important works on *mikkyō* iconography. He also showed a strong devotion to the esoteric deity Fudō Myōō 不動明王. Some scholars believe that it was through the efforts of both Ennin and Enchin that Tendai was in effect transformed into an esoteric school, with their having given minimal attention to traditional study of the Chinese Tiantai tradition.[22]

Eventually two groups emerged that dedicated themselves to esoteric study: the Sanmon 山門 lineage traced itself to Ennin and to Enryakuji (on top of Mount Hiei), while the Jimon 寺門 lineage traced itself to Enchin and to Onjōji 園城寺 (at the base of Mount Hiei). The two lineages did not fully split until the late 10th century, and while the long-term cause was more than a century of conflict over what group of monks would control the abbacy (*zasu* 座主) of Enryakuji, the immediate cause was Ryōgen's efforts to impose "unity and organization" on the monastic community on Mount Hiei[23] (see "Ryōgen"). While Ryōgen may have aimed to create unity, he did so by restoring one lineage and suppressing the other, resulting in "a schism that never healed."[24] Each lineage was composed of diverse groups and was not simply homogenous. The Jimon lineage seems to have had closer connections with the Shingon lineage of Tōji 東寺, and aspects of its ritual system were integrated into the mountain-based asceticism of native Japanese Shugendō practice. The Kamakura Shogunate appears to have favored the Jimon lineage because of its connections to particular court figures. Onjōji had no subtemples but had three imperial ones (Jpn. *monzeki* 門跡). Taimitsu cannot be described as a single, monolithic tradition because there was no centralized institution to represent the various groups that practiced Tendai esoteric Buddhism. In fact, some early documents describe medieval Japanese Tantrism as having three lineages: Tōji (from Kūkai), Sanmon, and Jimon. And although until Saichō's death most lineages traced themselves to Ennin, some scholars note that after the Tendai monk Kōkei 皇慶 (also pronounced Kōgyō, 977–1049) died, some Taimitsu groups traced their history through Tōmitsu lineages as well.[25]

Differences between the lineages were less about doctrine than about elements of practice such as mantras, mudras, altar size and orientation, what deity was enshrined, and what offerings were used. Such ritual details became closely guarded secret knowledge transmitted from teacher to disciple.[26] Although they shared some doctrinal and ritual elements, the two main Taimitsu lineages constructed specific liturgies in competition with each other.[27]

Various ritual sublineages also developed within Taimitsu (such as the Taniryū 谷流 and Kawaryū 川流), each with its own anthology of texts that embodied the ritual capital of the lineage.[28] Since many aristocrats had been ordained as Tendai monks, and because, whether due to family connections or otherwise, monks were commonly asked to perform rites for aristocrats and members of the royal court, some ritual lineages developed strong connections with particular family lines. In fact, rival schools of esoteric Buddhist ritual were commonly grounded in hereditary factions within the aristocracy. This pattern of aristocratic power relations got transplanted into the clerical world as more nobles took "holy orders."[29]

Annen. Unlike Ennin and Enchin, Annen (案然 841–889?) neither traveled to China nor became abbot of Enryakuji. Few details are known about his biography, but it is clear that he authored many texts on esoteric Buddhism that became important for later tradition. He likely studied under Ennin for many years and for a briefer period under Enchin. It appears that while he had great respect for Ennin, there may have been tensions between Enchin and him. Annen's writings state that Ennin had a broader understanding of *mikkyō* due to his having studied under eight teachers in China compared to Enchin's one. We have few recorded noteworthy disciples of Annen, and it is reasonable to assume that during his lifetime he was not a major teacher of the Taimitsu lineage. We do not have much knowledge of his activities, and the *Genkōshakusho*, a 14th-century compilation of Buddhist history, has only a brief entry about him.[30]

As an innovative thinker, however, it can be said that Annen was as important to the development of Japanese esoteric Buddhist doctrine as was Kūkai. His influence extended even into Tōmitsu lineages and had an impact on the writings of the Shingon monks Saisen and Kakuban.[31] He authored over one hundred works and wrote an extensive catalog of all the texts brought from China by the Japanese esoteric Buddhist masters (*Hakke hiroku* 八家秘録). Annen also contributed substantially to discussions of "original enlightenment" (*hongaku* 本覚) theory, especially regarding the view that "even grasses and trees possess Buddhahood" (*sōmoku jōbutsu* 草木成仏). His many writings, including six ritual manuals, helped to formulate new doctrines and to systematize esoteric practice. His chief texts were *Shingonshū kyōjigi* 真言宗教時義, which, among other foci, emphasized the infinite temporal aspect of Buddha Dainichi's teaching, and *Taizō kongō bodaishin ryaku mondōshō* 胎蔵金剛菩提心略問答抄, a commentary on the *Treatise on Bodhimind* (*Bodaishinron* 菩提心論, purported to be a Chinese translation of a text by the Indian master Nāgāruna), one of the central texts Kūkai used to buttress his definition of the unique qualities of esoteric Buddhism. These were later considered by Edo period scholars to be as comprehensive as Zhiyi's massive *Fahua men'i* 法華門義.[32] He also employed the *Yūgikyō* 瑜祇経 (*Kongōbu rōkaku issai yūga yūgikyō* 金剛峯楼閣一切瑜伽瑜祇経, a text in the *Kongōchōkyō* corpus) in a novel manner that emphasized its ritual importance.[33] Kūkai also richly employed this text in his writings but did not elaborate on its ritual value. Annen's interpretations impacted both later Taimitsu and Tōmitsu traditions.[34]

An important teacher of Annen was Henjō 遍昭 (817–890), grandson of Emperor Kanmu and a Tendai monk who had studied under both Ennin and Enchi. Henjō was the first Tendai monk appointed to the Sōgō (monastic administrative council) and his appointment represented a significant change in the Tendai school's attitude toward this bureau. Henjō was very important in terms of establishing better relations with Nara monks, which had suffered since Saichō's time.[35]

Annen's writings went so far as to assert that Tendai ought to focus as much on *mikkyō* as did the Tōmitsu lineages, and he even adopted the name "Shingon" for Tendai esoteric Buddhism. While he intended this term in the broader sense of a lineage focused on mantra, this choice of terminology nonetheless expressed his view that esoteric practice was at the heart of Tendai, not just side by side with exoteric study and practice.

Annen is usually considered the great systematizer of Tendai esoteric Buddhist doctrine. Although Tendai esoteric ritual continued to develop after his death, its doctrine reached its culmination with Annen.[36] Annen was also the first monk in the Tendai school to interpret the monastic precepts in the light of esoteric Buddhism.[37] Some of his administrative reforms were taken to heart in Tōmitsu lineages as well. It appears that one of his interests might have lain in creating an esoteric Buddhism that could span the Tendai–Shingon gap.

Ryōgen. Although he is not acknowledged to have written important doctrinal works, Ryōgen 良源 (912–985) was a great ritual innovator, an apparently savvy esoteric entrepreneur, and a Tendai monk who demonstrated that good relations with Nara clergy were possible. He studied Buddhist philosophy with masters from the Tōdaiji and Yakushiji temples in Nara and was trained in esoteric Buddhism by Kakue 覚慧 (872–954).

Due to Enchin's twenty-three-year tenure as abbot during the early 10th century, his ritual lineage prevailed in Taimitsu and continued to do so for half a century. Yet Ryōgen favored Ennin's lineage, as did others such as Henjō and Annen, and he was influential in restoring the supremacy of Ennin's line. A schism grew between the two lineages while cooperation weakened.

Ryōgen developed very close relations with the Fujiwara clan, having conducted esoteric rituals for Fujiwara no Tadahira (880–949), a powerful and influential noble that headed the Fujiwara's Northern House from 909.[38] His son, Morosuke, continued asking for Ryōgen's ritual favors, such as praying for his father after his death and prayers to secure the birth of his own male offspring. Ryōgen became famous and aristocrats donated funding to construct new monastic buildings for him on Mount Hiei. He also created new rituals to respond to fears of ghosts—not a minor social or political concern in the mid-Heian period—and in general helped to bring esoteric rites largely back into use for private families. Such practices had been prohibited in the late Nara period because the government sought to limit the activities of *hijiri* (itinerant Buddhist practitioners) who operated outside officially sanctioned religious institutions. However, the increased decentralization of the state apparatus from the mid-Heian period likely contributed to the reemergence of such rites. By the 10th century, Taimitsu rituals had become a kind of thaumaturgical support for the religiopolitical apparatus of aristocrats and were in vogue in their circles.[39]

Some of Ryōgen's innovations included creating a new Tendai ceremony involving seven healing buddhas (previously, the only buddha used for healing ceremonies was Yakushi Nyorai 薬師如来). Shingon monks later copied this practice. He also developed a ceremony for the protective deity Fudō Myōō 不動明王 that required five separate platforms for related deities. Rituals with Fudō were commonly used to vanquish evil spirits as well as living enemies. From Ryōgen's time forward elaborate ceremonies with multiple platforms requiring more monks than before increasingly became the standard, and his five-platform Fudō rite monopolized the market for such rituals. It seems the rite was even successful at vanquishing its own religious competitors.

Ryōgen also performed astrological rituals, which often focused on preventing heavenly anomalies from adversely impacting the particular star responsible for an emperor's well-being. He performed these for two emperors as well as for Fujiwara Kanemichi to recover from illness, the success of which earned him an appointment as Bishop.[40]

In spite of his having nurtured a major schism, Ryōgen's successes at consolidating aspects of Taimitsu practice, constructing new buildings, expanding the repertoire of available liturgies, and establishing solid connections with court figures who sought rituals were adequate grounds for Neil McMullin to assert that Ryōgen was "probably the most important figure in the history of Mount Hiei," after Saichō.[41]

Taimitsu Contributions. After Saichō, esoteric Buddhism in the Tendai school had two chief concerns in the arena of doctrine: (1) creating an effective taxonomy regarding the relationship between exoteric and esoteric teachings, and (2) articulating the role of the *Soshitsuji-kyō* practice in relation to the mandalas of the two realms.[42] Gauging the tradition's success on these two fronts is a complex task and would depend on one's perspective, but it is clear that both Ennin and Annen made significant theoretical contributions. Ennin's distinction between principle (*ri* 理) and practice (*ji* 事) circumvented Kūkai's hermeneutical criterion (that only teachings from the dharma-body buddha are esoteric) by affirming that true esotericism combines the highest understanding of reality with the embodied practice of the three mysteries. Annen's approach was different. He expanded the understanding of the dharma-body buddha by emphasizing (in his *Shingonshū kyōjigi*) this buddha's infinite temporal and spatial dimensions, thereby affirming Kūkai's view while also enhancing it.

Regarding the *Soshitsuji-kyō*, the Tendai insistence on the importance of this text derived from a renewed emphasis on it by the communities in China in which Ennin and Enchin had studied. While this text existed in Japan during Kūkai's lifetime, he did not consider it important. Its ritual significance in later Chinese esoteric Buddhist circles, however, attracted the attention of Tendai exegetes. One way to understand the complex Tendai hermeneutics regarding this text is to see that while the Shingon school's view of the nonduality of the Two Realms (Diamond and Womb, of the two mandalas) was based on its claim that Kūkai had received transmission of the two mandalas simultaneously, the Taimitsu position was that these should be considered two distinct transmissions that necessitated a third "accomplished class" of ritual transmission to completely unify the two.[43] Interpretations like this made by Tendai exegetes were complicated by the fact that the *Soshitsuji-kyō* is primarily a ritual text that does not offer much doctrinal explanation that might serve to clarify its placement. There also is no mandala or icon that accompanies it, unlike the mandalas of the Two Realms linked with the two textual corpora emphasized in Shingon. Thus, while the history of its usage in Taimitsu traditions was subject to various internal debates and innovations, it was precisely in this arena of innovation that Taimitsu flourished.

TŌMITSU

It is instructive to note that the use of the term "Tōmitsu" to refer to Shingon esoteric Buddhism, originally based as it was at the Tōji temple in Kyoto (the *tō* 東 in each term, meaning "eastern," is the same), is used more by non-Shingon writers than by Shingon ones. For non-Shingon writers, such as scholars from the Tendai or other Japanese Buddhist traditions or scholars not identified with a particular school of Japanese Buddhism, Tōmitsu designates one of the two main esoteric Buddhist traditions in Japan. However, for Shingon writers, there has long been a tendency to see the term *mikkyō* as being primarily defined by Shingon Buddhism, and in this view it is implied that Taimitsu is a derivative form of Shingon *mikkyō*. Thus, it appears that for some writers of a Shingon persuasion, the division of esoteric Buddhism in Japan into Tōmitsu and Taimitsu traditions embodies a rhetoric of inequality: Shingon (the so-called Tōmitsu) is the original *mikkyō* and Tendai its offshoot. This perspective is easily visible in many popular and even some scholarly publications in Japanese on *mikkyō* that are focused almost entirely on the Shingon Buddhism created by Kūkai. The implication here, rarely made explicit, is not that Taimitsu is not *mikkyō* but rather that Shingon is the prototype *mikkyō* and Taimitsu a spin-off.

Interestingly, there is another distinction often made in Shingon scholarship between "pure" (*jun* 純) and "mixed" (*zō* 雑) *mikkyō* that further affirms the superior nature of Shingon practice. According to this discourse, the pure forms of *mikkyō* manifest a genuine intention to attain buddhahood in this lifetime (Jpn. *sokushin jōbutsu* 即身成佛) at their core, to which "this worldly" benefits such as healing, warding off harm, affecting the gender of a fetus, or bringing rain are said to be secondary. This rhetorical strategy aims to preserve a spiritual sanctity for a certain Mahāyāna Buddhist orientation that is presumably dedicated, above all, to achieving enlightenment for the sake of all sentient beings. This is not to say, however, that Shingon writers have accused the Taimitsu tradition of being "mixed." Rather, both these traditions adopted this rhetoric to distinguish their lineages from those not based on the doctrines and rituals deriving from certain texts (such as the *Dainichi-kyō*, *Kongōchō-kyō*, and *Soshitsuji-kyō*) that are all understood to have been preached by the dharma-body buddha Dainichi. Although the *junmitsu/zōmitsu* terminology came after him, Kūkai employed a similar delimiter when he declared certain *dhāraṇī* (sacred formulae) commonly used in his day not to be true esoteric Buddhism because these practices were not taught by the dharma-body buddha.

Kūkai's initial rhetorical framing turned out to be a remarkably successful strategy. Monks and lay aristocrats in the court were deeply impacted by his theories and rituals, and they quickly took root across wide sectors of Japanese elite society. Saichō's initial attempt to develop a strong esoteric component for his new Tendai school was based entirely on Kūkai's expertise, and some later Tendai monks adopted Kūkai's interpretations heartily. Saichō's eventual protest (in letters to Kūkai and elsewhere) that the *Lotus Sutra* teaching of the One Vehicle was also esoteric and thus as advanced as Kūkai's Shingon teachings was an argument that was hard for later Tendai apologists to continue to defend. Some established monks, such as Tokuitsi 徳一 (d. 843) of the Hossō school, disputed Kūkai's claim about the role of the dharma-body, but there was never a strong or unified opposition to his broader program. Thus, Shingon's beginnings were very productive. Kūkai was given responsibility for developing the Tōji 東寺 temple at the southern entrance to the capital (Kyoto), and he established a new platform (*kaidan* 戒壇) for administering the esoteric precepts, or rules of monastic conduct, at Tōdaiji in Nara. He was also granted imperial permission to establish a Shingon monastery on Mount Kōya, several days' travel south of Kyoto, and was given charge of Takaōsanji on the outskirts of Kyoto. Just before Kūkai's death in 834, he was also successful in getting a chapel for esoteric services (Shingon'in) placed in the imperial palace. The services became known as the "Latter Seven-day Rite" (Jpn. *go-shichinichi mishuhō* 後七日御修法). Kūkai first performed them in the Central Affairs Ministry in the palace and later in the Shingon chapel. They were performed in the palace during the second week of the first month every year until 1871 and was then revived in 1883 and moved to Tōji. Kūkai's ability to promote Shingon practice at major temples in Nara and in the new capital was testament to his sociopolitical skills and his careful articulation of doctrine. Unlike Saichō, he did not get into lengthy debates with powerful monks from the Nara schools, such as Tokuitsu, nor with the members of the Office of Monastic Affairs (*Sōgō* 僧綱). His vision to essentially graft esoteric Shingon practices onto existing ones succeeded so well that contemporary Japanese scholarship commonly uses the phrase "exoteric–esoteric system" (*kenmitsu seido* 顕密制度) to refer to the entirety of Japanese Buddhism's cultural presence, in its combination of both monastic and political action, from Kūkai's time until the early modern period. Kūkai's institutional activities were matched by his prolific writings that detailed his understanding of *mikkyō*. As mentioned (see "Early Taimitsu and Kūkai"), the early Tendai school was deeply indebted to Kūkai's articulation of the unique role that esoteric ritual played in deciphering and employing the power of the "preaching of the dharma-body." In the Shingon school, this indebtedness lasted centuries. While it is clear that Kūkai's promotion of Shingon laid the foundation for all later manifestations of Japanese *mikkyō*, during the Heian period it was primarily only in the Tendai school that doctrinal development emerged. Ennin and Annen in particular created novel and impactful theories that allowed Tendai esotericism to flourish after Saichō's death. These innovations were apparently needed in order to distinguish their *mikkyō* lineages from those of Shingon. But since there was no such need for distinction for the Shingon school—and because, unlike Saichō, Kūkai focused extensively in his writings on matters of esoteric doctrine and practice—innovations on the Shingon side did not emerge until around the 12th century. Thus, post-Kūkai, Tōmitsu doctrinal development languished compared to the energetic growth within Taimitsu.

Original Tōmitsu Theories. The extent to which many of the ideas in Kūkai's doctrinal works were original to him is uncertain, since his main teacher in China, Huiguo 慧果 (743–805), left no writings. It is clear that Kūkai took many ideas from some key Vajrayāna texts such as the Chinese translations of the *Vajraśekhara-sūtra* and the *Mahavairocana-sūtra*, and from a commentary on the *Awakening of Faith in the Mahāyāna* (Jpn. *Daijō kishinron* 大乗起信論), called in Japanese the *Makaenron* 摩訶衍論 (widely considered in his day and since to be apocryphal). Regardless, because Kūkai's writings had immense impact on the early development of *mikkyō* teachings in Japan and influenced many aspects of Tōmitsu teachings, a summary of his key ideas is in order.

Perhaps the cornerstone of Kūkai's doctrinal edifice is the theory of the "preaching of the Dharma by the Dharma-body" (*hosshin seppō* 法身説法). The standard Mahāyāna interpretation was that the buddha possessed three "bodies," among which the dharma-body is formless, without shape or speech, and represents the buddha's deepest wisdom of ultimate reality. The buddha's two "form" bodies (Skt. *sambhoga-kāya* and *nirmāna-kāya*) communicate with beings on various levels. Kūkai's idiosyncratic proposition that the silent dharma-body preaches possessed doctrinal shock value and he exploited this with force. He claimed that the consecrated practice of the three secrets of *mudrā*, *mantra*, and *mandala* (based on having undergone formal initiation, *kanjō* 灌頂) enables practitioners to receive directly from the essence of enlightened wisdom (the dharma-body) the purest qualities of buddhahood. Such consecrated practice cuts through the language-based mediation by which the other two form bodies teach the Dharma and is thus the direct, unmediated manifestation of ultimate reality via a kind of nondual communication. This view is best articulated in his early *Treatise Distinguishing the Two Teachings, Exoteric and Esoteric* (*Benkenmitsu nikyōron* 弁顕密二教論). In later texts such as *The Meaning of Attaining Buddhahood in This Very Body* (*Sokushin jōbutsu-gi* 即身成仏儀), he clarifies that the three secrets practice brings the body, speech, and mind of a practitioner into a state of nondual union (*yūga* 喩伽) with the same three aspects of an enlightened buddha. Further, the consecrated practice of *mudrā*, *mantra*, and *mandala* provide one with the interpretive technology for deciphering a code naturally embedded in all phenomena so that, for example, one comes to see all conventional sounds, sights, and thoughts as natural expressions of ultimate reality. This idea is most clearly expressed in his *The Meaning of Voice, Word and Reality* (*Shōji jissō-gi* 声字実相儀). He also elaborates on these concepts in his *Secret Key to the Heart Sūtra* (*Hannya shingyō hiken* 般若心経秘鍵) and *The Meaning of the Syllable "Hum"* (*Unjigi* 吽字義).[44]

In his later years, Kūkai produced his magnum opus, the *Treatise on the Ten Stages of Mind of the Secret Mandala* (*Himitsu mandara jūjūshinron* 秘密曼荼羅十住心論) and its subsequent condensed version, *Precious Key to the Secret Treasury* (*Hizō hōyaku* 秘蔵宝鑰). These texts outlined his vision of a hierarchical classification of "mind states" (*jūshin* 住心) that range from a beastly human mentality to the highest enlightened state of a buddha. The fourth through tenth stages represent the spiritual fruits of practicing in accordance with different Buddhist teachings. Stages eight through nine accord with the teachings of the Japanese Buddhist schools of Tendai, Kegon, and Shingon, respectively, a ranking that Tendai exegetes frequently contested. Kūkai's doctrinal classifications possessed a Janus-like quality of both exclusivism and inclusivism because, while he consistently championed Shingon esotericism as the best path to buddhahood, he also averred that esoteric hermeneutics affirm that within every teaching are hidden features through which one can access the highest realization.

Through these texts and other less systematic writings, Kūkai presented a thorough portrait of what he saw as the characteristics of *mikkyō*. For several generations, members of his lineage added little of note to his formulations. His disciples and their successors did, however, manage to put into place strong institutional moorings that established Tōmitsu as an enduring component of the Japanese religious landscape. The roots of this institutional development were effectively planted during Kūkai's lifetime at Tōji, Takaōsanji, Kōyasan, and Tōdaiji. Thus, from the start, Shingon had a wider base than did Tendai and was much better accepted as a normative Buddhist teaching in Nara. This strong foundation seems to have emerged from various sources: Kūkai's skillful ecumenical approach to doctrine that acknowledged the value of other teachings; his congenial attitude toward building and maintaining relationships; and his familial connections with Nara monks from his own Saeki clan in Shikoku. His strengths in these areas offered him a relative advantage over Saichō, who criticized some Nara monks as being Hīnayānist and as lacking adequate knowledge of Buddhist scripture, who alienated the Sōgō council with his antagonist insistence on the need for an exclusive ordination platform for Mahāyāna practitioners, and whose ancestry was of fairly recent Chinese origin. Couple these facts with Saichō's limited understanding of esoteric scripture and ritual and the absence of any clear texts by him on these topics, and it is easy to see why Shingon (Tōmitsu) practice took off as quickly as it did, and Saichō's best disciples went to Kūkai to study *mikkyō* in order to build their own Taimitsu programs. It took more than a full generation, with creative innovations in doctrine and practice, for Taimitsu to catch up with and then, by some accounts, to surpass Tōmitsu. In the meantime, Shingon monks maintained effective relationships in all the venues established by Kūkai that helped assure the long-term relevance of esoteric practice in Japan.

Tōmitsu Developments. After returning from China in 806, Kūkai developed what was for a while a cooperative relationship with Saichō from 809, and was invited by Saichō, together with eminent Nara monks and high-ranking aristocrats, to offer a *kanjō* initiation at

Takaosanji in 812. In 816, he received imperial permission to begin constructing a monastery on Mount Kōya; in 822, he fulfilled a wish to construct a hall for esoteric *kanjō* at Tōdaiji'in; in 823, he was given supervision of the construction of the Tōji temple in Kyoto; in 834, he established an esoteric chapel called Shingon'in in the imperial palace (where the first month of every year Shingon monks performed rites to protect the emperor), and in 835, his Kongōbūji monastery was granted regular ordinands. Until his death in 835, he was exceedingly busy promoting his new *mikkyō* on multiple fronts.

Kūkai's disciples maintained all these commitments and also entertained frequent requests for rituals at court, such as prayers for rain and rituals for exorcism. Unlike Tendai, the early Shingon school was based in a variety of temple complexes, including three in Kyoto, one in Nara, plus Koyasan, so administrative demands were high and impulses to consolidate were natural. Strife eventually manifested around the time of the monk Kangen 観賢 (854–925), who himself was at different times in charge of Kōyasan, Tōji, and Ninnaji 仁和寺 (western Kyoto), with particular tensions arising between Kōyasan and Tōji over which would be the headquarters temple (*hon* 本) and which the subsidiary (*matsu* 末). Tōji received an imperial order to be the headquarters temple in 919. Tensions also derived from temples having support from different aristocratic patrons. Kangen was responsible for getting Kūkai's posthumous title Kōbōdaishi and for preserving an important text written by Kūkai recording his studies in China (the *Sanjūjōsasshi* 三十帖冊子, a designated national treasure).

Kūkai's immediate disciples included his brother Shinga 真雅 (801–879), nephew Shinnen 真然 (804–891, trained under Shinga), Jichie 実慧 (786–847), Shinzei 真済 (800–860), Jōgyō 常暁 (d. 867), Shūei 宗叡 (809–884), and Taihan (泰範 b. 778). Shinnen and Shinzei helped construct buildings at Kōyasan, with Shinnen garnering important support from donated lands. Shinzei managed the Shingon'in at the imperial palace, bestowed refuge vows to Emperor Montoku, and edited the important collection of Kūkai's letters and *ganmon* 願文 (votive documents) known as the *Shōryōshū* 性霊集. Jichie assisted with developing the grounds at Koyasan and traveled to China to report Kūkai's death. Jōgyō and Shūei both brought back important materials from travels to China as official government envoys (*kentōshi* 遣唐使), such as the *Taigen[sui] hō* 太元帥法 text (ritual for vanquishing enemies) and new copies of the two mandalas. All of these disciples except Jichie and Taihan were initially ordained while they were students of Kūkai. Jichie eventually managed Jingōji at Mount Takao but was originally from Daianji 大安寺 in Nara, a temple where Kūkai had studied and with which he maintained strong contacts. Taihan was originally a student of Saichō who had been sent, with Enchin, to study with Kūkai but who never returned to Mount Hiei.[45]

Later Tōmitsu Developments. Another student of Shinga's, Shōbō 証宝 (832–909, posthumously Rigen Daishi 理源大師), established the Daigōji 醍醐寺 temple near Kyoto. Like Kūkai, Shōbō studied extensively in Nara, both Hossō and Sanron teachings, and had close contacts with the many monks there who valued extended practice in the mountains (*sanrin shugyō* 山林修行). Shōbō consolidated the tradition of "combined study" of Shingon and Sanron at the Tōnan'in 東南院 at Tōdaiji and is regarded as the founder of the Ono 小野 lineage of Shingon. Daigōji became a powerful Tōmitsu center that garnered so much imperial support that it was referred to as the "three-generation family temple of [Emperor] Murakami." As Hayami Tasuku notes, the esoteric–exoteric combined study pattern became the model for

Nara Buddhism: "Mikkyō became a non-sectarian view of Buddhism in general . . . The doctrines of different schools differed little, but in practice each group championed its own secret method. Prayer (*kitō* 祈祷) Buddhism became the heart of aristocratic Buddhism."[46]

After a devastating fire at Kōyasan in 994, the monk Ningai 仁海 (951–1046) worked toward reconstruction and persuaded the very powerful Fujiwara Michinaga to visit on a pilgrimage. Perhaps on Michinaga's coattails, Kōyasan became a favorite destination for regents and received donations of many landed estates in support.

Tōmitsu doctrinal scholarship languished during the first few centuries after Kūkai, and the first noteworthy emergence is often said to be the writings of Kakuban 覚鑁 (1095–1143, posthumously Kōgyō-Daishi 興教大師). After studying at Kōfukuji and Tōdaiji in Nara, Kakuban moved to Kōyasan. He attempted to unify the two lineages of Ono 小野 and Hirosawa 広沢 and became the chief priest (*zasu* 座主) at Kongōbūji and the Daidenbō'in at Mount Kōya. It seems that his connections with noble families in Kyoto helped him gain influence in Kōyasan, and he used his position to attempt to relocate the center of Shingon from Tōji to Kōyasan. His political efforts brought strong opposition, along with the burning of the Daidenbō'in, and he fled with followers to Negoro-ji 根来寺 in Wakayama prefecture. His writings focused a great deal on the role of the Buddha Amitābha (Jpn. *Amida*) in Shingon practice. While some have suggested he was attempting to incorporate Pure Land doctrines into Shingon, it seems reasonable to see his work rather as more concerned with forging an esoteric perspective on the Pure Land teachings (he affirmed that the Pure Land is to be realized in this life). Kakuban's writings proffered esoteric interpretations of Amida's name along the lines of Kūkai's hermeneutics of *mantra* syllables.[47] His writings were influential, and the group at Negoro-ji became the start of the Shingon School of New Doctrine (*shingi shingon shū* 新義真言宗). Nearly a century after Kakuban's death, the Shingon monk Raiyū 頼瑜 (1226–1304) followed in his footsteps. Raiyū studied at Kōyasan and at Ninnaji, as well as at Tōdaiji and Kōfukuji in Nara. He wrote detailed commentaries on many of Kūkai's works. In 1284, he also left Mount Kōya for Negoroji with a group of disciples, marking the formal beginning of the Shingon School of New Doctrine.

Two more important scholar-monks in medieval Tōmitsu tradition were Gōhō 杲宝 (1306–1362) and Yūkai 宥快 (1345–1416). Both were based predominantly in Kōyasan. Gōhō was not only a scholar of Tōmitsu but also wrote about the history of *mikkyō* in Japan, of both Tendai and Shingon forms. His extensive use of documents for narrating detailed history was rare in his day. Gōhō also penned criticisms of Zen Buddhist practice. Yūkai was a remarkably prolific author of commentaries on Kūkai's works and on some of the Chinese texts central to Kūkai's presentation of *mikkyō*, such as the *Dainichi-kyō* and its commentary, and the *Bodaishinron* and *Shakumakuenron*. His scholarship was one of the marks of the revival of Shingon doctrinal work in the Muromachi period and has remained vital to modern sectarian scholarship as well.[48]

In 1585, the Negoroji monastery was burned by Toyotomi Hideyoshi as part of his attack on the powerful Buddhist establishments. In the aftermath, divisions emerged between the more permanent and more temporary monks of Negoroji. The group that relocated to Hasedera in Nara became the Buzan 豊山 lineage, while the group relocated to Chishaku'in in Kyoto became the Chizan 智山 lineage. It was at this point that extant Tōmitsu schools came to be called Kōgi (old doctrine 古義) Shingon, while the newer Buzan and Chizan groups were called Shingi (new doctrine).

LEGACIES OF BOTH TAIMITSU AND TŌMITSU

It is important to note how central a role *mikkyō*, whether in its Tendai or Shingon forms, has played in Japanese religious and political history. The following are some comments from contemporary scholarship.

Historian Hayami Tasuku writes about an early 9th-century shift wherein national Buddhism began to take on an esoteric character:

> What is significant in the path of esoteric ritual's mainstreaming into "nation protecting Buddhism" is what happened in the sixth month of 830 when all across the nation, because of spreading disease, monks were ordered to read the *Kongō hannyakyō* 金剛般若経 [*Diamond Sūtra*] and perform the Yakushi 薬師 [medicine buddha] repentance. Beginning with this, for the next ten years the rites for national protection took the shape of the former during the day and the latter at night. Of course repentance was originally an individual act to regret past negative deeds and to promise not to repeat them, but in Japan it became linked with native purification [*harae*] significance and assumed the communal form of thaumaturgic ritual chanting . . . Then in the latter half of the ninth century the nation protecting rites were no longer documented as "repentance" but rather as the "chanting of Shingon *dhāraṇī*" . . . Thus the establishment of Shingon-esoteric practice happened not so much via independent performances but as an accompaniment to the chanting of scripture for national protection.[49]

Not only was the need to address widespread disease likely one cause for the flourishing of *mikkyō* but so also was political turmoil from the mid-Heian period.[50] Esoteric ritual found a welcome response to its ritual practices that were aimed at securing personal advantage in political relationships. The new *mikkyō* offered by both Taimitsu and Tōmitsu may have possessed elements that assured progress on the path to buddhahood, but it also preserved strong continuities with so-called mixed esotericism (*zōmitsu* 雑密) in terms of practical benefits. Its capacity for broad application was well received.

Hayami further reminds us that the format of supplementing existing court ceremony with esoteric rites by conjoining "chanting *sūtra* in the day, mantra at night" was Kūkai's expressed intention for establishing the Shingon'in at the palace. This *shichinichi mishihō* (Latter Seven-day Rite) became the standard model for the practice of nation-protecting rituals in both Shingon and Tendai lineages. It was after this paradigm had taken root that the development of rites on an individual basis emerged, with Ryōgen's prolific activity (see the section "Ryōgen") being a fine example.

And as Allan Grapard makes clear, in early Japan there existed not only a shared soteriological and liturgical paradigm among Buddhist institutions, but also a common recognition among power holders that the work of Buddhist specialists was a potent social and political force. Referring to the symbiotic relationship between "worship" and "administration" (*saisei* 祭政), he writes:

> Kūkai established esoteric Buddhism at court by positing himself as the ritual guarantor of imperial legitimacy . . . [T]he overwhelming concern of early ninth-century courtiers was to establish the supremacy of the imperial house.[51]

Furthermore, Taimitsu and Tōmitsu alike soon found homes for their practices in Kyoto and in Nara, and eventually throughout the nation. As Fabio Rambelli notes:

> The Nara establishment soon realized the ideological and ritual importance of the new mikkyō as an instrument of political and economic control, and adopted it in a sort of surreptitious paradigm shift. Esoteric Buddhism became in this way an essential feature of pre-modern Japanese life.[52]

And finally, Carl Bielefeldt attests to the enduring impact of the *mikkyō* paradigm on Japanese Buddhist history overall:

> For its own part, the esoteric tradition itself tended to conceive of Buddhahood in cosmological terms, as the hidden macrocosm of which the human world was the manifest embodiment. An elaborate system of homologies was developed between the properties of the Buddha realm and the physical features of Japan, between the deities of the Buddhist pantheon and the local gods of Japan, between the virtues of the cosmic Buddha and the psychophysical characteristics of the individual, and so on. The chief means of communication between the two realms was ritual practice—recitation of spells and prayers, performance of mystic gestures, repentance, sacrifice, pilgrimage, and the like—through which the forces of the other realm were contacted and channeled into this world, and the people and places of this world were mystically empowered by (or revealed as) the sacred realities of the Buddha realm . . . This cosmological style of religion is often now held up as one of the key unifying forces of Japanese Buddhism.[53]

Bielefeldt adds a more historiographical comment:

> Historians of the [premodern] period warn against a narrow focus on the novel teachings of the new Kamakura movements, often preferring to see them against the background of an older, broader religious style of thought and practice that permeated the medieval Buddhist world—a style we may loosely call *mikkyō* . . .[54]

Both Taimitsu and Tōmitsu forms of *mikkyō* practice have had powerful impacts on Japanese religion in particular and society in general. Since the fundamental operating model for each tradition was nearly identical, we can generalize that tantric Buddhism's influence in Japan has been, and in many ways continues to be, immense. As the writings of Tamura Yoshirō, Sueki Fumihiro, and Jaqueline Stone frequently emphasize, the gaps between Heian (794–1185) and Kamakura (1185–1333) period Buddhism are not as sharp as previous narratives stressing discontinuity have suggested. Among the many factors promoting historical continuity, the various tantric features of *mikkyō*, with their accompanying theological and political ramifications, should be seen as significant.

REVIEW OF LITERATURE

While the topic of the two kinds of Japanese esoteric Buddhism might seem relatively obscure, there is a solid body of materials in English for initial research. Naturally there is much more in Japanese, though its conceptual purview is often limited by sectarian orientations. On Taimitsu traditions, an excellent survey that is thorough in historical spread, topical range, and critical perspective is "Taimitsu: The Esoteric Buddhism of the Tendai School" by Lucia Dolce.[55] Neil McMullin's article "The Sanmon–Jimon Schism in the Tendai School of Buddhism: A Preliminary Analysis" addresses important issues related to the schism resulting in the Jimon and Sanmon lineages.[56] Paul Groner's essay is also rich on early developments, and his book on Ryōgen offers a thorough treatment of this later monk's significant contributions.[57] The two most recent detailed Japanese monographs are by Ōkubo Ryōshun, *Taimitsu kyōgaku no kenkyū* and *Saichō no shisō to tendai mikkyō*, the former being broader while the latter focuses on Saichō's role.[58]

Curiously, the Tōmitsu tradition is less richly covered in English, one reason being that studies tend to focus on Kūkai alone. Abé's *The Weaving of Mantra* remains the best source for grasping how Kūkai worked within the religious and political worlds to ground esoteric Buddhist rhetoric at the center of imperial ideology.[59] David Gardiner's dissertation places Kūkai's contributions in some additional pan-Asian Buddhist doctrinal and historical contexts.[60] A solid source on later Tōmitsu developments is Hendrik van der Veere's *A Study into the Thought of Kougyoudaishi Kakuban: With a Translation of His* Gorin kuji myō himitsushaku on Kakuban's extensive treatment of the role of Amida (Amitābha) in Japanese esoteric Buddhist practice.[61] In Japanese, perhaps the best survey remains Matsunaga's *Mikkyō no rekishi* (surprisingly not out of date), with Yoritomi's more recent chapter in Tachikawa and Yoritomi's edited volume *Nihon no mikkyō* coming next.[62]

Both English and Japanese scholarship has moved in recent years to help break down problematic assumptions of more traditional studies. Three assumptions are that post-Nara esoteric Buddhism is substantially different from that of Nara (the "pure" *junmitsu* versus "mixed" *zōmitsu*); that Taimitsu and Tōmitsu traditions were independent and isolated; and that the "reformations" of Kamakura Buddhism essentially jettisoned *mikkyō* elements. Scholars point to the presence of this-worldly aims of much of Heian and later *mikkyō* in spite of the rhetoric that its *junmitsu* nature orients it primarily to the attainment of buddhahood (*jōbutsu*). Recent scholarship also illuminates the deep connections, mostly via patronage, that both Taimitsu and Tōmitsu monastic practice had with political and economic forces driving the aristocratic class. Studies also reveal how powerful was the esoteric Buddhist paradigm that sacralized the entire material world as an expression of the cosmic Buddha Dainichi, and how this theological orientation was not lost on the founders of the new Kamakura schools. Their Zen, *Lotus Sutra* (by Nichiren), and Pure Land models may have offered streamlined practices, but these were imprinted with *mikkyō* assumptions in various ways. Research is increasingly revealing that these various boundaries, taken for granted in earlier scholarship, operated more as convenient rhetorical devices that supported various sectarian interests.

A chief area that remains little studied is the development of texts and practices in both traditions during the medieval period. Dolce in particular has sketched some fruitful paths for future study in Taimitsu.[63] She helpfully points out that factors limiting such research include traditional emphasis on the founder Saichō; a focus on the core teachings of Chinese Tiantai; and the relatively scattered nature of relevant texts, which for the most part are not gathered in a single collection. Equally unstudied is the myriad of ways the two traditions borrowed from one another such that the sectarian boundaries appear more nominal than substantive.

FURTHER READING

Abé, Ryūichi. *The Weaving of Mantra*. New York: Columbia University Press, 1999.

Beghi, Clemente. "The Dissemination of Esoteric Scriptures in Eighth Century Japan." In *Esoteric Buddhism and the Tantras in East Asia*. Edited by Charles Orzech, 661–682. Leiden, The Netherlands: Brill, 2011.

Dolce, Lucia. "Taimitsu: The Esoteric Buddhism of the Tendai School." In *Esoteric Buddhism and the Tantras in East Asia*. Edited by Charles Orzech, 744–767. Leiden, The Netherlands: Brill, 2011.

Dolce, Lucia, with Shinya Mano. "Godai'in Annen." In *Esoteric Buddhism and the Tantras in East Asia*. Edited by Charles Orzech, 768–775. Leiden, The Netherlands: Brill, 2011.

Ford, James. "Exploring the Esoteric in Nara Buddhism." In *Esoteric Buddhism and the Tantras in East Asia*. Edited by Charles Orzech, 776–792. Leiden, The Netherlands: Brill, 2011.

Groner, Paul. *Saichō: The Establishment of the Japanese Tendai School*. Honolulu: University of Hawai'i Press, 1984.

Groner, Paul. "Annen, Tankei, Henjō, and Monastic Discipline in the Tendai School: The Background of the *Futsū jubosatsukai kōshaku*." *Japanese Journal of Religious Studies* 14, no. 2–3 (1987): 129–159.

Groner, Paul. *Ryōgen and Mount Hiei: Japanese Tendai in the Tenth Century*. Honolulu: University of Hawai'i Press, 2002.

Hayami, Tasuku 速水侑. *Heian kizoku shakai to bukkyō* 平安貴族社会と仏教. Tokyo: Yoshikawa kōbunkan, 1975.

Hayami, Tasuku 速水侑. *Nihon bukkyōshi: kōdai* 日本仏教史：古代. Tokyo: Yoshikawa kōbunkan, 1986.

Katsumata Shunkyō 勝又俊教. *Mikkyō no nihonteki tenkai* 密教の日本的展開. Tokyo: Shunjūsha, 1981.

Kiuchi, Gyōō 木内堯央. *Tendai mikkyō no keisei* 天台密教の形成. Tokyo: Keisuisha, 1984.

Kushida Ryōkō 櫛田良洪. *Shingon mikkyō seiritsu katei no kenkyū* 真言密教成立過程の研究. Tokyo: Sankibō Busshorin, 1964.

Matsunaga Yūkei 松長有慶. *Mikkyō no rekishi* 密教の歴史. Kyoto: Heirakuji shoten, 1969.

Matsunaga Yūkei 松長有慶. *Shingonshū: Nihon no bukkyō, hito to oshie* 真言宗：日本の仏教、人と教え. Tokyo: Shōgakkan, 1986.

McMullin, Neil. "The Sanmon–Jimon Schism in the Tendai School of Buddhism: A Preliminary Analysis." *Journal of the International Association of Buddhist Studies* 7, no. 1 (1984): 83–105.

Misaki Ryōshū 三崎良周. *Taimitsu no kenkyū* 台密の研究. Tokyo: Sobunsha 創文社, 1988.

Ōkubo Ryōshun 大久保良峻. *Taimitsu kyōgaku no kenkyū* 台密教学の研究. Tokyo: Hōzōkan, 2004.

Ōkubo Ryōshun 大久保良峻. "The Identity between the Purport of the Perfect and Esoteric Teachings." *Japanese Journal of Religious Studies* 41, no. 1 (2014): 83–102.

Ōkubo Ryōshun 大久保良峻. *Saichō no shisō to tendai mikkyō* 最澄の思想と天台. Kyoto: Hōzōkan, 2015.

Shimizutani Kyōjun 清水谷恭順. *Taimitsu kyōgaku no kenkyū* 台密教学の研究. Kyoto: Hōzōkan, 2004.

Sonoda Kōyū 薗田香融. *Tendai-shū: Nihon no bukkyō, hito to oshie* 天台宗：日本の仏教、人と教え. Tokyo: Shōgakkan, 1986.

Sueki, Fumihiko 末木文美士. *Heian shoki bukkyōshisōshi no kenkyū* 平安初期仏教思想史の研究. Tokyo: Shunjūsha, 1995.

Tachikawa Musashi 立川武蔵, and Yoritomi Motohiro 頼富元宏. *Nihon no mikkyō* 日本密教. Tokyo: Shunjūsha, 2000.

Togano'o Shōun 栂尾祥雲. *Togano zenshū* 栂尾全集. Vol. 1, *Himitsu bukkyōshi* 秘密仏教史. Koyasan, Japan: Koyasan University Press, 1959.

van der Veere, Hendrik. *A Study into the Thought of Kougyoudaishi Kakuban with a Translation of His* Gorin kuji myō himitsushaku. Leiden, The Netherlands: Hotei Publishing, 2000.

NOTES

1. Carl Bielefeldt, *Dogen's Manuals of Zen Meditation* (Berkeley, CA: University of California Press, 1990), 165.
2. See James Ford, "Exploring the Esoteric in Nara Buddhism," in *Esoteric Buddhism and the Tantras in East Asia*, ed. Charles Orzech (Leiden, The Netherlands: Brill, 2011), 776–792; and Clemente Beghi, "The Dissemination of Esoteric Scriptures in Eighth Century Japan," in *Esoteric Buddhism and the Tantras in East Asia*, ed. Charles Orzech (Leiden, The Netherlands: Brill, 2011), 661–682.
3. Gyōō Kiuchi 木内堯央, *Tendai mikkyō no keisei* 天台密教の形成 (Tokyo: Keisuisha, 1984), 66–70 on first two *kanjō*; and Paul Groner, *Saichō, The Establishment of the Japanese Tendai School* (Honolulu: University of Hawai'i Press, 1984), 67.
4. Paul Groner, *Saichō, The Establishment of the Japanese Tendai School* (Honolulu: University of Hawai'i Press, 1984), 57.
5. The next two paragraphs are indebted to Groner, *Saichō*, 44–64.
6. Groner, *Saichō*, 58–61; see also Misaki Ryōshū 三崎良周, *Taimitsu no kenkyū* 台密の研究 (Tokyo: Sobunsha, 1988), 42–58. For a thorough critique of Tendai claims regarding the degree to which Saichō received a "legitimate" esoteric transmission, see Jinhua Chen, "The Formation of Early Esoteric Buddhism in Japan: A Study of the Three Esoteric Japanese Apochrypha" (PhD diss., McMaster University, 1997).
7. Groner, *Saichō*, 83–87.
8. On their relationship and split, see Ryūichi Abé, "Saichō and Kūkai: A Conflict of Interpretations," *Japanese Journal of Religious* Studies 22, no. 1–2 (1995): 103–136; and David L. Gardiner, "Kūkai and the Beginnings of Shingon Buddhism in Japan" (PhD diss., Stanford University, 1994), 194–218. Many other excellent resources exist in Japanese.
9. Groner, *Saichō*, chaps. 6 and 7, 88–168.
10. See Edwin O. Reischauer, *Ennin's Diary: The Record of a Pilgrimage to China in Search of the Law* (New York: Ronald Press, 1955); and *Ennin's Travels in T'ang China* (New York: Ronald Press, 1955).
11. See Paul Swanson, *Foundations of T'ien-tai Philosophy: The Flowering of the Two Truths Theory in Chinese Buddhism*, annotated ed. (Fremont, CA: Asian Humanities Press, 1989).
12. Much of this paragraph is indebted to Lucia Dolce's excellent article, "Taimitsu: The Esoteric Buddhism of the Tendai School," in *Esoteric Buddhism and the Tantras in East Asia*, ed. Charles Orzech (London: Brill, 2011), 744–767.
13. On the "dharma-body," see the section "Original Tōmitsu Theories."
14. Ōkubo Ryōshun 大久保良峻, "Saichō, Kūkai no kaikaku 最澄空海の改革," in *Nihon bukkyō no so* 日本仏教の礎, ed. Sueki Fumihiro 末木文美士 (Tokyo: Kosei Shuppan, 2010), 183.
15. Stanley Weinstein, "Aristocratic Buddhism," in *Cambridge History of Japan*, ed. Donald H. Shively and William H. McCullough, vol. 2, *Heian Japan* (Berkeley, CA: University of California Press, 1999), 481.
16. Hayami Tasuku 速水侑, *Nihon bukkyōshi: kodai* 日本仏教史:古代 (Tokyo: Yoshikawa kobunkan, 1986), 178.
17. Dolce, "Taimitsu," 759–761.
18. Ōkubo Ryōshun, "Saichō, Kūkai no kaikaku," 186.
19. Ōkubo Ryōshun,"Saichō, Kūkai no kaikaku," 189.
20. Ōkubo Ryōshun, "Saichō, Kūkai no kaikaku," 189.
21. Ōkubo Ryōshun, "Saichō, Kūkai no kaikaku," 186. For details on Enchin's years in China, see also Onō Katsutoshi 小野勝年, *Nyūtōguhō gyōreki no kenkyū: Chishōdaishi Enchin hen*, 入唐求法行歴の研究: 智証大師円珍 (Kyoto: Hōzōkan, 1982–1983).
22. Weinstein, "Aristocratic Buddhism," 483.

23. Neil McMullin, "The Sanmon-Jimon Schism in the Tendai School of Buddhism: A Preliminary Analysis," *Journal of the International Association of Buddhist Studies* 7, no. 1 (1984): 83–84.
24. McMullin, "The Sanmon-Jimon Schism in the Tendai School of Buddhism," 99.
25. Hayami, *Nihon bukkyōshi: kodai*, 178; and Jacqueline Stone, *Original Enlightenment and the Transformation of Medieval Japanese Buddhism* (Princeton, NJ: Princeton University Press, 1999), 109–110.
26. Stone comments on the increase of privatization in medieval Japan, whether of wealth, political power, artistic skills, or religious knowledge, and suggests that the model of esoteric Buddhist initiations was influential in this process. See her *Original Enlightenment*, 108–109.
27. Dolce, "Taimitsu."
28. Dolce, "Taimitsu."
29. Stone, *Original Enlightenment*, 110.
30. Much of this paragraph comes from Paul Groner, "Annen, Tankei, Henjō, and Monastic Discipline in the Tendai School: The Background of the *Futsū jubosatsukai kōshaku*." *Japanese Journal of Religious Studies* 14, no. 2–3 (1987): 132–133, 143.
31. Lucia Dolce with Shinya Mano, "Godai'in Annen," in *Esoteric Buddhism and the Tantras in East Asia*, ed. Charles Orzech (Leiden, The Netherlands: Brill, 2011), 768–775.
32. Groner, "Annen, Tankei, Henjō," 152.
33. Taishō Shinshū Daizōkyō 大正新修大藏經, ed. Takakusu Junjirō 高楠順次郎 (Tokyo: Taishō issaikyō kankōkai, reprint edition, 1962), vol. 18, no. 867.
34. Dolce, "Taimitsu," 774.
35. Groner, "Annen, Tankei, Henjō," 138–150; and Groner, *Saichō*, 284–285.
36. Groner, "Annen, Tankei, Henjō," 154.
37. Groner, "Annen, Tankei, Henjō," 154.
38. Groner, *Ryōgen*, 66–68.
39. Stone, *Original Enlightenment*, 150.
40. Groner, *Ryōgen*, 90–92.
41. McMullin, "The Sanmon-Jimon Schism in the Tendai School of Buddhism," 89.
42. Dolce, "Taimitsu," 754.
43. Dolce, "Taimitsu," 774.
44. On Kūkai's doctrinal views of the uniqueness of the dharma-body's teaching, see Gardiner, "Kūkai and the Beginning of Shingon Buddhism in Japan"; and Ryūichi Abé, *The Weaving of Mantra* (New York: Columbia University Press, 1999).
45. On the early development of Shingon, see Matsunaga Yūkei 松長有慶, *Mikkyō no rekishi* 密教の歴史 (Kyoto: Heirakuji shoten, 1969); and Yoritomi Motohiro 頼富本宏, "Nihon mikkyō no seiritsu to tenkai 日本密教の成立の展開," in *Nihon no mikkyō* 日本の密教, ed. Tachikawa Musashi 立川武蔵 (Tokyo: Shunjūsha, 2005), 23–73.
46. Hayami, *Nihon bukkyōshi*, 171–172.
47. On Kakuban's interpretations of Kūkai's theory's Hendrik van der Veere, *A Study into the Thought of Kōgyōdaishi Kakuban with a translation of* his Gorin kuji myō himitsushaku (Leiden: Hotei Publishing, 2000), Yoshida Kōseki 吉田宏哲, "Kakuban 覚鑁, in *Shingonshū: Nihon no bukkyō: hito to oshie* 真言宗：日本の仏教、人と教え, ed. Matsunaga Yukei 松長有慶 (Tokyo: Shogakkan, 1985), 161–206, and James H. Sanford, "The Breath of Life: The Esoteric Nembutsu *Vision: Kakuban*," in *Tantric Buddhism in East Asia*, ed. Richard K. Payne (Boston: Wisdom Publications, 2006), 161–189.
48. Yoritomi 頼富本宏, "Nihon mikkyō no seiritsu to tenkai" 日本密教の成立と展開, 61–63.
49. Hayami, *Nihon bukkyōshi*, 172.
50. See William H. McCullough, "The Heian Court, 794–1070," in *The Cambridge History of Japan*, vol. 2, ed. Donald H. Shively and William H. McCullough (Cambridge, UK: Cambridge University Press, 1999), 20–96.

51. Allan Grapard, "Precepts for an Emperor," in *Tantra in Practice*, ed. David Gordon White (Princeton, NJ: Princeton University Press, 2000), 147–148.
52. Fabio Rambelli, "True Words, Silence, and the Adamantine Dance: On Japanese Mikkyō and the Formation of the Shingon Discourse," *Japanese Journal of Religious Studies* 21, no. 4 (1994), 384.
53. Carl Bielefeldt, "Japan," in *Encyclopedia of Buddhism*, vol. 1, ed. Robert E. Buswell Jr. (New York: Macmillan Reference, 2004), 390.
54. Bielefeldt, "Japan," 389.
55. Dolce, "Taimitsu," 744–767.
56. Neil McMullin, "The Sanmon–Jimon Schism in the Tendai School of Buddhism,": 83–105.
57. Paul Groner, "Annen, Tankei, Henjō," 129–159.; and Groner, *Ryōgen*.
58. Ōkubo Ryōshun 大久保 良峻, *Taimitsu kyōgaku no kenkyū* 台密教学の研究 (Tokyo: Hōzōkan, 2004); and Ōkubo Ryōshun 大久保 良峻, *Saichō no shisō to tendai mikkyō* 最澄の思想と天台 (Kyoto: Hōzōkan, 2015).
59. Abé, *The Weaving of Mantra*.
60. Gardiner, "Kūkai and the Beginning of Shingon Buddhism in Japan."
61. van der Veere, *A Study into the Thought of Kōgyōdaishi Kakuban*.
62. Matsunaga Yūkei 松長有慶, *Mikkyō no rekishi* 密教の歴史 (Kyoto: Heirakuji Shoten, 1969); and Yoritomi 頼富本宏, "Nihon mikkyō no seiritsu to tenkai."
63. Dolce, "Taimitsu."

David L. Gardiner

TANTRIC REVIVAL IN CHINA

BACKGROUND OF THE TANTRIC REVIVAL

While the sun was setting on China's final imperial dynasty, a number of Buddhists were attempting to resurrect what they believed to be an extinct facet of Chinese religiosity. The "Tantric Revival in China" 密教復興運動 is a term used by scholars to refer to esoteric Buddhism's rise in popularity in China during the late Qing dynasty (1664–1912) and early Republican period (1912–1949).[1] The first rise in popularity was centered in eastern China and was focused on Japanese esoteric Buddhism, whereas the second was centered near Beijing and concentrated on Tibetan Vajrayāna. However, the story of this revival began much earlier and is still being written by Buddhists throughout the Sinosphere in the 21st century.

Esoteric Buddhism is a form of initiatory Buddhism that developed over a long period of time in India during the 6th to 12th centuries CE.[2] While esoteric Buddhism—of which tantric Buddhism is one kind—is a form of Mahāyāna, its emphasis on complex rituals and master-to-disciple transmission of those rituals are what distinguish it from other forms of Buddhism. As Richard K. Payne succinctly stated, esoteric Buddhism is "the form of Buddhism that presents itself as constrained by concerns for the transmission of its powerful psycho-spiritual technologies only to those capable of using those technologies properly."[3] Esoteric Buddhist transmission is formalized via an initiatory ordination often translated into English as "empowerment" (Ch. 灌頂 Skt. *abhiṣeka*).[4]

Esoteric Buddhism originally gained popularity in China during the Tang dynasty (618–907).[5] The form of esoteric Buddhism that existed in China during that time was propagated primarily by Śubhākarasiṃha (637–735), Vajrabodhi (671–741), and

Amoghavajra (705–774) and is referred to as "Tang-dynasty esotericism" (*tangmi* 唐密), "the esoteric school" (*mizong* 密宗), or more commonly "Zhenyan" (真言)—the last of these is an early Chinese translation of the Sanskrit term "mantra." The proliferation of esoteric Buddhism during the Tang dynasty "overwhelmed the Chinese—and indeed East Asian—religious consciousness" and was so influential within Chinese circles that at the height of its popularity "the only texts being translated [from Sanskrit into Chinese] were esoteric ritual manuals."[6]

However, this popularity was relatively short-lived, and East Asian sectarian understandings of the nature of esoteric Buddhism during the Tang dynasty conflict with the scholarly consensus in the early 21st century. According to sectarian understandings—which the tantric revivalists accepted—sometime during the early Song dynasty 宋朝 (960–1269) the chain of esoteric initiation was interrupted, and its spiritual technologies became subsumed under other Buddhist movements, popular religion, and Daoism. As esoteric Buddhist claims to religious authority are based on the belief that no esoteric Buddhist school or lineage can "spring into being *ex nihilo* but must be able to trace its origin back through several generations of master-to-student transmission," this spelled the end for esoteric Buddhism in China and the disappearance of the Zhenyan lineage.[7]

Most academic scholars argue, in contrast to this view of history, that esoteric Buddhism did not exist as an independent Buddhist "school" (Ch. *zong* 宗) during the Tang and that the spiritual technologies prevalent within esoteric Buddhism "have been a staple of Chinese Buddhist monastic practice since its inception."[8] Instead, the historical record seems to indicate that it was Japanese Buddhists who first retroactively viewed Zhenyan as a distinct Buddhist lineage based on Japanese Buddhist sectarian perceptions.[9] The revivalists accepted this Japanese view because of historical occurrences related to Sino-Japanese interaction that scholars and practitioners largely agree upon.

While esoteric Buddhism was enjoying its height of popularity during the Tang dynasty, the Japanese figure Kūkai 空海 (formally titled Kōbō Daishi 弘法大師; 774–835) traveled to China and studied the esoteric dharma under a student of Amoghavajra named Huiguo 惠果 (746–805). After receiving multiple levels of empowerment, Kūkai returned to Japan where what he had learned in China became the basis of the form of Japanese Buddhism known as "Shingon," which was the Japanese pronunciation of the Chinese characters for "Zhenyan." Although this occurred over one thousand years ago, Shingon remains one of Japan's largest Buddhist faith communities.[10] The Japanese sectarian perception of Tang-dynasty Zhenyan as a distinct school similar to Japanese Shingon deeply influenced Chinese beliefs about their own past, as there is textual evidence for "a Chinese awareness that the transmission of the 'Esoteric Teachings' (Chn. Mijiao/Jpn. Mikkyō 密教) had survived in Japan."[11]

Relatedly, other forms of esoteric Buddhism—whose origins represent developments in Indian esoteric Buddhism subsequent to Zhenyan—later made their way to other locations such as Tibet, where forms of esoteric and tantric Buddhism, such as Vajrayāna, arose. Thus, although no recognized chains of esoteric Buddhist transmission existed within a strictly Chinese tradition for over a thousand years, they have continuously played major roles in the Japanese and Tibetan Buddhist landscapes. This, coupled with Chinese Buddhist acceptance of Japanese sectarian perceptions of Tang-dynasty Zhenyan, is why these two locations became the soil from which the tantric revival in China would eventually sprout.

THE BIRTH OF THE TANTRIC REVIVAL IN CHINA

The Chinese revival of esoteric Buddhism was initiated by none other than the great Buddhist reformer Taixu 太虛 (secular name: Lu Peilin 呂沛林; 1890–1947).[12] His goal was to create a modernized form of Buddhism that encapsulated all forms of Buddhism and would meet the needs of the modern world. This comprehensive vision demanded the inclusion of esoteric Buddhism.[13] However, as Chinese forms of Buddhism lacked a recognized chain of esoteric Buddhist transmission because of the fissure that occurred during the Song dynasty, he had to set his sights beyond the confines of Chinese Buddhism. Thus, he encouraged his students to travel to Japan and Tibet in order to study esoteric Buddhism. He additionally recommended the publication of *The Outline of Esoteric Buddhism* (*Mijiao gangyao* 密教綱要), originally written in Japanese by the Shingon priest Gonda Raifu 權田雷斧 (1846–1934) and translated into Chinese by Wang Hongyuan 王弘願 (1876–1937), a lay Buddhist who played an important role in the early days of the tantric revival.[14] The publication of this translation gained the esteem of its author, and in 1924 Gonda traveled to China with a number of his Shingon colleagues and gave a number of Chinese Buddhists esoteric empowerments and invited a number of them—including Wang—to come to Japan to receive more in-depth training. After returning from Japan as a fully ordained Shingon priest, Wang began propagating the esoteric dharma and ordaining his own disciples.

Despite the initial success of resurrecting Chinese esoteric Buddhism by receiving Japanese Shingon transmission, the Japanese-oriented part of the tantric revival has been referred to as "short-lived" because the font from which Chinese Buddhists drew in order to resurrect esoteric Buddhism subsequently switched to Tibet.[15] Nevertheless, a number of Japanese-oriented esoteric Buddhist organizations in Hong Kong, such as the Hong Kong Mantra School for Lay Buddhists (https://www.buddhistmantra.org.hk/?lang=en) 香港佛教眞言宗居士林, are living products of the popularity that Japanese esoteric Buddhism enjoyed in China during this time.[16]

Although Taixu originally displayed enthusiasm for the study of Shingon Buddhism and encouraged a number of his disciples to pursue it in earnest, he was not interested in studying it himself. In fact, he declined the offer to do so.[17] In contrast, Taixu not only instructed a number of his students to study Buddhism in Tibet but also received Tibetan Buddhist empowerment and even "regarded himself as a disciple" of one of the key Tibetan propagators of Buddhism at the time, the Panchen Lama (1883–1937).[18] However, owing in part to differences in ecclesiastical hierarchical structures, the tantric revival went in a direction that Taixu had not intended.[19]

Although Taixu's interests did not cause the decline of interest in Japanese esoteric Buddhism and the subsequent surge in Chinese attraction to Tibetan Buddhism, they somewhat mirror one another. While the only known living remnants of the original Japanese-oriented revivalists' efforts are confined to Hong Kong, the attractiveness of Tibetan Buddhism among Chinese religionists has yet to wane. Instead, it has extended beyond China's borders and can be found throughout the Sinosphere. Of particular interest is the importation of Tibetan Buddhism to Taiwan. This importation has been periodized into three phases: the Mainlander Transmission (1949–1979) that followed the arrival of the Nationalist Party, the first Tibetan Exile Transmission (1980–1997) in the wake of the visits of a large number of diasporic Tibetan lamas, and the second Tibetan Exile Transmission (which started in 1980) that began after the Dalai Lama's first visit to the island.[20]

Although the growing interest in Tibetan Buddhism among Chinese religionists was originally related to the effort to revive Chinese esoteric Buddhism—namely Tang-dynasty Zhenyan—that is no longer the case. As its popularity spread, Tibetan Vajrayāna came to be perceived as a distinct tradition to adopt independently (rather than a medium for resurrecting Zhenyan) or the font from which to create a hybrid form of Buddhism that scholars have referred to as "Sino-Tibetan Buddhism."[21] Thus, rather than representing the fruition of a "revival" of Chinese esoteric Buddhism, the spread of Tibetan Buddhism eventually superseded it. Consequently, the earlier goal of the tantric revival did not materialize during this period. However, as we will see in the following sections, the spread of Tibetan Buddhism in Taiwan fostered the revival of the tantric revival and caused it to go full circle by reinvigorating interest in Japanese esoteric Buddhism and renewing the desire to resurrect Tang-dynasty Zhenyan. This led to the birth of a movement referred to as "Neo-Zhenyan" or "Zhenyan Revivalism" that has spread from Taiwan to Hong Kong, Malaysia, the United States, and even back to China.[22]

THE REVIVAL'S REVIVAL

The later revival of the Chinese tantric revival began in Taiwan in the early 1970s, during what Abraham Zablocki referred to as the "Mainlander Transmission" of Tibetan Buddhism to Taiwan.[23] In the wake of World War II and the Chinese Civil War, Taiwan's sovereignty changed hands from Japan to the Kuomintang (KMT) 國民黨, who later retreated from China to Taiwan after their defeat at the hands of the Chinese Communist Party. With the intention of eventually retaking the Chinese mainland, the KMT involved itself in the affairs of the minorities on the outskirts of the People's Republic of China. While this fostered a tense relationship between the KMT and the exilic Tibetan government in Dharamshala, lamas living in China who were not politically affiliated with Dharamshala began to establish religious centers in Taiwan.

The propagator of Tibetan Buddhism most relevant to our discussion that came over during this time was Elder Gongga 貢噶老人 (secular name: Shen Shuwen 申書文; 1903–1997).[24] Elder Gongga was a female disciple of the Karma Kagyü master Gangkar Rinpoché (Gongga Hutuketu 貢噶呼圖克圖; 1893–1957).[25] Gangkar Rinpoché was one of many Tibetan teachers who helped spread Tibetan Buddhism in China during the Tantric Revival by giving initiation to "famous officers, warlords, wealthy traders, and intellectuals."[26] Gongga studied with Gankar Rinpoché during the Tantric Revival. Gongga—who is most famous for her posthumous mummification into a golden Flesh Body Bodhisattva Relic 肉身菩薩—left China in 1958 and in 1960 made her way to Taiwan, where she was instrumental in spreading Tibetan Buddhism. Originally from Beijing, she spent years in various retreats throughout Tibet and China before going to Taiwan. Despite her influence, she did not receive full monastic ordination until the age of seventy-seven in 1980.[27] She initially set up a center in Taipei and later opened another in Tainan, the Gongga Temple 貢嘎寺. Both are still extremely active.

Elder Gongga is credited with being one of the first Buddhist masters to openly propagate Tibetan Buddhism in southern Taiwan. This occurred in 1960 during a ten-day retreat attended by hundreds, all of whom received an introductory form of empowerment. This event represents one of the first times that Tibetan Buddhism had been publicly taught in southern Taiwan and was a key event in its early propagation.[28] It was also the spark that rekindled the revival of Tang-dynasty esoteric Buddhism and the Japanese-oriented direction of the tantric revival.

Elder Gongga's retreat took place at Zhuxi Temple (see figures 1–3)—Taiwan's oldest Buddhist monastery—and was organized by its secretary, Wuguang 悟光 (Dharma name: Quanmiao 全妙, secular name: Zheng Jinbao 鄭進寶; 1918–2000).[29] Wuguang was a Chan 禪 monk with a complex biography. Before becoming a Buddhist, Wuguang had spent years pursuing the practice and study of Daoist internal and external alchemy, spirit mediumship, exorcism, and Kundalini yoga. He first came to Zhuxi Temple as a construction worker when Zhuxi Temple was undergoing renovations and decided to enter the monkhood on the advice of Zhuxi Temple's abbot at the time.[30] Before this, Wuguang had made a living as a bamboo furniture maker and as a merchant sailor who reportedly had "a reputation for pugnacity that was known all along the South China coast."[31] He was also married and had six children. This multifaceted life earned him the title of "heavenly vagabond" 太空流浪人.[32]

According to Wuguang's autohagiography, his interest in Tibetan Buddhism, and what led him to invite Elder Gongga to officiate the retreat at Zhuxi Temple, sprang out of a personal religious crisis. After spending some time as a monk, he believed himself to be unfit for monkhood and came to feel as though he was leading a double life.[33] Externally, he was a devoted

Figure 1. Modern façade of Zhuxi Temple's inner courtyard.
Source: Image by author, 2013.

Figure 2. Modern façade of Zhuxi Temple.
Source: Image by author, 2013.

Chan monk while internally he was wracked with doubts and regretted ever becoming a monastic. Seeking solace, Wuguang entered into a personal secluded retreat in his room at Zhuxi Temple. Wuguang reports that a lay devotee visited him during the fourth month of this retreat and informed him that a master of Tibetan Buddhism from China had recently been coming to Tainan. She was in search of an established Buddhist community that would allow her to teach the Dharma but had been turned down by every temple in Tainan that she had approached.

Wuguang became interested in the possibility of learning from this master as he was unfamiliar with Tibetan Buddhism: an interest intertwined with the hope for the potential to reinvigorate his religious practice. This Tibetan master was none other than the female Elder Gongga. During the retreat, Wuguang became a disciple of Elder Gongga and then began studying Karma Kagyü esoteric rituals.[34] Following the retreat, Wuguang secured a place within Zhuxi Temple for Gongga and her followers to live and practice. He set them up in the dormitory which Wuguang himself had helped construct. To ensure her privacy, he designated a place for Gongga to stay near the monastery's ossuary stūpa 靈骨塔, which people avoided because of its association with death.[35]

Wuguang's tutelage under Elder Gongga and her followers' presence at Zhuxi Temple were short-lived. There are conflicting reports given for their falling out. Wuguang states that he became disillusioned with Elder Gongga after she appointed a new disciple to lead the community behind his back and that a number of Elder Gongga's followers in Tainan perceived it as a slight to Wuguang, as he had contributed so much to the community and had been Elder Gongga's assistant during lectures. Wuguang wrote that, in order to avoid creating ripples within the community, he decided not to defend his position and therefore severed his ties.

Elder Gongga's followers give a different version of the story, stating that the falling out was rooted in differences in Buddhist practice. As some Tibetan Buddhist rituals involve the ingestion of meat—which is forbidden in orthodox Chan Buddhism—Wuguang eventually banned the practice of Tibetan Buddhism at Zhuxi Temple.[36] Whichever account is closer to the truth, Elder Gongga and her disciples' departure from Zhuxi Temple does not seem to mark the end of Wuguang's involvement within the community as there is evidence that he continued to practice with them even after their departure.[37]

Sometime after this episode, Wuguang went into retreat once more, but this time in a small concrete hut near a mountaintop waterfall in Kaohsiung's rural Liugui District 高雄六龜區. It is reported that Wuguang discovered the existence of Tang-dynasty Zhenyan while studying the Chinese *Tripiṭaka* during this retreat. Seeking an esoteric Buddhist alternative to Tibetan Vajrayāna, he traveled to Japan in 1971 to study Shingon, the Japanese descendant of Zhenyan founded by Kūkai. There, Wuguang received Shingon empowerment and was ordained as a priest (Skt. *ācārya*). Upon returning to Taiwan the following year, he began to accumulate quite a following and started ordaining a number of his disciples as Shingon priests. When news of this reached his colleagues back in Japan, they ordered him to desist.[38] His refusal to do so led him to sever ties to Japan and found the first known independent—and self-perpetuating—Chinese esoteric Buddhist lineage since Zhenyan's chain of transmission had disappeared over a thousand years prior. Wuguang named his fledgling lineage the Mantra (Zhenyan) School Bright Lineage (MSBL 真言宗光明流).

As we will see in the following sections, the symbolism, architecture, and praxis of the MSBL were designed in a way to bolster its relationship to Tang-dynasty Chinese esoteric Buddhism. Moreover, a number of Wuguang's disciples—and rivals—followed suit and began establishing Zhenyan lineages throughout East Asia.

THE MANTRA SCHOOL BRIGHT LINEAGE

Wuguang's MSBL, which has over six thousand converts as well as branches and splinter groups in several countries, had very humble beginnings.[39] Upon returning to Zhuxi Temple after studying in Japan, Wuguang set up an esoteric sanctuary in accordance with Shingon tradition near the ossuary where Elder Gongga and her followers had previously resided.[40] Although he did not have an organization built around him, he was already a charismatic leader with a developed following as his days were spent catering to "a stream of people seeking help in various ways."[41] It was to this unorganized flock that Wuguang began teaching the esoteric dharma. We are also told it was just a year later, in 1973, that Wuguang relocated the Shingon altar and his esoteric evangelizing to a small back-alley popular religious shrine named Longshan Hall 龍山內院, less than two miles away from Zhuxi Temple. After the relocation, Wuguang's following steadily grew while he continued to periodically visit Kōyasan.[42] These trips came to a halt after he refused to quit independently ordaining his disciples in Taiwan, and thus the MSBL was officially born.

In 1980, an equally humble branch was established in Kaohsiung's Zuoying District 左營區. In 1983, the MSBL joined the Kaohsiung chapter of the Buddhist Association of the Republic of China (BAROC) 中國佛教協會, the Kaohsiung Buddhist Association 大高雄

佛教會.[43] The same year, a large plot of land in Kaohsiung's Neimen District 內門區 was purchased with the intention of constructing a large central monastery. It took sixteen years for the temple to be completed (in 1999), during which time the MSBL Hong Kong branch was opened in 1990, and another has since been opened in Taiwan's capital city, Taipei 台北.

The MSBL's head temple 本山 in Neimen, the Temple of Universal Brightness 光明王寺 (literally "Temple of the Luminous Wisdom King," hereafter TOUB), usually houses around fifteen monastics (see figures 3 and 4). The structure was designed to resemble Tang-dynasty Buddhist architecture in order to proclaim the rebirth of Tang-dynasty Zhenyan. Owing to its rural location—and the fact that it is nestled inside a small mountain cove within a large mountaintop, flat-floor valley named Mt. Five Wisdoms 五智山—it is usually a quiet and serene place. However, it becomes quite crowded on Buddhist holidays and the anniversary of Wuguang's birthday and passing and during a camp for the children of MSBL members in the summer.

Although Wuguang's MSBL is the first known successful revival of esoteric Chinese Buddhism, it was not the last. In fact, one of Wuguang's very own students went on to follow in his steps by receiving esoteric empowerment, severing ties with his teachers, and then establishing a new Chinese esoteric Buddhist lineage.

Figure 3. Main gate of the Temple of Universal Brightness.
Source: Image by author, 2015.

Figure 4. Front of Temple of Universal Brightness.
Source: Image by author, 2015.

THE SAMANTABHADRA LINEAGE

The Zhenyan Samantabhadra Lineage 真言宗普賢流 is an esoteric Buddhist movement with branches throughout Taiwan, the Pescadores Islands, and Hong Kong as well as loose followings in China and New Zealand. It was founded in the late 1990s by one of Wuguang's former disciples, Chesheng 徹聖 (secular name: Chen Shenghua 陳聖華; 1938–). Chesheng received empowerment and was ordained as a Zhenyan priest by Wuguang in 1983. The lineage is based in Taiwan's third largest city, Taichung 台中. Its headquarters, the Medicine Buddha Hall 藥師院, is located on the first floor of an apartment building adjacent to Chesheng's house (see figures 5 and 6). In the early 21st century, the Samantabhadra Lineage boasts an estimated 150 ordained priests and 1,000 converts.

The Medicine Buddha Hall is usually a quiet place, although there are often a handful of priests-in-training practicing rituals as part of their studies. However, a number of major annual events are held at the Medicine Buddha Hall, such as the Buddha Bathing Ceremony (see figures 7–9), an art and calligraphy exhibition, and retreats held especially for members from the Hong Kong branch.[44]

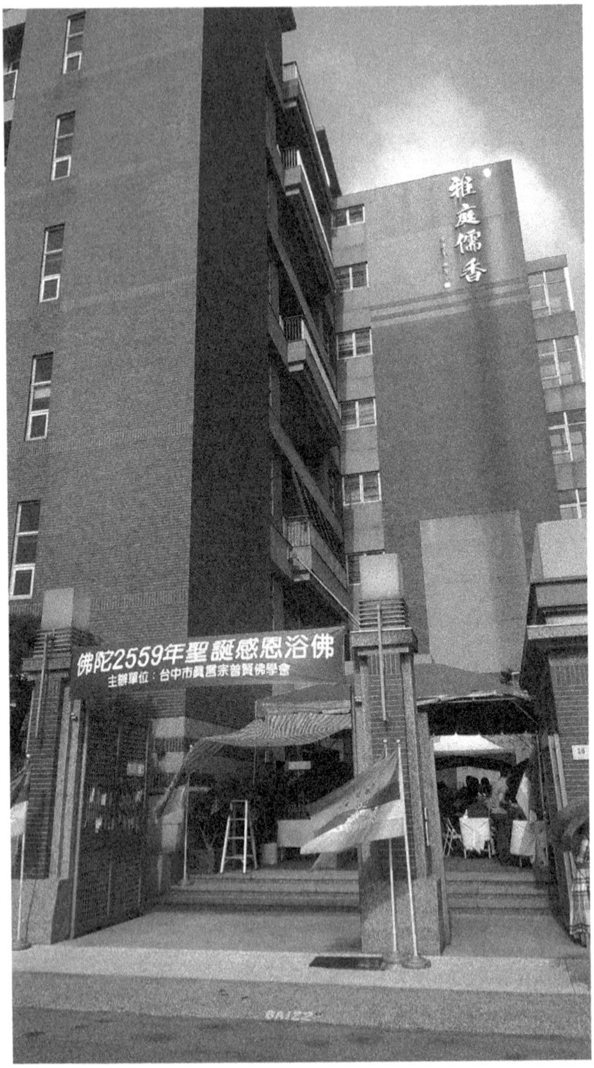

Figure 5. Medicine Buddha Hall.
Source: Image by author, 2015.

Despite the connection between Chesheng and Wuguang, Chesheng is not a member of the MSBL. Rather, his Samantabhadra Lineage represents an offshoot of Wuguang's MSBL. Although the Samantabhadra Lineage was officially founded after Wuguang's death, even during Wuguang's life there was tension between Chesheng, Wuguang, and the MSBL.[45] Chesheng has never been to the TOUB as his studies under Wuguang and subsequent break from him predate the temple's construction. There is little love between the MSBL and the Samantabhadra Lineage. Nevertheless, Chesheng—occasionally—quotes Wuguang during lectures and proudly displays his empowerment certificates signed by Wuguang in the main sanctuary of his lineage's headquarters. Unlike Wuguang,

Figure 6. Entrance to Medicine Buddha Hall.
Source: Image by author, 2015.

Chesheng is not a monk, but a layman. His lineage is similarly dominated by lay, rather than monastic, leadership. This is but one difference between the MSBL and the Samantabhadra Lineage.

Whereas the MSBL's praxis and symbols draw heavily upon Japanese Shingon and sparingly from Tibetan Karma Kagyü, the Samantabhadra Lineage draws heavily from both.[46] This difference may be directly related to a mutual connection between the groups' founders: Elder Gongga. Like Wuguang, Chesheng began studying esoteric Buddhism in earnest under Elder Gongga in the 1980s. This was before he began studying with Wuguang. Although he never received empowerment from Gongga, Chesheng does claim to be her dharma heir because of a series of dreams he had where he claims Elder Gongga ordained him as an esoteric Buddhist priest.[47] Thus, Chesheng claims a dual-esoteric dharma transmission: one Japanese from Wuguang and the other Tibetan from Elder Gongga. Thus, the Samantabhadra Lineage is simultaneously a first- and second-generation descendant of the original tantric revival in China.

Similar to how both Wuguang and Chesheng formed their ownesoteric Buddhist organizations after finding a way to connect themselves to Tang-dynasty Zhenyan after receiving empowerment within the Shingon chain of transmission, the following figure—who once studied under Chesheng—began to amass a following of esoteric Buddhist practitioners after receiving Shingon empowerment in Japan.

Figure 7. Devotees bathing the Buddha.
Source: Image by author, 2015.

KŌYASAN MURYŌKŌ-IN BRANCH TEMPLE

The Kōyasan Muryōkō-in Branch Temple 無量光院 is headquartered in Taipei in the apartment of its founder, Guru Rongyong 融永 (secular name: Chou Wen-Kuei 周文魁; dates unknown). Rongyong also oversees another branch in nearby Taoyuan 桃園 and two in Malaysia: one in Kuala Lumpur and another in Puchong.[48] Rongyong received empowerment from Habukawa Shōdō 土生川正道, abbot of Muryōkō-in 無量光院 at Kōyasan in Japan. Thus, Rongyong is in fact a Shingon—not Zhenyan—priest. However, that is only part of the story. Before studying in Japan under Habukawa, Rongyong was a member of the Samantabhadra Lineage. In fact, it is reported that he entered the one-hundred-day retreat

Figure 8. Buddha Bathing ceremony.
Source: Image by author, 2015.

Figure 9. Homa ritual during Buddha bathing ceremony.
Source: Image by author, 2015.

that leads to empowerment but then—for reasons that are disputed—left in the middle.[49] After this, Rongyong broke away from the Samantabhadra Lineage and severed his connection with them entirely.

In addition to being connected to the original tantric revival in China via Chesheng, Rongyong has a master's degree from Huafan University's 華梵大學 department of Asian humanities. His master's thesis, entitled "An Investigation of the Shingon Heritage and the Revival of Tang-Esoteric Buddhism during the Early Years of the Republic," is on the Japanese-oriented figures of the Tantric Revival.[50] This shows Rongyong's concern with the Sinic reclamation of the dharma-transmission chain of Tang-dynasty Zhenyan. Even though Rongyong claims that he has not broken away from Japan as Wuguang did in an attempt to thoroughly Sinicize this chain, he is not against the idea of eventually ordaining his own priests without Japanese oversight.[51]

THE XIU MING SOCIETY

The Xiu Ming Society 修明堂 was founded in Hong Kong in 1996. It is headquartered in a large complex called Mt. Dharma propagation 弘法山, which houses the main temple, the Hall of the Grandmaster 大師堂. Combined, these names are a clear reference to Kūkai, who was posthumously called the "Grandmaster of Dharma-propagation," Kōbō Daishi 弘法大師. Its training center is called the Chinese Hong Kong Esoteric Buddhist Enlightenment Training Hall 中華港密修明佛院. The founder and spiritual head is Li Kuiming 李居明, who also goes by the English name Edward Li (Dharma name: Chehao 徹豪).[52] Li is from Hong Kong and received empowerment from Wuguang in 1982.[53] Seeking to connect himself more directly to Shingon, he traveled to Japan where he received empowerment at Kōyasan in 1997.

It is difficult to estimate the number of Li's followers, as following Li's teachings is a more complex affair than being a member of the MSBL or Samantabhadra Lineage. Li has a very pronounced online presence, including a professional website of the temple,[54] his own YouTube Channel,[55] an online store,[56] Facebook page,[57] and a fan club named "Li Kuiming's Fan Club" 李居明大師超級 FANS 會[58] that has a Flickr account.[59] Through the use of multimedia and social media, Li has made himself extremely famous throughout the Chinese-speaking world. He frequently appears on television, produces many books and DVDs, and even has his own radio show.

Although Li writes prolifically about esoteric Buddhism, the majority of his books, DVDs, and CDs have almost nothing to do with Buddhism of any form whatsoever. The topics which he most commonly teaches are feng shui 風水, magical practices to accumulate wealth and good fortune, dream interpretation, divination, and even romantic love.

Although his approach radically differs from Wuguang's, Li states that all of this was inspired by the responsibility that Wuguang gave to him:

> I made a great resolution after my master Wuguang passed away. I was initially very low-key in my propagation of [the esoteric Dharma], but I made up my mind to raise my voice after ten years. Why? To provide the masses with the opportunity to join in the assembly of Esoteric Buddhist Priests, to raise the esteem of the Buddha and ensure the future

propagation of Zhenyan in China. Right now, Eastern Esotericism is a Japanese national treasure that they do not propagate to outsiders. My master [Wuguang] was able to obtain Chūin-ryū 院流[60] transmission, this was truly his karmic reward. While bringing the esoteric Dharma back to China, Master Wuguang would say that it was his responsibility to establish an eastern esoteric root temple in Kaohsiung. Twice he referred to me as the "Vanguard of Luminosity" and gave me permission to wear the purple robes.[61]

Although Li went to Kōyasan to supplement the esoteric credentials he received from Wuguang, here he states that his mission is the same as Wuguang's, namely to revive Chinese esoteric Buddhism. He also attributes his more commercial approach to the mission and status that Wuguang gave him as embodied in the purple robe. Whether or not this is true, Li demonstrates a misunderstanding of the meaning of the purple robe that he claims Wuguang allowed him to wear. This robe is meaningless outside of the Japanese ecclesiastical system, and being granted permission to wear it—which Wuguang officially was by his Japanese teachers—does not make one a successor. However, Li—and the majority of Han religionists who were the intended audience of this claim—would likely associate this with the "granting of the bowl and robe" in Chan succession stories.[62] According to these stories, Chan masters designate their successor by handing over their begging bowl and monastic robe. Of these, the robe is the more important.[63]

Despite these propagational stories, it is critical to note that Li draws upon Wuguang—not the Japanese priests from whom he received empowerment—as the source of the inspiration for his commercial and propagational endeavors as well as his priestly authority. Nevertheless, Li has entirely broken away from the MSBL.

THE MAHĀ PRAṆIDHĀNA KUTA MANTRAYĀNA

The Mahā Praṇidhāna Kuta Mantrayāna (MPKM) is based in Bukit Mertajam, Penang in northern Malaysia.[64] Unlike all of the other groups discussed thus far, the MPKM presents itself not as an offshoot of or different lineage from the MSBL, but as an extension thereof. This is despite the fact that the MSBL in Taiwan does not recognize it as such. It is run out of two spaces: an administrative office and an independent temple. The temple's name is the Mahā Praṇidhāna Parvata Sahasra Prabha Rajya Samghārāma 大願山千光王寺 ("The Great Vow Mountain Temple of the Lord of a Thousand Rays of Illuminosity"). The public face of the MPKM is Xiongyu 雄宇 (secular name: Tan Yinghao 譚英豪, Dharma name: Xuanyu 玄宇). Xiongyu was not a student of Wuguang, but traveled to the MSBL's head temple in 2007 and studied the MSBL's dharma there. He refers to himself as an MSBL priest, but those in the MSBL who know of him say that he was not ordained as a priest, but simply took refuge there.

Xiongyu's teacher and the head of the MPKM, Xiongyao 雄曜, claims to have received empowerment from the MSBL as well. Xiongyu states that his teacher Xiangyao is the person who got him interested in esoteric Buddhism in general and Wuguang in particular. He said it was the books that Xiongyao had brought back with him from Taiwan that got him interested.[65]

The liturgy of the MPKM is the same as that of the MSBL. They celebrate the same holidays and use the liturgical texts that can be found at both the Samantabhadra Lineage's Medicine Buddha Hall and the MSBL centers. Likewise, the MPKM runs more festive, family-oriented activities.

According to Xiongyu, the MPKM does not "currently" provide empowerment in Malaysia without the oversight of the MSBL. His characterizing this situation as "currently" makes it seem like this could happen in the future. If it does, this could mark a new chapter in the history of the tantric revival by creating a new independent and self-sustaining Zhenyan lineage.

FU DONG JI

Fu Dong Ji 不動寺 (Mandarin pronunciation: *Bu dong si*) is located in the Qinglong Mountain complex 青龍山 in Pingtung County's rural Gaoshu Township 屏東縣高樹鄉 in southern Taiwan.[66] It was founded in 1984 by Venerable Weili 惟勵法師 (1931–2016). Weili was a Taiwanese Chan monk who repeatedly traveled to Kōyasan, Japan in the 1970s and 1980s to receive training and eventual ordination as a Shingon priest. Fu Dong Ji's religious practice represents a hybridization of Chinese Chan and Pure Land with Japanese Shingon and a unique meditation composed by Weili that represents a hybridization of Chan meditation and Shingon A-seed Syllable 阿字觀 meditation.[67] The architecture and iconography at Fu Dong Ji display a mixture of Japanese and Chinese Buddhist elements. Examples include the complex's main gate and ossuary (see figures 10–12), a statue of Kūkai

Figure 10. Entrance gate to Fu Dong Ji.
Source: Image by author, 2018.

Figure 11. Ossuary at Fu Dong Ji.
Source: Image by author, 2018.

Figure 12. Main gate and ossuary of Fu Dong Ji.
Source: Image by author, 2018.

(see figure 13), another of Acala 不動明王—the Shingon deity the complex is named after (see figure 14)—and a Japanese-styled many-jeweled stūpa 多寶塔 (Skt. *prabhūtaratna-stūpa*), as it has a square base and circular second floor (see figures 15 and 16). This design differs from the more common East Asian design whose different levels are all square. This sort of structure began appearing in Japan during the Heian period 平安時代 (794–1185) and has always been associated with esoteric Buddhism.[68] As the many-jeweled stūpa design is a Japanese phenomenon, the presence of one in Taiwan, in a monastic complex run by Taiwanese Buddhists, is truly remarkable.[69] It is also an explicit reference to the community's ties to Japanese esoteric Buddhism.

In contrast to the other tantric revivalists thus far discussed, Weili never officially broke away from Japan. Instead of presenting his community as a new religious movement or a resurrection of Tang-dynasty Zhenyan, he refrained from creating a new chain of esoteric Buddhist transmission as he did not ordain his own disciples as priests. This enabled him to sustain ties with his Japanese colleagues, who oftentimes visited Fu Dong Ji during his lifetime.

Though not related to Wuguang through lineage, Weili did interact with Wuguang in the 1970s and 1980s. However, as their approach to tantric revivalism differed, they never established an official relationship. Nevertheless, toward the end of his life, Weili did ordain a number of his closest disciples on Taiwanese soil, thus following in the footsteps of Wuguang and his disciples.

Figure 13. Statue of Kūkai at Fu Dong ji.
Source: Image by author, 2014.

Figure 14. Statue of Acala at Fu Dong Ji.
Source: Image by author, 2014.

One of Weili's ordained disciples, Jianming 見明 (dates unknown), is a nun who lives at Fu Dong Ji and is Weili's successor (see figure 17).

FROM TAIWAN TO MICHIGAN

Chen Kuan 成觀 (Pinyin: Cheng Guan, secular name: Yu Jen-Tai; 1947–) is a Taiwanese Chan monk who received Shingon empowerment in Japan in 1996.[70] He oversees two hybrid exoteric-esoteric, Sino-Japanese Buddhist centers. The first, the Maha-Vairocana Temple 大毘盧寺 in Taipei, was founded in 1991. The second, the American Buddhist Temple 遍照寺, was originally founded in Cleveland, Ohio in 1993 but relocated to Howell, Michigan the following year. Chen is looking to expand and is seeking donations to procure land in a more rural area to construct a monastic complex which will be called the Neo-Carefree Garden Buddhist Canon Translation Institute 新逍遙園譯經院, which is the name of his publishing company.

In his autohagiography, Chen states that his interest in esoteric Buddhism was initiated by the growing popularity of esoteric Buddhism in Taiwan.[71] He believed that this trend was motivated by an unwholesome interest in magic and decided to study esoteric Buddhism in order to offer a more wholesome and less worldly oriented form.[72] His international presence, which enabled him to establish a foothold in America, is rooted in his graduate studies. From 1979 to 1982, Chen was a fellow in the English department at Texas Christian University. Prior to that, he taught high school English in Taiwan.

Figure 15. Stupa at Fu Dong Ji.
Source: Image by author, 2014.

Figure 16. Bell and many-jewewled stūpa at Fu Dong Ji.
Source: Image by author, 2018.

Figure 17. Jianming, Weili's successor, performing an esoteric Buddhist *homa* ritual.
Source: Video by author, 2018.

FROM CHINA TO PENNSYLVANIA

Unlike all of the other groups thus far, the Sino Esoteric Buddhism Association 中華唐密世界同修會 was founded by an individual from China. Moreover, this individual does not claim to propagate an esoteric Buddhism transmission that was routed through Japan. Instead, he claims that his chain of esoteric Buddhist transmission predates that of Kūkai's and in fact survived—secretly—in China for over 1,500 years.

Jinke Xuanlei 金珂玄雷 (1958–) was born in Yizhou 宜州, Guangxi Autonomous Region 廣西壯族自治區, where he claims to have received esoteric Buddhist empowerment from a mysterious individual named Jinyin 金音 (dates unknown) after ten years of studying and practicing in the mountains. Remarkably, Jinke claims that his chain of esoteric Buddhist transmission remained unbroken in China since the Tang dynasty. Moreover, he claims that his lineage split from that upon which Shingon is based before Kūkai ever stepped foot in China, as he claims to be the direct successor of Huilang 慧朗 (?–781), a student of Amoghavajra and colleague of Kūkai's teacher, Huiguo.[73] While Huiguo is still venerated, Jinke considers Huilang the "third patriarch" of esoteric Buddhism and the true torchbearer of Tang-dynasty Chinese esoteric Buddhist transmission.[74] Interestingly, scholarship from 2019 has shown that Huilang was in fact Amoghavajra's key disciple and essential successor, although Huiguo plays such a prominent role in Shingon.[75]

More importantly, whereas the Japanese Shingon sectarian understanding of Zhenyan—as well as that of the other figures explored thus far—proclaims that esoteric Buddhist transmission disappeared from China after the Tang dynasty, Jinke asserts not only that it continued to exist but that it was both practiced and propagated in secret until he decided to emerge as a public figure. The secret to esoteric Buddhism's survival, according to Jinke, was in fact its secrecy. Whereas non-esoteric forms of Buddhism were propagated openly, "the Chinese imperial families had always believed in Sino Esoteric Buddhism" but were bound by vows of secrecy. Hence, the common misconception—as he portrays it—that esoteric Buddhism disappeared from China.[76]

Jinke's self-coined emergence occurred in several stages. In 1983, he claims that he "emerge[d] from his practice in the mountains to visit a number of remote and poverty stricken (sic) regions" where he "helped and healed thousands of afflicted for free, propagated Buddha-Dharma and gave salvation to those in torment."[77] In 1985, he is said to have received monastic Buddhist ordination at Mt. Wutai in order to "conform to the societal norms of the time."[78] In 1993, Jinke emerged for the final time to propagate the dharma on a global scale. Since then, Jinke has been working to make a name for himself. In 2015, as reported in the *Daily Mail* and *Buddhistdoor Global*, Jinke and his disciples painted a portrait of the prime minister of India, Narendra Modi, and the president of the People's Republic of China, Xi Jinping, holding hands in a gesture of friendship.[79] Jinke and his disciples had wished to present the painting as a gift to Modi during his historic visit to China in 2015, but they were not given the opportunity to do so.[80]

Over the past few years, Jinke has attempted to establish a headquarters in America. At one point, he sought to construct "the world's tallest Mahāvairocana Buddha Statue," the key deity of Shingon Buddhism, in Lancaster, California.[81] After that plan did not come to fruition, he procured land in the Poconos in rural East Stroudsburg, Pennsylvania, where construction of the Jinyin Temple of Sino Esoteric Buddhism began. However, the outbreak of a fire, property taxes, and other unanticipated expenses delayed construction.[82] Nevertheless, the community has already begun hosting events in the space, which are regularly advertised on their Facebook page.[83]

Delimiting the Boundaries of Tantric Revivalism and Neo-Zhenyan. As demonstrated, although the first phase of the tantric revival that was limited primarily to the Chinese mainland did not accomplish its original goal of resurrecting Tang-dynasty esoteric Buddhism, the second phase of the revival has seen the birth of multiple Chinese esoteric Buddhist lineages. Moreover, the second phase of the revival came full circle, and the interest in Tibetan Buddhism led to a resurgence in the desire to resurrect Zhenyan via obtaining Shingon empowerment. Although the figures and communities discussed in this article represent different approaches, they are united in their belief that they practice an ancient form of Buddhism that disappeared over a thousand years ago.

The interest in Japanese Shingon is not limited to revivalists. In addition to the communities discussed here, there are Buddhists in Taiwan who have traveled to Japan, received empowerment, and then returned to Taiwan to spread the esoteric dharma that they learned abroad. However, such figures are not attempting to resurrect Zhenyan, for they choose to remain under the auspices of Japanese figures in Japan. One example is Huaihai Yuanzhi 懷海圓智, the abbot of a Shingon temple in Taichung that remains under Japanese direction, the Kōyasan Jūkon-in 高野山住嚴院 (see figures 18 and 19).

Figure 18. Exterior of the Kōyasan Jūkon-in.
Source: Image by author, 2013.

In addition to sending his students to Japan for training and ordination, Huaihai's temple regularly hosts Japanese Shingon priests who stay in Taiwan for weeks at a time in order to train Taiwanese adherents. Moreover, Huaihai attempts to replicate the experience of studying and worshipping in a Japanese setting, as even the clothes that students wear during rituals are imported from Japan. Whereas almost all of the figures we have looked at have attempted to Sinicize the Shingon that they teach, Huaihai remains a purist. In fact, one of his main criticisms of modern Tantric revivalists is their incorporation of non-Japanese elements into their religious practices.[84] Whereas Huaihai attempts to accurately transmit Japanese Shingon to his students, the revivalists are creating new forms of Buddhism that incorporate Japanese, Tibetan, and Taiwanese elements into their liturgy, practice, and even ritual utensils.[85]

Figure 19. Exterior of the Kōyasan Jūkon-in.
Source: Image by author, 2013.

REVIEW OF LITERATURE

The majority of the existing literature on the tantric revival in China focuses on the first phase that occurred during the late Qing dynasty and early Republican period. Holmes Welch was perhaps the first scholar to discuss this phenomenon and explore Taixu's motivations for initiating it, and Luo Tongbing has shown how controversies related to giving esoteric Buddhist empowerment to lay Buddhists played a role in Taixu's eventually distancing himself from esoteric Buddhism.[86] Erik Shicketanz gave a detailed historical account of the Japanese-oriented facet of the early revival, and Bill Mak explored how the interplay between politics and religion factored into the establishment of Shingon communities in Hong Kong.[87] Ester Bianchi composed an informative piece that delves into both the Japanese- and Tibetan-oriented currents.[88] Moreover, Bianchi has shown that although the spread of Tibetan Buddhism did not represent the actualization of the restoration of Tang-dynasty esoteric Buddhism and that this spread was halted during the Cultural Revolution (1966–1976), there has since been a resurging interest in Tibetan Buddhism in China, and a number of its propagators were educated by the earlier revivalists.[89] The volume edited by Monica Esposito, *Images of Tibet in the 19th and 20th Centuries*, and another edited by Matthew Kapstein, *Buddhism between China and Tibet*, contain additional articles that investigate the complexities of the revival's early phase.[90]

The work of Fabienne Jagou, which explores the life and impact of Elder Gongga, is critical to understanding how the importation of Tibetan Buddhism to Taiwan helped to revive the tantric revival. Of particular importance is her book *Gongga Laoren (1903–1997): Her Role in the Spread of Tibetan Buddhism in Taiwan*.[91] Additionally, the volume which she edited, *The Hybridity of Buddhism: Contemporary Encounters between Tibetan and Chinese Traditions in Taiwan and the Mainland*, contains a number of important pieces on the history and significance of Tibetan Buddhism in Taiwan.[92]

In terms of the later phase of revival in Taiwan and the actualization of the revival's original goal of resurrecting Tang-dynasty Esoteric Buddhism, Cody Bahir has thoroughly explored the life and ideology of Wuguang and the history of a number of other groups in East Asia.[93] In the early 21st century, the only other published scholarly treatises on this phenomenon are three master's degree theses that were written in Mandarin.[94]

With the increasingly globalized nature of the tantric revival and the unremitting emergence of fledgling Zhenyan communities, there may very well be a number of communities that have yet to be noted by scholars.

PRIMARY SOURCES

In addition to establishing new Buddhist communities, many of the revival's architects have been prolific authors. Elder Gongga, who introduced both Wuguang and Chesheng to esoteric Buddhism, left an account of her own religious devotion.[95] Similarly, in an autohagiography that gives a detailed account of his life, Wuguang explains his reasons for wanting to revive Zhenyan.[96] Chesheng, Wuguang's former student and head of the Samantabhadra Lineage, penned a treatise that describes his understanding of esoteric Buddhism and that is given to all new disciples.[97] Likewise, Edward Li has articulated his perception of esoteric Buddhism and explained how to apply its teachings to life in the modern world.[98] Weili, founder of Fu Dong Ji, wrote an introduction to esoteric Buddhism that details his view of the history, practice, and theology of Shingon.[99] Chen Kuan, who founded hybrid esoteric communities in both Taiwan and Michigan, detailed his studies of esoteric Buddhism and explains why he was attracted to this form of Buddhism.[100] These sources help explain what unites, and differentiates, these figures and their respective communities.

FURTHER READING

Bahir, Cody R. "Buddhist Master Wuguang's (1918–2000) Taiwanese Web of the Colonial, Exilic and Han." *e-Journal of East and Central Asian Religions* 1 (2013): 81–93. http://dx.doi.org/10.2218/ejecar.2013.1.737.

Bahir, Cody R. "Replanting the Bodhi Tree: Buddhist Sectarianism and Zhenyan Revivalism." *Pacific World: Journal of the Institute of Buddhist Studies* (Third Series) 20 (2018): 95–129.

Bianchi, Ester. "The Tantric Rebirth Movement in Modern China: Esoteric Buddhism Re-vivified by the Japanese and Tibetan Traditions." *Acta Orientalia Academiae Scientiarum Hungaricae* 57, no. 1 (2004): 31–54.

Bianchi, Ester. "A Religion-oriented 'Tibet Fever': Tibetan Buddhist Practices among the Han Chinese in Contemporary PRC." In *From Mediterranean to Himalaya—A Festschrift to Commemorate the 120th Birthday of the Italian Tibetologist Giuseppe Tucci*. Edited by Dramdul and Francesco Sferra, 347–374. Beijing: China Tibetology, 2014.

Bianchi, Ester. "Sino-Tibetan Buddhism: Continuities and Discontinuities; The Case of Nenghai's Legacy in the Contemporary Era." In *Chinese and Tibetan Esoteric Buddhism*. Edited by Yael Bentor and Meir Shachar, 300–318. Leiden, The Netherlands: Brill, 2017.

Esposito, Monica, ed. *Images of Tibet in the 19th and 20th Centuries*. Paris: École Française d'Extrême-Orient, 2008.

Jagou, Fabienne, ed. *The Hybridity of Buddhism: Contemporary Encounters between Tibetan and Chinese Traditions in Taiwan and the Mainland*. Edited by Fabienne Jagou. Paris: École Française d'Extrême Orient, 2018.

Jagou, Fabienne. *Gongga Laoren (1903–1997): Her Role in the Spread of Tibetan Buddhism in Taiwan*. Leiden, The Netherlands: Brill, 2021.

Kapstein, Matthew T., ed. *Buddhism between China and Tibet Kapstein*. New York: Wisdom Publications, 2009.

Schicketanz, Erik. "Wang Hongyuan and the Import of Japanese Esoteric Buddhism to China during the Republican Period." In *Buddhism across Asia: Networks of Material, Intellectual and Cultural Exchange*. Vol. 1. Edited by Tansen Sen, 323–347. Singapore: Institute of Southeast Asian Studies, 2014.

NOTES

1. See Ester Bianchi, "The Tantric Rebirth Movement in Modern China: Esoteric Buddhism Re-vivified by the Japanese and Tibetan Traditions," *Acta Orientalia Academiae Scientiarum Hungarica* 57, no. 1 (2004): 31–54; and Erik Schicketanz, "Wang Hongyuan and the Import of Japanese Esoteric Buddhism to China during the Republican Period," in *Buddhism across Asia: Networks of Material, Intellectual and Cultural Exchange*, ed. Tansen Sen (Singapore: Institute of Southeast Asian Studies, 2014), 1.323–1.347.
2. Ronald M. Davidson, *Indian Esoteric Buddhism: A Social History of the Tantric Movement* (New York: Columbia University Press, 2002), 3, 25–26.
3. Richard K. Payne, "Introduction," in *Tantric Buddhism in East Asia*, ed. Richard K. Payne (Boston: Wisdom Publications, 2006), 8.
4. See Abé Ryūichi, *The Weaving of Mantra: Kūkai and the Construction of Esoteric Buddhist Discourse* (New York: Columbia University Press, 1999), 124.
5. Ryūichi, *Weaving of Mantra*, 25; and Robert H. Sharf, *Coming to Terms with Chinese Buddhism: A Reading of the Treasure Store Treatise*, Kuroda Institute Studies in East Asian Buddhism 14 (Honolulu: University of Hawai'i Press, 2002), 268.
6. John R. McRae, *Seeing through Zen: Encounter, Transformation, and Genealogy in Chinese Chan Buddhism* (Berkeley, Los Angeles, and London: University of California Press, 2003), 70, 71.
7. Erik J. Hammerstrom, "The Heart-of-Mind Method: Legitimating a New Buddhist Movement in 1930s China," *Nova Religio: The Journal of Alternative and Emergent Religions* 17, no. 2 (2013): 13.
8. For an exploration on the development and use of this term, see Jimmy Wu, "Revisiting the Notion of Zong: Contextualizing the Dharma Drum Lineage of Chan Buddhism," *Chung-Hwa Buddhist Journal* 26 (2013): 113–151; and Sharf, *Coming to Terms*, 264.

9. For a thorough overview on the issues regarding esoteric Buddhism within East Asian contexts, see Charles D. Orzech, Henrik H. Sørensen, and Richard K. Payne, "Introduction: Esoteric Buddhism and the Tantras of East Asia: Some Methodological Considerations," in *Esoteric Buddhism and the Tantras of East Asia*, ed. Charles D. Orzech, Henrik H. Sørensen, and Richard K. Payne (Leiden, The Netherlands: Brill, 2011), 3–18.
10. Ian Astley, "The Study of the Esoteric Buddhist Tradition in Japan," in *Esoteric Buddhism in Japan: Selected Papers from Two SBS Gatherings on Esoteric Buddhism*, ed. Ian Astley-Kristensen (Copenhagen and Aarhus: Seminar in Buddhist Studies, 1994), 1.
11. Jeffrey Kotyk, "The Medieval Chinese Vision of Japan: Buddhist Perspectives in the Tang and Song Periods," *Studies in Chinese Religions* 6, no. 4 (2020): 360–385.
12. Luo Tongbing, "The Reformist Monk Taixu and the Controversy about Exoteric and Esoteric Buddhism in Republican China," in *Images of Tibet in the 19th and 20th Centuries*, ed. Monica Esposito (Paris: École Française d'Extrême-Orient, 2008), 433.
13. Holmes Welch, *The Buddhist Revival in China* (Cambridge, MA: Harvard University Press, 1968), 198.
14. For more information, see Schicketanz, "Wang Hongyuan and the Import of Japanese."
15. Bing Chen, "The Tantric Revival and its Reception in Modern China," in *Images of Tibet in the 19th and 20th Centuries*, ed. Monica Esposito (Paris: École Française d'Extrême-Orient, 2008), 394.
16. For more information on the popularity of Japanese esoteric Buddhism in Hong Kong, see Bill M. Mak, "The Career of Utsuki Nishū 宇津木二秀 in Hong Kong during the Japanese Occupation Period (1941–1945)," *Journal of the Royal Asiatic Society Hong Kong Branch* 55 (2015): 57–82.
17. See Bianchi, "Tantric Rebirth Movement," 36.
18. Chen, "Tantric Revival," 398.
19. See Tongbing, "Reformist Monk Taixu," 438–457.
20. Abraham Zablocki, "The Taiwanese Connection: Politics, Piety, and Patronage in Transnational Tibetan Buddhism, in *Buddhism between Tibet and China*, ed. Matthew T. Kapstein (Boston: Wisdom Publications, 2009), 385–390.
21. Monica Esposito coined this term in reference to this phenomenon in 1990. For more information, see Ester Bianchi, "Sino-Tibetan Buddhism: Continuities and Discontinuities: The Case of Nenghai's Legacy in the Contemporary Era," in *Chinese and Tibetan Esoteric Buddhism*, ed. Yael Bentor and Meir Shachar (Leiden, The Netherlands: Brill, 2017), 300–318.
22. The only extensive studies on the state of the Japanese-oriented examples of the tantric revival in the early 21st century are Cody R. Bahir, "Buddhist Master Wuguang's (1918–2000) Taiwanese Web of the Colonial, Exilic and Han," *e-Journal of East and Central Asian Religions* 1 (2013): 81–93; Cody R. Bahir, "Reenchanting Buddhism via Modernizing Magic: Guru Wuguang of Taiwan's Philosophy and Science of "Superstition" (PhD diss., Leiden University, 2017); Cody R. Bahir, "Reformulating the Appropriated and Relinking the Chain: Challenges of Lineage and Legitimacy in Zhenyan Revivalism," in *The Hybridity of Buddhism: Contemporary Encounters between Tibetan and Chinese Traditions in Taiwan and the Mainland*, ed. Fabienne Jagou (Paris: École Française d'Extrême Orient, 2018), 91–108; Cody R. Bahir, "Replanting the Bodhi Tree: Buddhist Sectarianism and Zhenyan Revivalism," *Pacific World: Journal of the Institute of Buddhist Studies* (Third Series) 20 (2018): 95–129; and Cody R. Bahir, "Taiwanese Tantra: Guru Wuguang's Art of Yogic Nourishment and the Esoteric Path," in *Buddhism & Medicine: Modern and Contemporary Voices*, ed. Pierce Salguero (New York: Columbia University Press, 2019), 137–146.
23. Zablocki, "Taiwanese Connection," 386.
24. For more about Elder Gongga, see Fabienne Jagou, *Gongga Laoren (1903–1997): Her Role in the Spread of Tibetan Buddhism in Taiwan* (Leiden, The Netherlands: Brill, 2021).
25. See Monica Esposito, "rDzogs chen in China: From Chan to 'Tibetan Tantrism' in Fahai Lama's (1920–1991) Footsteps," in *Images of Tibet in the 19th and 20th Centuries*, ed. Monica Esposito (Paris: École

Française d'Extrême-Orient, 2008), 476. About Gangkar Rinpoché, see Carmen Meinert, "Gangkar Rinpoché between Tibet and China: A Tibetan Lama among Ethnic Chinese in the 1930s to 1950s," in *Buddhism between China and Tibet*, ed. Matthew T. Kapstein (New York: Wisdom Publications, 2009), 215–240.

26. Chen, "Tantric Revival," 409.
27. See Douglas Gildow and Marcus Bingenheimer, "Buddhist Mummification in Taiwan: Two Case Studies," *Asia Major* (3rd Series) 15, no. 2 (2002): 95; and Fabienne Jagou, "Tibetan Relics in Taiwan: A Link between Past, Present, and Future," in *The Hybridity of Buddhism: Contemporary Encounters between Tibetan and Chinese Traditions in Taiwan and the Mainland*, ed. Fabienne Jagou (Paris: École Française d'Extrême Orient, 2018), 67–89.
28. Lo Wei-shu 羅娓淑, "A Study of the Development of Chongqing Temple in Tainan and Its Relationship to the Development of Tibetan Buddhism in Southern Taiwan 台南重慶寺的發展歷程與南台灣藏傳佛教發展關係 研究," *Chung-Hwa Buddhist Journal* 20 (2007): 316–317.
29. For the history of Zhuxi Temple see, Lu Jiaxing 盧嘉興, "*Taiwande diyizuo siyuan-zhuxisi* 臺灣的第一座寺院—竹溪寺 [Taiwan's First Monastery-Zhuxi Temple]," *Taiwan fojiao shilunji* (8)–*taiwan fojiao pian* 8 (1979): 233–254.
30. This period of reconstruction is memorialized in a stele that stands at Zhuxi Temple.
31. Shinzen Young, *Break Through Pain: A Step-by-Step Mindfulness Meditation Program for Transforming Chronic and Acute Pain* (Boulder, CO: Sounds True, 2004), 75.
32. Guo Yongkun 郭永坤, "*Da Kaohsiung fojiaohui suoshu siyuan tuanti jianjie* 大高雄佛教會所屬寺院團體簡介, [Profile of the Member Monasteries of the Buddhist Association of Kaohsiung]" (2010).
33. Unless otherwise noted, details from Wuguang's life come from his autohagiography that he read at the opening ceremony of his lineage's head temple in 2000. See Wuguang 悟光, *Cangsang huiyilu* 滄桑回憶錄 [Memoir of Trials and Tribulations] (handwritten manuscript, 1999) (http://www.mantrabright.org/index.php?option=com:%20lyftenbloggie&view=entry&id=5&Itemid=29).
34. Wei-shu, "Study of the Development," 316–317.
35. Huang Hui Li 黃慧琍, "The First Research of Tibetan Traditional Buddhism Development—Base on the Tibetan Tradition Buddhism Group in Tainan Area, 藏傳佛教在台發展初探--以台南地區的藏傳佛教團體為研究對象" (MA thesis, National University of Tainan, 2000), 54.
36. Fabienne Jagou, "Tibetan Buddhism in the Tainan Area: A Case Study of Two Karma bKa'rgyud School Monasteries," paper presented at the Third International Conference on Tainan studies with the theme Religion in Transformation in the Tainan Area, National Museum of Taiwan Literature, October 21, 2012.
37. See Bahir, "Replanting the Bodhi Tree," 105.
38. Bahir, "Master Wuguang's Taiwanese Web," 87.
39. On a refuge certificate from April 27, 2014, it states that Wuguang's successor has officiated over 835 MSBL ceremonies, a number that does not include refuge ceremonies conducted by other MSBL members in Hong Kong and Malaysia. Wuguang himself performed over 5,000.
40. Shinzen Young, personal correspondence, October 24, 2014.
41. Shinzen Young, personal communication, October 24, 2014.
42. Personal interview with Chesheng, July 2013.
43. Personal correspondence with an MSBL monastic on behalf of Huiding, June 22, 2016.
44. The center in Hong Kong is named the Zhenyan Samantabhadra Lineage Life Education Center (*Zhenyanzong puxianliu shengming jiaoyu xuehui* 真言宗普賢流生命教育學會) (http://www.ple.org.hk/).
45. See Chesheng 徹聖, *Shengyi xinyao azi yi* 勝義心要阿字義 [Explanation of the A-seed Syllable] (Taichung: Zhenyanzong Puxianliu Foxuehui, n.d.), 12.

46. See Bahir, "Reformulating the Appropriated."
47. Chesheng, *Bairi guanxinjing jiangyi* 百日關心經講義椎擊三要訣勝法解合輯本 [Collection of Explanatory Lectures on the Three Essentials from the Hundred Day Heart Sutra Retreat] (Taichung: Zhenyanzong puxianliu foxuehui, 2003), 88–107.
48. Muryōkō-in Taiwan Beitsuin (http://koyasan.org.tw/index.php).
49. Interview with a high-ranking member of the Samantabhadra Lineage, January 2014.
50. Chou Wen-Kuei, "An Investigation of the Shingon Heritage and the Revival of Tang-Esoteric Buddhism during the Early Years of the Republic 民初自日本回傳真言宗阿闍黎復興唐密之考察" (MA thesis, Huafan University, 2012).
51. Interview with Rongyong, December 2013.
52. Owing to Kuiming's Hong Kong setting, it should be noted that the character 居 is transcribed according to the Cantonese pronunciation that Kuiming himself uses; however, in Jyutping it is actually *geoi*.
53. Edward Li (Li Kuiming 李居明), *Mizong xinyang yu xiuchi*, 密宗信仰与修持 [The Practice of Esoteric Buddhism] (Beijing: Hualing chubanshe, 2010), foreword.
54. See Dashi Tang (http://www.lifedevotee.com).
55. The channel is named "Edward Li 李居明 (https://www.youtube.com/channel/UCWYlRSA5YFeZt9S18NhdTxw)."
56. See Xiumingtang Flagship Store (http://www.xyycgs.com/xiumingtangqijiandian) 修明堂旗舰店.
57. See Li Kuiming 李居明 (https://www.facebook.com/李居明-559501650810365/).
58. The URL, Li Kui Ming Fan Club (http://www.likuimingfansclub.com) redirects to a more professional looking website found at Li Kui Ming (http://www.likuiming.com/index.html).
59. See Li Kui Ming Fan Club (https://www.flickr.com/photos/likuimingfansclubcollections/).
60. Chūin-ryū 院流 is a particular branch of Shingon and the one that Wuguang was initiated into.
61. Edward Li, *Mizong qi meng* 密宗启蒙 [Elementary Esoteric Instructions] (Beijing: Hualing chubanshe, 2010), foreword.
62. Photographs of Wuguang's certificates detailing his ecclesiastical position can be seen in Wuguang, *Fojiao zhenyanzong jishenchengfo guan* 佛教真言宗即身成佛觀 [Contemplation on Becoming a Buddha in this Body] (Kaohsiung: Paise wenhua, 1991), front endpapers. For a thorough treatment of purple robes, see Duncan Williams, "The Purple Robe Incident and the Formation of the Early Modern Sōtō Zen Institution," *Japanese Journal of Religious Studies* 36, no. 1 (2009): 27–43.
63. See John Kieschnick, *The Impact of Buddhism on Chinese Material Culture* (Princeton, NJ: Princeton University Press, 2003), 110.
64. Formerly the Mahā Praṇidhāna Parvata Mantrayāna.
65. The contents of this section are based on data gathered through correspondence with Xiong on December 24 and 25, 2016.
66. This transliteration, which seems to represent a hybrid Chinese-Japanese pronunciation, is that used on the community's official Facebook page. See Qinglong Shan Fu Dong Ji 青龍山 不動寺 (https://www.facebook.com/FDJTW).
67. For more information on the traditional Japanese version, see Richard K. Payne, "Ajikan: Ritual and Meditation in the Shingon Tradition," in *Re-visioning "Kamakura" Buddhism*, ed. Richard K. Payne, 219–248. Studies in East Asian Buddhism, 11. Honolulu: University of Hawaii Press, 1998. Weili's hybrid Sino-Japanese, Chan-Shingon meditation is explained in Weili, *Yizi Chan: Azi guan yujia mengxiangfa* (Taipei: Jingyin chuban she, 1995).
68. Hugo Munsterberg, *The Arts of Japan: An Illustrated History* (Rutland, VT, and Tokyo: Charles E. Tuttle, 1988), 144.
69. Although there are textual references to many-jeweled stūpas that predate this design's Japanese debut, there are no existent examples. See Paul Groner, "Kōen and the 'Consecrated Ordination' within

Japanese Tendai," in *Buddhist Monasticism in East Asia: Places of Practice*, ed. James A. Benn, Lori Meeks, and James Robson (London and New York: Routledge, 2014), 197; and the only other one known to exist in Taiwan was constructed by a Taiwanese Chan monk, Weili 惟勵 (1931–2016), who, like Wuguang, received Dharma transmission *abhiṣeka* in Japan. See below, "Part 9: Fu Dong Ji."

70. The Chinese characters for Cheng's secular name are not known. However, their anglicization thereof can be seen on his bachelor's degree from National Taiwan Normal University. See Chen Kuan 成觀, *Wode xuemi licheng* 我的學密歷程 [The Course of My Esoteric Studies] (Taipei: Xin xiayaoyuan yi jingyuan, 2013), 31.
71. The temple's website can be found here: American Buddhist Temple (http://www.abtemple.org/).
72. Kuan, *Wode xuemi licheng*, 10–13.
73. For more information on Huilang, see Charles D. Orzech, "After Amoghavajra: Esoteric Buddhism in the Late Tang," in *Esoteric Buddhism and the Tantras of East Asia*, ed. Charles D. Orzech, Henrik H. Sørensen, and Richard K. Payne (Leiden, The Netherlands, and Boston: Brill, 2011), 321.
74. Sino Esoteric Buddhist Association, *First Silk Road (Dunhuang) International Cultural Expo Exhibition of Jinke Mandala Art* 首屆"絲綢之路"敦煌國際文化博覽會金剛曼荼羅文化藝術國際交流展 (Beijing: Sino Esoteric Buddhist Association, n.d.), 48.
75. Geoffrey C. Goble, *Chinese Esoteric Buddhism: Amoghavajra, the Ruling Elite, and the Emergence of a Tradition* (New York: Columbia University Press, 2019), 187–188.
76. Sino Esoteric Buddhist Association, "A Brief Introduction to the Vajra Master Jinke Xuanlei (https://www.jinyintemple.org/vajra-master-1)."
77. Sino Esoteric Buddhist Association, *To Spread the Buddha-Dharma Around the World, Light of Wisdom from the Buddha Shina through the Universe: Documentations of the Initiatives Taken by the Vajra Master Jinke Xuanlei of Sino Esoteric Buddhism to Spread the Buddha's Teachings* 法音傳世界佛光照大千:中華唐密金珂玄雷金剛上師弘法事迹匯編 (Beijing: Sino Esoteric Buddhist Association, n.d.), 6.
78. Sino Esoteric Buddhist Association, *To Spread the Buddha-Dharma*, 6.
79. Anathan Krishnan, "The Art of Diplomacy: Chinese Buddhist Master Paints "Unique" Portraits of Modi ahead of Historic Visit," *Daily Mail India*, May 11, 2015; and BD Dipananda, "President Xi Jinping and PM Narendra Modi on 'Canvas': Representing Sino-Indian Buddhist Cultural Bonds," *Buddhistdoor Global*, May 27, 2015.
80. Sutirtho Patranobis, "Chinese Buddhists paint Modi and Xi Together, Depict Sino-India Cultural Ties," *Hindustan Times*, May 10, 2015.
81. Sino Esoteric Buddhist Association, "May East Stroudsburg, Pennsylvania Become a More Beautiful Place—An Introduction of Jinyin Temple." This story was also picked up by several news outlets, but Jinke and his organization were not named. See NA, "Company Wants to Build Giant Buddha in Lancaster," *Associated Press News*, June 18, 2017. Also see Matt Sheehan, "A California Mayor Hopes China Will Save His Town from Meth Labs and Neo-Nazis, *Vice News*, May 30, 2017.
82. Bill Cameron, "Challenges in Building Temple," *Pocono Record*, April 20, 2019; and Bill Cameron, "Jinyin Temple Mulls Change in Plans after Setbacks," *Pocono Record*, April 21, 2019.
83. See Jinyin Temple of Sino Esoteric Buddhism Facebook Page (https://www.facebook.com/JinyinTempleUSA/).
84. Huaihai Yuanzhi 懷海圓智, *Fojiao mimi: mimi fojiaode xin shiye* 佛教秘密: 秘密佛教的新視 [Esoteric Buddhism: A New Vision for Esoteric Buddhism] (Taichung: Yiqie zhizhi guocha wenchuang, 2013), 48–51.
85. See Bahir, "Reformulating the Appropriated," 91–108; and Bahir "Replanting the Bodhi Tree," 95–129.
86. Welch, *Buddhist Revival in China*, 196–198; and Tongbing, "Reformist Monk Taixu," 433–471.
87. Schicketanz, "Wang Hongyuan and the Import of Japanese," 1.323–1.347; and Mak, "Career of Utsuki Nishū 宇津木二秀," 57–82.

88. Bianchi, "Tantric Rebirth Movement," 31–54.
89. Ester Bianchi, "A Religion-Oriented 'Tibet Fever': Tibetan Buddhist Practices among the Han Chinese in Contemporary PRC," in *From Mediterranean to Himalaya. A Festschrift to Commemorate the 120th Birthday of the Italian Tibetologist Giuseppe Tucci*, ed. Dramdul and F. Sferra (Beijing: China Tibetology 2014), 347–374; and Bianchi, "Sino-Tibetan Buddhism," 300–318.
90. Monica Esposito, ed., *Images of Tibet in the 19th and 20th Centuries* (Paris: École française d'Extrême-Orient, 2008); and Matthew T. Kapstein, ed., *Buddhism between China and Tibet* (New York: Wisdom Publications, 2009).
91. Jagou, *Gongga Laoren (1903–1997)*.
92. Fabienne Jagou, ed., *The Hybridity of Buddhism: Contemporary Encounters between Tibetan and Chinese Traditions in Taiwan and the Mainland* (Paris: École Française d'Extrême Orient, 2018).
93. Bahir, "Buddhist Master Wuguang's," 81–93; Bahir, "Reenchanting Buddhism via Modernizing Magic"; Bahir, "Reformulating the Appropriated," 91–108; Bahir, "Replanting the Bodhi Tree," 95–129; and Bahir, "Taiwanese Tantra," 137–146.
94. Gu Zhengli 顧正立, "Study on Shingon Buddhism of Guangmingwang Temple at Wuzhishan, Kaohsiung 高雄市五智山光明王寺之真言宗信仰研 究" (MA thesis, Huafan University, 2012); Li Yongbin 李永斌, "Master Wu Light Esoteric Ideological Research 悟光法师密教思想研究" (MA thesis, Northwest University, 2011); and Kao Hsi-chun 高璽鈞, Wu-Kuang's Journey of Religious Enlightenment and His Ultimate Choice (1918–1972) 釋悟光的宗教修學經歷與抉擇 (1918–1972) (MA thesis: National Sun Yat-sen University, 2017).
95. Gongga 貢噶, *Bai yunjian de chuanqi: Gongga laoren shan xiuxing ji* 白雲間的傳奇: 貢噶老人 雪山修行記 [A Legends from White Clouds: Records of Elder Gongga's Mountaintop Cultivation] (Taipei: Zheng fayan, 1993).
96. Wuguang, *Cangsang huiyilu*.
97. Chesheng, *Shengyi xinyao azi yi*.
98. Li, *Mizong xinyang yu xiuchi*.
99. Weili 惟勵, *Mijiao lilun yu shijian* 密教理論與實踐 [The Theory and Practice of Esoteric Buddhism] (Taipei: Jingyin chuban, 1995).
100. Chen Kuan, *Wode xuemi licheng*.

Cody R. Bahir

THERAVĀDA BUDDHISM

HISTORY OF THE TERM

The term *theravāda* first appears in the *Dīpavaṃsa*, a Sri Lankan Buddhist chronicle probably written in the later parts of the 4th century CE. In this text, *theravāda* is introduced as a synonym for *theriya*, the Pāli correlative of Sanskrit *sthavira* or *sthāviriya*. With these Sanskrit terms the Buddhist Sanskrit tradition of India denoted a specific lineage or group of lineages into which the Buddhist sangha ("monastic community") had subdivided during the first centuries.[1] The compound *theravāda* is exclusively attested in Sri Lankan literature and has no equivalent in Indian Buddhist literature. The corresponding Sanskrit term *sthaviravāda* is only attested in Sanskritized passages of later Sinhala literature from Sri Lanka.[2] In a different meaning the term *theravāda* occasionally appears in some Pāli commentaries, not to denote a specific "school tradition," but as a collective reference to exegetical views (*vāda*) of eminent masters, or elders, (*thera*) of the past.[3] From the *Dīpavaṃsa* onward the term *theravāda* is used by Sri Lankan historiographers as a synonym for *theriya nikāya, theranikāya,* and *theravaṃsa.* All these terms denote a *nikāya,* which these authors claim to embody the only lineage of the sangha transmitting the original teaching of the Buddha. The *theras* ("elders") whose legacy these terms refer to are the five hundred *arhats* who are believed to have codified the Buddha's words one year after his death. It must, however, be kept in mind that truthfulness to the master's teaching was claimed by *all* Buddhist *nikāyas.* Hence, the orthodoxy claim of the Theravādins has to be seen as a polemical statement within an ongoing "sectarian" controversy.

Mainland Indian Understandings of Sthavira. At least since the 2nd century CE Indian sources have reflected the plurality of juridical and exegetical traditions within the sangha as the result of a historical differentiation process. The history of the sangha was thereby reconstructed as a series of splits that produced several genealogically interrelated but institutionally autonomous and mutually exclusive lineages (*nikāya, kula,* or *samaya*). Due to the complex and partly contradictory nature of the sources, this differentiation process is not fully clear to us, neither historically nor with respect to the distinguishing criteria. Different sets of monastic precepts (*prātimokṣā*)—and the resultant impossibility of monks and nuns ordained in different *nikāyas* to perform *vinaya* rituals (*vinaya-karman*) together—constitute the formal and probably oldest criterion of *nikāya* division. But the earliest available sources also associate specific doctrinal and exegetical viewpoints with each lineage. A number of these sources, especially the early ones (e.g., *Samayabhedoparacanacakra* by Vasumitra, *Nikāyabhedavibhaṅga* by Bhāvya), report that an initial split in the sangha gave rise to two principal factions: the Sthavira Nikāya and the Mahāsāṃghika Nikāya. All other *nikāya* formations are, then, interpreted as subsequent spinoffs within one of these two main branches. Most lists give the number eighteen as the total amount of *nikāyas,* but the names and pedigrees differ. The occasion and reasons for the initial split also vary. Vasumitra (2nd cent. CE?) assigns the following eleven *nikāyas* to the Sthavira branch:[4]

1. Sarvāstivāda
2. Haimavata
3. Vātsīputrīya
4. Dharmottarīya
5. Bhadrāyanīya
6. Saṃmatīya
7. Channagirika
8. Mahīśāsaka
9. Dharmaguptaka
10. Kāśyapīya
11. Sautrāntika

The majority of these names are also known from other sources, including inscriptions in which specific monastic settlements identify their *nikāya* affiliation. Even in the early lists it is unclear whether the authors considered the "original" Sthaviras to still be extant as a separate group. Vasumitra mentions that the "original Sthaviras" (*pūrvasthavira*) had later changed their name into Haimavata.[5] So he seems to think that the Haimavata Nikāya more directly continued the tradition of the Sthaviras who had originated from the first split. Vasumitra does not refer to a separate *nikāya* in Sri Lanka or to their claim of continuing the original Sthavira lineage (see the section on "Sri Lankan Understandings of Theriya/Theravāda"). Bhavya (4th cent.) cites three different *nikāya* genealogies, apparently compiled from three older sources.[6] One of them, probably a Sarvāstivāda version, repeats Vasumitra's list. The second one, which is perhaps of Mahāsāṃghika origin, speaks of a threefold original split (Sthavira, Mahāsāṃghika, Vibhajyavāda) and informs us that the "Sthaviras come in two forms: the schools of the Sārvāstivādins and the Vātsīputrīya." Also here, the Sthaviras have no distinct life as a separate tradition, and they are not identified with the Haimavatas. The third list, which seems to be a Saṃmitīya account, likewise distinguishes between Haimavatas and the "original Sthaviras" (*pūrvasthavira*). *Pūrvasthavira* is not a separate lineage but an umbrella term for the Sarvāstivāda and the Vātsīputrīya *nikāyas*. Hence, it seems that for the early Indian doxographers the term *sthavira* was basically a superordinate category and a historical "parent" of some of the extant lineages of their times, rather than a self-referential name of a specific living *nikāya*.

By the 7th century the Sri Lankan tradition had succeeded in holding its ground, claiming that *their* group comprised "the" Sthaviras. In this period the idea of an initial split between Sthaviras and Mahāsāṅghikas was given up in favor of the notion of four equally ancient and legitimate root-*nikāyas* (*catur mahānikāya* or *āryanikāya*) from which the remaining groups developed. The *locus classicus* is Vinītadeva's *Samayabhedoparacanacakranikāyabhedopadarśan asaṃgraha* (8th cent.):[7]

1. Mahāsāṃghika
2. Sarvāstivāda
3. Sthavira
4. Saṃmatīya

In this list, the name *Sthavira* is reserved for the Sri Lankan lineage with its three sub-*nikāyas* (see the section on "History of the Sri Lankan Theriyas before the Reform"). Obviously, other *nikāyas* that were previously considered (or considered themselves) members of the Sthavira branch had given up that name as an identity marker. Vinītadeva distributes them between the Sarvāstivāda and Saṃmitīya branches, thus leaving the Sri Lankan lineages the only representatives of the Sthaviras. This fourfold list seems to de-emphasize the competition around the authenticity claims among the *nikāyas* by assigning an equal degree of genuineness and legitimacy to all four principal branches. This more diplomatic genealogy appears to have been widespread in India and ultimately entered Chinese and Tibetan literature. It was also known in Sri Lanka and seems to have been accepted by the generally more cosmopolitan Abhayagiri sub-*nikāya*. However, the authors of the Mahāvihāra sub-*nikāya*, with one exception, stuck to the more antagonizing twofold list, with the help of which this group's sole claim to authenticity could be formulated (see the section on "History of the Sri Lankan Theriyas before the Reform").[8]

As early as the first half of the 7th century, the Chinese pilgrim Xuanzang assigned each Buddhist monastery he visited in India to one of these four *nikāyas*. If his empirical observations and Vinītadeva's theoretical model are linked, it seems that by the 7th century the recognizable Sthavira monasteries of mainland India—which according to Xuanzang were predominantly located in South India—were considered institutions affiliated with one of the three monastic centers in Sri Lanka's capital, Anurādhapura.

Sri Lankan Understandings of Theriya/Theravāda. It is useful to set up some terminological conventions to illustrate the history and identity formation of the Sri Lankan traditions. Terms like *theravāda*, *theriya*, *sthavira*, and *sthaviravāda* are used as synonyms in Sri Lankan source material.[9] To facilitate this discussion, these are singled out and given a specific meaning to form a clear-cut nomenclature for analytical purposes:

- **Sthavira** is used for the monastic faction said to have arisen from the assumed first split in the sangha and as a collective category for the *nikāyas,* which are deemed to have emerged from the "original" Sthavira faction.
- **Indian proto-Theriya** denotes the historically obscure Indian tradition that transmitted the ordination tradition and the canonical material to Sri Lanka. This hypothetical lineage must have used *vinaya* and *abhidhamma* material different from other Sthavira lineages that ultimately developed into the known *Vinaya* and *Abhidhamma Piṭakas* of the Pāli Canon. It is possible that this lineage was already using some form of Pāli.
- **Sri Lankan proto-Theriya** refers to the Sri Lankan tradition *before* it started to promote itself under a distinct *nikāya* name.
- **Theriya (Nikāya)** represents the Sri Lankan tradition *after* it started to identify itself as a distinct *nikāya* named Theriya, Theravāda, or Theravaṃsa.
- **Theriya sub-*nikāyas*** denotes the three sublineages into which the Sri Lankan tradition had eventually split between the 1st century BCE and the 4th century CE. As there is no Pāli word for "sub-*nikāya*," their individual lineage names are given here as:
  - Mahāvihāra(-vāsin) Nikāya,
  - Abhayagiri(-vāsin) Nikāya,
  - Jetavana(-vāsin) Nikāya.
- **Theravāda Buddhism** (as a Pāli-English hybrid compound) is reserved for the modern discourse.

From the 4th century CE at the latest, the Sri Lankan traditions had started to proclaim themselves as the only true successors of the "original" Sthaviras and to propagate the view that only this lineage represented the teaching of the Buddha without any alterations. In this terminology, they claim the substantial identity of the following sequence:

1. the Buddha and his original teaching →
2. 500 Arhats of the 1st "council" (*saṅgīti*) →
3. original Sthaviras of the Sthavira/Mahāsāṅghika split →
4. Indian proto-Theriyas (according to tradition identical with the tradition of Moggalliputta Tissa of Pāṭalīputra →
5. Sri Lankan proto-Theriyas (according to tradition identical with the lineage founded by Mahinda Thera in Anurādhapura) →
6. Sri Lankan Theriyas (according to tradition there is no difference between 5 and 6)

   From the 5/6th century onward, Pāli texts would add

7. → Sri Lankan Mahāvihāravāsin Nikāya (according to the literature of this tradition there is no difference between 5, 6 and 7).

It must be highlighted that this genealogy is configured from a retrospective "sectarian" viewpoint of Sri Lankan authors. Virtually all items and links are historically questionable and have been challenged by other Buddhist traditions.[10] From this "sectarian" standpoint the *Dīpavaṃsa* (4th cent.) presents all other *nikāyas,* no matter whether subsumed under the Sthavira or Mahāsāṅghika branches, as "split-teachings" (*bhinnavāda*) that had distorted the Buddha's original message.[11] The Sri Lankan Theriyas were themselves split into three sub-*nikāyas*. It is likely that each of them claimed to continue the old Sthavira lineage exclusively for themselves and denied the validity of the claims of the other two. The Mahāvihāra Nikāya certainly formulated such a radically exclusivist self-image from the *Mahāvaṃsa* (5th–6th cent.) onward.[12] It is not known how the Abhayagiri and Jetavana Nikāyas regarded the matter because their literature has been lost. But we can be certain that they would, at least, not have agreed to point seven above (that is, that the Mahāvihāravāsins are the only true heirs of the Buddha's original teaching). More diplomatic articulations of Theriya identity show up occasionally. Hence, institutional claims to sole authenticity seem to have been challenged by more moderate camps, perhaps especially by those engaged in translocal Buddhist exchange or attempting to establish Sri Lanka as a cosmopolitan Buddhist center.[13]

During the first seven centuries of Buddhist history—this is almost the complete time before the *Dīpavaṃsa* was composed—Sri Lankan sources provide little evidence of any awareness of institutional diversities. Neither are local sub-*nikāyas* mentioned, nor is the rest of the Buddhist world presented as heterogeneous.[14] The first testimony of a Sri Lankan monastery positioning itself in the field of *nikāya* diversity is given in two inscriptions found in Nāgārjunikoṇḍa (Āndhra, central east India) dated to the mid-3rd century. Therein a monastic community from Sri Lanka identifies itself as: "the teachers who are Taṃbapaṇṇaka (Sri Lankan) Theriyas."[15] The inscription adds that they are Vibhajjavādins ("Analysts") and "dwellers of the Mahāvihāra" (*mahāvihāravāsin*). This testimony shows that the Sri Lankan tradition had by then started to associate itself with the Sthavira branch of the *nikāya* classification system. Any denial of authenticity for other *nikāyas* at least of the Sthavira branch was apparently not (yet?) implied. It also appears that this inscription understood Vibhajjavāda (Skt. *vibhajyavāda*) as a subgroup within the Sthavira branch, rather than a *nikāya* name in its own right as it appears in Bhavya's second list (see the section on "Mainland Indian Understandings of Sthavira"). Vibhajjavāda could have denoted an abstract class of those Sthavira-related *nikāyas* sharing a common "analyst" (*vibhajja*) approach to doctrinal exegesis.[16] The term *mahāvihāravāsin* in one of the inscriptions is identical to the unabbreviated *nikāya* name of the Sri Lankan Mahāvihāra(vāsin) Nikāya and indicates that the Sri Lankans represented their own tradition as split into sub-*nikāyas* by the 3rd century.[17]

The *Dīpavaṃsa* (4th cent.) contains the oldest known systematic account of the *nikāya* differentiation composed by Sri Lankan authors. Its genealogical scheme closely resembles the one by Vasumitra and might be directly or indirectly derived from it.[18] Based on this genealogy, the *Dīpavaṃsa* states that not only the Mahāsāṅghikas and their sublineages, but also the Sthavira-related *nikāyas* had adulterated the original dharma and *vinaya* of the Buddha. In other words, all *nikāyas* subsumed under the Sthavira-branch were interpreted as *breakaways* from the original Sthaviras. Yet, unlike Vasumitra, the compilers of the *Dīpavaṃsa* make it completely clear that the original Sthaviras still existed; they did not split *into* new lineages, but new lineages had split *from* them. With this logic the compilers of the *Dīpavaṃsa* unfold the idea that the tradition of the original Sthaviras remained untouched and intact throughout all separation processes and merely expanded geographically: During the time of the Indian king Aśoka their tradition had been brought to Sri Lanka where it still flourished. The *Dīpavaṃsa* is silent on any other remaining successors of the "original" Sthaviras in India or elsewhere, but insists that the eleven *nikāyas* of the Sthavira branch were breakaways and, therefore, not "real" Sthaviras—though some of them were widespread and masterminded much of the Buddhist scene in India and beyond. Finally, the *Dīpavaṃsa* states that the "real" Sthavira tradition expanded to several other countries, too, during the time of Aśoka.[19] However, the fate of those offshoots remains unclear as they are not mentioned again (see also the sections "International Relations before the Reform" and "The Story of the Third Council and the Lineage of Patriarchs).

The Sri Lankan concept of *theravāda* is essentially a polemic by which Sri Lankan Buddhist authors set themselves apart from the Buddhist *nikāyas* of India. Right from the start, the Sri Lankan interpretation of *nikāya* history is tightly connected to the notion of Sri Lanka as the "(island guided by) the light of the *dhamma*" (*dhammadīpa*), chosen by the Buddha himself to bear his "true" teaching, namely the tradition of the Theriyas.[20] This demarcation strategy is further developed in subsequent Pāli literature like the *Kathāvatthu-Atthakathā*, in which certain doctrinal viewpoints are defined as constitutive for the "real" Sthaviras. Several passages in the Pāli commentaries composed since the 5th century appear to indicate a less exclusivist understanding of the terms *theriya* and *theravāda*. Taken together they seem to allude to a more integrative concept of a Sthavira identity shared by several *nikāyas* in opposition to the *nikāyas* of the Mahāsāṃghika branch.[21]

In the 5th–6th-century chronicle *Mahāvaṃsa*, the term *Theravāda* is exclusively claimed for the author's own sub-*nikāya* of the Sri Lankan Theriyas. The *Mahāvaṃsa* is the first text referring to the disintegration of the Sri Lankan lineage into three sub-*nikāyas* even though it states that these splits had occurred several centuries in the past. The paucity of early sources—including the otherwise "*nikāya* aware" *Dīpavaṃsa*—leaves room for doubt as to when the rivalry between the Mahāvihāra, Abhayagiri, and Jetavana monasteries of the ancient Sri Lankan capital began and at what point they had started to view themselves as separate *nikāyas*. Certainly the author of the *Mahāvaṃsa* considers the other two *nikāyas* as renegade breakaways and denies that they are "true" Theriyas. Notwithstanding this polemical statement, there is no reason to doubt that the Abhayagirivāsins and the Jetavanavāsins considered themselves as legitimate representatives of the Theriya Nikāya.[22]

The *Mahāvaṃsa* also introduces a story significant for the modern (mis)understanding of the Theravāda concept in which a series of kings in the 4th century introduced a "heresy" (*adhamma*) from India, which had been strictly rejected by the Mahāvihāra Nikāya but widely accepted by the other two *nikāyas*.[23] In 1928, the Sri Lankan historian S. Paranavitana had, correctly or not, identified this "heresy" with Mahāyāna Buddhism.[24] This junction of arguments—the Mahāvihāra's sole claim to represent authentic "Theravāda" and Paranavitana's emphasis on this group's historical opposition against "Mahāyāna Buddhism"—is one of the keys to the modern model of Theravāda and Mahāyāna as two mutually exclusive variants of Buddhism.[25]

HISTORY OF THE SRI LANKAN THERIYAS BEFORE THE REFORM

If we assume that the multiple influences that doubtlessly shaped the early centuries of the Sri Lankan sangha and its canon were actually dominated by *one* more or less fixated tradition, it is still unclear which part of India this tradition originally came from; that is, where the Indian "proto-Theriyas" were situated. All we can say is that such a tradition must have used

Pāli as the language of a collection of authoritative texts that were similar (but surely not identical) to the collection called the Pāli Canon today. Decisive are the *Vinaya* and *Abhidhamma/ Abhidharma Piṭakas,* which incorporate the most *nikāya*-specific contents of early Buddhist literature. So far, no traces of an Indian lineage transmitting a canon with these characteristics have been found. Even for the language called Pāli today, testimonies are very rare on Indian soil.[26]

Based on lost older sources, the *Dīpavaṃsa* narrates a story about the Indian king Aśoka (3rd cent. BCE) during whose regency a number of Buddhist missionaries were sent to different parts of the known world.[27] According to this legend, the monk Mahinda, allegedly Aśoka's own son, was sent to Sri Lanka and converted the whole kingdom in the course of a few days.[28] This story would point to Pāṭaliputra, Aśoka's capital in the Magadha district in northeastern India, as the origin of the tradition. Scholars have doubted the historicity of this story for a number of reasons and tried to localize the origins of the Sri Lankan tradition in different parts of India, such as the Central Indian Vidiśa or Vanavāsa (modern Karnataka).[29] Some scholars have tried to identify or at least suggest a close relationship of the Sri Lankan Theriyas with some of the known Indian *nikāyas,* most prominently the Mahīśāsakas and other groups who promoted the idea that the Buddha's original teaching was a *vibhajyavāda* ("analyst viewpoint").[30] It is, of course, possible—indeed likely—that some of the Sthavira-derived *nikāyas* listed by Vasumitra and others go back to the same ancestor lineage as the Sri Lankan Theriyas (i.e., to what we have called "Indian proto-Theriyas"). If this is true, these lineages would probably have possessed *Vinaya* and *Abhidhamma Piṭakas* similar (but almost certainly not identical) to the ones known from the Pāli Canon. However, it must be borne in mind that historical relatedness can be very different from historical identity discourses. Although some of these *nikāyas* may have been close sister lineages from a historical viewpoint, the Sri Lankan Theriyas have rhetorically distanced themselves from all of them at least from the time of the *Dīpavaṃsa* and have denied that these lineages are as authentic as their own.

That Buddhism found footing in Sri Lanka roughly during the time of the Indian emperor Aśoka is commonly accepted, even if the quick island-wide conversion act depicted in the Mahinda story is doubtful and was challenged by a picture of a more gradual diffusion of Buddhism through the various principalities into which Sri Lanka was divided in this period.[31] The establishment of a unified kingdom in the 2nd century BCE seems to have had a centralizing effect on Buddhism on the island. The major monastic estates of the capital Anurādhapura, lavishly supported and extended by generations of kings, started to view themselves as the centers of Sri Lankan Buddhist learning and custodians of the tradition. An antagonism between the Mahāvihāra and the Abhayagiri, the two largest monasteries, may have set in early (according to the *Mahāvaṃsa* as early as the 1st cent. BCE).[32] This competition may have been one factor that led the Mahāvihāra tradition to "close" the canon of what its leadership regarded to be authentic buddha-word.[33] We do not know exactly when the closure of this so-called Pāli Canon occurred. Most scholars believe that the canonical collection of the Mahāvihāra Nikāya did not change very much after it was first written down—an event dated to the 1st century BCE by the *Mahāvaṃsa.*[34] The inventory of the canon seems to have been fluid to a certain degree before that time. What we know is that the canonical collection became contested in the 4th century CE when a stock of formerly unknown texts from India were promoted as authentic buddha-word in Sri Lanka.[35] There is good reason to assume that these newly introduced texts belonged to the literary stream that later would be termed

Mahāyāna literature. The *Mahāvaṃsa* has it that the monks of the Mahāvihāra vigorously rejected their authenticity, whereas the monks of the Abhayagiri—and later the Jetavana—adopted and worshiped them.[36]

The dispute about the authenticity of Mahāyāna literature and practice seems to have deepened the rivalries among the Sri Lankan sub-*nikāyas*. From the 7th century onward Sri Lanka became an internationally renowned center for Mahāyāna and esoteric (tantric) Buddhism and seems to have played a central role for the establishment of the esoteric Zhenyan school 真言 in China.[37] Many archaeological remains of Mahāyāna and tantric practice dating to this period (statues, *dhāraṇī* inscriptions, manuscript pages of Mahāyāna sutras, epigraphical eulogies to Avalokiteśvara, etc.) have been found scattered all over the island. It is possible that the Abhayagiri and Jetavana traditions had been key for the spread of Mahāyāna in Sri Lanka. But this does not necessarily mean that the Mahāvihāra and their large island-wide network of lineage-affiliated monasteries had forever and in its totality resisted any Mahāyāna and tantric influence, as later "neo-orthodox" texts like the *Nikāyasaṅgraha* would claim.[38] Regardless of the extent of their doctrinal and practical differences, antagonisms among the sublineages characterized Sri Lankan religious history until the Abhayagiri and Jetavana Nikāyas became institutionally extinct in the 12th century and were swallowed by the Mahāvihāra lineage. Apart from citations and a few disputed works attributed to the Abhayagiri, their literature was lost after that time.[39] Rivalries among the sub-*nikāyas* were not confined to the religious field, but included the competition for political influence and economical resources. The administrative responsibility for monuments connected to the Sri Lankan Buddhist cultural memory (e.g., Mihintale, Thūpārāma, bodhi tree), as well as the discursive control over history writing and identity politics, seem to have been special battlegrounds of these "intersectarian" conflicts. In the period of continuous warfare between Sri Lanka and the South Indian Coḷas since the 10th century, these tensions seem to have weakened over time.

In favor of a simplified Theravāda versus Mahāyāna opposition, it is often forgotten that the Abhayagiri and Jetavana Nikāyas were "sub-sects of Theravāda" (as Bechert puts it).[40] These two sadly lost sub-*nikāyas* likely regarded themselves as true representatives of the lineage brought to Sri Lanka by Mahinda. Archaeological remains prove that they practiced a Mahinda cult with regular commemorative Mahinda festivals. Furthermore, all three together were deemed by Indian doxographers as constituting "the" Theriyas (Sthaviras). In modern literature, however, Theravāda is predominantly used as a synonym for "Hīnayāna," in silent continuation of the Mahāvihāra Nikāya's alleged Hīnayāna-purism (see the section "From Theriya Nikāya to Theravāda Buddhism " on the emergence of this anachronism). In most of the premodern literature this connection was unknown. The words *sthavira, theriya,* and *theravāda* were commonly understood as a family relationship among monastic communities, not as a doctrinal or soteriological orientation. It is only some texts emerging from the Mahāvihāra lineage that promote a conceptual nexus between "true" Theriyas and a rejection of non-Pāli–based teachings. At least in the case of the Abhayagiri and Jetavana Nikāyas, it is highly likely that monks following a Pāli-based Śrāvakayāna orientation were living together in the same monasteries with monks who had taken the bodhisattva vow and worshiped Mahāyāna sutras—both of them were ordained in the same Theriya-sublineage. The Chinese pilgrim Xuanzang was using the compound *mahāyāna-sthaviras* to describe monks of the latter type. On this background, a statement like "Theravāda is a Śrāvakayāna-only tradition, restricted to the Pāli Canon and accepting only one *buddha* and only one *bodhisattva*" must have sounded counterfactual, even absurd in 7th- through 9th-century Sri Lanka, although such an idea may well have been propagated as a normative statement by certain hardliners (who could perhaps be found in all three sublineages). Nevertheless, modern scholars have tended to use the term *Theravāda* as a doxographic (rather than institutional) category, limiting the term to the Mahāvihāra's vision of "Buddhist orthodoxy" as formulated in the majority of extant literary products of this lineage. This static doctrinal concept of Theravāda is generally considered the conceptional opposite of the likewise rather clear-cut and static idea of Mahāyāna.[41] To confuse the picture even more, this idealized opposition pair is widely used by scholars to describe the religious history of Sri Lanka (and, in extension, Buddhist history in general), classifying the Abhayagiri and Jetavana lineages as partly or fully "non-Theravāda" and "heterodox."[42]

INTERNATIONAL RELATIONS BEFORE THE REFORM

The Sri Lankan Theriyas—probably of all three sublineages—kept close contact to other Buddhist *nikāyas* in the Indian mainland in whose religious discourses they were involved but from which they also strictly demarcated themselves (although we can be sure in this latter matter only for the Mahāvihāra sublineage). During the first millennium CE, Sri Lanka's connections with South India seem to have been particularly strong, but their presence in Buddhist strongholds of northeast India like Bodhgayā and Nālandā is also evidenced.[43] Further direct and indirect contacts to important Buddhist centers in other parts of India (e.g., Sāñchī, Gandhāra) are likely. Occasionally, Theriya literature—probably of Abhayagiri provenance—has been cited in mainland-Indian Buddhist Sanskrit texts.[44] In the second half of the first millennium CE, international religious contacts included China, Java, and probably mainland Southeast Asia.[45] A 9th-century manuscript of the Pāli *vinaya* was discovered in Nepal, perhaps a testimony of Sri Lankan missionary activities in the northeastern parts of the Indian subcontinent.[46] The influence of a Theravāda monk on Tibetan Buddhist literature in the 13th century seems to have been a singular occasion.[47] Some of these international relations might have been dominated by individual sublineages. At least the connection to Java can be traced only to the Abhayagiri sub-Nikāya.

It is debated whether or not independent Theriya communities existed in countries other than Sri Lanka, and whether and up to what time the Sri Lankans were aware of them and maintained contact with them. Due to the limited material remains of early Buddhist India, this question cannot be answered beyond doubt.

Autonomous Theriya communities have obviously existed in some Dravidian-speaking areas of South India. These hosted several respected Buddhist scholars who produced a number of Pāli commentaries after the 5th century that were incorporated into the literary inventory of the Sri Lankan Mahāvihāra sublineage. Thus, they seem to have been closely interconnected to the monasteries of Anurādhapura, and it is likely that their lineage origins ultimately go back to Sri Lanka.[48] The same might be true for Theriya communities that seem to have existed in Āndhra around the middle of the 1st millennium CE. At least we know from inscriptions that Sri Lankan Theriyas were active in regions of Āndhra in the 3rd century.[49] It is, however, also possible the other way round, that is, the proto-Theriyas were present in Āndhra and Tamil

Nadu before they diffused into Sri Lanka where they ultimately formed the self-conscious Theriya Nikāya through a long history of South Indian–Sri Lankan entanglement. This theory might provide an explanation for the odd fact that the Sri Lankans had never translated the canonical Pāli texts into Sinhala but used Pāli as their liturgical language: A Dravidian origin of the Sri Lankan lineage would imply that the island had received the Pāli texts from speakers of a non-Indo-European language, who might already have treated the Pāli—a North Indian idiom not easily translated into South Indian languages—as a sacrosanct medium.[50]

Theriya communities can also be traced in the Pyu kingdom of Śrīkṣetra in Lower Burma and in the Mon dominion of Dvāravatī in Thailand between the 5th and 8th centuries (see the section "Early Theriyas among the Pyu and Mon").

REFORM OF PARĀKRAMABĀHU I

After a long history of religious, political, and economic competition, the three sub-*nikāyas* of the Sri Lankan Theriya lineage were finally reunited by a so-called *sāsana*-reform enforced by king Parākramabāhu I (1153–1186). It is not completely clear what precisely this act had effected. It seems, per *Cūḷavaṃsa* and *Nikāyasaṃgraha,* that the king had empowered the leaders of a certain community of forest-dwelling monks of the Mahāvihāra Nikāya to "purify" all three sublineages (i.e., to exclude those monks they deemed unworthy) and to force all the remaining monks of the Abhayagiri and Jetavana lineages to be reordained under the Mahāvihāra *vinaya.*[51] A unified hierarchy of monastic administration and leadership headed by a *saṅgharāja* ("king/head of the order") was probably established right after the unification act. Some scholars emphasize that the reform had primarily juridical and administrative effects but did not change the doctrinal divergence among the formerly separate groups. This might explain the persistence of Mahāyāna tendencies in later Theriya literature. However, the reordination of their members is tantamount to the loss of the institutional autonomy of the Abhayagiri and Jetavana Nikāyas, which ceased to exist as separate entities. From this moment onward, the Theriya/Theravāda tradition was de facto represented only by members of the Mahāvihāra lineage.[52] Obviously this unification act was effectuated by a "conservative" camp of the Sri Lankan sangha embodied in a group of ascetic hardliners belonging to the Mahāvihāra Nikāya. In the following centuries the sangha leadership (*kāraka-saṅgha*) was spearheaded by *saṅgharājas* belonging to the rigorous forest-dwelling fraternities, who executed further *sāsana*-reforms frequently. Binding guidelines (*katikāvata*) for monastic practice, etiquette, and education were issued, their transgression threatened with punishment by state power.[53] At least in the long run, this strict hierarchical control of the sangha was certainly a factor for the broad implementation of a Mahāvihāra vision of a pure Pāli-based Śrāvakayāna-only "orthodoxy," which some authors of this *nikāya* had demanded for centuries. The famous Abhayagiri libraries whose wealth of Mahāyāna and Tantric literature had formerly attracted pilgrims from all over the Buddhist world, have almost completely vanished. Mahāyāna Buddhas and Bodhisattvas were transformed into protector deities acceptable within a Śrāvakayāna pantheon.[54] Albeit traces of Mahāyāna influence can still be found in later Buddhist literature in Sinhala and Pāli, the Buddhist authors of post-12th-century Sri Lanka are largely oriented toward the authority of the canonical Pāli literature, the classical Mahāvihāra commentators like Buddhaghosa (5th cent.), and Dhammapāla (7th cent.).

Parākramabāhu's reform was preceded by an earlier sangha purification under the rule of King Vijayabāhu (1055–1110), apparently performed with the help of monks from Burma. The sources for this incident are problematic and difficult to judge. But perhaps this earlier "reboot" of the Sri Lankan sangha had already leveled some of the tensions among the sub-*nikāyas*. After Parākramabāhu's reform the connections with Southeast Asia intensified and the "neo-orthodox" approach of the post-Parākramabāhu Mahāvihārins gained a footing in Burma, Thailand, and Cambodia.

THE THERIYAS OF SOUTHEAST ASIA

Early Theriyas among the Pyu and Mon. Starting with the 12th century, the religious links among Sri Lankans, Burmese, Thais, and Khmer are well documented. A possible earlier history of the Theriya Nikāya in Southeast Asia is, however, obscure.

A number of Pāli inscriptions were found in Lower Burma and Thailand between the 5th and 8th centuries. They were set up by the Pyu people of the Śrīkṣetra kingdom (Burma) and the Mon people who reigned in the kingdom of Dvāravatī (Thailand). Some of these inscriptions clearly refer to dogmatic material otherwise only known from Sri Lankan canonical and postcanonical literature.[55] While a multiplicity of Buddhist traditions left their traces in early Burma and Thailand, a Pāli-using community with resemblances to the Sri Lankan Theriyas was obviously among them. It is not clear whether this material is linked with Sri Lanka or South India, or possibly both. Comparison of further architectural and art-historical evidence points to a well-established exchange triangle connecting Āndhra, Sri Lanka, and Southeast Asia from at least the 4th century onward.[56] Some scholars keep the possibility open that these early Theriya activities in Southeast Asia go back to a Sri Lanka-unrelated Indian Theriya culture, the exact location and extent of which have not yet been discovered.[57] This problem largely overlaps with the unclear whereabouts of the "Indian proto-Theriyas"—the hypothetical Indian lineage that brought Buddhism to Sri Lanka in the first place, and perhaps to other regions where their traditions still might have existed for several centuries.

The early Pāli-using Buddhist communities in Southeast Asia (a) were directly related to the Sri Lankan Theriyas, (b) were indirectly affiliated with them and mediated through their South Indian settlements, or (c) represented a Sri Lanka–independent offshoot of the Indian proto-Theriyas. In any case, a Theriya or Theriya-like tradition of the Buddhist sangha yielded an important, perhaps partly dominant, influence among the Pyu and Mon. Thus, when fresh Sri Lankan influxes entered Southeast Asia in the form of "neo-orthodox" Mahāvihāra monks of the post-Parākramabāhu period, much of the intellectual, liturgical, and ritual commodities in their luggage may already have been familiar to the societies of Myanmar and Thailand, even if these regions were meanwhile dominated by new ethnic groups who had succeeded and partly assimilated the old Pyu and Mon cultures.

Expansion of the Neo-Orthodox Mahāvihāra Saṅgha into Southeast Asia. From the 11th to 13th centuries the Bamar (Burmese) and Thai formed kingdoms in Southeast Asia that ultimately developed into modern-day Myanmar and Thailand. Much of the premodern religious history of these quickly shifting dominions is characterized by tensions between the continuity of older Theriya lineages inherited from the Pyu and Mon cultures and fresh influxes from Sri Lanka. The "neo-orthodox" verve of the Sri Lankan post-Parākramabāhu Mahāvihāra seems to have attracted the Burmese and Thai aristocracy. Kings sought to increase their control over the religious institutions in their realms by repeated reformation acts that implemented Sri Lanka–style "neo-orthodox" lineages challenging the old, established religious traditions that were in place. The relative success of the Sri Lanka–oriented lineages soon encompassed the Khmer cultures further east in the territory of modern Cambodia. The religious mixture of divergent forms of Buddhism, Brahmanism, and autochthonous religions, which in principle characterizes Myanmar, Thailand, Laos, and Cambodia up to the present day, included the coexistence of "reformed" and "unreformed" Theriya lineages. The latter dissociated themselves from the newly established "Sīhaḷa Nikāya" (Sri Lankan lineage), emphasizing the long history of Pāli-based Buddhism in the region.

Myanmar (Burma): Was There a Theriya Lineage in Myanmar from the Time of Aśoka? In 1479 King Dhammazedi of the Mon kingdom Rāmañña in Lower Burma issued the well-known Kalyāni inscriptions that identify his kingdom as the ancient Suvaṇṇabhūmi, where two Buddhist missionaries, Soṇa and Uttara, had allegedly been sent in the 3rd century BCE when Aśoka reigned in India (see also the section "The Story of the Third Council and the Lineage of Patriarchs").[58] The inscription claims that Buddhism—which, even if not explicitly named, implicitly means the Theriya lineage—had been present in the Mon kingdom of Lower Burma ever since. A later source (*Mahayazawingyi*, 18th cent.) states that this Buddhist tradition of the ancient Mon kingdom was transplanted to Upper Burma in the 11th century after the Bamar (Burmese) built the first Burmese empire around the city of Pagan. King Aniruddha (Anawrahta) of Pagan was converted by the monk Shin Arahan from Lower Burma. Aniruddha invaded Thaton, the capital of the Mon kingdom, and captured a copy of the Pāli canon by force. Henceforth, the ancient Mon tradition of Buddhism (i.e., Theriya) was the main religion of the Pagan empire, replacing the Buddhism of the mysterious "Ari" (perhaps *tantrikas* or forest-dwelling monks) prevalent in Pagan before.

This narrative nexus has widely informed modern scholarship on Burmese religious history: Pagan, one of the predecessors of modern Myanmar, acquired the Theriya tradition from an ancient Mon culture, which itself had been converted in the time of Aśoka. The story renders the Buddhists of early Burma—and, thereby, the roots of the "unreformed" *nikāyas* of later times—a parallel "sister lineage" to the Sri Lankan Theriyas (in our nomenclature, an independent child of the "Indian proto-Theriyas"). However, this information is based on rather late imaginations of the past and is dependent on Sri Lankan sources that had been imported in the course of the continuous influence of post-Parākramabāhu Mahāvihāra monks during the Pagan period. Actually, there is no evidence of Buddhism in Burma before the 4th century CE. Thereafter it was practiced in several varieties along with Brahmanism and autochthonous religions by the Pyu (see the section "Early Theriyas among the Pyu and Mon") and further east by the Mon in the northern territory of modern Thailand. The claim that Burma was converted to Buddhism in the time of Aśoka is as late as the 15th century, when Dhammazedi adapted the story of Soṇa and Uttara almost verbatim from the *Mahāvaṃsa* and interpreted Lower Burma as the target country of their missionary activity. Aung-Thwin has denied the existence of an early Mon kingdom in Lower Burma and argues that the Pāli-based Buddhism in early Pagan was a direct heritage of the Pyu culture, which the Burmese had gradually swallowed from the 9th century.[59] Similarly Assavavirulhakarn argues that "Theravāda" (i.e., the Theriya tradition in our terms) in Southeast Asia was neither as old as the story Soṇa and Uttara suggests, nor was it first introduced when the Pagan emperors encouraged the establishment of a Sri Lanka–oriented "Sīhaḷa Nikāya" in the late 12th century. Rather, the establishment of a Sri Lanka–affiliated *nikāya* in Pagan represents an attempt to purify a Theriya lineage that has been present in Southeast Asia since the heydays of Śrīkṣetra and Dvāravatī after the 5th century.[60]

Sri Lankan "Neo-Orthodox" Influence in Myanmar. The Sīhaḷa Nikāya was founded in Pagan when Burmese monks returned home from Sri Lanka in 1190 and established a new order, modeled after the Sri Lankan Mahāvihāra lineage, recently reformed by Parākramabāhu I. It did not replace other Buddhist traditions, but established itself as a major force within a plurality of Buddhist communities, among others: the older Theriya lineages—whether they were inherited from the Pyu or "robbed" from the Mon. During the following centuries fresh lineages from Sri Lanka were reintroduced several times in the kingdoms succeeding Pagan after its breakdown in the late 13th century. These were partly connected to efforts of kings to purify and unify the sangha in their realms, as discussed earlier. A major step toward the dominance of Sri Lankan–style Theriya traditions in Burma was achieved in 1476 when King Dhammazedi had all monks in his Mon kingdom in Lower Burma reordained into a monastic lineage obtained from a place near the Kalyāṇi river (southwestern Sri Lanka). The event is commemorated in Kalyāṇi inscriptions (named after the Sri Lankan river; see the section "Myanmar (Burma): Was There a Theriya Lineage in Myanmar from the Time of Aśoka?").

Thailand and Cambodia. While the Sīhaḷa Nikāya of Pagan rose in prestige and started to spread across Southeast Asia, the Thai broke away from the Khmer empire of Angkor and founded the independent kingdom of Sukhotai in northern Thailand (1279). Similar to Burma, Sukhotai and its successor, the kingdom of Ayutthaya, were practicing multiple religious traditions, including the Brahmanist and Mahāyāna cultures spread among the Khmer and apparently the Pāli-based Theriya tradition that was already part of the religious mix in the old Mon civilization of Dvāravatī (see the section "Early Theriyas among the Pyu and Mon"). The so-called Yogāvacara meditation practices—sometimes called "Tantric Theravāda"—still extant in modern Thai Buddhism might be an amalgamate going back to this mixture.[61] An inscription of 1287 by king Rāma Khamhaeng (1279–1298) shows that monks of the "Sri Lanka lineage" (*laṅkāvaṃsa*) were already present in the early years of Sukhotai. Fresh Sri Lankan communities gained influence over the older lineages during the 14th and 16th centuries. Also, in the Angkhor empire Sri Lankan–style Theriyas had been increasingly preferred by the kings since Jayavarman VII (1181–1220) over the earlier mixture of Brahmanism and Mahāyāna traditions.

Sīhaḷa versus non-Sīhaḷa nikāyas. As in the case of the monastic lineage(s) behind the Pāli inscriptions found on the old Pyu and Mon territories, scholars are reluctant to settle for linear explanations of the textual and practical repertoire of the older Burmese and Thai Buddhist traditions who rivaled the freshly imported Sīhaḷa lineages in the 11th to 13th centuries. The inherited Pāli material sets them up in the proximity of the Theriya lineage as known from Sri Lanka and might well go back to the early intercultural contacts between the Mon, Pyu, and Sinhalese. Concrete proof is lacking, which seems to be why most scholars address these forms of Buddhism in Southeast Asia in rather vague terms like a generic "Pāli Buddhism" or "some form of Theravāda."

There is good reason not to overemphasize the agency of Sri Lankans in early and even later Southeast Asian cultures. Even if the influence of the "neo-orthodox" strand of the post-Parākramabāhu Mahāvihāra Nikāya set lasting and increasingly dominant marks in the Buddhist environments of Burma, Thailand, Laos, and Cambodia from the late 12th century onward, the authority of those "Sīhala" factions sharing its lineage pedigree and purist Śrāvakayāna vision remained limited. In addition, especially Burma and Thailand developed into centers of (this vision of) a "Theriya orthodoxy" in their own right, equaling and periodically surpassing the Sri Lankan sangha with respect to scholarship and institutional integrity. Many ancient texts—and even the lineage of higher monastic ordination—would have been lost, especially during the periods of decay of Sri Lankan Buddhism under colonial rule (but also before), if they had not been reintroduced from Burma and Thailand repeatedly. Also, the so-called fifth and sixth "Buddhist Councils" that were important to pave the way of "Theravāda Buddhism" into modernity were convened in Burma, not Sri Lanka.

With regard to early Theriya activities among the Pyu and Mon, cultural contacts between Sri Lanka and Southeast Asia before the 11th century cannot be confirmed from the Sri Lankan side. Although, judged from archaeological material in Śrīkṣetra and Dvāravatī, such interactions are very likely, they did not leave any traces in the extant historiographical sources written in Sri Lanka. It is an informed speculation that this is due to the loss of the literary treasures of the Abhayagiri Nikāya that may have dominated these contacts.[62] Furthermore, that the new lineages introduced to Burma and Thailand in and after the 12th century were collectively called "Sīhaḷa" seems to indicate that their local opponents did emphatically *not* associate themselves with anything Sinhalese or Sri Lankan.[63] Even if it were true that their traditions emerged from direct or indirect historical relationships with Sri Lanka, this connection was forgotten and the emphasis of local roots and founding stories narrating an independent spread of Buddhism from India to Southeast Asia (Buddha visits, Soṇa and Uttara, Upagupta) governed their identity constructions. The terms *theriya* or *theravāda* played no role as identity markers—but this is true also for the "Sīhaḷa" lineages.[64] These terms were even rare in Sri Lanka itself before the 19th century (see the section "From Theriya Nikāya to Theravāda Buddhism").

DISTINCTIVE FEATURES OF THE THERIYA LINEAGE

Talking about "Theravāda Buddhism" in premodern history implies the presumption of a set of religious features (practices, customs, worldviews, attitudes, perspectives, sentiments, etc.) shaping the totality of "Theravāda culture." In assertion of such features, Collins identified a relatively stable "mental universe created by and within Pali texts" that he called "the Pāli imaginaire."[65] Skilling has, however, contradicted this idea and denied any exceptional degree of stability in Theravāda traditions, rather highlighting their flexibility and openness for change and invention.[66] Indeed, "Theravāda Buddhism"—if we understand this term as a religio-cultural complex rather than a juridically constituted network of ritually compatible monastic institutions—emerged from multiple social and historical contexts and did not cease to transform itself and to develop multiple faces scattered across its different local and temporal embodiments. The previous presentation of Theriya history should have made clear that even the widely assumed purist Śrāvakayāna ("Hīnayāna") orientation of "Theravāda" was rather a vision of particular groups—and especially of essentialist projections of modern religious (and scholarly) interpreters—than a historical reality.

From the narrower perspective of monastic *nikāya* identity, we find recurring key references around which formulations of a Theriya lineage-identity have condensed through the ages.

1. A collection of authoritative literature, commonly known as the "Pāli Canon," which includes the *vinaya* codex, constitutive for the ritual compatibility of monks and nuns of the Theriya Nikāya, and a specific *Abhidhamma Piṭaka*;
2. a succession of patriarchs reaching from the buddha to Moggaliputta Tissa (the alleged head of the so-called Third Council); and
3. the use of Pāli as liturgical and (partly) scholarly and poetic language.

The Pāli Canon. Like the other Buddhist *nikāyas*, the Theriya lineage distinguishes three divisions or "baskets" (Pāli *tipiṭaka*) of what they believe to be authentic "buddha word":

1. *Vinaya Piṭaka*: the basket of disciplinary norms of the sangha;
2. *Sutta Piṭaka*: the basket of discourses of the buddha (and some of his disciples);
3. *Abhidhamma Piṭaka*: the basket of systematic analyses of certain doctrinal topics.

Apart from being transmitted in a peculiar language—the partly artificial Middle-Indic dialect today known as Pāli—the canon of the Theriyas has certain specialties in terms of arrangement and content that set it apart from the canonical collections of other *nikāyas*. The existence of *nikāya*-specific versions of the canon has also been known to historical authors and served as a cornerstone of inter-*nikāya* polemics. Nevertheless, these differences must not be overestimated. Especially for the *suttas* (sutras), the comparison between the Pāli versions and parallel versions of other *nikāyas*—so far still available—show close similarities.

While all Buddhist lineages seem to have known four subgroups to the Sutta-Piṭaka (*Dīghanikāya*, *Majjhimanikāya*, *Saṃyuttanikāya*, and *Aṅguttaranikāya*), the Theriyas belonged to those lineages that accepted an additional fifth group—the *Khuddakanikāya*, or "Group of Small Texts." The *Khuddakanikāya* is a "varia" collection grouping together a number of texts of different genres, like the well-known *Jātakas* ("Rebirth Stories") and the *Dhammapada*. Only some of the other known lineages had a *Khuddakanikāya* (or *Kṣudrakāgama* in Sanskrit), but their contents vary, and other lineages in part transmitted parallels to the works in the Pāli *Khuddakanikāya* as stand-alone texts.[67] Generally there seems to be more variance with respect to *vinaya* and *abhidhamma* literature among the *nikāyas*.

The *Vinaya Piṭaka* is centered around the *pātimokkha*, a list of monastic rules, to which the rest of the voluminous *Vinaya Piṭaka* functions as commentary and narrativization. The Pāli (i.e., Theriya) version of the *pātimokkha* comprises 227 rules for monks and 311 rules for nuns. Ordination and the organization of monastic life on the basis of these 227/311 rules is constitutive for the integrity of the Theriya lineage. The *vinayas* of other lineages, as far as still available, have similar but not identical *pātimokkha* lists.[68] The Sarvāstivāda *vinaya*, for example, lists 263 rules for monks, the one of the Mahāsāṃghikas only 218. Monks and nuns of different lineages are, therefore, not ritually compatible and cannot participate in each others' *vinaya* acts (such as ordination ceremonies, confession rituals, etc.). In the broad outline the surviving *vinayas* of different *nikāyas* share many structural and material features that may go back to either a common ancestor predating the *nikāya* division or to mutual borrowing and leveling among the different lineages. Nevertheless, as the vast bulk of literature included in the *Vinaya Piṭakas* was developed over several centuries in their *nikāya*-specific contexts, they also differ in several respects. Comparative research on *vinaya* literature has increasingly challenged the earlier assumption that the Pāli *vinaya* was generally the most archaic version available.[69]

The seven books of the Pāli *Abhidhamma Piṭaka* are unknown from other traditions. However, doctrinal matrices shared with *abhidharma* literature of other *nikāyas* can be detected in some cases.[70] It is possible that some of those ancient *nikāyas*, of which only their names are known to us, possessed an *Abhidharma Piṭaka* similar to the one known from the Theriya lineage. According to the Theriyas, the *Abhidhamma Piṭaka* was preached by the Buddha himself. This was not accepted by all *nikāyas*; the Sarvāstivādins, for example, assigned the books in their *abhidharma* collection to individual authors.

At least since the composition of the *Dīpavaṃsa* the Theriyas have expressed their conviction to possess the only authentic transmission of the Buddha Word, even if the knowledge of the exact differences in parallel collections seem rather vague. Modern comparative research cannot confirm that the Pāli Canon in total is generally of greater antiquity (not to speak of higher authenticity) than the canons of other *nikāyas*.[71] Due to the extinction of the Abhayagiri and Jetavana Nikāyas, only the Mahāvihāra recension of the canonical literature survived. It is this version of the Theriya canon that is called the "Pāli Canon" today.

Is the Pāli Canon a "canon" at all? Canonization is always an act of censorship.[72] A canon defines a selection of authoritative works and thereby implies an exclusion of something "other," something "noncanonical" (either in the sense of "less valuable" or straightforwardly "wrong"). According to the Mahāvihāra sub-*nikāya*, the Pāli Canon, as transmitted by their lineage, is the *complete* buddha word, and, according to the *Nikāyasaṃgraha*, contains every single word uttered by the buddha between his enlightenment and his death.[73] The question of canonical status becomes more complicated for the Abhayagiri and Jetavana sub-*nikāyas*, which most probably transmitted, studied, and recited the same Pāli texts (only perhaps in slightly different recensions).[74] However, they also accepted certain Mahāyāna and tantric texts to be authentic Buddha Word. So it seems that the Pāli Canon was a canon in the full sense of the concept only for the Mahāvihāra lineage, while for the other sub-*nikāyas* it was only a part of the totality of buddha word, ready to be supplemented when additional texts surface. Some scholars speak of an "open canon" in such cases. Collins argued that the Mahāvihāra's act of "canonical closure" (i.e., the declaration of the completeness of the Pāli Canon) was a reaction to their growing tensions with the Abhayagiri tradition.[75]

Perhaps the early Theriyas in the multireligious environment of 5th- to 8th-century Southeast Asia followed a similar "open" approach to define the buddha word as the Abhayagiri and Jetavana Nikāyas in Sri Lanka did.

Another issue is the social function of the Pāli Canon as a focus of religious authority. Unlike modern notions of a canon might suggest, the Pāli Canon was hardly a direct source or point of reference for the Buddhist laity before the late 19th century when it was gradually made accessible in printed translations into vernacular languages and English. Even for specialists (i.e., Pāli-reading monks), it functioned as a formal point of reference rather than as a practical guideline of religious belief and practice. As Collins puts it: "only parts of the canonical collection have ever been in wide currency, and . . . other texts have been known and used, sometimes much more widely."[76] It makes sense to follow Collins's distinction of a "formal" and a "practical canon." The *canonical totality* of the Pāli Canon is a "formal" idea rather than a repertoire of equally important textual sources of social knowledge and values. The "practical canon"—the texts actually used for monastic education, recitation, and preaching—could contain selections of canonical material but also other sources. An example for the latter are the above-mentioned *katikāvatas* (cf., the section "Reform of Parākramabāhu I"); short, royal-enforced prescriptions of monastic behavior in Sinhalese vernacular that from the 12th century onward had to be learned and observed by Sri Lankan monks (rather than the vast and difficult-to-access Pāli texts of the *Vinaya Piṭaka*). From around the same time, vernacular story collections, so-called preaching books (*baṇa-pot*), were used as the paramount media to fashion religious subjects and to shape religious communities.[77]

The Story of the Third Council and the Lineage of Patriarchs. In all forms of Buddhism, lineages play important roles of institutional self-ascertainment and historical identity-building. Of special importance are successions of special masters who are entrusted with the custody of a certain aspect of Buddhist transmission or of the integrity of the sangha as a whole. For the Theriya Nikāya, the succession of *vinaya* patriarchs (*vinayapāmokkha*) has been of vital historical importance. This succession starts with Upāli who, according to tradition, was appointed as the first chief of the *vinaya* by Mahā-Kassapa, the disciple of the Buddha who presided over the first *saṅgīti* one year after the Buddha's *parivirvāna*. A *saṅgīti* is an act of communal recitation of the complete canon as a reconfirmation of the tradition's institutional unity; these rare instances were misnamed "councils" in English research literature. The Sri Lankan tradition names five *vinaya* patriarchs following each other up to Moggaliputta Tissa, who headed the third *saṅgīti* in Pāṭaliputra (northeast India) during the time of King Aśoka.[78] According to the story, it was convened after a crisis had been overcome that threatened the "true" teaching to become diluted with false tenets. After "non-Buddhists" (*tīrthakas*) who had infiltrated the sangha were excluded by Moggaliputta Tissa, the co-recital of the freshly purified canon was executed. The *saṅgīti* of Pāṭaliputra and the figure of Moggaliputta Tissa are only known to the Theriya tradition. For this lineage the account is an important founding story, as it is seamlessly connected to the moment when Buddhism was transplanted to non-Indian countries: Moggaliputta Tissa entrusts the freshly purified tradition to his pupils and sends them abroad as missionaries of less-civilized "borderlands" that did not yet have contacts with Buddhism. These so-called Aśoka missions are, likewise, only attested in Theriya sources.[79] Of the nine missionary groups sent forth on this occasion, one group, headed by Aśoka's son the monk Mahinda, travels to Sri Lanka and converts the country to Buddhism. Mahinda is counted as the 6th *vinaya* patriarch in Sri Lankan texts.

Only one other missionary is known from another tradition (Majjhantika, who went to Kashmir and is known to the Kashmirian Sarvāstivādins), but he is not connected to Aśoka or Moggaliputta Tissa at all.[80] So it seems, the story of the "Aśoka missions" is a specific Theriya narrative to position their own lineage within the "sacred geography" of an expanded Indocentric Buddhist World created by the famous Aśoka and centered around the blessed northeast Indian spaces where the Buddha once trod. The Sri Lanka missionary Mahinda is the actual hero of the story. The other missionary figures are peripheral figures and we hear nothing of them until King Dhammazedi of Lower Burma requires two of them, Soṇa and Uttara, for the history of his own kingdom in the 15th century (cf., "Myanmar (Burma): Was There a Theriya Lineage in Myanmar from the Time of Aśoka?").

Pāli. As far as we know, no other Buddhist *nikāya* has used the language we call Pāli today. Parallels to Pāli canonical material belonging to other *nikāyas* have been found in Sanskrit and a variety of Middle-Indic languages. They resemble the Pāli versions to varying degrees.

Pāli is a relatively recent name used for this language, which earlier sources call Māgadhī after the supposed origin of the Pāli version of the canon that is believed to have been brought by Mahinda from Magadha in northeast India.[81] Historically, however, Pāli is not identical to the language of Magadha. It is important to note that the Theriyas of Sri Lanka "rediscovered" Pāli as a writing language as late as the 4th century CE. Before that time, they had used it as a liturgical language for reading and reciting their canonical and some later imported postcanonical material. But everything composed in Sri Lanka before the 4th century had been written in the local vernacular, Sīhaḷa Prākṛt. This includes a vast bulk of commentaries produced since the introduction of Buddhism to the island. Perhaps some parts of the early commentarial material had been translated into Sīhaḷa Prākṛti from other Indian languages.[82] In accordance with the claim that the Pāli Canon is the Buddha's "original" word, the commentaries identify Pāli/Māgadhī as the Buddha's own mother tongue.

The *Dīpavaṃsa* seems to be the oldest text written in Pāli in Sri Lanka. Around a century later the work of the famous Mahāvihāra commentator Buddhaghosa (5th century) marks a turning point in the (re-)establishment of Pāli as a scholarly language. Buddhaghosa reworked some of the old commentaries in Sīhaḷa Prākṛt and translated them into Pāli. The reason for this switch is given in his commentary on the *vinaya*: "On account of the fact that this [older] exposition [of the *vinaya*] had been done in the language of the Island of Sīhala [Sri Lanka], and since the monks overseas cannot understand the meaning thereof, I shall now begin this exposition in conformity with the method of treatment found in the Sacred Texts [i.e., the language of the canon]."[83] Thus it seems that the "revival" of Pāli as a scholarly and poetical conversation medium by and after Buddhaghosa was connected to a self-confident program to extend the exegetical knowledge peculiar to the tradition of Sri Lanka into the wider Buddhist world. Perhaps this can be seen as a countermovement to the increasing importance of Sanskrit for translocal communication in this period.[84] Given the scarcity of Pāli outside of Sri Lanka, Norman asked who, in fact, could the addressees—Buddhaghosa's "the monks overseas"—have been: "Where outside the island did the monks live to whom the newly translated [commentaries] would be intelligible?"[85] On the other hand, Pāli is easy to understand for a Buddhist intelligentsia versed in other forms of Prākṛt, especially since Buddhaghosa used (developed?) a refined form of Pāli characterized by a somewhat Sanskritized grammar and the avoidance of the archaic forms that can still be found in the canonical scriptures. Indeed, the switch to Pāli roughly coincides with an increase of historical traces for Theriya activity in continental India and Southeast Asia.

RARITY OF THE TERM *THERAVĀDA* BEFORE MODERNITY

In contrast to the familiarity of the term in the modern discourse, *theravāda* and its semantic equivalents, *theriya, sthavira,* and so on, hardly occur in premodern sources. These terms are not to be found in canonical Pāli literature, and they are also rare in the commentaries.[86] Epigraphically they are not used in any inscription set up in Sri Lanka and appear in no premodern document from Southeast Asia.[87] Hence, in premodern times the terms *Theriya* and *Theravāda* appear to have been of very limited value for the Sri Lankans and of no value for Southeast Asian Buddhists—monk or lay—to identify themselves.

However, in Sri Lankan monastic settlements abroad, the phrases *taṃbapaṃṇika theriya* and *siṃghala sthavira* appear in inscriptions at, respectively, Nāgārjunikoṇḍa and Bodh-Gayā. This indicates that prior to the *Dīpavaṃsa* the term *theriya/sthavira* played a certain role as a denominator of Sri Lankan Buddhist identity at the major Buddhist pilgrimage centers of mainland India, where monasteries of several *nikāyas* existed side by side. The Sri Lankan *vaṃsa* literature, which provides by far the most references to the terms *theriya* and *theravāda,* uses these terms with a similarly demarcating function, but in a radicalized and globalized perspective. As described earlier, texts like *Dīpavaṃsa, Mahāvaṃsa, Vaṃsatthappakāsinī, Cūḷavaṃsa,* and *Nikāyasaṅgraha* unfold the identity of the Theriya lineage against the background of a historical image in which the Buddhist world had fallen apart into a multitude of "heresies," leaving the Theriyas as the only remaining custodians of the "true" teaching.

The concept of Theravāda was taken by modern scholars and Buddhist actors from the Pāli *vaṃsa* literature and transformed into a Buddhist denomination.

FROM THERIYA NIKĀYA TO THERAVĀDA BUDDHISM

The term *theravāda* had its first real boom in history when it started to replace the pejorative term *Hīnayāna* during the first half of the 20th century.[88]

The principle of a twofold classification of Buddhism was introduced by E. Burnouf in his groundbreaking *Introduction à l'histoire du Buddhism Indien* of 1844. The different style and content of the Pāli sources from Sri Lanka, Burma, and Siam compared to the Buddhist Sanskrit sources found in Nepal caused him to distinguish between a "Southern" and "Northern" school of Buddhism. In the following decades the geographical distinction was complemented by a terminology based on doctrinal developments, whereby "Hīnayāna" was recognized as an older and "Mahāyāna" as a younger form of the Buddhist creed. Nevertheless the "Northern" and "Southern" distinction remained the better-known standard until the end of the 19th century. Both distinction pairs, Southern/Northern and Hīnayāna/Mahāyāna, were adopted by Asian Buddhists who had just started to establish international Buddhist associations, with the intention to unify the Buddhists of Asia as a counterforce against the colonial and Christian powers of the West. The formulation of an integral unity of the individual national Buddhist traditions afforded meaningful intrareligious distinctions. For this purpose the word "Hīnayāna" was problematic. As a term originating in Mahāyāna rhetoric, it was unknown to the traditions of Sri Lanka and Southeast Asia. Moreover, as an inherently polemical expression connoting the inferiority of non-Mahāyāna Buddhism, the term *Hīnayāna* was unbearable as a self-designation and undermined the pride of the Pāli-using

Buddhists—especially since European scholarship had meanwhile come to the conclusion that the canonical Pāli texts were of greater antiquity than the Mahāyāna material of the "Northern school" and, thereby, "scientifically confirmed" the higher authenticity of the "Southern Buddhist Church."

As a replacement for "Hīnayāna," the term "Theravāda Buddhism" was first used by Allan Bennett, an English native who was ordained as a Buddhist monk under the name Ananda Metteyya in Burma in 1902.[89] Starting in 1903 Ananda Metteyya published a journal called *Buddhism* that served scholarly as well as missionary purposes. Among other topics, the journal took up the contentious question of a meaningful and historically appropriate nomenclature for the types of Buddhism spread in modern Asia. In accordance with the limited historical knowledge of the time, Buddhism was perceived to have "split" into two varieties in early India, whereby the "original" teaching was preserved in the Pāli texts. In the 6th issue of *Buddhism* (1908) Ananda Metteyya explains that the Sinhalese commentaries and chronicles (i.e., *Dīpavaṃsa* and *Mahāvaṃsa*) use the term Theravāda, the "Tradition of the Elders," for this "original" form of Buddhism. Theravāda, rather than "Southern" or "Hīnayāna" should, therefore, be used to denote the Sri Lankan and Southeast Asian traditions, who represented "orthodox" Buddhism "in all its ancient purity." With this argument, Metteyya is following the classical Mahāvihāra historiographers and takes their exclusivist authenticity claim as a historical fact. Hence, the well-known dualistic opposition between Theravāda and Mahāyāna as the two principal forms of Buddhism emerged as a historical projection oscillating between the modern desire to organize the field of religious diversity along the lines of "sects" or "denominations," the religious geography and politics of the 20th century, and ancient demarcative ideologies. Thereby historical Śrāvakayāna (Hīnayāna) cultures other than the one of the Theriyas (Theravādin) as well as Mahāyāna traditions within the Theriya lineage were eclipsed.

In the following decade T. W. Rhys Davids and his wife C. A. F. Rhys Davids—two of the most eminent Pāli scholars of the day, conversation partners of Ananda Metteyya, and occasional contributors to his journal—started to promote the terms "Theravāda" and "Theravāda Buddhism" in the scientific debate. In articles published in the second decade of the 20th century they identified Theravāda as the "original school" and the "Buddhist mother church," which preserved the Buddha's original philosophical message.[90] In a 1928 article, Sri Lankan scholar Senerat Paranavitana illustrated the centuries-long struggle of the Theravādins to preserve the pure teaching against the Mahāyāna with the example of the historical Mahāvihāra rivaling and finally defeating the Abhayagiri Nikāya.[91] The article follows the monopolization of Theriya/Theravāda lineage identity of the post-Parākramabāhu Mahāvihāra as formulated in the 15th-century *Nikāyasaṅgraha*, and fashions the historical lineage rivalries as the legitimate protection of an "orthodoxy" against a superstitious "heresy" practiced by the uneducated common folk. Through the victory of what he calls the "orthodox sect," Sri Lanka became what it still is today: "the homeland of the Theravāda."[92] The topos of a historical antagonism between a rational, philosophical, "original Buddhism" (from now on designated as "Theravāda Buddhism") and a superstitious, polytheistic Mahāyāna permeated scholarly works and Buddhist propaganda in the late 19th century.[93] The reductionist and historically incorrect model of Buddhism having split into two principal schools named Theravāda and Mahāyāna established itself as a scholarly master narrative in the following decades. This model gained further momentum with the likewise problematic association of Mahāyāna

Buddhism with the Mahāsāṅghikas and their sub-*nikāyas*. This often repeated theory reduces the complexities of the early *nikāya* formations and their entanglement with the Bodhisattvayāna/Mahāyāna movement to a handy but misconstrued story according to which an initial split between *nikāyas* (Sthaviras and Mahāsāṅghikas) ultimately resulted in the establishment of two principal varieties of Buddhism.

MODERN THERIYA SUB-NIKĀYAS

In the modern Buddhist world, identities and the relationships among different Buddhist groups are widely negotiated along the modern opposition pair Theravāda and Mahāyāna Buddhism. These are further subdivided into geographical (sub-)distinctions (e.g., Thai Theravāda Buddhism, Sri Lankan Theravāda Buddhism, Japanese Mahāyāna, Tibetan Buddhism) and further into schools (e.g., the Zen Buddhism, Amida Buddhism, Tendai, Shingon etc. of Japan; Nyingmapa, Gelukpa, Kagyüpa schools etc. in Tibet). The different *nikāya* affiliations of these Buddhist varieties, however, are hardly known to nonspecialists. This may in part reflect the fact that *vinaya* lineages decreased in importance in most Buddhist countries centuries ago. For the religious identity of lay Buddhists they seem to never have played a role because nonordained practitioners are not members of a *nikāya*. (On the question of whether it makes sense at all to identify a lay Buddhist under a *nikāya*-name, e.g., to call them "Theravāda Buddhists," see "The Question of a "Theravāda Laity".) To a certain degree the reduced importance of *nikāya* boundaries for the construction of Buddhist group identities is also due to the fact that only three of the ancient *vinaya* lineages have survived. These are distributed along rather clear-cut geographical lines, so that rivalries and conflicts on the institutional *vinaya* level are reduced to exceptional cases.[94] We can divide the Buddhist monastic world into three "*nikāya* zones:"

1. the Sino-Korean-Japanese zone ⟶ Dharmaguptaka Nikāya;
2. the Tibeto-Mongolian zone ⟶ Mūlasarvāstivāda Nikāya;
3. the Sri Lankan-Southeast Asian zone ⟶ Theriya Nikāya.

All other *nikāyas* mentioned in "Mainland Indian Understandings of Sthavira" have vanished. In the past, other *nikāyas* had also spread into Tibet and China. However, King Ral-pa-can (815–838) eliminated *nikāya* plurality in Tibet (and the inhomogeneity connected therewith) by a royal decree ordering that all Tibetan monks had to be ordained according the Mūlasarvāstivāda *vinaya*. A bit more than one century earlier the Dharmaguptaka *vinaya* had been superimposed on all monks of China by the Tang emperor Zongzong (656–710) after a period of eclectic use of several *vinaya* traditions.[95] After these homogenization acts, the *nikāya* concept no longer made sense for internal distinctions within the domains of Tibeto-Mongolian and Chinese-Korean-Japanese Buddhism.

In the "Theriya zone" matters remained different, although (or perhaps because?) the Theriya *vinaya* was more or less unrivaled in Sri Lanka from the very beginning. Nevertheless, it was *vinaya* terms like *nikāya* (less frequently *gaṇa* or *vāda*) that provided the paramount categories for the classification of institutional and doxo-practical differences within Sri Lanka and Southeast Asia. As far as is known, not even the *yāna* category—one of the most important classifiers of inner-Buddhist distinction in other parts of the Buddhist world—had entered Pāli literature before the 20th century, even though "Mahāyāna Buddhists" had been active in these countries. But this is a modern category that does not necessarily reflect the discourses and terminologies of the respective regions and periods. Consequently, the Sri Lankan historian Dharmakīrti II (15th century) describes the Mahāyāna and Vajrayāna traditions in India's and Sri Lanka's past within the demarcating categories available and familiar to him. For him they were independent, "heretical" *nikāyas* who had dissociated themselves doctrinally and institutionally from the Theriyas.[96] The example of Dharmakīrti II shows the continued use of the *nikāya* concept to organize discourses of inner-Buddhist differentiation and deviation within the "Theriya zone." It must be emphasized that the term always remained tied to *monastic groups* and was never used to denote a broader idea of a "sect" or movement resting on creeds or commitments shared by monastics and convinced laypeople.

The sangha of Sri Lanka, Myanmar, Thailand, Laos, and Cambodia is subdivided into several *nikāyas* (more accurately, sub-*nikāyas*).[97] Each of them emerged during or after the colonial period. As they all make use of the same *vinaya*—namely the one in the only remaining Theriya canon that survived the reform of Parākramabāhu—they all are genealogically affiliated with the ancient Sri Lankan Mahāvihāra lineage. Since they share the same canon and classical commentaries (*Atthakathā*), differences among the modern Theriya sub-*nikāyas* are less concerned with doctrinal issues or the inventory of *vinaya* rules, but deal with their interpretation and practical implementation. Often these *nikāyas* emerged as ascetic reform groups demanding a stricter observation of the *vinaya* rules than practiced in the majority of monasteries in their respective societies. However, *vinaya* questions have not always been pivotal for the formation of these monastic groups. As Carbine explains with reference to the modern *nikāyas* of Myanmar:

> As pointed out by various scholars, Burmese monastic traditions, as with monastic traditions in other Buddhist contexts, are famously given to a sectarianism deriving from local cults of personality, resistances to centralized authority, *vinaya*-based claims about the laxities of certain monks, as well as, in some cases, doctrinally oriented claims about the proper transmission of "what the Buddha taught."[98]

Taking the societies of Sri Lanka and Southeast Asia together, there are several dozens of contemporary Theriya sub-*nikāyas*. Some of these are nationwide institutions and consist of huge portions of the monks in the respective country, others are small and comprise only a few closely adjacent monasteries. The following description is not exhaustive and surveys primarily the major systems. Even the larger sub-*nikāyas* are primarily tied to national boundaries. In some cases certain sub-*nikāyas* of different countries can be more closely related than others—like the Thommayut Nikāya of Cambodia, which is technically a branch of the Thammayut Nikāya of Thailand—but are organized as autonomous entities with independent hierarchies, embedded in the religio-political administration of the respective state.[99] Hence, it makes sense to divide the extant sub-*nikāyas* into national sets of groups. We have to bear in mind that different *nikāyas*—even those directly competing with each other within the same area—are not necessarily antagonistic on all social levels. Theoretically, they are mutually exclusive and do not acknowledge each other's validity of ordination. However, in everyday life many monks do not stress *nikāya* boundaries in intermonastic collaboration, friendships, or even ritual participation.[100] Moreover, laypeople are rarely aware of the *nikāya* affiliation of the monks they interact with. Therefore, the term "sectarian" used by many scholars should be treated with care. Boundary awareness typically increases toward the higher ranks of the sangha hierarchy where institutional issues concerning authority, resources, and representation are more imminent.

Sri Lanka. None of the *nikāyas* extant in Sri Lanka today can claim a direct continuity with the ordination-lineage enforced by Parākramabāhu in the 12th century. It is claimed that the state of the sangha had deteriorated since the 15th century and during the colonial period, so that the validity of the ordination-lineage of the remaining monks had become increasingly doubtful. As a consequence the 18th and 19th century saw the rise of several new *nikāyas*, which were initiated by fetching fresh ordination traditions from either Myanmar or Thailand (to where the ancient Sri Lankan Mahāvihāra lineage of the Theriya Nikāya had been exported in an earlier period, cf. "Thailand and Cambodia"). At least formally this process can be seen as a complete reboot of the monastic tradition in Sri Lanka. The modern *nikāyas* are commonly classified under a tripartite scheme:

1. Siyam or Syāma Nikāya;
2. Amarapura Nikāya;
3. Rāmañña Nikāya.

The names refer to the places from which the ordination traditions of these lineages were originally fetched. The actual number of *nikāyas* is, however, much higher. Bechert lists more than thirty, most of which are sub-*nikāyas* into which the Siyam and Amarapura Nikāyas had split during the later 19th century.[101] The Siyam Nikāya is the oldest, founded in the mid-18th century by Välivițiyē Saraṇaṅkara (1698–1778) with the help of monks from Siam (hence the name). Following Saraṇaṅkara's repeated appeal, King Kīrtiśrī Rājasiṃha of Kandy (1747–1782) invited these Siamese monks to revive the monastic tradition of the country. From the beginning the Siyam Nikāya was closely tied to the noble families of Kandy in the Sri Lankan highlands, which was not yet under British colonial rule at that time.[102] Soon after its establishment, the Siyam Nikāya started to restrict the access to higher ordination to the members of the two highest castes, which effectively excluded the low-caste population of the coastal areas of Sri Lanka from becoming fully ordained monks. As a consequence, members of the wealthy, anglicized middle class along the west coast started independent lineages by fetching monastic ordinations from Burma. Due to their opposition to the Siyam Nikāya, these younger *nikāyas* are sometimes called "reform *nikāyas*." The Amarapura Nikāya was founded by Ambagahapițiyē Ñāṇavimalatissa in 1802 after his return from Myanmar where he was ordained by the Burmese *saṅgharāja* in the city Amarapura. The Rāmañña Nikāya followed in 1864 after Ambagahavattē Indāsabhavarañāna had received ordination in Lower Burma (Rāmañña). At present the three *nikāyas* are spread throughout Sri Lanka with the central highlands around Kandy still dominated by the Siyam Nikāya. The hierarchies of the various sub-branches are similarly organized, so that the authority of the Sri Lankan sangha as a total is distributed among more than thirty Mahānāyakas ("grand leaders," "head-monks") who preside over the individual branches. The position of a supreme *saṅgharāja* was reinstalled with the establishment of the Siyam Nikāya but stalled and vanished after Saraṇaṅkara's death in 1778.

Myanmar. During Ne Win's *sāsana* reforms in the 1980s, nine *nikāyas* were officially recognized in Myanmar/Burma. The vast majority of monks belong to the Thudhammā Nikāya. The name is derived from council of Sayadaws (monastic elders) installed by King Bodawpaya (1782–1819) at the end of the 18th century. These elders met in the Thudhammā Pavilion (Mandalay) to settle the *pārupaṇa-ekaṃsika* controversy, the question of whether a monk has to cover one or both shoulders in public, which had been debated among Burmese monks for the better part of the 18th century. However, until the middle of the 19th century it makes little sense to identify the Thudhammā Nikāya as a *nikāya* in the strict sense.[103] It was simply the collective of all Burmese monks, now headed by the council of Thudhammā Sayadaws. In the time of King Mindon (1853–1878), groups of monks started to separate from the majority and built autonomous *nikāyas*. From then on, the majority of monks who remained under the traditional jurisdiction of the Thudhammā Sayadaws became collectively known as Thudhammā Nikāya.

Most of these new *nikāyas* emerged as reformist groups who demanded a stricter adherence to the rules of the *vinaya* or who rejected the authority of the Thudhammā Sayadaws. One of the first *nikāya* to separate from the Thudhammā was the Dvāra Nikāya, which arose in Lower Burma in 1855.[104] The formal cause was a *sīmā* controversy and the dispute about the exact wording of a certain religious formula uttered at the beginning of religious acts. The actual conflict, however, evolved around the demand of a stricter observation of the *vinaya* rules. With a similar demand Shwegyin Sayadaw formed a reform group in Upper Burma around the same time. Ultimately the group was discharged by a *gaṇavimutti* act ("discharge by mutual agreement") of the Thudhammā leadership and established itself as Shwegyin Nikāya.[105] The Swegyin Nikāya is today the second largest *nikāya* of Myanmar (ca. 5 percent of the country's monks) and is organized by a strict internal hierarchy. Its head is appointed through the consent of the community and exercises the ultimate authority in questions of the orthodoxy of the group's doctrines and practices.[106] In the late 1880s the Hngetwiṅ Nikāya emerged from a group of meditators residing in the "cave of birds" (*hngetwiṅ*) in Sagaing Hill Range in Upper Burma. The group is today based in Mandalay and is rather small (ca. 1,000 monks). It is especially known for its association with *satipaṭṭhāna* meditation and its radical rejection of certain rituals, such as the popular Nat cult and the practice to offer flowers in front of Buddha statues. The likewise small Mahāyiṅ, Gado, and Veḷwun *nikāyas* arose from the followers of individual masters toward the end of the 19th century. They go back to what Carbine called "local cults of personality," rather than to *vinaya* conflicts. Two *nikāyas*—Anaukchaung-Dvāra and Mūladvāra—had split from the Dvāra Nikāya because of leadership conflicts. The religio-political act of 1980 determined that every Burmese monk had to belong to one of these nine *nikāyas*. The formation of new *nikāyas* was prohibited.

Thailand, Cambodia, and Laos. In 1836 the prince-monk and later king Mongkut of Siam (Thailand) founded the Dhammayuttika Nikāya (Thammayut Nikāya) as a stricter order, more akin to the principles of the *vinaya*. The plurality of older lineages was henceforth summarized under the name Mahānikāya. Dhammayuttika and Mahānikāya represent the principle subdivisions of the Theriya sangha in Thailand. The Mahānikāya is less a homogeneous formal *nikāya* than a superimposed umbrella term for several monastic traditions originating in the pre-Mongkut era. Though small in size, the Dhammayuttika Nikāya remained highly influential, especially because of its continued relationship to the royal family. Different from Sri Lanka and Myanmar, the sangha of Thailand is still headed by a *saṅgharāja* who, until recently, was nominated by a supreme monastic council and formally appointed by the king. The "Sangha Act" of 2017 allowed the king to appoint the *saṅgharāja* directly based on the prime minister's recommendations.

The administration of the sangha of Thailand and its more than 21,000 monasteries is strictly organized and maintained by a hierarchy of dignitaries below the *saṅgharāja*. The principal structure had evolved in the late 19th century, but frequently changed in important details in the 20th and 21st centuries, including the influence of state organs on the sangha's autonomy.[107] The Dhammayuttika Nikāya's representation in the organs of monastic self-administration used to be particularly strong in relation to the fact that only about 6 percent of the country's monks and novices belong to this *nikāya*.

The Dhammayuttika Nikāya of Thailand was also imported to Laos and Cambodia. In Cambodia the Thommayut Nikāya was founded in 1864 by a monk scholar who had studied in a Dhammayuttika monastery in Bangkok. As in Thailand, the majority continuing the older native tradition became subsequently known as Mahānikāya. In contrast to Thailand, both Cambodian *nikāyas* are separately organized and have one *saṅgharāja* each. In Laos only a small number of monasteries in the southern Champassak province, close to the boarders with Thailand and Cambodia, belong to the Thammayut Nikāya (Dhammayuttika Nikāya).

THE QUESTION OF A "THERAVĀDA LAITY"

Before the 20th century no Buddhist layperson had ever referred to him- or herself as a "Theravādin." It is fairly safe to say that the mere absence of any historical document of such a speech act does not prove the nonexistence of the speech act itself. However, given the history of the term *Theravāda* with its scarcity and primarily technical meaning in historical sources and its clearly identifiable reinterpretation and subsequent boom in the early 20th century (cf., "From Theriya Nikāya to Theravāda Buddhism"), we can safely assume that the term *Theravāda* never played a role for lay-Buddhist identity formation until about a century ago. Before that time *Theravāda*, as Skilling notes, "was not part of their everyday vocabulary."[108] Nonordained people never belonged to a *nikāya* and, if we can extend the contemporary situation into the past, never had any particular awareness of the *nikāya* affiliation of the monasteries within their reach. If lay Buddhists are addressed in premodern Pāli and Sinhala literature it is done so in generic terms like "the pious" (*śraddhāvat*), "the devotees" (*upāsaka/upāsikā*), or "the donors" (*dāyaka*). It was a more common scenario for lay families to be specifically attached to certain monasteries with which they had personal or family relationships or just because they lived close by, than that they favored or even had a sense of belonging to a specific *nikāya*.[109]

Monasteries played an important role as centers for religious education and ritual service providers in Sri Lankan and Southeast Asian societies. Therefore, laypeople's religious practice cannot completely be separated from the *nikāya* affiliation of the monastic community they interacted with. It surely had effects on their religious knowledge, practices, and routines.[110] Some monastic authors emphasized that the laity was to be instructed "in the correct way"; that is, in conformity with the doctrines and methods represented by their respective *nikāyas*.[111] There is, however, little evidence supporting the assumption that the laity was systematically endowed with doxographical competences which that have enabled them to recognize, scrutinize, and accept or reject the specific teaching systems advocated by individual *nikāyas*.

The question that characterizes a Theravāda layperson expects an answer referring to preconceived differences between Theravāda and other varieties of the Buddhist religion. Chances are that these expectations are in one way or another related to the modern distinction set Theravāda, Mahāyāna, and Vajrayāna Buddhism. The genealogy of this discourse reveals that the modern concept of Theravāda Buddhism is connected to formulations of doctrinal purity promoted by certain authors of the Sri Lankan Mahāvihāra tradition and reinforced—perhaps radicalized—by the "neo-orthodox" movement of 12th century. However, historically this vision of a pure, original Buddhism has been everything but a consistent and stable model of religious belief and practice. Consequently, it has not produced a homogeneous Buddhist laity (or monastic tradition) with identical characteristics shared by Sri Lankans, Burmese, Thai, and so on, even if we take only the period after Parākramabāhu and the implementation of the Sīhaḷa Nikāya in Southeast Asia into account. The transformative dynamics of the different local environments, the relational and permanently changing social, political, and religious discourses complicate the determination of what exactly constitutes the specifics of a Theravāda laity—or clergy, or society, or civilization. One way to harmonize the modern language use of the term *Theravāda* with historical analysis is to use the recurring benchmarks of Mahāvihārin orthodoxy claims as heuristic anchors and to understand them as transposable, flexible *modules* contributing to the texture of a society influenced by Mahāvihāra ideals. As Skilling suggests: "Let us propose instead dynamic autonomous histories, in which Theravādin or Mahāvihāra modules have evolved in plural societies, continually responding to the social needs of the historical moment."[112]

Examples for such modules might be the textual authority and liturgical power of canonical and exegetical Pāli literature, Śrāvakayāna soteriologies and cosmologies (like the notion that only one Buddha and one Bodhisattva can exist at the same time), and the reference to the Third Council for historical identity building. For a Theravāda laity, the question is how far these modules shape the religious knowledge, practice, and identity of nonordained people; how these are implemented in daily life; how they changed; and how they were challenged, complemented, superimposed, and replaced by religious alternatives and rivals. A comparative study with such a design is lacking.

Returning to the modern opposition set, the "neo-orthodox" influence has never completely eradicated Mahāyāna and Vajrayāna Buddhist "modules" in Sri Lanka or in Southeast Asia. In Sri Lanka, for example, the cult of Bodhisattvas like Avalokiteśvara and Samāntabhadra was transformed into worldly (*laukika*) protector deity cults during the 14th and 15th century but continued as such and even gained in popularity and political significance—an evident case of a former Mahāyāna-based practice overwritten by a Śrāvakayāna-compatible "Mahāvihāra module."[113] In the same period, selected Mahāyāna texts and Mahāyāna-related notions like the plurality of bodhisattvas, the *trikāya* doctrine, and the ideal of aspiring to Buddhahood (rather than Arhatship) were promoted in popular Sinhala preaching literature (*baṇapot*) and became known to the laity as standard features of mainstream Buddhism.[114] As Dharmakīrti II (15th cent.) informs us, some esoteric (Tantric) rituals continued to be practiced secretly up to his time "among the foolish, unlearned folks" (*lāmaka vū ajñānayan kerehi*).[115]

With the emergence of Buddhist Modernism in the late 19th and early 20th centuries the situation changed. The increased availability of traditional text resources and the increased knowledge of the religions of Asia and elsewhere enabled the laity—primarily the urbanized, generally anglicized intellectual segment—to scrutinize and reformulate the doctrinal and historical specificities of their own religious heritage. By the middle of the 20th century the distinction between Theravāda and Mahāyāna Buddhism provided the primary model used by Sri Lankan and Southeast Asian monks and laypeople to define their religious identities, affiliations, and commitments. Today the Theravāda/Mahāyāna opposition is taught in schoolbooks and invoked by virtually every tourist guide and guidebook (often in rather stereotypical tropes). The global discourse has also bestowed concepts like "folk religion" and "superstition" as new demarcating devices to purge imaginations of "authentic" Theravāda from unwanted elements. In the process of Buddhist modernism the authority to define what "Theravāda Buddhism" is and what it is not has shifted from an almost exclusive monastic interpretation sovereignty to a public discourse coproduced by monks and laypeople.[116]

Does it make sense to call a Buddhist layperson a "Theravāda Buddhist"? This is a complex question answered differently and to the greater part silently by scholars. Based on the presented information a tentative answer might be that it might make the most sense for the modern context when the term *Theravāda* is used as a demarcating, self-referential concept based on particular images of the past, concepts of religion, and constructions of the religious Self and Other. It makes perhaps the least sense for the time before Parākramabāhu's reform. For historical purposes, "Theravāda Buddhist" is a heuristic device of limited analytical accuracy and value, dependent on a decontextualization of historical authenticity claims of certain monastic groups whose exact notions, motives, and diversification are not entirely clear.

CONCLUSION

Before the 20th century not a single layperson and merely a tiny number of monastics would have identified themselves as Theravādin. The term was confined to specific contexts of genealogical ascertainment, ritual compatibility, and exegetical tradition-building of monastic communities. Even in those monastic contexts the term was far less frequent than its usage in modern studies and religious self-presentations suggests. With Ananda Metteyya's creation of "Theravāda Buddhism," the term Theravāda leaves the semantic boundaries of monastic lineage identity and becomes a *type* of Buddhism. The term connects to the scholarly program of the comparative study of religion.[117] In this context *Buddhism* was "discovered" as one of the important "World Religions." by early 19th century scholars, and "world religion" emerged in a productive dialogue between European and Asian philologists and historians and the protagonists of Buddhist "revival" movements in several Asian countries.[118] The latter movements, in turn, stood in the contexts of a growing resistance against colonialism in countries such as Sri Lanka and Burma. These Buddhist reformers of the late 19th and 20th centuries, often English-educated representatives of a wealthy middle class, shared the textual bias and the positivist historicist approach of academic researchers.[119] Hence, the idea of "Buddhism" fashioned in this dialogue was basically a propositional worldview, localized in the ancient textual corpora, shared by a community of "believers" (which now included both monastics and laypersons). The prime task of the Buddhist reformers of Asia was, consequently, the creation of a collective Buddhist consciousness by educating the "Buddhists" in their respective countries in the lore and principles of "their" religion—based on the ancient texts (now gradually made accessible in English and vernacular translations) and reinterpreted on the background of modern intellectual standards. Modern self-conscious Buddhists should know *that* they are Buddhist and *why* they are Buddhists (rather than Christian, Hindu, atheist, etc.).[120] The "Theravāda Buddhists" are now conceptualized as the entirety of believers in the doctrines of the Pāli Canon.

FURTHER READING

The following list of publications is meant as a first access to cultural scholarship on Theravāda. It is far from complete—a task impossible for the thematic scope of this article. The list presents some of the most important studies in "Theravāda culture," sorted under general headings. Primarily, monographs are listed, especially on topics not covered in detail within this article. Journal articles and book chapters as well as philological/textual studies and Theravāda Buddhism in the West have been omitted.

HISTORY, MONASTIC HISTORY

Adikaram, E. W. *Early History of Buddhism in Ceylon*. Migoda, Sri Lanka: D. S. Puswella, 1953.

Ariyapala, M. B. *Society in Mediaeval Ceylon: The State of Society in Ceylon as Depicted in the Saddharma-Ratnāvaliya and other Literature of the Thirteenth Century*. 3rd ed. Colombo, Sri Lanka: Department of Cultural Affairs, 1997.

Assavavirulhakarn, Prapod. *The Ascendancy of Theravāda Buddhism in Southeast Asia*. Bangkok: Silkworm Books, 2010.

Aung-Thwin, Michael A. *The Mists of Rāmañña: The Legend That Was Lower Burma*. Honolulu: University of Hawai'i Press, 2005.

Deegalle, Mahinda. "Buddhist Preaching (Ban.a) in Sri Lanka. Sinhala Religious Rhetoric in the Popularization of Theravāda." *Sri Lanka Journal of Buddhist Studies* 5 (1996): 30–41.

Geiger, Wilhelm. *Culture of Ceylon in Medieval Times*. Wiesbaden: Otto Harrassowitz, 1960.

Gunawardana, R. A. L. H. *Robe and Plough: Monasticism and Economic Interest in Early Medieval Sri Lanka*. Association of Asian Studies, Monographs and Papers, 35. Tucson: University of Arizona Press, 1979.

Harris, Ian. *Cambodian Buddhism: History and Practice*. Honolulu: University of Hawai'i Press, 2005.

Panabokke, Gunaratne. *History of the Buddhist Sangha in India and Sri Lanka*. Colombo, Sri Lanka: University of Kelaniya, 1991.

Schalk, Peter, and Astrid von Nahl, eds. *Buddhism among Tamils in Pre-Colonial Tamilakam and Īlam: Extension and Conclusions*. Vol. 3. *Acta Universitatis Upsaliensis*. Uppsala: Uppsala Universitet, 2013.

Stargardt, Janice. *The Ancient Pyu of Burma: Early Pyu Cities in a Man-Made Landscape*. Vol. 1. Cambridge, UK: Pacsea, 1990.

EDUCATION, SCHOLARSHIP

Berkwitz, Stephen C. *Buddhist History in the Vernacular: The Power of the Past in Late Medieval Sri Lanka*. Brill's Indological Library, 23. Leiden: Brill, 2004.

Blackburn, Anne M. *Buddhist Learning and Textual Practice in 18th Century Lankan Monastic Culture*. Princeton, NJ: Princeton University Press, 2001.

Blackburn, Anne M., and Jeffrey Samuels, eds. *Approaching the Dhamma: Buddhist Texts and Practices in South and Southeast Asia*. Seattle: BPS Pariyatti Editions, 2003.

Deegalle, Mahinda. *Popularizing Buddhism: Preaching as Performance in Sri Lanka*. Albany: State University of New York Press, 2006.

Fischer, Silke Yasmin. *Erzähltradierung als Interpretationsprozess: Eine diachrone Analyse zweier staatlicher Buddhismus-Religionsbücher aus Sri Lanka*. Wiesbaden: Harrassowitz, 2011.

McDaniel, Justin. *Gathering Leaves and Lifting Words: Histories of Buddhist Monastic Education in Laos and Thailand*. Seattle: University of Washington Press, 2008.

MONASTIC LIFE, COMMUNITY

Blackburn, Anne M., and Jeffrey Samuels, eds. *Approaching the Dhamma: Buddhist Texts and Practices in South and Southeast Asia*. Seattle: BPS Pariyatti Editions, 2003.

Bunnag, Jane. *Buddhist Monk, Buddhist Layman: A Study of Urban Monastic Organization in Central Thailand*. Cambridge, UK: Cambridge University Press, 1973.

Carbine, Jason A. *Sons of the Buddha. Continuities and Ruptures in a Burmese Monastic Tradition*. Religion and Society, 50. Berlin: De Gruyter, 2011.

Carrithers, Michael. *The Forest Monks of Sri Lanka: An Anthropological and Historical Study*. Oxford University South Asian Studies Series. Delhi: Oxford University Press, 1983.

Cook, Joanna. *Meditation in Modern Buddhism. Renunciation and Change in Thai Monastic Life*. Cambridge, UK: Cambridge University Press, 2010.

Falk, Monica Lindberg. *Making Fields of Merit: Buddhist Female Ascetics and Gendered Orders in Thailand*. Copenhagen: NIAS Press, 2007.

Gombrich, Richard F. *Buddhist Precept and Practice: Traditional Buddhism in the Rural Highlands of Ceylon*. Delhi: Motilal Banarsidass, 1991.

Holt, John C., and Jacob N. Kinnard, eds. *Constituting Communities: Theravāda Buddhism and the Religious Cultures of South and Southeast Asia*. Albany: State University of New York Press, 2003.

Mendelson, E. Michael. *Sangha and State in Burma. A Study of Monastic Sectarianism and Leadership*. Ithaca, NY: Cornell University Press, 1975.

Samuels, Jeffrey. *Attracting the Heart: Social Relations and the Aesthetics of Emotion in Sri Lankan Monastic Culture*. Honolulu: University of Hawaiʻi Press, 2010.

Schedneck, Brooke. *Thailand's International Meditation Centers: Tourism and the Global Commodification of Religious Practices*. Religion in Contemporary Asia Series, 3. London: Routledge, 2017.

Tambiah, Stanley Jeyaraja. *The Buddhist Saints of the Forest and the Cult of Amulets: A Study in Charisma, Hagiography, Sectarianism, and Millennial Buddhism*. Cambridge Series in Social Anthropology, 49. Cambridge, UK: Cambridge University Press, 1984.

RITUAL, PRACTICE

Holt, John Clifford. *Theravāda Traditions: Buddhist Ritual Cultures in Contemporary Southeast Asia and Sri Lanka*. Honolulu: University of Hawaiʻi Press, 2017.

Langer, Rita. *Buddhist Rituals of Death and Rebirth: Contemporary Sri Lankan Practice and its Origins*. Routledge Critical Studies in Buddhism. Abingdon, UK: Routledge, 2007.

Swearer, Donald K. *Becoming the Buddha: The Ritual of Image Consecration in Thailand*. Princeton, NJ: Princeton University Press, 2004.

Trainor, Kevin. *Relics, Ritual, and Representation in Buddhism: Rematerializing the Sri Lankan Theravāda Tradition*. Cambridge Studies in the Religious Traditions, 10. New York: Cambridge University Press, 1997.

SOCIETY, POLITICS

Bechert, Heinz. *Buddhismus, Staat und Gesellschaft in den Ländern des Theravāda-Buddhismus. 1: Grundlagen, Ceylon (Sri Lanka)*. 2nd ed. Schriften des Instituts für Asienkunde in Hamburg, 5. Frankfurt: Alfred Metzner, 1966.

Bechert, Heinz. *Buddhismus, Staat und Gesellschaft in den Ländern des Theravāda-Buddhismus. 2: Birma, Kambodscha, Laos, Thailand*. Schriften des Instituts für Asienkunde in Hamburg, 17/2. Wiesbaden: Harrassowitz, 1967.

Hayashi, Yukio. *Practical Buddhism Among the Thai-Lao: Religion in the Making of a Region*. Kyoto Area Studies on Asia, 5. Kyoto: Kyoto University Press, 2003.

Ishii, Yoneo. *Sangha, State, and Society: Thai Buddhism in History*. Monographs of the Center for Southeast Asian Studies. Honolulu: University of Hawai'i Press, 1986.

Mendelson, E. Michael. *Sangha and State in Burma: A Study of Monastic Sectarianism and Leadership*. Ithaca, NY: Cornell University Press, 1975.

Smith, Donald Eugene. *Religion and Politics in Burma*. Princeton, NJ: Princeton University Press, 1965.

Spiro, Melford Elliot. *Buddhism and Society: A Great Tradition and Its Burmese Vicissitudes*. New York: Harper & Row, 1972.

Tambiah, Stanley S. *World Conqueror and World Renouncer: A Study of Buddhism and Polity in Thailand Against a Historical Background*. Cambridge Studies in Social and Cultural Anthropology, 15. Cambridge, UK: Cambridge University Press, 1976.

Taylor, Jim. *Forest Monks and the Nation-State: An Anthropological and Historical Study in Northeastern Thailand*. Singapore: Institute of Southeast Asian Studies, 1993.

CULTURE, IDENTITY, GENDER

Bartholemeusz, Tessa. *Women Under the Bo Tree: Buddhist Nuns in Sri Lanka*. Cambridge, UK: Cambridge University Press, 1994.

Falk, Monica Lindberg. *Making Fields of Merit: Buddhist Female Ascetics and Gendered Orders in Thailand*. Copenhagen: NIAS Press, 2007.

Gombrich, Richard F. *Buddhist Precept and Practice: Traditional Buddhism in the Rural Highlands of Ceylon*. Delhi: Motilal Banarsidass, 1991.

Hansen, Anne Ruth. *How to Behave: Buddhism and Modernity in Colonial Cambodia, 1860–1930*. Honolulu: University of Hawai'i Press, 2007.

Hayashi, Yukio. *Practical Buddhism Among the Thai-Lao: Religion in the Making of a Region*. Kyoto Area Studies on Asia, 5. Kyoto: Kyoto University Press, 2003.

Holt, John Clifford. *The Buddhist Viṣṇu: Religious Transformation, Politics, and Culture*. New York: Columbia University Press, 2004.

Holt, John Clifford. *The Religious World of Kīrti Śrī*. Oxford: Oxford University Press, 1996.

Holt, John Clifford. *Spirits of the Place: Buddhism and Lao Religious Culture*. Honolulu: University of Hawai'i Press, 2009.

Kemper, Steven. *Presence of the Past: Chronicles, Politics, and Culture in Sinhala Life*. Ithaca, NY: Cornell University Press, 1991.

Skilling, Peter, et al., eds. *How Theravāda is Theravāda? Exploring Buddhist Identities*. Chiang Mai, Thailand: Silkworm Books, 2012.

ETHNICITY, CONFLICT

Abeysekara, Ananda. *Colors of the Robe: Religion, Identity, and Difference*. Columbia: University of South Carolina Press, 2008.

Bartholomeusz, Tessa. *In Defence of Dharma: Just-War Ideology in Buddhist Sri Lanka*. London: Routledge/Curzon, 2002.

Deegalle, Mahinda, ed. *Buddhism, Conflict and Violence in Modern Sri Lanka*. Routledge Critical Studies in Buddhism. London: Routledge, 2006.

Harris, Ian Charles. *Buddhism in a Dark Age: Cambodian Monks under Pol Pot*. Honolulu: University of Hawai'i Press, 2013.

Holt, John Clifford, ed. *Buddhist Extremists and Muslim Minorities: Religious Conflict in Contemporary Sri Lanka*. Oxford: Oxford University Press, 2016.

Jackson, Peter A. *Buddhism, Legitimation, and Conflict: The Political Functions of Urban Thai Buddhism*. Singapore: Institution of Southeast Asian Studies, 1989.

Jerryson, Michael K. *Buddhist Fury: Religion and Violence in Southern Thailand*. Oxford: Oxford University Press, 2011.

Kemper, Steven. *Presence of the Past: Chronicles, Politics, and Culture in Sinhala Life*. Ithaca, NY: Cornell University Press, 1991.

Ling, Trevor. *Buddhism, Imperialism, and War. Burma and Thailand in Modern History*. London: Allen and Unwin, 1979.

Smith, Bardwell L., ed. *Religion and the Legitimation of Power in Sri Lanka*. South and Southeast Asia Studies. Chambersburg, PA: Anima Books, 1978.

Smith, Bardwell L., ed. *Religion and the Legitimation of Power in Thailand, Laos, and Burma*. South and Southeast Asia Studies. Chambersburg, PA: Anima Books, 1978.

Tambiah, Stanley J. *Buddhism Betrayed? Religion, Politics and Violence in Sri Lanka*. Chicago: University of Chicago Press, 1992.

COLONIALISM, MODERNITY, MODERNISM

Almond, Philip C. *The British Discovery of Buddhism*. Cambridge, < UK: Cambridge University Press, 1988.

Berkwitz, Stephen C. *Buddhist Poetry and Colonialism: Alagiyavanna and the Portuguese in Sri Lanka*. Oxford: Oxford University Press, 2013.

Blackburn, Anne M. *Buddhist Learning and Textual Practice in 18th Century Lankan Monastic Culture*. Princeton, NJ: Princeton University Press, 2001.

Bond, George D. *The Buddhist Revival in Sri Lanka: Religious Tradition, Reinterpretation and Response*. Columbia: University of South Carolina Press, 1988.

Bond, George Doherty. *Buddhism at Work: Community Development, Social Empowerment and the Sarvodaya Movement*. Bloomfield, CT: Kumarian Press, 2004.

Carbine, Jason A. *Sons of the Buddha: Continuities and Ruptures in a Burmese Monastic Tradition*. Religion and Society, 50. Berlin: De Gruyter, 2011.

Gombrich, Richard, and Gananath Obeyesekere. *Buddhism Transformed: Religious Change in Sri Lanka*. Princeton, NJ: Princeton University Press, 1988.

Hansen, Anne Ruth. *How to Behave: Buddhism and Modernity in Colonial Cambodia, 1860–1930*. Honolulu: University of Hawai'i Press, 2007.

Harris, Elizabeth J. *Theravāda Buddhism and the British Encounter: Religious, Missionary and Colonial Experience in Nineteenth-Century Sri Lanka*. Routledge Critical Studies in Buddhism. London: Routledge, 2006.

Harris, Ian Charles. *Buddhism in a Dark Age: Cambodian Monks under Pol Pot*. Honolulu: University of Hawai'i Press, 2013.

Marston, John Amos. *History, Buddhism, and New Religious Movements in Cambodia*. Honolulu: University of Hawai'i Press, 2004.

Mackenzie, Rory. *New Buddhist Movements in Thailand: Towards an Understanding of Wat Phra Dhammakāya and Santi Asoke*. Routledge Critical Studies in Buddhism. Abingdon, UK: Routledge, 2007.
Schedneck, Brooke. *Thailand's International Meditation Centers: Tourism and the Global Commodification of Religious Practices*. Routledge Religion in Contemporary Asia Series, 3. London: Routledge, 2017.
Schober, Juliane. *Modern Buddhist Conjunctures in Myanmar: Cultural Narratives, Colonial Legacies, and Civil Society*. Honolulu: University of Hawai'i Press, 2010.
Smith, Bardwell L., ed. *Tradition and Change in Theravāda Buddhism*. Leiden: Brill, 1973.
Strathern, Alan. *Kingship and Conversion in Sixteenth-Century Sri Lanka Portuguese Imperialism in a Buddhist Land*. Cambridge, UK: Cambridge University Press, 2007.
Turner, Alicia Marie. *Saving Buddhism: The Impermanence of Religion in Colonial Burma*. Honolulu: University of Hawai'i Press, 2014.
Young, R. F., and Somaratna, G. P. V. *Vain Debates: The Christian-Buddhist Controversies of Nineteenth Century Ceylon*. Publications of the De Nobili Research Library, 23. Vienna: De Nobili Research Library, 1996.

NOTES

1. Hermann Oldenberg, *The Dipavamsa: An Ancient Buddhist Historical Record* (Delhi: Williams & Norgate, 1992), 5.10 and 5.30–54 (hereafter cited in text as Dīp).
2. This is in particular the *Nikāyasaṅgraha* by Jayabāhu Dharmakīrti (14th-15th century) and the *Saddharmaratnākaraya* by his pupil Vimalakīrti (15th century).
3. Rupert Gethin, "Was Buddhaghosa a Theravādin? Buddhist Identity in the Pali Commentaries and Chronicles," in *How Theravāda is Theravāda? Exploring Buddhist Identities*, ed. Peter Skilling et al. (Chiang Mai: Silkworm Books, 2012), 1–66.
4. Samayabhed-c 95. Vasumitra, *Samayabhedoparacanacakra* [The cycle of the formation of the schismatic doctrines], trans. Keishō Tsukamoto (Taishō Volume 49, Number 2031). BDK English Tripit.aka, 76-I (Berkeley, CA: Bukkyō Dendō Kyōkai, Numata Center for Buddhist Translation, and Research, 2004), 95 (hereafter cited as Samayabhed-c).
5. Samayabhed-c, 94.
6. Cf. Lance S. Cousins, "On the Vibhajjavādins: The Mahiṃsāsaka, Dhammaguttaka, Kassapiya and Tambapaṇṇiya Branches of the Ancient Theriyas," *Buddhist Studies Review* 18, no. 2 (2001): 155–160. Bhavya's work *Tarkajvālā* is only extant in Tibetan translation, edited and translated by Malcolm David Eckel, *Bhāvaviveka and His Buddhist Opponents*, Harvard Oriental Series, 70 (Cambridge, MA: Harvard University Press, 2008).
7. For further references in Indian Sanskrit literature, see Peter Skilling, "Theravāda in History," *Pacific World: Journal of the Institute of Buddhist Studies*, 3rd ser., no. 11 (Fall 2009): 67.
8. The exception is the 7th-century Pāli commentator Dhammapāla, who mentions the fourfold scheme in his subcommentary on Buddhaghosa's *Sumaṅgalavilāsinī*); see Lily de Silva, *Dıghanikāyaṭṭhakathāṭıkā Lınatthavaṇṇanā*, 3 vols. (London: Pali Text Society, 1970), 3:372 (hereafter cited as Sv-pṭ).
9. The occurrences of these terms and their meanings in early Pāli literature were comprehensively discussed by Gethin, "Was Buddhaghosa a Theravādin?" As Gethin (p. 6) correctly remarks, the term *sthaviravāda*, the Sanskrit equivalent to *theravāda*, is not evidenced in any Sanskrit text or translations into other languages (Tibetan, Chinese, etc.). However, it is not a "ghost-word" coined by modern scholars, as claimed in some recent publications. It appears frequently in later Sinhala texts (cf., note 2).
10. For example, the Mahāsāṅghikas have claimed that *they*, not the Sthaviras, continued the original dharma and *vinaya*. See Janice J. Nattier and Charles S. Prebish, "Mahāsāṃghika Origins: The Beginnings of Buddhist Sectarianism," in *History of Religions* 16 (1976), 237–272. Likewise, each *nikāya* of the

Sthavira branch would have asserted that it transmits the teaching of the original Sthaviras, just as it was disputed among the Sri Lankan sub-*nikāyas* which of them represents the lineage of the Sri Lankan Theriyas in its purest form (Jonathan S. Walters, "Buddhist History," in *Querying the Medieval: Texts and the History of Practices in South Asia*, ed. Ronald Inden, Jonathan Walters, and Daud Ali (Oxford: Oxford University Press, 2000), 99–164.

11. Dīp 36.29–37.57; Wilhelm Geiger, ed., *The Mahāvaṃsa* (London: Pali Text Society, 1908), 5.1–21 (hereafter cited as Mhv); and *Nikāyasaṃgraha*, ed. Sanat Nānāyakkāra, *Nikāya Saṃgrahaya* (Dehivala, Sri Lanka: Bauddha Saṃskṛtika Madhyasthānaya, 1997), 7.13–27 (hereafter cited as Nikāya-$s_{(N)}$).
12. Mhv 5.13. On the allegedly broken ordination lineage of the Abhayagiri Nikāya see Mhv 33.95–98. Its and the Jetavana Nikaya's later betrayal of the Mahāvihāra and their "apostasy" from the "true doctrine" is depicted in a lengthy conspiracy story in Mhv 37; see also Jonathan S. Walters, "Mahāsena at the Mahāvihāra: On the Interpretation and Politics of History in Pre-Colonial Sri Lanka," in *Invoking the Past. The Uses of History in South Asia*, ed. Daud Ali (Oxford: Oxford University Press, 1999), 322–366.
13. Cf. note 21. The Sri Lankan communities were certainly involved in inter-*nikāya* cooperation. The diplomatic concept of the four *mahānikāyas* (see the section on "Mainland Indian Understandings of Sthavira") appears to have provided an intellectual tool for comparative studies of Buddhist literature of divergent *nikāya* provenience. The clearest example is a 9th-century Sanskrit inscription found at the Abhayagiri monastic compound stating that twenty-five members of each of the four *mahānikāyas* lived together in a certain building of the Abhayagiri monastery on a regular basis (but cf. Heinz Bechert, "The Nikāya-s of Mediaeval Sri Lanka and the Unification of the Saṅgha by Parākramabāhu I," in *Studies on Buddhism in Honour of Professor A. K. Warder*, ed. N. K. Wagle and F. Watanabe (Toronto: University of Toronto, 1993), 15 for an opposing view). Gunawardana compared this situation to North Indian Buddhist universities like Vikramaśīla in which members of different nikāyas engaged in comparative studies of their respective teachings; see R. A. L. H. Gunawardana, *Robe and Plough: Monasticism and Economic Interest in Early Medieval Sri Lanka*, Association of Asian Studies, Monographs and Papers, 35 (Tucson: University of Arizona Press, 1979), 250–254.
14. This statement concerns primarily epigraphical sources. Literary sources composed in Sri Lanka become accessible only from the 4th century onward. Older strata of Sri Lankan Buddhist literature can be reconstructed only indirectly and with a high degree of uncertainty through later citations and adaptations. There are two literary representations of the wider buddhist world in the form of accounts of the historical development of Buddhism after the buddha's death: one is the mentioned *Dīpavaṃsa*; the other is included in the *vinaya* commentary *Samantapāsādikā* (5th century). Both are based on lost older material and seem to have used different sources; Frank Perera, "The Early Historiography of Ceylon," PhD diss., University of Göttingen, Göttingen, Germany, 1979. Albeit slightly younger, the *Samantapāsādikā* seems to be based on source material representing an older stage of the account of Buddhist history than the *Dīpavaṃsa*'s sources. It is noticeable that the *Samantapāsādikā* knows of no different forms or lineages of Buddhism but the *Dīpavaṃsa* presents the later history of Buddhism as a process of secession. For the sake of completeness, it must be mentioned that stories about the so-called three councils *(saṅgīti)* are, indeed, older than the *Dīpavaṃsa*, but these do not paint a heterogeneous picture of the buddhist world. They are narratives about "solved crises" within the sangha, which did not produce lasting rival institutions.
15. J. Ph. Vogel, "Prakrit Inscriptions from a Buddhist Site at Nagarjunikonda," *Epigraphia Indica* 20 (1933): 1–37.
16. Cousins, "On the Vibhajjavādins." To be exact, Cousins assumes that "Vibhajjavāda"—the "analyst viewpoint"—is a common denominator of the *abhidharma* systems of traditions, which decidedly dissociated themselves from the "everything exists" (*sarvam asti*) theory of the Sarvāstivādins and those groups who postulated a transcendent bearer of personality (*pudgalavāda*). He supposes that the Vibhajjavādins included the Mahīśāsakas, Kāśyapīyas, Dharmaguptakas, and the Sri Lankan lineage (Tambapaṇṇiyas).

17. See, however, the alternative interpretation that *mahāvihāra* denotes a local monastery of Nāgārjuṇīkoṇḍa by D. C. Sircar and A. N. Lahiri, "Footprint Slab Inscription from Nagarjunikonda," in *Epigraphia Indica* 33 (1959–1960): 249. Jonathan S. Walters warns that the term *mahāvihāravāsin* here needs not necessarily be identical to the term familiar from later Sri Lankan literature (Jonathan S. Walters, "Mahāyāna Theravāda and the Origins of the Mahāvihāra," in *The Sri Lanka Journal of the Humanities* 23, no. 1–2 ([1997]), pp. 100–119).
18. Cousins, "On the Vibhajjavādins," 151.
19. Dīp 159–160.
20. On the semantics of the term *dhammadīpa,* often mistranslated as "island of the dhamma" and charged with modern nationalist projections, see Peter Schalk, "Semantic Transformations of the Dhammadipa," *Buddhism, Conflict and Violence in Modern Sri Lanka,* ed. Mahinda Deegalle, Routledge Critical Studies in Buddhism (London: Routledge, 2006), 86–92, particularly p. 89 on the "sectarian" implications of the term.
21. Gethin discusses traces in early Pāli commentaries assuming a certain degree of unity among the different *nikāyas* of the Sthavira branch (as opposed to the Mahāsāṅghika-related *nikāyas*) or even the concept of a "broader" Theriya community, which incorporated several *nikāyas* of the Sthavira branch (Gethin, "Was Buddhaghosa a Theravādin?," 13–20).
22. Heinz Bechert, "Buddha-Feld und Verdienstübertragung: Mahāyāna-Ideen im Theravāda-Buddhismus Ceylons," *Bulletin de la Classe des Lettres et des Sciences morales et politiques* 5, sér. 62 (1976): 27–51.
23. Mhv 36.41, 110–117; 37.1–31. The story of this "heresy" is much elaborated in Nikāya-s$_{(N)}$ 14.18–17.28. This latter text also relates the Abhayagiri Nikāya's later adoption of further "heresies" (Nikāya-s$_{(N)}$ 21.15–24.5), two of which are clearly offshoots of what the Indian tradition called Vajrayāna, whereas the Sri Lankan text speaks of these two "heresies" as the "Vajraparvata Nikāya" and the "Teaching of the Blue Robe" (*nīlapaṭadarśana*).
24. Senerat Paranavitana, "Mahāyānism in Ceylon," *Ceylon Journal of Science* 2 (1928): 35–71; but see Peter Skilling, "Vaidalya, Mahāyāna, and Bodhisatva in India: An Essay Towards Historical Understanding," in *The Bodhisattva Ideal: Essays on the Emergence of Mahāyāna,* ed. Bhikkhu Nyanatusita (Kandy: Buddhist Publication Society), 69–164. See also, note [35].
25. Sven Bretfeld, "Resonant Paradigms in the Study of Religion and the Emergence of Theravāda Buddhism," *Religion* 42, no. 2 (2012): 273–297.
26. Oskar von Hinüber, "Epigraphical Varieties of Continental Pāli from Devnimori and Ratnagiri," in *Buddhism and Its Relation to Other Religions: Essays in Honour of Dr. Shozen Kumoi on His Seventieth Birthday,* ed. Kosho Mitzutani (Kyoto: Heirakuji Shoten, 1985), 185–200.
27. Dīp 159–160, similar and more detailed in Buddhaghosa's *Samantapāsādikā*; see Nicholas Abedheera Jayawickrama, *Inception of Discipline and Vinaya-Nidāna: Being a Translation and Edition of the Bāhiranidāna of Buddhaghosa's Samantapāsādikā, the Vinaya Commentary,* Sacred Books of the Buddhists, 21 (Bristol, UK: Pali Text Society, 1962), 63–72 (hereafter cited as Sp$_{(J)}$).
28. Dīp 12–16; the account is confusing and seems to loosely patch together several sources. A more homogeneous account of Mahinda's conversion of the country is given in Mhv 13–20 and Sp$_{(J)}$ 73–107.
29. Erich Frauwallner, *The Earliest Vinaya and the Beginnings of Buddhist Literature,* Serie Orientale Roma, 8 (Rome: Giovanni Bardi, 1956). Frauwallner localized the origins in Vidiśa. Cousins, "On the Vibhajjavādins," 167–168, places them in Vanavāsa. An important key to this question would be the original home of the Pāli language, which is likewise unclear. On the different suggested origins of Pāli, see Oskar von Hinüber, "The Oldest Literary Language of Buddhism," in *Selected Papers on Pāli Studies,* ed. Oskar von Hinüber (Oxford: Pali Text Society, 2009), 181.
30. On the Theriyas being the Sri Lankan wing of the Mahīśāsakas see André Bareau, *Les sectes bouddhiques du petit véhicule,* Publications de l'École Française d'Extréme-Orient. (Saigon: École Française d'Extréme-

Orient, 1955). On the idea of a multi-nikāya alliance constituting the vibhajjavādins see Cousins, "On the Vibhajjavādins."

31. R. A. L. H. Gunawardana,"Prelude to the State: An Early Phase in the Evolution of Political Institutions in Ancient Sri Lanka," *Sri Lanka Journal of the Humanities* 8 (1982): 1–39, and Robin A. E. Coningham, "Monks, Caves and Kings: A Reassessment of the Nature of Early Buddhism in Sri Lanka," *World Archaeology* 27, no. 2 (1995): 222–242.
32. Mhv 33.96 relates that the monks of the Abhayagiri formed a "faction" (*pakkha*)—obviously a legal unit separate from the Mahāvihāra—due to a *vinaya* dispute. The text makes clear that "these monks [had] split from the Theravādins" (*te theravādīhi pabhinnā bhikkhavo*, Mhv 33.98) by this act.
33. Steven Collins, "On the Very Idea of the Pāli Canon," *Journal of the Pāli Text Society* 15 (1990): 89–126.
34. Mhv 33.100–101.
35. A contemporary Sinhala inscription calls these texts *vayatuḍalaka pot* "Vayatuḍala books"; see Sirimal Ranawella, "Jētavanārāma Fragmentary Slab Inscription of King Mahāsena, in *Sinhala Inscriptions in the Colombo National Museum*, ed. Sirimal Ranawella, Spolia Zeylanica: Bulletin of the National Museum of Sri Lanka, 42 (Colombo: Department of National Museums, 2005), 3–5). The *Mahāvaṃsa* associates a foreign teaching tradition (*vāda*) to these scriptures and renders the term into Pāli as *vetullavāda*. Several scholars have assumed that this teaching tradition was an early form of Mahāyāna Buddhism (see also, note [24]). The fact that various Mahāyāna sūtras have been known and worshiped in Sri Lanka seems to confirm this assumption (cf. Heinz Bechert, "Mahāyāna Literature in Sri Lanka: The Early Phase," in *Prajñāpāramitā and Related Systems: Studies in Honor of Edward Conze*, ed. Lewis Lancaster, Berkeley Buddhist Studies Series, 1 (Berkeley: University of California Press, 1977), 361–368; and Heinz Bechert, *Eine regionale hochsprachliche Tradition in Südasien: Sanskrit-Literatur bei den buddhistischen Singhalesen*, Veröffentlichungen zu den Sprachen und Kulturen Südasiens, Heft 37 (Wien: Österreichischen Akademie der Wissenschaften, 2005), 59–68. It is, however, far from clear which texts the term *vayatuḍalaka pot* actually referred to in the 4th century.
36. Cf. note [23].
37. Bechert, "Mahāyāna Literature in Sri Lanka"; John Holt, *Buddha in the Crown: Avalokiteśvara in the Buddhist Traditions of Sri Lanka* (New York: Oxford University Press, 1991); Walters, "Buddhist History"; Rangama Chandawimala, *Buddhist Heterodoxy of Abhayagiri Sect: A Study of the School of Abhayagiri in Ancient Sri Lanka* (Saarbrücken: Lambert Academic Publishing, 2013); and Jeffrey Roger Sundberg and Rolf Giebel, "The Life of the Tang Court Monk Vajrabodhi as Chronicled by Lü Xiang: South Indian and Śrı Laṅkān Antecedents to the Arrival of the Buddhist Vajrayāna in Eighth-Century Java and China— Recent Research on Esoteric Buddhism," *Pacific World: Journal of the Institute of Buddhist Studies* 13 (2011): 129–222.
38. Jayabāhu Dharmakīrti's *Nikāyasaṅgraha* (cf. note [2]) presents the Mahāvihāra lineage as heroes of Buddhist "orthodoxy" who have resisted any "heretic" teaching arriving in Sri Lanka throughout history (cf. note [23]). This teleological imagination of the Mahāvihāra's role in the history of Buddhism is widely informed by the "neo-orthodox" agenda of the post-Parākramabāhu period (see section on "Reform of Parākramabāhu I"), but was hardly scrutinized by modern scholarship.
39. Peter Skilling, "Vimuttimagga and Abhayagiri: The Form-Aggregate According to the Saṃskṛtāsaṃskṛtaviniścaya," *Journal of the Pali Text Society* 20 (1994171–210); Peter Skilling, "A Citation from the Buddhavaṃsa of the Abhayagiri School," *Journal of the Pali Text Society*, New Series 18 (1993): 165–175; Kate Crosby, "History versus Modern Myth: The Abhayagirivihāra, The Vimuttimagga and Yogācāra Meditation," *Journal of Indian Philosophy* 27 (1999): 503–550; and K. R. Norman, "The Literary Works of the Abhayagirivihārins," in *Kalyāṇamitta: Professor Hajime Nakamura Felicitation Volume*, ed. V. N. Jha (Delhi: Sri Satguru Publications, 1991), 41–50.

40. Bechert, "Mahāyāna Literature in Sri Lanka," 362. In our nomenclature we would have to say *Theriya*.
41. Cf., e.g., Jonathan A. Silk, "What, If Anything, Is Mahāyāna Buddhism? Problems of Definitions and Classifications." *Numen* 49, no. 4 (2002): 355–405, for a more complex understanding of Mahāyāna.
42. Chandawimala, *Buddhist Heterodoxy of Abhayagiri Sect*. For a more dynamical understanding of Theravāda as a multifaceted, contested discourse of institutional identity-building, see for example, Walters, "Mahāyāna Theravāda and the Origins of the Mahāvihāra"; Walters, "Buddhist History"; and Bretfeld, "Resonant Paradigms in the Study of Religion and the Emergence of Theravāda Buddhism."
43. Gunawardana, *Robe and Plough*, 262–271; for Bodhgayā, see also Vincent Tounier, "Mahākāśyapa, His Lineage, and the Wish for Buddhahood: Reading Anew the Bodhgayā Inscriptions of Mahānāman," *Indo-Iranian Journal* 57 (2014): 1–60.
44. Skilling, "A Citation from the Buddhavaṃsa of the Abhayagiri School"; and Skilling, "Vimuttimagga and Abhayagiri."
45. On contacts with China, see G. S. M. Weerasinghe, *A History of the Cultural Relations Between Sri Lanka and China: An Aspect of the Silk Rout*,. The Central Cultural Fund (Colombo: The Ministry of Cultural Affairs of Sri Lanka, 1999). The famous Abhayagiri branch in Java has been discussed by Jeffrey Roger Sundber,. "The Abhayagirivihāra's *pāṃśukūlika* Monks in Second Lambakaṇṇa Śrı Laṅkā and Śailendra Java: The Fluorescence and Fall of Influential Esoteric Buddhist Adepts," *Pacific World: Journal of the Institute of Buddhist Studies*, 3rd ser., 16 (2015): 49–185, among others. For early contacts to mainland Southeast Asia see section on "Early Theriyas among the Pyu and Mon."
46. Oskar von Hinüber, *The Oldest Pāli Manuscript: Four Folios of the Vinaya-Piṭaka from the National Archives, Kathmandu*, Untersuchungen zur Sprachgeschichte und Handschriftenkunde des Pāli, 2 (Berlin: Akademie der Wissenschaften und der Literatur, geistes- und sozialwissenschaftliche Klasse, 1991).
47. Peter Skilling, "Theravadin Literature in Tibetan Translation," *Journal of the Pali Text Society* 19 (1993): 69–201.
48. Peter Schalk, ed., *Buddhism among Tamils in Pre-Colonial Tamilakam and Ilam*. Part 1, *Prologue: The Pre-Pallava and the Pallava Period*, Historia Religionum Series, 19 (Uppsala: Uppsala University, 2002) 387–395.
49. The Sri Lankan Pāli commentators of the 5th century often refer to an *Andhaka-Aṭṭhakathā* ("Commentary of Āndhra"), which may have been a text by an established Theriya community in Āndhra. If this is true, the Theriyas of this region were at least independent enough from Sri Lanka to develop their own exegetical tradition. But their differences may have even been more grave. From citations in a *vinaya* commentary of the Mahāvihāra (*Samantapāsādikā*), P. Kieffer-Pülz concluded that the *Andhaka-Aṭṭhakathā* was composed in Pāli and based on a *vinaya* closely related but not identical to the one transmitted by the Sri Lankan lineage. So even if the lineage behind the *Andhaka-Aṭṭhakathā* was a "sister-lineage" of the Sri Lankan Theriyas and had developed from the same root—*ikāya* (i.e., the Indian proto-Theriyas)—there is good reason to assume that they have not acknowledged each other's ordination tradition; see Petra Kieffer-Pülz, "Zitate aus der Andhaka-Aṭṭhakathā in der Samantapāsādikā," in *Studien zur Indologie und Buddhismuskunde: Festgabe des Seminars für Indologie und Buddhismuskunde für Professor Dr. Heinz Bechert*, Studien zur Indologie und Buddhismuskunde, Festgabe des Seminars für Indologie und Buddhismuskunde für Professor Dr. Heinz Bechert, ed. Reinhold Grünendahl, Jens-Uwe Hartmann, and Petra Kieffer-Pülz. Indica et Tibetica Series, 22 (Bonn, Germany: Harrassowitz, 1993), 171–212.
50. Cousins, "On the Vibhajjavādins," 167, is opting for this possibility.
51. The *Cūḷavaṃsa* contains two accounts of this event; see [Cūḷv = Dhammakitti., in *Cūḷavaṃsa*., ed. Wilhelm Geiger, 2 vols. (London: Pali Text Society, 1925–1927. 1925–1927)]. 73.12–22 and 78.5–27 (hereafter cited as Cūḷv). William Geiger attributes these accounts to two different sources; see Geiger,

trans., *The Cūḷavaṃsa: Being the More Recent Part of the Mahāvaṃsa*, English translation by C. Mabel Rickmers, Vol. 2 (London: Pali Text Society, 1929), 102n2.

52. Bechert, "The Nikāya-s of Mediaeval Sri Lanka and the Unification of the Saṅgha by Parākramabāhu I."
53. The *katikāvatas*, so far still available, have been edited and studied by Nandasena Ratnapala, *The Katikāvatas: Laws of the Buddhist Order of Ceylon from the 12th Century to the 18th Century* (Munich, Germany: Kitzinger, 1971).
54. Holt, *Buddha in the Crown.*
55. Peter Skilling, "The Advent of Theravāda Buddhism to Mainland South-East Asia," *Journal of the International Association of Buddhist Studies* 20, no. 1 (1997): 93–107.
56. Janice Stargardt, *The Ancient Pyu of Burma: Early Pyu Cities in a Man-Made Landscape*, Vol. 1 (Cambridge, UK: Pacsea, 1990); and Prapod Assavavirulhakarn, *The Ascendancy of Theravāda Buddhism in Southeast Asia* (Bangkok: Silkworm Books, 2010).
57. Skilling, "Advent of Theravāda Buddhism to Mainland South-East Asia"; and Crosby, "History versus Modern Myth." Skilling talks about "continental Sthaviras" in this sense, see Skilling, "Theravadin Literature in Tibetan Translation," 150, and "On the School-Affiliation of the 'Patna *Dhammapada*,'" *Journal of the Pali Text Society* 23 (1997): 99.
58. Taw Sein Ko, *The Kalyānı Inscriptions Erected by King Dhammacetı at Pegu in 1476 A.D. Text and Translation*, Archaeological Survey of India, Rangoon, 1892, 2–3.
59. Michael A. Aung-Thwin, *The Mists of Rāmañña: The Legend That Was Lower Burma* (Honolulu: University of Hawai'i Press, 2005).
60. Assavavirulhakarn, *Ascendancy of Theravāda Buddhism in Southeast Asia*, 192. Note that Assavavirulhakarn does not follow Aung-Thwin's thesis that there was no Mon culture in Burma before the rise of the Pagan empire.
61. On this tradition, see Kate Crosby, "Tantric Theravāda: A Bibliographic Essay on the Writings of François Bizot and Others on the Yogāvacara Tradition," *Contemporary Buddhism* 1, no. 2 (2000): 141–198.
62. See Skilling, "Advent of Theravāda Buddhism to Mainland South-East Asia"; Crosby, "History versus Modern Myth"; and Crosby, "Tantric Theravāda" for a discussion of speculations in this direction.
63. Skilling, "Advent of Theravāda Buddhism to Mainland South-East Asia," 101.
64. Peter Skilling, "Introduction," in *How Theravāda is Theravāda? Exploring Buddhist Identities*, ed. Peter Skilling et al. (Chiang Mai, Thailand: Silkworm Books, 2012), xiii–xxx.
65. Steven Collins, *Nirvana and other Buddhist Felicities: Utopias of the Pali Imaninaire*, Cambridge Studies in Religious Traditions, 12 (Cambridge, UK: Cambridge University Press, 1998) 41.
66. Peter Skilling, "King Rama I and Wat Phra Chetuphon: The Buddha-Śāsanā in Early Bangkok," in *How Theravāda is Theravāda? Exploring Buddhist Identities*, ed. Peter Skilling et al. (Chiang Mai, Thailand: Silkworm Books, 2012), 297–354.
67. The complex history of the *Khuddakanikāya/Kṣudrakāgama* was studied by Etienne Lamotte, "Problèmes concernant les textes canoniques 'mineurs,'" in *Journal Asiatique* 244 (1956): 249–264. Also in the Theriya tradition its status and content was historically unstable to a certain degree (cf. Oskar von Hinüber, *A Handbook of Pāli Literature*, 2nd ed., Vol. 2, *Indian Philology an South Asian Studies* (Berlin: Walter de Gruyter, 2000), 41–43).
68. Theoretically, each *nikāya* must have possessed its own peculiar *Vinaya Piṭaka*. This is what formally constitutes a *nikāya*. Apart from the Pāli version, the *vinayas* of the following *nikāyas* have been preserved in Chinese or Tibetan translation: Mahāsāṃghika (Chinese), Sarvāstivāda (Chinese), Dharmaguptaka (Chinese), Mahīśāsaka (Chinese), and Mūlasarvāstivāda (Tibetan, partly Chinese). Parts of the Mūlasarvāstivāda and the Lokottara-Mahāsāṃghika *vinaya* have also survived in Sanskrit.
69. As early as 1976, Nattier and Prebish convincingly argued that the Theriya account of the first *nikāya* split was not historically accurate. A comparison of sources on the relationship between Sthaviras and

Mahāsāṃghikas cannot confirm that the Sthaviras represented a conservative "orthodoxy" opposing a "lax" monastic faction (i.e., the Mahāsāṃghikas) who wanted to change the *vinaya* into something more "easygoing." Rather, the opposite seems to have been the case (see Nattier and Prebish, "Mahāsāṃghika Origins").

70. Erich Frauwallner, "Abhidharma-Studien I–V," in *Wiener Zeitschrift für die Kunde Südasiens*, (1963–1973), 7–17.
71. For a summary of questions on the history and concept of the Pāli Canon, see K. R. Norman, *A Philological Approach to Buddhism*, The Bukkyō Dendō Kyōkai Lectures 1994, The Buddhist Forum, 5 (Berkeley, CA: Institute for Buddhist Studies, 2012), 131–148. For an overview of its structure and content, see K. R. Norman, *Pāli Literature: Including the Canonical Literature in Prakrit and Sanskrit of all the Hınayāna Schools of Buddhism*, A History of Indian Literature, 7.2 (Wiesbaden, Germany: Harrassowitz, 1983); and von Hinüber, *A Handbook of Pāli Literature*.
72. Aleida Assmann and Jan Assmann, eds., *Kanon und Zensur*, Beiträge zur Archäologie der literarischen Kommunikation, 2 (Munich: Fink, 1987).
73. Nikāya-$s_{(N)}$ 12.10–13.8.
74. See Bechert, "Buddha-Feld und Verdienstübertragung," 29, for a refutation of speculations that the Abhayagiri might have transmitted a canon in Sanskrit.
75. Collins, "On the Very Idea of the Pāli Canon."
76. Collins, 103.
77. Stephen C. Berkwitz, *Buddhist History in the Vernacular: The Power of the Past in Late Medieval Sri Lanka*, Brill's Indological Library, 23 (Leiden, The Netherlands: Brill, 2004); and Mahinda Deegalle, *Popularizing Buddhism: Preaching as Performance in Sri Lanka* (Albany: SUNY Press, 2006).
78. The story of the third *saṅgīti* occurs in *Dīpavaṃsa* (Dīp 7.34–43 and 44–59, two versions), *Mahāvaṃsa* (Mhv 5.267–282), *Samantapāsādikā* ($Sp_{(J)}$ 37–62), *Kathāvatthu-atthakathā* (Kv-a 5-7), and several later texts, such as the *Nikāyasaṃgraha* (Nikāya-$s_{(N)}$ 8.1–11.13).
79. Alleged confirmations of these missions in Aśoka inscriptions have been misinterpreted by earlier scholarship. Cousins, "On the Vibhajjavādins," on the other hand, speculates that the story of the "Aśoka missions" was a shared tradition among the *nikāyas* constituting the Vibhajjavāda group as he understands it (see note [16]). Also, Michael Willis reckons with them as a historical fact; see Willis, "Buddhist Saints in Ancient Vedisa," *Journal of the Royal Asiatic Society* 11, no. 2 (2001): 219–228.
80. The case of Majjhima who was sent to the Himalaya is a special historical problem (Willis, "Buddhist Saints in Ancient Vedisa").
81. On the history of the terms *pāḷibhāsā* and *pāḷi*, see Kate Crosby, "The Origin of Pāli as a Language Name in Medieval Theravāda Literature," *Journal of the Centre for Buddhist Studies, Sri Lanka* 2 (2004): 70–116.
82. K. R. Norman, "The Role of Pāli in Early Sinhalese Buddhism," in *Buddhism in Ceylon and Studies on Religious Syncretism in Buddhist Countries*, ed. Heinz Bechert (Goottingen: Vandenhoeck & Ruprecht, 1978), 28–47 and 34–35.
83. Jayawickrama, *Inception of Discipline and Vinaya-Nidāna*, 2.
84. See Sheldon Pollock, *The Language of the Gods in the World of Men. Sanskrit, Culture and Power in Premodern India* (Berkeley: University of California Press, 2006).
85. Norman, "Role of Pāli in Early Sinhalese Buddhism," 43–44.
86. Gethin, "Was Buddhaghosa a Theravādin?"
87. Skilling, "Introduction," xix–xx.
88. For a detailed study of these terminologies and the social impact of these terms, see Todd LeRoy Perreira, "Whence Theravāda? The Modern Genealogy of an Ancient Term," in *How Theravāda is Theravāda? Exploring Buddhist Identities*, ed. Peter Skilling et al. (Chiang Mai, Thailand: Silkworm Books, 2012), 443–571.
89. Perreira, "Whence Theravāda?" 550.

90. Bretfeld, "Resonant Paradigms in the Study of Religion and the Emergence of Theravāda Buddhism," 290.
91. Paranavitana, "Mahāyānism in Ceylon."
92. Bretfeld, "Resonant Paradigms in the Study of Religion and the Emergence of Theravāda Buddhism," 292.
93. This topos was elaborated in a somewhat later Buddhist nationalist account that presents worldwide civilization history as culminating in Sri Lankan Theravāda Buddhism; see D. C. Vijayawardhana, *Dharmavijaya: The Revolt in the Temple, Composed to Commemorate 2500 Years of the Land, the Race and the Faith* (Colombo, Sri Lanka: Daily News Press, 1953).
94. In modern Thailand, for example, where Mahāyāna monasteries of Chinese and Vietnamese migrants remain outside of the centralized administration of monastic institutions; Heinz Bechert, *Buddhismus, Staat und Gesellschaft in den Ländern des Theravāda-Buddhismus.2: Birma, Kambodscha, Laos, Thailand*. Schriften des Instituts für Asienkunde in Hamburg, 17.2 (Wiesbaden: Harrassowitz, 1967), 188). Another inter-*nikāya* conflict in modern times is the reintroduction of a female ordination lineage into the Theriya-order from China (see note [97]).
95. Ann Heirman, "Vinaya: From India to China," in *The Spread of Buddhism*, ed. Anne Heirman and Stefan-Peter Bumbacher (Leiden, The Netherlands: Brill, 2007), 167–202.
96. He calls them "Vaitulya Nikāya and Vajraparvata Nikāya" (Nikāya-s$_{(N)}$ 21.15–24.5).
97. For global comparisons the classification Theravāda Buddhism, Mahāyāna Buddhism, and Vajrayāna/Tantric Buddhism are common in modern "Theravāda countries," while the *nikāya* concept is pretty much reduced to the internal differentiation processes giving rise to monastic sublineages within the Theriya Nikāya. The difference between the Theriya Nikāya and the other still extent *nikāyas* (Dharmaguptaka and Mūlasarvāstivāda) rarely plays a role. One important exception is the debate about the reintroduction of a female ordination-lineage in Sri Lanka and other Theriya countries. The succession of *bhikkhuṇī* (nun) ordination was interrupted, and therefore lost, in the Theriya lineage several centuries ago. Modern attempts to revive this tradition with the help of Chinese nuns have time and again been blocked with the argument that Chinese *bhikkhuṇīs* belonged to the Dharmaguptaka Nikāya, which, by definition, uses another *vinaya* than the Theriya monks. Therefore new communities of fully ordained nuns in Sri Lanka would be institutionally and ritually incompatible with the local monk communities. For a detailed study of this topic, see Bhikkhu Bodhi, *The Revival of Bhikkhunı Ordination in the Theravāda Tradition* (Penang, Malaysia: Inward Path, 2009).
98. Jason A. Carbine, *Sons of the Buddha: Continuities and Ruptures in a Burmese Monastic Tradition*, Religion and Society, 50 (Berlin: De Gruyter, 2011), 74.
99. However, international "sub-*nikāya* relationships" can shape the authority structures of local conflicts. An example is the Sīmā dispute of Balapiṭiya (Sri Lanka) in the mid-19th century, in which the Burmese Saṅgharāja Ñeyyadhamma was invoked to settle a quarrel on a complex *vinaya* question between two camps in the Sri Lankan Amarapura Nikāya. The Amarapura Nikāya of Sri Lanka was founded with the help of a Burmese ordination tradition and is technically a branch of the Burmese Saṅgharāja's lineage. The expertise exchanged between Sri Lankan and Burmese *vinaya* specialists in this matter is currently studied by Petra Kieffer-Pülz (www.adwmainz.de/projekte/der-streit-um-die-sima-von-balapitiya/projektbeschreibung-project-description.html).
100. Cf. Carbine, *Sons of the Buddha*, 80.
101. Heinz Bechert, *Buddhismus, Staat und Gesellschaft in den Ländern des Theravāda-Buddhismus*, Vol. 1, *Grundlagen, Ceylon (Sri Lanka)*, 2nd ed, Schriften des Instituts für Asienkunde in Hamburg, 5 (Frankfurt: Alfred Metzner, 1966), 263–265.
102. The complex contexts of the emergence of the Siyam Nikāya have been studied in detail in Anne M. Blackburn, *Buddhist Learning and Textual Practice in 18th Century Lankan Monastic Culture* (Princeton, NJ: Princeton University Press, 2001).

103. Cf. Bechert, *Buddhismus, Staat und Gesellschaft in den Ländern des Theravāda-Buddhismus*, 21; and Carbine, *Sons of the Buddha*, 75.
104. E. Michael Mendelson, *Sangha and State in Burma: A Study of Monastic Sectarianism and Leadership* (Ithaca, NY: Cornell University Press, 1975), 92–96.
105. Mendelson, *Sangha and State in Burma*, 96–102. However, see Heinz Bechert, *Buddhismus, Staat und Gesellschaft: In den Ländern des Theravāda-Buddhismus*, Neuausgabe mit Supplementen sowie Personen- und Sachregister, 2nd ed., Vol. 2, *Birma, Kambodscha, Laos, Thailand. Veröffentlichungen des Seminars für Indologie und Buddhismuskunde der Universität Göttingen*, 8 (Göttingen, Germany: Seminar für Indologie und Buddhismuskunde, 2000), 326.
106. Carbine, *Sons of the Buddha*, 76.
107. A concise overview of the legal history until the late 1960s is given in Bechert, *Buddhismus, Staat und Gesellschaft in den Ländern des Theravāda-Buddhismus*, 184–189.
108. Skilling, "Introduction," xix.
109. Predilections for certain monastic lineages are evidenced for some kings. For example King Sena I (846–866) of the second Lambakaṇṇa dynasty of Sri Lanka seems to have been an ardent follower of Tantric practices maintained by the Abhayagiri Nikāya at that time. Therefore this king entered Mahāvihāra history as "Sena, the madman." His successor Sena II (866–901) seems to have abolished those practices in favor of a Mahāvihāra-based Śrāvakayāna (Nikāya-$s_{(N)}$ 23–24). But even Sena II is never called a Theravādin, Śrāvakayānin, Mahāvihārin, or similar.
110. Bechert refers the modern example of the Burmese Hngetwiṅ Nikāya, whose radical rejection of offerings to the Buddha had impacts on the ritual practice of the laity (Bechert, *Buddhismus, Staat und Gesellschaft*, 330).
111. An example can be found in Hammalawa Saddhatissa, ed., *Upāsakajanālaṅkāra: A Critical Edition and Study* (London: Pali Text Society, 1965); hereafter cited as Upās. This Pāli handbook of religious education for Buddhist laypeople was probably written not long after Parākramabāhu's reform (12th century). The author highlights (Upās 357) that his work is based on the methods of the Mahāvihāra "unmixed with the standpoints of other *nikāyas*" (*nikāyantaraladdhīhi*). Indeed, the text occasionally refutes divergent standpoints but rarely identifies their promoters by name. On one occasion a deviant viewpoint is attributed to the "Mahāsaṅghikas and Abhayagirivāsin" (Upās 292). Some scholars have argued that the work was generally implicitly arguing against Abhayagiri doctrines, especially as one of its main references was perhaps written by an Abhayagiri author. K. R. Norman has rejected this view; Norman, "Literary Works of the Abhayagirivihārins," 211–215). Be that as it may, we can conclude that the author emphasized that his handbook of lay-education followed the "correct" teaching tradition of his *nikāya* and makes his readers aware of opposing views without, however, systematically instigating them against concretely named rivals.
112. Skilling, "Introduction," xxii–xxiii.
113. Holt, *Buddha in the Crown*, 91–124.
114. Paranavitana, "Mahāyānism in Ceylon," 70; Rangama Chandawimala, "The Impact of the Abhayagiri Practices on the Development of Theravada Buddhism in Sri Lanka," PhD thesis, University of Hong Kong, 2007, p. 100. The works in question—the texts of Guruḷugōmī (12th century), the *Pūjāvaliya* (12th century), the *Saddharmālaṅkāraya* (15th century), the *Saddharmaratnākaraya* (15th century)—self-proclaim to have been written in order to communicate the principles of Buddhism to the "uneducated," who are unable to read Pāli and Sanskrit. If this is so, we may wonder if at least some Mahāyāna ideas had ever been more popular among the Sri Lankan laity than *after* the triumph of the Mahāvihāra-oriented "neo-orthodoxy"!
115. Nikāya-$s_{(N)}$ 22.24–26.

116. On this change of authority structures see Sven Bretfeld, "Buddhistische Laien, buddhistische Profis. Religiöse Individualisierung als Folge einer Neuverteilung religiösen Wissens in Sri Lanka," in *Transformierte Buddhismen* 1 (2008), 108–135.
117. Hans G. Kippenberg, *Die Entdeckung der Religionsgeschichte. Religionswissenschaft und Moderne* (Munich: Beck, 1997).
118. The post-orientalist argument of Buddhism as a Western product was highlighted in Tomoko Masuzawa, *The Inventions of World Religions: Or, How European Universalism was Preserved in the Language of Pluralism* (Chicago: University of Chicago Press, 2005). For a comprehensive survey of modern Buddhist movements, see David L. McMahan, *The Making of Buddhist Modernism* (Oxford: Oxford University Press, 2008).
119. See, for example, Philip C. Almond, *The British Discovery of Buddhism* (Cambridge, UK: Cambridge University Press, 1988); and Elizabeth J. Harris, *Theravāda Buddhism and the British Encounter: Religious, Missionary and Colonial Experience in Nineteenth-Century Sri Lanka*, Routledge Critical Studies in Buddhism (London: Routledge, 2006).
120. Bretfeld, "Resonant Paradigms in the Study of Religion and the Emergence of Theravāda Buddhism," 284–285.

Sven Bretfeld

THÍCH NHẤT HẠNH IN THE CONTEXT OF THE MODERN DEVELOPMENT OF VIETNAMESE BUDDHISM

INTRODUCTION

Many Vietnamese Buddhist monastics, both in Vietnam and overseas, will assert that Thích Nhất Hạnh's teachings and organization are not Buddhist, or at least are not Vietnamese Buddhist. This view is also reflected in the academic assessment given by Nguyen and Barber that the " 'New Age'-style Zen and rituals created by him . . . do not have any affinity with or any foundation in traditional Vietnamese Buddhist practices."[1] Instead this article argues that, while representing a modernist, globalist interpretation of Buddhism, Thích Nhất Hạnh's development is rooted in the Vietnamese Buddhist experience of the 20th century, and therefore focuses more on the first part of his life, before he was exiled from Vietnam and recreated himself as a Zen master in the West. While something of his career in the West is discussed, the focus is on his pre-exile period. There are two reasons for this: the first is that the earlier developments are fundamental for understanding his overall trajectory; and the second is that most of the source material for the post-exile period is more accessible and available in English, whereas a critical understanding of the earlier material requires access to sources that are harder to track down and require an ability to read Vietnamese.

The article starts with the historical context of the Buddhist developments in Vietnam in the 20th century. It then provides a biographical account of Thích Nhất Hạnh's life before it discusses two of the features for which Thích Nhất Hạnh is most known: as an engaged Buddhist and as a Zen master. The purpose of the article is not to deny either of these, but instead to contextualize these portrayals.

VIETNAMESE BUDDHISM IN THE TWENTIETH CENTURY

In the 1920s a movement emerged in Vietnam in response to the challenges of French colonialism, Catholic missionary pressures, modernism, and globalization. International connections were made with other reformers, with the Chinese Buddhist reformer Taixu being particularly influential.[2] His essays on "Humanistic Buddhism" (*renjian fojiao* [人間佛教] in Chinese and *Nhân gian Phật giáo* in Vietnamese) argued that Buddhism needed to shift from a focus on the dead to the living. His ideas of the need for Buddhists to be active in society had a great impact among the Vietnamese reformers and laid the groundwork for Buddhist activism against the war in the 1960s.

Another important impulse was to establish Buddhism as a "world religion," which was a Buddhist response to the globalization of the idea of "religion" as a differentiated system.[3] This resulted in the creation or hardening of orthodoxies and the reification of sects within the religion. It led to multiple processes, some of which included the discursive unification of Buddhism as a single religion with different national and sectarian divisions, stressing the importance of the historical buddha as the "founder" of the religion, and the original teachings of the buddha as the central doctrine. Orientalist scholarship expressed that the original teachings of the historical buddha had been degraded over time. Mahāyāna Buddhism was particularly targeted as fantastical and devotional, while Theravada Buddhism was upheld as being closer to true Buddhism.[4] Meanwhile, Japanese Zen Buddhists, such as Shaku Sōen and D. T. Suzuki, sought to show that Zen was not only worthy of being considered as a religion on par with Christianity, but also superior to Christianity in its compatibility with modernity and scientific rationalism.

In the 1920s reformers in the main urban centers of Vietnam started to restructure Buddhism.[5] A principal concern was to make Buddhism more accessible to lay Buddhists by forming associations and publishing religious texts and magazines. Monastic schools were founded, and monks started to give talks to lay Buddhists, defining and explaining a Buddhist orthodoxy. Thích Nhất Hạnh was born at a time when the reform movement in Vietnam was getting started, and from the beginning he was steeped in these reformist ideas.

BIOGRAPHY OF THÍCH NHẤT HẠNH

Information on Thích Nhất Hạnh's background and childhood is very limited. Beyond some anecdotes of his childhood found in his books *Bông Hồng cài Áo* and *At Home in the World,* he does not write about his life before renunciation or of his family.[6] These two sources are not biographical in nature and give no details that help to understand his background, whether his family was rich or poor, farmers, scholars, or government officials. He was born Nguyễn Xuân Bảo in 1926 in central Vietnam, likely in the area of Huế.[7] At the age of sixteen he became an aspirant at Từ Hiếu Pagoda in Huế. Further details of his life before renunciation are not known. Thích Nhất Hạnh gives a taste of his early years at Từ Hiếu in a series of short essays he published in the magazine *Phật giáo Việt Nam* (Vietnamese Buddhism) in 1957 under the pen name Tâm Quán. These were later collected and published in the book *Tình Người* in 1964 and translated into English as *My Master's Robe* in 2002. The image he gives of life as a novice shows that he spent a good part of his time doing manual labor at the monastery. He does not dwell on the religious practices at the pagoda, but what is mentioned seems to conform with the syncretic practice typical of pagodas in Vietnam: chanting sutras, making offerings to the Buddha, and meditation (although the prevalence of meditation is inconsistent and likely was not practiced by most Vietnamese monastics).

After three years at Từ Hiếu, Thích Nhất Hạnh received ordination and went to study at Báo Quốc Pagoda, a thirty-minute walk from Từ Hiếu. This school was the main institution that the reform association for central Vietnam (Hội An Nam Phật Học) founded to train monastics in the Buddhist orthodoxies that they were developing, divesting Buddhism of what reformers saw as cultural accretions and superstitious practices.[8] The purpose of this reform organization, like others elsewhere in Vietnam, was to disseminate information about Buddhism, including sutras, philosophy, and Buddhist history; to develop schools that would enable monastics to be able to speak authoritatively about Buddhism and interact with contemporary society; and to give Buddhism an organizational coherence.[9] The school taught not only Buddhist subjects, but also psychology, English and Chinese literature, and Sanskrit. Thích Nhất Hạnh was therefore exposed to the ideas of the Buddhist reform movement from the beginning of his monastic life. The modernist notions of Buddhism that he encountered there were important for his development, including his calls for the unification and modernization of Buddhism throughout Vietnam in the 1950s, his peace activism in the 1960s, and his reinvention as a Zen master in the 1970s.

Thích Nhất Hạnh finished his studies at the Báo Quốc Institute of Buddhist Studies around 1948 and received full ordination in 1949.[10] At some point he made his way to Saigon. For a year he lived in Long Vĩnh Pagoda with Thích Quảng Đức, the monk who shocked the world when he set himself on fire in 1963 to protest the repression of Buddhists by President Ngô Đình Diệm.[11] During this initial period in Saigon he started his literary career. In 1956, the Buddhist General Association (Tổng hội Phật giáo Việt Nam) started a journal called *Phật giáo Việt Nam* (Vietnamese Buddhism), published out of Ấn Quang Pagoda. At the start it was directed by senior monk Thích Huệ Quang, with Thích Nhất Hạnh as editor, but when Thích Huệ Quang died later that year Thích Nhất Hạnh took over as director.[12] It folded in 1959 after publishing twenty-eight issues, ostensibly because of financial reasons.[13] By then, Thích Nhất Hạnh had already left the magazine.

Thích Nhất Hạnh, himself, wrote many of the articles, publishing under a number of pseudonyms. He used Tâm Quán to write biographical pieces about his time as a novice at Từ Hiếu Pagoda; he used Dã Thảo when he wrote about Western literature; he used Thạc Đức when writing about contemporary news items and issues related to Buddhism and the people in northern and southern Vietnam; he used Phương Bối to write about Buddhist teachings; and reserved the use of Thích Nhất Hạnh for poems.[14] Other than the few poems published under his name, the use of pen names likely inhibited name recognition until he became more renowned for his peace activism in the 1960s. This is reflected in Chân Không's account of her first meeting with him. She describes meeting the "prominent monk" Thích Mãn Giác in 1959, who then recommended that she read Thích Nhất Hạnh's book, but she describes how she was uninterested in reading books from an "unknown author."[15]

This productive period in Saigon, when he established himself as a progressive young Buddhist thinker, ended in 1957 in disillusionment after clashing with the more conservative older monks. Thích Nhất Hạnh writes:

> And all of us . . . still can't find our place in the Buddhist organization. We have earned a reputation for spreading anti-doctrinal ideas, as extremists and saboteurs. We are useless to the system and to tradition. We have a small voice. We talk about unifying Buddhism; about modernizing ritual music, education, propagating Dharma; about a humanistic [*nhân bản*] and national Buddhism. We have pursued these for almost eight years. We have sown these seeds with great effort. In the meantime, we have met all kinds of denunciation, jealousies and stubborn obstacles. Still, we are not discouraged or disappointed. Some seeds have started to sprout. Along with dissatisfaction in the status quo, the sense of a national Buddhism gradually emerges.[16]

The details of the conflict are unclear, but Thích Nhất Hạnh writes that he had been forced to leave the editorship because of the views he was publishing. This is a puzzling statement, given that the themes of Buddhist unity and social engagement had been central discourses of the Buddhist reform movement publications since the early 1930s. For example, in 1937 the main Buddhist magazine in northern Vietnam (then Tonkin), published an article titled "Buddhism for this World" (*Nhân-gian Phật-giáo*).[17] In *Vietnam: Lotus in a Sea of Fire,* Thích Nhất Hạnh himself acknowledges that a call for social engagement had been around in Vietnam since the 1930s.[18] The institutions for teaching monks, including the one he attended as a novice in Huế, were based on the ideas of the reform movement, as were the journals that emerged in the late 1920s and 1930s. The journal that that he edited in the 1950s, *Phật giáo Việt Nam,* was part of that tradition of Buddhist reform. It is therefore unclear how he was forced to leave the magazine solely based on advocating for humanistic Buddhism and Buddhist unification.

After leaving *Phật giáo Việt Nam,* Thích Nhất Hạnh bought a piece of land in August 1957 in the Blao district of Lâm Đồng Province in the Central Highlands to build the Phương Bối retreat. It served as a gathering place for a group of like-minded monastics and lay Buddhists over a two-year period. Thích Nhất Hạnh's description of this time paints an idyllic community life, where friends would visit for periods before returning to Saigon to take care of various projects. One notable frequent visitor was Thích Thanh Từ, who was only a couple of years older than Thích Nhất Hạnh and has played a prominent role in reviving Zen (*Thiền*) practice in Vietnam.[19] By his account, it seems that his focus during this period was on his writing, but between the time he left *Phật giáo Việt Nam* in 1957 and when he returned from his studies in the United States in 1964 he published little: one article entitled "Chân-lý Không Nam trong Văn-tự, Danh-ngôn" (The truth doesn't lie in writings or saying) and a book called *Để Hiểu Đạo Phật* (To Understand Buddhism), which was mostly taken from essays previously published in *Phật giáo Việt Nam.*[20]

Aside from the chores of building and maintaining the center, meditation was a principal Buddhist activity, according to the English translation of his book about that period, *Nẻo Về của Ý.*[21] Notably, though, these activities are not recorded in the original Vietnamese version published in 1966. The English translation also records that during this period he was writing about "a new, 'engaged' Buddhism."[22] However, once again, mention of engaged Buddhism is missing from the original passage in *Nẻo Về của Ý.* Overall, Thích Nhất Hạnh describes the time at Phương Bối retreat as being regenerative.

In the summer of 1960, the reality of the events in Vietnam started to encroach on the peacefulness of Phương Bối. Sister Diệu Âm, who had provided the finances to buy the land, became ill and another member of the community was arrested.[23] Thích Nhất Hạnh was advised by friends to return to Saigon, where he started to teach classes at Trúc Lâm, Xá Lợi and Ấn Quang Pagodas.[24] In the fall of 1961, with the Diệm regime putting pressure on Thích Nhất Hạnh and his fellow activists, Thích Nhất Hạnh decided to accept a fellowship to study comparative religion at Princeton University, with encouragement from friends.[25]

He studied and taught in the United States for two years, starting at Princeton before moving to Columbia University, where he took up a position as a teaching and research assistant. By 1963, the situation in Vietnam had become dire. President Diệm, who was a Catholic, had been steadily increasing pressure on Buddhists. In May 1963 there was a major incident when eight Buddhists were killed and four were wounded by police during a protest. A month later an elderly monk, Thích Quảng Đức, set himself on fire in protest on a street in Saigon. This started a chain of events that led to a coup and the assassination of Ngô Đình Diệm later that year.[26] It also started what became known as the Buddhist struggle movement, which morphed from an opposition to Ngô Đình Diệm's anti-Buddhist policies to a more general protest against the war, American involvement, and the succession of presidents that followed.

Although Thích Nhất Hạnh was still in New York when this was all erupting, he became increasingly concerned about the situation back home.[27] He tried to bring awareness of the plight of the Buddhists in Vietnam to the world by staging a hunger strike for five days while the United Nations General Assembly debated the human rights issue in Vietnam.[28] The events of 1963 not only presented a window for strengthening and unifying Buddhism in South Vietnam, but also opened the door for escalating American military presence.[29] Thích Nhất Hạnh received a cable from one of the leading activist monks in South Vietnam and a classmate from Huế, asking him to return home to Vietnam to help rebuild Buddhism. Thích Nhất Hạnh agreed, returning back to Vietnam on December 16, 1963.[30]

A month after his return, the Unified Buddhist Church (UBC) was founded to unite Buddhists in southern Vietnam. Despite the name, the UBC was not united, as two leading figures, Thích Trí Quang and Thích Tâm Châu, struggled for control and held different views on the correct course of action. Thích Trí Quang, a monk from Huế who was six years older than Thích Nhất Hạnh, led the radical anti-war faction, while Thích Tâm Châu, who had escaped the Communist regime in North Vietnam, represented the conservative mainstream position that was strongly anti-Communist.[31]

The period after returning to Vietnam was when he developed his ideas of engaged Buddhism, which subsequently became one of his most recognized features in the West. At the Executive Council meeting of the UBC in January 1964 Thích Nhất Hạnh proposed a three-point plan calling for the UBC to: (a) publicly call for the end of hostilities in Vietnam; (b) establish a Buddhist university (a goal that was shared by other progressive monks, like Thích Thiên Ấn[32]); and (c) develop a school to train social workers that could bring social change guided by Buddhist teachings. His proposal was not heeded, though there was consensus that a university was needed.[33] Several monks, including Thích Nhất Hạnh, established Vạn Hạnh Buddhist University (Viện Đại Học Phật giáo Vạn Hạnh) in February 1964, as the first university focused on higher education for Buddhist monastic and lay Buddhists.[34] The university started off using pagodas as classrooms and run by volunteers and had both an arts college and a school of Buddhist studies.[35] Thích Trí Thủ was installed as the rector, Thích Minh Châu was the vice rector, and Thích Thiên Ấn was the headteacher.[36]

In September 1965, Thích Nhất Hạnh started the School of Youth for Social Service (SYSS—Thanh Niên Phụng Sự Xã Hội), as an additional department at Vạn Hạnh University. Thích Nhất Hạnh, influenced by the humanistic Buddhist ideas that the Buddhist reform movement had been promoted, founded the SYSS as an expression of engaged Buddhism, which he was starting to write more about in this period.[37] The activities of the SYSS represented what Thích Nhất Hạnh described as a third force, which was not on either the American/South Vietnamese side, nor the side of the Communist National Liberation Front, but instead sought a withdrawal of American forces and a peace settlement between the two sides. The SYSS was active in setting up hospitals, caring for refugees, conducting disaster relief, and working for peace.[38] While Thích Nhất Hạnh took the nominal leadership role, his student Cao Ngọc Phương, who later was ordained with the name Thích nữ Chân Không, was a substantial driving force.

Thích Nhất Hạnh wrote prolifically during this period on issues of social action and peace. He also started to make connections with Western peace activists and drew international attention. The journal of the UBC, called *Thiện Mỹ*, was launched in October 1964, with Thích Nhất Hạnh invited to be the editor. The journal focused on contemporary Buddhism and Buddhist activism.[39] In the journal Thích Nhất Hạnh wrote a series of articles called "Buddhism in Life" (Phật Giáo đi vào Cuộc đời) in which he "expressed a desire to build, a new and progressive Buddhist society as well as the nation's aspirations for peace."[40] It may be in this series of articles that he first announced the formation of the SYSS. As a result of the announcement, a thousand young people applied to the school and three hundred were accepted.[41] The journal ran until June 1966, the month after Thích Nhất Hạnh left for the United States on a speaking tour. At the same time, Thích Nhất Hạnh was also the editor of the weekly Buddhist newspaper *Hải Triều Âm*, which reported on issues related to culture, news, and debates of the Institution for the Propagation of Faith (Viện Hóa Đạo) of the UBC. The weekly ran from April 1964 until it was shut down a year later because of its criticism of government policies.[42]

Two students of Thích Nhất Hạnh founded Lá Bối press in 1964 to print and disseminate the works of Thích Nhất Hạnh and like-minded writers. Sister Chân Không writes that in the following two years it published twelve books by Thích Nhất Hạnh and twenty by other authors.[43] One was *Đạo Phật đi vào Cuộc đời, và Những Tiểu luận Khác* [Buddhism in life and other essays], which Devido cites as the "first explication of 'Engaged Buddhism,'" but was banned for being too controversial.[44] Taken as a whole, his writings in this period show that the main themes of Thích Nhất Hạnh's intellectual focus was on promoting the idea of Buddhist activism and a desire for peace in Vietnam. Included in the writings were nationalist expressions of how Buddhism was linked to the Vietnamese people.[45] In a lecture delivered at Vạn Hạnh University in 1965 he outlined the need for Vietnam to be self-reliant and not dependent on foreign assistance, and also that Buddhism was what he called a "latent force," since it was followed by the majority of people in South Vietnam and was trusted.[46] These basic ideas would become the core themes of *Vietnam: Lotus in a Sea of Fire*, published in 1967.

With increasing American involvement in the war in 1965, Thích Nhất Hạnh's energy expanded beyond calling for Buddhists to be engaged in the world by performing social work, to advocating more forcefully for a peaceful resolution to the conflict. Thích Nhất Hạnh wrote a letter to Martin Luther King Jr., dated June 1, 1965, in which he explained that the enemy of the struggle movement was not men, but, "intolerance, fanaticism, dictatorship, cupidity, hatred and discrimination which lie within the heart of man," and linked the struggles of the monks who set themselves on fire to the struggle for racial equality in the United States.[47] With an introductory letter from Martin Luther King, Jr. in hand, the Clergymen's Emergency Committee of the American Fellowship of Reconciliation visited Vietnam and met with Thích Nhất Hạnh.[48] In their report to Congress upon returning, the committee said:

> [Thích Nhất Hạnh] recognized that communism was an evil, but war was even a greater evil, and he could not understand how justice could be established on the dead body of peace. Buddhism carries great spiritual reserves which if ever tapped for social change could make a far more profound and benign revolution than any Marx ever advocated.[49]

The publication of Thích Nhất Hạnh's book of poems devoted to peace, *Chắp Tay Nguyện Cầu cho Bồ câu Trắng hiện* (Put your hands together and pray for the white dove), sold four thousand copies in less than a week.[50] However, the government also banned this book and ordered all copies to be seized. It earned him condemnation as a Communist by the government of South Vietnam, but was simultaneously denounced by Radio Peking, Radio Hanoi, and the Voice of the National Liberation Front, which saw him as a puppet of America.[51]

The chancellor of Vạn Hạnh University, Thích Minh Châu, was part of the pro-American faction of the UBC, and while the SYSS was funded through private donations, Vạn Hạnh received a significant amount of money from government sources. Another major source of funding came from the Asia Foundation, which Topmiller suggested could have been funneling money from the Central Intelligence Agency (CIA).[52] In May 1966, Thích Nhất Hạnh travelled to the United States to give a lecture at Cornell University.[53] Thích Minh Châu, dissatisfied with SYSS's promotion of anti-government, anti-American, and pacifist messages, took Thích Nhất Hạnh's absence as an opportunity to sever affiliation between the SYSS and Vạn Hạnh University.[54]

The students and workers of the SYSS started to be targeted by both the Communists and agents of the South Vietnamese state. In June 1966 grenades were thrown into a campus dormitory of the SYSS, injuring two students. A grenade was also thrown into Thích Nhất Hạnh's room, but fortunately he had left two weeks previously.[55] It became clear that Vietnam was no longer safe for Thích Nhất Hạnh. As Hassler noted at the time: "he is continually excoriated by the Saigon radio and press as 'Communist,' while Radio Hanoi, smarting under the knowledge of the popularity of his appeals for peace among the people of Vietnam, labels him a 'tool of the Pentagon.'"[56] Mary Emeny, who worked with Thích Nhất Hạnh, wrote that the final straw seemed to have been the publication of *Vietnam: Lotus in a Sea of Fire*, leading to permanent exile.[57] He was not to return to Vietnam for forty years.[58]

The year 1966 marks the beginning of a shift in Thích Nhất Hạnh's orientation from a Vietnamese Buddhist monk to a global Zen Buddhist leader. For several years after his exile, Thích Nhất Hạnh continued to work on trying to achieve peace in Vietnam. He delivered *A Proposal for Peace* at a press conference in Washington on June 1, 1966, which put forward his five-point plan for peace that called for: (a) all bombing in the North and South to stop; (b) offensive action by U.S. Forces to cease; (c) a demonstration of the United States' intention to withdraw troops; (d) a statement by the US to support a government that was truly representative of the will of the Vietnamese people; and (e) the United States to provide assistance for Vietnam to rebuild.[59]

Based on the lectures and presentations, during his tour, Thích Nhất Hạnh wrote *Vietnam: Lotus in a Sea of Fire*, with a Vietnamese edition published in Paris in 1966 and an English translation published in New York in 1967. The book starts by presenting a brief, idealized, history of Vietnamese Buddhism that highlights Zen as "by far the most important sect" in Vietnam and claims that "In Vietnam there are many Zen monasteries," while conceding a page later that most people actually practice Pure Land Buddhism, with a little Zen mixed in.[60] The book then proceeds to outline the dire situation for most Vietnamese as a result of the war and American involvement before outlining his "third way," which called for the United States to withdraw from the war so that the North and South could work out a peace process on their own. The book was initially aimed at an American audience, but the Vietnamese version evidently was popular in Vietnam, despite being banned.[61] The book cemented Thích Nhất Hạnh's importance as a voice in the West for Vietnamese aspirations for peace. By the end of 1966, the Fellowship for Reconciliation that had sponsored his tour declared it a success, having been able to get his book published, and taken him on a successful speaking tour.[62]

In January 1968 the Viet Cong and the North Vietnam People's Army launched the Tet Offensive, and while it was a military defeat for the Communists, it was a public relations coup, as it led to the United States starting to look for ways to disengage from the war. Preliminary peace talks began in Paris in May. In 1969 the Overseas Vietnamese Buddhist Association held a conference in Paris, out of which was born the Vietnamese Buddhist Peace Delegation, and Thích Nhất Hạnh was nominated as the chair.[63] He had studied in the United States, spoke both English and French, and had strong ties with peace activists throughout the West, so it was a logical choice. Together with Sister Chân Không, they set up an office in Paris, where they edited and printed a newsletter in English, French, and Vietnamese, called *Le Lotus*.

Thích Nhất Hạnh advocated for a "Third Solution" that was neither supporting the National Liberation Front, the Communist force, or the American-backed South Vietnamese government. In an interview with the Center for the Study of Democratic Institutions, he explains: "We Buddhists believe that peace in Vietnam cannot be established through a military victory for either side. The only kind of solution we can envision is one that can help both sides save face. We call this the Third Solution."[64]

The peace talks continued intermittently until 1973, when the Paris Peace Accord was finally signed, effectively removing the United States from active engagement in the war. During this period, Thích Nhất Hạnh continued to actively promote his Third Solution, to little effect. As one reporter wrote: "Thích Nhất Hạnh, the saffron-robed Buddhist, who with his neutralist co-religionists, offered highly moral but ineffectual advice from the sidelines."[65] When the accord was finally signed, the South Vietnamese Government denied Thích Nhất Hạnh permission to return to Vietnam, so he became a permanent exile in France.

Following the signing of the Peace Accord, Thích Nhất Hạnh withdrew from activity. An internal document of the US Department of State reported in 1974 that he remained quiet in Paris, with little contact with Buddhists in Vietnam or other Vietnamese organizations that were "anti-government of Vietnam." He continued to advocate, but since the US forces were gone—which had been his main goal—he was left with "a general appeal to 'humanitarianism.' "[66]

Together with Cao Ngọc Phương, he continued to work to bring relief to the Vietnamese people, raising money to help orphans and widows.

From the period following the signing of the Paris Peace Accord, Thích Nhất Hạnh's writings reflect a renewed focus on Buddhism, and a movement to reinvent himself as a Zen master. This trend started with his book *Nẻo Vào Thiền Học* (The way into the study of Zen), later translated as *Clefs pour le Zen* in 1973 and *Zen Keys* in 1974.[67] In it he not only discusses some basic Zen concepts, but also introduces the idea of mindfulness, which was to become one of his central themes. Two years later he published one of his most famous books, *The Miracle of Mindfulness*.[68] From this point on the majority of his writing focuses on meditation, mindfulness, and Zen.

Thích Nhất Hạnh was on a trajectory to becoming an international Buddhist leader, with a network of centers spreading around the world. While the main focus of his followers has been the practice of mindfulness meditation, Thích Nhất Hạnh has continued to work on issues related to fostering peace and healing wounds. He conducted a walking meditation at the Vietnam Veterans Memorial in Washington and worked with American veterans of the conflict in Vietnam.[69] He gave dharma talks and taught meditation in prisons and continued to advocate for peace and issues surrounding race.

After living half of his seventy-nine years in exile, Thích Nhất Hạnh returned home to Vietnam in 2005. He led a large pilgrimage of Vietnamese and Western convert followers on a tour of Vietnam at the invitation of the Vietnamese government. Particularly in northern Vietnam, he was not as well-known as he was overseas, but he nonetheless drew large crowds of curious Vietnamese Buddhists. He spoke about themes for which he was famous in the West, including mindfulness and how the Pure Land is within each of us; how Buddhism should be approached as a practice rather than a religion; and that one could practice mindfulness without converting to Buddhism.[70]

The 2005 tour was controversial. A number of Vietnamese Buddhist monastics I spoke with in the West at the time saw his acceptance of the invitation as a tacit statement of support for the Vietnamese Communist government. Thích Viên Định wrote a letter to Thích Nhất Hạnh on behalf of the Unified Buddhist Church of Vietnam (UBCV; formerly the UBC) suggesting that he did not fully understand the situation in Vietnam.[71] Nonetheless, Thích Nhất Hạnh argued that engagement would be more productive. During the tour, Thích Nhất Hạnh tried to meet with Thích Quảng Độ, the head of the UBCV, who was under house arrest at Thanh Minh Pagoda in Ho Chi Minh City, but Thích Quảng Độ refused to meet with him.

A legacy of the trip was that Thích Nhất Hạnh was allowed to establish a permanent community of his organization in Lâm Đồng Province, in the Central Highlands, not far from his former Phương Bối retreat. It was also agreed that his home pagoda, Từ Hiếu, would become a center for implementing the sort of reforms that he had developed in the West.[72]

He returned again in 2007. As with his first return trip, this one was also controversial, with the same criticism being levelled at him by the UBCV. At the center of controversy for this trip was a "Grand Requiem" ceremony held for the victims of the war on both sides. The UBCV was dismayed that Thích Nhất Hạnh would do this, feeling that it was a betrayal, particularly since the leaders of the UBCV continued to be under house arrest by the Communist government.[73] A spokesperson for the UBCV wrote in a statement: "In fact, Marxism-Leninism, and the advent of Communism in Vietnam are the root causes of the deaths of millions of

Vietnamese – the very people that Thich Nhat Hanh is asking us to pray for today."[74] The Vietnamese government also initially pushed back against the ceremonies because Thích Nhất Hạnh's organization wanted to call them "Grand Requiem for Praying Equally for All to Untie the Knots of Unjust Suffering." The Vietnamese officials objected that both sides could not be considered equal, so a compromise was reached by calling them a more innocuous "Grand Requiem for Praying."[75]

Thích Nhất Hạnh took the opportunity this time to advocate for religious freedom. There were reports that in a private meeting with President Nguyễn Minh Triết, Thích Nhất Hạnh urged for easing restrictions on religion, introducing a ten-point proposal for religious reforms. His comments were subsequently made public.[76] By October the following year the government accused him of distorting religious policies, and that some of his followers were living at Bát Nhã without permission. Perhaps under pressure from the government, the abbot of Bát Nhã asked his followers to leave. In June 2009, utilities were cut and the next month a mob overran the monastery. The government required that they leave the monastery by September 2, but they refused, and by the end of that month his followers were forcibly expelled.[77] In response, Thích Nhất Hạnh published a letter to President Nguyễn Minh Triết condemning the actions against his followers.[78]

In 2014 Thích Nhất Hạnh had a stroke leaving him unable to speak but still alert and able to communicate. In October 2018, at his request, he returned to his home pagoda, Từ Hiếu, in order to spend his remaining days. According to several accounts, he spent his last days in his room, still unable to speak, with the words "returning" written in calligraphy above his bed.[79] He died in 2022.

ZEN MASTER THÍCH NHẤT HẠNH, THE ENGAGED BUDDHIST

Thích Nhất Hạnh has been primarily known as a pioneer of "engaged Buddhism" and a Zen master. These two aspects, while attributed to him simultaneously, are in some ways representative of two different phases of his life: he was principally concerned with carrying forward the ideas of the Buddhist reform movement while in Vietnam; he gradually shifted his persona to be a Zen master once exiled. The way he has mostly been represented by his followers is through a teleological ascription of these aspects to his earlier life. Scholars like King and Hunt-Perry and Fine, for their part, have mostly been uncritical in accepting the hagiographic narrative.[80] The purpose here is not to dispute that he is either one of these things, but instead argue for the need to contextualize him as a Vietnamese Buddhist monk.

Thích Nhất Hạnh as an Engaged Buddhist Leader. Thích Nhất Hạnh has frequently been credited for coming up with the term "engaged Buddhism." However, accounts have often exaggerated claims of Thích Nhất Hạnh as being unique in leading an engaged Buddhist movement in Vietnam in the 1960s. King, who has written the most substantively about Thích Nhất Hạnh, calls him "the most important ideological leader of the Vietnamese 'struggle movement.' "[81] This reading seems to come from an uncritical overreliance on the English translations of Thích Nhất Hạnh's early writings, and secondary insider accounts, which impose a new "engaged Buddhism" onto an older reformist "Humanistic Buddhism." So, for example, in the Vietnamese language original of *Nẻo Về của Ý*, written in 1966, he describes his activities while at the Phương Bối retreat in this way:

> Although we had a lot of time to explore the mountains and jungle, many days of camping, many opportunities to engage in literary criticism, and although all of these activities were very interesting, we also spent a lot of time in studying, researching and writing.[82]

However, in *Fragrant Palm Leaves* (the English translation published in 1998) the parallel passage reads:

> Though we spent many days exploring the forest, reciting poetry, and just enjoying ourselves, we also devoted hours and hours to studying, discussing, and writing *about a new, "engaged" Buddhism.*[83]

In the same year he wrote *Nẻo Về của Ý*, he also published the Vietnamese version of *Vietnam: Lotus in a Sea of Fire* (called *Hoa Sen trong Biển Lửa*). In the later English translation, he uses the term "engaged Buddhism" to describe the activities of the Buddhist struggle movement, the SYSS, and their non-violent activities. He writes, "In the 1930's, the Buddhist scholars had already discussed the engagement of Buddhism in the modern society and called it Nhan Gian Phat Giao, or engaged Buddhism."[84] The Vietnamese version, published a year earlier, merely calls it by the term "Humanistic Buddhism."[85] As a direct descendent to the Buddhist reform movement, he was prominent in bringing the ideas of Buddhist engagement with society to prominence in the West, but in doing this he was not so much an innovator as he was an heir and transmitter.

Despite King's assertion of Thích Nhất Hạnh's prominence in the struggle movement, his centrality is exaggerated in the insider accounts on which King relies. Thích Nhất Hạnh was still studying and teaching in the United States as it was getting started and monks started immolating themselves in protest; he was in exile in the West when it came to a halt. Declassified CIA records show that there was little interest in Thích Nhất Hạnh compared to other Buddhist leaders. Jerrold Schecter's detailed contemporaneous account of the struggle movement also makes no mention of Thích Nhất Hạnh.[86] While Thích Nhất Hạnh was active during the struggle movement, it is therefore difficult to conclude that he was as central as King asserts.

Thích Nhất Hạnh and his followers were not political activists protesting the government, as were most of the militant Buddhists of the struggle movement, but instead engaged in social work, helping the poor and supporting people who had been displaced by the war, and calling for peace in his written work. After his exile he became prominent in the Western media during his 1966 speaking tour, cementing his image as an engaged Buddhist. From the late 1970s, although he took periodic stands for peace, for the most part, his "engagement" consisted of writing and speaking to groups that were in need of finding a way to deal with their difficult situations—notably veterans and convicts. His main focus, though, was on building his international organization and writing books that might be characterized as being about therapeutic Zen, aimed at helping people overcome issues in their daily lives, by reducing stress and anger.[87]

Based on this evidence three points can be made about Thích Nhất Hạnh as an engaged Buddhist. The first is that it was rooted in the reformist teachings from which he emerged. The second is that, while he was active in Vietnam, he was not uniquely so. Finally, it is a mischaracterization to say that Buddhist engagement has been the central focus of his career. As Temprano notes, accounts of Thích Nhất Hạnh as an engaged Buddhist characterize him this way in isolation, ignoring that the Order of Interbeing (the organization he founded and lead) and its activities, was at its core not really focused on engaged Buddhism, especially not in contrast to organizations like Tzu Chi.[88]

Thích Nhất Hạnh as Zen Master. While the academic focus on Thích Nhất Hạnh has been his work as an engaged Buddhist, descriptions in popular media and by his organization stress his persona as a Zen master.[89] Groups scattered around the world that are part of Thích Nhất Hạnh's Order of Interbeing mostly engage in meditation as their central practice, and mindfulness as a way to address the various stresses of daily modern life. This focus on meditation and mindfulness as a daily practice is also a central topic of many of his publications. This characterization of Thích Nhất Hạnh is therefore not surprising, but, like his persona as an engaged Buddhist, it needs to be understood in context.

A critical understanding of what makes Thích Nhất Hạnh a Zen master is particularly important since he and his organization has apparently tried to project this Zen identity into his past, when there are legitimate questions about how Zen fit into his life pre-exile. His disciples have placed an emphasis on Thích Nhất Hạnh being part of an unbroken Lâm Tế (Rinzai) Zen lineage, having received direct transmission from his master, and referring to Từ Hiếu as their "root temple."[90]

Most mentions of him in Western academic literature accept the label of "Zen master" without any critical examination.[91] This construction has been called into question by Nguyen and Barber, who point out that claims of direct transmission in a Zen lineage are problematic, since there was no one in Vietnam from whom he could receive this transmission, since there was no living Zen tradition in Vietnam.[92] Furthermore, Thích Nhất Hạnh was not known as a Zen master in Vietnam, but only came to be seen that way after relocating to the West.[93] Buddhism in Vietnam has not placed much emphasis on lineages in the past. Vietnamese Buddhism, as practiced throughout Vietnam and in almost all pagodas in the Vietnamese diaspora, is remarkably consistent in being a form of Buddhism that may combine some Zen elements but is primarily based on Pure Land devotionalism.

The Vietnamese fascination with Zen has deep roots. In the 14th century a historical record of Buddhism in Vietnam was compiled, entitled the *Thiền Uyển Tập Anh*. The text adopts the form of Chinese Ch'an transmission of the lamp texts, which describes the biographies of eminent Zen monks in three Zen lineages from the 6th to the 13th century.[94] After a thorough critical analysis of the text, however, Cuong Tu Nguyen concludes that the actual content of the stories is either borrowed from Chinese texts or represents a Buddhism that mixed meditation, asceticism, magic, thaumaturgy, and ritualism.[95] The Zen veneer of the *Thiền Uyển Tập Anh* indicates an elite fascination with Chinese culture and a desire to legitimize Vietnamese Buddhism by emulating Chinese forms.[96] He concludes that there are "no Zen monasteries, no sizeable Zen communities (we can even say *no* Zen communities), no recognizable Zen monasticism or practices as in the case of Japan or Korea."[97]

Trần Văn Giáp rediscovered the *Thiền Uyển Tập Anh* in 1927 and uncritically used it to write a Vietnamese Buddhist history published in 1932 in the *Bulletin de l'École Française d'Extrême Orient*. This Zen history asserted a national identity to Vietnamese Buddhism and fit well with the reformist narrative. It was accepted wholesale and repeated by all other subsequent accounts of Vietnamese Buddhist history, including the one written by Thích Nhất Hạnh under the pen name Nguyễn Lang.[98] In the 1960s, the Zen history that Trần Văn Giáp brought to light was bolstered by the translation of a number of Suzuki's works, reinforcing elite convictions that Zen represented the pinnacle of Buddhism.[99]

Thích Nhất Hạnh's identification with Zen is best understood through his participation in these currents that were taking place in Vietnam in the 1960s, but he does not start to construct himself as a Zen master until his exile. After he realizes that he has become permanently exiled, his writing starts to shift from a focus on peace to Zen and meditation. A passage in *Nẻo Về của Ý* includes an observation while studying in the United States that Zen would be more attractive in the West than Pure Land Buddhism.[100] Before his exile, Thich Nhat Hanh does not seem concerned with Zen in any way. It is possible that finding himself in exile, and with peace activism no longer needed or possible, his thoughts went to how to establish himself in the West. At this point the overseas Vietnamese community was small, and it does not seem that he had strong connections with those living in France. This meant that he had to become a teacher for Westerners, and at this point he may well have drawn on his earlier observation about the suitability of Zen for Westerners. The conclusion to draw from this discussion is that Thích Nhất Hạnh has had an indisputable impact as a Zen teacher in the West. His teachings about mindfulness have had a broad impact, extending beyond the boundaries of Buddhism. He has had a valuable and positive influence on many people through his demystifying approach. Further, the main activities of his organization center on the practice of Zen meditation. Nonetheless, when attempts are made to legitimize his Zen identity through recourse to attributions to a Zen lineage and "lamp transmission," questions appropriately arise. The truth is that Zen in Vietnam, while rooted in historical fascinations, is a modern construction that only started in the 1960s as a sectarian practice.

CONCLUSION

Thích Nhất Hạnh is undoubtedly one of the most important Buddhist figures of the 20th century. As a teacher of Zen, he was a prolific author of a wide range of books dealing with themes like the importance for making Buddhism relevant to the modern world, the need for Buddhists to be engaged in society, and a vast literature focused on mindfulness as a contemplative method for dealing with the vicissitudes of contemporary life. He also built up an international organization notable for breaking down one of the most often noted division between "ethnics" and "convert" Buddhists; for his modernist take on Buddhism has been attractive to both a large number of Westerners as well as overseas Vietnamese. On the global scene he made a tremendous impact to the engaged Buddhism movement, contributing not only the label, but also the understanding of contributing to peace activism and reconciliation.

While he received justifiable acclaim for these activities, the way he has been portrayed in popular media and in hagiographical literature has also given the impression that he stands separate from the Vietnamese Buddhist tradition and its developments in the 20th century. This article has aimed to re-center him within the Vietnamese Buddhist context. While the teachings of Thích Nhất Hạnh, and the organization he has developed, do not resemble the standard ways and forms of Vietnamese Buddhism, they are very much grounded within the experience of Buddhism in Vietnam. The Buddhist reform movement in Vietnam followed the lead of international reformist concerns of unifying Buddhists and creating rationalized organizations; creating orthodoxies by founding schools, publishing and holding public Dharma talks for the laity; and calling for Buddhists to become active in society. Thích Nhất Hạnh took up these central concerns of the Vietnamese Buddhist reformers and pushed forward with them to address the issues in Vietnam and then to make Buddhism more appropriate for Western converts. All of his activities and innovations stem from these initial reformist impulses. In the 1950s he wrote about the need for Buddhism in Vietnam to modernize, to be involved in society, and to unify. At the beginning of the 1960s he was concerned with publishing, teaching, and establishing a Buddhist university with other like-minded activist monks. As the war gripped Vietnam, he became more involved with development issues as the head of the School of Youth for Social Services. Working with poor and the refugees led naturally to an increasing focus on peace activism. His time in the United States gave him important skills that allowed him to become the international mouthpiece of the Vietnamese Buddhists' call for an end to the fighting. When his peace activism ended with the signing of the Paris Peace Accord, he shifted from his role as an engaged Buddhist to become a Zen master. Again, this focus reflected the currents that had been running through the Buddhist milieu in southern Vietnam.

Thích Nhất Hạnh was an innovative Buddhist leader who had a wide international impact. It is a mistake, however, to think that Thích Nhất Hạnh does not reflect Vietnamese Buddhism. To be sure, the innovations he has brought to Buddhist teachings are more reflective of globalist, modernist trends that privilege individual experience over collective ritual, and meditation over devotional reliance on external supernatural forces (like celestial Buddhas). Nonetheless, in doing this, he has been part of the reformist tradition and has been perhaps the most successful proponent of the reform spirit that got started in the decade he was born.

REVIEW OF LITERATURE

There are few critical works that have been written about Thích Nhất Hạnh. The two main essays that include biographical information on Thích Nhất Hạnh, by King and Hunt-Perry and Fine are both focused on Thích Nhất Hạnh as an engaged Buddhist, and both rely almost exclusively and uncritically on either Thích Nhất Hạnh's English writings or on his close associate and follower, Chân Không's, book.[101] Chân Không's biographical account of her work with Thích Nhất Hạnh is, indeed, the most extensive account of Thích Nhất Hạnh's activities in the 1960s and onwards, but it must be approached critically, as an insider account rather than a critical examination of his life. Additionally, Chapman wrote one chapter on Thích Nhất Hạnh's return visit to Vietnam in 2005, after thirty years of exile.[102] There are no other critical academic works that deal with the life of Thích Nhất Hạnh in a sustained way, although Thích Nhất Hạnh figures prominently in Phạm Văn Minh's account of the struggle movement between 1963 and 1966.[103] Topmiller's study of the same period has considerably less to say about Thích Nhất

Hạnh, suggesting that in his estimation Thích Nhất Hạnh was not particularly prominent. McHale and Woodside offer studies of the Buddhist reform movement that influenced Thích Nhất Hạnh.[104] Only DeVido's two essays on the period draw explicit parallels between the ideas of the reform movement and the development of Thích Nhất Hạnh's ideas.[105]

PRIMARY SOURCES

Aside from Chân Không's account, the best source for understanding Thích Nhất Hạnh comes from his own extensive writings. However, while an impressively prolific writer, he has only directly written about his life in three works: in *My Master's Robe* he describes his life as a novice monk at Từ Hiếu Pagoda in Huế; in *Fragrant Palm Leaves* he describes the period from when he left his post as editor of *Phật giáo Việt Nam* in 1957, to just before his exile from Vietnam in 1966; and in *At Home in the World* he provides a series of anecdotes from his life, from childhood to his exile in the West. While all three are interesting, none are written as an autobiography that comprehensively details his life. Instead, they provide clues and glimpses into his life while being intended to either give lessons and insights or serve to establish or reinforce his status as both a Zen master and engaged Buddhist. It is notable that the English translations do this second function to a greater extent than the original Vietnamese versions.

While Thích Nhất Hạnh was a prodigious writer, much of what he has written are variations on particular themes: peace activism; mindfulness and how it can be harnessed to deal with life problems; interfaith dialogue; interbeing; and writings about Buddhist doctrine. His most famous work on the Vietnamese conflict and his "Third Solution" is *Vietnam: Lotus in a Sea of Fire,* which was written to raise awareness in the West of the terrible impact of the war. Likely his most famous work, *The Miracle of Mindfulness* lays out the principles of mindfulness meditation in daily activity and was written as a practice for the young activists in the School of Youth for Social Services. *Being Peace* integrates themes of mindfulness and peacebuilding, and was published when (and was partially responsible for) Thích Nhất Hạnh rising fame in the West. Written in the same year, *Interbeing* lays out the Fourteen Precepts of his organization and explains the concept of interbeing, which is the foundational principle for his ideas of engaged Buddhism and peace building. In *Living Buddha Living Christ* Thích Nhất Hạnh stresses that religious experience, rather than doctrine, is the meeting point for the two faiths, and the importance of compassion and wisdom in both. Additionally, Thích Nhất Hạnh wrote commentaries about several sutras, the Buddha and other Buddhist themes. *Zen Keys* is probably his most important statement about Zen, written primarily for a Western audience. In *The Heart of the Buddha's Teaching* Thích Nhất Hạnh comments on key Buddhist teachings, like the Middle Way, the Four Noble Truths, the Eightfold Path, and the Three Jewels.

NOTES

1. Cuong Tu Nguyen and A. W. Barber, "Vietnamese Buddhism in North America: Tradition and Acculturation," in *The Faces of Buddhism in America*, eds. Charles S. Prebish and Kenneth K. Tanaka (Berkeley, CA: University of California Press, 1998), 131.

2. Elise DeVido, "Buddhism for This World: The Buddhist Revival in Vietnam, 1920–51 and Its Legacy," in *Modernity and Re-enchantment: Religion in Post-Revolutionary Vietnam*, ed. Philip Taylor (Singapore: Institute of Southeast Asian Studies, 2007), 250–296; "The Influence of Chinese Master Taixu on Buddhism in Vietnam," *Journal of Global Buddhism* 10 (2009): 413–458; and Alexander B. Woodside, *Community and Revolution in Modern Vietnam* (Boston: Houghton Mifflin, 1976), 192.
3. Peter Beyer, *Religions in Global Society* (Abingdon, UK: Routledge, 2006).
4. John S. Harding, *Mahāyāna Phoenix: Japan's Buddhists at the 1893 World's Parliament of Religions* (New York: Peter Lang, 2008), 96.
5. Woodside, *Community and Revolution*, 193.
6. Thích Nhất Hạnh, *Bông Hồng cài Áo* [A rose for your pocket] (Saigon: Lá Bối, 1962), which was translated as a bilingual edition in 1983, titled: *A Flower for You*; and *At Home in the World: Stories and Essential Teachings from a Monk's Life* (Berkeley, CA: Parallax Press, 2019).
7. Thích Nhất Hạnh does not mention his birthplace in any writings. Willis claims that he was born in Quảng Ngãi. In the setup of a 1966 article written by Thích Nhất Hạnh in the *New York Review of Books*, he is described as having been born in Dalat. King describes him as having been born in southern Vietnam while Hunt-Perry and Fine write that he was born in central Vietnam, but none of these sources is, unfortunately, any more reliable than the Vietnamese Wikipedia entry that has him born in Hue. Nor is the biography on the website for the Order of Interbeing, which also states that he was born in central Vietnam. See Jennifer Schwamm Willis, "Introduction," in *A Lifetime of Peace: Essential Writings by and about Thích Nhất Hạnh*, ed. Jennifer Schwamm Willis (New York: Marlowe, 2003), xi; Thích Nhất Hạnh, "A Buddhist Poet in Vietnam," *The New York Review of Books*, June 9, 1966a; Sallie B. King, "Thich Nhat Hanh and the Unified Buddhist Church of Vietnam: Nondualism in Action," in *Engaged Buddhism: Buddhist Liberation Movements in Asia*, eds. Christopher S. Queen and Sallie B. King (Albany: State University of New York Press, 1996), 322; and Patricia Hunt-Perry and Lyn Fine, "All Buddhism is Engaged: Thich Nhat Hanh and the Order of Interbeing," in *Engaged Buddhism in the West*, ed. Christopher S. Queen (Boston: Wisdom Publications, 2000), 36.
8. Trần Đại Vinh, Nguyễn Hữu Thông, and Lê Văn Sách, *Danh Lam Xứ Huế—The Celebrated Pagodas of Hue* (Huế, Vietnam: Nhà Xuất Bản Nhà Văn, 1993), 162.
9. Woodside, *Community and Revolution*, 193.
10. Hunt-Perry and Fine, "All Buddhism is Engaged," 38.
11. Thích Nhất Hạnh, *Vietnam: Lotus in a Sea of Fire* (New York: Hill and Wang, 1967), 1.
12. Nguyễn Đại Đồng, *Lược khảo Báo chí Phật giáo Việt Nam (1929–2008)* [Survey of Vietnamese Buddhist periodicals (1929–2008)] (Hanoi: Nhà xuất bản Tôn giáo, 2008), 145.
13. Nguyễn Đại Đồng, *Lược khảo Báo chí Phật giáo Việt Nam*, 148.
14. Chân Không, *Con Đường Mở Rộng: 52 Năm theo Thầy Học Đạo và Phụng sự* [The Road Opens Wide: 52 Years Following the Master Study and Service], chapter 4.
15. Chân Không, *Learning True Love: Practicing Buddhism in a Time of War* (Berkeley, CA: Parallax Press, 2007), 24.
16. Thích Nhất Hạnh, *Nẻo Về của Ý* [The return of an idea] (Ho Chi Minh City, Vietnam: Nhà Xuất bản Văn hóa Sài Gòn), 45. All translations of Vietnamese language sources are the author's.
17. Đ.N.T., "Nhân-gian Phật-giáo" [Buddhism for this world], *Được Tuệ* 55 (February 15, 1937): 3–9.
18. Thích Nhất Hạnh, *Vietnam*, 42.
19. Alexander Soucy, "Nationalism, Globalism and the Re-Establishment of the Trúc Lâm Thiền Buddhist Sect in Northern Vietnam," in *Modernity and Re-enchantment: Religion in Post-revolutionary Vietnam*, ed. Philip Taylor (Singapore: Institute of Southeast Asian Studies, 2007), 342–370; "Vietnamese Traditions," in *Oxford Handbook of Contemporary Buddhism*, ed. Michael Jerryson (New York: Oxford University Press, 2016), 177–195; and *Zen Conquest: Buddhist Transformations in Contemporary Vietnam* (Honolulu: University of Hawai'i Press, 2022).

20. Thạc Đức, "Chân-lý Không Nằm trong Văn-tự, Danh-ngôn" [The truth doesn't lie in writings or sayings], *Nguyệt san Phật giáo Việt Nam* 25–26 (1958): 21–24; and Phương-Bối, "Để Hiểu Đạo Phật" [To understand Buddhism] (Dalat, Vietnam: Phật Học Viện Trung phần, 1959). It is possible that he published other essays and/or books under a pseudonym other than the known ones he employed in *Phật Giáo Việt Nam*.
21. Thích Nhất Hạnh, *Fragrant Palm Leaves: Journals 1962–1966* (New York: Riverhead Books), 38, 39.
22. Thích Nhất Hạnh, *Fragrant Palm Leaves*, 51.
23. Thích Nhất Hạnh, *Nẻo Về của Ý*, 78–79.
24. Chân Không, *Learning True Love*, 29.
25. Chân Không, *Learning True Love*, 30.
26. Robert J. Topmiller, *The Lotus Unleashed: The Buddhist Peace Movement in South Vietnam, 1964–1966* (Lexington: The University of Kentucky Press, 2006), 2.
27. Marjorie Hope and James Young, *The Struggle for Humanity: Agents of Nonviolent Change in a Violent World* (Maryknoll, NY: Orbis Books, 1971), 195.
28. Chân Không, *Learning True Love*, 41.
29. Topmiller, *The Lotus Unleashed*, 5.
30. Chân Không, *Learning True Love*, 47.
31. Jerrold Schecter, *The New Face of the Buddha: Buddhism and Political Power in Southeast Asia* (London: Victor Gollancz, 1967), 162.
32. Thích Đồng Bổn, "Hòa Thượng Thích Thiên Ân (1925–1980)" [The Most Venerable Thích Thiên Ân (1925–1980)]. In *Tiểu sử Danh Tăng Việt Nam Thế kỷ XX—Tập II* [Biography of Famous Vietnamese Monks of the Twentieth Century, Vol. 2] (Hanoi, Vietnam: Nhà xuất bản Tôn giáo, 2002).
33. Sister Chân Không, *Learning True Love*, 48.
34. The university was named after one of Vietnam's most eminent historical monks of the Lý dynasty, Vạn Hạnh (d. 1025).
35. Kenneth W. Morgan, "The Buddhists: The Problem and the Promise," *Asia* 4 (Winter), Box 01, Folder 18, Gary Larsen Collection, Vietnam Center and Sam Johnson Vietnam Archive, Texas Tech University, 1966, 81.
36. Thích Đồng Bổn, "Hòa Thượng Thích Thiên Ân."
37. John Donnell, "Vietnam's Youth Associations: Social Commitment and Political Promise," Document 0721005002, John Donnell Collection, The Vietnam Center and Sam Johnson Vietnam Archive, Texas Tech University, 1969, 34.
38. Morgan, "The Buddhists: The Problem and the Promise," 81; and Topmiller, *The Lotus Unleashed*, 138.
39. Nguyễn Đại Đồng, *Lược khảo Báo chí Phật giáo Việt Nam*, 166–167.
40. Nguyễn Đại Đồng, *Lược khảo Báo chí Phật giáo Việt Nam*, 167.
41. Chân Không, *Learning True Love*, 70.
42. Nguyễn Đại Đồng, *Lược khảo Báo chí Phật giáo Việt Nam*, 155–156.
43. Chân Không, *Learning True Love*, 71.
44. Thích Nhất Hạnh, *Đạo Phật đi vào Cuộc đời, và Những Tiểu luận Khác* [Buddhism in life and other essay] (Saigon: Lá Bối, 1964). Elise DeVido, "Thích Nhất Hạnh," *Oxford Bibliographies*, 2014.
45. See, for example, Dã Thảo, "Vấn đề Mâu thuẫn giữa Quyền lợi Phật giáo và Quyền lợi Dân tộc" [The issue of conflict between Buddhism's interests and the people's rights] *Hải Triều Âm* 20 (September 3, 1964): 3.
46. Thích Nhất Hạnh, "Policy and Method: Basic Concepts of Movement of Youth for Social Service," lecture presented at University of Van-Hanh, School of Youth for Social Service, Saigon, August 1, 1965.
47. Thích Nhất Hạnh, *Chắp Tay Nguyện Cầu cho Bồ câu Trắng hiện* [Put your hands together and pray for the white dove] (Saigon: Lá Boi, 1965), 1.

48. Chân Không, *Learning True Love*, 84.
49. CIA (Central Intelligence Agency). "Congressional Record: Senate." Document Number CIA-RDP67B00446R000300130016-8, August 10, 1965.
50. Thích Nhất Hạnh, *Chắp Tay Nguyện Cầu*.
51. Thích Nhất Hạnh, *Vietnam*, 77.
52. CIA, "Congressional Record: Senate," 165n88.
53. *Viet Report*, "To Quang, To Lyndon." Document 6-20-15DC-116-UA17-149000056. Texas Tech University, the Vietnam Center & Sam Johnson Vietnam Archive, June/July 1966, 2 and 31.
54. Donnell, "Vietnam's Youth Associations," 34–35; and Phạm Văn Minh, *Vietnamese Engaged Buddhism: The Struggle Movement of 1963–1966* (Westminster, CA: Văn Nghệ, 2002), 263.
55. Phạm Văn Minh, *Vietnamese Engaged Buddhism*, 268.
56. Alfred Hassler, "Afterward," in *Vietnam: Lotus in a Sea of Fire*. ed. Thích Nhất Hạnh (New York: Hill and Wang, 1967), 100.
57. Mary Emeny, "Letters from Mary Emeny Collection," Document 0840101001, Mary Emeny Collection, The Vietnam Center and Sam Johnson Vietnam Archive, Texas Tech University, 1996, 17.
58. It is difficult to gauge Thích Nhất Hạnh's fame and influence in Vietnam before his exile without doing a more extensive search of newspapers and Buddhist journals from South Vietnam of the time, which the author has been unable to undertake up to this point. It seems that his prominence in this period has been overstated in the literature generated from within his own organization, and assumed by the few academic accounts that have uncritically repeated these claims.
59. Thích Nhất Hạnh, *Love in Action: Writings on Nonviolent Social Change* (Berkeley, CA: Parallax Press, 1993), 55.
60. Thích Nhất Hạnh, *Vietnam: Lotus in a Sea of Fire* (New York: Hill and Wang, 1967), 4, 5.
61. Chân Không, *Learning True Love*, 72.
62. Fellowship of Reconciliation, "Letter to Members and Supporters of the Fellowship by the National Chairman," Social Movements Collection, Vietnam Center and Sam Johnson Vietnam Archive, Texas Tech University, November 4, 1966, 1.
63. Chân Không, *Learning True Love*, 126–129.
64. Center for the Study of Democratic Institutions, "The Third Solution: A Neutral Coalition: A Discussion with Thích Nhất Hạnh," in *Vietnam: Matters for the Agenda*. Occasional Paper 1, no. 4, Vietnam Center and Sam Johnson Vietnam Archive, Texas Tech University, 1968, 6.
65. Scott Sullivan, "Paris Talks: Years of Sound, Fury, at Last Signifying Peace," *Baltimore Sun*, January 24, 1973, 17.
66. US Embassy. "Activities of South Vietnamese Buddhist, Thích Nhất Hạnh." April 29, 1974. Document number 1974PARIS10352. US National Archives, 2.
67. Thích Nhất Hạnh, *Nẻo Vào Thiền Học* [The way into the study of Zen] (Saigon, Vietnam: Lá Bối, 1971).
68. Thích Nhất Hạnh, *Miracle of Mindfulness: A Manual on Meditation* (Boston: Beacon Press, 1975).
69. Anne Cushman, "Healing the Wounds of War," *The Mindfulness Bell*, Fall 1991.
70. John Chapman, "The 2005 Pilgrimage and return to Vietnam of Exiled Master Thích Nhất Hạnh," in *Modernity and Re-enchantment: Religion in Post-Revolutionary Vietnam*, ed. Philip Taylor (Singapore: Institute of Southeast Asian Studies, 2007), 318–319, 321.
71. *Buddhist Channel*, "Buddhist Monk Requests Thích Nhất Hạnh 'To See True Situation in Vietnam,'" January 24, 2005.
72. Chapman, "2005 Pilgrimage," 329.
73. Kay Johnson, "The Fighting Monks of Vietnam," *Time*, March 2, 2007.
74. Vo Van Ai, "Statement by Vo Van Ai, UBCV International Spokesman, on the visit of Thích Nhất Hạnh and the International Delegation of Plum Village to Vietnam," February 20, 2007.
75. Johnson, "The Fighting Monks of Vietnam."

76. Human Rights Watch, "Vietnam: Sharp Backsliding on Religious Freedom: Harsh Crackdown on Followers of Buddhist Peace Activist Thích Nhất Hạnh," October 18, 2009.
77. Human Rights Watch, "Vietnam"; John Ruwitch, "Vietnam's Not-so-Simple Eviction of Buddhist Monks and Nuns," *Reuters*, October 5, 2009.
78. *BBC News Tiếng Việt*, "Thiền sư Thích Nhất Hạnh Lên Tiếng" [Zen Master Thích Nhất Hạnh Speaks Out], October 5, 2009.
79. Liam Fitzpatrick, "The Monk Who Taught the World Mindfulness Awaits the End of This Life," *Time*, January 24, 2019.
80. Sallie B. King, "Thich Nhat Hanh and the Unified Buddhist Church of Vietnam: Nondualism in Action," in *Engaged Buddhism: Buddhist Liberation Movements in Asia*, eds. Christopher S. Queen and Sallie B. King (Albany: State University of New York Press, 1996), 321–363; *Being Benevolence: The Social Ethics of Engaged Buddhism* (Honolulu: University of Hawai'i Press, 2005); *Socially Engaged Buddhism* (Honolulu: University of Hawai'i Press, 2009); and Hunt-Perry and Fine, "All Buddhism is Engaged."
81. King, *Socially Engaged Buddhism*, 4.
82. Thích Nhất Hạnh, *Nẻo Về của Ý*, 76.
83. Thích Nhất Hạnh, *Fragrant Palm Leaves: Journals 1962–1966* (New York: Riverhead Books, 51), emphasis added).
84. Thích Nhất Hạnh, *Vietnam: Lotus in a Sea of Fire*, 1967, 42.
85. Thích Nhất Hạnh, *Hoa Sen trong Biển* Lửa, 36.
86. Jerrold Schecter, *The New Face of the Buddha: Buddhism and Political Power in Southeast Asia* (London: Victor Gollancz, 1967).
87. see, for example, Thích Nhất Hạnh, *Anger: Wisdom for Cooling the Flames* (New York: Riverhead Books, 2001); Thích Nhất Hạnh, *Work: How to Find Joy and Meaning in Each Hour of the Day* (Berkeley, CA: Parallax Press, 2012).
88. Victor Gerard Temprano, *The Scholar and the Sage: Sallie B. King, David Loy, and Thích Nhất Hạnh* (MA Thesis, McGill University, Montréal, 2012), 55.
89. For example, Liam Fitzpatrick, "The Monk Who Taught the World Mindfulness Awaits the End of This Life," *Time*, January 24, 2019; and Tim Ward. "Look to your own culture, Zen master advises," *The Globe and Mail*, January 13, 1996, C18.
90. Pháp Dụng, "A Letter to Friends About Our Lineage," March 25, 2006.
91. The appellation of "Zen master" is ubiquitous in academic literature. See, for example, Phil Henry, *Adaptation and Developments in Western Buddhism: Socially Engaged Buddhism in the UK* (London: Bloomsbury, 2013), 92, 123; King, "Thich Nhat Hanh and the Unified Buddhist Church of Vietnam," 321; *Being Benevolence*, 11; *Socially Engaged Buddhism*, 4; David L. McMahan, *The Making of Buddhist Modernism* (New York: Oxford University Press, 2008), 150; and Scott A. Mitchell, *Buddhism in America: Global Religion, Local Contexts* (London: Bloomsbury, 2016), 78.
92. Nguyen and Barber, "Vietnamese Buddhism," 309n.9.
93. Nguyen and Barber, "Vietnamese Buddhism," 131.
94. Cuong Tu Nguyen, *Zen in Medieval Vietnam: A Study and Translation of the* Thiền Uyển Tập Anh (Honolulu: Kuroda Institute, University of Hawai'i Press, 1997), 3.
95. Cuong Tu Nguyen, "Rethinking Vietnamese Buddhist History: Is the *Thiền Uyển Tập Anh* a 'Transmission of the Lamp' Text?," in *Essays into Vietnamese Pasts*, eds. K. W. Taylor and John K. Whitmore (Ithaca, NY: Southeast Asia Program, Cornell University, 1995), 103.
96. Nguyen, *Zen in Medieval Vietnam*, 60.
97. Nguyen, *Zen in Medieval Vietnam*, 98.
98. Nguyễn Lang, *Việt Nam Phật giáo Sử luận* [Vol. 1]; *Việt Nam Phật giáo Sử luận* [Essay on the history of Vietnamese Buddhism, Vol. 2] (Paris: Lá Bối, 1978); and Nguyen, "Rethinking Vietnamese Buddhist History," 82–83.

99. Nguyen and Barber, "Vietnamese Buddhism," 131.
100. Thích Nhất Hạnh, *Nẻo Về của \Lửa*, 135.
101. King, "Thich Nhat Hanh and the Unified Buddhist Church of Vietnam"; Hunt-Perry and Fine, "All Buddhism is Engaged"; and Chân Không, *Learning True Love*, 7.
102. Chapman, "2005 Pilgrimage."
103. Phạm Văn Minh, *Vietnamese Engaged Buddhism.*
104. Shawn Frederick McHale, *Print and Power: Confucianism, Communism, and Buddhism in the Making of Modern Vietnam* (Honolulu: University of 'Hawai'i Press, 2004); and Woodside, *Community and Revolution.*
105. DeVido, "Buddhism for This World"; and "Influence of Chinese Master Taixu."

Alexander Soucy

THREE TURNINGS OF THE WHEEL OF DOCTRINE (DHARMA-CAKRA)

CYCLES OF BUDDHIST TEACHINGS

According to Buddhist tradition, the buddha, Siddhārtha Gautama (*c.* 485–405 BCE), attained awakening (*bodhi*) in Bodhgaya in modern day Bihar after six years of meditative practice following his decision to renounce his royal heritage and become a wandering ascetic. His final life was the culmination of countless previous births, during which he engaged in prodigious acts of merit-making and meditation practice, leading to progressively greater wisdom and skill in teaching in accordance with the soteriological needs of various audiences. As a result of his newfound realization, he understood the workings of the world as well as how karma (Pāli *kamma*) and rebirth operate, and he freed himself from cyclic existence (*saṃsāra*). Initially fearing that what he had realized was too profound to be understood by others, he decided to pass into nirvana without teaching, but the god Brahmā remonstrated with him, pointing out that there were some people whose minds were only clouded with slight degrees of ignorance (*avijjā*; Skt. *avidyā*) and who would comprehend and profit from his instructions.

As a result, the buddha embarked on a forty-year ministry, which began in Sarnath, near Varanasi in modern day Uttar Pradesh, where five former companions were engaged in ascetic practices in hopes of attaining liberation (*mokkha*; Skt. *mokṣa*). As he approached, they noticed a change in his demeanor: he radiated calm and understanding, and they asked him to share what he had learned. In response, he delivered a sermon referred to as the *Discourse Turning the Wheel of Doctrine (Dhamma-cakka-pavattana-sutta)*, in which he laid out what would become the essential tenets of his dharma (doctrine).[1] The buddha claimed that he was not an innovator: he had rediscovered fundamental truths about reality that were also understood by all past buddhas and that are true at all times and for all types of beings.

This first "wheel of doctrine" emphasized the four "noble truths" (*ariya-sacca*; Skt. *ārya-satya*): (a) that all life involves suffering (*dukkha*; Skt. *duḥkha*); (b) the origin (*samudaya*) of suffering; (c) that suffering can be brought to cessation (*nirodha*); and (d) the path (*magga*; Skt. *mārga*) for ending suffering, which involves a comprehensive reorientation of one's ideas and beliefs, practice of morality and cultivation of positive attitudes, and meditative techniques aimed at attaining mental calm and comprehension of the true nature of reality. The buddha also taught that all compounded phenomena (*saṅkhata*; Skt. *saṃskṛta*) are impermanent (*anicca*; Skt. *anitya*) and thus subject to constant change and that all things are in a constant process of interdependent causation (*paṭicca-samuppāda*; Skt. *pratītya-samutpāda*). Another important component of the "first wheel" of teachings was the "middle way" (*majjhimā-paṭipadā*; Skt. *madhyama-pratipad*)—the path to liberation requires that one avoids extreme asceticism as well as hedonism. The notion later became a cornerstone of Buddhist philosophy, an injunction against falling into extreme views, most importantly reificationism (*sassata-vāda*; Skt. *śāśvata-vāda*) and annihilationism (*uccheda-vāda*).

This discourse became one of the most influential sermons attributed to the buddha by his followers and encoded doctrines that became foundational for the religion that developed from teachings and practices that Buddhists traced back to him. The myriad schools and orders that regard themselves as adhering to his dharma accept the *Discourse Turning the Wheel of Doctrine* as an articulation of core principles, but not all view it as his final or most profound teaching. Several hundred years after the buddha's passing, a new corpus of discourses (sutra) began to circulate in India, and their adherents claimed that these had been taught by the buddha during his lifetime but were reserved for a small coterie of advanced students. Many of these were entitled "Perfection of Wisdom discourses" (*Prajñāpāramitā-sūtra*), and they purported to constitute a new and superior cycle of teaching, a "second wheel of Dharma." They retained the core teachings of the "first wheel," but often provided new interpretations, and they described practices that were purportedly more powerful and effective than those of the preceding dispensation. The ideal of the *arhat* who seeks a personal nirvana, valorized in the Pāli canon, was denigrated in the Perfection of Wisdom discourses as selfish. They portray the bodhisattva as the supreme Buddhist practitioner, a being motivated by compassion who follows the path to liberation in order to release others from suffering.

In addition, the Perfection of Wisdom discourses subject all phenomena to a thoroughgoing critique based on analysis of their "emptiness" (*śūnyatā*) of intrinsic existence (*svabhāva*). All produced phenomena come into being due to causes and conditions external to themselves, change from moment to moment, and pass away. This is true of the minute dharmas that are the building blocks of complex objects, and it is equally true of the buddha's teachings: they were propounded for particular purposes and aimed at certain types of beings in order to help them make progress on the path to liberation; but like everything produced by causes and conditions, the words of the buddha lack inherent existence and are empty. Thus the Perfection of Wisdom critique undermined the belief of naïve practitioners who attributed an inherent truth value and reality to the buddha's words. In the new cycle of teachings, Buddhist doctrines were characterized as heuristic devices promulgated for specific purposes, but once a practitioner has fully comprehended their purport, they should be left behind. Woncheuk (원측; Ch. Yuance 圓測, 613–696) argues that the key difference between the first two wheels is that in the former dispensation the buddha focused on entities such as dharmas and made unambiguous statements about doctrines based on the four noble truths, but emptiness was "hidden." In the second wheel, emptiness was the focus, and the buddha indicated that the categories and doctrines elucidated in the first wheel lacked substantial existence and are empty.[2]

HĪNAYĀNA AND MAHĀYĀNA

The Perfection of Wisdom discourses relegated the teachings of the "first wheel" and their ideal of the *arhat* to an "Inferior Vehicle" (Hīnayāna) and referred to their path as the "Greater Vehicle" (Mahāyāna). The chronological discrepancy between the time of the buddha's passing and the intervening centuries before these purportedly superior texts began to circulate in India was explained away by claiming that the buddha taught them during his lifetime but realized that there was no one who could adequately interpret them. He arranged for them to be hidden in the undersea realm of the *nāgas* (beings with human heads and serpent bodies that inhabit watery places) until the birth of the sage Nāgārjuna (*c.* 150–250 CE). After Nāgārjuna received the texts, he began to compose treatises that elucidated the buddha's intent. He is widely regarded in Buddhist Mahāyāna traditions as the founder and most influential exegete of the Madhyamaka (Middle Way) school, whose core doctrines are based on the Perfection of Wisdom corpus.

The notion of successive wheels of doctrine became well-established in Mahāyāna circles, but was rejected by those who were characterized as "Hīnayānists." They viewed the Mahāyāna "sutras" (a term denoting a discourse authentically originating with the historical buddha) as forgeries, and not particularly well-crafted ones. The Mahāyāna sutras were often much longer than those of the Pāli canon, they contained doctrines and practices not attested in sources regarded as authoritative by their rivals, and the historical discrepancy between the buddha's death and the appearance of the new teachings was regarded by non-Mahāyānists as clear evidence of their spuriousness.

Factions also developed among communities that accepted the Perfection of Wisdom discourses as normative, along with other Mahāyāna works. Once the principle of a wheel of doctrine that supersedes an earlier dispensation was generally accepted, it was perhaps inevitable that this hermeneutical move would be further extended and that groups who identified as Mahāyānists but regarded coreligionists as propounding doctrines that were inferior to their own would relegate their rivals to a "second wheel" and characterize their own path as constituting a superior "third wheel of doctrine."

The *locus classicus* for the three wheels of doctrine schema is the 3rd–4th century *Discourse Explaining the Thought* (*Saṃdhinirmocana-sūtra*), which became the main scriptural source for Yogācāra (Yogic Practice), the other major school of Indian Buddhism.[3] This is a mature work of Buddhist philosophy and meditation theory that presupposes centuries of doctrinal development. It purports to be the buddha's final word on these matters, and it puts forward a comprehensive vision of the dharma that has a place for the first two wheels, which are conceived as skillful teachings (*upāya-kauśalya*) appropriate to certain types of practitioners with similar proclivities. The relationship between the three wheels is one of supervenience: the third wheel is only possible because of the foundation of the other two, and its distinctive tenets build on and require those of the first and second wheels.

Robert Thurman has argued that the three wheels schema is chronological: the buddha began teaching first wheel doctrines, then switched to second wheel discourses, and then in the latter part of his life focused on the third wheel.[4] This is not, however, how the schema is presented in the *Discourse Explaining the Thought* or other Mahāyāna works that discuss it, and it has no basis in any of the extant hagiographies of the buddha's life. The three wheels are cycles of teaching, and all are interconnected. The second wheel would lack specificity without the first because these discourses critique first-wheel tenets and develop a vision of the path in which they are integrated, but as preliminaries to the higher teachings of the second wheel. Similarly, the third wheel is described as a "wheel of good differentiations" (*legs par rnam par phye ba'i 'khor lo*) that sorts out exactly what the buddha intended in the first and second wheels, clearing up ambiguities and establishing his final intention.[5] This is presumably why the seminal sutra of this cycle is entitled *Discourse Explaining the Thought*. Chokro Lügyeltsen (Cog ro klu'i rgyal mtshan, *c.* 9th century) comments that the title

> is designated according to the level of meaning. This *sūtra* definitely delineates the meaning of the profound thought and indirect thought of the Tathāgata [Buddha] and cuts all the knots of the afflictive obscurations (*kleśāvaraṇa*) and the cognitive obscurations (*jñeyāvaraṇa*). Here, "*Ārya-saṃdhinirmocana*" is designated as the name of the *sūtra*. . . . With respect to that, "*ārya*" means "one who is very distanced from all sinful nonvirtuous qualities." "*Saṃdhi*" refers to the profound thought and indirect thought of the Tathāgata. Also, in one sense the meaning of the words refers to the knots of the afflictive obscurations and the cognitive obscurations. "*Nirmocana*" refers to definitive delineation. It refers to "definitive delineation of the profound thought and indirect thought of the Tathāgata." Also, in one sense the meaning of the words means to cut completely: this refers to "completely cutting all of the knots of the afflictive obscurations and the cognitive obscurations." With respect to that, if the meaning of the words is brought together in a general way: it definitely disentangles the profound thought of the Tathāgata, and it cuts all of the knots of the afflictive obscurations and the cognitive obscurations; thus, it both explains his thought and completely cuts knots.[6]

The *Discourse Explaining the Thought* employs a number of literary and doctrinal tropes to present itself as the buddha's final word. Unlike the discourses of the Pāli canon and many Mahāyāna sutras, it is set in a celestial palace, and not one of the sites in north India that were the venues of other sermons delivered to audiences mainly comprising ordinary human (and some nonhuman) followers reported in canonical sources. The palace is only accessible to the most advanced practitioners, which ensures that the level of teaching will be appropriate to this type of audience, and not beginners. Throughout the text, its instructions are declared to be impossible for "children" (or beginners: *bāla*) to comprehend. All of the interlocutors are tenth level (*bhūmi*) bodhisattvas, which implicitly indicates that their questions will focus on rarified aspects of the later stages of the path and advanced doctrines. Much of the text is concerned with apparent discrepancies and contradictions in teachings attributed to the buddha. The interlocutors often preface their questions by stating: "Blessed One, in the past you said X, then you said not-X; what were you thinking when you said this?" The format of the questions assumes both that all the discourses attributed to the buddha were in fact spoken by him and that there must be some underlying thought behind them. In the first several chapters, the buddha provides often subtle explanations to reconcile these issues, and the seventh chapter describes a hermeneutical model for comprehensively understanding the hidden intention behind the voluminous corpus of discourses attributed to the founder of their religion by Indian Buddhists.

BUDDHIST HERMENEUTICS ACCORDING TO THE *DISCOURSE EXPLAINING THE THOUGHT*

Chapter seven opens with the bodhisattva Paramārthasamudgata reflecting on the Buddha's teachings: he begins with a review of pronouncements regarding the four truths and elements of the path found in Hīnayāna sources and then considers subsequent discourses that apparently undermine them:

> The Bhagavan [Buddha] has also said that all phenomena lack inherent existence, that all phenomena are unproduced, unceasing, quiescent from the start, and naturally in a state of nirvana. Then I thought, "Of what was the Bhagavan thinking when he said this?"[7]

The Buddha responds by explaining his hidden intentions in terms of three types of absence of intrinsic nature: absence of intrinsic nature in terms of character; absence of intrinsic nature in terms of production; and ultimate absence of intrinsic nature. These refer respectively to three characters (*trilakṣaṇa*): (a) the imputational character (*parikalpita-lakṣaṇa*); (b) the other-dependent character (*paratantra-lakṣaṇa*); and (c) the thoroughly real character (*pariniṣpanna-lakṣaṇa*). Woncheuk comments that Paramārthasamudgata's question implies that the two sets of teachings regarding absence of intrinsic nature in terms of character and production are mutually contradictory (*phan tshun 'gal ba*); the meaning of the query is: "Bhagavan, with respect to the statements concerning such things as nonentityness, of what were you thinking?"[8]

The first character comprises things that beings believe to be real but are in fact illusory, such as the notion of an enduring self (*ātman*): *parikalpita* is "a character posited as names and symbols, but it does not subsist by way of its own character." The other-dependent character refers to whatever "arises through the force of other conditions and not by itself." Phenomena that come into being in dependence on causes and conditions exist conventionally, but they are not ultimately real, and so they "lack intrinsic existence in terms of production."[9] The thoroughly real character is the way things really are: it is how the other-dependent is perceived when the false superimpositions of the imputational character no longer appear.

The buddha expands on this by stating that correctly understanding the third character is a crucial factor in the path to liberation: it is a "purifying object of observation" (*viśuddhālambana*), the ultimate truth (*paramārtha*), the absence of self of phenomena (*dharma-nairātmya*), and it is an "ultimate lack of intrinsic existence."[10] When meditators take it as the focal point of their practice, it serves to eliminate mental afflictions and helps them to attain advanced states of realization and ultimately liberation from the round of birth and death. It is "all-pervasive and unitary"; it is always the same, and it is exactly what it appears to be when correctly understood, and so it can aid practitioners in their soteriological goals. Woncheuk comments that it abides in "permanent, permanent time and everlasting, everlasting time," and it is uncompounded, unproduced, and unceasing.[11]

Its constancy is the most important aspect of the thoroughly real character, and so Gadjin Nagao is mistaken in claiming that the three natures schema is based on a "principle of convertibility."[12] According to Nagao, the efforts of meditators transform the other-dependent character and bring about the actualization of the thoroughly real. No Indian Yogācāra sources of which I am aware support this notion; if the final nature were something created by human activity, it could not serve its primary function as a purifying object of observation. It would be the result of meditation practice, rather than its focal and facilitating object. This is also the consensus of the commentators on the *Discourse Explaining the Thought*, all of whom equate it with the ultimate truth and suchness (*tathatā*). Chokro Lügyeltsen explains that

> due to correctly knowing suchness, the ultimate, the selflessness of phenomena, which is a character that is everywhere of one taste, one perceives it. . . . Because superiors (*ārya*) know the other-dependent character by way of a superior's knowledge and perception, that which completely awakens, which is perceived as being inexpressible, is thoroughly established suchness, the ultimate, the selflessness of phenomena, and it has a character that is everywhere of one taste. Therefore, it is an antidote to exaggerated pride in terms of apprehended objects, this ultimate that has a character that is everywhere of one taste.[13]

According to Woncheuk, "through the power of observing this object, one also attains mental purification." He adds that a purifying object of observation has three aspects: (a) it is permanently changeless; (b) it is a nature of virtue and happiness; and (c) it manifestly accomplishes everything: "Because the ultimate truth is free from sameness and difference, you should know that it is a purifying object of observation. Why is this? Because through the power of observing this object one obtains mental purification."[14]

THE PROBLEM OF NIHILISM

Following the discussion of the three characters and three non-entitynesses, the *Discourse Explaining the Thought* states that the "second wheel" teachings in which the buddha issued blanket pronouncements that all phenomena are unproduced, unceasing, quiescent from the start, and naturally in a state of nirvana were made with the three characters in mind, although they were not expressly articulated. As a result, some of the buddha's followers fell to an extreme of nihilism and thought he was denying the reality of anything at all and that his teachings were devoid of meaning. Because of this, it was necessary to initiate a third wheel of dharma, one that is supervenient on the previous two and that differentiates exactly what is being negated and what is not.

> Superimposing the intrinsic existence of the imputational onto the intrinsic existence of the other-dependent and the thoroughly real, sentient beings subsequently attribute conventions of the character of the intrinsic existence of the imputational to the intrinsic existence of the other-dependent and the thoroughly real. To the extent that they subsequently attribute such conventions, their minds are infused with conventional designations. . . . Due to these causes and conditions, in the future [this view of] the intrinsic existence of the other-dependent proliferates. Based on this, the afflictive obscurations give rise to further afflictions. . . . For a long time, sentient beings will wander, transmigrating among hell beings, or animals, or hungry spirits (*preta*), or gods, or *asuras*, or humans. They will not pass beyond cyclic existence.[15]

The buddha then indicates that he teaches a progression of cycles of doctrine: the first wheel is articulated for trainees with a particular set of predispositions, and it is superseded by the second wheel, which undermines some of the implicit assumptions of certain audiences. Finally, in the third wheel he clearly differentiates his final intention for the benefit of the most advanced students. The buddha then explains how the soteriological process works:

> I initially teach doctrines starting with the lack of intrinsic existence in terms of production to those beings who have not generated roots of virtue, who have not purified obstructions, who have not ripened their continuums, who do not have much conviction, and who have not completed the accumulations of merit and wisdom. When they hear those doctrines, they understand dependently originated compounded phenomena as impermanent. They know them to be phenomena that are unstable, unworthy of confidence, and changeable, whereupon they develop aversion and antipathy toward all compounded phenomena.[16]

Realizing that grasping after the dependently arisen phenomena of cyclic existence leads to suffering and continued rebirth, the buddha's followers turn away from them and thus engage in ethical behavior, the foundation of subsequent practice. They attain virtuous qualities that were not previously part of their psychophysical continuums. They then purify cognitive obscurations and develop unswerving faith in the buddha and his dharma, and as a result they advance in cultivation of merit (*puṇya*) and wisdom (*prajñā*). Despite such positive outcomes, these trainees do not fully understand the absence of intrinsic existence in all phenomena, and so the buddha introduces them to the perspective of the second wheel. After they hear the discourses of absence of intrinsic existence, second wheel practitioners develop thoroughgoing aversion to compounded phenomena and thus make further progress in eliminating afflictive obscurations and cognitive obscurations, the two primary obstacles to attainment of buddhahood. Thus they are able to attain nirvana, but this is not the final goal, according to the buddha: his followers should understand that there is finally only one vehicle (*ekayāna*), that of the bodhisattva who works tirelessly for the benefit of others.

Chokro Lügyeltsen comments that all will eventually develop the aspiration to benefit others:

> Because the causes of unsurpassed, perfect awakening are thoroughly ripening sentient beings and ripening the qualities of a buddha for oneself, those who do not perform those two activities lack the causes of buddhahood at that time. However, this is merely a difference in practice; it does not come from the nature of the mind. Therefore, they are referred to as "those who proceed solely to pacification" for as long as they have not attained the lineage of transformation into unsurpassed awakening and do not exert themselves in this.[17]

He adds that like all beings, they have the mental capacity to pursue the Mahāyāna path. Their Hīnayāna practices are not a dead end: because they attain advanced meditative states, when they make the transition to Mahāyāna, they will enter the path at the eighth bodhisattva level (*bhūmi*) and then progress quickly toward buddhahood.[18]

Second wheel trainees become overly attached to the teachings of absence of intrinsic existence and to their own progress on the path, and as a result fail to fully grasp the centrality of compassion for attainment of final liberation. There is an underlying purpose to all of the buddha's teachings, even if it is not apparent to his followers: "My disciplinary doctrine is explained well, is complete, and is taught with a very pure thought. With respect to this well-taught doctrine, degrees of conviction appear among sentient beings."[19] The buddha further explains that the instructions of the first two wheels are of "interpretable meaning" (*neyārtha*): they were delivered for specific audiences that would benefit from them, but they do not represent the "definitive meaning" (*nītārtha*). Interpretable teachings serve pragmatic purposes: they help students to develop conviction in the buddha and his dharma and get them started on the path to liberation. According to Pudön (Bu ston rin chen grub, 1290–1364), the aim of this cycle of instruction is to remove the misconceptions of students who received the teachings of the first two wheels and had fallen into one of the two extremes.[20]

Almost as an aside, the buddha indicates that this schema is not comprehensive and does not encompass all of his followers: some particularly intelligent and perceptive bodhisattvas have the ability to understand his hidden thought in all of the instructions they hear, and so they do not require the differentiations of the third wheel. Moreover, Tsongkhapa (Tsong kha pa blo bzang grags pa, 1357–1419) is probably correct in his assertion that the three wheels are not pertinent to all of the buddha's pronouncements.[21] Only doctrines that might require interpretation or that are subjects of dispute are included, and not clear-cut and unambiguous statements, such as the buddha's Vinaya statements regarding the details and configurations of monastic robes.

THE PROGRESSION OF THE THREE WHEELS

Paramārthasamudgata then summarizes the main outlines of the three wheels of doctrine, and he adds that they are not truly discrete: the buddha skillfully integrates third wheel teachings in all of his instructions, but so subtly that only the most advanced listeners can discern them. He compares this process to adding spice to food or the background of a painting: third wheel elements pervade all aspects of the dharma, but only trainees with a high level of realization are aware of the third wheel teachings. Woncheuk comments that these teachings, like a painting's canvas, are more than mere additions: they are the basis for everything else.[22] Like a spice that gives a recipe its distinctive flavor, definitive tenets pervade the entire dharma and are of "one taste" in all the buddha's discourses.[23] Paramārthasamudgata describes the process of doctrinal development:

> Initially, in the Varanasi area, in the Deer Park called Sages' Teaching, the Bhagavan taught the aspects of the four noble truths for those who were genuinely engaged in the [Śrāvaka] vehicle. The wheel of doctrine you turned at first is wondrous. Similar doctrines had not been promulgated before in the world by gods or humans. However, this wheel of doctrine that the Bhagavan turned is surpassable, provides an opportunity for dispute, is of interpretable meaning, and serves as a basis for dispute. Then the Bhagavan turned a second wheel of doctrine that is more wondrous still for those who are genuinely engaged in the Great Vehicle, because of the aspect of teaching emptiness, beginning

> with the lack of inherent existence of phenomena, and beginning with their absence of production, absence of cessation, quiescence from the start, and being naturally in a state of nirvana. However, this wheel of doctrine that the Bhagavan turned is surpassable, provides an opportunity for dispute, is of interpretable meaning, and serves as a basis for dispute. Then the Bhagavan turned a third wheel of doctrine, possessing good differentiations, and exceedingly wondrous, for those genuinely engaged in all vehicles, beginning with the lack of inherent existence of phenomena, and beginning with their absence of production, absence of cessation, quiescence from the start, and being naturally in a state of nirvana. Moreover, that wheel of doctrine turned by the Bhagavan is unsurpassable, does not provide an opportunity for dispute, is of definitive meaning, and does not serve as a basis for dispute.[24]

The buddha agrees with Paramārthasamudgata's summary and adds that the teachings of the third wheel comprehensively differentiate the meaning behind the other two wheels and constitute his final thought. Trainees who comprehend them and put them into practice will generate vast amounts of merit and will make rapid progress on the path. The sutra then reports that many members of the audience had breakthrough experiences as a result of being present at the auspicious occasion of the definitive teaching of the third wheel of Dharma.

Penjor Lhündrup (Dpal 'byor lhun grub, 1561–1637) explains that third wheel teachings are "unsurpassable" (*bla na ma mchis pa*; Skt. *anuttara*) because there are no other sutras of definitive meaning that are superior to them. They "do not provide an opportunity for dispute" because there is no opportunity for opponents validly to argue about them in terms of the literal readings of their teachings. They are of definitive meaning because "they need not be interpreted as something else and are definitive as that meaning."[25] Tsongkhapa contends, however, that while there is no basis for controversy according to the sutra, this

> should be taken as meaning that because the text indicates the existence or nonexistence of entityness, there is no place for controversy when scholars analyze whether the meaning of the *sūtra* is or is not delineated in this way; it does not indicate that there are no other controversies.[26]

Despite the clear hierarchy implied in the *Discourse Explaining the Thought*, Tsongkhapa—for whom the "second wheel" Madhyamaka teachings are definitive—refers to the buddha's statement that some advanced trainees are able to comprehend his final intention without requiring the third wheel's instructions as evidence that the specific audience of the third wheel comprises students who are actually at a lower level than the most intelligent second wheel trainees, who he contends are advanced Mādhyamikas. He claims that the buddha is referring to Mādhyamikas as the sharpest trainees, and by implication Yogācāras, the main audience for the sutra, are inferior in their understanding. According to Tsongkhapa,

> while the latter two wheels are similar in their instructions beginning with absence of intrinsic existence as the subject of expression, the difference in the presentation of the teaching is that the middle wheel does not differentiate what has intrinsic existence and

> what does not . . . because the latter wheel differentiates these, it is "possessed of good differentiations."[27]

In other words, Yogācāras need to have the buddha's intention spelled out for them in detail, while the "sharp trainees" (viz., the most perceptive Mādhyamikas) comprehend the "one taste" of the definitive aspects of the buddha's final thought in whatever they hear. For those who are able to perceive the basis in the buddha's thought (*dgongs gzhi*), there is no contradiction. These advanced practitioners are not the intended audience of the *Discourse Explaining the Thought*. Benjor Lhündrup explains that for the "special trainees" of the third wheel,

> stemming from the subject matter of absence of inherent existence and so forth, the Buddha differentiated well the particulars of true establishment and non-true establishment with regard to the three: imputations, other-dependent natures, and thoroughly real natures; and thoroughly real natures are the third wheel, the wheel of doctrine of good differentiation.[28]

This is an interesting bit of doxographic jiujitsu that attempts to turn the tables on adherents of the third wheel by using aspects of the *Discourse Explaining the Thought* to yield a result different from what its hierarchical ordering of doctrines apparently intended.

THE THREE WHEELS OF DOCTRINE AND BUDDHIST HERMENEUTICS

The three wheels of doctrine schema has been described as an important contribution to Mahāyāna Buddhist hermeneutics, one that provides a model for differentiating interpretable and definitive doctrines, but its scope is rather limited. As presented in the *Discourse Explaining the Thought*, it pertains to "second wheel" teachings in which the buddha made blanket pronouncements about emptiness, but no attempt is made to extend this model to other aspects of the vast plethora of teachings attributed to the buddha. Some exegetes characterize the "third wheel" as comprising doctrines associated with Yogācāra presented in the sutra, including the "foundational consciousness" (*ālaya-vijñāna*) and "cognition only" (*vijñapti-mātratā*), but this link is not made in the text itself. It could be argued that by implication any doctrines in the *Discourse Explaining the Thought* are aspects of the buddha's final thought because the treatise presents itself as a response to bodhisattvas at the highest levels of the path regarding matters of concern to them and others with similar advanced attainments, but this connection is not made explicitly.

Some exegetes extend the purview of third wheel teachings to include sutras that also contain statements to the effect that everything is cognition only (or "mind only": *citta-mātra*, a term that is used in many Tibetan doxographical works to designate Yogācāra). Other late Mahāyāna works such as the *Discourse of the Lion's Roar of Queen Śrīmālā* (*Śrīmālādevī-siṃhanāda-sūtra*; Ch. *Shengman shizi hou yisheng dafangbian fangguang jing* 勝鬘師子吼一乘大方便方廣經) that discuss the doctrine of "embryonic buddhahood" (*tathāgatagarbha*; Ch. *rulai zang* 如來藏, the notion that all beings have an innate potential for attainment of awakening) are often included within the third wheel, even though this concept is not found in the *Discourse Explaining the Thought*.

Some Tibetan exegetes associated Vajrayāna or tantric Buddhism with the third wheel. In his doxographical work *Freedom from Extremes Accomplished through Comprehensive Knowledge of Philosophy*, Daktsang Sherap Rinchen (Stag tshang Shes rab rin chen, 1405–1477), for example, characterizes it as a supplementary, practice-oriented component of the buddha's third wheel dispensation: "Mantra [Vajrayāna] is applied as an aid and support for the path of the third wheel, and in that way the teaching of Mantra is thus supplied in addition to the lower teachings."[29]

The three wheels schema is primarily a polemical device put forward in the sutra as a means of relegating some Mahāyānists to inferior status and characterizing others who viewed doctrines and practices that would later come to be associated with the developed Yogācāra school as superior. This sort of move was emulated by other Buddhist schools that developed in East Asia and that valorized particular texts as the Buddha's final teaching and based their tenets and practices on them. In East Asia, this practice is referred to as "classification of tenets" (*panjiao* 判教, an abbreviation of *jiaoxiang panshi* 教相判釋, "differentiation of the characteristics of tenets"). In East Asia, where many schools regarded a particular sutra as the supreme teaching, that text would be placed in the highest position and those valorized by rival traditions would be ranked in descending order. For example, Zhiyi 智顗 (538–597), the leading scholar of the Tiantai 天台 school, divided the buddha's teachings into five periods:

(1) The Avataṃsaka Period (Huayan shi 華嚴時), which began immediately after his attainment of awakening, when he delivered the *Flower Ornament Discourse* (*Avataṃsaka-sūtra*; Ch. *Dafangguang fo huayan jing* 大方廣佛華嚴經); this encapsulated the essence of his understanding and is referred to by Huiguan 慧觀 (*c.* 4th–5th century) as the "sudden" (*dun* 頓) teaching, but it was too abstruse for all but the most advanced listeners.

(2) The Deer Park Period (Luyuan shi 鹿苑時; also referred to as the "Āgama Period" [Ahan shi 阿含時] because these teachings were compiled in scriptural collections called Āgamas)—roughly corresponding to the "first wheel of doctrine"—during which the Buddha decided to propound doctrines that could be widely understood.

(3) The Extensive Period (Fangdeng shi 方等時), during which he taught the "extensive" (*vaipulya*) discourses of early Mahāyāna with the intention of converting Hīnayānists to Mahāyāna.

(4) The Wisdom Period (Bore shi 般若時), in which he revealed the Perfection of Wisdom discourses and emphasized the doctrine of emptiness.

(5) The Lotus-Nirvana Period (Fahua niepan shi 法華涅槃時), during which the Buddha delivered the *Lotus Sutra* (*Saddharma-puṇḍarīka-sūtra*; Ch. *Miaofa lianhua jing* 妙法蓮華經, commonly shortened to *Fahua jing* 法華經) and the *Discourse of the Great Final Release* (*Mahāparinirvāṇa-sūtra*; Ch. *Da banniepan jing* 大般涅槃經).

In these treatises, he informs students that there is finally only one vehicle, and these instructions bring together all the major threads of his previous doctrines. This classification system characterizes the teachings of the *Flower Ornament Discourse* as the most advanced dispensation of the buddha, but Tiantai's own core scripture, the *Lotus Sutra*, represents his mature thought and is the teaching best suited to Mahāyāna practitioners, a comprehensive presentation of doctrine and practice. The subject of East Asian classification systems would require a separate entry, but it is worth noting that they adopt the *Discourse Explaining the Thought*'s polemical move of finding a place for all of the teachings attributed to the buddha by various groups of followers within a hierarchical structure that valorizes one particular strand as the highest and most complete while relegating those of opponents to more elementary and less developed strata.

REVIEW OF LITERATURE

The "three wheels of doctrine" schema is an important trope that appears in numerous Mahāyāna sources, but there has been surprisingly little study of it in secondary literature. Blumenthal's "Three Turnings of the Wheel of Dharma" provides a short summary that reflects Tibetan interpretations, and Thurman's "Buddhist Hermeneutics" discusses it in the context of an overview of Buddhist hermeneutics.[30] Problems with Thurman's presentation were noted above, particularly his assertion that the schema is chronological. This is not how it is presented in the *Discourse Explaining the Thought*, the apparent *locus classicus* for the schema. Powers' *Hermeneutics and Tradition in the Saṃdhinirmocana-sūtra* contains several chapters on the context and doctrinal ramifications of the *Discourse's* formulation of the three wheels, along with material from the two largest commentaries on the text, Chokro Lügyeltsen's (Chok ro klu'i rgyal mtshan/Byang chub rdzu 'phrul) *Explanation of the Superior Discourse Explaining the Thought* and Woncheuk's voluminous *Expansive Explanation of the Superior Discourse Explaining the Hidden Thought*, both of which discuss the three wheels at length.[31] Neither of these has been translated, but Powers translates or summarizes most of the passages from these two works that discuss the three wheels or related concepts.[32]

The *Discourse* has been translated into English by Powers, based on the sDe dge Tibetan version and canonical commentaries.[33] Powers' thesis "The Concept of the Ultimate (*don dam pa, paramārtha*) in the '*Saṃdhinirmocana-sūtra*': Analysis, Translation, and Notes" contains a translation of the Stok Palace edition, along with extensive notes on textual variations in other Tibetan versions, including one in the Old Tibetan style.[34] Both of Powers' translations rely heavily on the commentaries of Woncheuk and Chokro Lügyeltsen, along with those of Jñānagarbha and Asaṅga.[35] Keenan's *The Scripture on Explanation of the Underlying Meaning* is an exacting translation from Xuanzang's Chinese version (Taishō vol. 16, #676), and Cleary's *Buddhist Yoga: A Comprehensive Course* is a looser translation from the Chinese that presents the *Discourse* as a textbook for meditation.[36] Lamotte's French translation, *Saṃdhinirmocana Sūtra: L'explication des mystères*, the first Western language rendering of the *Discourse*, is mainly based on a Tibetan text housed in the Bibliothèque Nationale in Paris, which he compares with the Chinese versions.[37]

The most comprehensive analysis of the conceptually related doctrine of three natures (or characters) is Boquist's *Trisvabhāva: A Study of the Development of the Three-Nature-Theory in Yogācāra*, which examines how it is presented in the *Discourse Explaining the Thought*, the *Descent into Laṅkā Discourse* (*Laṅkāvatāra-sūtra*), and several Yogācāra philosophical treatises.[38]

The three wheels of doctrine schema is central to Tsongkhapa's interpretation of Yogācāra hermeneutics, which he presents in *Essence of Good Explanations Regarding the Interpretable and the Definitive* (*Drang nges legs bshad snying po*), which inspired at least a dozen commentaries by later Gelukpas.[39] Thurman translates and analyzes Tsongkhapa's text, in *Tsong Khapa's Speech of*

Gold in the Essence of True Eloquence, as does Hopkins, in *Emptiness in the Mind-Only School of Buddhism*, which also discusses the commentarial literature.[40] Hopkins's *Reflections on Reality: The Three Natures and Non-Natures in the Mind-Only School* explores the social and doctrinal context of the three natures doctrine, presenting both Gelukpa interpretations and critiques by rival traditions, particularly the Jonangpa.[41] In the third volume of his study of *Essence of Good Explanations* and its reception by Tibetan scholars, Hopkins explores some of the issues that arose during the centuries of commentary and critique following its publication.[42]

FURTHER READING

Buescher, Hartmut. *The Inception of Yogācāra-Vijñānavāda*. Vienna: Österreichische Akademie der Wissenschaften, 2008.

Doboom Tulku, L. T. "The Twelve Scriptural Categories." In *Sutra of the Wise and the Foolish*. Translated by Alexander Berzin. Dharamshala, India: Library of Tibetan Works and Archives, [1974] 2009. http://www.berzinarchives.com/web/en/archives/sutra/level2_lamrim/initial_scope/safe_direction/twelve_scriptural_categories.html.

Lipman, Kennard. "Nītārtha, Neyārtha, and Tathāgatagarbha in Tibet." *Journal of Indian Philosophy* 8, no. 1 (March 1980): 87–95.

Lopez, Donald S., ed. *Buddhist Hermeneutics*. Honolulu: University of Hawai'i Press, 1988.

Mathes, Klaus-Dieter. *A Direct Path to the Buddha Within: Gö Lotsāwa's Mahāmudrā Interpretation of the Ratnagotravibhāga*. Boston: Wisdom Publications, 2008.

Powers, John. *Two Commentaries on the Saṃdhinirmocana-sūtra by Asaṅga and Jñānagarbha*. Lewiston, NY, and Queenston, ON: Edwin Mellen Press, 1992.

Powers, John. "The Term '*Saṃdhinirmocana*' in the Title of the *Saṃdhinirmocana-sūtra*." *Studies in Central and East Asian Religions* 4 (1992): 52–62.

Powers, John. *Wisdom of Buddha: The Saṃdhinirmocana-sūtra*. Berkeley, CA: Dharma Publishing, 1995.

Powers, John. "*Saṃdhinirmocana-sūtra*." In *Brill Encyclopedia of Buddhism*. Edited by Jonathan Silk, 240–248. Leiden, the Netherlands: E. J. Brill, 2015.

Powers, John. "Three Turnings of the Wheel of Doctrine (Dharma-Cakra)." In *Oxford Bibliographies in Buddhism*, July 21, 2016. https://doi.org/10.1093/obo/9780195393521-0163.

Powers, John. "Buddhist Hermeneutics." In *History of Indian Philosophy*. Edited by Purushottama Bilimoria, 40–48. London: Routledge, 2017.

Ruegg, David Seyfort. "Purport, Implicature, and Presupposition: Sanskrit *Abhiprāya* and Tibetan *Dgoṅs pa/Dgoṅs gźi* as Hermeneutical Concepts." *Journal of Indian Philosophy* 13, no. 4 (1985): 309–325.

Schmithausen, Lambert. *The Genesis of Yogācāra-Vijñānavāda: Responses and Reflections*. Tokyo: International Institute for Buddhist Studies of the International College for Postgraduate Buddhist Studies, 2014.

Snellgrove, David. *Indo-Tibetan Buddhism: Indian Buddhists and their Tibetan Successors*. Boston: Shambhala Publications, 1987.

Steinkellner, Ernst. "Who Is Byaṅ chub rdzu 'phrul? Tibetan and Non-Tibetan Commentaries on the *Saṃdhinirmocanasūtra*: A Survey of the Literature." *Berliner Indologische Studien* 4, no. 5 (1989): 238–241.

NOTES

1. *Discourse Turning the Wheel of Doctrine* (*Dhamma-cakka-pavattana-sutta*), *Saṃyutta-nikāya* 56.1, in *The Saṃyutta-nikāya of the Sutta-piṭaka*, vol. 5, ed. Léon Feer (London: Pali Text Society, 1973–1980), 420–423.

2. Woncheuk (Tib. Wen tshegs; Ch. Yuance 圓測), *Expansive Explanation of the Superior Discourse Explaining the Hidden Thought* [*Ārya-gambhīra-saṃdhinirmocana-sūtra-ṭīkā*; Tib. *'Phags pa dgongs pa zab mo nges par 'grel pa'i mdo'i rgya cher 'grel pa*], n.d., 133.4.
3. *Discourse Explaining the Thought* [*Saṃdhinirmocana-sūtra*; Tib. *Dgongs pa nges par 'grel pa'i mdo*; Ch. *Jieshenmi jing* 解深密經]. sDe dge #106, mDo sde, vol. *ca*: 1b1–55b7.
4. Robert A. F. Thurman, "Buddhist Hermeneutics," *Journal of the American Academy of Religion* 46, no. 1 (1978): 19–39.
5. Tsongkhapa (Tsong kha pa blo bzang grags pa), *Essence of Good Explanations Regarding the Interpretable and the Definitive* [*Drang nges legs bshad snying po*] (Sarnath, India: Pleasure of Elegant Sayings Printing Press, 1979), 26.11.
6. Chokro Lügyeltsen (Cog ro klu'i rgyal mtshan/Byang chub rdzu 'phrul), *Explanation of the Superior Discourse Explaining the Thought* [*Ārya-saṃdhinirmocana-sūtrasya-vyākhyāna*; Tib. *'Phags pa dgongs 'grel nges par 'grel pa'i mdo'i rnam par bshad pa*], vol. *cho*: 8.
7. *Discourse Explaining the Thought*, sDe dge: 31.
8. Woncheuk, *Expansive Explanation of the Superior Discourse*, vol. *ti*: 552.4.
9. *Discourse Explaining the Thought*, sDe dge: 33.
10. *Discourse Explaining the Thought*, sDe dge: 21.5.
11. Woncheuk, *Expansive Explanation of the Superior Discourse*, vol. *ti*: 567.6.
12. Gadjin M. Nagao, "The Buddhist World-View as Elucidated in the Three-Nature Theory and Its Similes," *The Eastern Buddhist* 16, no. 1 (1983): 1–18.
13. Chokro Lügyeltsen, *Explanation of the Superior Discourse*, vol. *cho*: 112.5.
14. Woncheuk, *Expansive Explanation of the Superior Discourse*, vol. *thi*: 406.2.
15. *Discourse Explaining the Thought*, sDe dge: 36.
16. *Discourse Explaining the Thought*, sDe dge: 36.
17. Chokro Lügyeltsen, *Explanation of the Superior Discourse*, vol. *cho*: 240.3.
18. Chokro Lügyeltsen, *Explanation of the Superior Discourse*, vol. *cho*: 241.3.
19. *Discourse Explaining the Thought*, sDe dge: 39.
20. Pudön (Bu ston rin chen grub), *The History of Buddhism (Chos ḥbyung); Part I: The Jewellery of Scripture; Part II: The History of Buddhism in India and Tibet*, trans. Eugene Obermiller (Wiesbaden, Germany: Harrassowitz Verlag, 1931), part II: 51–54.
21. Tsongkhapa, *Essence of Good Explanations*, 28.
22. Woncheuk, *Expansive Explanation of the Superior Discourse*, vol. *thi*: 108.2.
23. Woncheuk, *Expansive Explanation of the Superior Discourse*, vol. *thi*: 209.2.
24. *Discourse Explaining the Thought*, sDe dge: 48–49.
25. Benjor Lhündrup (Dpal 'byor lhun grub), *Lamp for the Teaching: Difficult Points in Essence of Good Explanations* [*Legs bshad snying po'i dka' 'grel bstan pa'i sgron me*] (Delhi: Rong tha mchog sprul rnam pa gnyis, 1969), 31.5.
26. Tsongkhapa, *Essence of Good Explanations*, 27.2.
27. Tsongkhapa, *Essence of Good Explanations*, 25.
28. Benjor Lhündrup, *Lamp for the Teaching*, 30.3.
29. Daktsang Sherap Rinchen (Stag tshang Shes rab rin chen), *A Commentary on the Treatise Freedom from Extremes Accomplished through Comprehensive Knowledge of Philosophy* [*Grub mtha' kun shes nas mtha' 'bral sgrub pa zhes bya ba'i bstan bcos rnam par bshad pa legs bshad kyi rgya mtsho*], in *Collected Works of Taktsang Lotsawa* [*Stag tshang lotsāwa shes rab rin chen gyi gsung 'bum pod dang po*], Vol. I: Dpal brtsegs bod yig dpe rnying zhib 'jug khang (Beijing: China Tibetology Press, 2007), 353.
30. James Blumenthal, "Three Turnings of the Wheel of Dharma," *Mandala Magazine* 10, no. 1 (2008).
31. John Powers, *Hermeneutics and Tradition in the Saṃdhinirmocana-sūtra* (Leiden, the Netherlands: E. J. Brill, 1993).

32. John Powers, "The Concept of the Ultimate [*don dam pa, paramārtha*] in the '*Saṃdhinirmocana-sūtra*': Analysis, Translation, and Notes," PhD Diss., University of Virginia, 1991.
33. John Powers, *Wisdom of Buddha: The Saṃdhinirmocana-sūtra* (Berkeley, CA: Dharma Publishing, 1995).
34. Powers, "The Concept of the Ultimate."
35. Jñānagarbha, *Commentary on Just the Maitreya Chapter from the Superior Discourse Explaining the Thought* [*Ārya-saṃdhinirmocana-sūtra-ārya-maitreyakevala-parivarta-bhāṣya*; Tib. *'Phags pa dgongs pa nges par 'grel pa'i mdo las 'phags pa byams pa'i le'u nyi tshe'i bshad pa*], n. d., sDe dge #4033, Sems tsam, vol. *bi*: 318b1–345a7; and Asaṅga, *Commentary on the Superior Discourse Explaining the Thought* [*Ārya-saṃdhinirmocana-bhāṣya*; Tib.*'Phags pa dgongs pa nges par 'grel pa'i rnam par bshad pa*], n. d., sDe dge #3981, mDo 'grel, vol. *ngi*: 1b1–11b5.
36. John P. Keenan, *The Scripture on Explanation of the Underlying Meaning* (Berkeley, CA: Numata Center, 2000); and Thomas Cleary, *Buddhist Yoga: A Comprehensive Course* (Boston: Shambhala, 1995).
37. Étienne Lamotte, *Saṃdhinirmocana Sūtra: L'explication des mystères* (Louvain, Belgium: Bureaux de Recueil, Bibliothèque de l'Université, 1935).
38. Ålt Boquist, *Trisvabhāva: A Study of the Development of the Three-Nature-Theory in Yogācāra* (Lund, Sweden: Department of History of Religions, University of Lund, 1993).
39. Tsongkhapa, *Essence of Good Explanations.*
40. Robert A. F. Thurman, *Tsong Khapa's Speech of Gold in the Essence of True Eloquence* (Princeton, NJ: Princeton University Press, 1984); and Jeffrey Hopkins, *Emptiness in the Mind-Only School of Buddhism: Dynamic Responses to Dzong-ka-ba's The Essence of Eloquence: Volume 1* (Berkeley: University of California Press, 1999).
41. Jeffrey Hopkins, *Reflections on Reality: The Three Natures and Non-Natures in the Mind-Only School* (Berkeley: University of California Press, 2002).
42. Jeffrey Hopkins, *Absorption in No External World: 170 Issues in Mind-Only Buddhism* (Ithaca, NY: Snow Lion Publications, 2005).

John Powers

TIBETAN BOOK OF THE DEAD (*BARDO THÖDOL*)

HISTORY OF THE TEXT

The Tibetan source-text for the *Tibetan Book of the Dead*, the *Bardo Thödol*, was standardized as a cohesive set of works in the 17th century by Rigdzin Nyima Dragpa (Rig 'dzin nyi ma grags pa; 1647–1710), who was a well-known "treasure revealer."[1] This version has since been redacted in multiple editions throughout various lineage traditions both inside and outside Tibet, with Dragpa's version considered to be the general standard for the textual corpus; however, other versions of the liturgy can be found to vary in order and content.[2]

This collection was drawn from Karma Lingpa's revealed treasure (*gter ma*), *The Profound Teaching of the Peaceful and Wrathful Deities: Natural Liberation through Enlightened Intention* (*Zab chos zhi khro dgongs pa rang grol*). This cycle of Nyingma teachings is based on the mandala scheme of the one hundred peaceful and wrathful deities (*zhi khro rigs brgya*) according to the *Guhyagarbha Tantra* system. This treasure literature is attributed to Padmasambhava, considered the originator of the Nyingma tradition in Tibet, who produced the work in the 8th century. According to tradition, his consort Yeshe Tsogyal (Ye shes mtsho rgyal; 757–817) wrote down the teaching and subsequently had the text buried in a cave at Gampodar Mountain in the region of Dakpo in Tibet.

Although the *Peaceful and Wrathful Deities* of the so-called Karling tradition was disseminated from the 15th century onward, the form that the collection took was most likely based on materials gathered by Karma Lingpa himself. It was revised and systematized by Karma Lingpa's successors, including his father, Nyida Sangye (Nyi zla sangs rgyas), and his son, Nyida Chöje (Nyi zla chos rje). The collection was passed on through various lines of transmission, and the *Bardo Thödol* compilation in particular continues to be utilized by adherents of various sects of Buddhism in Tibetan and Himalayan regions to this day.

After the content of the *Bardo Thödol* was initially revealed, it was taught by Karma Lingpa in and around the area of Dakpo, eventually spreading to other Tibetan regions such as Kongpo, a significant location for the origin myths of the empire (7th–9th centuries), which were dominated by stories of ancient death rites. It was no coincidence that it was this location where the *Bardo Thödol* tradition flourished, given the region's strong association with traditional funerary rituals associated with the early kings of Tibet.[3] In fact, Gyarawa Chökyi Gyatso (Rgya ra ba nam mkha' chos kyi rgya mtsho; b. 1430), the abbot of Menmo monastery in Kongpo, was responsible for forming the first easily reproducible liturgical program for the *Bardo Thödol* literature. This is where the rituals associated with the manual became standardized and began to be disseminated throughout the rest of Tibet, mainly in communities associated with the Nyingma and Kagyü (bka' brgyud) lineages, and where it soon became a primary source for funerary rites. In the 17th century, the collection was edited by Rigdzin Nyima Dragpa, who produced the version that we now commonly refer to as the *Bardo Thödol*.

The basic structure of the *Bardo Thödol* collection includes instructions on cultivating basic awareness of the nature of our minds within this life, methods for recognizing signs of impending death, an explanation of the dying process and dissolution of the bodily elements, and guidance on how to avoid untimely death. The primary utility of the work is found in its manual of instructions for the newly dead, which is to be read out to the deceased in order to help them successfully traverse the intermediate state before their next rebirth by recognizing the ultimate nature of their minds and thus the nature of appearances within the intermediate state existence. This is what is referred to in the title *Liberation through Hearing* (*Thödol, thos grol*). The collection further includes aspirational prayers for the deceased, a masked play illustrating the intermediate state experience, and finally instructions on attaching mantras to the deceased to encourage liberation through wearing (*brtags grol*).[4]

The "book" was most likely originally spread in the form of copies of handwritten manuscripts, since xylographs (wood-block prints) were not the standard means of text production in Tibet until the 18th century. These manuscripts were presumably commissioned by lamas and monastic institutions for ritual use, as well as by wealthy lay individuals who desired to accrue the merit from sponsoring text copying, a common practice in Tibet by that time.[5] Some of the various manuscript editions were eventually set down as block prints, which is the form of the *Bardo Thödol* text that became the basis for the *Tibetan Book of the Dead*.

HISTORY OF TRANSLATIONS

Walter Y. Evans-Wentz first coined the title *Tibetan Book of the Dead* with his 1927 Oxford University Press publication of significant portions of a version of the *Bardo Thödol*. This title was based on the *Egyptian Book of the Dead*, a name which also did not equate with a single text from Egypt, but rather referred to a collection of traditional funerary rites and incantations that were traditionally buried with the dead and often varied in content. A version of these funerary manuals was translated in 1842 by Karl Richard Lepsius (1810–1884), who was the first to come up with the name.[6]

As for the *Tibetan Book of the Dead,* the publication was based on a set of block-prints originally acquired by Major W. L. Campbell in 1919 from Gyantse, Tibet. Later that same year he passed these texts on to Evans-Wentz, who subsequently commissioned Kazi Dawa Samdup (1868–1923), an English and Tibetan teacher and interpreter based in Sikkim, to translate the collection. The Tibetan collection, *The Great Liberation through Hearing in the Intermediate State,* upon which the *Tibetan Book of the Dead* is based, is sometimes referred to nowadays by its Tibetan name, the *Bardo Thödol* (*Bar do thos grol chen mo*). After its initial publication, it was immediately noticed in spiritualist and psychologist circles, leading to the famous psychologist Carl Jung (1875–1961) providing his own commentary to the work; however, he was later criticized for his apparent rereading of the text to suit his own views of the unconscious.[7] Evans-Wentz himself was highly influenced by the 19th-century spiritualist thought of Theosophy, which is apparent in his liberal interpretations of Dzogchen and tantric terminology found within the work.[8] His limited knowledge of Tibetan Buddhism led to multiple misinterpretations and conflations of views that were at times more in line with the Indian Vedānta tradition.

Since Evans-Wentz's edition of Kazi Dawa Samdup's rendering of the *Bardo Thödol* was published, numerous editions and translations into Western languages have also used this title to attract a popular Western readership. Although they take advantage of the title *Tibetan Book of the Dead,* other translators have included their own selection of texts taken from the *Bardo Thödol* cycle of instructions that deviate to varied degrees from Evans-Wentz's 1927 work. Among the European-language translations of the *Tibetan Book of the Dead,* the famous Tibetologist Giuseppe Tucci (1894–1984) was the first to translate Evans-Wentz's work into Italian; his work is noteworthy because it included the first attempt to discuss the textual history of the *Bardo Thödol,* recognizing that the dissemination of the compilation in Tibet was varied and of ambiguous origin.[9] Chögyam Trungpa (1939–1987), a Tibetan lama who was famous in the United States and the United Kingdom for presenting Tibetan Buddhism to a Western audience, worked with his student Francesca Fremantle to publish the first new translation of the *Bardo Thödol* passages since Evans-Wentz.[10] This version attempted to make the language more accessible to a general audience and included a psychological commentary by Chögyam Trungpa. Francesca Fremantle later published her own supplementary book in order to provide further explanation to the concepts found in the text and updated translations of the work.[11]

The third English translation of selected passages from the *Bardo Thödol* was made by the Tibetologist Robert Thurman.[12] This publication included additional translations of two works from the *Bardo Thödol* literature that were not included in either of the previous English editions, and has since remained one of the most popular versions of the *Tibetan Book of the Dead.* The scholar and translator Gyurme Dorje translated and published the first full English translation of Rigdzin Nyima Dragpa's entire collection of the *Bardo Thödol,* which includes an additional nine chapters from Evan-Wentz's version, and also includes translations of two related works found in Karma Lingpa's larger treasure cycle, *Peaceful and Wrathful Deities.*[13]

The style of this translation is notably different from that of Evans-Wentz, providing clear and accurate renderings of Nyingma terminology, demonstrating Dorje's strong grasp of the Tibetan Buddhist tradition. This work has been generally well reviewed and includes a foreword by the Fourteenth Dalai Lama, as does Thurman's publication. The full collection was also translated into French by Philippe Cornu for his doctoral thesis, which was subsequently published.[14] A new translation of the *Tibetan Book of the Dead* by Elio Guarisco is the most recently published, based on the commentary of Namkhai Norbu, a well-known Dzogchen teacher, and is intended to be an updated version based on Tucci's Italian edition.[15]

DYING AND DEATH IN TIBETAN BUDDHISM

Although it is the best-known Tibetan death manual in the West, the literature associated with the *Tibetan Book of the Dead* is only one example of an extensive Buddhist textual tradition relating to dying and death. Death has been a core object for contemplation and practice for Buddhists over the centuries, as is demonstrated in Buddhist literature. It was even Siddhārtha Gautama's realization that every sentient being would inevitably die that motivated him to seek enlightenment and eventually become the buddha. Death in Buddhism is equated with the reality of impermanence; that is, anything that arises eventually ceases, such as thoughts, emotions, and the physical world, including our own bodies. Death is considered to be the cessation or the exhaustion of circumstances that enable a phenomenon to occur, and thus itself a cause for a new phenomenon to arise; therefore, each moment arises from the death of the previous moment. The centrality of death to the Buddhist view of reality is present not only in its philosophy but also in its meditative practices. All major Buddhist schools encourage followers to contemplate the reality of death, the uncertainty of when it will happen, and the preciousness of this life. These reminders are intended to motivate a practitioner to utilize this lifetime to cultivate understanding of the Buddhist teachings and awareness of the impermanent nature of reality in order to attain liberation from the idea of an unchanging or undying self.

In later tantric Buddhist traditions, death is a central object of meditation. A yogi is instructed to remain in charnel grounds, drink from skull-cups, and wear the ash from human cremations. An intimate and immediate exposure to death is meant to facilitate meditation practice and reduce the relative dualistic notions of purity and impurity, and even of life and death, which are said to be exactly what binds one to the cyclic existence of birth and death. The moment of death itself becomes an opportunity for awakening and total enlightenment, and a yogi's profession is to prepare for this occasion. A tantric practitioner trains in complex rituals and meditation techniques that are often intended to induce experiences that mimic the process of dying. According to the *Bardo Thödol*, in the Higher Yoga (*yogāniruttara*) tantric system of Indo-Tibetan Buddhism, the primary practices are concerned with manipulating and dissolving the subtle energies of the body in order to simulate the stages of dying. This is done both to utilize this experience to attain meditative realization and to prepare for the moment of death, leading to a favorable rebirth or the attainment of full buddhahood and liberation from cyclic existence.[16]

When Buddhism initially entered Tibet in the 7th century CE during its early diffusion (*snga dar*) with the help of imperial patronage, tantric Buddhism was already well established in India. When Buddhism flourished again in the 11th–13th centuries during its later diffusion (*phyi dar*) in Tibet, tantric Buddhism had become highly institutionalized in India, and famous tantric adepts were systematically transferring their lineage traditions to Tibetans who consequently developed their own syncretized tantric traditions. A notable example of this phenomenon is the transmission of the Six Yogas of Nāropa (*Nā ro'i chos drug*) from India to Tibet through the Indian *mahāsiddha* Nāropa (Nā ro pa; 1016–1100) and the Tibetan translator Marpa Chökyi Lodrö (Mar pa chos kyi blo gros; 1012–1097).[17] The Six Yogas is a tantric program that combines various tantric practice traditions that eventually became the primary method of approaching tantra for the Kagyü school of Tibetan Buddhism, which developed its own commentarial and ritual tradition based on these teachings.[18] The Six Yogas system itself also echoes many themes found within the *Bardo Thödol* literature, including detailed instructions on how to attain liberation in the intermediate state (*bar do chos*), as well as the practice instructions for transferring one's consciousness (*'pho ba chos*) to a higher realm at the time of death, which is also described in the *Bardo Thödol*.

Buddhist notions surrounding dying and death have produced an entire genre of Tibetan literature, philosophy, iconography, and ritual. The medium that influences popular Tibetan Buddhist notions of the process of dying and the postmortem state is primarily funerary rituals, which are predominately maintained and carried out by the monastic institutions. Another source for conceptualizing the framework for death within Tibet and the Himalaya is the popular folk tradition of *delog* (*'das log*) bards, who recount delog stories of those who travel to and return from the intermediate state (*bar do*) between death and rebirth.[19] Examining these cultural and religious popular expressions concerning death clearly illustrates the significance of mortality in Tibetan Buddhism, and one better comprehends the philosophical and social paradigms from which the *Bardo Thödol* developed.

THE INTERMEDIATE STATE (*ANTARĀBHAVA; BAR DO*)

As illustrated by the title of the *Bardo Thödol*, *The Great Liberation through Hearing in the Intermediate State* (*Bar do thos grol chen mo*), the primary concern of this collection is liberation while one is in the postmortem intermediate state or bardo (*antarābhava*; *bar do*). In the Tibetan Buddhist tradition, this concept of an intermediate state most often refers to the in-between existence experienced during the transitional period from the moment of death to the moment of conception. However, this term has also been used to express all transitional experiences throughout life; for example, the experience of sleeping is an intermediate state between the moments of falling asleep and waking, and even the moment of death itself is considered an intermediate state between life and the after-death experience. Generally, adherents of Tibetan Buddhism consider people always to be in a transitional state between one experience and another. However, this type of notion of an intermediary state of existence did not originate in Tibet, nor was it always the primary model of the afterlife for Tibetans.

The notion of intermediate states of existence was asserted by some of the early Indian Buddhist schools such as Sarvāstivāda, although the concept was not supported by many traditions, including the Theravāda, and it may have had some conceptual roots in the Vedic tradition of India.[20] Vasubandhu (*c*. 4th century CE) is known to be the first popular Buddhist supporter of the concept of intermediate states of existence, discussed in the third chapter of his *Abhidharmakośabhāṣya*, titled *Exposition of the World* (*Lokanirdeśa*). In this famous work on Abhidharma, Vasubandhu outlines four intermediate states: birth, the state between birth and dying, death, and the state between death and rebirth. The intermediate state is also advocated in several sutras, including the *Garbhāvakrāntinirdeśa Sūtra*, which was the primary influence for the notion of the intermediate state found in the *Yogācārabhūmi*, a definitive text for the Yogācāra school of Buddhism.[21]

Vasubandhu also advocated that the intermediate being is a *gandharva*, or "smell-eater."[22] While the *gandharva* does not necessarily represent a soul or true self, as these concepts are rejected in Buddhist tenets, the being represents the form or body that the mental continuum takes, which is subject to karma and made up of aggregates (*skandha*; *phung po*). This being is driven to its next birth when, seeing its potential parents copulating, it becomes driven by its oedipal feelings to enter the womb of the mother at the point of conception. The period of remaining in the intermediate state is generally understood to last forty-nine days. During this time, it is said the bardo being repeatedly experiences the dissolution process of the gross and subtle levels of consciousness, only to arise again in its intermediate state existence. This pattern occurs every seven days for a total of seven weeks, until the individual finally takes rebirth in one of the six realms of existence that is determined by its karma.[23]

Indian Buddhist tantric traditions eventually integrated the notion of an after-death intermediate existence into their soteriological framework, which resulted in instructions designed to prepare yogis to be able to carry out certain tantric practices in the intermediate state between death and rebirth with one's "illusory body" (*sgyu lus*), the ephemeral tantric body one possesses that is made up of channels (*nāḍī*; *rtsa*), wind (*prāṇa*; *rlung*), and drops (*bindu*; *thig le*).[24] Although not much is known about the reception of the concept of the intermediate state during the early diffusion of Buddhism into Tibet, it is clear that by the time of the later diffusion these well-developed tantric understandings were systematically incorporated into Buddhist tantric systems, as can be seen in the Six Yogas of Nāropa literature, where one of the Six Yogas or practices is the yoga of the intermediate state (*bar do chos*).[25]

The model of four intermediate states was taken up by Tibetan commentators, but there were various alternative presentations, including threefold and sixfold divisions. We find in the *Bardo Thödol* literature a sixfold division of the intermediate state existences. These states include the bardo of birth and living (*skye gnas bar do*), the bardo of dreams (*rmi lam bar do*), the bardo of meditation (*bsam gtan bar do*), the bardo of death (*'chi kha bar do*) which occurs during the dissolution process of the physical and mental elements, the bardo of reality-itself (*'chos nyid bar do*) which is the moment all coarse and subtle types of consciousness cease and one is confronted with the actual luminosity (*'od gsal*) of reality itself, and the bardo of becoming (*srid pa bar do*) which is the state between death and rebirth. While there is precedent for the other bardo states in other Buddhist traditions, the bardo of reality-itself appears to be particularly a Dzogchen innovation.[26]

Tantric practice instructions such as those found in the Six Yogas system outline methods for engaging in meditative practices in this life which prepare one for recognizing reality and the nature of mind, particularly during the dying stages, at the moment of death when the ultimate luminosity manifests, and during the post-mortem state of existence. These preparations are cultivated in order to enable oneself to merge the luminosity experienced during meditation, referred to in many texts as the "child luminosity" (*bu 'od gsal*), with the "mother luminosity" (*ma 'od gsal*) of ultimate reality that naturally manifests during the bardo of reality itself. If a yogi succeeds at merging the mother and child luminosities, he will essentially be liberated from his karmic conditions and there will be no need to traverse the bardo of becoming.[27] However, if the yogi does not succeed in merging, he may faint when confronted with the ultimate or mother luminosity, only to regain consciousness within the bardo of becoming. Nevertheless, the tantric practices cultivated in this life can help practitioners to recognize the nature of the many appearances in the intermediate state as merely projections of their own minds. This recognition can lead to liberation from the intermediate state and thus from being bound to one's next birth and continuing the cycle of existence (*saṃsāra*; *'khor ba*), instead leading one to full liberation (*nirvāṇa*; *mya ngan las 'das pa*). However, if one does not sufficiently train in practices that will lead to this recognition, the deceased can become disoriented, confused, and likely terrified by the many sensory manifestations occurring in the bardo of becoming.

The potentially terrifying experiences that one may encounter in the intermediate state are illustrated in depth within the Tibetan bard tradition of *delog* (*'das log*) accounts. *Delog* means "one who returns from beyond," a popular figure in Tibetan folklore. A *delog* is a person (usually a woman) who dies an untimely death, traverses the intermediate state, and then returns to this life to share her or his experiences with the living. While both the *Bardo Thödol* literature and the *delog* bards give detailed descriptions of the intermediate state, the *delog* experiences have tended to focus on the negative aspects of traversing the bardo when one has behaved negatively in this life, thus serving as a reminder for ethical behavior according to lay Buddhist principles (e.g., not stealing, not consuming intoxicants, not killing).[28] Although *delog*s convey the terrors of the after-death experience while the *Bardo Thödol* largely concentrates on death as an occasion for liberation, the *delog* tradition still acts as a popular medium by which Tibetans shape ideas about death and the intermediate state, further informing their preparations for the postmortem experience.

TIBETAN FUNERAL RITES

Death as a rite of passage was crucial to Tibetan conceptual frameworks of reality long before Buddhism entered Tibet. Thus, funerary rituals as they are found today in Tibet and the Himalaya reflect a complex history of ideas and practices that has formed a hybridized ritual system rooted in both Buddhist and pre-Buddhist traditions. Although relatively little is known about pre-Buddhist conceptions and practices relating to death, textual evidence found at the Dunhuang caves suggests that early Tibetan funerary rites and rituals to guarantee safe passage for the kings (*btsan po*) to the heaven-realm above (*dgung dgu gshegs*) were considered central to the duties of court priests (referred to as *bon po*). It is clear that the Tibetans believed in a realm of the dead, and that the dead or ancestral spirits (*mtshun*) were not necessarily benevolent toward the living and were thus contained within tombs. Elaborate rituals were designed to appease the dead in order to avoid inauspicious circumstances, including the use of effigies as ransoms (*glud*), as well as animal and likely human sacrifices. Before Buddhism entered Tibet in the 7th century, the dead, those who had lost their life force (*bla*), were considered unable to return to the land of living and remained within their realm of existence indefinitely.[29]

As Buddhism entered imperial Tibet systematically under the auspices of King Songtsen Gampo (Srong btsan sgam po; *c.* 617–*c.* 649), Tibetans began to negotiate certain ritual practices that were considered incompatible with Buddhist principles, particularly the use of living sacrifices. Although there existed antagonism within the Tibetan court between the *bon po* priests and the Buddhist ritual priests throughout the course of the empire (effectively ending in the 9th century), syncretic ritual programs eventually developed, incorporating Buddhist and indigenous beliefs regarding the afterlife. Bardo rituals (*bar do cho ga*) and liturgy were systematized by the 13th century, and these programs were designed primarily to purify an individual's negative karma during the dying and postmortem states in order to redirect his or her path toward a better rebirth (i.e., toward the god realms, human realm, or a buddha's pure land). The literature of the *Bardo Thödol* is exemplary of this intention, and the more the text is recited, the more beneficial it is for the dying or deceased, particularly if it is read by a lama or yogi in the presence of the corpse.

Many standard ritual programs for the dead that developed in Tibet are based on an early text translated from Sanskrit, *The Tantra on the Elimination of All Evil Rebirths* (*Sarvadurgatiparśodhana*).[30] While various traditions stemmed from this work, the practices tend to follow a common structure which includes such basic elements as prayers and rituals to avoid untimely death, supplication prayers to Buddhist masters and buddhas to aid in guiding one toward a better rebirth, deity meditation, rituals to save individuals from the lower realms, and instructions for bodily disposal. Another important element of most Tibetan Buddhist funerary rites is the practice of mind transference (*'pho ba*) to a higher realm, which is ideally to be carried out by a realized Buddhist master as close to the moment of death as possible.[31] All of the basic elements mentioned above are present within the *Bardo Thödol*.

Scholars have tended to approach studies of Tibetan Buddhist funerary rituals from an anthropological perspective.[32] They map their observations of such funerary rites in order to outline the complex process from the time of death through the ceremonies that take place during the forty-nine-day bardo period. According to these accounts, after death, in many regions of Tibet and the Himalaya, the body is often bound and continuously watched out of concern that the corpse may be possessed by demonic forces and rise again as a zombie (*ro langs*).[33] If the family has the financial means, monks are commissioned to perform prayers and standard practices such as mind transference and purification rituals. This is the time when the *Bardo Thödol* is traditionally to be read aloud next to the dead. The corpse often remains within the home of the deceased until an ideal time for bodily disposal is determined by an astrologer. There are various options for bodily disposal within the Tibetan region that relate to the elements: earth burial (*sa sbas gtong ba*), water burial (*chu bskyur*), cremation (*ro sregs*), and sky burial (*bya rgod 'don*).[34] In Tibet, a sky burial is considered to be spiritually ideal, and includes offering one's body through having the corpse cut into pieces and fed to vultures. However, this form of disposal is not available in all regions, and so cremation is the most common practice, particularly in the Buddhist communities of India and Nepal. In Tibetan custom, certain individuals are also mummified (*pur phung bzos*), particularly lamas of high status.

During a cremation ceremony, offerings are made to the deceased and are thrown onto the fire while monks perform certain rituals and prayers depending on the family's particular Buddhist affiliation. If the individual is considered a realized being, it is common to find reports of miraculous signs occurring during the funeral rite which signify a saintly death in Tibet, including rainbows, visions of buddhas, the sound of conch shells, and a rain of flowers. A saintly figure in Tibetan areas will also often leave relics behind, including pearl-like stones, teeth, and parts of the skull. These relics will be enshrined in special containers, especially in reliquary structures known as *stūpas* (*mchod rten*).[35]

PADMASAMBHAVA AND THE NYINGMA (*RNYING MA*) TRADITION

The *Bardo Thödol*, while purportedly revealed by Karma Lingpa in the 14th century, is said to have been originally authored by the famous Tibetan saint Padmasambhava (8th century), a semi-historical figure in Tibetan tradition whose name means "one born from a lotus." This Buddhist yogi and saint came from the land of Oḍḍiyāna (likely to be the present-day Swāt valley) and was invited by King Trisong Detsen (Khri srong lde btsan; 742–797) in order to fully transmit Buddhism to Tibet. Padmasambhava (also referred to by Tibetans as Guru Rinpoche) is perhaps the most revered figure in Tibetan Buddhism, as he is widely worshipped among all the major schools and is credited with subjugating the malevolent spirits of Tibet that were creating obstacles to the establishment of Buddhism. Legend claims that he never died, but instead traveled westward once his tasks in Tibet were completed. He is said to have possessed supreme magical powers, and is considered by many Tibetan Buddhists to have been a buddha and the emanation of the bodhisattva of compassion, Avalokiteśvara, and the celestial buddha Amitābha.[36]

Padmasambhava is also known to have imparted many teachings to disciples throughout Tibet and the Himalaya, the highest teachings of which are the Dzogchen (also referred to in the Nyingma tradition as Atiyoga or primordial yoga) instructions, which aim to engender direct recognition of awareness (*rig pa*) and the natural state of reality as naturally empty and luminous.[37] Many of the treasure teachings Padmasambhava transmitted claim to come directly and indirectly from the primordial buddha Samantabhadra (*kun tu bzang po*). He also received extensive instructions on the Dzogchen tantras from his guru Śrī Siṃha. Padmasambhava is thus considered by many to be the founder of Tibetan Buddhism and the central figure of the school known as Nyingma, meaning "ancient ones." The tradition that stemmed from his teachings is considered to be the oldest Buddhist school surviving in Tibet.

The Nyingma tradition maintains unique tantric teachings and rituals as well as Dzogchen instructions, many of which are included within their core collection of canonical works, the *Collection of Nyingma Tantras* (*Rnying ma'i rgyud 'bum*). This collection consists of many works that were translated into Tibetan during the early diffusion of Buddhism in the imperial era. Many of these works were not adopted into the canonical collections of what were later referred to as the "newer schools" (*gsar ma*), which were established during the later diffusion of Buddhism. Most Nyingma works were not included in the canons of the *Translated Words* (bKa' 'gyur) or the *Translated Treatises* (bsTan 'gyur) because they lacked an established Indian source, a conscious concern for many adherents of the newer schools such as the Kadam, Sakya, and Kagyü. Many of these rejected texts were, however, preserved within the Nyingma canon, including the *Guhyagarbha Tantra*, a central tantra to the Nyingma and the tantric tradition in which the *Bardo Thödol* literature developed.

Padmasambhava is said to have foreseen the degeneration of Buddhism in Tibet, and thus to have concealed many treasure teachings both in the ground (*sa gter*) as well as in the mind-streams of disciples (*dgongs gter*), which were sometimes revealed in the form of pure visions (*dag snang*). There are some Indian precedents for the custom of hiding teachings for the benefit of later generations, particularly within the Mahāyāna tradition. In Tibet, this means of providing innovative teaching cycles attributed to Padmasambhava and other buddhas has been largely associated with the Nyingma school. The practice of treasure revealing is a common phenomenon for realized Nyingma masters and is still carried out to this day. The authenticity of these systems of teachings has been questioned by more orthodox Tibetan teachers, who believed Buddhist teachings must be traced directly to Indian teachers in order to be considered authoritative and in line with the Buddha's instructions. Despite this concern, there have also been instances of revealed treasure teachings from other Tibetan Buddhist traditions, particularly from the Kagyü school. However, these teachings are not as central to their practice systems as they are to the Nyingma followers.[38]

Many of the treasure teachings that were concealed in the ground were written down by Padmasambhava's consort Yeshe Tsogyal, including *The Profound Teaching of the Peaceful and Wrathful Deities: Natural Liberation through Enlightened Intention*, within which the *Bardo Thödol* literature is contained. Padmasambhava imparted these instructions after Trisong Detsen requested that he give a quintessential teaching on tantra which would enable an individual to attain buddhahood within one lifetime. These teachings were given to the translator Chokrolui Gyaltsen (Cog ro klu'i rgyal mtshan; 8th century), after which Padmasambhava had them buried at Gampodar mountain in Dakpo for the benefit of future generations. This cycle of teachings on the peaceful and wrathful deities, from which the *Bardo Thödol* originated, was discovered by the treasure revealer Karma Lingpa, which was prophesied by Padmasambhava, a common claim for treasure revealers of the Nyingma tradition.

THE *GUHYAGARBHA TANTRA* AND THE 100 PEACEFUL AND WRATHFUL DEITIES (*ZHI KHRO RIGS BRGYA*)

The iconography described in the *Bardo Thödol* and associated meditative practices is derived from the Tibetan Buddhist tantric tradition that is concerned with the use of esoteric meditative practices, deity worship, and ritual techniques associated with a particular mandala system. A mandala is a geometric depiction of a particular buddha or deity universe, and is designed to be a representational aid for one's practice.[39] Tantric literature is often set within a particular cosmogenic mandala. The tantric liturgical program of the *Bardo Thödol* is based on the *Guhyagarbha Tantra* (*The Essence of Secrets Tantra*) and its associated mandala of the 100 peaceful and wrathful deities (*zhi khro rigs brgya*).[40] This is a primary tantra studied by the Nyingma tradition of Tibetan Buddhism, and its mandala system is central to various treasure teachings maintained by the tradition.

The works included in the Nyingma canon, the *Collection of Nyingma Tantras* (*Rnying ma'i rgyud 'bum*), are divided into Atiyoga, Anuyoga, and Mahāyoga. The *Guhyagarbha Tantra* is included here in the Mahāyoga class of tantras, which are considered to focus on the generation phase of tantric practice (Anuyoga tantras focus on the completion phase practices, and Atiyoga includes the Dzogchen tantras). Despite this classification, the *Guhyagarbha Tantra*

Figure 1. Mandala Depiction of the 100 Peaceful and Wrathful Deities of the Bardo. Tibet, 18th century.
Source: Rubin Museum of Art. Image from Himalayan Art Resources.

has also been linked with Dzogchen principles in various treasure literature and commentaries by famous Nyingma masters, including Longchen Rabjam (Klong chen rab 'byams; 1308–1363) and Mipham Gyatso (Mi pham rgya mtsho; 1846–1912).[41] This is due largely to the fact that the content of the associated tantric literature focuses on directly realizing the primordial nature of our minds as pure and naturally luminous (*'od gsal*). The authenticity of this tantra has been questioned by conservative Tibetan scholars, such as the translator Gö Khugpa Lhetse ('Gos lo tsā ba khug pa lhas btsas; 11th century), who did not believe it resembled other Indian tantras and could not trace a direct Indian lineage of the text.[42] Other Tibetan scholars, including Gö Lotsawa Zhonu Pal ('Gos lo tsā ba gzhon nu dpal; 1392–1481), assert that a Sanskrit version of the tantra was accounted for at Samye Monastery by the Kashmiri paṇḍita Śākyaśrībhadra (1127–1225).[43] Although there is currently no extant Sanskrit manuscript, the *Guhyagarbha Tantra* is nonetheless a highly influential tantra of the Tibetan Nyingma tradition and has given rise to a multitude of commentaries and associated treasure literature, including the *Bardo Thödol*.

The mandala that is described in the *Guhyagarbha Tantra* is a set of forty-two peaceful (*zhi*) deities and fifty-eight wrathful (*khro*) deities.[44] The central figures of the mandala are the primordial buddha Samantabhadra with his consort Samantabhadri. These figures are considered the ultimate source for all Buddhist teachings and for buddhahood itself. The rest of the ninety-eight deities consist of their retinue or emanations. The two primordial buddhas are directly surrounded by the five celestial buddhas together with their consorts. The rest of the peaceful retinue is made up of eight male and eight female bodhisattvas, six buddhas of the six realms, and four male and four female gatekeepers (*sgo ba*). The fifty-eight wrathful deities are made up of the five tantric deity emanations of the buddhas along with their consorts, surrounded by eight female and eight animal-headed deities, four female wrathful gatekeepers, and twenty-eight yoginis. Some scholars have interpreted these deities as symbols or archetypes of the pure nature of our psychological processes. From the Dzogchen perspective, all of these figures are merely projections of our minds, appearances which are pervaded by luminosity (*'od gsal*) and are ultimately expressions of the pure nature of our psycho-physical aggregates. They are said to be directly encountered as one traverses through the bardo, according to the *Bardo Thödol* and associated literature, and if one is able to recognize their true nature, one can be liberated from the bardo and ultimately attain buddhahood.

WESTERN INTERPRETATIONS

The *Tibetan Book of the Dead* is essentially a Western invention based on selections from the *Bardo Thödol*. No text actually titled *Tibetan Book of the Dead* ever existed in Tibet, and the selections taken from the *Bardo Thödol* were chosen by Walter Y. Evans-Wentz himself and had never made up a cohesive work in Tibet. A plurality of Tibetan funerary texts could have been given the same title, but it is these passages of the *Bardo Thödol* that have come to represent how the West understands Tibetan notions of dying, death, and the process of taking rebirth.

The first published edition of the *Tibetan Book of the Dead* in 1927 primarily consisted of annotations and an introduction by Evans-Wentz, with a preface by Sir. John Woodroffe, a British follower of Hindu tantrism residing in India. Evans-Wentz liberally interpreted the material of the *Tibetan Book of the Dead* from the perspective of his theosophical belief system, based on Helena Blavatsky's (1831–1891) *The Secret Doctrine.*[45] Blavatsky herself had knowledge of Buddhist philosophy, claiming to have spent seven years in Tibet with a secret order instructing her on "esoteric Buddhism."[46] This experience directly influenced her spiritual views and subsequently those promoted by the Theosophical Society, which maintained eclectic and perennialist notions of the nature of the divine, humanity, and the cosmos.[47] Their notoriety and emphasis on the study and incorporation of Asian esoteric traditions meant that the Theosophical Society greatly influenced Western ideas of Asian religious doctrines, especially in terms of Hinduism and Buddhism. Despite this mutual influence of interpretation between the first English presentation of the *Bardo Thödol* and prominence of religious esotericism found in early 20th century theosophical circles, doctrinal differences between tantric Buddhism and theosophy were largely ignored by Evans-Wentz. This synthetic presentation of Tibetan Buddhism has continued to influence subsequent translations, commentaries, and reformulations not only of the *Bardo Thödol,* but also of general Western understandings of Tibetan Buddhist funerary traditions.[48]

Since Carl Jung (1875–1961) produced his "Psychological Commentary," which appeared in English in the third edition of the *Tibetan Book of the Dead* (1949), further psychological interpretations have emerged from popular culture and Western scholarship.[49] The message of these commentaries, for the most part, accords with Jung's understanding that the text should be read as a psychological account of unconscious tendencies. The third edition also includes a foreword by the German-born Lama Anagarika Govinda (1898–1985), who also supported a psychological interpretation of the *Bardo Thödol* that claims that the text describes the death of the ego. Jung's and Govinda's interpretation was further maintained by scholars and spiritualists who have read the work as a manual for the living to transform their psychological experiences.[50]

Timothy Leary (1920–1996), a famous proponent of the use of psychedelic drugs to expose the consciousness to higher states of reality, also provided his own interpretation of the text, based on popular Western psychological interpretations of ego death. Leary, together with Ralph Metzner and Richard Alpert, published *Psychedelic Experience: A Manual Based on the Tibetan Book of the Dead* (1964), which restructured the text as a guide for a drug-induced experience.[51] The book has also been interpreted as a literary work, providing an alternative to reading it as a literal account of the afterlife.[52] This Western tradition of liberally interpreting the text as symbolic or metaphoric has continued through the various popular readings of the *Tibetan Book of the Dead.*[53]

New-Age spiritualists in America have continued the tradition of Evans-Wentz's theosophical rendering, often combining the instructions with Hindu, pagan, or even Christian belief systems to fit their own dispositions and beliefs. However, it is important to note that New Age as well psychological interpretations may dilute the sociohistorical and religious context from which the *Bardo Thödol* literature developed.[54] The intended function of the *Tibetan Book of the Dead* is to act as a ritual guide for the deceased, based on the belief in an afterlife existence and eventual rebirth that can be positively influenced by the living. Although from an ultimate perspective the appearances of deities in the bardo state as described in the *Tibetan Book of the Dead* are merely projections of our primordially luminous minds, on a relative level they are not necessarily any less real than any experience we may encounter throughout our lives, according to Tibetan Buddhist principles.

The *Tibetan Book of the Dead* has had a direct as well as indirect influence on popular culture in the West, as illustrated by John Lennon's song "Tomorrow Never Knows" and Gaspar Noé's 2009 film *Enter the Void*. Two documentary films on the *Tibetan Book of the Dead* have also been produced for a Western audience. In 1984 Hiroaki Mori and Yukari Hayashi produced a two-part documentary on the book, narrated by Leonard Cohen, offering a unique and notable introduction to ways in which the text is utilized both in the Himalaya as well as in the West. In 2007, the History Channel aired the documentary film *Tibetan Book of the Dead*.

REVIEW OF LITERATURE

The various editions and renderings of the *Tibetan Book of the Dead* have traditionally included interpretive commentary or introductions by spiritualists such as Walter Evans-Wentz or Lama Govinda, psychologists such as Carl Jung, or scholars such as Donald Lopez.[55] These introductory notes and annotations contain a wealth of valuable information on the historicity of the *Bardo Thödol* in Tibet, the wider religious context of Tibetan Buddhism, and the Western reception and reinterpretation of the text(s). Apart from these introductions and the available translations of *Bardo Thödol* literature into European languages, Tibetologists have also devoted considerable attention to the collection and its history both in Tibet and in translation. Bryan Cuevas has provided the most exhaustive treatment of the historical developments of the various Tibetan traditions of the *Tibetan Book of the Dead* literature, and Donald Lopez has covered the history and reception of the book in the West.[56] Gyurme Dorje, who published the first complete English translation of the entirety of works included within the *Bardo Thödol*, provides a useful and brief account of the literary history of this cycle of texts, as well as a glossary and tables which aid in conceptually mapping out the content of the *Tibetan Book of the Dead*.[57] This work also includes translations of Buddhist instructions on related preliminary practices and the tantric yoga of consciousness transference (*'pho ba*) to be performed at the time of death.

In terms of psychological (re)interpretations of the *Tibetan Book of the Dead* based on Jung's psychological commentary, which recommends a "reverse reading" of the described mental process of dying, Timothy Leary and colleagues offer the best-known publication that draws upon this theme by redesigning the book as a manual for drug-induced explorations of the ego and psyche.[58] Chögyam Trungpa, a popular Tibetan guru in America during the 1970s and 1980s, further echoed this prominent Western understanding that the purpose of the text(s) is to elucidate psychological processes that occur throughout this life, rather than taking the work to be a literal description of the after-death experiences.[59] While this was the dominant interpretation seen in commentaries, rereadings, and retranslations of the 1960s and 1970s within popular culture and spiritual circles, by the 1990s this type of reading of the *Tibetan Book of the Dead* and associated literature was also picked up by academics who were attempting to provide comparative or literary interpretations of the book.[60] These studies have tended to examine the *Tibetan Book of the Dead* apart from its sociohistorical and religious contexts, rarely acknowledging how the text(s) and the philosophical content are actually interpreted and practiced by Tibetans themselves. This point has recently been brought to light and critically examined by scholars such as Peter Bishop and Donald Lopez.[61]

Within the field of Tibetology, scholars continue to be fascinated by the complexity of rituals, practices, and doctrines associated with death in Tibet. This is due in part to the primacy of the funerary tradition in Tibet's pre-Buddhist indigenous religious practices and its later, elaborate manifestations syncretized with Buddhist doctrine. As Tibet was largely cut off from the rest of the world until the mid-20th century, many ancient shamanistic practices were preserved within mainstream Buddhist rituals, allowing for direct access into ancient practices. This is reflected by the fact that Tibetological investigations into Tibetan traditions related to dying and the dead have been primarily anthropological observations of funeral practices.[62] There have also been a few notable textual studies into the doctrinal interpretation of death and the dead by such scholars as David Germano and Tadeusz Skorupski.[63]

Although Nyingma funerary manuals have been the primary resource for Tibetological studies of belief systems related to death and the afterlife, until recently the history and doctrine of the Nyingma tradition was perhaps the least studied of all the major schools of Tibetan Buddhism. This may be due partly to the fact that, unlike the other major schools of Tibetan Buddhism, Nyingma lacks a clear hierarchal or institutional structure.[64] Since the turn of the 21st century, there has been a strong surge in Nyingma studies with prominent scholars such as Jacob Dalton, Janet Gyatso, Robert Mayer, Cathy Cantwell, and Orna Almogi all making valuable contributions toward understanding Nyingma literature and its history.[65] Also, Dorji Wangchuk, Gyurme Dorje, Dan Martin, Henk Blezer, and Sam van Schaik have all made important contributions toward investigating the *Guhyagarbha Tantra* and its associated literature.[66] It should finally be noted that perhaps the most intriguing aspect of the *Tibetan Book of the Dead* literature is that the conceptual framework and terminology for the *Bardo Thödol* is based on the Nyingma's Dzogchen tradition. Dzogchen, although little understood by Western spiritualists or academics, has received some notable attention from scholars including Sam van Schaik, Samten Karmay, and David Higgins.[67]

PRIMARY SOURCES

The *Tibetan Book of the Dead* is essentially based on a collection of Tibetan literature known as the *Bardo Thödol* or as *The Great Liberation through Hearing in the Intermediate State* (*Bar do thos grol chen mo*). Various editions of this text are available in Tibetan, and have been outlined by Bryan Cuevas.[68] This collection is part of a larger corpus of Tibetan treasure literature, *The Profound Teaching of the Peaceful and Wrathful Deities: Natural Liberation through Enlightened Intention* (*Zab chos zhi khro dgongs pa rang grol*). This treasure text is based on the *Guhyagarbha Tantra*, which is also extant in Tibetan in various editions. Various editions of all three of these textual collections and associated commentaries can be easily accessed online through the Tibetan Buddhist Resource Center (TBRC) (https://www.tbrc.org).[69]

DIGITAL MATERIALS

University of Virginia. The Tibetan Book of the Dead (http://explore.lib.virginia.edu/exhibits/show/dead). This website is a digital version of a special collections exhibition from the University of Virginia Library, curated by Bryan Cuevas. Although the website is difficult to navigate, it provides good examples of the Tibetan textual traditions of death and dying, particularly according to the *Bardo Thödol* tradition.

Bardo: Tibetan Art of the Afterlife (http://www.rmanyc.org/bardo). The physical exhibition of bardo iconography is located at the Rubin Museum of Himalayan Art, New York City, which can be toured via the website. This collection includes sculptures of the Peaceful and Wrathful Deities, illuminated manuscripts, three-dimensional mandalas, and so forth that illustrate Tibetan depictions of the bardo experiences between death and rebirth.

Himalayan Art Resources. Subject: Guhyagarbha Tantra (Peaceful & Wrathful Deities) (http://www.himalayanart.org/search/set.cfm?setid=2179). This website is an indispensable source for iconographic information on Tibetan and Himalayan art and contains an outline, iconography, and useful links relevant to the *Guhyagarbha Tantra*.

FURTHER READING

Bishop, Peter. "A Landscape for Dying: The *Bardo Thödol* and Western Fantasy." In *Constructing Tibetan Culture: Contemporary Perspectives*. Edited by Frank Korom, 47–72. St.-Hyacinthe, Quebec: World Heritage, 1997.

Blezer, Hank. *Kar gling zhi khro: A Tantric Buddhist Concept*. CNWS Publications 56. Leiden, The Netherlands: CNWS, 1997.

Cuevas, Bryan J. *The Hidden History of the* Tibetan Book of the Dead. New York: Oxford University Press, 2003.

Dorje, Gyurme. "The *Guhyagarbhatantra* and Its Fourteenth Century Tibetan Commentary: *Phyogs bcu mun sel*." PhD diss., University of London, 1987.

Dorje, Gyurme, trans. *The Tibetan Book of the Dead: The Great Liberation by Hearing in the Intermediate States*. Edited by Graham Coleman and Thupten Jinpa. London: Penguin, 2006.

Evans-Wentz, Walter Y. *The Tibetan Book of the Dead*, or *The After-Death Experiences on the Bardo Plane, According to Lama Kazi Dawa-Samdup's English Rendering*. Translated by Kazi Dawa Samdup. Oxford: Oxford University Press, 2000a.

Evans-Wentz, Walter Y., trans. *The Tibetan Book of the Great Liberation, or The Method of Realizing Nirvana through Knowing the Mind*. Oxford: Oxford University Press, 2000b.

Fremantle, Francesca, and Chögyam Trungpa, eds. and trans. *The Tibetan Book of the Dead: The Great Liberation through Hearing in the Bardo*. Clear Light Series. Boston: Shambhala, 1975.

Germano, David. "Dying, Death, and Other Opportunities." In *Religions of Tibet in Practice*. Edited by Donald S. Lopez Jr., 458–493. Princeton, NJ: Princeton University Press, 1997.

Gouin, Margaret. *Tibetan Rituals of Death: Buddhist Funerary Practices*. Routledge Critical Studies in Buddhism. New York: Routledge, 2010.

Gyatso, Janet. "Drawn from the Tibetan Treasury: The *gTer ma* Literature." In *Tibetan Literature: Studies in Genre*. Edited by José Cabézon and Roger P. Jackson, 147–169. Ithaca, NY: Snow Lion, 1996.

Imaeda, Yoshiro. "The Bar do thos grol, or 'The Tibetan Book of the Dead': Tibetan Conversion to Buddhism or Tibetanisation of Buddhism?" In *Esoteric Buddhism at Dunhuang: Rites and Teachings for This Life and Beyond*. Edited by Matthew Kapstein and Sam van Schaik, 145–158. Leiden, The Netherlands: Brill, 2010.

Jung, Carl G. "Psychological Commentary." In *The Tibetan Book of the Dead; or, The After-Death Experiences on the Bardo Plane: According to Lama Kazi Dawa-Samdup's English Rendering*. Edited by Walter Y. Evans Wentz and Kazi Dawa Samdup, xxxv–lii. 3d ed. Oxford: Oxford University Press, 1949.

Lauf, Detlef Ingo. *Secret Doctrines of the Tibetan Books of the Dead*. Boulder, CO: Shambhala, 1997.

Leary, Timothy, Ralph Metzner, and Richard Alpert. *The Psychedelic Experience: A Manual Based on the Tibetan Book of the Dead*. London: Penguin Classics, 2008 [1964].

Lopez, Donald S., Jr. "The Book." In *Prisoners of Shangri-La: Tibetan Buddhism and the West*. Edited by Donald S. Lopez Jr., 46–85. Chicago: University of Chicago Press, 1998.

Lopez, Donald S., Jr. *The Tibetan Book of the Dead: A Biography*. Lives of Great Religious Books. Princeton, NJ: Princeton University Press, 2011.

Rinpoche, Dudjom. *Nyingma School of Tibetan Buddhism: Its Fundamentals and History*. Translated by Gyurme Dorje and Matthew Kapstein. Boston: Wisdom, 2002.

Thurman, Robert. *The Tibetan Book of the Dead: Liberation through Understanding in the Between*. New York: Bantam, 1994.

Wicks, Robert. "The Therapeutic Psychology of 'The Tibetan Book of the Dead.'" *Philosophy East and West* 47, no. 4 (1997): 479–494.

NOTES

1. For an overview of Rigdzin Nyima Dragpa's life story, see *Treasury of Lives: Nyima Drakpa*.
2. For more on the various available Tibetan editions of the *Bardo Thödol*, see the first half of the chapter "Conclusion: Manuscripts and Printed Texts," in *The Hidden History of the* Tibetan Book of the Dead, ed. Bryan Cuevas (New York: Oxford University Press, 2003), 205–210.
3. *Hidden History*, 18.
4. The full set of the *Bardo Thödol* collection has been translated in Gyurme Dorje, trans., *The Tibetan Book of the Dead: The Great Liberation by Hearing in the Intermediate States*, ed. Graham Coleman and Thupten Jinpa (London: Penguin, 2006).
5. For more on the significance of written works in Tibet, see Kurtis Schaeffer, *The Culture of the Book in Tibet* (New York: Columbia University Press, 2009).
6. John Taylor, ed., *Journey Through the Afterlife: Ancient Egyptian Book of the Dead* (Cambridge, MA: Harvard University Press, 2010).
7. Donald Lopez Jr., "The Book," in *Prisoners of Shangri-La: Tibetan Buddhism and the West*, ed. Donald S. Lopez Jr. (Chicago: University of Chicago Press, 1998), 46–85.
8. For more on the life of Walter Evans-Wentz, see Ken Winkler, *Pilgrim of the Clear Light: The Biography of Dr. Walter Evans-Wentz* (2d ed.; Bangkok: Booksmango, 2013 [1982]).
9. Giuseppe Tucci, trans.,*Il Libro Tibetano del Morto* (Turin: UTET, 1949).
10. Francesca Fremantle and Chögyam Trungpa, eds. and trans., *The Tibetan Book of the Dead: The Great Liberation through Hearing in the Bardo* (Boston: Shambhala, 1975).
11. Francesca Fremantle, *Luminous Emptiness: Understanding the Tibetan Book of the Dead* (Boston: Shambhala, 2001).
12. Robert Thurman, *The Tibetan Book of the Dead: Liberation through Understanding in the Between* (New York: Bantam, 1994).
13. Gyurme Dorje, trans., *The Tibetan Book of the Dead*.
14. Philippe Cornu, trans., *Le Livre des Morts Tibétain: La grande libération par l'écoute dans les états intermédiaires* (Paris: Buchet/Chastel, 2009).
15. Elio Guarisco, *The Tibetan Book of the Dead: Awakening upon Dying*, ed. Nancy Simmons (Berkeley: Shang Shung, 2013).
16. David Germano, "Dying, Death, and Other Opportunities," in *Religions of Tibet in Practice*, ed. Donald S. Lopez Jr. (Princeton: Princeton University Press, 1997), 458–493.
17. On the story of how Marpa received teachings from Indian *mahāsiddhas* including Nāropa, see Nalanda Translation Committee, trans., *The Life of Marpa the Translator: Seeing Accomplishes All*, composed by Tsangnyön Heruka (Boulder, CO: Shambhala, 1982).
18. Ulrich Kragh, "Prolegomenon to the Six Doctrines of Nā ro pa: Authority and Tradition," in *Mahāmudrā and the Bka'-brgyud Tradition: Proceedings of the Eleventh Seminar of the International Association for*

Tibetan Studies, ed. Roger Jackson and Matthew Kapstein (Andiast, Switzerland: International Association for Tibetan Studies, 2011), 131–177.

19. Bryan Cuevas, *Travels in the Netherworld: Buddhist Popular Narratives of Death and the Afterlife in Tibet* (Oxford: Oxford University Press, 2008).
20. Bryan Cuevas, "Predecessors and Prototypes: Towards a Conceptual History of the Buddhist Antarābhava," *Numen* 43, no. 3 (1996): 263–302.
21. Robert Kritzer, "Childbirth and the Mother's Body in the Abhidharmakośabhāṣya and Related Texts," in *Indo tetsugaku bukkyō shisō ron shū: Mikogami Eshōkyōju shōju kinen ronshū* (Kyoto: Nagatabunshodō, 2004), 1009–1085. See also Robert Kritzer, *Garbhāvakrāntisūtra: The Sūtra on Entry into the Womb* (Studia Philologica Buddhica, Monograph Series 31; Tokyo: International Institute for Buddhist Studies, 2014).
22. For more on the classic Indian notion of a *gandharva* being, see Alex Wayman, *The Vedic Gandharva and Rebirth Theory* (Pune, India: Bhandarkar Oriental Research Institute, 1997).
23. Margaret Gouin, "The 49 Days," in *Tibetan Rituals of Death: Buddhist Funerary Practices* (Routledge Critical Studies in Buddhism; New York: Routledge, 2010), 97–99.
24. Alex Wayman, *The Buddhist Tantras: Light on Indo-Tibetan Esotericism* (Delhi: Motilal Banarsidass, 1990 [1973]).
25. Jamgön Kongtrul, "Intermediate State," in *The Treasury of Knowledge Book Eight, Part Four: Esoteric Instructions*, trans. Sarah Harding (Ithaca, NY: Snow Lion, 2007), 194–202.
26. Bryan Cuevas, "Transitions: The Buddhist Intermediate State," in *Hidden History*, ed. Cuevas, 39–68.
27. On the notion of merging types of luminosity in Tibetan tantric traditions, see Casey Kemp, "Merging Ignorance and Luminosity in Early Bka' brgyud *Bsre ba* Literature," in *Toward a History of Tibetan Mahāmudrā Traditions*, ed. Klaus-Dieter Mathes (Zentralasiatische Studien 44; Andiast, Switzerland: International Institute for Tibetan and Buddhist Studies, 2015), 35–50.
28. Françoise Pommaret, *Les revenants de l'au-delà dans le monde tibétain: Sources littéraires et tradition vivante* (Paris: CNRS, 1989).
29. Bryan Cuevas, "Beginnings: Funeral Ritual in Ancient Tibet," in *Hidden History*, ed. Cuevas, 27–38.
30. Tadeusz Skorupski, "The *Cremation Ceremony* According to the Byang-gTer Tradition," *Kailash* 9, no. 4 (1982): 361–376. See also Tadeusz Skorupski, *The Sarvadurgatipariśodhana Tantra: Elimination of All Evil Destinies, Sanskrit and Tibetan Texts with Introduction, English Translation and Notes* (Delhi: Motilal Banarsidass, 1983); Leonard van der Kuijp, "Notes Apropos of the Transmission of the *Sarvadurgatipariśodhanatantra* in Tibet," *Studien zur Indologie und Iranistik* 16/17 (1992): 109–125; and Zeff Bjerken, "On Mandalas, Monarchs, and Mortuary Magic: Siting the *Sarvadurgatipariśodhana Tantra* in Tibet," *Journal of the American Academy of Religion* 73, no. 3 (2005): 813–841.
31. For a detailed account of the significance of the practice of transference (*'pho ba*) in Kagyü and Nyingma traditions, see Ching Hsuan Mei, "The Development of 'Pho ba Liturgy in Medieval Tibet," PhD diss., Universität Bonn, 2009.
32. For example, some anthropological accounts have investigated the kinds of influence indigenous religious traditions and Buddhism have on Himalayan funerary rites. See Charles Ramble, "Status and Death: Mortuary Rites and Attitudes to the Body in a Tibetan village," *Kailash* 9, no. 4 (1982): 333–359; and Michael Vinding, "The *Thakalis* as Buddhists: A Closer Look at their Death Ceremonies," *Kailash* 9.4 (1982): 291–318.
33. Turrell Wylie, "Ro-Langs: The Tibetan Zombie," *History of Religions* 4, no. 1 (1964): 69–80.
34. Margaret E. Gouin, "Disposal of the Body," in *Tibetan Rituals of Death: Buddhist Funerary Practices*, ed. Gouin (Routledge Critical Studies in Buddhism; New York: Routledge, 2010), 46–78.
35. Dan Martin, "Pearls from Bones: Relics, Chortens, Tertons and the Signs of Saintly Death in Tibet," *Numen* 41, no. 3 (1994): 273–324.

36. For insights into the early sources for the legendary figure Padmasambhava, see Jacob Dalton, "The Early Development of the Padmasambhava Legend in Tibet: A Study of IOL Tib J 644 and Pelliot tibétain 307," *Journal of the American Oriental Society* 124, no. 4 (2004): 759–772.
37. For more on the Dzogchen view and tradition, see John Pettit, "Tibetan Buddhist Traditions and the Great Perfection," in *Mipham's Beacon of Certainty: Illuminating the View of Dzogchen, the Great Perfection,* ed. John W. Pettit (Boston: Wisdom, 1999), 71–100.
38. For more on treasure literature in Tibet, see Janet Gyatso, "Drawn from the Tibetan Treasury: The gTer ma Literature," in *Tibetan Literature: Studies in Genre,* ed. José Cabezón and Roger Jackson (Ithaca, NY: Snow Lion, 1996), 147–168.
39. For more on the significance of the mandala in Tibet, see Martin Brauen, *Mandala: Sacred Circle in Tibetan Buddhism* (New York: Rubin Museum of Art, 2009).
40. For a full translation of the *Guhyagarbha Tantra,* see Lama Chönam and Sangye Khandro, *The Guhyagarbha Tantra: Secret Essence Definitive Nature Just As It Is* (Ithaca, NY: Snow Lion, 2011).
41. Jamgön Mipham, *Luminous Essence: A Guide to the Guhyagarbha Tantra,* trans. Dharmachakra Translation Committee (Ithaca, NY: Snow Lion, 2009).
42. Sam van Schaik, "In Search of the Guhyagarbha Tantra," in *Early Tibet.*
43. Dan Martin, "Illusion Web: Locating the *Guhyagarbha Tantra* in Buddhist Intellectual History," in *Silver on Lapis: Tibetan Literary Culture and History,* ed. Christopher Beckwith (Bloomington, IN: Tibet Society, 1987), 175–220.
44. Henk Blezer, *Kar gling Zhi khro: A Tantric Buddhist Concept* (School of Asian, African, and Amerindian Studies 56; Leiden, The Netherlands: Research School CNWS, 1997).
45. Helena Blavatsky, *The Secret Doctrine* (Los Angeles: Theosophy Company, 1947 [1888]).
46. Donald Lopez Jr., "Foreword," in *The Tibetan Book of the Dead or The After-Death Experiences on the Bardo Plane, According to Lama Kazi Dawa-Samdup's English Rendering,* trans. Kazi Dawa Samdup (Oxford: Oxford University Press, 2000).
47. See further Peter Washington, *Madame Blavatsky's Baboon: A History of the Mystics, Mediums, and Misfits Who Brought Spiritualism to America* (New York: Schocken, 1993).
48. Donald Lopez Jr., *The Tibetan Book of the Dead: A Biography* (Lives of Great Religious Books; Princeton, NJ: Princeton University Press, 2011).
49. Originally published in 1935 in *Das Tibetanische Totenbuch* and translated into English by R. F. C. Hull. See Carl G. Jung, "Psychological Commentary," in *The* Tibetan Book of the Dead; *or, The After-Death Experiences on the Bardo Plane: According to Lama Kazi Dawa-Samdup's English Rendering,* ed. and trans. Walter Y. Evans Wentz and Kazi Dawa Samdup (3d ed.; Oxford: Oxford University Press, 1949), xxxv–lli.
50. Robert Wicks, "The Therapeutic Psychology of 'The Tibetan Book of the Dead,'" *Philosophy East and West* 47, no. 4 (1997): 479–494.
51. Timothy Leary, Ralph Metzner, and Richard Alpert, *The Psychedelic Experience: A Manual Based on the Tibetan Book of the Dead* (London: Penguin Classics, 2008).
52. Ralph Flores, "Final Emergency Reading: *The Tibetan Book of the Dead,*" in *Buddhist Scriptures as Literature: Sacred Rhetoric and the Uses of Theory,* ed. Flores (Albany: State University of New York Press, 2008 [1964]), 163–182.
53. For an example, see E. J. Gold, *American Book of the Dead* (San Francisco: Harper, 1995).
54. Peter Bishop, "A Landscape for Dying: The Bardo Thodol and Western Fantasy," in *Constructing Tibetan Culture: Contemporary Perspectives,* ed. Frank Korom (St-Hyacinthe, Quebec: World Heritage, 1997), 47–72.
55. Carl G. Jung, "Psychological Commentary," in *The* Tibetan Book of the Dead; *or, The After-Death Experiences on the Bardo Plane: According to Lama Kazi Dawa-Samdup's English Rendering,* ed. and trans. Walter Y. Evans Wentz and Kazi Dawa Samdup (3d ed.; Oxford: Oxford University Press, 1949), xxxv–lli;

Donald Lopez Jr., "Foreword" and "Afterword," in *The Tibetan Book of the Dead or The After-Death Experiences on the Bardo Plane, According to Lama Kazi Dawa-Samdup's English Rendering*, trans. Kazi Dawa Samdup (Oxford: Oxford University Press, 2000), A–Q, 243–253.

56. Cuevas, *Hidden History*; and Lopez, *The Tibetan Book of the Dead: A Biography*.
57. Gyurme Dorje, "A Brief Literary History of the Tibetan Book of the Dead," in *The* Tibetan Book of the Dead: *The Great Liberation by Hearing in the Intermediate States*, ed. Graham Coleman and Thupten Jinpa (London: Penguin, 2006), xxvi–xlix.
58. Leary, Metzner, and Alpert, *Psychedelic Experience*.
59. Francesca Fremantle and Chögyam Trungpa, eds. and trans., *The Tibetan Book of the Dead: The Great Liberation through Hearing in the Bardo* (Clear Light Series; Boston: Shambhala, 1975).
60. See for example Christopher Carr, "Death and Near-Death: A Comparison of Tibetan and Euro-American Experiences," *Journal of Transpersonal Psychology* 25, no. 1 (1993): 59–110; and Ralph Flores, "Final Emergency Reading: *The Tibetan Book of the Dead*," in *Buddhist Scriptures as Literature: Sacred Rhetoric and the Uses of Theory*, ed. Flores (Albany: State University of New York Press, 2008 [1964]), 163–182.
61. Lopez, "The Book"; and Peter Bishop, "A Landscape for Dying: The Bardo Thodol and Western Fantasy," in *Constructing Tibetan Culture: Contemporary Perspectives*, ed. Frank Korom (St-Hyacinthe, Quebec: World Heritage, 1997), 47–72.
62. See note 33.
63. David Germano, "Funerary Transformation of the Great Perfection (*Rdzogs chen*)," *Journal of the International Association of Tibetan Studies* 1 (2005): 1–54; and Tadeusz Skorupski, "The *Cremation Ceremony* According to the Byang-gTer Tradition," *Kailash* 9, no. 4 (1982): 361–376.
64. The most extensive reference available on Nyingma teachings and history in English is Dudjom Rinpoche, *The Nyingma School of Tibetan Buddhism: Its Fundamentals and History*, translated and edited by Gyurme Dorje and Matthew Kapstein (2 vols.; Somerville: Wisdom, 2002).
65. Jacob Dalton, "Recreating the Rnying ma School: the Mdo dbang Tradition of Smin grol gling," in *Power, Politics, and the Reinvention of Tradition in Seventeenth and Eighteenth Century Tibet*, ed. Bryan Cuevas and Kurtis Schaeffer (Leiden, The Netherlands: Brill, 2006), 91–101; Janet Gyatso, "Logic of Legitimation in the Tibetan Treasure Tradition," *History of Religions* 33, no. 2 (1993): 97–134; Robert Mayer, "gTer ston and Tradent: Innovation and Conservation in Tibetan Treasure Literature," *Journal of the International Association of Buddhist Studies* 36/37 (2015): 227–242; Cathy Cantwell, "Different Kinds of Composition/Compilation Within the Dudjom Revelatory Tradition," *Journal of the International Association of Buddhist Studies* 36/37 (2015): 243–280; and Orna Almogi, "The Materiality and Immanence of Gnosis in Some rNying-ma Tantric Sources," in *Yogic Perception, Meditation and Altered States of Consciousness*, ed. Eli Franco and Dagmar Eigner (Vienna: Verlag der Österreichischen Akademie der Wissenschaften, 2009), 241–262.
66. Dorji, Wangchuk, "An Eleventh-Century Defense of the Authenticity of the Guhyagarbha Tantra," in The Many Canons of Tibetan Buddhism, ed. Helmut Eimer and David Germano (Leiden, The Netherlands: Brill, 2002), 265–292; Gyurme Dorje, "The *Guhyagarbhatattvaviniṣcayamahātantra* and its XIVth century Tibetan Commentary *phyogs bcu mun sel*," PhD diss., School of Oriental and African Studies, University of London, 1987; Martin, "Illusion Web"; and Blezer, *Kar gling Zhi khro*; van Schaik, "In Search of the Guhyagarbha Tantra."
67. Sam van Schaik, *Approaching the Great Perfection: Simultaneous and Gradual Approaches to Dzogchen Practice in the Longchen Nyingtig* (Boston: Wisdom, 2004); Samten Karmay, *The Great Perfection (rDzogs chen in Tibetan): A Philosophical and Meditative Teaching of Tibetan Buddhism* (Leiden, The Netherlands: Brill, 2007); and David Higgins, *The Philosophical Foundations of Classical Rdzogs chen in Tibet: Investigating the Distinction Between Dualistic Mind (sems) and Primordial Knowing (ye shes)* (Wiener

Studien zur Tibetologie und Buddhismuskunde 78; Vienna: Arbeitskreis für Tibetische und Buddhistische Studien, 2013).

68. Bryan Cuevas, "Conclusion: Manuscripts and Printed Texts," in *Hidden History*, ed. Cuevas, 205–210.
69. Tibetan Buddhist Resource Center.

Casey Alexandra Kemp

TIBETAN BUDDHISM AND THE GESAR EPIC

BUDDHISM AND THE EPIC

Much of the Gesar/Geser epic's milieu and ethos suggests a pastoralist/warrior culture in which institutional/monastic Buddhism is not well established. The extent to which Buddhism is central to the epic's style, orientation, theater, and ideological pieties varies across tellings. In general one can say that the outlying Buryat and Ladakhi traditions display less overt Buddhist influence, while the eastern Tibetan tradition, where Gesar has been embraced within certain sections of institutional Vajrayāna Buddhism (especially since the late 19th century), is most imbued with explicitly Buddhist pieties. This observation suggests that the Buddhism of the epic represents a relatively late interpretative layer, while the archaic core of the epic lies in a secular folkloric orientation only lightly touched by Buddhist influence. The question of the epic's origins, however, remains uncertain. Based on the mentions of Gesar and his warriors in the Tibetan mytho-historical text known as *Lang kyi poti séru* (*Rlangs kyi po ti bse ru*,[1] which probably underwent its final redaction in the 15th century), Tibetan and Mongolian scholars tend to consider the epic's origins lying in far northeastern Tibet and the inner Asian trade routes during the 11th and 12th centuries, which was a period of intense competition between rival nomadic confederacies for control over the lucrative horse trade between China and inner Asia. How the tradition spread, and why it became particularly embedded in Buryatia (far to the north) and Ladakh (far to the west), remain, however, poorly understood, and the subject of speculation. Clearly the epic in its various regional traditions is a bricolage of different mythic, legendary, folkloric, and religious elements. To search for a unitary origin would therefore be misguided.

One striking feature that one finds in all tellings of the Gesar/Geser epic, whether oral or literary, and from all the regions of the epic's dissemination, is a core black/white dualism. The epic is presented as a continuation in the human chivalric realm of the perennial cosmic battle between the forces of the White Side or *karchok* (*dkar phyogs*) and the Dark Side or *nakchok* (*nag phyogs*). This feature is particularly notable in the far western Ladakhi and Burushaski oral traditions, the far eastern oral traditions among the Monguor and Gyalrong peoples, and the northern traditions of Buryatia. But it is also found prominently in the more elaborated, overtly Buddhist, and literarily influenced eastern Tibetan traditions. One often finds this motif most elaborated in the episodes of the epic dealing with the divine mission and birth of the epic hero. Here the hero is sent by the gods of the White Side to defeat the demonic forces of the Dark Side who have come to dominate the middle land of humans. This black/white dualism is a very common trope in Tibetan Buddhist conversion legends. The White Side represents the virtuous and liberating Buddha dharma, while the

Dark Side represents the demonic forces of ignorance and obstruction. So whether this dualism comes into the epic's "pool of tradition"[2] as a Tibetan Buddhist motif, or whether it represents part of an older religiously indeterminate Eurasian mythic strata (seen not only in Indian Vedic religion but also in Zoroastrian and Manicheian religions and in the shamanically tinted epic traditions of the Turkic peoples of central Asia and the Siberian steppe, as well as in the dualist mythology of Tibetan Bon), shall perhaps never be known with any certainty. Certainly in contemporary eastern Tibetan culture, the struggle between *karchok* and *nagchok* is interpreted by most tellers (oral and literary) as a Buddhist paradigm. There the central mission of the divinely sent hero is interpreted as an explicitly Buddhist mission—the conversion of the demonically influenced tribes and leaders to the liberating righteousness of Buddhism.

However, though Gesar in this broad sense is portrayed as a Buddhist hero and Ling as a Buddhist society, the cultural milieu of the epic, even in the eastern Tibetan tradition, is one in which institutional/monastic Buddhism is not well established. The individual clans and tribes in the epic are generally depicted as having their own ritualists, *amchö* (*a mchod*) or *lama* (bla ma), and the heroes regularly perform rites of *sang* (*bsang*) smoke purification and defer major decisions to the prognostications of divination or *mo* (*mo*). But mentions of monastic communities are markedly absent, even within the model "home" society of the (avowedly Buddhist) Lingpas.

As noted in the work on the Gesar epic by Samten Karmay,[3] the eastern Tibetan epic's pool of tradition suggests a cultural milieu that owes considerably to the traditions of Tibetan Bon. For example, a central role is played in the epic by Gesar's female protectress or "aunt" Ané Gungmen Gyelmo (A ne dgung sman rgyal mo) or Manene, a figure with considerable resonance in Bön as a primordial female deity linked to the mythical origins of the *sang* (*bsang*) smoke-purification rite,[4] which is a mainstay of Tibetan popular religion. The epic tradition also gives prominence to the *drala* (*dgra bla/sgra bla/dgra lha*) and *werma* (*wer ma*) classes of warrior spirits who empower weaponry and armor, making swords unnaturally sharp and arrows unnaturally swift and so on. These Tibetan spirit categories have no obvious Indic or Buddhist antecedents, but are prominently represented in the Bön tradition. The eastern Tibetan epic tradition also has a central emphasis on the three-tiered spirit world of *lha* (*lha*) gods of the sky above, *lu* (*klu*) netherworld spirits below, and *nyen* (*gnyan*) mountain-dwelling divinities in the middle, all three of whom unite behind the hero and are his main spirit-world supports. Also, the rhapsodic style of invocation in which the *chantefable* epic is performed has much in common—in both style and content—with Tibetan traditions of spirit invocation used by diviners (*mo ma*) and mediums (*lha pa*). All of these features suggest that the epic tradition is grounded first and foremost in what R. A. Stein dubbed Tibet's "nameless religion" preserved not by Buddhist institutionalism, but by the folk beliefs and practices of the laity. Naturally, however, in the predominantly Buddhist societies in which the epic has flourished, this folkloric orientation has also absorbed many explicitly Buddhist pieties. So in most modern tellings, for example, the gods of the upper realm who send the hero on his divine mission are assimilated to the buddhas and bodhisattvas of Mahāyāna Buddhism. But in general one can say that the Buddhism of the epic appears to be just a part of the epic's pool of tradition, rather than its primary source or inspiration. The suggestion that the epic has pre-Buddhist roots was also made by the early Tibetologist A. H Francke, who collected oral versions of the epic in Ladakh in the early 20th century and published them as *A Lower Ladakhi Version of the Kesar Saga*.[5] These versions, he observed, make no explicit reference to Buddhism, though they do depict the hero representing the White Side in its eternal battle with the Dark Side.

Buddhism in the epic is therefore primarily a Buddhism of aspiration, rather than one of descriptive or concrete institutional reality. A recurrent theme in the eastern Tibetan epic is the hero retiring into periods of meditative absorption, and then being roused once again to action by the dream-visitation-exhortations of his protecting goddess Manene. But it is very unusual for the hero's Buddhist practice to be described with any specificity. As such, the Buddhism of the epic is free from institutional, sectarian, or historical bias. The deities evoked by the heroes and heroines of Ling in their songs, for example, do not tend to be protectors associated with particular specific lineages or teachings, but are more often deities shared across Tibetan Buddhist traditions. And it is very rare to find explicit mentions within the epic of specific historical or religious figures drawn from Tibet's rich store legend and myth. The main exception to this absence of "historical" figures from the epic narrative is that in modern times—and especially since the 19th century—Padmasambhava has increasingly come to occupy a central role in the epic plot in many tellings, not only as the architect of the hero's divine mission, but also as the hero's main personal guide. This development continues to gather momentum today. The seminal textual version of the epic that gives pride of place to Padmasambhava in its narrative is the so-called Lingtsang Xylograph.[6] This text was composed in the early 20th century by a Nyingmapa monk under the patronage of the religious king of the eastern Tibetan principality of Lingtsang. This three-volume version integrates local oral and literary traditions concerning Gesar with the hero's Buddhist apotheosis, which had been greatly elaborated in late 19th century by the dozens of Gesar ritual texts authored by the highly influential and prolific lama Ju Mipham Namgyel Gyatso ('Ju mi pham rnam rgyal rgya mtsho; 1846–1912). The Lingtsang Xylograph version also gives a prominent place in the narrative to the 15th-century sage Thangthong Gyalpo (Thang mthong rgyal po). The idiosyncracy of this cameo appearance is probably connected to the important role played by Thangthong Gyalpo in the religious history of the neighboring eastern Tibetan kingdoms of Lingtsang and Derge. It also hints at the possibility that Thangtong Gyalpo, well known as a pioneer of the Tibetan opera *ache lhamo* (*a lce lha mo*) art form, may also have played a role in the development and popularization of the epic as a performative tradition. There is, however, no further corroborating evidence of this.

In general, therefore, one can say that the predominant ethos of the eastern Tibetan epic tradition is explicitly Buddhist, but not sectarian. The victory of the tribe of Ling over its adversaries is the victory of the White Buddha dharma—along with its civil law (Khrims) based on the ten virtues—over the heresies of its opponents, namely the tribes of Hor (Hor), Düyül (Bdud yul), Takzik (Stag gzig), Khache (Kha che), and so on, who are generally depicted in a variety of idiosyncratic and fanciful ways as Bönpos or other kinds of non-Buddhists.

The model of conflict one finds in the epic is also a blend of overtly Buddhist paradigms and those of less clearly Buddhist origin. In many tellings, especially in those epic texts authored by Buddhist monks, the Buddhist paradigm of demon taming is often evoked. Gesar is often depicted as bearing the "wrathful gaze for taming Rudra," the archetypal demon of Tibetan Vajrayāna, and his enemies, when killed, are often said to be "liberated." However, the model of conflict also gives pride of place to the Tibetan concept of *la* (Bla), sometimes translated as "soul," which again finds elaborate expression in Bön tradition, but is not a Buddhist concept. In order to defeat an enemy, the epic hero must first weaken the opponent by separating him from the "supports" of his *la*, which can be portable shrines, boxes, stones, or wild and domesticated animals. By killing the opponent's soul-supporting animals, and tricking him into desecrating or destroying his own soul-supporting shrines and objects, the hero weakens the enemy's power and charisma and renders him an object of ridicule, thus making him susceptible to defeat and his followers open to conversion to Ling and the forces of the White Side. This emphasis on *la* in the context of battle and conflict resonates strongly with myths and legends of early pre-Buddhist Tibet, in particular with the myth of Drigum Tsenpo (Dri gum btsan po), an early figure in the lineage of the Yarlung Pugyal dynasty who ruled Tibet during its imperial period.

In his conflicts with foes, the hero is also aided by warrior spirits known as *drala* and *werma* mentioned earlier, which are also often the objects of propitiation when the warriors of Ling perform their *sang* rituals of smoke purification. These warrior spirits, which are often associated through their names with carnivorous wild animals, are not categories with Buddhist origins but are prominent in Bön tradition. They are, however, also incorporated to some degree within Nyingmapa tantric traditions, which include, for example, the "five deities of the head" ('Go ba'i lha lnga), of whom the *drala* are often counted as one, in the entourages of certain wrathful Buddhist tantric divinities.

Where the Buddhism of the epic is most evident is in the invocations made by the heroes in their songs. Gesaric songs follow a formulaic pattern in which the character first calls upon his or her own favored divinities to "bear witness" (Mkhyen), then introduces him- or herself followed by the place of action, before continuing into the main import of the song. While the opponents of Ling typically invoke an idiosyncratic panoply of hybrid "worldly" spirits such as the *tsen* (Btsan), *lu* (klu), *te'u rang* (The'u rang), and so on, the heroes of Ling, and especially Gesar himself, invoke the buddhas and boddhisattvas as well as the paternal lords of the three-tiered spirit world of *lha, lu,* and *nyen*. Particularly prominent among the Buddhist deities invoked by the hero in many tellings are the Buddhas of the Five Families (Rigs lnga) and particularly the "three bodies" (Sku gsum) triad of the Padma family of Compassionate Buddhas, namely Amitābha, Avalokiteśvara, and Padamasambhava, who have a particular resonance in Tibet's wider Buddhist conversion mythology, as reflected in the Tibetan *chö jung* (Chos 'byung) genre of religio-mythic historiography.

The heroines of Ling, especially Gesar's queen Drukmo ('Brug mo), also regularly invoke the female bodhisattva Tārā as their main divinity. It is rare, however, to find the heroes of Ling invoking specific tantric deities beyond these. A major exception to this is Gesar's villainous uncle Trothung (Khro thung), who in many tellings invokes the wrathful form of Tamdrin/Hayagriva (Rta mgrin) as his tutelary deity in his songs. In fact, Throthung is often the character most explicitly portrayed in the epic as a tantrist. But he is a vainglorious and fickle figure, whose loyalties are also often portrayed as Bönpo. On account of his practices, Throthung has considerable magical power, but his exercise of magic regularly backfires, landing him in all sorts of sticky and humiliating situations. So while Gesar represents the genuinely enlightened lord, Trothung as his foil represents the vain egotistical tantrist, with all the confusions that incorrect and unscrupulous tantric practice can entail.

THE PALIMPSEST OF GESAR'S BUDDHIST APOTHEOSIS

In general terms, one might suggest that Gesar's divinity in the epic is a heroic palimpsest. In the first place he is a tribal warrior-hero with a band (or *comitatus*) of loyal knights embedded in a clan social structure. The formal setting in which this role is most clearly expressed is the tribal assembly, which is a recurrent theme in the epic's pool of tradition. Typically the assembly is convened by the blowing of the "white conch of the law" and the beating of the "drum of the law" and the sending out of messages of summons far and wide. At the assembly all the people of Ling (including the "father-uncles," "mother-aunts," lamas and diviners, elders, and children), as well as all the leaders of the tribes and clans that have joined the ever-swelling ranks of Ling, are seated according to rank and status on animal-hide seats suitable to their station. Gesar himself is seated at their center on a golden throne. But Gesar's role in the epic as a tribal lord is not a straightforward one. For his chivalric station in the epic is mirrored by what might be called his "shamanic" station as the lord and tamer of the unruly spirit world. This might also be called his "tantric" station, since tantrism in Tibetan Buddhism is centrally involved with taming the spirit world and the forces of nature. And sometimes Gesar is even depicted wearing the tantrist's initiation crown. But since he does not tend to be explicitly tied to specific tantric practices, cycles, or lineages, and since his spirit-taming adventures are performed through heroic solo missions and magical shape-shifting journeys, rather than through magical ritual, the term "shamanic" might be a more suitable than "tantric" in this context.

As a chivalric-shamanic lord historicized as an ancestral hero of the Dong *(Ldong)* tribal lineage in large parts of eastern Tibet, especially the regions around the Upper Yellow (Rma chu), Upper Yalong (Rdza chu), and Upper Yangtze ('Bri chu) Rivers, Gesar also came to be venerated as a kind of local ancestral protector deity *(srung ma)* in a manner akin to other worldly local gods of place know as *yul-lha (yul lha)* or *zhidak (zhi bdag)*. In keeping with his status as culture-hero, his position as a protector tends to have a political note—he is a protector not so much of the dharma, but of the place: the people, clan, family, livestock, and horses. His support is particularly supplicated in times of competition, travel, trade, gambling, conflict, and sickness. He is even, as befits the merging of the figures of Gesar and Guandi (the Chinese general-turned- imperial-protector deity) during the Qing dynasty, considered a protector of the nation, however that might be construed (Tibetan nation, Buryat nation, Mongolian nation, Manchu Imperium, etc.).

As a protector he is propitiated in a manner akin to mountain deities, primarily by means of the *sang* offering rite of purifying smoke, which can also be combined with offerings of alcohol, food, and sometimes also meat. However, unlike most *zhidak* or *yul-lha*, Gesar is not associated with any specific mountain, though he is held to have a special relationship with the mightiest of the *yul-lha* of northeastern Tibet, Magyal Pomra (Rma rgyal spom ra). It is from this mountain deity, according to some tellings of the epic, that he obtains his magical weapons and armor.

Gesar's further sanctification as an enlightened being or buddha follows a similar (though not identical) trajectory to the parallel sanctification of other "worldly" protectors in Tibetan Buddhism. However, unlike typical narratives concerning the apotheoisis of the Tibetan *damchen* (dam can) "oath-bound" deities that are propitiated across the Tibetan cultural world as protectors of the Buddhist dharma, Gesar was never "bound by oath," nor converted from a pre-Buddhist to Buddhist form. Instead his divinity is primordial: it derives from his status in the epic tradition as a son of the "gods above" (Gong ma'i lha). In a Buddhist register, the sky gods of the upper realm are merged and assimilated, to varying degrees, with the buddhas and the bodhisattvas of Mahāyāna Buddhism.[7] As a prince of the upper realm sent to the middle world of humans to bring order and justice there, Gesar thus comes to be considered an enlightened being from the outset, who requires no binding by oath nor conversion to be a protector of the faith. Instead the tropes of conversion and binding by oath that one finds in the Gesar epic are not in *his* being bound by oath by Padmasambhava (as with so many other narratives of native Tibetan protective divinities) but rather are tropes used of Gesar's own enlightened activities: it is he who binds by oath and (more often) "liberates" (the Buddhist euphemism for righteous killing) his demonic and non-Buddhist tribal foes. In this way Gesar is unusual as a native Tibetan protective divinity. And his role thus becomes parallel to that of Tibetan Buddhist civilization's archetypal tamer of demons and converter of the native spirit world, namely Padmasambhava himself. So Gesar is not a subject of Padmasmabhava, but rather a place holder for him. And by being Padmasambhava's emissary or manifestation, Gesar is also thereby tied to the wider Buddhist national mythology concerning the conversion and salvation of the barbarous snowlands of Tibet by means of the repeated interventions of its patron Bodhisattva Avalokiteśvara, of whom Padmasambhava (and thence Gesar) is but one incarnation.

This unusual position renders Gesar's role and status as a Buddhist protector rather fluid. Unlike a typical *yul-lha* or *zhidak*, he is not tied to any specific locality or community. And unlike a *dam-chen*, he has not been bound by oath by any outside or superior force. Being unrestricted in terms of locality makes Gesar suitable as the "destined deity for all the black-haired highlanders of Tibet." He is also described as an enemy-vanquishing warrior deity or *drala* as per the modern Nyingmapa usage of this term, which is somewhat distinct from the more archaic and Bönpo-esque use of the term within the epic. Gesar is also sometimes described as a "wealth god" (Nor lha) of both Tibet and China. This latter status is likely connected to the association nurtured during the Manchu Qing dynasty between Gesar and the Chinese martial deity Guandi.[8]

However, in contemporary eastern Tibetan epic tradition, Gesar's primary sanctity is undoubtedly furnished by his association with Padmasambhava. It is this close association—whereby Sengchen Norbu Drandul (Seng chen nor bu dgra 'dul, as Gesar is often known) effectively becomes a folkloric place holder for Padmasambhava, whose violent activities are assimilated to the tantric demon taming of Vajrayāna Buddhism—which in recent times has come to subsume other facets of Gesar's heroic identity. Early texts suggest that in earlier religious interpretations of Ling Gesar's "place" in Tibetan civilizational discourse, he was initially more often identified as a placeholder for the 8th-century Tibetan king Trisong Deutsen (Khri srong lde'u btsan), Padmasambhava's secular patron. But gradually this association came to be subsumed by a more direct association between Gesar and Padmasambhava himself.

The association between Gesar and Padmasambhava dates back certainly as far as the mid-17th century (when Gesar epic texts start to appear in Tibetan), and perhaps earlier. Clearly, it was greatly bolstered by the epic's literary tradition, since like all forms of Tibetan literature, written versions of the Gesar epic tend to be the work of monk-authors. Today the association between Gesar and Padmasambhava thoroughly suffuses the oral epic tradition of eastern Tibet. Early Gesar texts that appear to promote the association include, for example, the *Takzik Norgyé* (*Stag gzig nor 'gyed*, a text attributed to Dzogtrül Pema Rigzin; Rdzogs sprul Padma rig 'dzin; 1625–1697),[9] which is currently our oldest datable Gesar epic text. Its setting is an assembly at which Gesar is distributing the wealth and tribute accrued from his victory over Takzik, to the assembled throngs of Ling and its many other incorporated subjects of the four directions. When Gesar addresses this assembly, his first appeal (in the invocatory section of his song) is to Pema Jungné (Padma 'byung gnas/Padmasambhava). Then, when introducing himself (as per the epic's performative conventions) he declares,

As for me, if you know me not,
In the early part of life, known as the vagrant child Joru,
I was the terror (lit: "tiger-demon") of the pika of Lower Ma
In the middle part [of life], known as the military-commander Drandul,
I was the annihilator of the demon Hor
In the latter part of life, known as a Buddha of the Three Times,
I am one who sets beings on the path to liberation.
I am the king of Tibet and the World,
I am the *lama* who guides departed souls
I am the inner counsel of worldly chiefs
I am the *drala* (enemy-defeating god) of men![10]

Later in the same song, when praising the many treasures he has accrued, he declares that among them are those which had been concealed by Orgyan Pema (Padmasambhava), which only he has been able to "bring out," since he, the Great Lion King, is "a *trulku* [bodily manifestation] of the great master of Orgyan," and the "summation of the Three Bodhisattva Lords."[11]

In another relatively early literary Gesar text (probably dating from the 18th century) known as *Tsawa'i Namthar*,[12] Gesar's association with Padmasambhava and his apotheosis as a buddha (as an incarnation of the Three Bodhisattva Lords) is also celebrated. Its opening verse of praise describes the hero thus:

By morning a slaying slaughterman,
By evening a lama who guides [departed souls].
A buddha who has gone beyond the earth.
Pillar of the pristine blue sky,
Peg that holds fast the earth's foundation.
Executioner who tames Rudra,
Neck-yoke of Yellow Hor,
Bludgeon of Black Demons,
Destined god of Tibet and the World.
In the holy dharma, he is Śakyamuni
In the secret *mantrayāna*, he is Padmasambhava.
With perfect wisdom and method, he is Jamyang (Manjuśrī)
With loving-kindness and compassion, he is Chenrézik (Avalokiteśvara)
With magical power, he is Chaknadorjé (Vajrapāṇi).
Son of the magically-manifesting primordial *werma*
Son of the swift primordial *drala*.
Master of enjoyment, he is a prince of the *lu* [water spirits below]
Master of magic, he is son of king of *lha* [gods above]
Summation of heroic skill, he is son of king of *nyen* [mountain divinities in the middle].[13]

In the *Horling Yülgyé*, a seminal Gesar epic text from Kham that dates from the 1730s (though it comes down to us only in a version further edited in the early 1960s),[14] the association between Gesar and Padmasambhava is not at all prominent, perhaps reflecting the source of this version in the early 18th-century oral recitations of "some twenty bards" that the author took as his base. However, the same Buddhist associations do also appear in this text, albeit rather late (halfway through the second volume). Here, Gesar is presented as an "emissary" (pho nya) of Padmasambhava, but also as a "manifestation" (sprul pa) of his secular patron, the Tibetan emperor Trisong Deutsen:

> Gesar, King of the World, Sengchen Norbu Drandul,
> Manifestation of the Three Bodhisattva Lords (Rigs gsum mgon po rnam sprul)
> Emissary of Lopön Padma,
> Manifestation of Trisong Deutsen,
> Lord of the World
> *Drala* of the Tibetan Snowlands
> Protective Guardian of the White Side
> Subduing Slayer of the Dark Side
> Chief who advances righteousness and snuffs out evil,
> Military commander who smashes enemies and promotes his kin
> And so on.[15]

THE EPIC OF GESAR AND THE CULT OF GESAR

Ritual texts of smoke purification (Bsang) propitiating Gesar as a protective deity and as an enlightened being start to appear in Tibetan as early as our earliest epic texts. It is safe to assert that this ritual cult was an outgrowth of an existing oral epic tradition that was already well developed. Because the early epic texts we have tend to be the work of monastic authors, it is sometimes hard to draw a clear line between the epic, on the one hand, and the verses of praise to Gesar used in a ritual context, on the other. Given the symbiotic relationship between the epic and the cult, one way of understanding the relationship is that the cult replaces the *polyphony* of the epic—many bards, many heroes, many characters, many consorts, many deities, and many demons—with the *univocal,* authoritatively "realized" (mostly as "pure vision" or "mind treasure") verses of praise and invocation. As such in the cult of Gesar we only ever really encounter the hero himself and his entourage. His enemies are largely absent, as is his villainous uncle Trotung, who is a central character and protagonist in the epic. Instead, in the cult, we are presented with the univocal praise of the single deified hero: Gesar as an icon.

There are a number of "cross-over" texts that, while presenting themselves as narrative epic texts, have more the character of ritual background myths. One example is the "pure vision" (Dag snang) text by the fifth Lelung incarnation Zhépé Dorjé (Sle lung lnga pa Bzhad pa'i rdo rje; 1697–1740).[16] This text provides a mythic backstory for the two texts of ritual propitiation of Gesar by the same author. The vision apparently came to Lelung in 1729 and presents a theogony of Gesar as the son of a primordial goddess after her sexual union with a *nyen* mountain divinity. This text is particularly interesting in light of Ju Mipham's later development of a Buddhist cult of Gesar as a *yidam* (Yi dam) tutelary deity, because the name that Lelung uses for Gesar is Gesar Dorjé Tsegyal (Rdo rje rtshe rgyal), the same name later used by Ju Mipham in his liturgical elaborations of the ritual cult of Gesar. Lelung's text seems to be our earliest textual attestation of this name or "form" of Gesar.

Another "cross-over" text that bridges the epic tradition and the Buddhist cult is the *Nyaling dzogpa chenpo* (*Dmyal gling rdzogs pa chen po*),[17] a self-proclaimed *terma* (*gter ma*) or "treasure" text, in which Gesar goes to the hell realms (*dmyal gling*) to liberate tormented beings there. Both stylistically and in content, this text owes more to its Nyingmapa religious "pool of tradition" than it does to the Gesar epic's warrior-heroic "pool of tradition."[18] It is said that in some communities in Amdo, this text is recited ritually in a manner akin to the *Bardo Tödröl* (*Bar do thos sgrol*) or the *Tibetan Book of the Dead*, for guiding the wandering souls of the recently deceased. The original author of this text is said to have been be the "lama of Den" Chökyi Wangchuk (Chos kyi dbang phyugs), and it was then rediscovered in Golok in the late 18th or early 19th century by a "descendent of Ling" named Rigdzin Draktsel Dorjé (Rig 'dzin grags rtsal rdo rje).

As stated earlier, the ritual cult of Gesar is best considered an outgrowth from the epic tradition, but the ritual cult (see below) has also nourished and determined the directions in which the mobile oral and literary epic tradition has developed, especially in eastern Tibet. A good example of an influential (near canonical) epic text that explicitly cites a ritual/liturgical text as its chief source and inspiration is the *Ta-gyu norbu chadün* (*Rta rgyugs nor bu cha bdun*), which is the third volume (the "horse race") of the Lingtsang Xylograph. The author of this text, who was the abbot of the small Nyingmapa monastery adjoining the palace of the Lingtsang king (*rgyal po*) in the early 20th century, states explicitly both in his prologue and in the colophon, that his inspiration in writing the volume was to elucidate the Mipham-authored prayer to Gesar known as the *The Symbolic Secret Jewel* (*Brda gsang nor bu*).

Many prominent contemporary tellers and authors of the epic in eastern Tibet have been particularly influenced in their tellings by the recent charismatic lama Khenpo Jikmé Phuntsok ('Jigs med phun tshogs; 1933–2004), who identified himself as an incarnation of one of the lesser heroes from the Gesar epic tradition. In keeping with the traditions cemented by Ju Mipham in the 19th century, Khenpo Jikphun adopted Gesar as both a symbol and an important enlightened protector of the Dzogchen-infused eastern Tibetan *ri-mé* (*ris med*) or nonsectarian Buddhist tradition. Contemporary authors of Gesar epic texts such as Guru Gyeltsen (Gu ru rgyal mtshan) from Gabdé (Sga bde), and Tendzin Drakpa (Bstan 'dzin grags pa) from Chikdril (Gcig dril), both in the Golok ('Go log) region, are examples of devout Nyingmapa *ngakpas* (sngags pa) or lay *māntrin* practitioners devoted to Khenpo Jikphun who have made careers as authors of new Gesar epic texts, describing them as *mind treasures* (*dgongs gter*).

GESAR RITUALS

It is hard to say with certainty when Tibetan Gesar ritual texts started to emerge. The earliest texts appear to date from the 17th century.[19] However, the main body of Gesar ritual texts date from the 18th, 19th, and 20th centuries, and continue to be composed today. The form in which Gesar is often ritually propitiated is Gesar Dorje Tsegyal, "the *Vajra* Lord of Life." The earliest attested use of this "tantric" title for Gesar is in the early 18th-century visionary text of the fifth Lelung Rinpoche mentioned earlier. A two-volume compendium of ritual texts devoted to Ling Gesar dating from the 18th and 19th centuries was published in India in 1971 by the eighth Khamtrül Rinpoche as the *Ling Gesar Drupkor* (*Gling ge sar sgrub skor*).[20] The earliest texts in this collection are visionary texts attributed to Lharik Dechen Yeshe Rölpatsel

(Lha rigs bde chen ye shes rol pa rtsal), a Dzogchen practitioner about whom little is known, though he appears to have lived in the 18th–19th centuries. Other authors of texts in this collection include many of the most famous eastern Tibetan lamas associated with the late 19th-century *rimé* (nonsectarian) revival: the fifth Khamtrül Drupgyü Nyima (Khams sprul lnga pa Sgrub brgyud nyi ma; 1781–1847), Do Khyentse Yeshe Dorje (Rdo mkhyen brtse ye shes rdo rje; 1800–1859), Jamgön Kongtrül Lodrö Thaye ('Jam mgon kong sprul blo gros mtha' yas; 1813–1899), Nyagla Pema Dündul (Nyag bla Padma bdud 'dul; 1816–1872), Jamyang Khyentse Wangpo ('Jam dbyang mkhyen brtse dbang po; 1820–1892), Chogyur Lingpa (Mchog gyur gling pa; 1829–1870). But by far the most prominent author in this collection is Ju Mipham Namgyel Gyatso ('Ju mi pham rnam rgyal rgya mtsho; 1846–1912), who authored no fewer than forty-five Gesar ritual texts. These texts span Mipham's long and prolific career. The earliest was composed when he was only thirteen years old (1859) and the latest when he was around sixty.

Mipham's Gesar corpus is extensive and wide ranging. As elucidated in recent research by Gregory Forgues (*Journeys to Freedom* it covers a range of popular folk rituals in which Gesar is invoked. Mipham also establishes Gesar as a tantric tutelary deity or *yidam* (*yi dam*) for the "four activities" (pacifying, enriching, magnetizing, and subjugating), and in particular he celebrates Gesar as a vehicle for specifically Dzogchen teachings. Gesar's position in the "lower vehicles" as a messenger of Padmasambhava and a symbol of efficacy in apotropaic rituals is thus combined with a further symbolism in the "highest vehicle" of Dzogchen, in which he symbolizes the "direct" path to Buddhist realization through bare recognition of the ineffable ground of all phenomena. Devotional practices directed at Gesar, such as recitation of an unattributed *terma* verse of praise known simply as the *Drala Töpa* (*Dgra lha bstod pa*) or "Praise for the *drala*," are also sometimes used as preliminary practices for Dzogchen teachings.

As shown by Forgues,[21] taking Mipham's famous prayer known as the *Sol-lo Chenmo* (full name: *Gsol mchod phrin las myur 'grub*) as an example, Gesar is depicted as a *rigdzin* (*rig 'dzin*), "holder of sheer knowing," and as a *yidam*. In the prayer he is described inter alia as the "combined embodiment of the magical manifestation of the peaceful and wrathful deities of the Three Bodhisattva Lords" (line 17) the "face of all the Buddhas" (line 19); the "chief of the guardians and dharma protectors" (line 22); "the precious essence of the ocean of wealth gods" (line 23); the "supreme king of the *drala*"(line 24); and in many different formulations, as the "slayer of all the spirits of the Dark Side" (eg line 34).[22] The range of rituals covered by Mipham's Gesar texts is impressive. His Gesar rituals include the following:

supplications and offerings (*gsol mchod/ gsol 'debs*)
smoke-purification offerings (*bsang mchod*)
sādhanas (*sgrub thabs*)
guru yogas (*bla ma'i rnal 'byor*)
rituals to summon good fortune (*g.yang 'gug/ g.yang sgrub*)
instructions for improving *prāna* by preparing and raising prayer flags (*rlung rta*)
rituals for attaining wealth (*nor sgrub*)
rituals for the fulfillment of pledges (*bskang gsol*)
divination rituals (*pra chog*)
rituals for overcoming enemies (*dgra 'dul*)
rituals for attaining the (wish-fulfilling) "whip" (*lcag sgrub*)

"heart-essence" Dzogchen practice texts (*snying thig*)
religious advice/pith instructions/ upadeśa (*man ngag*),
tantric rituals to magnetize (*dbang sdud*)
rituals to restore harmony (*yo bcos*),
rituals of life-force entrustment (*srog gtad*)

It was also Mipham who established the connection between Gesar and the millenarian Shambhala mythology of the Kālacakra Tantra by identifying Gesar with *Kalkin* Raudra Cakrin, the future *rigden* (*rigs ldan*) king of Shambhala. This identification is found, for example, in Mipham's *Drandul Norbu Nyingtig* (*Dgra 'dul nor bu snying thig*).

Mipham was also influential in shaping the ritual masked dances or *cham* (*'cham*) performed in Gesar's honor at many monasteries. In particular he is said to have designed the masks for the Gesar *cham* performed annually at Dzogchen monastery in Kham. He is also said to have helped design the statues of Gesar and his companions in the Gesar temple erected at the alleged site of Gesar's birth at the village of A-shu, which was part of the historic kingdom of Lingtsang, today part of Derge county in the Kandze Tibetan autonomous prefecture of Sichuan province. This temple, founded in the early years of the 20th century, may have been the first temple exclusively devoted to Gesar (rather than to the merged forms of Gesar and Guandi). Since then many further temples have been built, especially in the Golok Tibetan autonomous prefecture of Qinghai province.

In recent decades, the Buddhist cult of Gesar has been continued and further developed by a variety of Tibetan lamas, many of whom come from the "Gesar country" around the Dri, Ma, and Dza Rivers of northern Kham and Golok. Prominent among them in the global dissemination of Tibetan Buddhism since the 1950s have been Chogyam Trungpa, Tarthang Tulku, and Namkha Drimed (who practices Gesar divination). Most influential in the contemporary eastern Tibetan development of the cult has been Khenpo Jikmé Phuntsok, and many others since then.

THE CULT OF LING GESAR AND THE SCHOOLS OF TIBETAN BUDDHISM

In a devotional/ritual context, Ling Gesar is today considered a predominantly Nyingma deity—a wish-fulfilling *yidam* in a mounted-warrior *drala* form with a strong association with Padmasambhava as a tamer of the unruly spirit world. However, the Buddhist cult of Gesar in Tibet has always been primarily a *regional* phenomenon, rather than one determined by sectarian affiliation. In central Tibet, the cult of Gesar is weak and in many places nonexistent, whereas throughout Kham and Amdo, the cult is particularly strong. In eastern Tibet, Gesar's apotheosis has been an explicitly *ri-mé* or "nonsectarian" phenomenon, and there are many Nyingma, Kagyü, and Sakya monasteries that perform Gesar dances and rituals and maintain Gesar shrines in these areas. Among the Kagyüpa an association is nurtured between Gesar and Milarepa. In Mongolia, Geser Khan has also been embraced at various times as a Buddhist protector, mostly by Gelukpas. This is connected in part to the merging of the figures of Gesar, Guandi, and Begtse during the Qing dynasty. The Ladakhi Kesar tradition, in contrast, does not appear to have developed a Buddhist cult in the same way.

Although the Tibetan Gesar cult is sometimes presented as embracing "Buddhism and Bön without distinction," there is no evidence of a cult of Ling Gesar in Tibetan Bön religion. It seems that while Buddhists often regard the cult of Gesar as being tinged with Bön elements—in particular with regard to the hero's "parentage" among primordial sky deities, his connections to the spirits of the Upper Middle and Lower realms, and his association with the archaic warrior spirits the *drala* and *werma*—Bönpos for their part consider Gesar an explicitly Buddhist figure, who if anything is hostile to Bön, and they do not take part in his apotheosis. An exception to this are the three volumes of Gesar texts authored by a *rimé* Bönpo chief named Wangchen Nyima (Dbang chen nyi ma) in the early 20th century.[23]

There is an abiding impression among scholars that the cult of Gesar is anathema to the Gelukpa school. This, however, seems to be a simplification. It is true that monks in Drepung Monastery, one of the most important seats of the Geluk school, are discouraged from reading or listening to the Gesar epic. It is said that this proscription is connected to the cult of the protector Pehar, who is particularly associated with the Nechung Oracle located right next to Drepung in Lhasa. The protector Pehar is associated by legend with Namte Karpo, an inner Asian deity hostile to Buddhism who was converted into the Buddhist protector Pehar by Padmasambhava. In the Gesar epic, Namte Karpo is the favored deity of several of Gesar's main adversaries (such as the Horpas). There is a concern that to read or recite Gesar near the Nechung oracle could therefore anger Pehar, and that this could have negative consequences. A less cultic explanation of the proscription is simply that the Gesar epic is to be avoided because it is a waste of time: the epic as the collective product of generations of often illiterate storytellers is considered an ill-informed mess, particularly in its apparent religious pieties, and is therefore not a suitable material subject of distraction for monastics.

Despite this proscription in Drepung, however, it would be misleading to regard the cult of Gesar as having no place in the Geluk world. In Geluk tradition the association between Gesar with the wealth deity and guardian of the north, Vaisravana, is the primary point of reference for whatever sanctity the figure of Gesar enjoys. In Mongolia, where the Geluk school of Tibetan Buddhism was dominant since the 16th century, the propitiation of Geser as an enlightened protector flourished. In part this appears to be a legacy of the Qing dynasty's merging of the cults of Gesar with the Chinese imperial protector-deity Guandi. The Guandi temple established in Lhasa in 1793 after the Qing expulsion of the Gorkha invasion, which was curated by the Gelukpa monks of the neighboring Kundeling Monastery, also doubled as a Gesar temple for the Tibetans, at which government ritual observances involving both the Manchu Imperial representatives (known as *ambans*) and officials of the (Geluk-aligned) Tibetan government took part.

The notion that Gelukpas in general were hostile toward the cult of Gesar as a protector was roundly dismissed by the Mongolian scholar and lama Bâmbyn Rintchen as an "absurd thesis."[24] In favor of Rintchen's assertions on this point, it is worth observing that we have Gesar *thangkas* depicting the epic hero surrounded by yellow-hatted (Geluk) lamas. George Roerich in his 1942 article observed,

> In Amdo among the followers of the dGe-lugs-pa sect one often hears the unexpected statement that Tsong-kha-pa himself, the Tibetan Reformer, had once been the chaplain (a-mchod) of King Kesar of Ling.[25]

We also know that the Reting Regent, Gelukpa ruler of Tibet during the minority of the present Fourteenth Dalai Lama, was himself very keen on Gesar as a protector figure and even supported a personal Gesar bard, in the person of Champasangta (Byams pa gsang bdag), who would later become the knowledgeable informant of both R. A. Stein and Rene de Nebesky-Wojkowitz, two of the foremost pioneers of western Tibetology. The Reting Regent himself was also involved in the sponsorship of a Gesar text by the third Jamtrul Rinpoche (a relatively minor Nyingmapa Kham lineage) in the 1920s.

So although it would be wrong to assert outright that a Buddhist cult of Gesar is anathema to the Geluk school of Tibetan Buddhism, it is fair to say that the ethos of the Buddhist cult of Gesar leans toward the Nyingma and Kagyü schools of Tibetan mysticism.

REVIEW OF LITERATURE

The epic of Gesar became an object of study for Tibetan scholars relatively recently. The only premodern Tibetan scholarly treatment of the epic came in the letters of Sumpa Khenpo (Sum pa mkhan po Ye shes dpal 'byor; 1704–1788) to the sixth Panchen Lama (Blo bzang dpal ldan ye shes; 1738–1780).[26] However, since the incorporation of Tibet into the People's Republic of China in the 1950s, the study of Gesar as a folk hero has been supported by state patronage, and as a result the academic study of the epic has flourished, with scores of Tibetan- and Chinese-language books on various facets of the epic being published. Collection, transcription, and publication of the oral recitations of living bards have also been prioritized by the Gesar research institutes established in all Chinese provinces with Tibetan populations (particularly Tibetan Autonomous Region, Sichuan, Qinghai, Gansu, and Yunnan). R. A. Stein's monumental work on the epic, his 1959 *Recherches sur l'Épopée et le Barde au Tibet,* has also been published in Chinese translation. Despite this tremendous growth in scholarly attention being lavished on the epic, its religious interpretation and the epic's relationship to Tibetan Buddhism have not been foregrounded.

Western scholarship on the Tibetan Gesar epic began late. In the 19th century there was a limited amount of Russian scholarship focused mainly on Mongolian traditions, and an abridged German translation is the earliest rendition of the epic in any European language.[27] This was an abridged translation of the Mongiolian-language version of the epic that had been sponsored by the Kangxi emperor in 1716 entitled *Arban ĵü-ün eĵen Geser qagan-u toguji.* Schmidt's German translation was later published in an anonymous and unannotated English translation as *Gesar! The Epic Tale of Tibet's Great Warrior-King.*[28] Scholarship on the Mongolian Geser tradition is dominated by the German-language work of Walther Heissig. Interesting structuralist ethnographic theories concerning the social function of the Geser epic in Buryatia, and its relationship to hunting and shamanizing, are found in the various works (mostly in French) by Roberte Hamayon.[29]

The earliest Western scholarship on the Tibetan-language Gesar traditions focused on the Ladakhi versions and was undertaken by A. H. Francke in the early 20th century. Francke was particularly interested in the non-Buddhist character of the recitations he collected, and he considered the epic cycle a nature myth of pre-Buddhist origin. In 1931 a Burushaski version of the epic from the Gilgit region was published by Lorimer, which had much in common with the Ladakhi traditions.[30] In the same year, the French mystic Mme David-Neel published her retelling of the entire epic,[31] based on a variety of oral and literary sources collected during her sojourns in eastern Tibet. Her version remains unsurpassed as a Western-language literary treatment of the eastern Tibetan Buddhist narrative traditions concerning Ling Gesar. In 1942 George Roerich published an account of the epic and its associated culture based on research undertaken in eastern Tibet.[32]

The greatest milestone in Western study of the epic came in the 1950s when the epic became the main object of research of the great French Tibetologist R. A. Stein. His magnum opus was the magisterial *Recherches sur l'Épopée et le Barde au Tibet* published in 1959. It surveyed all the versions and sources on the epic available at that time, utilizing not only Tibetan sources but also Chinese and Mongolian. Stein's study was studiously literary and explored the many layers of intertextuality found in the epic, giving many insights into the evolution of the Gesar epic as a Tibetan literary genre dominated by monk-authors. He also made an insightful ethnographic study of traditional Gesar bards and their clothes and accoutrements. In 1965 a lengthy study of the epic was published in German by Matthias Hermanns as *Das National-Epos der Tibeter gling König Ge sar*. The work is rather poorly referenced but contains interesting material, including a translation of a manuscript version of the epic from Guide in Amdo. Hermanns took the view that the epic's origins were pre-Buddhist and lay in the warrior-pastoralist culture of the ancient inner Asian tribes. A collection of comparative literary studies by Siegbert Hummel of various apparently Indo-European mythical themes and motifs found in the Gesar cycle have been translated into English and published together as *Eurasian Mythology in the Tibetan Epic of Ge-sar*.

In recent decades significant Western-language contributions to the study of Gesar have been made by Samten Karmay,[33] Geoffrey Samuel,[34] and S. G. FitzHerbert, though material appearing in Tibetan and Chinese now far outstrips that which is available in Western languages. On the Buddhist cult of Gesar, pioneering recent research has been undertaken by Gregory Forgues, whose work includes full translations of several Mipham-authored Gesar ritual texts.[35]

FURTHER READING

TRANSLATIONS/WESTERN LANGUAGE VERSIONS

Anon. *Gesar! The Epic Tale of Tibet's Great Warrior King*. Berkeley, CA: Dharma Publishing, 1991.

Blondeau, Anne-Marie, and Anne Chayet, trans. *L'Épopée Tibétaine de Gesar: Manuscript Bon-po Fonds A. David-Néel du Musée Guimet: Présentation et Traduction*. Paris: Editions Findakly, 2014.

David-Neel, Alexandra, and Lama Yongden. *The Superhuman Life of Gesar of Ling the Legendary Tibetan Hero, as Sung by the Bards of his Country*. London: Rider and Co., 1933.

Francke, A. H. *A Lower Ladakhi Version of the Kesar Saga*. New Delhi. Asian Educational Services, 2000.

Guillaume, Jacques, and Chen Zhen. *Une Version rGyalrong de l'Épopée de Gesar*. Osaka: National Museum of Ethnology, 2010.

Kornman, Robin, Sangye Khandro, and Lama Chonam, trans. *The Epic of Gesar of Ling: Gesar's Magical Birth, Early Years and Coronation as King*. Boston: Shambhala, 2012.

Lorimer, D. L. R. "An Oral Version of the Kesar Saga from Hunza." *Folklore* 42, no. 2 (1931): 105–140.

Penick, Douglas J. *The Warrior Song of King Gesar*. Boston: Wisdom Books, 1996.

Richtsfeld, Bruno. "Geburt und Jugend des Helden im Gesar-Epos der Monguor (VR China, Provinz Qinghai." *Anthropos* 101, no. 2 (2006): 473–498.

Stein, Rolf A. *L' Épopée Tibetaine de Gesar dans sa Version Lamaïque de Ling*. Paris: Presses Universitaires de France, 1956.

SELECTED SCHOLARSHIP

FitzHerbert, Solomon George. "Constitutional Mythologies and Entangled Cultures in the Tibeto-Mongolian Gesar Epic: The Motif of Gesar's Celestial Descent." *Journal of American Folklore* 129, no. 513 (2016): 297–326.

FitzHerbert, Solomon George. "An Early Tibetan Gesar *bsang* Text." *Archiv Orientální* 84 (2016): 1–60.

Forgues, Gregory. *Journeys to Freedom: A Transdisciplinary and Transcultural History of the Tibetan Gesar Rituals and Practices*. Leiden, The Netherlands: Brill, 2020.

Gcod pa don 'grub and Snying bo tshe ring. *gCod pa don 'grub dang snying bo tshe ring gi ched rtsom phyogs bsgrigs*. Xining: mTsho sngon mi rigs dpe skrun khang, 2004.

Hummel, Siegbert. *Eurasian Mythology in the Tibetan Epic of Ge-sar*. Translated by Guido Vogliotti. Dharamshala: Library of Tibetan Works and Archives, 1998.

Kapstein, Matthew, and Charles Ramble, eds. *The Many Faces of King Gesar: Homage to Rolf A. Stein*. Leiden, The Netherlands: Brill, 2022.

Karmay, Samten. "Gesar: the Epic Tradition of the Tibetan People." *Bulletin of the Department of Sanskrit and Indian Studies, Harvard University* 2, no. 3 (1992): 25–30.

Karmay, Samten. "The Theoretical Basis of the Tibetan Epic." *Bulletin of the School of Oriental and African Studies* 55, no. 2 (1993): 234–246.

Karmay, Samten. "The Social Organization of Ling and the Term 'phu-nu'in the Gesar Epic." *Bulletin of the School of Oriental and African Studies* 55, no. 2 (1995): 303–313.

Samuel, Geoffrey. "The Origins and Meaning of the East Tibetan Epic." In Ihara and Yamaguchi, eds., *Proceedings of the 5th IATS Conference (1989)*. Narita, 1992.

Stein, Rolf A. *Recherches sur l'Épopée et le Barde au Tibet*. Paris: Presses Universitaires de France, 1959.

Stein, Rolf A. "Introduction to the Gesar Epic." *Tibet Journal* 6, no. 1 (1981): 3–14.

NOTES

1. *Rlangs kyi po ti bse ru*, Gangs can rig mdzod 1 (Lhasa: Bod rang skyong ljongs spyi tshogs tshan rig khang bod yig dpe rnying dpe skrun khang, 1986).
2. On the concept of "pool of tradition" in the context of oral traditions of epic recital, see Lauri Honko "Text as Process and Practice: The Textualization of Oral Epics," in *Textualization of Oral Epics*, ed. Lauri Honko, Trends in Linguistics, Studies and Monographs 128 (Berlin: Mouton de Gruyter, 2000), 3–54.
3. Karmay's collected articles on the Gesar epic are found in Samten Karmay, *The Arrow and the Spindle: Studies in History, Myths, Rituals and Beliefs in Tibet*, vol. 1 (Kathmandu: Mandala Book Point, 1998).
4. Samten Karmay, "The Local Deities and the Juniper Tree: a Ritual for Purification (*bsang*)," in Karmay, *Arrow and Spindle*, 380–412.
5. A. H. Francke, *A Lower Ladakhi Version* of *the Kesar Saga* (New Delhi: Asian Education Services, 2000).
6. The three volumes of the "Lingtsang Xylograph" were authored by Gyurmé Thubten Jamyang Drakpa (Gyur med Thub brtan 'jam dbyangs grags pa) in the early 20th century. The titles of the three volumes are *Lha gling gab tse dgu skor*; *'Khrungs gling me tog ra ba*; and *Rta rgyugs nor bu cha bdun*. The Tibetan texts have been republished in many editions, in many countries. For example: R. A. Stein, trans., *L'Epopée Tibetaine de Gesar dans sa Version Lamaique de Ling* (Paris: Presses Universitaires, 1956); Kunzang Tobgyel and Mani Dorji, eds., *The Epic of Gesar,'Dzam gling ge sar rgyal po'i rtogs brjod*, vol. 1 (Thimphu, Bhutan: Kunzang Tobgyel, 1979); editions of the individual volumes published by Si kron mi rigs dpe skrun khang, Chengdu, in 1980, 1981, 1999; editions of the individual volumes published by Kan su'u mi rigs dpe skrun khang, Lanzhou, 1981; editions of the individual volumes published by Mtsho sngon zhing chen ge sar zhib 'jug khang, Xining, 1986. A full English translation of the three volumes is now available as R. Kornman, Sangye Khandro, and Lama Chonam, trans., *The Epic of Gesar of Ling: Gesar's Magical Birth, Early Years and Coronation as King* (Boston: Shambhala, 2012).
7. Solomon George FitzHerbert, "Constitutional Mythologies and Entangled Cultures in the Tibeto-Mongolian Gesar Epic: The Motif of Gesar's Celestial Descent," *Journal of American Folklore* 129, no. 513 (Summer 2016): 297–326.

8. See R. A. Stein, *Recherches sur l'Épopée et le Barde au Tibet* (Paris: Presses Universitaires de France, 1959).
9. *Stag gzig nor 'gyed* by rDzogs sprul Padma rig 'dzin (1625–1697). Editions: Lhasa: Bod ljongs mi dmangs dpe skrun khang, 1980, 2008; in *Mnga ris gser rdzong* (Chengdu: Mi rigs dpe skrun khang), 177–233. Dzogtrul Pema Rigdzin is best known for having founded Dzogchen Monastery in Kham in the 1650s with patronage from the ruler of Derge, Sanggyé Tenpa (Sangs rgyas brtan pa). The location of this monastery is very close to the historic seat of the royal family of Lingtsang, who claimed descent from Gesar's nephew in the epic, Drala Tsegyal, and played significant role in the elevating the status of the epic in Tibetan society. Pema Rigzin is also remembered as a chief disciple of Karma Chagmé (Karma chags med) and was himself considered a reincarnation of Lang Pelgi Senge (Rlangs dpal gyi seng ge).
10. *Takzik Norgyé*, 5–6.
11. *Takzik Norgyé*, 8.
12. (*Tsa wa'i namthar*) *'Phags pa'i yang sprul mi yi seng ge skyes bu nor bu dgra 'dul gyi mdzad pa las spros pa'i yan lag dor te rtsa ba'i rnam thar*. Editions: woodblock print held in British Library (no date); woodblock print in the library of Rai Bahadur T. D. Densapa, Gangtok, Sikkim (no date); published as Tashi Tsering, ed., *Gling rje ge sar gyi rtsa ba'i mdzad pa mdor bsdus dang slob dpon chen po'i rnam thar chen mo nas zur phyung snying bsdus 'ga' zhig* (Dharamshala: Library of Tibetan Works and Archives, 1981).
13. Tsawa'i Namthar fols. 5–7.
14. *Hor gling g.yul 'gyed* (2 vols.); original author (1730s): Derge *zhabdrung* Ngawang Tenzin Phuntso (Ngag dbang bstan 'dzin phun tshogs); edited 1960–1962 by the Qinghai Province People's Literature and Art Association; editions: Xining, 1962 (*stod cha* only); Thimphu, Bhutan, Kunzang, Tobgyel, 1979 (as vols. 3 and 4 of *The Epic of Gesar/'Dzam gling ge sar rgyal po'i rtogs brjod*); Xining, Mtsho sngon mi rigs dpe skrun khang, 1979, 1997; Lhasa, Bod ljongs mi dmangs dpe skrun khang, 1980; and Beijing, Mi rigs dpe skrun khang, 2000 (as vols. 4 and 5 of the *Gling sgrung gces bstus* series).
15. Horling Yülgyé, 2.330.
16. The fifth Lelung's Pure Vision: *Dag snang ge sar gyi gtam rgyud le'u 'o* by Sle lung Bzhad pa'i rdo rje, TBRC W22130.
17. *Dmyal gling rdzogs pa chen po*. Editions: *Gling rje ge sar rgyal po' mdzad sgrungs las dmyal ba'i le'u: An Episode from the Gesar Epic Cycle Recounting the King of Ling's Conquest of Hell* (Himachal: New Thobgyal Monastic Centre, 1973); D. G. Khochen Tulku, ed., *Dmyal gling rdzogs pa chen po: The dMyal gling Episode of the Gesar Epic Recounting the Conquest of the Realm of the Dwellers of Hell* (Dehra Dun: 1977); and Kunzang Tobgyel and Mani Dorji, eds., *Dmyal gling rdzogs pa chen po thos pa rang grol ngan song chos kyi pasakula glu*, vol. 31 of *The Epic of Gesar,'Dzam gling ge sar rgyal po'i rtogs brjod* (Thimphu, Bhutan: Kunzang Tobgyel, 1984); *Dmyal gling rdzogs pa chen po* (Chengdu: Si kron mi rigs dpe skrun khang, 1980, 1987, 1994).
18. For Lauri Honko's concept of "pool of tradition" see note 3 above.
19. Solomon George FitzHerbert, "An Early Tibetan Gesar *bsang* Text" *Archiv Orientální* 84 (2016): 1–60.
20. Don brgyud nyi ma, ed., *Gling ge sar gyi sgrub skor*, 2 vols. (Palampur: Sungrab Nyamso Gyunphel Parkhang, 1971), TBRC W27926.
21. Gregory Forgues, "Materials for the Study of Gesar Practices" (MA diss., University of Vienna, 2011).
22. Lines 17, 19, 22, 23, 24, and (e.g.,) 34.
23. The three volumes by the Bönpo chief Wangchen Nyima text are held in the Alexandra David-Neel Collection at the Musée Guimet in Paris. Although the presentation of the epic here uses Bönpo spellings for the warrior-spirits *sgra bla*, Gesar is nevertheless depicted in this version as a Buddhist hero. The three volumes have recently been published in facsimile along with a full French translation in Anne-Marie Blondeau and Anne Chayet, trans., *L'Épopée Tibétaine de Gesar: Manuscript Bon-po Fonds A. David-Néel du Musée Guimet: Présentation et Traduction* (Paris: Editions Findakly, 2014).
24. Bâmbyn Rintchen, "En Marge du Culte de Guesser Khan en Mongolie," *Journal de la Societe Finno-Ougrienne* 60 (1958): 7.

25. George N. Roerich, "The Epic of King Kesar of Ling," *Journal of the Asiatic Society of Bengal* 8, no. 7 (1942): 286.
26. This exchange is translated in full in Solomon George FitzHerbert, "On the Tibetan Ge-sar Epic in the Late 18th Century: Sum-pa mkhan-po's letters to the Sixth Paṇ-chen Bla-ma," *Études Mongoles, Sibériennes, Centralasiatiques & Tibétaines* (online journal) 46 (2015). Available at https://emscat.revues.org/2602.
27. I. J. Schmidt *Die Thaten des Vertilgers der Zehn Uebel in den zehn Gegenden, des verdienstvollen Helden Bogda Gesser Chan; eine mongolische Heldensage, nach einem in Peking gedruckten Exemplare aufs neu abgedrukt* (St. Petersburg, 1839, re-edition Berlin: Auriga Verlag, 1925).
28. (Berkeley, CA: Dharma Publishing).
29. Her magnum opus is Roberte Hamayon, *La Chasse à l'Âme: Esquisse d'une Theorie du Chamanisme Sibirien* (Nanterre: Societe d'Ethnologie, 1992). For an English-language treatment of how the epic fits with her theory of shamanism, see Roberte Hamayon, "The Dynamics of the Epic Genre in Buryat culture: a Grave for Shamanism, a Ground for Messianism," in *Epic Adventures: Heroic Narrative in the Oral Performance Traditions of Four Continents*, eds. Jan Jansen and Henk Maier (Utrecht: VockinginVorm LIT Verlag, 2004), 53–65.
30. D. L. R. Lorimer, "An Oral Version of the Kesar Saga from Hunza," *Folklore* 42, no. 2 (1931): 105–140.
31. Alexandra David-Neel and Lama Yongden, *La Vie Surhumaine de Guésar de Ling, le Héros Thibétain: Racontée par les Bardes de son Pays* (Paris: Adyar, 1931). Then translated into English and published as *The Superhuman Life of Gesar of Ling the Legendary Tibetan Hero, as Sung by the Bards of his Country* (London: Rider and Co, 1933).
32. George Roerich, "The Epic of King Kesar of Ling," *Journal of the Asiatic Society of Bengal* 8, no. 7 (1942): 277–311.
33. Karmay's collected essays on the epic are found in Samten Karmay, *The Arrow and the Spindle: Studies in History, Myths, Rituals and Beliefs in Tibet*, vol. 1 (Kathmandu: Mandala Book Point, 1998).
34. Samuel's most influential contributions on the subject of the Gesar epic are found in Geoffrey Samuel, ed., *Tantric Revisionings: New Understandings of Tibetan Buddhism and Indian Religion* (Delhi: Motilal Banarsidas. 2005).
35. Forgues's book on the cult of Gesar is, at the time of writing, forthcoming (*Journeys to Freedom*, Leiden, The Netherlands: Brill). For the thesis on which it is based see note 22 above.

Solomon George FitzHerbert

TIBETAN BUDDHIST POWER OBJECTS

THE UBIQUITY AND DIVERSITY OF POWER OBJECTS IN TIBETAN BUDDHISM

Material and sensory objects ascribed with the power to impact human lives and environments are an integral part of Tibetan religious life. Tibetan Buddhist traditions typically feature a wide diversity of such objects. These can range from pills, cords, amulets, relics, ritual implements, and other small portable items; to the middle-sized goods of hats, masks, portable statues and reliquaries, paintings, and the like; all the way up to larger immobile items such as massive statues and reliquaries, shrines, geological formations, and even entire valleys. What binds items together under the rubric of "power objects" is the belief that they are potent enough to impact anyone and anything that comes into contact with them, and that such potency derives in some measure from their previous relationships with buddhas, bodhisattvas, tantric deities, ritual masters, yogis, or some other similarly charged person, place, or thing.

Owing to this widespread set of beliefs, one of the most immediately visible features of Himalayan Buddhist traditions is the practice of aspirants bringing themselves into direct physical contact with these kinds of objects. Such contact is typically made through touching, eating, wearing, prostrating, circumambulating, making offerings, conducting elaborate rituals, or most often, a combination thereof.

These practices, moreover, are not just popular among the laity. They are also commonly performed and prescribed by religious specialists as diverse as monastic hierarchs, monks, nuns, tantric ritual specialists, and itinerant yogis, regardless of Buddhist, Bön, or sub-sectarian affiliation or persuasion. Physical human interactions with power objects are therefore immediately observable at any of the pilgrimage sites, monasteries, temples, and hermitages scattered across the Himalayan region. Tales of how power objects acquire astounding powers of animation and agency—hats taking flight, books talking, masks weeping, statues standing, barley grains suspended in mid-air, and so on—also abound in Tibetan Buddhist narrative and pilgrimage literature. Tibetan Buddhist liturgical texts focused on such objects also often explicitly frame such displays of animated matter as signs of a ritual operation's success.

The goals of interacting with power objects are manifold. These range from the pragmatic aims of protection against misfortune; healing; longevity; successful conception and childbirth; and increased wealth, power, intelligence, and influence to the more transcendent aims of the accumulation of positive karma; the purification of negative karma; the consequent freedom from negative future rebirths; or even the final liberation from rebirth in saṃsāra as a whole. Sometimes the goal depends on the type of object concerned, but more often interaction with one and the same object promises the full spectrum of goals, depending on a number of mitigating factors, such as the level of spiritual development of the person interacting with the object, the master who consecrated it, and others. But contact with objects of power is not unequivocally positive in nature. Power objects can also be employed with the aim of subjugating or destroying enemies, seducing consorts, persuading leaders, sowing enmity between rival factions, and vanquishing armies, among other coercive or violent goals.

Interactions with powerful objects have therefore also had pronounced social and political aims and overtones. Ritual and other interactions with sites or smaller formations believed to house local deities—often through the medium of a dagger, scepter, or other ritual object—have historically served as the dynamic by which Himalayan Buddhist masters have subjugated local landscapes and converted their human and non-human inhabitants to Buddhism. Power objects have consequently become important touchstones in the formation of communal identity and institutional prestige—points of pride and markers of identity for Buddhist institutions, pilgrimage sites, and communities.

The use of power objects to subjugate landscapes, vanquish enemy armies, and garner prestige has made them particularly important in the political arena. Highly revered relics, along with a whole range of other objects featuring in rites performed with the aim of protecting polities, have been a galvanizing force in the formation of Tibetan Buddhist states. Power objects were especially active in this role during the middle of the 17th century, with the rise of the Ganden Potrang (Dga' ldan pho brang) government, the state of Sikkim, and the state of Bhutan.

Himalayan Buddhists' interactions with powerful objects have long been observed by scholars. Yet the factors that gave rise to this practice, its rationale among Himalayan Buddhists, and its implications in social and political domains have thus far, with few notable exceptions, received attention only in passing. This relative scholarly neglect of power objects has only been acknowledged in the past few decades, as Buddhist studies has begun to inflect the humanities-wide turn toward the approaches of material culture studies and social history. This shift has given new impetus for Buddhist studies scholars to begin focusing their attention on the roles powerful objects have played in the lives of Himalayan Buddhists.

ORIGINS

The origins and history of the Tibetan fascination with Buddhist power objects follows the trajectory of the Tibetan importation and assimilation of Buddhist traditions as a whole. A popular narrative tradition recounting Tibet's first encounter with Buddhism has it that a casket containing a group of five objects and texts—two Buddhist sutras, a mold engraved with a *dhāraṇī* formula, the mantra of Avalokiteśvara, and a golden reliquary (Tib. *mchod rten*, Skt. *stūpa*)—fell from the sky onto the roof of the palace of the Tibetan king Lha Thotori Nyentsen (Lha tho tho ri gnyan btsan).[1] No one at the court was able to read the sutras or understand the import of the other objects, but the king and his retainers nonetheless presumed them auspicious, named them the "Secret Potency" (*gnyan po gsang ba*), and instituted their worship. The fruit of this veneration for the Secret Potency was that the king, then sixty-one years old, reverted to a sixteen-year-old youth and lived to the ripe old age of 120. The king was also given a prophecy that the Secret Potency would be understood after five generations. This would correspond, as Tibetan historiographical tradition claims, with what Tibetans regard as the first concerted royal effort to import Buddhist traditions to Tibet in the 7th century under Emperor Songtsen Gampo (Srong btsan sgam po).

Although this narrative became popular in Tibet only after the 10th century, it is nonetheless quite revealing about historical conceptions concerning what constitutes an object of power among Buddhists in Tibet and India.[2] Most notably, here it is not just material objects, strictly speaking, that are included in the Secret Potency but scriptural books too, as well as shorter linguistic condensations of doctrine and practice known as *dhāraṇī* and mantra. And although the detail of the narrative in which the Tibetan court treats written materials as objects to be worshiped rather than read and interpreted speaks to the assumption that Tibetans were illiterate at the time of this event, it also reflects the practice, prevalent already in India, of Buddhists treating linguistic formulations, including scriptural books, as power objects in their own right, above and beyond whatever propositional content they might contain and communicate.

Buddhist practices centering on particularly esteemed objects believed to possess, accrue, and communicate power are thus by no means a Tibetan innovation. Belief in the powers of material objects to bring about transformations in the conditions of beings and environments has an ancient pedigree in Indian Buddhism. Distinct emphases on the interaction with material forms, or, conversely, the cultivation of discursive meanings in the efficacy of Buddhist practice stem in some measure from the dual nature of what Buddha Śākyamuni left to the world: his teachings, the dharma, which he dispensed in a teaching career that spanned about forty-five years, and which came to form the most voluminous set of scriptures of any major world religion; and his physical remains, which were distributed in the form of relics and enshrined in reliquaries throughout India and the rest of the Buddhist world. These two forms—one linguistic and one bodily—would be the primary media by which Buddhists would continue to access the presence of the buddha's awakening in the world.

These two modes of the buddha's ongoing presence are reflected in two overlapping cultic orientations in Indian Buddhism. One tendency, which Gregory Schopen has termed the "cult of the book," foregrounds the physical object of the scriptural book itself as the center of Buddhist cultic life.[3] This orientation finds expression repeatedly throughout many Mahāyāna sutras in the promise to fulfill pragmatic and soteriological aims, including bringing the buddha into presence, simply through the copying, reciting, preaching, carrying, or wearing of scriptural books.[4] The other tendency is the cult of the stupa, or reliquary, which centers more on it and its institutional settings as the venue through which to best feel the presence of the buddha in one's pursuit of the religious life.[5]

These two orientations were fused in an approach that combined the veneration of scriptural books, including short linguistic formulas known as *dhāraṇī* that encapsulate larger scriptures, with the worship of relics and their reliquaries.[6] This fusion is reflected in a series of identifications—between the buddha's speech, Buddhist scriptural books, the buddha's physical remains, images made in his likeness, and the content of ultimate awakening itself—such that visits to structures or venues that feature Buddhist scriptures, relics, reliquaries, and statues, individually or in combination, could mean encountering the buddha himself and partaking of his awakened presence.

When this combination of features was wed to the bodhisattva ethic, there also developed the practice, expressed in a number of Mahāyāna sutras and *śāstras*, of bodhisattvas making aspirations to materialize in whatever form is needed to benefit beings. This practice entails the notion that the process of perfecting this resolve over multiple lifetimes—which is tantamount to traversing the entirety of the Mahāyāna Buddhist path—will result in its actualization, such that just seeing the forms of highly realized bodhisattvas, hearing their voices or names, eating their flesh, or otherwise coming into sensory contact with them has the potential to heal beings, plant positive sensory impressions in their minds, and lead them eventually to salvation.[7] This development enabled Buddhists to continue revealing novel forms of awakened presence, far away from India, and long after the historical Buddha Śākyamuni and his immediate followers had passed.

In later Indian Buddhist *dhāraṇī* and tantra texts, the category of power objects expanded to include a wider range of mundane effects—including destructive aims—and even the direct purification of negative karma. It became a standard feature of *dhāraṇī* and tantra texts to prescribe numerous techniques for producing material objects, such as images, talismans, amulets, potions, powders, pills, medicines, and other contraptions or devices. Owing to the belief that these various and sundry material objects were all extensions of awakened intentionality—either as manifestation of the awakened resolve of bodhisattvas or through consecration rituals that infuse them with the power of buddhas and bodhisattvas—they purport to address a panoply of mundane and soteriological concerns through physical, sensory contact alone.[8] Following the familiar Buddhist pattern, moreover, these items are almost invariably formed not just from material substances but also in combination with linguistic forms such as *dhāraṇī* and mantras, which, much like *dhāraṇī*, were often construed as condensations of larger scriptural formulations and equivalent to the mind-stream of their corresponding buddhas.

The combination of elements that form Buddhist power objects can be clearly witnessed in Tibetan Buddhist funerary practice and reliquary construction.[9] When a Tibetan Buddhist master passes away, his body is typically left for several days seated upright in meditation posture in a state known as *thukdam* (*thugs dam*). During this time, the master's vital signs of heartbeat, brain activity, and breathing have all ceased, but other vital signs remain, such as warmth, coloration, and physical flexibility. It is believed that a master's ability to enter and abide in this state at death is the concrete fruition of his mastery of the processes of death and rebirth through previous training. It is also believed that during this period his awakened altruistic consciousness, now relatively unfettered by physical constraints but not yet fully departed from his body, is particularly accessible to the living.

Once this period has come to an end—which is typically signaled by the emission of blood from one nostril and mucus or lymph from the other—his body is preserved on salt for several weeks, during which time it becomes a locus of ritual activity and contemplative practice, before it is cremated in a ceremony patterned directly after reliquary construction and consecration. After the body has been cremated, the master's close associates sift through the remains in search of relics. These can consist of crystal pellets; inexplicably unburned parts of the body, like the tongue, heart, or skull; mantra syllables that have self-arisen on remaining pieces of bone; and other objects and indicators.[10] The ash and the rest of the physical remains, along with a portion of the relics, are then interred within a reliquary accompanied by scriptural books, *dhāraṇī* and mantra formulas, and relics of previous masters and buddhas, among other items.[11] It is through physical interactions with such a reliquary and its mixture of elements, in addition to the study and practice of a deceased master's teachers (which are often compiled, edited, and published for the occasion), that one is deemed capable of receiving his salvific blessings and assimilating his awakened mind, in addition to more pragmatic effects. Moreover, the master's body fluids, along with the salt that preserved his body, are, by the logic of contiguity, deemed power objects in their own right and are accordingly distributed among the faithful. Relics of deceased masters also have the tendency to multiply and become animated in response to human veneration.

This particularly Tibetan Buddhist funerary procedure was clearly culled from Indian Buddhist precedents. But several elements, such as the practice of *thukdam*, the preservation of the body on salt for a period, and perhaps others, seem to be Tibetan adaptations, although it is difficult to know for certain. All this suffices to say that Indian Buddhists were deeply invested in the cult of power objects, long before Tibetans became Buddhist. Indian Buddhist traditions instilled this fascination among converts—central Asians, Chinese, and then Tibetans—as Buddhist traditions spread north beyond their land of origin. Throughout this process, host cultures, which, like all human cultures, would have already formulated specific beliefs about power objects, assimilated and adapted Indian Buddhist practices and ideas about power objects according to their own cultural sensibilities.

There is also considerable evidence that trade in relics, images, scriptural books, and other portable power objects was an important impetus behind the circulation of Buddhist thought and practice across Asia in the ancient world.[12] With the spread of Buddhism, Buddhist pilgrimage circuits and merchant trade routes would become one and the same.[13] Trade in Buddhist power objects could have enabled itinerant clergy points of entry for the establishment of Buddhist monasteries and hermitages along these routes. In this light, the Tibetan story of the Secret Potency might then very well be read, as Dudjom Rinpoche and other Tibetan masters before him had, as a mythic rendering of an early royal encounter with such objects through the intercession of itinerant monks who arrived in Tibet from neighboring Buddhist countries.[14]

KEY TERMS AND RUBRICS

As Tibetans assimilated Buddhist traditions through the translation of scriptures and the foundation of monastic institutions beginning in the 8th and 9th centuries, they coined a number of terms to designate power objects—both the objects themselves and the power that inheres in them. The most prevalent general terms for objects and places of power are "receptacle" (*rten*), "abode" (*gnas*), and "substance" (*rdzas*).

Receptacle. The term "receptacle" (pronounced "*ten*" in Tibetan), otherwise rendered as "basis" or "support," is perhaps the most pervasive general term applied to items believed to concentrate power. The broad application of this term to power objects is perhaps best illustrated by its use in tantric descriptions of mandala palaces and their resident deities—the mandala palace serves as the "receptacle" or "support" (*rten*) residence, where the deities dwell as the "supported" (*brten pa*) residents.[15] Moreover, the tantras most commonly practiced by Tibetans, along with their commentaries, tend to explain the mandala residence not as an inert venue for deities but as an expression of gnosis in its own right, on par with the deities it houses.[16] Nonetheless, there is evidence in polemical exchanges from the 16th century onward that a sector of Tibetan exegetes understood this Tibetan term, when applied to a broader range of objects, to signal an inert "representation" or "prop" for the recollection of doctrinal values, rather than a living nexus of awakened presence.[17] The term in fact allows for both senses, even as Tibetan doctrinal experts debated about which understanding should be construed as primary. In practice, however, the logic of representation consistently gives way to the logic of presence. Rather than signify some value extrinsic to them, such objects are unequivocally treated in Himalayan Buddhist contexts as loci for the concentration of power and influence.

Beyond the scope of mandala palaces, "receptacles" are most commonly categorized as three-fold (*rten gsum*):

1. Receptacles of awakened body (*sku rten*), which are statues, paintings, and other kinds of images of buddhas, bodhisattvas, or masters
2. Receptacles of awakened speech (*gsung rten*), namely, scriptural books, mantras, and other auditory or written sacred media
3. Receptacles of awakened mind (*thugs rten*), which primarily signals reliquaries (Tib. *mchod rten*, Skt. *stūpa*).[18]

Tibetan Buddhist shrines, temples, and institutions are not considered fully qualified focal points or venues of ritual interaction and contemplative practice unless they include instances of all three types. And lest one narrow the semantic range of the term *ten* to a mere "symbol" or "representation" of the buddha, as it might appear to function in the context of Buddhist shrines, "receptacles" are also focal points of consecration rituals—locations that buddhas and bodhisattvas are called to inhabit.[19] Further along these lines, the phrase "receptacle of awakened body" or "one who possesses a receptacle of awakened body" (*sku rten pa*) can also refer to the bodies of Tibetan Buddhist oracles that Buddhist protectors inhabit and speak through to guide their human followers.[20]

Abode. The term "abode" or "site" (*gnas*, pronounced "*né*") functions more unambiguously to signal the residence of a deity or some other non-human spirit entity, or alternatively, a place marked by the visitation of a previous buddha, bodhisattva, or saint.[21] The term thus tends to refer to special locations—rocks, trees, springs, rivers, lakes, mountains, caves, or other geological formations—said to either house or be equated with a particular entity, Buddhist or non-Buddhist. But when *né* designates where a past buddha, bodhisattva, or master visited, such places are often marked by the traces of their illustrious past visitors, typically through imprints of their hands, feet, or body miraculously left in stone or other local objects. Moreover, *né* can also feature an image or some other sign of a buddha's or bodhisattva's presence that has miraculously "self-arisen" (*rang byon*), typically by gradually appearing in stone without human artifice. Shared perceptions of the transformative power of *né* account for their popularity as important places of pilgrimage, where pilgrims seek a range of goals—pragmatic and soteriological.[22] The Tibetan term *né* is hence used in common colloquial Tibetan to designate "pilgrimage place." Moreover, *né* also appear in Buddhist tantric scriptures as the "power places" associated with the deities of a given mandala, which are often said to be scattered throughout the landscape of South Asia. By analogy, the term also figures as the key energy nodes distributed throughout the subtle yogic body of beings. Thus, like a number of similar terms and concepts in tantric Buddhism, the word *né* operates simultaneously on the levels of macrocosm, microcosm, and mesocosm, connecting by homologous structures cosmos, landscape, and person.[23]

Substance. "Substance," or "*dzé*" in Tibetan, tends to designate smaller objects, such as pills, amulets, and ritual instruments, but can also refer more generally in the same way that "receptacle" does to a "basis" for the concentration of power and presence. The terms "receptacle" and "substance" are often joined together in another typology of the three receptacles of awakened body, speech, and mind that applies specifically to objects at use in tantric rituals.[24] According to this rubric, substances that are receptacles of awakened body include not only images depicting buddhas but also the hand implements and adornments for tantric deity images as well as ritual daggers, vases, and other ritual instruments.[25] Substances that are receptacles of awakened speech include the thigh bone trumpets, skull drums, rosaries, and other sound-related implements.[26] Substances that are receptacles of awakened mind include the skull cups (*kapāla*), hand gestures (*mudrā*), staffs (*khaṭvāṅga*), crystals, mirrors, caskets, and other items that feature in tantric initiations and other tantric ceremonies.[27] There is also a special class of substance that includes supports of awakened mind for dharma protectors. These typically include the knives, swords, clubs, and other weapons that these fierce beings are depicted as brandishing in their protective functions.[28]

Other rubrics, such as "the triad of outer, inner, and secret," are also common ways of organizing both receptacles and substances. Some of these categories have taken on wider valences and come to have lives of their own. "Inner receptacle" (*nang rten*), for instance, came to refer collectively to all the power objects interred within a statue or reliquary as part of its consecration. Since such contents prominently feature multiple copies of *dhāraṇī* formulas rolled-up and stuffed within the inner cavities of the object to be consecrated, the terms "*dhāraṇī* receptacle" (*gzungs rten*) and "*dhāraṇī* filling" (*gzungs gzhug*) are sometimes also used to refer to the contents as a whole, or the receptacle containing them, even though relics and other objects and substances of power are often interred alongside *dhāraṇīs*.[29] The filling of a statue or reliquary with such objects is believed to enliven it and make it a proper conduit for the blessings and power of past buddhas, bodhisattvas, and masters.[30]

Similarly, "inner receptacle" can also refer to all the power objects in the holdings of a particular hermitage, monastery, lama estate (*bla brang*), or pilgrimage site. Catalogues (*dkar chag*) of such "inner receptacles"—whether they are related to statues, reliquaries, pilgrimage sites, or monastic institutions—are important records of power objects, as they tend to include not just lists of items but also descriptions of their receptacle's construction and historical narratives of each item's import and how each came to reside in its current location.[31]

Oath Substance. The sense of the term "substance" as receptacle comes from Buddhist tantric scriptures, where substance is also typically paired with the term *samaya* (*dam tshig*) to form in Tibetan translation the compound "*damdzé*" (*dam rdzas*).[32] This term most likely entered Tibetan as a translation of the Sanskrit compound *samaya-dravya* of Indian Buddhist scriptures. *Samaya* (*dam tshig*), the first term in the compound *samaya-dravya*, is a key concept in tantric Buddhist traditions. It refers to a set of prescriptions and prohibitions bestowed orally by a tantric master to his or her circle of tantric initiates, the oath made by initiates to observe those precepts, the ongoing commitment of observing them in practice, and the magical bond that forms through this process, the maintenance of which ensures the integrity and efficacy of a practice that master and initiates have in common.[33] As such, *samaya* has a semantic range that includes "precept," "oath," "commitment," and "magical bond."

Samaya also has a pronounced material component. Initiates often receive *samaya* precepts in conjunction with their consumption of a drop of *samaya* water, which, in some senses, is interchangeable with the precepts themselves.[34] The proper observance of *samaya* by a group of initiates is often said to be sufficient to enable the actualization of the associated practice, whereas transgressions of *samaya*, even when committed by a single member of the group, is said to result in negative rebirth for the perpetrator and deleterious effects for the entire group, including their master. These different outcomes are expressed in ritual settings in terms of the *samaya* water. As the material correlate of tantric vows, the drop is said to remain in the heart, where it alternately confers bliss upon those who properly observe the precepts and incinerates those who do not.[35] Simply put, then, *samaya* constitutes a set of regulatory observations, encapsulated in material form, which are instrumental in the formation and maintenance of communal bonds among initiates, between them and their master, and through him and their shared practice to associated deities, buddhas, past masters, and more.

When applied to *dravya* (*rdzas*), or "substance," *samaya* and its bond-forming capacities take on even more markedly material and sensory dimensions. The compound *samaya-dravya* appears relatively few times in the translated sutras and tantras (*bka' 'gyur*) but gains greater frequency in the translated commentarial treatises (*bstan 'gyur*). This Indian commentarial literature most generally uses it to signify the tantric sacraments of "five meats" (Tib. *sha lnga*,

Skt. *pañcamāṃsa*) and "five ambrosias" (Tib. *bdud rtsi lnga*, Skt. *pañcāmṛta*), which make up an enumeration of ten *samaya-dravya*, a list with its own variations across the extant Indian tantric literature.[36]

The semantic range of the term *damdzé* appears to have expanded considerably in Tibet. In a creative adaptation upon the term *samaya-dravya* from the Indian Buddhist context, it came to denote a much broader range of objects and substances—including the traditional Indian tantric five ambrosias and five meats; edible sacra of all kinds; amulets; larger items, such as particularly revered statues; and other images and objects believed to possess transformational power.

Moreover, although the term "oath substance" is generally defined as "a material object that has been transformed by mantra," its wider semantic range in Tibet means that oath substances are often regarded as extensions or materializations of awakened buddhas and bodhisattvas and thus treated in practice as though they possess their own transformational properties, above and beyond their ritual treatment.[37] It is in this sense that oath substance has often been used in Tibet interchangeably with "receptacle" to signal a material substrate for the concentration of transformative power.

Treasure Substance. The kind of substance that perhaps best typifies innovative Tibetan approaches to power objects is "Treasure substance" (*gter rdzas*), often regarded as a special subcategory of oath substance.

In the 11th century, as Tibetans were systematizing Indian Buddhist scriptural traditions to form uniquely Tibetan lineages and institutions, visionary masters, otherwise known as Treasure revealers (*gter ston*) that belonged mostly to lineages that would soon coalesce into the Nyingma (Rnying ma) tradition, began to unearth revelations with a demonstrably material and sensory focus.[38] These "Treasure substances," as they were called, include a range of potent materials that the Nyingma tradition (and, to a lesser extent, the Bön and Kagyü traditions) maintains were concealed by the 8th-to-9th-century Indian tantric master Padmasambhava, his consort Yeshé Tsogyal, and others throughout the Tibetan landscape for later destined Treasure revealers to retrieve and implement anew when the time for their peak efficacy is reached.[39] These items—typically excavated along with Treasure teachings that explain their histories, benefits, and modes of preparation—are, among other things, statues, relics, clothing, ritual objects, gems, medicines, or even entire valleys or lands. Moreover, these substances are also often presented as including the fluids, flesh, bone, hair, nails, clothes, or handiwork of Padmasambhava and other awakened buddhas and bodhisattvas from the past and are thus presumed to have their own intrinsic powers to impact beings and environments. Human ritual treatment, however, is typically still required to activate or direct the power of these items. The power of these objects, once augmented and unleashed by ritual mediation, is most often expressed in terms of newly acquired properties of animation that confound the senses. Treasure substances are depicted in narratives as multiplying; boiling; wafting fragrant odors; emitting lights; flying; producing dreams and visionary encounters with deities, masters, and buddhas; and other outcomes that typically amaze, astound, and inspire audiences and participants.[40] Liturgies are also explicit that such events are telltale signs of the success of ritual performances focused on these items.[41]

By the 14th century, many of these objects came to be categorized according to a four-fold typology, in which the mode of contact or efficacy was used to refer to the objects themselves, or, alternatively, to a special object, text, person, or location endowed with all four. One thus encounters objects such as (1) miniature statues, said to be crafted by the hands of past masters, as well as special mantra or *dhāraṇī* formulas that promise "liberation through seeing"; (2) a range of mantra or *dhāraṇī* textual formulas and instruction manuals that promise "liberation through hearing"; (3) instruction manuals, diagrams, or mantra or *dhāraṇī* formulas that prescribe their manufacture into powerful amulets that can confer "liberation through wearing"; and (4) especially potent pills made of the relics of past masters and other materials that can grant "liberation through tasting."[42] One or another of these categories also included a number of other items, such as ritual daggers, hats, vases, water, gems, garments, and so forth, that similarly promise "liberation" to whomever comes into physical, sensory contact with them.

The 14th century was also witness to the first public critiques among Tibetans of the claim that encounters with special objects are so potent that they can bring "liberation." These criticisms came from prestigious Buddhist hierarchs who seemed to have seen in such claims a gross exaggeration of the potency of objects described in scriptural sources, at the expense of the mind and efforts put toward its purification on the Buddhist path. These early criticisms resurfaced with greater force in the 16th and 17th centuries, thus compelling Nyingma exegetes to provide more robust doctrinal justifications for their efficacy.[43] Perhaps as a testament to the success of these Nyingma rebuttals, objects that liberate and their categories continued to proliferate. One thus encounters a rubric of six modes of liberation (*grol ba drug*), in which "touching" (*reg pa*) and "smelling/sensing" (*tshor ba*), or sometimes "recollecting" (*dran pa*), are added to the previous set of four: "seeing," "hearing," "wearing," and "tasting." Also prevalent was an enumeration of eight means of "liberation," in which "wearing" appears first, followed in turn by liberation through "seeing," "hearing," "touching," "tasting," "recollecting," "understanding," and "sensing."[44] The proliferation of such categories appears to reach its apex in the 19th century with a rubric of eleven modes of liberation—a typology developed by Jamgön Kongtrul Lodrö Tayé (1813–1899) to include each and every different sensory and discursive mode of contact with particularly powerful objects.[45]

The Nyingma school has promoted the belief that interactions with these kinds of objects are special techniques belonging to the Great Perfection tradition that can grant "buddhahood without meditation" (*ma bsgoms sangs rgyas*). There has also been a pronounced tendency to concentrate these media into a single item and to distribute their efficacy to other persons, places, or things. It has thus become commonplace to encounter special objects, instructions, persons, and locations said to have the capacity to liberate through all four modes; these are dubbed as those "endowed with the four modes of liberation" (*grol ba bzhi ldan*). Here, liberation through "wearing" and "tasting" are sometimes replaced by liberation through "touching" and "recollecting," apropos of the type of object involved (i.e., whether it is something that can be "worn" or "tasted"). Great Perfection literature tends to describe individuals endowed with the four liberations—that is, someone with whom any kind of sensory contact brings others spiritual progress—as having the capacity to provide the highest form of beneficial action in the world. Theoretically, this capacity is achievable only by sublime beings who have perfected themselves for the welfare of others. The fluidity of efficacious power between persons, places, and things can also be seen clearly in the category of "liberation through seeing." By the middle of the 17th century this rubric subsumed sacred places, visionary experiences, insight into ultimate reality, persons who experienced such insight, as well as any artistic products consecrated by such a person.[46]

The charisma of certain objects, texts, and persons believed to liberate through sensory contact alone meant also that possession of liberation-through-senses objects became a popular component of institutional prestige even outside Nyingma circles. The monasteries and institutions of other sectarian groups, such as the Sakya school's Shalu (Zhwa lu) monastery, among several other examples, gained considerable fame for their possession of relics, reliquaries, texts, or other objects similarly dubbed as items that could purify immeasurable negative karma and sometimes even bring liberation, simply through sensory contact.[47]

Despite the semantic shift of oath substance from its earlier, more limited usage as a translation for the Sanskrit term *samaya-dravya*, the association of substance with oath taking captures something fundamental about how it and other material media of power function in the lives of the people who use them. "Receptacles," "abodes," and "substances" are all value-laden transactional items; that is, they function as meaningful units of exchange and points of interaction between human beings. Exchanges of and interactions with power objects in Tibetan Buddhist societies bind people together under a shared rubric of aesthetic and moral values. Such objects function as particularly efficacious "sensational forms," which mobilize people into communal "aesthetic formations," through shaping individual aesthetic sensibilities into common, recognizable patterns, or collective habits.[48] In conjunction with their displays of animation, power objects shape sensibilities based primarily on the sense faculty through which they are accessed, whether it be through sight, sound, taste, touch, thought, or more often, a combination thereof. And owing to the social dynamic of intensive exchange and interaction with such valued objects, they have often become a galvanizing force for the formation of Himalayan Buddhist communities, institutions, and states.

THEORIES OF EFFICACY

An understanding of power objects as sensory media that bind invites speculation about the various styles of binding enacted by them and the implications of their binding properties upon the religious sensibilities of individuals and their formation into communities. There is not a great deal of theoretical speculation among Tibetan Buddhist writers about what constitutes the power of power objects, how and why certain things become imbued with power, and what their main uses ought to be. Moreover, even when Tibetans have theorized on these issues, they have been far from unanimous in their appraisals. Nonetheless, key in all such considerations is the relationships between power objects and human beings. Such relationships can be summed up as threefold: (1) how buddhas, bodhisattvas, or masters figure in the formation of power objects; (2) how ritual masters and participants treat power objects in subsequent tantric ritual settings; and (3) how people exchange or interact with such objects outside of these ritual settings.

Jinlap and Tu. Regardless of the nature of human involvement in their creation and use, it is unequivocally accepted as a basic assumption in Tibetan cultural contexts that objects are powerful when they possess a concentration of "*jinlap*" (*byin rlabs*) and "*tu*" (*mthu*), which are most commonly rendered into English as "blessings" and "power," respectively. However,

Tibetans have often been at loggerheads over how, exactly, humans imbue such objects with "blessings" and "power"; whether objects become "imbued" at all and might instead be either the natural material manifestations of previous sainthood, or, on the contrary, inert props for the recollection and communication of doctrinal values; and what the range of their powers might include.

The tensions surrounding the human involvements with power objects is expressed well by the term "oath substance." Although the term is typically defined as "a material object that has been blessed/transformed/charged by mantra," the wider semantic range of "oath substance" in Tibet, particularly as it applies to the subset of Treasure substance, means that such objects are often regarded as extensions or materializations of awakened buddhas and bodhisattvas and thus treated in practice as though they possess their own transformational properties, above and beyond their subsequent ritual treatment.[49] The overlap between tantric power objects and medicinal substances is also telling in this regard—oath and Treasure substances often include a range of medicinal substances with healing properties that are believed to be intrinsic to their material make-up and therefore independent in large part from ritual treatment. And yet, both Treasure substances and medicinal substances, regardless of their intrinsic powers, are common focal points of ritual practice, the logic being that ritual practice can augment and concentrate their potencies, as well as channel them toward specific ends.

A primary factor that complicates further an accurate assessment of the efficacy of power objects is that the concepts of *jinlap* and *tu*—the active ingredients, as it were, in power objects—are far from transparent. For instance, "blessings" is a rather poor rendering for the combination of reciprocity and transformational power conveyed by the Tibetan term *jinlap* or its longer participial form, *jingyi lapa* (*byin gyis brlabs pa*). The terms *jinlap* and *jingyi lapa* were probably first used in Buddhist contexts as translations of the Sanskrit term *adhiṣṭhāna*, which has a semantic range that includes (1) "basis"; (2) "vow" and "resolve"; and, most salient for the present context, (3) "mastery" and "power."[50] However, the term *jinlap* is taken by Martin as having been rendered indirectly from the previous rendering of *adhiṣṭhāna* into Chinese as 加持 (*jia chi, kaji*).[51] Martin speculates that the Tibetan term might therefore be etymologized as "received" (*rlabs*) "by way of" (*gyis*) "giving" (*byin*), a set of notions that connotes well the relational and dynamic sense of transformational possibilities that emerges in encounters with objects said to possess *jinlap*. However, the term *jin* (*byin*) on its own seems to have already conveyed notions associated with "power," "charisma," "majesty," and "radiance" in earlier pre-Buddhist contexts, where it often appears alongside *tu* (*mthu*)—"power/force"—as an associated quality of persons, places, or things.[52]

Later Tibetan Buddhist discourses also tend to centrally frame these phrases in terms of power. *The Great Tibetan-Tibetan-Chinese Dictionary* offers the following doctrinal definition of the noun *jinlap*: "the capacity or power present within the object/content of Dharma that constitutes the path of a noble one."[53] This same dictionary defines the verbal sense of *jingyi lapa* more generally as "to be transformed by radiant energy into something powerful, or to cause power to enter and emerge."[54] Taken as separate entries, *jin* appears therein as "a capacity or power that can transform the attitude, perception, and so forth of others," while the noun *lap*, for its part, is defined as a "wave," or "degree of capacity or power."[55] Moreover, the verb *lopa* (*rlob pa*) appears therein as, "to give/do/make and to transform," with *jingi lopa* (*byin gyis rlob pa*) given as an example.[56]

Most idiomatic usages of *jinlap* construe it as overwhelmingly positive in nature—something that is highly sought after in interactions not only with powerful objects and places, but also in encounters with powerful people such as revered lamas and in engagements with powerful rituals like initiations. It can be observed in such interactions that *jinlap* is often likened to a stream or rain of divine ambrosia that flows vertically from above to anoint everything that falls under its influence.[57]

Nonetheless, there is also a considerable degree of moral ambiguity in the term. Another influential dictionary defines *jinlap* as "transformative power," whether it be a change for the better or the worse, in which case its English rendering as "blessing" would appear too limited in scope, and "power" or "empowerment" might be more fitting.[58]

Further along these lines, in addition to *jinlap* being defined in terms of transformative capacity and power, Tibetan Buddhist writers also directly use the word "*tu*" (*mthu*) alongside it as a related property that such objects are said to possess or acquire.[59] The term *tu* is primarily defined as "force" (*stobs*) but has the secondary meaning of "black magic" or "sorcery" (*ngan sngags*, literally, "evil mantra"); this may mark a transition between the general meaning of power as the ability to simply make an impact and its more restricted sense as the ability to exert coercive or destructive power over others.[60] These Tibetan senses of the term *tu* predate its usages in Buddhist texts.[61] It stands to reason, then, that the term first entered Buddhist contexts as a rendering for a range of Sanskrit lexical items—*prabhāva, anubhāva, bala, sāmarthya, sthāma, pratibala, śakti,* and so on—which similarly convey various nuances of "power," "authority," "strength," "efficacy," "force," "ability," "might," "dynamism," "energy," and related qualities, typically, but not exclusively, as they are possessed by people, gods, or other living beings.[62] The term *prabhāva,* for its part, appears in a number of Mahāyāna Buddhist texts to refer to the "powers of a bodhisattva," which include their supernormal cognitions (Tib. *mngon par shes pa,* Skt. *abhijñā*), wonder-working (Tib. *rdzu 'phrul,* Skt. *ṛddhi*), and so on. Moreover, the Sanskrit term for "wonder-working," *ṛddhi,* has also sometimes been rendered by the Tibetan *tu,* indicating a slippage in the term's valances from powers, to abilities, to the public display of those potencies in the perspectives of others.[63] The other Sanskrit terms rendered by *tu,* however, tend to be more general in sense. Like their indigenous Tibetan counterpart, they acquire positive or negative connotations depending primarily on context.

Regardless of its positive or negative impact, something (or someone, or somewhere) imbued with *jinlap* and *tu*—a "receptacle of *jinlap*" (*byin rten*), as it were—has a contagious effect upon any person, place, or thing that comes into contact with it.[64] *Jinlap* and *tu* flow between entities and can therefore be acquired, concentrated, and channeled toward specific ends.

A THREE-FOLD TYPOLOGY OF POWER OBJECTS

When taking stock of the full range of power objects and how people variously interact with them inside and outside ritual precincts, their workings can be characterized in terms of ongoing oscillations between two ideal-typical poles. At one extreme are the objects of geological formations like potent springs or mountains; forms such as deity images "self-arisen" in stone; traces of previous masters' hands, feet, and bodies in the form of prints left in stone or metal; relics of past buddhas, bodhisattvas, or saints; and edible Treasure substances or substances with pronounced medicinal properties. These are treated as potent embodiments of power in and of themselves; that is, ritual treatment can only unleash, augment, and direct their power. These kinds of objects exert influence directly upon others and operate largely through physical proximity, touch, ingestion, or some other mode of contact.

At the opposite pole are materials used in initiation rituals and other ceremonies primarily as iconic or symbolic props for the representation and communication of extrinsic meanings. These materials are usually artifacts but may also be natural objects, such as crystals, grass, or other substances. These kinds of objects function primarily through the combined sensory media of vision and speech, where verbal exegesis tends to play a particularly active role.

A third category of material, the most prevalent variety, straddles these two categories. This type includes objects whose presumed intrinsic properties and the categories to which they belong may or may not mark them as somewhat efficacious, but which take on amplified powers through the mediations of complex ritual proceedings and interpretative operations. This category includes the statues, deity images, ritual implements, oblations, musical instruments, clothing articles, and other ritual paraphernalia that typically feature in Tibetan rituals and often undergo consecration before use. Objects are consecrated through a densely choreographed combination of contemplative exercises, mantra recitations, and physical operations, often featuring other sacred objects. Sometimes elements of such consecrations are also integral to their manufacture.

Tantric Buddhist rituals all use, to varying degrees, a combination of contemplative exercises (Skt. *samādhi*, Tib. *ting nge 'dzin*), linguistic formulas (Skt. *mantra*, Tib. *sngags*), and material substances (Skt. *dravya*, Tib. *rdzas*) as media through which the master of ceremonies can make manipulations in himself, others, and the wider world. Material substances, as the most tangible component of this triad, often serve as the key locus in the processes of concentrating and directing the power felt necessary to bring about such changes. This is true whether a ritual's explicit aim is pragmatic or transcendent in scope. This means that any ordinary object or setting can in theory be consecrated and imbued with efficacious power. And once so imbued, it can function to direct the flow of efficacious power into other persons, places, and things.

In light of these observations, there is heuristic value in provisionally demarcating three categories of objects:

1. Objects deemed powerful and efficacious in and of themselves
2. Objects with less *a priori* power, and which therefore require more diverse means to create or augment power during their manufacture, ritual treatment, and use
3. Initiation props, offering substances and other objects treated largely as devoid of intrinsic power and used primarily to condense meanings and communicate those discursively to others.

In this typology, the operations of discursive signification and intrinsic material power of categories three and one, respectively, operate in a sense as ideal types, occupying poles along a continuum of material power and immaterial meaning, where one or another mode is emphasized without negating the other but incorporating it. In practice, this means that the intrinsic power of objects never severs objects from their symbolic associations; at the same time, objects used primarily for their symbolic valences can also accrue and transmit power during ritual settings through physical contact. In other words, the roles of objects as symbols or power substances are not only commensurable but mutually interact to ensure the efficacy of rites that incorporate them.

It is also important to keep in mind that whatever else object-oriented rites may do, they are explicitly executed to "pacify" disease, "enrich" patrons, "repel" enemies, "initiate" students, and so on. The principles of efficacy at work in each ritual, even while emphasizing the ideal types of intrinsic material power or symbolic signification, also include a full spectrum of other mechanisms that run the gamut between these poles. These principles are as varied as directives about incorporation, ingestion, and contact; patterns of resemblance; category inclusion; aesthetic values; discursive knowledge; exegesis; and other elements. More often than not, several principles overlap or are compounded in a single object. This condensation of principles of efficacy in objects—regardless of whether physical contact or discursive signification is emphasized in each case—is a key factor that ensures that these rites can meet their intended aims. It also means that Tibetan Buddhists can interact with one and the same power object for a diversity of pragmatic and transcendent goals.

SOCIOPOLITICAL IMPLICATIONS

Objects of power have been influential not only within ritual precincts but also in the social and political dynamics that occur in their vicinity. The Jowo Śākyamuni statue, for instance, housed in the Jokang Temple in Lhasa, appears variously throughout Tibetan history in prophecies, biographies, histories, and other writings as a focal point of prognostications and affairs of state that implicate the fate of all Tibetans. On this account, the Jowo Śākyamuni statue has been aptly described as the national palladium of Tibet.[65] Interactions with and control over this and other power objects have been instrumental for Tibetan political leaders in securing the symbolic authority to rule Tibet.[66]

The force of power objects in sociopolitical affairs was particularly pronounced during the flurry of Tibetan Buddhist state formation that transpired in the middle of the 17th century with the founding within a single short decade of three different Tibetan Buddhist polities: the Ganden Potrang (Dga' ldan pho brang) in Central Tibet and the states of Sikkim ('Bras ljongs) and Bhutan ('Brug gzhung) bordering Tibet to the south.[67]

Power objects and rituals centered on them were instrumental for the Fifth Dalai Lama Ngawang Lozang Gyatso (1617–1682) in accruing the symbolic capital for the office of Dalai Lama and building the authority of the Ganden Potrang state that he and the successive Dalai Lama incarnations would head from 1642 to the middle of the 20th century. As the first Dalai Lama to occupy the position of leader of the Ganden Potrang state, the religious and political career of the Fifth Dalai Lama was focused in large part upon fusing within his persona the constellation of elements thought essential for the legitimacy of a Tibetan Buddhist ruler and his polity.[68] Architecture, art, ritual, and literature provided the sensory and discursive forms that would bind these elements together and impress their authenticity and power upon the Tibetan populace.[69] As part of this broader project, the Fifth Dalai Lama also inherited Treasure substances and other power objects through his multiple involvements with Tibet's contemporaneous Treasure revealers and implemented rites featuring them in the service of the state. Vestiges of these rituals continue in the ceremonies centered on the Fourteenth Dalai Lama Tenzin Gyatso.[70]

A similar formula of state creation also played out in Sikkim, as founding figures created in the 1640s and 1650s compelling narratives, temples, reliquaries, statues, murals, performances, and other images and objects that could connect people with one another under a rubric of shared values that would define the new state and its relationship with the territory and populace.[71] Here too, power objects were central: an effigy-focused exorcism rite and a Treasure vase–centered offering rite still feature today as the crowning calendrical rituals performed every Tibetan New Year at Sikkim's Drakar Tashiding, considered the very center of the kingdom's sacred landscape.[72]

The formation of the state of Bhutan in the 1640s follows a similar pattern. Here, however, it was the possession of a particularly revered relic—a "self-arisen" image of Avalokiteśvara in his Khasarpaṇi aspect that formed from the remains of a past master—that would secure for Bhutan's first leader, the Zhabtrung Ngawang Namgyel (1594–1651), the necessary legitimacy to install himself as ruler of the region.[73] The self-arisen Kharsarpaṇi image is honored to this day as the national palladium of Bhutan.

When reflecting back on the story of the Secret Potency from the vantage point of these later sociopolitical developments, it becomes immediately apparent how enduring the theme of power objects has been in Tibetan Buddhist conceptions of righteous kingship and rule.

REVIEW OF LITERATURE

The study of Tibetan Buddhist power objects is still in its infancy. A number of scholarly works broach the topic of power objects in Tibetan Buddhism but mostly only in passing and usually as ancillary to discussions of other broader topics. When scholars have treated power objects, their approach has been primarily ethnographic. Textual historical treatments have only emerged relatively recently, and these too are often accompanied by ethnographic observations.

The dearth of research focused on Tibetan Buddhist power objects and the primacy of the ethnographic approach in their study is probably because power objects are one of the most conspicuous but least theorized features of Tibetan Buddhist traditions. Even a casual visit to Tibetan Buddhist cultural regions invariably entails encounters with power objects and Tibetan interactions with them. Yet, aside from catalogues of the contents of specific statues and reliquaries or inventories of the holdings of specific hermitages and monasteries, there are relatively few primary textual sources in Tibetan that more broadly explicate their significance and use. Studying power objects textually thus calls for tracing them thematically through a wide swathe of genres—narrative, scriptural, liturgical, bibliographical, polemical, philosophical, and others—while attending to the sociohistorical contexts of their production and use. Ethnographic fieldwork is nonetheless an important complement to textual studies. Without firsthand observations it is difficult to get a clear sense of the many roles such objects play in the lives of real Tibetan Buddhists and textual passages about power objects might remain obscure.

As illustrated by the threefold typology presented in this article, the complex roles of power objects in the lives of Tibetan Buddhists are best understood when specific items are analyzed in relation to the full range of other meaningful ritual objects, sacra, and powerful substances at use in particular contexts. Moreover, Tibetan Buddhist treatments of power objects are typically adaptations of Indian Buddhist practices. Taking stock of particularly Tibetan conceptions of power objects thus also requires appreciation of Indian Buddhist precedents, exploration of indigenous Tibetan conceptions and practices, and comparison with how the neighboring lands of central, east, and southeast Asia have also appropriated Indian Buddhist power objects. The works of John Kieschnick and Fabio Rambelli provide particularly useful points of comparison with Tibetan Buddhist cultural regions by presenting broad, thematic considerations of how Buddhist attitudes and treatments of objects in China and Japan, respectively, variously influenced material cultural and historical developments within those two countries.[74] Moreover, Stanley Tambiah's work on the cult of Buddhist amulets in Thailand is an important potential inspiration for analysis of the roles of amulets in Tibetan cultural regions, where, like Thailand, amulets are ubiquitous.[75] However, with few minor exceptions notwithstanding, the cult of amulets in Tibetan Buddhism has thus far received nearly no sustained scholarly attention.[76]

Owing to their centrality in Buddhist practice, there have been a number of important studies of relics, reliquaries, and images in Indian Buddhism and other Asian Buddhist contexts that have aided significantly in the understanding of Tibetan Buddhist power objects.[77] The first scholarly publications focused squarely on power objects in Tibetan Buddhism have followed suit to produce textual and ethnographic studies of how relics, reliquaries, and associated consecration rituals are conceptualized and performed in Himalayan societies. The works of Yael Bentor and Martin were pioneering in this regard, offering a range of considerations of how Tibetans viewed and used relics and reliquaries in a variety of contexts.[78] As an extension of this early interest, researchers have also begun to bring scholarly attention to relic pills and other edible concentrations of power. Moreover, owing to the prominent roles of power objects in Tibetan Buddhist sociopolitical affairs, these dynamics have also received some attention by historians of Tibetan Buddhist state formation.

Despite the scarcity of studies focused squarely on power objects, there is a cluster of topics in the study of Tibetan Buddhism that touch upon many of the same themes. For instance, studies of ritual, pilgrimage, and medicine in Tibetan Buddhist societies sometimes address issues related to the study of power objects, such as conceptions of material efficacy and the relationships between powerful objects and human mediations and interactions.

Since power objects tend to feature in rituals, studies of Tibetan Buddhist ritual have shed light on the nature and role of power objects in Tibetan Buddhist societies. These studies were initially ethnographic in scope. Only relatively recently has ritual emerged as a more common topic of study from a textual perspective too.[79] Nonetheless, whether textual or ethnographic in approach, most studies of Tibetan rituals tend to treat ritual objects and accoutrements only in passing and purely in descriptive terms, without considering the broader roles they play in Tibetan societies, inside and outside ritual settings.

Ethnographic and textual studies of Tibetan Buddhist pilgrimage have also yielded some insights into the workings of power objects. These too were purely ethnographic at first but have since been combined with textual approaches to yield rich results. However, studies of pilgrimage practices in Tibetan Buddhist societies typically focus only on the "abodes" of pilgrimage sites and tend therefore to treat these in relative isolation from the wider phenomenon of power objects.

The study of Tibetan medicine has also been a promising area through which to tangentially explore broader conceptions and treatments of Tibetan Buddhist power objects. One setback, however, is that with some notable exceptions medicine in Tibet is often treated in relative isolation from the fuller range of fields of knowledge concerned with power objects.[80] Yet, in Tibetan Buddhist cultural contexts medicine is often embedded in logics that also pertain to tantric practice as a whole, in which the intrinsic material efficacy of objects can be augmented (or depleted) through human ritual and contemplative mediations. Traditional Tibetan medicine thus often operates alongside other curative power objects, like reliquaries, consecrated longevity pills, and the like. In local contexts these things all tend to circulate together within a local "health-care system," where Tibetan medicine can operate in conjunction with astrology, oracular healing, Buddhist rituals and doctrine, allopathic medicine, and perhaps other models of embodiment, pathology, and healing.[81]

FURTHER READING

STUDIES THAT FOCUS ON POWER OBJECTS IN TIBETAN BUDDHISM

Bentor, Yael. "On the Indian Origins of the Tibetan Practice of Depositing Relics and *dhāraṇīs* in Stūpas and Images." *Journal of the American Oriental Society* 115, no. 2 (1995): 248–261.

Bentor, Yael. *Consecration of Images and Stupas in Indo-Tibetan Tantric Buddhism*. Leiden, The Netherlands: E. J. Brill, 1996.

Cantwell, Cathy. "The Medicinal Accomplishment (*sman sgrub*) Practice in the Dudjom *Meteoric Iron Razor* (*gnam lcags spu gri*) Tradition: Reflections on the Ritual and Meditative Practice at a Monastery in Southern Bhutan." *Journal of the Oxford Centre for Buddhist Studies* 8 (2015): 49–95.

Cuevas, Bryan. "Illustrations of Human Effigies in Tibetan Ritual Texts: With Remarks on Specific Anatomical Figures and Their Possible Iconographic Source." *Journal of the Royal Asiatic Society* (Third Series) 21, no. 1 (January 2011): 73–97.

Diemberger, Hildegard. "Holy Books as Ritual Objects and Vessels of Teaching in the Era of the 'Further Spread of the Doctrine' (*bsTan pa yang dar*)." In *Revisiting Rituals in a Changing Tibetan World*. Edited by Katia Buffetrille, 9–42. Leiden, The Netherlands: Brill, 2012.

Dokhampa, Rigzin N. "Origins of the Bumchu (bum chu) of Drakar Tashiding (Brag dkar bKra shis sdings)." *Bulletin of Tibetology* 39, no 1. (May 2003): 25–30.

Garrett, Frances. "The Alchemy of Accomplished Medicine (*sman sgrub*): Situating the Yuthok Heart Essence (G.yu thog snying thig) in Literature and History." *Journal of Indian Philosophy* 37 (2009): 207–230.

Garrett, Frances. "Eating Letters in the Tibetan Treasure Tradition." *Journal of the International Association of Buddhist Studies* 32, no. 1–2 (2010): 85–114.

Garrett, Frances. "Tapping the Body's Nectar: Gastronomy and Incorporation in Tibetan Literature." *History of Religions* 49, no. 3 (February 2010): 300–326.

Gayley, Holly. "Ontology of the Past and Its Materialization in Tibetan Treasures." In *The Invention of Sacred Tradition*. Edited by James R. Lewis and Olav Hammer, 213–239. Cambridge, UK and New York: Cambridge University Press, 2007.

Gayley, Holly. "Soteriology of the Senses in Tibetan Buddhism." *Numen* 54 (2007): 459–499.

Gentry, James Duncan. *Power Objects in Tibetan Buddhism: The Life, Writings, and Legacy of Sokdokpa Lodrö Gyeltsen*. Boston and Leiden, The Netherlands: Brill, 2017.

Germano, David, and Kevin Trainor, eds. *Embodying the Dharma: Buddhist Relic Veneration in Asia*. Albany: State University of New York, 2004.

Loseries-Leick, Andreas. "The Use of Human Skulls in Tibetan Rituals." In *Tibetan Studies: Proceedings of the 5th Seminar of the International Association for Tibetan Studies, Narita 1989*. Vol. 1. Edited by Shōren Ihara and Zuihō Yamaguchi, 159–173. Narita-shi: Naritasan Shinshoji, 1992.

Martin, Daniel. "Crystals and Images from Bodies, Hearts and Tongues from Fire: Points of Relic Controversy from Tibetan History." In *Tibetan Studies: Proceedings of the 5th Seminar of the International Association for Tibetan Studies, Narita 1989*. Vol. 1. Edited by Shōren Ihara and Zuihō Yamaguchi, 183–191. Narita-shi: Naritasan Shinshoji, 1992.

Martin, Daniel. "Pearls from Bones: Relics, Chortens, Tertons and the Signs of Saintly Death in Tibet." *Numen* 41 (1994): 273–324.

Martin, Daniel. "Tables of Contents (*dKar chag*)." In *Tibetan Literature: Studies in Genre*. Edited by José Cabezón and Roger Jackson, 500–514. Ithaca, NY: Snow Lion, 1996.

Mullard, Saul. "Brag dkar bkra shis sdings kyi sku 'bum: The Text, the Author, the Stupa and Its Importance in the Formation of Religious Politics in Sikkim." *Bulletin of Tibetology* 39, no. 1 (2003): 13–24.

Skorupski, Tadeusz. *Tibetan Amulets*. Bangkok: White Orchid Books, 1983.

STUDIES OF BROADER TOPICS THAT TOUCH UPON POWER OBJECTS AND RELATED ISSUES

HISTORY

Sørensen, Per K., and Guntram Hazod, in cooperation with Tsering Gyalbo. *Rulers on the Celestial Plain: Ecclesiastic and Secular Hegemony in Medieval Tibet; A Study of Tshal Gung-thang*. 2 vols. Veröffentlichungen zur Sozialanthropologie 361. Vienna: Verlag der Österreichischen Akademie der Wissenschaften, 2007.

RITUAL

Beyer, Stephan. *The Cult of Tārā: Magic and Ritual in Tibet*. Berkeley, CA: University of California Press, 1978.

Cabezón, José, ed. *Tibetan Ritual*. Oxford and New York: Oxford University Press, 2010.

Garret, Francis, et al. "Narratives of Hospitality and Feeding in Tibetan Ritual." *Journal of the American Academy of Religion* 81, no. 2 (June 2013): 491–515.

Kind, Marietta. *Mendrub: A Bönpo Ritual for the Benefit of All Living Beings and for the Empowerment of Medicine Performed in Tsho, Dolpo*. Kathmandu: Vajra Publications, 2012.

Kohn, Richard J. *Lord of the Dance: The Mani Rimdu Festival in Tibet and Nepal*. Albany: State University of New York Press, 2001.

Nebesky-Wojkowitz, Réne de. *Demons and Oracles of Tibet*. Delhi: Book Faith India, 1998.

Ortner, Sherry B. *Sherpas through Their Rituals*. Cambridge, UK: Cambridge University Press, 1978.

Stablein, William. "The *Mahākālatantra*: A Theory of Ritual Blessings and Tantric Medicine." PhD diss., Columbia University, 1975.

PILGRIMAGE

Huber, Toni. *The Cult of Pure Crystal Mountain: Popular Pilgrimage and Visionary Landscape in Southeast Tibet*. New York: Oxford University Press, 1999.

Huber, Toni. "Putting the Gnas back into Gnas-Skor: Rethinking Tibetan Buddhist Pilgrimage Practice." In *Sacred Spaces and Powerful Places in Tibetan Culture: A Collection of Essays*. Edited by Toni Huber, 77–104. Dharamshala: Library of Tibetan Works and Archives, 1999.

Huber, Toni. *The Holy Land Reborn: Pilgrimage and the Tibetan Reinvention of Buddhist India*. Chicago: University of Chicago Press, 2003.

McKay, Alex, ed. *Pilgrimage in Tibet*. Richmond, UK: Curzon Press, 1998.

MEDICINE

Adams, Vincanne, Mona Schrempf, and Sienna Craig. *Medicine between Science and Religion: Explorations on Tibetan Grounds*. Oxford and New York: Berghahn Books, 2010.

Craig, Sienna. *Healing Elements: Efficacy and the Social Ecologies of Tibetan Medicine*. Berkeley, CA: University of California Press, 2012.

Craig, Sienna R., and Barbara Gerke. "Naming and Forgetting: Sowa Rigpa and the Territory of Asian Medical Systems." *Medical Anthropology Theory* 3, no. 2 (2016): 87–122.

Gyatso, Janet. *Being Human in a Buddhist World: An Intellectual History of Medicine in Early Modern Tibet*. New York: Columbia University Press, 2015.

NOTES

1. Dudjom Rinpoche, *The Nyingma School of Tibetan Buddhism*, trans. Gyurme Dorje and Matthew Kapstein (Boston: Wisdom Publications, 1991), 508–509.
2. Sam Van Schaik, "A New Look at the Tibetan Invention of Writing," *Old Tibetan Documents Online Monograph Series* 3 (2011): 46.
3. Gregory Schopen, "The Phrase 'sa pṛthivīpradeśaś caityabhūto bhavet' in the *Vajracchedikā*," in *Figments and Fragments of Mahāyāna Buddhism in India: More Collected Papers* (Honolulu: University of Hawaii Press, 2005), 25–62.
4. Schopen, "The Phrase."
5. Kevin Trainor, *Relics, Ritual and Representation* (Cambridge, UK: Cambridge University Press, 1997).
6. Schopen traces this tension and cites the *Saddharmapuṇḍarīka-sūtra* (Lotus Sutra) as the classic formulation of its resolution. Schopen, "The Phrase," 41.
7. Paul Demiéville, *Buddhism and Healing: Demiéville's Article "Byō" from Hōbōgirin*, trans. Mark Tatz (Lanham, MD, New York, and London: University Press of America, 1985), 46–50. For a detailed discussion of this theme as it appears in Śāntideva's *Śikṣāsamuccaya*, see Susanne Mrozik, *Virtuous Bodies: The Physical Dimensions of Morality in Buddhist Ethics* (Oxford and New York: Oxford University Press, 2007), 37–59.
8. See, for instance, David Gray, *The Cakrasamvara Tantra (The Discourse of Śrī Heruka) (Śrīherukābhidhāna): A Study and Annotated Translation* (New York: American Institute of Buddhist Studies, 2007); and G. W. Farrow and I. Menon, *The Concealed Essence of the Hevajra Tantra with the Commentary Yogaratnamala* (Delhi: Motilal Banarsidass, 1992). See also Wiesiek Mical, trans., "The Tantra of Caṇḍamahāroṣaṇa" (2006) and the many other tantras that are beginning to appear in English translation courtesy of *84000: Translating the Words of the Buddha*.
9. For a particularly rich study of Tibetan reliquaries and their consecration rituals, see Yael Bentor, *Consecration of Images and Stupas in Indo-Tibetan Tantric Buddhism* (Leiden, The Netherlands: E. J. Brill, 1996).
10. For details about this practice and historical controversies among Tibetans about what counts as a bona fide relic, see Daniel Martin, "Pearls from Bones: Relics, Chortens, Tertons and the Signs of Saintly Death in Tibet," *Numen* 41 (1994): 273–324; and Daniel Martin, "Crystals and Images from Bodies, Hearts and Tongues from Fire: Points of Relic Controversy from Tibetan History," in *Tibetan Studies: Proceedings of the 5th Seminar of the International Association for Tibetan Studies, Narita 1989*, vol. 1, ed. Shōren Ihara and Zuihō Yamaguchi (Narita-shi: Naritasan Shinshoji, 1992), 183–191.
11. For a presentation and analysis of the catalogue of a recently constructed reliquary, see Dan Martin, "Tables of Contents (*dKar chag*)," in *Tibetan Literature: Studies in Genre*, ed. José Cabezón and Roger Jackson (Ithaca, NY: Snow Lion, 1996), 500–514. For a brief discussion of Indian precedents for the

close association between Buddha's physical remains and his bequeathal of the dharma; the role of this relationship in the formation of the notion of *dharmakāya*; and the cult of relics, stupas, and *dhāraṇīs*, see Yael Bentor, "On the Indian Origins of the Tibetan Practice of Depositing Relics and Dhāraṇis in Stūpas and Images," *Journal of the American Oriental Society* 115, no. 2 (April–June 1995): 248–261.

12. Susan Whitfield, *Silk, Slaves, and Stupas: Material Culture of the Silk Road* (Oakland: University of California Press, 2018).
13. Whitfield, *Silk, Slaves, and Stupas*, 85.
14. Van Schaik, "A New Look," 47–48.
15. For details on how these terms function in traditional Tibetan presentations of tantric Buddhist deity yoga practice, see Shechen Gyaltsap IV and Kunkyen Tenpe Nyima, *Vajra Wisdom: Deity Practice in Tibetan Buddhism*, trans. Dharmachakra Translation Committee (Boston: Shambhala, 2012). Here these terms are rendered as the "support" or "supportive" celestial palace and the "supported" deities, respectively.
16. Gyaltsap and Nyima, *Vajra Wisdom*.
17. James Duncan Gentry, *Power Objects in Tibetan Buddhism: The Life, Writings, and Legacy of Sokdokpa Lodrö Gyeltsen* (Boston and Leiden, The Netherlands: Brill, 2017), 171–290.
18. Martin, "Tables of Contents," 504.
19. Bentor, *Consecration of Images*, 56–58.
20. John Vincent Bellezza, *Spirit-Mediums, Sacred Mountains and Related Bon Textual Traditions in Upper Tibet: Calling Down the Gods* (Boston and Leiden, The Netherlands: Brill, 2005).
21. Toni Huber, "Putting the Gnas Back into Gnas skor: Rethinking Tibetan Pilgrimage Practice," in *Sacred Spaces and Powerful Places in Tibetan Culture: A Collection of Essays*, ed. Toni Huber (Dharamshala: Library of Tibetan Works and Archives, 1999), 77–104.
22. Toni Huber, *The Cult of Pure Crystal Mountain: Popular Pilgrimage and Visionary Landscape in Southeast Tibet* (New York: Oxford University Press, 1999).
23. Huber, *Cult of Pure Crystal Mountain*, 39–57.
24. Bkra shis rgya mtsho et al., *Gsang rnying rgyan dang rol mo'i bstan bcos*, ed. Bu byung dbang 'dus (Lhasa: Bod ljongs bod yig dpe snying skrun khang, 1996), 46–98.
25. Bkra shis rgya mtsho et al., *Gsang rnying rgyan*, 69–77.
26. Bkra shis rgya mtsho et al., *Gsang rnying rgyan*, 77–88.
27. Bkra shis rgya mtsho et al., *Gsang rnying rgyan*, 89–91.
28. Bkra shis rgya mtsho et al., *Gsang rnying rgyan*, 92.
29. Krang dbyi sun et al., *Bod rgya tshig mdzod chen mo* (Chengdu: Mi rigs dpe skrun khang, 1993), 2507.
30. Bentor, "On the Indian Origins."
31. Martin, "Tables of Contents."
32. The compound *dam rdzas* is an abbreviation of the full form *dam tshig gi rdzas*.
33. Although there is no systematic or consistent list of tantric *samayas* in Indian sources, Tibet's Nyingma school generally stipulates twenty-eight *samayas*, divided into three main and twenty-five subsidiary *samayas*, whereas Tibet's New Schools generally have fourteen main and eight subsidiary *samayas*, which protect against a corresponding number of downfalls (Sam van Schaik, "The Limits of Transgression: The *Samaya* Vows of Mahāyoga," unpublished paper). For more on tantric *samaya* from a relatively recent traditional source, see Jamgön Kongtrul Lodrö Tayé, *The Treasury of Knowledge Book Five: Buddhist Ethics*, trans. International Translation Committee (Ithaca, NY: Snow Lion, 2003), 215–306.
34. Jacob Dalton, *The Taming of the Demons: Violence and Liberation in Tibetan Buddhism* (New Haven, CT and London: Yale University Press, 2011), 60–61.
35. This role of "*samaya* water" (*dam tshig gi chu*) is spelled out with great clarity in the majority of "initiation liturgies" (*dbang chog*) belonging to the "highest yoga tantra class" (*bla med rgyud sde*).

36. Despite such variations, Christian Wedemeyer states that the five fleshes, or five meats, as he translates the term, typically include beef, dog, elephant, horse, and human flesh, and the five ambrosias tend to include human feces, urine, blood, semen, and marrow or flesh. See Christian Wedemeyer, *Making Sense of Tantric Buddhism: History, Semiology, and Transgression in the Indian Traditions* (New York: Columbia University Press, 2013), 106.
37. "*dam tshig gi rdzas te sngags kyis byin gyis brlabs pa'i dngos po*," in Krang dbyi sun et al., *Bod rgya tshig mdzod chen mo*, 1248.
38. Although this refers to Treasure substances in particular, and not to the texts that these typically accompany, the rationale of the Treasure tradition as a whole can be characterized in terms of an emphasis on materiality, a distributed sense of agency, and the pronounced presence of political overtones. See Gentry, *Power Objects*, 46–68. To account for this material-inflected emphasis of Tibetan Treasure traditions, Holly Gayley has insightfully termed Treasures "materializations of the past." See Holly Gayley, "Ontology of the Past and Its Materialization in Tibetan Treasures," in *The Invention of Sacred Tradition*, ed. James R. Lewis and Olav Hammer (Cambridge, UK and New York: Cambridge University Press, 2007), 213–239.
39. Although this constitutes the general scenario for most Treasures, the Nyingma school also includes among its ranks other Treasure concealers, such as Songtsen Gampo, Vimalamitra (8th century), Yeshé Tsogyel, and Prince Mutri Tsenpo, among others. See Janet Gyatso, "The Logic of Legitimation in the Tibetan Treasure Tradition," *History of Religions* 33, no. 2 (November 1993): 98n2. Moreover, Treasures are not just the preserve of the Nyingma school. They also feature among the authoritative teachings of other schools, including Bön (Gyatso, "Logic of Legitimation," 98n2). For a detailed traditional account of the Nyingma school's Treasure tradition, see Tulku Thondup Rinpoche, *Hidden Teachings of Tibet: An Exploration of the Terma Tradition of Tibetan Buddhism*, ed. Harold Talbott (Boston: Wisdom Publications, 1986).
40. Gentry, *Power Objects*, 56–133.
41. Gentry, *Power Objects*, 291–356.
42. Gentry, *Power Objects*, 259–284 and 296–316; and Holly Gayley, "Soteriology of the Senses in Tibetan Buddhism," *Numen* 54 (2007): 459–499.
43. Gentry, *Power Objects*, 171–290.
44. Lha btsun nam mkha' 'jigs med, "Lo rgyus rin po che 'od zer stong gi phreng ba," in *Sprin gyi thol glu*, vol. 1 (Gangtok: S. N., 1975), 176.3–4.
45. Padma gar dbang blo gros mtha' yas pa'i sde, "Thugs sgrub bar chad kun sel las/Longs sku 'dro 'dul gyi las rim grol ba gcu gcig gi lag len gsal byed ngo mtshar rgya mtsho," in *mChog gling gter gsar*, vol. 2 (*ka*) (Paro: Lama Pema Tashi, 1982–1986), 253–291.
46. Lha btsun nam mkha' 'jigs med, "Lo rgyus rin po che," 177.4–178.4.
47. Skal bzang and Rgyal po, *Zha lu dgon gyi lo rgyus* (Lhasa: Bod ljongs mi dbang dpe skrun khang, 1987), 34–42. See also Benjamin Wood, *The Jeweled Fish Hook: Monastic Exemplarity in the Shalu Abbatial History* (PhD diss., University of Toronto, 2012) for more on this aspect of Shalu monastery's institutional prestige.
48. Birgit Meyer, "Introduction: From Imagined Communities to Aesthetic Formations; Religious Mediations, Sensational Forms, and Styles of Binding," in *Aesthetic Formations: Media, Religion, and the Senses*, ed. Birgit Meyer (New York: Palgrave Macmillan, 2009), 1–28.
49. "*dam tshig gi rdzas*," in Krang dbyi sun et al., *Bod rgya tshig mdzod chen mo*, 1248.
50. Ryōzaburō Sakaki, ed., *Bonzō kanwa shiyaku taikō Mahāvyutpatti*, 2 vols. (Kyōto: Shingonshū Kyōto Daigaku, 1916–1925), 1: entries 1580–1584, 4264, and 4305; and J. S. Negi, *Tibetan-Sanskrit Dictionary* (Sarnath: Central Institute of Higher Tibetan Studies, 1993), 9:3827 and 3834 also records *jinlap* (*byin rlabs*) and *jingyi lapa* (*byin gyis rlabs pa*) as translations for the Sanskrit *adhiṣṭhāna*. See also Franklin

Edgerton, *Buddhist Hybrid Sanskrit Grammar and Dictionary*, 2 vols. (Delhi: Motilal Banarsidass, 1970), 2:12–13.

51. Martin, "Pearls from Bones," 274. Martin's source for this judgment is Hisao Inagaki, "Kūkai's Sokushin-Jōbutsu-Gi (Principle of Attaining Buddhahood with the Present Body)," *Asia Major* 17, no. 2 (1972): 194. Inagaki describes how Chinese translators rendered the Sanskrit term *adhiṣṭhāna* into the two-character term 加持 (*jia chi*), whose first character can mean "to support," "to add," or "to apply," and whose second character can mean "to hold," "to control," "to preserve," and "basis." Inagaki states that this rendering signals, according to the interpretation of Kūkai, both the transformational "power on the part of the Buddha and also the response to and reception of it on the part of the practitioner." Although this interpretation appears to loosely accord well with general Tibetan understandings of how *jinlap* functions, as an etymology it demands that one follow Martin and take *jin* (*byin*) as the Tibetan verb "to give, add, mix," a gloss that conflicts with Tibetan treatments of the term (see the following) as it appears in the compound *jinlap*. Furthermore, even if Martin's etymology is in fact correct, the similarity between the Chinese and Tibetan terms could also reflect a common "meaning translation" inherited from Indian exegetes instead of a Tibetan rendering of a Chinese translation.
52. Rolf A. Stein, *Rolf Stein's Tibetica Antiqua, with Additional Materials*, trans. and ed. Arthur P. McKeown (Leiden, The Netherlands and Boston: Brill, 2010), 68–71, 86, 93, 113–114, 126, 138, 156, 239.
53. "*byin rlabs/'phags pa'i lam chos kyi don gang yin pa la gnas pa'i nus pa'am mthu/*," in Krang dbyi sun et al., *Bod rgya tshig mdzod chen mo*, 1885.
54. "*byin gyis brlabs pa/gzi byin gyis nus ldan du sgyur ba'am/nus pa 'jug par byed pa dang/thon par byed pa/*," in Krang dbyi sun et al., *Bod rgya tshig mdzod chen mo*, 1884.
55. "*gzhan gyi bsam pa dang snang ba sogs bsgyur thub pa'i nus pa'am mthu/*," in Krang dbyi sun et al., *Bod rgya tshig mdzod chen mo*, 1884; and "(1) *chu sogs 'gul skabs byung ba'i gnyer ma/* (2) *nus pa dang/mthu stobs kyi tshad/*," in Krang dbyi sun et al., *Bod rgya tshig mdzod chen mo*, 2733–2734.
56. "*gnang ba dang bsgyur ba/*," in Krang dbyi sun et al., *Bod rgya tshig mdzod chen mo*, 2741.
57. Martin Mills, *Identity, Ritual and State in Tibetan Buddhism: The Foundations of Authority in Gelukpa Monasticism* (London and New York: RoutledgeCurzon, 2003), 160, 180–181.
58. Padma Rdo rje et al., *Dag yig gsar bsgrigs* (Xining: Mtsho sngon mi rigs dpe skrun khang, 2014), 534. More specifically, it defines the compound *jinlap* primarily as "a term for power, capacity, and so forth that can transform the attitude, perception and so forth of others" (*gzhan gyi bsam pa dang snang ba sogs bsgyur thub pa'i mthu dang nus pa sogs kyi ming*). It also gives the exact same definition for the term *jin* (p. 534) on its own and offers examples indicating that it can signal either positive or negative transformations (*mi ngan pas byin gyis brlabs/mi gzi byin can/lus la gzi byin chags pa zhes pa lta bu*). Further along these lines, it defines the verb *lob* as a transitive, volitional verb meaning, "to transform [something] into something else" (*gzhan du bsgyur ba*; p. 760). In contrast, Dung dkar Blo bzang 'phrin las, *Dung dkar tshig mdzod chen mo* (Beijing: Krung go'i bod rig pa dpe skrun khang, 2002), 1487, defines *jinlap* as unequivocally positive in impact: "*jin* is capacity and *lap* is the transformation of something negative into something positive, such that based on that capacity, something negative transforms into something positive" (*byin ni nus pa dang rlabs ni ngan pa bzang por 'gyur ba ste nus pa de la brten nas ngan pa bzang por 'gyur ba la'o*). Thub bstan bsam sgrub, *Mdo gzhung chen mo tshig mdzod* (Delhi: Sherig Parkhang, 2005), 491, alternatively defines *byin rlabs* (and *byin gyis brlabs pa*) as, "Charisma/majesty that transforms or renders the mind-stream workable" and offers the following doctrinal etymology (*sgra bshad*): "'*jin*' means charisma and '*lap*' means to transform, thus signaling that the mind-stream of disciples is transformed or rendered workable through the charisma of the object of refuge" (*gzi byin sgyur ba'am/shes rgyud las rung du byed pa/sgra bshad ni/byin zhes pa gzi byin dang/rlabs zhes pa sgyur ba'i don yin pas/skyabs yul gyi gzi byin gyis gdul bya'i shes rgyud sgyur ba'am las rung byed pa'i don yin/*). Moreover, it gives

the secondary definition of "blessed/empowered substance" (*byin gyis brlabs pa'i rdzas*), without explaining how the cognitive sense of the primary definition might relate to material substance.

59. Objects are often described as possessing *jinlap* and *tu*. Alternatively, *tu* is used in the compound *jinthu* (*byin mthu*), which is parsed as "the force or potency of *jinlap*." "*byin labs kyi stobs sam nus pa*," in Krang dbyi sun et al., *Bod rgya tshig mdzod chen mo*, 1884.
60. Krang dbyi sun et al., *Bod rgya tshig mdzod chen mo*, 1210. For a discussion of *tu* as "black magic" or "sorcery," see Nicolas Sihlé, *Rituels bouddhiques de pouvoir et de violence: La figure du tantriste tibétain* (Turnhout, Belgium: Brepols, 2013), 217–219.
61. Stein, *Tibetica Antiqua*, 68–71, 86, 113–114, 156, 156, 239.
62. Sakaki, *Bonzo kanwa*, 1:227, 653, 5153, 5154, 5155, 9334, 9367; and Negi, *Tibetan-Sanskrit Dictionary*, 4:2110.
63. Negi, *Tibetan-Sanskrit Dictionary*, 4:2110.
64. "*byin rten/byin rlabs kyi rten/*," in Krang dbyi sun et al., *Bod rgya tshig mdzod chen mo*, 1884.
65. Per K. Sørensen, "Control over the lHa-sa Mandala Zone: Geo-Political Schemes, National Monuments, Flood Control Politics and Ideological Battlefield," in *Rulers on the Celestial Plain: Ecclesiastic and Secular Hegemony in Medieval Tibet: A Study of Tshal Gung-thang*, by Per K. Sørensen and Guntram Hazod, in cooperation with Tsering Gyalbo, Veröffentlichungen zur Sozialanthropologie 361 (Vienna: Verlag der Österreichischen Akademie der Wissenschaften, 2007), 2:401–552.
66. Sørensen, "Control over the lHa-sa Mandala Zone."
67. For comparisons between these state formations, see John Ardussi, "Formation of the State of Bhutan ('Brug gzhung) in the 17th Century and Its Tibetan Antecedents," in *The Relationship between Religion and State (chos srid zung 'brel) in Traditional Tibet: Proceedings of a Seminar Held in Lumbini, Nepal, March 2000*, ed. Christoph Cüppers (Lumbini: Lumbini International Research Institute, 2004), 33–48.
68. For a detailed account of the Fifth Dalai Lama's life and literary works, see Kurtis R. Schaeffer, "The Fifth Dalai Lama," in *The Dalai Lamas: A Visual History*, ed. Martin Brauen (Chicago: Serindia, 2005), 64–91.
69. For a general discussion of the role in this process of rituals, narratives, and architectural forms associated with Avalokiteśvara and the Tibetan dynastic period, see Derek F. Maher, "The Dalai Lamas and State Power," *Religion Compass* 1–2 (2007): 266–267. The function of rituals and festivals centering upon the Fifth Dalai Lama in the Ganden Potrang government's efforts to legitimate the Dalai Lama's rule over Tibet is explored by Yumiko Ishihama, "On the Dissemination of the Belief in the Dalai Lama as a Manifestation of the Bodhisattva Avalokiteśvara," in *The History of Tibet: The Medieval Period*, ed. Alex McKay (London: RoutledgeCurzon, 2003), 538–553; and Kurtis Schaeffer, "Ritual, Festival, and Authority under the Fifth Dalai Lama," in *Power, Politics and the Reinvention of Tradition: Tibet in the Seventeenth and Eighteenth Centuries*, ed. Bryan J. Cuevas and Kurtis R. Schaeffer (Leiden, The Netherlands: Brill, 2006), 187–202. For a discussion focused on the role of monumental architecture in this process, particularly the Potala Palace of Lhasa, see Anne Chayet, "The Potala, Symbol of the Power of the Dalai Lamas," in *Lhasa in the Seventeenth Century: The Capital of the Dalai Lamas*, ed. Françoise Pommaret (Leiden, The Netherlands: Brill, 2003), 39–52.
70. One such vestige could be witnessed in Taklung Tsetrül Shedrup Trinlé Nyinchezangpo (1926–2015), the hierarch of the Northern Treasure tradition and incarnation of Rindzin Gödem, regularly presiding over the public long-life ceremonies dedicated to the Fourteenth Dalai Lama Tendzin Gyatso until Taklung Tsetrül's death in 2015.
71. Saul Mullard, *Opening the Hidden Land: State Formation and the Construction of Sikkimese History* (Leiden, The Netherlands: Brill, 2012) relates copious details about how commissioning monumental sacred architecture and establishing regular ritual performances throughout Sikkim formed a major part of Sikkim's founding figures' efforts to create a Tibetan Buddhist kingdom.
72. Rigzin N. Dokhampa, "Origins of the Bumchu (bum chu) of Drakar Trashiding (Brag dkar bKra shis sdings)," *Bulletin of Tibetology* 39, no 1. (2003): 25–30. For more details on the long and storied history

of Tibetan lamas' involvements with Tashiding, see Mélenie Vandenhelsken, "Tibetan Masters and the Formation of the Sacred Site of Tashiding," *Bulletin of Tibetology* 42, nos. 1–2 (2006): 65–90.

73. Ardussi, "Formation of the State of Bhutan," 13.
74. John Kieschnick, *The Impact of Buddhism on Chinese Material Culture* (Princeton, NJ: Princeton University Press, 2003); and Fabio Rambelli, *Buddhist Materiality: A Cultural History of Objects in Japanese Buddhism* (Stanford, CA: Stanford University Press, 2007).
75. Stanley Tambiah, *The Buddhist Saints of the Forest and the Cult of Amulets* (Cambridge, UK: Cambridge University Press, 1984).
76. Notable exceptions include Gentry, *Power Objects*, 236–259; and Tadeusz Skorupski, *Tibetan Amulets* (Bangkok: White Orchid Books, 1983).
77. Important examples include Paul Mus, *Barabadur: Esquisse d'une histoire du bouddhisme fondée sur la critique archéologique des textes*, 2 vols. (Hanoi: Imprimerie d'Extreme-Orient, 1935); Anna Libera Dallapicccola and Stephanie Zingel-Avé Lallemant, eds., *The Stūpa: Its Religious, Historical, and Architectural Significance* (Wiesbaden: Steiner, 1980); John Strong, *The Legend of King Aśoka: A Study and Translation of the Aśokāvadāna* (Princeton, NJ: Princeton University Press, 1983); Gregory Schopen, "Burial 'Ad Sanctos' and the Physical Presence of the Buddha in Early Indian Buddhism: A Study in the Archaeology of Religions," *Religion* 17 (1987): 193–225; Daniel Boucher, "The *Pratītyasamutpādagāthā* and Its Role in the Medieval Cult of the Relics," *Journal of the International Association of Buddhist Studies* 14, no. 1 (1991): 1–27; Trainor, *Relics, Ritual*; and John Strong, *Relics of the Buddha* (Princeton, NJ: Princeton University Press, 2004).
78. Bentor, *Consecration of Images*; Bentor, "On the Indian Origins"; Martin, "Tables of Contents"; Martin, "Pearls from Bones"; and Martin, "Crystals and Images."
79. For a useful overview of Tibetan ritual and its study, see José Cabezón, ed. *Tibetan Ritual* (Oxford and New York: Oxford University Press, 2010).
80. For instance, Janet Gyatso, *Being Human in a Buddhist World: An Intellectual History of Medicine in Early Modern Tibet* (New York: Columbia University Press, 2015), offers insightful analysis of the role of tantric contemplative traditions in the historical development of Tibetan medicine.
81. Mills, *Identity, Ritual and State*, 168. Mills borrows his notion of "health-care system" from Arthur Kleinman, *Patients and Healers in the Context of Culture* (Berkeley, CA: University of California Press, 1980) and applies it to his fieldwork with Tibetan Buddhists in Ladakh.

James Duncan Gentry

TIBETAN MEDICINE AND ITS BUDDHIST CONTEXTS

HISTORICAL OVERVIEW

Tibetan medicine developed as a synthesis of Indian, Chinese, and Greco-Arab medical systems, within an overall Buddhist theoretical grounding. The multicultural character of Tibetan medicine is emphasized in Tibetan medical histories starting from the earliest extant exemplar of this genre, the Tibetan medical history by Cheje zangton shigpo (Che rje zhang ston zhig po), dating to the early 13th century. Cheje sets medical knowledge within what he terms "The Seven Schools" (*lugs bdun*), referring to both divine and human realms.[1] Within the human realm, the list refers to medical systems from: India, Kashmir, Urgyan (in present-day Pakistan), Nepal, Arabo-Persian (Stag gzig), Dolpo, Uighur (Hor), Tangut/Xixia (Me nyag), Khotan, Byzantium (Phrom), China, and Tibet.[2] Variations of this list became practically standard in subsequent Tibetan medical histories. Medical histories portray the earliest stage of Tibetan medicine as its most multicultural.

The earliest extant sources on Tibetan medicine come from what is known as the "library cave" in Dunhuang. These medical manuscripts, dating to the 9th or 10th century, are largely practice-oriented, but nevertheless include important information for understanding some of their theoretical assumptions. The main therapy that is mentioned in these early manuscripts is moxibustion (*me btsa'*, the heating of particular locations on the body), but there are also references to bloodletting, fumigation, massage, horn cupping, as well as uses of materia medica, mostly from plants, minerals, and animal substances.

The Four Treatises. The text known as *Four Treatises* (also known as *Four Tantras*, or *Gyushi/Rgyud bzhi*), thought by scholars to have been compiled in the 12th century, is regarded as the locus classicus of Tibetan medicine and has remained the core of its instruction in the 21st century. The *Gyushi* begins with an account of how the Buddha, manifesting as the Medicine Buddha, gave the teaching encompassed in the text. The origin and history of the *Four Treatises* have been the focus of heated debates in Tibet for centuries. Traditional views ascribe the text to the Medicine Buddha and claim it was written down in Sanskrit, then hidden inside a column of the Samye Monastery, to be found when the time was ripe for its teaching. According to this account, Drapa Ngonshe (Grwa pa Mngon shes) "found" the text and Yuthog Yonten Gonpo (G.yu thog yon tan mgon po) the younger recompiled it in its current form. Other views deny any Sanskrit original and ascribe the text to a Tibetan author—either the older or the younger Yuthog Yonten.

Scholars agree that the *Four Treatises* is a native Tibetan text that has incorporated and synthesized elements from the Indian, Chinese, and Greco-Arab medical systems, combined with a Buddhist theoretical grounding. The *Gyushi* presents the same medical doctrine from four different perspectives.

The *Four Treatises*, or *Four Tantras*, includes:

1. The *Root Tantra* (*Rtsa rgyud*)—a general outline in brief of the principles of Tibetan medicine, diagnosis, and treatments. It discusses the humors and humoral imbalances that give rise to illness.
2. The *Explanatory Tantra* (*Bshad rgyud*)—it elaborates on the theoretical basis of Tibetan medicine and discusses topics such as embryology, anatomy, channels of the body, pathology, diet and conduct, medications, external therapies, diagnosis, and medical ethics.
3. The *Instructional Tantra* (*Man ngag rgyud*)—it focuses on the practical application of medical theories and discusses specific treatments for particular illnesses.
4. The *Subsequent Tantra* (*Phyi ma rgyud*)—a further elaboration on diagnosis through pulse examination, urine analysis and observation of the tongue, the preparation of medicines, inner cleansing procedures, and discussion of external therapies, such as bloodletting, moxibustion, massage, and minor surgeries.

THE GOLDEN AGE OF TIBETAN MEDICINE

The 17th century was a period of great development of Tibetan medicine.

Under the rule of the Fifth Dalai Lama, Ngawang Lozang Gyatso (Ngag dbang blo bzang rgya mtsho, 1617–1682), and his regent, Desi Sangye Gyatso (Sde srid Sangs rgyas rgya mtsho, 1653–1705), who both had a keen interest in medicine, several monumental enterprises in the field of medicine took place. The first college specializing in medical training was established on the Iron Hill (Chagpori; Lcags po ri). The Fifth Dalai Lama also sought out medical experts from abroad and supported foreign medical scholars to translate new medical texts from India, both for his own well-being but also with a view of broadening Tibetan medicine's repertoire of diagnostic, therapeutic, surgical, and pharmacological tools.

The endeavors of the Fifth Dalai Lama were continued by his regent, Desi Sangye Gyatso. Sangye Gyatso composed the *Blue Beryl* (*Bai dūrya sngon po*), an important commentary of the *Gyushi*, and commissioned a set of seventy-nine medical paintings, whose purpose was to aid in the understanding and remembering of the content of the *Blue Beryl* and the *Gyushi*. Sangye Gyatso also composed a seminal work on the history of Tibetan medicine, the *Mirror of Beryl* (*Gso ba rig pa'i khog 'bugs*), as well as one on astral knowledge, the *White Beryl* (*Bai dūrya dkar po*).

TIBETO-MONGOL-BURYAT MEDICINE IN THE COURT OF THE RUSSIAN TSAR

A fascinating chapter in the history of Tibetan medicine is its adoption as part of military medicine in Saint Petersburg and among the Russian elite in the early 20th century. This transmission path illuminates how Tibetan medicine moved along with Tibetan Buddhism across cultures: from Tibet to Mongolia, from Mongolia to Buryatia (18th century), to Saint Petersburg (18th and 19th centuries), then on to Poland and Switzerland in the 20th century.[3]

This transmission began when Tibeto-Mongol medicine was transmitted along with Buddhism at the end of the 17th century to Buryatia, situated around Lake Baikal in southern Siberia. Sultim Badmayev (d. *c.* 1873), who studied Tibetan medicine in the Aginsky Datsan Buryat Buddhist monastery, became famous around 1850, after reportedly successfully treating an epidemic of typhoid among the Russian troops who were stationed in Buryatia. Sultim Badmayev was then invited to Saint Petersburg, where he not only received an important position in the military hospital, but also became godson of Tsar Alexander II, and established a private pharmacy and clinic in Saint Petersburg. His younger brother, Zhamsaran, soon joined him. Zhamsaran was baptized into the Russian Church as Pyotr Aleksandrovich Badmayev and became the godson of Alexander III, the tsar's son and heir. This allowed him to later become physician of the rich and powerful in Saint Petersburg. He also spearheaded the links with the Thirteenth Dalai Lama during the Great Game, via the Buryat tutor of the Dalai Lama, Agvan Dorzhiev.

Tibetan medicine continued to thrive in Saint Petersburg through the work of two of Pyotr Badmayev's nephews: Ossor Badmayev, later baptized as Nikolay Nikolayevich Badmayev, and Zhamyan Badmayev, later to be baptized as Vladimir Nikolayevich Badmayev, and both having Tsar Nikolay II as their godfather. Probably in 1917, Vladimir Nikolayevich Badmayev fled to Poland, where he renamed himself Wlodzimierz Badmajeff and became the physician of leaders and famous artists. Wlodzimierz Badmajeff positioned Tibetan medicine as an alternative to scientific biomedicine, as a holistic path toward a better life.

The Polish government legalized the production of his Tibetan herbal medications, but when Wlodzimierz Badmajeff died, Tibetan medicine died in Poland, too. A book by Cyrill

(Johannes) von Korvin-Krasinski (1905–1992), which was based on the knowledge of the Badmayev family, influenced the Swiss businessman Karl Lutz (1923–1995) and with the help of Wlodzimierz Badmajeff's son, Peter Badmajew (b. 1929), the Swiss pharmaceutical company Padma was established.[4] Padma AG has been an established company in Switzerland since 1969, producing herbal medicines and food supplements based on Tibetan medical formulas.

The 20th Century. The Thirteenth Dalai Lama (Thupten Gyatso, Thub bstan rgya mtsho, 1876–1933), following the example of the Fifth Dalai Lama, made important contributions toward promoting medical education. In 1916, he established the Mentsikhang (Institute of Medicine and Astrology) in central Lhasa. The Chagpori Medical College was destroyed by the People's Liberation Army (PLA) in March 1959. In 1961, following the Tibetan exile, a sister institute to Lhasa Mentsikhang was set up in Dharamshala. At the same time, the Lhasa Mentsikhang was officially incorporated into the Chinese communist healthcare system and from then on was increasingly biomedicalized. The Dharamshala Men-Tsee-Khang includes a Tibetan medical college, a clinic, a large pharmacy, a museum, and a translation department. In 1992, in commemoration of the Lhasa Chagpori, Trogawa Rinpoche (1931–2005) established the Chagpori Tibetan Medical Institute in Darjeeling, in northeast India. In 1994, Samdhong Rinpoche, then vice chancellor of the Central University for Tibetan Studies (CUTS, since renamed the Central Institute of Higher Tibetan Studies), established a department for the study of Tibetan medicine, a step that has been crucial in the official recognition of *Sowa Rigpa* in India.[5]

In the 21st Century. *Sowa Rigpa* is presently recognized as an integral part of national healthcare systems in China, Bhutan, Mongolia, and India. India was the latest addition to this list, when in 2010 the government of India officially recognized Tibetan medicine as an "Indian system of medicine," bringing to the fore important debates concerning issues of cultural heritage and minority politics.[6]

The globalization of Tibetan medicine in the 21st century has resulted in various forms of interplay between traditional forms of *Sowa Rigpa* and the crucial quest for legitimization and licensing, which is taking different forms across its range of locations both in Asia and the West.

Particularly because of its inherent integration of Buddhism and its views of the links between body and mind, along with an increasing global need of new approaches to mental health and well-being, there is a growing interest in Tibetan medicine and the contribution it could make to global health in these areas. Approaches to body-mind, well-being, and meditation—all deriving from the Tibetan understanding of *lüng* (*rlung*), usually rendered into English either as "wind" or as "vital energy"—are making their mark on Western methods of treatments. *Trulkhor ('khrul 'khor,* or *'phrul 'khor*), combining both physical movements and breathing to stabilize and regulate one's *lüng*, once taught only to advanced practitioners of Tibetan Buddhism, is now increasingly practiced and used within conventional biomedical settings in the United States.[7]

PHYSIOLOGY AND PRACTICE

The Three Nyepa ("Humors"). The basic view of health and illness as they are manifested in the *Gyushi* is based on the notion of the three *nyepa* (*nyes pa*), usually translated as "humors," but which literally means "fault" or "trouble." These correspond to the Ayurvedic concept of the three *doṣa*, as they are termed in Sanskrit. In a medical context, the three *nyepa* refer both to the potential causes of trouble or illness, as well as to illness itself.

The three *nyepa* are: wind (*rlung*; pronounced *lüng*), bile (*mkhris pa*; pronounced *tripa*), and phlegm (*bad kan*; pronounced *peken*). The translation of *nyepa* to humors is problematic, as are the terms for each of the three (wind, bile, and phlegm): they are not precise or unequivocal translations. It ought to be pointed out that the mere choice of translating the *nyepa* into humors not only conveys meanings but also creates meanings that are removed from their original ones and establishes an a priori link with Greco-Arab medicine where there isn't necessarily one.

Several chapters in the first and second parts of the *Four Treatises* depict the body in its healthy condition, described in the Tibetan sources as an "unaltered state." In this state, the three *nyepa* support and maintain the functions of the body. As long as the three *nyepa*, along with the seven body constituents and the three waste products, are in a state of balance, the body will remain healthy. Any of the *nyepa* can be in a state of imbalance, which can be a state of excess, deficiency, or disturbance. Factors that may cause the *nyepa* to be imbalanced could include inappropriate nutrition, lifestyle, or behavior.

When out of balance, any of the three *nyepa* can cause illness. Hence, there can be illnesses that are due to bile imbalance, phlegm imbalance, wind imbalance, or, more commonly, a combination of two *nyepa*. Among the three *nyepa*, wind (*rlung*) is considered particularly important.

The Tibetan term *rlung* has a host of other meanings, too: *rlung* refers to outer wind, or breeze, as well as to the air, and breath. *Rlung* has a key role in both what in Western terms would be defined as the mental realm, as well as somatic motility. According to the *Four Treatises*, the general functions of the winds are inhalation and exhalation, moving the limbs, and responsibility for different substances within the body. *Rlung* is also responsible for all types of mental and verbal activities. The basic notion that the human body contains channels through which *rlung* flows is shared by Tibetan medicine and Tibetan tantric Buddhism. Subtle forms of *rlung* constitute part of meditative practices aimed at controlling the subtle forms of mind.

In Tibetan medicine, diverse symptoms—such as memory weakness, constipation, dizziness, or shivering—can all be diagnosed as resulting from an imbalanced *rlung*. A complex method of diagnosis establishes the underlying cause of ambiguous symptoms. Once these symptoms are diagnosed as resulting from, for example, excess of wind, they could all be, in principle, treated in the same way.

Diagnosis. The process of diagnosis in Tibetan medicine involves detailed questioning, observation, and feeling the pulse. The questioning procedure will try to establish not only the natural tendencies of the patient but also immediate causes of any disorders. The physician will enquire about the patient's symptoms, diet, and lifestyle. Thus, for example, a stress-related lifestyle is seen as promoting *rlung* illnesses. The visual examination includes observing the tongue and urine, as well as the eyes and skin of the patient. The *Four Treatises* describes how a tongue of those with wind, bile, or phlegm disorders would look, as well as how their urine would appear. Unlike other elements of Tibetan medicine, which have parallels in Indian- or

Chinese-derived medical traditions, urine analysis appears to have derived from a Greco-Persian-Arabic tradition.[8]

The main diagnostic method of Tibetan medicine is an elaborate system of pulse diagnosis, taken at three different locations near each wrist. In the interpretation of all these diagnostic signs, the age of the patient will be taken into account, as well as the season, since according to the theoretical principles of *Sowa Rigpa*, natural tendencies change according to one's age and according to the season. These diagnostic methods require great skill and much practice, but are able to provide considerable important information about the patient.

Treatments. According to the level of severity of the disorder, an assigned treatment would first involve a change of diet and recommendations regarding lifestyle. The next level would involve prescribing multicomponent herbal medication, moxibustion, yogic, and meditative practices, and finally various detoxifying treatments. This is the case at least in theory. In practice, treatments vary according to the laws and practices of the particular country in question. In Asia, treatments often include medications in the first instance, while Tibetan doctors generally do not prescribe yogic and meditative practices in a clinic situation, though they may refer patients to a Buddhist lama who would perhaps teach those, or recommend ritual treatments. In the West, because of strict legal regulations, *Sowa Rigpa* practitioners are often limited to treat primarily with diet and massage. Tibetan medicine also recommends bathing in thermal baths or spring waters, massages, and oil applications—particularly for controlling wind and in aiding relaxation. Cupping therapy is also used in Tibetan medicine, especially for back and shoulder pain caused by stress, as well as for cases of shortness of breath or chest pain. The main difference between Tibetan medicine and biomedicine in determining treatment is that in Tibetan medicine advice regarding nutrition, medication, and lifestyle is specific to an individual's constitution.

Moxibustion (*me btsa'*) is a therapeutic method in which small cones of the mugwort plant are burned on specific points of the body. Moxibustion is often prescribed for general phlegm disorders, such as digestion problems, joint pains, mild arthritis, or insomnia. Moxibustion has a long history of being a quick and easy type of therapy, which can be performed at the household level: from the earliest extant Tibetan moxibustion manuscripts from Dunhuang (9th or 10th century) to present-day testimonials of it being used in Tibetan households.

Tibetan pharmacology is based on the notion that the nature of the five elements is the same in the body, in disease, in food, and in medicinal substances. Tibetan doctors seek to understand how body and mind relate and interact with substances deriving from plants, animals, minerals, and so on. Foods and materia medica are classified according to six tastes, eight potencies, and seventeen qualities, which balance one's disturbed *nyepa*s.

LINKS WITH BUDDHISM

Tibetan medicine exemplifies a unique link between medicine and Buddhism. Medical knowledge was brought to Tibet along with Buddhism along its many paths from India and Central Asia. Tibetan medical theory integrates Buddhist notions at its very core: the three *nyepa* are seen to be linked with the three Buddhist mental poisons: wind (*rlung*) with desire or attachment, bile (*mkhris pa*) with hatred or anger, and phlegm (*bad kan*) with delusion or ignorance.

Tibetan Buddhist accounts maintain that medicine was taught by Buddha Śākyamuni, the founder of Buddhism. Medicine is categorized as one of the five "major sciences" (*rig gnas che ba*).[9] It is worth noting here that the Tibetan term *rig gnas*, which is usually translated as "science," also means art, culture, or a field of knowledge. From a Mahāyāna point of view, the study of these fields of knowledge has been described as essential in the path of the bodhisattva's striving toward omniscience. This omniscience is considered in Buddhist literature both as a means of helping others and a way of knowing oneself.[10]

In Tibetan medicine, a subcategory of what may be termed "Buddhist medicine," and particularly "tantric Buddhist medicine," the knowledge and application of how to preserve one's health, is an important aspect of one's spiritual path. The positive effects of physical health on one's spiritual development are already recorded in the earliest Buddhist Pali literature, such as the *Majjhima Nikaya*. Already in early Buddhist writing, health is seen as an individual's finest possession and the difficulty of engaging in meditative practices if one's body is in constant pain is also pointed out.

From early on in Buddhism, knowledge of the body—as well as maintaining and restoring health—has been given soteriological significance. This has been particularly developed in tantric Buddhism, the Buddhist variant that reached Tibet. In this context, four aims are discussed: prevention of illness, cure of illness, securing longevity, and attaining spiritual liberation. Medical practice was incorporated into the monastic syllabus.

The conceptualizations of body and mind as found in Tibetan tantric Buddhism are also at the heart of Tibetan medical theory. Tantric Buddhist soteriology elaborates the relationship between mind, body, and spiritual liberation. Practically, this relationship manifests in the winds (*rlung*) and the way a practitioner learns to control them for the purpose of health maintenance, but ultimately, for the purpose of spiritual liberation. Tantric yogis engage in a variety of meditative practices in order to know and control one's *rlung*. Through these meditative practices, tantric yogis aim to refine their physical and subtle body.

In accordance with the basic theory of *Sowa Rigpa*, in both diagnosis and treatment the mind and the body are treated in tandem. According to Tibetan medicine, a healthy body will result in long life, spiritual and material well-being, and ultimately the potential of leading to the attainment of enlightenment.

INFLUENCE ON WESTERN UNDERSTANDINGS: MIND AND LIFE INSTITUTE MEETINGS

What began as private meetings between a group of scientists and the Fourteenth Dalai Lama, Tenzin Gyatso (Bstan 'dzin rgya mtsho), have grown to become very popular open events, attracting thousands of participants and have had significant impact on the emerging field of contemplative studies in the West. These meetings have resulted in highly influential trends in various fields such as psychology and neurological research.

The first Mind and Life meeting took place in 1987, as a result of an initiative by the late Dr. Francisco Varela (1946–2001), who was a neuroscientist and practicing Buddhist, together with Adam Engle, a businessman and a student of the Fourteenth Dalai Lama. A small group of leading scientists working on various aspects of cognitive sciences—many of them with an interest in Buddhism—engaged in dialogue with the Dalai Lama for a week. This first meeting explored many topics, which were dealt with in greater detail in subsequent years: these included topics like the links between Buddhism and neuroscience, experimental psychology, artificial intelligence, and philosophy of the mind. The meeting was documented in the book *Gentle Bridges: Conversations with the Dalai Lama on the Sciences of Mind.*[11] Research avenues that ultimately led to the extensive proliferation of mindfulness in the West can be traced to these meetings, such as the research of Jon Kabat-Zinn and Richard Davidson, who used scientific methodology to show that mindfulness meditation has a positive effect on the immune system.[12]

REVIEW OF LITERATURE

Alexander Csoma de Körös, who is considered the "father of Tibetology," was the first to write about the *Gyushi* in English.[13] Research into Tibetan medicine also developed in Russia in the 19th century, as a result of the significant presence of Tibetan medicine in Saint Petersburg (see the section "Tibeto-Mongol-Buryat Medicine in the Court of the Russian Tsar"). Pyotr Badmayev produced the first translation of the first two tantras of the *Gyushi* into any European language, published in Russian in 1898.[14] This, however, was more of a "cultural translation" than a direct translation: being a Russian Orthodox himself and keen to show that *Sowa Rigpa* should be considered a medical science, Pyotr Badmayev removed whatever he considered to be too Buddhist or "mystical."

In 1981, Fernand Meyer, a pioneering leading scholar of Tibetan medicine, published the important study *Gso-ba Rig-pa: Le système médical tibétain* that brought a comprehensive overview of Tibetan medicine to a Western audience for the first time.[15]

Sections of the *Gyushi* were translated into English by various scholars through the years: Terry Clifford translated the psychiatric chapters (chapters 77–79 of the Third Tantra) in 1984, and Barry Clark published a translation of the first and second tantra in 1995.[16] In 2008, 2011, and 2017, the Translation Department of the Dharamshala Men-Tsee-Khang published very useful English translations, along with the original Tibetan, of the first, second, fourth, and parts of the third tantras.[17]

A formidable collaboration between Russian and European scholarship along with substantial editorial effort brought about the 1992 publication of the Tibetan Medical Paintings, commissioned by Sangye Gyatso, regent of the Fifth Dalai Lama of the 17th century.[18] This important publication is based on the unpublished texts in Russian of the late Professor Yuri Parfionovitch (1921–1990), along with the work of Fernand Meyer and Gyurme Dorje. The elaborate two-volume publication provides excellent reproductions of the set of Tibetan medical paintings, copied in Ulan-Ude in the 1920s from an original set that was created between 1687 and 1703, together with an excellent introduction and synopses of the topics of each medical painting.

Bodies in Balance: The Art of Tibetan Medicine, edited by Theresia Hofer, which came out to accompany a major exhibition on Tibetan medicine in the Rubin Museum of Art in New York in 2014, is one of the best overviews of Tibetan medicine in the English language, with chapters written by specialists on multiple angles of Tibetan medicine.[19]

The main perspectives from which Tibetan medicine is studied nowadays are: anthropology, history, Buddhist studies, and the emerging field of contemplative studies.[20]

Available literature in English and other European languages also includes books by leading practitioners. Particularly worthy of mention in this context are the books by Yeshi Dhonden, former personal physician of the Fourteenth Dalai Lama.[21]

In the last few decades, most of the work on Tibetan medicine has been conducted by medical anthropologists, such as Vincanne Adams, Geoffrey Samuel, Mona Schrempf, Sienna Craig, Barbara Gerke, Theresia Hofer, Tatiana Chudakova, Craig Janes, Laurent Pordié, Stephan Kloos, Martin Saxer, Colin Millard, and Calum Blaikie.[22] Their work deals with the various ways in which Tibetan medicine is evolving as a result of encounters with modernity, with exile, its changing links with Buddhism—and how all these play out with the TAR and other locations in the People's Republic of China; in the Tibetan exiled community in China; and in other locations where *Sowa Rigpa* is practiced: India, Nepal, Bhutan, Mongolia, Buryatia (south Siberia), Europe, and the United States, through investigating socioeconomic perspectives, ritual and economic issues of recognition, and cultural heritage.

PRIMARY SOURCES

ENGLISH TRANSLATIONS OF THE GYUSHI

First and Second Tantra

The Basic Tantra and the Explanatory Tantra from the Secret Quintessential Instructions on the Eight Branches of the Ambrosia Essence Tantra. By Yuthog Yonten Gonpo. Translated by the Translation Department, Men-Tsee-Khang, Dharamshala. Dharamshala, India: Men-Tsee-Khang Publications, 2008; 2nd ed. 2011.

Clark, Barry. *The Quintessence Tantras of Tibetan Medicine.* Ithaca, NY: Snow Lion, 1995.

Third Tantra (First Twenty-Seven Chapters)

The Oral Instruction Tantra from the Four Tantras of Tibetan Medicine. Dharamshala, India: Men-Tsee-Khang Publications, 2017.

Fourth Tantra

The Subsequent Tantra: From the Four Tantras of Tibetan Medicine. Dharamshala, India: Men-Tsee-Khang Publications, 2011; 2nd ed. 2015.

DIGITAL AND VISUAL MATERIALS

FILMS

Reichle, Franz, dir. *The Knowledge of Healing.* New York: Icarus Films, 1997.

Saxer, Martin, dir. *Journeys with Tibetan Medicine* (https://vimeo.com/122821844). Cham, Switzerland: Impuls Home Entertainment, 2006. The documentary was released at the Solothurn Film Festival in January 2005.

WEBSITES

Institute of Medicine and Astrology (http://www.men-tsee-khang.org/) (Dharamshala Men tsee khang).

Mind and Life Institute (https://www.mindandlife.org/).

FURTHER READING

Adams, Vincanne, Mona Schrempf, and Sienna Craig, eds. *Medicine between Science and Religion: Explorations on Tibetan Grounds*. New York: Berghahn, 2011.

Chaoul, Alejandro. *Tibetan Yoga for Health and Well-Being: The Science and Practice of Healing Your Body, Energy and Mind*. Carlsbad, CA: Hay House, 2018.

Craig, Sienna. *Healing Elements: Efficacy and the Social Ecologies of Tibetan Medicine*. Berkeley, CA: University of California Press, 2012.

Craig, Sienna, Mingji Cuomu, Frances Garrett, and Mona Schrempf, eds. *Studies of Medical Pluralism in Tibetan History and Society*. Andiast, Switzerland: International Institute for Tibetan and Buddhist Studies GmbH, 2010.

Garrett, Frances. "Buddhism and the Historicising of Medicine in Thirteenth-Century Tibet." *Asian Medicine: Tradition and Modernity* 2, no. 2 (2007): 204–224.

Garrett, Frances. *Religion, Medicine and the Human Embryo in Tibet: Becoming Human*. London: Routledge, 2008.

Gerke, Barbara. *Long Lives and Untimely Deaths: Life-span Concepts and Longevity Practices among Tibetans in the Darjeeling Hills, India*. Leiden, The Netherlands: Brill, 2011.

Gyatso, Janet. *Being Human in a Buddhist World: An Intellectual History of Medicine in Early Modern Tibet*. New York: Columbia University Press, 2015.

Hofer, Theresia, ed. *Bodies in Balance: The Art of Tibetan Medicine*. New York: Rubin Museum of Art, 2014.

Karmay, Samten. "The Four Tibetan Medical Treatises and Their Critics." In *The Arrow and the Spindle: Studies in History, Myths, Rituals and Beliefs in Tibet*. By Samten Karmay, 228–237. Kathmandu: Mandala Book Point, 2009 (first published 1997).

Kloos, Stephan. "The Recognition of Sowa Rigpa in India: How Tibetan Medicine Became an Indian Medical System." *Medicine Anthropology Theory* 3, no. 2 (2016): 19–49.

Meyer, Fernand. *Gso-ba Rig-pa: Le système médical tibétain*. Paris: CNRS, 1981.

Meyer, Fernand. "Theory and Practice of Tibetan Medicine." In *Oriental Medicine: An Illustrated Guide to the Asian Arts of Healing*. Edited by Jan van Alphen and Anthony Aris, 109–141. London: Serindia, 1995.

Meyer, Fernand, Kenneth Holmes, and Khenpo Troru Tsenam. "Tibetan Medicine Today." In *Oriental Medicine: An Illustrated Guide to the Asian Arts of Healing*. Edited by Jan van Alphen and Anthony Aris, 143–153. London: Serindia, 1995.

Parfionovitch, Y., F. Meyer, and Gyurme Dorje, eds. *Tibetan Medical Paintings: Illustrations to the Blue Beryl Treatise of Sangye Gyamtso (1653–1705)*. 2 vols. London: Serindia Publications, 1992.

Pordié, Laurent, ed. *Tibetan Medicine in the Contemporary World: Global Politics of Medical Knowledge and Practice*. London: Routledge, 2008.

Ramble, Charles, and Ulrike Roesler, eds. *Tibetan and Himalayan Healing: An Anthology for Anthony Aris*. Kathmandu: Vajra Publications, 2015.

Samuel, Geoffrey. "The Subtle Body in India and Beyond." In *Religion and the Subtle Body in Asia and the West: Between Mind and Body*. Edited by Geoffrey Samuel and Jay Johnston, 33–47. Abingdon, UK: Routledge, 2013.

Samuel, Geoffrey. "Subtle-Body Processes: Towards a Non-Reductionist Understanding." In *Religion and the Subtle Body in Asia and the West: Between Mind and Body*. Edited by Geoffrey Samuel and Jay Johnston, 249–266. Abingdon, UK: Routledge, 2013.

Sangyé Gyatso, Desi. *Mirror of Beryl: A Historical Introduction to Tibetan Medicine*. Translated by Gavin Kilty. Boston: Wisdom, 2010.

Saxer, Martin. *Manufacturing Tibetan Medicine: The Creation of an Industry and the Moral Economy of Tibetanness*. New York: Berghahn Books, 2013.

Schaeffer, Kurtis. "Textual Scholarship, Medical Tradition and Mahāyāna Buddhist Ideals in Tibet." *Journal of Indian Philosophy* 31 (2003): 621–641.

Scrempf, Mona, ed. *Soundings in Tibetan Medicine.* Leiden, The Netherlands: Brill, 2007.

Yeshi Dhonden. *Healing from the Source: The Science and Lore of Tibetan Medicine.* Translated and edited by B. Alan Wallace. Ithaca, NY: Snow Lion Publications, 2000.

Yoeli-Tlalim, Ronit. "Tibetan 'Wind' and 'Wind' Illnesses: Towards a Multicultural Approach to Health and Illness." *Studies in History and Philosophy of Biological and Biomedical Sciences* 41 (2010): 318–324.

NOTES

1. For a study of this work, see Dan Martin, "An Early Tibetan History of Indian Medicine," in *Soundings in Tibetan Medicine*, ed. Mona Scrempf (Leiden, The Netherlands: Brill, 2007), 307–325.
2. For a detailed analysis of the two Western components of this and similar lists, that is, stag gzig and phrom, see Dan Martin, "Greek and Islamic Medicines' Historical Contact with Tibet: A Reassessment in View of Recently Available but Relatively Early Sources on Tibetan Medical Eclecticism," in *Islam and Tibet: Interactions along the Musk Routes*, ed. Anna Akasoy, Charles Burnett, and Ronit Yoeli-Tlalim (Farnham, UK: Ashgate, 2011), 117–143. See also Ronit Yoeli-Tlalim's "On Urine Analysis and Tibetan Medicine's Connections with the West," in *Studies of Medical Pluralism in Tibetan History and Society*, ed. Sienna Craig et al. (Halle, Germany: International Institute for Tibetan and Buddhist Studies GmbH, 2010), 195–211; and Ronit Yoeli-Tlalim, "Re-visiting 'Galen in Tibet,'" *Medical History* 56, no. 3 (July 2012): 355–365.
3. The following section is based on: Martin Saxer, "The Journeys of Tibetan Medicine," in *Bodies in Balance: The Art of Tibetan Medicine*, ed. Theresia Hofer (New York: Rubin Museum of Art, 2014), 246–256; and Martin Saxer, "Tibetan Medicine and Russian Modernities," in *Medicine between Science and Religion: Explorations on Tibetan Grounds*, ed. Vincanne Adams, Mona Schrempf, and Sienna Craig (Oxford: Berghahn, 2011), 57–80.
4. Cyrill von Korvin-Krasinski. *Die Tibetische Medizinphilosophie: Der Mensch als Mikrokosmos* (Zurich: Origo, 1953).
5. Stephan Kloos, "The Recognition of Sowa Rigpa in India: How Tibetan Medicine Became an Indian Medical System," *Medicine Anthropology Theory* 3, no. 2 (2016): 19–49.
6. See Kloos. "The Recognition of Sowa Rigpa in India," 19–49.
7. See Alejandro Chaoul, *Tibetan Yoga for Health and Well-Being: The Science and Practice of Healing Your Body, Energy and Mind* (Carlsbad, CA: Hay House, 2018).
8. Ronit Yoeli-Tlalim, "On Urine Analysis and Tibetan Medicine's Connections with the West," in *Studies of Medical Pluralism in Tibetan History and Society*, ed. Sienna Craig et al. (Andiast, Switzerland: International Institute for Tibetan and Buddhist Studies GmbH, 2010), 195–211.
9. The other four are the inner science (i.e., *nang rig pa*, or Buddhism), epistemology and logic (*gtan tshigs rig pa*), grammar (*sgra rig pa*), and arts and crafts (*bzo rig pa*). For an overview of the ten Buddhist sciences in Tibetan Buddhist literature, see David S. Ruegg, "Science religieuse et sciences séculières en Inde et au Tibet: Vidyāsthāna indo-bouddhiques et rig gnas indo-tibétains," in *Ordre spirituel et ordre temporel dans la pensée bouddhique de l'Inde et du Tibet* (Paris: Collège de France, Institut de civilisation indienne, 1995), 93–147. See also Vesna A. Wallace, *The Inner Kālacakratantra: A Buddhist Tantric View of the Individual* (Oxford: Oxford University Press, 2001), 43–55.
10. See, for example, Bu ston Rinpoche (1290–1364) quoting the *Sūtralaṁkāra*. Bu ston, *Jewellery of Scripture*, trans. E. Obermiller (New Delhi: Paljor Publications, 2000), 52. On this topic, see also Kurtis Schaeffer, "Textual Scholarship, Medical Tradition and Mahāyāna Buddhist Ideals in Tibet," *Journal of Indian Philosophy* 31 (2003): 621–641.

11. Hayward, Jeremy W,. and Francisco J. Varela, eds., *Gentle Bridges: Conversations with the Dalai Lama on the Sciences of Mind* (Boston and London: Shambhala, 1992).
12. See, for example, R. Davidson, J. Kabat-Zinn, et al., "Alterations in Brain and Immune Function Produced by Mindfulness Meditation," *Psychosomatic Medicine* 65 (2003): 564–570.
13. Alexander Csoma de Körös, "Analysis of a Tibetan Medical Work," *Journal of the Asiatic Society of Bengal* 37 (January 1835): 1–20.
14. Pyotr Aleksandrovich Badmayev, *O Sisteme Vrachebnoy Nauki Tibeta (On the System of the Medical Sciences of Tibet)* (Saint Petersburg, Russia: Nadezhda Skoropetschatnaja,1898). Discussed in Martin Saxer, "The Journeys of Tibetan Medicine."
15. Fernand Meyer, *Gso-ba Rig-pa: Le système médical tibétain* (Paris: CNRS, 1981).
16. Terry Clifford, *Tibetan Buddhist Medicine and Psychiatry: The Diamond Healing* (York Beach, ME: Samuel Weiser, 1984); and Barry Clark, *The Quintessence Tantras of Tibetan Medicine* (Ithaca, NY: Snow Lion, 1995).
17. *The Basic Tantra and the Explanatory Tantra from the Secret Quintessential Instructions on the Eight Branches of the Ambrosia Essence Tantra*, by Yuthog Yonten Gonpo, trans. the Translation Department, Men-Tsee-Khang, Dharamshala (Dharamshala, India: Men-Tsee-Khang Publications, 2008; 2nd ed. 2011); *The Subsequent Tantra: From the Four Tantras of Tibetan Medicine* (Dharamshala, India: Men-Tsee-Khang Publications, 2011; 2nd ed. 2015); and *The Oral Instruction Tantra from the Four Tantras of Tibetan Medicine* (Dharamshala, India: Men-Tsee-Khang Publications, 2017).
18. Yuri Parfionovitch, Fernand Meyer, and Gyurme Dorje, eds., *Tibetan Medical Paintings: Illustrations to the Blue Beryl Treatise of Sangye Gyamtso (1653–1705)*, 2 vols. (London: Serindia Publications, 1992).
19. Theresia Hofer, ed., *Bodies in Balance: The Art of Tibetan Medicine* (Seattle: University of Washington Press, 2014).
20. For contemplative research, see the Journal of Contemplative Studies. https://contemplativejournal.org/#/.
21. Yeshi Dhonden, *Healing from the Source: The Science and Lore of Tibetan Medicine*, trans. B. Alan Wallace (Ithaca, NY: Snow Lion Publications, 2012).
22. See for example: Vincanne Adams, Mona Schrempf, and Sienna Craig, eds., *Medicine between Science and Religion: Explorations on Tibetan Grounds* (New York: Berghahn, 2011); Sienna Craig, *Healing Elements: Efficacy and the Social Ecologies of Tibetan Medicine* (Berkeley, CA: University of California Press, 2012); Barbara Gerke, *Long Lives and Untimely Deaths: Life-span Concepts and Longevity Practices among Tibetans in the Darjeeling Hills, India* (Leiden, The Netherlands: Brill, 2011); Laurent Pordié, ed. *Tibetan Medicine in the Contemporary World: Global Politics of Medical Knowledge and Practice* (London: Routledge, 2008); Martin Saxer, *Manufacturing Tibetan Medicine: The Creation of an Industry and the Moral Economy of Tibetanness* (New York: Berghahn Books, 2013); Calum Blaikie, "Positioning Sowa Rigpa in India: Coalition and antagonism in the quest for recognition," *Medicine, Anthropology and Theory* 3, no. 2 (2016): 50–86; Stephan Kloos, *Tibetan Medicine among the Buddhist Dards of Ladakh* (Vienna: Wiener Studien zur Tibetologie und Buddhismuskunde, 2004); Theresia Hofer, *Medicine and Memory in Tibet: Amchi Physicians in an Age of Reform* (Seattle: University of Washington Press, 2018); Geoffrey Samuel and Jay Johnston, eds., *Religion and the Subtle Body in Asia and the West: Between Mind and Body* (Oxon: Routledge, 2013); Tatiana Chudakova, "Contingent Efficacies in Buryat Tibetan Medicine," *Asian Medicine* 10, no. 1–2 (2015): 249–272; Craig Janes, "The Transformations of Tibetan Medicine," *Medical Anthropology Quarterly* 9, no. 1 (1995): 6–39; and Colin Millard, "Bon Medical Practitioners in Contemporary Tibet: The Continuity of a Tradition," *East Asian Science, Technology and Society* 7, no. 3 (2013): 353–379.

Ronit Yoeli-Tlalim

TIBETAN VISIONARY BUDDHISM

DEFINING "VISION" AND "VISIONARY BUDDHISM"

Buddhist traditions are full of visual elements, ranging through contemplative practices that involve visualization, philosophies that investigate the nature of appearances, literary descriptions of pure lands, and visual arts that depict deities and divine worlds. For many Buddhists, the category of "seeing" has also been one of the key metaphors for "knowing," and so Buddhist epistemologies have often used it as a starting point for exploring the problems and possibilities of perception.

Tibetan religious traditions have taken particular delight in the visual. In an initial encounter with religion in Tibetan worlds, one is likely to take note of the vibrant aesthetics of Tibetan temples, the distinctive Tibetan artistic styles, and a widespread enthusiasm for seeing or encountering sacred sites and people. Some of the hallmark practices in Tibetan religion also involve feats of visualization; these may take the form of exoteric meditations for cultivating compassion where one visualizes hosts of perceived enemies, or esoteric practices like "generation stage" tantra where one visualizes oneself as a deity dwelling in an elaborate mandala.

Tibetan Buddhists also have a wide variety of traditions that could be more properly called "visionary," as a way of distinguishing them from other metaphorical, literary, artistic, and visualized practices of seeing. "Visionary" here refers to experiences of seeing, in which images arise spontaneously to the eyes, rather than being deliberately constructed in the mind. Some of these visionary practices have more practical purposes: textual revelation, prognostication, communication with deities, devotional encounters, the seeking of blessings or protection, or signs and contemplations related to dying. Other visionary practices (and these frequently overlap with the first category) are more closely tied to the Buddhist soteriological project and involve the meditative cultivation of visionary experiences thought of as crucial parts in the attainment of buddhahood.

As a whole, there is a great diversity among Tibetan visionary practices. Some involve visions said to occur without intentional cultivation, while others evoke visions through meditative practice; some involve immediate and fully formed visions, while others result in visions that develop over days or weeks; some occur to untrained laypeople, and others to religious specialists; some are thought of as transcendent or otherworldly, while others are simply functions of human physiology.

Taken together, it can be useful to think of these practices of seeing as a type of "visionary Buddhism"; the term may help to indicate the interrelation between diverse practices of seeing and to distinguish them from other types of visual practice. Caution is certainly warranted in the use of the term. First, visionary Buddhism does not correspond to any particular native term and may not represent a category through which Buddhists themselves organize or view their own traditions. Even the term "Buddhism" can be troublesome here, in that visionary practices are key parts of the Bön tradition, a Buddhist school that does not always map neatly onto the category "Buddhism" as many understand it. Neither does visionary Buddhism refer to any systemized school, philosophy, or technique. Rather, it should be thought of as an arena in which Buddhists of various types, times, and places have used spontaneous visual experiences to pursue Buddhist goals.

CONNECTIONS TO INDIAN BUDDHIST THEORY AND PRACTICE

While Tibetan practices of vision are often esoteric, and may be the purview of advanced practitioners, they are nonetheless grounded in mainstream Buddhist ideas. Tibetan visionary traditions are well aware of the Buddhist caution that the eyes can be sources of error that perpetuate *saṃsāra*. However, visionary traditions are also inspired by Indian Buddhist literature that suggests higher possibilities for the eyes: that the eyes may become divine or be used to perceive fundamental truths.

Ordinary Eyes as Sources of Straying and Error. Buddhist thought has commonly been wary of the eyes, given how easily the visual world can become a source of distraction, attachment, or immorality. Restraint of the eyes is a part of the *vinaya*, and monastics vow to gaze downward with the eyes not wandering.[1] Buddhist ethical literature contains numerous other cautions about guarding the eyes: not staring lustfully, not winking at women or gazing into their eyes, not eavesdropping, and not watching military activity.[2]

Outside of ethical discussions, the ordinary eyes are often portrayed as sources of illusion and error, as parts of a perceptual system that can look at a rope and mistake it for a snake. Though the eyes and the visual consciousness are thought of as non-conceptual, the data they provide to the mental consciousness is a major source of mental proliferation and conceptuality. This conceptual thought, in turn, helps to reinforce what Buddhists identify as our primary ignorance: the ignorant perception of a true "self" or "identity" in beings and objects. This, in turn, leads to the mental poisons of attachment and hatred, and so the eyes are one of the major features in the perpetuation of *saṃsāra*.

In Buddhist soteriology, the realization of emptiness—that no such inherent self or identity exists—is said to be the way out of *saṃsāra* and suffering. Though meditations on emptiness may be described as practices of "higher seeing" (*lhag mthong, vipaśyanā*) or as routes through a "path of seeing" (*mthong lam, darśana-mārga*), the realization of emptiness is explicitly one that does not involve the senses. A normative Mahāyāna claim is that the ultimate cannot be experienced by consciousness or the senses. This is famously expressed in Chandrakīrti's statement that the ultimate "cannot be taught directly, as it is inexpressible and just not an object of consciousness."[3]

Thus, one clear inheritance of Tibetan visionary practices is the idea that the eyes, in their ordinary dimension, are not essential parts of the spiritual path. At best they may be useful for creating a feeling of revulsion for the world, as when the Buddha saw the "four sights" that led to his renunciation. Yet overall they serve as gateways to the distractions, desires, and misperceptions that bind beings to the ordinary world.

Transcendent Eyes as Sources of Power and Insight. Yet these are not the only ways that mainstream Buddhist traditions have treated the eyes. Buddhist scriptures also describe higher visual faculties that can see more than just the forms of the ordinary world. One of these faculties is the "divine eye" (*lha'i mig, divya-cakṣu*), descriptions of which appear frequently in Buddhist literature. Vasubandhu, for instance, in his famous commentary to the *Treasury of Abhidharma* describes this eye as a type of worldly superpower attained by meditation, in which a practitioner's eyes are transformed to become like those of a form realm god.[4]

Rather than being sources of immorality or error, these divine eyes grant one the ability to perceive objects that cannot be seen by the ordinary eye: forms that are in other universes, or that are extremely subtle, or that are obscured. It also affords the ability to "see" into others' karma (to see in what realms they will be born, and what particular karmic deeds propel them there), along with the related ability to see the immaterial beings who are in the intermediate state between births.

Buddhist literature also contains descriptions of visual powers that are even more transcendent than these divine eyes. The *Perfection of Wisdom Sūtra in 25,000 Lines* discusses a famous series of "five eyes" that bodhisattvas and buddhas attained through the practice of the perfection of wisdom. These are: (a) a "fleshy eye" that can see for hundreds or thousands of leagues across space, and can see thousands of other world systems; (b) a "divine eye" that can "see" the specific effects of karma; (c) an "eye of insight" that is the bodhisattva's insight into emptiness; (d) a "dharma eye" that allows the bodhisattva to see others' level of spiritual development, or to see their personal histories, and thus to see how best to assist them; and (e) a "buddha eye," which is a buddha's ultimate realization itself.[5]

Reviewing all these kinds of transcendent eyes make it clear that mainstream Indian Buddhist texts, in both Pāli and Sanskrit, accept the possibilities of visual faculties that are much more powerful than the ordinary eyes. Some of these are more metaphorical "eyes" that would seem to provide types of insight, rather than types of visual perception. But others are clearly visual faculties that are essential qualities of buddhas and bodhisattvas and represent distinctively Buddhist attainments. This background is later drawn upon by visionary practitioners in Tibet, who evoke, modify, and reinvent these types of seeing in new settings.

Practices of Direct Encounter. Beyond theory, it is also possible to find descriptions of visionary practice in Indian Buddhist sources. One important example comes from the Mahāyāna scripture known as the *Sūtra of the Samādhi of Direct Encounter with the Buddhas of the Present.*[6] Its quest for "direct encounter" is based on the practice of "recollection of the Buddha," in which one contemplates the qualities of the Buddha. The sutra combines this with lengthy retreats, long periods of wakefulness, and philosophical contemplation, in the hopes of seeing Buddhas. As the sutra explains:

> Bhadrapāla, it is like this: If a man who has eyes turns his face upward to look in the space of the clear, cloudless, midnight sky, he will see the forms of many stars there. It is the same, Bhadrapāla, for *bodhisattva-mahāsattvas* who are supported by the buddhas and abide in this *samādhi*: because they are immersed in this cognition of space and are blessed with a cognition of the buddhas, due to the power of the buddhas and the cultivation of this *samādhi*, if they gaze to the east, to another world system, then many buddhas will appear to their eye sense-power, with little effort.[7]

This practice would neatly fit within the parameters of "visionary Buddhism" as defined in the quotation, in that it aims for a visionary experience with the actual eyes, and it expects the visions to arise spontaneously, or "with little effort." Reading a little further into the scripture, the practice could also be placed in the "soteriological" category, as the practitioner is urged to contemplate the nature of the visions and realize their ultimate nature:

> When those bodhisattvas have thoroughly cultivated this *samādhi*, those bodhisattvas see those Tathāgatas with little effort. Having seen them, they pose questions [to the Tathāgatas], and are delighted when their questions are answered. They think: "Did these Tathāgatas come from anywhere? Or did I go anywhere?" Through this, they realize: "Those Tathāgatas did not come from anywhere. And my body also has not gone anywhere either!" Perceiving this, they think: "These three worlds are nothing but mind! Why is that? It is because however I conceptualize things, that is how they appear!"[8]

While the *Samādhi of Direct Encounter* does not seem to have been popular among Tibetan advocates of visionary practice, many features of the practice it describes would become hallmarks of Tibetan visionary Buddhism. In particular, the eyes are used here to bridge the gap between the relative and the ultimate, or between appearance and emptiness. That is, the initial aim is the production of visionary appearances, but the very arising of those visions becomes an opportunity to contemplate the nature of appearance itself and to realize them as ultimately empty.

VISIONARY BUDDHISM IN TIBET: WORLDLY AIMS

Among the practices of vision found in Tibetan religion, one type is those that have more this-worldly orientations, whose goals are located within samsara rather than representing attempts to transcend *saṃsāra*. This is a diverse group of practices ranging through the fields of divination, decision making, communication with deities, revelation, blessings, healing, protection, and so forth. These do appear alongside more soteriological visionary practices and may themselves give way to transcendent experiences and realizations. Still, as a heuristic device they can be distinguished by noting that their immediate goals differ from visionary practices whose ultimate aim is liberation.

Divination, Decision Making, and Mediums. One of the major functions of vision in the Tibetan world has been for matters of divination. A widespread variety is a category of practices known as *prasenā*.[9] In essence, these are ritual practices in which one attempts to gain knowledge of the past, present, or future; their prototypical form involves a spontaneous vision appearing on an empty or reflective surface, such as a mirror, a lake, a sword, the sky, or even the ritualist's thumbnail. The practitioner may be ritually prepared or empowered, or may empower someone else such as a young girl, resulting in the ability to see visions that reveal information about the past, present, or future. *Prasenā* is not a single ritual but rather a diverse class of rituals that may involve reflective surfaces, child mediums, consultations with oracles, descent of deities, exorcism of malevolent beings, and so forth. These types of rituals were known in Indian Buddhist sources like the *Questions of Subāhu Tantra*, which made its way into Tibet in the 8th century; native Tibetan descriptions of rituals going under the term *prasenā* date back to the 8th and 9th centuries.[10]

A *prasenā* ritual, combined with exorcism of malevolent beings, features in one of the foundational Tibetan Buddhist narratives: Padmasambhava's opening the way for Buddhism to enter Tibet. In the version of the story told in the *Testament of Wa*, malevolent deities are preventing the establishment of Buddhism, and it is through a *prasenā* ritual that Padmasambhava was able to identify and later subdue them.[11]

A contemporary example of the visionary *prasenā* can be found in the discovery of the Fourteenth Dalai Lama (Bstan 'dzin rgya mtsho; b. 1940). As part of the search for the Dalai Lama's reincarnation, the regent Reting Rinpoche performed a *prasenā* at Lake Lhamo Lhatso. The ritual is said to have resulted in some visionary clues appearing on the surface of the lake: a series of letters, a monastery, and an image of an unusual house arise on the surface of the lake. These were used to direct the search for the young Fourteenth Dalai Lama, who was found in the foretold house in the vicinity of Kumbum Monastery.[12]

Visionary prognostications may also be parts of broader practices that involve oracles and spirit mediums. Mediums (*lha pa, lha babs mkhan*) commonly use mirrors as one of their ritual implements and may employ them during the descent of an oracle. In some cases the oracle who possesses the medium may appear in the mirror, or visions appearing in the mirror may be used to reveal hidden information. In some instances, the medium may be asked to describe what is seen in the mirror; alternatively, mediums themselves may make interpretations of mirror appearances and then recommend techniques to achieve aims such as removal of obstructions and healing.[13]

Outside of mediumship, such visionary divinations may be used by ritualists for more ordinary decision making, providing information to clients, or making critical choices in times of danger.[14]

Finally, visionary divination also becomes important as a metaphor in visionary yoga practices. Particularly in Kālacakra literature, the spontaneity of an image appearing in a prognostic mirror becomes a metaphor for the spontaneity of visionary yogic experience. In this way it becomes a key image for expressing the distinctive features of vision, and to contrast it with conceptual and deliberately evoked visualizations.

Prophecies, Warnings, Blessings, and Instructions. In Tibetan religious worlds, vision is not always deliberately produced through ritual but may also occur on its own time. A rich set of examples from a life punctuated by such visions can be found in the secret biography of the Fifth Dalai Lama (Ngag dbang blo bzang rgya mtsho; 1617–1682) and in a summary of his experiences entitled *Visions and their Significance*.[15] The text catalogs visionary experiences that began in the Dalai Lama's youth and continued throughout his life. In his account, these were not deliberately produced (as when a ritualist performs a *prasenā*) but came when deities saw fit to intervene, including a gap of ten years when he had no visions to report.

The Fifth Dalai Lama was of course an elite figure—one of Tibet's most famous politicians, scholars, and meditators—so while many of his experiences may be unique, they are also illustrative of the types of vision found in Tibetan worlds. Much of his catalog describes visionary encounters with religious figures: lamas, tutelary deities, protectors, *ḍākinīs*, and buddhas. Most of these were fully formed images of beings who were recognizable to him (Padmasambhava, the goddess Palden Lhamo, and so forth), but some were unformed, mysterious, even fearful.

The divine figures in his visions typically bring him some prophetic content or instructions: they bring signs of future success, warnings of coming obstacles, or messages about duties that should be performed. At other times, the deities give teachings and transmissions, and confer empowerments and blessings. Some of these encounters turned into contemplative states, resulting in profound meditative experiences.[16]

The Fifth Dalai Lama's catalog reveals several features of Tibetan visionary practices in general. First, they extend across a wide range of concerns, including protection, prophecy, blessing, and healing, and are not just limited to the spheres of yoga and contemplation on the nature of appearances. This range of concerns also include politics: the Fifth Dalai Lama at times had visions of the great past emperor Songtsen Gampo (Srong btsan sgam po; *c.* 605–649), who provided assurance of the Dalai Lama's own success in ruling, and informed him of rituals and offerings that needed to be carried out.[17] Visions of other figures made recommendations about governance, or provided signs, advice, and protection related to military conflicts.[18] It is widely known that the Tibetan government employed state oracles for decision making, but here is also evidence of a visionary component to a ruler's own decision making.

The text also reveals something about Tibetan public skepticism of visions. In the opening of his secret catalog of visions, the Fifth Dalai Lama states that he did not detail his visions in his ordinary autobiography, as doing so would have created too much suspicion. Speaking of the records of his visions, he warns that "the erudite should not read this work, if they do, they will be embarrassed."[19] Thus while receiving visions can be important for a religious career and can authenticate someone as having a unique connection to deities, visions are not universally accepted and may also serve to create suspicion.

The Dalai Lama's work also indicates that there is a strong connection between vision and ritual. Although his visions do not seem to have been deliberately evoked, they frequently occurred during ritual performance, as when the Namgyal monks were performing a ritual to Palden Lhamo, and the goddess herself appeared to the Dalai Lama.[20] Further, many of the instructions he received in vision pertained to ritual duties: visionary deities informed him of necessary ritual duties and recommended rites to perform.

Finally, in his example one can also see a close connection between vision and the arts. In the Tibetan world, vision may prompt the creation of literature, as experiences are written down, and those writings may inform and direct the later visions of those who read them. Similarly, there is also a small but very vibrant genre of painting that depicts visions, and the Fifth Dalai Lama wrote that his catalog of visions was intended in part to benefit "those who wish to do drawings and paintings of the heavens."[21]

Signs of Death and Post-Death Experiences. The process of dying is commonly said to entail a series of visionary appearances that serve as "internal signs" of dying. As the elemental and wind energies that enliven one's body sequentially dissolve, one is said to experience a series of luminous appearances, resembling a mirage, smoke, fireflies, and a butter lamp.[22] In many cases, these are not regarded as miraculous appearances but are simply epiphenomena that occur when the body's coarse components cease to function. Alternatively, the visions may be seen as the dawning of an inner luminous awareness that was formerly locked away in the ordinary body.

Following death, one is said to enter the intermediate state, where one has a series of fully formed visionary experiences: now not just sparks of light, but mandalas and peaceful and wrathful deities, accompanied by states of awe and terror. These are famously described in the

Tibetan Book of the Dead.[23] These visions are part of religious cultures that prepare for death, in which practitioners receive introductions and instructions about dying, and study its related experiences and physiology. Oral advice is also read to the deceased, in the hopes that the deceased may realize the post-death imagery of their own mind, and thus attain a favorable rebirth or liberation.

Textual Revelation. Visionary experience plays a part in the revelation of texts known as "treasures" (*gter*). In the Nyingma and Bön traditions, a text may be concealed by a past master (such as the 8th-century Padmasambhava); the text could be hidden away in a physical location or concealed in the recesses of a disciple's mind. At the appropriate time, perhaps centuries later, the text is unearthed from the location or memory in which it was initially concealed. The role of vision in this process can be seen in written descriptions of treasure discoveries, and in accounts from contemporary treasure revealers.[24] Prior to discovering a treasure, the revealer may have visionary or dreamlike experiences that represent intuitions of the revelation to come. In addition, they may have encounters with past masters like Padmasambhava, who affirm their worthiness to reveal treasures or provide auspicious signs. The act of discovery may also be marked by visions, with miraculous appearances or visitations hinting at an oncoming revelation and its physical location, or the text itself may be received in vision.[25]

A related type of visionary revelation is called "pure vision" (*dag snang*).[26] This type of scriptural production is distinguished from treasure revelation in that the texts are not said to have been concealed but rather acquired in vision directly from their sources. Such revelations are said to occur through direct experiences of buddhas, within meditative experiences, or within dreams and may take place in one's own world or involve travels to pure lands.

Creating Visions: Illusions, Deceptions, and Contests. Creating (rather than receiving) miraculous appearances (*cho 'phrul*) is a frequent trope in Tibetan narrative literature and religious histories, and sometimes takes the form of battles in which the opponents use illusions. For instance, in Bön narratives about Tönpa Shenrab (Ston pa gshen rab), his archenemy Khyabpa Lakring (Khyab pa lag ring) tries to deceive or destroy him with illusions: sending Shenrab false images of his teachers and family; or hosts of deceptive goddesses and demons; or emanations of fires, floods, and storms. Shenrab sees through these with his insight into their illusory nature, but he also counters them with miraculous manifestations of his own. Such narratives make comments about the deceptive nature of appearances but also suggest how an exalted being may make skillful use of such visionary appearances.

Similarly, one of the more entertaining features found in Tibetan narratives is the illusion contest, as when Bönpos and Buddhists are portrayed as competing for superiority in a contest organized by Emperor Trisong Detsen (Khri srong lde brtsan; 742–*c*. 800 CE). This is an attempt to solve a religious rivalry (and attain royal support) through a contest of miraculous displays and magical power (*rdzu 'phrul dang mthu rtsal*). In Shardza Tashi Gyaltsen's (Shar rdza bkra shis rgyal mtshan; 1859–1934) account, the participants demonstrate their prowess by striking the sun and moon together like cymbals, making rainbow drawings in space, cutting off and reattaching their heads, throwing thunderbolts in space, and so forth.[27] The ability to create such appearances is valued not in itself, but rather as a marker of true inner accomplishments, and thus indicates the efficacy and authenticity of one's own tradition.

VISIONARY BUDDHISM IN TIBET: SOTERIOLOGICAL AIMS AND VISIONARY YOGAS

Practitioners across Tibet's religious sects have used meditative techniques that are designed to induce visions. These are particularly apparent in practices related to the *Kālacakra Tantra*, and in the Bön and Nyingma contemplative traditions known as the Great Perfection. Such practices may be closely related to the types of vision discussed in the "Visionary Buddhism in Tibet: Worldly Aims" section above: instructions for their practice may be revealed in treasure texts or visions, and their practitioners may also engage in visionary techniques of divination or have significant visionary experiences outside of meditative practice. Still, visionary meditation can be distinguished from these as its practitioners see their ultimate aims as being "transcendent" rather than mundane and view it as being a key part of the Buddhist path to enlightenment.

Visionary Practices in the Kālacakra Tantra. The tantric Kālacakra tradition, which entered Tibet as early as the 11th century, contains a series of visionary perfection-phase practices known as the "six yogas."[28] These use two basic techniques, called "night yoga" and "day yoga," to induce types of sensory deprivation. In the first, the practitioner prepares a completely dark room in which to meditate; the second uses an outdoor shelter that gives an unobstructed view of the empty sky. In these settings, the practitioner holds the body in specified postures, and eventually visionary experiences begin. At first, one is said to have visions of unstructured lights: images such as sparks and fireflies (just as in the signs of death). Eventually, these culminate in a fully formed vision of a goddess known as the "Great Seal" or "Great Consort," who is perceived both in the body and in the sky. The vision of the Great Seal is described as an "empty form" (*stong gzugs, śūnyatā-bimba*), meaning that it is empty of intrinsic existence but is nonetheless luminous and able to be seen. In its accounts of vision, Kālacakra literature explains that practitioners perceive these empty form visions not with the ordinary eyes, but with the transcendent five eyes.[29]

When the Great Seal is present, the practice then starts to resemble the "blazing and dripping" type of sexual yoga that is common in Buddhist perfection-phase practices: a fire ignites at the practitioner's navel, melts a reservoir of seminal nuclei located at the forehead, and these drip down the central channel, creating sensations of bliss as they pass through the various energy wheels. However, this Kālacakra yoga is described as being carried out in a visionary context rather than a visualized or physical one. Practitioners are instructed to abandon the "Action Seal" (meaning an actual physical consort) and to also avoid meditations involving a "Gnostic Seal" (a visualized consort). Rather, one is told to embrace the "Great Seal" (the visionary consort), as union with this empty-form goddess is the true path to buddhahood.

Kālacakra visionary yogas could thus be seen in part as rethinking and critiquing two hallmark tantric practices: visualization and sexual yoga. (But overall Kālacakra tradition does contain plenty of both of these.) Arising late in the history of Indian Buddhism, Kālacakra seems to have looked back on preceding tantric practice with concern about the "impurity" of physical sexual yoga, and with suspicion of the deliberate, effortful conceptuality of visualization practices. As its alternative, it offers a visionary consort, said to be capable of producing a bliss that can burn away the physical atomic structure of the body, and leave it as a pure empty form, just like the body of the visionary Great Seal herself.

Visionary Practices in the Great Perfection. The dark-room and sky-gazing techniques can also be found in the Great Perfection, as parts of the contemplative techniques it calls "direct transcendence" (*thod rgal*). As in Kālacakra, these are practices in which immersion in light or darkness leads to a series of unfolding visions, beginning with unstructured lights and culminating in visions of buddhas and mandalas. In the Great Perfection context, the practices are largely devoid of sexual content. A distinctive discourse in the Great Perfection describes a set of light-channels in the body, which form part of the physiological matrix for visionary experience. A key idea here is that the body contains a pure luminous "awareness" (*rig pa*) locked away at the heart region, like a lamp concealed in a vase. A set of energy channels connects the heart to the eyes. When a practitioner uses the appropriate bodily postures and contemplative techniques, the radiance of awareness is said to rise up through those channels to the gateway of the eyes, such that it can be seen in the practitioner's vision. The goal of these practices is often described in terms of "recognition": vision provides a moment where one can determine that external visions are simply the lighting up of one's internal awareness, and this determination can lead to the end of dualistic perception.

Great Perfection literature contains numerous detailed descriptions of these experiences, organized around schemes like the "four visions."[30] In the first of these visions, the "vision of awareness' immediacy" (*rig pa mngon sum gyi snang ba*), one's internal awareness, comes directly into view as moving spots of light called "seminal nuclei" (*thig le*) and linked chains of lights called "the little linked lambs of awareness" (*rig pa lu gu rgyud*), named after the appearance of a string of lambs on a mountainside. These appear against a radiant blue background called "the expanse" (*dbyings*). Second, in the "vision of the intensification of experience" (*nyams gong nas gong du 'phel ba'i snang ba*), the visions become more continuous, numerous, and diverse: taking different shapes and assembling in simple configurations. Third, in the "vision of awareness' optimization" (*rig pa tshad la phebs pa'i snang ba*), the lights then organize themselves into a mandala of one hundred peaceful and wrathful deities: the expanse becoming a buddhafield, the seminal nuclei becoming inestimable mansions, and the linked lambs becoming buddha-bodies. Fourth, in the "vision of exhaustion within reality" (*chos nyid zad pa'i snang ba*), the visions dissolve back to the expanse, providing an image of appearances resolving into emptiness.

Visionary Practice and Philosophical Views. Literature describing such visions often presents visionary practice as an alternative way to contemplate and realize emptiness. Great Perfection traditions, for instance, refer to visions as a type of "higher seeing" (a term more commonly used for meditations on emptiness) or as a "path of seeing" (a term typically used for one's first direct experience of emptiness).[31] Visions of course appear to the eyes of the practitioner, but they do so in a way where it is clear that those appearances have no substantial reality. Kālacakra's visionary Great Seal, for instance, is often identified with the goddess Prajñāpāramitā; encounters with this goddess are then described as being encounters with the ultimate: "The Great Seal is the defining characteristic of all phenomena, their lack of inherent nature. It is [also] endowed with all supreme aspects, and is [the goddess] Prajñāpāramitā, the mother who gives birth to the buddhas."[32] Such visionary objects are empty, but this can also be understood as a type of luminous insubstantial "fullness," in which appearances do not contradict an object's ultimate empty nature. The fact that such realizations involve acts of seeing suggests that, for some Buddhists, the ultimate may not simply be the purview of an internal insight, but that it may be encountered in the external world, through the gateway of the eyes.

REVIEW OF LITERATURE

"Visionary Buddhism" is not a distinct field of study that possesses its own literature. Nonetheless, there are several overlapping bodies of work though which one can pursue its study. First among these would be translations of primary sources and analyses of traditions that employ visionary techniques. These sources do not treat their subjects purely through the lens of visionary practice but rather analyze the broader ritual and contemplative projects of which vision is a part. Such studies have been produced by several interrelated groups: academic scholars, contemporary Tibetan religious teachers, and Western Buddhist practitioners. Beginning in the late 1990s a wide selection of reliable and thorough treatments of the Kālacakra and Great Perfection traditions began to appear, along with materials on post-death experiences.[33]

Other studies have focused on visionary individuals and localized practices rather than on broad traditions. Such studies incorporate biography and narrative accounts of vision.[34] Other studies have presented vision and visionaries ethnographically, as well as in studies of material culture, visual art, and contemporary politics.[35]

In the 2000s, the subjects of "sensing," "seeing," and "vision" became popular subjects for thematic studies and comparative projects in Buddhist studies.[36]

Studies of Buddhist epistemological traditions also provide important background for understanding visionary practice. This is a well-developed literature that has been one of Buddhist studies specialties; it presents philosophical studies and intellectual histories inspired by Buddhist *pramāṇa* literature, major Indian Buddhist thinkers, and Tibetan scholastic traditions.[37] The Tibetan "mind and awareness" (*blo rig*) literature is also useful here.[38]

Finally, there are bodies of literature that are outside of (and perhaps unaware of) Buddhist studies on vision, but that nonetheless add importantly to the understanding of the topic. The first of these is scientific studies of unusual visual phenomena. While one would not want to reduce Buddhist visionary phenomena to these issues, it is nonetheless informative to explore topics like entoptic lights, Charles Bonnet syndrome, and the relationships between vision and sensory deprivation.[39] Second, there is a growing body of literature in the field of visual studies, by which visionary Buddhist material could be informed, and to which it could contribute.[40]

PRIMARY SOURCES

In the Kālacakra tradition, the two primary textual sources are the root *Kālacakra Tantra* and its immense commentary *Stainless Light*.[41] An early Tibetan commentary that focuses on matters of visionary experience can be found in the works of Yumo Mikyo Dorjé (Yu mo mi bskyod rdo rje; 11th century).[42]

In the Great Perfection, two bodies of literature have been very important in the understanding of visionary practices. These are the *Seventeen Tantras* (from the Nyingma Tradition) and the *Oral Tradition from Zhang Zhung* (from the Bön tradition).[43] Works by Longchenpa (Klong chen pa) and Drugyelwa (Bru rgyal ba) are good starting points for delving into the Tibetan commentarial traditions on those works.[44]

FURTHER READING

Achard, Jean-Luc. *The Six Lamps: Secret Dzogchen Instructions of the Bön Tradition.* Boston: Wisdom Publications, 2017.

Elkins, James. *How to Use Your Eyes.* New York: Routledge, 2000.

Gentry, James D., ed. *Revue d'Études Tibétaines* 50, special issue on "Tibetan Religion and the Senses," June 2019.

Germano, David. "Poetic Thought, the Intelligent Universe, and the Mystery of Self: The Tantric Synthesis of Rdzogs Chen in Fourteenth Century Tibet." PhD thesis, University of Wisconsin, 1992.

Hatchell, Christopher. *Naked Seeing: The Great Perfection, the Wheel of Time, and Visionary Buddhism in Renaissance Tibet.* New York: Oxford University Press, 2014.

Harrison, Paul, trans. *The Samādhi of Direct Encounter with the Buddhas of the Present: An Annotated English Translation of the Tibetan Version of the Pratyutpanna-Buddha-Saṃmukhāvasthita-Samādhi-Sūtra, with Several Appendices Relating to the History of the Text.* Tokyo: International Institute for Buddhist Studies, 1990.

Karmay, Samten. *Secret Visions of the Fifth Dalai Lama: The Gold Manuscript in the Fournier Collection.* London: Serindia Publications, 1988.

Kilty, Gavin, ed. and trans. *Ornament of Stainless Light: An Exposition of the Kālacakra Tantra.* Boston: Wisdom Publications, 2004.

Merabet, Lotfi, Denise Maguire, Aisling Warde, Karen Alterescu, Robert Stickgold, and Alvaro Pascual-Leone. "Visual Hallucinations During Prolonged Blindfolding in Sighted Subjects." *Journal of Neuro-Ophthalmology* 24, no. 2 (2004): 109–113.

Ramachandran, V. S. *Phantoms in the Brain: Probing the Mysteries of the Human Mind.* New York: William Morrow, 1998.

Wallace, Vesna. *The Inner Kālacakratantra: A Buddhist View of the Tantric Individual.* Oxford: Oxford University Press, 2001.

NOTES

1. See the *So sor thar ba'i mdo* (*Prātimokṣa-sūtra*), D2, 18a.6. Related discussions from Pāli sources can be found in the *Discourse on the Foundations of Mindfulness* (*Satipaṭṭhāna Sutta*, MN 10); and see Bhikku Ñāṇamoli and Bhikku Bodhi, trans., *The Middle Length Discourses of the Buddha: A New Translation of the Majjhima Nikāya* (Boston: Wisdom Publications, 1995), 153.
2. For discussions of these, see Ṭhānissaro Bhikkhu, *The Buddhist Monastic Code I: The Pāṭimokkha Rules Translated & Explained by Ṭhānissaro Bhikkhu* (Valley Center, CA: Metta Forest Monastery, 2007), 62, 102, 111, 203, 347.
3. From *Commentary on the "Supplement to [Nāgārjuna's] 'Treatise on the Middle Way'"* (*dBu ma la 'jug pa'i bshad pa, Madhyamakāvatārabhāṣya*), D3862, 255a.6. For translation and discussions related to this passage, see Kevin Vose, *Resurrecting Candrakīrti: Disputes in the Tibetan Creation of Prāsaṅgika* (Boston: Wisdom Publications, 2008), 86.

4. D4089, vol. khu, 64b.3. See Louis de La Valée Poussin (trans.), *Abhidharmakoṣabhāṣyam of Vasubandhu*, trans. from the French by Leo M. Pruden (Berkeley, CA: Asian Humanities Press, 1988), 1176.
5. This is based on a lengthy description found in the *Perfection of Wisdom in 25,000 Lines* (*Shes rab kyi pha rol tu phyin pa stong phrag nyi shu lnga pa, Pañcaviṃśatisāhasrikā-prajñāpāramitā*), D0009, vol. ka, 72a.3.
6. D0133. Paul Harrison has translated and written extensively on this text. See Paul Harrison, trans., *The Samādhi of Direct Encounter with the Buddhas of the Present: An Annotated English Translation of the Tibetan Version of the Pratyutpanna-Buddha-Saṃmukhāvasthita-Samādhi-Sūtra, with Several Appendices Relating to the History of the Text* (Tokyo: International Institute for Buddhist Studies, 1990).
7. D0133, ch. 5, 17a.3. Translated while consulting Harrison's translation, 49.
8. D0133, ch. 3, 15a.2. Translated while consulting Harrison's translation, 42.
9. Tibetanized in forms like *pra, pra se na, pra ti se na, pra phab pa*. For notes on the history of the Tibetan form of this term, see Bill McGrath, "Tantric Divination and Empirical Diagnosis: A Genealogy of Channel Prasenā Rituals in the Tibetan Medical Tradition," in *Knowledge and Context in Tibetan Medicine*, ed. William McGrath (Leiden, The Netherlands: Brill, 2019).
10. See McGrath, "Tantric Divination," for discussion of the *Questions of Subāhu Tantra*, analysis of the Tibetan assimilation of *prasenā*, and discussions of medical versions of *prasenā* rituals.
11. See Pasang Wangdu and Hildegard Diemberger, *Dba'-Bzhed: The Royal Narrative Concerning the Bringing of the Buddha's Doctrine to Tibet* (Vienna: Verlag der Österreichischen Akademie der Wissenschaften, 2000), 55; and see McGrath, "Tantric Divination," 275.
12. Dalai Lama, *Freedom in Exile: The Autobiography of the Dalai Lama* (New York: Harper Collins, 1990), 11, 216; and see Lama Chime Radha, "Tibet," in *Oracles and Divination*, ed. Carmen Blacker and Michael Lowe (London: Random House, 1981), 9.
13. For discussion and examples, see John Vincent Bellezza, *Calling Down the Gods: Spirit-Mediums, Sacred Mountains and Related Bon Textual Traditions in Upper Tibet* (Leiden, The Netherlands: Brill, 2005), 68ff, 355, 437; and see Hildegard Diemberger's discussion of "Divination with mirrors and lakes," in her article "Female Oracles in Modern Tibet," in *Women in Tibet*, ed. Janet Gyatso and Hanna Havnevik (New York: Columbia University Press, 2005), 133.
14. See Lama Chime Radha, "Tibet," 11–12.
15. *Mthong ba don ldan*. See Samten Karmay's full presentation of this in *Secret Visions of the Fifth Dalai Lama: The Gold Manuscript in the Fournier Collection* (London: Serindia Publications, 1988).
16. Karmay, *Secret Visions of the Fifth Dalai Lama*, 45, 55.
17. Karmay, *Secret Visions of the Fifth Dalai Lama*, 36, 49, 55, 59.
18. Karmay, *Secret Visions of the Fifth Dalai Lama*, 29–30, 38, 47, 55.
19. Karmay, *Secret Visions of the Fifth Dalai Lama*, 27.
20. Karmay, *Secret Visions of the Fifth Dalai Lama*, 35.
21. For examples from the Great Perfection tradition, see Ian Baker and Thomas Laird, *The Dalai Lama's Secret Temple: Tantric Wall Paintings from Tibet* (New York: Thames & Hudson, 2000); and Karmay, *Secret Visions of the Fifth Dalai Lama*, 28.
22. There are various formulations of these signs. For examples, see Lati Rinbochay and Jeffrey Hopkins, *Death, Intermediate State and Rebirth* (Ithaca, NY: Snow Lion Publications, 1985), 32; and Christopher Hatchell, *Naked Seeing: The Great Perfection, the Wheel of Time, and Visionary Buddhism in Renaissance Tibet* (New York: Oxford University Press, 2014), 335.
23. Gyurme Dorje (trans.), *The Tibetan Book of the Dead: The Great Liberation by Hearing in the Intermediate States* (New York: Viking, 2006).
24. See Janet Gyatso, "The Logic of Legitimation in the Tibetan Treasure Tradition," *History of Religions* 33, no. 1 (1993): 97–134; and Antonio Terrone, "Bya Rog Prog Zhu, the Raven Crest: The Life and

Teachings of Bde Chen 'Od Gsal Rdo Rje, Treasure Revealer of Contemporary Tibet" (PhD thesis, University of Leiden, 2010), 164, 197.

25. See discussions of these various types of visionary signs and experiences in Janet Gyatso's articles, "Signs, Memory and History: A Tantric Buddhist Theory of Scriptural Transmission," *Journal of the International Association of Buddhist Studies* 9, no. 2 (1986): 7–35; and Gyatso, "The Logic of Legitimation."
26. See Tulku Thondup, *Hidden Teachings of Tibet: An Explanation of the Terma Tradition of the Nyingma School of Buddhism* (London: Wisdom Publications, 1986), 90. See also Janet Gyatso, "Genre, Authorship, and Transmission in Visionary Buddhism: The Literary Traditions of Thang-Stong Rgyal-Po," in *Tibetan Buddhism: Reason and Revelation*, ed. Steven Goodman and Ronald Davidson (Albany: State University of New York Press, 1992); and see also Dudjom Rinpoche, *The Nyingma School of Tibetan Buddhism: Its Fundamentals and History*, trans. and ed. Gyurme Dorje and Matthew Kapstein (Boston: Wisdom Publications, 1991), I.747.
27. This is Shardza quoting the *Srid rgyud*, in his own *Legs bshad rin po che'i mdzod*; and see Samten Karmay, *The Treasury of Good Sayings: A Tibetan History of Bon* (Oxford, UK: Oxford University Press, 1972), 88.
28. See Vesna Wallace, *The Inner Kālacakratantra: A Buddhist View of the Tantric Individual* (Oxford, UK: Oxford University Press, 2001), 203; and see Giacomella Orofino, "On the Ṣaḍaṅgayoga and the Realisation of Ultimate Gnosis in the Kalacakratantra," *East and West* 46 (1996): 127–143.
29. See discussions and translations related to this in Hatchell, *Naked Seeing*, 108ff.
30. *snang ba bzhi*. The descriptions here are from *Stringing a Garland of Pearls* (*Mu tig phreng ba brgyus pa*), 136ff; this commentary to the *Tantra of the Blazing Lamps* (*Sgron ma 'bar ba'i rgyud*) is found in the "Lhasa" edition of the Nyingma bKa' ma, published by Tsering Gyatso, volume Be (105). Here I have also used David Germano's unpublished translation of Longchenpa's *Treasury of Words and Meanings*, chapter 8, 264ff.
31. *lhag mthong*, *vipaśyanā*. The term in this context has the sense of "superior sights" or "higher sights," as it refers to the three basic ways that awareness is encountered in direct transcendence practice, which are "sound, light, and rays"; and *mthong lam*, *darśana-mārga*; see *The Twenty-One Nails* (*Gzer bu nyi shu rtsa gcig gi gzhung*), in *History and Doctrine of Bon-Po Niṣpanna Yoga*, repr. by Lokesh Chandra and Tenzin Namdak (New Delhi: International Academy of Indian Culture, 1968), ZZNG, 511; and Gyerpungpa's commentary (*Gzer bu nyer gcig gi 'grel pa*), in *History and Doctrine*, repr. by Chandra and Namdak, ZZNG, 554ff.
32. From *Stainless Light* (*Dri ma med pa'i 'od*, *Vimalaprabhā*), D0845, 409a.2. See further comments on this in Christopher Hatchell, "Visual Worlds II: Buddhist Practices of Visualization and Vision," *Religion Compass* 7, no. 9 (2013), 349–360. See also Hatchell, *Naked Seeing*, 102, 165.
33. See Vesna Wallace's works, including *The Inner Kālacakratantra*. See also Gavin Kilty (ed. and trans.), *Ornament of Stainless Light: An Exposition of the Kālacakra Tantra* (Boston: Wisdom Publications, 2004); Samten Karmay, *The Great Perfection: A Philosophical and Meditative Teaching of Tibetan Buddhism* (London: E.J. Brill, 1988); David Germano, "Poetic Thought, the Intelligent Universe, and the Mystery of Self: The Tantric Synthesis of Rdzogs Chen in Fourteenth Century Tibet" (PhD thesis, University of Wisconsin, 1992); Tenzin Wangyal, *Wonders of the Natural Mind: The Essence of Dzogchen in the Native Bon Tradition of Tibet* (Barrytown: Station Hill Press, 1993); Lopon Tenzin Namdak, *Bönpo Dzogchen Teachings According to Lopon Tenzin Namdak*, trans. and ed. John Myrdhin Reynolds (Kathmandu: Vajra Publications, 2006); Jean-Luc Achard, *The Six Lamps: Secret Dzogchen Instructions of the Bön Tradition* (Boston: Wisdom Publications, 2017); see also his series of Zhangzhung Nyengyü Studies, beginning with *The Three Precepts* (München: Naldjor Institute for Movement, 2005); and Dorjé, trans., *The Tibetan Book of the Dead*; and Bryan J. Cuevas, *The Hidden History of the Tibetan Book of the Dead* (Oxford: Oxford University Press, 2003).

34. Karmay, *Secret Visions of the Fifth Dalai Lama*; Bellezza, *Calling Down the Gods*; Terrone, "Raven Crest"; Sarah Jacoby, *Love and Liberation: Autobiographical Writings of the Tibetan Buddhist Visionary Sera Khandro* (New York: Columbia University Press, 2014); and Suzanne Bessenger, *Echoes of Enlightenment: The Life and Legacy of the Tibetan Saint Sönam Peldren* (New York: Oxford University Press, 2016).
35. David Germano, "Re-Membering the Dismembered Body of Tibet: Contemporary Tibetan Visionary Movements in the People's Republic of China," in *Buddhism in Contemporary Tibet*, ed. Melvyn C. Goldstein and Matthew Kapstein (Berkeley: University of California Press, 1998); Ian Baker and Thomas Laird, *The Dalai Lama's Secret Temple: Tantric Wall Paintings from Tibet*; and James Duncan Gentry, *Power Objects in Tibetan Buddhism: The Life, Writings, and Legacy of Sokdokpa Lodrö Gyeltsen* (Leiden, The Netherlands: Brill, 2016).
36. "Revue d'Études Tibétaines 50: Tibetan Religion and the Senses" (June 2019); and Hatchell, *Naked Seeing*.
37. Georges Dreyfus, *Recognizing Reality: Dharmakīrti's Philosophy and Its Tibetan Interpretations* (Albany: State University of New York Press, 1997); Jeffrey Hopkins, *Meditation on Emptiness* (London: Wisdom Publications, 1983); and John D. Dunne, *Foundations of Dharmakīrti's Philosophy* (Boston: Wisdom Publications, 2004).
38. Lati Rinpoche, *Mind in Tibetan Buddhism: Oral Commentary on Ge-shay Jam-bel-sam-pel's Presentation of Awareness and Knowledge*, ed. and trans. Elizabeth Napper (Ithaca, NY: Snow Lion Publications, 1980).
39. For popular sources, see Vilayanur S. Ramachandran, *Phantoms in the Brain: Probing the Mysteries of the Human Mind* (New York: William Morrow, 1998); Oliver Sacks, *Hallucinations* (New York: Alfred A. Knopf, 2012); James Elkins, *How to Use Your Eyes* (New York: Routledge, 2000), 232, 238; for more technical sources, see Stephen H. Sinclair, Madelynn Azar-Cavanagh, Keith A. Soper, Ronald F. Tuma, and Harvey N. Mayrovirz, "Investigation of the Source of the Blue Field Entoptic Phenomenon," *Investigative Ophthalmology & Visual Science* 30, no. 4 (1989): 668–673; Kenneth Gold and Peter V. Rabins, "Isolated Visual Hallucinations and the Charles Bonnet Syndrome: A Review of Literature and Presentation of Six Cases," *Comprehensive Psychiatry* 30, no. 1 (1989): 90–98; and Lofti Merabet, Denise Maguire, Aisling Warde, Karen Alterescu, Robert Stickgold, and Alvaro Pascual-Leone, "Visual Hallucinations During Prolonged Blindfolding in Sighted Subjects," *Journal of Neuro-Ophthalmology* 24, no. 2 (2004): 109–113.
40. See James Elkins, *Visual Studies: A Skeptical Introduction* (New York: Routledge, 2003).
41. The *Kālacakra Tantra* (*Mchog gi dang po'i sangs rgyas las phyung ba rgyud kyi rgyal po dpal dus kyi 'khor lo zhes bya ba, Paramādibuddhoddhṛta-śrīkālacakra-nāma-tantrarājā*) can be found in various editions of the Tibetan canon, including the Dergé edition (text number D0362 and D1346). Puṇḍarīka's *Stainless Light* (*Bsdus pa'i rgyud kyi rgyal po dus kyi 'khor lo'i 'grel bshad rtsa ba'i rgyud kyi rjes su 'jug pa stong phrag bcu pa bcu gnyis pa dri ma med pa'i 'od ces bya ba, Vimalaprabhā-nāma-mūlatantrānusāriṇī-dvādaśasāhasrikā-laghukālacakratantrarājaṭīkā*) is numbered D0845 and D1347.
42. See the text *Stong nyid gsal sgron* in the collection *The Cycle of the Four Radiant Lamps* (*Gsal sgron skor bzhi*) (Gangtok, India: Sherab Gyaltsen and Lama Dawa, 1983). Note that in this published edition the author is misidentified as A-wa-dhū-ti-pa-bsod-nams.
43. *Rgyud bcu bdun*, found in the various editions of the *Collected Tantras of the Ancients* (*Rnying ma rgyud 'bum*). See in particular the text *Tantra of the Blazing Lamps* (*Sgron ma 'bar ba'i rgyud*), mTshams brag edition of the *Rnying ma rgyud 'bum*, vol. 12 (na), 467–491. See also the commentary to this text, *Mu tig phreng ba brgyus pa*, in the "Lhasa" edition of the Nyingma bKa' ma, published by Tsering Gyatso, volume Be (105), 15–325. For the *Zhang zhung snyan rgyud*, see *History and Doctrine*.
44. Among his famous "Seven Treasuries" (*Mdzod bdun*), see his *Treasury of Words and Meanings* (*Tshig don mdzod*) (Gangtok, India: Sherab Gyaltsen and Khyentse Labrang, 1983); and see his *Commentary on the Intended Meaning of the Six Lamps* (*Sgron ma drug gi dgongs don 'grel pa*), in *History and Doctrine*, 355–422.

Chris Hatchell

TRANSMISSION OF BUDDHIST MEDIA AND TEXTS

MEDIA THEORY

The buddha is reported to have told his followers to spread his message far and wide, in various languages, and by implication, media, and so it has been.[1] With the possible exception of Jainism, Buddhism is the oldest extant proselytizing religion, and its great success must be attributed in part to its willingness to utilize all the latest developments in media technology to spread its message. Not only was the oral tradition successfully deployed in Buddhism, but the oldest dated printed book in the world is the Buddhist *Diamond Sūtra* that reads (according to the Gregorian calendar): "Printed on 11 May 868 by Wang Chieh, for free general distribution, in order in deep reverence to perpetuate the memory of his parents."[2] Elsewhere in the Buddhist world, countless thousands of hours were spent by literate monks, and sometimes even laypeople, copying manuscripts by hand on such media as palm leaves, birch bark, silk, and mulberry paper to gain merit and preserve the dharma.[3] In contemporary society, Buddhism continues to explore the use of new popular media. In the late 20th century, the music stores of Asia were filled with tape cassette recordings of monks delivering sermons or reciting Buddhist texts. Currently, the Pali, Chinese, and Tibetan canons are available on the internet for all to read, and on September 15, 2014, a search for "Buddhism" in the Apple iTunes store yielded more than four hundred applications for smartphones. This proliferation is augmented by the thousands of Buddhist websites, blogs, and podcasts related to Buddhism that populate the internet.[4]

Media technologies, namely the material systems by which people communicate, do not merely transmit information, but shape the message by accelerating, retarding or blocking different features of a communication.[5] All media have their own particular constraints, as well as affordances specific to them.[6] As media historian Paul Heyer has explained,

> The transformation of basic information into knowledge is not a disembodied process. It is powerfully influenced by the manner of its material expression. In other words, the medium is never neutral. How we organize and transmit our perceptions and knowledge about the world strongly affects the nature of those perceptions and the way we come to know the world.[7]

As communication technologies improve and allow people to communicate more widely and efficiently, they have the potential to change the way society develops as new ideas are afforded the ability to spread more effectively. Writings allow exposure to a greater variety of ideas than orality because far more written works can be taken from one place to another than could possibly be transmitted orally. Beyond this, print and electronic media greatly expand on the breadth, volume, and efficiency of communication. As such, the intellectual developments in a society are closely tied to the shape of available communications media.

In the oral world in which Buddhism started, most people would only have come into contact with ideas espoused by someone with whom they had had personal contact, whereas today many Buddhists living, for instance, in a small town in middle America, may have learned everything they know about the religion from the Internet and may have never actually met another Buddhist in person. These situations engender very different dynamics. Jeremy Rifkin has compiled a comprehensive study that looks at how different forms of consciousness arise in large measure due to the changes in the ways that humans connect and communicate with each other. He holds that revolutions in consciousness occur in tandem with changes in media technology that allow our senses to expand further and further beyond our immediate environment. As our "temporal and spatial orientation is recalibrated . . . we undergo a process of reinterpreting our new environments and social context in an effort to locate our place and purpose in the new scheme of things."[8] Likewise, seminal media theorist Walter Ong famously opined that media technology "asserts its effects simultaneously on quite diverse sensoria, from the highly visualist sensorium of technological cultures veering toward new organizations in sound, to the sensoria of primitive cultures which have not yet crossed the threshold of literacy," and these effects are felt particularly acutely in the realm of religion and its associated textual landscape.[9]

Media theory holds that a full picture of society must include a detailed analysis of its communications and media environment, along with a careful and nuanced analysis of the various modalities of each stage of communication. For example, there are significant differences between primary orality in which writing is not known or used at all, and secondary orality, where writing is known but oral discourse is still the main form of expression. Writing, too, can be used in many different ways, which Paul Griffiths has helpfully identified as composition, display, and storage, and the effects of each mode can be quite different.[10] The social and psychological effects of writing also vary depending on whether it is done by hand, printed with a press, or reproduced electronically. Furthermore, each form of communication necessitates different social institutions to ensure its transmission through time and space. Therefore, a better understanding of Buddhism and its textual traditions can be expected to emerge through an investigation of its relationship to media technologies.

THE ORAL STAGE

The buddha lived at some point between the 6th and 4th centuries BCE in northeast India, probably before writing was used in that region.[11] Therefore, all of his sermons were most likely retained and passed on through an oral tradition that used some techniques associated with the sophisticated tradition of Vedic memorization, and added some of its own methods.[12] Although there has been some debate about the presence of writing in India at this time, it is quite clear that even in the unlikely case that writing was known, it was not used for recording or transmitting religious texts.[13] Writing implements, manuscripts, or the act of reading are never mentioned in the canonical Pali texts, even though every conceivable aspect of monastic life at the time is described in the *Vinaya*. As Rhys Davids and Oldenberg point out in their introduction to the *Vinaya*,

> Every movable thing, down to the smallest and least important domestic utensils, is in some way or other referred to, and its use is pointed out . . . But nowhere do we find the least trace of any reference to manuscripts, much less of inks, or pens, or styles, or leaves or other writing materials. And we do find, on the contrary, passages which show the

> difficulties which arose every time that the memorial tradition by word of mouth of any of the sacred texts was interrupted, or threatened to be interrupted.[14]

Furthermore, traditional chronicles even as late as the 15th-century Thai *Mūlasāsana* also speak of the religious texts as traditionally having been transmitted orally:

> The religion which was established in our land of Thailand ought to be understood in the hearts of the wise, learned people as follows: Mahā Upāli learned the *Vinaya* from the very mouth of the Buddha and thus it is said that Upāli was the first [in the line of transmission]. Then came Dasako, who was the second . . . then came all the noble people . . . who passed it down far and wide from one generation to the next and without end.[15]

The Pali *Suttas* all begin with the phrase *evaṃ me sutaṃ*, "Thus have I heard," pointing, again, toward their oral origin. The term *bahussuta* is commonly used to describe a learned person, which literally means "one who has heard much" and not "one who is widely read" as often found in a literate society. Monks would spend many hours of each day memorizing texts, and much of their training and the very organization of the early sangha was structured to foster the memorization and transmission of the teachings. Traditionally, two main tasks were assigned to the monks, ideally, according to their propensities: *vipassanādhura* "bearing the tradition of meditation" and *ganthadhura* "bearing the textual tradition." Among the monks charged with *ganthadhura*, the actual memorization of the texts was assigned to specialists called *bhāṇakas* who were divided into several groups responsible for the different bodies of texts, perhaps some specializing in *Vinaya* and others in specific *Nikāyas*.[16] The longer texts themselves were often divided into *bhāṇavāras*, being recitation sections that were probably so designated to help in the mental organization of the vast amount of material that these monks were required to remember. Some *bhāṇakas* demonstrated such facility with the texts that they were granted the title of *tipiṭakadhara* or "bearer of the canon," as an acknowledgement of their extensive achievements in memorization. The monks who attended the early councils where the texts were collected and edited, for example, are generally referred to in chronicles as *tipiṭakadhara*.[17] In a world where an important measure of social value was derived from the amount of texts that one knew, there would have been great prestige associated with this title, and there are many accounts of rulers throughout Asia honoring those who bore large portions of the dharma in their head. For example, in a passage about the bringing of Buddhism from central to northern Thailand in the 7th century, the *Jinakālamālī* chronicle lists the five hundred *tipiṭakadhara* monks—whose job it was to deliver the oral tradition of Buddhist texts to the region—separately from the rest of the noble retinue that made the journey.[18] The sophisticated tradition of oral recitation and transmission is still extant, and the *Guinness Book of World Records* notes that the largest confirmed amount of text ever memorized by a human being is the Theravāda Buddhist canon, or *Tipiṭaka*, covering 16,000 printed pages, that was recited over several weeks by a Burmese monk in 1974.[19] Vibrant preaching traditions that continue some of the *bhāṇaka* practices are still found in Southeast Asian Buddhist communities, where learned monks wish to communicate the texts and teachings of Buddhism in a way that engages the community.[20]

Monastic rules were also introduced to deal with the vagaries of oral transmission. For example, a passage in the *Vinaya* allows a monk to interrupt his otherwise sacrosanct rains retreat (*vassa*) if a person who knew a text was ill and there was thus some danger of its disappearance:

> In case, O Bhikkhus, an upāsaka . . . knows how to recite a celebrated suttanta. If he sends a messenger to the Bhikkhus (saying) 'Might their reverences come and learn this suttanta; otherwise this suttanta will fall into oblivion' . . . then you ought to go.[21]

In addition to the the institutional features that coalesced around the oral tradition, the texts themselves were designed for memorization, and a number of their formal features developed to facilitate this process.[22] Powerful and effective mnemonic features are found in these texts such as the repetition of certain standardized passages, formulaic composition of key ideas and accounts, various kinds of poetic meter, and the copious use of numbered lists. One of the simplest ways to make a text more easily memorable is to preserve it in a verse form, and that is exactly how many of the early Buddhist texts were indeed preserved. Texts such as the *Dhammapada* and *Sutta Nipāta* were entirely in verse, and many others have metrical cores that were (perhaps later) expanded upon to provide more information and context.

In the *Mahāparinibbāna Sutta,* there are numerous occasions where the Buddha, having witnessed some event or other, utters a related verse (*udāna*) on the spot. It is very possible that such metrical passages may have served as the early core of the work around which narratives were embellished to give rise to the texts available now. For example, at one point the Buddha comes to the river Ganges and sees people looking for boats and making rafts as they attempt to get to the other side. He uses his magical powers to teleport to the far shore and then utters this verse: "when they want to cross the sea, lake or pond, people make a bridge or raft—the wise have crossed already."[23] It is easy to see how the surrounding story could have been composed based upon this core verse that had been passed down for some time.

The *Saṅgīti Sutta* of the *Dīgha Nikāya* contains an unusually frank discussion of the problems of oral transmission, along with a solution, which is that the teachings should be recited communally by the faithful to preserve them. Numbered lists are used here to facilitate their memorization, and this method is used widely in other collections such as the *Aṅguttara Nikāya,* which is organized around the thematic numbers that appear in the discourses. Sāriputta in the *Saṅgīti Sutta* addresses the monks, saying

> . . . this Dhamma has been well proclaimed by the Lord, the fully enlightened One. And so we should all recite it together without disagreement, so that this holy life may be enduring and established for a long time, thus to be for the welfare and happiness of the multitude, out of compassion for the world, for the benefit, welfare and happiness of devas and humans. And what is this Dhamma that has been well proclaimed by the Lord? There is one thing that was perfectly proclaimed by the Lord . . . What is this one thing? "All beings are maintained by nutriment. All beings are maintained by conditions. There are two things that were perfectly proclaimed by the Lord . . . Which are they? 'Mind and body', 'Ignorance and craving for existence' . . .

and so on, up to ten things.[24] This is an excellent example of the way in which the content of the text conforms to the medium. Of course, even the decision to end at the number ten is a function of having ten fingers on which to keep track of the various features of the Dhamma that are enumerated in this *sutta*.

Peter Skilling points out that the Sarvāstivādin version of this *Saṃgītisūtra* eventually developed into an *Abhidharma* text as the rudimentary lists were codified more thoroughly and systematically. He points out that here "we see how the early imperative to preserve the Dharma led to the drawing up of itemized and structured compendia of basic categories set within a narrative frame, and, in at least one case, how it led further to the production of an Abhidharma text. Going further, we may, at least in part, count the Abhidharma as a product of the concern for accurate preservation."[25]

THE HANDWRITTEN STAGE

The great Buddhist king Aśoka was the first in India to use writing in any appreciable way starting around the middle of the 3rd century BCE. Aśoka seems to have recognized the power of this new medium and had royal proclamations inscribed on rocks and pillars at key points throughout his kingdom, many of which promoted the dharma and communicated Buddhist ethics to the people.[26] A great many of the examples of early writing in India in the centuries after Aśoka are likewise Buddhist in nature, such as donative inscriptions on *stūpas* at Bhārhut.[27] While Aśoka is held to have sponsored the third Buddhist council to redact the texts, this council did not produce any written documents, but rather ended up with a group of edited texts that were still maintained through the mechanism of oral transmission. The Pali Canon is traditionally believed to have been finally written down at the Fourth Council in Śrī Laṅkā during the 1st century BCE.[28] If true, this would certainly be among the earliest organized projects in South Asia to transmit any religious texts in writing, cementing the close relationship between writing and Buddhism in the regional context. Other early projects appear also to have been Buddhist in nature, such as the possible production of Gāndhārī Buddhist manuscripts in the northwest around this time.[29]

Both literary and archeological evidence exist for the early Buddhist manuscript tradition, and much of it comes, in fact, from China. Early translations of sutras from the 2nd and 3rd centuries CE make it clear that written copies were used as the exemplars, and writers from the period such as Chu Shih-Hsing speak of having been able to acquire written *Prajñāpāramitā* texts.[30] There are also physical examples of early written texts from Gandhāra on birch bark dating to at least the 1st century CE, and possibly even to a few decades before the Common Era.[31] The oldest known Pali manuscript consists of twenty gold leaves inscribed with various canonical passages that were buried in a reliquary from the Pyu center of Śrī Kṣetra in Burma dated to the 5th or 6th century CE.[32]

Indic Buddhist texts began to be translated into Chinese in the 2nd century CE and, from that point on, a steady flow of Indian texts arrived in China and were translated over many centuries in what is the most extensive episode of cultural transmission in history. These texts included mainstream Buddhist works from several non-Mahāyāna sects as well as Mahāyāna texts and were largely written on silk or paper rolls. There was no central authority dictating what was and was not to be considered canonical, and the collections of texts became quite immense and came to include texts that were original Chinese products as well.[33] During the Tang period, complete copies of certain versions of the canon probably made their way to Japan, perhaps as early as the late 7th century.[34] Like rulers elsewhere in the Buddhist world, Japanese emperors sponsored the copying of sutras to gain merit and solidify their reign in the eyes of the faithful. By the 10th century, copying had become so important and revered in Japan that inks began to be made of powdered gold and silver and were applied in a striking way to dark blue paper, as had been done a few centuries earlier in China as well. In the early 14th century, various versions of Tibetan translations of Buddhist texts, both sutras (*mdo*) and *śāstras* (*bstan bcos*), were collected at the Kadampa (*bka' gdams pa*) monastery of Narthang (*snar thang*), and compiled into an important manuscript edition of the Kangyur (words of the buddha), although other versions have been compiled over time as well.

The main material used in South and Southeast Asia for writing has been palm leaves upon which letters were usually carved with a stylus and then inked, although ink was written with pens in the Gandhāran region as well. One or two holes are generally bored into the palm leaves through which a string or stick is put to hold the leaves together. Another common early material from the north is birch bark, a pliable natural material that holds the written word well. Sometimes, wooden boards have been used as protective covers for the manuscript bundles, and they have been painted or carved with varying degrees of ornamentation.[35]

Manuscripts have played a variety of different roles in Buddhist history including as supports for the words of texts, objects of worship, and symbols of power and prestige. The offering of fruit to a manuscript in a *pūja* ceremony, the procession of a manuscript through the city on the back of an elephant, or the enshrinement of a manuscript in a royal compound to mark the ruler's support of the dharma have been just as central to the lived reality of Buddhism as has reading the text to learn the doctrine. Over time, the initial ambivalent attitudes toward writing changed such that manuscripts came to be treated as physical embodiments of the teachings of the buddha. Many rulers sponsored manuscript production projects to strengthen their legitimacy in hopes of being seen as ideal dharmic rulers who were defenders and supporters of the faith, rather than out of a desire to supply the centers of monastic learning with better or more copies of the canonical texts.[36] Many manuscripts bear vernacular colophons written by the scribe that often provide information about the circumstances surrounding the production of the manuscript and the aspirations to gain merit or reach *nibbāna* on the part of the scribes and donors, who ranged from royal to monastic to lay.[37] Explicit hopes that the manuscript will be used by others to learn more about the dharma are infrequent. Copying the Tripiṭaka was used in China as well as other Asian countries to shore up the legitimacy of the rulers as seen by one early act of the first Sui emperor Wen (r. 581–604 CE) who, during the reunification of China after years of division and strife, commissioned forty-six copies of the Tripiṭaka to be distributed among various Buddhist temples around the country.[38]

The cultic function of manuscripts cannot be overemphasized, especially in light of the modern tendency to view them as repositories of knowledge and nothing more. Gregory Schopen was one of the first to write about the idea that written Buddhist texts began to serve as symbols of the Buddha himself and as such were viewed as objects of worship in Mahāyāna Buddhism.[39] However, this position was also taken eventually by mainstream schools as well, and by the 2nd century CE, more generally

> manuscripts were understood and treated as relics. The status of written representations of the words of the Buddha (*buddhavacana*) as dharma-relics (dharma-*śarīra*), functionally equivalent to bodily relics of the Buddha or other Buddhist venerables, is widely acknowledged in Buddhist tradition. Thus, the essential motivation for interring manuscripts is obvious; it was a form of relic dedication.[40]

This attitude is attested throughout the Buddhist world. For example,

> In the Mongolian language, the word *nom*, . . . designates both the Buddha Dharma and a book, implying the Mongols' nondifferentiating view of the two. The second line in the opening, salutary words found at the beginning of many Mongolian Buddhist texts, which reads: "I pay homage to the Dharma (*nom*)," implies one's homage to both, Dharma and the book. The Mongols' reverence for Buddhist scriptures is also expressed in their texts of dedication to different Buddhist sutras and in texts prescribing the methods of worshipping sutras, making offerings to them, and giving them alms as if they were living sagely ascetics.[41]

In China, the texts were often kept on revolving octagonal shelves, and it was thought that merit could be gained by merely turning the cabinet around. In reference to texts in China, Natasha Heller says,

> A text might be copied not primarily for one's own use, but as a means to generate merit, very often on behalf of someone else. Nor was a single copy necessarily the aim: a text could meritoriously be copied multiple times. Textual copying could also be coupled with bodily discipline, as in the case of those who copied out sutras in their own blood . . . The urge to disseminate scriptures, and for the state to benefit from the spiritual capital thereby generated, was also a factor in large-scale printings of the Buddhist canon, as in the case of imperial printings of the canon in the Northern Song.[42]

Christoph Emmrich writes of the Nepalese tradition of restoring, emending and improving a Mahāyāna *Prajñāpāramitā* text as a way of creating merit.[43] Throughout the Buddhist world, *stūpas* and images with Pali or Sanskrit texts inside them such as the *ye dhammā* credo have also been found, where the written text has been thought of as providing sacred power to the artifact.[44]

As with any new technology, it seems that different sectors of society held different attitudes toward orality and writing. These attitudes were determined by social and psychological factors, as well as practical considerations pertaining to the physical features of different media. Often a particular medium was central to one's social position, such as orality in the case of the *bhāṇakas*. The attitude of these monks toward writing would certainly have been affected by the degree to which they saw writing as a threat to their position. Likewise, monks belonging to traditions more amenable to the written word would have naturally had other opinions. Rulers also had different perspectives on orality and writing that depended at least in part on their view of the utility of these technologies for stabilizing their rule.

Once writing came to be used, by no means did it supplant the oral transmission of Buddhist teachings. A lively oral tradition remained in place for centuries, as it still is today to some extent.

In the Aśokan inscriptions, there are a number of references to the importance of listening to the texts.[45] The early Gāndhārī manuscript collections include texts whose terse formulations and extensive use of abbreviations make it clear that they were used to support memorization, rather than as primary instantiations of the text.[46] Even as late as the 5th century, Chinese monk Faxian had difficulty finding written scriptures in Northern India but still found monks skilled in the oral tradition.[47] A colophon of a Thai *paritta* manuscript from 1677, to give but one late example, specifically says that it ought to be learned by heart.[48] With respect to the situation in Central Asia, Anne Klein has compiled a record of the oral scholarship of a contemporary Tibetan teacher who stands within a rich living tradition of oral transmission of primary and commentarial texts.[49]

BUDDHIST INSCRIPTIONS

In addition to the Aśokan inscriptions, the earliest written attestations of Buddhism in India are inscriptions on *stūpas* and railings that label the iconography sculpted thereon, such as what is seen at Bhārhut from the 2nd century BCE.[50] While the texts of these early inscriptions are generally donative in nature, quotes or paraphrases of canonical passages and other textual passages are also sometimes found in early inscriptions.[51] The earliest examples of writing in mainland Southeast Asia stem from the middle of the first millennium in such locations as the Mon polity of Dvāravatī in central Thailand and the Pyu center of Śrī Kṣetra in Burma and are, by and large, associated with Buddhism. Particularly notable are the Dvāravatī *dhammacakka* inscriptions dating from about the 7th century CE. They are the most extensive Pali language inscriptions found in early mainland Southeast Asia and include selections from the *Dhammacakkappavattana*, *Dhammapada*, and *Visuddhimagga* carved into the spokes or felloe of some of the wheels. It is important to note that most of these wheels would have been placed high on top of a pillar, making it impossible for anyone to actually read these inscriptions. This suggests that they were written to accentuate the powers of the local rulers who sponsored them, or to provide apotropaic functions protecting the area, rather than to spread knowledge of the teachings of the buddha.[52]

In China, numerous sutras were inscribed on stone in different regions to preserve the texts for posterity in the face of the less permanent media such as silk and bamboo.[53] Perhaps the most remarkable store of Buddhist inscriptions consists of thousands of stones inscribed with a wide variety of Buddhist texts in Chinese, some of which are the oldest extant versions, and deposited in caves in the Fang Shan region southwest of Beijing. These texts were carved during the Tang, Chin, and Liao periods (the early 7th century through the late 12th century) and comprise an enormous corpus of hundreds of Buddhist texts that were evidently made to ensure the continuity of the tradition as well as to make merit.[54] A more recent epigraphic megaproject was the inscribing of the Tipiṭaka into hundreds of marble slabs at Kuthodaw in Myanmar under the sponsorship of King Mindon in 1868 as the expansion of British power threatened the security of the religion.[55]

WRITING AND THE BIRTH OF MAHĀYĀNA

Buddhism's use of the technology of writing affected not only the transmission of the religion but also the very way that its doctrines developed. Richard Gombrich has controversially argued that writing allowed the Mahāyāna doctrines to survive and flourish despite their departure from the orthodox notions that formed the backbone of Buddhism until then.[56] This is because in the preliterate world, a complicated tradition of oral transmission sanctioned by the Sangha was required to transmit the lengthy texts of Buddhism, and therefore a sect would not wish to expend precious mnemonic resources on preserving texts that were not accepted by the entire community. Writing, however, provides the opportunity to record, preserve, and transmit heterodox ideas that do not conform to the tradition as it is preserved orally.

There is little doubt that, unlike mainstream Buddhism, early Mahāyāna made use of writing from the very beginning, and was expert at driving people to maintain and copy these documents. Already in the earliest strata of Mahāyāna texts such as the *Prajñāpāramitā* literature, for example, passages like this one are common:

> . . . if someone else were to learn this perfection of wisdom, recite and study it, and wisely attend to it, would reveal it to others, and would honour, revere, and worship, with flowers, etc. . . . a written copy of it; then [he] would on that account beget . . . merit.[57]

There is also a strong association of wisdom (*prajñā*), which is a pillar of Mahāyāna Buddhism, with books and manuscripts as exemplified in early iconographic portrayals of the goddess *Prajñāpāramitā*, who is usually shown holding a manuscript. This must have served as a powerful engine driving the replication of these texts and teachings during the formative years of Mahāyāna. Many centuries later, these attitudes are reflected in some Theravāda works as well, such as the 14th-century *Saddhammasaṅgaha*, which praises the writing down of texts and compares each syllable to a buddha image.[58] However, an even longer chapter in this text cites the many advantages of listening to the Dharma.

In addition to their promulgation, there may be a connection between the very evolution of three of the key doctrines of Mahāyāna Buddhism and writing as well: compassion for all (*karuṇā*), emptiness (*śūnyatā*), and the transcendent status of a buddha. Many media theorists hold that writing tends to diversify one's social world by extending networks of communication such that one is more likely to encounter strangers—or at least their ideas—and those heterogeneous encounters commonly lead to more toleration, a broadening of vistas and eventually compassion for others.[59]

The central idea of *śūnyatā* or emptiness also may have a connection to the use of writing because of the more abstract and unnatural aspects of this medium. The human mind evolved to use verbal language. All human societies utilize speech, and all healthy babies will begin over the course of the first few years of their lives to use speech and to learn it naturally, even if they are not actively taught how to communicate in this way. Literacy is an entirely different matter and does not come naturally. Its unnaturalness forces the user to recognize the artificiality and arbitrariness of the signs employed in a way that speech does not. Speaking wholly engages one in the flow of communication without needing to pause and reflect on the communicative process. However, when reading, the vast majority translate the marks on the page into silent speech in their head and then process the data from there, rather than directly from the written words. Thus, the artifice and socially constructed nature of writing is far more obvious than that of speech, which promotes the idea that there is no necessary connection between a written word and its meaning. Once the connection between signifier and signified has been severed in this way, it also becomes much easier to unshackle the meaning of the spoken word from the sounds associated with it, thereby destroying one of the foundations of essentialist thinking, just as Mahāyāna and in particular Madhyamaka Buddhism is attempting to do with the concept of *śūnyatā*.

Prior to the development of writing, the transcendence of the buddha was downplayed, and sacred sites in Buddhism tended to be associated with places where the buddha himself had lived or preached, or where items that he had personally owned were located. However, with the association of books with the *dhammakāya*, a location where a book containing Buddhist texts had been placed could now become sacralized as well.[60] As David McMahan points out:

> The fact that anywhere the text was placed could now become a sacred place equivalent to those associated with the life of the Buddha had the effect of de-emphasizing the significance of the specific, localized, and temporal presence of Śākyamuni. Sacred space was now mobile. This is perhaps the beginning of a marked tendency in the Mahāyāna ... toward a more general dislocation of the sacred from the locus of the "historical" life of Śākyamuni in favor of more abstract and unlocalizable understandings of the sacred and of the Buddha.[61]

If the buddha is now conceived as a fully transcendent being who pervades all places at all times, then the written word mimics more closely the true nature of the buddha, for it does not unfold along one dimension in strict temporal sequence as does speech but rather persists through time and expands along multiple dimensions. It can be stated with some confidence, then, that the use of writing played an important role in the success and spread of Mahāyāna Buddhism, as well as in the development and acceptance of some key features of Mahāyāna ideology.

THE BLOCKPRINTING STAGE

The very first mechanically mass-produced words related to Buddhism were on coins minted in the 2nd century CE by the Kuṣāṇa emperor Kaniśka. These coins bear a picture on the reverse accompanied by text in Greek letters saying "Boddo," thus identifying the figure as the buddha.[62] Moving a few centuries later in history, printing evolved in monasteries during the heyday of the religion in the Tang dynasty (618–907 CE). Like writing, printing was also deeply entwined with the practice of Buddhism. It is likely that the admonition to generate merit by copying the Mahāyāna texts inspired Buddhists during this period to carve the pages of sacred texts such as the *Lotus Sutra* and the *Diamond Sūtra* onto wooden blocks and print many copies in what were the first complete printed books anywhere in the world.[63] The very oldest known examples of printing, however, are not complete sutras but rather *dhāraṇīs* that were printed in Japan between 764 and 770, inspired by the idea that those who place *dhāraṇīs* inside many *stūpas* will have a long life, get good karma and vanquish their enemies.[64]

In 972, the Sung dynasty ordered more than 5,000 scrolls containing texts based on those found in the 8th-century K'ai Yüan Buddhist Catalogue to be carved into 130,000 blocks for xylographic printing, and when this was complete in 983 CE, the Chinese canon was effectively standardized. Here, the interaction between the shape of the religion and the communication technologies that were used to transmit the texts is apparent, as the availability of printing led to the fixing of the canon. Once carved, these blocks essentially became the official canon. There were, of course, a few slightly different versions based on different xylographic projects, but generally, the constant growth of the canon came to a halt at this point.

The vagaries of time and the violence of the 13th-century Mongol invasions have ensured that no complete copy of the canon from this time survived in China, but happily a copy was brought to Korea early on, where another set of woodblocks was carved from 1010 to 1030. Although this set was also burnt by the Mongols, the monk Sugi and his team were able to reconstruct it with editorial improvements from 1236 to 1251, and these woodblocks still survive. Later, Kubilai Khan commissioned a repair of damaged printing blocks from the Chin edition that came to be known as the Hung Fa edition. In northern China, the Khitan Liao dynasty also produced a printed canon in the 11th century and presented a copy to the Koryŏ court, among others. Manchu and Tangut canons were also produced based on the early Chinese canons. During the tumult accompanying the overthrow of the Yuan dynasty many of the canons were severely damaged and therefore yet another edition was prepared by Emperor Hung Wu, founder of the Ming Dynasty, which was printed in Nanjing. In 1410, the Yongle emperor of the Ming dynasty sponsored a woodblock printed edition of the Tibetan Kangyur canon, and there have been a number of editions of different lineages since then in Tibet.

Most of the various early Chinese editions were bound as scrolls, while some were accordion-folded books. While the accordion books were more awkward to handle than scrolls, they were easier to use. The twin problems of ergonomics and readability were solved with the Leng Yen (Wan Li) edition begun in 1589 that was bound like a codex, but each page was printed only on one side and was folded over so that the folded end became the outer edge of the book. The Leng Yen edition was recarved and printed in Japan in 1681 in a project headed by the Ōbaku Zen Master Tetsugen, who also constructed a repository at the lead Ōbaku monastery in Kyoto, Mampuku-ji, to house the blocks (which still exist). This Ōbaku edition became quite popular during the Edo period (1603–1868), helping to support the Buddhist resurgence at that time. After printing became popular, handwritten manuscripts continued to be made largely for ceremonial and artistic reasons, still employing the gold and silver inks, which could not be used for printing. In Japan, there were even "one-day" transcriptions in which the emperor would organize thousands of people each to write a portion of the canon at the same time, thereby completing the entire corpus in one day.[65]

THE MOVABLE TYPE STAGE

An early but somewhat impractical form of ceramic movable type was developed in China in the 11th century; however, it was not used extensively to publish Buddhist texts, as far as is known. Metal movable type was developed in Korea at least by 1234, as Mongol threats, political intrigue, and weakness of the Sung, which had previously provided many texts to Korea, combined to greatly damage Korea's literary collections. They therefore needed to produce a few copies of many different texts to replenish their archives, rather than many copies of a few texts which are better suited to xylography.[66] Some Buddhist texts, especially of the Sŏn

(Ch'an) school were made, but this form of printing was used largely for Confucian texts during the Joseon (Yi) Dynasty from 1392. In Japan during the early Edo period a movable type edition of the *Tripiṭaka* was printed known as the Tenkai edition, based on Chinese exemplars, and completed in 1648.

The problem with movable type when used to print Chinese characters is that, while the preparation of each page is somewhat less laborious than carving it from scratch from a block of wood, so many different characters are required that not many instances of each character can be made. Typically, once a page has been printed, some of the characters used in that page will need to be used in the next page, so the printing form would often be broken down and the characters reused. If further pages needed to be printed, the whole page would have to be typeset once again.

Modern printing employing European technology has been used to transmit Buddhist texts as well, ironically employed at first in the 18th and 19th centuries by Christian missionaries to help those who wished to refute Buddhism to learn more about its mistaken doctrines.[67] The modern printed canon was not introduced until the 19th century, and the very first volumes were in Roman letters published by the Pali Text Society starting in 1881. However, a Thai script version of the entire canon was completed in Thailand in 1893 under the sponsorship of King Chulalongkorn, while it took several more decades for the Pali Text Society to complete the project it had started in the 1880s. In Cambodia, the use of printing presses for Buddhist books was prohibited until the 1920s out of the fear that mass production may diminish their sacred value.[68] The Korean copy of the Sung era Chinese canon served as the basis for the Japanese *Taishō* printed edition of the Chinese canon (*Dazangjing* or *Daizokyo* in Japanese pronunciation), which was originally published in the 1920s and remains the scholarly standard, being kept in university libraries all over the world.

Complete published translations of the Tipiṭaka into the local languages of Southeast Asia emerged only in the second part of the 20th century. A Burmese edition was commenced in 1962 by the Ministry of Religious Affairs, a Khmer edition in 1969 by the Institute Bouddhique, and a Thai edition in 1971 by the Ministry of Religious Affairs and Ministry of Education, all using modern printing techniques. There has not yet been a complete published translation of the *Tipiṭaka* in Lao, although a few *Nikāya* volumes were produced in the early 1970s before the fall of the Royalist government to the Marxists.[69]

One of the most profound changes ushered in by print has been a reinterpretation of Buddhism along lines similar to those of Protestant Christianity, which itself emerged during the printing revolution in Europe. Like what transpired in Christendom, in many traditional Buddhist countries there has been a turn inward toward an individualized conception of the spiritual quest, as private reading of printed texts has come into vogue. There has also been a rise in emphasis on meditation, stronger criticism of excessive ritual, and a suspicion of "later accretions" to the original Buddhist teachings.[70]

ANALOG ELECTRONIC MASS MEDIA

Buddhism has always taken advantage of the latest means for getting its message across, and it has also been profoundly affected by changing media technologies. When radio was introduced in Asia, it was eagerly taken up by Buddhist preachers to communicate sermons and canonical readings to the masses and helped to allow people in remote villages to gain access to the teachings of the leading preachers and scholars of the day. Tape cassettes were also used for this purpose.[71] Such modern media have radically changed the shape of Buddhism by, among other things, affecting the authority of the monks who previously were the sole guardians of the sacred texts. Until these relatively recent developments, most common people in Buddhist countries had access to the teachings of the religion only through the sermons given by local monks. Now, they could access the teachings from their own home on television, radio, or in printed books, which has led to a growing interest among laypeople in meditation as well as renewed interest in the original canonical texts which often place less emphasis on the kind of merit generating rituals that have been the backbone of local Buddhist practice throughout Asia for centuries.[72]

DIGITAL MEDIA TECHNOLOGIES

In contemporary society, Buddhism is still at the forefront of media technology. Buddhists and scholars of Buddhism were among the first people to establish internet-based discussion forums, the oldest of which is Buddha-L. Buddha-L came into being in 1991, at which point there were few discussion forums to use as a model. The *Journal of Buddhist Ethics*, founded in 1994 was the first peer-reviewed online journal in religious studies and has been a model for many other online journals established since that time.[73] The Buddhist Studies WWW Virtual Library was another early resource, from 1992, containing such things as bibliographies, biographies, directories, Buddhist electronictexts, poetry, and sermons. Buddhist magazines aimed at practitioners, such as the *Lion's Roar* and *Tricycle*, reside on robust and well-trafficked websites that are often visited by those seeking information about Buddhist texts, beliefs, and practices, and in particular how they relate to life in contemporary society.

Presently, contemporary Buddhist media technologies generally consist of websites, virtual worlds, smartphone apps, and even video games.[74] Buddhanet is a particularly popular and helpful website with information for the serious student about all forms of Buddhism, including primary and secondary textual sources, full-text e-books, Buddhist art, and extensive links to other Buddhist sites. It exemplifies the way that contemporary digital media are being used to shape, strengthen, and transmit Buddhism. As the website states: "In this way, an ancient tradition and the information superhighway will come together to create an electronic meeting place of shared concern and interests." Another important area is Buddhist blogs, which have exploded in popularity over the last several years.[75]

An example of a virtual world is Second Life, a three-dimensional immersive, interactive world housed in cyberspace, and accessed via the internet. Through on-screen representations, called *avatars*, millions of Second Life users explore virtual worlds, communicate and socialize with one another, as well as create, sell and purchase virtual goods. Interestingly, a sizable percentage of Second Life users practice a form of Buddhism that centers on Zen-inspired silent online meditation.[76] At the Buddha Center in Second Life, there are links to eBooks covering a wide variety of Buddhist topics for avatars—and their human controllers—to read. At the Utopia Library of World Religions in Second Life, copies of selected Theravāda *Suttas* as well as Zen works, such as Dogen's *Mountains and Waters Sūtra*, are available. Second Life also has virtual prayer wheels with mantras written on them that can be spun by the avatar.

These new technologies raise the question of the karmic efficacy of producing or ritually engaging with virtual Buddhist texts. Anthropologist Jessica Falcone has dealt with this question and found through interviews that, "the distinction in belief about the magical/sacred properties of holy objects in Second Life has more to do with one's views about holy objects in general, and much less to do with the mediated platform of Second Life itself." Many of those she interviewed in Second Life asserted that there was some efficacy and spiritual significance imparted to sacred objects in Second Life, though less than in actual life. "This argument counters the conventional wisdom that virtual things are just unreal, pixilated non-objects that are unable to do actual religious work. In fact, actual objects are always already more virtual than we thought, and virtual objects are more actual than we may expect."[77]

Much Buddhist digital media utilize the encyclopedic affordance for the storage and transmission of scripture, and other documents. For instance, in the late 1990s, The Vipassana Research Institute (VRI), founded by wealthy Indo-Burmese businessman S. N. Goenka, produced a CD-ROM containing the entire Pali canon based on the Burmese 1956 edition produced at the sixth council to honor 2,500 years since the buddha's nirvana, and numerous other projects have put the dharma into digital form. The VRI edition allows the text to be read in a variety of scripts, including Latin, Devanagari, Sinhalese, Burmese, Thai and even Mongolian. Other digital repositories exist as well: for instance, a Thai edition of the Pali canon from 1928 was put on a CD-ROM by Mahidol University in honor of the Thai king's 60th birthday in 1988, and the Access to Insight website has published a great many English versions of the texts online. Currently, there are many searchable databases with enormous collections of Buddhist texts, including the Chinese canon as well as the Tibetan canon. The International Dunhuang Project contains thousands of digitized images of manuscripts and blockprints recovered from the caves of Dunhuang as well as other places along the Eastern Silk Road. Digitized collections of Northern Thai and Lao manuscripts, many of them Pali or vernacular Buddhist texts, are also available and are fully searchable online. Lewis Lancaster is working with a team at the Electronic Cultural Atlas Initiative to develop a high dimensional visualization system to assist in analyzing text structure and patterns based on the digitized Chinese canon

Digital media can greatly facilitate the analysis of texts and are likely to revolutionize the study of Buddhism. Lewis Lancaster reports that it took him two years in the 1960s to manually search through seven different Chinese translations of a *Prajñāpāramitā* text looking for occurrences of certain words that would help him determine the nature of the Sanskrit originals. When the Korean version of the Chinese canon was digitized, Lancaster performed an automated search for these same terms. It took only twenty minutes to find a few word occurrences that he had missed as well.[78] The powers of digital technology are bound to assist our understanding of Buddhist texts in many ways in the future.

REVIEW OF LITERATURE

A few book-length studies of the different media used by Buddhists to transmit the texts over time have been published. A particularly helpful introductory narrative is by Kogen Mizuno, who covers the early oral tradition and then looks at the introduction of writing, xylography and then modern printing with a focus on Japan.[79] Günter Grönbold has produced a work that covers a range of manuscript traditions throughout Asia, and Paul Harrison and Jens Uwe

Hartmann have edited the proceedings of a conference about Indic Buddhist manuscripts.[80] A number of books and articles also deal with various aspects of Buddhist media. Mark Allon has examined the mnemonic functions of various stylistic features of the Pali texts in a book length study, and there are a number of good articles that examine other oral aspects of early Buddhism, most notably by Steven Collins, Frank Hoffman, K. R. Norman, Bhikkhu Anālayo, and Alexander Wynne.[81] More details about orality in the Indian context are supplied by Ludo Rocher, who focuses on the Brahmanical tradition.[82] The classic study of oral composition and the role of formulas and other mnemonic aids by Albert Lord focuses on the traditions of Serbian bards but is of relevance to Buddhist studies as well. [83]

Richard Salomon provides an excellent introduction to early writing in India in the first part of his study of Indian epigraphy, while Harry Falk has conducted the most sustained and detailed study of the rise of writing in India.[84] The most useful study, including introductory material, detailed textual analysis and high-quality photographs of early manuscripts from 2nd-century Gandhāra, has been headed by Richard Salomon.[85] Richard Gombrich has written a much-cited article that focuses on the role played by writing in the development of Mahāyāna Buddhism, and a more detailed account of writing's effects on Mahāyāna ideology is provided by David McMahan.[86] Berkwitz, Schober, and Brown have edited a collection that focuses on Buddhist manuscript cultures in all parts of Asia, which provides the best available overview of the topic, focusing on the physical production of these artifacts, as well as their position in different societies and their effects on developments in Buddhism.[87] The beginnings of writing in China are dealt with by Tsuen Hsuin Tsien, although he focuses largely on pre-Buddhist writing.[88] Gregory Schopen wrote a seminal article about the cultic aspects of books and manuscripts in the Mahāyāna tradition that has been very influential.[89] With respect to the interface between the written and oral traditions, Daniel Veidlinger provides the most detailed analysis with respect to Thailand but with implications for all Buddhist cultures in which written and oral texts are both in use.[90] Philip Clart and Gregory Scott have edited a volume about print culture in China from 1800 that has chapters on Buddhist printing and the role it played in community development.[91] Peter Skilling provides a succinct glimpse of the various Tibetan canons, their translation and preservation.[92]

Modern digital media and their effects upon Buddhist practice and belief in contemporary times are the subject of Gregory Grieve and Daniel Veidlinger's edited volume, and Lewis Lancaster has also written a great deal about digital means for preserving, transmitting and analyzing Buddhist texts.[93]

Most theorizing about the effects of media on the dissemination and interpretation of texts has been done in relation to Western culture, but many of these insights are salient to Buddhist studies as well. For a classic introduction to media theory, see Walter Ong; and for a more updated framework that takes the Internet into account, see Marshall Poe.[94] Heidi Campbell has written more generally about how new media affect religion.[95]

FURTHER READING

Allon, Mark. *Style and Function: A Study of the Dominant Stylistic Features of the Prose Portions of Pāli Canonical Sutta Texts and Their Mnemonic Function.* Tokyo: International Institute for Buddhist Studies of the International College for Advanced Buddhist Studies, 1997.

Bechert, Heinz. "The Writing Down of the Tripitaka in Pali." *Wiener Zeitschrift fur de Kunde Sudasiens* 36 (1992): 45–53.

Berkwitz, Stephen, Juliane Schober, and Claudia Brown, eds. *Buddhist Manuscript Cultures*. New York: Routledge, 2009.

Clart, Philip, and Gregory Scott, eds. *Religious Publishing and Print Culture in Modern China 1800–2012*. Berlin: De Gruyter, 2014.

Collins, Steven. "Notes on Some Oral Aspects of Pali Literature." *Indo-Iranian Journal* 35 (1992): 121–135.

Falk, Harry. *Schrift im Alten Indien*. Tübingen, Germany: Gunter Narr, 1993.

Gombrich, Richard. "How the Mahāyāna Began." In *The Buddhist Forum*. Edited by Tadeusz Skorupski, 21–31. London: University of London, 1990.

Grieve, Gregory, and Daniel Veidlinger. *Buddhism, the Internet and Digital Media: The Pixel in the Lotus*. New York: Routledge, 2015.

Grönbold, Günter. *Die Worte des Buddha in den Sprachen der Welt: Tipiṭaka, Tripiṭaka, Dazangjing, Kanjur (Eine Ausstellung aus dem Bestand der Bayerischen Staatsbibliothek)*. Munich: Bayerische Staatsbibliothek, 2005.

Harrison, Paul, and Jens-Uwe Hartmann, eds. *From Birch Bark to Digital Data: Recent Advances in Buddhist Manuscript Research*. Papers presented at the conference "Indic Buddhist Manuscripts: The State of the Field," Stanford, California, June 15–19, 2009. Vienna: Verlag der Österreichischen Akademie der Wissenschaften, 2014.

Hundius, Harald. "The Colophons of Thirty Pali Manuscripts from Northern Thailand." *Journal of the Pali Text Society* 14 (1990): 1–174.

Hoffman, Frank. "Evam Me Sutam: Oral Tradition in Nikāya Buddhism." In *Texts in Context*. Edited by Jeffrey Timm, 195–220. Albany: SUNY Press, 1991.

Lancaster, Lewis. "Buddhism in the Digital Age." *Hsi Lai Journal of Humanistic Buddhism* 4 (2003): 79–86.

Lord, Albert. *The Singer of Tales*. Cambridge, MA: Harvard University Press, 1960.

McMahan, David. "Orality, Writing and Authority in South Asian Buddhism: Visionary Literature and the Struggle for Legitimacy in the Mahāyāna." *History of Religions* 37, no. 3 (1998): 249–274.

Mizuno, Kogen. *Buddhist Sutras*. Tokyo: Kosei, 1982.

Norman, K. R. *A Philological Approach to Buddhism*. Lancaster, UK: Pali Text Society, 2006.

Ong, Walter. *Orality and Literacy: The Technologizing of the Word*. London: Routledge, 1982.

Poe, Marshall. *A History of Communications: Media and Society from the Evolution of Speech to the Internet*. Cambridge, UK: Cambridge University Press, 2011.

Rocher, Ludo. *Orality and Textuality in the Indian Context*. Philadelphia: University of Pennsylvania, 1994.

Salomon, Richard. *Indian Epigraphy: A Guide to the Study of Inscriptions in Sanskrit, Prakrit and the Other Indo-Aryan Languages*. Oxford: Oxford University Press, 1998.

Schopen, Gregory. "The Phrase *sa pṛthivīpradeśaś caityabhūto bhavet* in the *Vajracchedikā*: Notes on the Cult of the Book in Mahāyāna." *Indo-Iranian Journal* 17 (1975): 147–181.

Skilling, Peter. "From bKa' bstan bcos to bKa' 'gyur and bsTan 'gyur." In *Transmission of the Tibetan Canon*. Edited by Helmut Eimer, 87–111. Vienna: Osterreichischen Akademie der Wissenschaften, 1997.

Tsien, Tsuen Hsuin. *Written on Silk and Bamboo: The Beginnings of Chinese Books and Inscriptions*. Chicago: University of Chicago Press, 2004.

Veidlinger, Daniel. *Spreading the Dhamma: Writing, Orality and Textual Transmission in Buddhist Northern Thailand*. Honolulu: University of Hawaii Press, 2006.

Veidlinger, Daniel. "When a Word Is Worth a Thousand Pictures: Mahāyāna Influence on Theravada Attitudes Towards Writing." *Numen* 53, no. 4 (2006): 405–447. Available online. http://www.researchgate.net/journal/0029-5973_Numen.

NOTES

1. Herman Oldenberg and T. W. Rhys Davids, trans., *Vinaya Texts Vol. III* (Oxford: Clarendon, 1885), 150–151.
2. Chang Shao Lee, *Popular Buddhism in China* (London: Commercial Press, 1940), 9.
3. The best source for information on all aspects of manuscript production and usage across the Buddhist world is *Buddhist Manuscript Cultures*, eds. Stephen Berkwitz, Juliane Schober, and Claudia Brown, (New York: Routledge, 2009).
4. For a collection of essays on various aspects of Buddhism and new media, see Gregory Grieve and Daniel Veidlinger (eds.), *Buddhism, the Internet and Digital Media: The Pixel in the Lotus* (New York: Routledge, 2015).
5. The most famous (and still very useful) early examples of this way of approaching media are Harold Innis, *The Bias of Communication* (Toronto: University of Toronto Press, 1951) and Marshall McLuhan, *Understanding Media: The Extensions of Man* (New York: McGraw Hill, 1964).
6. Marshall Poe, in *A History of Communications* (Cambridge, U.K.: Cambridge University Press, 2011), looks at various approaches to communication studies and highlights eight key attributes that pertain to media. He then identifies the different levels to which each attribute is expressed in different kinds of media. These attributes are accessibility, privacy, fidelity, volume, velocity, range, persistence and searchability. Some media afford easy searchability, for example, whereas others do not; a book is far more searchable than a scroll, and a webpage is again more searchable than a book. A stone inscription is more persistent than a paper book, which is more persistent than a spoken sentence. These media attributes greatly affect the way that society develops. For example, Poe holds that media that have a low accessibility lead to societies that are elitist, whereas ones with high accessibility lead to more egalitarian values.
7. Paul Heyer, *Communications and History: Theories of Media, Knowledge and Civilization* (New York: Greenwood Press, 1988), xiv.
8. Jeremy Rifkin, *The Empathic Civilization: The Race to Global Consciousness in a World in Crisis* (New York: Jeremy Tarcher/Penguin, 2009), 182.
9. Walter Ong, *The Presence of the Word: Some Prolegomena for the Cultural and Religious History* (New York: SUNY Press, 1967), 11.
10. Paul Griffiths, *Religious Reading: The Place of Reading in the Practice of Religion* (Oxford: Oxford University Press, 1999).
11. The exact dates of the Buddha are an area of dispute. The best forum for discussion of the various issues involved is Heinz Bechert (ed.), *When Did the Buddha Live? The Controversy on the dating of the Historical Buddha: Selected Papers Based on a Symposium Held under the Auspices of the Academy of Sciences in Göttingen* (Delhi: Sri Satguru, 1995). For a summary and discussion of the scholarship dealing with the origins of writing in India, see Richard Salomon, *Indian Epigraphy: A Guide to the Study of Inscriptions in Sanskrit, Prakrit and the Other Indo-Aryan Languages* (Oxford: Oxford University Press, 1998), 10–14. There are two main schools of thought on this issue: the most common view holds that the lack of clear archeological and literary evidence for writing before the Mauryan period is proof that it was unknown before around 300 BCE, and a minority view holds that some obscure pre-Mauryan literary allusions are in fact referring to writing and that the sophistication of early urban society in India also suggests that writing must have been in use.
12. Two very good catalogues of techniques used in oral transmission and their triumphs and challenges in the early Indian context are Ludo Rocher, *Orality and Textuality in the Indian* Context (Philadelphia: University of Pennsylvania, 1994) and Frits Staal, *The Fidelity of Oral Tradition and the Origins of Science* (Amsterdam: North Holland, 1986). The most comprehensive analysis of methods of oral memorization and transmission specific to the Pali texts is Mark Allon, *Style and Function: A Study of the Dominant*

Stylistic Features of the Prose Portions of Pāli Canonical Sutta Texts and Their Mnemonic Function (Tokyo: International Institute for Buddhist Studies of the International College for Advanced Buddhist Studies, 1997).

13. Jack Goody, "Oral Composition and Oral Transmission: The Case of the Vedas," in *Oralita*, eds. Bruno Gentili and Guiseppe Paioni (Rome: Edizioni dell' Ateneo, 1980), 7–18.
14. Herman Oldenberg and T. W. Rhys Davids, trans., *Vinaya Texts Vol. I* (Oxford: Clarendon, 1881), xxxii–xxxiv.
15. Bamphen Rawin, ed., *Mūlasāsanā Samnuan Lan Na* (Chiang Mai: Social Research Institute, 1995), 175 (author's translation).
16. E. W. Adikaram, *Early History of Buddhism in Ceylon* (Migoda: D. S. Puswella, 1946), 24.
17. For an analysis of the valences of the term *tipiṭakadhara* see Daniel Veidlinger, *Spreading the Dhamma: Writing, Orality and Textual Transmission in Buddhist Northern Thailand* (Honolulu: University of Hawaii Press, 2006), 31–36.
18. See Buddhadatta, ed., *Jinakālamālīpakaraṇaṃ* (London: Pali Text Society, 1962), 73.
19. Norris McWhirter, ed., *The Guinness Book of World Records* (New York: Sterling, 1986), 22.
20. Two studies of preaching in Southeast Asia are particularly noteworthy. Justin McDaniel, *Gathering Leaves and Lifting Words* (Seattle: University of Washington Press, 2008) explores the way oral and written texts have been used to educate monks and laypeople in Thailand and Laos, and Mahinda Deegalle, *Popularizing Buddhism: Preaching as Performance in Sri Lanka* (Albany: SUNY Press, 2006) looks at the continuities and innovations that have been made by preachers on the island.
21. Herman Oldenberg and T. W. Rhys Davids, trans., *Vinaya Texts Vol. I* (Oxford: Clarendon, 1881), 304–305.
22. See Steven Collins, "Notes on Some Oral Aspects of Pali Literature," *Indo-Iranian Journal* 35 (1992): 121–135.
23. Maurice Walshe, *Thus Have I Heard: The Long Discourses of the Buddha* (London: Wisdom, 1987), 239.
24. Walshe, *Thus Have I Heard*, 481.
25. Peter Skilling, "Redaction, Recitation, and Writing: Transmission of the Buddha's Teaching in India in the Early Period," in *Buddhist Manuscript Cultures*, eds. Stephen Berkwitz, Juliane Schober, and Claudia Brown (New York: Routledge, 2009), 54.
26. The standard reference on Aśokan inscriptions is Eugen Hultzsch, *Inscriptions of Aśoka* (Oxford: Clarendon, 1925), though other inscriptions have been discovered since. Richard Salomon discusses the extant literature on these inscriptions and provides a brief summary of their history, location and contents in *Indian Epigraphy*, 133–140. Harry Falk, *Aśokan Sites and Artefacts: A Source-book with Bibliography* (Mainz: Philipp von Zabern 2006) and Patrick Olivelle, ed., *Aśoka in History and Historical Memory* (Delhi: Motilal Barnasidass, 2009) also cover the latest developments in Aśokan studies.
27. A helpful summary of the scholarship on early inscriptions from the Śuṅga to the Gupta periods (2nd century BCE—4th century CE) can be found in Richard Salomon, *Indian Epigraphy*, 141–145. References to detailed examinations of the contents of these inscriptions can be found therein.
28. The seminal account of the writing down of the *Tipiṭaka* during the fourth council in Lāṅka can be found in the *Mahāvaṃsa* 33.100. This event is also recounted in other traditional Pali chronicles such as the *Sāsanavaṃsa* from Burma. For more information see Daniel Veidlinger, *Spreading the Dhamma*, 25. Steven Collins suggests that the stated timing of the writing down of the canon is indeed appropriate, for there was then a growing rivalry between the Mahāvihāra and the Abhayagiri monasteries, and the fixing of the canon by the Mahāvihāra would have helped to establish their hegemony with respect to the religion. See Steven Collins, "On the Very Idea of the Pali Canon," *Journal of the Pali Text Society* 15 (1990): 98.
29. Richard Salomon, "Gāndhārī Manuscripts in the British Library, Schøyen and Other Collections," in *From Birch Bark to Digital Data: Recent Advances in Buddhist Manuscript Research: Papers Presented at the*

Conference "Indic Buddhist Manuscripts: The State of the Field," Stanford, June 15–19, 2009, eds. Paul Harrison and Jens-Uwe Hartmann (Vienna: Verlag der Österreichischen Akademie der Wissenschaften, 2014), 9.

30. Kogen Mizuno, *Buddhist Sutras* (Tokyo: Kosei, 1982), 163.
31. Richard Salomon, *Ancient Buddhist Scrolls from Gandhāra* (Seattle: University of Washington Press, 1999), 154. For more recent developments see Mark Allon, "Recent Discoveries of Buddhist Manuscripts from Afghanistan and Pakistan and their Significance," in, *Art, Architecture and Religion Along the Silk Roads: Proceedings from the Fifth Conference of the Australian Society for Inner Asian Studies (A.S.I.A.S.). Macquarie University, November 27th to 28th, 2004,* ed. Ken Parry (Turnhout: Brepols, 2008), 153–178.
32. Janice Stargardt, "The Oldest Known Pali Texts, 5th–6th century: Results of the Cambridge Symposium on the Pyu Golden Pali Text from Śrī Kṣetra, 18–19 April 1995," *Journal of the Pali Text Society* 21 (1995): 199–213.
33. Robert Buswell, *Chinese Buddhist Apocrypha* (Honolulu: University of Hawaii Press, 1990).
34. Kogen Mizuno, *Buddhist Sutras,* 167.
35. An excellent survey of the physical appearance of books and manuscripts with full color pictures and clear descriptions is Jeremiah Losty, *The Art of the Book in India* (London: The British Library, 1982). For a focus on Thai books, which are generally representative of those found in Southeast Asia, see Henry Ginsburg, *Thai Manuscript Painting* (Honolulu: University of Hawaii Press, 1989).
36. For example, a 15th-century king from northern Thailand sponsored a council to redact the canonical texts which were then stored in a library at a royal monastery. However, the library was apparently so little used that it soon became dilapidated due to inattention until his grandson was able to prepare a new building for the texts. See Buddhadatta, ed., *Jinakālamālīpakaraṇaṃ* (London: Pali Text Society, 1962), 115.
37. The most extensive study of manuscript colophons in the Theravāda tradition is Harald Hundius, "The Colophons of Thirty Pali Manuscripts from Northern Thailand," *Journal of the Pali Text Society* 14 (1990): 1–174. Other studies of colophons can be found in Heinz Braun, "The Colophons of Burmese Manuscripts," *Journal of the Pali Text Society* 27 (2002): 147–153 and Oskar von Hinüber, "Die Kolophone Der Gilgit-Handschriften," *Studein Zur Indologie und Iranistik* 5–6 (1980): 49–82.
38. Kogen Mizuno, *Buddhist Sutras,* 165.
39. Gregory Schopen, "The Phrase *sa pṛthivīpradeśaś caityabhūto bhavet* in the *Vajracchedikā:* Notes on the Cult of the Book in Mahāyāna," *Indo-Iranian Journal* 17 (1975): 147–181.
40. Richard Salomon, "Why Did the Gandhāran Buddhists Bury their Manuscripts?" in *Buddhist Manuscript Cultures,* eds. Stephen Berkwitz, Juliane Schober and Claudia Brown (New York: Routledge, 2009), 30.
41. Vesna Wallace, "Diverse Aspects of the Mongolian Buddhist Manuscript Culture and Realms of its Influence," in *Buddhist Manuscript Cultures,* eds. Stephen Berkwitz, Juliane Schober, and Claudia Brown (New York: Routledge, 2009), 90.
42. Natasha Heller, "Between Zhongfeng Mingben and Zhao Mengfu: Chan Letters in the Manuscript Context," in *Buddhist Manuscript Cultures,* eds. Stephen Berkwitz, Juliane Schober, and Claudia Brown (New York: Routledge, 2009), 110.
43. Christoph Emmrich, "Emending Perfection: Prescript, Postscript, and Practice in Newar Buddhist Manuscript Culture," in *Buddhist Manuscript Cultures,* eds. Stephen Berkwitz, Juliane Schober, and Claudia Brown (New York: Routledge, 2009), 149.
44. For examples and discussion of the ritual uses of written sacred verses see Daniel Boucher, "The *Pratītyasamutpādagāthā* and Its Role in the Medieval Cult of the Relics," *Journal of the International Association of Buddhist Studies* 14, no. 1 (2001): 1–27; Yael Bentor, "On the Indian Origins of the Tibetan Practice of Depositing Relics and Dhāraṇīs in Stūpas and Images," *Journal of the American Oriental Society* 115 (1995): 248–261; and Daniel Veidlinger, *Spreading the Dhamma,* 190–197.

45. Steven Collins, "Notes on Some Oral Aspects of Pali Literature," *Indo-Iranian Journal* 35 (1992): 121–122.
46. Richard Salomon, *Ancient Buddhist Scrolls*, 165.
47. James Legge, trans., *A Record of Buddhistic Kingdoms: Being an Account by the Chinese Monk Fa Hien* (Oxford: Clarendon, 1886), 98.
48. Oskar von Hinüber, "Chips from Buddhist Workshops: Scribes and Manuscripts from Northern Thailand," *Journal of the Pali Text Society* 22 (1996): 53.
49. Anne Klein, *Path to the Middle: The Spoken Scholarship of Kensur Yeshey Tupden* (Albany: SUNY Press, 1994).
50. Peter Skilling, "Redaction, Recitation, and Writing," 65.
51. For example, an explication of the Four Noble Truths is found in a 5th-century inscription from Guntupalle, Andhra Pradesh, that echoes a passage in *Dhammapada*, for which see Peter Skilling, "A Buddhist Verse Inscription from Andhra Pradesh," *Indo-Iranian Journal* 34 (1991): 239–246. Other examples of the *pratītyasamutpāda* formula from Gandhāra can be found in Oskar von Hinüber, *Beiträge zur Erklärung der Senavarma-Inschrift* (Stuttgart: Franz Steiner Verlag, 2003), 1.
52. Robert Brown, *The Dvāravatī Wheels of the Law and the Indianization of Southeast Asia* (Leiden, The Netherlands: Brill, 1996), 96–120.
53. For a brief survey of some key Buddhist inscriptions in China, see Tsuen-Hsuin Tsien, *Written on Bamboo and Silk: The Beginnings of Chinese Books and Inscriptions* (Chicago: University of Chicago Press, 2004), 85–88.
54. Lewis Lancaster, "The Rock Cut Canon in China: Findings at Fang-Shan," in *The Buddhist Heritage*, ed. Tadeusz Skorupski (Tring: Institute of Buddhist Studies, 1989), 143–156.
55. Mark Allon, Wendy Reade, Chris Clark, Ian McCrabb, Tamara Ditrich, Royce Wiles, and Bob Hudson, "The Kuthodaw Pagoda Marble-stelae Inscriptions, Mandalay, Myanmar: Conservation, Photographing, and Study of a Neglected Recension of the Pali Buddhist Canon," *Bulletin of the Chuo Academic Research Institute (Chuo Gakujutsu Kenkyūjo Kiyō)* 45 (2016): 222–249.
56. Richard Gombrich, "How the Mahāyāna Began," in *The Buddhist Forum*, ed. Tadeusz Skorupski (London: University of London, 1990), 21–31.
57. Edward Conze, trans., *The Large Sutra on Perfect Wisdom* (Berkeley: University of California Press, 1975), 248.
58. See Chapter 10 in Bimala Churn Law, trans., *Saddhammasaṅgaha: A Manual of Buddhist Historical Traditions* (Calcutta: University of Calcutta, 1963).
59. For example, see Marshall Poe, *A History of Communications: Media and Society from the Evolution of Speech to the Internet* (Cambridge, U.K.: Cambridge University Press, 2011), 89.
60. Gregory Schopen, "The Phrase *sa pṛthivīpradeśaś caityabhūto bhavet* in the *Vajracchedikā*: Notes on the Cult of the Book in Mahāyāna," *Indo-Iranian Journal* 17 (1975): 147–181.
61. David McMahan, "Orality, Writing and Authority in South Asian Buddhism: Visionary Literature and the Struggle for Legitimacy in the Mahāyāna" *History of Religions* 37, no. 3 (1998): 260.
62. John Rosenfield, *The Dynastic Art of the Kushans* (Berkeley: University of California Press, 1967), 76–77.
63. The oldest printed copy of the *Diamond Sūtra (Vajracchedikā)* is dated to 868 ce. See Yong You, *The Diamond Sutra in Chinese Culture* (Hacienda Heights, CA: Buddha's Light Publishers, 2010).
64. Robert Sewell, "The First Printed Text in the World, Standing Tall and Isolated in Eighth-Century Japan: Hyakumantō Darani," *Journal of the Rutgers University Libraries* 60 (2003): 117–128.
65. Kogen Mizuno, *Buddhist Sutras*, 171.
66. Pow-key Sohn, "Early Korean Printing," *Journal of the American Oriental Society* 79, no. 2 (1959): 98.
67. The history of the early European engagement with Buddhist texts can be found in J. W. de Jong, *A Brief History of Buddhist Studies in Europe and America* (Delhi: Sri Satguru, 1987), chapter one.

68. George Chigas, *Tum Teav: A Translation and Analysis of a Cambodian Literary Classic* (Phnom Penh: Documentation Center of Cambodia, 2005), 30.
69. Justin McDaniel, *Gathering Leaves and Lifting Words: Histories of Buddhist Monastic Education in Laos and Thailand* (Seattle: University of Washington Press, 2008), 51.
70. For two good studies of the effects of print on Buddhist modernism in Asia, see Richard Gombrich and Gananath Obeyesekere, *Buddhism Transformed: Religious Change in Sri Lanka* (Princeton, NJ: Princeton University Press, 1988), 110–124, and Anne Hansen *How to Behave: Buddhism and Modernity in Colonial Cambodia* (Honolulu: University of Hawaii Press, 2007).
71. David Engel and Jaruwan Engel, *Tort, Custom and Karma: Globalization and Legal Consciousness in Thailand* (Stanford, CA: Stanford University Press, 2010), 88.
72. On meditation, see Erik Braun, *The Birth of Insight: Meditation, Modern Buddhism, and the Burmese Monk Ledi Sayadaw* (Chicago: University of Chicago Press, 2013); and David McMahan on the canonical texts in *Buddhist Modernism* (New York: Oxford University Press, 2008).
73. Charles Prebish, "Online Peer-Reviewed Journals in Buddhism: The Birth of the Journals of Buddhist Ethics and Global Buddhism," in *Buddhism, Digital Media and the Internet: The Pixel in the Lotus*, eds. Gregory Grieve and Daniel Veidlinger (New York: Routledge, 2015), 79–92.
74. Louise Connelly, "Toward a Typology and Mapping of the Buddhist Cyberspace," in *Buddhism, Digital Media and the Internet: The Pixel in the Lotus*, eds. Gregory Grieve and Daniel Veidlinger (New York: Routledge, 2015), 58–78.
75. Beverley McGuire, "The Way of the Blogisattva: Buddhist Blogs on the Web," in *Buddhism, Digital Media and the Internet: The Pixel in the Lotus*, eds. Gregory Grieve and Daniel Veidlinger (New York: Routledge, 2015), 204–220.
76. Gregory Grieve, *Cyber Zen: Imagining Authentic Buddhist Identity, Community and Practices in the Virtual World of Second Life* (New York: Routledge, 2017).
77. Jessica Falcone, "Our Virtual Materials: The Substance of Buddhist Holy Object in a Virtual World," in *Buddhism, Digital Media and the Internet: The Pixel in the Lotus*, eds. Gregory Grieve and Daniel Veidlinger (New York: Routledge, 2015), 173–190.
78. Lewis Lancaster, "Buddhism in the Digital Age," *Hsi Lai Journal of Humanistic Buddhism* 4 (2003): 84.
79. Kogen Mizuno, *Buddhist Sutras*.
80. Günter Grönbold, *Die Worte des Buddha in den Sprachen der Welt: Tipiṭaka, Tripiṭaka, Dazangjing, Kanjur (Eine Ausstellung aus dem Bestand der Bayerischen Staatsbibliothek)* (Munich: Bayerische Staatsbibliothek, 2005); and Paul Harrison and Jens-Uwe Hartmann, eds., *From Birch Bark to Digital Data: Recent Advances in Buddhist Manuscript Research*. Papers presented at the conference "Indic Buddhist Manuscripts: The State of the Field," Stanford, California, June 15–19, 2009 (Vienna: Verlag der Österreichischen Akademie der Wissenschaften, 2014).
81. Mark Allon, *Style and Function: A Study of the Dominant Stylistic Features of the Prose Portions of Pāli Canonical Sutta Texts and Their Mnemonic Function* (Tokyo: International Institute for Buddhist Studies of the International College for Advanced Buddhist Studies, 1997); Steven Collins, "Notes on Some Oral Aspects of Pali Literature," *Indo-Iranian Journal* 35 (1992): 121–135; Frank Hoffman, "Evam Me Sutam: Oral Tradition in Nikāya Buddhism," in *Texts in Context* ed. Jeffrey Timm (Albany: SUNY Press, 1991), 195–220; K. R. Norman, *A Philological Approach to Buddhism* (Lancaster, U.K.: Pali Text Society, 2006); Bhikkhu Anālayo, "Oral Dimensions of Pāli Discourses: Pericopes, other Mnemonic Techniques, and the Oral Performance Context," *Canadian Journal of Buddhist Studies* 3 (2007): 5–33; and Alexander Wynne, "The Oral Transmission of Early Buddhist Literature," *Journal of the International Association of Buddhist Studies* 27.1 (2004): 97–127.
82. Ludo Rocher, *Orality and Textuality in the Indian* Context (Philadelphia: University of Pennsylvania, 1994).

83. Albert Lord, *The Singer of Tales* (Cambridge, MA: Harvard University Press, 1960).
84. Richard Salomon, *Indian Epigraphy*; and Harry Falk, *Schrift im Alten Indien* (Tübingen, Germany: Gunter Narr, 1993).
85. Richard Salomon, *Ancient Buddhist Scrolls*.
86. Richard Gombrich, "How the Mahāyāna Began," 21–31; and David McMahan, "Orality, Writing and Authority in South Asian Buddhism," 249–274.
87. Stephen Berkwitz, Juliane Schober, and Claudia Brown, eds., *Buddhist Manuscript Cultures* (New York: Routledge, 2009).
88. Tsuen Hsuin Tsien, *Written on Bamboo and Silk: The Beginnings of Chinese Books and Inscriptions* (Chicago: University of Chicago Press, 2004)
89. Gregory Schopen, "The Phrase *sa pṛthivīpradeśaś caityabhūto bhavet* in the *Vajracchedikā*: Notes on the Cult of the Book in Mahāyāna," *Indo-Iranian Journal* 17 (1975): 147–181.
90. Daniel Veidlinger, *Spreading the Dhamma*.
91. Philip Clart and Gregory Scott, eds., *Religious Publishing and Print Culture in Modern China 1800–2012* (Berlin: De Gruyter, 2014).
92. Peter Skilling, "From bKa' bstan bcos to bKa' 'gyur and bsTan 'gyur," 87–111.
93. Grieve and Veidlinger, eds., *Buddhism, Digital Media, and the Internet*, 79–86.
94. Walter Ong, *Orality and Literacy: The Technologizing of the Word* (London: Routledge, 1982); and Marshall Poe, *A History of Communications: Media and Society from the Evolution of Speech to the Internet* (Cambridge: Cambridge University Press, 2011).
95. Heidi Campbell, *When Religion Meets New Media* (London: Routledge, 2010).

Daniel Veidlinger

TRI SONGDETSEN

THE LIFE OF TRI SONGDETSEN

Tri Songdetsen's life was marked by conflict and tragedy. His birth is recorded in the *Old Tibetan Annals'* entry for the Tibetan year spanning the spring of 742 to the spring of 743. In its matter-of-fact style, the *Annals* states that Emperor (*btsan po*) Songdetsen was born in Drakmar (Brag dmar), and that his mother, Mangmojé Shiteng of the Nanam clan (Sna nam za Mang mo rje Bzhi steng), died.[1] One assumes from this that she died in childbirth, but it should also be said that the prince was born into a world of plague and pestilence. Just one year previous, the *Annals* records the entombment of the prince Lhébon (Lhas bon) and the Chinese princess Jincheng Gongzhu, who died in 739 and early 740, respectively.[2] Their deaths have generally been attributed to a disease thought to have been brought to Tibet by refugees, among them many Buddhist monks fleeing persecution in Central Asia.[3] Whether just or unjust, laying the blame at the feet of foreign Buddhist monks signaled a nativist antipathy toward the foreign religion, a point with which Tri Songdetsen would later have to contend in acting as Buddhism's champion.

At the time of his death in 739, Prince Lhébon appears to have been the only son and presumably the crown prince of the emperor, Tri Détsuktsen (Khri Lde gtsug rtsan; 704–*c.* 755). Despite the tragedy of his mother's death, Tri Songdetsen's birth three years after the prince's death was fortuitous in preserving the royal succession. As the only clear heir to his father, Tri Songdetsen also staved off the sort of succession struggle that his father went through as a baby in 705, when, following the death of his father Tri Düsong (Khri 'Dus srong; 676–704), Tri Détsuktsen's supporters deposed his elder brother Lha Belpo (Lha Bal po), after which Tri Détsuktsen's grandmother effectively ruled the country in his stead until 712.[4] Even in the apparent absence of a rival brother, however, Tri Songdetsen's succession was still a contested and bloodstained affair. There is a rather fascinating lacuna in both extant versions of the *Old Tibetan Annals* between the years 747 and 755. When the *Annals* resumes its account in the latter year, it appears to be describing the "mopping up" of a revolution led by two councilors, Lang Nyézik (Lang Myes zigs) and Bel Dongtsap ('Bal Ldong tsab), who assassinated Emperor Tri Détsuktsen and set up their own regime. By 755, however, Lang and Bel are dead, their property is being confiscated, and their supporters are being rounded up and punished.[5] The *Annals* does not record the funeral and entombment of Tri Détsuktsen, however, which would customarily be noted two years after an emperor's death. Assuming the veracity of the later tradition, according to which his tomb stands in the royal burial ground of Chonggyé ('Phyong rgyas), on Mura Hill just below the large and commanding tomb of his son Tri Songdetsen, the clear implication is that Tri Détsuktsen was assassinated in 753 at the latest.[6] Given that the *Old Tang Annals* records Tri Détsuktsen's death in 755, it is unlikely that he died many years earlier than this.[7] We can therefore assume that the councilors Lang and Bel ruled Tibet for one to two years from 753 to 754. This temporary overthrow of the monarchy—the only such interregnum known in the history of the Tibetan Empire—would account for the lacuna in the official administrative record during this time, assuming that their revolt was already underway in 748, where the gap in the *Annals* begins.

One cannot overestimate the impact of this revolt both on Tri Songdetsen and on Tibet as a whole. Even in the civil war of the 690s, the powerful Gar (Mgar) clan was unable to overthrow the Tibetan emperor—a point that is celebrated in the *Old Tibetan Chronicle* to emphasize the insuperable power of the Tibetan emperors.[8] Breaking the sacred contract between emperors and their councilors, Lang and Bel's revolt had the potential to permanently undermine the imperial ideology upon which the Tibetan Empire depended. It is against this backdrop of royal weakness and ministerial usurpation that Prince Songdetsen, aged fifteen by Tibetan reckoning, assumed the emperorship with the regnal name Tri Songdetsen in the summer of 756.[9] Living through this crisis—which claimed the life of his father, put him in serious danger, and saw the Tang win many border skirmishes with Tibet—Tri Songdetsen embarked on a war footing. For the remainder of his reign Tibet took full advantage of Tang weakness during and after the An Lushan rebellion to seize control over the four garrisons and annex Tang territories in the Gansu corridor.[10]

At home, Tri Songdetsen was also fighting battles with his councilors, though these seem to have been of an ideological rather than a military variety. He describes these in two of his edicts recorded in a 16th-century Tibetan Buddhist history.[11] These paper edicts, which appear to be genuine in their content if not in their imperfectly reworked and updated orthography, accompanied a short edict inscribed on a pillar to mark the consecration of Samyé Monastery, in all likelihood in the year 779.[12] The second of the paper edicts goes into some narrative detail about the background to the legal act of royally endowing Samyé Monastery and binding all of the high-ranking councilors to support the Buddhist religion.[13] It recounts how shortly after Tri Songdetsen's father was assassinated, some councilors hastily passed a law banning the practice of Buddhism, arguing that its foreign gods and customs were unsuitable for Tibet. The edict states that matters changed when Tri Songdetsen reached the age of twenty (i.e., 761). What is fascinating is that the law against the practice of Buddhism was not reversed based on royal decree or on the triumph of reason, but on the basis of signs and omens. When no ritual could reverse bad omens, which persisted for several months, they finally abated and turned positive after the law against Buddhism was abandoned and Buddhist practice was allowed.

In the edict's narrative, the adoption of Buddhism was a deliberate process that was discussed with different religious teachers and in the face of several doubts about its compatibility with traditional Tibetan beliefs and, notably, whether or not it would be a threat to Tibet's traditional methods of governance. Some, adopting the same line of argument that seems to have precipitated both the law against Buddhism and its repeal, feared that the practice of Buddhism would bring on disease and famine in Tibet. In order to set things right, Tri Songdetsen convened a council in c. 761 at which he addressed his vassals and councilors. Though the emperor called this a "consultation," he was also clear that the point of the council was to secure support for Buddhism and to quash dissent.[14] It ended, in fact, with all of Tri Songdetsen's vassals and councilors swearing never to persecute Buddhism, but to increasingly uphold and support it.[15]

In the first edict, which closes with a list of the "signatories"— that is, those who are sworn to support Buddhism upon the consecration of Samye Monastery in *c.* 779—Tri Songdetsen presents the consecration of the monastery and official support for Buddhism as a remedy for what he refers to as the unrest that followed his father's death.[16] In this way, the young emperor effectively aligns—rightly or wrongly—the opponents of Buddhism with political adversaries that remained from the revolution that resulted in his father's assassination. Reciprocally, one can clearly see that those who swore to uphold the Dharma were also pledging their allegiance to Tri Songdetsen.

The way in which Tri Songdetsen deftly wielded Buddhism as a marker of royal allegiance can certainly be read in the context of the ministerial revolt that resulted in his father's assassination, and the young emperor's consolidation of power following this crisis. Notably, and in keeping with one of the core principles of Tibetan rhetoric and persuasion, Tri Songdetsen is at pains to emphasize the temple building and other Buddhist activities of his forbears, and to thus present his support for Buddhism as having royal precedent in Tibet. At the same time, it is abundantly clear that his reign is a dividing line such that one can speak of Tibetan Buddhism before Tri Songdetsen and Tibetan Buddhism after Tri Songdetsen. Indeed Tri Songdetsen's successors advanced his vision such that Buddhism became increasingly central to the culture of the Tibetan Empire.

The conflict and tragedy that marked Tri Songdetsen's life did not end with his victory in founding Samyé Monastery and establishing a Buddhist Sangha in Tibet. Besides the doctrinal disputes attending the Tibetan assimilation of various forms of Buddhism from India, Central Asia, and China, the end of Tri Songdetsen's reign was marred by a battle for succession between his sons. Interrogating the accounts of various Old Tibetan and Classical Tibetan sources, it appears that Tri Songdetsen had four sons.[17] His first son, born in the summer of 760—just prior to the time that the emperor successfully reversed the law against practicing Buddhism—appears to have died young. Concerning his three subsequent sons, Tri Songdetsen either abdicated in favor of, or ruled jointly with, Munetsen (Mu ne brtsan) from c. 797 until this son was assassinated c. 798. There followed an unfortunate struggle involving Tri Songdetsen and his two remaining sons, the elder, Muruktsen (Mu rug brtsan), and the younger, Desong (Lde srong), which would not be resolved until after their father's death. In the face of violent opposition from Muruktsen, Tri Songdetsen groomed his younger son, Desong, and ruled jointly with him until passing away c. 800. At this point, however, Tri Songdetsen's chosen heir was not yet well established, and elder brother Muruktsen ousted Desong and ruled Tibet for approximately two years before Desong retook the throne c. 802. Two years later, it appears that Muruktsen died, and only Desong, now enthroned as Tri Desongtsen (Khri Lde srong brtsan), remained of Tri Songdetsen's royal progeny.[18] Tri Desongtsen would rule Tibet until 815. During his reign he sponsored the translation of Buddhist scriptures from India and extended his father's patronage of Buddhism. He was succeeded by his own devout son Tri Tsukdétsen (Khri Gtsug lde brtsan; r. 815–841), alias Relpachen (Ral pa can).

THE BUDDHISM OF TRI SONGDETSEN

In his edicts, Tri Songdetsen introduces the core of Buddhist doctrine as he understood it, or as he wished to present it to a potentially skeptical audience. Specifically, he emphasizes karma and transmigration. In his first edict, he clearly states that there is no one who has not been born before, and that beings will be reborn in good or bad stations depending on their deeds. He also introduces the buddha, the dharma, and the Sangha.[19] Tri Songdetsen explains the Buddhist cosmology of the six classes of beings with reference to the Tibetan belief in a tripartite universe consisting of an above, a below, and a between, each populated by various beings such as gods (*lha*), *lu* spirits (*klu*) , and humans, respectively. Mapping the one cosmology onto the other, he states that the gods are above in the heavens; the hell beings are under the earth; and demigods, humans, animals, and hungry ghosts (*pretas*) are between, on the earth. With reference to karma, he explains that it consists of good deeds resulting in virtue (*dge ba*), and wicked deeds resulting in sin (*sdig pa*). The core of virtue is the practice of the ten virtues and the avoidance of the ten non-virtues, and the accumulation of virtue leads to buddhahood, bodhisattvahood, and so on. There is also the accumulation of transcendent virtue and wisdom, based on the four noble truths, the twelve links of dependent origination, the practice of the ten perfections, and the thirty-seven practices of a bodhisattva.[20]

Among the Buddhist commentaries preserved in the commentarial part of the Tibetan Buddhist canon (*Tenjur; Bstan 'gyur*) are several that are attributed to Tri Songdetsen. In the longest of these, *The Authentic Proof of the Scriptures* (*Bka' yang dag pa'i tshad ma*), Tri Songdetsen emphasizes causality and karma in the process of transmigration and rebirth. The emperor's exposition appears to delight in its embrace of Buddhist scholasticism and reasoned argumentation.[21] This is perfectly in keeping with Tri Songdetsen's argument in the second of his edicts: addressing objections that Buddhism is incompatible with traditional Tibetan customs, and charges that it might cause disease and famine, Tri Songdetsen does not rebut these head-on and claim that the practice of Buddhism will bring forth good health and good harvests—though these claims are made vigorously elsewhere—but rather gives a short discourse on karma and rebirth. In urging his subjects to embrace Buddhism, the emperor was also thrusting upon them a new type of reasoned discourse and a cosmopolitan model of elite learning.[22]

Tri Songdetsen's initial support of Buddhism was directed largely at establishing a Sangha in Tibet. Samyé Monastery played host to some of the first Tibetans to be ordained as monks. Led by the abbot Śāntarakṣita (725–*c.* 788), a famous Indian Buddhist teacher from Vikramaśīla Monastery, Samyé also constituted a royal center. Not only was it built near Tri Songdetsen's birthplace in Drakmar, but its architecture and layout emphasized the synergy between Buddhism and kingship. The message that Tri Songdetsen sent with the consecration of this monastery and with his edicts was heard clearly by Tibet's aristocratic families, whose scions were ordained as monks and thus gave rise to a new and important figure within the Tibetan imperial bureaucracy: the monk-councilor.

The Sangha was bureaucratized to a high degree, and leading monks were appointed to official posts, such as that of the "representative of the *bhagavan*" (*bcom ldan 'das kyi ring lugs*).[23] One monk additionally held the privilege of serving as the emperor's *kalyāṇamitra* or "spiritual friend." Besides acting as the emperor's spiritual tutor or preceptor, the *kalyāṇamitra* oversaw, or exercised jurisdiction over the Buddhist temples and monasteries in the region from Samyé to Lhasa (Lha sa).[24] The importance of this office is evident in that fact that Tri Songdetsen's son and chosen heir, Tri Desongtsen, was tutored in his youth by the *kalyāṇamitra*-monk Nyang Tingédzin (Myang Ting nge 'dzin), who in turn became one of the first of Tibet' highly powerful monk-councilors. A generation later, he would be succeeded by Drenka Pelgyiyönten (Bran ka Dpal gyi yon tan), a Buddhist monk who served as Tibet's chief councilor, and who presided over the 821–822 peace treaty with the Tang.[25]

Tri Songdetsen's edicts emphasize temple building, both that of his ancestors, beginning with Songtsen Gampo, and his own efforts in founding Samyé Monastery. The latter, which still stands in southern Tibet, persists as Tri Songdetsen's most visible achievement, and a monument to his successful struggle to transplant the roots of Buddhism into Tibetan soil. The monastery is a visual representation of the Vajradhātu mandala with its central figure, the primordial Buddha Vairocana. This Buddha is prominent in statuary of the late imperial period, where he is clearly associated with the figure of the Tibetan emperor.[26] The layout of Samyé Monastery, which also represents Buddhist cosmology more generally, deftly wielded Buddhist iconography to further align Tri Songdetsen with the religion that he supported and protected.[27]

Tri Songdetsen's reign also saw the production of translations of Buddhist scriptures from Chinese and Sanskrit into Tibetan. At the outset, such translations were carried out piecemeal, by students of various teachers from China, India, and Central Asia, based on their own interests and needs. In this way, some of the most important sutras, such as the *Ratnamegha* and the *Laṅkāvātara*, were first translated into Tibetan.[28] With Tri Songdetsen's patronage of Buddhism, this process gathered pace such that more and more translations were produced. In this environment, there was no lexicographic standard for all scriptoria to follow, either with respect to common terms such as the Sanskrit *sūtra*—initially translated with *dar ma*, and only later with *mdo*—or with regard to rendering Sanskrit case endings in Tibetan.[29] In the manner of an archetypal Buddhist monarch, Tri Songdetsen appears to have made moves to standardize and centralize such practices. These efforts were only realized later, during the reign of Tri Desongtsen, who also ordered the creation of a catalog of all translations of Buddhist scriptures extant in Tibet.[30] In drawing on the expertise of various translators' colleges, and on a central committee who standardized lexicographic practices, Tri Desongtsen no doubt built upon the foundations that had been laid by his father.

Although the first catalog of Tibet's Buddhist translations, the *Lhenkarma* (Lhan dkar ma), was not produced until c. 812, it included many scriptures translated during the reign of Tri Songdetsen. Notable in this respect is the fact that the text with pride of place as the first entry in the catalog is the longest Perfection of Wisdom sutra, the *Śatasāhasrikāprajñāpāramitā-sūtra*, embodying the totality of Indian Madhyamaka philosophy.[31] This well reflects Tri Songdetsen's emphasis on philosophical reasoning. This is not to say, however, that tantric Buddhism was absent from Tri Songdetsen's interests or from Tibetan Buddhism during his reign. While it is true that the official protocols for translation published under successor Tri Desongtsen include an injunction not to produce translations of tantras without royal permission, this is not to rule out royal interest in such texts. Indeed, among the translations recorded in the *Lhenkarma Catalog* is the *Sarvadurgatipariśodhana*, a tantra which, in addition to being the basis for Buddhist funeral rites, also includes technologies for purifying misdeeds and for supporting kings.[32] Some later representations of Tri Songdetsen, as we shall see, in fact emphasize his status as a tantric king, a view that may have already been held by those who appreciated the symbolism of Samyé Monastery.

The *Lhenkarma Catalogue*, the non-extant *Chimpuma (Mchims phu ma) Catalogue*, and the recently unearthed *Pangtangma ('Phang thang ma) Catalogue* represent three successive records of Tibetan imperial holdings of Buddhist texts.[33] Their internal organization represents an early attempt at a Tibetan canonical doxography, with various distinctions being made, for example, between types of sutras based on length, genre (e.g., "*Avataṁsaka* class," "*Ratnakūṭa* class," or Hīnayāna), and on source language (e.g., Chinese). There are also several divisions of *dhāraṇī* and commentaries, as well as one section on tantra, one on vinaya, and one on logic.[34] Another section contains compositions by Tri Songdetsen and other Tibetan authors, demonstrating at once the importance of this king as a Buddhist figure, and the emergence of a distinction between Indian and Tibetan compositions that would play an increasing role in debates over canonicity in Tibetan Buddhism.

In his more public and performative aspect, Tri Songdetsen well fit the profile of a traditional Buddhist monarch. This is most evident in his presiding over the famous Council of Tibet or Council of Lhasa, an effort to establish which form of Buddhism was most appropriate for Tibet. The council of Tibet can be viewed as the culmination of the consultation process that began *c.* 761 when the law against Buddhism was overturned. In the first instance, the conflict was largely over quelling opposition to Buddhism as such, and the council involved Tri Songdetsen compelling his councilors to swear not to curb or destroy Buddhism's prospects in Tibet. This was essentially repeated or ratified with the consecration of Samyé Monastery and with the accompanying edicts, in which the councilors once again swore to uphold the religion of the buddha. But once Samyé was consecrated and populated with its first Tibetan monks, the process of deliberation begun in c. 761 became less a question of whether Buddhism should be followed and more a matter of how and in what form it should be practiced.

To this end, Tri Songdetsen sent queries to some of the greatest Buddhist masters of India and China. A few of their responses, including short expositions on the nature of Buddhism and Buddhist practice from such luminaries as Tankuan, have been passed down.[35] This sort of exploratory reconnaissance came to a head in approximately 792, when the Indian Buddhist teacher Kamalaśīla and several of the Tibetan monks at Samyé confronted the Chinese Chan teacher Moheyan (alias Hashang Mahāyāna) and his followers. The exact nature of this confrontation, and even its outcome, remain contentious matters. The traditional Tibetan account has it that Moheyan and his followers were defeated in a face-to-face debate at Samyé Monastery, after which Moheyan was sent back to China, Chan was discredited, and the form of Indian Buddhism espoused by Kamalaśīla was embraced in Tibet.[36] A contemporary Chinese account by one of Moheyan's disciples, on the other hand, claims that Moheyan won the debate.[37] Moreover, many scholars have pointed to the persistence of Chan in Tibet after the council.[38] To this one can add that some have expressed doubt that a face-to-face debate ever took place, arguing that this would be practically and linguistically very difficult, and that the discourse likely took place through the medium of writing.[39] What is not in dispute, however, is that Tri Songdetsen presided over the exercise, and wielded the power to choose which form of Buddhism Tibet should embrace. Even more indisputable is the fact that from around this time onward, Tibet's translation and transmission activities were directed more toward Sanskrit texts and Indian teachers than Chinese texts and Chinese teachers.

KING-CENTRIC REPRESENTATIONS OF TRI SONGDETSEN, 9TH–12TH CENTURIES AND BEYOND

One can distinguish three main types of representations of Tri Songdetsen which, while roughly succeeding each other chronologically, have each been transmitted to the present day.[40] The first comprises self-representations in his edicts, the inscribed eulogy in the Chonggyé Bridge Inscription, and the eulogy in the *Old Tibetan Chronicle*. The second type includes posthumous representations from the 9th through the 11th centuries that expand upon Tri Songdetsen's Buddhist legacy and emphasize his role in establishing Buddhism in Tibet, with the primary example being the early Tibetan Buddhist history called the *Bazhé* (*Sba bzhed*). The third type, from approximately the 12th century onward, subordinates Tri Songdetsen as an important but secondary character in the story of the taming and conversion of Tibet by the yogin Padmasambhava. Generically, the first and second types of representations fed into the genre of religious historiography (*chos 'byung*), and informed standard narrations of Tri Songdetsen's reign such as one finds in the famous 14th-century Tibetan Buddhist history, *The Mirror Illuminating the Royal Genealogies* (*Rgyal rabs gsal ba'i me long*).[41] The third type of representation, on the other hand, is generally articulated in hagiographies of Padmasambhava, beginning in earnest with the *Zanglingma* (*Bka' thang Zangs gling ma*) "revealed" by Nyangrel Nyima Özer (Nyang ral Nyi ma 'Od zer; 1124–1192).

The closest thing to a self-representation of Tri Songdetsen is found inscribed on a pillar that stands near the royal burial ground of Chonggyé.[42] This inscribed pillar was most likely erected on the occasion of Tri Songdetsen's entombment, c. 802, two years after his death. Like the pillar erected near the tomb of his son, the inscription publishes a royal eulogy that encapsulates the emperor's life according to a standard literary format.

This literary form is also found in the royal eulogies collected in the *Old Tibetan Chronicle*.[43] The eulogy to Tri Songdetsen, as is typical, opens with an evocation of the royal ancestor, introduces the person being eulogized, the reason for the eulogy, and the existence of a more detailed paper document recording his deeds. The eulogy then proceeds to a *res gestae* mentioning how Tri Songdetsen conquered in the four directions while benefiting his people and embracing the good religion, that is, Buddhism. It ends with a summation, including his posthumous name and title, "the sacred god, Great *Bodhi*" (*'phrul gyi lha* Byang chub chen po), supposedly bestowed upon him by the people. While this literally means "Mahābodhi," as in the name of the temple that stands at the site of the buddha's enlightenment in Bodhgaya, India, it may be an abbreviation for "great bodhisattva" or "*bodhisattva mahāsattva*" (*byang chub sems dpa' sems dpa' chen po*).[44] In any case, Tri Songdetsen's posthumous name echoes his own pen name, Jangchup Dzuntrül (Byang chub rdzu 'phrul), which he used in signing colophons to his Buddhist commentaries.[45]

Although these praises, including the posthumous name, were only published after his death, Tri Songdetsen may have had some hand in their drafting.[46] Even so, the restrictive genre of eulogy is such that it leaves little room for innovation. Where Tri Songdetsen's eulogy differs from those of his predecessors as recorded in the *Old Tibetan Chronicle* is in its emphasis on Buddhism. Not only did he embrace Buddhism in order to give it to all of his people, but, the eulogy states, he was also a "great Dharmarāja" (*chos rgyal chen po*).[47] This clearly presents him both as the ideal Tibetan emperor, and as the ideal Buddhist sovereign, connecting him not only with his forefathers but implicitly with other great Buddhist kings such as Aśoka.

Other 9th- and 10th-century representations of Tri Songdetsen, which are truly posthumous and where there is little question of self-portraiture or self-mythologization, develop and expand the Buddhist themes in his eulogy. In the eulogy to Tri Songdetsen found in the *Old Tibetan Chronicle*, this even takes on a messianic flavor: "Establishing the Dharma, he embraced everyone with his compassion, liberated them from birth and death, and delivered them eternally."[48] This further elaboration on the inscribed eulogy may reflect a posthumous development in Tri Songdetsen's mythologization, added in the telling and redaction of the *Old Tibetan Chronicle*. Another document that keeps close to the outlines of Tri Songdetsen's life as revealed by his edicts and by his eulogy inscription is a short text called "The Sutra that Came Down from Heaven" (*Gnam babs kyi dar ma*—recalling that *dar ma* here translates the Sanskrit *sūtra*, not dharma).[49] It celebrates two emperors, Songtsen Gampo and Tri Songdetsen, and mentions some biographical details of the latter, for example, his advocacy for Buddhism after its decline following the death of his father. Written in seven-syllable verse, the text glorifies the reigns of these emperors as a golden age when people were virtuous, healthy, and prosperous, and when there was a great harmony characterized both by the practice of Buddhism and the upholding of Tibet's ancestral traditions.

Further posthumous depictions develop Tri Songdetsen's image as a Buddhist ruler. A mid-9th-century prayer from Dunhuang, for example, praises Tri Songdetsen as a great king alongside Aśoka, Kaniṣkā, and Harṣa Śīlāditya.[50] A rock inscription in eastern Tibet that likely postdates the 10th century refers to Tri Songdetsen as "the emperor, the bodhisattva," thus making explicit what may have been implicit in Tri Songdetsen's pen name and posthumous name.[51]

The Prophecy of the Khotanese Arhat (*Li yul dgra bcom gyi lung bstan pa*), the earliest manuscript of which dates to the 9th or 10th century, includes a prophecy that a bodhisattva will take birth as the king of Tibet and will support the Sangha, build temples and monasteries, and patronize Buddhism there. This is arguably the earliest reference to a Tibetan emperor as an emanation of an arya-bodhisattva, to be distinguished from the use of "bodhisattva" as a title, or in the sense of a buddha-to-be, as in a *Jātaka* tale.[52]

Another Dunhuang manuscript, possibly dating to the 10th century, also refers to Tri Songdetsen as being "of a bodhisattva lineage." Furthermore, this text equates him with King Dza (Rdza), an important figure in *Mahāyoga* tantric lineages.[53]

One further posthumous representation of Tri Songdetsen stands between the early and later refigurations. This is the pseudepigraphical letter of Buddhaguhya/Buddhagupta, supposedly sent to Tri Songdetsen by way of politely refusing his invitation to come and teach in Tibet.[54] For a letter by an Indian teacher based near Mt. Kailash, it displays a very odd amalgamation of accurate and inaccurate knowledge about the Tibetan royal line, the names of Tibetan religious figures, and standard Tibetan forms of royal praise. Whether its core contained an actual letter from Buddhaguhya or not is debatable, but in the manner in which it has come down in the Tibetan canon, it is most likely the work of a Tibetan some centuries removed from the lifetime of Tri Songdetsen. Notably, it salutes Tri Songdetsen as being of an unbroken bodhisattva lineage with Songtsen Gampo, who is saluted as the embodiment—actually, "the body" (*sku*)—of Avalokiteśvara. Buddhaguhya further refers to Tri Songdetsen as "belonging to the uninterrupted lineage of manifestations" (*sprul pa'i rgyud ma chad pa'i nang*).[55] This may be one of the earliest articulations of the belief that Songtsen Gampo was an emanation of Avalokiteśvara. It does not seem, however, to equate Tri Songdetsen with Mañjusrī, despite an opening invocation to this bodhisattva. If anything, a firmer emanational line is drawn between Tri Songdetsen and Songtsen Gampo and, by extension, Avalokiteśvara.

The most important development during this early phase of representation was the extension of Tri Songdetsen's edicts into a longer account concerning the fate of Buddhism during his reign. Just as the Samyé edicts drew on earlier accounts and on the *narratio* to earlier binding decisions such as that enacted by Tri Songdetsen at his council in 761 to promote the acceptance of Buddhism, the Samyé edicts informed later accounts arising out of similar situations. The council of Tibet may constitute one such example, as may a grant supposedly given to Selnang of the Ba clan (Sba Gsal snang) for his service to the Buddhadharma in Tibet.[56] With the collapse of the monarchy, this clan took on the role of caretaker of this narrative tradition, which came to be known as the *Bazhé* (*Sba bzhed*), or *Testament of the Ba Clan.*[57]

The earliest extant version of the *Testament of the Ba Clan* bears the subtitle *"Text of the Royal Narrative Concerning How the Buddhist Religion Came to Tibet"* (*Sangs rgyas kyi chos bod khams su ji ltar byung ba'i bka' mchid kyi yi ge*), where "royal narrative" is the same generic term that describes one of Tri Songdetsen's two Samyé edicts. This earliest version, like later versions of the *Bazhé*, is centered on the reign of Tri Songdetsen and closely echoes his edicts and eulogies while adding quite a lot of further detail regarding the construction and consecration of Samyé Monastery, the council of Tibet, and the leading roles played by Ba clan members in the Tibetan assimilation of Buddhism. Several influential religious histories relied on the *Bazhé*'s account for their narrations of Tri Songdetsen's reign, and the *Bazhé* in turn expanded itself on the model of such histories, appending short vignettes of Tri Songdetsen's predecessors and successors. Its core nevertheless remained the narration of the reign of Tri Songdetsen.

In this way, Tri Songdetsen's administrative acts in support of Buddhism, and their attendant *narratios*, initially composed in the context of a conflict with his councilors and in the shadow of his father's assassination, fed into the creation of Tibet's unique form of religious historiography. To this one can also add influences from eulogies, praises, administrative genres, Khotanese religious histories, ritual texts, and Tibet's chronicle-epic tradition, but there is no question that Tri Songdetsen, and his context of conflict and advocacy, is strongly implicated in the birth of Tibetan Buddhist historiography.

YOGIN-CENTRIC REPRESENTATIONS OF TRI SONGDETSEN, 12TH–14TH CENTURIES AND BEYOND

In the 11th and 12th centuries, an emerging Tibetan *Heilsgeschichte*, in which Avalokiteśvara was identified as the patron bodhisattva of Tibet, interacted in dynamic ways with the earlier, royalist tradition of Buddhist historiography represented by the *Bazhé*. The initial focal point of the new devotional and narrative dispensation, articulated in revealed "treasure" (*gter ma*) literature, was Emperor Songtsen Gampo, who was refigured as an emanation of Avalokiteśvara. Subsequently, however, there was a shift in emphasis to a second figure, the yogin Padmasambhava, who was presented as a demon-tamer chiefly responsible for civilizing and converting Tibet during the reign of Tri Songdetsen.[58] The change in focus from Songtsen Gampo to Padmasambhava mirrored a parallel movement whereby, after the collapse of the monarchy and with the rise of tantric ideals, the lama or religious hierarch came to displace the king as the center of spiritual and secular power in Tibetan culture. This movement is acted out in various ways in the portrayals of Emperor Tri Songdetsen in the hagiographies of Padmasambhava. Here, the emperor is no longer the main agent in bringing Buddhism to Tibet but is overshadowed by the powerful displays of Padmasambhava, whose disciple he becomes. Simultaneously, Tibetan Buddhists articulated a sort of emanational hierarchy for their most treasured religious kings, flanking Songtsen Gampo (the emanation of Avalokiteśvara) with Tri Songdetsen, who was identified with the bodhisattva Mañjusrī, and Tri Tsukdétsen (alias Relpachen), who was refigured as an emanation of Vajrapāṇi. These representations of Tri Songdetsen as a disciple of Padmasambhava and as an emanation of Mañjusrī remain the most salient in Tibetan religious memory and have tended to exist unproblematically alongside one another and in conversation with the more "kingly" representations such as those transmitted in the *Bazhé*.

Relics, objects, and texts associated with the imperial period were revealed and revered as "treasure" (*gter ma*) from the 11th and 12th centuries onward, giving rise to a genre of revealed or inspired Buddhist apocrypha. As part of this process, Emperor Songtsen Gampo was identified as an emanation of Avalokiteśvara, and became an increasingly important site of memory and devotion. The most important such treasures that expressed and disseminated this refiguration of Songtsen Gampo were the *Kachem Kakölma* (*Bka' chems ka khol ma*) and the *Mani Kambum* (*Ma Ni bka' 'bum*).[59]

Devotion to Avalokiteśvara also informed the subsequent and enduring turn in treasure literature toward the figure of the tantric-adept Padmasambhava. On an ontological level, the shift to a new protagonist in Tibet's *Heilsgeschichte* entailed no essential change: Padmasambhava is an emanation of the Buddha Amitābha, to whose "family" Avalokiteśvara belongs. While Padmasambhava is somewhat peripheral to the *Bazhé*'s narrative and, unlike Śāntarakṣita, is not mentioned in any of Tri Songdetsen's writings, he emerged in some circles as a central devotional figure. This process was certainly in motion by the 10th century and may have begun as early as Padmasambhava's lifetime.[60] The full flowering of the devotional mythologizing of

Padmasambhava took place in the 12th century with the appearance of the *Zanglingma* hagiography "revealed" by Nyangrel Nyima Özer. Here, Padmasambhava is the central protagonist, and the narrative follows him from his appearance or miraculous birth in Oddiyana through his sojourns in India and Tibet to his departure from Tibet to tame demons elsewhere.[61]

Within this narrative, Tri Songdetsen is clearly subordinate to Padmasambhava, a fact illustrated by the popular topos of the meeting of the emperor and the yogin. This topos, found also in connection with Tri Songdetsen's meeting with other tantric masters such as Vairocana and Vimalamitra, trades on the protocols of who should bow to whom. Within Tibetan imperial culture and court etiquette, there is no doubt that one prostrates to the emperor. In the 12th-century milieu of Nyangrel Nyima Özer and thereafter, however, the figure of the lama or yogin reigned supreme, and it was to him that one should show obeisance. These two vectors of respect come together in dramatic fashion in the *Zanglingma* when Padmasambhava refuses to bow to Tri Songdetsen, and the emperor in turn refuses to bow to Padmasambhava. Padmasambhava then resolves the situation by bowing, but simultaneously using his magical powers to set fire to Tri Songdetsen's robes. Duly chastened, the emperor then bows to Padmasambhava.[62]

The narrative amplifies the portrait of Padmasambhava given in the *Bazhé* such that he plays a central role in taming the demons of Tibet, preparing the ground for the foundation of Samyé Monastery, giving instruction to Tri Songdetsen, performing miracles, and concealing "treasures" for future generations to reveal. His only failures are inevitably due to his being curtailed or thwarted by Tri Songdetsen, who is either at the mercy of his wary councilors, or who is himself vacillating in one way or another. When Padmasambhava leaves Tibet, therefore, he gives a prophecy that details not only how well everything would have turned out had he not faced such obstacles, but also the consequences that the failings of Tri Songdetsen, his councilors, and others will have for Tibet's future.[63] Much of this comes in the form of advice directed at various sectors of Tibetan society, and in this it closely resembles the pseudepigraphical letter of Buddhaguhya.

Seen in the context of earlier, "kingly" depictions of Tri Songdetsen, the hagiography of Padmasambhava essentially dethrones the emperor in favor of the yogin. In the context of treasure literature, it also marks a shift in emphasis from the figure of the king, Songtsen Gampo, to that of the yogin, Padmasambhava. There is a third demotion, which happens on an emanational level. During this period, various of Tibet's best-remembered emperors were being identified as emanations of bodhisattvas. This was a matter of negotiation, however, and it remained in flux for some time, both with regard to which emperors were highlighted and with respect to which bodhisattvas' emanations they represented. This is evident, for example, in the letter of Buddhaguhya, which appears to identify Tri Songdetsen as belonging to a lineage of emanations of Avalokiteśvara. The *Zanglingma*, however, along with most subsequent works, introduces Tri Songdetsen as an emanation of the bodhisattva of wisdom, Mañjusrī. Later versions of the *Zanglingma* also depict the emperor dissolving into the heart of Mañjusrī upon his death, echoing a similar scene in narrations of the life of Songtsen Gampo.[64] Assimilating Tri Songdetsen to Mañjusrī also shunts him somewhat to the side as being peripheral to the narrative of the fate of Buddhism in Tibet through its patron bodhisattva Avalokiteśvara.

The yogin displaces the king in one further sense in Nyangrel Nyima Özer's work. Nyangrel himself, the champion of the Padmasambhava hagiography, was identified as a reincarnation of Tri Songdetsen. His depictions, therefore, are of his own past life as this emperor. Furthermore, Nyangrel's present incarnation as a lama is an improvement on, not to say the perfection of, his previous incarnation as an emperor. In this fashion, claiming Tri Songdetsen as a previous incarnation adds to Nyangrel's legacy and prestige, and puts him in close proximity to the previous guru, Padmasambhava, to whom he can show obeisance by proxy in debasing his past, kingly self.[65]

Many other Tibetan lamas and religious hierarchs, notably the Fifth Dalai Lama Ngawang Losang Gyatso (Ngag dbang Blo bzang Rgya mtsho'; 1617–1682), adopted a similar strategy, claiming Tri Songdetsen among their previous incarnations.[66]

The *Zanglingma*'s depiction of Tri Songdetsen informed later Padmasambhava hagiographies, such as the popular 14th-century *Pema Katang* (*Padma Bka' thang*) of Orgyen Lingpa (O rgyan gling pa; b. 1323) and the *Katang Sertreng* (*Bka' thang Gser phreng*) of Sanggyé Lingpa (Sangs rgyas gling pa; 1340–1396). It also found itself in dialogue with historical works such as the *Bazhé* and the *Chöjung Metok Nyingpo Drangtsi Chü* (*Chos 'byung me tog snying po sbrang rtsi'i bcud*), the latter also attributed to Nyangrel. In the course of their elaboration and transmission over centuries, these works, particularly the *Bazhé* and the *Zanglingma*, increasingly borrowed from each other and from other sources in order to further develop their narratives. As a result of Padmasambhava's growing centrality to Tibet's national mythos, and his emergence as the main figure of the Nyingma (Rnying ma) school of Tibetan Buddhism, the depiction of Tri Songdetsen the disciple remains the abiding one within Tibetan cultural memory, and within Tibetan Buddhism more generally.

Finally, mention should be made of a non-Buddhist counter-representation of Tri Songdetsen within the Tibetan Bön religion. Its earliest articulation is arguably that found in the *Drakpa Lingdrak* (*Bsgrags pa gling grags*), a Bön history that may date to as early as the 12th or 13th century. In its organization, it resembles the extended *Bazhé*, with a core narrative concerning Tri Songdetsen, and short vignettes of the reigns of previous and subsequent Tibetan emperors.[67] Its narration of the reign of Tri Songdetsen is like a mirror image of that of the *Bazhé* in that it covers the same basic events but narrates them in an opposite manner, casting Tri Songdetsen, Padmasambhava, and Śāntarakṣita as villains who embrace a perverse religion and endanger the traditional Bön religion of Tibet. The Bön depiction embellishes the yogin-centric Buddhist depiction of Tri Songdetsen's vacillation to good effect, showing him as sometimes supporting Bön and sometimes supporting Buddhism, sometimes in the sway of councilors and sometimes in the sway of priests, but in the end persecuting the Bön religion and its adherents. This depiction, like the Buddhist refiguration articulated from the twelfth century onward, has been transmitted up to the present and continues to circulate as a dissenting counter-representation of Tri Songdetsen.[68]

REVIEW OF LITERATURE

Buddhological and Tibetological scholarship has traditionally followed the dominant Tibetan Buddhist narrative in approaching Tri Songdetsen as an auxiliary to Padmasambhava. This is due partly to the youth of these disciplines, and partly to the influence that translations of

Padmasambhava's hagiography have exerted on the study of Buddhism and of Tibetan literature in the West.[69] In this way, the disciplines received and transmitted, somewhat uncritically at first, the traditional Tibetan Buddhist narrative concerning Padmasambhava and Tri Songdetsen. Tibetan Buddhists worldwide remain familiar with the depiction of Tri Songdetsen as a disciple of Padmasambhava, and are often unaware of the more recent critical reappraisal of the role of Tri Songdetsen in establishing Buddhism in Tibet, or of the existence of Old Tibetan sources written prior to the emergence of Tibet's grand Buddhist framing narrative in the 11th and 12th centuries.

From the late 1960s onward, the figure of Padmasambhava was subjected to scholarly scrutiny, such that it became a matter of debate whether any such person ever existed.[70] Around the same time, the field of Old Tibetan studies matured as scholars focused on imperial Tibetan inscriptions and on Tibetan Dunhuang manuscripts as sources for the study of Tibetan history, religion, and culture. This served as a corrective in some sense, since Tri Songdetsen looms large in these early sources, while Padmasambhava is relatively obscure. As the field of Tibetology marshaled its sources, and as more and more Tibetan histories and hagiographies appeared due to the flight of Tibetans into exile in India and Nepal, advances during this period were cautious and piecemeal. Many focused on contradictions between earlier and later accounts or between Tibetan and Chinese sources in an attempt to discern accurately the broad outlines of Tibet's history.[71]

Another strand of research, emphasizing the Tibetan kings, and the nature of Tibetan sacred kingship, also informs developments in the understanding of Tri Songdetsen. This can be traced back to seminal works by Giuseppe Tucci and Erik Haarh, and more recently to Matthew Kapstein's study of the Tibetan assimilation of Buddhism during the imperial period.[72] Most recently, scholars of Old Tibetan studies, notably Lewis Doney, have turned their attention to representations of Tri Songdetsen in the earliest sources, and have emphasized his importance as a pivotal figure in the Tibetan adoption of Buddhism.[73]

PRIMARY SOURCES

Many of the primary sources for the study of Tri Songdetsen exist in translation. In particular, Hugh Richardson, W. South Coblin, Li Fang-Kuei, and many others have translated the Old Tibetan inscriptions and Tri Songdetsen's edicts. Dunhuang manuscripts relevant to Tri Songdetsen have also been subject to translation and study. Those wishing to consult images and rubbings of the inscriptions can refer to a recent collection of new transliterations of the inscriptions by Nathan Hill, Kazushi Iwao, and Tsuguhito Takeuchi.[74] Their introduction to each inscription gives references to translations and secondary literature, and also to published rubbings and photographs, including those on the Tibet Album (http://tibet.prm.ox.ac.uk) website operated by the Pitt Rivers Museum.

Many of the Dunhuang manuscripts relevant to Tri Songdetsen, including the *Old Tibetan Annals* and the *Old Tibetan Chronicle*, are available online in searchable transliterations on the Old Tibetan Documents Online websites (http://otdo.aa.tufs.ac.jp). One can also consult high-quality digital images of these manuscripts on the websites of the International Dunhuang Project (http://www.idp.bl.uk), Gallica (http://www.gallica.bnf.fr), and Artstor (http://www.artstor.org).

For classical Tibetan sources relevant to Tri Songdetsen, one is even better served by well-annotated translations and studies of key histories and hagiographies. The earliest extant version of the *Bazhé* exists in English translation, accompanied by photographic reproductions of the manuscript.[75] Per Sørensen's annotated translation of the influential 14th-century history *The Mirror Illuminating the Royal Genealogies* features heavy annotation that cross-references this history's account with those of the most important Tibetan Buddhist histories.[76] Nyangrel Nyima Özer's *Zanglingma* hagiography of Padmasambhava, so influential to the changing depiction of Tri Songdetsen from the twelfth century onward, is the subject of a recent study by Lewis Doney that includes a long introduction and photographic reproductions of manuscripts representing the earliest extant version of the *Zanglingma*.[77] An English translation of a later version of the hagiography was published by Erik Pema Kunsang.[78]

DIGITAL MATERIALS

The Tibet Album (http://tibet.prm.ox.ac.uk).
Old Tibetan Documents Online (http://otdo.aa.tufs.ac.jp) (new website; previous website available here (http://otdo.aa.tufs.ac.jp).
International Dunhuang Project (http://www.idp.bl.uk).
Gallica (http://www.gallica.bnf.fr).
Artstor (http://www.artstor.org).

FURTHER READING

Bacot, Jacques, Frederick W. Thomas, and Charles G. Toussaint. *Documents de Touen-houang relatifs à l'histoire du tibet*. Paris: Librarie Paul Geuthner, 1940–1946.

Chetsang, Drikung Kyabgon. *A History of the Tibetan Empire. Drawn from the Dunhuang Manuscripts*. Translated by Meghan Howard, with Tsultrim Nakchu. Dehra Dun: Songtsen Library, 2011.

Doney, Lewis. "Emperor, Dharmaraja, Bodhisattva? Inscriptions from the Reign of Khri Srong lde brtsan." In *Current Issues and Progress in Tibetan Studies*. Edited by Tsuguhito Takeuchi et al., 63–84. Kobe, Japan: Kobe City University of Foreign Studies, 2013.

Doney, Lewis. "Nyang ral Nyi ma 'od zer and the Testimony of Ba." *Bulletin of Tibetology* 49.1 (2013): 7–38.

Doney, Lewis. "Early Bodhisattva-Kingship in Tibet: the Case of Tri Songdetsen." *Cahiers d'Extrême-Asie* 24 (2015): 29–47.

Dotson, Brandon. "'Emperor' Mu-rug-btsan and the *'Phang thang ma Catalogue*." *Journal of the International Association for Tibetan Studies* 3 (2007): 1–25.

Dotson, Brandon. "Tri Songdetsen." In *Oxford Bibliographies Online: Buddhism*. Edited by Richard Payne. New York: Oxford University Press, 2011.

Haarh, Erik. "The Identity of Tsu-chi-chen, the Tibetan 'King' Who Died in 804 AD." *Acta Orientalia* 25 (1960): 121–170.

Kapstein, Matthew T. *The Tibetan Assimilation of Buddhism: Conversion, Contestation, and Memory*. Oxford: Oxford University Press, 2000.

Kollmar-Paulenz, Karénina. "The Buddhist Way into Tibet." In *The Spread of Buddhism*, part 8, vol. 16. Edited by Anne Heirman and Stephan-Peter Bumbacher, 303–340. Leiden, The Netherlands: Brill, 2007.

Li, Fang Kuei, and W. South Coblin. *A Study of the Old Tibetan Inscriptions*. Taipei: Academia Sinica, 1987.

Richardson, Hugh E. *A Corpus of Tibetan Inscriptions*. London: Royal Asiatic Society, 1985.
Schaeffer, Kurtis, Matthew T. Kapstein, and Gray Tuttle. *Sources of Tibetan Tradition*. New York: Columbia University Press, 2013.
Scherrer-Schaub, Cristina. "A Perusal of Early Tibetan Inscriptions in Light of the Buddhist World of the 7th to 9th Centuries A.D." In *Epigraphic Evidence in the Pre-Modern Buddhist World*. Edited by Kurt Tropper, 117–165. Vienna: Arbeitskreise für Tibetische und Buddhistische Studien, 2014.
Seyfort Ruegg, David. *Buddha-Nature, Mind, and the Problem of Gradualism in a Comparative Perspective: On the Transmission and Reception of Buddhism in India and Tibet; Jordan Lectures in Comparative Religion*. London: School of Oriental and African Studies, 1989.
Sørensen, Per K. *Tibetan Buddhist Historiography: The Mirror Illuminating the Royal Genealogies*. Wiesbaden, Germany: Harrassowitz, 1994.
Stein, Rolf. *Rolf Stein's Tibetica Antiqua with Additional Materials*. Translated and edited by Arthur McKeown. Leiden, The Netherlands: Brill, 2010.
Wangdu, Pasang, and Hildegard Diemberger. *dBa' Bzhed: The Royal Narrative concerning the Bringing of the Buddha's Doctrine to Tibet*. Vienna: Austrian Academy of Sciences Press, 2000.

NOTES

1. Brandon Dotson, *The Old Tibetan Annals: An Annotated Translation of Tibet's First History* (Vienna: Austrian Academy of Sciences Press, 2009).
2. Dotson, *The Old Tibetan Annals*.
3. Matthew T. Kapstein, *The Tibetan Assimilation of Buddhism: Conversion, Contestation, and Memory* (Oxford: Oxford University Press, 2000).
4. Kapstein, *The Tibetan Assimilation of Buddhism*.
5. Dotson, *The Old Tibetan Annals*.
6. Jampa L. Panglung, "Die metrischen Berichte über die Grabmäler der tibetischer Könige. Ihre Überlieferung und ihr Beitrag zur Identifizierung," in *Tibetan Studies: Proceedings of the 4th Seminar of the International Association for Tibetan Studies*, ed. H. Uebach and J. Panglung, 321–368 (Munich: Bavarian Academy of Sciences Press, 1989).
7. S. W. Bushell, "The Early History of Tibet: From Chinese Sources," *Journal of the Royal Asiatic Society* 12 (1880): 435–541; Paul Pelliot, *Histoire ancienne du tibet* (Paris: Adrien Maisonneuve, 1961).
8. Hugh E. Richardson, "The Mgar Family in Seventh-Century Tibet," in *Reflections on Tibetan Culture: Essays in Memory of Turrell V. Wylie*, ed. L. Epstein and R. Sherburne (New York: The Edwin Mellen Press, 1989), 49–57.
9. Dotson, *The Old Tibetan Annals*.
10. Christopher I. Beckwith, *The Tibetan Empire in Central Asia: A History of the Struggle for Great Power among Tibetans, Turks, Arabs, and Chinese during the Early Middle Ages* (Princeton, NJ: Princeton University Press, 1993).
11. Hugh E. Richardson, "The First Tibetan *chos-'byung*," *Tibet Journal* 5, no. 3 (1980): 62–73; W. South Coblin, "A Reexamination of the Second edict of Khri-Srong-Lde-Btsan," in *Reflections on Tibetan Culture: Essays in Memory of Turrell V. Wylie*, ed. L. Epstein and R. Sherburne (New York: The Edwin Mellen Press, 1989), 165–185; Matthew T. Kapstein, "The Conversion Edict of Tri Songdetsen," in *Sources of Tibetan Tradition*, ed. K. Schaeffer, M. T. Kapstein, and G. Tuttle (New York: Columbia University Press, 2013), 60–64.
12. Hugh E. Richardson, *A Corpus of Tibetan Inscriptions* (London: Royal Asiatic Society, 1985); Li Fang Kuei and W. South Coblin, *A Study of the Old Tibetan Inscriptions* (Taipei: Academia Sinica, 1987).
13. Coblin, "A Reexamination of the Second Edict of Khri-Srong-Lde-Btsan"; Kapstein, "The Conversion Edict of Tri Songdetsen."

14. Lewis Doney, "Emperor, Dharmaraja, Bodhisattva? Inscriptions from the Reign of Khri Srong lde brtsan," in *Current Issues and Progress in Tibetan Studies*, ed. T. Takeuchi et al. (Kobe, Japan: Kobe City University of Foreign Studies, 2013), 63–84.
15. Coblin, "A Reexamination of the Second Edict of Khri-Srong-Lde-Btsan"; Kapstein, "The Conversion Edict of Tri Songdetsen."
16. Richardson, "The First Tibetan *chos-'byung*"; Kapstein, "The Conversion Edict of Tri Songdetsen."
17. Erik Haarh, "The Identity of Tsu-chi-chen, the Tibetan 'King' Who Died in 804 AD," *Acta Orientalia* 25 (1960): 121–170.
18. Brandon Dotson, "'Emperor' Mu-rug-btsan and the *'Phang thang ma Catalogue*," *Journal of the International Association for Tibetan Studies* 3 (2007): 1–25.
19. Richardson, "The First Tibetan *chos-'byung*"; Kapstein, "The Conversion Edict of Tri Songdetsen."
20. Coblin, "A Reexamination of the Second Edict of Khri-Srong-Lde-Btsan."
21. Kapstein, *The Tibetan Assimilation of Buddhism*, 45–46; Matthew T. Kapstein, "Causes and Signs," in *Sources of Tibetan Tradition*, ed. K. Schaeffer, M. T. Kapstein, and G. Tuttle (New York: Columbia University Press, 2013), 118–123.
22. Kapstein, *The Tibetan Assimilation of Buddhism*.
23. Helga Uebach, "On Dharma-Colleges and Their Teachers in the Ninth Century Tibetan Empire," in *Indo-Sino-Tibetica: Studi in Onore Di Luciano Petech*, ed. P. Daffinà (Rome: Bardi, 1990), 393–417.
24. Dotson, "'Emperor' Mu-rug-btsan and the *'Phang thang ma Catalogue*."
25. Hugh E. Richardson, "Great Monk-Ministers of the Tibetan Kingdom," in *High Peaks, Pure Earth: Collected Writings on Tibetan History and Culture, by Hugh E. Richardson*, ed. M. Aris (London: Serindia, 1998), 140–148.
26. Amy Heller, "Buddhist Images and Rock Inscriptions from Eastern Tibet, VIIIth to Xth Century, part IV," in *Tibetan Studies: Proceedings of the 7th Seminar of the International Association for Tibetan Studies, Graz 1995*, ed. H. Krasser (Vienna: Austrian Academy of Sciences Press, 1997), 385–403; Kapstein, *The Tibetan Assimilation of Buddhism*; Michael Walter, *Buddhism and Empire* (Leiden, The Netherlands: Brill, 2009).
27. Giuseppe Tucci, "The Simbolism [*sic*] of the Temples of bSam yas," *East and West* 6, no. 4 (1956): 279–281; Kapstein, *The Tibetan Assimilation of Buddhism*.
28. Cristina Scherrer-Schaub, "Enacting Words: A Diplomatic Analysis of the Imperial Decrees (*bkas bcad*) and Their Application in the *sGra sbyor bam po gnyis pa* Tradition," *Journal of the International Association of Buddhist Studies* 25, no. 1–2 (2002): 263–340.
29. Rolf Stein, "Tibetica antiqua I: Les deux vocabularies des traductions Indo-Tibétaine et Sino-Tibétaine dans les manuscrits de Touen-Houang," *Bulletin de l'École Française d'Extrême-Orient* 72 (1983): 150–236; Rolf Stein, *Rolf Stein's Tibetica Antiqua with Additional Materials*, trans. and ed. A. McKeown (Leiden, The Netherlands: Brill, 2010).
30. Adelheid Herrmann-Pfandt, *Die lHan kar ma: Ein früher Katalog der ins Tibetische übersetzten buddhistischen Texte* (Vienna: Austrian Academy of Sciences Press, 2008).
31. Marcelle Lalou, "Les texts Bouddhiques au temps du roi Khri-Sroṅ-lde-bcan," *Journal Asiatique* 241 (1953): 313–353; Herrmann-Pfandt, *Die lHan kar ma*.
32. Zeff Bjerken, "Of Mandalas, Monarchs, and Mortuary Magic: Siting the Sarvadurgatipariśodhana Tantra in Tibet," *Journal of the American Academy of Religion* 73.3 (2005): 813–841.
33. Dotson, "'Emperor' Mu-rug-btsan and the *'Phang thang ma Catalogue*."
34. Georgios Halkias, "Tibetan Buddhism Registered: A Catalogue from the Imperial Court of 'Phang thang," *Eastern Buddhist* 36, no. 1–2 (2004): 47–105; Kawagoe Eishin, *dKar chag 'Phang thang ma* (Sendai, Japan: Tōhoku indo chibetto kenkyū kai, 2005).
35. Werner Pachow, *A Study of the Twenty-Two Dialogues on Mahāyāna Buddhism/Ta-sheng erh-shih-erh wen chih yen-chiu* (Taipei: Tung-ch'u ch'u-pan-she, 1993).

36. *Giuseppe Tucci, Minor Buddhist Texts, Part II: First Bhāvanākrama of Kamalaśīla; Sanskrit and Tibetan Texts with Introduction and English Summary* (Rome: Istituto Italiano per il Medio ed Estremo Oriente, 1958); David Seyfort Ruegg, *Buddha-Nature, Mind, and the Problem of Gradualism in a Comparative Perspective: On the Transmission and Reception of Buddhism in India and Tibet; Jordan Lectures in Comparative Religion* (London: School of Oriental and African Studies, 1989); Pasang Wangdu and Hildegard Diemberger, *dBa' Bzhed: The Royal Narrative concerning the Bringing of the Buddha's Doctrine to Tibet* (Vienna: Austrian Academy of Sciences Press, 2000); Matthew T. Kapstein, "Chinese and Indian Buddhists at Samyé," in *Sources of Tibetan Tradition*, ed. K. Schaeffer, M. T. Kapstein, and G. Tuttle (New York: Columbia University Press, 2013), 142–150.
37. Paul Demiéville, *Le concile de Lhasa: Une controverse sur le quiétisme entre Bouddhistes de l'Inde et de la Chine au VIIIe siècle de l'ère Chrétienne* (Paris: Presses Universitaires de France, 1952).
38. Sam van Schaik, *Tibetan Zen: Discovering a Lost Tradition. Stories Told by the Dunhuang Cave Manuscripts* (Boston, MA: Snow Lion Publications, 2015).
39. Yoshiro Imaeda, "Documents tibétains de Touen-Houang concernant le concile du Tibet," *Journal Asiatique* 263 (1975): 125–146.
40. Brandon Dotson, "Tri Songdetsen," in *Oxford Bibliographies Online: Buddhism*, ed. R. Payne (New York: Oxford University Press, 2011).
41. Per K. Sørensen, *Tibetan Buddhist Historiography: The Mirror Illuminating the Royal Genealogies* (Wiesbaden, Germany: Harrassowitz, 1994).
42. Richardson, *A Corpus of Tibetan Inscriptions*; Li and Coblin, *A Study of the Old Tibetan Inscriptions*; Doney, "Emperor, Dharmaraja, Bodhisattva?"
43. Brandon Dotson, "The Unhappy Bride and her Lament," *Journal of the International Association for Bon Research* 1 (2013): 199–225.
44. Doney, "Emperor, Dharmaraja, Bodhisattva?"
45. Ernst Steinkellner, "Who Is Byaṅ chub rdzu 'phrul? Tibetan and non-Tibetan Commentaries on the Saṃdhinirmocanasūtra," *Berliner Indologische Studien* 4–5 (1989): 229–252.
46. Brandon Dotson, "Naming the King: Accession, Death, and Afterlife through the Re-, Un-, and Nick-naming of Tibet's Kings," *Cahiers d'Extrême-Asie* 24 (2015): 1–27.
47. Richardson, *A Corpus of Tibetan Inscriptions*; Li and Coblin, *A Study of the Old Tibetan Inscriptions*; Doney, "Emperor, Dharmaraja, Bodhisattva?"
48. Jacques Bacot, Frederick W. Thomas, and Charles G. Toussaint, trans., *Documents de Touen-houang relatifs à l'histoire du tibet* (Paris: Librarie Paul Geuthner, 1940–1946); Drikung Kyabgon Chetsang, *A History of the Tibetan Empire. Drawn from the Dunhuang Manuscripts*, trans. M. Howard, with T. Nakchu (Dehra Dun, India: Songtsen Library, 2011).
49. Rolf Stein, "Tibetica antiqua IV: La tradition relative au début du Bouddhisme au Tibet," *Bulletin de l'École Française d'Extrême-Orient* 75 (1986): 169–196; Stein, *Rolf Stein's Tibetica Antiqua*; Hugh E. Richardson, "'The Dharma [*sic*] That Came Down from Heaven': A Tun-huang Fragment," in *Buddhist Thought and Asian Civilization: Essays in Honor of Herbert V. Guenther on His Sixtieth Birthday*, ed. L. S. Kawamura and K. Scott (Emeryville, CA: Dharma Publications, 1977), 62–73.
50. Sam van Schaik and Lewis Doney, "The Prayer, the Priest, and the Tsenpo: An Early Buddhist Narrative from Dunhuang," *Journal of the International Association of Buddhist Studies* 30, no. 1–2 (2007): 175–217.
51. Heller, "Buddhist Images and Rock Inscriptions from Eastern Tibet";Lewis Doney, "Early Bodhisattva-Kingship in Tibet: the Case of Tri Songdetsen," *Cahiers d'Extrême-Asie* 24 (2015): 29–47.
52. Frederick William Thomas, *Tibetan Literary Texts and Documents Concerning Chinese Turkestan* (London: Luzac, 1935).
53. Samten Karmay, "King Tsa/Dza and Vajrayāna," in *Tantric and Daoist Studies in Honour of R. A. Stein*, vol. 1, ed. M. Strickmann (Brussels: Institut Belge des Hautes Études Chinoises, 1981), 192–211; Yoshiro Imaeda, "Un extrait tibétain du *Mañjuśrīmūlakalpa* dans les manuscrits de Touen-houang," in *Nouvelles*

contributions aux études de Touen-houang à la mémoire de Paul Demiéville, ed. M. Soymié (Geneva, Switzerland: Librairie Droz, 1981), 303–320; Rolf Stein, "Tibetica Antiqua III: À propos du mot gcug-lag et de la religion indigène," *Bulletin de l'École Française d'Extrême-Orient* 74 (1985): 83–133; Stein, *Rolf Stein's Tibetica Antiqua*.

54. Siglinde Dietz, *Die buddhistische Briefliteratur Indiens: Nach dem tibetischen Tanjur herausgegeben, übersetzt und erläutert* (Wiesbaden, Germany: Harrassowitz, 1984); David Snellgrove, *Indo-Tibetan Buddhism: Indian Buddhists and their Tibetan Successors* (Boston, MA: Shambhala, 1987).
55. Snellgrove, *Indo-Tibetan Buddhism*.
56. Philip Denwood, "Some Remarks on the Status and Dating of the *sBa bzhed*," *Tibet Journal* 15 (1990): 135–148; Per K. Sørensen, "Preface: *dBa'/sBa bzhed*: The dBa'[s]/sBa [Clan] Testimony Including the Royal Edict (*bka' gtsigs*) and the Royal Narrative (*bka' mchid*) Concerning the bSam yas Vihāra," in *dBa' bzhed*, by P. Wangdu and H. Diemberger, ix–xv (Vienna: Austrian Academy of Sciences Press, 2000).
57. Wangdu and Diemberger, *dBa' bzhed*.
58. Ronald Davidson, *The Tibetan Rennaissance: Tantric Buddhism in the Rebirth of Tibetan Culture* (New York: Columbia University Press, 2005).
59. Kapstein, *The Tibetan Assimilation of Buddhism*; Ronald Davidson, "The Tibetan Kingly Cosmogonic Narrative and Tibetan Histories: Indian Origins, Tibetan Space, and the *bKa' chems ka khol ma* Synthesis," *Lungta* 16 (2003): 64–84.
60. Jacob Dalton, "The Early Development of the Padmasambhava Legend in Tibet: A Study of IOL Tib J 644 and Pelliot tibétain 307," *Journal of the American Oriental* Society 124.4 (2004): 759–772; Cathy Cantwell and Robert Mayer, "Representations of Padmasambhava in Early Post-Imperial Tibet," in *Tibet after Empire: Culture, Society and Religion between 850–1000*, ed. C. Cüppers, R. Mayer, and M. Walter, 19–50 (Lumbini, Nepal: Lumbini International Research Institute, 2013); Lewis Doney, *The Zangs gling ma: the First Padmasambhava Biography. Two exemplars of its Earliest Attested Recension* (Andiast: International Institute of Tibetan and Buddhist Studies, 2014).
61. Doney, *The Zangs gling ma*.
62. Lewis Doney, "Nyang ral Nyi ma 'od zer and the Testimony of Ba," *Bulletin of Tibetology* 49.1 (2013): 7–38.
63. Doney, *The Zangs gling ma*.
64. Doney, *The Zangs gling ma*.
65. Daniel Hirshberg, *Remembering the Lotus-Born: Padmasambhava in the History of Tibet's Golden Age* (Boston, MA: Wisdom Publications, 2016).
66. Per K. Sørensen, "The Dalai Lama Institution: its Origins and Genealogical Succession," *Orientations* (September 2005): 53–60.
67. For a short précis of its contents, see Per Kvaerne, "Religious Change and Syncretism: The Case of the Bon Religion of Tibet," in *Bon, Buddhism and Democracy: The Building of a Tibetan National Identity*, ed. P. Kvaerne and R. Thargyal (Copenhagen: Nordic Institute of Asian Studies, 1993), 7–26.
68. Samten Karmay, *The Treasury of Good Sayings: A Tibetan History of Bon* (Oxford: Oxford University Press, 1972).
69. Gustave-Charles Toussaint, *Le Dict de Padma* (Paris: E. Leroux, 1933); Kenneth Douglas and Gwendolyn Bays, trans., *The Life and Liberation of Padmasambhava (Padma bka'i thang)* (Emeryville: Dharma Publishing, 1978); Erik Pema Kunsang, trans., *The Lotus-Born: The Life Story of Padmasambhava* (Boston, MA: Shambhala, 1993).
70. F. A. Bischoff, "Padmasambhava est-il un personnage historique?," in *Proceedings of the Csoma de Koros Symposium*, edited by L. Ligeti (Budapest: Akademiai Kiado, 1978), 27–33; Anne-Marie Blondeau, "Analysis of the Biographies of Padmasambhava According to Tibetan Tradition: Classification of Sources," in *Tibetan Studies in Honour of Hugh Richardson*, ed. M. Aris and A.S. Suu Kyi (Warminster: Aris and Philips, 1980), 45–52.

71. Haarh, "The Identity of Tsu-chi-chen"; Erik Haarh, *The Yar-Luṅ Dynasty* (Copenhagen: Gad, 1969); Christopher Beckwith, "The Revolt of 755 in Tibet," in *Contributions on Tibetan Language, History and Culture*, ed. E. Steinkellner and H. Tauscher (Vienna: University of Vienna Press, 1983), 1–16; Dotson, "'Emperor' Mu-rug-btsan and the *'Phang thang ma Catalogue*."
72. Giuseppe Tucci, "The Secret Characters of the Kings of Ancient Tibet," *East and West* 6 (1955): 197–205; Erik Haarh, *The Yar-Luṅ Dynasty* (København: Gad, 1969); Kapstein, *The Tibetan Assimilation of Buddhism*.
73. Lewis Doney, Transforming Tibetan Kingship: the Portrayal of Khri Song lde brtsan in the Early Buddhist Histories (D.phil. thesis: School of Oriental and African Studies, 2011); Doney, "Emperor, Dharmaraja, Bodhisattva?," Doney, "Early Bodhisattva-Kingship in Tibet." See also Walter, *Buddhism and Empire*.
74. Kazushi Iwao, Nathan Hill, and Tsuguhito Takeuchi, *Old Tibetan Inscriptions* (Tokyo: Tokyo University of Foreign Studies, 2009).
75. Wangdu and Diemberger, *dBa' bzhed*.
76. Sørensen, *Tibetan Buddhist Historiography*.
77. Doney, *The Zangs gling ma*.
78. Kunsang, *The Lotus-Born*.

Brandon Dotson

TSANGPA GYARE (1161–1211), FOUNDER OF THE DRUKPA KAGYÜ SCHOOL

WHO WAS TSANGPA GYARE?

Tsangpa Gyare (Gtsang pa rgya ras Ye shes rdo rje, 1161–1211, see Figure 1) was one of the most relevant figures in the history of the southeastern Himalayas. He founded the Drukpa Kagyü ('Brug pa bka' brgyud) school in the 12th century, and one of his later reincarnations succeeded in establishing one nation that would be called Druk Yul ('Brug yul), that is, Bhutan. However, he has not received much attention from Western academia, mainly because of lack of access to primary sources.

Although Buddhism is said to have spread from Tibet into the lands of current Bhutan in the 7th and 8th centuries, the full-scale propagation began from the 12th or 13th centuries when many schools, such as Kagyü (Bka' brgyud), Sakya (Sa skya), and Nyingma (Rnying ma), started to send their missionaries to Bhutan. In 1616, Shabdrung Ngawang Namgyal (Zhabs drung Ngag dbang rnam rgyal, 1594–1651), the 17th head abbot of the Drukpa Kagyü school,[1] moved from the Drukpa Kagyü head monastery Ralung (Ra lung), located in the region of western Tsang, to western Bhutan. Eventually, he founded a nation called Druk Yul, meaning "the country governed by the Drukpa Kagyü school." Subsequently, this school has traditionally participated, in various forms and to varying degrees, in the government of the country.

The founder of the Drukpa Kagyü school was Tsangpa Gyare, who will be examined in this article. Several modern scholars have written introductions to his life, but their accounts do not tally.[2] The author has examined different pieces of information contained in Gyare's available biographies and chapters dedicated to him in chronicles,[3] while another paper by him introduces findings obtained during a field research trip conducted in places related to Tsangpa

Figure 1. Tsangpa Gyare.
Source: Photo by Seiji Kumagai.

Gyare.[4] This article integrates this philological and field information to reexamine Tsangpa Gyare's life, presenting both:

(1) a historical mapping of Tsangpa Gyare according to both the spiritual lineage of pre-/reincarnations and dharma lineages (master and disciple relationship); and
(2) an examination of Tsangpa Gyare's life.

In order to understand the life and personality of this figure, we need to examine his own works and sources referring to him. This article thus also introduces bibliographical information about Tsangpa Gyare.

TSANGPA GYARE'S BIOGRAPHIES AND CHRONICLES REFERRING TO HIM

This article examines seven available biographies of Tsangpa Gyare, three of which were composed by his direct disciples: Sanggyebum, Martun, and Lorepa:

1. Biography composed by Sanggyebum (Sangs rgyas 'bum 'Bras mo jo btsun, b. 12/13th century).
2. Biography composed by Martun (Mar ston, 12–13th century).
3. Biography composed by Lorepa (Lo ras pa Dbang phyug brtson 'grus, 1187–1250).
4. Biography composed by Gyalthangpa (Rgyal thang pa Bde chen rdo rje, b. 13th century?).

5. Biography composed by Mangala Bhadra (Ra'i bande Mangala Bhadra, Ra Bkra shis bzang po, during/after 13th or 15th centuries).
6. Biography composed by Pema Karpo (Pad ma dkar po, 1527–1592).
7. Anonymous biography (no date).

The article also refers to four chronicles and one doxography mentioning Tsangpa Gyare:

1. *Lho rong chos 'byung*, composed by Tatsag Tsewanggyal (Rta tshag Tshe dbang rgyal, 15th century) in 1446.
2. *Deb ther sngon po*, composed by Gö Lotsawa Zhönnupel ('Gos lo tsa wa Gzhon nu dpal, 1392–1481) in 1476.
3. *Chos 'byung bstan pa'i Padma rgyas pa'i nyin byed*, composed by Pema Karpo in 1581.
4. *Thu'u bkwan grub mtha'*, composed by Tukwan Lobzang Chökyi Nyima (Thu'u bkwan Blo bzang chos kyi nyi ma, 1737–1802) in 1802.
5. *Lho 'brug chos 'byung*, composed by Gendün Rinchen (Dge 'dun rin chen, 1926–1997) in 1972.

HISTORICAL MAP OF TSANGPA GYARE

How did Tsangpa Gyare's personality and thoughts develop? This section historically maps Tsangpa Gyare according to the lineage of his pre-incarnations/reincarnations and to the lineage and sub-lineages of masters and disciples of the Kagyü school.

We shall first examine the lineage of Tsangpa Gyare's pre-incarnations. Sørensen and Haoran pointed out the fact that Dorje Lingpa Senge Sherab (Rdo rje gling pa Seng ge shes rab, 1238–1287) and Pökyapa Senge Rinchen (Spos skya pa Seng ge rin chen, 1258–1313) were regarded as the reincarnations of Darma Senge Sangye Wonre (Darma seng ge Sangs rgyas dbon ras, 1177–1237).[5] Before Darma Senge, there was a tradition that considered his uncle Tsangpa Gyare to be the reincarnation of Gampopa (Sgam po pa Bsod nams rin chen; Dwags po lha rje, 1079–1153), although there is a gap of eight years between them. There are at least six traditions about his pre-incarnation found in biographies and chronicles examined in this article.[6] All traditions commonly regarded Naropa as one of the pre-incarnations of Tsangpa Gyare, as follows:

(1) Tsangpa Gyare's biography composed by Martun:
Naropa→Ashedhana→Gampopa→Tsangpa Gyare
(2) Tsangpa Gyare's biography composed by Gyalthangpa:
Naropa→Śrībhadra→Siddhiprajñā→anonymous reincarnation→Tsangpa Gyare
(3) Tsangpa Gyare's biography composed by Pema Karpo:
Amitabuddhikīrti→Avalokiteśvara→Puṇḍarīka→Songtsen Gampo→Naropa→Kālacakrapāda→Candraprabhakumārabhūta→Tsangpa Gyare
(4) Anonymous biography of Tsangpa Gyare:
Naropa→Ashedhana→anonymous reincarnation→Dewe Junne→Tsangpa Gyare
(5) *Lho rong chos 'byung*:
Naropa→Shadhaka→Dewe Junne→Tsangpa Gyare
(6) *Lho 'brug chos 'byung*:
Naropa→Gampopa→Tsangpa Gyare.

No one was recognized as Tsangpa Gyare's reincarnation just after his death. The thirteenth head abbot of the Drukpa Kagyü school, Gyalwangje Kunga Penjor (Rgyal dbang rje Kun dga' dpal 'byor, 1428–1476), was officially confirmed as his next reincarnation around two hundred years after his death.[7]

After the death of Gyalwangje, Jamyang Chökyi Trakpa ('Jam dbyangs chos kyi grags pa, 1478–1523) was recognized as the third reincarnation of Tsangpa Gyare. The fourth reincarnation, Pema Karpo, became one of the greatest scholars of the Drukpa Kagyü school and was thus called "the omniscient" (*kun mkhyen*).

After the death of Pema Karpo, there occurred a conflict between two candidates for the fifth reincarnation of Tsangpa Gyare. One was the seventeenth head abbot of the Drukpa Kagyü school, Shabdrung Ngawang Namgyal, who belonged to the Gya (Rgya) clan and thus had a blood relationship with Tsangpa Gyare. The other was Paksam Wangpo (Dpag bsam dbang po, 1593–1641), the son of a leader in the Chonngye ('Phyong rgyas) region. The governor of Tsang intervened in the conflict and finally recognized Paksam Wangpo as the genuine reincarnation of Pema Karpo.[8] Shabdrung finally left the head monastery in Ralung and moved to western Bhutan in order to avoid the conflict, and the Drukpa Kagyü school was thus divided into the so-called Northern Drukpa Kagyü school (Byang 'brug) and Southern Drukpa Kagyü school (Lho 'brug).

The Northern Drukpa Kagyü school has remained up to the current (twelfth) reincarnation of Tsangpa Gyare ('Brug chen or Rgyal dbang 'brug pa), Jigme Pema Wangchen ('Jigs med Padma dbang chen, b. 1963), who is active mainly in Ladakh.

Belonging to the Southern Drukpa Kagyü school, Shabdrung Ngawang Namgyal founded the nation called Druk Yul, which is referred to as Bhutan or Bhootan by Westerners.[9] Shabdrung has been regarded as the reincarnation of Tsangpa Gyare and Pema Karpo in Bhutan. Several decades after Shabdrung's death, three types of emanation (i.e., those of body, speech, and mind) appeared, but their lineages gradually declined.[10] The lineage of Tsangpa Gyare's reincarnations (Rgyal dbang 'Brug pa, See Figure 2) is as follows.[11]

Here we map Tsangpa Gyare according to the lineage of masters and disciples. Drukpa Kagyü is one of the subschools of the Dagpo Kagyü school.

1. Marpa Chökyi Lodrö (Mar pa Chos kyi blo gros, 1012–1097)
2. Milarepa (Mi la ras pa, 1052–1135)
3. Gampopa Sonam Rinchen (Sgam po pa Bsod nams rin chen or Dwags po lha rje, 1079–1153)
4. Phagmo Drupa (Phag mo gru pa Rdo rje rgyal po, 1110–1170)
5. Ling Repa Pema Dorje (Gling ras pa Padma rdo rje, 1128–1188)
6. Tsangpa Gyare Yeshe Dorje (1161–1211)

The Ralung Monastery (Ra lung dgon pa) and the Druk Monastery ('Brug gi dgon pa or 'Brug Se ba byang chub chos gling) became head monasteries of the Drukpa Kagyü school. The list of abbots of both monasteries, all of them belonging to the Gya clan up to Shabdrung Ngawang Namgyal, goes as follows:[12]

1. Tsangpa Gyare Yeshe Dorje (1161–1211)
2. Darma Senge Sangye Wonre (1177–1237)
3. Shönnu Senge (Gzhon nu seng ge, 1200–1266)
4. Nyima Senge (Nyi ma seng ge, 1251–1287)
5. Pökyapa Senge Rinchen (1258–1313)

1. Tsangpa Gyare Yeslle Dorje (b.1161-d.1211): 1st abbot of the Drukpa Kagyu school

2. Gyalwangje Kunga Penjor (b.1428-d.1476): 13th abbot of the Drukpa Kagyu school

3. Jamyang Chökyi Drakpa (b.1478-d.1523)

4. Pema Karpo (b.1527-d.1592)

Northern Drukpa Kagyu school

5. Paksam Wangpo (b.1593-d.1641)

6. Mipham Wangpo Ngagkyi Wangchuk (*Mi pham dbang po Ngag gi dbang phyug*, b.1641-d. 1717)

7. Kagyu Trinle Shingta (*Dkar brgyud 'Phrin las shing rta*, b.1718-d.1766)

8.Kunzig Chökyi Nangwa (*Kun gzigs Chos kyi snang ba*, b.1768-d.1822)

9. Jigme Mingyur Wanggi Gyalpo (*'Jigs med Mi 'gyurd bang gi rgyal po*, b.1823-d.1883)

10. Mipham Chökyi Wangpo (*Mi pham Chos kyi dbang po*, b.1884-d.1930)

11. Tenzin Khyenrab Gelek Wangpo (*Bstan 'dzin* mkhyen rab Dge legs dbang po, b.1931-d 1960)

12. Jigme Pema Wangchen (b.1963-present)

Southern Drukpa Kagyu school

5. Shabdrung Ngawang Namgyal (b.1594-d.1651)

Three types or reincarnation (i.e., those of body, speech and mind)

Figure 2. Tsangpa Gyare reincarnation lineage.

6. Senge Gyalpo (Seng ge rgyal po, 1289–1326)
7. Kunga Senge (Kun dga' seng ge, 1314–1347)
8. Lodrö Senge (Blo gros seng ge, 1345–1390)
9. Sherab Senge (Shes rab seng ge, 1371–1392)
10. Yeshe Rinchen (Ye shes rin chen, 1364–1415)
11. Namkha Pelzang (Nam mkha' dpal bzang, 1398–1425)
12. Sherab Zangpo (Shes rab bzang po, 1400–1438)
13. Gyalwangje Kunga Penjor (1428–1476)
14. Ngawang Chögyal (Nga dbang chos rgyal, 1465–1540)
15. Ngawang Tenpe Gyaltsen (Ngag dbang Bstan pa'i rgyal mtshan, 1506–1538)
16. Mipham Chökyi Gyalpo (Mi pham Chos kyi rgyal po, 1543–1604)
17. Shabdrung Ngawang Namgyal (1594–1651)
18. Paksam Wangpo (1593–1641)
19. Mipham Wangpo Ngagkyi Wangchuk (1641–1717)
20. Kagyü Trinle Shingta (1718–1766)
21. Kunzig Chökyi Nangwa (1768–1822)
22. Jigme Mingyur Wanggi Gyalpo (1823–1883)

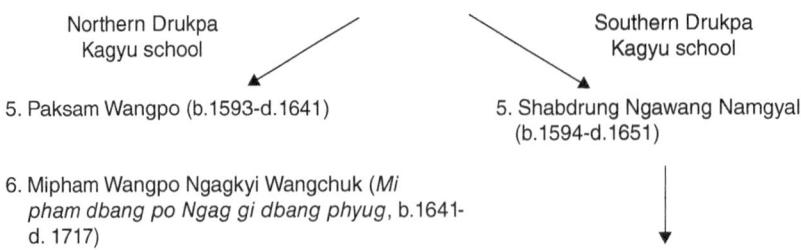

23. Mipham Chökyi Wangpo (1884–1930)
24. Tenzin Khyenrab Gelek Wangpo (1931–1960)
25. Jigme Pema Wangchen (b. 1963)

LIFE OF TSANGPA GYARE

The previous section mapped Tsangpa Gyare according to the lineage of his pre-incarnations/reincarnations and the dharma lineage of the Kagyü school. This section focuses on his life as narrated in his biographies and as accounted for in chronicles.

Tsangpa Gyare is said to have been born on the morning of the fifteenth of the first month of summer (*dbyar zla ra ba*) in 1161.[13] His birthplace (see Figure 3) seems to have been a village of the Gya clan in Saral (Sa ral) in Khule (Khu le) at the bottom of the Hawo Kangzang mountain (Ha 'o gangs bzang) in the upper Nyang region (Myang stod) of the eastern Tsang (Gtsang) region in central Tibet.[14]

Tsangpa Gyare was the youngest of seven brothers. His father was called Gyazurpo Tsape (Rgya zur po tshab pe) and his mother Marza Tarki (Mar za dar skyid).[15] Tsangpa Gyare's childhood name was Yungdrungpel (G.yung drung dpal), and he was also called Pelnag (Dpal nag, black auspicious [boy]) by his family members and fellow villagers.

Regarding his family structure,[16] there is no description of his father's lineage's connections to China in Tsangpa Gyare's biographies. However, such references can be found in the

Figure 3. Tsangpa Gyare's birthplace.
Source: Photo by Seiji Kumagai.

monastic history composed by Pema Karpo,[17] and in the *chos 'byung* (historical account of Buddhism) *Lho 'brug chos 'byung* (98: 8–11),[18] and have been confirmed during my field research.[19] The *Lho 'brug chos 'byung* gives the names of Tsangpa Gyare's six brothers: Lhanyen (Lha gnyan), Lhabum (Lha 'bum), Kelden (Skal ldan), Jotsul (Jo tshul), Gompe (Sgom pad), and Mangtsen (Mang btsan). In his birthplace Saral there are currently no inhabitants; only ruins remain. According to local tradition, past inhabitants of Saral moved to the current village of Chudu (Chu 'dus) nearby.[20]

Tsangpa Gyare's family seems to have had a strong relationship with the Bön tradition.[21] Actually, it is said that both Buddhist and Bönpo monks performed rituals at the moment of his birth and educated Tsangpa Gyare as a child.

Among his elder brothers, Kelden seems to have been his tutor. Kelden took Tsangpa Gyare to see the Bön master (*slob dpon bon*) with whom Tsangpa Gyare studied during his childhood. He kept up a relationship with the Bön master and learned from him even after having himself become a Buddhist novice monk. While the master seems to have belonged to the Bön religion, he must have taught Buddhism to Tsangpa Gyare because there is no mention of Bönpo doctrines in his education. Also, there are no traces of either Bön religion or thinking in his collected works. We may thus deduce that Tsangpa Gyare learned only Buddhism from his Bönpo master.

The biographies and annals state that Tsangpa Gyare was a noble, handsome, and wise child. He is said to have pleased people by building temples, teaching dharma, and conducting himself as a bodhisattva. Such episodes prove that Tsangpa Gyare was wise and had the right personality to become a monk.

In the ruin of his mother's house (see Figure 4), we can find a "square rock" (*rdo leb gru bzhi pa*, see Figure 5) or a "dice-like rock" (*pha bong cho long 'dra ba*) on which Tsangpa Gyare is said to have sat and taught children from the village, as referred to in several biographies.[22]

The biographies and annals give few descriptions of his father, while they refer to many positive episodes of his mother;[23] namely, that she experienced many auspicious signs when Tsangpa Gyare was born. His mother probably influenced Tsangpa Gyare and formed his character much more than his father. However, she passed away when he was only seven or eight years old (1167 or 1168).

Tsangpa Gyare had the aspect of a fully ordained monk while he was a retreat meditator wearing a thin cotton cloth, called Re[pa] (*ras [pa]*) in Tibetan. He seems to have renounced the secular world at around age twelve.[24] The master who cut Tsangpa Gyare's hair when he renounced the world is known as Tathangpa (Rta thang pa).[25]

Tsangpa Gyare received the dharma name Sherab Dutsi Korlo (Shes rab bdud rtsi 'khor lo). He was also called Sherab Pel (Shes rab dpal). Sherab Dutsi Korlo seems to be his full dharma name, while Sherab Pel is presumed to be a compound name incorporating his dharma name, Sherab Dutsi Korlo, and his secular name, Yungdrungpel.

After his renunciation, Tsangpa Gyare studied both sutras and tantras with many scholars and masters.[26] He studied Vajrayāna Buddhism, including tantras, meditation practices, and rituals, as well as Sūtrayāna Buddhist texts, such as Pramāṇa, Madhyamaka, and Pāramitā. His collected works also prove that he deeply understood both Sūtrayāna and Vajrayāna Buddhism.[27]

Tsangpa Gyare's biographies state that he studied the Great Perfection (*rdzogs chen*), but he did not write any treatise on it. He may not have written about doctrines belonging to other

Figure 4. Ruin of Marza Tarki's house.
Source: Photo by Seiji Kumagai.

Figure 5. Square rock on which Tsangpa Gyare sat when teaching local children.
Source: Photo by Seiji Kumagai.

schools, but he studied them as part of his general education. He received education from a Bönpo master, but no works on the Great Perfection or Bönpo doctrine are found in his collected works.

Tsangpa Gyare's main master was Ling Repa.[28] He seems to have begun studying with Ling Repa when he was around twenty-one to twenty-three years old. Ling Repa appreciated Tsangpa Gyare's skills and so educated him with rigor.

One day, Ling Repa lost a debate with Tsangpa Gyare. This made him appreciate Tsangpa Gyare's high intelligence even more, yet intending to avoid unnecessary trouble, he asked him to refrain from debating with his other disciples.[29] This episode shows that Tsangpa Gyare was not only a great meditation practitioner but also an excellent philosophy scholar. At the same time, it depicts a delicate and somehow distant relationship with the other disciples of Ling Repa, whose humble personality was also revealed through this story.

Later, Tsangpa Gyare often asked Ling Repa for permission to leave for meditation, but Ling Repa hardly ever allowed it. Because of his frequent requests, Ling Repa finally granted him permission to leave for meditation and gave him all the required oral transmissions in advance.

At the age of twenty-eight (in 1188), when he was coming back from Karchu (Mkhar chu) in the Lhodak (Lho brag) region after finishing his meditation, Tsangpa Gyare was informed that Ling Repa had died and so he rushed to his side. Tsangpa Gyare strongly regretted that he was not with his master when he passed away because he had left for meditation against Ling Repa's wish.

Most of his biographies and annals give the year 1193 (age thirty-three) for Tsangpa Gyare's full ordination from multiple masters, Zhang (Zhang G.yu brag pa Brtson 'grus grags pa, 1122–1193) and Zepa (Bzad pa) being the main ones.[30]

The biographies and annals concordantly state that the Longdol Monastery (Klong rdol dgon pa) was founded, fulfilling Master Zhang's prophecy.[31] On the other hand, there are several traditions about the year of its foundation: 1189, 1193, and 1194 (when Tsangpa Gyare was aged twenty-nine, thirty-three, and thirty-four. Whatever the truth of the matter, the Longdol Monastery was certainly founded early in his monastic career.

According to local information obtained at the Ralung Monastery, the Longdol Monastery is situated near the current Dolma Lhakhang in Nyethang. There used to be a small temple there, but only a meditation cave remains today.[32]

The Ralung Monastery (see Figures 6–11) is located in the east end of the upper Nyang near the boundary between the regions of Tsang and Lhokha.[33] It is said that the monastery was founded following the prophecy of a deity (*yi dam*). Tsangpa Gyare built the monastery of Ralung, which became a head monastery belonging to the Drukpa Kagyü school.[34] Only the biography composed by Gyaltangpa gives the year 1196 (when Tsangpa Gyare was thirty-six) for its foundation, while the other biographies do not mention its foundation year.[35] According to this tradition, the Ralung Monastery was founded a little after the Longdol Monastery.

Local tradition insists that the monastery was founded in 1193 and that around five thousand monks used to live in it, while currently there are less than twenty monks left.[36] The twelfth Drukchen, Jigme Pema Wangchen, belonging to the spiritual lineage of Paksam Wangpo, is regarded to be the current abbot of the Ralung Monastery though he is active

Figure 6. Ralung Monastery as it is today.
Source: Photo by Seiji Kumagai.

Figure 7. Ruin of former monastery and monks' dormitories.
Source: Photo by Seiji Kumagai.

Figure 8. Wall painting of former Ralung Monastery and stupa.
Source: Photo by Seiji Kumagai.

mainly in Ladakh. Interestingly, there is also a photograph of Shabdrung Ngawang Namgyal, Paksam Wangpo's rival, in the main temple, which shows the great respect in which they hold him. Current Ralung monks think that Shabdrung was not exiled to Bhutan because of his political defeat, but that he instead voluntarily moved there to avoid the unnecessary conflicts foreseen in a prophecy.

The Druk Monastery (see Figure 12), origin of the name of the Drukpa Kagyü school, was founded to the southwest of Lhasa, fulfilling Ling Repa's prophecy.[37] Most of the biographies and annals give the year 1205 (when Tsangpa Gyare was forty-five) for its foundation, that is to say, the monastery was founded in his later years.[38]

The Druk Monastery is the place where Tsangpa Gyare died in 1211, so many relics of his, such as his monk's robe and shoes, remain there.

The monastery was taken over by Paksam Wangpo after Shabdrung moved to Bhutan. The current monastery was rebuilt after its destruction during the Cultural Revolution.

Tsangpa Gyare continued to edify and educate his disciples and left many testaments as oral instructions into his later years. He died in 1211 (aged fifty-one).[39] Upon his death, it is said that there appeared many auspicious signs, such as a wonderful fragrance, the appearance of a rainbow, and the disposition of his twenty-one vertebrae recreating the shape of Avalokiteśvara. Tens of thousands of disciples are said to have gathered to attend his funeral. He thus seems to have gradually become popular because of his successful edification and education of his young disciples.

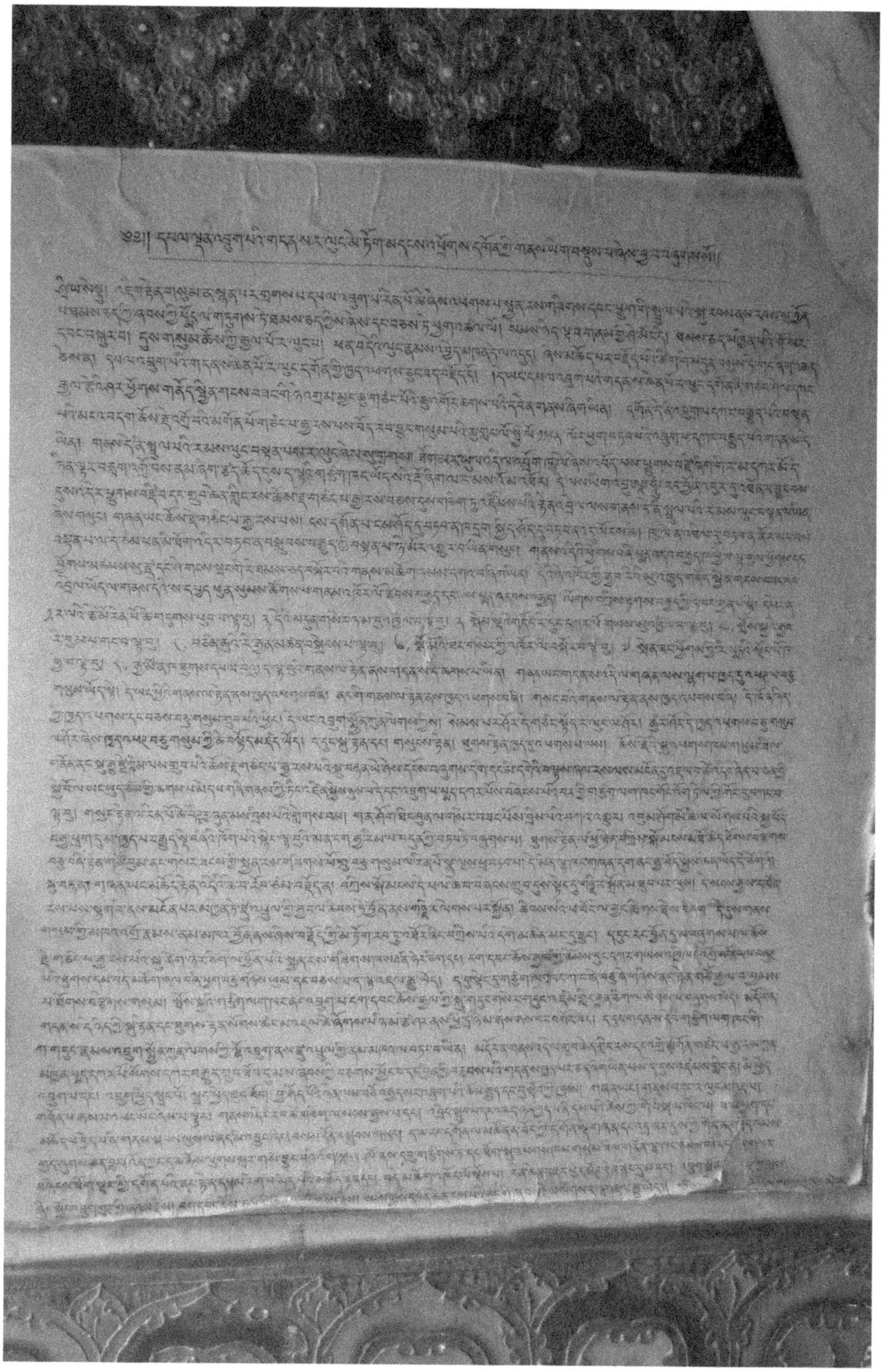

Figure 9. Document of the history of Ralung Monastery preserved at the monastery.
Source: Photo by Seiji Kumagai.

Figure 10. New building of Ralung Monastery as it is today.
Source: Photo by Seiji Kumagai.

Figure 11. New stupa of Ralung Monastery.
Source: Photo by Seiji Kumagai.

Figure 12. Druk Monastery as it is today.
Source: Photo by Seiji Kumagai.

COLLECTED WORKS AND CHARACTERISTICS OF TSANGPA GYARE

Tsangpa Gyare composed many works during his life. The author of this article is currently elaborating an integrated version of the collected works of Tsangpa Gyare by mutually compensating the omitted works and comparing variants found in different versions of overlapping works.[40]

As seen in Table 1, Tsangpa Gyare cultivated many genres, such as Sūtrayāna philosophy and instruction as well as Mahāmudrā and Vajrayāna meditation.[41] We can thus see that he was a person of various talents. This proves that the descriptions of Tsangpa Gyare's versatility in his biographies are not an exaggeration.

This article has historically mapped and examined the life of Tsangpa Gyare. As stated in another article by the same author, Tsangpa Gyare had the characteristics of: (1) a Vajrayāna practitioner, (2) a scholar monk of Sūtrayāna, (3) an educator, and (4) a poet or man of culture.[42] These aspects are proved by his biographies as well as by his own works.

Such an ideal religious practitioner attracted monks, yogis, local leaders, and the general public. He also produced many disciples. His activities resulted in the future prosperity and development of the Drukpa Kagyü school in the regions of Ü, Tsang, and Lhokha.

Unfortunately, his life and characteristics seem to have been forgotten because of the reduced availability of his collected works, while Drukpa Kagyü masters such as Pema Karpo, Drukpa Kunlek, and Shabdrung Ngawang Namgyal became popular and left many works,

Table 1. Categories of Tsangpa Gyare's Works

Category	Number
i) Biography	4 works
ii) Philosophy	6 works
iii) Mahāmudrā	3 works
iv) Meditation	12 works
v) Practice	5 works
vi) Instruction	4 works
vii) Ritual	2 works
viii) Spiritual songs	2 works
ix) Treatise for practical purposes	2 works

biographies, and episodes. It is important to understand the life history and features of Tsangpa Gyare in order to fully understand the basis of the Drukpa Kagyü school and also the thinking and traits of later popular Drukpa Kagyü monks.

DISCUSSION OF THE LITERATURE

The first Western academic paper focusing on Tsangpa Gyare's life was published by Dan Martin in 1979.[43] Between the 1960s and the 1970s, both the head monasteries of the Drukpa Kagyü school, the Ralung Monastery and the Druk Monastery, were destroyed during the Cultural Revolution, and the Northern Drukpa Kagyü school was on the verge of extinction. Since Bhutan had just opened the country to foreigners in 1974, its national Buddhist school, the Southern Drukpa Kagyü school, had barely been studied academically in the 1970s. At that period, when the Drukpa Kagyü school was unknown to scholarship, Martin's paper had a significant value as a pioneering work. However, it was too short to offer detailed information about Tsangpa Gyare's life. It also includes fundamental mistakes, such as incorrect dates for the foundation of the Ralung Monastery and the Druk Monastery.

The first paper which gave wrong years for the foundation of the two head monasteries was that published by David Snellgrove in 1968; it did not refer to any primary sources.[44] Unfortunately, later researchers, including Martin, continued to quote this misinformation, although they could have confirmed the right dates by referring directly to the different biographies of Tsangpa Gyare.

W. Blythe Miller's paper, published in 2005, provided more profitable information than Martin's and analyzed the relationship between Master Ling Repa and his disciple Tsangpa Gyare in detail.[45] However, Miller also included a mistake, stating that the Ralung Monastery was founded jointly by Ling Repa and Tsangpa Gyare in 1180.[46] As explained in notes 34 and 35 of the present article, Tsangpa Gyare had not become Ling Repa's disciple by 1180; therefore, it was not possible for them to have founded the monastery jointly at that time. The foundation year should be instead 1196, as mentioned here.

In a paper published in 2018, Seiji Kumagai referred to seven different biographies of Tsangpa Gyare and different dharma annals, corrected the wrong information given by previous researchers, and reexamined Tsangpa Gyare's life.[47] That paper overlooked relevant information concerning the pre-incarnations of Tsangpa Gyare which is now included in the present article. In another work, Kumagai reported his discovery of ruins associated with Tsangpa Gyare, such as his birthplace and his childhood house, and included their pictures.[48] Kumagai also published a paper addressing all collected works of Tsangpa Gyare and explaining their characteristics.[49] The present article critically analyzes such academic sources.

PRIMARY SOURCES

Chos 'byung bstan pa'i Padma rgyas pas'i nyin byed. Composed by Padma dkar po Nga dbang nor bu (1527–1592) in 1581. In *Tibetan Chronicle of Padma-dkar-po*. Edited by Lokesh Chandra, 1–619. Śata-piṭaka Series, Indo-Asian Literatures 75. New Delhi, India: International Academy of Indian Culture, 1968.

Chos rje 'gro ba'i mgon po gtsang pa rgya ras kyi rnam par thar ba. Composed by Rgyal thang pa Bde chen rdo rje.

(Anonymous edition) *Chos rje 'gro ba'i mgon po gtsang pa rgya ras kyi rnam par thar pa* (Work Number of Tibetan Buddhist Resource Center (TBRC): W1KG2849).

(Palampur edition) *Chos rje rin po che gtsang pa ye shes rdo rje'i rnam par thar pa*. In *Dkar brgyud gser 'phren: A Thirteenth Century Collection of Verse Hagiographies of the Succession of Eminent Masters of the 'Brug-pa Dkar-brgyud-pa Tradition*, 485–525. Palampur, India: Sungrab Nyamso Gyunphel Parkhang, 1973 (TBRC's Work Number: 23436).

Chos rje 'gro ba'i mgon po gtsang pa rgyal sras kyi rnam par thar ba. Composed by Mar ston.

(Dehradun edition) *Chos rje 'gro ba'i mgon po gtsang pa rgyal sras kyi rnam par thar ba*. In *Bka' brgyud gser phreng chen mo: Biographies of Eminent Gurus in the Transmission Lineage of Teachings of the 'Ba'-ra Dkar-brgyud-pa Sect*. Vol. 1 (Ka), 412–451. Dehradun, India: Ngawang Gyaltsen and Ngawang Lungtok, 1970 (TBRC's Work Number: W19231).

Chos rje gtsang pa rgya ras kyi rnam thar. Composed by Sangs rgyas 'bum 'Bras mo jo btsun.

(Palampur edition) *Gtsang pa rgya ras kyi rnam thar*. In *Rwa lung dkar brgyud gser 'phreng: Brief Lives of the Successive Masters in the Transmission Lineage of the Bar 'Brug-pa Dkar-brgyud-pa of Rwa-lun*. 4 vols., 1: 397–452. Palampur, India: Sungrab Nyamso Gyunphel Parkhang, 1975–1978 (Reproduced from a set of prints from the 1771–1772 Spuns-than xylographic blocks.) (TBRC's Work Number: 19222).

(Thimphu edition) *Chos rje gtsang pa rgya ras kyi rnam thar*. In *Dkar brgyud gser gyi 'phren ba: A Collection of Biographical Materials on the Lives of the Masters of the Rwa-lun Tradition of the 'Brug-pa Dkar-brgyud-pa Tradition in Tibet and Bhutan*. 3 vols., 1: 379–431. Thimphu, Bhutan: Tango Monastic Community, 1982 (TBRC's Work Number: 23861).

Chos rje rin po che gtsang pa rgya ras pa'i rnam thar mgur 'bum dang bcas pa. Composed by Lo ras pa Dbang phyug brtson 'grus.

(Leh edition) *Chos rje rin po che gtsang pa rgya ras pa'i rnam thar mgur 'bum dang bcas pa*. In *Dkar brgyud ser 'phreng: A Golden Rosary of Lives of Eminent Gurus*, 270–293. Leh, India: Sonam W. Tashigang, 1970 (TBRC's Work Number: 30123).

Chos rje rin po che gtsang pa rgya ras pa'i rnam thar mgur 'bum dang bcas pa. (Anonymous)

(Bhutanese edition) *'Brug lugs gsung rab phyogs bsdebs las chos rje gtsang pa rgya ras kyi bka' 'bum glegs bam ka pa bzhugs so* and *'Brug lugs gsung rab phyogs bsdebs las chos rje gtsang pa rgya ras kyi bka' 'bum glegs bam kha pa bzhugs so*. Vol. 1 (Ka). Thimphu, Bhutan: Bhutanese Monastic Body, 2011, 1.1–53.6.

(Ladakhi edition) *The Collected Works (Gsuṅ-Bum) of Gtsaṅ-pa Rgya-ras Ye-śes-rdo-rje: Reproduced from Rare Manuscripts and Blockprints Belonging to Various Lamas and Notables of Ladakh*. Darjeeling, India: Kargyud Sungrab Nyamso Khang, 1972, 243–293 (TBRC's Work Number: 26076).

Deb ther sngon po (*Bod kyi yul du chos dang chos smra ba ji ltar byung ba'i rim pa*). Composed by 'Gos lo twa wa gzhon nu dpal between 1476 and 1478. Ed. Chandra (1974).

Gdan sa chen po ra lung gi khyad par 'phags pa cung zad brjod pa ngo mtshar gyi gter. Composed by Padma dkar po Nga dbang nor bu. In *Collected Works of Kun-mkhyen Padma-dkar-po*. Vol. 4. Darjeeling, India: Kargyu Sungrab Nyamso Khang, 1973, 175–205 (TBRC's Work Number: W10736).

'Gro ba'i mgon po gtsang pa rgya ras pa'i rnam par thar pa ngo mtshar dad pa'i rlabs phreng. Composed by Padma dkar po Nga dbang nor bu.

(Darjeeling edition) *'Gro ba'i mgon po gtsang pa rgya ras pa'i rnam par thar pa ngo mtshar dad pa'i rlabs phreng*. In *Collected Works of Kun-mkhyen Padma-dkar-po*. Vol. 3. Darjeeling, India: Kargyud Sungrab Nyamso Khang, 1973, 1–109 (TBRC's Work Number: W10736).

(Kathmandu edition) *'Gro ba'i mgon po gtsang pa rgya ras pa'i rnam par thar pa ngo mtshar dad pa'i rlabs phreng*. Kathmandu, Nepal: Gam po pa library, 2007/2013 (TBRC's Work Number: W1KG15852).

Lho 'brug chos 'byung (*Lho phyogs nags mo'i ljongs kyi chos 'byung*). Composed by Dge 'dun rin chen in 1972. Thimphu, Bhutan: KMT, 2004.

Lho rong chos 'byung (*Dam pa'i chos kyi byung ba'i legs bshad lho rong chos 'byung*). Composed by Rta tshag Tshe dbang rgyal in 1446. Lhasa, Tibet: Bod ljongs bod yig dpe rnying dpe skrun khang, 1994.

Lho'i chos 'byung (*Lho'i chos 'byung 'phro mthud 'jam mgon smon mtha'i 'phreng ba*). Compiled by Bstan 'dzin chos rgyal (?–1761) in 1759. Thimphu, Bhutan: KMT, 2004.

Rje gtsang pa rgya ras kyi rnam thar. Composed by Ra'i bande Mangala Bhadra (Ra bKra shis bzang po, after/during the 13th or 15th cen.).

(Bhutanese edition) *'Brug lugs gsung rab phyogs bsdebs las chos rje gtsang pa rgya ras kyi bka' 'bum glegs bam ka pa bzhugs so* and *'Brug lugs gsung rab phyogs bsdebs las chos rje gtsang pa rgya ras kyi bka' 'bum glegs bam kha pa bzhugs so*. Thimphu, Bhutan: Bhutanese Monastic Body, 2011, 2 (Kha): 1.1–244.6.

(Ladakhi edition) *The Collected Works (Gsuṅ-Bum) of Gtsaṅ-pa Rgya-ras Ye-śes-rdo-rje: Reproduced from Rare Manuscripts and Blockprints Belonging to Various Lamas and Notables of Ladakh*. Darjeeling, India: Kargyud Sungrab Nyamso Khang, 1972, 1–242 (TBRC's Work Number: 26076).

Thu'u bkwan grub mtha' (*Grub mtha' thams cad kyi khungs dang 'dod tshul ston pa legs bshad shel gyi me long*). Composed by Thu'u bkwan Blo bzang chos kyi nyi ma in 1802. Gansu, China: Kun su'i mi rigs dpe krun khang, 1984.

FURTHER READING

Ardussi, John. *Bhutan before the British: A Historical Study*. PhD diss., Australian National University, 1977.

Aris, Michael. *Bhutan: The Early History of a Himalayan Kingdom*. Warminster, UK: Aris & Phillips, 1979.

Baillie, Luiza Maria. "Father Estevao Cacella's Report on Bhutan in 1627." *Journal of Bhutan Studies* 1 (1999): 1–35.

Chandra, Lokesh. *The Blue Annals*. New Delhi, India: International Academy of Indian Culture, 1974.

Imaeda, Yoshiro. *Histoire médiévale du Bhoutan*. Tokyo, Japan: Toyo Bunko, 2011.

Kumagai, Seiji. "History and Current Situation of the Sa skya pa school in Bhutan." In *Bhutanese Buddhism and Its Culture*. Edited by Seiji Kumagai, 127–139. Kathmandu, Nepal: Vajra, 2014.

Kumagai, Seiji. "Introduction to the Biographies of Tsangpa Gyare (1161–1211), Founder of the Drukpa Kagyü School." In *Buddhism, Culture and Society in Bhutan*. Edited by Seiji Kumagai, 9–34. Kathmandu, Nepal: Vajra, 2018.

Kumagai, Seiji. "A Report on Some Physical Evidences and Oral Transmission about Tsangpa Gyare (1161–1211) Collected at the Ralung Monastery and the Druk Monastery in Tibet." In *Vajrayana Buddhism in the Modern World: Proceedings of the Second Vajrayana Conference, 28–30 March 2018, Thimphu*, 34–48. Thimphu, Bhutan: Centre for Bhutan Studies & GNH Research, 2018.

Kumagai, Seiji, Gawa Thupten, and Akinori Yasuda. "Introduction to the Collected Works of the Founder of the *Drukpa Kagyu* (*'Brug pa bKa' brgyud*) School: Tsangpa Gyare (gTsang pa rgya ras, 1161–1211)." In *Buddhism without Borders: Proceedings of the International Conference on Globalized Buddhism, Bumthang, Bhutan May 21–23, 2012*. Edited by Karma Ura and Dendup Chophel, 36–52. Thimphu, Bhutan: Centre for Bhutan Studies, 2012.

Martin, Dan. "Gling-ras-pa and the Founding of the 'Brug-pa School." *Tibet Society Bulletin* 13 (1979): 56–69.

Miller, W. Blythe. "The Vagrant Poet and the Reluctant Scholar: A Study of the Balance of Iconoclasm and Civility in the Biographical Accounts of Two Founder of the 'Brug pa bka' brgyud Lineages." *Journal of the International Association of Buddhist Studies* 28, no. 2 (2005): 369–410.

Miller, W. Blythe. " 'Brug pa'i lo rgyus zur tsam: An Analysis of a Thirteenth Century Tibetan Buddhist Lineage History." *Tibet Journal* 31, no. 3 (2006): 17–42.

Phuntsho, Karma. *History of Bhutan*. Noida, India, and London, UK: Random House India, 2013.

Roerich, George. *The Blue Annals*, 2nd ed. Delhi, India: Motilal Banarsidas, 1996.

Smith, E. Gene. "Foreword." In *Tibetan Chronicle of Padma-dkar-po*. Edited by Lokesh Chandra, 1–8. New Delhi, India: International Academy of Indian Culture, 1968.

Snellgrove, David. *A Cultural History of Tibet*. New York: F. A. Praeger, 1968.

Sørensen, Per K., and Hou Haoran. "The Invention of the Reincarnation Lineage of 'rGyal dbang 'Brug chen.'" In *Buddhism, Culture and Society in Bhutan*. Edited by Seiji Kumagai, 35–67. Kathmandu, Nepal: Vajra, 2018.

Vitali, Roberto. "Glimpses of the History of the Rgya Clan with Reference to Nyang Stod, Lho Mon and Nearby Lands (7th–13th Century)." In *The Spider and the Piglet: Proceedings of the First International Seminar on Bhutan Studies*. Edited by Karma Ura and Sonam Kinga, 6–20. Thimphu, Bhutan: Centre for Bhutan Studies, 2004.

NOTES

1. As will be explained later, the way to count the number of head abbots belonging to the Drukpa Kagyü school differs according to different researchers. This article uses the method of Yoshiro Imaeda, *Histoire médiévale du Bhoutan* (Tokyo, Japan: Toyo Bunko, 2011), 206–208, who provides a detailed family tree of the Rgya clan.
2. The brief introduction of Tsangpa Gyare by modern scholars such as Dan Martin, "Gling-ras-pa and the Founding of the 'Brug-pa School," *Tibet Society Bulletin* 13 (1979): 56–69; W. Blythe Miller, "The Vagrant Poet and the Reluctant Scholar: A Study of the Balance of Iconoclasm and Civility in the Biographical Accounts of Two Founder of the 'Brug pa bka' brgyud Lineages," *Journal of the International Association of Buddhist Studies* 28, no. 2 (2005): 369–410; and W. Blythe Miller, " 'Brug pa'i lo rgyus zur tsam: An Analysis of a Thirteenth Century Tibetan Buddhist Lineage History," *Tibet Journal* 31, no. 3 (2006): 17–42, enables us to grasp the outline of his life. However, these authors refer to only a few biographies and do not examine relevant information found in different biographies and chronicles. Tsangpa Gyare's life, integrating such diverse information, is reexamined in Seiji Kumagai, "Introduction to the Biographies of Tsangpa Gyare (1161–1211), Founder of the Drukpa Kagyü School," in *Buddhism, Culture and Society in Bhutan*, ed. Seiji Kumagai (Kathmandu, Nepal: Vajra, 2018), 9–34.
3. See Kumagai, "Introduction to the Biographies of Tsangpa Gyare (1161–1211)."
4. Seiji Kumagai, "A Report on Some Physical Evidences and Oral Transmission about Tsangpa Gyare (1161–1211) Collected at the Ralung Monastery and the Druk Monastery in Tibet," in *Vajrayana Buddhism in the Modern World: Proceedings of the Second Vajrayana Conference, 28–30 March 2018, Thimphu* (Thimphu, Bhutan: Centre for Bhutan Studies & GNH Research, 2018), 34–48.
5. Per K. Sørensen and Hou Haoran, "The Invention of the Reincarnation Lineage of 'rGyal dbang 'Brug chen'," in *Buddhism, Culture and Society in Bhutan*, ed. Kumagai, 43–46.
6. Note that Kumagai, "Introduction to the Biographies of Tsangpa Gyare (1161–1211)," 15–17, lacks the information of pre-incarnations given in the biography composed by Gyalthangpa, *Chos rje rin po che gtsang pa ye shes rdo rje'i rnam par thar pa*, in *Dkar brgyud gser 'phren: A Thirteenth Century Collection of Verse Hagiographies of the Succession of Eminent Masters of the 'Brug-pa Dkar-brgyud-pa Tradition* (Palampur, India: Sungrab Nyamso Gyunphel Parkhang, 1973), 489.4–490.2; and the biography composed by Pema Karpo, *'Gro ba'i mgon po gtsang pa rgya ras pa'i rnam par thar pa ngo mtshar dad pa'i rlabs phreng* (Darjeeling, India: Kargyud Sungrab Nyamso Khang, 1973–1974), 5.3–11.6.
7. According to Sørensen and Haoran, "The Invention of the Reincarnation Lineage of 'rGyal dbang 'Brug chen'," 46–47, there was also another tradition which regarded Jamyang Kunga Senge ('Jam dbyangs Kun dga' seng ge, 1314–1347) as the reincarnation of Tsangpa Gyare prior to Gyalwangje Kunga Penjor, who is generally regarded as the first reincarnation after Tsangpa Gyare's death.
8. Michael Aris, *Bhutan: The Early History of a Himalayan Kingdom* (Warminster, UK: Aris & Phillips, 1979), 206; Imaeda, *Histoire médiévale du Bhoutan*, 34–36; and Karma Phuntsho, *History of Bhutan* (Noida, India, and London, UK: Random House India, 2013), 212–217.
9. Regarding the name of Bhutan, see Aris, *Bhutan*, xxiv–xxv.
10. Imaeda, *Histoire médiévale du Bhoutan*, 162–165.
11. Concerning the lineage of the Northern Drukpa Kagyü school, see John Ardussi, *Bhutan before the British: A Historical Study*, PhD dissertation, Australian National University (1977), 548.
12. As mentioned, we follow here Imaeda, *Histoire médiévale du Bhoutan*, 206–208, regarding the number of head abbots. Other scholars use different systems. For example, Karma Phuntsho, *History of Bhutan*, 212, omits Namkha Pelzang but adds Mipham Tenpe Nyima (Mi pham Bstan pa'i nyi ma, 1567–1619) after Mipham Chökyi Gyalpo, that is, he regards Shabdrung Ngawang Namgyal as the 17th abbot and Gyalwangje Kunga Penjor as the 12th.
13. Gyaltangpa, in his biography, gives the date as the "eighth." See Kumagai, "Introduction to the Biographies of Tsangpa Gyare (1161–1211)," 22.

14. According to the present local tradition, Saral and Khule are believed to be different villages: Saral is the place of Tsangpa Gyare's mother's family; Khule is the place of the current Ralung Monastery near his birthplace. Thus, the interpretation of these two toponyms seems to have changed over time. See Kumagai, "A Report on Some Physical Evidences and Oral Transmission," 36.
15. Gyaltangpa, in his biography, names her Mar Darmakyi (Dmar dar ma skyid). We can presume her name to be "a Tibetan (*gdong dmar*) who rejoices (*skyid*) in Buddhism (*dar ma*)."
16. Regarding the family composition, see Kumagai, "Introduction to the Biographies of Tsangpa Gyare (1161–1211)," 22.
17. See Pema Karpo's *Gdan sa chen po ra lung gi khyad par 'phags pa cung zad brjod pa ngo mtshar gyi gter*, in *Collected Works of Kun-mkhyen Padma-dkar-po*, vol. 4 (Darjeeling, India: Kargyu Sungrab Nyamso Khang, 1973), 198.1–199.1. Pema Karpo explained that the Gya clan was descended from Lhaga (Lha dga'), who is traditionally regarded to have escorted with Luga (Klu dga') the Buddha image brought to Tibet by Kong-jo. See also Ardussi, *Bhutan before the British*, 108, and Aris, *Bhutan*, 12–13. Regarding the Gya clan, see Roberto Vitali, "Glimpses of the History of the rGya Clan with Reference to Nyang Stod, Lho Mon and Nearby Lands (7th–13th century)," in *The Spider and the Piglet: Proceedings of the First International Seminar on Bhutan Studies*, ed. Karma Ura and Sonam Kinga (Thimphu, Bhutan: Centre for Bhutan Studies, 2004), 6–20.
18. This work was originally compiled by Dge 'dun rin chen in 1972. See *Lho 'brug chos 'byung (Lho phyogs nags mo'i ljongs kyi chos 'byung)* (Thimphu, Bhutan: KMT, 2004), 98: 8–11: *gang las 'khrungs pa'i gdung ni jo bo Sha'kya mu ne gdan 'dren pa'i rgya nag po'i gyad stobs po che lha dga'i gdung rabs las/yab zas gtsang lta bu'i rgya zur po tshab pe dang/*. (The lineage in which [Tsangpa Gyare] was born is the powerful Chinese lineage of Lhaga which brought [the statue of] Śākyamuni [to the Jokhang Monastery]. From the lineage, his father Gyazurpo Tsape and . . .)
19. See Kumagai, "A Report on Some Physical Evidences and Oral Transmission."
20. See Kumagai, "A Report on Some Physical Evidences and Oral Transmission."
21. Regarding the influence of the Bön religion, see Kumagai, "Introduction to the Biographies of Tsangpa Gyare (1161–1211)," 22–23.
22. See Kumagai, "A Report on Some Physical Evidences and Oral Transmission."
23. Regarding the information of Tsangpa Gyare's mother, see Kumagai, "Introduction to the Biographies of Tsangpa Gyare (1161–1211)," 23.
24. Regarding the information of Tsangpa Gyare's renunciation, see Kumagai, "Introduction to the Biographies of Tsangpa Gyare (1161–1211)," 24.
25. According to Kumagai, "Introduction to the Biographies of Tsangpa Gyare (1161–1211)," 24, Gyaltangpa and Mangala Bhadra regard Tathangpa to be a master of the Bön religion. The *Lho rong chos 'byung* states that Tsangpa Gyare renounced in front of a Bön master at age 12 (in 1172) and then renounced again in front of the Buddhist master Tathangpa at age 13 (in 1173).
26. Regarding his studies after renunciation, see Kumagai, "Introduction to the Biographies of Tsangpa Gyare (1161–1211)," 25–26.
27. Seiji Kumagai, Gawa Thupten, and Akinori Yasuda, "Introduction to the Collected Works of the Founder of the Drukpa Kagyü (*'Brug pa bKa' brgyud*) School: Tsangpa Gyare (gTsang pa rgya ras, 1161–1211)," in *Buddhism without Borders: Proceedings of the International Conference on Globalized Buddhism, Bumthang, Bhutan May 21–23, 2012*, ed. Karma Ura and Dendup Chophel (Thimphu, Bhutan: Centre for Bhutan Studies, 2012), 50.
28. Regarding his studies under Ling Repa, see Kumagai, "Introduction to the Biographies of Tsangpa Gyare (1161–1211)," 26–27.
29. Regarding the debate with Ling Repa, see Kumagai, "Introduction to the Biographies of Tsangpa Gyare (1161–1211)," 25–26.
30. Regarding Tsangpa Gyare's full ordination, see Kumagai, "Introduction to the Biographies of Tsangpa Gyare (1161–1211)," 27. Furthermore, according to Kumagai (same page), the biography composed by

Gyaltangpa gives the year 1178 (when Tsangpa Gyare was 18) for his full ordination, but this seems too early.

31. Regarding the foundation of the Longdol Monastery, see Kumagai, "Introduction to the Biographies of Tsangpa Gyare (1161–1211)," 27–28.
32. See Kumagai, "A Report on Some Physical Evidences and Oral Transmission."
33. Regarding the foundation of the Ralung Monastery, see Kumagai, "Introduction to the Biographies of Tsangpa Gyare (1161–1211)," 28.
34. Ardussi, *Bhutan before the British,* 108, says that Ling Repa owned a small hermitage in Ralung, but I could not find any reference to this fact in his biography. He did own a monastery in Naphu (Sna phu). Miller, "The Vagrant Poet and the Reluctant Scholar," 377, says that the Ralung Monastery was "founded jointly by Ling Repa and Tsangpa Gyare" without reference to any primary sources. If they had jointly founded the Ralung Monastery, it would have been from the period when Tsangpa Gyare became Ling Repa's disciple (1181–1183) to Ling Repa's death (1188). However, no description of the foundation of Ralung Monastery during these periods is found in any of the seven biographies referred to in this article. On the other hand, the biography composed by Gyaltangpa gives the year 1196 (when Tsangpa Gyare was 36), that is, eight years after Ling Repa's death, for the foundation of the monastery.
35. Modern scholars such as David Snellgrove, *A Cultural History of Tibet* (New York: F. A. Praeger, 1968), 137; Martin "Gling-ras-pa and the Founding of the 'Brug-pa School," 67n34; and Phuntsho, *History of Bhutan,* 210, give the year "1180" (when Tsangpa Gyare was 20) for the foundation of the Ralung Monastery, but none of them refer to any primary sources. However, the year 1180 is not reasonable because Tsangpa Gyare had not met Ling Repa at that time. Most of the monasteries founded by Tsangpa Gyare were built after 1193, when he had been fully ordained.
36. See Kumagai, "A Report on Some Physical Evidences and Oral Transmission."
37. Regarding the foundation of the Druk Monastery, see Kumagai, "Introduction to the Biographies of Tsangpa Gyare (1161–1211)," 28.
38. Modern scholars such as Snellgrove, *A Cultural History of Tibet,* 137; and Martin "Gling-ras-pa and the Founding of the 'Brug-pa School," 67n34, adopt the year 1193 (when Tsangpa Gyare was 33) given by the *Deb ther sngon po.* E. Gene Smith, "Foreword," in *Tibetan Chronicle of Padma-dkar-po,* ed. Lokesh Chandra (New Delhi, India: International Academy of Indian Culture, 1968), while Aris, *Bhutan,* 172, adopts the year 1189 for the foundation of the Druk Monastery without reference to any primary sources. It is more reasonable to follow the year of 1205 given by all biographies examined in this article.
39. Regarding the death of Tsangpa Gyare, see Kumagai, "Introduction to the Biographies of Tsangpa Gyare (1161–1211)," 29–30. The biographies and annals give the same year (1211), date (25th), and time (evening) but different months for his death: the second month of summer (*dbyar zla 'bring po*), the last month of summer (*dbyar zla tha chung*), the first month of autumn (*ston zla ra ba*), and the second month of autumn (*ston zla 'bring po*). That is to say: there are four different traditions regarding the month of Tsangpa Gyare's death.
40. Regarding further detailed information about his works, see Kumagai, Thupten, and Yasuda, "Introduction to the Collected Works."
41. Regarding the contents of his collected works, see Kumagai, Thupten, and Yasuda, "Introduction to the Collected Works," 50. Please note Table 1 has to be revised, due to the need to acknowledge the heterogeneous nature of texts that were thought to be monothematic.
42. See Kumagai, "Introduction to the Biographies of Tsangpa Gyare (1161–1211)," 30–31.
43. Martin, "Gling-ras-pa and the Founding of the 'Brug-pa School."
44. Snellgrove, *A Cultural History of Tibet.*
45. Miller, "The Vagrant Poet and the Reluctant Scholar."
46. Miller, "The Vagrant Poet and the Reluctant Scholar," 377.

47. Kumagai, "Introduction to the Biographies of Tsangpa Gyare (1161–1211)."
48. Kumagai, "A Report on Some Physical Evidences and Oral Transmission."
49. Kumagai, Thupten, and Yasuda, "Introduction to the Collected Works."

Seiji Kumagai

TZU CHI

INTRODUCTION

The Buddhist Compassion Relief Tzu Chi Foundation was founded in 1966 as a global humanitarian nongovernmental organization (NGO), with formidable phalanxes of volunteers and professionals in the fields of charity, relief, medicine, education, and cultural production, together with the Tzu Chi Buddhist School and a monastic lineage called the Jing Si Dharma Lineage.[1] This article uses the term "Tzu Chi" in a narrow sense and a broader sense. In the narrow sense, "Tzu Chi" will refer to the "Tzu Chi Foundation" (aka the Mission of Charity), which is the largest mission and the one in consultative status with the United Nations Economic and Social Council (UN-ECOSOC). "Tzu Chi" in a broader sense could refer to all or selected mission(s) depending on the context: there are three other missions—Mission of Medicine, Mission of Education, and Mission of Culture—each with their own organization structures. In the 1990s, four additional endeavors were launched: international relief, bone marrow donation, community volunteerism, and environmental protection. Together these are Tzu Chi's "Four Missions and Eight Footprints."

As of 2021, Tzu Chi has provided humanitarian aid to people in 122 countries and regions. There are Tzu Chi volunteers in sixty-six countries and regions across the continents of Asia, Europe, Africa, North America, and South America as well as Oceania.[2] Tzu Chi missions rely on ten million certified volunteers and paid professionals to carry out its global missions.[3] In 2020, the Tzu Chi Foundation's income was NT$6,182,291,198 (US$210,197,901) and expenditures were NT$7,222,969,446 (US$245,580,961), with assets of NT$131,022,132,138 (US$4,454,752,492).[4] Compared with many other international aid groups, the Tzu Chi Foundation is very asset-rich. Other international organizations like Catholic Relief Services, for example, have far higher incomes (US$923,592,000) and expenditures (US$913,016,000) but relatively modest assets of US$555,059,000.[5]

But all these achievements started with one person, the Taiwanese *bhikkhunī* Cheng Yen.[6]

MASTER CHENG YEN AND THE PEOPLE OF TZU CHI

Wang Jinyun was born in Qingshui, Taichung County, Taiwan, in 1937, and was adopted by her paternal uncle and aunt who owned various properties and managed movie theaters in the area. When she was twenty years old, her adoptive father died suddenly of a stroke: this precipitated a spiritual crisis for her. For the next several years, as described in an authorized biography, she searched "for a place to take refuge, seeking the origin and boundaries of life, looking for the answers to the riddle of impermanence."[7] This time period involved pivotal encounters that would shape her whole life. At Ciyun Temple, located near her home, she met the Abbess Venerable Xiudao and decided to become a *bhikkhunī*. Jinyun took the tonsure under the direction of a lay teacher but still needed to receive full ordination as a *bhikkhunī*. In the spring of 1963, aged twenty-six, she traveled to Taipei's Linji Temple for ordination but was rejected because she lacked a monastic tonsure master. When she stopped by the nearby Huiri Lecture Hall to buy the *Complete Works of Master Taixu*, she met Huiri's founder, the distinguished scholar Venerable Yinshun 印順 (1906–2005). He agreed to sponsor her for ordination and gave her the dharma name Cheng Yen 證嚴 and dharma title Hui Chang 慧璋.

She made a silent vow to follow his exhortation: "at all times do everything for Buddhism, do everything for sentient beings (*wei fojiao, wei zhongsheng* 為佛教, 為眾生). She took to heart his teachings to build a Pure Land in this world, rather than focus on attaining a better rebirth.[8] (See section "Tzu Chi School of Buddhism and Jing Si Dharma Lineage" for more information about Cheng Yen's Buddhist thought.)

Cheng Yen went to the small city of Hualian on Taiwan's east coast and continued her spiritual cultivation, mainly based at Puming Temple. She quickly gained *bhikkhunī* disciples and lay followers through her public lectures on the Earth Treasury Sūtra and Lotus Sutra. She declined several offers to become the abbess of temples elsewhere; rather, she and her followers remained in Hualian and vowed to be self-sufficient through farming and handicrafts.

Cheng Yen soon found the specific direction for her vow "to do everything for Buddhism and do everything for sentient beings." First, she witnessed how the lack of adequate medical resources in the Hualian area perpetuated the vicious cycle between poverty and illness. Second, a conversation with three Catholic nuns convinced her that Buddhism as a religion of compassion should do more to help society, such as building schools and hospitals. In 1966 Cheng Yen and her disciples, including *bhikkhunīs* and laypersons, founded the "Buddhist Overcoming-Difficulties Compassion Relief Merit Association" (Fojiao kenan ciji gongdehui) to serve the poor, ill, and victims of disasters. Cheng Yen and her monastic disciples reside and work at the Still Thoughts Abode and follow the self-reliant principle: "a day without work is a day without food."[9] In the early days, Cheng Yen and her disciples made baby shoes and candles and produced bean powder to make a living and finance their charity work. In addition, to fund the charity and relief work and as daily dāna practice, Cheng Yen asked lay members to donate a few coins every day.

From the start, Master Cheng Yen had *bhikkhunī* disciples and female lay disciples. First, in a conservative society, it is more proper for a *bhikkhunī* to work with laywomen and vice versa. Second, the cult of Guanyin (Avalokiteśvara) historically has been important in Taiwan at least since the 17th century, attested not only by the number of temples dedicated to her, but also in the numbers of lay devotees (both male and female) who practiced *zhaijiao* 齋教, the so-called "vegetarian religions."[10] In Chinese culture Avalokiteśvara is usually gendered female, and women especially were drawn to Guanyin's salvationist powers. C. Julia Huang relates the story of the "Guanyin miracle," when a young Cheng Yen (still a laywoman) prayed to Guanyin to heal her mother, and her mother recovered.[11] The research of Liu Meiling (Shi Dechi) discusses the influence of Guanyin on Cheng Yen during the time (as laywoman) she spent at Ciyun Temple, a temple centered on Guanyin devotion.[12]

In her many lectures, Cheng Yen has instructed her followers to emulate Guanyin: the thousand-armed, thousand-eyed Bodhisattva of Compassion who hears and sees all and aids those in need. "We will become Guanyin's watchful eyes and hands, and the world won't ever call us Buddhists a passive group again."[13]

In addition, Cheng Yen skillfully linked the so-called "feminine" virtues of compassion, nurturance, empathy, selflessness, self-sacrifice, patience, and warmth to Buddhist virtues. Women who become Tzu Chi members have opportunities to learn new skills in counseling, health care, publishing and other mass media, public speaking, organization, foreign travel, and foreign languages. In this way, Tzu Chi extended women's purported nurturing and healing roles from home to society, as well as provided avenues for women to gain new knowledge and a new voice. Indeed, a number of scholars have argued that one main reason for Tzu Chi's success is its empowerment of women, and such empowerment is Tzu Chi's great contribution to contemporary Buddhism in Taiwan and worldwide.[14]

During the 1980s–1990s Taiwan experienced the transition from authoritarian to democratic rule, the growth of the middle class, and the flowering of NGOs and religious groups of all kinds, as André Laliberté and Richard Madsen have discussed.[15] For Tzu Chi, these were also years of major transition. Its evolution from an informal "merit association" to foundation began in 1979 when Cheng Yen voiced her intention to build a hospital in Hualian. Taiwan's east coast lacked adequate medical services, and Cheng Yen insisted that medical services were crucial to mitigate the vicious cycle of illness and poverty. The decision to build a hospital, which opened in 1986, was momentous for Cheng Yen and her supporters for the following reasons: first, the "merit association" needed to systematize its operations and reorganize its structure in order to obtain legal standing as a foundation. Second, to build a hospital required vast resources: land, funding, and qualified personnel. Third, to build a hospital required difficult negotiations with Taiwan's government on all levels. Fourth, in the 1970s and 1980s the majority of doctors, dentists, engineers, and architects in Taiwan were male, some of whom became Tzu Chi members. Thus the gender component of Tzu Chi changed from primarily female to mixed gender in various ratios depending on what part of the enterprise is analyzed. As C. Julia Huang wrote: "Since the mid-1990s, Tzu Chi has been a far cry from a women's group; instead, it is a microcosm that represents Taiwan's diverse social strata."[16]

Of special note is that in the early 1990s, a new group for laymen was formed—the Tzu Cheng Faith Corps, *cicheng dui* 慈誠隊—originally to serve as traffic guards after the Tzu Chi junior college of nursing opened in 1989. As C. Julia Huang writes, the Ten Tzu Chi Precepts appeared at this time and consist of the traditional Buddhist Five Precepts: (a) No killing, (b) No stealing, (c) No fornication, (d) No lying, and (e) No drinking, plus five precepts "customized by Cheng Yen to protect the ideal Tzu Chi men from the common bad habits attributed to Taiwanese masculinity"—that is, (f) No smoking or use of narcotics or betelnut, (g) No gambling, (h) Practice filial piety and develop pleasant manners and speech, (i) Abide by traffic laws (i.e., as a good citizen and to prevent harm to others), and (j) No participation in political activities or demonstrations.[17] The Tenth Precept is controversial for its seemingly dim view of democracy and of politics as something chaotic and corrupted. The background was that in the early 1990s, Taiwan's democracy burst forth onto the streets and interparty brawls broke out in the Legislative Yuan. In this context, the Tenth Precept's purpose seems not only to maintain so-called "political neutrality" for instrumental reasons, but also to cultivate equanimity of mind, *upekkhā*.

At any rate, according to Tzu Chi's own literature, Corpsmen "emphasized organization and discipline and were strong and vigorous. Because of their participation, Tzu Chi became more efficient and its public image was greatly elevated." This wording is typical of 1990s gender norms in Taiwan.[18] Research is needed to ascertain how gender norms have changed in the Tzu Chi Organization as new generations take part and Tzu Chi works with international groups that take varying stances in gender discourse.

In the late 1990s Tzu Chi organized its volunteers according to neighborhood to facilitate communication, resource-sharing, and rapid mobilization for urgent needs, but most importantly, to build a new community by holding lectures and classes and offering service opportunities. Persons of any religious, cultural, or national background can become volunteers. Commissioners—*weiyuan* 委員 (female and male)—are the most dedicated Tzu Chi lay members: they receive several years' training and have a good record of volunteering and fundraising. Many Commissioners are professionals in various fields, especially in business, who offer their funds, time, and business and political connections to Tzu Chi organizations. As of 2020, the numbers of Commissioners and Tzu Cheng Faith Corpsmen was highest in Taiwan followed by Malaysia, then the United States.[19]

RESTRUCTURING

Over the years, few openly criticized Tzu Chi because the organization contributed so greatly to Taiwan and the world. However, some charity groups alleged they could not compete with Tzu Chi due to its large size and fame; some people resented Tzu Chi's aid provision to China and other overseas destinations, and others disapproved of placing Jing Si Aphorisms and other Tzu Chi symbols in public schools rebuilt by Tzu Chi.[20] In 2015, just before the fiftieth anniversary of its founding, the Tzu Chi Foundation faced strong public opposition about a land-development plan and an alleged lack of transparency about their finances. The original "spark" was a controversy over Tzu Chi's US$40.4 million purchase of land in an environmentally protected area located in a Taipei suburb. The Tzu Chi Foundation, the city government, local residents, environmental groups, and the media clashed with each other. Tzu Chi canceled this project, originally planned for a disaster-coordination center.[21] Moreover, some reports criticized Tzu Chi for owning "too much" land and property. One source valued Tzu Chi holdings in Greater Taipei alone at US$1.27 billion in 2015. Heated debates followed in public discourse about reforming laws regarding religious groups in Taiwan because religious groups are tax-exempt and "the government has turned a blind eye to the management of religious bodies."[22]

Faced with this unprecedented public critique, the Tzu Chi Foundation employed the accounting firm KPMG to conduct a thorough auditing of the company and provide advice on restructuring, while Lee & Li Attorneys at Law provided legal advice.[23] The goals were to realize "organizational optimization, financial transparency, social responsibility, and sustainability," and craft a Mission Statement. At the same time, in 2015, the Tzu Chi Foundation incorporated the UN Sustainable Development Goals (SDGs) into their development plans. In 2016, the Foundation appointed a new board of directors and CEO. The chair of the board of directors is Cheng Yen.

Table 1 shows the organizational structure of Tzu Chi's Mission of Charity. As of 2022, details about how the offices coordinate or the operational decision-making process within the Mission of Charity or among the other missions was not public information. The Mission

Table 1. Organizational Structure of the Buddhist Compassion Relief Tzu Chi Foundation's Mission of Charity (2020)

Supervisors	Board of Directors	Sustainable Development Committee
Auditing Office	Chairperson	Asset Management Committee
Legal Affairs Office	CEO Dept. of	Office of the Chairman
Construction	Finance	Long-Term Care Promotion Center
Management	Relations	Office of the CEO
Resources	Humanitarian	Compilation
		Literature
		Development

Source: Office of the CEO, Buddhist Compassion Relief Tzu Chi Foundation.

of Charity is the largest in scope and wealth among the four missions and allocates money to the other three missions of medicine, education, and culture as needed. Each mission has its own organizational structure led by a CEO. Master Cheng Yen is the chair of the board of directors of all four missions. Large branches like Tzu Chi USA are their own foundations and report to Tzu Chi's board of directors. Branches of other sizes report to the Department of Religious Culture and Humanitarian Aid. An in-depth discussion of the organizational structure is beyond the scope of this article; however, if readers compare the 2020 organizational structure of Tzu Chi's Mission of Charity with the organizational structures from 1993 and 1999, one will discover, among other things, that the Tzu Chi Organization grew considerably during these years.[24] An "international office" appeared in 1999, and its international affairs are now on a global scale. Since 2016, the CEO is no longer a position held by Cheng Yen.

TZU CHI HIGHLIGHTS

Mission of Charity's Work. Tzu Chi's emotional and financial relief measures include the following: long-term emotional support and/or financial assistance for chronic cases of illness or poverty, and ongoing emotional care for the bereaved, for orphans, elders, and for persons with disability or illness, in both home and institutional settings such as prisons.

Tzu Chi disaster relief is generally divided into three types: short-term crisis relief (material aid and medical care) to persons after accidents and disasters, and mid- and long-term projects, including the building of schools, homes, and providing job training. Tzu Chi aid is not one-way: in Taiwan and overseas, many recipients of Tzu Chi aid donate funds, labor, and material when they are able to, and some become Tzu Chi members and Commissioners.

Tzu Chi began international relief in 1991, by providing help to children orphaned during the Persian Gulf War and to flood victims in Bangladesh and China. International relief not only provides emergency materials like food, clothing, grain seeds, and medical materials, it goes further to rebuild houses and schools, set up water supply systems, and offer free medical clinics.

In 2008, Tzu Chi assisted with relief and reconstruction after the Sichuan Wenchuan earthquake, and in 2010 Tzu Chi was the first overseas NGO to officially establish a nation-wide charity in China. In addition to building schools, clinics, and homes after disasters, local programs focus on the environment (vegetarianism and recycling) and on providing scholarships to students.

The Mission of Medicine: The Tzu Chi Medical Foundation. One of Cheng Yen's early vows was to improve medical care in rural Taiwan. Tzu Chi runs seven hospitals in Taiwan, a clinic in Suzhou, China, and a hospital in Jakarta, Indonesia. In addition, Tzu Chi founded its International Medical Association in 1996, comprised of fourteen thousand medical professionals who provide free medical services in twenty-four countries.

Tzu Chi also took the lead in shaping a public discourse on illness, dying, and death—previously taboo topics—through publications, community classes, and public advocacy. In particular, Tzu Chi is a pioneer in the field of hospice care in Taiwan. Tzu Chi's work in medicine and "end of life" issues has convinced families to donate their own or loved ones' bodies, which Tzu Chi members call "Silent Mentors," for medical research and education.

Another noteworthy accomplishment is their bone marrow registry. Overcoming popular taboos and former legal restrictions against blood and bone marrow donations in Taiwan, Tzu Chi founded their bone marrow registry in 1993, and it became the largest in Asia. In 2002, the registry expanded to become the Tzu Chi Stem Cell Center. The center operates a marrow donor registry, an umbilical cord blood bank, and an immunogenetic research laboratory.

The Mission of Education: The Tzu Chi Education Foundation. As of 2021, the Tzu Chi Foundation in Hualian is comprised of a comprehensive school system, from preschool to high school, as well as Tzu Chi University and the Tzu Chi University of Science and Technology, and, a secondary school in Tainan, Taiwan. Overseas, there are seventy-five Tzu Chi schools in eight countries: England, Canada, the United States, Australia, Malaysia, Indonesia, Thailand, and Singapore. All the schools emphasize service learning and provide scholarship assistance.

The Mission of Culture: The Tzu Chi Culture and Communication Foundation. Tzu Chi's media operations include Da Ai TV, Da Ai Radio, Chinese- and foreign-language publications, *Rhythms Monthly*, and Jing Si Publications. Tzu Chi programming includes Master Cheng Yen's dharma lectures; Tzu Chi-related activities around the world; Buddhist history; programs about art, family life, and vegetarian cooking, to give some examples. Most programming is available on Tzu Chi-affiliated websites and on Youtube.

Environment Protection. Tzu Chi has promoted environmental awareness, recycling, and conservation to a greater extent than other Buddhist groups in Taiwan. Tzu Chi started its recycling campaign in 1990, ten years before Taiwan's government began its recycling programs. Tzu Chi operates recycling stations in both Taiwan and overseas. In 2008 Tzu Chi founded an affiliate body called the "Great Love Technology Company" that sells environmentally friendly clothing and household items, in particular turning plastic bottles collected by Tzu Chi recycling stations into fabric for blankets, clothing, tote bags, and luggage. All proceeds are said to fund Tzu Chi's charitable missions.

What are the sources for Cheng Yen's environmental ethics, and more, for her cosmology? First, Cheng Yen seems to have been inspired by "Gaia theory": the Earth is a living and breathing organism. Second, as a Buddhist and a believer in Chinese correlative cosmology, in her view many "natural" disasters are man-made, not only due to human abuse of the environment but also from humanity's "accumulated negative karma" and general human moral depravity, which upsets cosmological harmony. In Buddhism, ignorance, greed, and hatred are the three poisons, while wisdom, generosity, and lovingkindness are the cures. For Cheng Yen, purifying human hearts is the key to building a Pure Land on Earth, all the more urgent in these times of climate crises and environment disasters caused by humans. Third, there is a component from the Confucian tradition. Cheng Yen believes social and global change will occur most meaningfully by cultivating individual morality, self-restraint, and the powers of empathy. She uses the phrase *keji, fuli* 克己復禮 from the *Book of Rites* and the *Analects*, "to overcome one's desires and revive courtesy." This means to not only reduce one's needs and consumption habits, but also to shape harmonious ties of mutual respect among people.[25]

Vegetarianism. Obeying the First Buddhist Precept of "no killing" and also practicing compassion for all sentient beings, all monastic disciples in the Tzu Chi organization and many laypersons are vegetarians, and Tzu Chi always encouraged eating less or no meat. However, in recent years, their vegetarianism campaign is broader and more intense for the following reasons: for environmental protection; to prevent zoonotic diseases; and for sustainable living and food security. Tzu Chi directly links the killing and consumption of animals to climate crises and zoonotic diseases like SARS and COVID-19.[26]

Tzu Chi Foundation and the United Nations. The Tzu Chi Foundation has a number of affiliations with the United Nations, mediated by its Tzu Chi United Nations Task Force. On July 19, 2010, the Buddhist Tzu Chi Foundation became an NGO in Special Consultative Status with the UN-ECOSOC. On January 9, 2019, it was granted accreditation by the United Nations Environment Programme, as an observer to sessions of the United Nations Environment Assembly and its subsidiary organs. In December 2021, the UN Interagency Task Force on Religion and Sustainable Development's Multifaith Advisory Council appointed Tzu Chi Foundation as its co-chair.

Tzu Chi's affiliations with the United Nations are significant in at least three ways: First, because Taiwan does not belong to the United Nations, Tzu Chi can strengthen the international profile of Taiwan. Second, having United Nations affiliations provide many new networks and resources within (and outside of) the UN to the Tzu Chi Foundation. Third, such affiliations allow Tzu Chi to share their networks and resources with other groups. Their *Annual Reports* and *Sustainability Reports* illustrate the degree to which the Tzu Chi Foundation in its external presentation has entered global development discourse and has adopted its jargon *du jour* such as engagement, empowerment, stakeholders, initiatives, partnerships, good governance, community holistic care, compassionate technologies, grassroots empowerment, risk management, and sustainable social responsibility. All Tzu Chi missions articulate how their activities align with the UN SDGs.[27]

Refugees. Of particular note is Tzu Chi's work with refugees, often collaborating with the UNHCR, the United Nations Refugee Agency. In 2021, Tzu Chi helped refugees in ten countries: Serbia, Turkey, Jordan, Thailand, Malaysia, Australia, Canada, France, England, and the

United States.[28] From the start of the 2022 war in Ukraine, Tzu Chi assisted Ukrainian refugees in Poland and neighboring countries. For all refugee work, Tzu Chi local branches in these countries or in nearby countries work with governments and/or other NGOs and coordinate with the Tzu Chi Foundation in Taiwan. In addition to distributing food, clothes, and medical care, Tzu Chi stresses education so that refugees might have a better future. Some examples of Tzu Chi's aid to refugees include the following: In Turkey, Tzu Chi's Turkish branch established El-Menahil School (primary, middle, and high school) in Istanbul for Syrian refugees. A total of 2,300 students attend the school, which employs Syrian refugees as teachers and staff. Tzu Chi Turkey also aids Syrian refugee students to attend college. In Jordan, Palestinians and refugees from Syria and Iraq receive medical care and educational support. Thailand has refugees from fifty countries, and Tzu Chi provides refugees jobs as translators. In Malaysia, Tzu Chi aids refugees from Myanmar, Syria, Yemen, Iraq, Pakistan, Afghanistan, Somalia, Sri Lanka, Palestine, Iran, India, and more. Tzu Chi supports the Madrasah Hashimiah, a religious school for Rohingya children, and provides other educational opportunities for stateless children in Malaysia.[29]

Rebuilding Schools. Another admirable accomplishment is how Tzu Chi rebuilds schools. After a major earthquake in Taiwan on September 21, 1999, Tzu Chi rebuilt fifty damaged or destroyed schools. Architects and other professionals donated their time, money, and materials to this project. The schools were "built green"—that is, to conserve water and other resources, sort and recycle waste, recycle rainwater for use in restrooms, utilize natural light and ventilation, and protect the plants and natural landscapes of each school. Tzu Chi has also built schools in China, Thailand, Indonesia, Philippines, Myanmar, Haiti, and Iran. As of 2019, Tzu Chi built or rebuilt 232 schools in sixteen countries.[30]

COVID-19 Action. In January 2020, Tzu Chi Foundation in Hualian established the Global Unified Command Center to coordinate information and supplies on both domestic and international levels.[31]As of June 20, 2021, the Tzu Chi Foundation provided COVID-19 aid to 125 countries and regions in Asia (including Taiwan), Oceania, the Americas, Africa, and Europe. Such aid included masks, PPE, and other medical supplies, food, and daily necessities.[32]

Of particular note is Tzu Chi's cooperation with fifty-nine NGOs as they provide relief in India, Nepal, Bhutan, Bangladesh, Sri Lanka, Laos, and Cambodia. In India, Tzu Chi works with Catholic groups and other Buddhist groups.[33] In addition, scientists at Tzu Chi University and Academia Sinica together with Taipei Tzu Chi hospital developed COVID-19 test kits based on IgM/IgG immune responses and donated these to countries in need. Furthermore, the Tzu Chi Foundation bought five million doses of Pfizer-BioNTech COVID-19 vaccine and donated them to the Taiwan government for distribution to the public.

SUSTAINABILITY

There comes a day when all organizations, particularly those with charismatic founders, must face hard questions concerning their long-term sustainability. The Tzu Chi enterprise must determine how each part will play a role. Who are the future members and leaders? To what extent will Tzu Chi take root in local societies among non-Chinese communities? And will the Tzu Chi Foundation successfully recruit young people as both volunteers and professionals? Will Tzu Chi recruit enough professionals from around the world with training in many fields of expertise? Since 1992, students in colleges and junior colleges in Taiwan and around the world have formed branches in the Tzu Chi Youth Friendship Association to train students for community volunteering and environmental protection activities. In light of ageing populations and declining birth rates in many parts of the world including Taiwan, will future generations be able and willing to provide enough time and money to maintain global Tzu Chi operations?

As for the *bhikkhunīs* of the Pure Abode, will they take on more diversified roles in the future? Some *bhikkhunīs* are being trained to represent Tzu Chi in the public sphere, such as at conventions and government meetings including those overseas, while others will continue to record Master Cheng Yen's lectures and writings, produce scholarship on Tzu Chi, hold classes for both other *bhikkhunīs* and laypersons, teach in universities, participate in all aspects of Pure Abode management, and engage in production to support the Pure Abode, including producing products such as herbal teas, salves, organic snacks, organic soaps, and ceramics.

The key challenges are how to better organize all four missions as one entity; how to better coordinate Taiwan's operations with operations overseas; and how to develop the Jing Si Dharma Lineage and the Tzu Chi School of Buddhism as the threads that bind Tzu Chi together.

Tzu Chi School of Buddhism and Jing Si Dharma Lineage. Since 2006, Cheng Yen and the Tzu Chi Foundation have been developing the Tzu Chi School of Buddhism and the Jing Si Dharma Lineage. What is Cheng Yen's religious background?

Like many born and raised in Taiwan, she was familiar, to a various extent, with the worship of Guanyin and of the Queen Mother of the West as well as Pure Land practices. She decided her future path as a Buddhist nun when she spent time among nuns at Ciyun Temple near her home. Unlike some other leading monks in Taiwan with graduate degrees and/or training at Buddhist institutes in China or Taiwan, Cheng Yen did not receive a higher education nor study at a Buddhist institute. In 1963, in a chance encounter at his Huiri Lecture Hall in Taipei, Master Yinshun sponsored her for ordination, and Cheng Yen vowed to dedicate her life "all for Buddhism, all for sentient beings." Though Cheng Yen did not formally study with Master Yinshun, she considers him her life-long mentor, 導師. She studied the works of Taixu, Yinshun, and Buddhist sutras as they became available outside of Buddhist institutes, temple libraries, or private collections—for example, she bought her copy of the *Lotus Sutra* 妙法蓮華經 from a layperson in 1960.

Cheng Yen as well as Hsing Yun (b. 1927), founder of Fo Guang Shan (1967), and Sheng Yen (1931–2009), founder of Dharma Drum Mountain (1989), built the large transnational Buddhist organizations based in Taiwan that claim to propagate *renjian fojiao*, "Buddhism for the human realm," usually translated as "Humanistic Buddhism."[34] Taiwan's economic take-off (1970s–1980s) and democratization (1980s), as well as globalization from the 1990s enabled all three organizations to grow rapidly.

Each founder has paid homage to the masters who formulated *renjian fojiao*, Taixu and Yinshun. Taixu (1890–1947) was the major figure in China's Buddhist reformation movement in the early 20th century. Like reformist Buddhists in Sri Lanka, India, Southeast Asia, and Japan of the late 19th and early 20th centuries, Taixu and his reformist colleagues aimed to reinterpret Buddhist teachings and practices, to strengthen Buddhist institutions not only to meet the challenges of the modern world, but to assert national identity and to promote an ethics to improve people's lives.[35]

In a 1933 essay on how to establish *renjian fojiao*, Taixu wrote:

> *Renjian fojiao* is not a Buddhism in which you leave the human realm and become a god or ghost, or for everyone to take monastic vows, go to a temple, or become an eremite in the forest. It's a Buddhism which, in accordance with Buddhist teachings, reforms society, helps humankind to progress, and improves the whole world.[36]

Yinshun (1906–2005), the esteemed Chinese Buddhist scholar and teacher, and Taixu's student in China, wrote many articles for Taixu's Buddhist journal, *Hai Chao Yin*. He was also chief editor of Taixu's *Complete Works* and was Taixu's biographer. Yinshun was part of an exodus of Chinese monks to Taiwan after 1949. In particular, the Buddhist Association of the Republic of China (BAROC) and other monks from China, in different ways, sought to establish in Taiwan the "orthodox Chinese Buddhism" they had known in China. To do so, BAROC extirpated the influence of Japanese Buddhism and extant Chinese Buddhist institutions and muted the influence of *zhaijiao* vegetarian cults' leaders in Buddhist circles.[37]

For his part, based in Taiwan after 1952, Yinshun focused on teaching and scholarship: early Indian Buddhism, Madhyamaka studies, and Chan. His writings on *renjian fojiao* and his Pure Land research stressed the bodhisattva path to create a Pure Land on Earth. Unlike Taixu, he did not draw up blueprints for the socially engaged Bodhisattva. However each leader—Cheng Yen, Hsing Yun, and Sheng Yen—has interpreted what the Bodhisattva path should be. Each group has utilized mass media to promulgate the dharma in creative ways, and carries out charity to one degree or another, but global humanitarianism has been the Tzu Chi organization's focus; Fo Guang Shan's is education, Chinese Buddhist scholarship, Buddhist art and music, and worldwide promotion of the *bhikkhunī* order; and Dharma Drum Mountain has advanced the field of Chinese Buddhist scholarship and developed its own Chan School.[38]

However, Cheng Yen stresses that the legacy of Tzu Chi is not only its humanitarian contributions to the world, but also to "transmit the Jing Si Dharma Lineage and promote the Tzu Chi School of Buddhism," 傳承「靜思法脈」, 弘揚「慈濟宗門」. In 2006, Master Cheng Yen first announced the formation of the Jing Si Dharma Lineage and the Tzu Chi School of Buddhism, followed by a formal declaration in 2016 to coincide with the fiftieth anniversary of Tzu Chi Benevolent Association. The year 2006 was crucial for the Tzu Chi organization: not only was it the fortieth anniversary of the founding of the Buddhist Overcoming-Difficulties Compassion Relief Merit Association, but it was also the year in which the "Four Missions and Eight Footprints"—missions of charity, medicine, education, and culture, international relief, bone marrow donation, community volunteerism, and environmental protection—were established and began to flourish. In that year, Cheng Yen also declared her intention to establish the Tzu Chi School of Buddhism and the Jing Si Dharma Lineage, and since then, the dharmic foundation for the School and Lineage as well as the Lineage organizational structure continue to be developed.

While in-depth research is still required, three interlinked reasons for establishing this School and Lineage were: (a) to map the future of the Tzu Chi organization overall after the charismatic founder Cheng Yen's eventual passing and to transform personal devotion to the Master to identification with a School and Lineage; (b) to clarify Cheng Yen's similarities and differences with the teachings of Master Yinshun and other Buddhist groups; and (c) to strengthen Buddhist institutions globally, for without a solid dharmic foundation, Tzu Chi might become solely a secular humanitarian NGO-NPO, and however noble that might be, Cheng Yen's vow is not only to work "for sentient beings," but to work "for Buddhism."

As Cheng Yen explained:

> You say what is the Tzu Chi School? It is the Buddha dharma brought into daily life, and the Buddha dharma truly utilized in life. Look at the *Sūtra of Infinite Meanings*: "after suffering is removed [from people], they can then spread the Buddha dharma [on how to remove suffering]." After we help [those who suffer], we'll be their companion until they feel at ease in body and mind, and at the same time they can help others in the same way. This is what is called saving humanity.[39]

In Chinese, *zong* 宗 means "school" or "sect." Cheng Yen explains the Tzu Chi School through the terms *zongjiao* 宗教, "religion," and *zongzhi* 宗旨, "aim":

> Our aim, *zongzhi*, is kindness, compassion, joy and equanimity to sacrifice for the human world and to save all sentient beings. "Zong" 宗 is the aim, and "jiao" 教 is "education"; we educate sentient beings for the sake of Buddhism, and make people believe in righteousness and stir up their compassionate hearts. "Compassion and joy" is our School, "honesty and faithfulness" is our Dharma Lineage, all realized through bodily practice [i.e., not remaining on the abstract or philosophical level].[40]

Master Cheng Yen differentiates the Tzu Chi School of Buddhism from Chan and Pure Land practices. She argues that Chan is difficult to practice correctly, and she believes that she is not qualified to teach Chan, since her meditation practice has not approached the realm of enlightenment, *chanjing* 禪境. As for Pure Land practices, such as chanting and visualizations, she explained she has not had time to develop these because her whole life has been dedicated to serving sentient beings in this world.[41]

As for the Jing Si Dharma Lineage, it includes dedicated laypersons; the *bhikkhunī* disciples of Cheng Yen who, in accordance with the Dharmagupta Vinaya, uphold 348 precepts; and a new group called Pure Practitioners, 清修士, *qingqiushi*. In 2006, Master Cheng Yen raised the idea of "Pure Practitioners" as a third category between monastic and lay, whose members devote their lives to service with Tzu Chi and ensure a steady pool of talent for the Foundation's missions, since volunteers come and go and monastics have their own duties, restrictions, and schedules. Furthermore, according to Buddhist monastic codes, a *bhikkhunī* such as Cheng Yen cannot have monk disciples, so male "Pure Practitioners" are the closest equivalent. Pure Practitioners are female and male disciples, some from the ranks of Tzu Chi youth, who uphold the Tzu Chi Ten Precepts, take a vow of chastity, and work for the various Tzu Chi missions including Tzu Chi University. Fundraising for Tzu Chi missions is optional. In the years following 2006, a group of devout female and male laypersons from Taiwan, Malaysia, Singapore, and other places developed the rules and structure of this unique order. The first ordinations took place at the Pure Abode in Hualian in 2019, and many Pure Practitioners reside there, where Cheng Yen, her *bhikkhuni* disciples, and Foundation affiliates live and work.[42] A comparison of the "Pure Practitioners" with the *anagārika* in Theravada Buddhism would be instructive, because the latter is also a group that moves between the monastic and lay realms.

The Tzu Chi School of Buddhism's core texts, termed the "Jing Si Dharma Treasury," include the following, all of which Master Cheng Yen has lectured upon and written about for many years. She has had particular affinity with the *Threefold Lotus Sutra*, which includes the *Sūtra of Infinite Meanings*, the *Lotus Sutra*, and the *Sūtra of Meditation on the Universal Worthy Bodhisattva*, ever since she read (when still a laywoman) a Japanese-language commentary on the *Threefold Lotus Sutra*. The term "Still Thoughts," *Jing Si*, from the *Sūtra of Infinite Meanings*, is fundamental to Cheng Yen's vision and Tzu Chi's missions.

> With minds tranquil and clear, vows vast as the universe, Bodhisattvas remain unwavering for countless kalpas . . . Infinite Dharma-doors readily appear in front of them. They attain great wisdom and thoroughly comprehend all Dharma.[43]

Her commentaries on the following Sutras are published in Chinese. Key teachings include the bodhisattva path, making vows, the importance of filial piety, self-discipline, and repentance. The works include: the *Sūtra of Infinite Meanings* 無量義經; the *Lotus Sutra* 妙法蓮華經; the *Medicine Buddha Sūtra* 藥師經 (The Twelve Great Vows); *Sūtra of the Eight Realizations of Great Beings* 佛說八大人覺經; *Thirty-Seven Practices to Enlightenment* 三十七道品偈誦釋義; *Sūtra of Profound Gratitude to Parents* 父母恩重難報經; *Sūtra of the Buddha's Bequeathed Teaching* 佛垂般涅槃略說教誡經; *Earth Treasury Sūtra* 地藏菩薩本願經; *Sūtra of Forty-Two Chapters* 四十二章經; and the *Compassionate Samadhi Water Repentance* 慈悲三昧水懺.[44]

In sum, Tzu Chi's greatest challenge is to articulate its distinct school of Buddhism and harmonize this with its identity as a powerful international humanitarian NGO.[45] The Tzu Chi Foundation's *2021 Annual Report* begins with words from the founder, Cheng Yen, yet the term "Buddhism" only appears seven times in the entire report, of which two instances are as a part of Tzu Chi Foundation's name. If "from the door of charity to the door of Buddhism," *shanmen ru fomen* 善門入佛門, is the essence of the Tzu Chi School, Tzu Chi can further elucidate the notion of "good works as skillful means," how "good works" in the Buddhist sense and the many definitions of "altruism" are related, including altruism as social justice; and how good works lead to wisdom and to enlightenment in self and others.[46]

In this vein, might Cheng Yen and her disciples build upon the Master's notion of 身體力行 *shenti lixing*? "Practice what you preach" is too simplistic a translation. Because compared with other Buddhist groups, "the body" is key for Tzu Chi: energetic bodies infused by compassion that save ill and broken bodies so that they may stand up and save others, somewhat like the New Testament lesson "take up your mat and walk." And "Silent Mentors" are "holy bodies," a form of dāna that save others. Compassion for animals' lives as well, as seen in Tzu Chi's vigorous promotion of vegetarianism. Tzu Chi also disciplines the body: uniforms based on rankings and roles, as well as group devotions expressed in sign language, drama, and song.[47] A deeper exploration of the *Medicine Buddha Sūtra*'s and the *Lotus Sutra*'s "gift of the body" might develop the notion of *shenti lixing* as a "bodily practice of compassion."[48] As Ruben Habito suggests, to the 13th-century Japanese Buddhist priest Nichiren, Śākyamuni Buddha was a constant living presence due to Nichiren's "habitual reading of the *Lotus Sutra*, not just in a conceptual manner, but in a very immediate and experiential—one could say—bodily manner."[49] Yet no matter what the organizational and philosophical configuration, Tzu Chi is a model for humanitarians and Buddhists alike on how to relieve suffering, nurture hope, and build community through the bodhisattva path.

REVIEW OF LITERATURE

In 1981 the Tzu Chi Cultural Mission published a biography of Cheng Yen written by Chen Huijian called *Zhengyan fashi de Ciji shijie* [Venerable Zheng Yan's World of Ciji]. The book was republished in 1984 and 1989, and then again in 2000 with the title: *Zhengyan fashi de ciji shijie: Hualian ciji gongdehui de yuanqi yu chengzhang* [Master Zheng Yan's World of Ciji: The Origin and Growth of Hualian's Ciji Merit Association]. As far as is known, the 1981 book was the first about Cheng Yen and the Tzu Chi Merit Association authorized by them. The author was a well-known lay Buddhist writer and editor, who for a time was editor-in-chief of a Tzu Chi magazine. The book is based on interviews and takes an emic and nonanalytic approach, but preserves details about the early days that might have otherwise been forgotten. A 1997 collection of photographs contains useful biographical material.[50] Pan Xuan, an author of numerous publications about Cheng Yen and Tzu Chi for the Tzu Chi organization, wrote a history of Cheng Yen and Tzu Chi, translated into English as *50 Years on the Bodhisattva Path*.[51] It gives a general overview in Tzu Chi's typical fashion via the personal stories of volunteers, professionals, and aid recipients, interwoven with teachings by Cheng Yen.

Anthropologist Lu Hwei-syin is a pioneer in gender studies in Taiwan and since the early 1990s published many works about women and gender in Tzu Chi.[52] In 1998 the anthropologists Robert P. Weller and C. Julia Huang published an important article about the rise of Tzu Chi in the contexts of women and charity work, Buddhist history in Taiwan, new religions, and growth of the public sphere.[53] Their article opened paths for research on Tzu Chi. Works about Buddhist history in Taiwan written in English or other languages besides Chinese or Japanese were rare until Charles B. Jones's 1999 book, *Buddhism in Taiwan: Religion and the State, 1660–1990*. The book gives a good overview of Buddhism in Taiwan from the later Imperial era, through the Japanese colonial era, then the post-1949 period of the Republic of China on Taiwan. Tzu Chi is one group that Jones discusses in the context of Taiwan's 1980s religious efflorescence, along with Fo Guang Shan (and the waning of BAROC influence at that time). Sociologist Richard Madsen's 2007 book discussed how Tzu Chi and other Buddhist groups like Fo Guang Shan and Dharma Drum Mountain flourished due to democratization and growth of the middle class.[54]

Sociologist André Laliberté's 2004 book on the politics of Buddhist organizations in Taiwan discussed "Tzu Chi's humanistic Buddhism and the avoidance of politics," by which he meant that Tzu Chi members eschew participation in party politics, elections, campaigns, political protest, and lobbying.[55] Tzu Chi's Tenth Precept says, "do not participate in political activities and demonstrations," and as Laliberté explains, maintaining social order and purifying people's hearts is the priority for Tzu Chi members, not to sully oneself in the messy business of democratic political process.[56] Cheng Yen wrote: "Concern about national affairs means this: do your work well, conduct yourself well, and follow the rules you should abide by as a citizen, in order to help suffering people in the world."[57]

However, it is evident that Tzu Chi members are politically savvy in the following ways: They work with government bodies, with the United Nations and other supranational bodies, faith-based and nonfaith-based NGOs, and businesses. First, with government offices in Taiwan from the central to local level (including Ministries of Foreign Affairs and Defense); second, with international humanitarian organizations like UNHCR, InterAction, FEMA, and the Red Cross; third, they cooperate with disaster-management bodies in the National Applied Research Laboratories, and National Disaster Prevention, and Relief Science and Technology Center; fourth, they coordinate with companies in fields of information and systems like Chunghwa Telephone, Taiwan Mobile, Asia Pacific Telecom, IBM, ASUSTeK Computer, and CTCB Bank; and fifth, they work with other philanthropic groups, professionals of all types including scholars, and businesses in all sectors. Many Tzu Chi members and Commissioners work with these entities or have other socioeconomic connections around the world.[58]

In the field of anthropology, C. Julia Huang's *Charisma and Compassion: Cheng Yen and the Buddhist Tzu Chi Movement*, based on extensive fieldwork, gives an excellent overview of the Tzu Chi's founding and development (and description of life at the Pure Abode) in Taiwan and overseas as of the mid-2000s, and a helpful explanation of the groupings and identity-construction of the volunteers. She provides a thorough exploration of charisma, leadership, and organization-building with regards to Cheng Yen and Tzu Chi, and details Tzu Chi's special appeal to women. The chapter entitled "Weeping and Musical Corporeality" is an ethnographic tour de force. However, due to rapid developments in recent years, a number of topics need to be explored more thoroughly, namely:

1. Weberian theories of charismatic leadership and bureaucratization in Chapter 2—Cheng Yen as Charismatic Leader of a Fluid Organization and Shapeless Bureaucracy—need to be revisited.
2. Deeper exploration of "the gift," sacrifice, discipline, and power.
3. Gender ratios and roles in Tzu Chi.
4. The reasons for Tzu Chi's overseas expansion need to be explained. They include more than a growing "diaspora" of ethnic Chinese middle-class or proselytization by a Buddhist group, but are also due to the interplay of Tzu Chi with international NGOs and the central role of Tzu Chi USA.
5. The Buddhist identity of Tzu Chi: the Tzu Chi School and Jing Si Dharma Lineage should be critically analyzed.

In the field of history, Elise Anne DeVido's 2010 book focuses on the contributions of Taiwan's *bhikkhunīs* and laywomen to Buddhism and civil society and includes three chapters on Cheng Yen and Tzu Chi. The book analyzes how gender and Buddhism are interlinked in Taiwan and discusses the relation between *renjian fojiao* and the growth of Taiwan's Buddhism. But this work needs updating to reflect changing gender roles in Taiwan and changes in Tzu

Chi's global organization, as well as the current situation of *bhikkhunīs* and their organizations in Taiwan.

Exploration of Tzu Chi as a "New Religious Movement" with reference to Rodney Stark's "Ten Propositions" is the focus of sociologist Yu-Shuang Yao's 2012 book.[59] Readers can learn about Tzu Chi in the context of Taiwan's rich religious landscape, as well as the social background of members and recruitment strategy, and about Cheng Yen's leadership style and the teachings and practices that she developed. Yet due to the ten-year gap between dissertation and book, the author missed new scholarship, and the book makes perplexing statements like: Tzu Chi's "continued international appeal seems doubtful" and "the absence or at least unimportance of many traditional Buddhist teachings and practices has made the Tzu Chi movement one of the most secular religions in the Chinese Buddhist world, perhaps indeed in the Buddhist world anywhere."[60] And though the book's title includes the term "Engaged Buddhism," there is no discussion of it in the book.

Studies on special topics include "Silent Mentors"; case studies of Tzu Chi activities in separate countries; and Tzu Chi's environmental ethics. First, scholars from diverse academic fields have written on "Silent Mentors."[61] Second, regarding case studies of Tzu Chi groups in Southeast Asia, scholars are going beyond the "overseas-Chinese diffusion" thesis. Chengpang Lee (2020) takes a nuanced and comparative approach to analyze the growth of Tzu Chi in Malaysia, Indonesia, Singapore, and the Philippines.[62] Aranya Siriphon and Sunanta Yamthap (2019) examine the Chiang Mai (Thailand) Tzu Chi School.[63] Arnold L. Lau and Jayeel S. Cornelio published an important study about Tzu Chi volunteers in the Philippines who are Catholic and non-Chinese.[64] And Aristotle C. Dy has compared the localization of Humanistic Buddhism by Tzu Chi and Fo Guang Shan in the Philippines.[65]

The Buddhist Tzu Chi Foundation published its first history of a Tzu Chi branch, *Xinjiapo cijishi* [History of Tzu Chi Singapore], and other such histories will follow.[66] Ooi Tan Lee looks at Buddhist revitalization in Malaysia via transnational Buddhist groups like Tzu Chi.[67] Chengpang Lee and Ling Han stress that environmental protection is central to Tzu Chi's "theology-practice system," and studies of Tzu Chi can advance the field of comparative environmental ethics.[68]

The following are selected works on the Tzu Chi School of Buddhism and Jing Si Dharma Lineage and are mostly in Chinese; works in other languages are sorely needed. Buddhist studies specialists should provide critical analysis of the Tzu Chi School of Buddhism and Jing Si Dharma Lineage. Readers should start with the papers of the Fourth Tzu Chi Forum (2016) on "The Universal Value of Buddhism and the Dharma Path of Tzu Chi."[69] Scholars from Taiwan, including Pure Abode *bhikkhunīs,* and abroad contributed papers. Some contributions are academic in nature, others are field reports by Tzu Chi professionals, and others are personal reflections. Her Rey-sheng's contribution to the volume is a rigorous analysis of the development of the Tzu Chi School.[70] In another article, Lin Chien-te compares the "Yinshun School" and the "Tzu Chi School" from the point of view of Buddhology.[71]And in 2021, the Tzu Chi Foundation and several universities launched the Yin-Cheng Distinguished Lecture Series on Buddhism for scholars from different disciplines to explore topics in contemporary Buddhism.[72]

Helpful for comparison with Tzu Chi, a book by Jimmy Yu discusses the question of *zong* (school) and details how the monk Sheng Yen founded Dharma Drum Mountain and developed a new Chan School as part of Sheng Yen's interpretation of Taixu's ideas on the "humanistic pure land."[73]

In sum, since 2010 Tzu Chi in all aspects has developed dramatically due to its affiliations in the United Nations, relentless globalization with its positive and negative forces, the climate crisis and environmental emergencies, and the 2015–2016 restructuring and preparation for long-term sustainability. Each of the following topics deserve in-depth treatment, whether in Chinese or other languages, and require use of sources in Chinese and multiple languages as well as fieldwork: Tzu Chi and the United Nations; environmental work; refugees; interfaith humanitarianism (Buddhist, Christian, Muslim); Tzu Chi and COVID-19 action; Tzu Chi and disaster prevention and relief; Tzu Chi and vegetarianism; Taiwan's *bhikkhunīs*; Tzu Chi's "Pure Practitioners"; Youth; Humanistic Education; Tzu Chi media productions; and the politics of Tzu Chi in Taiwan and overseas in relation to government bodies, e.g., with the United Nations and other supranational bodies, faith-based and nonfaith-based NGOs, and business circles. More comparative studies of Tzu Chi with other global Buddhist organizations are needed. Even more interdisciplinary studies on all these topics are necessary, and are best achieved through collaborative research projects.

PRIMARY SOURCES

An annotated bibliography is sorely needed for Cheng Yen's writings. Her major works can be found on Tzu Chi's Jing Si Books website (https://www.jingsi.com/) and to a limited extent on Amazon. Most are in Chinese, and some are translated into English and Japanese.

Since 1982, Cheng Yen has published her *Daily Journal* that includes her dharma talks, record of daily meetings, and her travels in Taiwan to places related to Tzu Chi missions and to Tzu Chi branches. Scholars can find these journals in Tzu Chi Digital Collection Resource Network (https://tcdata.tzuchi-org.tw).

The series of volumes *Jing Si Aphorisms* (sometimes translated as *Still Thoughts Aphorisms*) are the best-known of Cheng Yen's works, due to their clear illustration of how Buddhist and Confucian wisdom can be applied in everyday life and to extend compassion to the wider society and to the earth. As of 2019, the *Aphorisms* were translated into eighteen languages and have sold seven million copies.[74]

Her commentaries on the *Sūtra of Infinite Meanings* (English translation published in 2021) and on the *Lotus Sutra*—the texts that have inspired her work for decades—are for scholars and advanced students of Buddhism.

In her book on the "Modern-day Bodhisattva Practitioner," Cheng Yen introduces the Tzu Chi School of Buddhism and explains how spiritual cultivation is best accomplished through alleviation of sentient beings' suffering by putting sutra teachings into action. This book is also a succinct story of Tzu Chi missions interspersed with Tzu Chi volunteers' experiences.

The book *Realizing Principles through Propriety: Cultivating a Humanistic Character* shows how the Chinese philosophical ideas of 禮*li* (propriety) and 理*li* (principles) are as important to Cheng Yen as the *Lotus Sutra*'s teachings on equality of all sentient beings, and the centrality of the bodhisattva vow. "Realizing Principles through Propriety" is the English translation of

有禮達理, and these core values inform Cheng Yen's ideas about "humanistic culture"—the culture of respecting humanity to bring harmony and peace to oneself, society, and the world. Lastly, to understand Tzu Chi as a global NGO/NPO, one must consult its *Annual Reports, Yearly Almanacs*, and *Sustainability Reports*; these are professionally prepared and audited. See "*Tzu Chi Foundation and the United Nations*" section for more information.

Shih, Cheng Yen. 靜思法髓妙蓮華 [Cheng Yen's Teachings on *Lotus Sutra*]. Taipei: Jing Si Mission of Culture, 2019–2022.
Shih, Cheng Yen. 證嚴上人衲履足跡 *Zhengyan Shangren nalu zuji* [*Daily Journal of Dharma Master Cheng Yen*]. Taipei: Tzu Chi Culture. Published four times annually, 1996–Present (with different titles from 1982–1996).
Shih, Cheng Yen. 靜思語典藏版 [*Jing Si Aphorisms Collectors' Edition*]. In English, French, German, and Italian, with Chinese appended. Taipei: Tzu Chi Culture, 2013.
Shih, Cheng Yen. *The Path to Truth for the Modern-Day Bodhisattva Practitioner*. Translated by Tzu Chi USA Editorial Team. Taipei: Jing Si Publishing, 2014.
Shih, Cheng Yen. *Realizing Principles through Propriety: Cultivating a Humanistic Character*. Translated by Dharma as Water Editorial Team. Taipei: Jing Si Publishing, 2017.
Shih, Cheng Yen. *Teachings and Commentary on the Sūtra of Infinite Meanings*: Volumes I and II. Translated by Dharma as Water Editorial Team. Taipei: Jing Si Publishing, 2021.

ONLINE SOURCES

In order to consolidate the copious amount of information available on Tzu Chi organizations' numerous websites, in 2020 the Tzu Chi Foundation launched the Tzu Chi Digital Collection Resource Network (Chinese). Register for an account to access this free searchable database, updated regularly. Categories include: Images; Books; Periodicals; Community Volunteers Documentation; and Tzu Chi official websites.

Researchers should also consult Tzu Chi organization's major websites:

IN ENGLISH

The main site for global Tzu branches is organized geographically. The organizations' reports can also be accessed here, including *Annual Reports, Yearly Almanacs*, and *Sustainability Reports*.

The website dedicated to the Principles of the Jing Si Dharma Lineage and Tzu Chi School of Buddhism is divided into three categories: Faith, Vows, Practice.

IN CHINESE

The Tzu Chi website in Taiwan is organized topically, and includes information about Tzu Chi School of Buddhism and Jing Si Dharma Lineage.

法脈宗門綱要 *Famai zongmen gangyao* [Principles of the Jing Si Dharma Lineage and the Tzu Chi School of Buddhism] is divided into three categories: Faith, Vows, Practice.

靜思 *Jing Si* [Still Thoughts]. This website has specific sources on Jing Si Abode, Jing Si Lineage, and information on Tzu Chi Missions.

慈濟思想論述學術研究 *Ciji sixiang lunshu xueshu yanjiu* [Academic Research on Tzu Chi Thought]. This website has books and articles related to research on Tzu Chi, including the Tzu Chi Forum.

See the Da Ai media productions website for a guide to their news broadcasts, TV serial dramas, and cultural performances.

FURTHER READING

Chen, Xinji. *Jingwai shehui zuzhi yu zhongguo dalu hefaxing de jianli: yi Ciji jijinhui weili* [Establishing Legality of Foreign Social Organizations in Mainland China: A Case Study of Tzu Chi Foundation]. Taipei: Zhizhi Xueshu, 2013.

DeVido, Elise Anne. *Taiwan's Buddhist Nuns*. Albany: State University of New York Press, 2010.

Her, Rey-sheng, Mutsu Hsu, and John Hoffmire, eds. *The Buddhist Renaissance: The Philosophy and Practice of the Tzu Chi Dharma Path*. Taipei: Rhythms Monthly, 2020.

Hsu, Mutsu, Jinhua Chen, and Lori Meeks, eds. *Development and Practice of Humanitarian Buddhism: Interdisciplinary Perspectives*. Hualian, Taiwan: Tzu Chi University Press, 2007.

Huang, C. Julia. *Charisma and Compassion: Cheng Yen and the Buddhist Tzu Chi Movement*. Cambridge, MA: Harvard University Press, 2009.

Huang, C. Julia. "Scientific and Sacramental: Secularization of Buddhism and Sacralization of Medical Science in Tzu Chi (Ciji)." *Journal of Global Buddhism* 18 (2017): 72–90. https://doi.org/10.5281/zenodo.1248036.

Huang, C. Julia, and Robert P. Weller. "Merit and Mothering: Women and Social Welfare in Taiwanese Buddhism." *Journal of Asian Studies* 57, no. 2 (1998): 379–396.

Jones, Charles B. *Buddhism in Taiwan: Religion and the State, 1660–1990*. Honolulu: University of Hawaii Press, 1999.

Jones, Charles B. *Taixu's "On the Establishment of the Pure Land in the Human Realm": A Translation and Study*. New York: Bloomsbury Academic, 2020.

Laliberté, André. *The Politics of Buddhist Organizations in Taiwan: 1989–2003*. London: RoutledgeCurzon, 2004.

Lau, Arnold Lindros, and Jayeel Serrano Cornelio. "Tzu Chi and the Philanthropy of Filipino Volunteers." *Asian Journal of Social Science* 43 (2015): 376–399.

Lee, Chengpang. "The Forgotten Bonds: A Coevolutionary Framework on the Diffusion of Tzu Chi in Four Southeast Asian Countries." *American Behavioral Scientist* 64, no. 10 (2020): 1471–1484.

Lee, Chengpang, and Ling Han. "Becoming INGO: A Case Study on Taiwan's Tzu-Chi in the United States." *Voluntas* 31 (2020): 1201–1211.

Lee, Chengpang, and Ling Han. "Recycling Bodhisattva: The Tzu-Chi Movement's Response to Global Climate Change." *Social Compass* 62, no. 3 (2015): 311–325.

Lin, Chien-te (Kent). "Churu yu shengsu zhijian—fojiao cishan shiyezhi chubu sikao" [Passing through the Holiness and the Worldliness: An Exploration on the Buddhist Charity Enterprise]. *Xuanzang Foxue Yanjiu* 28 (September 2017): 105–136.

Lou, Yu-lieh, and Herman B. Leonard, eds. *Ciji zongmen de pushi jiazhi* [The Universal Value of Tzu Chi School of Buddhism]. Taipei: Jingdian Zazhi, 2017.

Lu, Hwei-syin. " 'The Bodhisattva's Path' as Gender-Neutral Practices: A Case Study of the Buddhist Tzu Chi Community in Taiwan." In *The Bloomsbury Research Handbook of Chinese Philosophy and Gender*. Edited by Ann A. Pang-White, 357–376. London: Bloomsbury Academic, 2016.

Madsen, Richard. *Democracy's Dharma: Religious Renaissance and Political Development in Taiwan*. Berkeley: University of California Press, 2007.

Pan, Xuan. *50 Years on the Bodhisattva Path*. Taipei: Tzu Chi, 2019.

Reinke, Jen. *Mapping Modern Mahāyāna: Chinese Buddhism and Migration in the Age of Global Modernity*. Berlin: De Gruyter Oldenbourg, 2021.

Wang, Pen-jung. *For Buddhism, for Sentient Beings: The Buddhist Practice of Tzu Chi's Missions*. Taipei: Rhythms Monthly, 2022.

Yan, Ho-dan, Chi-yin Wu, and Ruey-fa Lin. "Social Entrepreneurship and Charismatic Leadership: Master Cheng Yen and the Tzu Chi Foundation." *International Journal of Innovation and Regional Development* 8, no. 2 (July 2018): 136–158. https://doi.org/10.1504/IJIRD.2018.10013233.

NOTES

1. *Tzu* 慈 means "compassion," and *Chi* 濟, "relief." The legal name in Chinese is *Caituan faren zhonghua minguo fojiao ciji cishan shiye jijinhui* 財團法人中華民國佛教慈濟慈善事業基金會 that translates as "Buddhist Compassion and Relief Philanthropic Foundation of the Republic of China (ROC)." But the latter translation is not used in their official publications; instead, renderings include the following: Taiwan Buddhist Compassion Relief Tzu Chi Foundation; Buddhist Compassion Relief Tzu Chi Foundation; Buddhist Tzu Chi Foundation; Tzu Chi Foundation, Taiwan; or Tzu Chi Foundation. If a place name is stated in their publications, it is "Taiwan," not "ROC." Whether "Taiwan" and "Buddhist" are used depends on the political and religious context in which "Tzu Chi" is operating.
2. Buddhist Tzu Chi Foundation, *Inspiring Great Love around the World* (Hualian, Taiwan: Department of Literature and History, Buddhist Tzu Chi Foundation, 2021), 6–9.
3. Buddhist Tzu Chi Foundation, *Holding Together, Building Hope* (Hualian, Taiwan: Tzu Chi Foundation, 2019), 10.
4. Buddhist Tzu Chi Foundation, *Tzu Chi Annual Report, 2020* (Hualian, Taiwan: Tzu Chi Foundation, 2021), 91–92.
5. RSM Audit & Tax Consulting, *Catholic Relief Services: U.S. Conference of Catholic Bishops and Affiliates, Consolidated Financial Report, September 30, 2020* (Maryland: RSM, 2021), 3 and 5.
6. As a rule, this article will use *Hanyu pinyin* for the Chinese but will use the Wade-Giles system for "Tzu Chi," "Cheng Yen," etc., used by the organization, and "Taipei" as conventionally rendered.
7. Liu King-pong, ed., *Lotus Flower of the Heart: Thirty Years of Tzu Chi Photographs* (Taipei: Still Thoughts Cultural Mission, 1997), 33.
8. For more information about Yinshun, see William Yau-nang Ng, "Yin Shun's Interpretations of the Pure Land," *Journal of Chinese Philosophy* 34, no. 1 (March 2007): 25–47.
9. A phrase traditionally attributed to Chan Master Baizhang of the Tang Dynasty.
10. Yu-chen Li, "The Religiosity and Leadership of Taiwanese Bhiksuni Leaders: Guanyin and Bhiksunis Fuhui and Zhengyan," in *Bridging Worlds: Buddhist Women's Voices across Generations*, ed. Karma Lekshe Tsomo (Taipei: Yuan Chuan Press, 2004), 97.
11. C. Julia Huang, *Charisma and Compassion: Cheng Yen and the Buddhist Tzu Chi Movement* (Cambridge, MA: Harvard University Press, 2009), 19.
12. Meiling Liu, 劉美玲(釋德雲), 自力更生之寺院經濟型態研究:以慈濟靜思精舍為例 [*Zili gengsheng zhi siyuan jingji xingtai yanjiu: yi ciji jingshe weili*], "Study on the Economic Type of Self-Reliance Temples: A Case Study of Tzu Chi's Jing Si Abode," MA Thesis (Linmei Village, Taiwan: Foguang University, Department of Buddhist Studies, 2020), 43–44.
13. Barbara E. Reed, "Guanyin Narratives: Wartime and Postwar," in *Modern Taiwan: Tradition and Innovation in a Changing Society*, ed. Philip Clart and Charles B. Jones (Honolulu: University of Hawaii Press, 2003), 199.

14. See Lu Hwei-syin, "Gender and Buddhism in Contemporary Taiwan: A Case Study of Tzu Chi Foundation," *Proceedings of the National Science Council, Part C: Humanities and Social Sciences* 8, no. 4 (1998): 539–550.
15. André Laliberté, *The Politics of Buddhist Organizations in Taiwan, 1989–2003: Safeguard the Faith, Build a Pure Land, Help the Poor* (London: Routledge/Curzon, 2004); and Richard Madsen, *Democracy's Dharma: Religious Renaissance and Political Development in Taiwan* (Berkeley: University of California Press, 2007).
16. Huang, *Charisma and Compassion*, 75.
17. Huang, *Charisma and Compassion*, 72–77, quotation is from p. 75.
18. Liu, *Lotus Flower of the Heart*, 26, 133.
19. Buddhist Tzu Chi Foundation, *2020 Tzu-Chi Almanac* (Hualian, Taiwan: Tzu Chi Foundation, 2021), 636–639.
20. In fact according to *2020 Annual Report*, p. 86, the expenditures of the Tzu Chi Foundation were 62 percent of the total for Taiwan and 38 percent of the total for its international offices.
21. "City Officials, Neihu Residents Welcome Tzu Chi's Project Pullback," *Focus Taiwan*, March 16, 2015.
22. "United Daily News: Tzu Chi Row Reflects Three Social Changes," *Focus Taiwan*, March 3, 2015.
23. Buddhist Tzu Chi Foundation, *Buddhist Compassion Relief Tzu Chi Foundation Vision Statement: Gone through Half a Century, Striding into the Future* (Hualian, Taiwan: Tzu Chi Foundation, 2016).
24. Huang, *Charisma and Compassion*, 52–55.
25. A 2020 book gives a good overview of Tzu Chi's environmental work since 1990. Shih Cheng Yen Shih, *Ciji huanbao sanshi: yong guwode shuangshou zuo huanbao* [Tzu Chi Environmental Protection at Thirty: Do Recycling with Clapping Hands] (Taipei: Jing Si Renwen, 2020).
26. Teresa Chang, trans., "Words from Dharma Master Cheng Yen—It's Time to Be a Vegetarian," Tzu Chi Culture and Communication Foundation, March 2021.
27. See, for example, Buddhist Tzu Chi Foundation, *Sustainability Report, 2018–2019* (Hualian, Taiwan: Tzu Chi Foundation, 2020), 21–23.
28. Buddhist Tzu Chi Foundation, *2021 Tzu-Chi Almanac* (Hualian, Taiwan: Tzu Chi Foundation, 2021), 545.
29. Buddhist Tzu Chi Foundation, *Holding Together*, 12–42.
30. Elise Anne DeVido, *Taiwan's Buddhist Nuns* (Albany, NY: State University of New York Press, 2010), 49–46; and Buddhist Tzu Chi Foundation, *Tzu Chi Annual Report, 2019* (Hualian, Taiwan: Tzu Chi Foundation, 2020), 2.
31. Buddhist Tzu Chi Foundation, *Sustainability Report, 2018–2019*, 8–13.
32. Buddhist Tzu Chi Foundation, *Inspiring Great Love*, 48–57; and "Tzu Chi COVID-19 Relief Effort Updates across Southeast Asia," Tzu Chi Center, June 29, 2021.
33. "COVID-19 Relief in India and Southeast Asia: Compassion Knows no Borders," Tzu Chi Center, May 26, 2021; and "Tzu-Chi's COVID-19 Aid to India: Bringing People Together, a Testament to Human Generosity and Kindness," Tzu Chi Center, May 14, 2021.
34. If one chooses the English terms "humanism" or "humanistic," one should consider the long intellectual history of these terms from pre-Socratic times onward, as well as the history of Confucian ideas about the primacy of the human realm.
35. See DeVido, *Taiwan's Buddhist Nuns*, 93–101.
36. Jiang Canteng, "Cong rensheng fojiao dao renjian fojiao" [From "Buddhism for Human Life" to "Buddhism for the Human Realm"], in *Taiwan fojiao yu xiandai shehui* [Taiwanese Buddhism and Modern Society], ed. Canteng Jiang (Taipei: Dongda, 1992), 180.
37. For more details, see Charles B. Jones, *Buddhism in Taiwan: Religion and the State, 1660–1990* (Honolulu: University of Hawaii Press, 1999), 97–115, 137–152.

38. See the books by Stuart Chandler, *Establishing a Pure Land on Earth: The Foguang Buddhist Perspective on Modernization and Globalization* (Honolulu: University of Hawaii Press, 2004); Jens Reinke, *Mapping Modern Mahāyāna: Chinese Buddhism and Migration in the Age of Global Modernity* (Berlin: De Gruyter Oldenbourg, 2021); and Jimmy Yu, *Reimagining Chan Buddhism: Sheng Yen and the Creation of the Dharma Drum Lineage of Chan* (New York: Routledge, 2022). For more information on different aspects of Taiwan's *renjian fojiao* and some discussion of the Tzu Chi organization, see ORE entries on Fo Guang Shan; Buddhist Missionaries; Taixu; Hsing Yun; and Engaged Buddhism.
39. "慈濟故事50-以苦為師慈濟" [The Tzu Chi Story 50—Establishing the Tzu Chi School of Buddhism], Da Ai TV, October 5, 2019.
40. "Famai zhengchuan, zongmen zhengli" [Rightly Transmit the Lineage, Rightly Establish the School], Principles of the Jing Si Dharma Lineage and Tzu Chi School of Buddhism, October 7, 2016.
41. "Famai zhengchuan, zongmen zhengli."
42. An early work on both Tzu Chi Youth Pure Practitioners is Wang Yuping, *Rang shijie hexie: quanqiu ciqing yu qingxiushide shijianzhilu* [Let the World Be Reconciled: Global Ci Ji Youth and Pure Practitioners' Path of Practice] (Taipei: Tianxia Wenhua, 2012). A brief piece on the Pure Practitioners is "Qingxiushi zhongshen fengxian jingshe wei jia" [Pure Practitioners Life-Long Dedication to the Pure Abode as Home], October 17, 2019.
43. CBETA 電子佛典集成 » 大正藏 (T) » 第 9 冊 » no. 0276» 第 1 卷無量義經德行品第一[0384B04]: 靜寂清澄，志玄虛漠，守之不動億百千劫，無量法門悉現在前；得大智慧，通達諸法. Translation in Pan Xuan, *50 Years on the Bodhisattva Path* (Taipei: Tzu Chi, 2019), 448.
44. Buddhist Tzu Chi Foundation, "Faith," 2022.
45. See Chien-te (Kent) Lin, "Churu yu shengsu zhijian—fojiao cishan shiyezhi chubu sikao" [Passing through the Holiness and the Worldliness: An Exploration on the Buddhist Charity Enterprise], *Xuanzang Foxue Yanjiu* 28 (September 2017): 105–136.
46. See this important work that explores "the economy of goodness" through comparative study of different traditions of altruism. Her Rey-sheng, *Shan jingji: jingjide lita sixiang yu shijian* [The Economy of Goodness: The Philosophy and Practices from the Perspectives of Altruism] (Taipei: Lianjing, 2020).
47. C. Julia Huang's *Charisma and Compassion* has insights into the many aspects of the "Tzu Chi body," 11–12, and "Weeping and Musical Corporeality," 124–152, 175–183.
48. Or, "embodied compassion in action" suggested by a peer reviewer.
49. See Ruben Habito, "Bodily Reading of the Lotus Sutra: Understanding Nichiren's Buddhism," Japanese Journal of Religious Studies 26, no. 3–4 (1999): 298.
50. Liu, *Lotus Flower of the Heart.*
51. Xuan, *50 Years on the Bodhisattva Path.*
52. For example, Hwei-syin Lu, "Gender and Buddhism in Contemporary Taiwan," 539–550; and Hwei-syin Lu, *Renqinghua da'ai: duomianxiang de cij gongtongti* [Great Love with Human Feelings: The Multi-Faceted Tzu Chi Community] (Taipei: Nantian Books, 2011). See a description in Chinese of Hwei-syin Lu's research and a list of her publications here.
53. C. Julia Huang and Robert P. Weller, "Merit and Mothering: Women and Social Welfare in Taiwanese Buddhism," *Journal of Asian Studies* 57, no. 2 (1998): 379–396.
54. Madsen, *Democracy's Dharma.*
55. Laliberté, *The Politics of Buddhist Organizations in Taiwan, 1989–2003*, 86–105.
56. Laliberté, *The Politics of Buddhist Organizations*, 98–100.
57. Shih Cheng Yen, "九到十一日和合互協聚眾力 [*Jiu dao shiyiri hehe huxie juzhongli*]," *Tzu Chi Monthly* 576, February 25, 2016.
58. Buddhist Tzu Chi Foundation, *Sustainability Report, 2015* (Hualian, Taiwan: Tzu Chi Foundation, 2020), 26–27.

59. Yu-Shuang Yao, *Taiwan's Tzu Chi as Engaged Buddhism: Origins, Organization, Appeal and Social Impact* (Leiden, the Netherlands: Brill, 2012).
60. Yao, *Taiwan's Tzu Chi as Engaged Buddhism*, 227, 229.
61. See Lu Hwei-Syin, "Sanctification of the Corpse, Transcendence of the Death: The Religious and Cultural Phenomena of Tzu Chi's Body Donation," *Journal of Life-and-Death Studies* 11 (2011): 89–174; Rey-Sheng Her, "The Silent Mentors of Tzu Chi," *Journal of the Oxford Centre for Buddhist Studies* 4 (2013): 47–74; Scott Santibañez, Debra Boudreaux, Guo-Fang Tseng, and Kimberly Konkel, "The Tzu Chi Silent Mentor Program: Application of Buddhist Ethics to Teach Student Physicians Empathy, Compassion, and Self-Sacrifice," *Journal of Religion and Health* 55, no. 5 (October 2016): 1483–1494; Hung-Chieh Chang, "The Normalisation of Body Gifting in Taiwan," *Biosocieties* 11, no. 2 (2016): 135–151; and Rachel Douglas-Jones, "'Silent Mentors': Donation, Education and Bodies in Taiwan," *Medicine Anthropology Theory* 4, no. 4 (October 2017): 69–98.
62. Chengpang Lee, "The Forgotten Bonds: A Coevolutionary Framework on the Diffusion of Tzu Chi in Four Southeast Asian Countries," *American Behavioral Scientist* 64, no. 10 (2020): 1471–1484.
63. Aranya Siriphon and Sunanta Yamthap, "Religious Practices and Syncretization: The Tzu Chi Missions in the Northern Thai Border," *Regional Journal of Southeast Asian Studies* 4, no. 1 (January 2019): 20–40.
64. Arnold Lindros Lau and Jayeel Serrano Cornelio, "Tzu Chi and the Philanthropy of Filipino Volunteers," *Asian Journal of Social Science* 43, no. 4 (2015): 376–399.
65. Aristotle Chan Dy, "Buddhist Modernism in the Philippines: Emerging Localization of Humanistic Buddhism," *Religions* 13, no. 3 (2022): 220.
66. Tzu Chi Foundation Compilation Office, *Xinjiapo cijishi* [History of Tzu Chi Singapore] (Taipei: Jingdian zazhi, 2020).
67. Ooi Tan Lee, *Buddhist Revitalization and Chinese Religions in Malaysia* (Amsterdam: Amsterdam University Press, 2020).
68. Chengpang Lee and Ling Han, "Recycling Bodhisattva: The Tzu-Chi Movement's Response to Global Climate Change," *Social Compass* 62, no. 3 (2015): 311–325.
69. Yu-lieh Lou and Herman B. Leonard, eds., *Ciji zongmen de pushi jiazhi* [The Universal Value of Tzu Chi School of Buddhism] (Taipei: Jingdian Zazhi, 2017).
70. Rey-Sheng Her, "Zhengyan shangren li ciji zongmen zhi sixiang tixi" [Zhengyan Shangren's Establishment of the Tzu Chi School's System of Thought], in Lou and Leonard, *Ciji zongmen de pushi jiazhi*, 185–282.
71. Jiande (Kent) Lin, "Yinshun xuepai yu ciji zongmen: shilun yinshun sixiang dui cijizhiye kaizhan zhi keneng qifa" [An Investigation of Possible Inspiration the Tzu Chi Foundation Might Gain from the Thought of Yinshun], *Xuanzang Foxue Yanjiu* 17 (March 2012): 93–134.
72. See Yin-Cheng Network for Buddhist Studies (Tzu Chi Foundation). Accessed October 15, 2022.
73. Jimmy Yu, *Reimagining Chan Buddhism: Sheng Yen and the Creation of the Dharma Drum Lineage of Chan* (New York: Routledge, 2022).
74. Tzu Chi Culture and Communication Foundation, "Wise Words for a Good Life: Three Decades of Jing Si Aphorisms," November 2019.

Elise Anne DeVido

V

THE VAJRAKĪLA TANTRAS

VEDIC ANTECEDENTS

According to the first book of the *Ṛgveda,* the demiurge Indra employed a *kīla*-like weapon before the world came into being in order to slay the primordial cosmic serpent Vṛtra, within whose coils were trapped "the waters of life."[1] As the primeval ocean was released life began, thus revealing the *kīla* as an instrument of paradox: a weapon having the power of both life and death. As a religious emblem it appears to kill and yet it creates life.

It is also said that during his act of creating the world, Indra pinned down the earth and propped up the heavens. Prior to that, earth and heaven were not separated. Thus the spike can be seen to possess a cosmic dimension as a weapon that spans both earth and heaven. The special function of its lower part is to stabilize the earth, while its upper part leads to the realm of the gods.[2]

These early themes remained discernible through the centuries within the complex mythology of the Buddhist *kīla*. The idea of a spike that kills and liberates, a spike that strikes into the earth and reaches up to heaven, became absorbed into Buddhism and eventually arose as the focal point of a tantric cult dedicated to the worship of the esoteric deity Vajrakīla, who bears as his special symbol the ancient pointed spike adopted as a powerful instrument of ritual and magic.

A preliminary step toward the Buddhist assimilation of the *kīla* was probably the annual circumscription of an area within which the sangha would have been expected to remain for the duration of the summer season rains retreat. As the monks were engaged in pegging out the boundaries of their sacred domicile with wooden stakes and lengths of cord, they would undoubtedly have wished those boundaries to remain secure against the onslaughts of Māra, who could be relied upon to try and disturb their meditations. Thus, as the stakes were hammered into the ground, the myth of Indra versus Vṛtra may have come to mind and been recast in Buddhist form.

Any demarcation of a circumference automatically creates a center and, for all practical purposes, a wooden stake is again the natural implement with which to mark out the central spot. In the section concerning the delineation of the mandala in chapter eleven of the *Sarvatathāgatatattvasaṃgraha Tantra* (STTS 91) it is written: "Having pierced the acacia wood spike in the centre of the maṇḍala, make a double-threaded string (and) with that, one should delineate (the circle). On that occasion, this is the "heart essence" of the kīla; Oṃ Vajrakīla, you must nail down. Transfix all obstructors! Hūṃ phaṭ!"

SACRED ARCHITECTURE

Indian treatises on temple architecture describe a number of operations for which the use of wooden pegs is required. For the most part these pegs are nailed into the earth in order to establish the outline of the building to be constructed, and the texts describe the distances that are required to lie between these wooden pegs and the manner in which the whole area is to be divided up by further stakes and lengths of string so as to facilitate the delineation of the full temple plan upon the ground.

The initial prescription in such treatises is to locate, by astrological methods, the earth-dwelling *nāga* spirit within whose domain the architects wish to construct their edifice. It is then possible to stabilize the building site by fixing that *nāga* with a *kīla* judiciously driven into the earth.[3]

Throughout this process, the *kīla* serves as both boundary marker and holder of the center, where "center" refers not to a single point but to a vertical axis rising up through the highest point of the temple spire to the heavens above. Having stabilized the ground below, the upright line of the peg itself also acts as a conduit to the realm of the gods.

Linking the placement of the *indrakīla* with the establishment of the *bodhimaṇḍa*, quoting from the *Pūjāvaliya*, Lily de Silva says: "[it] is a great fortress protected by the majestic wall of the ten pāramitā, extending up to the cupola of the Brahmā world. Even Māra with his vast array of forces could not get past this formidable barrier."[4] The later tantric rites of *kīlana*, in which an area is sanctified by nailing it down with a group of ten *kīla*, establish just such a formidable barrier against Māra and his hordes, surrounding and enclosing the sacred palace (or fortress) of the *bodhimaṇḍala*. In the rite of initiation through which this protective power is transmitted, these ten *kīla* are explicitly associated with the ten *pāramitā* or perfections of practice on the path to enlightenment.

Even in its most simple form, the rite of striking pegs into the four corners of a site marking out the ground plan of a stupa or *vihāra* is regarded as establishing a protective boundary (Skt. *rakṣācakra*) capable of repelling all harm.[5] As it says in the *Āryamañjuśrīmūlakalpa*: "Having prepared kīla of acacia wood, empowered by 108 recitations of mantra, they should be embedded in the four directions. That is the way in which the boundaries are sealed."[6]

This idea may have been established in Buddhist practice at a remarkably early period, because literary evidence for the use of the *kīla* as a magical implement is to be found in the *dhāraṇī*, some of which conceivably date right back to the 3rd or 4th centuries BCE, and the earliest extant pegs of this type, in which the form of the *kīla* unambiguously reflects its identification with a wrathful divinity, are believed to have been carved in the 1st century BCE. They were discovered by the archaeologist and explorer Sir Marc Aurel Stein among the debris associated with the ancient watchtowers situated at the southwest extremity of the frontier defense system to the north of Dunhuang. Together with other artifacts discovered there, Stein describes a number of *kīla* to which were originally attached loops of string. He describes these items as resembling tent pegs and exhibiting evident signs of having been pegged into the ground and yet "certainly not strong enough to have served as real tent pegs." Some of these pegs bore Chinese inscriptions that could only make sense if read as personal names, but no indication is given as to whether they might be the personal names of men or gods. The evidence put forward by Stein for dating these finds to the 1st century BCE seems overwhelming.[7]

The theme of the apotropaic spike, having come to the surface in the early *dhāraṇī*, was subsequently developed extensively within the *kriyā*- and *yogatantra* of the later periods. Throughout this time spikes came to be employed increasingly in rituals of mundane sorcery, which seem to have posed no moral dilemma for their perpetrators, even within a Buddhist context.

Although the "heart essence" mantra of Vajrakīla is to be found in the fundamental *yogatantra Sarvatathāgatatattvasaṃgraha Tantra* (STTS) and, as pointed out by authorities on tantric practice, "the mantra is the god," the absolute deification of the sacred spike and its transformation into an awesome god of terrible wrath seems not to have been finally completed until the period of the "unexcelled yoga tantra" (Skt. *yoganiruttaratantra*). By this time the spike that brought death and destruction to its opponents came also to be regarded as the harbinger of liberation, a bestower of *nirvana*. As a symbol of absolute stability, the paradoxical nature of the magic spike is expressed in the religious myth and ritual of the deity, which everywhere depicts chaos as the natural condition of *samsara*. The mandala of the deified spike is a bloody charnel ground, in the center of which dwells the god in a palace of skulls, astride a throne of demonic corpses. His sanguinary sport (Skt. *līlā*) is the archetype of violent behavior, leading to a distinct antinomian trend in the religious ideals of his worshippers.

CONQUEST OF EVIL AND THE BIRTH OF VAJRAKĪLA

The received mythology of Vajrakīla, however, describes the archetypal struggle and final conquest of evil as against neither of the early demons (Māra and Vṛtra) but as the buddhas versus Rudra, reflecting the competition for patronage and power between the Buddhists and Śaivites (followers of Rudra). An early version of this myth is to be found in the fundamental text of the *yogatantra* class, with more developed portrayals in the later texts of Cakrasaṃvara and other Heruka manifestations.[8] The premier account, however, is given in the *Sūtra of the Gathered Intention* (*mDo dgongs pa 'dus pa*).[9]

According to this myth, during a previous eon of moral decline when Rudra, the arch demon of pride or egoism, held sway over the entire triple world, all the buddhas of the cosmos, unable through peaceful means to convince Rudra of the error of his ways, empowered a manifestation of great wrath in order to destroy him. At the time of his downfall, all of the males in the retinue of Rudra were killed and all of the females were raped. This is given a wholesome interpretation in the symbolic philosophy of the tantra where the masculine element is equated with creative imagination which, when perverted in the form of stubborn false views and pride, must be destroyed. The feminine element is said to be the "empty" (Skt. *śūnya*) nature of all manifestation and this is to be penetrated by the vajra mind (vajra = penis) in search of wisdom. The rape of Rudra's demonic wife by the buddhas' wrathful manifestation resulted in the immediate birth of a son called Vajrakumāra (Vajra Youth), half *heruka* buddha and half *rākṣasī* demon. This "Son of Heruka," also known as Vajrarākṣasa in remembrance of his maternal line, was the first earthly embodiment of Vajrakīla. He was both ugly as a demon and beautiful as a buddha. Outwardly violent and inwardly tranquil, he was noble, base, arrogant, and loving, a divine mystery as full of contradictions as his Vedic namesake.

The *Chronicles of Profound Fierce Mantra* (*Drag sngags zab pa'i lo rgyus*) states: "As for his name Vajra, this signifies the unborn dharmatā. His name Kumāra signifies freedom from old age and decrepitude. That itself is the uncontrived and unmistaken truth which is impartial and does not fall to any side."[10] And the *Black Razor Tantra* (BRT) says: "This is the form of the wisdom manifestation of all the buddhas, the unbearable configuration of blazing wrath that emanates from the very nature of the vajradharmadhātu."

When the monstrous body of the demon Rudra was conquered and hurled from the peak of Mount Malaya, it was scattered into the eight directions. The four divisions of his trunk (head, heart, intestines, and genitals) landed in the cardinal quarters, and his four limbs fell down in the intermediate directions. These areas are renowned in the myths as the eight great charnel grounds (*aṣṭamahāśmaśāna*) and they define the very mandala of Vajrakīla himself.

THE NATURE OF THE CONQUEROR

In chapter two of the *mūlatantra Black Razor Tantra* (BRT) it is written:

> In that place the bhagavat Mahāśrīvajrakumāra spoke these words: "Kyai! Pay attention to this, all you hosts here assembled! In the mighty charnel ground of the natural condition, reflected forms, like the images in a mirror or the moon in water, abide in the sphere of natural meaning without being covered by the stains of the afflictions. The teacher is like a miraculous display in the sky, teaching the Dharma of fierce mantra in the supreme charnel ground of the natural state." Thus he spoke.

And in chapter three:

> [When it is said that] he is the supreme son of all tathāgata, the word "son" means that he comes without birth from the dharmatā and "supreme" means that he is the spontaneous fulfilment of enlightened activity. He is the son of all of them in order to destroy Rudra. The "son" is the unborn vajra son.

Thus the deity Vajrakīla is presented as a numinous aspect of vibrant enlightenment, a potent force in the struggle against evil, immanent in a variety of (essentially illusory) forms. As "the son of the buddhas," he is a contrivance of enlightened wisdom (Skt. *prajñā*) specifically brought forth as a method (Skt. *upāya*) to overthrow the forces of darkness.

Appropriating the form and adornments of the conquered enemy, Vajrakīla is invariably dressed in the "spoils of war," those grisly clothes and ornaments of the charnel ground that were originally stripped from the body of the defeated Rudra and have subsequently been worn by all *heruka*. His clothing includes an upper garment of human skin, a cloak of elephant skin, and a skirt of tiger skin. Among his ornaments are the fivefold set made of bone associated with the five buddha families, numerous snakes encircling his limbs and body, a crown of five dry skulls, a necklace of fifty freshly severed heads, a belt of splintered bones, and so on. He is also characterized by the "ten attributes of glory" (Tib. *dpal gyi chas bcu*), which demonstrate his magnificent power and authority, and he paints his face with the "three ointments" (Tib. *byug pa'i rdzas gsum*): the dust of human ashes (Tib. *thal chen tshom bu*) on his forehead, drops of blood (Tib. *rakta'i thig le*) upon his cheeks, and a smear of fat (Tib. *zhag gi zo ris*) across his chin.[11] He is erotic and sensual. His captivating nine modes of dance (Skt. *navanāṭaka*) are at once alluring and repulsive and his dwelling is a gruesome palace made of skulls.[12]

Dark blue in color, representing the spacious nature of his primordially pure mind, the deity Vajrakīla has a ferocious white face on the right side of his head that destroys the afflictions of anger. His left red face annihilates all impurities of desire, and his central blue face vanquishes ignorance. Each face has an unblinking third eye in the center of its forehead, so that none of these mental defilements may pass by unnoticed.

Generally described as sporting in non-duality with his spouse, in his right hands he holds a nine-pronged vajra indicating his mastery of the nine *yāna* and the ten *bhūmi*, and a five-pronged vajra showing his possession of the five *jñāna*. In his left hands he holds a blazing mass of wisdom fire and a *khaṭvāṅga*, proclaiming his mastery of all techniques of yoga. With his final pair of hands he rolls a *kīla*, and the sky is filled with his vajra wings.

According to the tradition of the *Guhyagarbha Tantra*, his three faces indicate the destruction of the three poisons and the attainment of the three *kāya*.[13] His six arms show the ability to liberate beings in the six realms and his four legs symbolize his four modes of activity (Skt. *catvāri karmāni*) as well as the liberation of beings from the four kinds of birth (egg, womb, moisture, and miraculous). To this should be added that Vajrakīla simultaneously tramples down the four Māras: *skandha*, *kleśa*, *mṛtyu*, and *devaputra*.

His wild dance in the flames of wisdom that consume the appearances of the world demonstrates his passionate commitment to the vow of universal salvation, and icons of the deity depict an incestuous image of the union of Vajrakīla and his erotic playmate, his "simultaneously born" (Skt. *sahaja*) sister. This passionate embrace is to be read as a symbol of chastity—an image of desire fulfilled, not one of lustful yearning. Hinting at the yogic technique of coitus reservatus, Vajrakīla's perpetual union with his consort marks the end of desire, just as their wild dance in the doomsday fire signifies the end of the tormenting heat of *kleśa*. The elemental interplay of sex and death is depicted here in an icon of extreme violence, the most powerfully destructive element of which is described in the tantras as the non-dual pounding thrust of their conjoined sexual organs.

THE TANTRAS OF VAJRAKĪLA

The *Necklace of Gems* (*Nor bu'i do shal*), composed by Trinley Dudjom ('Phrin las bdud 'joms, 1725–1789) as an introduction to the doctrines of Vajrakīla for a group of his disciples about to become initiated into the cult, states at the outset the author's belief that a single Vajrayāna empowerment encompasses within itself every aspect of the path and goal.[14] However, "for those who cannot grasp this immensity within a single maṇḍala," he says that the buddha taught the two vehicles known as "the causal vehicle of dialectics" (Tib. *mtshan nyid rgyu yi theg pa*) and "the resultant vajra vehicle" (Tib. *'bras bu rdo rje'i theg pa*). The teachings of the former are contained within the *sutra* and those of the latter within the tantra.

These two vehicles of cause and result may, alternatively, be considered under three rubrics as "the vehicle that controls the source of suffering" (Tib. *kun 'byung 'dran pa'i theg pa*), "the vehicle of the outer tantra of austere awareness" (Tib. *phyi dka' thub rig pa'i rgyud kyi theg pa*), and "the vehicle of overpowering means" (Tib. *dbang bsgyur thabs kyi theg pa*).[15] Each of these three *yāna* has three divisions, and thus there are the nine vehicles of the: (1) Śrāvaka, (2) Pratyekabuddha, and (3) bodhisattva, who are followers of the Hīnayāna and Mahāyāna *sutras* that control the source of suffering through renunciation, wisdom, and compassion; (4) Kriyātantra, (5) Ubhayatantra, and (6) Yogatantra, which, by means of austere awareness, gradually transform the universe and its inhabitants into a sacred mandala populated with deities; and (7) Mahāyogatantra, (8) Anuyogatantra, and (9) Atiyogatantra, which, respectively, emphasize the skillful means of the generation stage (Skt. *utpattikrama*), the discriminative awareness of the completion stage (Skt. *saṃpannakrama*), and the pristine cognition free of duality that is the great perfection of the final result. Within this ninefold scheme, the canon of Vajrakīla embodies the skillful means (Skt. *upāya*) of the Yoganiruttaratantra, a general term for the teachings of the seventh, eighth, and ninth vehicles. Generally in rNying ma literature these three are known as "the inner tantra," within which category the doctrines of Vajrakīla pertain mostly to Mahāyoga but are not limited by this.[16] As it is said:

> Generated in accord with Mahāyogatantra,
> One meditates upon him on the path of Anuyoga
> As the illusory nature of the mind itself.
> He is finally perfected as the result of Atiyoga,
> Quite effortlessly. Free of origination and cessation.[17]

According to traditional accounts, the doctrines of Vajrakīla were first taught among the heavenly (Skt. *deva*) and subterranean (Skt. *nāga*) spirits before being transmitted to the human realm. They were subsequently propagated in India by Indrabhūti, Dhanasaṃskṛta, Śrīsiṃha, Prabhahasti, and an unnamed *kāpālika* brahmin. Kīla chronicles, such as the *Concise History* written by Tsang Kenchen (gTsang mkhan chen) and the *History of the Meteoric Razor* (*gNam lcags spu gri lo rgyus chos 'byung*) by bDud 'joms Rin po che, say that these Vajrakīla doctrines were taught by Indrabhūti to Dhanasaṃskṛta, who then passed them on to Padmasambhava, Vimalamitra, and Śīlamañju.[18] These three companions additionally received teachings from Prabhahasti. Furthermore, the doctrines of Vajrakīla are said to have been taught in Khotan by Vairocana, who studied in India under Śrīsiṃha. Unfortunately, however, no pertinent Indic text survives from this period and only very little is known of the masters who were responsible for the transmission of the *kīla* doctrines during that far-off epoch.

VAJRAKĪLA STUDIES

In recent years a great surge of interest has been shown in the rNying ma tantras in general and the tantras of Vajrakīla in particular by international scholars, both Tibetan and non-Tibetan.

Tradition holds that Padmasambhava introduced a very large body of Vajrakīla teachings to Tibet, as practiced to this day within all schools, especially those of the rNying ma and Sa skya, for in the *Hundred Thousand Tantras of the Early Translation Period* (*rNying ma'i rgyud 'bum*, NGB) alone are more than forty-one major treatises filling three entire volumes.[19] The popularity of these doctrines was such that countless "treasure texts" (Tib. *gter ma*) have subsequently been brought forth by appointed "revealers of hidden treasure" to supplement those originally taught, and a recent project to gather together all of these teachings and texts resulted in a published compilation of over 1,300 texts in forty-five large volumes.[20]

Over the years, an increasing number of English-language books have carried passing references to either the deity Vajrakīla or to symbolic *kīla* as encountered in Tibetan iconography or ritual. Of particular note is the classic *Oracles and Demons of Tibet* by René de Nebesky-Wojkowitz, for the large number of instances cited in this text clearly demonstrate the ubiquity of the ritual *kīla* as a magic weapon throughout the entire realm of Tibetan tantrism. The first monograph on such items was by John Huntington (*The Phur-pa: Tibetan Ritual Daggers*), in which a number of ritual *kīla* are described in terms of length, weight, material of manufacture, and so on.[21]

An important early study was made by Bischoff and Charles Hartman on the manuscript from Dunhuang listed as "Pelliot tibétain 44," said to be "possibly the oldest document in existence referring to Padmasambhava" and considered by Prof. Giuseppe Tucci as a major proof of the siddha's historicity.[22] Its theme is the summoning of the *Kīla Vidyottama Tantra* from Nālandā University to the Asura cave in Nepal. In their introduction to the text, the translators deal with the problem of the widespread assertion in Tibetan literature that the Sanskrit term for *phur ba* is *kīlaya* (with or without a long i), when all dictionaries and Sanskrit works agree the word to be *kīla* (or *kīlaka*). This would seem to be due to an indiscriminate use by Tibetans of the dative singular *kīlāya*. This form would have been familiar to them in the simple salutation "namo vajrakīlāya" ("homage to Vajrakīla"), from which it could easily be assumed by those unfamiliar with the technicalities of Sanskrit that the name of the deity is Vajrakīlāya instead of Vajrakīla. It should also be noted that the term (*vajra*)*kīlaya* is frequently found in Sanskrit texts (as well as in virtually every *kīlanamantra*), legitimately used as the denominative verb "to spike," "transfix," "nail down," and so on.

Many Tibetan monasteries host annual "festivals of great attainment" (Tib. *phur pa sgrub chen*) in honor of Vajrakīla, and various international Buddhist groups led by Tibetan lamas in far-flung parts of the world have translated the ritual practice texts of Vajrakīla into English and other languages, publishing them privately for their own group meditations.

Major academic studies of Vajrakīla literature have been made by Martin Boord, Cathy Cantwell, and Robert Mayer. Other academic studies of a more general nature that have a particular bearing on the subject of wrathful tantric deities include the works of Jacob Dalton, Gyurme Dorje, and Rob Linrothe (see the bibliography of "Secondary Sources").

CONTENTS OF THE TANTRAS

The Kīla Vidyottama Tantra. At one time, it is said, the *mahāsiddha* Padmasambhava dispatched two messengers to his guru Prabhahasti requesting assistance to tame certain obstacles that were disturbing his meditation practice in Nepal. His guru responded by sending him "the Kīla Vidyottama Tantra in one hundred thousand sections," a set of teachings so massive that his two messengers could barely carry it.[23] A text by the name of *Vidyottama Tantra* (*Āryavidyottama mahātantra*) is found in all editions of the bKa' 'gyur (P. 402), but this is not the one referred to here. If there ever was in India such a text or collection of texts bearing this name and focused on the doctrines of Vajrakīla, then it was lost long ago. More probably, however, the name is intended generally as *locus ascriptus* for the store of ideas pertaining to the deity without reference to a particular presentation of precepts. It may thus serve as a generic term for the vast conglomeration of individual treatises such as those currently found in Tibet (the title pages of many of which proclaim their descent from such a matrix) as well as to the oral tradition that accompanies them. Also, it is not necessary to assume that this huge volume of teachings was ever written down on paper, for mystics the world over have always been capable of reading volumes into a few key words or sentences. The staggering weight of the doctrines conveyed at this time may simply be a metaphor for their great importance. The ambiguity of the various Kīla chronicles tends to confirm this hypothesis, for the title occurs as an article of faith in almost every Vajrakīla lineage, despite an acknowledgment of their discrete inceptions and the absence of any such named text.

The doctrines of Vajrakīla were at one time rejected as spurious by various teachers of the "new schools" (Tib. *gsar ma*) on the grounds that no original Sanskrit texts could be produced in evidence of their authenticity. All such opposition is said to have been crushed, however, when Kunga Gyaltsen (Sa skya Paṇḍita Kun dga' rgyal mtshan, 1182–1252) is said to have discovered in Shangsreg zhing (Shangs sreg zhing) a Sanskrit text that belonged to Padmasambhava himself. This short text, the *Vajrakīla-mūlatantrakhaṇḍa* (VKMK), now known only through Sa skya Paṇḍita's Tibetan translation (*rDo rje phur pa rtsa ba'i rgyud kyi dum bu*), includes many key elements that arise again and again in the literature of the cult as a whole, and it is included in the tantra section of the canonical "Translated Words of the Buddha" (bKa' 'gyur P. 78).[24]

Doctrinal Themes in the Vajrakīla Tantras. Although the tantras of Vajrakīla are many in number, in brief it is said that there are two types—root tantra and explanatory tantra. According to the most authoritative commentary on the texts and practices of Vajrakīla, the root tantra (Skt. *mūlatantra*) is the *rTsa thung rdo rje khros pa* and there are 108 explanatory tantras including the *gSang rgyud* (*Guhya Tantra*), the *Khrag 'thung rtsa ba'i rgyud*, and so on.[25]

The stage of generation (Skt. *utpattikrama*) is taught in the *Kīlaguhya Tantra*, and the completion stage (Skt. *saṃpannakrama*) is fully revealed in the *Kīlanirvāṇa Tantra*.

From the standpoint of ultimate truth (Skt. *paramārthasatya*), its followers claim that the teachings of Vajrakīla encompass all the teachings of dharma, including the twelve categories of *sutra* teachings (Skt. *dharmapravacana*), the precious Tripitaka, the three trainings, the four classes of tantra, and so on.[26]

With regard to the twelve categories of buddha-word: because the tantra texts are divided into two categories, *sutra* and commentary, there are *sutra* of Vajrakīla. Because the fundamental texts are composed in verse, there is verse (Skt. *gāthā*). As evidenced by an abundance of examples, there are hymns of praise (Skt. *geya*). Because of the way in which Rudra was subjugated, there are marvelous stories (Skt. *adbhutadharma*). Because there are introductions to all of the tantric traditions, there are introductions (Skt. *nidāna*). And so it goes with the rest.

Then, as for the Tripitaka: since the doctrines of Vajrakīla are manifest in a manner beyond the reach of the rational mind, they pertain to "the basket of philosophical and psychological analyses" (Skt. *abhidharma piṭaka*). Since they teach many fundamental and secondary vows, they pertain to "the basket of regulations of good conduct" (Skt. *vinaya piṭaka*). And, since they demonstrate both relative and ultimate truths, they pertain to "the basket of discourses" (Skt. *sūtra piṭaka*).

With regard to the three trainings: because the Vajrakīla doctrines contain many teachings concerning the bestowal of wise counsel and the protection of vows, there is training in morality (Skt. *śīla*). Training in wisdom (Skt. *prajñā*) is demonstrated by the teachings on voidness, and the many meditations (Skt. *dhyāna*) on the generation and completion stages reveal training in meditation (Skt. *samādhi*).

Furthermore, the deeds to be performed with body and speech are revealed in *kriyātantra*, and those to be done with the mind are taught in *yogatantra*. Activities of both body and mind are revealed in *ubhayatantra*, and the enjoyment of the five meats and five nectars constitute the teachings of the *niruttaratantra*.

HIGHER RITES LEADING TO THE ATTAINMENT OF UNSURPASSED AWAKENING (*BODHICITTA*)

Before beginning the practice of Vajrakīla, the yogin should prepare himself by receiving initiation and taking vows, select an auspicious location and suitable helpmates, familiarize himself with the proper series of ritual activities, and choose an astrologically propitious time to begin. As it is written in the *Tongue of Flames Tantra* (*Kī la ya me lce gsang ba'i rgyud*):

> Place and person, retinue, activity and time,
> When these five excellences are present
> All one's deeds, whatever is wished for, will be accomplished.

Then the yogin embarks upon the seven steps of the prior approach (Tib. *sngon 'gro*, Skt. *pūrvaṅgama*) to the triple mandala: (1) establishing the boundaries, (2) opening the symbolic doors, (3) paying homage to the symbols, (4) applying the sect-marks, (5) confessing sins, (6) the descent of blessings, and (7) sanctifying the three articles. These constitute the general preliminaries for all magical rites, both peaceful and fierce.

With regard to the method of establishing the boundaries: outwardly there is the ceremonial performance of the ritual, inwardly there is the annihilation of difficult circumstances and obstructions, and secretly there is one's realization, be it subtle or coarse.

With regard to the nature of the boundaries: there is the essential boundary of the view, the personal boundary of generating oneself as the deity, and the protective boundary of mantra and *mudrā*.

Secured within these boundaries, the yogin opens the doors to the mandala and pays homage to the deities within. Then, in order to bring himself into alignment with his brothers in the cult of Vajrakīla, he applies spots of blood to the raised areas of both cheeks and the bridge of his nose, draws three lines upon his forehead with a handful of human ashes, and draws a vajra and half-moon upon his heart with a smear of fat. In this manner the yogin creates a vajra connection and demonstrates his allegiance to the group.

Purifying himself by a confession of all his faults, the yogin seeks the personal blessing of all the mandala deities, and then he sets out three sacred *samaya* substances upon the altar: to the right he places white *amṛta* (nectar), to the left he places red *rakta* (blood), and in the center he places a blue *bali* (offering cake). Each of these has an important significance within the cult and, being blessed, is said to bestow great blessings.

The preliminaries having been completed, the main practice begins with generating the triple *samādhi* of the basis, known as the *samādhi* of "thusness" (Skt. *tathatā*), the all-illuminating *samādhi* (Skt. *samantāvabhāsa*), and the *samādhi* of the cause (Skt. *hetu*). From this primary cause arises the divine mandala palace of Vajrakīla and his retinue, the pure symbolism (Skt. *viśuddhi*) of which is expounded upon in the *Guhya Tantra*:

The utterly pure nature of the maṇḍala palace
Will now be explained by me in total purity.
The arising of the vajra tent
Is a sign that it cannot be impeded by outer obstacles (*vighna*).
Its being adorned by a retinue of obedient servants
Is a sign that it cannot be harmed by inner demons (*māra*).
Its being clearly situated within the triangular dharmodaya[27]
Symbolises its origin from the dharmadhātu.
The fact that it is created of the four elements
Shows that it is located within the lotuses ("sky") of the four mothers.
The fact that the palace is perfectly square
Symbolises the equality of buddhas and sentient beings.
The fact that it also has four doors
Symbolises the four foundations of mindfulness (*smṛtyupasthāna*)
And the four door-keepers are the five powers (*bala*).
Generating [the palace] with four triumphal archways
Is a sign of the four strenuous exertions (*saṃyakprahāṇa*).
Its having four "wheels of doctrine" (*dharmacakra*) [over the doorways]
Symbolises the four bases of miracle power (*ṛddhipāda*).
The offering goddesses of the five sensual qualities
Are a sign that the five faculties (*indriya*) are nourished and vitalised.

The necklaces and half-necklaces
Are explained as the seven branches of enlightenment (*bodhyaṅga*).
Its being adorned with eight pillars
Is explained as the noble eightfold path (*āryāṣṭāṅgamārga*).
The fivefold line [of the palace walls] is the five wisdoms
And the triangle [in the center] is the three [doors to] liberation.
Thus it is the perfect representation of all the teachings of cause and effect.

Having completed the generation of the mandala palace of residence, the yogin's next task is to generate the three groups of deities that dwell within: the fundamental assembly of the primordial state (Tib. *bdag nyid*), which has the nature of the *dharmakāya*; the assembly of wrathful kings in the ten directions, which has the nature of the *saṃbhogakāya*; and the assembly of material *kīla*, which has the nature of the *nirmāṇakāya*.

According to the Vajrakīla tantras, there are four causal beings of deity generation: In the beginning, when entering into solitary retreat, the yogin who has developed firm faith in his personal deity (Skt. *iṣṭadevatā*) is the pledge being (Skt. *samayasattva*). After that there is the meditation being (Skt. *samādhisattva*), who is generated by means of the three ritual meditations on the three *samādhi*. Then there is the divine wisdom being (Skt. *devajñānasattva*), which is the invited wisdom being, similar in form to oneself.[28] When those two are indissolubly united as one, that is the non-dual wisdom being (Skt. *advayajñānasattva*). When any one of these meditative steps is omitted in the generation, it is said to be non-meditation. The true state of meditation is not achieved so long as those four are incomplete.

With regard to the various guises in which the generated forms arise, from a certain perspective these are not really to be discriminated, for they arose following the teachings of authentic tantra. In the twelfth chapter of the *Guhya Tantra*, it is taught that the supreme Vajrakumāra has one thousand heads, one thousand arms, and one thousand times ten million eyes. In chapter four of the *Kīlanirvāṇa Tantra* it is taught that, when he subjugated Rudra, Vajrakumāra manifested nine heads and eighteen arms. In the root tantra of *Vajra Wrath* and so on, Vajrakumāra is taught with three heads and six arms. And according to the various tantra derived from the *Kīla Tantra in Twelve Chapters*, Vajrakumāra is taught with a single face and two arms. Therefore one must meditate in accordance with whatever teachings one has received. Similarly, the ten wrathful kings and so on are also taught in various guises.

As for the violent nature of the generated deities: their divine "wrath" is not the same as the anger of *māra* and *rākṣasa* demons. On the contrary, it manifests as a skillful means for the disciplining of those beings to be converted and one therefore meditates upon the deities by means of compassion and with a profundity of intellect. The supremely intelligent yogin meditates upon the deities as primordially pure. The one of mediocre intelligence meditates upon the deities as mere details of form, and the one of inferior capacity meditates upon the deities until he has achieved "divine pride" (Skt. *devatāhaṃkāra*), for it is just through divine pride that the follower of mantra becomes what is called "one on the path of the gods" (Tib. *lha lam pa*, Skt. **devapanthaka*).

With regard to the various levels of generation: the beginner generates what he knows as the deity. As it is said, "Meditating upon consciousness as the vajra [deity]."[29] One with a little experience meditates upon himself as the deity, in accordance with the words, "One must generate oneself in the form of the [deity's] body."[30] The mature practitioner meditates upon the aggregates of his person (Skt. *skandha*) as deities. As it is said, "Having established the aggregates as vajra."[31] One who has reached the final end of his practice meditates upon his entire environment as divine. As it is said, "[The whole of] existence is the deity Vajrakīla/ All who exist are Vajrakīla deities."[32]

It is stated in the *rTsa rgyud rdo rje khros pa*:
One's own mind, the Vajrakumāra of the base,
Is all-pervading, just as oil pervades the sesame seed.
Comprehending this is the great wonder of buddhahood.
Advancing forward, the Vajrakumāra of the path,
One attains wisdom and means, the three "buddha bodies" (kāya) and the five wisdoms.
One must engage in yoga uninterruptedly like the flow of a river.
Clear perception (abhisamaya), the Vajrakumāra of the result,
Is possessed of five kāya and nine wisdoms.
Thus the unmistaken realization is manifestly attained.
Achieving the base, the path, and the result,
One sees the face of the dharmakāya free of all mental propositions.

Also in the same tantra it is explained that one should meditate upon the yoga of the generation stage and the yoga of the perfection stage in unison:

Shining awareness refutes the view of nihilism (ucchedavāda).
Not grasping at this as reality refutes the view of eternalism (śāsvatavāda).
Completely ascertaining indissoluble appearance/emptiness,
One meditates in the manner of perfect non-arising.

Thus is explained the fundamental *dharmakāya* assembly of the primordial state, consisting of the yogin meditating upon himself as the central deity Vajrakumāra in union with his consort.

With regard to the *saṃbhogakāya* assembly of wrathful kings, it is taught in the *Guhya Tantra*:

Idle speech and falsehood, murder, wrong views and slander,
Taking what is not given, abusive words and a desire to harm,
Greed and sexual misconduct—these are the ten areas
Which the wrathful kings and queens arise to purify.

And their ten consorts are said to embody the ten perfections: knowledge, wisdom, morality, meditation, skill in means, enthusiastic perseverance, generosity, prayer, strength, and patience.

With regard to the *nirmāṇakāya* assembly of genuine Kīla sons, this is clearly defined in the words of a ubiquitous liturgical verse that describes the *nirmāṇakāya* as "the wisdom embodiment of all the buddhas."[33] This *nirmāṇakāya* is, in fact, the handheld material spike made of metal or wood that the yogin always carries on his person and with which he performs his sacred rituals for the benefit of all beings. In order for this material object to arise as "the wisdom embodiment of all the buddhas" and function as a *nirmāṇakāya* deity, it must receive a full series of consecrating empowerments (Skt. *abhiṣeka*), analogous to those received by the yogin himself as he embarked upon his religious career.

Thus, just as a king, even though he be possessed of retinue and wealth of enjoyments, is not truly entered into lordliness if the royal personage lacks charisma, so too, the Supreme Son must have his body, speech, and mind blessed as single-pointed wisdom. Therefore the yogin should meditate upon the syllable "hūṃ" on each of the three edges of the sharp-pointed blade, a syllable "phaṭ" on each of its three sides, and a white syllable "A" at the tip.

Furthermore, in the same way that a king, even though he be possessed of great charisma, does not truly become king if he is not anointed on the head with rites of consecration, here also, the empowerment of the five buddha families is required. Thus the yogin should imagine the five fingers of his right hand to be the lords of the five families, standing upon solar discs generated from the syllable "MA," and the five fingers of his left hand to be their five female consorts upon lunar discs generated from "A." Then he brings the fathers and mothers together in union and as the nectar (Skt. *bodhicitta*) of their union melts into the Supreme Son, the empowerment is received.

Then, just as the king must wear armor when going to war, in order to protect the *kīla* from the spells of his enemies, the yogin should recite the prescribed mantra and pour seeds of black or white mustard over the *kīla* as he imagines that the body becomes covered in armor, free of even the slightest chink.

When the king goes to battle, even though he is wearing armor he must also have a sharp-pointed weapon. So the yogin now tempers the tip of the *kīla* spike by holding it in the smoke of burning incense and, as smoke rises up from the incense, he imagines the *kīla* to become possessed of a savagely sharp tip—unbearably powerful, unassailable, unconquerable.

Just as that king requires his sharp-tipped weapon to be fierce in fighting against the enemy, now the yogin recites the *raktamantra* and anoints the spike with blood. Thus the *kīla*, the color of dark red smoke, is contemplated to have the power to conquer at a touch. As it is written in the root tantra:

> In order to grind the arrogant ones to dust,
> Smear with the blood of goat, dog and pig.

Just as a king who has conquered his opponents in battle must then take control of his enemy's territory, similarly, in the rites of the *kīla*, the yogin recites "*samaya tiṣṭha lhan*" and meditates upon establishing the separation of good and evil in the hearts of the enemies and obstructers. As it is written in the tantra:

> The quintessence of all the important pith instructions
> Is to mark out the border between vice and virtue.

LOWER RITES AIMED AT THE DESTRUCTION OF ENEMIES AND OBSTRUCTERS

The quintessence of the lower rites is the offering (Skt. *pūjā*) of union and slaughter, where "union" refers to the sexual union of the male and female wrathful deities, and "slaughter" refers to the "liberation" of the enemies and obstructers. In the performance of the rite, furthermore, the five fingers of the right hand are to be generated as the five fierce buddhas, and the five fingers on the left are to be generated as their five female consorts. Then, in the inconceivable space of the sex organs of the males appears a *hūṃ* that transforms into a vajra with blazing tip, and the yogin should imagine that the inconceivable sex organs of the females appear as triangular iron mortars, arisen from the syllable "E." Dragging forth the enemies and obstructers, they are placed within those mortars and, as one recites, "They must be pounded by the blazing vajra pestles," they are rebuked and pressed down by the vajra in one's hand.[34] Reciting a mantra, the bodies of the enemies and obstructers are pounded to fine particles, while their consciousness is absorbed into the tip of the vajra and raised up to take rebirth on the path to enlightenment in one of the buddha-fields. As a result of this, from the causal seed of ignorance develops the resultant fruit of five skull cups full of meat, and these are offered to the lords of the fundamental *dharmakāya* mandala of the primordial state. The yogin should then imagine that the leftovers are consumed by the deities of the other two mandala, while he himself appropriates the enemies' remaining life force and glory to enhance his own longevity.

The purpose of these lower rites is the annihilation of enemies and obstructers and, in this regard, the tantras teach that all the enemies and obstructers are subsumed within the "ten categories of those to be killed" (Tib. *bsgral ba'i zhing bcu*). This group of ten includes enemies of the guru, those who threaten the lives of mantra-holders, or those who bring dishonor to the Triple Gem and so on. As it is written in the *Phur pa khrag 'thung rtsa ba'i rgyud*:

> Those who bring dishonour to the Triple Gem,
> Cause harm to the Buddhist religion,
> Embezzle the property of the saṅgha,
> Slander the Mahāyāna,
> Place the life of the guru in danger,
> Sow discord among the vajra assembly,
> Interrupt the attainment of siddhi and
> Turn away from that which is sacred (i.e. abandon their vows),
> Cruel demons (rākṣasa) devoid of compassion
> Who profess the perverted views of non-Buddhists,
> Adversaries of those who strive in religious practice (sādhaka).
> These are the ten kinds of being who must be destroyed.

SYNOPSIS

In general, there is a division into four varieties of *kīla*, corresponding to four types of person who penetrate the extreme. As it is written in the root tantra:

> The kīla of wisdom awareness
> Is implanted in the realm free of subject and object.
> Success is measured in radiant realization

And the fruit is the attainment of the unborn dharmakāya.
If this is not successfully realised, one roams in saṃsāra.
The kīla of boundless compassion
Is implanted into beings with love and compassion.
Success is the realization of the non-duality of self and others
And the result is the attainment of the saṃbhogakāya.
Failing this, one falls into the demonic state of Rudra.
The kīla of higher bodhicitta
Is implanted in the pure depths of the mother's sky.
The measure of its success is an insubstantial bliss,
The result of which is to gain the indivisible three bodies (trikāya).
If this is not successfully realised, one shores up the banks of saṃsāra.
The material kīla of visible characteristics
Are the kīla of pacification, enrichment, control and the wrathful rites.
As it says in the *Guhya Tantra*:
Silver or any variety of white wood
Are materials for the kīla of pacification.
Gold or any variety of yellow wood
Are materials for the kīla of increasing virtue.
Copper or any variety of red wood
Are materials for the controlling kīla of supreme speech.
Iron or any variety of black wood
Are materials for the kīla of the wrathful rites.
It is written in the *Kīlanirvāṇa Tantra*:
"Kī" is the sphere beyond creation
And "la" means without cessation.
"Kī" stands for the dharmadhātu
And "la" is the wisdom of awareness.
Non-dual nirvāṇa, transcending suffering,
The mental essence of mind itself is the kīla,
The very truth of truth itself is the kīla,
Kīla is the essential characteristic of the sky.
If one meditates with clarity, generation is achieved.
If it is non-dual, union is achieved.
If the realization is resplendent, success is achieved.
If all mental factors are under control, slaying is achieved.

Thus there are two broad categories: absolute *kīla* and relative *kīla*. With regard to the first type, it is written in the tantra:

The true meaning of the kīla is the wisdom of awareness,
The sphere of which is said to be the entire dharmadhātu.

The second type, relative *kīla*, are those made of the five types of metal or wood, and one of these is to be carried on the person of the initiated yogin at all times. They are described in the *Kīlanirvāṇa Tantra*:

The upper knot on the kīla handle is the dharmakāya,
And the lower knot is the saṃbhogakāya.
The tip is the nirmāṇakāya.
So, from head to tip it is without fault and
It should be properly fashioned in three-edged form.

Initiates into the cult of Vajrakīla are urged to strive for supreme and perfect enlightenment for the benefit of all living beings and are cautioned that it would be a grave mistake to follow only the path of the yoga of generation because this would lead to rebirth as Rudra or as a god in the realm of desire. Thus, it is said, it is very important to engage in the methods of the completion stage, in which that which has been emanated is reabsorbed, that which has been assembled is dissolved, the focus of one's awareness is "thusness" itself, and one perseveres in the view that the body of the deity is the absence of self-nature (Skt. *niḥsvabhāva*) within a manifest appearance of light, which is the indivisible unity of clear appearance and emptiness. This is the seal of the *nirmāṇakāya*. The speech of the deity is the quiescent sound of the dharma, which is the indivisible unity of sound and emptiness. This is the seal of the *saṃbhogakāya*. The mind of the deity is great bliss, which itself is the indivisible unity of awareness and emptiness. This is the seal of the *dharmakāya* and, subsequently, the practitioner should hold firmly to the pride of himself as the deity Vajrakumāra, bringing benefit to all he meets whether he be walking, standing, sitting, or lying down.

REVIEW OF LITERATURE

Native Tibetan scholars recognize two distinct genres of literature related to *guhyamantra*: root texts (*tantra*), in which the mythology of the deity is to be found, and texts outlining the "means of attainment" (Skt. *sādhana*), by means of which a yogic practitioner can attain the status of the deity. Commentaries written by lineage holders focus almost exclusively on the *sādhana* texts, often drawing on the root *tantra* for support, and such studies may deal with the history of the practice, listing the important masters of the lineage and their enlightened activities and so on, or they may seek to clarify points of ritual procedure or the order of service and so on. Lineage masters may also compose additional liturgy that becomes incorporated into the *sādhana*, so that the transmitted text grows with time, but the *tantra* are never expected to be altered in any way.

As a result of the Chinese Communist takeover of Tibet in the latter half of the 20th century and the subsequent diaspora of a large number of Tibetan religious teachers, the religious practice of Vajrakīla has been spread throughout the world. This is reflected in the currently available literature, which is heavily weighted in favor of ritual meditation manuals (*sādhana*), privately published in Tibetan Buddhist centers around the world. Due to the traditional tantric code of secrecy, however, these volumes of translated invocations, praises, prayers, and ritual activity are not easily obtained without first visiting the various centers and receiving initiation and permission from a recognized authority. A small number of commentaries on ritual practice, on the other hand, originating in a similar manner outside of Tibet, have become publicly accessible in recent years. Examples include the oral teachings given by Khenpo Namdrol Rinpoche at Kunzang Palyul Chöling, Poolsville, Maryland, United States, in June 1995, subsequently published as *Vajrakilaya*; and a compilation of oral instructions on the practice of Vajrakīla delivered in the early 1990s in Colorado, New Mexico, and Florida by Khenchen Palden Sherab and Khenpo Tsewang Dongyal, eventually published as *The Dark Red Amulet*.[35]

In contrast to this strong bias toward *sādhana* within the religious community, the academic world has taken a much greater interest in the tantra texts.

A particularly interesting exception to this is an in-depth study by René de Nebesky-Wojkowitz of an instruction manual for the performance of a sacred dance featuring Vajrakīla and his vast retinue of emanations and assistant deities, in which the teachings of the *tantra* are brought vividly to life.[36] The main text was written by the Fifth Dalai Lama, a keen proponent of the Vajrakīla tantras, who is known to have organized just such a dance as part of the preliminary preparations of the Red Hill site before embarking on the construction of the Potala Palace, and this study by Nebesky-Wojkowitz includes a brief outline of the history of such dances, from both the historical and mythological points of view.

Groundbreaking philological and historiographical work on the tantras of Vajrakīla has been done by Cathy Cantwell and Robert Mayer (see "Primary Sources" and "Secondary Sources"). Their long period of collaborative research has shed a bright light on the reception of the Kīla cult in Tibet and its place in the canon of the early schools, the *rNying ma'i rgyud 'bum* (NGB). As well as offering useful summaries of the contents of the texts studied, by close analysis of the manuscripts of a range of Vajrakīla texts, Cantwell and Mayer have revealed the lines of transmission and geographical spread of these texts and produced valuable critical editions.

PRIMARY SOURCES

Almost all of the primary sources in Tibetan language have been gathered together in a compendium of forty-five volumes entitled *dPal chen kī la ya'i chos skor phyogs bsgrigs*, published by the Bod kyi shes rig zhib 'jug khang, Chengdu, 2002. This is available electronically as W24051 on the TBRC (http://www.tbrc.org/) website.

For academic studies of some early Tibetan material, without English translation, see:

Cantwell, Cathy, and Robert Mayer. *The Kīlaya Nirvāṇa Tantra and the Vajra Wrath Tantra: Two Texts from the Ancient Tantra Collection*. Vienna: Austrian Academy of Sciences Press, 2007.

Cantwell, Cathy, and Robert Mayer. *Early Tibetan Documents on Phur pa from Dunhuang*. Vienna: Austrian Academy of Sciences Press, 2008.

SECONDARY SOURCES

Bischoff, F. A., and C. Hartman. "Padmasambhava's Invention of the Phur-bu: Ms. Pelliot Tibétain 44." In *Études tibétaines dédiées à la mémoire de Marcelle Lalou*. Edited by A. Macdonald, 11–27. Paris: Adrien Maisonneuve, 1971.

Boord, Martin J. *A Bolt of Lightning from The Blue: The Vast Commentary of Vajrakīla That Clearly Defines the Essential Points; Annotated Translations, Including the* Phur 'grel 'bum nag *as Transmitted to Ye-shes mtsho-rgyal*. Berlin: Edition Khordong, 2002.

Boord, Martin J. *Vajrakīla Texts of the Northern Treasures Tradition* . Berlin: Wandel, 2010–.

Cantwell, Cathy. "To Meditate upon Consciousness as Vajra: Ritual 'Killing and Liberation' in the rNying-ma-pa Tradition." In *Tibetan Studies: Proceedings of the 7th Seminar of the*

International Association for Tibetan Studies, Graz 1995. Vol. 1. Edited by Helmut Krasser et al., 107–118. PIATS 7. Vienna: Österreichische Akademie der Wissenschaften, 1997.

Cantwell, Cathy, and Robert Mayer. "A Dunhuang Phurpa Consecration Rite: IOL Tib J 331. III's Consecrations Section." In *Chinese and Tibetan Tantra at Dunhuang*. Edited by Matthew Kapstein and Sam van Schaik, Studies in Central and East Asian Religions, special edition, 248–276. Leiden, The Netherlands: Brill.

Dalton, J. P. *The Taming of the Demons: Violence and Liberation in Tibetan Buddhism*. New Haven, CT, and London: Yale University Press, 2011.

Davidson, R. M. "Reflections on the Maheśvara Subjugation Myth." In *The History of Tibet*. Vol. 2. Edited by A. McKay, 206–232. London: RoutledgeCurzon, 2003.

Dorje, Choying Tobden, *The Complete Nyingma Tradition from Sūtra to Tantra: Books 15–17; The Essential Tantras of Mahāyoga*. 2 vols. Translated, introduced, and annotated by Gyurme Dorje. Boulder, CO: Snow Lion, 2016.

Dorje, Gyurme, "The Guhyagarbhatantra and Its XIVth Century Commentary, *phyogs-bcu mun-sel*." PhD diss., School of Oriental and African Studies, University of London, 1988.

Fremantle, Francesca. "A Critical Study of the Guhyasamāja-Tantra." PhD diss., School of Oriental and African Studies, University of London, 1971.

Huntington, John C. *The Phur-pa: Tibetan Ritual Daggers*. Ascona: Artibus Asiae, 1975.

Huntington, John C., and Susan L. Huntington. "The John C. and Susan L. Huntington Archive of Buddhist and Related Art: A Photographic Research and Teaching Archive (http://www.huntingtonarchive.org/)." 1995–2006.

Kapstein, Matthew. *The Tibetan Assimilation of Buddhism: Conversion, Contestation and Memory*. Oxford: Oxford University Press, 2000.

Karmay, Samten G. "An Open Letter by Pho-brang Zhi-ba-'od to the Buddhists in Tibet." *The Tibet Journal* 5, no. 3 (1980): 3–28.

Karmay, Samten G. *Secret Visions of the Fifth Dalai Lama*. London: Serindia, 1988.

Linrothe, Rob. *Ruthless Compassion: Wrathful Deities in Early Indo-Tibetan Esoteric Buddhist Art*. London: Serindia, 1999.

Marcotty, Thomas. *Dagger Blessing: The Tibetan Phurpa Cult; Reflections and Materials*. Delhi: B. R. Publishing, 1987.

Mayer, Robert. "Observations on the Tibetan Phur-pa and the Indian Kīla." In *Buddhist Forum*. Vol. 2. Edited by Tadeusz Skorupski, 163–192. London: School of Oriental and African Studies, 1991.

Mayer, Robert. *A Scripture of the Ancient Tantra Collection: The* Phur-pa bcu-gnyis. Oxford: Kiscadale, 1996.

Nebesky-Wojkowitz, René de. *Oracles and Demons of Tibet: The Cult and Iconography of the Tibetan Protective Deities*. s'Gravenhage: Mouton, 1956.

Silva, Lily de. "The Symbolism of the Indrakīla in the Parittamaṇḍapa." In *Studies in South Asian Culture*. Vol. 7. Edited by Leelanda Prematilleke, Karthigesu Indrapala, and Johanna E. van Lohuizen de Leeuw, 229–252. Leiden, The Netherlands: Brill, 1978.

Snellgrove, David. *Indo-Tibetan Buddhism: Indian Buddhists and Their Tibetan Successors*. London: Serindia, 1987.

Tucci, Giuseppe. *Indo-Tibetica*. 4 vols. in 7 parts. Satapitaka Series 347–353. Delhi: Aditya Prakashan, 1998–1995.

Wayman, Alex. "Notes on the Phur-bu." *Journal of the Tibet Society* (http://www.digitalhimalaya.com/collections/journals/jts/index.php) 1 (1981): 79–86.

Yeshe Tsogyal. *The Life and Liberation of Padmasambhava (Padma bka'i thang), Rediscovered by Terchen Urgyan Lingpa.* Translated by Gustave-Charles Toussaint (French), and Kenneth Douglas and Gwendolyn Bays (English). Emeryville, CA: Dharma Publishing, 1978.

ABBREVIATIONS

BRT
Black Razor Tantra. Tibetan text and English translation to be found in Boord, Martin. *A Bolt of Lightning from the Blue: The Vast Commentary of Vajrakīla That Clearly Defines the Essential Points; Annotated Translations, Including the* Phur 'grel 'bum nag *as Transmitted to Ye-shes mtsho-rgyal.* Berlin: Edition Khordong, 2002, 3.

MMK
Mañjuśrīmūlakalpa. Edited by Ganapati Sastri. 3 vols. Bibliotheca Indo-Buddhica Series 57–59. Trivandrum, 1925.

NGB
rNying ma'i rgyud 'bum. Collected tantras of the rNying ma tradition.

NSTB
The Nyingma School of Tibetan Buddhism: Its Fundamentals and History, by 'Jigs bral ye shes rdo rje. Translation and annotation by Gyurme Dorje and Matthew Kapstein. 2 vols. Boston: Wisdom Publications, 1991.

P
Peking bKa'-'gyur and bsTan-'gyur Catalogue and Index of the Tibetan Tripiṭaka, kept in the library of Otani University, Kyoto. Edited by Daisetsu Teitaro Suzuki. Tokyo: Suzuki Research Foundation, 1962.

STTS
Sarvatathāgatatattvasaṁgraha. Edited by Lokesh Chandra. Delhi: MLB, 1987.

T
Taisho edition of the Chinese Tripiṭaka, *Taisho Issaikyo.* Edited by Takakusu Junjoro and Watanabe Kaigyoku. Tokyo, 1924–1929.

TBRC
Buddhist Digital Resource Center (formerly Tibetan Buddhist Resource Center) online database.

VKMK
Vajrakīlamūlatantrakhaṇḍa. Tibetan text and English translation to be found in Boord, Martin. *A Bolt of Lightning from the Blue: The Vast Commentary of Vajrakīla that Clearly Defines the Essential Points; Annotated Translations, Including the* Phur 'grel 'bum nag *as Transmitted to Ye-shes mtsho-rgyal.* Berlin: Edition Khordong, 2002, 2.

NOTES

1. The name Vṛtra derives from the Sanskrit root *vṛ* with the sense of "to surround, enclose, obstruct." Hence the noun *vṛtra* means restrainer, enemy, or hostile host. It also stands as "the name of the Vedic

personification of an imaginary malignant influence or demon of darkness and drought supposed to take possession of the clouds, causing them to obstruct the clearness of the sky and keep back the waters." Monier Monier-Williams, *Sanskrit-English Dictionary*. See F. B. J. Kuiper, "Cosmogony and Conception: A Query," *History of Religions* 10 (1970): 91–138; and cf. S. Kramrisch, *The Presence of Śiva* (Princeton, NJ: Princeton University Press, 1981), 29ff.

2. A function often ascribed to mountains, popularly regarded in Indo-Tibetan culture as natural manifestations of the *indrakīla*. An apotropaic aspect of the spike is also to be noted in the Atharvaveda ritual of hammering acacia pegs into the ground in order to drive out demons of illness. Ganesh Umakant Thite, *Medicine: Its Magico-Religious Aspects According to the Vedic and Later Literature* (Poona: Continental Prakashan, 1982), 148.
3. Robert Mayer, "Observations on the Tibetan Phur-ba and the Indian Kīla," in *Buddhist Forum*, vol. 2, ed. Tadeusz Skorupski (London: School of Oriental and African Studies), 167. This practice of *vāstuvidyā* is condemned as a vile art in the *Dīgha Nikāya* I.9, II.87, and so on. According to Trevor Ling, its purpose was to ascertain before building a house whether or not the site is haunted by spirits. Trevor Ling, *Buddhism and the Mythology of Evil* (London: George Allen & Unwin, 1962), 19.
4. Lily de Silva, "The Symbolism of the Indrakīla in the Paritta Maṇḍapa," in *Studies in South Asian Culture*, vol. 7, ed. L. Prematilleke, K. Indrapala, and J. E. van Lohuizen de Leeuw (Leiden, The Netherlands: Brill), 248.
5. All that has a terrible aspect (Skt. *ghora*) is traditionally regarded in India as *vighna*: an impediment, obstacle, interruption, hurdle, difficulty, or trouble. Indeed, the vast size of the problem of *vighna* led to its being associated with the boundary or circumference, which, it is said, the Vedic Prajāpati finally overcame by taking control of the center (an inconceivable subtlety totally devoid of extension) so that "the very root of (demonic) arrogance and conceit, viz. the vast size, ceased to have any meaning." Vasudeva Saran Agrawala, "The Meaning of Gaṇapati," *Journal of the Oriental Institute* 13, no. 1 (1963): 1–4.
6. Ganapati Sastri, ed., *Mañjuśrīmūlakalpa*, 3 vols., Bibliotheca Indo-Buddhica Series 57–59 (Trivandrum, 1925), 693.
7. Marc Aurel Stein, *Serindia*, 5 vols. (Oxford, 1921). Stein's description of the watchtower and his finds is to be found in vol. 3:644–651, and the *kīla* themselves are depicted in vol 4: plate 52. More recent photographs of two of those *kīla*, currently housed in the British Museum, are to be seen in Roderick Whitfield and Anne Farrer, *Caves of the Thousand Buddhas: Chinese Art from the Silk Route* (London: British Museum, 1990), 174.
8. Lokesh Chandra, ed., *Sarvatathāgatatattvasaṁgraha* (Delhi: MLB, 1987), 6, quoted extensively in David Snellgrove, *Indo-Tibetan Buddhism: Indian Buddhists and Their Tibetan Successors* (London: Serindia, 1987), 134ff; and Giuseppe Tucci, *Indo-Tibetica*, vol. 1: *The Stūpa*, Satapitaka Series 347 (Delhi: Aditya Prakashan, 1988), 135ff.
9. This text is found in vol. 16. of the mTshams brag edition of the *rNying ma'i rgyud 'bum* [Collected tantras of the rNying ma tradition] edited by Rdo rje thogs med in 46 vols. and published by the National Library of Bhutan, Thimpu, in 1982. Accounts in English are to be found in Jacob Dalton, *The Taming of the Demons: Violence and Liberation in Tibetan Buddhism* (New Haven, CT, and London: Yale University Press, 2011), appendix A; Gyurme Dorje, *The Guhyagarbha Tantra*, chapter 15; and Douglas and Bays, *The Life and Liberation of Padmasambhava: Padma bka'i thang, Rediscovered by O rgyan gling pa*, trans. Gustave-Charles Toussaint (French) and Kenneth Douglas and Gwendolyn Bays (English) (Emeryville, CA: Dharma Publishing, 1978), chapters 5–6.
10. *Drag sngags zab pa'i lo rgyus* [Chronicles of profound fierce mantra]. A treasure text revealed by Rigzin Godem (Rig 'dzin rgod kyi ldem 'phru can) in 1366. TBRC W27295, 161–166.
11. Makara heads worn as epaulets express his blazing glory, the sun and moon worn in his hair show the simultaneity of *prajñā* and *upāya*, his protruding fangs demonstrate the annihilation of birth and death, his vajra wings symbolize the fulfilment of all wishes, his upraised hair shows the reversal of *saṃsāric* tendencies, his coat of vajra indicates absolute authority, his military jacket of rhinoceros

hide symbolizes the invincibility of buddhahood, his aura of flames burns up malevolent forces, his girdle of knives cuts through any opposing tendency, and the vajra worn on the crown of his head shows his own immutability. Gega Lama, *Principles of Tibetan Art* (Antwerp: Karma Sonam Gyamtso Ling, 1981), 390.

12. These nine modes, originating in ancient Indian treatises on dance and drama, are interpreted in Alex Wayman, *Yoga of the Guhyasamājatantra* (Delhi: Motilal Banarsidass, 1977), 327–328.
13. Dorje, *Guhyagarbha Tantra*, 118.
14. 'Phrin las bdud 'joms, *Nor bu'i do shal*[Necklace of gems], In dpal chen kI la ya'i chos skor phyogs bsgrigs. TBRC W24051. 13: 667–700. [khreng tu'u]: si khron zhing chen mi rigs zhib 'jug su'o, bod kyi shes rig zhib 'jug khang , 2002.
15. These three divisions are said to have been outlined in the *anuyoga* text *sPyi mdo dgongs pa'i 'dus pa* and elaborated by teachers in the sMin grol gling tradition. Gyurme Dorje, *Guhyagarbha Tantra*, 18.
16. They are found under that heading, for example, in the *rNying ma'i rgyud 'bum* [Collected tantras of the rNying ma tradition].
17. *Phur 'grel 'bum nag*, available in three recensions on the TBRC (Buddhist Digital Resource Center [formerly Tibetan Buddhist Resource Center]) website, and translated in Martin Boord, *A Bolt of Lightning from the Blue: The Vast Commentary of Vajrakīla That Clearly Defines the Essential Points; Annotated Translations, Including the* Phur 'grel 'bum nag *as Transmitted to Ye-shes mtsho-rgyal* (Berlin: Edition Khordong, 2002).
18. The *Phur pa'i chos 'byung bsdus pa* is to be found in gTsang mkhan chen, *rDo rje phur pa'i chos 'byung* (Darjeeling: Taklung Tsetrul, 1979), 161–196. *gNam lcags spu gri lo rgyus: dPal rdo rje phur bu bdud 'joms gnam lcags spu gri'i lo rgyus chos kyi byung tshul mdo tsam spros pa skal bzang rna ba'i dga' ston*, vol. 10 (Tha), in bDud 'joms Rin po che, *'Jigs bral ye shes rdo rje: The Collected Writings and Revelations of H. H. bDud-'joms Rin-po-che 'Jigs bral ye shes rdo rje*, 25 vols. (Kalimpong: Dupjung Lama, 1979–1985), 11–75. An electronic version is now available from the TBRC as W20869.
19. The large cycle of Vajrakīla doctrines adhered to by the Sa skya school is said to have been taught by Padmasambhava to 'Khon klu dbang srung and subsequently transmitted from generation to generation within the 'Khon family. 'Khon dKon mchog rgyal po (1034–1102) eventually abandoned the rNying ma tradition in disgust at its later degeneracy, founding his own school at Sa skya in 1073. All other religious groups in Tibet, both Buddhist and Bon, also transmit the teachings of Vajrakīla to a greater or lesser extent. According to the catalog of this collection prepared by Elichi Kaneko (Tantras of the Nyingmapa Tradition / Ko Tantora zenshu kaidai mokuroku), Tōkyō: Kokusho Kankōkai, Shōwa 57, 1982), volumes 27, 28, and 29 consist entirely of Kīla texts.
20. *dPal chen kī la ya'i chos skor phyogs bsgrigs* (Chengdu: Bod kyi shes rig zhib 'jug khang, 2002). This is available electronically as W24051 on the TBRC website.
21. René de Nebesky-Wojkowitz, *Oracles and Demons of Tibet: The Cult and Iconography of the Tibetan Protective Deities* (s'Gravenhage: Mouton, 1956); and John Huntington, *The Phur-pa: Tibetan Ritual Daggers* (Ascona: Artibus Asiae, 1975).
22. F. A. Bischoff and Charles Hartman, "Padmasambhava's Invention of the Phur-bu: Ms. Pelliot Tibétain 44," in *Études tibétaines dédiées à la mémoire de Marcelle Lalou*, ed. A. Macdonald (Paris: Adrien Maisonneuve, 1971), 11–28.
23. Keith Dowman, "A Buddhist Guide to the Power Places of the Kathmandu Valley," *Kailash Journal* 8, no. 3–4 (1981): 251. Most sources stipulate Prabhahasti as the actual donor of the teachings at that time, thus confirming him as the personal preceptor of Padmasambhava. 'Jigs bral ye shes rdo rje says that Padmasambhava studied the Kīla doctrines eighteen times under Prabhahasti's tutelage. 'Jigs bral ye shes rdo rje, *The Nyingma School of Tibetan Buddhism: Its Fundamentals and* History, 2 vols., trans. and annotated by G. Dorje and Matthew Kapstein (Boston: Wisdom Publications, 1991), 1:481.

24. Full text and English translation of the VKMK are to be found in Boord, *A Bolt of Lightning from the Blue*, 79–90. See also the image of an 8th-century statue of Vajrakīla included in the Huntington Archives.
25. *Phur 'grel 'bum nag*, available in three recensions on the TBRC website, and translated in Boord, *A Bolt of Lightning from the Blue*, 110–344. gTing skyes NGB, vol. 27 (ŚA), 317, in 17 folios. Also referred to as the *Root Tantra of Vajra Wrath*.
26. Here "ultimate truth" refers to the doctrines of Buddhism.
27. Taking the form of a downward pointing triangle (or tetrahedron), or else a pair of interlocking triangles (or tetrahedra), this is a symbol of space as "the origin of all phenomena" (Skt. *dharmodaya*).
28. The wisdom being is summoned to unite with the yogin himself, known as the "pledge being" (Skt. *samayasattva*).
29. "*rnam par shes pa rdo rjer bsgom.*" *Vajrakīlamūlatantrakhaṇḍa* (VKMK); and *Black Razor Tantra* (BRT), 3. Full Tibetan text and English translations of VKMK and BRT are found in Boord, *A Bolt of Lightning*.
30. "*sku yi dbyig tu bdag bskyed cig.*" VKMK; and BRT, 3.
31. "*phung po rdo rjer gtam byas nas.*" VKMK; and BRT, 3.
32. "*srid pa rdo rje phur bu'i lha.*" VKMK; and BRT, 3.
33. "*sangs rgyas kun gyi ye shes sku.*" VKMK; and BRT, 3.
34. "*brdungs shig rdo rje 'bar ba'i gtun.*" VKMK; and BRT, 3.
35. Khenpo Namdrol, *Vajrakilaya* (London: Dharmakosha, 1997); and Ven. Khenchen Palden Sherab Rinpoche and Ven. Khenpo Tsewang Dongyal Rinpoche, *The Dark Red Amulet* (Ithaca, NY: Snow Lion, 2008).
36. René de Nebesky-Wojkowitz, *Tibetan Religious Dances: Text and Translation of the 'Chams yig* (The Hague: Mouton, 1976).

Martin Boord

VINAYA RULES FOR MONKS AND NUNS

DEFINING *VINAYA*

Buddhist texts state that the buddha himself laid the foundations of the Buddhist monastic community. According to tradition, he invited his first disciples to join him by saying, "Come, O monk" (Skt. *ehi bhikṣu*; Pāli *ehi bhikkhu*). As the community started to grow, a more complex ordination system developed. First, a candidate takes refuge in the buddha, the doctrine (dharma), and the community (*sangha*); then he asks permission to go forth. As a novice (Skt. *śrāmaṇera*; Pāli *sāmaṇera*), he is obliged to follow ten precepts. With some very small variations according to textual traditions, he should refrain from:

(1) Killing.
(2) Stealing.
(3) Engaging in unchaste behavior (sex).
(4) Lying.
(5) Drinking alcohol.
(6) Wearing flowers, perfume, or jewels.
(7) Singing, dancing, or making music, or attending performances.

(8) Using a high or large bed.
(9) Eating after noon.
(10) Handling gold, silver, or other valuables.

Boys who are able to chase away annoying crows may be allowed to enter the monastic community from the age of seven, but the standard minimum age for going forth is between twelve and fifteen. This indicates that going forth is far from easy, and novices must be able to display that they are strong enough to survive the rigors of monastic life before they are allowed to undertake it. It is only at the age of twenty that a novice is allowed to become a full member of the monastic community—a monk (Skt. *bhikṣu*; Pāli *bhikkhu*). In addition to respecting all of the monastic precepts, each monk is expected to assume several duties within the community.[1]

As the Buddhist community continued to expand, it was felt there was a need for more guiding principles and rules. Consequently, a number of monks started to expand the so-called *vinaya* texts—writings that *guide* or *direct* the community. Various *vinaya* traditions developed as members of the monastic community traveled across the Indian subcontinent. While these traditions were all fundamentally similar, they also contained some remarkable differences, and disagreements over the precepts they espoused led to some significant divisions among monastic communities.[2] The *vinaya* texts thus became identity markers for a number of different schools. According to tradition, at one time there were eighteen of these schools, but many of the texts are not extant, and after Buddhism declined in India only six full *vinayas* survived. It is uncertain when the *vinaya* schools came into being. The Buddhist texts traditionally date these developments to soon after the demise of the buddha. The first inscriptions attesting to the geographical distribution of certain schools date mostly from the 1st century CE on.[3]

The core texts of *vinaya* monastic discipline for each school are a list of rules (Skt. *prātimokṣa*; Pāli *pāṭimokkha*) and a set of formal procedures. In all of the traditions, the *prātimokṣa* is recited every two weeks during a ceremony called *poṣadha* (Pāli *uposatha*). Monks and nuns (Skt. *bhikṣuṇī*; Pāli *bhikkhunī*) each have their own distinctive *prātimokṣas*. Originally designed to provide an opportunity to confess any offenses, the *poṣadha* developed into a ceremony during which loyalty to the *vinaya* rules was declared, as defined by the *prātimokṣa*. It is important to note that the *prātimokṣa* did not include every rule from the outset; rather, rules were formulated and incorporated gradually in response to each occasion when the behavior or attitude of a monk or nun was considered to be inappropriate. This process continued long after the demise of the buddha until each of the schools finally produced the definitive version of its own particular *prātimokṣa*, possibly to distinguish itself from the other traditions.[4] Nevertheless, all of the traditions continued to attribute all of their regulations to the buddha himself.

The rules of the *prātimokṣa* are introduced and discussed in detail in explanatory chapters (*vibhaṅgas*) for monks (*bhikṣuvibhaṅgas*) and nuns (*bhikṣuṇīvibhaṅgas*). Formal procedures, on the other hand, are explained in chapters that are traditionally called *vastus* or **skandhakas* (or *khandhakas* in the Pāli tradition). Apart from expositions on ceremonies and procedures, these include a wealth of short guidelines on many aspects of daily monastic life. The *vibhaṅgas*, together with the *vastus*/**skandhakas*, constitute what is generally known as a school's full *vinaya*.

Four of the six full *vinayas* that survive to this day are extant only in Chinese versions (translated as *lü* 律—"rule" or "law"):

- *Mishasai bu hexi wufen lü* 彌沙塞部和醯五分律 (T.1421),[5] Mahīśāsaka *vinaya*;
- *Mohesengqi lü* 摩訶僧祇律 (T.1425), Mahāsāṃghika *vinaya*;
- *Sifen lü* 四分律 (T.1428), Dharmaguptaka *vinaya*; and
- *Shisong lü* 十誦律 (T.1435), Sarvāstivāda *vinaya*.

The other two full *vinayas* are:

- Pāli *vinaya*; and
- *Genbenshuoyiqieyou bu pinaiye* 根本說一切有部毘奈耶 (T.1442–T.1451), Mūlasarvāstivāda *vinaya*.[6]

The Chinese *vinayas* were translated in the 5th century CE, and all four are still consulted frequently. A Theravāda *vinaya* written in Pāli was also translated into Chinese at the end of the 5th century, but this translation was never presented to the emperor and was subsequently lost.[7] At the beginning of the 8th century, the monk Yijing 義淨 (635–713) translated large parts of the Mūlasarvāstivāda *vinaya* into Chinese. A Tibetan translation and many Sanskrit sections of this *vinaya* are also extant, with the Tibetan version considered the most complete text of the Mūlasarvāstivāda school.[8]

It is not evident to define the *rules* given in the *prātimokṣa* as *rules*, *prescriptive precepts*, or even *guidelines*. When transgressed, one might refer to them as *rules*, as is the case in this article; but when taken as guidelines for monastics on what to do and especially on what not to do, *prescriptive precepts* is probably a more suitable term.[9] The most essential *rules* are contained within each tradition's *prātimokṣa*, with the total number varying from school to school. In the three *vinaya* traditions that are still practiced in the 21st century—Pāli *vinaya* (in South and Southeast Asia), Dharmaguptaka *vinaya* (in East Asia), and Mūlasarvāstivāda *vinaya* (in the Tibetan traditions)—there are 227, 250, and 249/262 (depending on the branch) rules for monks and 311, 348, and 358/371 rules for nuns, respectively. These are presented in the *vibhaṅgas* in descending order of gravity.[10]

The most serious transgressions are known as *pārājika* offenses. Breaking any of these rules results in permanent exclusion from full monastic status (in the non-Pāli traditions, a minor position may be retained within the monastic community).[11] There are four *pārājika* rules for monks, concerning sexual intercourse, killing, stealing, and lying about spiritual achievements. Nuns must abide by all of these rules plus an additional four: two relating to improper behavior with a man; one regarding concealing another nun's offenses; and one concerning provision of assistance to a suspended monk.

The rules in the second category (Skt. *saṃghāvaśeṣa*/*saṃghātiśeṣa*; Pāli *saṃghādisesa*) essentially address various lesser forms of misconduct, most prominently sexual or quarrelsome behavior that may cause divisions within the *sangha* (monastic community). Violation of one of these rules may lead to temporary exclusion. There are thirteen rules for monks and between seventeen and twenty for nuns, depending on the tradition.

The third category of rules—*aniyata*—is applicable only to monks. It comprises just two rules relating to a monk who is accused of improper behavior by a female lay follower. If found guilty, the monk is punished according to the gravity of his offense.

The fourth category (Skt. *naiḥsargika-pāyantikā* and variants; Pāli *nissaggiya-pācittika*) contains thirty rules for monks and between thirty and thirty-three for nuns, depending on the tradition. It concerns objects that are unlawfully obtained and therefore must be surrendered.

The most voluminous chapter is the fifth (Skt. *pāyantikā* and variants; Pāli *pācittika*), which includes between 90 and 92 rules for monks and between 141 and 210 rules for nuns. It covers a wide variety of issues that may arise within a community, such as unchaste behavior, adherence to worldly matters and luxury, incorrect teachings, and troublemaking. The offender may atone for any of these offenses with confession. Punishments are relatively light.

The sixth category (Skt. *prātideśanīya*; Pāli *pāṭidesaniya*) comprises four rules for monks and between eight and eleven for nuns. These all concern gifts of food that may or may not be accepted. All offenses should be confessed and, as above, some light punishments may be administered.

The seventh category (Skt. *śaikṣa*; Pāli *sekhiya*) consists of rules "of good conduct." The precepts in this category vary considerably in content and number from school to school. Many of them relate to etiquette regarding clothing and food, and any contravention of a rule is considered a minor offense. Therefore, transgression generally has few, if any, consequences, although some admonishment may be deemed appropriate.

Rather than listing potential offenses and the associated punishments, the eighth and final category covers "rules for settling disputes" (Skt. *adhikaraṇaśamatha*; Pāli *adhikaraṇasamatha*). Essentially pieces of advice regarding the resolution of conflict within the community, these are explained extensively in other parts of the *vinaya*. This chapter is not recited during the *poṣadha* ceremony.

In all of the *bhikṣu-* and *bhikṣuṇīvibhaṅgas*, most of the rules of the *prātimokṣa* are preceded by introductory stories that explain why each individual rule was formulated. However, these stories are written some time after the rule was drafted, so their connection is often rather tenuous. They certainly should not be viewed as historical accounts; rather, they express the values that the compilers of the *vinayas* considered important. The rules themselves are generally followed by word-for-word explanations that analyze the terms used as well as discussions of various possible scenarios and the effect they may have on the gravity of the offense. Any exceptions are then enumerated. Finally, a handful of rules conclude with some supplementary information. While this is the usual format in which the rules are presented, it is important to note that one or more of the aforementioned elements may be omitted; for instance, the rules of etiquette are often rather brief.

In addition to the *bhikṣu-* and *bhikṣuṇīvibhaṅgas*, the *vinayas* contain chapters (*vastus*, *skandhakas*, *khandhakas*) that discuss myriad rules and regulations relating to the monastic community as a whole. There is a marked contrast between the *vastus* in the Mahāsāṃghika *vinaya* and those in the other full *vinayas*, so the latter five schools are considered as a single branch of *vinaya* and are known collectively as the Sthavira *vinayas*.[12] According to tradition, these two discrete groups developed as a result of a major schism that occurred around a century after the demise of the buddha. The *vastus*, which are arranged thematically, discuss issues such as ordination, penances, and disputes as well as more routine business, such as food, clothing, and medicine. As a result, they are important sources for the study of material culture.

Finally, some of the *vinayas* include supplementary sections, such as the Pāli *Parivāra* (which contains summaries and analyses of certain rules for teaching purposes) and the Mūlasarvāstivāda *Uttaragrantha* (which clarifies various aspects of monastic discipline).[13]

THE SPREAD OF *VINAYA*

South and Southeast Asia. When Buddhism started to spread, most prominently to the south and the east, new circumstances developed and questions arose relating to how to organize the monastic community on the basis of the *vinaya* rules. First in the south (modern-day Sri Lanka) and then in the southeast (modern-day Cambodia, Laos, Myanmar, and Thailand), the Pāli *vinaya* was viewed as the most authoritative source. Subsequently, *vinaya* commentaries written in Sri Lanka were held in the highest regard and became standard reference works throughout the whole of South and Southeast Asia. These commentaries are supplemented by compilations and manuals on various subjects. An excellent overview of these texts is provided by Petra Kieffer-Pülz, who identifies three important categories: first, early commentaries compiled before the 4th–5th century CE (only quotations in later commentaries have survived); second, the so-called *aṭṭhakathās* ("explanations of the meaning"), written in Pāli and based on the earlier commentaries; and, third, subcommentaries (*ṭīkās*) on important issues discussed in the *aṭṭhakathās*.[14] According to Kieffer-Pülz, the earliest sub-commentary likely dates to the 10th century.

The most important *vinaya* commentary is the *Samantapāsādikā* (4th–5th century CE), which is traditionally attributed to the monk Buddhaghosa, but in reality was probably written by several authors.[15] It discusses a wealth of *vinaya* cases in detail and contains countless references to earlier commentaries and opinions. Consequently, it became an authoritative standard text in the Pāli tradition.

East Asia. While the Pāli tradition achieved preeminence in South and Southeast Asia, the monastic communities in Central Asia and China adopted a different stance. The monastics in these regions eagerly translated many Buddhist texts, including the *vinaya* texts, into local languages, although Sanskrit remained an esteemed Buddhist language, especially in Central Asia.

All of the *vinaya* traditions are broadly similar, but they display some notable differences with respect to interpretation of and attitudes toward certain practices. The *prātimokṣa* that is recited at the bimonthly *poṣadha* ceremony, and accepted by every new member of the monastic community at the ordination ceremony, serves as a bond between all of the followers of that particular *vinaya* tradition. Therefore, the *prātimokṣa* texts that started to reach China in the 3rd century CE were documents of supreme importance. Subsequently, when four full *vinayas* were translated into Chinese within a few decades of each other at the start of the 5th century, there was a sudden profusion of monastic guidelines that could be used to underpin the formation of Chinese monastic life. Therefore, it is unsurprising that a number of Chinese masters soon started commenting on these texts. One of them was the 7th-century *vinaya* master Daoxuan 道宣 (596–667), who strongly favored unification of all the *vinaya* traditions in China. At the start of the 8th century, this notion was adopted by the imperial government, when the emperor imposed that only the Dharmaguptaka *vinaya* should be used for ordinations. Ever since, all Chinese ordinations and monastic discipline have been based on this text's guidelines. However, this does not mean that all of the other *vinaya* traditions suddenly became redundant or irrelevant in China. It is obvious from Daoxuan's commentaries that he studied all of the *vinaya* texts that were available to him. Although he emphasized that the Dharmaguptaka *vinaya* is the principal *vinaya* text and the one on which the first Chinese ordinations were based, he suggested that other *vinaya*s should be consulted as and when necessary.[16]

Although masters such as Daoxuan were deeply influenced by the Indian *vinayas*, they were also strongly attracted to a new movement—commonly called Mahāyāna—that reached China in the very early stages of Chinese Buddhism. A central concept in Mahāyāna Buddhism is the bodhisattva—"a being oriented towards enlightenment." This features in the so-called birth stories (*jātakas*) of the buddha, which explain that he perfected attributes such as generosity and morality in many earlier lives as a bodhisattva. However, the concept is extended in Mahāyāna Buddhism, which teaches that many bodhisattvas live in countless different worlds and can offer help to all living beings. Furthermore, it was accepted that everyone has the potential to be a bodhisattva, as every living being possesses at least some buddha-nature, and thus the germs of enlightenment. Mahāyāna Buddhists become bodhisattvas as soon as they arouse the "mind of enlightenment" (*bodhicitta*). The rules of moral conduct for these bodhisattvas were articulated in several Mahāyāna texts.[17]

The most influential text on bodhisattva rules is the *Fanwang jing* 梵網經, the *Brahmā's Net Sutra* (T.1484), which in the second of its two fascicles contains fifty-eight precepts.[18] Although, traditionally, Kumārajīva was credited with translating the *Fanwang jing* from Sanskrit into Chinese in 406, the text was actually composed in China, probably around the middle of the 5th century.[19] It is uncertain when it started to play an important role in Chinese Buddhism, but Paul Groner suggests this must have occurred within one or two centuries of its compilation.[20] The second fascicle, with its list of precepts, was certainly circulating as a discrete text by the end of the fifth century. It enumerates ten major and forty-eight minor precepts, with the focus firmly on appropriate behavior for monastics and lay followers. The ten major precepts emphasize:

- No killing.
- No stealing.
- No improper sexual conduct.
- No lying.
- No selling alcohol.
- No discussion of others' faults.
- No praising oneself and denigrating others.
- No stinginess.
- No resentment.
- No denigration of the three jewels (the buddha, dharma, and *sangha*).

Some of the so-called minor precepts also had a significant influence on East Asian Buddhism, such as one that prohibits the eating of meat and some pungent herbs (including garlic), and another that encourages compassion for all living beings. Violation of a bodhisattva precept is usually punished by some kind of bad karmic effect, rather than a sanction imposed by the monastic community.

After the bodhisattva guidelines were drafted, they sometimes formed part of a formal, ordination-like ceremony at which a bodhisattva vow was declared. However, among Chinese monastics, even up to the present day, ordination based on the traditional *vinaya* texts has invariably preceded this rite.[21]

In addition to the precepts in the *Fanwang jing*, other bodhisattva rules gained influence within the Yogācāra school. One text of major significance was the *Bodhisattvabhūmi*, attributed to the Indian master Asaṅga (fl. 4th century CE).[22] This included a set of major and minor precepts for monastic bodhisattvas, with a focus on inappropriate attitudes such as attachment to material wealth, angry feelings (such as those that lead to murder), belittling the buddha, dharma, or *sangha*, or causing unrest within the Buddhist community. Although the *Fanwang jing* eventually became the most important bodhisattva text in China, and as such was incorporated within the ordination ceremony, these Yogācāra rules exerted considerable influence, too, especially when the monks Tanwuchen 曇無讖 (Dharmakṣema; 385–433) and Guṇavarman (367–431) translated two separate versions of the *Bodhisattvabhūmi* into Chinese: respectively the *Pusa dichi jing* 菩薩地持經 (T.1581) and the *Pusa shanjie jing* 菩薩善戒經 (T.1582 and T.1583).[23] Very influential also was the *Bodhisattvabhūmi* translation made halfway *through* the 7th century by the famous Chinese master Xuanzang 玄奘. It is incorporated as the fifteenth section in Xuanzang's translation of the *Yogācārabhūmiśāstra* (Treatise on the Stages of Yogic Practice), traditionally attributed to Asaṅga or to a group of scholars including Asaṅga: *Yuqie shi di lun* 瑜伽師地論 (T.1579).[24]

Finally, building on the foundation of several centuries of *vinaya* texts and compilations, a new genre called "the rules of purity"—*qing gui* 清規—started to develop in China from the 8th century onward. While the *qing gui* clearly rely on earlier compendia of disciplinary rules, the principal aim was different as the focus shifted to the practical organization of large public monasteries.[25] When this is combined with the fact that Buddhism in India gradually declined—in marked contrast to the situation in China, where a number of large monasteries, particularly those that were influenced by Chan practices, still enjoyed strong public support—the *qing gui* also mark the end of a continuous flow of Buddhist influx from India to China. Hereafter, China, and especially its Chan monasteries, would become the example to be emulated, at least for a number of influential Japanese traveler monks.

Buddhist tradition attributes the first rules of purity to the monk Baizhang Huaihai 百丈懷海 (749–814). However, although he may well have had some interest in drafting regulations for his own monastery, none of the rules later ascribed to him was unique; rather, they reflect a growing demand for regulations among all of the large Chinese monasteries.[26] The oldest extant code is the *Chanyuan qing gui* 禪苑清規, *The Pure Rules for the Chan Monastery* (W 111, pp. 875–942), compiled by Changlu Zongze 長蘆宗賾 (?–1107?) in 1103.[27] These rules have been updated regularly and have become paradigmatic for the organization of all Chinese public monasteries, regardless of school affiliation.[28] They did not replace earlier *vinaya* rules but rather supplemented them by offering practical administrative guidelines. The most important updates are:

- The *Ruzhong riyong* 入眾日用, *Daily Life in the Assembly* (W 111, pp. 943–947), a monastic text compiled by the Chan monk Wuliang Zongshou 無量宗壽 in 1209.[29]
- The late 13th-century *Conglin jiaoding qing gui zongyao* 叢林校定清規總要, *Essentials of the Revised Rules of Purity for Major Monasteries*, compiled by the monk Jinhua Weimian 金華惟勉 (W 112, pp. 1–55).
- The *Chanlin beiyong qing gui* 禪林備用清規, *Auxiliary Rules of Purity for Chan Monasteries*, compiled by the monk Zeshan Yixian 澤山弌咸 (W 112, pp. 56–149) in 1311.

- The highly influential *Chixiu Baizhang qing gui* 敕修百丈清規, *Baizhang's Rules of Purity Revised on Imperial Order*, compiled by Dongyang Dehui 東陽德輝 between 1335 and 1343 (T.2025).[30]

All of these texts outline the ideal organization of a Buddhist monastery, as envisaged by their authors and compilers. Once again, the primary focus is on China's largest monasteries. These institutions comprised only a small fraction of the active monasteries in the medieval period, but they set a benchmark for others to follow in terms of practice and behavior that ultimately became a normative ideal.[31] They significantly inspired all local monastic regulations (*guiyue* 規約) that, together with the expansion of Buddhist monasteries, equally were compiled in order to set a standard for a specific monastery.

Given the manner in which the *vinaya* texts came into being, and their distribution across diverse Indian and Chinese regions, it would be misleading to view them as firsthand accounts of Buddhist lives and actors of the time they refer to. On the other hand, one should not be overly dismissive of them. Not only the compilers and authors, but also the readers of these texts must have been familiar with the ideas, practices, and objects that are mentioned within them. They also reveal the ways in which monastic masters wanted Buddhist practitioners to behave. In this context, it is important to remember that the *vinaya* guidelines were presented to—and accepted by—practitioners as the express wishes of either the buddha himself or of most inspirational masters. Therefore, while modern historical research calls their origins into question, they were and remain of the utmost importance as guiding principles. They "provide us with rich insights into how the canonical authors/redactors, the monastic lawmakers, envisaged the [. . .] Buddhist experience."[32]

VINAYA IN JAPAN

The Chinese disciplinary guidelines soon became the model to follow throughout East Asia, and especially in Japan, Korea, and Vietnam. That said, each region developed its own unique traditions. This was most evident in Japan, where the Indian *vinaya* texts were gradually supplanted by an exclusive focus on bodhisattva ethics. In this way, the country's Buddhists adopted a strong Mahāyāna identity. This was especially notable in the Japanese Tendai school, which rejected any ordination based on the *vinaya*s and concentrated solely on bodhisattva precepts, using the *Fanwang jing* as the solitary basis for ordination of both monks and lay believers. The founder of the Tendai school, the famous monk Saichō (767–822), is credited with initiating this development.[33]

Some of the Japanese monks who commented on the precepts, most notably Annen (841–?), asserted that they were merely pragmatic means to obtain a higher goal that varied according to each person's faculties and attributes.[34] The widespread acceptance of such statements meant that Japan developed a more relaxed attitude toward the precepts than other East Asian regions. For instance, it was acceptable for Japanese monks to marry and consume alcohol. Moreover, this much less strict approach was reinforced by the concept of emptiness. As Paul Groner explained, "Because good and evil could be seen as empty, an advanced bodhisattva might not have to observe the precepts."[35] The difference between violation and observance of the precepts—if any—thus became a major subject of debate in Japan, whereas it attracted far less attention among Buddhists in the rest of East Asia.

VINAYA IN TIBET

In Tibet, while the Mūlasarvāstivāda *vinaya* became the standard text for monastic ordination, detailed knowledge of *vinaya* generally relies on a commentary—the *Vinayasūtra* of the Indian monk Guṇaprabha (fl. 7th century)—and a number of subcommentaries. The *Vinayasūtra* thus became the most important text in Tibetan Buddhism, and it was studied in all of the major schools. However, there was also a focus on the (Yogācāra) *Bodhisattvabhūmi* as well as a commentary on that text by the monk Tsongkhapa (*c.* 1357–*c.* 1419), the founder of the highly influential Gelukpa (dGe-lugs-pa) school.[36]

Of central importance in the Tibetan tradition are the so-called *chayik* (*bca' yig*)—"guidelines"—which were promulgated for specific monasteries.[37] These reflect the influence of a variety of secular legal documents, proclamations by earlier masters, and Buddhist regulations, including *vinaya* precepts, with the inspiration for them sometimes coming from oral sources.[38] *Chayik* address routine issues such as the governance of monasteries, the duties of monastic managers, the decision-making process in the monastery, and ritual activities as well as inappropriate behavior, including corruption and political scheming. They also offer guidance on the judicial, economic, and social organization of the monastery.[39] *Chayik* thus reveal the pragmatic efforts of individual monastic communities to regulate themselves and establish their respective positions in wider society. It is important to note that laypeople are also addressed in these guidelines and urged to respect certain rules. As Berthe Jansen points out, this highlights the importance of Tibetan monkhood for the laity of that region.[40]

CONTEMPORARY DISCUSSIONS OF *VINAYA*

The foundations of the precepts for monks and nuns were laid in the first centuries of Buddhism, then shaped as the monastic order started to spread. As mentioned in the defining *vinaya* section, three major *vinaya* traditions are used for ordination purposes in modern times: the Pāli tradition in South and Southeast Asia; the Mūlasarvāstivāda tradition in the Tibetan regions; and the Dharmaguptaka *vinaya* in East Asia (with the exception of Japan). In their various contexts, the original rules have been supplemented with regional traditions, be it bodhisattva rules in Japan, Tibetan *chayik*, Chinese rules of purity, or influential commentaries, manuals, or (supra)local guidelines written by inspirational monastic masters. Finally, at certain times, in certain places, Asian governments have imposed strict control over their respective monastic communities, causing the *sangha* to lose authority. Equally, though, other monastics have been granted much more freedom to organize their institutions and their way of life as they see fit. Indeed, on occasion, they have gained control over the state. It is important to bear in mind that monastic regulations invariably evolve within a context of wider society that has a significant influence over the way in which they are discussed and drafted. In addition to guiding members of the monastic community, they must inspire trust and confidence among laypeople. They help to shape the *sangha*'s identity, so they are subject to constant efforts to fit in, work with, and present a positive image to lay society, while avoiding any resentment or animosity. This has resulted in perpetual discussions about and refinements to the regulations.

In Theravāda Buddhism, for instance, notwithstanding an ongoing clear division between monastics and laypeople, several countries have adopted the practice of temporary ordination. In Thailand, for instance, the tradition is that every male Buddhist joins the monastic community as a novice or even a monk, and therefore abides by the *vinaya* rules, for a period of time. Thereafter, no stigma is attached to any subsequent decision to leave the *sangha*.[41] Consequently, there is widespread knowledge of monastic life—and the rules that govern it—throughout society. Furthermore, qualifications earned as a monk or personal contacts made within the monastery often prove useful after a former monastic has returned to lay life.

Nevertheless, the distinctions between monks and laypeople remain explicit. In her study on Thai urban monastic organization, Jane Bunnag draws attention to the most important identifying markers of Thai monks: monastic robes, shaven heads, strict adherence to celibacy, no food after noon (a rule that is strictly enforced in Theravāda countries, but less so in other Buddhist regions), and reliance on donations.[42] In general, monastics also endeavor to speak, walk, or eat in a calm and dignified manner at all times. It is important to note that ordination, including temporary ordination, is exclusively male in Thailand, although it is estimated that around one hundred Thai female practitioners have obtained full ordination abroad.[43] In Thailand itself, the term *mae chi* is used to describe women who lead a monastic life that is separate from the officially recognized (male) *sangha*. They usually follow a set of eight to ten rules that are similar to those for novices and may live alongside monks in a monastery, in "nunneries," temporarily in a forest, or in private houses. They wear white robes and their heads are shaven.[44]

In the 21st century, there has been a striking resurgence of *vinaya* discipline in China and Taiwan, inspired by the growing conviction that this may help Buddhism to reverse decades of decline. A similar movement flourished in the first half of the 20th century, although at that time, the focus was on modernization, including calls to embrace Japan's more secular model.[45] However, those demands were ultimately rejected in favor of a traditional Chinese interpretation of *vinaya* that dates back to the 7th-century *vinaya* master Daoxuan. As Ester Bianchi puts it: "In an age of alleged decline of the monastic order and of great changes in the rest of society, many Buddhist leaders considered it necessary to strictly adhere to the disciplinary standards to enhance the religious authority and political legitimacy of the Buddhist *sangha*."[46] Most leading Chinese Buddhists advocate the traditional combination of the Dharmaguptaka *vinaya* and the *Fanwang jing* bodhisattva rules (although some have suggested a reappraisal of the *Yogācāra* rules). The thinking is that this approach reinforces the link to original Buddhism (a claim that is similarly made in Theravāda counties, which enjoy a high reputation as a result), while also facilitating smooth integration with secular Chinese society. Moreover, detailed knowledge of *vinaya* has enhanced the reputations of individual members of the monastic community. The most prominent *vinaya* master of the first half of the 20th century was Hongyi (1880–1942). Once an artist, he turned to monastic life in his thirties and thereafter devoted himself to the study of *vinaya*.[47] His works have since become standard points of reference for contemporary monasteries. Similarly, the likes of Xuyun 虛雲 (*c.* 1864–1959), Yinguang 印光 (1861–1940), Xingci 興慈 (1881–1950), and Tanxu 倓虛 (1875–1963), whose efforts to promote traditional Chinese disciplinary codes have been studied by Daniela

Campo, "advocated and carried on a regeneration of Buddhist religious practices chiefly based on the reinstatement and observance of Chinese Vinaya."[48]

This reinforcement of traditional Chinese disciplinary codes, including *vinaya*, is an integral aspect of contemporary Chinese monastic life in the 21st century, just as it was in the early 20th century. *Vinaya* is once again a major component of monastic education, and the *sangha*'s reputation relies on it. Awareness of *vinaya* rules is thus growing steadily. In the words of Wu Yin 悟因 (b. 1940), abbess of the Taiwanese Luminary Nunnery (*Xiangguang nisengtuan* 香光尼僧團):[49]

> The ten advantages [a traditional set of ten reasons to observe the Buddhist precepts] are for us to implement and realize. Although we are not yet liberated, we are protected by the devoted practitioners of the past. Our present opportunity to practice the Dharma is due to their kindness. They worked hard to observe the precepts and practice the Dharma, so that society and the individuals in the world benefit and have faith in the Dharma. It is now our time. We have the responsibility to observe the precepts and practice the Dharma, so that the Buddhadharma will exist for those in future generations. Through our efforts, we can bring purity to the world and become the hope of others. We can prolong the existence of the Three Jewels [buddha, dharma, *sangha*] in the world. This is our responsibility.[50]

The revival of *vinaya* rules—and especially *vinaya* ceremonies—also transformed China into the principal role model for the ordination of nuns, given that women are not ordained in the Theravāda (with some exceptions) and Tibetan traditions.

NUNS AND *VINAYA*

According to tradition, the first ordained nun was the buddha's stepmother, Mahāprajāpatī (Pāli Mahāpajāpatī). Her story appears in most of the *vinaya*s as well as some other early Buddhist texts.[51] Although Mahāprajāpatī is accordingly seen as the first Buddhist nun, it is likely that the story of her ordination was added to the canon some time after the establishment of a community of nuns.[52] Nevertheless, her admission into the Buddhist monastic order and her acceptance of the basic rules of the female monastic community constitute significant points of reference for the development of the first Buddhist nunneries. Initially, so the story goes, the buddha denied Mahāprajāpatī's full ordination as a nun, although he later informed the monk Ānanda that women could become arhats and thus obtain enlightenment. Many accounts also highlight the fact that Mahāprajāpatī was the buddha's stepmother and stress the debt he owed her for everything she had done on his behalf.[53] Following further mediation by Ānanda, the buddha finally permitted women to enter the Buddhist monastic order, as long as they were prepared to accept eight fundamental rules (Skt. *gurudharma*; Pāli *garudhamma*) that effectively made the nuns' order (Skt. *bhikṣuṇīsaṃgha*; Pāli *bhikhhunīsaṃgha*) subservient to the monks' order (Skt. *bhikṣusaṃgha*; Pāli *bhikkhusaṃgha*). According to tradition, the buddha stipulated these rules on the occasion of Mahāprajāpatī's acceptance into the order. However, many researchers assert that they were actually formulated some time after the first order of nuns was founded.[54] They differ slightly from *vinaya* to *vinaya*. In modern times, the majority of *bhikṣuṇī*s observe the rules that are stipulated in the Dharmaguptaka *vinaya* (T.1428, p. 923a26–b21):

1. Even when a nun has been ordained for one hundred years, she must rise up from her seat when seeing a newly ordained monk, and she must pay obeisance.
2. A nun may not revile a monk by saying that he has done something wrong.
3. A nun may not punish a monk, nor admonish him, whereas a monk may admonish a nun.
4. After a woman has been trained as a probationer for two years, the ordination ceremony must be conducted in the monks' order. (Later [T.1428, pp. 924c4–926a26], the *vinaya* clarifies that the ceremony should take place first in the nuns' order, then in the monks' order.)[55]
5. When a nun has committed a *saṃghāvaśeṣa* offense, she must undertake the penance in both orders.[56]
6. Nuns must ask monks for instruction every two weeks.
7. Nuns cannot spend the summer retreat (rainy season) in a place where there are no monks.
8. At the end of the summer retreat, nuns must conduct the *pravāraṇā* ceremony in the monks' order.[57]

The story of Mahāprajāpatī's ordination casts women as soteriologically equal to men, but institutionally inferior. It also introduces an additional stage in the training toward full ordination. While there are only two steps toward full ordination for male candidates (novice, then fully ordained monk), their female counterparts progress through three steps: novice (Skt. *śrāmaṇerī*; Pāli *śrāmaṇerī*), probationer (Skt. *śikṣamāṇā*; Pāli *sikkhamānā*), and fully ordained nun. The probationer stage comprises two years of extra training before the candidate is permitted to request full ordination.[58]

Until very recently, only the Dharmaguptaka tradition—which is followed by nuns in China, Taiwan, Vietnam, and Korea—accepted that women could be fully ordained. In addition, dual ordination (that is, into both the *bhikṣuṇīsaṃgha* and the *bhikṣusaṃgha*) and the training of probationers have been widely discussed in East Asia. The former has not been practiced continuously throughout Buddhist history, while probationer ordination has been even less common and possibly never institutionalized.[59] In the 21st century, dual ordination is becoming more widespread, but the subject of probationers remains a matter of debate.[60] Observance of the eight *gurudharmas* has also been discussed, with the prevailing opinion being that, while they should continue to be respected, the views of contemporary society must be taken into consideration, too.[61]

Meanwhile, in the other *vinaya* traditions, the ordination of women has become a major issue. For instance, in Sri Lanka, the monastic community seems to have reached a widely accepted consensus that the full ordination of nuns should be permitted.[62] Elsewhere, including Tibet, discussions remain ongoing. Such debates highlight the significance of *vinaya*, in local as well as regional contexts.[63]

REVIEW OF LITERATURE

Detailed study of *vinaya* initially focused on editing and translating texts, primarily those in the Pāli tradition. The major foundational work was conducted by several British scholars who were associated with the Pāli Text Society, founded by Thomas William Rhys Davids (1843–1922) in

1881. Rhys Davids, a British civil servant based in Sri Lanka, was a keen student of Pāli Buddhism. Together with the German Indologist Hermann Oldenberg (1854–1920), he undertook the huge task of translating the whole Pāli *vinaya*.[64] Oldenberg also published a detailed edition of the same text.[65] Later, an elaborate and still much-consulted translation of the Pāli *vinaya* was published by Isaline Blew Horner (1896–1981), president of the Pāli Text Society from 1959 until her death in 1981.[66] She also wrote an influential monograph on women in Buddhism, bringing the topic of female Buddhists to the fore.[67] The other traditions have attracted far less attention, and full English translations of their *vinayas* are yet to appear.

Further studies concentrated on the development of *vinaya*. For a time, one particularly influential work was Erich Frauwallner's attempt to establish when the first *vinaya* was formulated.[68] However, from the end of the 20th century on, most researchers reject the notion of a core *vinaya* text. Rather, the focus has shifted to the gradual evolution and dissemination of the major *vinaya* traditions. For instance, Oskar von Hinüber, one of the most prominent *vinaya* researchers, published a concise and intriguing study on the development of the Pāli *vinaya*, maintaining the strong German tradition in *vinaya* studies.[69] Japanese scholars, such as Akira Hirakawa (1915–2002), who wrote extensively on the rules for both monks and nuns, have similarly conducted important *vinaya* research.[70] In addition, several detailed overviews of extant *vinaya* texts have appeared over the course of the last forty years.[71]

As *vinaya* studies continued to develop, researchers started to engage in thorough examinations of specific topics and individual *vinaya* chapters. One notable field of study in this respect is women in *vinaya*, including the revival of full ordination for women in South and Southeast Asia as well as Tibet.[72] Other highly detailed research has focused on the *poṣadha* and *pravāraṇā* ceremonies, legal regulations, and comparing the various traditions' *prātimokṣa* rules.[73] Local disciplinary rules have also been studied in depth, as have East Asian bodhisattva rules and the Chinese "rules of purity."[74] Finally, studies that are firmly rooted in local contexts, such as Tibet, have started to appear in recent years.[75]

The *vinaya* texts contain a wealth of information on everyday monastic and lay life, which makes them invaluable resources for material culture scholars. Gregory Schopen, who has published several inspirational studies in this field, has been instrumental in linking *vinaya* to archaeological and epigraphical material. His work has also enhanced appreciation of the importance of self-representation among members of the monastic community.[76] In the same vein, the *vinaya* texts' guidelines on such issues as bodily practices and family relations have been studied in depth.[77]

Finally, a very recent trend in scholarship has focused on the so-called revival of *vinaya* texts, particularly in China, and has questioned whether *vinaya* rules are compatible with modern society in a globalizing world.[78]

FURTHER READING

Anālayo. *The Foundation History of the Nuns' Order*. Bochum and Freiburg: Projekt Verlag, 2016.

Andrews, Susan, Jinhua Chen, and Cuilan Liu, eds. *Rules of Engagement: Medieval Traditions of Buddhist Monastic Regulations*. Bochum and Freiburg: Projekt Verlag, 2017.

Bianchi, Ester. "Yi jie wei shi 以戒為師: Theory and Practice of Monastic Discipline in Modern and Contemporary Chinese Buddhism." *Studies in Chinese Religions* 3, no. 2 (2017): 111–141.

Bodiford, William M. *Going Forth: Visions of Buddhist Vinaya*. Honolulu: University of Hawai'i Press, 2005.

Clarke, Shayne. *Family Matters in Indian Buddhist Monasticisms*. Honolulu: University of Hawai'i Press, 2013.

Clarke, Shayne. "Vinayas." In *Brill's Encyclopedia of Buddhism*: Vol. 1, *Literatures and Languages*. Edited by Jonathan A. Silk, 60–87. Leiden, The Netherlands: Brill, 2015.

French, Rebecca Redwood, and Mark A. Nathan, eds. *Buddhism and Law: An Introduction*. Cambridge, UK: Cambridge University Press, 2014.

Groner, Paul. "The Bodhisattva Precepts." In *The Oxford Handbook of Buddhist Ethics*. Edited by Daniel Cozort and James Mark Shields, 29–50. Oxford: Oxford University Press, 2018.

Jansen, Berthe. *The Monastery Rules: Buddhist Monastic Organization in Pre-modern Tibet*. Oakland: University of California Press, 2018.

Prebish, Charles S. "The *Vinaya*." In *Brill's Encyclopedia of Buddhism*:Vol. 1, *Literatures and Languages*. Edited by Jonathan A. Silk, 96–115. Leiden, The Netherlands: Brill, 2015.

Schopen, Gregory. *Buddhist Monks and Business Matters: Still More Papers on Monastic Buddhism in India*. Honolulu: University of Hawai'i Press, 2004.

Yifa. *The Origins of Buddhist Monastic Codes in China: An Annotated Translation and Study of the Chanyuan qinggui*. Honolulu: University of Hawai'i Press, 2002.

NOTES

1. See, among others, Christopher Lamb, "Rites of Passage," in *Buddhism*, ed. Peter Harvey (London: Continuum, 2001), 151–160. For the age of novices, see Ann Heirman, "How to Deal with Dangerous and Annoying Animals: A *Vinaya* Perspective," *Religions* 10, no. 2 (2019): 113.
2. For a basic overview, see John S. Strong, *Buddhisms, An Introduction* (London: Oneworld, 2015), 199–219.
3. For a detailed overview of the evolution and spread of the early schools, see Petra Kieffer-Pülz, "Die buddhistische Gemeinde," in *Der Buddhismus*. Vol. 1, *Der indische Buddhismus und seine Verzweigungen*, ed. Heinz Bechert et al. (Stuttgart: Kohlhammer, 2000), 285–302.
4. Oskar von Hinüber, *Das Pātimokkhasutta der Theravādin*, Studien zur Literatur des Theravāda-Buddhismus (Stuttgart: Franz Steiner Verlag, 1999), 89–91.
5. T. stands for *Taishō shinshū daizōkyō* 大正新修大蔵經, 85 vols, ed. Junjirō 高楠順次郎 and Watanabe Kaigyoku 渡邊海旭 (Tokyo: Taishō Issaikyō Kankōkai, 1924–1934). This anthology is the most widely used collection in Buddhist studies.
6. In addition to the six full *vinaya*s, the chapter for nuns (*bhikṣuṇīvibhaṅga*) of the Mahāsāṃghika-Lokottaravādins is extant, preserved in a transitional language between Prākrit and Sanskrit; see Gustav Roth, *Bhikṣuṇī-Vinaya, Including Bhikṣuṇī-Prakīrṇaka and a Summary of the Bhikṣu-Prakīrṇaka of the Ārya-Mahāsāṃghika-Lokottaravādin* (Patna, India: Kashi Jayaswal Research Institute, 1970), lv–lvi. It has never been translated into Chinese. For a translation into French, see Édith Nolot, *Règles de discipline des nonnes bouddhistes, le bhikṣuṇīvinaya de l'école Mahāsāṃghika-Lokottaravādin* (Paris: Collège de France, 1991).
7. See Ann Heirman, "Vinaya from India to China," in *The Spread of Buddhism*, ed. Ann Heirman and Stephan-Peter Bumbacher (Leiden, The Netherlands: Brill, 2007), 190–192.
8. For a detailed overview and discussion of extant *vinaya* texts, see Shayne Clarke, "Vinayas," in *Brill's Encyclopedia of Buddhism*. Vol. 1, *Literatures and Languages*, ed. Jonathan A. Silk (Leiden, The Netherlands: Brill, 2015), 60–87.
9. On this issue in 21st-century Theravāda Buddhism, see Nirmala Salgado, "On the Question of 'Discipline' (*Vinaya*) and Nuns in Theravāda Buddhism," *Religions* 10, no. 2 (2019): 98.
10. For a short discussion of the *prātimokṣa*, see Peter Harvey, *An Introduction to Buddhism: Teachings, History and Practices*, 2nd ed. (Cambridge, UK: Cambridge University Press, 2013), 289–294.

11. Shayne Clarke, "The Existence of the Supposedly Non-existent *Śikṣādattā–śrāmaṇerī*: A New Perspective on *Pārājika* Penance," *Buddhist Studies* [*Bukkyō kenkyū* 佛教研究] 29 (2000): 149–176.
12. Ernst Frauwallner, *The Earliest Vinaya and the Beginnings of Buddhist Literature* (Rome: Istituto Italiano per il Medio ed Estremo Oriente, 1956); and Clarke, "Vinayas," 61–63.
13. Clarke, "Vinayas," 60, 76–81.
14. Petra Kieffer-Pülz, "Vinaya Commentarial Literature in Pali," in *Brill's Encyclopedia of Buddhism*, 430–449.
15. Oskar von Hinüber, *A Handbook of Pāli Literature* (Berlin: Walter de Gruyter, 1996), 103–105; and Kieffer-Pülz, "Vinaya Commentarial Literature," 431.
16. Tōru Funayama, "The Acceptance of Buddhist Precepts by the Chinese in the Fifth Century," *Journal of Asian Studies* 38, no. 2 (2004): 113–115; Ann Heirman, "Vinaya from India to China," 192–195; and Ang Zou, "The Life of Daoxuan, According to Others and in His Own Words" (PhD diss., Ghent University, 2018), 168–188.
17. For a compact general introduction, see Paul Demiéville, "Bosatsukai 菩薩戒," in *Hōbōgirin, Dictionnaire encyclopédique du bouddhisme d'après les sources chinoises et japonaises*, Vol. 2, ed. Paul Demiéville (Tokyo: Maison Franco-Japonaise, 1930), 142–147.
18. For an English translation, see Charles Muller and Kenneth Tanaka, *The Brahmā's Net Sutra* (Moraga, CA: Bukkyo Dendo Kyokai, 2017).
19. Paul Groner, "The *Fan-wang ching* and Monastic Discipline in Japanese Tendai: A Study of Annen's *Futsū jubosatsukai kōshaku*," in *Chinese Buddhist Apocrypha*, ed. Robert Buswell (Honolulu: University of Hawai'i Press, 1990), 253–257; Funayama, "The Acceptance of Buddhist Precepts," 110–113; Paul Groner, "The Bodhisattva Precepts," in *The Oxford Handbook of Buddhist Ethics*, 34–36. For a discussion on the success of the *Fanwang jing*, see William Chu, "Bodhisattva Precepts in the Ming Society: Factors behind their Success and Propagation," *Journal of Buddhist Ethics* 13 (2006): 1–36.
20. Groner, "The *Fan-wang ching*," 278.
21. For details of bodhisattva ordination, see, among others, Paul Groner, "The Ordination Ritual in the Platform Sūtra within the Context of the East Asian Buddhist Vinaya Tradition," in *Fo Kuang Shan Report of International Conference on Ch'an Buddhism* (Kaohsiung: Fo-kuang shan, 1990); and Yamabe Nobuyoshi, "Visionary Repentance and Visionary Ordination in the Brahmā Net Sūtra," in *Going Forth. Visions of Buddhist Vinaya: Essays Presented in Honor of Professor Stanley Weinstein*, ed. William M. Bodiford (Honolulu: University of Hawai'i Press, 2005), 17–39.
22. For a study, see Michael Zimmermann, "The Chapter on Right Conduct in the *Bodhisattvabhūmi*," in *The Foundation for Yoga Practitioners: The Buddhist Yogārcārabhūmi Treatise and Its Adaptation in India, East Asia, and Tibet*, ed. Ulrich Timme Kragh (Cambridge, MA: Harvard University Press, 2013), 862–883.
23. Funayama, "The Acceptance of Buddhist Precepts," 104–109; and Groner, "The Bodhisattva Precepts," 32–34.
24. On Yogācāra rules in China, see, among others, Sheng-Yen, "On the Temporal and Spatial Adaptability of the Bodhisattva Precepts, with Reference to the Three Cumulative Pure Precepts," in *Buddhist Behavioral Codes and the Modern World: An International Symposium*, ed. Charles Wei-hsun Fu and Sandra A. Wawrytko (Westport, CT: Greenwood Press, 1994), 3–50.
25. Yifa, *The Origins of Buddhist Monastic Codes in China* (Honolulu: University of Hawai'i Press, 2002), 3-98; and Yifa, "From the Chinese Vinaya Tradition to Chan Regulations, Continuity and Adaptation," in *Going Forth: Visions of Buddhist Vinaya*, 124–129.
26. For a discussion, see, among others, Jinhua Jia, "The Creation and Codification of Monastic Regulations at Mount Baizhang," *Journal of Chinese Religions* 33 (2005): 39–59.
27. W stands for *Wan xuzang jing* 卍續藏經 (Supplement to the Canon), Vol. 150, ed. Xinwenfeng Bianshenbu 新文豐編審部 (Taipei, Taiwan: Xinwenfeng chubanshe, 1975). Changlu Zongze's compilation was translated into English by Yifa in *Buddhist Monastic Codes in China*, 112–220.

28. For a general study, see Wang Dawei 王大伟, *Song Yuan chanzong qinggui yanjiu* 宋元禅宗清规研究 (Study of Chan pure rules in Song and Yuan dynasties) (Beijing: Zongjiao wenhua chubanshe, 2013).
29. For an introduction to this text and a translation, see T. Griffith Foulk, "Daily Life in the Assembly," in *Buddhism in Practice*, ed. Donald S. Lopez (Princeton, NJ: Princeton University Press, 1995), 147–208.
30. For an English translation of the *Chixiu Baizhang qing gui*, see Shohei Ichimura, *The Baizhang Zen Monastic Regulations* (Berkeley, CA: Numata Center for Buddhist Translation and Research, 2006).
31. For a discussion, see John Kieschnick, "Buddhist Monasticism," in *Early Chinese Religion, Part Two: The Period of Division (220–589 AD)*, ed. John Lagerwey and Lü Pengzhi (Leiden, The Netherlands: Brill, 2010), 545–549, 573–574.
32. Cf. Shayne Clarke (on Indian *vinaya*), "Monks Who Have Sex: *Pārājika* Penance in Indian Buddhist Monasticism," *Journal of Indian Philosophy* 37, no. 1 (2009): 36.
33. Paul Groner, *Saichō: The Establishment of the Japanese Tendai School* (Honolulu: University of Hawai'i Press, 2000).
34. Groner, "The Bodhisattva Precepts," 38–40. Groner argues that the focus was thus on spiritual potential rather than ethical behavior.
35. Groner, "The Bodhisattva Precepts," 44.
36. Berthe Jansen, "Monastic Organizational Guidelines," in *Brill's Encyclopedia of Buddhism*, 442–449. For a translation of Tsongkhapa's commentary, see Mark Tatz, *Asaṅga's Chapter on Ethics, with a Commentary of Tsong-Kha-Pa. The Basic Path to Awakening, the Complete Bodhisattva* (Lewiston, NY: Edwin Mellen, 1986). On the fascinating influence of Gelukpa guidelines in a modern Chinese monastic environment in Sichuan Province, see Ester Bianchi, *The Iron Statue Monastery, "Tiexiangsi," a Buddhist Nunnery of Tibetan Tradition in Contemporary China* (Florence: Leo S. Olschki Editore, 2001), 86–103.
37. The term *bca' yig* is sometimes translated as "constitution." See Ter Ellingson, "Tibetan Monastic Constitutions: The bca' yig," in *Reflections on Tibetan Culture: Essays in Memory of Turrell V. Wyllie*, ed. Lawrence Epstein and Richard F. Sherburne (Lewiston, NY: Edward Mellen Press, 1990), 205–207, 216–219. Nevertheless, Berthe Jansen argues that *chayik* has greater significance, wider than merely "constituting" a monastic community, so she prefers the English term "guideline." She also notes that *chayiks* were equally written outside of strict monastic settings. See Berthe Jansen, *The Monastery Rules: Buddhist Monastic Organization in Pre-modern Tibet* (Oakland: University of California Press, 2018), 15–16.
38. Ellingson, "Tibetan Monastic Constitutions," 207–213; and Jansen, *Monastery Rules*, 14–30.
39. Jansen, *Monastery Rules*, 11.
40. Jansen, *Monastery Rules*, 115–147.
41. Strong, *Buddhisms*, 321–326.
42. Jane Bunnag, *Buddhist Monk, Buddhist Layman: A Study of Urban Monastic Organization in Central Thailand* (Cambridge, UK: Cambridge University Press, 1973), 29–36.
43. Martin Seeger, *Gender and the Path to Awakening: Hidden Histories of Nuns in Modern Thai Buddhism* (Chiang Mai, Thailand: Silkworm Books, 2018), 18.
44. For a recent study, see Seeger, *Gender and the Path to Awakening*.
45. Ester Bianchi, "Yi jie wei shi 以戒為師: Theory and Practice of Monastic Discipline in Modern and Contemporary Chinese Buddhism," *Studies in Chinese Religions* 3, no. 2 (2017): 112–113.
46. Bianchi, "Theory and Practice of Monastic Discipline," 113.
47. For a detailed study of his life, see Raoul Birnbaum, "Two Turns in the Life of Master Hongyi, a Buddhist Monk in Twentieth-Century China," in *Making Saints in Modern China*, ed. David Ownby, Vincent Goossaert and Ji Zhe (Oxford: Oxford University Press, 2017), 161–208.
48. Daniela Campo, "A Different Buddhist Revival: The Promotion of Vinaya (*jielü* 戒律) in Republican China," *Journal of Global Buddhism* 18 (2017): 131.
49. On Wu Yin and the Luminary Nunnery, see Chün-fang Yü, *Passing the Light: The Incense Light Community and Buddhist Nuns in Contemporary Taiwan* (Honolulu: University of Hawai'i Press, 2013).

50. Wu Yin, *Choosing Simplicity: Commentary on the* Bhikshuni Pratimoksha (Ithaca, NY: Snow Lion Publications, 2001), 60–61.
51. For a comparison of these texts, see Anālayo, *The Foundation History of the Nuns' Order* (Bochum and Freiburg: Projekt Verlag, 2016).
52. For a discussion, see, among others, Ute Hüsken, "The Legend of the Establishment of the Buddhist Order of Nuns in the Theravāda Vinaya-piṭaka," *Journal of the Pali Text Society* 26 (2002): 46–65; Liz Williams, "A Whisper in the Silence: Nuns before Mahāpajāpatī?" *Buddhist Studies Review* 17, no. 2 (2000): 167–173; and Jin-il Chung, "Ursprung und Wandel der Aufnahme von Frauen in den buddhistischen Orden nach der kanonischen Uberlieferung—eine Randbemerkung," *Annual of the Sanko Research Institute for the Studies of Buddhism* 37 (2006): 12–14.
53. These aspects of Mahāprajāpatī's story have been researched in detail by Reiko Ohnuma, "Debt to the Mother: A Neglected Aspect of the Founding of the Buddhist Nuns' Order," *Journal of the American Academy of Religion* 74, no. 4 (2006): 861–901.
54. For a discussion, see, among others, Isaline Horner, *Women under Primitive Buddhism: Laywomen and Almswomen* (New York: E. P. Dutton, 1930), 118–161; Hüsken, "The Legend of the Establishment," 46–65; Anālayo, *The Foundation History*, 91–116. For an interesting debate on the foundation of the first nuns' communities, see Oskar von Hinüber, "The Foundation of the Bhikkhunīsamgha: A Contribution to the Earliest History of Buddhism," *Annual Report of the International Research Institute for Advanced Buddhology at Soka University for the Academic Year 2007*, 11 (2008): 3–29; and, partially in response to the latter article, Anālayo, "Theories on the Foundation of the Nuns' Order: A Critical Evaluation," *Journal of the Centre for Buddhist Studies, Sri Lanka* 6 (2008): 105–142.
55. For details, see Ann Heirman, *"The Discipline in Four Parts": Rules for Nuns According to the Dharmaguptakavinaya* (Delhi, India: Motilal Banarsidass, 2002), 75–79.
56. On the interpretation of this rule, see Ann Heirman, "Gurudharma: An Important Vinaya Rule," *Indian Journal of Buddhist Studies* 10, no. 1–2 (1998): 18–26; and Heirman, *The Discipline in Four Parts*, 63–65.
57. The *pravāraṇā* (or invitation; Pāli *pavāraṇā*) ceremony is held at the end of the summer retreat. Every monk/nun is expected to invite his/her fellow-monks/nuns to point out his/her wrongdoings, if any, whether seen, or heard, or even suspected.
58. On this training, see, among others, Heirman, *The Discipline in Four Parts*, 67–75.
59. For a discussion, see Ann Heirman, "Where Is the Probationer in the Chinese Buddhist Monasteries?" *Zeitschrift der Deutschen Morgenlandischen Gesellschaft* 158, no. 1 (2008): 105–137.
60. For details, see Ester Bianchi, " 'Transmitting Precepts in Conformity with the Dharma': Restoration, Adaptation and Standardization of Ordination Procedures," in *Buddhism after Mao: Negotiations, Continuities, and Reinventions*, ed. Ji Zhe, Gareth Fisher, and André Laliberté (Honolulu: University of Hawai'i Press, 2019).
61. See Ann Heirman and Tzu-Lung Chiu, "*Gurudharma* in Taiwanese Buddhist Nunneries," *Buddhist Studies Review* 29, no. 2 (2012): 273–300; and Tzu-Lung Chiu and Ann Heirman, "The *Gurudharmas* in Buddhist Nunneries of Mainland China," *Buddhist Studies Review* 31, no. 2 (2014): 241–272.
62. See, in particular, Anālayo, "The Revival of the *Bhikkhunī* Order and the Decline of the Sāsana," *Journal of Buddhist Ethics* 20 (2013): 137–162. Anālayo (p. 161) further points out that, based on internal evidence within the Pāli *vinaya*, it may be said that "*bhikkhus* are permitted to ordain *bhikkhunī*s in a situation [. . .] when no *bhikkhunī* order able to confer higher ordination is in existence."
63. For a discussion, see, among many others, Martin Seeger, "The Bhikkhunī Ordination Controversy in Thailand," *Journal of the International Association of Buddhist Studies* 29, no. 1 (2006): 155–183; Ann Heirman, "Buddhist Nuns: Between Past and Present," *Numen* 58 (2011): 603–631; Jampa Tsedroen, "Buddhist Nuns' Ordination in the Mūlasarvāstivāda Tradition: Two Possible Approaches," *Journal of Buddhist Ethics* 23 (2016): 165–246; and numerous contributions by Anālayo, a summary of which can be found in Anālayo, "*Bhikṣuṇī* Ordination," in *The Oxford Handbook of Buddhist Ethics*, 129–130.

64. Thomas William Rhys Davids and Hermann Oldenberg, trans., *Vinaya Texts* (London: Oxford University Press, 1882).
65. Hermann Oldenberg, ed., *The Vinaya Piṭakaṃ: One of the Principal Buddhist Holy Scriptures in the Pāli Language* (London: Williams and Norgate, 1879–1883).
66. Isaline Blew Horner, trans., *The Book of Discipline* (London: Luzac, 1938–1966).
67. Isaline Blew Horner, *Women in Early Buddhist Literature* (Kandy, Sri Lanka: Buddhist Publication Soçiety, 1961).
68. Eric Frauwallner, *The Earliest Vinaya and the Beginnings of Buddhist Literature* (Rome: Istituto per il Medio ed Estremo Oriente, 1956).
69. Oskar von Hinüber, *Das Pātimokkhasutta der Theravādin, Studien zur Literatur des Theravāda-Buddhismus* (Stuttgart, Germany: Franz Steiner Verlag, 1999).
70. Akira Hirakawa 平川彰, *Ritsuzō no kenkyū* 律蔵の研究 (A Study of the Vinaya–Piṭaka; Tokyo: Sankibō Busshorin, 1970); and Akira Hirakawa 平川彰/, *Bikuni-Ritsu no kenkyū* 比丘尼律の研究 (A Study of the Vinaya for Nuns; Tokyo: Shunjūsha, 1998).
71. These bibliographical works include, for instance, Akira Yuyama, *Systematische Übersicht über die buddhistische Sanskrit-Literatur, Erster Teil: Vinaya-Texte* (Wiesbaden, Germany: Franz Steiner Verlag, 1979); Shayne Clarke, "Vinayas," in *Brill's Encyclopedia of Buddhism*, 60–87; and Charles Prebish, *A Survey of Vinaya Literature* (Taipei: Jin Luen Publishing House, 1994; London: Routledge, 1996). There is an interesting review of the latter by Jan Willem de Jong: "Charles S. Prebish, *Survey of Vinaya Literature*," *Indo-Iranian Journal* 41, no. 2 (1998): 179–182.
72. Akira Hirakawa, with Zenno Ikuno and Paul Groner, *Monastic Discipline for the Buddhist Nuns: An English Translation of the Chinese Text of the Mahāsāṃghika-Bhikṣuṇī-Vinaya* (Patna, Thailand: Kashi Jayaswal Research Institute, 1982); Ute Hüsken, *Die Vorschriften für die Buddhistische Nonnengemeinde im Vinaya-Piṭaka der Theravādin* (Berlin: Dietrich Meier Verlag, 1997); Édith Nolot, *Règles de discipline des nonnes bouddhistes. Le Bhiksunīvinaya de l'école Mahāsāmghikalokottaravādin. Traduction annotée, commentaire, collation du manuscript* (Paris: Diffusion de Boccard, 1991); Heirman, "*The Discipline in Four Parts*"; and Anālayo, *Foundation History of the Nuns' Order*.
73. Petra Kieffer-Pülz, *Die Sīmā. Vorschriften zur Regelung der buddhistischen Gemeindegrenze in älteren buddhistischen Texten* (Berlin: Dietrich Reimer Verlag, 1992); Haiyan Hu-von Hinüber, *Das Poṣadhavastu: Vorschriften für die buddhistische Beichtfeier im Vinaya der Mūlasarvāstivādin***s** (Reinbek, Germany: Dr. Inge Wezler Verlag für Orientalistische Fachpublikationen, 1994); Jin-il Chung, *Die Pravāraṇā in den kanonischen Vinaya-Texten der Mūlasarvāstivādin und der Sarvāstivādin* (Göttingen, Germany: Vandenhoeck & Ruprecht, 1998); and Wang Pachow, *A Comparative Study of the Prātimokṣa: On the Basis of Its Chinese, Tibetan, Sanskrit and Pāli Versions*, rev. ed. (Delhi, India: Motilal Banarsidass, 2000).
74. On East Asian *vinaya* interpretations and additions, see, among others, William M. Bodiford, *Going Forth: Visions of Buddhist Vinaya*; Yifa, *Origins of Buddhist Monastic Codes*.
75. See, for instance, Jansen, *The Monastery Rules*.
76. Gregory Schopen, *Bones, Stones, and Buddhist Monks: Collected Papers on the Archaeology, Epigraphy, and Texts of Monastic Buddhism in India* (Honolulu: University of Hawai'i Press, 1997); Gregory Schopen, *Buddhist Monks and Business Matters: Still More Papers on Monastic Buddhism in India* (Honolulu: University of Hawai'i Press, 2004); Gregory Schopen, *Figments and Fragments of Mahāyāna Buddhism in India: More Collected Papers* (Honolulu: University of Hawai'i Press, 2005); and Gregory Schopen, *Buddhist Nuns, Monks, and Other Worldly Matters: Recent Papers on Monastic Buddhism in India* (Honolulu: University of Hawai'i Press, 2014).
77. Ann Heirman and Mathieu Torck, *A Pure Mind in a Clean Body: Bodily Care in the Buddhist Monasteries of Ancient India and China* (Ghent, Belgium: Academia Press, 2012); and Shayne Clarke, *Family Matters in Indian Buddhist Monasticisms* (Honolulu: University of Hawai'i Press, 2013).

78. For an interesting discussion, see Ester Bianchi, "Yi jie wei shi 以戒為師: Theory and Practice of Monastic Discipline in Modern and Contemporary Chinese Buddhism," *Studies in Chinese Religions* 3, no. 2 (2017): 111–141.

Ann Heirman

VISUALIZATION/CONTEMPLATION SUTRAS (GUAN JING)

Modern studies typically treat the six visualization/contemplation sutras as a specific group or genre of Mahayana scriptures in East Asia Buddhist canons. Doing so can help to frame their study in a way that cuts across typical sectarian boundaries. It is important, however, to also recognize the sutras as individual narratives, each featuring different objects of devotion and showing varied approaches to practice. This article will thus first address three themes—contemplation/visualization, recitation, and repentance—that occur repeatedly across them, then summarize the narratives and some key points for each sutra individually. The six sutras will be identified from here by abbreviated English titles and their individual scripture numbers in the *Taishō* canon (T).[1] In addition to these six sutras, visualization/contemplation sutras devoted to Mañjuśrī and Avalokiteśvara (or Avalokitasvara) are listed in premodern Chinese Buddhist catalogs as lost scriptures. However, a few studies since 2010 have investigated evidence among extant scriptures for their possible preservation in whole or in part, and these will be addressed in the "Review of Literature" section.

Visualization, Meditation, Contemplation. How best to render the key term *guan* 觀 in the visualization/contemplation sutras—which is fundamental to their scholarly identification as a specific group—is a vexed question. Among East Asian–language Buddhist scriptures more broadly, the term often renders "insight" (Sk. *vipaśyanā*) in a common twofold classification of meditation methods as calming (Sk. *śamatha*; Ch. *zhi* 止) and insight. However, few researchers think that this is the context here, and there is no consensus on an Indic-language equivalent for *guan* in the visualization/contemplation sutras.[2]

That said, *guan* does commonly indicate an active "looking" and related concepts, such as viewing, observing, contemplating, and discerning. In this regard, the term is similar to "seeing" and its cognates in English, which can refer variously to sensory and cognitive processes linked to sight, whether physically or metaphorically. This is surely part of the basis for rendering *guan* in the sutras as "visualize" or "visualization," which became the most common English-language renderings after art historian Alexander Soper's seminal 1959 analysis of the sutras. There, Soper explicitly defines *guan* (or *kuan*) as "a systematic building-up of visual images, each as complete and precise as possible, in a sequence from the simple toward the complex."[3]

Influenced in part by Soper, many subsequent art historians have examined paintings, sculptures, inscriptions, and other material evidence for Buddhist practices at cave sites in China and Central Asia with reference to the visualization/contemplation sutras. Among those studies, many characterize the practices using the rubric of "visualization." Such characterizations may be correct, and there certainly is material evidence from the caves that points that way.[4] However, the common understanding of *guan* as "visualization" gets more complicated when the individual sutras and the Chinese texts themselves are analyzed.

For example, Soper, Nobuyoshi Yamabe, and Cuong Mai all argue that the *Maitreya Contemplation Sutra* does not offer any particular program of "visualization," even while they primarily use that term to render *guan* for the visualization/contemplation sutras.[5] But the *Maitreya Contemplation Sutra* does recognize what it teaches as *guan*, however the term is chosen to be rendered in English. This can be seen in both the outer and an alternative interior title for the scripture (T 452 14:418b4; 420c17–18). It can also be seen in the sutra's use of a stock phrase that is considered characteristic of the visualization/contemplation sutras, on "performing the *guan* this way . . .," to punctuate certain sections, as well as in other injunctions to "perform this *guan*" (419c7; 420b25).[6] More broadly, Yamabe argues that among the six visualization/contemplation sutras, only two can really be considered practical visualization manuals, the *Samādhi Sea Sutra* and the *Amitāyus Contemplation Sutra*. Even here, Yamabe's own painstaking analyses of the *Samādhi Sea Sutra* show that the "visualization-manual-proper portion" is concentrated in just one of the twelve chapters (chapter 3). He further argues that, there and elsewhere in the text, any visualization processes are often fragmentary or obscured by the profuse narrative elements.[7]

Such caveats notwithstanding, the relative presence of "concrete techniques of visualization" serves all the same as one of the yardsticks by which Yamabe (and Soper before him) assesses the relative dating of the visualization/contemplation sutras or their status as "primary" or "secondary/later" sutras within the group.[8] To be clear, Yamabe is a skilled and careful philologist, and this is not the only criteria he uses. But the question merits asking: if only a minority of the *guan* sutras actually display the characteristics of a "visualization program," how valuable is "visualization" as a standard for measuring where individual sutras fit within the group and what *guan* means in this context?

Further challenges to understanding *guan* as "visualization" are raised by Robert Sharf's provocative 2001 essay, "Visualization and Mandala in Shingon Buddhism," and recent studies by Eric Greene. Sharf contests a widely held notion in the study of East Asian esoteric Buddhism that mandalas function as aids to visualization. Sharf refers primarily to the idea that Shingon practitioners use, or should use, the mandala as a kind of prop to help fix images of the contemplated deities in their "mind's eye" during rituals. He argues instead that this notion is supported by neither the ritual manuals nor the ethnographic evidence for Shingon rituals.[9] Sharf does qualify his remarks by noting that images and other physical objects are used as foci for "meditative visualizations" in different Buddhist contexts, and his analysis in that study centers on different contexts than the visualization/contemplation sutras.[10] That the study does, however, have ramifications for research on the sutras is evidenced by Sharf's argument that "visualization" is a dubious rendering for *guan* (Jp. *kan*) and related Sino-Japanese Buddhist terms that use the character as part of a compound. He argues that such terms often refer to procedures that are "more discursive, literary, or tropical than they are visual or graphic," and he accordingly opts instead for such terms as think, imagine, contemplate, or discern to designate the "mental component" of the rites he examines.[11]

Sharf's arguments in turn have influenced Greene's studies of the visualization/contemplation sutras and the related 5th-century Chinese meditation manuals.[12] Greene, however, takes the decentering of "visualization" a step further. He does so through a kind of genealogical tracing of the term in Western-language scholarship, especially as it applies to the meditation manuals and visualization/contemplation sutras. Greene shows that, although there was at least one example before Soper of translating *guan* in the title of the visualization/contemplation sutras as "visualizing" or "visualization," Soper was the first to explicitly argue that the practices in the sutras should be understood as "visualization." [13] Before this, *guan* was more typically rendered simply as "meditation," which does not necessarily imply the kind of systematic and precise mental construction (or reconstruction) of specified visual images that Soper's definition does.

Of course, the term "meditation" in Western-language analyses of Buddhism has also been scrutinized, with many scholars recognizing that it too does not correspond to any single Indic-language equivalent.[14] And as a translation of *dhyāna*, one of the Indic-language Buddhist terms most frequently rendered as "meditation," "meditation" is a questionable rendering for *guan* in the visualization/contemplation sutras.[15] First, by the time of their compilation, *dhyāna* was commonly rendered by the Chinese transliteration *chan* 禪, the translation *ding* 定, or their combination as *chanding* 禪定.[16] Second, even when these terms are used in the visualization/contemplation sutras, there is little suggestion that they are synonymous with *guan*.

For example, in the *Maitreya Contemplation Sutra*, the opening query by the monk Upāli specifically depicts Maitreya as *not* having practiced "meditative concentration" (*chanding*). That setup for the Buddha's ensuing delineation of the "contemplation" is significant because it exemplifies a difference between the visualization/contemplation sutras and the near-contemporary Chinese meditation manuals with which they show affinities. Whereas the meditation manuals show much concern with meditation characterized as *chan*, or *dhyāna*, and most of the attributed translators of the visualization/contemplation sutras are recognized as *chan* specialists, the practice is not typically emphasized in the visualization/contemplation sutras.[17] The characterization of Maitreya in the opening query to the *Maitreya Contemplation Sutra*, for example (which the Buddha never explicitly denies), is clearly in the breach. Similarly, the opening questions to the *Samantabhadra Contemplation Sutra* frame the Buddha's ensuing discourse as one for practitioners who do not "cut off the afflictions," an achievement frequently posited as a fruit of meditative concentration. Shortly thereafter, the Buddha assures his audience that even practitioners who have not entered *samādhi* (meditative concentration) will be able to see Samantabhadra by reciting and upholding the *guan* that he urges them to study.[18]

Thus, at various points in the visualization/contemplation sutras, the promoted practices are contrasted with the practices or achievements of meditative concentration. To be sure, this is not always the case. For example, the *Samādhi Sea Sutra* sometimes supports such a contrast and other times recommends the practice of *chan*.[19] In the *Bhaiṣajyarāja Contemplation Sutra*, the mind's ability to "roam in meditative concentration" (*chanding*) is eighth among the ten blessings that monks, nuns, and male and female lay practitioners can attain through practice of the *dhāraṇī* taught by Bhaiṣajyasamudgata, one of the two brother bodhisattvas who is the object of devotion in the sutra. Later in that sutra, ordinary people bound by their afflictions who wish to see Bhaiṣajyarāja, the elder brother, after the buddha's nirvana are urged to cultivate four things, with meditative concentration as the third.[20] Such examples notwithstanding, there are enough instances among the visualization/contemplation sutras of distinctions drawn with *dhyāna* and other "meditation" practices to suggest the merit of Soper's pursuit of an alternative translation for *guan*. Moreover, the sutras do emphasize visionary practices. Many passages urge practitioners to clearly contemplate, visualize, or discern (*guan* 觀); imagine or envision (*xiang* 想); and see (*jian* 見) the designated features of the deities and their pure lands or heavens, which are often depicted with vivid visual imagery. In that regard, a translation of *guan* related to "vision" makes sense.

The problem, however, is that the *guan* taught in these sutras embrace more than visual phenomena, including auditory and didactic elements. Some passages do appear to urge the kind of precise visual replication of phenomena in the mind's eye that is typically understood by "eidetic contemplation," and which is integral to many uses of "visualization" in English.[21] But other passages, as Greene has argued, point more toward any resulting vision as confirmation of the success of one's practice, and these visions do not always mirror the phenomena described. In other words, visions that *differ* from the described characteristics or specific object of one's contemplation can also confirm one's progress along the path.[22] For these various reasons, many scholars prefer to render *guan* as "contemplation."[23] This article also suggests that "contemplation" has the advantage of a rubric for *guan* that could include, but not be limited to, practices commonly understood as "visualization."

RECITATION

Scholars have long recognized that the visualization/contemplation sutras are intimately connected to the development in China of practices of calling on (*nian* 念) and reciting the names of buddhas and bodhisattvas. An emphasis on such practices is clear in all of the sutras, including the *Ākāśagarbha Contemplation Sutra*, which is sometimes omitted from comparative analyses due to its brevity.[24] Moreover, Fujita Kōtatsu argues for the *Amitāyus Contemplation Sutra* and the remaining sutras:

> one should note the Chinese-tinged terms that can be detected in these passages—for example, "reciting the name" [*chengming* 稱名] of the buddha or bodhisattva. Since the same term also appears in the *Ākāśagarbha Contemplation Sūtra* . . ., the idea of reciting such a name is common to all the contemplation sūtras under discussion. However, as most of the occurrences of name-recitation cannot be traced back to Sanskrit texts, the idea is considered to have originated primarily within the religious milieu of Chinese translations of Buddhist scriptures.[25]

There are also increasing suggestions in Western-language scholarship of the significance of recitation more broadly for interpreting *guan* in the sutras. This article suspects that the late Luis Goméz formed an important link in this development, even though he is not often cited for this in the scholarship on the visualization/contemplation sutras. In a telling footnote to his 1996 introduction to the Chinese versions of the "Larger" and "Shorter" *Sukhāvatīvyūha sutras*, when referring to the *Amitāyus Contemplation Sutra* ("the Meditation Sutra"), Goméz suggests:

> Again, the term "meditation" (*guan*) is at best problematic. In this case, the term *guan* is often translated as "visualization." As I read the sutra, it is not about visualization or

> mental concentration, but about dedicated and constant repetition of verbal imagery—a sort of narrative rehearsal (*anusmṛti?*). This practice overlaps with certain forms of meditation but also overlaps with other rituals of remembrance and devotion. In practice, the Meditation and the Shorter Sutras often provide the content for chanting and recitation, rather than for silent meditations. The ritual and devotional context in which one finds these sutras fits somewhere between reciting or rehearsing a narrative, chan[t]ing a litany, imagining a narrative setting, and meditating.[26]

These keen observations prefigure related ones on *guan* (or *kuan*) in Sharf's 2001 essay "Visualization and Mandala" and on the visualization/contemplation sutras in his 2002 book, *Coming to Terms with Chinese Buddhism*. In the conclusion to the 2001 essay, Sharf pointedly notes for Shingon rituals that "the *kansō* [觀想], or 'contemplative,' material in the rites is often more discursive than visual. These contemplations are treated not so much as guided meditations, but rather as liturgical recitations."[27] In the 2002 book, Sharf comments on "the centrality of invocation in the so-called *kuan-ching* 觀經, or 'discernment sūtras,' " which "describe elaborate invocation procedures involving the use of icons, mantra, visualization, and other elements often associated with Tantra."[28] Again here, Sharf's sights are principally set on different contexts than the visualization/contemplation sutras themselves, and he does not deny elements of "visualization" within them. But the shared challenging of the translation of "visualization" for *guan* and related compounds, paired with the emphasis on recitation, invocation, and other liturgical procedures for practices understood as *guan*, do suggest continuity with Goméz's views. It seems likely that some of these same concerns then extend, at least in part, via Sharf to Greene.

Increasing recognition of the importance of chanting and recitation for the visualization/contemplation sutras (beyond the issue of "reciting the names") comes from other directions as well. For example, Yamabe investigates a chanting manual found in Dunhuang, the *Sūtra on the Major and Minor Bodily Marks* (*Xianghao jing* 相好經), which was based on the *Samādhi Sea Sutra*. Examining the evidence from this and similar liturgical texts, including a chanting manual based on the *Pratyutpanna-sūtra* and the *Amitāyus Contemplation Sutra*, he argues that visualization and chanting were inseparably connected in Dunhuang, Turfan, and elsewhere.[29]

Similarly, regarding the *Maitreya Contemplation Sutra* ("MVS"), Mai argues that "Recitation of the MVS is not opposed to visualization of Tuṣita, in whatever way the latter may have been carried out."[30] That said, his analysis of the text emphasizes recitation as the likely means by which the *guan* was actually carried out. Mai argues that "The ritual recitation of the text is itself the method of 'constantly keeping Tuṣita in mind,' " and he offers a broader sense of *guan* in the text as referring to such recitation before an image of Maitreya while making vows to direct the ensuing merit.[31] Here, however, it should be recognized that the *Maitreya Contemplation Sutra* never explicitly refers to recitation of the *guan* or to the performance of it before an image. These elements are instead inferred by Mai based on his assessment of the likely ritual context and more general injunctions in the text. By contrast, the *Samantabhadra Contemplation Sutra* does refer to reciting the *guan*, as will be seen in the section "*Samantabhadra Contemplation Sutra*." That passage thus lends support to recitation as part of what it means to "perform this *guan* correctly" in the visualization/contemplation sutras (to invoke their common refrain).

REPENTANCE

All six visualization/contemplation sutras celebrate, to varying degrees, the efficacy of the practices they promote for repenting and extinguishing sins. For example, Fujita's charts of distinctive terminological affinities among them feature "eliminating the sins" of tremendous numbers of eons of "birth and death" as the second key phrase, immediately following the one on "reciting the names" of the buddhas or bodhisattvas.[32] Like the "reciting the name" emphasis, this holds true for the *Ākāśagarbha Contemplation Sutra* as well, which is omitted from Fujita's charts due to its brevity.

Moreover, turning to the terminology of "repentance" (*chan* 懺 or *chanhui* 懺悔), one can point to several salient passages among the sutras. For example, chapter 3 of the *Samādhi Sea Sutra*, on the "Contemplation of [the Buddha's] Bodily Marks," refers to monks, nuns, and male and female lay practitioners who commit such grave sins as the four fundamental offenses (Sk. *pārājika*) or the five heinous crimes. Such people are urged to practice repentance single-mindedly six times per day. Prostrating themselves before the buddha, they should eulogize him and his virtuous deeds, then "recite the repentance rite." However, true to the nature of the chapter, that section devotes the most attention to contemplation of the light from the mark of the white curl between the buddha's eyebrows as the means to extinguish the sins, deferring details of formal proceedings (*jiemo* 羯磨) for expiation to "separate records."[33]

Given the *Amitāyus Contemplation Sutra*'s well-known emphasis on extinguishing sins, it is somewhat surprising that the specific language of "repentance" does not come up much. The term only appears twice. First is during the frame story, when two ministers of King Ajātaśatru chastise him for intending to kill his mother, Vaidehī. After hearing their reproach, he repents and locks her up rather than killing her.[34] The second is when Vaidehī first entreats the buddha to show her a place of rebirth that will be free of sorrows and afflictions, a land of "pure karma." In doing so, she prostrates herself before the buddha, begs him to take pity on her, and repents.[35] Similarly, the *Maitreya Contemplation Sutra*, although also promoting its practices for overcoming sins, only refers to "repentance" once: the buddha explains to Upāli that those who violate the precepts and perpetrate evil deeds can quickly have those deeds purified by hearing Maitreya's name, prostrating themselves, and sincerely repenting. The sutra then adds that "it will be the same for the various groups in future generations" (T 452 14:420b6–9).

The pace of references to repentance picks up, however, in the *Bhaiṣajyarāja Contemplation Sutra*. The sutra links repentance to the *dhāraṇīs* taught by the two brother bodhisattvas, as well as to devotion to many of the same sets of buddhas and bodhisattvas designated in the *Ākāśagarbha Contemplation Sutra*. The buddha calls attention to sentient beings who want to extinguish transgressions of the four grave precepts, obtain repentance for the five heinous crimes or the ten evil deeds, or extinguish the grave sin of slandering the dharma. He first urges such beings to diligently recite the spells of the bodhisattvas Bhaiṣajyarāja and Bhaiṣajyasamudgata. He then exhorts them to also pay reverence to the buddhas of the ten directions, the fifty-three buddhas, the thousand buddhas of this auspicious eon, and the thirty-five buddhas. Following this, practitioners should "universally venerate all the countless buddhas of the ten directions." They are then ready to perform the actual repentance rites: "At the six times of day and night, with their minds and imaginations clear and sharp like flowing water, they should perform the repentance rites. Following this, they should fix their thoughts and call to mind the pure material bodies of the two bodhisattvas Bhaiṣajyarāja and Bhaiṣajyasamudgata" (T1161 20:664a29–b8).

Toward the end of the sutra, after delineation of the sutra's names, a much simpler method is taught for "purifying" many of those same evil deeds. Here, the buddha tells Ānanda:

> After my nirvana, if there are monks and nuns who hear this sutra and sincerely take joy in it, even for a moment, the four grave evil deeds will all be purified. If there are male or female lay practitioners who hear this sutra and sincerely take joy in it, even for a moment, if they have violated the five precepts or broken the eight precepts of abstinence, this will quickly be purified. If there are kings of countries, great ministers, *kṣatriyas*, householders, *vaiśyas* (merchants), *śūdras* (peasants or serfs), brahmans and the like, or any others who hear this sutra, if even for a moment they sincerely take joy in it, the five heinous crimes and ten evil deeds will all be purified. (T1161 20:666b8–14)

In light of these passages—as well as the fact that the first two names the buddha provides for the sutra's teachings are "Elimination of the Sins and Obstructions" and the "Divine Spell of Repentance for Evil Deeds"—the significance of repentance and purification of sins for understanding this "Contemplation" is clear.[36]

Among the six visualization/contemplation sutras, however, repentance and purification of sins come most clearly to the fore with the two attributed to Dharmamitra, the *Samantabhadra Contemplation Sutra* and *Ākāśagarbha Contemplation Sutra*. Whether or not either of those texts is properly attributed to Dharmamitra, their attribution to the same translator may reflect not only their general status as visualization/contemplation sutras—or Dharmamitra's renown as a meditation specialist—but their shared emphasis on repentance.

The basic process in the *Samantabhadra Contemplation Sutra* is that practitioners are repeatedly enjoined to contemplate the wondrous forms and transformations of Samantabhadra and the other stipulated buddhas and bodhisattvas and to "see" them and their teachings. The contemplations proceed in stages, whose success is determined by the resulting visions and encounters. Yet each success along the way is only partial, revealing particular deities or aspects of them, but with more still to come. At those points, practitioners are urged to redouble their acts of veneration, repentance, and scriptural recitation and study. After doing so, they can then see the next aspect, deity, or set of deities in the sequence and/or hear their teachings more directly. The central role played by repentance is evident not only in the sutra's repeated injunctions to confess and repent, but in the very structure of successively purifying the sins of the six sense organs. In subsequent Buddhist traditions, most notably the Tiantai master Zhiyi's 智顗 (538–597) influential systemizations of meditative practices, the repentance for purifying the sense organs would become one of the most celebrated aspects of the sutra.

Zhiyi famously classified and systemized diverse meditation traditions for his monastic community as four types of *samādhi*: constantly sitting, constantly walking, both sitting and walking, and neither sitting nor walking. As Daniel Stevenson explains, the *Samantabhadra Contemplation Sutra* and the chapter on the "Exhortations of the Bodhisattva Samantabhadra" in the *Lotus Sutra* formed the basis for Zhiyi's twenty-one-day "Lotus Samādhi" practice. Zhiyi grouped this within the category of both sitting and walking.[37] Repentance practices from the *Ākāśagarbha Contemplation Sutra* also receive mention within Zhiyi's fourfold system, in this case under the category of neither sitting nor walking. Specifically, Zhiyi mentions an "Ākāśagarbha" practice of cleaning the latrines for 800 days that is featured in the sutra. The category within which this is embedded centers on *samādhi* and repentance practices that do not readily fit into the preceding three categories, and Zhiyi explains these as the cultivation of *samādhi* "wherever one's mind is directed" (*sui ziyi* 隨自意).[38]

In the *Ākāśagarbha Contemplation Sutra*, the latrine-cleaning practice only comes as a kind of last resort after a series of other penitential and contemplative acts are undertaken (T 409 13:677c16–c18). These include, among others, paying reverence to the buddhas of the ten directions, calling on the names of the thirty-five buddhas and Ākāśagarbha, and envisioning or imagining (*xiang*) the bodhisattva's form as well as the sounds that his transformations produce. Only when practitioners do not receive visionary confirmation of the extinction of sins in dreams, in seated meditation, or through perception of a "voice in the sky" are they enjoined to undertake the longer penance of cleaning the latrines.

Many of those preceding practices—which are all framed in the context of repentance—may strike contemporary readers as more clearly meditative, contemplative, or visionary than the latrine cleaning that Zhiyi cites as an example of *samādhi* "wherever one's mind is directed." But even within the *Ākāśagarbha Contemplation Sutra* itself, continuity, rather than rupture, with the preceding practices is suggested by the conclusion to the latrine cleaning. At this point, the penitents are instructed to bathe, pay reverence to the thirty-five buddhas, and chant Ākāśagarbha's name for an additional twenty-one days, then to retake the precepts while calling on Mañjuśrī and the bodhisattvas of the current "auspicious eon" to serve as witnesses.[39] Although Zhiyi's classification of the latrine practice stands as an example of a later, creative reformulation, it helps underscore a more general point about the visualization/contemplation sutras. While the sutras at times tout the rewards of their practices for those *not* specifically cultivating *dhyāna* or *samādhi*, the contemplations they preach remain intimately joined to such traditional categories of meditative practice and attainment. That even the apparently mundane practice of latrine cleaning could be considered "*samādhi*" drives this point home.

THE SIX VISUALIZATION/CONTEMPLATION SUTRAS

This section examines each of the six sutras in turn, summarizing their translator attributions and their narratives, with a focus on what is covered by the term *guan* in the sutras.

***Samādhi Sea Sutra*, T 643.** The translation of the *Samādhi Sea Sutra* into Chinese is attributed to the Indian monk Buddhabhadra in the early 5th century CE. As with all the traditional translator attributions for the visualization/contemplation sutras, however, modern scholars have questioned that attribution. That said, the early-5th-century dating for the Chinese text tends to be supported. Although various earlier scholars posited a Gandhāran (northwest India) origin for the text, Yamabe—the leading specialist of the sutra in Western-language scholarship—raises strong doubts on that hypothesis. He contrastingly suggests that the sutra was likely written originally in Chinese, but composed in the Turfan area of Central Asia, where Indian and Chinese Buddhist traditions mixed freely in the 5th century.[40]

The *Samādhi Sea Sutra* is by far the longest of the six visualization/contemplation sutras. Partly due to its length and the challenges posed by many unusual passages, the sutra has not yet been translated into any Western language. However, Yamabe's 1999 PhD dissertation, the most comprehensive study to date, and Soper's 1959 art historical study provide valuable summaries.[41] The text is divided into twelve chapters, with the titles of most featuring particular objects of meditation or contemplation. The twelve chapters, along with their starting points in the *Taishō* edition, are: (1) "The six similes" (T 643 15:645c6); (2) "Enumeration of the Objects of Contemplation" (647b15); (3) "Contemplation of [the Buddha's] Bodily Marks" (648c24); (4) "Contemplation of the Buddha's Heart" (668b15); (5) "Contemplation of the Four Types of Limitless Mind" (674b5); (6) "Contemplation of the Four Types of Deportment [of the Buddha]" (675b16); (7) "Contemplation of [the Buddha's] Horse-King Organ" (683b5); (8) "Past-Life Deeds" (687b5); (9) "Contemplation of Images" (690a2); (10) "Calling to Mind the Seven Buddhas [of the Past]" (693a11); (11) "Calling to Mind the Buddhas of the Ten Directions" (693c28); and (12) "Secret Practice of the Contemplation of the Buddha" (695b8).[42]

This framework largely adopts the form of the 5th-century Chinese meditation manuals. However, as Yamabe's analysis suggests, so many narrative elements are interspersed within the discussions of the buddha's bodily marks and other objects of contemplation that the structure of the underlying meditative practice is often obscured.[43] To highlight a few narratives that have received particular scholarly attention, chapter 6, on the buddha's four types of deportment—walking, standing, sitting, and lying down—includes discussion of knowing the seated buddha by contemplating (*guan*) his "emanation" (*xing* 影). Notably, this discussion does feature the kind of systematic build-up of visual images that scholars often understand *guan* to mean in the visualization/contemplation sutras. Here, this includes contemplating or observing an image (*xiang* 像) of the buddha—likely referring to a physical image—and creating a mental image (*xiang* 想) or vision of the seated buddha. But any lines between the two kinds of images are well blurred when the practitioner "invites" the physical image to sit down, then creates further visions of a pure white rock cave and a rock wall into which the buddha leaps (T 643 15:681b15–22). And to get to this specific contemplation, the sutra first takes the audience through longer stories of the buddha's subjugation of *nāgas* (snake-like deities) and female demons at what became the famous Buddha "Emanation" or "Shadow" cave of Nagarahāra, in the Gandhāra area.[44]

Similarly, chapter 7 is ostensibly devoted to contemplation or visualization of one of the buddha's bodily marks, his "horse-king organ," referring to his usually hidden male organ. But virtually the entire chapter is devoted to entertaining stories of court ladies and prostitutes who doubt his potency and endowments (and are variously pleasantly surprised or ashamed by what they find) and of rival Jain ascetics who had similar doubts. The Jains, who would go naked as part of their ascetic practices and had initially challenged the buddha, are also ashamed when the buddha out-endows them. They thus repent, and they too become his disciples.[45]

These examples help show that, here and elsewhere in the sutra, one may question how much the focus really is on "visualization"—at least as that term is typically understood—and how much instead is on storytelling. Even so, Yamabe, who well recognizes these caveats, does consider "Buddha visualization" (as he renders *guanfo* 觀佛) to be the sutra's main topic. And there is no doubt that the sutra's discussions of *guanfo* and *nianfo* 念佛 (calling the buddha to mind) influenced many later Tiantai, pure land, and other East Asian Buddhist masters.[46]

Yamabe interprets *guanfo* as referring to visualization of the buddha, primarily through use of a statue, and he offers that definition more generally for Chinese Buddhist texts.[47] There certainly are passages in the *Samādhi Sea Sutra* that lend themselves to such an interpretation. The instructions on contemplating the buddha's cave emanation provide one such example. Other prominent examples include injunctions to enter a stupa and to contemplate or make offerings to buddha images as an aid to one's repentances and contemplations, which are often interlinked. One such instance completes the contemplation of the buddha's emanation, or the seated buddha, for those who still cannot see it; another occurs within an entire chapter devoted to the "Contemplation of Images" (or the "Visualization of Statues," as Yamabe renders it).[48]

As suggestive as such passages and sections are in the *Samādhi Sea Sutra*, however, for interpreting the use of *guan* more broadly across the visualization/contemplation sutras, a closer look at the remaining ones is warranted.

***Amitāyus Contemplation Sutra*, T 365.** The *Amitāyus Contemplation Sutra* is the best known of the visualization/contemplation sutras, and there are numerous Western-language translations. This is in part due to the scripture's adoption as one of the three fundamental Pure Land sutras by Japanese Pure Land schools that emerged in the Kamakura period (1185–1333). Those schools ultimately produced a vast amount of sectarian scholarship, a tradition that continues to influence interpretations of the visualization/contemplation sutras. As Kenneth Tanaka points out, however, at least forty commentaries on the *Amitāyus Contemplation Sutra* were produced from the Sui (*c.* 581–618) to the Song period (960–1279), the majority of which were compiled before 800 CE.[49] In addition, at least 150 copies of the sutra have been identified from the Dunhuang cave archives, whose manuscripts only date up to the early 11th century.[50] Deep interest in this particular visualization/contemplation sutra thus clearly has roots in China well predating the emergence of the Japanese Pure Land schools.

The Chinese translation is traditionally attributed to Kālayaśas between 424 and 442, and Kālayaśas was apparently one of many meditation specialists from "the Western regions" (India or Central Asia) teaching in south China in the Liu Song dynasty (420–479 CE).[51] This translation attribution has also been contested, however. Fujita, whose analyses of the provenance of this and the other visualization/contemplation sutras have been influential, suggests that "there is as yet no compelling reason to reject this claim."[52] But even here, similar to Yamabe's theories on the *Samādhi Sea Sutra*, Fujita suggests that while the foreign translator orally transmitted a Central Asian contemplation practice, perhaps from the Turfan area, the sutra in its written form was composed in China. He thus adopts what he calls a "compromise" Central Asian and Chinese compilation theory.[53]

The *Amitāyus Contemplation Sutra* centers on a sequence of sixteen contemplations. Śākyamuni Buddha is said to have taught these to Queen Vaidehī, after she had been imprisoned by her evil son Ajātaśatru and requested instruction on rebirth in a place free of sorrows and afflictions. In doing so, she beseeches the buddha to teach her how to contemplate (*guan*) such a "place of pure karma."[54] When the buddha manifests such pure lands presided over by all the buddhas of the ten directions, Vaidehī conveys her wish to be reborn in Amitāyus's

Land of Utmost Bliss (i.e., his Pure Land). In response, the buddha instructs her to "fix your thoughts and clearly contemplate that [buddha] land."[55] Elaborating, he explains:

> I, the Thus Come One (Sk. *tathāgata*), shall now teach you, Vaidehī, and all sentient beings of the future how to contemplate the Western Land of Utmost Bliss. By the power of the Buddha, you will be able to see that Pure Land as clearly as if looking at your own image in a bright mirror. Seeing the utmost beauty and bliss of that land, you will rejoice and immediately attain insight into the non-arising of all *dharmas*.[56]

Vaidehī accordingly acknowledges having seen Amitāyus's Pure Land thanks to the buddha's power. She then asks how those "defiled and evil" sentient beings after the buddha's nirvana will be able to do so. The buddha thus delineates the sixteen contemplations on Amitāyus's Pure Land. Summary analyses are appended here, with a particular eye on what is included within the range of the key term *guan* in the sutra.

(1) Contemplation of the Sun. Queen Vaidehī, and all future sentient beings with the faculty of sight, are first told to direct their attention to the setting sun. They should "sit in the proper posture, facing west," then contemplate or observe (*guan*) and fix their minds on the sun, seeing its "setting form like a suspended drum." Having seen it thus, one should be able to "make it clear, whether your eyes are open or shut." Description of the first contemplation then closes with a stock phrase, typical of the visualization/contemplation and related scriptures, that caps all but the final, sixteenth contemplation: "Performing the contemplation this way is called correct contemplation. If one contemplates otherwise, it is called false contemplation."[57]

(2) Contemplation of the Water. After the first contemplation has been successfully accomplished, the buddha's attendant Ānanda, Vaidehī, and future practitioners are instructed to "envision and see (*xiang jian* 想見) the western direction as entirely flooded by water." The buddha then describes the transformations of the water into ice, then beryl, and the manifestation of other elements of the now jewel-adorned, crystalline landscape. Notably, the account concludes with a depiction of musical instruments, which, stroked by the breezes arising from a platform of light, "proclaim the truths of suffering, emptiness, impermanence, and no-self." The text makes explicit that these are sounds. Thus, in addition to the dazzling visual imagery, didactic and auditory elements are included within the contemplations.[58]

(3) Contemplation of the Ground. In contemplation two, the water envisioned permeating the Pure Land was already to be seen as transforming into a "beryl ground." Thus contemplations two and three are so closely linked that, as the buddha declares, "When the envisioning (*xiang* 想) of the water has been accomplished, it is called the general perception (*jian* 見) of the ground of the Land of Utmost Bliss." The contemplation of the ground here refers to the attainment of a state of *samādhi* in which the ground is seen "clearly and distinctly." Moreover, as part of the "correct contemplation," Ānanda is enjoined to expound the contemplation of the ground for future sentient beings. Crucially, those who carry out this contemplation will extinguish the evil karma that would otherwise bind them to rebirth for myriad eons, and they will assuredly be reborn in the Pure Land in their next life.[59] This assurance is repeated for many of the individual contemplations.

(4) Contemplation of the Jeweled Trees. This is one of the most purely visual of the contemplations. It prescribes contemplation of each of the jeweled trees adorning the Pure Land, from the trunks, through the branches and leaves, to the blossoms and fruits. As in many of the contemplations, the practitioners are urged to render all the envisioned objects "clear and distinct." But any vision is very much in motion, as the buddha indicates that within jeweled canopies (transformed from the lights emitted by the trees' fruits) are reflections of the *deeds* of all buddhas.[60]

(5) Contemplation of the Ponds. The buddha describes the ponds as made from the seven kinds of jewels, which issue forth from a wish-fulfilling jewel. The sound of the water's rippling is fine and subtle, "broadly proclaiming [the truths of] suffering, emptiness, impermanence, no-self, and the *pāramitās*" (the practices that bodhisattvas "perfect" on their way to enlightenment). The sound further eulogizes the auspicious marks of the buddhas, while the songs of jeweled birds, manifested from the light of a *maṇi* jewel, constantly praise the virtues of mindfulness (*nian*) of the buddha, the dharma, and the sangha.[61]

(6) "Collective" Contemplation. The buddha refers to this as a "collective contemplation" (*zong guan xiang* 總觀想). When complete, it is called the "general perception of the jeweled trees, jeweled ground, and jeweled ponds of the Land of Utmost Bliss." The objects actually depicted, however, are jeweled pavilions in which countless gods play heavenly music, with musical instruments in the sky that spontaneously sound their notes without even being struck, and those sounds' preaching mindfulness of the buddha, dharma, and sangha.[62] Thus while there are visual elements, the emphasis here is on sound.

(7) Contemplation of the Lotus Throne. In this contemplation, Amitāyus makes his first appearance, standing in the sky with the bodhisattvas Avalokiteśvara and Mahāsthāmaprāpta to his left and right. Once Vaidehī is able to see Amitāyus, she asks how future sentient beings can also see him. This prompts the buddha's depiction of the tremendous jeweled "flower throne" on which Amitāyus will sit. As is often the case for these objects of contemplation, the throne is described with dazzling visual imagery. But the throne itself is not a mere receptacle for Amitāyus, as it also *acts*, emitting golden lights that "transform in accordance with one's wishes and carry out the deeds of a buddha."[63]

(8) Contemplation of the Buddha Image. The buddha tells Ānanda and Vaidehī that once they have seen the lotus throne, they should "envision the buddha" (*xiang fo* 想佛).[64] This, he explains, is because:

> The buddhas, Thus Come Ones, have dharma-realm bodies that enter the minds and conceptions (*xin xiang* 心想) of all sentient beings. Thus when your mind envisions a buddha, this mind itself becomes the thirty-two marks and eighty secondary signs. This mind produces the buddha, and this mind is itself the buddha. (T 365 12:343a19–21)

The buddhas, he elaborates, thus "arise from the mind and conceptions, and because of this, you should single-mindedly fix your thoughts and clearly contemplate that buddha." To do so, practitioners are instructed to first envision Amitāyus's image (*xiag xiang* 想像). Whether their eyes are open or closed, they should see a jeweled image, sitting on the flower throne. After seeing the seated image, their "mind's eye" (*xinyan* 心眼) will open, and they will clearly see the various jeweled adornments of the Pure Land.

The practitioners can then envision seated images of the bodhisattvas Avalokiteśvara and Mahāsthāmaprāpta on Amitāyus's left and right. The images of the three deities emit golden lights that reveal images of buddhas, similarly with paired bodhisattvas, sitting under the trees of the Pure Land. The entire land is permeated with such images. After this vision is complete, "practitioners should hear the streams, lights, jeweled trees, ducks, geese, male and female mandarin ducks, and so on all preaching the wondrous Dharma." Moreover, they will constantly hear that dharma, whether in or out of meditation. When emerging from meditation, they should remember what they heard "and confirm it with the sutras. If it does not match, it should be called an illusion (*wangxiang* 妄想). If it matches, it is called the general perception of the Land of Utmost Bliss." Those who perform this contemplation of "envisioning the image" are assured again that they will remove the sins that would otherwise bind them to countless eons of rebirth. They are also told that they will "attain in their present bodies the *samādhi* of calling the buddha to mind" (*nianfo sanmei* 念佛三昧).[65]

This article suggests that the injunction to *confirm* with the sutras the perceptions from visionary practices is crucial to understanding the "visualization" or "contemplation" process. This is the case both for the *Amitāyus Contemplation Sutra* and elsewhere in the visualization/contemplation sutras. In other words, the process is not a passive one, in which one simply mirrors in one's mind what was prescribed, but one that requires active confirmation, including from "external" sources, such as the scriptures or a (human) teacher.[66]

(9) Contemplation of the Bodily Marks of the Buddha. The buddha teaches Ānanda and Vaidehī how to contemplate Amitāyus's auspicious bodily marks and light (an alternate name for this buddha is Amitābha, or "Immeasurable Light"). Amitāyus is depicted in incredibly colossal terms, with even the mark of the white tuft of hair between his eyebrows five times larger than the fabled Mt. Sumeru. The contemplation then proceeds from his blue eyes, through the light emitted from all the pores of his body, to the tremendous halo of light around him. Each light he emits "embraces and does not abandon those who call the buddha to mind." Those who see such lights and auspicious marks, including the myriad transformation buddhas and bodhisattvas manifested within them, "see all the buddhas of the ten directions." The buddha then adds: "Because they see the buddhas, this is called the *samādhi* of calling the buddha to mind."[67]

Those who have performed this contemplation will, in future lives, be reborn before the buddhas. But the sutra goes on to suggest that, even before then, having already seen Amitāyus and the countless buddhas through contemplation of the white tuft alone, they will receive predictions of their future buddhahood. This is an important detail because, given that the buddha addresses the contemplation to Queen Vaidehī as well as Ānanda, it suggests that women in their present lifetimes can receive predictions of future buddhahood (a position that not all scriptures support).

(10) Contemplation of Avalokiteśvara Bodhisattva. Avalokiteśvara is described in similarly colossal terms, with the contemplation proceeding from the mark of the mound atop his head to the "thousand-spoked wheel" on the soles of his feet. The buddha then adds that all of Avalokiteśvara's remaining bodily marks and signs are the same as the buddha's (likely referring to Amitāyus), except the mound on his head and "the mark of the uppermost, invisible part," which are not equal to those of the buddha. Also of note here is the buddha's proclamation that "just by hearing [Avalokiteśvara's] name, you will reap immeasurable merit; how much more so if you clearly contemplate him!"[68]

(11) Contemplation of Mahāsthāmaprāpta Bodhisattva. Mahāsthāmaprāpta is depicted in similar terms to Avalokiteśvara. After discussion of the lights Mahāsthāmaprāpta emits, his heavenly crown, and the mound on his head, the buddha declares, "His remaining bodily marks are the same as Avalokiteśvara's." However, a particular benefit promised for those who perform this contemplation (in addition to the usual removal of sins) is that they will "no longer be born from the womb" and can journey freely to the various pure lands.[69]

(12) Contemplation of One's Own Birth in the Land of Utmost Bliss. The buddha next instructs Ānanda and Vaidehī to arouse their imaginations and "see yourselves born in the Western Land of Utmost Bliss, sitting cross-legged in a lotus flower." After the lotus flower and their eyes open, they will "see buddhas and bodhisattvas filling the sky." They will also hear "the sounds and voices of the water, birds, and trees and of the buddhas, all proclaiming the wondrous Dharma." The practitioners are again urged to remember those teachings after they emerge from meditation. Once they have perceived these things, "it is called seeing Amitāyus's Land of Utmost Bliss," and the buddha refers to this as a comprehensive contemplation.[70]

(13) "Mixed" Contemplation. Here, the buddha instructs practitioners wishing to be born in the Western Land to first contemplate a 16-foot-high image (*xiang* 像) atop a pond. The buddha insists: "Just by envisioning an image of the buddha [Amitāyus], you will obtain immeasurable merit; how much more so if you also contemplate the buddha's complete bodily marks!" Because Amitāyus can change his form and manifest at will, he sometimes appears as a large body that fills the sky, and other times as a small one, 16 or 8 feet high. Regarding Avalokiteśvara and Mahāsthāmaprāpta, the buddha adds that they have the same bodies everywhere, and one can only tell them apart by looking at (*guan*) the marks on their heads. He calls this contemplation a "mixed" one (*za xiang guan* 雜想觀).[71]

(14–16) Contemplation of the Nine Grades of Rebirth. Contemplations fourteen through sixteen will be addressed collectively because they each follow the same pattern. These three contemplations are devoted to nine descending grades of practitioners born in the Pure Land, in three broad groups, and to the nature of the birth they attain there. Each of the three groups is similarly divided into three descending levels: high, middle, then low. So contemplation fourteen covers the three highest grades of rebirth; contemplation fifteen, the three middle grades; and contemplation sixteen, the three lowest grades.[72] The grades of rebirth are based on the practitioners' faith and deeds during their multiple lives.

The nine grades of rebirth have been one of the most widely debated aspects of this sutra, past and present. However, as this part in particular is unique among the visualization/contemplation sutras, further details will be omitted, except to note that some commentators consider only the first thirteen contemplations to constitute the "meditation" or "visualization" portion proper and these remaining three to belong to a different category.[73] That said, the *Taishō* text does show the same designation of *guan* referring to these latter three contemplations, and all but the sixteenth *guan* are capped with the stock phrase on correct and false performance of the contemplation. Instead, the final contemplation is immediately followed by reference to Vaidehī and her 500 female attendants having listened to the buddha's preaching. Accordingly, Vaidehī attains great awakening, and her attendants attain the aspiration for perfect enlightenment and rebirth in the Pure Land.[74]

***Bhaiṣajyarāja Contemplation Sutra*, T 1161.** As with the *Amitāyus Contemplation Sutra*, Kālayaśas is credited with the translation of the *Bhaiṣajyarāja Contemplation Sutra* between 424 and 442 CE. For the former sutra, however, Yamabe suggests that Kālayaśas's name may have been used simply "to lend an air of authority to the text," and by extension, that could be applied to the *Bhaiṣajyarāja Contemplation Sutra* as well. Both Yamabe and Julian Pas consider this to be a relatively late, "second-generation" visualization/contemplation sutra, although the general dating of the Chinese text to about the first half of the 5th century remains widely accepted (including by Yamabe and Pas).[75] Accorded a relatively minor status among the visualization/contemplation sutras, the sutra has not been the focus of many specific studies in contemporary scholarship. However, Raoul Birnbaum has analyzed the text and provided a full annotated English-language translation as part of his monograph on "The Healing Buddha," and many studies do address the sutra alongside analyses of one or more of the other visualization/contemplation sutras.[76]

The sutra centers on a pair of brother bodhisattvas, Bhaiṣajyarāja and Bhaiṣajyasamudgata, or Medicine King (Yaowang 藥王) and Medicine Lord (Yaoshang 藥上). The brother pair also appears in the *Lotus Sutra*, with the elder brother, Bhaiṣajyarāja, even receiving his own chapter (chapter 23), which is part of the basis for his greater popularity over his younger brother in Chinese scriptures.[77] As Inoue Hirofumi argues, however, the image of Bhaiṣajyarāja in the *Lotus Sutra* is rather different from that in the *Bhaiṣajyarāja Contemplation Sutra*. In the *Lotus Sutra*, Bhaiṣajyarāja is celebrated primarily as a devotee of the sutra and for the ardor of his practices, including self-immolation offerings of his whole body, then his arms after he was reborn. Here, the healing powers suggested by his name are attributed to the *Lotus Sutra* itself.[78] In the *Bhaiṣajyarāja Contemplation Sutra*, however, both brothers are the main objects of devotion, and their healing power and other benefits can be accessed through the mere hearing of their names, recitation of the *dhāraṇī* they teach, or contemplation of them.

Moreover, while likely drawing inspiration and perhaps a few passages from the *Lotus Sutra*, the *Bhaiṣajyarāja Contemplation Sutra* also shares many distinctive phrases and emphases with the visualization/contemplation sutras and the Pure Land sutras, especially the *Samādhi Sea Sutra* and the *Amitāyus Contemplation Sutra*.[79] These include, for example, contemplation of the merits of hearing and calling their names, the pure lands they will preside over, manifestations of the bodhisattvas in dreams and visions, their auspicious bodily marks, and the transformation buddhas and bodhisattvas produced from those marks.

***Maitreya Contemplation Sutra*, T 452.** The *Maitreya Contemplation Sutra* is noteworthy for having a Tibetan version, although that translation was based on the Chinese and thus does not attest to an Indic-language original.[80] Juqu Jingsheng 沮渠京聲 (d. 464 CE) is credited in the *Taishō* edition as the translator of the Chinese text, which he is traditionally said to have done in southern China between 439 and 455. However, the key primary source for this recognition is a bit ambiguous on his role. Sengyou's 僧祐 (445–518) generally esteemed bibliographic catalog, *A Compilation of Notices on the Translation of the Tripiṭaka* (*Chu sanzang ji ji* 出三藏記集; completed in 517), at one point indicates that in the southern territory ruled by the Song, Jingsheng "first issued the two contemplation sutras on Maitreya and Avalokiteśvara," which he had obtained in Turfan (T 2145 55:106c4–8). Although the reference to "issuing" or "producing" (*chu* 出) these sutras does often imply "translation," elsewhere in the catalog Sengyou indicates that "those two Contemplations had long been translated (*yi chu* 譯出) in Gaochang commandery [Turfan]" before Jingsheng brought them to the southern capital (T 2145 55:13a14–15). Thus these references may simply point to his reciting or otherwise transmitting a previously translated text. But whatever the actual status of Jingsheng's role, the paired indications here for the two contemplation sutras' roots in Turfan and the time frame for their "issuance" in southern China are noteworthy.

The buddha's discourse in the *Maitreya Contemplation Sutra* centers on the marvels of Tuṣita, the heaven into which Maitreya will be reborn before his subsequent rebirth in this world, when he becomes the next buddha. These dual themes of Maitreya's "ascent" to Tuṣita Heaven and his "descent" to this world have been widely treated as characteristic motifs for the East Asian Maitreya cult, and the *Maitreya Contemplation Sutra* is considered the foremost example of the ascent motif.[81] But the sutra also presupposes one of the leading scriptures exemplifying the descent motif, the *Sutra on Maitreya's Descent to Rebirth* (*Mile xiasheng jing* 彌勒下生經; T 453), which it refers to by name (T 452 14:420a8). Thus here, as in other instances of the cult, the two motifs are intertwined, even if the *Maitreya Contemplation Sutra* emphasizes the ascent motif.[82]

The buddha's prediction of Maitreya's rebirth in Tuṣita is prompted when the monk Upāli asks him,

> From long ago in the *vinaya* and various sutra collections, the World-Honored One taught that Ajita [Maitreya] would become the next buddha. This Ajita possesses an ordinary, foolish body and has not yet cut off the defilements (*lou* 漏). Where will he be reborn when his life ends? Although now he has left the household life, he does not cultivate meditative concentration (*chanding* 禪定) nor does he cut off the afflictions. [However,] the Buddha has predicted that he will attain buddhahood, without doubt. In what realm will he be reborn when his life ends?[83]

Despite Maitreya's posited lack of meditative practice and other attainments, the buddha responds to Upāli's query by predicting that Maitreya will be reborn in Tuṣita in twelve years and that the bodhisattva will ultimately attain supreme and perfect enlightenment. The buddha then depicts in rich sensual terms the panoply of deities and offerings awaiting Maitreya in Tuṣita. For example, immediately after his prediction, the buddha depicts myriad "heavenly sons" (or gods; *tianzi* 天子) there who, in order to make offerings to Maitreya, remove their sandalwood and *maṇi*-jewel crowns and make vows to attain their own predictions of enlightenment when Maitreya takes his place as buddha. In response, the crowns instantly transform into an equally tremendous number of palaces, made of the seven precious jewels (T 452 14:418c13–24). The transformations of the jewels and the countless, multicolored lights they radiate ultimately produce myriad "heavenly jewel maidens" (*tian baonü* 天寶女) who, in turn, make offerings of their jeweled necklaces and of musical melodies (T 452 14:418c24–29).

Significantly, those melodies are said to preach the "stage of non-regression" of a bodhisattva (T 452 14:418c29–419a1). Shortly thereafter, rows of jeweled trees rained down by dragon (or *nāga*) kings "broadly expound the dharmas of suffering, emptiness, impermanence, no-self, and the *pāramitās*" (419a5–7).[84] Then, a separately manifested group of heavenly maidens (*tiannü* 天女) sing and play melodies that "broadly expound the ten good deeds and the four great vows," and the "heavenly beings who hear this all generate the aspiration for the supreme Way" (419a14–20). Thus, much as in the contemplations of the Pure Land depicted in the *Amitāyus Contemplation Sutra*, here too aural and didactic elements are interspersed with the spectacular visual imagery. Moreover, the *Maitreya Contemplation Sutra* makes clear that the delights of Tuṣita await not only Maitreya, but anyone reborn there, with specific reference to the heavenly maidens awaiting them: "If one attains rebirth in Tuṣita Heaven, [they] will spontaneously receive these heavenly maidens as attendants."[85] Recognizing that such maidens produce melodies that preach, one can also recognize the close interplay between the sensual and the soteriological within those delights.

This main section on the marvels of Tuṣita is also notable for the absence of reference to Maitreya's presence. Thus, for example, one of the adornments awaiting him is a jewel- and gold-decorated "lion-throne," onto which countless heavenly sons and maidens make their own offerings of jeweled lotus blossoms (T 452 14:419b1–8). At this point, however, the throne is empty. Due to the sutra's emphasis on the heaven itself, some scholars have implicitly or explicitly questioned the level of devotion to Maitreya specifically. For example, Soper's seminal Western-language analysis of the visualization/contemplation sutras uses "Tuṣita Sūtra" as the abbreviated title, rather than featuring Maitreya's name.[86] Mai suggests that the sutra focuses more on the merits of Tuṣita,[87] and argues that the link between Maitreya and Tuṣita is relatively weak because Tuṣita is not created due to the bodhisattva's own vows, in contrast to pure lands, such as that of Amitābha (Amitāyus).[88] Most explicitly, Christoph Anderl suggests that "Maitreya himself does not play a significant role in the text."[89] However, two qualifications are warranted. First, the buddha's response to Upāli's opening question shows that most of the Tuṣita landscape and soundscape he depicts was created *in response to* Maitreya's anticipated rebirth there, as offerings to the bodhisattva. Second, the narrative does shift to focus more on devotion to Maitreya himself, right after the main section describing Tuṣita. Notably, this is where the term *guan* is first introduced in the sutra, and performance of the *guan* is framed as advice for those "who want to become Maitreya's disciple" (T 452 14:419c6–7).

That focus on the merits not only of Tuṣita but of devotion to Maitreya specifically continues through the rest of the sutra. Here, the buddha explains in more detail the conditions of Maitreya's ascent to and rebirth in Tuṣita as well as how followers can attain rebirth in the heaven and accompany Maitreya when he descends to become the next buddha (T 452 14:419c7–420c10). The methods for their doing so, however, do draw on practices typical of the visualization/contemplation sutras, cutting across specific objects of devotion: contemplating images of the particular buddhas and bodhisattvas as well as their bodily signs, calling on their names, repenting and extinguishing one's transgressions, and clearly imagining and seeing the stipulated visionary phenomena.

Samantabhadra Contemplation Sutra, T 277. The Indian monk Dharmamitra (356–442) is credited in the *Taishō* with the translation of the *Samantabhadra Contemplation Sutra*, as well as the *Ākāśagarbha Contemplation Sutra* (both between 424 and 442) and one of the Chinese meditation manuals.[90] All these attributions are contested. Even so, as with many of the visualization/contemplation sutras, the translator attributions are revealing in their designation of a practitioner renowned as a meditation specialist, with links to Central Asia, believed to have been active in China in the first half of the 5th century.[91] The *Samantabhadra Contemplation Sutra* was strongly influenced by the *Lotus Sutra*, particularly the chapter "Exhortations of the Bodhisattva Samantabhadra," which stands as the culminating chapter in Kumārajīva's (344–413) translation (T 262). In fact, the link between the scriptures was so clear that the *Samantabhadra Contemplation Sutra* has long been grouped with the *Lotus Sutra* and recognized as the "concluding sutra" of the *Threefold Lotus Sutra*.[92]

The sequence of questions that prompt the buddha's discourse in the *Samantabhadra Contemplation Sutra* are posed in unison by his disciples Ānanda and Mahākāśyapa and by the bodhisattva Maitreya:

> World-Honored One, after the Thus Come One's nirvana, how can sentient beings arouse the aspiration for enlightenment, practice the Mahayana Sutras of Great Extent, and consider the single-truth realm with right thought? How can they avoid losing the aspiration for supreme enlightenment? How, without cutting off the afflictions and separating from the five desires, can they also purify their sense organs and eliminate their sins? How, with the ordinary, pure eyes they received at birth from their parents and without cutting off the five desires, can they see things beyond their hindrances? (T 277 9:389c5–9)

The buddha responds by explaining how to study and follow the practices of Samantabhadra and eliminate sins (T 277 9:389c12–14). In doing so, he explicitly counsels those who wish to see Samantabhadra's material form, the stupa of the buddha Prabhūtaratna ("Abundant Treasures"), as well as Śākyamuni and the buddhas he emanates, and to purify the six sense organs, to "study this Contemplation (*guan*)."[93] Those who do will be able to see those wondrous forms. Moreover, even those "who have not yet entered into *samādhi*" will be able to see Samantabhadra by reciting and upholding it.[94] The amount of time it will take to see the bodhisattva varies according to the relative weight of the practitioners' hindrances, and the retribution for past deeds is not always the same. But it is for this very reason, the buddha explains, that he "teaches variously" to different practitioners (389c24–27).

The buddha next describes the form in which Samantabhadra appears in this world. In doing so, he pays particular attention to the six-tusked, pure white elephant that Samantabhadra rides and to the miraculous emanations from the elephant's own bodily marks. These include such manifested deities as "jade maidens" (*yunü* 玉女), who, like the "heavenly maidens" (*tennü*) in the *Maitreya Contemplation Sutra*, play musical instruments that preach doctrine. Here, however, the jade maidens are depicted as having crimson faces "whose radiance surpasses even that of heavenly maidens," and the doctrine they extol is "the way of one reality in the Mahayana," an implicit reference to *Lotus Sutra* teachings.[95] Also notable among the beings adorning the elephant is a transformation buddha who emits a ray of golden light from the mark between his eyebrows. The light enters in turn the elephant's trunk, eyes, ears, and head and ultimately transforms into a golden saddle with a jeweled pedestal supporting a lotus flower. There, Samantabhadra sits cross-legged, his body like a white jewel, emitting multicolored rays of light, each of which has their own transformation buddhas as attendants (T 277 9:390a22–b2).

The elephant then walks toward the practitioners, and this is when the jade maidens play their songs of praise for the one-reality teachings. In response, the practitioners rejoice and redouble their study and recitations of the scriptures and their acts of reverence. However, Samantabhadra's physical form is still not visible to them, and they next pray to the bodhisattva to "show me your physical form" (T 277 9:390b2–b8). The buddha then instructs them how to do so, through such methods as paying reverence to the buddhas in all directions six times per day, practicing repentance (*chanhui* 懺悔), reading and reciting Mahayana sutras, and reflecting on the meaning and practice of the Mahayana. They are also urged to regard all people like they would regard the buddha, and all beings like they would their parents (390b8–b11). When the practitioner finishes reflecting in this manner, Samantabhadra will send forth a light from the mark between his eyebrows and manifest many other signs, including the illumination of bodhisattvas in all directions, mounted on six-tusked white elephants, just like Samantabhadra. Again in response, the practitioners rejoice, this time praying to the illuminated bodhisattvas to teach them the dharma. The bodhisattvas respond in turn by teaching the Mahayana sutras and praising the practitioners in unison. Precisely at this point, the buddha declares: "This is called the first stage of first contemplating (*guan*) Samantabhadra."[96]

This section has explored in some detail the sutra through this first stage of the contemplation to help give its flavor and because it illuminates key themes addressed throughout: the merits of seeing and otherwise encountering Samantabhadra and the other buddhas and bodhisattvas; how veneration and repentance can help purify the six sense organs and extinguish sins, thereby enabling one to do so; and the importance of studying and reciting the Mahayana sutras. In context, these sutras are exemplified by the *Lotus Sutra*. Equally important, however, is that "reciting and upholding" this *guan* (Contemplation) itself is set up as the means to achieve those goals.[97]

Once having completed the first stage of the contemplation, and successfully "seen" (*jian* 見) these matters, practitioners are able to "keep in mind the Mahayana day and night without abandoning it, and in dreams, see Samantabhadra preaching them the Dharma." In doing so, the bodhisattva will remind them of phrases or verses they have forgotten. Samantabhadra will further enable them to keep in mind and see the buddhas of all ten directions (T 277 9:390b27–c3). However, in a recurring pattern throughout the sutra, even this exalted vision is not the culminating one, but just another step in the continuous process of invocation, veneration, repentance, and confirmation. Thus the buddha next depicts the practitioners as praying to see the buddhas not only with closed eyes but with open ones. Once the practitioners have completed the stipulated acts of veneration and repentance, and acquired the "*dhāraṇī* of revolution" (one of the *dhāraṇī* celebrated in the *Lotus Sutra*), they will first be able to see and hear the seven buddhas of the past in their dreams. After Samantabhadra explains to the practitioners their karmic conditions from past lives and induces them to confess all their sins, they attain "the *samādhi* in which the buddhas appear."[98]

Yet even that exalted *samādhi* does not lead to the clear vision of the buddhas they seek. Amid the ensuing visions, Samantabhadra teaches the practitioners in a dream "the method of repentance for purifying the six sense organs" (T 277 9:390c27–28). Only after following these and other teachings issued by Samantabhadra and the buddhas can they see clearly not only the pure lands, but the buddhas themselves (391a22–25). Accordingly, an unidentified "voice in the sky" advises them that although they can see these various buddhas, they cannot yet see Śākyamuni Buddha, the buddhas he emanates, or the stupa of Prabhūtaratna Buddha (391a26–29). This passage thus implicitly establishes these visions as trumping those of the various buddhas and their pure lands. Here, the text again shows the influence of the *Lotus Sutra,* which extols the pairing of Śākyamuni and Prabhūtaratna in Chapter 11 (T 262), "Emergence of the Jeweled Stūpa." Accordingly, once the practitioners further recite and study the Mahayana scriptures, "even in dreams" they can see Śākyamuni on Vulture Peak, including his preaching of the *Lotus Sutra* there (T 277 391a29–b2). The ability to see Śākyamuni and the buddhas emanated from him is ultimately linked to the method for repenting the sins of the eye organ (391c17–19). Then, after the practitioners again redouble their reading and recitations of the Mahayana sutras and further repent, they are able to see the stupa of Prabhūtaratna (391c23–392a7).

The sutra then proceeds in turn through the repentances for the sins of the ears, nose, tongue, and body and mind. The last two of these six sense organs, body and mind, are largely depicted together, but that section does engage in telling reflections on the mind. The buddhas of the ten directions are said to reach out with their right hands, pat the practitioners on the head, and explain that when one contemplates (*guan*) the mind, there is no mind except that which arises from distorted conceptions. The mind is just like the wind, with no place in which it can ground or abide. The buddhas thus ask rhetorically, "What is sin? What is virtue?" (T 277 9:392c21–c26). In this manner, the teaching on the contemplation of mind deconstructs the very "sins" that the sutra urges its audience to repent.

***Ākāśagarbha Contemplation Sutra,* T 409.** The translation of the *Ākāśagarbha Contemplation Sutra,* like that of the *Samantabhadra Contemplation Sutra,* is attributed to Dharmamitra. Apart from the *Samādhi Sea Sutra,* all six of the visualization/contemplation sutras are relatively small, one-fascicle texts. But the *Ākāśagarbha Contemplation Sutra* is especially brief. Scholars of the visualization/contemplation sutras typically relegate the *Ākāśagarbha Contemplation Sutra* to a peripheral status among them, in part due to its small size, but also to characterizations of it as "an unfinished draft."[99] However, that should not obscure recognition of the sutra's significance in medieval China for repentance practices.[100]

As with the *Maitreya Contemplation Sutra,* the *Ākāśagarbha Contemplation Sutra*'s framing questions are introduced by the monk Upāli, who was known for his expertise in the *vinaya,* or monastic discipline. The summary here will focus on these opening questions and the buddha's direct response to them, because these parts form the core of the specific "Contemplation" taught.

Upāli first points out that, in a certain sutra (likely referring to the *Ākāśagarbha Sutra* [*Xukongzang Pusa jing* 虛空藏菩薩經; T 405]), the buddha had taught that Ākāśagarbha could remove evil deeds and cure outcaste kings and outcaste monks of their evil behavior.[101] He then asks and prompts the buddha:[102]

> If they wish to be cured of such evil things, how should they contemplate (*guan*) Ākāśagarbha Bodhisattva? If they do see him, how can they dwell together [with the other monks], [join] the *poṣadha,* and [take part in] monastic affairs? If male lay practitioners

> break the five precepts or violate the eight precepts of abstinence; if ordained monks or nuns, male novices, female novices, or probationary nuns violate the four grave precepts (Sk. *pārājika*); if lay bodhisattvas transgress the six grave rules, or ordained bodhisattvas violate the eight grave precepts, such people are at fault. Previously, in the *vinaya*, the World-Honored One explained that they should definitely be expelled, cast away like broken rocks [that cannot be put back together]. But now, in that sutra, you have taught that the great compassionate Ākāśagarbha Bodhisattva can save one from all hardships, and you have also taught a spell that can remove sins and transgressions. If there is such a person [whose sins have been removed], how can this be made known? How can this be verified? (T 409 13:677b9–19).[103]

Given the concern with *vinaya* matters, Upāli is a fit interlocutor for the buddha's discourse. However, typical of the visualization/contemplation sutras, the concerns are explicitly extended to lay practitioners. Moreover, as Greene points out, the issue Upāli raises of how to "contemplate" or "visualize" (*guan*) Ākāśagarbha does not appear as such in the *Ākāśagarbha Bodhisattva Sutra*, which the *Ākāśagarbha Contemplation Sutra* in other aspects clearly builds from.[104] In this manner as well, the sutra reflects the extended use of *guan* across the visualization/contemplation sutras, as does the buddha's ensuing response.

The buddha first reassures Upāli and "all future upholders of the *vinaya*" that his compassionate vows do not abandon anyone, and he points to his teachings on the methods to cure sins in the *Sutra on Profound Merits (Shen gongde jing* 深功德經).[105] He instructs the penitents to put on "clothes of shame" and, for one to seven days, to pay reverence to the buddhas of the ten directions and call on the names of the thirty-five buddhas and Ākāśagarbha. When the Bright Star—usually understood as Venus—appears in the sky, they should kneel down, join their palms together, and plead to Ākāśagarbha to appear before them. The buddha then details how to envision (*xiang* 想) the bodhisattva at that time. Notable features include a wish-fulfilling jewel atop Ākāśagarbha's head, which, once visible, reveals the bodhisattva's heavenly crown. In that crown appear the forms or images (*xiang* 像) of the thirty-five buddhas and in the jewel, those of the buddhas of the ten directions. Ākāśagarbha's incredibly large body appears sitting cross-legged and holding in hand a wish-fulfilling jewel. That jewel in turn proclaims the sounds of the monastic rituals together with the *vinaya*.[106]

In this manner, the buddha's instructions move fluidly and rapidly from acts of veneration and repentance, to oral invocation, to visual features of the object of contemplation, then to sounds and didactic elements. The buddha's discourse is thus well on the way to answering the first of Upāli's questions, on how to contemplate Ākāśagarbha. It is the ensuing passages, however, that principally address Upāli's remaining questions, and these, too, should be understood as part of the contemplation.

The buddha explains that if the bodhisattva takes pity on the sentient beings, he will "assume the form of a monk and all kinds of shapes and forms." In dreams or during seated meditation, he will stamp their arms with the seal from a *maṇi* jewel. The seal features the letters or characters for "removal of sin" (*chuzui* 除罪). Once a monastic penitent obtains this sign, they can then "return to the monastic assembly and recite the precepts as before." This part clearly indicates that their monastic status has been restored and that they can again participate in the *poṣadha* rite of precept recitation and confession, one of Upāli's specific concerns. For male lay practitioners, obtaining the sign means that they "will not be hindered from being ordained" (T 409 13:677c7–11). (Note that neither here nor in Upāli's opening questions are female lay practitioners [*youpoyi* 優婆夷; Sk. *upāsikā*] specifically addressed, although in Upāli's questions, other categories of female practitioners are.)

If the practitioners do not receive the sign, then Ākāśagarbha will cause a voice to appear in the sky that proclaims: "Sins extinguished! Sins extinguished!" (*zuimie* 罪滅). If no voice is perceived, they will see Ākāśagarbha in a dream. The bodhisattva will instruct "monk so-and-so" or "male lay practitioner so-and-so" to perform further repentance rituals for one to forty-nine days. Then, "due to the power of paying reverence to the thirty-five buddhas and Ākāśagarbha Bodhisattva," the practitioner's sins will be rendered faint. At that point, "one who knows the Law" should have him plaster and otherwise maintain the latrines for 800 days, instructing him not to tell anyone about this. After the practitioner has completed this task, he should bathe, pay reverence to the thirty-five buddhas, and chant Ākāśagarbha's name. Prostrating himself before the twelvefold scriptures, he must explain his transgressions and evil deeds. Once he has performed repentance in this manner for another twenty-one days, the wise man must gather the practitioner's relatives and intimates.[107] Then, "before a buddha image, [they] should chant the names of the thirty-five buddhas[108] and call on Mañjuśrī and call on the bodhisattvas of this auspicious eon to serve as witnesses." At this point, the penitent essentially retakes the same precepts he originally did, but before this specific assembly of fellow practitioners and bodhisattvas. Finally, "due to the power of his austerities, his sinful deeds are forever removed," and he will not be hindered in his pursuit of the three kinds of awakening.[109]

The text then makes clear that this completes the "contemplation" in question, as the buddha next instructs Upāli to "uphold this teaching of the contemplation of Ākāśagarbha" and to explain it well for the sake of future shameless sentient beings and wicked people (T 409 13:677c23–25).

Much of the *Ākāśagarbha Contemplation Sutra* in the *Taishō* (which is based on the Second Koryŏ canon, completed *c.* 1251) are appendages to this contemplation, and they are not included in the "Old Song" (1104–1148), Yuan (1290), and Ming editions (1601).[110] (This is not to say that they are less significant for that; they are just less central for the analysis here.) These include such lists as the names of the thirty-five buddhas, fifty-three buddhas, and buddhas of the ten directions; in some cases, the text mentions the benefits of chanting the names. Also featured are the "Ākāśagarbha Bodhisattva *dhāraṇī*" and an explanation of the benefits of chanting his name and venerating him, which appears to be drawn primarily from the *Ākāśagarbha Bodhisattva Sutra*.[111] Notable as well is the *Jifayue sheku tuoluoni jing* 集法悅捨苦陀羅尼經 (*Dhāraṇī-sūtra* on Collecting the Joy of the Teachings and Getting Rid of Suffering), which centers on a past-life story of Śākyamuni as a horrible sinner.[112] Although also clearly an appendage to the "Contemplation" here, the story of even the buddha having needed to overcome past sins does fit the sutra's overall emphasis on repentance.

DISCUSSION OF THE LITERATURE

Due to space constraints, this review will focus on English-language literature. For a broader-ranging bibliographic guide, see David Quinter's article on the visualization/contemplation sutras in *Oxford Bibliographies in Buddhism*.[113]

Much of the literature on the sutras has been driven by interest in individual ones and/or issues of provenance. However, Soper's 1959 art historical study is seminal among Western-language studies treating the visualization/contemplation sutras as a group, and it features helpful summaries or other analyses of all but the *Ākāśagarbha Contemplation Sutra*.[114] Influenced in part by Soper, and increasingly by Yamabe, many subsequent art historical studies, especially on Buddhist cave temple sites in China and Central Asia, reference the visualization/contemplation sutras.[115] Cynthea Bogel also makes good use of the sutras in an art historical study of Japanese esoteric Buddhism.[116]

Leading studies of individual visualization/contemplation sutras include Birnbaum's annotated translation and analysis of the *Bhaiṣajyarāja Contemplation Sutra* within his monograph *The Healing Buddha*, originally published in 1979.[117] There have also been several translations of the *Samantabhadra Contemplation Sutra* amid a focus on the *Lotus Sutra*.[118] And as early as 1931, de Visser provided a thorough summary of the *Ākāśagarbha Contemplation Sutra* in a small, posthumously published volume on the Ākāśagarbha cult in China and Japan.[119] But historically, apart from Yamabe's many publications on the *Samādhi Sea Sutra*, most such studies have focused on the *Amitāyus Contemplation Sutra*. These include translations and analyses of significant medieval Chinese commentaries on the sutra by Tanaka, Pas, and Inagaki.[120] Inagaki also collaborated with Harold Stewart on an English-language translation of the sutra (one of many on the sutra, but singled out here for its accessibility and for Inagaki's longstanding work on the sutra).[121] Ducor and Loveday's 2011 French-language monograph on the sutra stands out for combining a careful textual analysis and translation with a thorough art historical study.[122] Also notable is Silk's 1997 essay on the frame story, which includes a provocative argument for an interweaving of Indian, Central Asian, and Chinese elements in the sutra's composition.[123]

Focus on the *Amitāyus Contemplation Sutra* has also driven Fujita's influential analyses of the provenance of the visualization/contemplation sutras, in which he assesses the evidence for both Central Asian and Chinese compilation and ultimately adopts a "compromise" theory of mixed compilation for the *Amitāyus Contemplation Sutra*.[124] Yamabe's studies of the *Samādhi Sea Sutra* strike related notes, as he argues for a "hybrid-apocrypha" theory of the sutra's original composition in Chinese, but *in* Central Asia, with many distinctly Indian elements. In many ways, Yamabe's ambitious 1999 dissertation on that sutra set a new standard for study of the visualization/contemplation sutras in the West, and his publications have influenced much Western-language scholarship on the sutras in the first two decades of the 21st century.[125]

While Yamabe's studies largely extend the focus on issues of the sutras' provenance (which is especially characteristic of Japanese scholarship), Mai's 2009 dissertation is notable for a different approach. He concentrates his analysis instead on the texts' Chinese *reception* and the process of "cult consolidation" evidenced therein. Although the dissertation is framed by an interest in the *Amitāyus Contemplation Sutra* in particular, Mai devotes successive chapters to the *Maitreya*, *Samantabhadra*, and *Amitāyus* contemplation sutras (chapters 5–7), giving each of them substantial weight.[126]

Two recent studies that also deal with provenance questions, but from a different direction, are Quinter's 2010 annotated translation and analysis of the *Mañjuśrī Parinirvāṇa Sutra* (*Wenshushili banniepan jing* 文殊師利般涅槃經; T 463) and Greene's 2012 dissertation, "Meditation, Repentance, and Visionary Experience." As part of their analyses, each author addresses one of the visualization/contemplation sutras traditionally considered lost. Based on the evidence from premodern Chinese Buddhist catalogs and analysis of the sutra's contents, Quinter argues that the common attribution of the *Mañjuśrī Parinirvāṇa Sūtra* to Nie Daozhen 聶道眞 as translator, and its corresponding dating to 280–312, is mistaken. Instead, he suggests that the sutra would be better grouped with the 5th-century milieu of the visualization/contemplation sutras, and it may well be connected to the *Mañjuśrī Contemplation Sutra* (*Wenshu guan jing* 文殊觀經) listed in Sengyou's 517 catalog as an anonymously translated, lost scripture.[127]

Similarly, the *Avalokiteśvara* (or *Avalokitasvara*) *Contemplation Sutra* (*Guanshiyin guan jing* 觀世音觀經) appears as extant in Sengyou's catalog but is listed as lost in 602 and later catalogs. However, Greene argues that the sutra may have survived in whole or part as the Upasena narrative in the *Avalokitasvara Invitation Sutra* (*Qing Guanyin jing* 請觀音經; T 1043), and appendix two of his dissertation features an annotated translation of that narrative.[128] Greene's studies, here and elsewhere, are also significant for his wide-ranging investigations of the Chinese meditation manuals linked to the visualization/contemplation sutras, as well as his revisionist appraisals of notions of "visualization" posited for both sets of scriptures.[129]

DIGITAL MATERIALS

The full Chinese texts of the six visualization/contemplation sutras can all be readily found via their *Taishō* (T) sequence number in the following two databases.

Chinese Buddhist Electronic Text Association (CBETA) (https://cbetaonline.dila.edu.tw/en/T0001_001)

The Chinese portion of the *Taishō Shinshū Daizōkyō*, volumes 1–55 and 85, is available here in searchable digital editions.

SAT Daizōkyō text database (https://21dzk.l.u-tokyo.ac.jp/SAT/index_en.html) features searchable digital editions of all the Chinese and Japanese Buddhist scriptures from the *Taishō*, volumes 1 to 85.

FURTHER READING

Abe, Stanley K. "Art and Practice in a Fifth-Century Chinese Buddhist Cave Temple." *Ars Orientalis* 20 (1990): 1–31.

Birnbaum, Raoul. *The Healing Buddha*. Rev. ed. Boston: Shambhala, 1989.

Bogel, Cynthea J. "Contemplations and Imagery: Issues Relevant to Ancient Japanese Esoteric Buddhist Icons, Ritual Practice, and Cultural Contexts." *Pacific World: Journal of the Institute of Buddhist Studies*, 3rd series, 12 (2010): 191–222.

de Visser, Marinus Willem. *The Bodhisattva Ākāśagarbha (Kokūzō) in China and Japan*. Amsterdam: Koninklijke Akademie van Wetenschappen, 1931.

Ducor, Jérôme, and Helen Loveday. *Le sūtra des contemplations du Buddha Vie-Infinie: Essai d'interprétation textuelle et iconographique*. Turnhout, Belgium: Brepols, 2011.

Fujita Kōtatsu. "The Textual Origins of the *Kuan Wu-liang-shou ching*: A Canonical Scripture of Pure Land Buddhism." Translated by Kenneth K. Tanaka. In *Chinese Buddhist Apocrypha*. Edited by Robert E. Buswell Jr., 149–173. Honolulu: University of Hawai'i Press, 1990.

Greene, Eric M. "Meditation, Repentance, and Visionary Experience in Early Medieval Chinese Buddhism." PhD thesis, University of California, Berkeley, 2012.

Greene, Eric M. "Visions and Visualizations: In Fifth-Century Chinese Buddhism and Nineteenth-Century Experimental Psychology." *History of Religions* 55, no. 3 (2016): 289–328.

Hsu, Eileen Hsiang-Ling. "Visualization Meditation and the *Siwei* Icon in Chinese Buddhist Sculpture." *Artibus Asiae* 62, no. 1 (2002): 5–32.

Inagaki, Hisao, and Harold Stewart, trans. *The Three Pure Land Sutras*. BDK English Tripiṭaka Series (Taishō Volume 12, Numbers 360, 365, 366). 2nd rev. ed. Berkeley, CA: Numata Center for Buddhist Translation and Research, 2003.

Katō, Bunnō, Yoshirō Tamura, Kōjirō Miyasaka, William E. Soothill, Wilhelm Schiffer, and Pier P. Del Campana, trans. *The Threefold Lotus Sutra: Innumerable Meanings, the Lotus Flower of the Wonderful Law, and Meditation on the Bodhisattva Universal Virtue*. New York: Weatherhill, 1975.

Kuo Li-ying. *Confession et contrition dans le bouddhisme chinois du Ve au Xe siècle*. Paris: École Française d'Extrême-Orient, 1994.

Mai, Cuong T. "Visualization Apocrypha and the Making of Buddhist Deity Cults in Early Medieval China: With Special Reference to the Cults of Amitābha, Maitreya, and Samantabhadra." PhD thesis, Indiana University, 2009.

Pas, Julian. *Visions of Sukhāvatī: Shan-Tao's Commentary on the* Kuan Wu-Liang-Shou-Fo Ching. Albany: State University of New York Press, 1995.

Quinter, David. "Visualizing the *Mañjuśrī Parinirvāṇa Sutra* as a Contemplation Sutra." *Asia Major*, 3rd series, 23, no. 2 (2010): 97–128.

Quinter, David. "Visualization/Contemplation Sutras." In *Oxford Bibliographies in Buddhism*. Edited by Richard Payne. New York: Oxford University Press, 2013. Updated in 2018. https://doi.org/10.1093/OBO/9780195393521-0137.

Sharf, Robert H. "Visualization and Mandala in Shingon Buddhism." In *Living Images: Japanese Buddhist Icons in Context*. Edited by Robert H. Sharf and Elizabeth Horton Sharf, 151–197. Stanford, CA: Stanford University Press, 2001.

Silk, Jonathan A. "The Composition of the *Guan Wuliangshoufo-Jing*: Some Buddhist and Jaina Parallels to Its Narrative Frame." *Journal of Indian Philosophy* 25, no. 2 (1997): 181–256.

Soper, Alexander Coburn. *Literary Evidence for Early Buddhist Art in China*. Ascona, Switzerland: Artibus Asiae, 1959.

Sponberg, Alan. "Meditation in Fa-Hsiang Buddhism." In *Traditions of Meditation in Chinese Buddhism*. Edited by Peter N. Gregory, 15–43. Honolulu: University of Hawai'i Press, 1986.

Sponberg, Alan. "Wŏnhyo on Maitreya Visualization." In *Maitreya, the Future Buddha*. Edited by Alan Sponberg and Helen Hardacre, 94–109. Cambridge, UK: Cambridge University Press, 1988.

Tanaka, Kenneth K. *The Dawn of Chinese Pure Land Doctrine: Ching-Ying Hui-Yüan's Commentary on the* Visualization Sutra. Albany: State University of New York Press, 1990.

Yamabe, Nobuyoshi. "*The Sūtra on the Ocean-Like Samādhi of the Visualization of the Buddha*: The Interfusion of the Chinese and Indian Cultures in Central Asia as Reflected in a Fifth Century Apocryphal Sūtra." PhD thesis, Yale University, 1999.

Yamabe, Nobuyoshi. "Practice of Visualization and the *Visualization Sutra*: An Examination of Mural Paintings at Toyok, Turfan." *Pacific World: Journal of the Institute of Buddhist Studies*, 3rd series, 4 (2002): 123–152.

Yamabe, Nobuyoshi. "Visionary Repentance and Visionary Ordination in the *Brahmā Net Sūtra*." In *Going Forth: Visions of Buddhist Vinaya*. Edited by William M. Bodiford, 17–39. Honolulu: University of Hawai'i Press, 2005.

NOTES

1. Translations of the full titles given in the summary, and the abbreviated titles used throughout this article, are adapted from Fujita Kōtatsu, "The Textual Origins of the *Kuan Wu-liang-shou ching*: A Canonical

Scripture of Pure Land Buddhism," trans. Kenneth K. Tanaka, in *Chinese Buddhist Apocrypha*, ed. Robert E. Buswell Jr. (Honolulu: University of Hawai'i Press, 1990), 149–173. "T" stands for *Taishō Shinshū Daizōkyō* 大正新脩大藏経, 100 vols., ed. Takakusu Junjirō 高楠順次郎 and Watanabe Kaigyoku 渡邊海旭 et al. (Tokyo: Taishō Issaikyō Kankōkai, 1924–35). References from the *Taishō* are identified here by text number then, as needed, by volume, page, register, and line numbers.

2. For a detailed investigation of various Indic-language terms that have been posited, and typically rejected, as possible equivalents to *guan* in the visualization/contemplation sutras (centering on its construction as *guanfo*), see Nobuyoshi Yamabe, "*The Sūtra on the Ocean-Like Samādhi of the Visualization of the Buddha:* The Interfusion of the Chinese and Indian Cultures in Central Asia as Reflected in a Fifth Century Apocryphal Sūtra" (PhD thesis, Yale University, 1999), 125–184.
3. Alexander Coburn Soper, *Literary Evidence for Early Buddhist Art in China* (Ascona, Switzerland: Artibus Asiae, 1959), 144.
4. See, for example, Stanley K. Abe, "Art and Practice in a Fifth-Century Chinese Buddhist Cave Temple," *Ars Orientalis* 20 (1990): 1–31; Eileen Hsiang-Ling Hsu, "Visualization Meditation and the *Siwei* Icon in Chinese Buddhist Sculpture," *Artibus Asiae* 62, no. 1 (2002): 5–32; Eileen Hsiang-Ling Hsu, "The Sengchou Cave and Early Imagery of Sukhāvatī," *Artibus Asiae* 71, no. 2 (2011): 283–323; Ning Qiang, "Visualization Practice and the Function of the Western Paradise Images in Turfan and Dunhuang in the Sixth to Seventh Centuries," *Journal of Inner Asian Art and Archaeology* 2 (2007): 133–142; Sunkyung Kim, "Seeing Buddhas in Cave Sanctuaries," *Asia Major*, 3rd series, 24, no. 1 (2011): 87–126. Kim's article is a mixed case, as it starts by urging caution on using "visualization" for such cave-site practices (87–88), then predominantly uses that rubric when referring to the visualization/contemplation sutras, and sometimes for the Xiaonanhai cave that is the article's focus. For examples of cave-site studies from Yamabe's work, focusing respectively on Toyok in Turfan and the Mogao caves in Dunhuang, see Nobuyoshi Yamabe, "Practice of Visualization and the *Visualization Sutra*: An Examination of Mural Paintings at Toyok, Turfan," *Pacific World: Journal of the Institute of Buddhist Studies*, 3rd series, 4 (2002): 123–152; and Yamabe, "Transformation Tableaux 'Based on' the Amitayus *Visualization Sutra:* Their Deviations from the Text," *Kristi* 1 (2008): 1–31.
5. Soper, *Literary Evidence*, 216; Yamabe, "Sūtra on the Ocean-Like Samādhi," 42, 56; Cuong T. Mai, "Visualization Apocrypha and the Making of Buddhist Deity Cults in Early Medieval China: With Special Reference to the Cults of Amitābha, Maitreya, and Samantabhadra" (PhD thesis, Indiana University, 2009), 205–206. Soper does suggest that for the *Maitreya Contemplation Sutra*, *guan* would be better rendered as "meditation" (216), while Mai's analysis clearly aims to complicate the understanding of "visualization." Mai's views will be addressed in the section on "Recitation."
6. The full phrase reads: "Performing the contemplation (*guan*) this way is called correct contemplation. If one contemplates otherwise, it is called false contemplation" (T 452 14:419c10; 420c9–10). On this phrase in the visualization/contemplation sutras and related scriptures, see, for example, Fujita, "Textual Origins," 164; Yamabe, "Sūtra on the Ocean-Like Samādhi," 181–182, 364–371; David Quinter, "Visualizing the *Mañjuśrī Parinirvāṇa Sutra* as a Contemplation Sutra," *Asia Major*, 3rd series, 23, no. 2 (2010), 118, 119–120.
7. See, for example, Yamabe, "Sūtra on the Ocean-Like Samādhi," 57, 231, 246.
8. See Yamabe, "Sūtra on the Ocean-Like Samādhi," 55–58, including 56n33.
9. Robert H. Sharf, "Visualization and Mandala in Shingon Buddhism," in *Living Images: Japanese Buddhist Icons in Context*, ed. Robert H. Sharf and Elizabeth Horton Sharf (Stanford, CA: Stanford University Press, 2001), 151–197, especially 151, 153, 156.
10. Sharf, "Visualization and Mandala," 154–155.
11. Sharf, "Visualization and Mandala," 163. Examples that Sharf gives (using the Japanese readings) include "*kan* 觀, *kansō* 觀想, *kansatsu* 觀察, *teikan* 諦觀, *kannen* 觀念." They also extend to related terms, such as *sō* 想, *nensō* 念想, and *shii* 思惟, that appear commonly within both the visualization/contemplation sutras and the esoteric texts he examines. See also Sharf, "Visualization and Mandala," 185–186.

12. In this article, the "Chinese meditation manuals" often linked to the visualization/contemplation sutras refer to: (a) *Meditation Manual by Dharmatrāta* (*Damoduoluo chan jing* 達摩多羅禪經; T 618), traditionally attributed to Buddhabhadra (359–429) between 398 and 421; (b) *Manual of the Samādhi of Sitting Meditation* (*Zuochan sanmei jing* 坐禪三昧經; T 614), attributed to Kumārajīva (344–413); (c) *Essential Explanation of the Methods of Meditation* (*Chanfa yaojie* 禪法要解; T 616), attributed to Kumārajīva; (d) *Abridged Essentials of Meditation* (*Siwei lüeyao fa* 思惟略要法; T 617), attributed to Kumārajīva; (e) *Essentials of the Meditation Manual Consisting of Five Gates* (*Wumen chanjing yaoyong fa* 五門禪經要用法; T 619), attributed to Dharmamitra (356–442); (f) *Manual of the Secret Essentials of Meditation* (*Chan miyaofa jing* 禪祕要法經; T 613), attributed to Kumārajīva; and (g) *Secret Essential Methods to Cure the Diseases Caused by Meditation* (*Zhi chanbing miyao fa* 治禪病祕要法; T 620), attributed to Juqu Jingsheng (d. 464). See Yamabe, "Sūtra on the Ocean-Like Samādhi," 59–60; Nobuyoshi Yamabe, "The Paths of Śrāvakas and Bodhisattvas in Meditative Practices," *Acta Asiatica* 96 (2009): 49–50. Yamabe's lists of the relevant manuals also include the Sanskrit "*Yogalehrbuch*" (Yoga Manual). Fragments of the manual were discovered in Central Asia, and the reconstructed text shows many parallels with the Chinese manuals and the *Samādhi Sea Sutra*.
13. Eric M. Greene, "Visions and Visualizations: In Fifth-Century Chinese Buddhism and Nineteenth-Century Experimental Psychology," *History of Religions* 55, no. 3 (2016): 313n90, cites: Bhikkhu Assaji, trans., *The Sutra of Visualizing the Buddha of Immeasurable Length of Life* (Hong Kong: International Buddhist Propaganda Association, 1939).
14. On this issue, see especially Alan Sponberg, "Meditation in Fa-hsiang Buddhism," in *Traditions of Meditation in Chinese Buddhism*, ed. Peter N. Gregory (Honolulu: University of Hawai'i Press, 1986), 15–21. This chapter is also helpful for understanding the *Maitreya Contemplation Sutra*, as is Sponberg's related study, "Wŏnhyo on Maitreya Visualization," in *Maitreya, the Future Buddha*, ed. Alan Sponberg and Helen Hardacre (Cambridge, UK: Cambridge University Press, 1988), 94–109.
15. The first English-language translation of the *Amitāyus Contemplation Sutra*, which has had long-standing influence, back-translated the Chinese title into Sanskrit as *Amitāyur-dhyāna-sūtra*. See J. Takakusu, "The Amitāyur-dhyāna-sūtra," in *Buddhist Mahāyāna Texts*, ed. F. Max Müller (New York: Dover, 1969), Part 2, 159–201 (original edition, Oxford: Clarendon, 1894).
16. *Chanding* can also translate (or be back-translated into) "*dhyāna* and *samādhi*." But that rendering still presupposes practices and states of meditative concentration, which is what is most important here.
17. See Eric M. Greene, "Meditation, Repentance, and Visionary Experience in Early Medieval Chinese Buddhism" (PhD thesis, University of California, Berkeley, 2012), 84–86.
18. See the section on the *Samantabhadra Contemplation Sutra* here and T 277 9:389c7–8, c21–24.
19. Greene, "Meditation, Repentance," 85.
20. See T 1161 20:661c7–c16; 663a9–16.
21. For an analysis of *guan* and related compounds as "eidetic contemplation" in esoteric Buddhism (which also takes into account other meanings), with reference to the visualization/contemplation sutras, see Cynthea J. Bogel, "Contemplations and Imagery: Issues Relevant to Ancient Japanese Esoteric Buddhist Icons, Ritual Practice, and Cultural Contexts," *Pacific World: Journal of the Institute of Buddhist Studies*, 3rd series, 12 (2010): 193–201.
22. See Greene, "Meditation, Repentance"; Greene, "Visions and Visualization"; and Eric M. Greene, "Atonement of *Pārājika* Transgressions in Fifth-Century Chinese Buddhism," in *Rules of Engagement: Medieval Traditions of Buddhist Monastic Regulation*, ed. Susan Andrews, Jinhua Chen, and Cuilan Liu (Bochum, Germany: Projektverlag, 2017), 369–408.
23. In addition to Greene's studies, see, for example, Raoul Birnbaum, *The Healing Buddha*, rev. ed. (Boston: Shambhala, 1989); Fujita, "Textual Origins"; Kuo Li-ying, *Confession et contrition dans le bouddhisme chinois du Ve au Xe siècle* (Paris: École Française d'Extrême-Orient, 1994); Quinter, "Visualizing the

Mañjuśrī Parinirvāṇa Sutra"; Jérôme Ducor and Helen Loveday, *Le sūtra des contemplations du Buddha Vie-Infinie: Essai d'interprétation textuelle et iconographique* (Turnhout, Belgium: Brepols, 2011).

24. For examples of "reciting the name" in the *Ākāśagarbha Contemplation Sutra*, see T 409 13:677b27 and 677c20–21. For examples from the remaining visualization/contemplation sutras, see Fujita's comparative tables of terminological parallels in "Textual Origins," 164, and in Fujita Kōtatsu 藤田宏達, *Genshi jōdo shisō no kenkyū* 原始浄土思想の研究 (Tokyo: Iwanami Shoten, 1970), 129. See also Quinter, "Visualizing the *Mañjuśrī Parinirvāṇa Sutra*," 118–119 (including 118n88).
25. Fujita, "Textual Origins," 160–161. See also Fujita, *Genshi jōdo shisō*, 129; Kagawa Takao 香川孝雄, "'Kanmuryōjukyō' no seiritsu mondai shikō『観無量寿経』の成立問題試考," *Bukkyō daigaku sōgō kenkyūjo kiyō* 仏教大学総合研究所紀要 1: *Jōdokyō no sōgōteki kenkyū bessatsu* 浄土教の総合的研究別冊: 26–28.
26. Luis O. Gómez, trans., *Land of Bliss: The Paradise of the Buddha of Measureless Light; Sanskrit and Chinese Versions of the Sukhāvatīvyūha Sutras* (Honolulu: University of Hawai'i Press, 1996), 245n15.
27. Sharf, "Visualization and Mandala," 195.
28. Robert H. Sharf, *Coming to Terms with Chinese Buddhism: A Reading of the Treasure Store Treatise* (Honolulu: University of Hawai'i Press), 264.
29. See Yamabe, "Sūtra on the Ocean-Like Samādhi," 216–217, Appendix 3 (especially 513, 554–557). For Yamabe's critical edition of the *Sūtra on the Major and Minor Bodily Marks*, see Appendix 4 there.
30. Mai, "Visualization Apocrypha," 239.
31. Mai, "Visualization Apocrypha," 236, 237.
32. Fujita, "Textual Origins," 164; Fujita, *Genshi jōdo shisō*, 127.
33. T 643 15:655b7–b24. See also Greene, "Meditation, Repentance," 294, on this section. Given the sutra's length, there are naturally other references to repentance; see the section "Samādhi Sea Sutra, T 643" for a few examples. The one here was simply chosen to underscore the interweaving of repentance and "visualization" or "contemplation."
34. T 365 12:341a29–b2; Hisao Inagaki and Harold Stewart, trans., *The Three Pure Land Sutras*, 2nd rev. ed. (Berkeley, CA: Numata Center for Buddhist Translation and Research, 2003), 66.
35. T 365 12:341b19–21; Inagaki and Stewart, *The Three Pure Land Sutras*, 67.
36. The latter two names the buddha provides for the *Bhaiṣajyarāja Contemplation Sutra* are "Nectar and Sublime Medicine for Curing the Afflictions and Illness," and "Contemplation (*guan*) of the Pure Material Bodies of Bhaiṣajyarāja and Bhaiṣajyasamudgata." See T 1161 20:666b4–7 for the full list of four.
37. See especially Zhiyi's *Fahua sanmei chan yi* 法華三昧懺儀 (Procedures for the Lotus Samādhi Repentance; T 1941) and Daniel B. Stevenson, "The Four Kinds of Samādhi in Early T'ien-t'ai Buddhism," in *Traditions of Meditation in Chinese Buddhism*, 67–72. For a broader-ranging analysis of the origins of the Lotus Samādhi rite, see Daniel B. Stevenson, "The T'ien-t'ai Four Forms of Samādhi and Late North-South Dynasties, Sui, and Early T'ang Buddhist Devotionalism" (PhD thesis, Columbia University, 1987), 188–214. For a translation based on a critical edition of Zhiyi's text, see Stevenson, "The T'ien-t'ai Four Forms," 468–537.
38. See Zhiyi's *Mohe zhiguan* 摩訶止觀, T 1911 46:15b18–19, for the reference to the "Ākāśagarbha" practice. The later Tiantai patriarch Zhanran 湛然 (711–782), commenting on this passage, elaborates on the practice and cites the "*Ākāśagarbha Sutra*." Based on the sutra excerpts he quotes, this refers to the *Ākāśagarbha Contemplation Sutra*; see *Zhiguan fuxing zhuan hongjue* 止觀輔行傳弘決, T 1912 46:196c17–197a13. See also the discussion of Zhiyi's fourth category of *samādhi* practice in Stevenson, "The Four Kinds of Samādhi," 72–84, and 94n83, which references the Zhanran comments.
39. T 409 13:677c18–c22. This passage also underscores the significance of the sutra for bodhisattva-precepts traditions beginning to flourish at the time, another point it shares with the *Samantabhadra*

Contemplation Sutra. See Nobuyoshi Yamabe, "Visionary Repentance and Visionary Ordination in the *Brahmā Net Sūtra*," in *Going Forth: Visions of Buddhist Vinaya*, ed. William M. Bodiford (Honolulu: University of Hawai'i Press, 2005), 17–39. On bodhisattva-precepts traditions in China more broadly then, see Tōru Funayama, "The Acceptance of Buddhist Precepts by the Chinese in the Fifth Century," *Journal of Asian History* 38, no. 2 (2004): 97–120.

40. Yamabe, "*Sūtra on the Ocean-Like Samādhi*."
41. See Yamabe, "Sūtra on the Ocean-Like Samādhi," especially 25–29; Soper, *Literary Evidence*, 184–195.
42. Translations of the chapter titles are based on the *Taishō* text (but omitting the term for "chapter" in each), with reference to the translations in Yamabe, "Sūtra on the Ocean-Like Samādhi," 25–26. The "Horse-King Organ" (*mawangzang* 馬王藏) could alternatively be translated as "Horse-King Treasury," and Yamabe renders the term as "Hidden Male Organ." That it indicates the Buddha's concealed penis, one of the thirty-two marks of a buddha, is clear in any case.
43. See Yamabe, "Sūtra on the Ocean-Like Samādhi," 246, which refers specifically to chapter 3 of the *Samādhi Sea Sutra* and "visualization" practice.
44. On the section on the "Buddha Emanation Cave" (alt. "Buddha Shadow" or "Buddha Image" cave), see Soper, *Literary Evidence*, 185–86, 191–192; Yamabe, "Sūtra on the Ocean-Like Samādhi," 263–298. For issues with the typical rendering of *ying* 影 in the cave's name as "Shadow," see Yamabe, "Sūtra on the Ocean-Like Samādhi," 263n1; Greene, "Meditation, Repentance," 223–224n68.
45. For the full four stories, see T 15:683b6-687a11. For analyses, see Yamabe, "Sūtra on the Ocean-Like Samādhi," 377–426; Nobuyoshi Yamabe, "The *Ocean Sūtra* as a Cross-Cultural Product: An Analysis of Some Stories on the Buddha's 'Hidden Organ,'" in *"The Way of Buddha" 2003: The 100th Anniversary of the Otani Mission and the 50th of the Research Society for Central Asian Cultures*, ed. Irisawa Takashi (Kyoto: Ryukoku University, 2010), 257–268; Nobuyoshi Yamabe, "Indian Myth Transformed in a Chinese Apocryphal Text: Two Stories on the Buddha's Hidden Organ," in *India in the Chinese Imagination: Myth, Religion, and Thought*, ed. John Kieschnick and Meir Shahar (Philadelphia: University of Pennsylvania Press, 2014), 61–80, 233–241.
46. For an efficient sampling of such influence, see the "Later Quotations" section in Yamabe, "Sūtra on the Ocean-Like Samādhi," 34–37.
47. Yamabe, "Sūtra on the Ocean-Like Samādhi," 127, 170, 353.
48. See T 643 15:681b29–c4 and 690c1–c6, respectively, for these passages. For a more detailed sampling of *Samādhi Sea Sutra* passages recommending images as aids to devotional practices, see Soper 1959, 188–192.
49. Kenneth K. Tanaka, *The Dawn of Chinese Pure Land Doctrine: Ching-ying Hui-yüan's Commentary on the* Visualization Sutra (Albany: State University of New York Press, 1990), xvii.
50. Vincent Eltschinger, "Pure Land Sūtras," in *Brill's Encyclopedia of Buddhism*, ed. Jonathan A. Silk, Oskar von Hinüber, and Vincent Eltschinger, Vol. 1, *Literature and Languages* (Leiden, The Netherlands: Brill, 2015), 221.
51. On such meditation specialists, see especially Greene, "Meditation, Repentance." On Kālayaśas numbering among them, see Greene, "Meditation, Repentance," 246.
52. Fujita, "Textual Origins," 156.
53. Fujita, "Textual Origins." See also Fujita Kōtatsu 藤田宏達, *Jōdo sanbukyō no kenkyū* 浄土三部経の研究 (Tokyo: Iwanami Shoten, 2007), 545, where he reaffirms his theories on the compilation.
54. T 365 12:341b16–21; Inagaki and Stewart, *The Three Pure Land Sutras*, 67. Translations from the *Amitāyus Contemplation Sutra* in this section are adapted from Inagaki and Stewart, *The Three Pure Land Sutras*, with modifications based on the *Taishō* text and for consistency with the present author's translations elsewhere in the article.
55. T 365 12:341c6; Inagaki and Stewart, *The Three Pure Land Sutras*, 67.

56. T 365 12:341c18–22; Inagaki and Stewart, *The Three Pure Land Sutras*, 68.
57. T 365 12:341c27–342a5; Inagaki and Stewart, *The Three Pure Land Sutras*, 69.
58. T 365 12:342a5–22; Inagaki and Stewart, *The Three Pure Land Sutras*, 69–70.
59. T 365 12:342a22–b1; Inagaki and Stewart, *The Three Pure Land Sutras*, 70.
60. T 365 12:342b1–22; Inagaki and Stewart, *The Three Pure Land Sutras*, 70–71.
61. T 365 12:342b23–c6; Inagaki and Stewart, *The Three Pure Land Sutras*, 71–72.
62. T 365 12:342c6–14; Inagaki and Stewart, *The Three Pure Land Sutras*, 72.
63. T 365 12:342c14–343a17; Inagaki and Stewart, *The Three Pure Land Sutras*, 72–73.
64. This article uses "the Buddha" (capitalized) to refer to Śākyamuni Buddha, who is considered the historical buddha, and "the buddha" (lowercase) when the referent is more ambiguous or likely refers to another buddha, such as Amitāyus.
65. T 365 12:343a18–b14; Inagaki and Stewart, *The Three Pure Land Sutras*, 73–75.
66. For related arguments, see Greene, "Meditation, Repentance," and Greene, "Visions and Visualizations."
67. T 365 12:343b15–c10; Inagaki and Stewart, *The Three Pure Land Sutras*, 75–76.
68. T 365 12:343c11–344a17; Inagaki and Stewart, *The Three Pure Land Sutras*, 76–77.
69. T 365 12:344a18–b14; Inagaki and Stewart, *The Three Pure Land Sutras*, 77–78.
70. T 365 12:344b14–b24; Inagaki and Stewart, *The Three Pure Land Sutras*, 78–79.
71. T 365 12:344b25–c8; Inagaki and Stewart, *The Three Pure Land Sutras*, 79.
72. T 365 12:344c9–345b7; Inagaki and Stewart, *The Three Pure Land Sutras*, 79–82; T 365 12:345b8–c9; Inagaki and Stewart, *The Three Pure Land Sutras*, 82–83; and T 365 12:345c10–346a26; Inagaki and Stewart, *The Three Pure Land Sutras*, 83–85.
73. See in particular Shandao 善導 (613–681) versus Huiyuan 慧遠 (523–592) and others on this; Yamabe, "Transformation Tableaux," 1–31. See Yamabe, "Transformation Tableaux," 2–3 for citations from premodern commentaries; the issue is related as well to paintings of scenes from the sutra addressed in Yamabe's article. See also Julian Pas, *Visions of Sukhāvatī: Shan-Tao's Commentary on the* Kuan Wu-Liang-Shou-Fo Ching (Albany: State University of New York Press, 1995), xiii, 47.
74. T 365 12:346a27–b2; Inagaki and Stewart, *The Three Pure Land Sutras*, 86.
75. Yamabe, "Sūtra on the Ocean-Like Samādhi," 53 and 51; Pas, *Visions of Sukhāvatī*, 43.
76. Birnbaum, *The Healing Buddha*, 35–51, 115–148.
77. On the greater popularity of the older brother, see Birnbaum, *The Healing Buddha*, 224–227.
78. Inoue Hirofumi 井上博文, "'Kan Yakuō Yakujō ni bosatsukyō' no kenkyū' 『観薬王薬上二菩薩経』の研究, Ryūkoku daigaku daigakuin bungaku kenkyūka kiyō 龍谷大学大学院文学研究科紀要 23 (2001): 1–3. On the healing powers of the *Lotus Sutra* in the "Medicine King" chapter, see T 262 9:54c23–26; Burton Watson, trans., *The Lotus Sutra* (New York: Columbia University Press, 1993), 288.
79. See Yamabe, "Sūtra on the Ocean-Like Samādhi," Appendix 1, 502–507; Inoue, "'Kan Yakuō Yakujō ni bosatsukyō' no kenkyū;'" and Inoue's modern Japanese annotated translation of the *Bhaiṣajyarāja Contemplation Sutra*, "'Kan Yakuō Yakujō ni bosatsukyō' to kanren kyōten" 『観薬王薬上二菩薩経』と関連経典, Ryūkoku daigaku bukkyōgaku kenkyūshitsu nenpō (龍谷大学仏教学研究室年報) 11 (2001b): 1–24.
80. Fujita, "Textual Origins," 155.
81. Miyata Noboru, "Types of Maitreya Belief in Japan," in *Maitreya, the Future Buddha*, 176–177; Richard Bowring, Richard McBride II, Miyaji Akira, and Jonathan Silk, "Maitreya," in *Brill's Encyclopedia of Buddhism*, ed. Jonathan A. Silk, Richard Bowring, Vincent Eltschinger, and Michael Radich, vol. 2, *Lives* (Leiden, The Netherlands: Brill, 2019), 303.
82. For two studies complicating the ascent/descent picture, see Jan Nattier, "The Meanings of the Maitreya Myth: A Typological Analysis," in *Maitreya, the Future Buddha*, 23–47; Sponberg, "Wŏnhyo on Maitreya Visualization," in *Maitreya, the Future Buddha*, 94–109.

83. T 452 14:418c5–9. Translations and paraphrases from the *Maitreya Contemplation Sutra* in this section are based on the *Taishō* text, but with reference to translations of various passages in Mai, "Visualization Apocrypha," chapter 5.
84. These same dharmas are later expounded through the instruments played by a group of "hundreds of thousands of heavenly maidens" (T 452 14:419b11–13).
85. T 452 14:419a29–b1. In contrast to Amitāyus's Pure Land, in which women are said to be transformed into men upon rebirth there, both women and men can be reborn in Tuṣita.
86. Soper, *Literary Evidence*, 215–216.
87. Mai, "Visualization Apocrypha," 163, 201, 208.
88. Mai, "Visualization Apocrypha," 225–226.
89. Christoph Anderl, "Miscellaneous Informal Remarks on Narrative Structures in Chinese Maitreya Accounts," in *Sun Changwu jiaoshou bashi huadan jinian wenji* 孙昌武教授八十华诞纪念文集, ed. Niang Jiayu 宁稼雨, Xiao Zhanpeng 肖占鹏, Zhan Ru 湛如, Pu Hui 普慧, and Zhang Peifeng 张培锋 (Tianjin, China: Baihua Wenyi Chubanshe, 2016), 124.
90. See *Essentials of the Meditation Manual Consisting of Five Gates* (T 619) for the meditation manual attributed to Dharmamitra, and Yamabe, "Sūtra on the Ocean-Like Samādhi," 84–100, for an analysis. Also, based primarily on evidence from the catalog section of Sengyou's *Compilations of Notices* (T 2145), some modern scholars conclude that the *Manual of the Secret Essentials of Meditation* (T 613) was first attributed to Dharmamitra (although Kumārajīva is listed as the translator in the *Taishō*). For the complications of that evidence, however, see Greene, "Meditation, Repentance," 115–116.
91. See especially Fujita, "Textual Origins." For more on Dharmamitra specifically, see Fujita, "Textual Origins," 152–153 and 156–157.
92. The "opening sutra" in the *Threefold Lotus Sutra* is the *Sutra of Innumerable Meanings* (*Wuliangyi jing* 無量義經; T 276), which is followed by the *Lotus Sutra* itself, then the *Samantabhadra Contemplation Sutra*. Translations in this section from the *Samantabhadra Contemplation Sutra* are based on the *Taishō* text, but benefitting from the translations of the *Threefold Lotus Sutra* in Bunnō Katō, Yoshirō Tamura, Kōjirō Miyasaka, William E. Soothill, Wilhelm Schiffer, and Pier P. Del, trans., *The Threefold Lotus Sutra: Innumerable Meanings, the Lotus Flower of the Wonderful Law, and Meditation on the Bodhisattva Universal Virtue* (New York: Weatherhill, 1975), and in Gene Reeves, trans., *The Lotus Sutra: A Contemporary Translation of a Buddhist Classic* (Boston: Wisdom, 2008).
93. The six sense organs in this sutra are those for the faculties of sight, hearing, smell, speech, touch, and thought. These are typically represented as the ears, nose, tongue or mouth, the body for tactile sensations, and the mind for thought. The faculty associated with the tongue is rendered as "speech" here because the corresponding section in the sutra emphasizes speech rather than taste (see T 277 9:392b16–27).
94. T 277 9:389c19–24. This interpretation of what is being "recited and upheld" differs from that in Katō et al., *Threefold Lotus Sutra*, 348, and Reeves, *Lotus Sutra*, 402, which each insert an additional reference to the "Great Vehicle" (Mahayana) that is not in the text at that point (389c22). "Mahayana" does appear in the next line, but both studies use that one reference twice to produce their renderings. Based on the grammar and narrative flow, the present author thinks that the contemplation (*guan*) is what is being recited and upheld. See also Mai, "Visualization Apocrypha," 278, and Greene, "Meditation, Repentance," 85, whose renderings concur.
95. For the jade maidens, see T 277 9:390a5–6 and 390b3–4. In the *Maitreya Contemplation Sutra*, in addition to heavenly maidens, jade maidens also make an appearance, at the close of the main section detailing the wonders of Tuṣita Heaven; see T 452 14:419b28–c1.
96. T 277 9:390b12–b26. The term translated in the final sentence here as "stage" (in keeping with various prior translations of the sutra), *jingjie* 境界, might be best understood as a "verificatory vision" that confirms that the practitioner's first contemplation of Samantabhadra has been successful. On this use of *jingjie*, see Greene, "Meditation, Repentance," 69; Greene, "Visions and Visualizations," 318–319.

97. Again, see T 277 9:389c19–24.
98. T 277 9:390c8–c23. "The *samādhi* in which the buddhas appear" (*zhu fo xianqian sanmei* 諸佛現前三昧) is one of the translations for the *pratyutpanna-samādhi*. The phrase can also be found in the *Samādhi Sea Sutra* (T 643 15:693c6–8; 695b10) and the *Amitāyus Contemplation Sutra* (T 365 12:346b3). On this *samādhi* and the principal texts outlining it, see Paul Harrison, "*Buddhānusmṛti* in the *Pratyutpanna-buddha-saṃmukhāvasthita-samādhi-sūtra*," *Journal of Indian Philosophy* 6, no. 1 (1978): 35–57; Paul Harrison, trans., *The Pratyutpanna Samādhi Sutra*, BDK English Tripiṭaka 25, no. 2 (Berkeley: Numata Center for Buddhist Translation and Research, 1998).
99. See Yamabe, "Sūtra on the Ocean-Like Samādhi," 50, which supports this characterization of the *Ākāśagarbha Contemplation Sutra* in Tsukinowa Kenryū 月輪賢隆, *Butten no hihanteki kenkyū* 仏典の批判的研究 (Kyoto: Hyakkaen, 1971), 118.
100. See Stevenson, "The T'ien-t'ai Four Forms of Samādhi," 230–232; Kuo, *Confession et contrition*, 136–138; Yamabe, "Visionary Repentance and Visionary Ordination," 32–33; Greene, "Atonement of *Pārājika* Transgressions," 389–403.
101. "Outcaste" here renders *zhantuoluo* 旃陀羅 (Sk. *caṇḍāla*). Greene, "Atonement of *Pārājika* Transgressions," 392n62, indicates that the reference is likely based on the *Ākāśagarbha Bodhisattva Sutra* (T 405), which likens those committing grave transgressions to *caṇḍāla*. For a recent study of *caṇḍāla* in Indian Buddhist literature, see Jonathan A. Silk, "Indian Buddhist Attitudes toward Outcastes: Rhetoric around *caṇḍālas*," *Indo-Iranian Journal* 63 (2020): 128–187, and 167 for a reference to that sutra.
102. Translations from the sutra in this section are based on the *Taishō* edition, but benefitting from the summary in Marinus Willem de Visser, *The Bodhisattva Ākāśagarbha (Kokūzō) in China and Japan* (Amsterdam: Koninklijke Akademie van Wetenschappen, 1931), 29–35; and the translations of key passages in Yamabe, "Visionary Repentance and Visionary Ordination," 32–33; and Greene, "Atonement of *Pārājika* Transgressions," 390–398.
103. *Poṣadha* (Ch. *busa* 布薩) refers to the monthly ceremonies of precept recitation and confession. For the monastic community, this is typically held twice per month, while the shared ceremony for monastics and lay practitioners is held six days per month. On the "broken rock" metaphor, see Greene, "Atonement of *Pārājika* Transgressions," 394 and 394n64, from which the translation of that sentence is adapted.
104. Greene, "Atonement of *Pārājika* Transgressions," 392–393n63.
105. The sutra states that the method is called "Determination of the *Vinaya*" (*Jueding pini* 決定毘尼), which signals its indebtedness to the *Upāli's Questions Sutra on Determination of the Vinaya* (Sk. *Vinaya-viniścaya-Upāli-paripṛcchā*). Yamabe identifies the earliest Chinese version of that sutra as the *Jueding pini jing* 決定毘尼經 (T 325). However, he attributes the visionary repentance and self-ordination methods that follow here primarily to the combination of the *Upāli's Questions Sutra* and bodhisattva-precepts traditions in Guṇavarman's translation of the *Bodhisattva Stage* (*Pusa dichi jing* 菩薩地持經 [T 1581]; *Pusa shanjie jing* 菩薩善戒經 [T 1582]). See Yamabe, "Visionary Repentance and Visionary Ordination," 28–33. See also his more detailed Japanese-language version of that essay: Yamabe Nobuyoshi 山部能宜, "'*Bonmōkyō*' ni okeru kōsōgyō no kenkyū: Toku ni zenkan kyōten to no kanrensei ni chakumoku shite"『梵網経』における好相行の研究: 特に禅観経典との関連性に着目して, in *Hokuchō zui tō chūgoku bukkyō shisōshi* (北朝隋唐中国仏教思想史), ed. Aramaki Noritoshi 荒牧典俊 (Kyoto: Hōzōkan, 2000), 205–269, especially 222–230.
106. T 409 13:677b20–c7. The phrase rendered here as "monastic rituals" (*zhongfa* 衆法) could alternatively be translated as "assembled (or many) teachings."
107. It is a bit ambiguous whether the "wise man" (*zhi zhe* 知者) refers to the penitent himself or to the previous "one who knows the Law" (or "one who knows the procedures"; *zhifa zhe* 知法者) instructing the practitioner to clean the latrines. Due to the similarity in phrasing, however, the latter interpretation

is opted for in this article. See also Greene, "Atonement of *Pārājika* Transgressions," 397, which renders both terms as "his [i.e., the practitioner's] preceptor."

108. The *Taishō* edition just indicates to "chant the names of the thirty-five buddhas" here, but other editions indicate to also "chant the name of Ākāśagarbha." See T 409 13:677n28.
109. T 409 13:677c11–c23. The "three kinds of awakening" (*san zhong puti* 三種菩提) refer to those of *śrāvaka* (auditors), pratyekabuddhas (solitary, self-enlightened buddhas), and buddhas.
110. See T 409 13:678n2 and n4.
111. See de Visser, *The Bodhisattva Ākāśagarbha*, 31–35, on those parts.
112. T 409 13:679c29–680b23. On that sutra's preservation here and within other texts, and for a critical edition and translation, see Jonathan A. Silk, "The *Jifayue sheku tuoluoni jing*: Translation, Non-translation, Both or Neither?," *Journal of the International Association of Buddhist Studies* 31, no. 1–2 (2008 [2010]): 369–420.
113. David Quinter, "Visualization/Contemplation Sutras," in *Oxford Bibliographies in Buddhism*, ed. Richard Payne (New York: Oxford University Press, 2013/2018).
114. Soper, *Literary Evidence*.
115. See, for example, Abe, "Art and Practice"; Hsu, "Visualization Meditation"; Hsu, "The Sengchou Cave"; Ning, "Visualization Practice"; Kim, "Seeing Buddhas in Cave Sanctuaries"; Angela F. Howard, "On 'Art in the Dark' and Meditation in Central Asian Buddhist Caves," *The Eastern Buddhist* 46, no. 2 (2015): 19–39.
116. Bogel, "Contemplations and Imagery."
117. Birnbaum, *The Healing Buddha*, 35–51, 115–148.
118. See, for example, Katō et al., *The Threefold Lotus Sutra*, 345–370; Reeves, *The Lotus Sutra*, 399–423; and Michio Shinozaki, Brook A. Ziporyn, and David C. Earhart, trans., *The Threefold Lotus Sutra: A Modern Translation for Contemporary Readers* (Tokyo: Kosei, 2019), 382–413.
119. de Visser, *The Bodhisattva Ākāśagarbha*, 29–35.
120. See Tanaka, "*The Dawn of Chinese Pure Land Doctrine*"; Pas, *Visions of Sukhāvatī*; Hisao Inagaki, trans., "Shan-tao's Exposition of the Method of Contemplation on Amida Buddha," Parts 1–3, in *Pacific World: Journal of the Institute of Buddhist Studies*, 3rd series, 1 (1999): 77–89; *Pacific World*, 3rd series, 2 (2000): 207–228; and *Pacific World*, 3rd series, 3 (2001): 277–288.
121. Inagaki and Stewart, *The Three Pure Land Sutras*, 63–87.
122. Ducor and Loveday, *Le sūtra des contemplations du Buddha Vie-Infinie*.
123. Jonathan A. Silk, "The Composition of the *Guan Wuliangshoufo-jing*: Some Buddhist and Jaina Parallels to Its Narrative Frame," *Journal of Indian Philosophy* 25, no. 2 (1997): 181–256.
124. In English, see Fujita, "Textual Origins."
125. Among Yamabe's studies, see, for example, "Sūtra on the Ocean-Like Samādhi" (his 1999 dissertation, which remains his most comprehensive work on the sutras); Yamabe, "Practice of Visualization and the *Visualization Sutra*"; Yamabe, "Visionary Repentance and Visionary Ordination"; Yamabe, "The Paths of Śrāvakas and Bodhisattvas"; Yamabe, "The *Ocean Sūtra* as a Cross-Cultural Product"; and Yamabe, "Indian Myth Transformed in a Chinese Apocryphal Text."
126. Mai, "Visualization Apocrypha."
127. Quinter, "Visualizing the *Mañjuśrī Parinirvāṇa Sutra*." For the listing in Sengyou's catalog, see T 2145 55:32c7.
128. See Greene, "Meditation, Repentance," 328–341, including 328n5, for the catalog references.
129. See especially Greene, "Meditation, Repentance" and "Visions and Visualizations."

David Quinter

W

WESTERN BUDDHISM AND RACE

DEFINING ORIENTALISM AND ORIENTALIST

Edward Said's landmark work, *Orientalism*, proves invaluable for locating the emergence of 19th-century Western Buddhist representations of Asian Buddhisms as less authentic forms of an "essential" and "pure" Buddhism. The emphases on textual translation and linguistics that led to the formation of oriental studies on Hinduism, Buddhism, and Islam have colonial encounters as their starting point and therefore are located in regimes of knowledge and power. Building on Foucault's assertation that discourse becomes knowledge, Said famously described "Orientalism" as "a Western style of dominating, restructuring, and having authority over the Orient."[1] Said further argued that this knowledge, supported by institutions and "regimes of truth," became an entire way of interpreting and understanding "Orientals," including their religions. This knowledge, shaped by cultural perceptions and widely circulated in scholarly networks, constituted a kind of discursive power exercised over objects of study that included non-Western, nonwhite Buddhists themselves. Orientalist scholarship formulated and employed a set of concepts by which the Orient could be made familiar for Europeans. Orientalist constructions of Buddhism also emerged in relation to social Darwinist and eugenicist conceptions of race that were prominent in Europe and the United

States. The constructions of race and racial difference in this era resulted in a collusive bifurcation between Europeans and non-Europeans, whereby the former was placed at the apex of culture and civilization. This demarcation reshaped the concept of race and ethnicity, becoming what theorist Homi Bhabha notes as "one of the most elusive and effective strategies of colonial power and knowledge."[2]

SCIENTIFIC RACISM

In *Racism*, Robert Miles states that prior to the age of exploration (early 15th century to early 17th century), group differences were largely based on religion, language, and geography. European colonialists identified themselves in terms of their religious identity (e.g., "Christian") or ties to a particular geographical or ethnic group (e.g., "English"), rather than in terms of a racial category such as "white." With the advent of the science of taxonomy in the 17th century, however, the modern conception of race emerged to dichotomize the differences between Europeans and non-Europeans.[3] François Bernier (1625–1688) was the first scientist to classify human beings into groups: Europeans, Negroes, Far Easterners, and Lapps. However, it was not until 1735 that the Swedish botanist Carolus Linnaeus (1707–1778) proposed a comprehensive system of categorizing humans that resembles the modern conception of race. In the 19th century, scientists built on the elaborate systems of human classification developed in the 18th century to further support the superiority of the European race over Native Americans, Africans, and other nonwhite races.[4] This pursuit of categorizing human beings would later become known as "scientific racism," or the manifestations of falsely constructed biases, purportedly based on evolution, which further substantiated the positional superiority of the white race and its morality. The "racial projects" of imperialism further divided whites from nonwhites and reinforced the concept of the West's positional superiority discussed by Said. While Europe came to function as the centerpiece of all societies, *others* were subjugated to the margins. By the end of the 19th century, scientific racism and evolutionary bias were implicit to the formation of racial categories, and white superiority became naturalized and entrenched in European notions of race.

ORIENTALIST CONSTRUCTION OF BUDDHISM

Said's study of orientalist scholars and the Eurocentric positional superiority perpetuated through the widespread acceptance of Victorian scholarly discourse proves invaluable to understanding the rearticulation of "orientalist Buddhism" as a scholarly phenomenon. In the context of Victorian Buddhism, characterizations of orientalist Buddhism and orientalist scholarship as superior to its Asian counterparts reflects the logics of colonialism and imperialism that sought to disenfranchise others by highlighting differences between white and nonwhite methodologies and practices. In other words, the promulgation of a putative bifurcation between "Asian Buddhism" and the "orientalist's Buddhism" reproduced the tendency to proclaim an essentialized difference between the East and the West, and between Asian and Western forms of Buddhism, Buddhists, and scholarship. Within the orientalist framework, the former was held to be to inferior and ignorant and the latter promoted as superior and scientific. Such simplistic characterizations are misleading and perpetuate the orientalist reliance on monolithic categories to maintain dominance.[5] This imperialist drive to categorize Indigenous peoples and cultures functioned in a strikingly similar acquisitional manner akin to the extraction of raw materials and other natural resources that colonists sought to acquire, possess, and exploit.[6] The extraction of knowledge, including many Buddhist sutras as sources of ancient wisdom, by colonial administrators and orientalists mined ideas from the contexts of non-Western practitioners and cultures to appropriate and filter the religion and philosophy through a Western framework, re-represented to Westerners to bolster the positional superiority of the West.

Among the founders of the study of Buddhism in the West, well-known linguists and historians such as Brian Houghton Hodgson, Eugene Burnouf, Thomas William Rhys Davids and Caroline Rhys Davids, Alexandra David Neal, and others contributed to the construction and reception of Buddhism as a predominantly textual tradition, with scant attention to the practice of the religion among the laity. John James Clarke argues that much of the early written sources on Buddhism from the 19th century contributed to the promulgation of Buddhism as an example of an "Oriental (Asian) wisdom," which could be deployed as a "corrective mirror" for the West by providing the means to revive the moral degradation of modern Europe.[7] Hodgson furthered the emergence of textual Buddhism as "the real Buddhism" by recovering, collecting, and bestowing Buddhist sutras to European linguists and the Asiatic Society of Bengal, a scholarly association composed initially of some thirty British civil servants working in Calcutta under the auspices of the East India Trading Company. Eugene Burnouf, the eminent linguist of Pali and Sanskrit, translated some 147 Sanskrit manuscripts into French, and his 1844 influential book, *Introduction a l'histoire du Buddhisme indien*, became the definitive work on Buddhism in the West for many years. Burnouf promoted the idea, common among Western orientalists, that the scientific methods by which they examined textual Buddhism was more legitimate for determining the essence of Buddhism than the lived Buddhism practiced by Asians.[8] The emphasis of textual translation facilitated the exclusion of rituals and practices of Asian Buddhism. This *transfer of power* from an original indigenous source to Eurocentric intellectual expertise became an integral part of the Western appropriation of Buddhism.

By the middle of the 19th century, the location of textual Buddhism and its discursive counterparts that were rooted within Western institutions and their scholarly reinterpretations of Buddhist texts had already been forged in the confluence of colonialism and imperialism. In direct correlation to the idea that *others* should be subjugated and relegated to the margins of legitimate forms of knowledge, native scholars of Buddhism were often discredited as they translated Sanskrit and Tibetan manuscripts for orientalist scholars.[9] Philip C. Almond thus argues that orientalist Buddhism

> provides a mirror in which is reflected an image not only of the Orient, but of the Victorian world also . . . [T]he essence of Buddhism came to be seen as expressed not "out there" in the Orient, but in the West through the control of Buddhism's own textual past.[10]

In effect, the first generation of orientalist scholars discounted Buddhist rituals and practices embodied in the sangha and practiced by the laity as nonscientific irrational forms of worship that had little place within the greater social sciences and reputable scholarship.

Through a network of European scholarly exchange, Sanskrit manuscripts such as the *Lotus Sutra* were sent by Hodgson to Paris, translated into French by Burnouf, and eventually traveled to the United States to be translated into English by transcendentalist Henry David Thoreau, in an article titled "White Lotus of the Good Law."[11] In this network of exchange from European scholars to American transcendentalists, Asian forms of Buddhism were further encoded with modernist values of individualism, freedom, and European romanticism. The pioneering works of orientalist scholars such as William Jones heavily influenced the literary writings of American transcendentalist poet Ralph Waldo Emerson and the poet Walt Whitman. Thus, Americans discovered a modernist Buddhism—one that prized meditation and individual freedom and was shaped by orientalist scholars and European romanticism—through the transcendentalists nearly fifty years before the first Buddhist teachers came to the World Parliament of Religions in Chicago in 1893.[12]

During the late Victorian era, new scientific discoveries called into question the ability of Protestant Christianity to rise to the challenge of science and rationalism; a resultant crisis of faith led some Euro-Americans toward more esoteric spiritual movements such as spiritualism, theosophy, and Buddhism. The Buddhism that appealed to Euro-Americans differed greatly from the popular and monastic forms of Buddhism practiced in Asian countries of origin; instead, the type of Buddhism that appealed in the United States was filtered through Orientalism and underwent a certain Protestantization to imbue it with similar structures to Christianity—such as an attractive founder, a sacred text, and a set of ethical rules.

In addition to the formation of Buddhism through orientalist and Protestant frameworks, toward the end of the 19th and early 20th centuries, Asian Buddhist missionaries such as Shaku Soen, Anagarika Dharmapala, and Daisetsu Teitaro Suzuki reshaped modern Buddhism in a reverse-missionary effort to spread Buddhism to the West. This Buddhist missionary effort, however, also displayed several characteristics that identified its roots in colonial encounters in Asia that promoted the religion as rational and scientific. Dharmapala, for example, asserted that Buddhism was a better religion for modern man because it was scientific and did not depend on the belief in miracles such as Jesus walking on water or turning water into wine, and other purportedly irrational aspects of Christianity. It is notable that many of the stories of the buddha's miraculous feats of levitation and his past life stories were left out of these newer constructions of Buddhism.

The orientalist, Protestant, and modernist influences of Buddhism are still quite evident in contemporary forms of Western Buddhism that include primarily white practitioners who continue to privilege meditation over chanting, merit-making, and other rituals that are viewed as examples of cultural accretions muddling the original teachings of the buddha. Ann Gleig notes, however, that such efforts to highlight authenticity of meditation as the original practices of the buddha at the expense of devotional rituals were not just a product of Orientalism and Buddhist modernist leanings. Instead, the relegation of Buddhist rituals, cosmology, and devotions to the sidelines of "real" Buddhism occurred as an "Asian reformist movement spanning a number of geographical areas and schools that demythologized Buddhism and reinterpreted it as a rational religion that was linked to social reform and nationalist movements."[13] This intentional effort on the part of Asian reformers emerged within the context of colonialism, thus complicating the tendency to assume that the demythologization of Buddhism was simply a result of Western scholarship. Similarly, Charles Hallisey argues that the orientalists' dismissal of the rituals and devotional practices of Asian Buddhists, their exclusion of vernacular source, and the input of native informants in the construction of Western Buddhism did not silence the voices of Asian specialists. Orientalist discourse about Buddhism was therefore not an entirely Western construct, but also reflected patterns of "intercultural mimesis," or "aspects of a culture of a subjectified people influenc[ing] the investigator to represent that culture in a certain manner."[14] Hallisey recounts Thomas Williams Rhys Davids's interactions with Ven Waskaduve Subhuti, Yataramulle Unnanse, and other monks who devoted their lives to scholarship rather than the rites and rituals of Buddhism. Rhys Davids's subsequent scholarship furthered the belief that Singhalese Buddhism was free of interpretive ritual. The Singhalese monks with whom Rhys Davids interacted were themselves partially "Westernized," and they saw their own religion from the perspective of Western scholarship.[15] The representation of early Buddhism as a tradition devoid of ritual and magic can be found not only in orientalist scholarship but also in native specialists' understanding of their own religious practices.

For "armchair" orientalist scholars, "true" Buddhism is devoid of rituals and other cultural accretions associated with Asian Buddhism. This attitude extended to the second-generation of the founders of Western Buddhism, many of whom worked in a thoroughly Buddhist environment within Asia, but still preferred textual Buddhism over rituals and practices of Asian Buddhists. Rhys Davids, scholar of the Pali language and the founder of the Pali Text Society, who lived and worked with his wife, Caroline, in Ceylon for many years, is the case in point. The Rhys Davids became captivated with Singhalese people and culture, learned the Singhalese language, and spent time with them. In his writing, however, Rhys Davids remained indifferent toward the religious practices of the Singhalese Buddhists, whom he saw on a daily basis. A Singhalese biographer, Ananda Wickremeratne, commented that

> as much as he loved Sinhalese Buddhists, he also felt that they had betrayed Buddhism. Their idolatry had led them to regard the Buddha as an all-powerful being—a God—just as other men had deified the progenitors of their faiths.[16]

Rhys Davids, Burnouf, and many other orientalists assumed that Asian Buddhists were trapped in their own cultural accretions and Asian Buddhism needed to be rescued from its degraded state within Asian cultures. In other words, Asian Buddhists were too incompetent to be guardians or caretakers of Buddhism, in part because they were ignorant of the original teachings of the buddha. The sacred texts and key teachings could be rescued or made invigorated with the aid of Western scholars and their superior analytical perspectives.[17] In short, Christian normativity underlies the academic discipline of Buddhist studies because Western scholars of Buddhism have focused far more on studying and translating sacred texts than on studying rituals, art, or material objects.

Perceptions of Buddhism in the 19th century were far more complex than a simple translation of Asian traditions into Western modes of knowledge; instead, the rise of Western Buddhism occurred through a global interchange of ideas between Asian Buddhist reformers, traditional scholarly monastics, Western scholars, Buddhist popularizers, and Buddhists traveling abroad from Japan and South and Southeast Asia. In "Seeking Sakyamuni: Travel and the Reconstruction of Japanese Buddhism," Richard Jaffe examines the travels of Kitabatake

Doryu (1820–1907), Shaku Kozen (1849–1924), and Shaku Soen (1859–1919), three Meiji-era Japanese Buddhists to South and Southeast Asia during the 1880s and 1890s. Japanese fascination with Buddhist sites in India was prompted by Kitabatake's journey to Bodh Gaya, and the travels of Kozen and Soen to Sri Lanka gave rise to a renewed interest in Sakyamuni as the founder of the Buddhist tradition. The Japanese emphasis on Sakyamuni was a response to orientalist projects to recover the historical buddha—an effort to find common ground with their Asian co-religionists and to reconsider the role of Sakyamuni in Japanese Buddhism itself. Unlike Burnouf, Sylvian Lei, Oldenberg, and other European scholars, Kitabatake, Kozen, and Soen were not armchair scholars relying on the circulation of knowledge among orientalists. For the Japanese clerics, Sakyamuni was not merely an object of scholarly study in the search for an authentic expression of Buddhism, but rather the foundation of Buddhist belief, worship, and practice. This Buddhist faith-inspired conviction gave Kozen and Soen greater impetus in their attempt to "save" Buddhism in Asia by building a coalition of Asian Buddhists to resist colonialism and the spread of Christianity in Asia.[18]

MISSIONARY ENCOUNTERS WITH BUDDHISM

While Burnouf, Rhys Davids, and other orientalists focused on textual Buddhist study to the exclusion of Buddhist rituals and practices, Protestant missionaries in Asia immersed themselves in local Buddhist communities and left detailed ethnographic records of Buddhist beliefs and practices. Although their understanding of Asian Buddhism was filtered through a Christian framework, their descriptions and recordings of temple life, rituals, and practices functioned as ethnographic data for future missionaries as a way to understand Buddhist beliefs and practices prior to their arrival. Far from being an objective field of knowledge about Buddhism, the information gathered served as a means to facilitate the conversion of Buddhist natives to Christianity. Thus, in seeking support and funds for their missions in Asia, American Protestant missionaries often focused on what they deemed the negative aspects of Asian cultures, which furthered the racialization of Asian difference. In China, for example, American Protestant missionaries often emphasized the misery caused by pagan culture: gambling, opium addiction, foot-binding, polygamy, infanticide, and other forms of depravities. For many missionaries, Chinese religions were held to display marks of paganism, and many associated Asian religions with a degenerate form of "Tauism [*sic*], Boodism [*sic*], ancestor worship, and opium addiction."[19] The assumption of Christian supremacy was deeply ingrained in these early missionaries who circulated ideas of Asian religious beliefs and practices as hopelessly superstitious and therefore in need of Christianity as a means to overcome and convert the natives.[20] In this manner, Christian missionization embedded itself in orientalist and colonial endeavors to assert their control over Asians.

The presence of Christian missionaries on the Asian continent in the 19th century can also be seen as a reflection of the messianic impulse of that period. The normative Western perception of "the White man's burden" was deployed to couple the purported benefits of Western civilization and Christian faith within non-Eurocentric cultures. In Burma, Sri Lanka, and India, missionary schools introduced Eurocentric forms of knowledge that emphasized particular European languages, histories, and vocations and effectively dislodged the local transmission of indigenous knowledge to the next generation.[21] In Burma, for example, prior to the establishment of missionary schools during the colonial era, monasteries (*phongyi kyaung*) had been the primary sites for the production of knowledge and culture, as well as the transmission of Buddhist values and the dissemination of a monastic way of life. With the advent of modern education under British colonialism, it was more advantageous for middle- and upper-class Burmese parents to send their children to missionary schools in order to secure their children's future as bureaucrats and civil servants. The underlying assumption of this colonial education was that one had to become a European or a Westerner in order to become a Christian. Many Westerners considered this responsibility as necessarily ordained by God; Westernized Christian natives were then perceived as "more civilized."[22] Furthermore, encounters between Christian missionaries and Buddhist monks and lay devotees took place on an unequal footing. The Christian assumption was that Christianity, a revealed religion, had access to the fullness of divine grace, whereas Buddhism, a gnostic religion, offered at best only partial glimpses of the divine reality.[23] The uniqueness and the finality of Christian beliefs were deemed unquestionably superior to the naturalistic beliefs and "superstitious" practices of Buddhism. Within this context, the missionaries' task was clear: to convert the Buddhists and other "pagans" to become Europeans and, thereby, Christians. By the 19th century, the cultural and religious assumptions of Europe were the norm throughout missionary schools and colonial institutions in Asia. This Eurocentrism presumed Christian supremacy and granted Europe positional superiority over other races and nationalities and their cultural and religious practices.

The new era of Buddhist studies began with the arrival of scholar missionaries in the middle of the 19th century. Many of these scholars could read and write in Pali and Sanskrit. Unlike the orientalist scholars, however, missionary scholars did not ignore the commentaries and other sources produced by Asians. For example, some of the works of Robert Spence Hardy—*Eastern Monachism* (1850) and *A Manual of Buddhism in Its Modern Development* (1852)—offered well-researched studies that drew upon a variety of Singhalese sources and texts. These texts were intended to help missionaries to gain a better understanding of Buddhism and became some of the main sources of information about Buddhism for many Westerners. Ironically, works such as *A Manual of Buddhism in Its Modern Development* ended up popularizing in the West the very religion they sought to displace in the East.[24]

CHRISTIAN NORMATIVITY IN WESTERN BUDDHISM

In *The Future of Faith*, Harvey Cox, professor emeritus of Harvard University, declares that our religious and cultural traditions shape our language and thought forms to the extent that "they seep into the marrow of our bones and the synapses of our brain."[25] He refers to this process as "living in a haunted house," whereby the convert's prior religious imagination continues to exert its influence, "suffus[ing] . . . Buddhism with Christian or Jewish overtones."[26] These remnants of the past religion haunt the present by exerting a subtle influence over decisions that people make in their everyday lives. Regardless of what culture, faith, and tradition they come from, their past will always haunt them. Many works of textual Buddhism developed by European scholars were similarly influenced, perhaps unconsciously, by Protestant assumptions about the location of "true" Christianity in the printed word of God. Scholars such as

Burnouf, who viewed a translated Buddhism as authoritative and more authentic than its Asian counterpart, seemed to depend more on his imagination as a Western linguist than on how Asian Buddhists actually practiced their own religion. In other words, Burnouf privileged orientalist Buddhism as more "authentic" by essentializing it in texts in a fashion similar to Protestant Christianity.

Gregory Schopen, professor of Buddhist studies at the University of California, Los Angeles, argues that the primacy of textual sources in Buddhist studies emphasized by orientalist and modern Buddhist scholars reflects Protestant suppositions rather than the values and history of Indian Buddhism. He thus broadened the field of Buddhist studies by studying material objects such as reliquaries, devotional inscriptions on stupas, and other archaeological evidence as legitimate sources of academic inquiry. Schopen reveals the methods whereby Western intellectual tradition assimilated the Protestant principle of *Sola Scriptura* and presumed that all other traditions could and should be approached from this perspective. Schopen illustrates how the Protestant assumption of the location of "true" religion in the printed sacred text "has determined the history of the study of Indian Buddhism and that—as the consequence—our picture of Indian Buddhism may reflect more of our own religious history and values than the history and values of Indian Buddhism."[27] Schopen brings to light the "haunted," yet deep-seated Christian normativity and Christian hegemony that operates within orientalist discourses of Buddhism. His analysis provides an important framework to understand how Christian supremacy informs racialized interpretations of Buddhism and the interconnection between Christian normativity and white supremacy.

Race and religion were and continue to be bound together to represent Buddhism through the lens of Protestantism, orientalism, colonialism, and scientific racism. Anglo-Protestant normativity came to haunt 19th-century scholarship by exerting subtle and not-so-subtle influence over assertions made about Buddhism, in general, and Asian Buddhism, in particular. The Christian upbringing of orientalist scholars and the Protestant emphasis on the printed word buttressed racialized claims that the locus of "true" Buddhism was found exclusively in textual Buddhism and not in the rituals and practices of non-European adherents. Such assertions continue through the 21st century, albeit with notable differences from contemporary scholars of Buddhism who engage critical race theory.[28]

Jeanne Hill Fletcher, a constructive theologian at Fordham University, has adapted Michael Omi and Howard Winant's concept of "racial project" or "what race means in a particular discursive practice and the ways in which both social structures and everyday experiences are racially organized, based upon that meaning."[29] Fletcher expands this concept to draw attention to the ways in which Christianity functions within the construction of whiteness. Using Fletcher's framework of a religio-racial project, we can see how the founding figures of the Western study of Buddhism delineated what constitutes "true" Buddhism by asserting that the essence of Buddhism was in the Pali and Sanskrit texts, translated and interpreted by orientalist scholars for the consumption of Westerners.[30] This was not the lived Buddhism of Asian Buddhists, but an orientalist Buddhism with the trappings of Protestantism. Buddhist converts and sympathizers in the United States of the late Victorian era gravitated toward this framework, as many former Protestants sought religious alternatives. This kind of Buddhism, constructed from the framework of their inherited faith, resonated with deeply held values within the recesses of their subconscious. In a classic example of Cox's "haunted house,"

Euro-Americans who left Protestantism to embrace Buddhism in the late Victorian era suffused their newfound faith with the "ghosts" (or framework and norms) of the religion in which they had been raised. While this process may be unconscious for many Euro-Americans, the connection between Christian normativity and whiteness is clearly evident in the experiences of Chinese and Japanese immigrants in the 19th-century United States.

RELIGION AND RACE IN AMERICA

When Burnouf published his landmark book, *Introduction a l'histoire du Buddhisme indien* in 1844, based on his encounters with orientalist scholars, it outlined how Chinese migrants had arrived in the United States to search for gold and, later in the 1850s, served as indentured workers to build the transcontinental railroad. They settled mainly in California and elsewhere on the West Coast. Because racial segregation was the norm, they were forcibly separated into racial and ethnic enclaves popularly referred to as Chinatowns; however, their religious differences also contributed to this racialized separation. Since Chinese indentured workers were not Christian, their Buddhist and syncretistic Chinese religious expressions were deemed alien religions, which further flamed anti-Chinese sentiment. Chinese immigrants, whose syncretic folk religion included Buddhist elements, established temples that were often mocked as "joss houses" and further denigrated their religious sites of worship as indices of their racial and religious difference and inferiority. Few whites visited these sites of worship, and when they did it was "only as tourists at some of the more public temples in Chinatown."[31] However, there were anti-Chinese vigilante groups that took pleasure in burning down these joss houses. Indeed, the "strangeness" of Chinese customs, the assumed unassimilability of their way of life, and the so-called superstitious elements embedded in their religion were precisely some of the rationales used by Senator Aaron Augustus Sargent when he argued before the Senate in 1878 to prohibit immigration from China to the United States. The primary motivation for this ban stemmed from the fear that the Chinese could not assimilate into a white Christian nation, due to their religion and ways of life. Religion and culture were deeply intertwined, and concepts of whiteness and Christianity were bound together to reflect the association of whiteness with Christianity and being American.[32] In short, the stereotypical depictions of Chinese as foreigners, unassimilable, and racialized others led to discrimination and violence; these views culminated in the first Chinese Exclusion Act, which was passed in 1882, restricting immigration from China and rendering Chinese people ineligible for naturalization. This was the first in a series of anti-Chinese and anti-Asian legislation including the Geary Act of 1892 and the Immigration Act of 1924 (which included the Asian Exclusion Act and National Origins Act).

Japanese immigrant laborers began arriving in Hawaii in the 1860s to work in sugarcane fields. Later, many moved to the mainland United States, where they worked mainly as farmers and fishermen. They brought their Buddhist traditions with them; the most prominent were the Higashi Honganji and Nishi Hongwanji branches of Jodo Shinshu sect, popularly known as "Shin Buddhism." These branches became known as the Buddhist Churches of America in the United States and Canada. In 1898, the Reverend Doctor Shuya Sonoda and the Reverend Kakuryo Nishijima arrived in San Francisco and, in 1890, they established the Buddhist Mission of North America, a precursor to the Buddhist Churches of America.

Identified as nonwhite and non-Christian, Japanese immigrants and their children experienced both racial and religious discrimination. They were characterized as unassimilable aliens based on their race and Buddhist religion, which was equated with being un-American. Moreover, following the outbreak of the Second World War and attacks on the US naval base at Pearl Harbor by Japanese naval planes on December 7, 1941, Japanese Americans became classified as a threat to US national security, and with the signing of Executive Order 9066 by President Franklin D. Roosevelt, over one hundred thousand Japanese Americans, a majority of whom were Buddhists, were rounded up and incarcerated in internment camps. In his book, *American Sutra: A Story of Faith and Freedom in the Second World* War, Duncan Ryūken Williams examines the near interchangeability between the categories of religion and race as they pertained to Japanese American Buddhists whose religious affiliation rendered them vulnerable to anti-Japanese American racial violence, loss of civil liberties, jobs, and properties despite their status as US citizens. Because their religious difference signified pro-Japanese sentiment, Japanese Buddhist priests were the first to be rounded up and arrested for suspicion of "anti-Americanness." Over 110,000 Japanese and Japanese Americans were incarcerated during World War II in camps that further marginalized Buddhists by limiting their ability to gather together, by prohibiting the use of Japanese during worship, and by refusing Japanese American soldiers a Buddhist funeral and burial. These anti-Buddhist actions signified the conflation of religious and racial identities that marked Japanese American Buddhists as hostile subjects. Thus, Japanese Americans endured relentless pressure to demonstrate their loyalty to the United States. Despite the hysteria, suspicion, and discrimination, Japanese American Buddhists sought to adapt their religious practices to prevailing Christian norms as a means of survival and as a symbol of their resilience. Hence, with the cooperation of white convert clergy, such as Julius Goldwater and Sunya Pratt, Japanese American Buddhists translated their services and service books into English, incorporated hymns, and introduced several adaptations as a form of survival and resilience in the face of extreme violence and anti-Japanese sentiment.[33]

In 1944, the Buddhist Mission of North America was intentionally renamed the Buddhist Churches of America at the Topaz War Relocation Center to avoid further racial hostility. As a result of anti-Buddhist discrimination in the camps, Shin Buddhist temples followed a model of adaptation to Protestant culture, which had begun in Japan prior to World War II. This involved adopting more Protestant forms of architecture and liturgy through the use of pews, setting gathas to hymns, introducing choirs, and Western musical instruments (e.g., organs).[34] In so doing, Japanese American Buddhists contributed to the survival and unique iteration of Buddhism in America. Like the many non-Christian traditions in the United States studied by Khyati Y. Joshi, Japanese American Buddhism needed to adapt to the forces of white Christian privilege and hegemony to sustain itself during and after the war.[35]

BUDDHIST MODERNISM

Buddhist modernism emerged in the context of 19th-century colonialism and included both Western efforts to translate the tradition to fit scientific, individualistic, and Romanticist leanings and Asian Buddhists who, in response to the threat of Western modernity, reaffirmed aspects of their native spiritual traditions over and against the perceived strengths of the West.[36]

The Burmese monk Ledi Sayadaw (1846–1923) was one such Asian Buddhist modernist who played a pivitol role in the revival of Burmese Buddhism and opened the practice of *vipassana* or insight meditation to the laity.[37] Within the context of British colonialism, Ledi Sayadaw and other Asian Buddhist modernists contributed to the promotion of a scientific, demythologized religion that valorized meditation and made rhetorical claims of textual purity. Religion was thus deeply connected to nationalistic movements of social reform in Asian modernist projects.[38] David L. McMahon also identifies the phenomenon of Buddhist modernism as a movement instigated both by Asian Buddhist sources and Western scholars who collectively sought to connect Buddhism with a science of the mind and rationalism, while preserving Buddhism's connections with meditation and mysticism, and its connections to nature.[39]

According to Ann Gleig, 20th-century Buddhist modernism in Asia included the following revisions: stricter monastic regulations; the revival of meditation; mass meditation movements for lay and monastics; the discarding of the popular forms of practice; claims to a pure tradition and teaching; further rejection of the strict separation between laity and monastics; claims that nirvana was attainable in this lifetime by monks and laity alike; and increasing popularization of Buddhist doctrine.[40] These Asian-inspired modernist transformations aligned with Western modernism's emphasis on individualism, freedom, and scientific inquiry, which, in turn, shaped American Buddhism and the rise of "American Buddhist meditation-based convert lineages in the 20th and 21st centuries."[41] While much of the American Buddhist meditation-based convert lineages share in modernist reifications of meditation as the most authentic forms of practices, and the privileging of white forms of knowledge and the perceived superiority of non-Asian white teachers and scholars, scholars like Gleig argue that American Buddhism can no longer be identified by and limited to distinctions between Western and Asian Buddhism and the association of meditation with convert Buddhists and popular Buddhism with Asian and Asian American forms of Buddhism. Instead, American Buddhism has matured beyond modernism to a postmodern form that includes the decontextualization of traditional Buddhism through the rise of technology and secularization and the simultaneous desire to revalorize traditional rituals, sangha, and cosmological structures ignored in modernist interpretations.[42]

MINDFULNESS

The rise of mindfulness as a scientific practice beloved among neuroscientists and business culture alike reflects one of the most recent developments of Western Buddhism as it pertains to the issue of race, for in the process of medicalizing and marketing mindfulness, its Asian roots needed to be severed. Ronald Purser argues that MBSR (mindfulness-based stress reduction) programs created by Jon Kabat-Zinn needed to decouple from Buddhism and avoid using words such as "mindfulness" and "meditation" in order to evade rejection by the medical establishment.[43] Wakoh Shannon Hickey's study of mindfulness, *Mind Cure: How Meditation Became Medicine*, traces the medicalization of mindfulness further back from the widely held belief that it originated in the 1970s. Instead, as Hickey argues, meditation as an efficacious "mind cure" originated in the late 19th and early 20th centuries through the efforts of women who believed that transforming one's mind could in turn transform external forms of suffering and oppression. However, in order to support mindfulness and meditation as a scientifically backed practice, its religious origins were largely suppressed and a more "universal" mindfulness was popularized.[44]

According to Ronald Purser, decoupling mindfulness from its Buddhist roots, rebranding it to fit into a nonreligious mold, and marketing mindfulness to patients in hospitals, students in schools, and people in other institutions as a secular therapeutic practice resulted in "privatizing mindfulness."[45] By removing explicit connections to spirituality and the sangha in order to focus on the benefits of the individual and personal needs, the popularization of mindfulness led to the further erasure of Asian and Asian American Buddhists and repacked this traditional Buddhist practice for mass consumption by a primarily upper-middle-class to upper-class white clientele. In so doing, the privatization and secularization of mindfulness cannot be decoupled from the politics of whiteness and white privilege within non-Buddhist and American Buddhist meditation-based convert lineages.[46]

BUDDHIST TAXONOMIES

The study of Buddhism in America has resulted in the creation, utilization, retirement, and recreation of several taxonomies of Buddhism by scholars attempting to account for the wealth of diversity of Buddhists in the United States. These taxonomies that often delineate between convert Buddhists (usually assumed to be white) and "ethnic" or Asian heritage Buddhists tend to obscure far more difference within and across different groups. In her essay "Two Buddhisms, Three Buddhisms, and Racism," Wakoh Shannon Hickey critiques the tendency to rely on these models that unwittingly reproduce the "unconscious White privilege" that drove their formation in the first place and argues that "a long American history of White racism, and minority groups' concomitant distrust, have contributed to the development of racially segregated Buddhist communities in the United States."[47] Hickey's study of the lineage of taxonomies indicates that "some of the *assumptions* underlying *taxonomies of American Buddhism* reflect *unconscious White privilege*,"[48] which shapes how we approach Buddhist difference. There is a historical tendency in American Buddhism to locate a fault line between Asian and Asian American Buddhists—who are often viewed as backward, insular, overly devotional, and less authentic—and convert Buddhists—largely determined to be white, educated, economically well-off meditators, with little interest in the ritual merit-making activities of popular Buddhists. Hickey traces the development of these various taxonomies beginning with Charles Prebish's "two Buddhisms" model, which distinguished between more stable forms associated with heritage Buddhists and convert Buddhists that developed following radical social change.

Paul Numrich later utilized a model of two Buddhisms that explicitly employed the labels "ethnic" and "immigrant" Buddhists in distinction to convert Buddhists, viewed predominantly as white practitioners. Such divisions were insufficient, for they did not account for Asian Americans who may have converted to Buddhism and obscured more integrated services that draw from Asian and non-Asian Buddhists. That white privilege operated in the use of the taxonomies came into stark relief when Helen Tworkov introduced her own model of two Buddhisms that distinguished between American Buddhism or white Buddhists and Asian American Buddhists that she placed under the category of Buddhists in America. In so doing, she infamously claimed that "Asian American Buddhists . . . so far . . . have not figured prominently in the development of something called American Buddhism."[49] Tworkov's remarks raised the ire of many Asian American Buddhists who had been living in America as Buddhists for over a century. The legacy of the two Buddhism's model continues to impact the popular view of Asian American Buddhists as somehow less worthy markers of American Buddhism, as Funie Hsu's 2016 essay title in *Lion's Roar* magazine attests—"We've Been Here All Along."[50]

For many scholars utilizing the two Buddhism's model and its subsequent variations, "ethnic Buddhist" tends to refer to Asian immigrant and Asian American Buddhists, while "convert Buddhist" usually denotes white practitioners. As scientific categorizations based on "race" generally carry with them negative connotations, many Western scholars of Buddhism have conveniently reduced race to "ethnicity," which is meant to be nonevaluative, or as not having any of the negative trappings that race ensues. Although the diffusion of tensions surrounding the discussion of race is, in part, one of the goals of using the term "ethnicity" over "race," it remains the case that race and racialization formed the construction and continued acceptance of the two-Buddhism typology in the first place.

EMERGENT SCHOLARSHIP

In an effort to disrupt the perpetuation of white privilege in the production of knowledge about Buddhism and Buddhists, several contemporary works have emerged to counter and transform the historical legacy of whiteness and white supremacy that have largely shaped the field. They largely fall under three subcategories: those focusing on (a) Asian American Buddhism and Buddhists; (b) critiques of Buddhism and whiteness through a critical race approach; and (c) the works of Black Buddhist scholars, teachers, and practitioners. Recent examples of these works include Duncan Ryūken Williams's *American Sutra: A Story of Faith and Freedom in the Second World War*, which reveals the adaptation and resilience of Japanese American Buddhists incarcerated during World War II and the racialization of their religion as un-American; and George Yancy and Emily McCrae's coedited volume, *Buddhism and Whiteness: Critical Reflections*, which brings the philosophy of race and critical whiteness studies to bear on the study and practice of Buddhism in the West. Also significant are the volumes *Radical Dharma: Talking Race, Love, and Liberation*, by Angel Kyodo Williams, Lama Rod Owens, and Jasmine Syedullah, and *Dharma Matters: Race, Women, and Tantra*, by Jan Willis, which explore race, gender, and the dharma in contemporary culture.[51]

FURTHER READING

Almond, Philip C. *The British Discovery of Buddhism*. Cambridge, UK: Cambridge University Press, 1988.

Bhabha, Homi. *The Location of Culture*. New York: Routledge, 1994.

Bogdan, Robert C., and Sari Knopp Biklen. *Qualitative Research for Education: An Introduction to Theory and Methods*. Needham Heights, MA: Allyn & Bacon, 1988.

Cheah, Joseph. *Race and Religion in American Buddhism: White Supremacy and Immigrant Adaptation*. New York: Oxford University Press, 2011.

Cheah, Joseph. "Buddhism, Race, and Ethnicity." In *Oxford Handbook of Contemporary Buddhism*. Edited by Michael Jerryson, 650–661. New York: Oxford University Press, 2017.

Clarke, John James. *Oriental Enlightenment: The Encounter between Asian and Western Thought*. New York: Routledge, 1997.

Cox, Harvey. *The Future of Faith*. New York: HarperCollins, 2009.

Fields, Rick. *How the Swans Came to the Lake: A Narrative History of Buddhism in America*. Boston: Shambhala, 1992.

Fletcher, Jeannine Hill. *The Sin of White Supremacy: Christianity, Racism, and Religious Diversity in America*. Maryknoll, NY: Orbis Books, 2017.

Gleig, Ann. *American Dharma: Buddhism beyond Modernity*. New Haven, CT: Yale University Press, 2019.

Gleig, Ann. "Undoing Whiteness in American Buddhist Modernism." In *Buddhism and Whiteness: Critical Reflections*. Edited by George Yancy and Emily McRae, 21–42. Lanham, MD: Lexington Books, 2019.

Goldberg, Ellen. "Buddhism in the West: Transplantation and Innovation." In *Buddhism in World Cultures: Comparative Perspectives*. Edited by Stephen C. Berkwitz, 285–310. Santa Barbara, CA: ABC-CLIO, 2006.

Gombrich, Richard, and Gannaneth Obeysekere. *Buddhism Transformed: Religious Change in Sri Lanka*. Princeton, NJ: Princeton University Press, 1988.

Hallisey, Charles. "Roads Taken and Not Taken in the Study of Theravada Buddhism." In *Curators of the Buddha: The Study of Buddhism under Colonialism*. Edited by Donald S. Lopez Jr., 31–61. Chicago: University of Chicago Press, 1995.

Hickey, Wakoh Shannon. "Two Buddhisms, Three Buddhisms, and Racism." *Journal of Global Buddhism* 11 (2010): 35–58.

Hickey, Wakoh Shannon. *Mind Cure: How Meditation Became Medicine*. New York: Oxford University Press, 2019.

Hsu, Funie. "We've Been Here All Along." *Lion's Roar* (Winter 2016). Accessed March 26, 2022. https://www.lionsroar.com/weve-been-here-all-along/.

Iwamura, Jane Naomi. "The Oriental Monk in American Popular Culture." In *Religion and Popular Culture in America*. Rev. ed. Edited by Bruce D. Forbes and Jeffrey H. Mahan, 23–43. Berkeley: University of California Press, 2005.

Jaffe, Richard M. "Seeking Sakyamuni: Travel and the Reconstruction of Japanese Buddhism." *Journal of Japanese Studies* 30, no. 1 (Winter, 2004), 65–96.

Joshi, Khyati. *White Christian Privilege: The Illusion of Religious Equality in America*. New York: New York University Press, 2020.

McMahon, David L. *The Making of Buddhist Modernism*. New York: Oxford University Press, 2008.

Miles, Robert. *Racism*. London: Routledge, 1989.

Omi, Michael, and Howard Winant. *Racial Formation in the United States*. 3rd ed. New York: Routledge, 2015.

Purser, Ronald E. *McMindfulness: How Mindfulness Became the New Capitalist Spirituality*. London: Repeater Books, 2019.

Said, Edward. *Orientalism*. New York: Vintage Books, 1978.

Schopen, Gregory. "Protestant." *History of Religions* 31, no. 1 (August 1991): 22–23.

Sharf, Robert H. "Buddhist Modernism and the Rhetoric of Meditative Experience." *Numen* 42, no. 3 (1995), 228–283.

Smith, Linda Tuhiwai. *Decolonizing Methodologies: Research and Indigenous Peoples*. London: Zed Books, 1999.

Suh, Sharon A. *Silver Screen Buddha: Buddhism in Asian and Western Film*. New York: Bloomsbury Academic, 2015.

Takaki, Ronald. *A History of Asian Americans: Strangers from a Different Shore*. Boston: Little, Brown, 1998.

Wickremeratne, Ananda. *The Genesis of an Orientalist: Thomas William Rhys Davids and Buddhism in Sri Lanka*. Columbia, MO: South Asia Books, 1985.

Williams, Duncan Ryuken. *American Sutra: A Story of Faith and Freedom in the Second World War*. Cambridge, MA: Harvard University Press, 2019.

Yancy, George, and Emily McRae, eds. *Buddhism and Whiteness: Critical Reflections.* Lanham, MD: Lexington Books, 2019.

Yandell, Keith, and Harold Netland. *Buddhism: A Christian Exploration and Appraisal.* Downers Grove, IL: Inter Varsity Press, 2009.

NOTES

1. Edward Said, *Orientalism* (New York: Vintage Books, 1978), 3.
2. Homi Bhabha, *The Location of Culture* (New York: Routledge, 1994), 126.
3. Robert Miles, *Racism* (London: Routledge, 1989), 19.
4. Tanya Maria Golash-Boza, *Race & Racisms: A Critical Approach* (New York: Oxford University Press, 2015), 23–26.
5. Keith Yandell and Harold Netland, *Buddhism: A Christian Exploration and Appraisal* (Downers Grove, IL: Inter Varsity Press, 2009), 80–81.
6. Linda Tuhiwai Smith, *Decolonizing Methodologies: Research and Indigenous Peoples* (London: Zed Books, 1999), 58–59.
7. Joseph Cheah, *Race and Religion in American Buddhism: White Supremacy and Immigrant Adaptation* (New York: Oxford University Press, 2011), 24.
8. Charles Hallisey, "Roads Taken and Not Taken in the Study of Theravada Buddhism," in *Curators of the Buddha: The Study of Buddhism under Colonialism,* ed. Donald S. Lopez Jr. (Chicago: University of Chicago Press, 1995), 4.
9. Philip C. Almond, *The British Discovery of Buddhism* (Cambridge, UK: Cambridge University Press, 1988), 13.
10. See Almond, *Discovery of Buddhism,* 13.
11. Robert Kuhn McGregor, "Henry David Thoreau: The Asian Thread," in *Thoreau's Importance for Philosophy,* ed. Rick Anthony Furtak, Jonathan Ellsworth, and James D. Reid (New York: Fordham University Press, 2012), 204; and Hallisey, "Roads Taken and Not Taken," 32.
12. Ellen Goldberg, "Buddhism in the West: Transplantation and Innovation," in *Buddhism in World Cultures: Comparative Perspectives,* ed. Stephen C. Berkwitz (Santa Barbara, CA: ABC-CLIO, 2006), 286–287.
13. Ann Gleig, *American Dharma: Buddhism beyond Modernity* (New Haven, CT: Yale University Press, 2019), 4.
14. Hallisey, "Roads Taken and Not Taken," 33.
15. For further information on the history of the encounters between the Singhalese and Westerners, see Richard Gombrich and Gannaneth Obeysekere, *Buddhism Transformed: Religious Change in Sri Lanka* (Princeton, NJ: Princeton University Press, 1988), 220–240.
16. Ananda Wickremeratne, *The Genesis of an Orientalist: Thomas William Rhys Davids and Buddhism in Sri Lanka* (Columbia, MO: South Asia Books, 1985), 198.
17. Jane Naomi Iwamura, "The Oriental Monk in American Popular Culture," in *Religion and Popular Culture in America,* rev. ed., ed. Bruce David Forbes and Jeffrey H. Mahan (Berkeley: University of California Press, 2005), 23–43.
18. Richard M. Jaffe, "Seeking Sakyamuni: Travel and the Reconstruction of Japanese Buddhism," *Journal of Japanese Studies* 30, no. 1 (2004): 73, 93.
19. Rick Fields, *How the Swans Came to the Lake: A Narrative History of Buddhism in America* (Boston: Shambhala, 1992), 72.
20. John James Clarke, *Oriental Enlightenment: The Encounter between Asian and Western Thought* (New York: Routledge, 1997), 44.

21. Juliane Schober, "Buddhist Visions of Moral Authority and Modernity in Burma," in *Burma at the Turn of the 21st Century*, ed. Monique Skidmore (Honolulu: University of Hawai'i Press, 2005), 115.
22. Justo L. Gonzalez, *The Story of Christianity: The Reformation to the Present Day*, vol. 2 (New York: HarperCollins, 1985), 305.
23. Martin J. Verhoeven, "Americanizing the Buddha: The World Parliament of Religions, Paul Carus, and the Making of Modern Buddhism" (PhD diss., University of Wisconsin, 1997), 89–90.
24. Clarke, *Oriental Enlightenment*, 74.
25. Harvey Cox, *The Future of Faith* (New York: HarperCollins, 2009), 129.
26. Cox, *The Future of Faith*, 129.
27. Gregory Schopen, "Protestant," *History of Religions* 31, no. 1 (August 1991): 22–23.
28. Reference Joseph Cheah, Sharon A. Suh, Ann Gleig, Jane Iwamura, to name a few.
29. Omi and Winant, *Racial Formation in the United States*, 3rd ed. (New York: Routledge, 2015), 56.
30. In *The Sin of White Supremacy*, Jeannine Hill Fletcher introduces "religio-racial project" as an adaptation of Michael Omi and Howard Winant's concept of "racial project": "what race means in a particular discursive context and the ways in which both the social structures and everyday experiences are racially organized, based upon that meaning." See Michael Omi and Howard Winant, *Racial Formation in the United States: From the 1960s to the 1990s* (New York: Routledge, 1994), 56. Fletcher expands the concept of "racial project" to "draw attention to the way religion functions within racial projects." See Jeannine Hill Fletcher, *The Sin of White Supremacy: Christianity, Racism, and Religious Diversity in America* (Maryknoll, NY: Orbis Books, 2017), 3.
31. Fields, *How the Swans Came to the Lake*, 75.
32. Cited in Fletcher, *The Sin of White Supremacy*, 1; see also Aaron Augustus Sargent, *Chinese Immigration. Speech of Hon. A. A. Sargent of California, in the Senate of the United States, March 7, 1876* (Washington, DC: Government Print Office, 1876), 23.
33. Duncan Ryuken Williams, *A Story of Faith and Freedom in the Second World War: American Sutra* (Cambridge, MA: Harvard University Press, 2019), 82–84, 236–237.
34. Ama Michihiro, *Immigrants to the Pure Land: The Modernization, Acculturation, and Globalization of Shin Buddhism, 1898–1941* (Honolulu: University of Hawai'i Press, 2011), 87–90.
35. Khyati Joshi, *White Christian Privilege: The Illusion of Religious Equality in America* (New York: New York University Press, 2020), 107–112.
36. Robert H. Sharf, "Buddhist Modernism and the Rhetoric of Meditative Experience," *Numen* 42, no. 3 (1995): 259.
37. Gleig, *American Dharma*, 23.
38. Gleig, *American Dharma*, 23.
39. David L. McMahon, *The Making of Buddhist Modernism* (New York: Oxford University Press, 2008).
40. Gleig, *American Dharma*, 22.
41. Gleig, *American Dharma*, 5.
42. Gleig, *America Dharma*, 11–12.
43. Ronald E. Purser, *McMindfulness: How Mindfulness Became the New Capitalist Spirituality* (London: Repeater Books, 2019), 66.
44. Wakoh Shannon Hickey, *Mind Cure: How Meditation Became Medicine* (New York: Oxford University Press, 2019).
45. Purser, *McMindfulness*, 65–82.
46. Ann Gleig, "Undoing Whiteness in American Buddhist Modernism," in *Buddhism and Whiteness: Critical Reflections*, ed. George Yancy and Emily McRae (Lanham, MD: Lexington Books, 2019), 22.
47. Wakoh Shannon Hickey, "Two Buddhisms, Three Buddhisms, and Racism," *Journal of Global Buddhism* 11 (2010): 5.

48. Wakoh Shannon Hickey, *Buddhism beyond Borders: New Perspectives on Buddhism in the United States*, ed. Scott Mitchell and Natalie Quli (Albany: SUNY Press, 2015), 39.
49. Helen Tworkov, "Many Is More," *Tricycle: The Buddhist Review*, 1, no. 2 (Winter 1991), 4.
50. Funie Hsu, "We've Been Here All Along," *Lion's Roar* (Winter 2016), accessed March 26, 2022.
51. Duncan Ryūken Williams, *American Sutra: A Story of Faith and Freedom in the Second World War* (Cambridge, MA: Harvard University Press, 2019); George Yancy and Emily McCrae, *Buddhism and Whiteness: Critical Reflections* (Lanham, MD: Lexington Books, 2019); Angel Kyodo Williams, Lama Rod Owens, and Jasmine Syedullah, *Radical Dharma: Talking Race, Love, and Liberation* (Berkeley, CA: North Atlantic Books, 2016); and Jan Willis, *Dharma Matters: Race, Women, and Tantra* (New York: Wisdom Publications, 2020).

Joseph Cheah and Sharon A. Suh

X

XUYUN

A MODERN EMINENT MONK: THE LIFE OF XUYUN ACCORDING TO HIS ANNALISTIC BIOGRAPHY

Xuyun's annalistic biography (i.e., following a year-by-year account) was initially published as an autobiography.[1] In 1951, Xuyun, who at that time was supposedly more than 100 years old, fell ill at the Dajue Chan 大覺禪 Monastery of Mount Yunmen 雲門 (district of Ruyuan, northern Guangdong Province), where he was serving as abbot, after an accident linked to the tense political climate of the Communist Land Reform campaign. His disciples, fearing the worst, asked him to recount the story of his life and then secretly sent their notes to Hong Kong, where Cen Xuelü 岑學呂 (1882–1963), a politician from Guangdong who had become Xuyun's disciple in 1937 and had left the mainland in the 1940s, edited the text. Because the narration of his life as told by Xuyun to his acolytes in 1951 stopped at the year 1949, from this moment and up until Xuyun's death in 1959, the events of his life were recorded by his disciples in the third person.

Following its initial publication in Hong Kong in 1953, the text went through several editions[2] before attaining its current, standardized (and, to date, final) version.[3] Since the 1960s, when a disciple published an English translation of this text,[4] the same portrait of Xuyun has also been available to Western readers and practitioners. Although it has been the object of recent critical studies,[5] the annalistic biography, notwithstanding its hagiographical tone and positive slant in Xuyun's favor, remains the normative source on this master to date—the following life story is based on this account. The composition of the annalistic biography, which is discussed in the succeeding section, confirms the continuity of Buddhist historiographical methods in the 20th century.

Ascetism and Awakening. Xuyun (family name Xiao 蕭, first name unknown) was born in 1840. His family was descended from illustrious ancestors and had lived in Hunan Province for many generations. In 1838, Xuyun's father, Xiao Yutang 蕭玉堂 began to serve as assistant magistrate of different prefectures in Fujian Province. At this point, his parents were both over 40 years old and feared that they would have no descendants. One day, his mother went to pray for a child at the Guanyin temple and made a vow to have the building and the temple bridge rebuilt. Shortly thereafter, an extraordinary dream announced to both parents the conception of a child. In due time, Xuyun's mother gave birth not to a child but to "a ball of flesh" (*routuan* 肉團) and died. The next day, an itinerant medicine man cut open the ball and extracted a baby, who was brought up by his father's concubine.

Xuyun was destined to continue two family lines, as his uncle, who had no children, also designated him as heir. However, the boy showed early signs of a religious vocation and ran away at the age of 17, well intentioned to become a monk. He was caught halfway and taken back home, where his marriage to two ladies was celebrated though (according to his biography) never consummated. Two years later, he escaped again, this time for good: in 1858, Xuyun received his tonsure at the Yongquan 湧泉 Monastery on Mount Gu (Gushan 鼓山, in Fujian Province),[6] and the following year, he was ordained as a monk by Master Miaolian 妙蓮 (ca. 1846–1907) at the same monastery.

After becoming a monk, Xuyun (known as Deqing 德清 at this time) was obliged to hide in caves for three years because his father had sent people far and wide to discover his whereabouts. He lived as a hermit and practiced austerities, wearing his clothes to shreds and letting his beard and hair grow long. His wanderings took him to a small temple on Mount Tiantai 天台 (in Zhejiang Province), where a master taught him the Chan method of penetrating the critical phrase (*kan huatou* 看話頭).[7] After training for five years on the critical phrase "Who is he who drags this corpse?,"[8] Xuyun departed to practice in the most renowned monasteries of Southeast China, including, in 1880–1881, Jinshan 金山 and Gaomin 高旻 (both in Jiangsu Province).

In 1882, Xuyun undertook a three-year pilgrimage, prostrating himself every three steps, from the island of Mount Putuo 普陀 to Mount Wutai 五台 (in Shanxi Province), sacred to the Bodhisattva Wenshu 文殊 (Mañjuśrī). When, during this pilgrimage, he found himself twice at death's door, the bodhisattva came to his assistance disguised as a beggar. From 1887 to 1894, Xuyun visited the most sacred places of Chinese Buddhism and also traveled to Tibet, Bhutan, India, Ceylon, and Burma. In 1895, over several weeks of constant meditation at the Gaomin Monastery, he achieved awakening upon hearing the sound of a teacup crashing to the ground.

Thereafter, Xuyun traveled to the Ayuwang 阿育王 Monastery in Ningbo (on the coast of Zhejiang Province). In order to repay his debt of gratitude to the mother he had never known, he burned off the ring finger of his left hand in front of the Buddha's relic preserved in this site. In 1900, he retired to the Zhongnan 终南 Mountains (in Shaanxi Province), where he had already lived from 1885 to 1887. At this point, his mastery of meditative techniques led him to enter prolonged states of meditative concentration (*ding* 定, *samādhi*). After the news spread, Deqing decided to change his name to "Xuyun" so as to avoid being overwhelmed by followers.

The Restoration Activity and the Rise to Eminence. In 1904, Xuyun obtained from local authorities the ruined site of the Boyu 鉢盂 Temple on Mount Jizu 雞足 (Rooster Foot Mountain), situated between Yunnan Province and Burma. He had already visited this wild region in 1889 and vowed to establish a monastic community there in order to counter the state of decadence of Buddhism.

Xuyun resumed his travels to solicit funds for the restoration of his temple, and in 1906 he obtained from the Guangxu emperor its official recognition and a complete collection of the Buddhist canon. He also committed to ensure the protection of the Chinese monastic community in broad terms. In fact, together with a few eminent Buddhist masters, he solicited an imperial edict granting the protection of monastic property from governmental expropriation and, in 1911, participated in the establishment of the first national Buddhist association in Shanghai (the General Association of Chinese Buddhism, *Zhonghua fojiao zonghui* 中華佛教總會). Xuyun also contributed to obtaining the ratification of the association's charter by Sun Yat-sen (Sun Zhongshan 孫中山, 1866–1925) as well as the agreement of the new president of the republic, Yuan Shikai 袁世凱 (1859–1916), to ensure the protection of monastic properties.

Xuyun subsequently returned to his site on Mount Jizu to complete its restoration. Renamed "Zhusheng Chan Monastery, Protector of the Country"[9] by the emperor, the temple became a refuge for the ferocious general Li Genyuan 李根源 (1879–1965), the warlord who ruled Yunnan Province. The master organized local offices of the General Association of Chinese Buddhism and, starting from 1919, was invited by local authorities to officiate civic rituals in the form of Services for the Deliverance of the Souls of Water and Land (*shuilu fahui* 水陸法會).[10]

In 1920, with the support of the new Yunnan governor, Tang Jiyao 唐繼堯 (1881–1927), Xuyun undertook his second monastic restoration. The new Huating Yunqi 華亭雲棲 Monastery, situated near the town of Kunming, became a model for religious practice in the province and a refuge for the civilian population when threatened by local militarists.

In 1929, Xuyun returned to Fujian to take charge of his old monastery on Gushan, which found itself without an abbot. The buildings of the Yongquan Monastery did not require extensive restoration work, so Xuyun focused on improving its organization and established an Institute of Buddhist Studies. In 1934, the sixth Chan patriarch, Huineng 惠能 (638–713), appeared to him three times in dreams to summon him to the restoration of the Nanhua 南華 Monastery of Caoxi 曹溪 (in Shaoguan, northern Guangdong Province). Huineng himself had directed this monastery for over 35 years, and the site had sheltered his mummified corpse over the centuries.[11] The monastery was in very poor condition. As had already been the case in the past, a miraculous event greeted the efficacy of Xuyun's action: the River Caoxi changed course to favor the restoration works.

Invitations to direct religious ceremonies, particularly in Canton and Hong Kong, helped Xuyun to raise the funds for the restoration of Nanhua Monastery. Although economic difficulties increased during the War of Resistance against Japan (1937–1945), the master sought to relieve the population, which had been hard hit by the hostilities, through donations and religious services. In 1936, the Nanhua Monastery received visits from national political representatives, including General Chiang Kai-shek 蔣介石 (Jiang Jieshi, 1887–1975). In 1942, Xuyun was invited to direct a great Mahākarunā Ceremony for the Protection of the Country and the Cessation of Calamities (*Huguo xizai dabei fahui* 護國息災大悲法會) in the temporary wartime capital of Chongqing. Popular participation in this event was enormous.

The Yunmen Incident and the Last Years. In 1944, Xuyun took up his position as abbot at the Yunmen Monastery in order to undertake its restoration. By now, his fame had surpassed Asian borders: in 1948, he temporarily welcomed at the monastery Ananda Jennings, an American disciple devoted to the study of Buddhism. Xuyun also took up his fundraising journeys again, performing rites and directing ceremonies in Canton, Hong Kong, and Macao.

In the spring of 1951, two years after the communist takeover, an "incident" happened at the Yunmen Monastery at the time of the transmission of the precepts: the local authorities of the Ruyuan district laid siege to the establishment searching for gold, arms, and "counterrevolutionaries." They confined and interrogated the monastic community, searched the buildings throughout, and took away the monastery's documents and all of Xuyun's writings and correspondence. About 20 monks, a few of whom went missing, were arrested. Locked up in a room, Xuyun was interrogated and repeatedly beaten by the military arm of the Public Security Bureau sent by the local authorities. Heavily injured, he entered a state of meditative concentration. When he awaked after 10 days, he recounted a dream to his attendants. He had gone to the Tushita Heaven of Maitreya Buddha, and the buddha had told him that, since his karmic link with the world had not ended yet, he had to go back. The siege of the monastery was raised after almost three months, when, solicited by demands coming from Xuyun's disciples in China and abroad, the central government sent a few members of a special commission to Yunmen in order to investigate the incident. (A censored account of the Yunmen incident appeared only in the 1957 and 1962 editions of the annalistic biography before being entirely expunged from the latest edition).[12]

In 1952, summoned by Buddhists and by the government of the People's Republic, Xuyun left the Yunmen Monastery for Peking, where he participated in a number of government-sponsored activities, including the meeting of the promoters of the Buddhist Association of China (*Zhongguo fojiao xiehui* 中國佛教協會).[13] Thereafter, he departed on a long journey to the Jiangnan area, the stronghold of Buddhism, in the south of the country. In Shanghai, he directed a Dharma Assembly for World Peace lasting 49 days and oversaw two meditation weeks (*chanqi* 禪七) at the Yufo Monastery. He then went to Hangzhou and Suzhou. Huge crowds of devotees gathered to meet and hear him on the occasion of the many ceremonies he directed.

In 1953, Xuyun returned to Peking for the opening ceremony of the Buddhist Association of China, of which he became honorary president. At the end of the year, he found a hermitage where he could retire in the twilight of his life, in the ruins of the Zhenru 真如 Monastery on

Mount Yunju 雲居 (in Jiangxi Province). However, as soon as he settled, monks began to arrive at the monastery from all over the country. (At this time, large monasteries were becoming less and less numerous and increasingly at the mercy of state politics.) Therefore, Xuyun had no other choice but to start restoring the buildings of Zhenru and clearing the land in order to lodge and feed the monastic community, which he did thanks to funds sent by devotees in China and overseas and by relying on the workforce of the monks. In 1954, he gave religious instructions to the community over a period of four months and the next year, employing the expedient of self-ordination (*zi shi shoujie fangbian* 自誓受戒方便) provided in the *Brahma's Net Sutra*,[14] he accomplished his last transmission of the precepts (and one of the last in the entire country).

In 1957, local authorities succeeded, in an underhanded way, in seizing the fields that the community of the Zhenru Monastery had cleared and cultivated over the years. Xuyun successfully complained to the government in Peking. However, according to his disciples who recorded the last years of his life, the resentment that he aroused among the local authorities led to the accusations of the following year. (An account of these events can be found only in the 1957 and 1962 editions of the annalistic biography.)

The next year, the master was accused of corruption, reactionary ideology, erroneous ideas, homosexuality, and other crimes during the antirightist movement and barely escaped political persecution. Again, all official documents of the monastery, as well as Xuyun's private correspondence and religious writings, were seized, never to be returned. At the end of these investigations, Xuyun was declared to be innocent. His health kept worsening, and as soon as the restoration of the Zhenru Monastery was completed, he passed away on October 13, 1959.

THE ELABORATION OF THE ANNALISTIC BIOGRAPHY OF MASTER XUYUN

Xuyun's life narrative is a model example of the Buddhist saint-making process illustrating the porosity of the boundary between biography, autobiography, and hagiography in modern times.[15] The portrait that the annalistic biography offers of this master corresponds to the template of the ideal eminent monk in medieval China: the three main themes that characterize the collected biographies of eminent monks[16]—namely, asceticism, erudition, and thaumaturgy[17]—are equally present in the representation of Xuyun. From the miraculous circumstances associated with his conception and birth to his encounters with the Bodhisattva Wenshu on Mount Wutai, the annalistic biography displays a wide selection of Buddhist hagiographical tropes. A case in point is Xuyun's extraordinary age: according to Chinese reckoning, he was supposedly 120 years old at the time of his death in 1959.

Although the annalistic biography of Master Xuyun is referred to only as an autobiography in the title of the first edition of 1953 (and in the title of the English translation) and although Xuyun's extraordinary age has been the subject of controversy and the object of recent critical studies,[18] the autobiographical nature of his life narrative has never been questioned. Even in its final version, his biography remains written mostly in the first person. However, this text was actually composed, for the most part, from existing materials, especially early biographies and articles from the Buddhist press.

Early biographies of this master began to appear in the 1920s and 1930s.[19] These accounts must have first circulated orally; their forewords and postscripts indicate that the materials on which they are based originated from anecdotes recounted by Xuyun, his comrades, or his disciples. Additional biographical data became available as Xuyun became famous, and his celebrity inspired new legends that circulated via oral traditions. These two processes evolved in parallel fashion in the phase preceding the final standardization of Xuyun's life narrative in the annalistic biography. As the last link in the chain of texts, the annalistic biography embraces and reorganizes all the available information in a coherent narrative. For instance, in order to pad out the years that have been added on to the master's life and to smooth away chronological inconsistencies, the editor Cen Xuelü altered the timeline of certain events, pushed back in time some episodes of Xuyun's life, and especially extended the period of Xuyun's spiritual apprenticeship by duplicating experiences on the basis of divergent accounts of the same event found in the early biographies.[20]

Articles from the Buddhist press of the 1930s and 1940s represent the second major source on which the annalistic biography is based. By the mid-1930s, Xuyun had already become a public figure. The contemporary Buddhist press contributed to his fame by publishing his early biographical accounts, his religious instructions, his photographs, and his writings (prefaces, calls for contributions, letters, and poems) as well as announcements of the dharma assemblies directed by him and news concerning the monasteries that he was restoring. At a time when the educated, urban, middle-class public typically believed in supernatural powers and phenomena, readers of the Buddhist press could also find accounts written by Buddhist laymen who had met him or had attended the extraordinary events occurring in his presence: sudden flowerings out of season, tree spirits seeking out Xuyun to receive the precepts, fragrances perfuming the air to mark his presence, animals refusing to eat meat after taking refuge in the Buddhist Law, and so forth. These events are understood as manifestations of "sympathetic resonance" (*ganying* 感應), namely, spontaneous wonders of the natural or the divine world responding to Xuyun's actions. In the annalistic biography, Cen Xuelü transcribed entire passages from these materials, often without citing his sources, or he included these documents in the form of appendices.[21] In other words, he treated these sources as the modern equivalent of the collections of miraculous stories that provided most of the material for the compilation of the *Biographies of Eminent Monks* in the medieval period.[22]

Cen also engaged in considerable alteration of available materials. He developed some episodes of Xuyun's life in order to illustrate their conformity to the Buddhist tradition and the Chan tradition in particular. For example, he injected the theme of water, full of symbolic meanings, as a background to different episodes leading to Xuyun's awakening. He also omitted some events that did not comply with an ideal picture of the master, as in the case of the monastic revolt that Xuyun provoked when he imposed by force a rigorous observance of the Chinese monastic rules to the community of Gushan Monastery in Fujian in the early 1930s.[23] Some other events, such as the Yunmen incident, were censored by the editor for political reasons. The Yunmen incident is very well known in Buddhist circles in China and abroad, and Xuyun's near-martyrdom during these events has, without a doubt, contributed to his mythologization: at the time, he was supposedly more than 100 years old and regarded as a spiritual authority and a religious model in China.

Along with his comrades, disciples, and biographers, Xuyun participated in different ways in his own saint-making process. Anecdotes that he recounted became part of oral traditions and biographical accounts. A few miraculous stories can be attributed to Xuyun himself, including the overestimation of his age: the master provided different, approximate indications of his age in various writings in the 1930s and 1940s; and, in 1952, in an interview for the Buddhist periodical *Xiandai foxue* 現代佛學 supported by the communist government, he affirmed publicly that he had been born in 1840.[24] In 1956, Xuyun also revised and annotated the first edition of his annalistic biography, therefore implicitly endorsing it. Finally, it appears that Xuyun deliberately tried to model his life on the ideal type of Buddhist sanctity represented by the lives of past eminent monks. In addition to his missing finger, Xuyun's long hair and beard betray his past as a hermit. Witnesses also repeatedly described several habits deriving from his extended ascetic experience, such as his exceptional (even for those days) frugality, his Herculean strength, his remarkable walking speed, and his endurance during long-distance hiking. Xuyun directed his charisma toward his religious entourage and Chinese devotees during his life—the recollections of his disciples bear testimony to the long-lasting bond tying them to their master's person and memory. This master has been so involved in his role as a patriarch of Buddhist tradition that he finally merged with it. Therefore, the aims underlying the composition of Xuyun's biography—to provide the Buddhist community with a model to follow and to illustrate to the lay community the proof of the efficacy of the Buddhist path—seem to have also been the aims that Xuyun had set for his own life and he entrusted the transmission of this religious ideal to his biography.

In 1951, given the circumstances, Xuyun probably recounted his life story in a very succinct or fragmentary way. However, Xuyun's annalistic biography cannot be considered an independent and unique work but rather should be seen as the result of a process of stratification originating in one or more oral traditions and successively written down. In the case of Xuyun (as in other cases), the saint-making process was a response to his increasing popularity. For several decades, accounts of Xuyun's life have been amplified and enriched following the criteria of the Buddhist hagiographic tradition. As the last player in the saint-making process, the editor Cen Xuelü collated, integrated, amended, exaggerated, embroidered, and reformulated all the information he had at his disposal according to standard religious historiographical methods.

The publication of the English translation of his annalistic biography in the 1960s allowed Xuyun's fame as a modern eminent monk to cross the Chinese borders and reach the Western world.

THE BUDDHIST LEADER

Based upon available sources, Xuyun appears as a complex, polyvalent religious figure combining hagiographical function and historical role—and escaping easy categorization. Severe ascetic and miracle worker, enlightened master and eminent abbot, authoritative teacher and political martyr, knowledgeable monk and influential leader: Xuyun represents a large spectrum of Buddhist practices and ideals responding to the religious needs of a very heterogeneous public. If the nature of his individual self can hardly be grasped, Xuyun's voluntary agency in shaping both his hagiographical image and historical role emerges clearly instead.

In effect, this master not only contributed to creating his own image by authoring a vision of himself and of his normative biography as shown in the previous section but also relinquished his eremitic disposition in order to endorse the roles of Buddhist leader and Chan master. In these capacities, he was able to play a fundamental role in the reconstruction and transmission of the Buddhist tradition in the first half of the 20th century and especially contributed in a lasting manner to its preservation during the Maoist period (1949–1976) and subsequent renewal. More specifically, Xuyun's comprehensive restoration of many historical sites of the Chan tradition, long-term engagement in the preservation of the rules of Chinese monasticism (the Chinese Vinaya), and systematic effort to ensure through dharma transmissions (*chuanfa* 傳法) the reproduction of Chinese Buddhism in general and of the Chan school in particular can be singled out among his most important contributions to modern Chinese Buddhism. The wide geographical reach of his action spanning different southern Chinese provinces also contributed to his visibility and influence in a Buddhist China often marked by regionalism.

For over five decades, Xuyun brought back to life many forgotten or declining sites of the Chan tradition,[25] including six large, important monasteries, in different provinces of South China. The physical restoration of monasteries was accompanied by the re-establishment of their economic autonomy and the reconstitution of their dispersed monastic communities and was followed by a program of institutional reform embracing education, religious practice, manual labor, and monastic discipline. In all his monasteries, Xuyun reintroduced daily ritual and meditation practice, annual meditation retreats, extended yearly ordination sessions, and largely forgotten practices prescribed by the Vinaya. He also composed monastic codes of rules (*guiyue* 規約) adapted to the different establishments and historical periods.[26]

His restoration activity was favored and supported by a number of contemporary political figures, especially military commanders, anti-Manchu revolutionaries, and members of the Guomindang, on whom Xuyun relied in order to favor the legitimation of Buddhism within the new sociopolitical conditions of 20th-century China. While these privileged connections, as well as his persistent defense of his monastic communities, caused him to fall out of favor with local authorities of Guangdong and Jiangxi provinces during the communist regime, on many occasions they were also instrumental in helping Xuyun to assert his authority as a Buddhist leader at both a local and a national level. For example, on the occasion of the revolt of the monastic community at Gushan in the 1930s, order was restored thanks only to the support of the master's political protectors.

It is especially at the time of the foundation of the Buddhist Association of China in 1952–1953 that Xuyun availed himself of his authority and his political connections—particularly of his relationship with the vice president of the communist government, Li Jishen 李濟深 (1885–1959), an ancient Guomindang official who was one of his longtime disciples—to enforce his vision of Chinese Buddhism. In effect, on this occasion, this master was instrumental in refuting attempts to modify the Chinese Vinaya so that monastics could marry, eat meat, and drink alcohol by revolutionary monastics advocating the union of the Buddhists under the aegis of the communists.[27] If, on one side, the promotion of high standards of conduct during the Republican period played an important role in the modern evolution of Chinese Buddhism by helping the monastic community strengthen its religious authority, social credibility, and political legitimation,[28] on the other side, the formal preservation of the rules of Chinese monasticism has permitted its reconstruction on a traditional basis starting from the partial opening of the country in the 1980s.

Because of his insistence on Buddhist orthodoxy conceived of as a set of moral values inherited from the past (especially ritual and religious practice and the observance of monastic rules), Xuyun is considered the epitome of the conservative monk as opposed to Taixu 太虛 (1890–1947), the promoter of a Western-inspired reform of Buddhism along modernist and socially oriented lines.[29] However, it appears that, just like a handful of other "conservative" Buddhist leaders, Xuyun did articulate a long-standing pattern of Buddhist revitalization within the new Buddhist institutions of the first half of the 20th century. Concerned about the instruction of the clergy, this master founded Buddhist seminaries in the last four monasteries he restored and he participated in the establishment of a number of Buddhist associations at both a local and a national level—seminaries for monks and national associations counted among the new institutions of modern Chinese Buddhism. Xuyun also realized, well before the 1949 communist takeover, the necessity for monks to provide for their own subsistence: since the 1930s, he encouraged his communities to cultivate the fields, and since the 1940s, he actually established Buddhist farms and led the monks in reclaiming the uncultivated land and practicing agriculture.[30] Xuyun ordained female monastics and occasionally allowed nuns to participate in meditation retreats; at times, he also permitted groups of laymen to join the daily religious practice of his monasteries. Far from the intellectual character of the Buddhist modernist movement, the sutra lectures, religious ceremonies, and public rituals he directed all over the country attracted huge numbers of followers and especially the common people. His ability to approach people at all levels is indeed one of the reasons that he achieved such celebrity during his lifetime.

THE CHAN MASTER

Xuyun, the most famous Chan master of modern China, acquired this reputation especially thanks to his expertise in meditation, to his training of a large number of disciples, and to his enterprise of re-establishing and transmitting the five dharma lineages of the Chan school. Xuyun was not the only reputed Chan master of his time. However, other renowned Republican Chan masters such as Laiguo 來果 (1881–1953), a former ascetic and Chan practitioner like Xuyun, instructed in meditation-only (male) monastics and only inside their monasteries—the same Gaomin Monastery for over 30 years, in the case of Laiguo—and transmitted the dharma to only a small number of disciples.

Recognized as an expert meditator ever since the news of his alleged awakening experience and prolonged states of meditative concentration spread, Xuyun centered his teaching on vows and practice. Besides reintroducing meditation practice in the monasteries that he restored, he led extended meditation retreats in other monasteries in China.[31] This master trained monastic and lay Buddhists in the *kan huatou* method of meditation, which he explained in a simple and direct language more comprehensible to the lay practitioners and the typical monks than the Buddhist idiom standardized over many centuries. That he was an expert Chan practitioner can be inferred from, among other things, the repeated publication and frenzied circulation of his religious and meditation instructions,[32] which were translated in many languages[33] and are still used by practitioners in Asia and the West.

Maintaining a posture that was coherent with the rhetoric of the Chan school, Xuyun also valued (and personally performed) manual and agricultural work as a form of practice: in the

1950s, when Buddhist monasteries were deprived of their conventional financial resources, the Zhenru Monastery on Mount Yunju was entirely rebuilt by the monks with recuperated materials. Though a Chan representative, Xuyun insisted on the efficacy of any Buddhist practice properly performed, an attitude that was in line with the antisectarian tendencies of Republican Buddhism; however, like other Chan masters, he reduced the Pure Land practice of repeating the name of the buddha (*nianfo*, Jap. *nembutsu*) to just a variant of *kan huatou* meditation.[34]

The relationship between master and disciple is of fundamental importance in the Chan school, and Xuyun did train a large number of disciples both in meditation practice and in the traditional lifestyle of large public monasteries. Beginning in the 1930s, he also formalized his master–disciple relationships by relying on dharma transmissions: Xuyun was the Chan master who accomplished the greatest number of dharma transmissions in the first half of the 20th century. In Chinese Buddhism, the transmission of dharma (or dharma transmission, *chuanfa* 傳法) is a religious entrustment by which a master formally recognizes the spiritual accomplishments of a disciple, names him as his heir, and confers upon him the authority to teach others. A dharma lineage (*famai* 法脈) is a line of spiritual descent claiming direct and uninterrupted filiation from a common ancestor through a succession of dharma transmissions.

In the late 19th century, a new historical narrative was transmitted to China from Japan attributing the decline of Chinese Buddhism to the loss of the many schools extant during what was considered its flourishing period: the Sui and Tang dynasties, from the late 6th century to the beginning of the 10th. The revival of lost schools therefore came to be equated with the revival of Buddhism.[35] As far as the Chan school is concerned, at the beginning of the 20th century, only two of its five branches existing during the Tang and Northern Song dynasties, the Linji and Caodong branches, were still extant along with their dharma lineages. Beginning in the mid-1930s, Xuyun undertook to reinstate one after another the three interrupted lineages of the Weiyang, Fayan, and Yunmen branches and to transmit their dharma to a large number of monks.[36] Like other Chan masters of the Republican era, he also transmitted the dharma of the two extant branches of the Chan school: the Linji branch and the Caodong branch. Xuyun would symbolically associate each one of the monasteries that he was restoring with a Chan branch, and in that monastery he would carry out most of the dharma transmissions of that specific branch. In the years that preceded and followed the communist takeover, he also particularly intensified dharma transmissions,[37] and while he refused to leave the country himself, he enjoined his more motivated disciples to establish these transmissions abroad.

Besides permitting him to acquire national and international visibility through his posterity, Xuyun's programmatic and systematic dharma transmissions created a heritage for Chinese Buddhism since his dharma lineages have been instrumental in the reassertion of this religious tradition in post-Mao China thanks to the religious, social, and political meanings associated with them. At the beginning of the 1980s, when ordination ceremonies were resumed after an interruption of more than 20 years, many of Xuyun's dharma heirs re-emerged to lead Buddhist reconstruction. The dharma transmission aroused in them, in the first place, a sense of belonging to the different traditions of Chan and the concern to preserve their sacred sites: almost all the monasteries restored by Xuyun in the first half of the 20th century, as well as many other Chan monasteries, were rebuilt by his dharma heirs since the 1980s and followed the same restoration pattern as their master's. While the reconstruction of Buddhist monasteries in post-Mao China was also undertaken in small temples in the south that did not have dharma lineages, dharma filiation to a charismatic figure such as Xuyun has greatly contributed to this enterprise. In the second place, since the end of the Maoist period, religious identity based on Xuyun's dharma lineages has also favored the creation of national and transnational networks. His disciples in China were able to undertake the religious reconstruction in part due to the ritual expertise and economic support provided by their expatriate comrades in Hong Kong, Taiwan, and the United States, many of Xuyun's dharma heirs having moved abroad before the communist takeover of 1949. Lastly, besides being a springboard for acceding to the highest positions within the Buddhist Association of China—from 2002 to 2015, the position of president was occupied by two of his dharma heirs: Yicheng 一诚 (1927–2017) and Chuanyin 传印 (b. 1927)—affiliation with Xuyun's prestigious dharma lineage today represents a religious and political credential for the abbotship of important public monasteries.[38]

Xuyun's dharma disciples include Master Jinghui 淨慧 (1933–2013), a well-known public figure of institutional Buddhism and the promoter of the Living Chan movement,[39] and Master Xuanhua 宣化 (1918–1995), the founder of the City of Ten Thousand Buddhas (Wanfocheng 万佛城) near San Francisco, one of the largest Buddhist temple complexes in the United States. Master Zhiding 知定 (Jy Din Shakya, 1917–2003), another dharma disciple of Xuyun whom he encouraged to leave China in 1949, arrived in 1956 in Hawaii, where he founded the Hsu Yun Temple in Honolulu. Since then, at least 30 temples and memorial halls have been named after Xuyun all over the world.[40]

The posterity of Xuyun's dharma transmissions shows the relevance of his legacy in post-Mao Buddhist reconstruction: Chinese Buddhism on the mainland is especially indebted to the pattern of Buddhist revitalization articulating Buddhist vows and religious practice within the new Buddhist institutions of the first half of the 20th century—a pattern that was particularly (though, of course, not exclusively) promoted and transmitted by Xuyun. If the legacy of Taixu's "Humanistic Buddhism" (*renjian fojiao* 人間佛教) or "Buddhism for human life" (*rensheng fojiao* 人生佛教) has been especially carried on and developed in Taiwan and is only recently making a moderate comeback to the mainland, many influential masters in Taiwan such as Shengyan 聖嚴 (1931–2009), the founder of the Buddhist organization Dharma Drum Mountain, and Weijue 惟覺 (1928–2016), the founder of the Buddhist transnational organization Zhongtai shan, also openly emphasize their dharma descendance from Xuyun.

In contemporary China, Xuyun remains a model for a Buddhist life centered on vows and practice—a model negotiating with and balancing the influence of Humanistic Buddhism—and the long-standing Buddhist ideals and moral values conveyed by his hagiographical representation continue to inspire and guide a great number of monastics.

REVIEW OF LITERATURE

Xuyun's extraordinary age has been the subject of controversy since at least 1959, when, after some private inquiries, the celebrated Chinese philosopher and man of letters Hu Shi (1891–1962) publicly refuted, during a conference in Taipei, the veracity of the information about

Xuyun's date of birth (and the charges of his father) contained in the annalistic biography.[41] Since 2000, Xuyun's age has also become the object of academic research, and different hypotheses based on the collation of available materials have been advanced concerning his date of birth, particularly by Master Yinshun (1905–2005)[42] and by scholars Wang Jianchuan,[43] Daniela Campo,[44] and Ye Bing.[45] The quest to assess the "real" age of Xuyun represents, more than an academic exercise, a questioning of the received tradition's authority. However, for the time being, Xuyun's age remains an open question, as no historical documentation prior to the 1910s can be found on this master. Other events of Xuyun's life have not yet been entirely elucidated for reasons linked to censorship and the inaccessibility of a number of governmental archival documents.

The most exhaustive publication on Xuyun to date is Ye Bing's *Xuyun heshang nianpu changbian* 虛雲和尚年譜長編, published in 2018 in Hong Kong. In this work, the received year-by-year narrative of Xuyun's Annalistic Biographic is supplemented by virtually all the materials made public and available on this master so far, including of the governmental kind.[46] Ye Bing puts Xuyun's age at the time of his death at 83.

Western scholarship on Xuyun includes references to this master contained in the works by Holmes Welch, especially testimonies and accounts from Chinese monks who emigrated to Hong Kong at the time of the communist takeover.[47]

In her monograph *La construction de la sainteté dans la Chine moderne: la vie du maître bouddhiste Xuyun*,[48] based on both historical documents and oral and written accounts by Xuyun's disciples, Daniela Campo deconstructs the religious biography of this master and reconstructs his historical biography as well as the genesis of his religious myth. In this work, Xuyun's life is also considered to be representative of the many ways that Chinese Buddhist communities lived in modern times and reacted to political and social changes.[49] Articles in English by the same author particularly explore Xuyun's reform of Gushan Yongquan Monastery in the 1930s[50] and Xuyun's Dharma lineages.

PRIMARY SOURCES

Xuyun's early biographies include the following:

- "Succinct Biography of Master Xuyun of Zhusheng Monastery of Mount Jizu in Yunnan": Ye Qingyan 葉青眼, "Yunnan Jizushan Zhusheng si Xuyun heshang lüezhuan 雲南雞足山祝聖寺虛雲和尚略傳," *Foyin* 8/9 (1924): 5–6; and
- "Report on the Chan Practices of Master Xu of Gushan": Wuzhu 無住, "Gushan Xugong chanxing shuwen 鼓山虛公禪行述聞," *Shijie fojiao jushilin linkan* 36 (1933): 2–10. This account was republished in booklet form: Zhu Shouzhuo 朱守拙, ed., *Xuyun laoheshang shiji jilüe* 虛雲老和尚事蹟紀略 (N.p., 1936). It also served as the basis for the portrait of Xuyun contained in the *Representative Enriched and Revised Collection of the Lineage of Gushan Patriarchs*, which is much shorter but contains further details and corrections: Baoguang 寶光, "Di baisanshi dai Xuyun chanshi 第百三十代虛雲禪師," in Xuyun 虛雲, ed., *Zengjiao Gushan liezu lianfang ji* 增校鼓山列祖聯芳集 (Fujian Gushan Yongquan chansi, 1936), 35–39.

The first edition of Xuyun's annalistic biography is the *Annalistic Autobiography of Master Xuyun* dating from 1953: Cen Xuelü 岑學呂, ed., *Xuyun heshang zishu nianpu* 虛雲和尚自述年譜 (Xianggang: Xuyun heshang fahui bianyin banshichu chuban, 1953). A second, identical edition appeared some months later, and a third enriched and revised edition, entitled *Annalistic Biography of Master Xuyun*, appeared in 1957: Cen Xuelü 岑學呂, ed., *Xuyun heshang nianpu* 虛雲和尚年譜 (Xianggang: Xianggang foxue shuju chuban, 1957). The 1962 edition contains the narrative of Xuyun's life up to the moment of his death in 1959; moreover, it has not been censured (as has the current version): Cen Xuelü 岑學呂, *Xuyun heshang nianpu* 虛雲和尚年譜 (Xianggang, 1962; republished in Cen Xuelü 岑學呂, ed., *Xuyun laoheshang nianpu fahui* 虛雲老和尚年譜法匯 [Shenzhen: Shenzhen yachang yanse yinshua youxian gongsi, 2004]).

What is left of Xuyun's writings, the *Dharma Collection of Master Xuyun*, also edited by Cen Xuelü, contains the dharma speeches (*fayu* 法語) in the classical language that Xuyun used to address the monastic community; part of his religious instructions (*kaishi* 開示) in the colloquial language used to guide monks and committed laymen in religious practice; a collection of literary pieces such as prefaces, postscripts, and other compositions; codes of rules (*guiyue* 規約) which Xuyun had formulated for his monasteries; a considerable number of poems of all kinds; and, finally, part of his correspondence: Xuyun 虛雲, *Xuyun laoheshang fahui* 虚云老和尚法汇 (Beijing: Huangshan shushe, 2005; first edition: *Xuyun heshang fahui* 虛雲和尚法彙 [Xianggang: Xuyun heshang fahui bianyin chu, 1953]).

A *Supplement to Master Xuyun's Dharma Collection* was edited by Jinghui: Jinghui 净慧, ed., *Xuyun heshang fahui xubian* 虚云和尚法汇续编 (Shijiazhuang: Hebeisheng fojiao xiehui yinxing, 1990).

DIGITAL MATERIALS

The 1962 edition of Xuyun's annalistic biography can be found on numerous websites, for example: 虚云和尚年谱 (http://www.lianhua33.com/xy4a.htm).

Besides published translations of his biography and selected religious instructions,[51] Xuyun's discourses and other materials in different Western languages can also be found on the Internet and especially on the website of the Zen Buddhist Order of Hsu Yun (http://www.hsuyun.org/index.html) founded in 1997 by Master Zhiding.

Remembrances of Xuyun by his direct disciples include the following:

Jy Din Shakya (Zhiding), *Empty Cloud: The Teachings of Xu Yun: A Remembrance of the Great Chinese Zen Master* (http://www.thezensite.com/ZenTeachings/Teishos/Remembering_Master_Xu_yun_Empty_Cloud.pdf).

Qixian 齐贤, "Huiyi Xuyun laoheshang diandi 回忆虚云老和尚点滴 (http://chan.bailinsi.net/2009/4/2009405.htm)", *Chan* 4 (2009).

Shaoyun 紹雲, *Xuyun laoheshang shentong shi xian* 虛雲老和尚神通示現 (2010): 绍云法师:虚云老和尚神通示现 (http://www.xuefo.net/nr/article3/26218.html)

Ye Bing 叶兵, ed., *Foyuan fashi dui Xuyun laoheshang de huiyi* 佛源法师对虚云老和尚的回忆: 佛源法师对虚云老和尚的回忆 作者: 叶兵 (https://xliang.gitbooks.io/buddhism-articles/content/0033.html)

Xuyun's life has also been adapted for a Chinese TV series of 20 episodes (*Bainian Xuyun* 百年虚云, 2009): 百年虛雲(高清) (https://www.youtube.com/playlist?list=PL699DE44BE9F1C94F).

FURTHER READING

Blofeld, John. *The Wheel of Life: The Autobiography of a Western Buddhist*. Rev. ed. London: Rider, 1987.[52]

Campo, Daniela. *La construction de la sainteté dans la Chine moderne: la vie du maître bouddhiste Xuyun*. Paris: Les Belles Lettres, 2013.

Campo, Daniela. "Imposing the Rules: Reform and Rebellion at Gushan Yongquan Monastery in the 1930s." *Studies in Chinese Religions* 3, no. 2 (2017): 142–174.

Campo, Daniela. "Bridging the Gap: Chan and Tiantai Dharma Lineages (*famai* 法脈) from the Republican Era to post-Mao China." In *Buddhism after Mao: Negotiations, Continuities, and Reinventions*. Edited by Ji Zhe, André Laliberté, and Gareth Fisher, 123–151. Honolulu: University of Hawai'i Press, 2019.

Cen Xuelü 岑學呂, ed. *Yunmen shanzhi* 雲門山志. Minguo nianjian Yunmen si paiyin ben, 1951.

Cen Xuelü 岑學呂, ed. *Yunju shanzhi* 雲居山志. Xianggang: Xianggang fojing liutongchu, 1959.

Cheung, Richard. *The Autobiography and Maxims of Chan Master Han Shan (1546–1623)*. Translated by Cheung Richard. Xianggang: Hong Kong Buddhist Book Distributor, 1995.

Gyatso, Janet. *Apparitions of the Self: The Secret Autobiographies of a Tibetan Visionary*. Princeton, NJ: Princeton University Press, 1998.

Ji Zhe. *Religion, modernité et temporalité: Une sociologie du bouddhisme chan contemporain*. Paris: CNRS Editions, 2016.

Kieschnick, John. *The Eminent Monk: Buddhist Ideals in Medieval Chinese Hagiography*. Honolulu: University of Hawai'i Press, 1997.

Luk, Charles (Lu K'uan Yü). *Ch'an and Zen Teaching: First Series*. Rev. ed. London: Rider, 1970.

Luk, Charles, ed. *Empty Cloud: The Autobiography of the Chinese Zen Master Xuyun*. Translated by Hunn Richard. Dorset, UK: Element Books Limited, 1988.

Ownby, David, Goossaert Vincent, and Ji Zhe, eds. *Making Saints in Modern China*. New York: Oxford University Press, 2016.

Shaoyun 紹雲, ed. *Xuyun laoheshang zai Yunju shan* 虛雲老和尚在雲居山. Xianggang: Xianggang yannanfei chuban youxian gongsi, 2002.

Welch, Holmes. *The Practice of Chinese Buddhism*. Cambridge, MA: Harvard University Press, 1967.

Welch, Holmes. *The Buddhist Revival in China*. Cambridge, MA: Harvard University Press, 1968.

Wu Pei-yi. *The Confucian's Progress: Autobiographical Writings in Traditional China*. Princeton, NJ: Princeton University Press, 1990.

Ye Bing 葉兵, ed. *Xuyun heshang nianpu changbian* 虛雲和尚年譜長編. Xianggang: Zhongguo wenming chubanshe, 2018.

NOTES

1. This article on Xuyun is especially based on my monograph *La construction de la sainteté dans la Chine moderne: la vie du maître bouddhiste Xuyun* (Paris: Les Belles Lettres, 2013) and on the chapter "Chan Master Xuyun: The Embodiment of an Ideal, the Transmission of a Model," in *Making Saints in Modern China*, ed. David Ownby, Vincent Goossaert, and Ji Zhe (New York: Oxford University Press, 2016), 99–136.
2. See the "Primary Sources" section.
3. Cen Xuelü 岑學呂, ed., *Xuyun fashi nianpu* 虛雲法師年譜 (Beijing: Zongjiao wenhua chubanshe, 1995). For the "annalistic biography" literary genre, see Denis C. Twitchett, "Chinese Biographical

Writing," in *Historians of China and Japan*, ed. W. G. Beasley and E. G. Pulleyblank (London: Oxford University Press, 1961), 113; for the "annalistic autobiography" literary genre, see Wu Pei-yi, *The Confucian's Progress: Autobiographical Writings in Traditional China* (Princeton, NJ: Princeton University Press, 1990), 32–41.

4. Richard Hunn, ed., and Charles Luk, trans., *Empty Cloud: The Autobiography of the Chinese Zen Master Xuyun* (Dorset, UK: Element Books Limited, 1988). The English version of Xuyun's biography was translated in many languages, including Polish and Italian: *Nuvola Vuota: Autobiografia di un maestro Chan* (Rome: Ubaldini Editore, 1990).
5. Campo, *La construction de la sainteté*; Ye Bing 葉兵, ed., *Xuyun heshang nianpu changbian* 虛雲和尚年譜長編 (Xianggang: Zhongguo wenming chubanshe, 2018).
6. He received the monastic names of Guyan 古岩 and Yanche 演徹 as well as the personal public name Deqing 德清.
7. For the *kan huatou* method, see Robert E. Buswell, "The 'Short-cut' Approach of K'an-hua Meditation: The Evolution of a Practical Subitism in Chinese Ch'an Buddhism," in *Sudden and Gradual: Approaches to Enlightenment in Chinese Thought*, ed. Peter N. Gregory (Honolulu: University of Hawai'i Press, 1987), 321–377.
8. *Tuo sishi shi shei* 拖死屍是誰.
9. Jishan Huguo Zhusheng chansi 雞山護國祝聖禪寺.
10. For this ritual, see Yifa, *The Origins of Buddhist Monastic Codes in China: An Annotated Translation and Study of the Chanyuan qinggui* (Honolulu: University of Hawai'i Press, 2002), 290–291n45; and Daniel B. Stevenson, "Text, Image, and Transformation in the History of the *Shuilu fahui*, the Buddhist Rite for Deliverance of Creatures of Water and Land," in *Cultural Intersections in Later Chinese Buddhism*, ed. Marsha Weidner (Honolulu: University of Hawai'i Press, 2001), 30–72.
11. For Huineng and his mummified corpse, see John J. Jørgensen, *Inventing Hui-neng, the Sixth Patriarch: Hagiography and Biography in Early Ch'an* (Leiden, The Netherlands: Brill, 2005); John Jorgensen, "Huineng," *Oxford Research Encyclopedia of Religion* (Oxford: Oxford University Press, 2021).
12. For a tentative reconstruction of the causes and events of the Yunmen incident, see Campo, *La construction de la sainteté*, 263–277; "Chan Master Xuyun," 121–125.
13. The Chinese Buddhist Association established in 1947 had followed the Nationalists to Taiwan.
14. *Fanwangjing* 梵網經 (*Brahmajāla-sūtra*), T. 1484, vol. 24, 1006c14–15; see Kuo Li-ying, *Confession et contrition dans le bouddhisme chinois du Ve au Xe siècle* (Paris: École Française d'Extrême-Orient, 1994), 40–45.
15. See Ben Van Overmeire, "Buddhism and Biography," in *Oxford Research Encyclopedia of Religion*, (Oxford: Oxford University Press, 2021).
16. Particularly, the *Biographies of Eminent Monks* (*Gaoseng zhuan* 高僧傳, T. 2059, vol. 50) compiled by Huijiao 慧皎 (497–554); the *Further Biographies of Eminent Monks* (*Xu gaoseng zhuan* 續高僧傳, T. 2060, vol. 50) compiled by Daoxuan 道宣 (596–667); the *Song Biographies of Eminent Monks* (*Song gaoseng zhuan* 宋高僧傳, T. 2061, vol. 50) compiled by Zanning 贊寧 (919–1001).
17. See John Kieschnick, *The Eminent Monk: Buddhist Ideals in Medieval Chinese Hagiography* (Honolulu: University of Hawai'i Press, 1997). For sanctity in China at the beginning of the medieval period, see Robert F. Campany, *Making Transcendents: Ascetics and Social Memory in Early Medieval China* (Honolulu: University of Hawai'i Press, 2009).
18. See the "Review of Literature" section.
19. See the "Primary Sources" section.
20. Campo, *La construction de la sainteté*, 87–116.
21. See, for example, Zhang Zhuoxian 張拙仙, "Yunqi shuang bai'e wangsheng ji 雲棲雙 白鵝往生記," *Haichao yin* 9, no. 1 (1928): 4–6 (republished in Cen, *Xuyun fashi nianpu*, 55–56 as Hong Xi, "Yunqi

shuang'e wangsheng ji") and Hu Yisheng 胡毅生, "Feitao ruiying ji 緋桃瑞應記," *Yuanyin yuekan* 1 (1947): 51 (republished in Cen, *Xuyun fashi nianpu*, 108–109).
22. Koichi Shinohara, "Two Sources of Chinese Buddhist Biographies: *Stupa* Inscriptions and Miracle Stories," in *Monks and Magicians. Religious Biographies in Asia*, ed. Phyllis Granoff and Koichi Shinohara (Delhi: Motilal Banarsidass, 1994), 119–228.
23. See Daniela Campo, "Imposing the Rules: Reform and Rebellion at Gushan Yongquan Monastery in the 1930s," *Studies in Chinese Religions* 3, no. 2 (2017): 142–174.
24. Shengyin 勝音, "Xuyun laoheshang fangwen ji 虛雲老和尚訪問記," *Xiandai foxue* 現代佛學 26/3, no. 2 (1952): 19, 32. Xuyun gave as his date of birth a day that, in the year 1840, did not exist.
25. Thirty-one sites overall, according to Ye, *Xuyun heshang nianpu changbian: xia*, 483–484.
26. The codes for the Yunqi Monastery and for the Yunmen Monastery can be found in Xuyun 虛雲, *Xuyun laoheshang fahui* 虚云老和尚法汇 (Beijing: Huangshan shushe, 2005), 292–318. The code for the Yongquan Monastery on Mount Gu is Xuyun 虛雲, "Gushan Yongquan si chongding andan guize (bingxu) 鼓山湧泉寺重訂安單規則 (並序)," *Haichao yin* 海潮音 11, no. 3 (1930): 22–25.
27. Campo, *La construction de la sainteté*, 294–314.
28. See Daniela Campo, "A Different Buddhist Revival: The Promotion of Vinaya (jielü 戒律) in Republican China," *Journal of Global Buddhism* 18 (2017): 129–154. Chinese Societies.
29. See on Taixu Don A. Pittman, *Toward a Modern Chinese Buddhism: Taixu's Reforms* (Honolulu: University of Hawaii Press, 2001); and Justin R. Ritzinger, *Anarchy in the Pure Land: Reinventing the Cult of Maitreya in Modern Chinese Buddhism* (New York: Oxford University Press, 2017).
30. For the set of regulations composed by Xuyun for the Dajue Farm on Mount Yunmen in Guangdong ("Nongchang zuzhi jianzhang 农场组织简章"), see Xuyun, *Xuyun laoheshang fahui*, 313–315.
31. See, for example, the meditation instructions he delivered over two meditation weeks at the Yufosi in Shanghai in 1952: Cen, *Xuyun fashi nianpu*, 154–181.
32. Different series of Xuyun's meditation instructions are contained in his annalistic biography and in the *Dharma Collection of Master Xuyun* also edited by Cen Xuelü: Xuyun, *Xuyun laoheshang fahui*.
33. English translations of Xuyun's religious instructions can be found in, for example, Charles Luk (Lu K'uan Yü), *Ch'an and Zen Teaching: First Series* (London: Rider, 1970), 19–117; Hunn and Luk, *Empty Cloud*, 156–187; Sheng Yen, *Attaining the Way: A Guide to the Practice of Chan Buddhism* (Boston and London: Shambhala Publications, 2006), 87–116.
34. Charles B. Jones, "Toward a Typology of Nien-fo: a Study in Methods of Buddha-Invocation in Chinese Pure Land Buddhism," *Pacific World: Journal of the Institute of Buddhist Studies*, 3rd series, no. 3 (2001): 232–233.
35. Erik Schicketanz, "Narratives of Buddhist Decline and the Concept of the Sect (Zong) in Modern Chinese Buddhist Thought," *Studies in Chinese Religions* 3, no. 3 (2017): 281–300.
36. For a description of this practice, see Daniela Campo, "Bridging the Gap: Chan and Tiantai Dharma Lineages (*famai* 法脈) from the Republican Era to Post-Mao China," in *Buddhism after Mao: Negotiations, Continuities, and Reinventions*, ed. Ji Zhe, André Laliberté, and Gareth Fisher (Honolulu: University of Hawai'i Press, 2019), 123–151.
37. Xuyun's Dharma disciples in all five Chan branches number 105, according to the overview in Ye, *Xuyun heshang nianpu changbian: xia*, 482.
38. See Campo, "Bridging the Gap."
39. See Ji Zhe, *Religion, modernité et temporalité: Une sociologie du bouddhisme chan contemporain* (Paris: CNRS Editions, 2016).
40. In China, Taiwan, Canada, the United States, Europe (Hungary), and Singapore: Ye, *Xuyun heshang nianpu changbian: xia*, 480.

41. For the ensuing international polemic that opposed Hu Shi to Cen Xuelü and to Chinese and overseas Buddhists, see Chen Jinguo 陳進國, "Hu Shi yu 'Xuyun heshang nianpu' de yi duan gong'an – yi 'bi hushuo ji' wei taolun zhongxin 胡適與虛雲和尚年譜的一段公案——以辟胡說集為討論中心," *Taiwan zongjiao xuehui tongxun* 臺灣宗教學會通訊 7, no. 1 (2001): 65–76.
42. Shi Yinshun 釋印順, "Gushan yu Xuyun heshang 鼓山與虛雲和尚," in *Yongguang ji* 永光集 (Beijing: Zhonghua shuju, 2011), 186–190.
43. Wang Chien-ch'uan 王見川, "Huan Xuyun yige benlai mianmu: ta de nianji yu shiji xinlun 還'虛雲'一個本來面目: 他的年紀與事蹟新論," *Yuanguang foxue xuebao* 圓光佛學學報 13 (2008): 169–188. See also Wang Chien-ch'uan 王見川, "Xuyun shengnian yu shiji bulun 虛雲生年與事蹟補論," in *Lishi, Yishu yu Taiwan renwen luncong (1): zongjiao minsu zhuanji* 歷史、藝術與台灣人文論叢 (1): 宗教民俗專輯, eds. Wang Huichen 王惠琛, Xiao Baifang 蕭百芳, and Wang Chien-ch'uan 王見川 (Taipei: Boyang wenhua, 2012).
44. Campo, *La construction de la sainteté*, 47–65; "Xuyun chanshi (yue 1864–1959) yu qi gaoling shenhua de jiangou 虚云禅师(约 1864–1959) 与其高龄神话的建构," *Hanyu foxue pinglun* 漢語佛學評論 4 (2014): 271–289.
45. Ye, *Xuyun heshang nianpu changbian*: *shang*, 2–11.
46. Such as published archival materials of the United Front from 1949 to 2009 (*Xin Zhongguo tongyi zhanxian liushinian dashiji* 新中国统一战线六十年大事记): Ye, *Xuyun heshang nianpu changbian*. I am very grateful to Prof. Xuan Fang 宣方, of the Renmin University of China, for sending this work to me.
47. Holmes Welch, *The Practice of Chinese Buddhism* (Cambridge, MA: Harvard University Press, 1967); *The Buddhist Revival in China* (Cambridge, MA: Harvard University Press, 1968); *Buddhism under Mao* (Cambridge, MA: Harvard University Press, 1972).
48. On Xuyun's biography, see in English by the same author "Chan Master Xuyun."
49. See also Eyal Aviv's unpublished paper "Religion, Historiography and Cultural Identity in the Debate over Xuyun's Biography."
50. Campo, *Imposing the Rules*; *Bridging the Gap*.
51. See notes 4 and 30.
52. In 1938, the English Buddhist John Blofeld (1913–1987) was permitted to live in the meditation hall of the Huating Monastery. A chapter of his book *The Wheel of Life*: *The Autobiography of a Western Buddhist* (London: Rider, 1959) is devoted to the memories of the nine months he spent in the monastery.

Daniela Campo

Z

ZHENTONG (OTHER-EMPTINESS)

VIEWS OF EMPTINESS AND BUDDHANATURE

The Tibetan term *zhentong* (*gzhan stong*; also phonetized *shentong*) refers to a diverse range of philosophical views and meditative experiences that assert understandings of the ultimate nature of reality to be emptiness (*śūnyatā*; *stong pa nyid*) devoid of everything other than (*gzhan*) the innate luminous essence (*garbha*; *snying po*) that pervades living beings, known as *buddhanature* (*tathāgatagarbha*; *de bzhin gshegs pa'i snying po*). The literal meaning of the term zhentong is to be *empty of other*; normative translations include "other-emptiness" and "emptiness of other," though "extrinsic emptiness" is more precise. A zhentong view expresses emptiness that is other than buddhanature, sometimes referred to as the *great emptiness* (*stong pa chen po*). Those who adhere to zhentong views maintain that the ultimate (*don dam*), while empty of everything that is not itself (*rang ma yin pas stong pa*), is not empty of itself (*rang stong ma yin*). The ultimate is understood to be a positive reality equated with buddhanature and pristine awareness (*ye shes*) that persists in a manner that is empty (*stong pa*), luminous (*gsal ba*), and permanently constant (*rtag pa*). In contrast, *rangtong* (*rang stong*) refers to views that assert emptiness that is devoid of an intrinsic nature (*svabhāva*). While zhentong is said to be beyond constructs of the intellect and cannot be understood in terms of deconstructive or reductive dialectics, an understanding of rangtong is arrived at through analytical negationist methods. Adherents to zhentong views are called "Zhentongpas," while adherents to rangtong views are called "Rangtongpas." Though rangtong and zhentong views are not inherently contradictory, and in fact were initially posited as complementary descriptions of relative and ultimate reality, Tibetan interpreters have fiercely debated the ontology of these modes of emptiness since the 14th century.

INDIAN BUDDHIST SOURCES FOR ZHENTONG

With the rise of the Mahāyāna at the dawn of the first millennium, the *Prajñāpāramitā* sutras and development of the Madhyamaka school, there was an emphasis on the Buddha's teaching of emptiness (*śūnyatā*; *stong pa nyid*). The Madhyamaka school articulated a deconstructive philosophy that analyzed the constituent components of the individual self and phenomena of the world, concluding that there is no autonomous, enduring, or permanent existence. This lack of an intrinsic nature (*svabhāva*; *rang bzhin*) to self and phenomena is explained to be the realization of emptiness. Buddhist sutras, however, including the *Śrīmālādevī-siṃhanāda Sūtra*, *Tathāgatagarbha Sūtra*, and *Laṇkāvatāra Sūtra*, set forth an understanding that there is an enlightened essence (*garbha*) called *tathāgatagarbha* (buddhanature) that endures within living beings and is continuously permanent. In addition to these Mahāyāna sutras, the *Ratnagotravibhāga*, popularly known as the *Uttaratantra* and one of the *Five Treatises of Maitreya*, expounded on buddhanature. Attributed to the Indian figure Maitreyanātha and his disciple Asaṅga (*c.* 4th–5th centuries), these five treatises comprise a range of doctrinal formulations that are situated in opposition to the highly apophatic discourse found within the *Prajñāpāramitā* sutras. Along with these sutras and the *Five Treatises of Maitreya*, the Indian zhentong canonical corpus includes the *Collection of Hymns* (*Bstod tshogs*) attributed to Nāgārjuna. In contrast to Nāgārjuna's *Collection on Reasoning* (*Rigs tshogs*), where he unequivocally relies on the *via negativa* method of Madhyamaka, his hymns provide a cataphatic appraisal of the ultimate. The later zhentong literary tradition in Tibet regularly cites these hymns, and specifically the *Dharmadhātustava* or *Praise to the Sphere of Phenomena*, as core sources for a positivist tradition in the works of Nāgārjuna.

To reconcile internal doctrinal paradoxes between the teaching of emptiness that expounds the lack of an intrinsic nature and that of buddhanature, which expounds a continuously permanent essence, Buddhist sutras put forth several hermeneutical schemes to interpret these different teachings. The *Saṃdhinirmocana Sūtra* organizes the Buddha Śākyamuni's teachings into a scheme of three distinct sets of teachings or *turnings*, not according to a historical framework of when they were taught, but according to doctrines. The first turning includes the Buddha's teachings on the Four Noble Truths, interdependence, and no-self. The second turning teachings are on emptiness, the understanding that phenomena are devoid of any intrinsic existence (*svabhāvaśūnya*). The third turning elucidates buddhanature, an innate luminous essence that pervades living beings. While there is a rough correlation to the historical progression of these teachings in Indian Buddhism, these three turnings are not a historical model of the Buddha's teachings but are meant to organize philosophical ideas.

With the reception of these Mahāyāna ideas and their correlative literature in Tibet from the 10th through 13th centuries, there arose different interpretations over which set of teachings are provisional in their meaning (*neyārtha*; *drang don*) and which are definitive in their meaning (*nītārtha*; *nges don*). As relatively late recipients of Indian Buddhism, Tibetan scholastic traditions elaborately systematized the Indian hermeneutical schemas and developed their own ways of interpreting Buddhist doctrines. Of consequence to this Buddhist discourse, two Tibetan exegetical systems emerged from two distinct interpretations of the *Five Treatises of Maitreya*, as they were translated from Sanskrit into Tibetan during the late 10th to early 11th centuries. These two systems of interpretation differ on the meaning of the *Five Treatises of Maitreya* and the *Uttaratantra* in particular. One system became known as the analytic system (*thos bsam gyi lugs*) established by Lotsāwa Loden Sherab (Lo tsā ba blo ldan shes rab), otherwise known as Ngok Lotsāwa (Rngog lo tsā ba, 1059–1109), and the other system was referred to as the meditative system (*sgom lugs*), established by Tsen Kawoché (Btsan kha bo che, b. 1021).[1]

ZHENTONG SCHOLARSHIP IN TIBET

In Tibet, there arose two distinct classifications of the Madhyamaka school of emptiness: (a) General Madhyamaka, which includes those whose views assert that there is no intrinsic nature (*niḥsvavhāvavādin*), namely the Prāsaṅgika and Svātantrika approaches to Madhyamaka or what is called Rangtong Madhyamaka; and (b) Great Madhyamaka, or what becomes known as Zhentong Madhyamaka, which includes those whose views of emptiness align positively with buddhanature.[2] The analytic system of interpreting Maitreya's treatises is associated with the General Madhyamaka, while the meditative system is associated with the Great Madhyamaka. Accordingly, these two subdivisions of Madhyamaka in Tibet align with the second and third turnings of the Buddha's teachings, respectively, making a clear division between interpretative traditions of Indian Mahāyāna canonical scriptures, including the *Five Treatises of Maitreya* and their views on the nature of reality.

By the 14th century, Tibetan scholars sought to reconcile and synthesize these two systems of Mahāyāna Buddhist thought that relied on distinct sets of Indian scriptures as their doctrinal basis. The Jonang Kālacakra scholar Dölpopa Sherab Gyaltsen (Dol po pa shes rab rgyal mtshan, 1292–1361)—known by the epithet, "the Buddha from Dölpo"—famously described the teachings of the second turning to be *rangtong* because these teach emptiness that is devoid of an intrinsic nature, while teachings of the third turning to be *zhentong* because these teach emptiness that is devoid of everything other than buddhanature. With this usage, Dölpopa formalized the technical language and an interpretive model for distinguishing two modes of emptiness: emptiness devoid of an intrinsic nature, and what is not empty of buddhanature. The Jonang exegetical tradition that follows Dölpopa asserts that while the rangtong teachings of the second turning are provisional in their meaning, zhentong teachings of the third turning are definitive in their meaning. In several of his works, including *The Fourth Council* (*Bka' bsdus bzhi pa*) and his *Letter to My Disciples* (*Slob ma la spring ba*), Dölpopa identifies the canonical literature of the Great Madhyamaka with what he calls the Dharma of the Perfect Eon.[3] Using the popularly conceived three Buddhist Councils (*bka' bsdu*) in India as recorded in early Sarvāstivāda sources and concepts of the Perfect Eon (*kṛtayuga*; *rdzogs ldan*) from Kālacakra cosmology, Dölpopa set forth an organizational framework for the history of zhentong. Dölpopa creatively interpreted sutras by means of tantras, and vice versa, identifying a corpus of definitive canonical Buddhist literature for Zhentong Madhyamaka that included twenty sutras, the *Five Treatises of Maitreya*, and the *Kālacakra Tantra*, along with the *Vimalaprabhā* and other commentarial works. This synthetic project culminated in his magnum opus, *Mountain Dharma: An Ocean of Definitive Meaning* (*Ri chos nges don rgya mtsho*), wherein he quoted extensively from these core sources to argue for the definitive meaning of zhentong. The zhentong view of emptiness as articulated by Dölpopa was furthered by several of his direct disciples, including Nyawon Kunga Pel (Nya dbon kun dga' dpal, 1285–1379), Drikung Lotsāwa Maṇikaśrījñāna ('Bri gung lo tsā ba, 1289–1363), Sazang Mati Paṇchen (Sa bzang ma ti paṇ chen, 1294–1376), and Choklé Namgyal (Phyogs las rnam rgyal, 1306–1386).[4] These scholars wrote expositions on zhentong as well as commentaries on the *Uttaratantra* and explanatory works on the Kālacakra from a zhentong view.

During the 15th and 16th centuries, following the period of Dölpopa's disciples in the 14th century, the Sakya scholar Shākya Chokden (Shākya mchog ldan, 1428–1507) was the most influential zhentong thinker.[5] Shākya Chokden characterizes rangtong and zhentong as two distinct systems of thought that describe two modes of emptiness, and he works to correlate Madhyamaka and Yogacārā thought with these two systems. Keeping with Tibetan divisions of Madhyamaka, he recognizes that these two systems determine emptiness differently, though he admits that they ultimately realize a shared view of reality within meditative equipoise.[6] According to Tāranātha's (1575–1635) *Twenty-One Profound Points* (*Zab don nyer gcig*), which deciphers the zhentong views of Dölpopa from those of Shākya Chokden, the critical distinction between their positions is that while Dölpopa takes nondual awareness to be permanently continuous, Shākya Chokden takes it to be impermanent.[7]

From the Seventh Karmapa Chödrak Gyatso (1454–1506) onward, a moderate zhentong position emerged and formed an identity within the Karma Kagyü order. This Kagyü zhentong is a distinct position that can be traced through the writings of the Third Karmapa Rangjung Dorjé (1284–1339), Seventh Karmapa, and the Eighth Karmapa Mikyo Dorjé (1507–1554). The Second Zharmapa Kachö Wangpo (1350–1405) posited a zhentong view in terms of conventional reality.[8] While Karmapa Chödrak Gyatso did not write extensively on zhentong, he articulated a view of the luminous nature of mind and buddhanature that is devoid of adventitious stains, and thereby *empty of other* or zhentong.[9] This position takes the basis of negation (*dgag gzhi*) to not be permanently continuous, but rather to be an unconditioned luminous buddhanature that persists in a series of moments; in contrast to the mainstream Jonang position of Dölpopa that presents an ultimate continuous reality (*rtag dngos*). In many respects, Karmapa Chödrak Gyatso's position closely aligns with Shākya Chokden's zhentong view.

After Dölpopa, Tāranātha was the most prolific Jonang author in the history of zhentong. Inspired by a vision of Dölpopa that led to insights about the intent of Dölpopa's thought, Tāranātha composed a series of zhentong works, beginning with the *Ornament of Zhentong* (*Gzhan stong dbu ma'i rgyan*). He went on to write several other important works that continue to be studied within the contemporary Jonang curriculum, including the *Essence of Zhentong* (*Gzhan stong snying po*), *Ascertaining the Two Systems* (*Tshul gnyis rnam par 'byed pa*), and his multivolume work, the *Supreme Vehicle of Madhyamaka* (*Dbu ma theg mchog*). Following his death in 1635, by the year 1650, the Ganden Potrang government headed by the Fifth Dalai Lama Ngawang Lobzang Gyatso (Ngag dbang blo bzang rgya mtsho, 1617–1682) confiscated Tāranātha's Takten Puntsok Ling (Rtag brtan phun tshogs gling) Monastery and converted the Jonang studies curricula to Geluk. Starting in 1658, the study of zhentong was prohibited and books on zhentong were banned in central Tibet. Despite the prohibition on zhentong by the government in central Tibet, disciples of Tāranātha fled to eastern Tibet where they revitalized the Jonang order in the Dzamtang, Gyarong, Ngawa, and Golok regions of Amdo.

By the 1720s, the Nyingma polymath Rikzin Tsewang Norbu (Rig 'dzin tshe dbang nor bu, 1698–1755) from Katok Monastery in Kham sought to revive zhentong. His efforts, along with those of his close friend Situ Paṇchen Chökyi Jungné (Si tu paṇ chen chos kyi 'byung gnas, 1699–1774), sparked a revival of interest in zhentong among Tibetan intellectuals in Kham. Other Nyingma scholars during this period wrote on zhentong, specifically Lochen Dharmaśrī (Lo chen dharma shrī, 1654–1718) at Mindroling Monastery in central Tibet.[10] The most ardent Nyingma champion of zhentong during this period was Tsewang Chökdrup (Tshe dbang mchog grub, 1761–1829), otherwise known as Katok Getsé Paṇḍita, who wrote several works on Zhentong Madhyamaka in the context of explaining Dzogchen and Nyingma expositions of Mahāyāna doctrine.[11] The celebrated Nyingma scholar Mipham Namgyal Gyatso (Mi pham rnam rgyal rgya mtsho, 1846–1912), though he wrote on zhentong, including *The Lion's Roar Affirming Zhentong* (*Gzhan stong khas len seng ge'i nga ro*), seems to take an ambivalent stance. For instance, he claims that the ultimate is unmistaken and intrinsically not empty in the context of seeing pure visions, that is, only from the perspective of sublime beings.[12]

With the rise of Rimé (*ris med*) ecumenicalism in eastern Tibet during the latter part of the 19th century, zhentong was posited as the basis for a social and intellectual vision of Tibetan Buddhism. Jamgön Kongtrul Lodrö Tayé ('Jam mgon kong sprul blo gros mtha' yas, 1813–1899) and his dear friend Jamyang Khyentsé Wangpo ('Jam dbyangs mkhyen brtse'i dbang po, 1820–1892), as the leading Rimé figures, positioned zhentong to be a critical marker and philosophical platform for their brand of ecumenicalism. Both Kongtrul and Khyentsé composed works on zhentong and supported conditions for the further transmission of zhentong in their Kagyü and Nyingma communities in Kham. Kongtrul was particularly influenced by the zhentong thinking of Shākya Chokden, Tāranātha, and the blend of zhentong and Mahāmudra expressed by the Seventh Karmapa Chödrak Gyatso. During his travels, Kongtrul visited the Dzamtang valley in Amdo where he studied with the Jonang scholar Ngawang Chöpel (Ngag dbang chos' phel, 1788–1865), and during one of his extended stays wrote his work *Light Rays of the Stainless Vajra Moon: Instructions on the View of Zhentong Madhyamaka* (*Gzhan stong dbu ma chen po'i lta khrid rdo rje zla ba dri ma med pa'i 'od zer*). This work fuses Kongtrul's Kagyü training with his study of Jonang presentations of zhentong and his insights from conversations with Jonang teachers, especially his understanding of tantra zhentong based on the Kālacakra sixfold yoga. Besides the *Stainless Vajra Moon*, which is his most focused work on zhentong views and meditation, Kongtrul elaborated on zhentong in his encyclopedic compendium *Treasury of Knowledge* (*Shes bya mdzod*). There are two presentations of zhentong in the *Treasury of Knowledge*, one in book six on the tenet systems of Buddhist philosophy, and the other in book seven on establishing the authentic view.[13] His most extensive presentation of zhentong is in book six on the *Frameworks of Buddhist Philosophy*, where his classification of the Madhyamaka philosophical system follows the order: Rangtong Madhyamaka, Svātantrika, Prāsaṅgika, Zhentong Madhyamaka, and Secret Mantra Madhyamaka.[14]

The most important Jonang scholar and author of zhentong during the 20th century was Khenpo Lodrö Drakpa (Blo gros grags pa, 1920–1975) from Tsangwa Monastery in

Dzamtang.[15] The Jonang scholars Bamda Tubten Gelek Gyatso ('Ba' mda' thub bstan dge legs rgya mtsho, 1844–1904) and his disciple Ngawang Tsoknyi Gyatso (Ngag dbang tshogs gnyis rgya mtsho, 1880–1940) either did not write explicitly on zhentong, as is the case of Bamda Gelek, or wrote compromised renderings of the essence (*ngo bo*) of buddhanature that were influenced by Geluk presentations.[16] Another prominent Jonang scholar of the early 20th century, Lobzang Chökdrub Gyatso (Blo bzang mchog grub rgya mtsho, *c.* 1840–1914), trained in the Geluk scholastic curriculum at Drepung Monastery where he acquired his Geshe degree but wrote explicitly on the definitive meaning of zhentong.[17] Inheriting the thought of these Jonang scholars, Khenpo Lodrö Drakpa sought to realign Jonang zhentong philosophical thinking with Dölpopa and Tāranātha. In his work, *The Fearless Lion's Roar*, otherwise known as the *Great Exposition on Zhentong* (*Gzhan stong chen mo*), Khenpo Lodrö Drakpa asserts zhentong with these mainstream Jonang presentations by systematically explaining the vital points for understanding the zhentong view as articulated by Dölpopa in his *Mountain Dharma*.[18] Unlike Dölpopa's synthetic presentation, however, he deciphers salient differences between sutra zhentong and tantra zhentong. In so doing, Khenpo Lodrö Drakpa, and the modern Jonang scholastic tradition that studies this line of thought, reclaims Dölpopa's vision while creatively reformulating zhentong.

There are numerous Tibetan proponents of zhentong philosophical thinking representative of the different orders of Tibetan Buddhism in the modern era, only some of which are translated into English. In *The Nyingma School of Tibetan Buddhism* (1991), Dudjom Rinpoche Jikdrel Yeshé Dorjé ('Jigs bral ye shes rdo rje, 1904–1987) follows Getsé Paṇḍita's presentation virtually verbatim to assert the definitiveness of the Great Madhyamaka.[19] The Kagyü teacher, Khenpo Tsultrim Gyamtso Rinpoche presents a zhentong method of meditative investigation and procedure in conversation with other Buddhist approaches in his *Progressive Stages of Meditation on Emptiness* (1988).[20] Within Tibet, and to a lesser extent abroad, Jonang scholars author new works on zhentong and continue their traditions of zhentong teachings.

THE RANGTONG/ZHENTONG DEBATES

With the rise of zhentong philosophical thought came historic polemic and controversy in Tibet. During Dölpopa's lifetime in the 14th century, despite his extensive quotations of authoritative Buddhist canonical sources, his zhentong view was disputed by contemporary Tibetan scholars, including Butön Rinchen Drub (Bu ston rin chen grub, 1290–1364). The most fervent disputes and refutations of zhentong, however, emerge in written form with the institutionalization of the Geluk order after Dölpopa's lifetime during the latter part of the 14th and early 15th centuries. One of the earliest written refutations of zhentong is by Kashipa Rinchen Dorjé (Rin chen rdo rje, d.u.) who criticizes Choklé Namgyal, one of Dölpopa's close disciples, and praises Tsongkhapa Lobzang Drakpa (Tsong kha pa blo bzang grags pa, 1357–1419). The fiercest critic of zhentong and the Kālacakra during this period was Tsongkhapa's principal teacher, the Sakya scholar Remdawa Zhonnu Lodrö (Red mda' ba gzhon nu blo gros, 1349–1412). In several of his works, including his *Explanation of the Intent of the Uttaratantra* (*Rgyud bla ma'i don bsdus*), a work that is not currently extant, his *Jewel Garland* (*Nor bu'i 'phreng ba*) and *Precious Lamp* (*Rin po che'i sgon me*), Remdawa criticizes the Jonang view of emptiness and the Kālacakra. During this period, Remdawa participated in public debates in the courtyard at Sakya Monastery, and on one occasion at Jonang, where he furthered his reactionary movement against zhentong and the Kālacakra.[21] Some of the specific philosophical points of disputation involved in these polemics were recorded in rebuttals by Dölpopa's students, including the *Lamp That Illuminates the Expanse of Reality* by Garungwa Lhai Gyaltsen (Gha rung ba lha'i rgyal mtshan, 1319–1402/1403).[22] There were also occasions where Dölpopa's disciples are said to have spread zhentong thought, such as an episode when Drigung Lotsāwa Maṇikaśrījñāna (1289–1363) successfully debated twenty-five scholars for four days at Gyantsé.[23] There were also scholars, including the Sakya scholar Gorampa Sonam Sengé (Go rams pa bsod nams sen ge, 1429–1489) in his *Distinguishing the Views* (*Lta ba'i san 'byed*), who criticized both Dölpopa's and Tsongkhapa's views.[24]

Written in 1801, perhaps the most well-known critique of zhentong is *The Crystal Mirror of Philosophical Systems* (*Grub mtha' shel gyi me long*) by the Geluk scholar Tukwan Lobzang Chökyi Nyima (Thu'u bkwan blo bzang chos kyi nyi ma, 1737–1802).[25] Tukwan's work criticizes a wide range of views that encompass Nyingma, Kadam, Kagyü, Jonang, Zhijé, Sakya, and Bön Tibetan traditions as well as non-Buddhist traditions that include classical schools of Hindu philosophy, Daoism, and traditions from Inner Asia, India, China, Mongolia, Khotan, and even Shambhala. His work is on the presentation of philosophical systems or tenets (*grub mtha'*) and rebuttal of their views, though it is more historical and comparative than many Tibetan writings in this genre. The chapter on the Jonang and their zhentong view is an oversimplified caricature that lacks a nuanced understanding of the philosophical subtleties of zhentong.[26] Tukwan begins his critique by claiming that Dölpopa Sherab Gyaltsen was "holy," yet he presented views that were literally identical to those of extremists and goes on to equate Jonang views of zhentong with Sāṃkhya, Mīmāṃsaka, and Vedānta schools of classical Hindu thought. He presents his criticism through the dialectics of debate, juxtaposing critics and defenders, and concludes with an attack against Shākya Chokden as a defender of zhentong. There was no formal written response by a Jonang author to the claims made by Tukwan. This suggests on the one hand that the so-called "rangtong versus zhentong" debate in Tibetan Buddhism was not a fully engaged polemics with opposite sides weighing their views against each other, and on the other, that despite this triumphalist exclusiveness by Geluk apologists, Jonang scholars were not aware or did not feel the need to engage in rhetorical exchange.

SUTRA AND TANTRA ZHENTONG

Throughout the history of zhentong thought, exponents of zhentong from different orders of Tibetan Buddhism agree that the Great Madhyamaka or Zhentong Madhyamaka is the pinnacle of the Buddha's sutra teachings. The term and concept zhentong emerged, however, as a description by Dölpopa Sherab Gyaltsen of his meditative experiences born from practicing the sixfold yoga (*ṣaḍaṅgayoga*; *rnal 'byor yan lag drug*) completion stage process of the *Kālacakra Tantra*.[27] Throughout his writings, Dölpopa emphasizes both sutra and tantra sources to explicate his view of zhentong, synthesizing passages from myriad sources in his *Mountain Dharma*. For Dölpopa, sutras validated views in the tantras, and vice versa, making both exoteric and esoteric Buddhist sources authoritative for zhentong.

Later Jonang exponents of zhentong, including Tāranātha and most explicitly in the writings of Khenpo Lodrö Drakpa, made distinctions between (a) sutra zhentong (*mdo'i gzhan stong*), based on the exoteric discourses of the Buddha; and (b) tantra zhentong (*sngags gi gzhan stong*), referring to expressions of zhentong based on Buddhist esoteric discourses.[28] The core sources for sutra zhentong are the ten *Essence Sūtras*, ten *Sūtras on Definitive Meaning*, and the *Five Treatises of Maitreya*. Tantra zhentong is most associated with a contemplative understanding that derives from the practice of the sixfold yoga completion stage of the Kālacakra but includes Buddhist tantric literature in general.[29] The core sources for tantra zhentong, cited by Dölpopa and later Jonang authors, are the *Bodhisattva Trilogy*, which consists of the definitive Indian commentaries on the *Kālacakra Tantra*, *Hevajra Tantra*, and the *Cakrasamvara Tantra*. Tibetan forefathers of sutra zhentong include Tsen Kawoché for his interpretation of the *Five Treatises of Maitreya* and of tantra zhentong, and Yumo Mikyö Dorjé (1038–1117) for his interpretation of the *Kālacakra Tantra*.

REVIEW OF LITERATURE

Western scholarship on zhentong first appeared in the 1960s and, with increasing interest and understanding of zhentong philosophical and contemplative thought, several important studies and translations have been published over the past few decades. The first significant contribution to the study of zhentong was David Seyfort Ruegg's 1963 article on the Jonang, which, based on *The Crystal Mirror of Philosophical Systems* by the Geluk scholar Tukwan Lobzang Chökyi Nyima (1737–1802), presents the Jonang and zhentong through the polemical lens of a critic.[30] While not representative of zhentongpa's thought, this article nonetheless sets the stage for academic inquiry into Zhentong Madhyamaka as well as the history of the rangtong–zhentong discourse in Tibet. In 1970, E. Gene Smith published his introduction to Jamgön Kongtrul's (1813–1899) encyclopedic *Treasury of Knowledge* in which he emphasizes the influence of zhentong on Kongtrul and Jamyang Khyentsé Wangpo (1820–1892) during their conception of Rimé ecumenicalism in eastern Tibet during the latter part of the 19th century.[31]

The contemporary Kagyü teacher, Khenpo Tsultrim Gyamtso Rinpoche's *Progressive Stages of Meditation on Emptiness* (1988), though not an academic work on zhentong, makes important distinctions between zhentong and Cittamātra, and the zhentong method of meditative investigation and procedure (86–88).[32] S. K. Hookham's *The Buddha Within* explicitly and exclusively addresses zhentong through a study of the *Uttaratantra*. However, the study makes mistakes and is flawed in many respects.[33]

The Buddha from Dolpo by Cyrus Stearns (1999), a study of the life and thought of the Jonang scholar Dölpopa Sherab Gyaltsen (1292–1361), is the first major contribution to the study of zhentong thought and history.[34] Stearns's book discusses Dölpopa's formulation of zhentong, surveys zhentong in Tibet before and after Dölpopa, and presents translations of two of Dölpopa's important zhentong works, the *General Commentary on the Doctrine* (*Bstan pa spyi 'grel*, 109–121) and *Fourth Council* (*Bka' bsdu bzhi pa*, 123–173), both with informative introductions.

John W. Pettit's *Mipham's Beacon of Certainty* (1999) is a study of the Nyingma scholar Mipham Gyatso's (1846–1912) exposition on Madhyamaka that includes a discussion on zhentong philosophy (111–114), Mipham's interpretation of zhentong and buddhanature (117–124), and the author's translation of Mipham's, *The Lion's Roar Proclaiming Extrinsic Emptiness*.[35] A review of Paul William's (2000) book *The Reflexive Nature of Awareness: A Tibetan Madhyamaka Defense* by Matthew Kapstein (2000), titled "We Are All Gzhan stong pas," in the context of a technical discussion on reflexive awareness (*svasaṃvedana; rang rig*), takes issue with Williams's characterization of Mipham Gyatso as a proponent of zhentong.[36]

Two articles by Klaus-Dieter Mathes (2000 and 2004) discuss Tāranātha's presentation of zhentong, giving attention to his use of the three natures scheme (*trisvabhāva*) in the *Essence of Zhentong*, and the twenty-one points that Tāranātha delineates to differentiate Shākya Chokden's view from that of Dölpopa, detailing important doctrinal topics in the study of zhentong.[37] In two volumes, Jeffrey Hopkins has translated Dölpopa's masterpiece *Mountain Dharma: An Ocean of Definitive Meaning*, as well as Tāranātha's *Essence of Zhentong*, which includes his translation of Tāranātha's *Twenty-One Profound Points* as an appendix.[38]

Based on Tāranātha's history of the Kālacakra, Michael Sheehy (2009) abbreviates the history of the Jonang Kālacakra lineage, giving a historical framework for the transmission of tantric zhentong in Tibet.[39] *When the Clouds Part* includes Karl Brunnhölzl's (2014) study of the meditative tradition of the *Uttaratantra* and zhentong in the Jonang, Kagyü, and Nyingma, and translations of several important instruction texts in this lineage, including those by the Eight Karmapa Mikyö Dorjé (1507–1554) and Jamgön Kongtrul.[40]

The most important publication to date on zhentong is *The Other Emptiness*, edited by Michael R. Sheehy and Klaus-Dieter Mathes (2019), an anthology of chapters contributed by leading international scholars on zhentong across the history of the Tibetan discourse.[41] The editor's introduction by Mathes and Sheehy overviews critical philosophical discussions and the literary history of zhentong.[42] Chapters give attention to the key proponents and moments in the development of this distinct strain of Buddhist thought in the Nyingma, Jonang, Kagyü, Sakya, and Kadam orders of Tibetan Buddhism.

DIGITAL MATERIALS

Jonang Foundation (https://jonangfoundation.org): Resources for understanding the history and thought of the Jonang order of Tibetan Buddhism. Includes an online library with translations of works on zhentong.

Treasury of Lives (https://treasuryoflives.org): A Biographical Encyclopedia of Tibet, Inner Asia, and the Himalaya: Brief biographies of key figures in the history of zhentong in Tibet.

Buddhist Digital Resource Center (BDRC) (https://library.bdrc.io): Digital library and encyclopedic resource for Tibetan literature. Includes scans and searchable electronic text for important works of Tibetan-language zhentong literature.

FURTHER READING

Brunnhölzl, Karl. *When Clouds Part: The Uttaratantra and Its Meditative Tradition as a Bridge between Sūtra and Tantra*. Ithaca, NY: Snow Lion Publications, 2014.

Burchardi, Anne. "A Look at the Diversity of the Gzhan stong Tradition." *Journal of the International Association of Tibetan Studies* 3 (2007): 1–24.

Hopkins, Jeffrey, trans. *Mountain Doctrine: Tibet's Fundamental Treatise on Other-Emptiness and the Buddha Matrix*. By Dö-bo-ba Śhay-rap-gyel-tsen. Ithaca, NY: Snow Lion, 2006.

Hopkins, Jeffrey, trans. *The Essence of Other-Emptiness*. By Tāranātha. Ithaca, NY: Snow Lion, 2007.

Kapstein, Matthew. "We Are All Gzhan stong pas." *Journal of Buddhist Ethics* 7 (2000): 105–125.

Kapstein, Matthew. "Zhentong Traces in the Nyingma Tradition: Two Texts from Mindroling." In *The Other Emptiness: Rethinking the Zhentong Buddhist Discourse in Tibet*. Edited by Michael R. Sheehy and Klaus-Dieter Mathes, 235–255. New York: State University of New York Press, 2019.

Kongtrul Lodrö Taye, Jamgön. *The Treasury of Knowledge: Frameworks of Buddhist Philosophy*. Translated by Elizabeth M. Callahan. Ithaca, NY: Snow Lion Publications, 2007.

Makidono, Tomoko. "Kong sprul on the Great Madhyamaka of Other-Emptiness: Theory and Practice." *The Indian International Journal of Buddhist Studies* 16 (2015): 151–191.

Mathes, Klaus-Dieter. "Tāranātha's Presentation of trisvabhāva in the gZhan stong snying po." *Journal of the International Association of Buddhist Studies* 23, no. 2 (2000): 195–223.

Mathes, Klaus-Dieter. "The Gzhan stong Model of Reality: Some More Material on Its Origin, Transmission, and Interpretation." *Journal of the International Association of Buddhist Studies* 34, no. 1–2 (2012): 187–223.

Mathes, Klaus-Dieter. "Tāranātha's *Twenty-One Differences with Regard to the Profound Meaning*: Comparing the Views of the Two Zhentong Masters Dolpopa and Shakya Chokden." In *The Other Emptiness: Rethinking the Zhentong Buddhist Discourse in Tibet*. Edited by Michael R. Sheehy and Klaus Dieter-Mathes, 197–233. New York: State University of New York Press, 2019.

Mathes, Klaus-Dieter. "Zhentong Views in the Karma Kagyu Order." In *The Other Emptiness: Rethinking the Zhentong Buddhist Discourse in Tibet*. Edited by Michael R. Sheehy and Klaus Dieter-Mathes, 115–144. New York: State University of New York Press, 2019.

Mathes, Klaus-Dieter, and Michael R. Sheehy. "The Philosophical Grounds and Literary History of Zhentong." In *The Other Emptiness: Rethinking the Zhentong Buddhist Discourse in Tibet*. Edited by Michael R. Sheehy and Klaus Dieter-Mathes, 1–27. New York: State University of New York Press, 2019.

Pettit, John W. *Mipham's Beacon of Certainty: Illuminating the View of Dzogchen, the Great Perfection*. Boston: Wisdom, 1999.

Sheehy, Michael R. "A Lineage History of Vajrayoga and Tantric Zhentong from the Jonang Kālacakra Practice Tradition." In *As Long as Space Endures: Essays on the Kalachakra Tantra in Honor of the Dalai Lama*. Edited by Edward A. Arnold, 219–235. Ithaca, NY: Snow Lion Publications, 2009.

Sheehy, Michael R. "Jonang." In *Oxford Bibliographies in Buddhism*. Edited by Richard Payne. New York: Oxford University Press, 2012. http://www.oxfordbibliographies.com/view/document/obo-9780195393521/obo-9780195393521-0097.xml.

Sheehy, Michael R. "The Dharma of the Perfect Eon: Dolpopa Sherab Gyaltsan's (1292–1361) Hermeneutics of Time and the Jonang Doxography of Zhentong Madhyamaka." In *The Other Emptiness: Rethinking the Zhentong Buddhist Discourse in Tibet*. Edited by Michael R. Sheehy and Klaus Dieter-Mathes, 65–93. New York: State University of New York Press, 2019.

Sheehy, Michael R. "The Zhentong Lion Roars: Dzamtang Khenpo Lodro Drakpa and the Jonang Scholastic Renaissance." In *The Other Emptiness: Rethinking the Zhentong Buddhist Discourse in Tibet*. Edited by Michael R. Sheehy and Klaus Dieter-Mathes, 351–377. New York: State University of New York, 2019.

Sheehy, Michael R. "Images of Emptiness in a Prognostic Mirror: Tantric Zhentong Visions of Thatāgatagarbha in Early Jonang Kālacakra Yoga Manuals." In *Buddha Nature Across Asia*. Edited by Klaus-Dieter Mathes and Casey A. Kemp, 229–260. Vienna: University of Vienna Press, 2022.

Sheehy, Michael R., and Klaus-Dieter Mathes, eds. *The Other Emptiness: Rethinking the Zhentong Buddhist Discourse in Tibet*. New York: State University of New York Press, 2019.

Smith, E. Gene. "'Jam mgon Kong sprul and the Nonsectarian Movement." In *Among Tibetan Texts: History of Literature of the Himalayan Plateau*. Edited by Kurtis R. Schaeffer, 235–272. Boston: Wisdom Publications, 2001.

Stearns, Cyrus. *The Buddha from Dolpo: A Study of the Life and Thought of the Tibetan Master Dolpopa Sherab Gyaltsen*. Ithaca, NY: Snow Lion, 2010.

RELATED ORE ARTICLES

Madhyamaka, https://doi.org/10.1093/acrefore/9780199340378.013.191
Tibetan Visionary Buddhism, https://doi.org/10.1093/acrefore/9780199340378.013.720

NOTES

1. Karl Brunnhölzl, *When Clouds Part: The Uttaratantra and Its Meditative Tradition as a Bridge between Sūtra and Tantra* (Ithaca, NY: Snow Lion Publications, 2014).
2. It should be noted that there are instances where adherents to Rangtong Madhyamaka also call their own system the "Great Madhyamaka" (dbu ma chen po).
3. Michael R. Sheehy, "The Dharma of the Perfect Eon: Dolpopa Sherab Gyaltsen's Hermeneutics of Tibet and the Jonang Doxography of Zhengong Madhyamaka," in *The Other Emptiness: Rethinking the Zhentong Buddhist Discourse in Tibet*, ed. Michael R. Sheehy and Klaus-Dieter Mathes (New York: State University of New York Press, 2019), 65–93. For a translation of the *Fourth Council* and its autocommentary, see Cyrus Stearns, *The Buddha from Dölpo: A Study of the Life and Thought of the Tibetan Master Dölpopa Sherab Gyaltsen* (Ithaca, NY: Snow Lion Publications, 2010).
4. On the zhentong tradition after Dölpopa, see Stearns, *Buddha from Dölpo*, 55–83.
5. Yaroslav Komarovski, *Visions of Unity: The Golden Paṇḍita Shakya Chokden's New Interpretation of Yogācarāra and Madhyamaka* (New York: State University of New York Press, 2011). For translations of Shākya Chokden's works on zhentong, see Yaroslav Komarovski, *Radiant Emptiness: Three Seminal Works by the Golden Paṇḍita Shakya Chokden* (Oxford: Oxford University Press, 2020); and Komarovski, *Visions of Unity*, 17–21.
6. Komarovski, *Visions of Unity*, 18.
7. On the distinction between Dölpopa's and Shākya Chokden's zhentong positions, see Klaus-Dieter Mathes, "Tāranātha's *Twenty-One Differences with Regard to the Profound Meaning*: Comparing the Views of the Two Zhentong Masters Dolpopa and Shakya Chokden," in Sheehy and Mathes, *The Other Emptiness*, 197–233; and also Jeffrey Hopkins, trans., *The Essence of Other-Emptiness*, by Tāranātha (Ithaca, NY: Snow Lion, 2007).
8. See Martina Draszczyk, "Buddha-Nature: 'Natural Awareness Endowed with Buddha Qualities' as Expounded by Zhamar Kacho Wangpo," in Sheehy and Mathes, *The Other Emptiness*, 145–169.
9. For details on Kagyü zhentong, see Klaus-Dieter Mathes, "Zhentong Views in the Karma Kagyü Order," in Sheehy and Mathes, *The Other Emptiness*, 115–144. For a comparative discussion see, Anne Burchardi, "A Look at the Diversity of the Gzhan stong Tradition," *Journal of the International Association of Tibetan Studies* 3 (2007): 1–24.
10. Matthew Kapstein, "Zhentong Traces in the Nyingma Tradition: Two Texts from Mindroling," in Sheehy and Mathes, *The Other Emptiness*, 235–255.
11. For a discussion on Getsé Paṇḍita's expositions on zhentong, see Tomoko Makidono, "Kaḥ thog Dge rtse Mahāpaṇḍita's Doxographical Position: The Great Madhyamaka of Other-Emptiness (Gzhan stong dbu ma chen po)," *Indian International Journal of Buddhist Studies* 12 (2011): 77–119; and Tomoko Makidono, *Dge-rtse Mahāpaṇḍita's Great Middle Way of Other-Emptiness*, Bibliotheca Tibetica et Buddhica 2 (Tokyo: Sankibo Busshorin, 2016).
12. Kapstein, "Zhentong Traces in the Nyingma Tradition," 236. There are several important studies on Mipham's zhentong view, including: John W. Pettit, *Mipham's Beacon of Certainty: Illuminating the View of Dzogchen, the Great Perfection* (Boston: Wisdom, 1999); Matthew Kapstein, "Mipham Namgyel: The

Lion's Roar Affirming Extrinsic Emptiness," in *Buddhist Philosophy: Essential Readings*, ed. Willian Edelglass and Jay L. Garfield (New York: Oxford University Press, 2009), 61–71; Douglas S. Duckworth, *Mipam on Buddha-Nature: The Ground of the Nyingma Tradition* (New York: State University of New York Press, 2008); Douglas Duckworth, "Zhentong as Yogācāra: Mipam's Madhyamaka Synthesis," in Sheehy and Mathes, *The Other Emptiness*, 257–272; and Dorji Wangchuk, "Where Buddhas and Siddhas Meet: Mipam's Yuganaddavāda Philosophy," in Sheehy and Mathes, *The Other Emptiness*, 273–322.

13. These are book six, part three and book seven, part three, respectively. For a translation see, Jamgön Kongtrul Lodrö Taye, *The Treasury of Knowledge: Frameworks of Buddhist Philosophy*, trans. Elizabeth M. Callahan (Ithaca, NY: Snow Lion Publications, 2007), 249–268; and Kongtrul Lodrö Taye, *Treasury of Knowledge*, 139–143.
14. For a translation, see Kongtrul Lodrö Taye, *Treasury of Knowledge*, 249–268.
15. Matthew Kapstein, "Introduction," in *Ngag dbang blo gros grags pa, Selected Historical and Doctrinal Writings of 'Dzamthang Mkhan-po Blo-gros-grags-pa*, 1, 1–58, and 2, 1–10 (Dharamsala: Library of Tibetan Works and Archives, 1993); and Michael R. Sheehy, "The Zhentong Lion Roars: Dzamtang Khenpo Lodro Drakpa and the Jonang Scholastic Renaissance," in Sheehy and Mathes, *The Other Emptiness*, 257–272.
16. For scholarship on these modern Jonang authors, see the following sources: Matthew Kapstein, "From Kun-mkhyen Dol-po-pa to 'Ba'-mda' dge-legs: Three Jo-nang-pa Masters on the Interpretation of the *Prajñāpāramita*," in *Reason's Traces: Identity and Interpretation in Indian and Tibetan Buddhist Thought* (Boston: Wisdom Publications, 2001), 301–316; Michael Sheehy, "The Zhentong Madhyamaka Writings of Ngawang Tsoknyi Gyatso (1880–1940)," in *Ngag dbang tshogs gnyis rgya mtsho: Ngag dbang tshogs gnyis rgya mtsho'i dbu ma gzhan stong phyogs bsgrigs*, ed. Michael R. Sheehy (Khreng tu'u, China: Si khron mi rigs dpe skrun khang, 2009), 1–5; Filippo Brambilla, "A Late Proponent of the Jo nang gZhan stong Doctrine: Ngag dbang tshogs gnyis rgya mtsho (1880–1940)," *Revue d'Etudes Tibétaines* 45 (2018): 5–50; and Sheehy, "Zhentong Lion Roars," 351–377.
17. Klaus-Dieter Mathes, "Blo bzang mchog grub rgya mtsho, the Dge bshes of Dza 'go (Amdo): A Jo nang Scholar Trained in the Dge lugs Tradition," in *Nonsectarianism (ris med) in 19th- and 20th-Century Eastern Tibet: Religious Diffusion and Cross-fertilization beyond the Reach of the Central Tibetan Government*, ed. Klaus-Dieter Mathes and Gabriele Coura (Leiden, The Netherlands: Brill, 2021), 165–200.
18. Michael R. Sheehy, *The Gzhan stong chen mo: A Study of Emptiness according to the Modern Tibetan Buddhist Jo nang Scholar 'Dzam thang Mkhan po Ngag dbang blo gros grags pa (1920–75)* (PhD diss., California Institute of Integral Studies, 2007).
19. Dudjom Rinpoche Jikdrel Yeshe Dorje, *The Nyingma School of Tibetan Buddhism: Its Fundamentals and History*, trans. and ed. Gyurme Dorje and Matthew Kapstein (Boston: Wisdom Publications, 1991), 169–189, 206–216.
20. Khenpo Tsultrim Gyamtso, *Progressive Stages of Meditation on Emptiness*, trans. Shenpen Hookham (Oxford: Longchen Foundation, 1988).
21. Stearns, *Buddha from Dölpo*, 55–60.
22. Dorje Nyingcha, "Buddha-Nature in Garungpa Lhai Gyaltsen's Lamp That Illuminates the Expanse of Reality and among Tibetan Intellectuals," in Sheehy and Mathes, *The Other Emptiness*, 95–113.
23. Cyrus Stearns, "Drigung Lotsāwa Maṇikaśrījñāna (https://treasuryoflives.org/biographies/view/Drigung-Lotsawa-Manikashrijnana/3936)," in *Treasury of Lives: A Biographical Encyclopedia of Tibet, Inner Asia, and the Himalaya* (2008).
24. José Ignacio Cabezón and Geshe Lobsang Dargyay, *Freedom from Extremes: Gorampa's "Distinguishing the Views" and the Polemics of Emptiness* (Boston: Wisdom Publications, 2007), 71–77.
25. Thuken Losang Chökyi Nyima, *The Crystal Mirror of Philosophical Systems: A Tibetan Study of Asian Religious Thought*, trans. Geshé Lhundub Sopa, ed. Roger R. Jackson (Boston: Wisdom Publications, 2009), 197–213.

26. Chökyi Nyima, *Crystal Mirror of Philosophical Systems*, 11.
27. Stearns, *Buddha from Dolpo*, 15–16; and Michael R. Sheehy, "Images of Emptiness in a Prognostic Mirror: Tantric Zhentong Visions of Tathāgatagarbha in Early Jonang Kālacakra Yoga Manuals," in Buddha Nature Across Asia, ed. Klaus-Dieter Mathes, and Casey A. Kemp (Vienna: University of Vienna Press, 2022), 229–260.
28. Michael R. Sheehy, "The Zhentong Lion Roars: Dzamtang Khenpo Lodro Drakpa and the Jonang Scholastic Renaissance," in Sheehy and Mathes, *The Other Emptiness*, 362–368.
29. Michael R. Sheehy, "A Lineage History of Vajrayoga and Tantric Zhentong from the Jonang Kālacakra Practice Tradition," in *As Long as Space Endures: Essays on the Kalachakra Tantra in Honor of H.H. the Dalai Lama*, ed. Edward A. Arnold (Ithaca, NY: Snow Lion Publications, 2009), 219–235.
30. Originally published in the *Journal of the American Oriental Society*, 1963. Republished in David Seyfort Ruegg, "The Jo nang pas: A School of Buddhist Ontologists according to the Crystal Mirror of Philosophical Systems (Grub mtha' shel gyi me long)," in *The Buddhist Philosophy of the Middle: Essays on Indian and Tibetan Madhyamaka* (Boston: Wisdom Publications, 2010), 289–231.
31. Originally published in *Kongtrul's Encyclopedia of Indo-Tibetan Culture* by the International Academy of Indian Culture, 1970. Republished in E. Gene Smith, " 'Jam mgon Kong sprul and the Nonsectarian Movement," in *Among Tibetan Texts: History and Literature of the Himalayan Plateau*, ed. Kurtis R. Schaeffer (2001), 247.
32. Gyamtso, *Progressive Stages*, 75–89.
33. Shenpen K. Hookham, *The Buddha Within: Tathāgatagarbha Doctrine according to the Shentong Interpretation of the Ratnagotravibhāga* (New York: State University of New York Press, 1991). For reviews of Hookham's work, see Robert M. Gimello, "Review of *The Buddha Within: Tathāgatagarbha Doctrine according to the Shentong Interpretation of the Ratnagotravibhāga* by S. K. Hookham," *The Journal of Asian Studies* 51, no. 3 (1992): 6246; and also, Paul Griffiths, "Review of *The Buddha Within: Tathagatagarbha Doctrine according to the Shentong Interpretation of the Ratnagotravibhaga* by Shenpen K. Hookham," *Journal of the American Oriental Society* 113, no. 2 (1993): 317–319.
34. Originally published by State University of New York Press, 1999. Republished as Stearns, *Buddha from Dölpo*. For a review, see Mark Tatz, "Review of *The Buddha from Dolpo: A Study of the Life and Thought of the Tibetan Master Dolpopa Sherab Gyaltsen* by Cyrus Stearns," *The Journal of the American Oriental Society* 121 (2001): 3.
35. Pettit, *Mipham's Beacon of Certainty*, 415–427.
36. Paul Williams, *The Reflexive Nature of Awareness: A Tibetan Madhyamaka Defense* (New York: Routledge, 2013): 199–206.
37. Klaus-Dieter Mathes, "Tāranātha's Presentation of trisvabhāva in the gZhan stong snying po," *Journal of the International Association of Buddhist Studies* 23, no. 2 (2000): 195–223. The 2004 article by Mathes was published in the *Journal of the International Association of Buddhist Studies* 27, no. 2 (2004): 285–328. It was republished as Mathes, "Tāranātha's *Twenty-One Differences*," 197–233.
38. Jeffrey Hopkins, trans., *Mountain Doctrine: Tibet's Fundamental Treatise on Other-Emptiness and the Buddha Matrix*, by Dö-bo-ba Shay-rap-gyel-tsen (Ithaca, NY: Snow Lion, 2006); and Hopkins, *Essence of Other-Emptiness*.
39. Sheehy, "Lineage History of Vajrayoga," 219–235.
40. Brunnhölzl, *When Clouds Part*, 123–150.
41. Michael R. Sheehy and Klaus-Dieter Mathes, eds., *The Other Emptiness: Rethinking the Zhentong Buddhist Discourse in Tibet* (New York: State University of New York Press, 2019).
42. Klaus-Dieter Mathes and Michael R. Sheehy, "*The Philosophical Grounds and Literary History of Zhentong*," in Sheehy and Mathes, *The Other Emptiness*, 1–27.

Michael R. Sheehy

Directory of Contributors

Saskia Abrahms-Kavunenko
New York University Shanghai
Mongolian Buddhism in the Democratic Period

Jean-Luc Achard
CNRS—Centre de recherche sur les civilisations de l'Asie orientale
The Bön Tradition of Dzogchen

Andrea Acri
Ecole Pratique des Hautes Etudes, PSL
Maritime Buddhism

Anna Ayse Akasoy
City University of New York Graduate Center
Muslim–Buddhist Relations and Buddhism in Muslim Sources until the Mongol Period

Michihiro Ama
University of Montana
American Buddhism during World War II Imprisonment
The Imamura Families and the Making of American Buddhism

Carol S. Anderson
Kalamazoo College
Four Noble Truths

James B. Apple
University of Calgary
Abhisamayālaṃkāra (Ornament for Clear Realization)
Gelukpa
Perfections (Six and Ten) of Bodhisattvas in Buddhist Literature

Naomi Appleton
University of Edinburgh
Jātaka

Paula Arai
Institute of Buddhist Studies
Domestic Dharma in Japan

Dan Arnold
University of Chicago
The Philosophical Works and Influence of Dignāga and Dharmakīrti

Norihisa Baba
University of Tokyo
Buddhaghosa

Cody R. Bahir
Kehilla Jewish High School
Tantric Revival in China

Cameron Bailey
Dongguk University
Guardian/Protector Deities in Tibetan Buddhism

Carl L. Bankston III
Tulane University
Southeast Asian Refugees in North America

Agata Bareja-Starzyńska
University of Warsaw
Jebtsundamba Khutugtus of Mongolia

T. H. Barrett
SOAS University of London
Buddhism and Print Culture in China

Mikaël Bauer
McGill University
The Six Nara Schools

Brian Baumann
University of California, Berkeley
Mongolian Buddhism in the Yuan Period

Stefan Baums
Ludwig Maximilians Universität München
Canon and Commentary in the Earliest Buddhist Manuscripts

Claudine Bautze-Picron
Centre National de la Recherche Scientifique
Imaging the Buddha in South Asia

Christopher Bell
Stetson University
Nechung: A Tibetan Buddhist Oracle

Stephen C. Berkwitz
Missouri State University
Narratives of Buddhist Relics and Images

Martin Boord
The Oriental Institute
The Vajrakīla Tantras

Thomas Borchert
University of Vermont
Monastic Education in Contemporary Asia
The Sangha as an Institution

Jørn Borup
Aarhus University
Buddhism and Globalization

Sven Bretfeld
Norges Teknisk Naturvitenskapeligt Universitet
Theravāda Buddhism

Jeffrey L. Broughton
California State University, Long Beach
Chan Literature

Courtney Bruntz
Southeast Community College
Pilgrimage in China

Megan Bryson
University of Tennessee
Buddhist Geography and Regionalism

Albion M. Butters
University of Turku
Longchenpa

Thomas Calobrisi
Graduate Theological Union and the Institute of Buddhist Studies
Early Modern European Encounters with Buddhism

Daniela Campo
University of Strasbourg
Xuyun

Joseph Cheah
University of St. Joseph
Western Buddhism and Race

Swati Chemburkar
Benaras Hindu University and Jnanapravaha
Prajñāpāramitā and Khmer Esoteric Buddhism in the 10th to 13th centuries

Clark Chilson
University of Pittsburgh
Naikan: A Meditation Method and Psychotherapy

Kate Crosby
King's College, London
Practices of Protection in the Pali World

Paul Crowe
Simon Fraser University
Buddhisms in Diaspora: The Canadian Context of Chinese Buddhism

Elise Anne DeVido
Duke University
Tzu Chi

K. L. Dhammajoti
Renmin University of China
Sarvāstivāda Abhidharma

James C. Dobbins
Oberlin College
D. T. Suzuki: A Biography
D. T. Suzuki: Ideas and Influences

Paul B. Donnelly
Northern Arizona University
Madhyamaka
Pilgrimage in Buddhist Tibet

Brandon Dotson
Ludwig Maximilians Universität München
Tri Songdetsen

Mélodie Doumy
The British Library
Dunhuang Texts

Cécile Ducher
Ecole Pratique des Hautes Etudes—Sciences Religieuses
Marpa Lotsawa Chökyi Lodrö

Douglas S. Duckworth
Temple University
Mipam

William Edelglass
Marlboro College and Emerson College
Buddhism and the Environment

Christoph Emmrich
University of Toronto
From Manuscript to Print in South and Southeast Asia

Mavis L. Fenn
University of Waterloo
Global Theravada Buddhism: Asian Foundations
Global Theravada: Transmission beyond Asia

Solomon George FitzHerbert
University of Oxford
Tibetan Buddhism and the Gesar Epic

Niklas Foxeus
Stockholm University
Buddhist Wizards (*Vidhyadhāra/Weizzā/Weikza*): Origins and History

Ruth Gamble
La Trobe University
The Reincarnation System in Central Asian Buddhism

David L. Gardiner
Colorado College
Tantric Buddhism in Japan: Kukai and Saicho
Tantric Buddhism in Japan: Shingon, Tendai, and the Esotericization of Japanese Buddhisms

Andrew Gebert
Waseda University
Sōka Gakkai

James Duncan Gentry
Harvard University
Tibetan Buddhist Power Objects

Suchandra Ghosh
University of Calcutta
Patronage of Buddhist Monasteries in Eastern India, 600–1300 CE

Ann Gleig
University of Central Florida
Engaged Buddhism

Geoffrey Goble
University of Oklahoma
Amoghavajra

Eric Goodell
Fo Guang University
Taixu

David B. Gray
Santa Clara University
Tantra and the Tantric Traditions of Hinduism and Buddhism

Georgios Halkias
University of Hong Kong
Pure Land Buddhism in Tibetan Contexts

Oren Hanner
University of Hamburg
Abhidharmakośabhāṣya (Treasury of Metaphysics with Self-Commentary)

Sarah Harding
Tsadra Foundation
Chöd: A Tibetan Buddhist Practice

Laura Harrington
Boston University
Mañjuśrī

Stephen E. Harris
Leiden University
Śāntideva's Introduction to the Practices of Awakening (*Bodhicaryāvatāra*)

Chris Hatchell
Coe College
Tibetan Visionary Buddhism

Ann Heirman
Ghent University
Vinaya Rules for Monks and Nuns

Ira Helderman
Vanderbilt University
Psychological Interpreters of Buddhism

John Holt
Bowdoin College
Sri Lanka's Sinhala Buddhist Guardian Deities: Satara Varan Devi

Eric Huntington
Rice University
Buddhist Cosmology

Roger R. Jackson
Carleton College
Mahāmudrā in India and Tibet

John Jorgensen
La Trobe University
Huineng

Casey Alexandra Kemp
University of Vienna
Secular Buddhism
Tibetan Book of the Dead (*Bardo Thödol*)

Matthew W. King
University of California, Riverside
Mongolian Buddhism in the Early 20th Century

Natalie Köhle
Hong Kong Baptist University
Buddhism and Healing in China

Seiji Kumagai
Kyoto University
Early History of the Drukpa Kagyü School
Tsangpa Gyare (1161–1211), Founder of the Drukpa Kagyü School

Pyi Phyo Kyaw
King's College, London and Shan State Buddhist University
Practices of Protection in the Pali World

Sonya S. Lee
University of Southern California
Buddhist Wall Paintings

Erberto Lo Bue
Università di Bologna
Buddhist Art and Architecture in Tibet

Jessica Locke
Loyola University Maryland
Ethics and Buddhism

Andrew Macomber
Oberlin College
Buddhism and Medicine in Premodern Japan

Kendall Marchman
University of Georgia
Fo Guang Shan
Hsing Yun

Nathan McGovern
University of Wisconsin, Whitewater
Esoteric Buddhism in Southeast Asia

Karin Meyers
Mangalam Research Center
Intention in the Pali Suttas and Abhidharma

Nathan Jishin Michon
Independent Scholar
Buddhist Chaplaincy

Scott A. Mitchell
Institute of Buddhist Studies
Buddhism and Media

Eisho Nasu
Ryukoku Daigaku
Rennyo
Ryōgen

Douglas Ober
University of British Columbia
Buddhism in Colonial Contexts

Sree Padma
Bowdoin College
Sri Lanka's Sinhala Buddhist Guardian Deities: Satara Varan Devi

Thomas Patton
City University of Hong Kong
Buddhist Wizards (*Vidhyadhāra/Weizzā/Weikza*): Contemporary Burma/Myanmar

Richard K. Payne
Institute of Buddhist Studies, Emeritus
Globalizing Tantric Buddhism
Homa: Tantric Fire Ritual
Secular Buddhism

Maurizio Peleggi
National University of Singapore
Art, Architecture, and National Memory-Making

Elisabetta Porcu
University of Cape Town
Japanese Buddhisms in Diaspora

John Powers
Deakin University
Bodhisattvabhūmi (The Bodhisattva Stages)
The Body of the Buddha
Three Turnings of the Wheel of Doctrine (Dharma-Cakra)

Aaron Proffitt
University at Albany, State University of New York
Shingon

David Quinter
University of Alberta
Visualization/Contemplation Sutras (Guan Jing)

Fabio Rambelli
University of California, Santa Barbara
Buddhism and Shinto

Jens Reinke
Leipzig University
Global Buddhism

Nicolas Revire
Thammasat University
The Study of Visual Culture in South and Southeast Asian Buddhism

Ulrike Roesler
University of Oxford
The Kadampa: A Formative Movement of Tibetan Buddhism

Richard Salomon
University of Washington
Epigraphy and the Study of Buddhism: South Asia's Northern Corridor

Jonathan Samuels
Austrian Academy of Sciences
Debate in the Tibetan Tradition

Monica Sanford
Independent Scholar
Buddhist Chaplaincy

Asuka Sango
Carleton College
Debate Traditions in Premodern Japan

Bee Scherer
Vrije Universiteit Amsterdam
Queering Buddhist Traditions

Jens Schlieter
Universität Bern
Buddhism and Bioethics

Sarah Shaw
University of Oxford
Buddhist Meditation and Contemplation

Michael R. Sheehy
University of Virginia
Zhentong (Other-Emptiness)

Mark Siderits
Illinois State University
Buddhist Philosophy as Philosophy
Nāgārjuna

Henrik H. Sørensen
Ruhr University Bochum
History of Buddhisms in China: The Nanbeicho Period (Late 4th Century to the Sui Dynasty)

Alexander Soucy
St. Mary's University
Thích Nhất Hạnh in the Context of the Modern Development of Vietnamese Buddhism

Jacqueline Stone
Princeton University
Nichiren

Sharon A. Suh
Seattle University
Buddhism in Film
Western Buddhism and Race

Stefania Travagnin
SOAS University of London
Humanistic Buddhism (Rensheng Fojiao 人生佛教 / Renjian Fojiao 人間佛教)

Katja Triplett
Leipzig University
Buddhism and Medicine in Japan

Ben Van Overmeire
Duke Kunshan University
Buddhism and Biography

Sam van Schaik
The British Library
Dzogchen

Daniel Veidlinger
California State University, Chico
Transmission of Buddhist Media and Texts

Kevin Vose
College of William & Mary
Candrakīrti's Middle Way Philosophy

Vesna A. Wallace
University of California, Santa Barbara
Buddhism and Medicine in India
Kālacakra-Maṇḍala: Symbolism and Construction

Michelle C. Wang
Georgetown University
Dunhuang Art

Elizabeth Williams-Oerberg
Independent Scholar
The Economics of Buddhism

Guang Xing
University of Hong Kong
Filial Piety in Chinese Buddhism

Ronit Yoeli-Tlalim
Goldsmiths University of London
Tibetan Medicine and Its Buddhist Contexts

Jimmy Yu
Florida State University
Sheng Yen

Chün-fang Yü
Columbia University
Avalokiteśvara: The Bodhisattva of Compassion

Index

Notes: Page numbers printed in boldface indicate a major discussion, while those followed by "*f*" indicate figures and illustrations and those followed by "*t*" indicate tables. For the benefit of digital users, indexed terms and table entries that span two pages (e.g., 52–53) may, on occasion, appear on only one of those pages.

AAR. *See* American Academy of Religion
Abaqa, 1642
Abatai Khan, 1647–1649, 1651–1654
Abbasid empire, 1636, 1668–1670, 1672, 1674–1679
Abe, Masao, 710
Abel-Rémusat, Jean-Pierre, 864–865, 876–877
  reputation of, 878, 881
Abe Ryūchi, 2334, 2336, 2359
Abe Yasurō, 345–346
Abhayagiri branch, of Theravāda Buddhism, 2429 n.45, 2433 n.109
Abhayagirivihāra, 1522
Abhayākaragupta, 23–24, 626–627
abhayamudrā, 1286–1287
Abhidhamma Piṭaka, 1882–1884, 2408–2409
Abhidharma Buddhism. See also *specific topics*
  Abhidhamma texts, 1880–1881, 1888, 1890–1892
  doctrine of, 2122 n.11
  emptiness in, 1457–1458
  Mahāyāna Buddhism and, 617–618, 630 n.3
  manuals for, 2097
  Mipam on, 1563
  Nāgārjuna and, 1454, 1689–1690
  orthodoxy in, 1701 n.10
  philosophy of, 529–530, 1819–1824, 1833
  scholarship on, 2093–2098 (*See also* Sarvāstivāda Abhidharma school)
  theory in, 1335
  translations of, 1298 n.16
  Vasubandhu on, 1–2, 1833, 2097
Abhidharmakośabhāṣya (*AKBh*) (*Abidatsuma kusharon*), 750–751
  content of, 5–9
  in digital materials, 12
  history of, 1819–1820
  notable commentaries on, 9–10

Abhidharmakośabhāṣya (AKBh) (*continued*)
physicians in, 246
scholarship on, 1–2, 11, 481, 2097, 2098*t*, 2100–2101, 2106–2107
textual history of, 2–5, 1401–1402
Vasubandhu and, 2111, 2113–2114
Abhidharma-mahāvibhāṣā (*MVŚ*)
on *nirvāṇa*, 2107–2108
Sarvāstivāda Abhidharma school and, 2093–2094, 2106, 2112–2113, 2121 n.1
scholarship on, 2093–2099, 2121 n.1 (*See also* Sarvāstivāda Abhidharma school)
soteriological analysis from, 2109–2110
Abhidharmasamuccaya, 1399–1400
Abhidharma theory, 1327–1335, 1690
Abhinavagupta, 2309
abhiññas, 511–512
Abhisamayālaṃkāra
content of, 18–23
controversies with, 25–29
Indian Buddhist commentaries on, 23–24
scholarship on, 17–18, 29–30, 1041
in Tibetan Buddhism, 24–25
Abidatsuma kusharon (*Abhidharmakośabhāṣya*), 750–751
Abisha, 304
abodes, 2509, 2513
academic education, 2138–2139, 2158–2160
Acala, 2378–2380, 2382*f*
Acceptance and Commitment Therapy (ACT), 1952
Account of Conduct (Zhaoqian), 54, 57
acculturation, 1357–1358
Acela Sutta, 1024–1025
Achard, Jean-Luc, 840
Acri, Andrea, 969, 1527–1528, 1927
ACT. *See* Acceptance and Commitment Therapy
action. See *karma*
action based ethics, 1329
active religion, 2137
Act on Monuments and Antiques, 76–77
Adamantine Dagger, 1478–1479
Adamek, Wendi Leigh, 821–823
adaptability, 766–767, 778, 1113–1115
adaptation, 184–185
Adhyārdhaśatika Prajñāpāramitā, 1906
Adikaram, E. W., 153
Adulyadej, Bhumipol, 2067–2068
Advaita Vedānta philosophy, 1464–1465, 1698
Advayasamatāvijayamahākalparāja, 1469 n.19
Advayavajrasaṃgraha (Shastri, H.), 1491
Advice on the Six Lamps (Drugom Yungdrung), 836
Advyasiddhī (Lakṣmīṅkarā), 1901
aesthetics, 1431–1432, 1488–1489, 2268. *See also* visual culture
"Aesthetics of Excess" (Heim), 1336
affinity narratives, 1722–1725
afflicted views (dṛṣṭi), 7–8
afflictive emotions, 977
Afghanistan, 632–633, 1604, 1624–1625, 1667–1668
African hypothesis, 864–865, 871
Agata Inukai Tachibana no Michiyo, 2198–2199, 2201
aggregates of matter (*rūpa*), 6
Agnew, Neville, 825
agnihotra, 1196 n.14
agnosticism, 2135
agriculture, 351–352
Agvan Dorjiev, 1609, 2020
Ahmad, Zahiruddin, 1656–1658
AIBS. *See* American Institute of Buddhist Studies
Aitken, Allison, 1445–1446
Aitken, Robert, 1814–1815
Aitkin, Anne, 910
Ajahn Brahm, 1081–1082
Ajahn Chah, 1081–1082, 1117–1118
Ajanta Caves, 944, 1368
Ajase (king), 288
Ajātaśatru (king), 557–560, 635, 1497
Akamatsu Kōshō, 1963, 1974, 2333–2334
Ākāśagarbha Contemplation Sutra, 2677, 2679–2681, 2693–2695
AKB. See *Abhidharmakośabhāṣya*
AKBh. See *Abhidharmakośabhāṣya*
Akihira, Fujiwara, 756–757
Akira Kurosawa, 404
Akiya Enosuke, 2215
Akizuki Ryōmin, 708
Akoṣbhya-vyūha Sūtra, 483
Akṣayamati, 2076–2077
Aksọbhya Buddha, 2180–2181
Akṣobhya-vyūha Sūtra, 482–483
Alaka Chattopadhyaya, 1407
Ālambanaparīkṣa (Dignāga), 1822, 1833
The Alchemical Body (White, D.), 2318
alcohol, 980, 1705–1706, 1709
Alexander, Franz, 1943–1945, 1950
Alexander II (tsar), 2529
Alexander the Great, 543–545, 1637
Alien Land Law, 13 n.5
all-accomplishing rite, 1423, 1423*t*
All-Creating King, 1444
The All-Creating Sovereign, 1478–1479
Alles, Gregory, 200
All-Illuminating Moon (Tupten Püntsok), 1756

Allione, Tsultrim, 694–695
Allon, Mark, 639, 2566–2567
Almogi, Orna, 2481
Almond, Philip C., 1939, 2709
Aloka Vihara Forest Monastery, 1117–1118
Alpert, Richard, 2479
Alphabetum barmanorum seu regni avensis, 1048
Alphabetum Tibetanum (Giorgi), 871, 879
Altan Khan, 1065, 1503–1504, 1583, 1644–1657, 1750, 2014–2015
Altan tobchi (Lubsangdandzin), 1657–1658
Altglas, Véronique, 200
altruism, 919–920
Altruism and Reality (Williams, P.), 986
Âm, Diệu, 2437–2438
Amarakosha (Amarasimha), 874–876
Amarasimha, 874–875
Ambedkar, B. R., 181, 384–385, 907–908, 984, 1053
Ambros, Barbara, 778–779
America. *See* United States
American Academy of Religion (AAR), 1982
American Buddhism, 34–41, 1313
American Dharma (Gleig), 1122–1123
American Institute of Buddhist Studies (AIBS), 1142, 1491
American Sutra (Williams, D.), 2716, 2719
American Theological Schools, 465
Ames, William, 1467
Amida Buddha, 43–47, 871–872, 1307, 1312, 1349–1350
Amida hisshaku, 2185–2186
Amidism, 1260
Amitābha
  depictions of, 277–278, 1971–1972, 1972*f*, 2180–2181
  family of, 1968–1969, 1968*t*
  images of, 938
  legacy of, 2184
  in Pure Land Buddhism, 557–560, 558*f*
  scholarship and, 85–86, 91, 271–272, 1960–1962, 1970–1971 (*See also* Pure Land Buddhism)
  in *Sukhāvatīvyūha Sūtras*, 1291
  in Tibet, 1970–1971
Amitābha Buddha in the Western Pure Land, 796, 797*f*
Amitāyus, 426–427, 427*f*, 429–430
Amitāyus Contemplation Sutra, 2675, 2677–2679, 2683–2688
Amitāyus Nine Deity Maṇḍala (Jetāri), 1972–1973
Amoghavajra
  biographical information about, 54–60, 1469 n.12, 1515–1517, 1527
  in China, 2363–2364
  in Japan, 58–59, 2177
  to Kūkai, 1524
  legacy of, 57–60, 1517, 2177, 2363–2364
  politics of, 1502–1503
  reputation of, 963, 1502–1503, 1519, 1522, 1524
  scholarship and, 53–54, 60–64, 1801 n.11, 1866–1867, 2175–2177, 2328–2329
  in Sri Lanka, 2176–2177
Among Tibetan Texts (Smith, E. G.), 1068–1069
Amritananda, Vajracarya, 877
Amstutz, Galen, 1357
amulets, 966
A myes zhab, 1397
Ân, Thích Thiên, 2438
Anālayo, Bhikkhu, 2566–2567
Analects (Huang Kan), 813
analog electronic mass media, 2564–2565
Ānanda, 1498, 2666, 2680, 2684–2687, 2691
Anandabodhi, Ayya, 1117
Anandadeva, 1795
Ananda Wickremeratne, 1101
Anaṅga, 1418–1419
Anaṅgavarman (prince), 1525
anarchy, 1260, 1442–1444
Anarchy in the Pure Land (Ritzinger), 2294–2295
anātmavāda (no-self), 1836–1837
Anawratha (king), 343
ancestry, 776–777, 790–792
ancient translations, 684–685
Anderl, Christoph, 657–658, 2690
Andersen, Paul Kent, 951
Anderson, Benedict, 77–78, 377–378, 1036–1037
Anderson, Carol, 1032–1033
Anderson, Richard, 233
Andhare, Shridhar, 1201–1202
Andreeva, Anna, 279, 302–303
Ané Gungmen Gyelmo, 2488–2489
Angkor National Museum, 1919–1923, 1922*f*
Angkor Wat, 84
Anglo-American society, 2129–2131, 2141
Anglo-Burmese War, 599, 1048–1049
Aṅguttara Nikāya
  medicine and, 245–246, 250, 252–253, 256
  scholarship and, 481, 888, 1319–1322
Aṇguttaranikāya, 995–997
aniconic iconography, 1294
aniconism, 2263
Anige (master), 1633–1634
animals, 1281–1282, 1329–1331
aniyatas, 2658
Anjirō, 865–866
AññāKoṇḍañña, 1020–1021

Annalistic Autobiography of Master Xuyun (Cen Xuelü), 2737
Annan, Kofi, 2165
Anne, 2047
Annen, 2183–2184, 2333, 2336, 2348–2349
annihilationism, 1694
Anningson, Ryan, 1311–1312
Anonymous History of the Autonomous Period, 1606–1607
Anquetil-Duperron, Abraham Hyacinthe, 872–873
Anshi, 2047
Ān Shìgāo, 635–638, 997, 1004–1005, 2096
Anthology of Pure Land Texts (Karma Chagme), 1974
Anthropological Studies in Theravāda Buddhism, 574–576
anthropology, 112 n.12, 574–575, 2484 n.32, 2626
anthropomorphic representations, 1273–1274
anti-colonialism, 923
antifetishism, 882
antiquities, 2267–2268
Anuruddha (king), 253–254, 1732. *See also* disciples
Anuttarayoga tantra, 1926
Anzhai jing, 1185
Aoyama Shundō Rōshi, 774
apocryphal texts, 1004–1005
Apoha (Siderits), 1838
apoha doctrine (Dignāga), 1823–1829, 1836–1838
App, Urs, 864–867, 869
Appadurai, Arjun, 200, 228–229, 240–241
Apple, James B., 27–28, 628–629, 1407
Appleton, Naomi, 1815, 2024
application, 1991
applied Buddhist ethics, 984–985
apprentice education, 1571
apps, 1016
apratisaṃkhyā-nirodha, 2105
Arabian Nights, 1678
Arab-Muslim conquests, 1668, 1670–1672
Ārāḍa Kālama, 121–122
arahantship, 978–979
Arai, Paula, 185, 778–779
The Arcanum, 129–130, 132
Archaeological Survey of India, 70–71, 1914
archaeology, 375, 889–890, 2569 n.11
architecture
  art and, 66–68, 77–78, 890
  Buddhist, 33 n.55, 75–77, 421–424, 437–444
  Dunhuang art and, 713 n.27, 781–784
  functions of, 440–441
  in Japan, 1308–1309
  rituals and, 2526 n.69, 2526 n.71
  sacred, 2636–2637
  of stupas, 2264–2265
  Xuanzang on, 1672
Ardussi, John, 845
Argentina, 1353–1355, 1357–1358
Arghun, 1642
Arguillère, Stéphane, 1442, 1446–1447
Fujiwara Arihira, 2046
Ariq-böke Khan, 1628–1629
Aris, Michael, 845, 2025
arising (*samudayo*), 1025–1026
Aristotle, 981
Ariyaratne, A. T., 895–896, 905–906, 916, 919
Ariyā-Weizzā Organization, 593–594, 596–597, 600, 603–604
Arjia Rinpoche, 1591
army, Taiwan, 2155–2157
Arnold, Dan, 1838
Arnold, Edwin, 181
Aronson, Harvey, 1956
Arslan, 1655
art. *See also* Dunhuang art
  Amitābha Buddha in the Western Pure Land, 796, 797*f*
  architecture and, 66–68, 77–78, 890
  Bodhisattva Guide of Souls, 790, 791*f*
  Buddhist, 67, 75–77, 421–424, 433–437, 443–444
  Christian, 425
  contemporary, 795–796
  dating, 112 n.9
  early Buddhist, 2272 n.18
  historians, 84
  historical evidence, 961–962
  history, 2265–2266, 2272 n.18
  iconography and, 230, 788
  imaging Buddha in, 1274–1278
  at "Inspired by Dunhuang," 796
  jātaka and, 1368–1369
  Jewish, 2262
  Khmer, 969
  Kṣitigarbha and the Ten Kings of Hell, 790–791, 792*f*
  light in, 1301 n.58
  Magic Competition murals, 783–784, 796–797
  Maṇḍala of Eight Great Bodhisattvas, 788–790, 789*f*
  materials, 433–437
  merit of, 1290–1292, 2268–2269
  new, 112 n.1
  New-Style Mañjuśrī, 793–794, 794*f*
  Panorama of Mount Wutai, 793, 793*f*
  pilgrimage and, 1869
  with pounces, 784, 785*f*
  religious, 66
  Sūtra on the Names of the Buddha, 784, 786*f*
  symmetry in, 1296 n.8

in Taiwan, 1633–1634
from Tang dynasty, 555–560
Tibetan, 112 n.8
tradition in, 425
to UNESCO, 795
Western, 66–67
"L'art gréco-bouddhique du Gandhāra" (Foucher), 1294
artifacts, 68, 72, 75–76, 112 n.4, 236, 633
Artinger, Brenna, 1119
Art of Central Asia, 802
The Arts of Contemplative Care (Giles, Miller, W.), 454–458, 471–472
Arugh (prince), 1635, 1657–1658
Ary, Elijah, 2025
Āryadeva, 615–616, 748–749, 1461–1462, 1498. *See also* Candrakīrti
Āryadeva the Brahmin, 686–688, 690
Āryamañjuśrīmūlakalpa, 2636–2637
āryas (Nobles), 531–532
Āryaśūra, 944, 1810, 2010–2011
Ārya-Śūra's Compendium of the Perfections, 1814–1815
Ārya Vimuktisena, 23–24
Asad, Talal, 2145
Asahara Saichi, 720, 722
āsanas, 2266–2267
Asanga, 23–24, 100–102, 2204, 2464, 2662, 2744
"Ascending to Heaven after Death" (Halkias), 1974
ascertainment, of sūtras, 2107–2110
asceticism, 2726–2727
Asceticism and Healing in Ancient India (Zysk), 260–261
Ashem vohū, 812
Asher, Frederick, 1786–1787
Ashikaga Takauji, 2185
Ashikaga Yoshimitsu, 2036, 2185
Ashin Jinarakkhita, 1078
Ashmolean Museum, 1908–1909, 1909*f*
Asia. See also *specific topics*
Asian Buddhism, 864, 2708–2712
Asian movements, 2126–2127
Asians, 470
Buddha images in, 1733–1734
Buddhist, 94
Christianity in, 2294–2295
colonialism in, 1074–1075
communities in, 1719–1720
contemporary, 1570–1580
culture in, 69, 83–84, 2130–2131
Esoteric Buddhism in, 64
Europe and, 73–74, 1941, 2137
higher education in, 1577–1578
Humanistic Buddhism in, 1261
ideology in, 1576–1577
immigration from, 408
inner-Asian Buddhist exchanges, 1083–1086
Japan and, 1075, 1299 n.31
maritime, 1513*f*, 1518–1521
modernity in, 1604–1607, 2126
Naikan in, 1709
national Asian traditions, 1077–1080
non-Asians and, 1080–1083
Pali Buddhism in, 2658, 2660
pilgrims in, 1292–1293
professional conservation in, 75–76
radio in, 2564–2565
relics in, 1720
religion in, 1622
Société Asiatique, 1814
Western Europe and, 367
women in, 1119–1121
after World War II, 2164
Asian Americans, 457
Asian languages, 98–100, 151–153
Asian Medical Systems (Huard), 279
Asilakkhaṇa Jātaka, 251
Asing Lama, 1645
Aśoka (king)
in China, 2071
in *Dīpavaṃsa*, 2400
inscriptions and, 932, 934, 2431 n.79, 2560, 2570 n.26
legacy of, 495, 498
Mahinda and, 194
Śākyamuni and, 933–934
scholarship on, 68, 70, 350, 633, 917, 1095, 1725–1726, 1732–1733, 1865
Theriya lineage and, 2405–2406
writing to, 2557
Aśoka Maurya, 861 n.2, 933–934
An Aspiration Prayer for the Pure Land Sukhāvatī (Karma Chagme), 1966, 1968
aspiration prayers, 1965–1968
An Aspiration Prayer to Sukhāvatī (various authors), 1966, 1970–1971
assimilative modern liberalism, 1122–1123
Assmann, Jan, 70
Association for Clinical Pastoral Education, 461
Association for Professional Chaplains, 461–462
Aṣṭasāhasrikā Prajñāpāramitā, 1521
Aṣṭasāhasrikā prajñāpāramitā manuscripts, 1044–1045, 1785–1786, 1788–1789, 1810–1811, 1923–1926
astrology, 1168, 1887–1888
Aṣṭsāhasrikā Prajñāpāramitā Sūtra (Vaidya), 125, 1899–1900

Aśvaghoṣa's Buddhacarita (Johnston), 125
Aśvaghoṣa's Discourse on the Awakening of Faith in the Mahayana, 703, 716
Ataka Yakichi, 706
Āṭānāṭiya Sutta, 481, 1879–1880, 1883
At Home in the World (Hanh), 2448
Atikūṭa, 1519
Atiśa Dīpaṃkaraśrījñāna
  legacy of, 1394, 1411, 1413 n.25, 1479, 1525, 1536
  reputation of, 1393–1401, 1404–1406, 1436–1437, 1519, 1546–1547, 2010–2011
  scholarship on, 1397–1399, 1406–1407, 1548
  (*See also* Kadampa)
Atiśa Dipaṅkaraśrījñāna, 626–627, 684–685
atiyoga, 834–835
ātman, 1–2, 9, 1953–1955
atomic weapons, 380
attachment, 7–8, 887
attainment (*samāpatti*), 5
Attainment of Gnosis, 1475
Attainment of Secrets, 1475
Attākaradeva (king), 1796
atṭhakathās, 2660
Atthasālinī (Buddhaghosa), 145, 147, 153
Atwood, Chris, 1198 n.47, 1203, 1386, 1614–1615
Auerback, Micah, 181–182
Augsburg confession, 867–868
Aung San, 225 n.98
Australia
  BLIA in, 1014
  Buddhist chaplaincy in, 469–470
  Cambodia and, 1102
  Canada and, 1116
  Europe and, 1590
  New Zealand and, 112 n.9
  nuns in, 907–908
  scholarship and, 1991
  South Africa and, 913
  U.S., and, 2137
authenticity, 236–240
authorship, 100–101, 147–148
autobiography, 185–186
Auto-commentary (Rangjung Dorjé), 2026
Auxiliary Rules of Purity for Chan Monasteries (Zeshan), 2662
Avadānaśataka, 1372
Avalokiteśvara
  to bodhisattvas, 83–84, 2687
  in China, 85–93
  depictions of, 1908–1909, 1914–1915, 1918
  devotion to, 2674
  donations by, 1785–1786
  as Guanshyin, 1517
  images of, 2518
  in India, 84
  in Japan, 93–94
  Mahākāśyapa and, 2175
  Mahāsthāmaprāpta and, 2685–2687
  Mañjuśrī and, 1970
  monasteries of, 943–944
  Padmasambhava and, 2491–2492
  Pure Land Buddhism and, 356
  references to, 961
  scholarship and, 94, 946, 1867–1868
  in South Asia, 84–85
  in Southeast Asia, 84–85
  statues of, 1587
  Tāranātha and, 100
  in Tibet, 1979 n.45
  to Tibetan Buddhism, 93–94
  triad of, 1903*f*, 1908
  Trisong Detsen and, 2583–2584
Avantivarman, 1788
Avataṃsaka, 483–484
Avataṃsaka period, 2463
Avataṃsaka Sutra, 85–86, 88–89, 1021–1022, 1039–1040, 1499, 1501–1502, 1866–1868
Avataṃsaka University, 2283
Aviṣahya Jātaka, 1806–1807
awakening, 2076–2077, 2643–2647
Awakening of Faith, 716–717, 2282
Awakening of Mahāvairocana Tantra (Wu-xing), 2311
awareness, 2551 n.31
Āyatanas, 2102*t*
Ayōttitācar, K., 1053
Ayurbarwada (emperor), 1635
Āyurveda, 245, 260–261, 267, 305
Ayushi Güüshi, 1651–1652
Ayushiridara (emperor), 1639
Azad, Arezou, 1469 n.26
Aziz, Barbara, 695

BAC. *See* Buddhist Association of China
Ba clan, 2582
Bacot, Jacques, 1553
Badiner, Allan Hunt, 362
Badmajeff, Wlodzimierz, 2529–2530
Badmajew, Peter, 2529–2530
Badmayev, Ossor, 2529–2530
Badmayev, Pyotr Aleksandrovich, 2529, 2534
Badmayev, Zhamyan, 2529
Badreddin Khan, 112 n.16
Bae Young-Kyun, 405–406
Bagan (king), 1048–1049

Bagyidaw (king), 599
Bahir, Cody, 1136–1137, 1139–1140, 1150, 2388
Bai Fazhu, 998
Bailey, H. W., 639, 820
Baisheng Dongfu, 2154–2155
Baizhang Huaihai, 2662
Baizhang's Ryles of Purity Revised on Imperial Order (Dongyang), 2663
Bakula Rinpoche, 908, 1589–1590, 2022
Bala (monk), 937–938
Balabhaṭṭa, 1794
al-Balādhurī, 1671–1674
Bālaputradeva (king), 947, 1525–1526
Baldanza, Kathlene, 1040
Bali, 963
Bamboo Grove Monastery, 212–213
Bâmbyn Rintchen, 2498
Bamda Tubten Gelek Gyatso, 2747–2748
Bandaranaike, S. W. R. D., 375
Bandito Khambo Lam, 1608
Bangkok National Museum, 74–75, 1805 n.108, 1908, 1919, 1920*f*, 1937 n.119
Bangladesh, 1099, 1783, 1793–1796, 1802 n.36, 1889–1890
Bang Vien inscription, 1902
Bankei, 706, 714–715
Bankston, Carl L., III, 2243
Banteay Neang inscription, 1902, 1906, 1913, 1916, 1918
Ban Tetsugyu, 2171 n.41
Ban Tetsugyu, Rōshi, 2160
Bao, Jieman, 1114–1115, 1122
Bảo, Nguyễn Xuân. *See* Hanh
Bảo Giám, 1039–1041
Baolin, 657–658
Baolin zhuan, 1230, 1237–1238
Baozhi, 88
Bapat, P. V., 153
Baptism, 1048
Barabudur stūpa, 960
Barber, A. W., 2434, 2445
Bardo Thödol. See *Tibetan Book of the Dead*
Bareja-Starsyńska, Agata, 1592, 1594, 1656–1657
Barker, Kristin, 911
Barnes, Gina, 2209
Barnett, L. D., 2088
Barnhart, Michael, 2088–2089
BAROC. *See* Buddhist Association of the Republic of China
Barrett, Timothy H., 328, 1037–1038
Barron, Richard, 841
Bartholomew, T., 1656–1657
Barua, Benimadhab, 639
Basic Ordinance of Mañjuśrī, 1473
Bastis, Madeline Ko-i, 461–462
Batbold, Sükhbaataryn, 1384
Batchelor, Martine, 2138–2139
Batchelor, Stephen, 2132–2133, 2136, 2138–2139, 2142, 2144–2145
Bat Cum inscription, 1804 n.79, 1906
Bat Cum temple, 1902–1904
Batụvantudāve, Don Andris de Silva, 1046–1047
Bauddha Praśnaya (Guṇānanda), 373–374
Bauer, Mikaël, 759, 2209
Baumann, Martin, 191, 195, 1072 n.9, 1087, 1118
Baums, Stefan, 639, 941*f*, 949–950
Bautze-Picron, Claudine, 1796–1797, 2269–2270
Bawden, Charles, 1386, 1604–1605, 1608
Bayly, Christopher, 383
Bazhé, 2585
BBS. *See* Budo Bala Sena
bca' yig (constitution), 2671 n.37
bDud 'joms Rin po che, 2640–2641
Beacon of Certainty (Mipam), 1562
Beastie Boys, 112 n.4, 226–227, 238–239
Beat Generation, 48, 723–724, 1081, 1311, 1313
Beauchamp, Tom L., 165–167
beautiful objects, 515–516
Bechert, Heinz, 2145, 2294–2295
Beck, Joko, 2142
Beckwith, Christopher, 1672, 1675–1676
Beek, Kimberly, 159 n.50, 237
Before and After Faith (Yoshimoto), 1703
Begtse, 1170–1172
Béguin, Gilles, 443–444, 2262–2263, 2269–2270
Behrendt, Kurt, 2269–2270
Beiner, Ruedi, 1708–1709
Being Peace (Hanh), 2448
Bel Dongtsap, 2574–2575
Bell, Charles, 1406–1407
Bell, Christopher, 1173–1174, 1755
Bell, Tevvy, 825
Belo Tsewang Kunkyab, 1541, 1545, 1553
Beltz, Johannes, 1927
Benares, 251
Benavides, Gustavo, 889
Bencaojing jizhu, 814
Bencao shiyi, 213
Benefit Beings! (Fisher), 471–472
Benjamin, Walter, 66–67
Benjor Lhündrup, 2461–2462
Benkenmitsu nikyōron (Kūkai), 2180
Bennet, Tony, 72
Bennett, Allan, 2413
Bentor, Yael, 821–823, 1208–1210, 2270, 2519

Berger, Patricia, 1386, 1656–1657
Berger, Peter, 1131
Berichte über das Leben des Atiśa (Eimer), 1407
Berke, 1642
Berkeley Bussei (magazine), 1311–1312
Berkwitz, Stephen C., 1140, 2567
Bernard, Jean Frédéric, 868–869, 871, 873, 875
Bernard, Pierre, 2314
Bernard of Clairvaux (Saint), 1447
Bernhard, Franz, 639
Bernier, François, 2708
Bersani, Leo, 1992–1993
Beyer, Peter, 200, 417, 1087
Beyer, Stephan, 1202–1203, 1210–1211
"Beyond Coping" (Bhikkhu Thanissaro), 1023–1024
Bha Bha Min group, 224 n.82
Bhadanta Vimuktisena, 23–24
Bhadraṇāga, Mahāsāmanta, 1790–1791
Bhadrapā, 1551
Bhagavad Gita, 2306
Bhaiṣajyarāja, 115–116, 247–250
Bhaisạjyarāja Contemplation Sutra, 2676–2677, 2679–2680, 2688
Bharhut, 932, 934–936, 935*f*, 2264
Bharhut Inscriptions (Lüders), 948–949
Bhattacharya, Gouriswar, 1783–1784
Bhattacharya, Kamaleswar, 1465
Bhavadevamahāvihāra, 1794–1795
bhāvanā, 519–522
Bhāviveka, 105–106, 623–626, 1459, 1467
Bhikkhu Anālayo, 1031
Bhikkhu Bodhi, 125, 911, 978, 1325, 2143
bhikkhunī disciples, 2623–2624, 2626–2627
Bhikkhuni Kusama, 1103–1104
bhikkhunī ordination, 1085–1086, 1577, 2614, 2621
bhikkhuni sangha, 1102–1104, 1119–1121. See also *specific topics*
bhikkhus, 1101–1104, 2672 n.62
Bhikkhu Sanghasena, 862 n.13, 863 n.48, 906, 908, 931 n.133
Bhikkhu Thanissaro, 1023–1026
Bhilsa Topes (Cunningham), 948
Bhutan, 694, 857, 1444, 2062–2063, 2595. *See also* Tsangpa Gyare
Bianchi, Ester, 1150, 2387–2388, 2665–2666
Bianhong, 1519
Bian Que, 209
The Bibliothèque nationale de France, 812, 817–818
Bidatsu, 266–267
Bielefeldt, Carl, 2341, 2358
Bigandet, Paul Ambroise, 1048–1049
The Big Lebowski (film), 403–404
Bihar, 1783–1786, 1792–1793, 1798–1800
bīja (seeds), 7–8, 1834–1835
Bimbisāra (king), 248–249, 251–252
Bingenheimer, Marcus, 1869
Bin Wei, 1864
bioethics
  biomedicine and, 161–163, 165–166, 168
  of cloning, 112 n.2
  consolidation of, 169–170
  of dependent origination, 113 n.18
  dignity and, 159 n.54
  ethics and, 163–164
  interdependence and, 159 n.47
  scholarship on, 164–172
The Biographies from the Ocean of Oath-Bound Protectors (Lelung Zhepe Dorje), 1161–1162
Biographies of Eminent Monks, 2730
Biographies of Exemplary Transcendents (Liu Xiang), 1864
biography. See also *specific topics*
  adaptation and, 184–185
  autobiography and, 185–186
  of Buddhaghosa, 144–145
  Buddhism and, 177–179, 186–187
  in China, 182–183
  of D. T. Suzuki, 701–702, 709–710, 725
  of Hanh, 2435–2443, 2449 n.7
  Lamotte on, 180, 184, 186
  of Ling Repa Pema Dorje, 848
  of Toda, 2221
  women and, 184–185
  of Xuyun, 2725–2731, 2735–2737
biomedicine, 161–163, 165–166, 168
Bira, Sh., 1386–1387
Birnbaum, Raoul, 213, 2688, 2696
al-Bīrūnī, 1679–1680
Bischoff, F. A., 2641
Bishop, Peter, 2480
Bizot, François, 578, 963–965, 969–970, 1890
Björk, 226
Bka' chems ka khol ma (pillar testament), 1399, 1404–1405
Bka' gdams chos 'byung, 1397
Bka' gdams glegs bam, 1397, 1399
Bka' gdams gsung gros thor bu (Lce sgom Shes rab rdo rje), 1396–1397
Bka' gdams pa. *See* Kadampa
Black, Indigenous, and People of Color, 1119, 2137–2138
Blackburn, Anne, 385–386, 576–577, 1528, 1580, 1891
Black Lives Matter Movement, 911
Black Razor Tantra (BRT), 2638–2639
Black Sect Esoteric Buddhism, 1138
Bladel, Kevin van, 1675–1676

blame, 2079
Blavatsky, Helena, 2478–2479
Blazing Flame, 1166
blessings, 2543–2544
Blezer, Henk, 2481
BLIA. *See* Buddha's Light International Association
Blissful Land (Amitābha), 1960–1961
Block, Jennifer, 450–451
blockprinting, 2562–2563
Blofeld, John, 2741 n.52
Bloom, Alfred, 1357
blo sbyong (mind training), 1403, 1405–1406
Blue Annals (Gö Lotsawa), 848, 1438–1439, 1485, 1540, 1553, 2026
The Blue Annals (Roerich), 694–695, 1406–1407
Blue Beryl (Sangye Gyatso), 2529
Blue Cliff Collection (Yuanwu), 665
Blum, Mark L., 2042–2043
Blumenthal, James, 2464
BMNA. *See* Buddhist Mission of North America
Bo Bo Aung, 590, 598–599, 601–602
Bodagama Chandima, 1084–1085
Bodawhypaya (king), 587
Bodaw Myanmar Aye, 600
Bodawpaya (king), 1048–1049, 2417
Bode, Mabel, 184–185
Bodhgaya (Bodh Gayā), 1789–1790
Bodh Gaya (Bodh Gayā), 936, 948–949
Bodhicaryāvatāra (BCA), 510, 1812
  chapter 5 of, 2082–2083
  chapter 6 of, 2083–2085
  chapter 7 of, 2085
  chapter 8 of, 2085–2087
  chapter 9 of, 2087
  dedication in, 2088
  generosity in, 2081–2082
  history of, 2088–2089
  Madhyamaka Buddhism and, 2087
  mental afflictions in, 2080–2081
  Śāntideva on, 2079–2080
  scholarship on, 980, 982, 1561–1562, 1810, 2076–2079
bodhicitta (awakening), 980, 2643–2647
bodhicitta types, 2079–2080
Bodhi College, 2138–2140
Bodhidharma, 186, 1518–1519
Bodhidharma Anthology, 648–649
Bodhipathapradīpa (Atiśa), 1401–1402, 1404
Bodhirājakumāra, 250
Bodhiruci, 55–56, 1205
bodhisattva, 979–980
bodhisattva-avadānas. See *jātaka*
Bodhisattva-bhūmi
  in Asian languages, 98–100
  context for, 97–98
  main features of, 109–110
  in modernity, 101–103
  scholarship and, 1812, 2662
  second section of, 108
  structure of, 103–108
  third section of, 109
  Yogācārā-Bhūmi and, 100–101
Bodhisattvabhūmi Sūtra, 1003
Bodhisattva Guide of Souls, 790, 791*f*
Bodhisattva Learning Center, 2293
Bodhisattva Never Disparaging, 2224
bodhisattvas. See also *specific topics*
  Avalokiteśvara to, 83–84, 2687
  Candrakīrti on, 1810
  in China, 85–93
  in *kālacakra-maṇḍala*, 1421*t*
  in monasteries, 2640, 2661–2666, 2668
  at Mount Wutai, 792–795
  pilgrimage and, 1866–1868
  progressions of, 21–22
  scholarship on, 87–88, 94, 1809–1814, 2640, 2661–2666, 2668, 2687
  tradition for, 2705 n.105
  training for, 20–21
"Bodhisattva Vow" (song), 226–227, 238–239
Bodhisena, 1519
bodies
  bodily devotion, 521–522
  body offerings, 691–692
  of Buddha, 113–116, 120, 125
  Buddhist path and, 116–118
  cultural logic of, 118–119
  healing and, 112 n.9
  karma and, 114
  in Mahāyāna Buddhism, 122–124
  meditation and, 520–521
  merit and, 286–292
  metamorphosed, 1281–1282
  physical pleasure and, 124–125
  in reincarnation system, 114–116
  science of, 205–207
  sexuality and, 120–122
  Zhiyi on, 277
Bodies in Balance (Hofer), 2534
Body Treasury, 1475–1476
Boeles, J. J., 969
Boġda Khaġan, 1383
Bogdanov, 1609
Bogd Gegeen. *See* Jebtsundamba Khutugtus

Bogd Khaan, 1583
Bogd Khaanate, 1604–1607, 1614
Bogel, Cynthea, 2696
Boisvert, Matthieu, 417
Boksal, 2249–2250
Bo Min Guang, 567–568, 569*f*, 572, 590, 593–595, 600–603
Bonds of the Dead (Rowe), 778–779
Bones of Contention (Ambros), 778–779
Bonneval, Arnold of, 1447
Bönpo Dzogchen, 144 n.32, 829–831, 835, 839–840, 1145
Bönpo lineage, 136
Bönpo monks, 2598–2600
Bönpo people, 2489, 2497–2498, 2502 n.23. See also *specific topics*
Bönpo school, 133
Bön religion, 2585
Bön tradition
  Bönpo tradition, 112 n.15, 835–836
  cults and, 344
  Dzogchen and, 130–135
  Dzogchen patriarchs in, 135–137
  in modernity, 112 n.8, 137–138
  in monasteries, 112 n.2
  Nyingmapas and, 112 n.7, 112 n.9
  rituals in, 112 n.6
  scholarship on, 2314, 2317, 2545–2546, 2549
  Shinto and, 342–344
  Snellgrove on, 112 n.1
  in Tibet, 127–130, 2314
Bönzhik Khyung-nak, 134
Bönzhik Yungdrung Lingpa, 134
book collecting, 144 n.37, 326–327
book formats, 814–815
A Book of Ceremonies for Use of Buddhists at Gatherings, 42
Book of Documents, 813
Book of Idols (al-Kalbī), 1670
Book of Omens, 810
Book of Patañjali (al-Bīrūnī), 1679
Book of Religious Communities and Beliefs (al-Shahrastānī), 1679–1681
"Book of the Bka' gdams," 1404–1405
Book of the Simple Physician (Kajiwara), 273, 275
Book of Vimalakirti, 809
Boord, Martin, 2641–2642
Bo Pauk Sein Sayadaw, 568, 571*f*
Bopp, Franz, 878
Boquist, Ålt, 2464
boran kammaṭṭhāna, 963–964
borderland complex, 498–499
Bortolin, Matthew, 400–401, 405–406
Borup, Jørn, 199–200, 1357, 2144–2145
Bōsan, 2049–2050
Boussemart, Marie-Stella, 1407
Bower Manuscript, 251
Bowring, Richard, 2336
Bo Yi, 999–1000
Brac de la Perrière, Bénédicte, 1891–1892
Bradley, F. H., 1831–1832
Brahmā, 1283*f*
Brahmajāla Sutta, 255
Brāhmaṇa Jātaka, 1806–1807
Brahmanical philosophy, 1515, 1822, 1836–1837, 2252
Brahmanic literature, 2248
Brahmā's Net Sūtra, 267–268, 2326–2327
Brahmins, 873
Braitstein, Lara, 1490
Bramadat, Paul, 417
Bramāyu, 119
Brancaccio, Pia, 2269–2270
Brassard, Francis, 2088–2089
Braun, Erik, 1892
Brazier, Caroline, 912
Brazier, David, 912
Brazil, 234–235, 1133–1135, 1353–1358
Breen, John, 346
Breitman, Barbara, 454
Brief Hagiography of Jokpa Jangchup Penden (Sangyé Gyatso), 1744–1745, 1748
The Brief Sukhāvatī Aspiration Prayer (Namchö Mingyur Dorje), 1966
Bringing Zen Home (Arai), 778–779
Britain. *See* England
British East India Company, 873
British Library, 632–633, 635–639, 816–817. See also *specific texts*
Broido, Michael, 1490
Brokaw, Cynthia, 328
Broken Blossoms (film), 398
'Brom ston Rgyal ba'i 'byung gnas, 1394, 1397–1401, 1404. *See also* Atiśa Dīpaṃkaraśrījñāna
Bronkhorst, Johannes, 11
Brooks, Phyllis, 821–823
Brough, John, 639
Brown, Robert L., 2269–2270, 2567
BRT. See *Black Razor Tantra*
Bruguier, Bruno, 1898–1899
Bru Gyelwa Yungdrung, 132
Bruner, Jerome, 1946–1947
Brunner, Hélène, 1212
Brunnhölzl, Karl, 29–30, 1490, 2751

Brussels Buddha, 941, 942*f*
Bsod nams lha'i dbang po, 1397
bSod nams rtse mo, 2077
Bubna-Litic, David, 2144–2145
al-budd, 1469 n.30, 1676–1678
Buddha. See *specific topics*
The Buddha (Oldenberg), 181
The Buddha and His Dharma (Ambedkar), 907–908, 1053
Buddhadāsa Bhikkhu, 359, 895–896, 906
The Buddha from Dolpo (Stearns), 2750
Buddhaghosa
  animals to, 1329–1330
  biography of, 144–145
  Devdas and, 1332
  Dhammapāla and, 1325
  ethics of, 978–979
  Heim on, 1300 n.49
  humans to, 119
  on intention, 1333
  on *Intention sutta*, 1323
  on karma, 1330, 1333–1334
  knowledge in, 1322–1323
  Pali Buddhism and, 150–151
  in Sanskrit, 151–153
  scholarship and, 117–118, 153–154, 978–979, 1027, 1032, 1336
  Seng Chao and, 533
  source materials for, 147–148
  typology of, 519
  Vasubandhu and, 117, 1327–1328, 1331–1332, 1334–1335, 1343 n.139
  Visuddhimagga and, 148–150
  works from, 145–147
Buddhaguptanātha, 1521
Buddhahood, 109
Buddha images
  in Asia, 1733–1734
  in Burma/Myanmar, 74
  contemplation of, 2685–2686
  history of, 1720–1721
  national memory-making and, 72–75
  in Sri Lanka, 67
  to Taliban, 66
  in Thailand, 66–67
  in World Heritage Sites, 33 n.56
  Xuanzang on, 1292
Buddhajīva, 1518–1519
Buddha Light International Organization, 2166–2167
"Buddha Loves You" (song), 226–227, 232
Buddhamitrā (nun), 937–938
Buddhananda, 941, 942*f*
Buddhanature, 2743–2744
Buddhāpadāna, 1807
Buddhapālita, 1459–1460
Buddharakṣita, 938
Buddha Sakyamuni, 69
Buddhaśira, 941
Buddha's Light International Association (BLIA), 1008–1010, 1014, 1219–1220
Buddha's Light TV, 1016
Buddhavaṃsa, 1372
The Buddha Within (Hookham), 2750
Buddhism. See *specific topics*
Buddhism (Mitchell, D.), 2061–2062
Buddhism, the Internet, and Digital Media (Veidlinger and Grieve), 240
"Buddhism, Meditation, and Global Secularisms" (McMahan), 2145–2146
Buddhism and American Cinema (Storhoff and Whalen-Bridge), 400–403, 405–406
Buddhism and Bioethics (Keown), 169–170
Buddhism and Ecology (Tucker and Ryūken Williams), 362
Buddhism and Healing (Demiéville), 213, 224 n.82
Buddhism and Healing in Medieval China and Japan (Salguero), 310
"Buddhism and Indian Medicine" (Unschuld), 214
Buddhism and Medicine (anthology), 310–311
"Buddhism and Popular Ritual in Mongolia" (Atwood), 1614–1615
Buddhism and Society (Spiro), 1890–1891
Buddhism and Whiteness (McCrae and Yancy), 2719
Buddhism-based new religious movements, 1355–1356
Buddhism between China and Tibet (Kapstein), 2387–2388
Buddhism Beyond Borders (Beek), 237
"Buddhism for the World" (Hanh), 2437
Buddhism Goes to the Movies (Green, R.), 232, 400–402, 405–406
Buddhism in Canada (Matthews), 417, 2243
Buddhism in Hawaii and An Outline of Buddhism (HHMH), 1308
"Buddhism in Life" (Hanh), 2439
"Buddhism in Mongolia After 1990" (Bareja-Starsyńska), 1594
Buddhism in Mongolian History, Culture, and Society (Wallace), 1595, 1615
Buddhism in Taiwan (Jones, C.), 1017, 2625
The Buddhism of Tibet (Waddell), 1406–1407
Buddhist apologists, 2128–2129
Buddhist architecture, 33 n.55, 75–77, 421–424, 437–444

Buddhist art, 67, 75–77, 421–424, 433–437, 443–444
Buddhist artifacts, 236
Buddhist Association of Canada, 411
Buddhist Association of China (BAC), 1248–1249, 1258–1259
Buddhist Association of the Republic of China (BAROC), 1017, 2369–2370, 2622
Buddhist Care for the Dying and Bereaved (Watts, J. and Tomatsu), 472
Buddhist Catechism (Olcott), 373–374, 1941
Buddhist chaplaincy
  in Australia, 469–470
  Clinical Buddhist Chaplaincy, 468
  core competencies of, 452–459
  cultural competencies in, 456–457
  education for, 159 n.54
  empathy in, 113 n.19, 452–454
  field of, 450–452
  globalization of, 459–470
  interfaith understanding in, 456
  in Japan, 467–468
  in Korea, 176 n.69, 466–467
  listening in, 454–456
  literature on, 112 n.9, 450
  to monks, 176 n.69
  narrative theology and, 144 n.37
  in North America, 159 n.45, 449–450, 460–465
  reflection and, 457–458
  scholarship on, 112 n.2, 159 n.50, 471–472
  in South Korea, 176 n.69, 466–467
  in Taiwan, 468
  in Thailand, 176 n.69, 465–466
  in United Kingdom, 468–469
  in Vietnam, 466
Buddhist Churches of America, 45–46, 1351–1352, 1989. *See also* Buddhist Mission of North America
Buddhist Compassion Relief Tzu Chi Foundation, 2613, 2617*t*, 2631 n.1. *See also* Tzu Chi
Buddhist Conquest of China (Zürcher), 1192
Buddhist cosmology, 114, 478–480, 486–487, 1886
Buddhist deity cults, 144 n.31
Buddhist fiction, 159 n.50, 237–238
Buddhist figures, 177, 186
Buddhist hell, 1996 n.24
Buddhist Hybrid English, 646
Buddhist Iconography (Loksh Chandra), 443–444
"Buddhistic Training" (Alexander), 1944
Buddhist images. *See* Buddhist relics
"Buddhist Influence on Early Taoism" (Zürcher), 1203–1204
Buddhist inscriptions, 933–934, 946–948, 2560
Buddhist literature, 428–429, 1802 n.35, 1809–1814
Buddhist logic, 1820–1821
A Buddhist Manual of Psychological Ethics of the Fourth Century bc (Rhys Davids, C.), 1939–1940
Buddhist Materiality (Rambelli), 240
Buddhist media
  analog electronic mass media, 2564–2565
  blockprinting for, 2562–2563
  digital media technology, 2565–2566
  four noble truths in, 2572 n.51
  handwritten stage of, 2557–2560
  in India, 2571 n.35
  inscriptions in, 2560
  media theory, 2553–2554
  with movable type, 2563–2564
  oral stage of, 2554–2557
  scholarship on, 2566–2567, 2569 n.11, 2569 n.6
  in Thailand, 2571 n.36
  writing and, 2560–2562, 2570 n.28, 2570 n.20
Buddhist Mission of North America (BMNA), 34–38, 40–43. *See also* Buddhist Churches of America
Buddhist modernism, 863 n.38
Buddhist morality, 595
Buddhist Moral Philosophy (Gowans), 986
Buddhist narratives, 1734–1736
Buddhist path, 116–118
Buddhist Peace Fellowship, 904, 910, 922–923
Buddhist philosophy
  integration and, 533–539
  scholarship on, 527–529
  tradition of, 529–533, 539–540
Buddhist Philosophy from 350 to 600 A.D., 1837
Buddhist Philosophy from 600 to 750 A.D., 1837
"A Buddhist Prayer Against Sickness" (Veith and Minami), 311
Buddhist Prophet Nichiren (Petzold), 1774
Buddhist psychology, 358–359
Buddhist relics
  affinity narratives and, 1722–1725
  authority narratives and, 1731–1734
  Buddhist narratives and, 1734–1736
  glorification narratives and, 1727–1731
  history of, 1719–1721
  prediction narratives and, 1725–1727
  scholarship on, 1736–1738
Buddhist Revival in China (Welch), 2294–2295
Buddhist Sculpture in Clay (Luczanits), 443–444
Buddhists in Canada (Boisvert), 417
Buddhist sites, 69–72, 1798*f*, 1800*t*
Buddhist soteriology, 2540
Buddhist studies, 239–240, 1015
Buddhist Tantra. *See* Mahāyāna Buddhist tantra

"The Buddhist Tantric Medicine in the *Kālacakratantra*" (Wallace), 260–261
Buddhist texts, 632, 811, 821–823, 1028, 2660
Buddhist Thought in India (Conze), 1814–1815
"Buddhist Training as an Artificial Catatonia" (Alexander), 1943–1944
Buddhist universities, 160 n.59
Buddhist wall paintings
  in Central Asia, 551–555
  Dunhuang art and, 555–560
  scholarship on, 542–543
Buddhist wizards
  in Burma/Myanmar, 564–567, 587–589, 601
  dhāt and, 225 n.83
  esoteric congregations with, 112 n.17, 159 n.53, 225 n.88, 595–598, 601
  to government, 601
  initiation of, 191 n.79
  as lived religion, 567–574
  prosperity Buddhism and, 601–602
  scholarship on, 112 n.2, 574–580, 584–585, 599–600, 602–604
  siddhis and, 144 n.35
  social status of, 593–595
  soteriology and, 584–585, 589–591
  taxonomies for, 591–593
  in Tibetan Buddhism, 585–586
Buddhist Yoga (Cleary), 2464
Buddho-Shinto relations, 340–341
Budge, Stephanie L., 1119, 1122
Budhila (teacher), 938
Budo Bala Sena (BBS), 1099, 1104
Bue, Erberto Lo, 443–444
Bugault, Guy, 1466
Bühler, Georg, 936–937, 948
Builders of the Third Civilization (Dator), 2226
Building a Religious Empire (Sullivan), 1068–1069
A Bull of a Man (Powers), 1993
Bunker, Emma, 1800 n.2, 1897, 1919, 1920*f*, 1927
Bunnag, Jane, 2665
Burke, Peter, 328
Burma/Myanmar
  Anglo-Burmese War, 599, 1048–1049
  authority in, 2560
  Buddha images in, 74
  Buddhism in, 1728–1729, 1952, 2716–2717
  Buddhist wizards in, 564–567, 587–589, 601
  Burmese vicissitudes, 1048–1049
  Ceylon and, 1100
  colonialism and, 112 n.7, 500, 591–592, 1571–1572, 1892
  COVID-19 in, 1885–1886
  culture of, 968, 1732, 1986
  East India and, 1280–1281
  England and, 589, 599, 1095–1097
  exclusionary practices in, 159 n.50
  history of, 2405–2406
  Islam in, 907, 919, 922, 1099
  language in, 112 n.1, 567–574
  modernity in, 2063–2064
  Mon kingdom in, 2405
  nats cults in, 343–344
  politics in, 571–572, 907
  Pyu kingdom in, 2403
  rebellion in, 225 n.90, 225 n.97
  religion in, 890–891
  scholarship on, 1884, 1891–1892
  Sri Lanka and, 76–77, 1100, 2236, 2292–2293
  Thailand and, 70, 1579, 1729–1730, 2068–2070, 2265–2266, 2404–2407, 2560
  Theravāda Buddhism in, 2417
Burmese Grammar (Judson, A.), 1048
Burmese Supernaturalism (Spiro), 1890–1891
Burnouf, Eugene. *See also* Western Buddhism
  for Buddhism, 113 n.23, 181, 1939
  classifications from, 2412–2413
  influences of, 875, 1505–1506
  Jesuit missionaries and, 878–881
  on religion, 864–865
  scholarship from, 881–882, 1076, 1081, 2709–2711, 2715
  translations by, 872–873, 1464, 1814
Burns, Susan, 310–311
Burton, Antoinette, 1103
Burton, David, 1698
Buryat Buddhism, 1469 n.8, 1600, 1603, 1608–1609, 1611
Bush, Eugene, 1990
Bush, George W., 2240
Bu-ston rin-chen-grub, 25
Buswell, Robert E., Jr., 503, 1027–1028, 1815
Butler, Judith, 1981, 1992. *See also* Queer Theory
Butön, 1444
Butön Rinchendrup, 1469 n.19, 1634, 2748–2749
Butters, Albion M., 1446–1447
Bya 'Chad kha ba, 1403
Byang chub 'od, 1398–1399
Bya yul ba Gzhon nu 'od, 1401
"Byō" (Demiéville), 213–214, 310

Cabezón, José Ignacio, 628–629, 1068–1069, 1993–1994
Cable Act, 13 n.5
Cadge, Wendy, 2243
Cage, John, 723–724
Caine, Kwai Chang, 398–399

Caine-Barret, Myokei, 912
caitya pillars, 1801 n.5, 1897–1899, 1908–1909, 1919–1923, 1926
Cakkavattisīhanāda Sutta, 888
Cakravāla, 479
cakravartin (universal ruler), 1279
Cakrin, Raudra, 2497
calculation exercises, 1713–1714
California, 802, 1008, 1012–1014, 1351–1353
calm (*samatha, śamatha*), 509–514, 518–520
Calm-and-Unhurried Hermitage (Wansong), 666
Cāmadevīvaṃsa, 1722, 1729
Cambodia. *See also* colonialism; Khmer Esoteric Buddhism
  Angkor National Museum in, 1919–1923, 1922*f*
  Angkor Wat in, 84
  Australia and, 1102
  China and, 2234
  culture of, 906–907, 1051–1053, 2236–2237
  demographics of, 2232
  historical documents from, 1802 n.29, 1802 n.47
  history of, 967, 1897, 1927
  Java and, 962
  Jayavarman VII in, 1519–1520
  Khmer Rouge regime in, 906–907, 1052–1053, 1101, 2233, 2237
  Laos and, 1096, 1100–1101, 1884, 2231–2232, 2235–2236, 2238–2239, 2242–2243, 2564
  monks in, 1114
  nationalism in, 378
  National Museum of Cambodia Phnom Penh, 1916, 1917*f*
  nuns in, 1102
  orthodoxy in, 963
  politics in, 2237
  refugees from, 1115–1116
  Siamese influences on, 161 n.63
  temples in, 1887
  Thailand and, 2214, 2406
  Theravāda Buddhism in, 2417–2418
  U.S., and, 2239
  Vietnam and, 2235, 2311
Cambodian Buddhism in the United States (Mortland), 2243
Cambyses II (emperor), 871
Cam domains, 1526–1527
Campbell, Heidi, 2567
Campbell, John R. B., 628–629
Campbell, Patricia, 231
Campbell, Robert Chodo, 453
Campbell, W. L., 2469
Campergue, Cecile, 894
Campo, Daniela, 2665–2666, 2735–2736
Cam Prajñāpāramitā, 1911
Canada
  Australia and, 1116
  Buddhist institutions in, 410–412
  Chinese Buddhist diaspora in, 412–413, 415–416
  Chinese Consolidated Benevolent Association in, 409
  Chinese religions in, 408–410, 417–418
  England and, 1112
  Fo Guang Shan in, 412
  Humanistic Buddhism in, 413–415
  immigration in, 112 n.5
  Japanese Buddhism in, 1353
  Jodo Shinshu Buddhist Temples of Canada, 1353
  Laos and, 1115–1116
  refugees in, 2235–2236
  scholarship on, 417, 2243
  temples in, 1115–1116
  Tzu Chi in, 413–414
  U.S., and, 36, 112 n.6, 112 n.8
  Vietnam and, 2239–2241
Candrabhānu (king), 1520
Candragarbha. *See* Atiśa Dīpaṃkaraśrījñāna
Candragupta II, 944
Candrakīrti
  ascension of, 626–627
  on bodhisattvas, 1810
  commentary from, 1464–1465
  on existence, 1691
  Gelukpa and, 1062
  on hypostatization, 1458
  in India, 626–627
  literary ambitions of, 615–616
  Longchenpa and, 1445
  on Madhyamaka Buddhism, 616–620, 1462–1463
  on "Mind-Only" Buddhism, 620–621
  Nāgārjuna and, 1467, 1488
  Prāsaṅgika and, 623–626
  Śāntarakṣita and, 1463
  scholarship and, 627–629, 630 n.6, 1460, 1485–1486
  in Tibetan Buddhism, 627
  on *timira*, 630 n.2
  translations of, 1462
  valid cognition to, 630 n.5
  on the world, 622–623
cannabis sativa, 1449 n.23
cannibalism, 1471 n.52
canons, early Buddhist manuscripts and, 634–637
Cantonese, 2392 n.52
Cantwell, Cathy, 821–823, 2481, 2641–2642, 2651
Cao Guangshun, 675–676
Caoqi Dashi zhuan, 1229–1230, 1237–1238
Cao Yijin, 787
Cao Yuanzhong, 787, 808
capitalism, 601–602, 888, 897, 920–921
Capra, Frank, 398
Carakasaṃhitā, 260–261

Carbine, Jason A., 2415, 2417
caregivers, 256–257
Carey, Felix, 1048
Carey, William, 1048
Cariyāpiṭaka, 1366–1367, 1372, 1807
Carpani, Melchiorre, 1048
Carpenter, Amber, 861 n.7, 1465
Cartelli, Mary Anne, 821–823
Carus, Paul, 702–703, 714, 716–717, 721, 1308, 1941, 1945–1946
Cārvāka school, 617
Casablanca (film), 405–406
Casanova, José, 2128
Casas, Roger, 1577
caste system, 181, 907–908
"Catalog and Revised Texts" (Baums), 949–950
Catalogue of All the Divisions of Dhāraṇī (Amoghavajra), 56–57
Catalogue of the Ancient Principalities, 813
catalogues, 819–821, 825
Catechism of the Christian Faith (Valignano), 866, 870
Cathechism of Religion (Judson, A. H.), 1049–1050
Catholicism, 181, 466, 708–709, 865–870, 2435
Catubhāṇavāra, 1883
Catuhśatakaśastra (Aryadeva), 1498
catuṣkoṭi (tetralemma), 536–537
Caucasian Buddhists, 1311–1312
causal efficacy, 1826, 1835–1836
causality, doctrine of, 2115–2118
Cave of Tidal Sounds, 1867–1868
caves. See *specific caves*
cave shrines, 713 n.27, 781–784
The Caves of Dunhuang (Whitfield, S.), 800
Cave Temples of Dunhuang (Getty Center), 802
Cave Temples of Mogao at Dunhuang (Whitfield, R.), 800
CCP. *See* Chinese Communist Party
Cecen Khan, 1377
celibacy, 1588–1589, 1983
Central Asia. See also *specific countries*
  Buddhist wall paintings in, 551–555
  China and, 1288, 2660–2663, 2674–2675
  collections from, 818–819
  homa in, 1202–1203
  India and, 2312
  Iran and, 939
  Khotanese-language materials from, 808–809, 820–821
  medicine in, 2532
  missionaries in, 85
  reincarnation system in, 2007–2008
  Silk Road in, 496
  Tibetan Buddhism in, 1038
  Tibet and, 1501–1505
  Xuanzang in, 1291
Central Intelligence Agency (CIA), 2232, 2440
The Central Philosophy of Buddhism (Murti), 1464–1465
central pillar caves, 781, 782*f*
Central Tibetan Administration, 1384
Cen Xuelü, 2725, 2729–2731, 2737
The Ceremonies and Religious Customs of the Various Nations of the World (Picart and Bernard, J. F.), 868–869, 871, 873
Cerensodnom, Dalantai, 1657–1658
Certeau, Michel de, 179
"Cetanā" (Karunaratna), 1336
Cetanā and the Dynamics of Volition in Theravāda Buddhism (Devdas), 1335–1336
Ceylon, 1096–1100. *See also* colonialism; Sri Lanka
Chabi, 1633–1634
'Chad kha ba Ye shes rdo rje, 1400–1401
Chagna Pandita, 1626, 1630
Chakesadhātuvaṃsa, 1722
Chak Lotsāwa Chöjepal, 1873
Chakna Dorje, 1625
Chakri dynasty, 2063–2064
Chaktung, 1549
Champasangta, 2498–2499
Chan Buddhism
  canonical texts in, 676
  Chan compendia, 667–670
  Chan records and, 674–675
  in China, 2072
  communism and, 2731–2733
  Confucianism and, 2279
  to Dharma Realm Buddhist Association, 1987
  discourse in, 2278–2279
  expressions in, 631 n.9, 674, 684 n.96
  Huineng and, 1238
  Humanistic Buddhism and, 2290–2291
  in Japan, 645
  Kamalaśīla on, 685–686
  mantras in, 2726
  meditation in, 1623–1624
  monks in, 1869–1871
  orthodox, 2368–2369
  Pure Land Buddhism and, 2733–2734
  scholarship and, 63, 93
  Shengyen for, 2160–2163, 2171 n.44
  Shingon Buddhism and, 2180–2181
  in Song dynasty, 664–665
  Taixu on, 2290–2291, 2298 n.9
  texts, 325–326
  tradition in, 2730
  in U.S., 2160–2163, 2170 n.38
  in Vietnam, 1987
  Xuyun in, 2733–2735
  Zen Buddhism and, 1027–1028, 2161

Chan Canon/Chan zang (Zongmi), 667–669
chandasi, 159 n.43
chanding, 2700 n.16
Chandler, Jeannine, 1146–1147
Chandler, Stuart, 1017, 1222
Chandra, Lokesh, 969
Chang, Garma C. C., 1490
Ch'angan, 1724–1725
Changchun Qiu Chuji, 1624–1627
Changjin, 2154
Changkya Rölpé dorjé, 1066–1067, 1380
Changkya rölpé dorjé yéshé tenpé drönmé, 1380
Changlu Zongze, 2662
Chang Shana, 796
Chang Shuhong, 796
Chang Yen, 2291
Chan literature
  Chan records and, 674–675
  compendia in, 646, 667–670
  flame-of-the-lamp records in, 656–661
  glossary for, 674
  letters in, 646, 671–672
  poetry in, 645, 661–664
  pretend dialogues in, 646, 672–673
  scholarship on, 645–656, 675–676, 684 n.97
  silence-and-illumination inscriptions in, 652–656
  in standards-with-comments collections, 664–667
  translations of, 683 n.88
  yulu genre in, 631 n.7, 645, 647–656
Chan Master Dufeng Shan of Tianzhen's Essential Sayings (Dufeng Benshan), 655–656
Chan Prolegomenon (Zongmi), 667–669, 674–675
chanting, 771–774, 1772–1773, 1881, 1883–1884
chanting manuals, 2678
chanting rituals, 776
Chanyuan qing gui, 2662
Chao Hui, 1086
Chao-Hwei, 1987, 1992
Chao Yuanfang, 211
Chapa Chökyi Sengé, 627, 732, 735–737, 744
chaplains, 449–450, 459–470. *See also* Buddhist chaplaincy
Chapman, John, 2447–2448
Charisma and Compassion (Huang), 2626
charismatic attainments, 2066
Charles V (king), 867
Charleux, Isabelle, 1615
Chart of the Doctrinal Points in Tiantai, 807
Châu, Thích Minh, 2440
Châu, Thích Tâm, 2438
Chavannes, Édouard, 823–824, 1468 n.3, 1527
Chayet, Anne, 443–444
chayik guidelines, 2664–2665, 2671 n.37
Cheah, Joseph, 1118–1119, 1122
Cheje zangton shigpo, 2527–2528
Ch'en, Kenneth, 993–994, 1192
Chen Duxiu, 2288
Chengguan (monk), 1867
Chengguang, 1235–1236, 1238
Chengxiu, J., 1387
Cheng Yen. *See* Shih
Chen Huijian, 2625
Chen Kuan, 2382, 2388
Chen Lüan, 1011
Chen Ming, 213
Chen Shui-bian, 1011
Chenxing Han, 1122
Chen Yan, 212
Chen Yinke, 213
Chen Yuan, 819
Chesheng, 1137, 1139–1140, 2371–2373, 2376, 2388
Chia, Jack Meng-Tat, 1222
Chiang Kai-shek, 2169 n.18, 2280–2281, 2728
CHIBS. *See* Chung-Hwa Institute of Buddhist Studies
Chicago Buddhist Temple, 1352–1353
Chidatsu, 2205
Chihō, 2205
Chikō, 2207
Childers, Robert C., 1814
Childress, James F., 165–167
Chimpuma Catalogue, 2579
China. See also *specific topics*
  Amoghavajra in, 2363–2364
  Aśoka in, 2071
  authority in, 2065–2066
  Avalokiteśvara in, 85–93
  bodhisattvas in, 85–93
  Buddhism in, 1667–1668, 2062–2063
  Buddhist Association of China, 1248–1249, 1258–1259, 1261–1262
  Buddhist Association of the Republic of China, 1017
  Buddhist biographies in, 182–183
  Cambodia and, 2234
  cannibalism in, 1471 n.52
  Central Asia and, 1288, 2660–2663, 2674–2675
  Chan Buddhism in, 2072
  China Institute, 796, 802
  Chinese Communist Party, 2154–2155
  Christianity in, 1074, 1437
  communism in, 25, 909, 1014, 1219, 1231, 1600–1601, 2008, 2650–2651, 2728, 2730–2731
  Communist Land Reform campaign in, 2725
  Confucianism in, 377–378, 993–994, 1436
  Cultural Revolution, 138, 424, 893, 1084, 1488–1489, 1576, 1718 n.35, 1745, 1873–1874
  culture of, 1002*t*, 1579, 2152–2153, 2664–2666
  Dalai Lama and, 2023–2024

Daoism in, 2314
Daoxuan in, 2665–2666
Datong in, 2294
Dharma transmissions in, 2734–2735
dynasties in, 1622–1628
Esoteric Buddhism in, 53–57, 2177
etiology in, 212–213
Europe and, 1039–1041
filial piety in, 1006
geopolitics of, 2160
government of, 1605, 1868–1869
healing in, 203–205, 213–215
hermits in, 69–70
history of, 354–357, 1181–1183, 1191
Hsing Yun in, 1218–1222
Huineng in, 1230
Humanistic Buddhism in, 1249–1253, 1258–1259, 1451 n.64
illness in, 204
imaging Buddha in, 1301 n.70
immigration from, 1012–1014, 1078
India and, 9–10, 54, 225 n.98, 1181–1182, 1368, 2663
Indonesia and, 54
influences from, 882
Islam in, 1860–1861, 1871–1873
Japan and, 4–5, 68, 83–84, 713 n.10, 751–752, 864–865, 1132, 1445–1446, 1768–1769, 2065, 2342–2343, 2728
Jueding pini jing in, 2705 n.105
Kagyu tradition in, 1939–1940
Korea and, 77, 645, 1348, 1709, 2667
Kūkai in, 2187
Laos and, 1574
Ling Gesar in, 2492
Madhyamaka Buddhism in, 1455–1456, 1470 n.33
Mahāyāna Buddhism in, 1078, 1445, 2174–2175
Maitreya cult in, 1191
Mañjuśrī in, 1501–1505
Mantra School Bright Lineage in, 2369
manuscripts in, 2559
after Mao, 1258–1259
Maoism in, 2731–2732, 2734–2735
medieval, 208
modern, 1873–1875
monasteries in, 2064–2065, 2726, 2732
Mongolia and, 1141, 1379, 1383–1384, 1592–1593, 1645–1656, 2563
mountains in, 1869–1871
Naikan in, 1709–1710
nationalism in, 2168 n.13, 2169 n.18
National Library of China, 815, 818–820
Northern Dipper homa in, 1203–1204
nuns in, 1102–1103, 1436–1437
One Belt, One Road initiative in, 795
ophthalmology in, 211–212
ordination in, 2068
Pali Buddhism and, 637
philosophy in, 1195 n.2
pilgrimage in, 792–795, 876, 1860–1864, 1873–1875
poetry from, 674–675
politics in, 2731–2733
print culture in, 144 n.37, 144 n.39, 319–328
printing in, 1038
Puguang from, 5–6
Qing dynasty in, 2280
reform in, 1079–1080, 2284, 2294–2295
relics from, 57–58
religion in, 1261–1262, 1861, 2369–2382
royalty in, 1038–1039
Russia and, 1383, 1605–1607
sacred places in, 1866–1868
Saichō and, 2343–2345
Śākyamuni in, 483
scholarship from, 675–676
secular Buddhism in, 2280–2281
Shengyen in, 2169 n.21
Shiji jing in, 482
Shingon Buddhism in, 2177
Siam and, 871–872
Sino Esoteric Buddhism Association in, 2384
Sino-Japanese War, 2152–2153, 2170 n.26
Soka Gakkai in, 2213
Song dynasty in, 2077
Southeast Asia and, 1299 n.31
Sri Lanka and, 2277–2278
Taisho Canon in, 1630
Taiwan and, 64, 1013–1014, 1219–1220, 1260, 1438–1439, 1443–1444, 2155–2157
Taixu in, 2127, 2154–2155
Tang Dynasty in, 2096
Tantric Buddhism in, 1135–1140
tantric revival in, 2363–2369, 2384–2388
temples in, 1869–1871
Thailand and, 1576, 2069
Tibetan Buddhism in, 5, 12, 61, 63, 1084, 1143
Tibet and, 112 n.5, 138, 1067–1068, 1092 n.53, 1132–1133, 1461–1462, 1591–1592, 1610
T'ien T'ai Buddhism in, 2224
tradition in, 2294, 2312
translations from, 3–4, 10
U.S., and, 1013
vinayas in, 2658
vinaya texts in, 1865
Yuan dynasty and, 1639–1646
Zen Buddhism and, 716–717, 724
Zhenyan school in, 963

Chinese Buddhism
apocryphal texts in, 1004–1005
communities with, 1077–1078
debt payments in, 1003–1004
filial piety in, 993–996
Han, 2163, 2165
Huineng in, 1231–1233
interpretations of, 1003, 1579
Mahāyāna Buddhism and, 2291
parables in, 993–994, 1005–1006
pilgrimage in, 1869–1871
scholarly refutations and, 999–1002
scholarship on, 996, 1006, 1866
sutras in, 996–999
in Taiwan, 2160, 2164–2165
to Taixu, 2292
Taixu and, 1076–1077
Theravāda Buddhism and, 998
Udayana and, 1724–1725, 1727
Chinese Buddhist diaspora, 412–413, 415–416
Chinese Buddhist Electronic Text Association, 328
Chinese Buddhist Learning (Taixu), 2290–2291
Chinese collections, 818
Chinese Communist Party (CCP), 2154
Chinese Consolidated Benevolent Association, 409
Chinese Exclusion Act, 1078–1079
Chinese-language materials, 806–807, 819–820
Chinese languages, 1963, 1978 n.31, 2208–2209, 2393 n.70
Chinese Magical Medicine (Strickmann), 296–297, 310
Chinese medicine, 211–213
Chinese Pacific Railway, 409–410
Chinese pilgrims, 1291
Chinese Poetry and Prophecy (Strickmann), 2056
"The Chinese Reception of Indian Medicine" (Unschuld), 213
Chinese religions, 408–410, 417–418
Chinese Socialist Party, 2280
Chinggis Khan
Eurasia and, 1640
in history, 1377, 1638, 1656–1657, 2019
legacy of, 1641, 1646
Möngke Khan and, 1637
Mongolian Buddhism and, 1469 n.15, 1622–1628
nationalism and, 1584
Qubilai Khan and, 1640
reputation of, 1636, 1641
Ching Zorigt Chin Wang Lama Badmadorj, 1606–1607
Chin Kung, 1084–1085
Chisan Kangaku-kai, 758
Chishō Daishi. *See* Enchin
Chisō, 305–306
Chisong Milin, 2154–2155
Chiterpa, 1542
Chitsū, 2205
Chiyū, 2205
Chizan lineage, 2356
Chö (Tenga Rinpoche), 695–696
Cho, Francisca, 232–234, 240, 400–401, 404–406
Chöd
commentary on, 691–692
Dukngel Zhijé and, 685–686
early development of, 690–691
eight practice lineages, 685
"gods and demons" in, 692
history of, 684–685
Jamgön Kongtrul Lodrö Tayé and, 685–687, 695–696
Machik Lapdröns and, 687–690
in modernity, 694
music in, 692, 694
rituals of, 691–694
scholarship on, 694–696
semantics in, 686–687
sources of, 686–694
in Tibetan Buddhism, 692
wisdom in, 687
"Chod" (Khenchen Thrangu Rinpoché), 695–696
The Chöd Practice (Tsering Wangdu Rinpoche), 695–696
Chödrak Gyatso, 1485, 2746–2747
Chödrak Zangpo, 1441–1443, 1447
Chödrön, Pema, 1999 n.75
Chödrub Gyatso, 2017–2018
Ch'oe Ch'iwŏn, 1230–1231
Choephel, David Karma, 4
Chōgaku, 2186
Chōgen, 290, 2185
Chögyal Pakpa, 731, 2013–2015
Chögyam Trungpa
global Buddhism and, 1082, 1087
scholarship and, 1144, 1553, 1950, 2021–2022, 2469, 2480, 2497
Chogyur Dechen Lingpa, 1970–1971
Choibalsan, Khorloogiin, 1613
Chöje Drukpa. *See* Tsangpa Gyare
Chōkaku, 2186–2187
Chokhor Gyatso, 1164–1165
Chöki Zangpo, 1470 n.39
Chokle Namgyal, 2745–2746, 2748–2749
Chokro Lügyeltsen, 2455–2459, 2464
Chokrolui Gyaltsen, 2476
Chökyi Dawa, 688
Chökyi Gyaltsen, 1064–1065, 2021

Chökyi gyelpo, 1376
Chökyi Gyeltsen, 1382, 2012
Chökyi Lodrö, 1542
Chongyuan, 1227–1228
Choompolpaisal, Phibul, 963–964, 1579
Chosgi odsir, 1635, 1657–1658
Chos rgyal 'phags pa blo gros rgyal mtshan, 1503–1504
Chou Yi-lang, 60
Chöwang, 1549–1550, 1553
Chöying Dorje, 839, 2015–2016, 2746
Choyin Rangdrol, 923
Chōzen, Paulo, 866
Chpār Rānsi, 1803 n.73, 1906–1907
Christianity. *See also* Protestant Christianity
  in Asia, 2294–2295
  Buddhism and, 722, 1594, 1648–1649
  Catholicism and, 865
  in China, 1074, 1437
  Christian art, 425
  Christian hymns, 226
  Christian literature, 452, 458
  Christian normativity, 2713–2715
  clergy in, 456
  colonialism and, 1183, 2711–2713
  Confucianism and, 1040–1041
  cosmology to, 485
  culture of, 1114
  Eastern philosophy and, 2479
  in Europe, 896, 1072 n.9, 1074
  evangelical, 456–457
  fundamentalist, 1148–1149, 1151
  God in, 455–456
  Islam and, 236, 1104, 1650
  in Japan, 35
  to Japanese Americans, 15 n.25, 46
  Judaism and, 159 n.45, 916–917, 1673–1674
  in Korea, 466, 1709
  lay, 567
  LGBTIQ+ in, 1986–1987
  liberal Protestant thought, 2127–2128
  medieval Christian nuns, 187
  in Middle East, 1668–1669
  missionaries for, 370–371, 373–374, 376, 865–870, 919, 1075–1077, 1136–1137, 1589–1590
  in Mongolia, 1593
  non-heritage Buddhism and, 1122
  proselytizing in, 1046
  Protestant, 1086–1087, 1890, 2710–2711
  protestant religious culture, 2137–2138
  Pure Land Buddhism and, 719
  relics in, 67
  religion to, 194
  science and, 485
  in Siam, 1100
  sin in, 2129
  in South America, 1355
  in South Korea, 466
  texts from, 812
  theology of, 1211
  tradition in, 453
  in U.S., 1311–1312, 1349, 1351–1352
  YMCA, 1075–1076
  Zen meditation and, 1081
  Zorastrianism and, 1672–1673
"Christianity as Model and Analogue in the Formation of 'Humanistic' Buddhism of Tai Xu and Hsing Yun" (Yu-Shuang and Gombrich), 1222
Chronicle of Padmasambhava (Ogyan Lingpa), 1746–1748
Chronicles of Japan, 292–293
Chronicles of Profound Fierce Mantra, 2638
Chronicles of the Copper Palace (Hirschberg), 2025
A Chronological Biography of Master Sheng Yen (Lin Qixian), 2166
The Chronology of Ancient Nations (al-Bīrūnī), 1679
Chuanfa, 656–658
Chuanxin fayao, 1218 n.83
Chuanyin, 2734–2735
Chūgoku bukkyō shi (Shigeo), 1192
Chuk Mor, 1078
Chulalongkorn Rama V (king), 1049–1050, 1883–1884, 2564
Chung-Hwa Institute of Buddhist Studies (CHIBS), 2162–2163
Chungyalpa, Dekila, 911
Chuogenglu (Tao Zongyi), 1657–1658
Chuon Nath, 1052–1053
Chushan Shaoqi, 670
Chu Shih-Hsing, 2557
Chuttiwongs, Nanadana, 84, 1925–1926
Chūzan, 2048–2049
CIA. *See* Central Intelligence Agency
CIA World Factbook, 2232, 2234
Cicuzza, Claudio, 1891–1892
Cihang, 1247–1248, 1250–1253, 1256, 1260
Cinema Nirvana (Sluyter), 400–401, 405–406
Cirebon shipwreck, 1524
citizenship, 13 n.5, 16 n.38, 176 n.69, 462–463
Citrakarmaśāstra, 2267
City of Ten Thousand Buddhas, 2735
civic engagement, 1257–1258
Cixi (emperor), 2020

Clark, Barry, 2534
Clark, John, 1698–1699
Clarke, Shayne, 1578–1579, 1994
Clart, Philip, 2567
Classic of Go, 814
Classic of the Conversion of the Barbarians, 812
Classic of the Mountains and Seas, 1861–1862
classification of tenets, 2463–2464
Clayton, Barbara, 986
Clear Ascertainment of the Three Vows, 1482–1483
clear comprehension, 1300 n.48
Clear Words (*Prasannapadā*), 615–618, 622–623, 627–628, 630 n.6, 1460
Cleary, J. C., 1238–1239, 2464
Cleaves, F. W., 1656–1658
clerical training, 2037
Clifford, Terry, 2534
climate change, 912
Clinebell, Howard, 451, 455–456
Clinical Buddhist Chaplaincy, 468
clinical pastoral education, 454–455, 461
Clippard, Seth Devere, 361–363
cloning, 112 n.2, 169–170. *See also* bioethics
Coblin, W. South, 2586
Code of Gentoo Laws (Halhed), 873
Code of Kami Law, 2200–2201
Coderey, Celine, 579–580
codified forms, 1276
Cœdès, George, 74, 587, 1050–1051, 1527, 1903
coexistent causes (*sahabhu hetu*), 2116
cognition (*saṃjñā*), 6, 575, 1831–1832, 1834–1836, 2111
cognitive behavioral therapy, 1952
cognitive intention, 1297 n.11, 1331–1333, 1335
Cognitively-Based Compassion Training, 985
Cohen, Leonard, 2480
Cold War, 575, 1073, 1079, 1570–1571, 2071–2072, 2226
Colebrooke, Henry Thomas, 875
Collected Annotations on the Classic of Materia Medica (Tao Hongjing), 213
Collected Tantras of the Ancients of the Tshamdrak Monastery, 841
Collected Tantras of the Nyingma, 833–834, 841, 1966
Collected Tantras of Vairocana, 833, 841
Collected Works (Rangjung Dorjé), 2026
Collected Works (Taixu), 2289–2290
Collected Writitngs on Shin Buddhism (D. T. Suzuki), 725
Collection of Hymns, 2744
Collection of Nyingma Tantras, 2475–2478
Collection of Precious Glories, 813
Collection of Records concerning the Tripitaka (Jiaojing), 5–6
collective contemplation, 2685
Collett, Alice, 185
Collins, Randall, 892
Collins, Steven, 576–578, 603–604, 1022–1023, 1371, 2407–2410
colonialism
  anti-colonialism, 923
  in Asia, 1074–1075
  Buddhism in, 367–369, 382–386
  Burma/Myanmar and, 112 n.7, 500, 591–592, 1571–1572, 1892
  Christianity and, 1183, 2711–2713
  colonial archaeology, 375
  colonial scholarship, 1032
  decolonization, 922–923
  England in, 369–375, 1096, 1886–1887, 2309
  France in, 375–378, 1040–1041, 1051–1052, 1100–1101, 1890
  global Buddhism in, 1075–1077
  global Theravāda Buddhism and, 1096–1104
  GMD and, 1445
  history of, 191 n.78, 1117
  Islam in, 159 n.55
  Japan and, 378–382, 1230–1231
  Lopez on, 864
  modernity and, 112 n.16, 113 n.20
  monks in, 225 n.83
  nationalism and, 916
  Osterhammel on, 112 n.7
  political imaginary in, 598–600
  postcolonial studies, 864
  psychology of, 113 n.21
  reincarnation system and, 2022–2023
  scholarship on, 377
  Seven Year's War and, 872
  in Sri Lanka, 1045–1047
  in Taiwan, 1252–1253, 1437
  translations in, 873–875
  Western, 501–503
Come, Come, Come Upward (film), 403–404
"Coming of Islam" (Azad and Kennedy), 1469 n.26
Coming to Terms with Chinese Buddhism (Sharf), 2678
Comintern. *See* Soviet Union
Commentary on the Meaning of the Bodhisattva Precepts (Guanding), 1003
commercialized Buddhisms, 234–235
commodities, 895
communal ethical action, 2287
communication studies, 2569 n.6
communism. See also *specific topics*
  CCP, 2154
  Chan Buddhism and, 2731–2733
  in China, 25, 909, 1014, 1219, 1231, 1600–1601, 2008, 2650–2651, 2728, 2730–2731
  Communist Land Reform campaign, 2725

geopolitics of, 1606–1611
in Hong Kong, 2734–2735
on Jebtsundambas, 1386
Leninism and, 1609, 1611–1612
politics of, 1873–1874, 2729
in Southeast Asia, 2233
in Vietnam, 190 n.71, 906–907
to Western imperialism, 192
Como, Michael, 294–295
Comparative Philosophy and the Philosophy of Scholarship (Tuck), 628–629, 1464
comparisons, in images, 326–328, 1281–1282
compassion, 113 n.19, 167, 452–454, 862 n.16, 985, 1990. See also *specific topics*
Compassionate Relief Organization, 2166–2167
compendia, 646, 667–670
Compendium of Chronicles (al-Din), 1636
Compendium of the Perfections (Āryaśūra), 1810
Compendium of the Principles of All the Tathāgatas, 1473
Compendium of the Teachings of Mani, 812
Compendium of the Topics of Abhidhamma (Anuruddha), 253–254
Complete Works of Master Taixu, 2613–2614
conative intention, 1297 n.11, 1323, 1331–1333, 1335
conceit (*māna*), 7–8
concentration, 509–514
Conception of Buddhist Nirvana (Shtcherbatsky), 1464–1465
"The Concept of the Ultimate" (Powers), 2464
conceptual construction, 1830
conceptualization, 1991
Le Concile de Lhasa, 821
Concu, Martino Dibeltulo. *See* Dibeltulo Concu, Martino
Condensed Sleeping Meditation for (Beholding) Amitābha (Jamyang Khyentse Chökyi Lodrö), 1966
conditioned factors (*cittavipra-yukta*), 6
conditioning factors (*saṅkhāra*), 1324–1326
Cone, Margaret, 1814–1815
conflict, 1678–1681
Confluences of Medicine in Medieval Japan (Shōzen), 310–311
Confucianism
Buddhism and, 747, 751
Chan Buddhism and, 2279
in China, 377–378, 993–994, 1436
Christianity and, 1040–1041
Confucian literature, 1039–1040
Daoism and, 999, 1001, 1190, 2208–2209
Datong in, 2286
filial piety and, 994–996, 1003
global Buddhism and, 1080–1081
history of, 748–751
Huineng and, 1238
Humanistic Buddhism and, 2294–2295
ideology of, 2288
in Japan, 751–753, 759, 777, 1762, 2202–2203
Marxism and, 1444
monasteries and, 2066
in Mongolia, 1631
mountains in, 1871
neo-Confucianism, 92–93, 267, 675–676, 2055
philosophy of, 701, 1260
pilgrimage in, 1871
politics and, 753–756
scholarship and, 85, 758
Sekitan rituals in, 748–749, 751–752, 759
to Taixu, 2288
tradition in, 2290
utopia in, 2279
Xiaojing in, 999–1000, 1002
Confucius, 999–1000
conjoined causes, 2116
connotations, 2265–2266
consciousness (*vijñāna*), 6, 519–520, 2028 n.19
consecration, 2305
consecration ceremonies, 2268
Consequences of Compassion (Goodman), 171–172
consequent action, 1342 n.116
consequentialism, 171–172, 981–983, 2077–2078, 2088–2089
constituting sanghas, 2066–2070
constitution (*bca' yig*), 2671 n.37
"Constructing American Buddhism" (Pierce), 1314
La construction de la sainteté dans la Chine moderne (Campo), 2736
constructive motivation, 2133–2134
constructivism, 1344 n.156
contemplation. *See also* visualization/contemplation sutras
of Avalokiteśvara bodhisattva, 2686–2687
of the bodily marks of the Buddha, 2686
of the Buddha Image, 2685–2686
collective, 2685
contemplative education, 2150 n.80
of the ground, 2684
guan and, 2674–2677, 2699 n.6
of the jeweled trees, 2685
of the Lotus Throne, 2685
of Mahāsthāmaprāpta bodhisattva, 2687
meditation and, 506–508, 522–523
mixed, 2687
of the nine grades of rebirth, 2687–2688
of one's own birth in the land of utmost bliss, 2687
of the ponds, 2685
in Pure Land Buddhism, 2684
repentance and, 2701 n.33
of the sun, 2684
of the water, 2684

Contemplation Sutra, 1354–1355
contemplative science, 984–985
contemporary art, 795–796
contemporary Asia, 1570–1580
Contemporary Buddhism (Crosby), 1121–1122
contemporary Buddhist ethics, 984–985
contestation, of tantra, 1148–1149
contests, 2545
conventional Buddhism, 618
Conze, Edward, 29–30, 1814–1815, 1897, 1899–1901, 1926–1927
Coomaraswamy, Ananda K., 1294, 2262
Cooper, David E., 1698–1699
Cooper, Paul, 1955–1956
Copp, Paul, 62–63, 821–823
coppersmiths, 434, 435*f*, 441
Corless, Roger, 1993–1994
Cornelio, Jayeel S., 2627
Cornu, Philippe, 2469–2470
Correct Dharma-Eye (Dahui), 666–667
Correct Dharma-Eye Depository (Dahui), 660
Cort, John E., 1201–1202
cosmology
  Buddhist, 114, 478–480, 486–487, 1886
  cosmic systems, 861 n.8, 1428–1431
  Cosmic Vairocana, 483
  cosmological time, 660
  in East Asia, 482–484
  of guardian/protector deities, 1158–1160
  in Hinduism, 481
  history of, 480–486
  in India, 480, 693
  Kālacakra, 2745–2746
  in Mahāyāna Buddhism, 482–484, 1038–1039
  Śākyamuni and, 112 n.4
  scholarship on, 481–482, 487
  secular Buddhism and, 2149 n.59
  in Southeast Asia, 484–485
  in Thailand, 486
  in Tibet, 486–487
  in Vajrayāna Buddhism, 484, 486
  Vasubandhu on, 6–7, 481–482, 484
  in Western science, 485–486
cosmopolitan Buddhism, 968, 1308–1309
court Buddhism, 497
Court Buddhism, 2198–2199
court debates, 730–731
Cousins, Lance, 963–964, 969–970, 1031, 1033, 2426 n.16
COVID-19
  Bodhi College during, 2139
  in Burma/Myanmar, 1885–1886
  SARS and, 2619
  tourism during, 192
  Tzu Chi during, 2620, 2628
  virtual communities during, 2138
Cowell, E. B., 1814
Cox, Collett, 3, 5–6, 639
Cox, Harvey, 2713–2715
Cozort, Daniel, 986
Crane, Cornelius, 707–708
craving, 887, 2087
creativity, 766–767, 1301 n.72
cremation ceremonies, 122–123, 2474–2475
CRISPR/Cas, 170
"Critical Investigation of Percepts" (Dignāga), 1833–1834, 1836
critical race theory, 930 n.120
"A Critical Study of the Guhyasamāja Tantra" (Fremantle), 1491
critical theory (CT), 1981
A Critique of Western Buddhism (Wallis), 2131–2132
Crosby, Kate
  Bizot and, 963–964
  scholarship from, 144 n.30, 959, 1104–1105, 1121–1122, 1891
  on tradition, 964, 967, 969–970
cross-cultural studies, 861 n.11
Crosson, J. Brent, 2128
Crowley, Aleister, 2314
Cruz v. Beto, 464
The Crystal Mirror of Philosophical Systems (Tukwan Lobzang Chökyi Nyima), 2749–2750
Csoma de Körös, Alexander, 1814
Csordas, Thomas J., 1131, 1150
CT. *See* critical theory
Cuba, 1088, 1357–1358
The Cuckoo of Awareness, 832–833, 841
Cuevas, Bryan, 2480
Cula-Maluṃkyovada Sutta, 1023–1024
Cūlavaṃsa, 144, 146, 153
Cullavagga X, 1101, 1105
Cullen, Christopher, 823–824
culminating insight, 22
"Cultivating an Appropriate Response" (Kinst), 455–456
cult objects, 2262–2263
Cult of Emptiness (App), 867
cult of Gesar, 2494–2495, 2497–2499
cult of traces, 66–68
cults
  Bha Bha Min group, 224 n.82
  Bön tradition and, 344

Buddhist deity, 144 n.31
cult objects, 2262–2263
cult of Gesar, 2494–2495, 2497–2499
cult of traces, 66–68
deities and, 1172–1173
devotional *weizzā*, 112 n.17, 601–602
esoteric congregations and, 595–598
Indo-European fire, 1199–1200, 1207
Kami, 332–341
local, 334–338, 341–345
Mahākāla as, 1631–1632
Maitreya cult, 1191
nats, 343–344
savior, 1514–1515
Schopen on, 2506
Tārā cult, 1203
Zhenwu cult, 1863–1864
cultural appropriation, 113 n.23
A Cultural History of Tibet (Snellgrove and Richardson), 1068–1069
Cultural Revolution, China. *See* China
Cunin, Olivier, 1927
Cunningham, Alexander, 70, 948–949, 1783
The Cup (film), 401
curatorship, 1051–1053
Curators of Buddha (Lopez), 864
Cutler, Joshua, 1815
Cutting-Off, 672–673
Cyrus the Great, 1637

Dacheng bensheng xindi guan jing, 997, 1003–1004
daemons, 1071 n.4
Dahui, 716
Dahui yulu (Dahui), 651–652
Dahui Zonggao, 184, 651–652, 660, 666–667, 671–672
Daigan Matsunaga, 1774
Daigo (emperor), 2184
Dai Hanqing, 2153–2154
Daijo. *See* Mahāyāna Buddhism
Daijō kishinron, 716–717. See also *Awakening of Faith*
daily chants, 771–773, 1073
Daily Life in the Assembly, 2662
daimandara (great mandala), 1769–1770
daimoku, 1762–1763, 1765–1773
Dainichi, 2352, 2359
Dai Nihon Bukkyō zensho, 759–760
Daishi-kō, 1351
Daishō, Tana, 37
Đại Việt sử ký toàn thư, 1039–1040
Daizong (emperor), 54–55, 57–60
Dajian. *See* Huineng
Dakmema, 1549–1550
Dakpo Kagyü. *See* Gampopa Sonam Rinchen
Dakpo Lharjé. *See* Gampopa Sonam Rinchen
Daktsang Sherap Rinchen, 2463
Dalai Lama. See also *specific Lamas*
authority of, 1742, 1748–1749
belief in, 85
China and, 2023–2024
exile of, 2008, 2021–2022
Gelukpa and, 1065–1068
gender and, 2027 n.5
in globalization, 1148–1149
goddesses and, 1750
Hanh and, 1022
history of, 1072 n.9, 1137–1140, 2014–2015, 2032 n.88, 2065–2066
Mind and Life Institute from, 1951–1952
Mind-Life Institute by, 1110 n.96
in modernity, 2022–2023
Mongolia and, 1376, 1384
Nechung monastery and, 1754–1755
oracles and, 1717 n.22, 1746–1748
prestige of, 2015–2017, 2020–2021
protests against, 1147–1148
Qing dynasty and, 2017–2018
scholarship on, 2028 n.8
sexual abuse by, 2022–2023
in Thailand, 1073
in Tibet, 94, 1132
in World War II, 1079–1080
The Dalai Lama and the Emperor of China (Schwieger), 1068–1069
The Dalai Lama and the Nechung Oracle (Bell, Christopher), 1173–1174, 1755
D'Alembert, Jean le Rond, 871–872, 875
Dalit Buddhism, 914–915, 923, 1053
Dalit rights, 907–908
Dalton, Jacob, 820, 1208, 2481, 2641–2642
Damdinsüren, Ts., 1386
Dampa Ritröpa, 132
Dampa Sangyé, 685–689
Dampa Sönam Gyaltsen, 1437–1438
Damrong Rajanubhab (prince), 74–75, 1050–1051
dana, 2130
Da Nang Museum, 1804 n.88
dānapāramitā, 1811
DANCE. *See* Dharma Action Network for Climate Engagement
dancers, 546*f*, 547
Daṇḍapāṇi, 121
Daṇḍin, 1552

Dante, 1642
Daoan (Dao'an), 1187–1188, 2284
Daodejing, 703, 716–717, 812
Daoism
  Buddhism and, 268–269, 993–994, 1184–1185, 1189
  in China, 2314
  Confucianism and, 999, 1001, 1190, 2208–2209
  Daoist Canon, 322–323
  in East Asia, 278
  Esoteric Buddhism and, 64, 1204–1205
  healing in, 209–210
  history of, 320
  immortality in, 91–92
  mountains in, 1861–1864
  Neo-Daoism, 1184
  pilgrimage for, 1861–1864
  printing and, 319–320
  qigong and, 1231
  rituals in, 2164
  scholarship on, 2168
  Shinto and, 2313, 2340
  in Taiwan, 2166–2167
  tradition in, 269
Daosheng, 1187
Daoshi, 210, 997–998
Daosui, 2326–2327
Daoxuan, 208, 210, 497–498, 2660–2661, 2665–2666
Daoyi, 57
Daoyuan, 1240
Daozhen (monk), 798
Daozhen, Nie, 2696–2697
Dargyay, Geshe Lobsang, 628–629
The Dark Red Amulet, 2650–2651
Dark Side (*nakchok*), 2487–2489
Darlington, Susan, 362–363
Darma Dodé, 2010
Darma Senge Sangye Wonre, 853–857, 854*f*, 859, 2594
Dārṣṭāntika-Sautrāntika doctrines, 2097, 2117–2118
Darwa Paṇḍita Agwangchoijurdondubbalsang, 1609
Daśabhūmika sūtra, 1810
Das National-Epos der Tibeter gling König Ge sar (Hermanns), 2500
Dāṭhāvaṃsa, 1722, 1729
dathu, 14 n.8
Datong, 2286, 2294
Dator, James, 2226
daurmanasya (mental pain), 2083–2084
David-Neel, Alexandra, 694–695, 2499, 2502 n.23
Davidson, Richie, 1951–1952
Davidson, Ronald, 969, 1201–1202, 1212–1213, 1515–1516, 2024
Davis, Gordon, 2078
Daxing, 909
Dayal, Har, 1506, 1814, 2088
Dayan Khan, Batu-möngke, 1641–1642, 1644–1645, 1647
Dayi, 1233–1234
Dayong, 1136
day yoga, 2546
Dazhi du lun, 1187
DBT. *See* Dialectical Behavior Therapy
death
  of Dongchu Denglang, 2162
  karma and, 2102–2103
  of Kūkai, 2347
  of Longchenpa, 1448 n.1
  mindfulness of, 518
  of Nāropā, 1547
  poetry at, 654
  post-death experiences, 2544–2545
  rebirth and, 2080
  of Saichō, 2345–2346
  of Taixu, 1437–1438
  in *Tibetan Book of the Dead*, 2470–2471
  of Toda, 2213
  of Tsangpa Gyare, 2595, 2612 n.39
Debate in Tibetan Buddhism (Perdue), 744
debates
  court, 730–731
  debate language, 735–737
  discourse in, 735–737
  doctrinal, 2050–2051
  education from, 743
  format of, 713 n.15, 740–743, 751–753
  group, 742
  in Japan, 747–751, 759
  monasteries and, 730–733, 737–738
  on Nikāyas, 1325–1326
  Ōwa debate, 754, 2047–2049
  as performance tradition, 756–758
  politicization of, 753–756
  Ryōgen in, 754, 2046–2049
  Samyé debate, 730
  scholarship on, 729–730, 743–745, 758–759
  scholastic, 738–740
  in Tibetan Buddhism, 729–730, 733–735
  topics for, 738–740
Deb ther dmar pa (Tshal pa Kun dg' rdo rje), 1657–1658
debt payments, 1003–1004
DeCaroli, Robert, 341–342, 1174
deception, 2545
Dechen Lingpa, 136–137
De Christiana expeditione apud Sinas (Ricci), 870
decillion, 1468 n.4
decision making, 2542–2543

Decleer, Hubert, 1553
decolonization, 922–923
deconstruction, 1992
deductive logic, 1821
Deeds of the Buddha, 120–122
Deeg, Max, 876, 1528
deep ecology, 357–358
Deep Times (Macy), 923
Deer Park period, 2463
Deguchi, Yasuo, 1466, 1699
Deguchi Tetsujyo, 2171 n.41
deities. *See also* guardian/protector deities
  Buddhist deity cults, 144 n.31
  cults and, 1172–1173
  healing, 208–210
  history of, 1274, 1902
  identity and, 1211
  in *kālacakra-maṇḍala*, 1418–1422
  in Khmer empire, 1923, 1924*f*
  in Khmer Esoteric Buddhism, 1801 n.15
  local, 341–344
  lokapala, 2247–2248
  lokottara (hypercosmic), 1159, 1167
  meditation and, 1424
  100 peaceful and wrathful, 2476–2478
  100 peaceful and wrathful deities, 2476–2478
  Padmasambhava and, 1159–1160, 1163
  plague, 292–298
  scholarship on, 1899–1901
  in Shinto, 336–337
  Śiva, 1163–1164
  in tantra, 1207
  in Tantric Buddhism, 1911, 1913*f*
  in Tibetan Buddhism, 1072 n.10, 1158–1160
  of worship, 1427–1428
Dekanduwala Bhikkhuni Training Centre, 1104
De La Vallée Poussin, Louis
  on Candrakīrti, 627–629
  on four noble truths, 1032–1033
  Lévi and, 29–30
  scholarship and, 4, 10, 1814, 2122 n.16
  Tibetan Buddhist manuscripts from, 820
Delek Gyatso, 1441
Deleo, Kristin, 454
Deleuze, Gilles, 1982
Delhey, Martin, 101, 1469 n.13
deliberation, 2104–2105
delog tradition, 2471, 2473
DeMartino, Richard, 707–708
Demiéville, Paul, 213–214, 224 n.82, 279, 310, 675–676, 821–823
democracy
  in Mongolia, 1582–1591
  Mongolian Buddhism and, 1591–1593
  politics of, 1593–1594
  religion and, 1593
  revolution and, 1582–1584
  socialism and, 1583–1584
Democracy According to the Buddhist Viewpoint (Emyō), 1305
Democracy's Dharma (Madsen), 1017
Demonic Divine (Linrothe), 1173–1174
demons. *See also* guardian/protector deities
  daemons and, 1071 n.4
  devil and, 691–692
  evil and, 2637–2638
  final age and, 296–298
  gods and, 692
  māra and, 2645
  philosophy of, 1158–1159
  scholarship on, 2641
  in Sri Lanka, 1167
  in Vajrayāna Buddhism, 2492
Deng Xiaoping, 1258
Dengyō Daishi, 2334
Denkarma Catalogue, 1963
Denmark, 1087
deontic elements, 2078
Department of Justice, U.S. (DOJ), 14 n.18, 38–39
Department of Public Instruction, 1306
Departures (film), 232, 403–404
dependent origination, 113 n.18
depression, 1714
Deqing. *See* Xuyun
Derrida, Jacques, 1982
De Silva, Padmasiri, 895–896
Désong, 2576–2577
Despeux, Catherine, 213, 823–824
Dessein, Bart, 3, 5–6
Dessì, Ugo, 1357
destruction, 2647–2648
Devadatta, 1365
Deva Khaḍga, 1794
Devānampiyatissa (king), 1095, 1732–1733
Devapāla (king), 947, 1786, 1791–1792, 1796
Devapāladēva (king), 1784
Devā Sutta, 995
Devdas, Nalini
  Buddhaghosa and, 1332
  on *cetanā*, 1301 n.62, 1344 n.146
  commentary from, 1326
  on creativity, 1301 n.72
  Heim and, 1335–1336, 1343 n.120, 1344 n.152
  scholarship and, 1299 n.31
  Sthiramati and, 1319

"The Development of Gcod Tradition" (Gyatso), 695
"The Development of the Pure Land Doctrine in Buddhism" (D. T. Suzuki), 719–720
deviant logic, 536–537
DeVido, Elise, 2439, 2447–2448, 2626–2627
devil (*māra*), 690–692, 1164, 2645
Devī Māhātmya, 1166–1167
Dézhin Shekpa, 1966, 2014
Dezong (emperor), 1230
Dge lugs pa, 1396
Dgon pa ba, 1401
Dgon pa pa Dbang phyug rgyal mtshan, 1397
Dhammacakkappavattana Sutta, 1021–1022, 1883
Dhammacetī (king), 343–344
Dhammagavesi, Ven. Pandita M., 1815
Dhammakaya monks, 895
Dhammapada, 2556
Dhammapāla, 1325
Dhammasami, Khammai, 1579
Dhammasaṅgaṇi, 1940–1941
Dhamma Walks, 361
Dhanasaṃskṛta, 2640–2641
Dhanavatī (nun), 937–938
dhāraṇī, 320–322, 947, 947*f*, 2505–2507, 2509–2512. *See also* power objects
Dhāraṇī for the Protection of All Children, 270
Dhāraṇī of the Heart of Ārya-Aparimitāyurjñāna, 1801 n.3, 1964, 2637
Dhāraṇī Sutra of the Thousand-Armed and Thousand-Eyed, 276
dharma. See *specific topics*
Dharma Action Network for Climate Engagement (DANCE), 912
Dharma Bums (Kerouac), 723–724
Dharmacakrapravartana Sutra, 1021–1022
dharma chronicles, 845–847, 862 n.28
Dharma Collection of Master Xuyun (Cen Xuelü), 2737
Dharma Drum Mountain, 2163–2165, 2621, 2625, 2627–2628
"Dharma Exemplified" (Po to ba Rin chen gsal), 1402
Dharma Gaia (Badiner), 362
Dharmaguptaka tradition, 151, 2667
Dharmaguptakavinaya, 1020–1021
Dharma-Jewel Platform Sutra (Fahai), 1224
Dharmakīrti
  Dignāga and, 535–536, 731–735, 1802 n.29, 1819–1828, 1836–1838
  epistemology of, 1462–1463, 1800 n.2, 1828–1836
  idealism of, 1801 n.7
  philosophy of, 537–538
  on rebirth, 1801 n.19
  scholarship and, 23–24, 529–530, 1499–1500, 1525, 1801 n.6
  Seng Chao and, 533
  studies with, 1518
Dharmakīrti II, 2414–2415, 2419–2420
Dharmakṣema, 99–100
Dharma Matters (Willis), 2719
Dharmamitra, 23–24, 2690–2691
The Dharma of Star Wars (Bortolin), 400–401, 405–406
Dharmapāla (king), 1526, 1790–1791
Dharmapala, Anagarika
  on globalization, 195, 916, 1075–1077, 1086–1087
  reputation of, 383–384
  scholarship and, 374, 1098–1099, 1148, 1787, 2256
  on secularism, 2127–2129
Dharma Rain (Kaza and Kraft), 362
Dharmarakṣa, 998–999
Dharmarakṣita, 938
Dharma Realm Buddhist Association, 412, 1987
Dharmaruci, 1519
dharmas, 2101–2106
Dharmasaṅgani lists, 1298 n.18
Dharmasaṅgīti Sūtra, 1812
Dharmāśoka (king), 1726
Dharmasvāmin, 1786–1787
Dharma transmissions, 2734–2735
Dharmatrāta, 2108
Dharmayaśas, 1518–1519, 1521–1522
Dharmmadatta, 1796
Dharmodgata, 115–116, 498–499
dharmology, 1991–1993
Dharmottara, 1830
dhāt, 225 n.83
Dhātus, 2102*t*
Dhātuvaṃsa, 1722, 1729
Dhonden, Yeshi, 2535
Dhvanvatari, 247
dhyāna (meditation), 2085–2087. *See also* meditation
diagnoses, etiology and, 268–270
diagnoses, in Tibetan medicine, 2531–2532
Dialectical Behavior Therapy (DBT), 1952
dialetheist interpretations, 1466
Dialogues of the Buddha (Rhys Davids, T. W.), 125
(great mandala) *diamandara*, 1769–1770
Diamond, Debra, 2317
Diamond Mountains, 498–499
Diamond Sutra
  history of, 321–322
  Huineng and, 1234–1235
  Lotus Sutra and, 815, 2562
  media and, 2553

Nirvana Sutra and, 1235
origins of, 816
Platform Sutra and, 1234–1235
scholarship on, 1234–1235, 1899–1900
diaspora
of Asians, 470
Buddhisms in, 408–415, 417–418
Chinese Buddhist, 412–413, 415–416
ethnicity and, 1359 n.2
immigration and, 1348–1351, 1359 n.7
Japanese Buddhisms in, 1347–1348
in Latin America, 1353–1355, 1357–1358
migration and, 1351–1353
new religious movements and, 1355–1356
religion in, 1347–1348
research and, 1356–1358
South Asia, 2311
in Tibet, 501
Dibeltulo Concu, Martino, 864, 879–880, 1135–1136, 1150
Dick, Roland, 1708–1709
dictionaries, 814
The Dictionary of Pastoral Care and Counseling, 450
Diderot, Denis, 871–873, 875
Diệm, Ngô Đình, 2436–2438
Diemberger, Hildegard, 2025
dietary treatments, 250
dietetics, 207–208
Difficult Points of Scriptures in General (Mirapa), 1562
Digambara tradition, 1202
digestive problems, 250
Dīgha Nikāya, 250, 253–255, 481, 2556–2557
digital materials, 12
digital media technology, 2565–2566
Dignāga
Dharmakīrti and, 535–536, 731–735, 1802 n.29, 1819–1828, 1836–1838
epistemology of, 623, 1828–1836
influences of, 623–625
philosophy of, 533, 625–626
scholarship on, 10, 621, 1499–1500, 1802 n.30
Vasubandhu and, 529–530
Dignāga Investigation of the Percept, 1838
Dignāga on the Interpretation of Signs (Hayes, R.), 1837
dignity, 159 n.54
dikpala tradition, 2249
Dillon, Michael, 1989–1990
al-Din, Rashid, 1636, 1657–1658
al-Din 'Ata Malik Juvaini ("Ala"), 1657–1658
Ding Fubao, 1236
Dīpaṃkaraśrījñāna. *See* Atiśa Dīpaṃkaraśrījñāna
Dīpaṃkara Śrījñāna, 731
Dīpavaṃsa, 147–148, 2394–2395, 2397–2400, 2409, 2411–2412
direct experience, 2140, 2541–2542
Dīrghāgama texts, 633–636
disciples
of Amida Buddha, 871–872
Ānanda and, 1498
bhikkhunī, 2623–2624, 2626–2627
of Buddha, 544*f*, 545–546
to Dölpopa, 2745–2746
of Kūkai, 2345, 2349
Malunkyaputta, 400
of Marpa Lotsawa, 1545–1546, 1550–1551
of Nāropā, 1542–1544
of Padmasambhava, 1436–1437
of Saichō, 2338 n.4, 2345–2350
scholarship and, 936, 1384–1385
of Taixu, 1136
disciplinary codes, 2063
Discourse Explaining the Thought, 102, 123–124, 2456–2465. *See also* three wheels of doctrine
Discourse of the Lion's Roar of Queen Śrīmālā, 2462
Discourse on Lamas, 2018
Discourse on the Eight Commands (Mipam), 1563
"Discourse on the Physical Characteristics," 117
"Discourse to Cankī," 116
"Discourse to Rohitassa," 125
Discourse Turning the Wheel of Doctrine. *See* three wheels of doctrine
discrimination, 1079
disease, 204–205, 210–211, 254, 270
"The Disease, the Cause, the Cure, the Medicine" (Gethin), 1023–1024
disengaged Buddhists, 920
disloyalty, 960–961
Dispeller of Objections (Nāgārjuna), 1455–1456
dissonance, 741–742
Distinction Between the Two Truths (Jñānagarbha), 1467
Distinguishing the Views (Gorampa), 1463, 2748–2749
diversity, 506–507, 1119, 1983–1987, 1991–1992
Divina Commedia (Dante), 1642
divination, 2542–2543
divine compassion, 2255
Divine Farmer's Classic of Materia Medica, 213
Divine Spell of the White-Robed Great Being, 86
Dixian, 1437, 2283
Dizang, 89–91
Dizang pusa benyuan jing, 999
Độ, Thích Quảng, 2442
doctrinal classification, 2291–2292

doctrinal debates, 2050–2051
doctrinal knowledge, 2175–2176
doctrinal studies, 2262
doctrinal themes, 2642–2643, 2655 n.19
doctrine, 601
La doctrine de Nichiren (Renondeau), 1774
"The Doctrine of Prajñāpāramitā" (Obermiller), 29–30
doctrines (*nitārtha*), 1–2
Documentation of Mongolian Monasteries (Teleki and Majer), 1594
Dodrupchen Jigme Tenpa Nyima, 1968
Dog-duty Ascetic sutta, 1326
Dōgen
  legacy of, 2565
  scholarship on, 268, 716, 751, 1236, 1774, 2055
  Shinran and, 2325, 2335, 2341
Dogsomyn Bodoo, 1608
Dohākośa, 1551–1552
Dōhan, 2186–2187
DOJ. *See* Department of Justice
Dokai, 2329
Dōkyō, 2202
Dolce, Lucia, 1774, 2336, 2358–2359
Dölpopa Shérab Gyeltsen
  as holy, 2749
  influences of, 2745–2746
  Longchenpa and, 1445
  scholarship on, 627–629, 1484, 1966, 1968, 2750 (*See also* zhentong)
  on sixfold yoga, 2749
  vision of, 2746–2747
Ḍombhipa, 1397
domestic Dharma
  in daily life, 767–768
  family and, 764, 776–777
  healing with, 773–776
  home altars for, 770–773, 772*f*
  in Japan, 764–766
  Mahāyāna Buddhism and, 766
  in modernity, 777–778
  protection practices with, 769–770
  in Pure Land Buddhism, 777
  rituals and, 766–767
  scholarship on, 778–779
donations, of images, 1796–1797
Dondogdulam (mistress), 1382
Döndrup Zangpo, 688. *See also* Machik Lapdrön
Doney, Lewis, 2586–2587
Dong Bang Sang, 408–409
Dongchu Denglang
  death of, 2162
  Dongshan Liangjie and, 2171 n.46
  Lingyuan and, 2161–2162
  scholarship and, 1438
  Shengyen and, 2158, 2170 n.35, 2171 n.40, 2171 n.46
  Taixu and, 2154–2155, 2158
  as teacher, 2158–2159
Đông Dương, 1526–1527
Dongshan Liangjie, 2171 n.46
Dong tribal lineage, 2491
Dongyang Dehui, 2663
Donjing Menhua Lu (Men Yuanliao), 1005–1006
Donnelly, Paul, 1873
donor communities, 784–788
donor monks, 936
donors, in inscriptions, 935, 938
Dönyö Dorje, 1064
Dorje, Gyurme, 2641–2642
Dorje, Wangchuk, 4
Dorje Dechen Lingpa, 1970–1971
Dorje Drakden. *See* Pehar
Dorjee, Penpa, 1068–1069
Dorje Lekpa, 1167–1171, 1173
Dorje Lingpa Senge Sherab, 2594
Dorje Pagmo, 1439–1441
Dorje Shugden, 1146–1148, 1151, 2020–2022
Dorjiev, Agvan, 1604
Dorji Wangchuk, 1442–1443, 1446, 2481
Dorsey, Roshi Issan, 1989
Dor-ta Darqan, 1625
Doryu, Kitabatake, 2711–2712
Dorzhiev, Agvan, 2529
doṣa, 205–207
Dōshō, 2204–2205
Dotson, Brandon, 823–824
Dott, Brian, 1864
"Double Headed Mongolian Buddhism" (Jadamba), 1595
doubt (*vicikitsā*), 7–8
Douglas, Mary, 229, 231
Douglas, Nik, 2314
Dowager Cixi (empress), 85
Down syndrome, 164–165
Dōzen-bō, 1760–1761
draftee films, 404–405
Dragonetti, Carmen, 1466–1467
Dragpa Gyaltsen, 1146, 2015
Dragpa Özer, 1440–1441
Dragpa Senge, 1441
Dragpa Sengge, 2012
Dragpa Tenpa Yarpel, 2022
Drakpa Lingdrak, 2585

Drala Töpa (Mipham), 2496
Drala Tsegyal, 2502 n.9
Drandul Norbu Nyingtig (Mipham), 2497
Drapa Ngönshechen, 688
"Dreadful Mystic Banquet" (David-Neel), 694–695
dreams, 620–621
Drège, Jean-Pierre, 824
Dreitlein, Thomas, 2339 n.25
Dremowa, 856
Drenka Pelgyiyönten, 2578
Dressler, Markus, 1571–1572
Dreyfus, Georges, 628–629, 744, 1068–1069, 1146, 1580, 1837
Drigum Tsenpo, 2489–2490
Drigung Lotsāwa Maṇikaśrījñāna, 2748–2749
Drikung Lotsāwa Maṇikaśrījñāna, 2745–2746
Drime Özer. *See* Longchenpa
Drogön Chögyel Pakpa Lodrö gyeltsen. *See* 'Phags pa lama
Droit, Roger-Pol, 864–865, 881
Drokmi Lotsāwa, 1538, 1542, 1552–1553
Dromtön Gyelwa Jungné, 1436–1437, 2010–2011
Dromtönpa, 1479
Drop of Mahāmudrā, 1474
Drott, Edward, 279, 285
Drowa Zangmo, 2011–2012
Drugom Yungdrung, 836
drugs, 1449 n.23, 1709
Drugyelwa, 2549
Dru Gyelwa Yungdrung, 132
Druk Desi, 2019
Drukmo (queen), 2490
Druk Monastery, 852–854, 857–858, 2602, 2606
Drukpa Kagyü school
  abbots in, 2610 n.1
  Darma Senge Sangye Wonre and, 853–856
  dharma chronicles and, 862 n.28
  at Druk Monastery, 2602, 2605*f*
  hagiography of, 845–847
  history of, 857–858, 2593–2594, 2597–2606
  Lingre Kagyü school and, 846–850
  Ling Repa Pema Dorje and, 850–851
  monasteries for, 2612 n.38
  Ralung monastery and, 2600–2602, 2606
  scholarship on, 858–859
  in Tibet, 862 n.17
  Tsangpa Gyare and, 851–853, 856–857, 861 n.5, 863 n.37, 2592–2593, 2606–2607
Drukpa Kunley, 845
Druk Yul. *See* Bhutan
D. T. Suzuki. *See* Suzuki Daisetsu Teitarō
Du'a, 1637
Đức, Thích Quảng, 2436
Ducher, Cécile, 1553
Duckworth, Douglas, 1567, 2088–2089
Ducor, Jérôme, 2696
The Dude and the Zen Master (Sluyter), 400–401
Dudjom, Trinley, 2640
Dudjom Rinpoche, 1988
Dudjom Rinpoche Jikdrel Yeshé Dorjé, 2748
Düdkyi Chöd Yul, 691
Dudül Dorje, 1970–1971
Duerlinger, James, 4
Dufeng Benshan, 655–656
Duff, David, 237
Du Fu, 1863
Dugu Pei, 1227–1229
Dukngel Zhijé (Dampa Sangyé), 685–686
Dulaf, Abū, 1676
Dülzinpa, 1062–1063
Duncan, Carol, 72
Dunhuang art
  for ancestry, 790–792
  architecture and, 713 n.27, 781–784
  Buddhist wall paintings and, 555–560
  donor communities and, 784–788
  historiography of, 796–798
  in modernity, 795–796
  Mount Wutai and, 728 n.35, 792–795
  multiculturalism in, 788–790
  scholarship on, 798–803
  "treaty temple" and, 713 n.26
Dunhuang Mogao ku neirong zonglu, 801
Dunhuang shiku neirong zonglu, 801
Dunhuang texts
  book formats with, 814–815
  from British Library, 816–817
  catalogues, 819–821
  documents, 128
  language in, 806–810
  literature, 796
  manuscripts and, 810–814, 831–833, 2586
  scholarship on, 816–826
  secular documents and, 812–814
  techniques in, 814–816
  in Tibet, 1964–1965
  translations of, 1964–1965
Dunne, John, 1837–1838
Durbodhālokā (Dharmakīrti), 23–24
Durkheim, Emile, 2256
Dushun, 1188, 2207–2208
Düsum Khyenpa Pakmodrupa, 1482, 2007–2008, 2011

Duṭagämunu (king), 1726
Dutch East India Company, 870–871
Dutt, Sukumar, 99, 2072
Duṭṭhagāmaṇi (king), 1099, 1724, 1731–1732
Du Xinfu, 144 n.39
Dy, Aristotle C., 2627
Dyer, Thomas, 462
"The Dynamics of Intention, Freedom and Habituation" (Meyers), 1336
Dza (king), 2582
dze. *See* substance
Dzogchen
  atiyoga and, 834–835
  Bonpo, 144 n.32, 829–831, 835–836, 839–840
  Bön tradition and, 130–135
  in Dunhuang manuscripts, 831–833
  in exile, 137–138
  history of, 829–831
  innovations, 2472
  instruction series for, 836–837
  interpretations of, 2469
  literature, 130–135
  Longchenpa and, 1436, 1445–1446
  meaning of, 130–131
  meditation and, 829–839
  in modernity, 839–840
  monks in, 129–130
  to Nyingma school, 134
  Nyingma tradition and, 128
  patriarchs, 135–137
  perspective, 2478
  philosophy of, 836
  practitioners of, 113 n.19
  principles, 2476–2478
  scholarship on, 840–841
  Seminal Heart texts and, 837–838
  teachings of, 1970–1971, 2475
  in *terma* collections, 838–839
  texts, 831–834
  in Tibet, 835–836, 1141
  Tibetan yoga and, 1144–1146
  tradition, 127–130, 1438–1439, 2481
Dzogtrul Pema Rigdzin, 2502 n.9
Dzongsar Jamyang Khyentse Rinpoche, 1988
Dzongsar Khyentse, 1142–1143, 2023

early Buddhism, 494–495, 889–893
early Buddhist art, 2272 n.18
early Buddhist ethics, 977–979
early Buddhist manuscripts
  canons and, 634–637
  commentary in, 637–639
  in history, 633–634
  miscellaneous texts and, 639
  research on, 632–633
  scholarship from, 639
early modern Europe, 864–875
Early Sino-Tibetan Art (Stoddard), 443–444
Early Temples of Central Tibet (Vitali), 443–444
East Asia. See also *specific countries*
  Buddhist canons of, 59–60
  Buddhists in, 86
  classification of tenets in, 2463–2464
  cosmology in, 482–484
  Daoism in, 278
  East Asian Mahāyāna Buddhism, 1987–1988
  education in, 713 n.10, 1572–1573
  engaged Buddhism in, 909–910
  environmental justice in, 354–357
  Europe and, 1042–1043
  footprints in, 69
  geopolitics of, 378–382
  Greater East Asian Buddhist Conference, 2281
  homa in, 1203–1205
  Madhyamaka Buddhism in, 1461–1462
  Strickmann on, 1212
  Sukhāvatī in, 1978 n.35
  tantra in, 2194 n.1
  Tibetan Buddhism in, 2
  tradition in, 17, 2313
  vinaya texts in, 2660–2663
  Zhenyan school in, 969
Eastern India. See also *specific regions*
  Bangladesh, 1793–1796
  Bihar, 1792–1793, 1798–1800
  Buddhist sites in, 1798*f*, 1800*t*
  culture of, 1789–1790, 1796–1797
  epigraphic mentions of, 1792
  Harikela area of, 1795–1796
  North Bengal, 1791–1792
  Samataṭa area of, 1794–1795
  scholarship on, 1781–1783
  South Bahir, 1788–1789
  territorial rulers of, 1800*t*
  West Bengal, 1792–1793
Eastern Monachism (Hardy), 2713
East India, 1280–1281, 1284–1285
East India Company, 370
Eastman, Elizabeth, 1133–1135, 1151
Eberhardt, Nancy, 1891
Eckel, Malcolm David, 1467
Eckhart, Meister, 722

eco-Buddhism, 359–361. *See also* environmental justice
Ecodharma Center, 913
École Française d'Extrême-Orient (EFEO), 377, 1898–1899
ecology. *See* environmental justice
economics
  of Buddhism, 885 n.62, 887–889, 893–898
  of early Buddhism, 889–893
  economic documents, 812–813
  economic epicenters, 891–893
  economic relations, 887–889
  of Jebtsundambas, 1384–1385
  merit economies, 890–891
  morality and, 895
Eddy, Glenys, 1141
Edelglass, William, 986, 2078
Edelman, Lee, 1992–1993
Eder, Jens, 184
Edgerton, Franklin, 1814
Edmunds, Albert J., 704
Edou, Jérôme, 695
education. See also *specific topics*
  academic, 2138–2139, 2158–2160
  apprentice, 1571
  Association for Clinical Pastoral Education, 461
  for Buddhist chaplaincy, 159 n.54
  clinical pastoral, 454–455, 461
  contemplative, 2150 n.80
  contemporary monastic, 1576–1577
  culture and, 2213, 2220–2222
  from debates, 743
  diversity in, 506–507
  in East Asia, 713 n.10, 1572–1573
  Fo Guang Shan and, 1014–1016
  of four noble truths, 1020–1022
  higher, 160 n.59, 239–240, 463, 702–706, 1015, 1577–1578
  in Hiroshima Prison, 1706
  informal, 2138–2139
  in Japan, 701–702, 751–753, 2215
  Kūkai studies, 2184–2185
  monastic, 737–738, 748–749, 1570–1580, 2283–2284
  Sangha Education Association, 2280
  scholar monks, 750–753, 756–757
  scholastic debates, 738–740
  in secular Buddhism, 2138–2139, 2150 n.80
  in Singapore, 1578
  in socialism, 1612–1613
  teachers, 1116–1117
  technology and, 1014–1016
  in Thailand, 1573
  with Theravāda Buddhism, 2433 n.114
  in Tibet, 1063–1064
  tradition and, 2131–2132
  to Tzu Chi, 2618, 2620
EFEO. *See* École Française d'Extrême-Orient
efficient causes (*kāraṇa hetu*), 2116
effort (*vīrya*), 2085
Efu Chin van Dondovdorji, 1379
Egypt, 367, 370, 870–871
Egyptian Book of the Dead, 2468–2469
Ehyō Tendai-shū (Kūkai), 2331–2332
eighteen elements (*dhātu*), 6
Eighteen Lectures on Dunhuang (Rong), 800, 825
Eightfold path, 507–508
Eimer, Helmut, 1407
Eisai, 268, 2187
Eisei, Imamura Gen'emon, 870–871
Eisenstein, Elizabeth, 1036–1037, 1048–1049
Eison (monk), 290, 1469 n.19
Eizon, 2186
Ekādaśamukhadhāraṇī, 1901
Ekajaṭi, 1167–1171
Eke Dagina, 1382
Ekottarāgama, 995, 997–998
Ekottarikāgama texts, 633–635
Elara (king), 1099
Elbegdorj, Tsakhiagiin, 1384
elder care, 773–776
Elder Gavaṃpati, 1728–1729
Elder Gongga, 1137, 1139–1140, 2366–2369, 2373, 2388
elderly monks, 2066
Eldershaw, Lynn P., 1144
Eliade, Mircea, 1650
Eljigidei, 1637
Ellison, Kosho Paley, 472
Eltschinger, Vincent, 1837
"Elucidation of the Knowable" ('Phags pa), 1630
Elverskog, Johan, 351–352, 1594–1595, 1603, 1615, 1648–1649, 1656–1658, 1677–1678
Elvin, Richard, 356
emanations, 2010–2011
Embodiment of the Guru's Realization (Sangye Lingpa), 838–839
embryology, 207
embryonic Buddhahood, 2462
Emended Commentary on Monastic Practices (Daoxuan), 208
Emeny, Mary, 2440
Emerson, Ralph Waldo, 715, 2710
emic languages, 172
eminent monks, 209–210

Emmerick, Ronald Eric, 820
Emmrich, Christoph, 1044–1045, 2559
Emory University, 985
emotions, 976–977
empathy, 113 n.19, 452–454
Empirical Omniscience, 21
empiricism, 1831, 2141
empowerment, 2175–2176
emptiness
in Abhidharma Buddhism, 1457–1458
compassion and, 862 n.16
descriptions of, 2028 n.11
D. T. Suzuki on, 717–718
existence and, 2087
form and, 395
in *King of Concentrations*, 1472–1473
"Mind-Only" Buddhism and, 668–669
Nāgārjuna on, 623–624, 1688–1689, 1691–1697
philosophy of, 1694–1696
realization of, 979–980
soteriological impact of, 1696–1697
teachings on, 619, 1701 n.8
Tsongkhapa on, 627
writing about, 2561–2562
in zhentong, 2743–2744
Emptiness in the Mind-Only School of Buddhism (Hopkins), 2464–2465
Emyō Imamura, 1303–1313, 1349–1350, 1357
Enchin, 303–304, 1233–1234, 2345–2351
Enchō, 2330, 2345
Encyclopedia of Indian Philosophy (Potter), 628–629, 1837
Encyclopedia of Mongolia and the Mongolian Empire (Atwood), 1386
Encyclopédie (d'Alembert and Diderot), 871–872
ending (*nirodho*), 1026–1027
enemies, 2647–2648
engaged Buddhism
in critical race theory, 930 n.120
in East Asia, 909–910
ethics of, 984
ethnocentric, 921–922
in Europe, 912–913
generational shifts in, 922–923
global, 904–913
Hanh and, 885 n.68, 905, 984, 2443–2446
hermeneutics, 913–916
in international groups, 913
mindfulness in, 920–921
in modernity, 918–919
scholarship on, 904, 916–919
in South Asia, 905–910
in Southeast Asia, 905–907
in Sri Lanka, 905–906, 921
tradition and, 919–920
in U.S., 910–912
Engaged Buddhism (Queen and King, S.), 916
Engendering Faith (Ruch), 2209
England
Anglo-Burmese War, 599, 1048–1049
Buddhism in, 1939
Burma/Myanmar and, 589, 599, 1095–1097
Canada and, 1112
in colonialism, 369–375, 1096, 1886–1887, 2309
empiricism in, 1831
feminism in, 1103
France and, 368–369, 1100
history of, 1104–1105
Pali Text Society in, 1032–1033
Regulating Act in, 873
Russia and, 1604
in Southeast Asia, 225 n.98
Sri Lanka and, 1075–1076
Engle, Adam, 2533–2534
Engler, Jack, 1954
engravings, 1239
enlightenment (*satori*), 340, 429–430, 715–716, 722, 974–975, 1354–1355
Enlightenment by a Single Means (Jackson, D.), 1490
Enni Ben'en, 2187
Ennin
Enchin and, 2345–2346, 2348–2351
Jimon lineage and, 2348
legacy of, 303–304
scholarship and, 1233–1234, 1864–1865, 2047, 2050, 2183–2184
Taimitsu and, 2345–2347
En no Gyōja, 2177
Enomiya-Lassalle, Hugo Makibi, 1081
Enryakuji, 2049–2050, 2053–2054
Entering the Middle Way (Candrakīrti), 1062, 1444
entertainment, 1015–1016
Enter the Void (film), 2480
Entrance to the Middle Way (Candrakīrti), 615–624, 626–628, 1485–1486
Entretiens de Lin-tsi (Demiéville), 675–676
Entsū Fumon, 485
environmental justice, 918, 2618–2619
approaches to, 359–361
in East Asia, 354–357
ethics of, 357–359

in India, 349–352
scholarship on, 361–363
in Tibet, 352–354
to Tzu Chi, 2618–2619
En'yū (emperor), 2053
epidemics, 292–296
epigraphy
Epigraphical Hybrid Sanskrit, 933, 937–938
first Buddhist inscriptions, 933–934
from Gandhāra, 938–943
from Gupta-Vākāṭaka period, 942–946
inscriptions and, 886 n.101, 936–943
inscription types, 932–933
in Khmer Esoteric Buddhism, 1906–1907
late Buddhist inscriptions, 946–948
from Mathurā, 937–938
monasteries and, 1792
from Palola dynasty, 886 n.83
scholarship on, 948–951, 2265
Schopen and, 949–950
scripts, 933
in South Asia, 932
from Śuṅga period, 934–936
Tsukamoto on, 861 n.5
typological survey of, 933–948
from Western Cave complexes, 936–937
epistemology
of Dharmakīrti, 1462–1463, 1800 n.2, 1828–1836
of Dignāga, 623, 1828–1836
in Hetucakraḍamaru, 1821
logic and, 1444, 1819–1824
of Nyingma tradition, 1564
philosophy and, 535–536, 739–740
representationalist, 1831
from Saṃghabhadra, 2110–2111
of Vasubandhu, 1802 n.29
Western, 538–539
Erb, Felix, 627–628
Erdene Shanzodba, 1606–1607
Erhard, Franz-Karl, 1446
Errington, Elizabeth, 941*f*
Esen Taishi, 1640–1641
Eshinni (nun), 93
Esoteric Buddhism. See also *specific topics*
in Asia, 64
Black Sect Esoteric Buddhism, 1138
in China, 53–57, 2177
creation of, 57
culture and, 56–57
Daoism and, 64, 1204–1205
Esoteric Tendai Pure Land practices, 2183
exoteric-esoteric Buddhism, 2208
guan in, 2700 n.21
in India, 63
in Japan, 2332, 2363, 2696
Kūkai and, 2333, 2364
legacy of, 58–60
Liu Benzun and, 64
in modernity, 64
popularity of, 2363
scholarship on, 60–63, 959, 961–962, 969, 1212–1213, 2194 n.1
Shingon Buddhism and, 2173–2175, 2177–2179
Shingon Esoteric Buddhism, 2355–2356
Shinto and, 338–340
in Southeast Asia, 959, 967–969
Tantric Buddhism and, 2340–2351
Tibetan Book of the Dead in, 2478–2479
Esoteric Buddhism in Mediaeval Maritime Asia (Acri), 1528
esoteric congregations, 112 n.17, 159 n.53, 225 n.88, 595–598, 601
esoteric Indian Buddhism, 1500–1501
esoteric *mahāmudrā*, 1477–1478
esoteric rituals, 318 n.113
esoteric scriptures, 1970–1971
Esposito, Monica, 2387–2388
Essays in Zen Buddhism (D. T. Suzuki), 706, 714–715, 725
Essence of Good Explanations Regarding the Interpretable and the Definitive (Tsongkhapa), 2464–2465
The Essence of Japanese Buddhism (Ryūsaku), 1309
The Essence of True Eloquence (Tsongkhapa), 1062
Essence of Zhentong (Mathes), 2751
Essential Formulas Worth a Thousand in Gold for Every Emergency (Sun Simiao), 211
Essential Mind Training (Jinpa), 1407
Essentials of Medicine, 279–280
Essentials of the Eight Schools (Gyōnen), 2198
Essentials of the Revised Rules for Purity for Major Monasteries (Jinhua), 2662
"Essential Trilogy" (Saraha), 1475–1476
Establishing a Pure Land on Earth (Chandler, S.), 1017, 1222
Establishing the Three Vows as Essentially One, 1563
estates (*labrangs*), 2013, 2015, 2021
Estève, Julia, 1897
Eternal Bön. *See* Bön tradition
eternalism, 1694–1695

ethics
action based, 1329
of altruism, 919–920
applied Buddhist, 984–985
applied Buddhist ethics, 984–985
bioethics and, 163–164
in biomedicine, 165–166
in *bodhisattva*, 979–980
of Buddhaghosa, 978–979
Buddhism and, 973–977, 980–986
Buddhist, 171–172, 977–979, 983–985, 1371
of cloning, 169–170
communal ethical action, 2287
of compassion, 862 n.16
of consequentialism, 981–983
contemplative science and, 984–985
contemporary Buddhist, 984–985
contemporary Buddhist ethics, 984–985
of CRISPR/Cas, 170
in cross-cultural studies, 861 n.11
early Buddhist, 977–979
eco-ethicists, 360
of engaged Buddhism, 984
of environmental justice, 357–359
ethical discipline, 2082–2083
ethical self-cultivation, 978–979
ethical theory, 2078
foundational, 915
greed, 359
of Humanistic Buddhism, 2735
in *Intention sutta*, 1329
from introspection, 2082
karma and, 861 n.8, 975–976, 995, 1695–1696, 2103
of Mahāyāna Buddhism, 838, 861 n.10, 979–980, 1403–1404
mercy killing, 171–172
in moral phenomenology, 982–983
in moral psychology, 976–977
in neuroscience, 172
organ donation, 171
of Pali Buddhism, 861 n.2
of particularism, 983–984
of rebirth, 2135
relics and, 1720–1721
religion and, 888
of Śāntideva, 863 n.32
scholarship on, 862 n.12, 977–980
sexual, 980, 1983–1984, 1996 n.24
in suffering, 861 n.7, 974–976
in Theravāda Buddhism, 997
virtue, 981–982
in Western scholarship, 172
Ethics in Early Buddhism (Kalupahana), 986
ethnic Buddhists, 1311–1312
ethnicity, 71–72, 1099, 1116, 1359 n.2, 1891, 2152, 2168 n.1, 2719
ethnic sectarianism, 1308–1313
ethnocentric engaged Buddhism, 921–922
ethnography, 567, 575, 2315–2316, 2518–2519
etiology, 212–213, 253–254, 268–270
eulogies, 933, 1290–1291, 1396, 1966
Eurasian Mythology in the Tibetan Epic of Ge-sar (Hummel), 2500
Europe. *See also* colonialism
Asia and, 73–74, 1941, 2137
Australia and, 1590
Buddhism in, 179, 881–882
China and, 1039–1041
Christianity in, 896, 1072 n.9, 1074
early modern, 864–875
East Asia and, 1042–1043
engaged Buddhism in, 912–913
Eurocentrism, 367
European Buddhist Union, 1986–1987, 1991
European languages, 9–10
European Romanticism, 2710
Goa and, 865
history of, 2712–2713
imperialism and, 1117
India and, 429–430, 874
Indo-European fire cults, 1199–1200, 1207
Indo-European languages, 885 n.56
Kundalini Yoga in, 2314
medieval history in, 177, 180
modernity in, 875–881, 2709
mythology in, 2500
Naikan in, 1709
North America and, 72, 897, 981, 1802 n.35, 2277–2278
printing in, 1036–1037
Protestant Christianity in, 2564
Romanticism in, 721–722
Russia and, 1600, 2534
Śākyamuni Buddha in, 181–182
scholarship and, 881–882, 2707–2708
Swedenborg Society in, 704–705
tourism from, 232
Treaty of Wesphalia in, 1649–1650
U.S., and, 1121, 1361 n.41, 1940, 1945, 2143, 2311
Victorian Buddhism in, 2128, 2708–2709
Western, 367, 1577
Zen Buddhism in, 707
evangelical Christianity, 456–457
Evans-Wentz, W. Y., 694–695, 839, 1945, 2468–2470, 2478–2480. See also *Tibetan Book of the Dead*
Events from Buddha's life, 1285, 1286*f*

evolutionary psychology, 2141–2142
exhibition catalogues, 825
exile, 1764–1767, 2008, 2021–2022
existence, 114, 2471–2473
exogenous disease agents, 296–298
exoteric-esoteric Buddhism, 2208
exoteric-esoteric systems, 2335
exoteric scriptures, 1965–1968
Expansive Explanation of the Superior Discourse Explaining the Thought (Woncheuk), 2464
expedition reports, 826
experiential authority, 2140
Expilly, Giuseppe, 1048
Explanation of the Intent of Uttaratantra (Remdawa), 2748–2749
"Explanation of the Path to Knowledge/Wisdom" (Ledi Sayadaw), 592–593
Explanation of the Superior Discourse Explaining the Thought (Chokro Lügyeltsen), 2464
Explanatory Tantra, 2528
Explication of Terms, 1864
Explication of Written Characters, 1864
Exposition of Benevolence (Tan Sitong), 2279
Exposition of the World (Vasubandhu), 2471–2472
The Expositor, 1328
Extensive period, 2463
Extensive Sport, 117–118, 121
Extinction Rebel Buddhists, 912
extracanonical Buddhist literature, 324–326
extremism, 1694
eyes, 2540–2541

Fabao, 10
The Faces of Buddhism in America, Bloom in, 1357
Facheng, 2096
factors (*dhātu-nirdeśa*), 5
faculties (*indriya*), 5–6
FAD. *See* Fine Arts Department
Fafang, 909, 1251, 1259
Fahai, 1224, 1236
faith, 231, 1606–1607, 2103
Falcone, Jessica, 2566
Faliang, 781
Falk, Harry, 949–952, 1294, 2567
family
 adaptability and, 778
 of Amitābha, 1968–1969, 1968*t*
 domestic Dharma and, 764, 776–777
 family caves, 787
 in Japan, 764–765
 karma, 777
 Khan, 1639–1646
 Khön, 1479–1480
 of Marpa Lotsawa Chökyi Lodrö, 1469 n.24
 registers, 812–813
 Tamanaha, 38
 of Xuanzang, 2176
 Zhang, 2152
family council (*ikkeshū*), 2037–2038, 2041–2042
Fan Chengda, 1869
Fanwang jing, 1002–1003, 2661–2662, 2665–2666
Fanyang Lu, 1232–1233
Farris, William Wayne, 293, 296
Faure, Bernard
 on Buddhist figures, 177, 186
 scholarship from, 301–302, 724, 821–823, 1238–1239, 1982, 1993, 2208–2209
Fausbøll, Viggo, 1814
Faxian
 legacy of, 84, 876, 1187, 1505–1506
 scholarship on, 1516–1519, 1522–1523, 1727, 1865
Fayuan Zhulin (Daoshi), 997–998
Fazang, 1003, 2207–2208
Fazun, 1136
The Fearless Lion's Roar (Khenpo Lodrö Drakpa), 2747–2748
Feeding Your Demons (Allione), 694
feelings (*vedanā*), 6
Feer, Léon, 1032–1033
Feichtinger, Christian, 232
Feixi, 53–54
feminism, 914–915, 930 n.120, 1103, 1294, 1982, 1989
Feniger, Siegmund, 1952–1953
Fenollosa, Ernest, 75
Ferguson, John, 579–580, 587–588
Fernandez, Marilyn, 46
fertility, 271
fiction, 159 n.50, 237–238
Fields of Merit Fomulae (Kitano), 273
Fifteen Year War, 381
50 Years on the Bodhisattva Path (Pan Xuan), 2625
The Fifty Stanzas on the Guru (Gurupañcāśikā), 2306
The Fifty Verse Poem (Āryadeva the Brahmin), 686
Fight Club (film), 402
Le figuier a cinq branches (Bizot), 963
Fihrist (al-Nadīm), 1676–1678
filial piety
 Buddhist sutras related to, 996–999
 in China, 1006
 in Chinese Buddhism, 993–996
 Confucianism and, 994–996, 1003
 in culture, 1005–1006
 philosophy of, 999–1004
 translations of, 1004–1005
Filliozat, Jacqueline, 1052–1053
Filliozat, Jean, 213, 2304

film, 397–406. See also *specific films*
film studies, 144 n.31, 232–234, 395
"Final Testament of the Tripiṭaka Monk" (Amoghavajra), 53–55
Finch, Kosho, 1134
Finding Rest in the Nature of the Mind (Longchenpa), 1143
Fine, Lyn, 2443, 2447–2448, 2449 n.7
Fine Arts Department, Thailand (FAD), 76–77
fine materiality (*rūpya-dhātu*), 6–7
Finot, Louis, 1052–1053, 1801 n.5, 1890
fire, 1198–1200, 1207, 1210, 1217 n.66
Fisher, Daniel Clarkson, 471–472
Fisker-Nielsen, Anne Mette, 2227
Fitzgerald, Timothy, 565, 2145
FitzHerbert, S. G., 2500
Five-Altar Rite, 300–301
Five Appeals to American Patriotism (HHMH), 1304–1305
five categories of matter (*rūpa*), 6
five-category subsumption, of *dharmas*, 2101–2106
Five Great Wisdom Kings, 300–301
Five Treatises of Maitreya, 101, 2744
flame-of-the-lamp records, 645, 656–661, 665
Flath, James, 1871
Flesh Body Bodhisattva Relic, 2366
Fletcher, Jeanne Hill, 2714–2715
Flood, Finbarr B., 1669–1670
Flood, Gavin, 2318
Flower Garland Sutra, 2201
Flower Ornament Discourse (Zhiyi), 2463–2464
Flowers on the Rock (Harding, Hori, and Soucy), 417–418
Flowing Bridges, Quiet Waters (Reynolds), 1715
Flug, Kostantin K., 818
Fo Guang Shan
  BLIA and, 1009–1010
  in Canada, 412
  education of, 1014–1016
  entertainment and, 1015–1016
  Fo Guang Shan Buddha Museum, 1011–1012
  history of, 113 n.20
  Hsi Lai Temple and, 1012–1014
  Humanistic Buddhism and, 1219–1221
  main campus, 1010–1012
  monasteries and, 1010–1012, 1015
  in North America, 1010, 1013
  in Philippines, 2627
  preservation of, 1219–1220
  properties, 1010–1014
  scholarship on, 196, 1016–1017, 2621, 2625
  structure of, 1008–1010
  in Taiwan, 1009, 1011
Foguoji (Faxian), 876
Fojiao yu rensheng (Zhang Mantao), 1261
folk Buddhism, 2232
Font, Bernat, 2150 n.74
footprints, 69
For a Chan Monk Seeking Instructive Sayings (Qianfeng), 663
Forbes, Bruce, 240
Foreign Devils on the Silk Road (Hopkirk), 800, 825
foreign ideology, 379
foreign language schools, 1306
Foreign Materia Medica (Hu bencao), 213
foreign relations, 2214
Forerunner of All Things (Heim), 1335–1336
Forest (Juefan), 669–670
forest monks, 970
Forgues, Gregory, 2496, 2500
form, 395
formations (*saṃskāra*), 6
Formigatti, Camillo, 1042–1043
forms of Buddha, 1277
Forty Years of Naikan (Satō), 1705
Fosheng daolitian weimu shuofa jing, 997–998
Foshuo Daaidao bannianhuan Jing, 998
Foshuo Fumu Enzhong Nanbao Jing. See *Fumu Enzhong Jing*
Foshuo pusa shanzi jing, 998
Foshuo weishengyuan jing, 999
Foshuo yulanpen jing, 998–999
Foster, Mary, 384, 1309
Foster, Nelson, 910
Foucault, Michel, 112 n.17, 172, 1982, 1997 n.38, 2002 n.119, 2707–2708. *See also* Queer Theory
Foucher, Alfred, 949, 1294, 2262, 2266
foul objects, 516
foundational ethics, 915
Foundation for the Preservation of Mahayana Tradition (FPMT), 196, 1140–1146, 1150, 1588, 1590
Foundation of Japanese Buddhism (Daigan and Matsunaga), 1774
Foundations of Dharmakīrti's Philosophy (Dunne), 1837–1838
"Foundations of Mindfulness Discourse," 113
Fourfold Seminal Heart (Longchenpa), 837–838
four great deeds, 1062–1063
The Four Hundred (Nāgārjuna), 1459
Four Hundred Stanzas (Āryadeva), 615–616. *See also* Candrakīrti
four mindfulnesses, 518–520
four noble truths
  absence of, 1030–1031

in Buddhist media, 2572 n.51
dukkhaṃ, 1024–1025
education of, 1020–1022
grammatical inconsistencies in, 1029
karma and, 979
nirodho, 1026–1027
in Pali Buddhism, 1023–1028
paṭipadā, 1027–1028
samudayo, 1025–1026
scholarship on, 1022–1028, 1032–1033
tradition of, 974–976
translations of, 1031–1032
variations on, 1028–1031
zhentong and, 2744
Fourth Council (Dölpopa Sherab Gyaltsen), 2745–2746, 2750
Four Treatises, 2528, 2531–2532
Foxeus, Niklas, 567–568, 579–580, 602–604
Foyuan, 1231
FPMT. *See* Foundation for the Preservation of Mahayana Tradition
Fragrant Palm Leaves (Hanh), 2448
France
in colonialism, 375–378, 1040–1041, 1051–1052, 1100–1101, 1890
EFEO, 1898–1899, 1937 n.117
England and, 368–369, 1100
Orientalism in, 377
in Seven Year's War, 872
translations from, 33 n.60
Vichy, 378–379
Francke, A. H., 2488–2489, 2499
Franco, Eli, 1837–1838
Franke, Herbert, 1656–1657
Frankl, Victor, 1714
Frasch, Tilman, 194, 1528
Fraser, Sarah E., 799–801
Frauwallner, Erich, 11
Frederick S. Wight Art Gallery, 802
"Freedom and Self Control" (Meyers), 1335–1336
Freedom from Extremes Accomplished through Comprehensive Knowledge of Philosophy (Vajrayāna), 2463
Frege scholarship, 1826
Fremantle, Francesca, 1491
Freud, Sigmund, 1943–1944, 1947–1948
Friar Bala, 1287–1288
Fromm, Erich
D. T. Suzuki and, 707–708, 723–724, 1947–1948, 1952
scholarship from, 1945, 1948–1949, 1953–1954
From the Heart Essence of Mitra (Mitrayogin), 1970–1971
From the Treasury of Mantras (Dorje Dechen Lingpa), 1970–1971
fruit, result (*phala*), 7–8, 18, 23, 2094, 2100
Fu Chi Ying, 1222
Fuchizawa Chimyo, 2171 n.41
Fudō Myōō, 308–309, 2055–2056, 2350
Fu Dong Ji, 2378–2382, 2383*f*, 2388
Fu Fang, 213
Fugita, Stephen S., 46
Fuhito (emperor), 2198–2199, 2201
Fuhito, Fujiwara no, 2200, 2202–2203
Fujikawa Bunko, 311
Fujikawa Yū, 277–278, 311
Fujimoto, Hogen, 464
Fujimoto Katsuyoshi, 297–298
Fujimura Bunyū, 33 n.53, 36–38, 42, 49
Fujita Kōtatsu, 2677, 2679, 2683, 2696
Fujiwara clan, 2350
Fujiwara Kanemichi, 2350
Fujiwara Tadahira, 2046–2047, 2053
Fukuzawa Yukichi, 1303–1304
Fuliang, 2207
Fuller, Paul, 914, 919, 921–922
Fuller, Robert C., 2126
Fumu enchong jing, 1185
Fumuen nanbao jing, 997, 1004–1005
Fumu Enzhong Jing, 994–997, 1004–1005
Funahashi, Issai, 4–5
Funaki Yoshimi, 2045–2046
functional intention, 1330–1331
fundamentalist Christianity, 1148–1149, 1151
Fundamental Stanzas on the Middle Way (Nāgārjuna), 615–616. *See also* Candrakīrti
Fundamental Wisdom of the Middle (Nāgārjuna), 1062
funeral rites, 2473–2475, 2481
Furui, Ryosuke, 1790
Furuta Shōkin, 708
Fūshinchō, 2333–2334
fusion philosophy, 534–535
Fussman, Gérard, 639, 949–950
The Future of Faith (Cox, H.), 2713–2714
Fuyu Zhanglao, 1626–1627

Gabaude, Louis, 1890
Gachen yéshé chöpel, 1380
Gaia theory, 2618–2619
Gajō, 2049–2050
Galambos, Imre, 824–825
Gampola period, of Sri Lanka, 2245–2246

Gampopa Sonam Rinchen, 1814–1815
incarnations of, 2594
Kyungtsangpa and, 1539–1540
Milarepa and, 1536
scholarship and, 692, 847, 986, 1481–1482, 1486–1487, 1489–1490, 1983–1984, 2011
Kyungtsangpa and, 1469 n.11
Gandaharan Buddhist Reliquaries (Jongeward, Errington, Salomon, and Baums), 941*f*
Gaṇḍavyūha Sūtra, 483–484
Gandenpa. *See* Gelukpa
Ganden Potrang government, 2504, 2517
Gandhāra
Buddha in, 1278, 1283–1284, 1288, 1294
scholarship and, 938–943, 1274–1275, 1283–1285, 1293
Gāndhārī, 495, 632–633, 636–637, 639. *See also* early Buddhist manuscripts
Gandhi, Mahatma, 909–910, 2292–2293
Ganeri, Jonardon, 11
Ganges Mahāmudrā, 1476–1477
Gangkar Rinpoche, 1137, 2366
Gangri Tókar, 1440
Gangteng Tulku, 1441–1442
Ganjin, 1517, 2201
ganying (sympathetic resonance), 86–87
Gaofeng Yuanmiao, 654–655
Gaofeng yulu (Gaofeng), 654–655
Gaoseng chuan (Huichao), 1189–1190
Gao Xingjian, 1231
Garab Dorjé Rinpoché, 694, 837
Garbhāvakāntisūtra (Kritzer), 260–261
Garbhāvakrānti, 253–254
Garden, Domnern, 2061–2062
Gardiner, David, 2335–2336, 2359
Garfield, Jay, 628–629, 983–984, 1465–1466, 1699, 2078
Garland of Jātaka (Āryaśura), 2010–2011
Garland of Views (Padmasambhava), 1563
Garrett, Frances, 2024
Garungwa Lhai Gyaltsen, 2748–2749
Gateway to Scholarship (Mipam), 1563
Gathara, 2253–2254
gathas (hymns), 1349–1350, 1966
Gathering of Intentions Sutra, 1163
Gautama Buddha, 1012, 1020, 1506, 2453–2454, 2470
Gautamīputra Śrīsātakarṇi (king), 937
Gayley, Holly, 185
Geary, Patrick, 187, 846
Gebert, Andrew, 2226
Gegegen, 1602–1603
Geldsetzer, Lutz, 1466
Gellner, David, 1148
Gellner, Ernest, 77–78
Gelukpa
Dalai Lama and, 1065–1068
history of, 1062–1063
influence of, 1485–1486, 1643
leadership of, 1643–1644
monasteries with, 1063–1065
philosophy of, 1061–1068
scholarship on, 1068–1070, 1071 n.3
school, 2498
Geluk tradition
history of, 1603, 1608, 1643–1644, 1646–1647, 1754–1755
scholarship and, 26–30, 713 n.14, 732–733, 737, 1171, 1601–1604, 2313
Genbō, 2201, 2205
gender
in Buddhism, 1101–1102
categories, 1984–1986
in contemporary monastic education, 1576–1577
Dalai Lama and, 2027 n.5
diversity, 1983–1986
equity, 913
gender studies, 2625
hierarchies in, 2066
scholarship on, 184–185
sexuality and, 1997 n.38
in sociology, 1983
Gendun Chokyi Nyima, 2023–2024
Gendün Chöpel, 383–384, 486, 1067, 1489–1490, 1553
Gendun Drupa, 1064, 1164–1165, 1649, 2014
Gendün Drup Pal Sangpo, 1062–1063
Gendun Gyatso, 1064, 1164–1165, 2014
Gendün Rinchen, 2594
genealogy, 1997 n.38
General Commentary on the Doctrine (Dölpopa Sherab Gyaltsen), 2750
General Madhyamaka, 2745
generational shifts, 922–923
generosity (dāna), 2081–2082
Genet, Jacques, 675–676
Genku (master), 1297 n.13
Genmei, 2199
Genmei Tennō, 275–276
genres, 631 n.7, 645–656, 664–665, 1363–1366
Genshin, 2047, 2051, 2055
Gensho, 2199
Genshō Tennō, 275–276
Gentle Bridges (Hayward and Varela), 2533–2534
Gentle Glory. *See* Mañjuśrī

Gentleman's Agreement (1907), 1078–1079
geography
  borderland complex, 498–499
  of early Buddhism, 494–495
  geo-cultural Tibet, 421–424
  geographical texts, 813
  regionalism and, 493–494, 496–498, 503
Geonka, S. N., 2566
Gere, Richard, 226
Geresenje, 1647–1648
Germano, David, 840, 1446–1447, 2481
Germany, 36, 101, 1072 n.9, 1708–1709
Germer, Christopher, 1952–1953
Gernet, Jacques, 821–823, 1237–1238
gers, 1586
Gesar! (Schmidt), 2499
Gesar, Ling (king)
  cult of, 2494–2495, 2497–2499
  depictions of, 2489–2490
  divinity of, 2491–2494
  in Nyingma tradition, 2495
  Padmasambhava and, 2492–2494, 2498
  rituals for, 2496–2497
  scholarship on, 1567, 2499–2500, 2502 n.9
  songs of, 2490
  in Tibetan Buddhism, 2494–2495, 2497–2499
Gesar epic. *See also* Ling Gesar
  apotheosis of, 2491–2494
  cult of Gesar and, 2494–2495, 2497–2499
  Karmay on, 2501 n.2
  Padmasambhava and, 2489
  rituals with, 2495–2497
  scholarship on, 1552, 1567
  Tibetan Buddhism and, 2487–2490, 2499–2500
  translations of, 2503 n.29
Geser Khan. *See* Gesar, Ling (king)
geshe (honorific), 737
Geshe degrees, 129–130, 137–138
Geshe Kyo Shakya Yeshé, 687
Geshe Lhundub Sopa, 1067–1068
Geshe Rabten, 1067–1068
Geshe Sopa, 1815
Geshu Han, 54–55
Gest, Guion M., 798–799
gestures, 2266–2267
Gethin, Rupert, 98, 153, 171–172, 1023–1024, 2149 n.59, 2427 n.21
Getse Paṇḍita, 2748
Getty Center, 802
Ghazan, 1642
Ghosanda, Maha, 906–907, 909–910
Ghost Dog (film), 403–404
Giác, Thích Mān, 2436
Giebel, Rolf, 1527–1528
Gien, 2205
Gihipaṭipatti, 1052–1053
Giles, Cheryl, 451, 457, 471–472
Giles, Lionel, 819
Gimaret, Daniel, 1469 n.30
Gimello, Robert M., 1027–1028
Ginsberg, Allen, 361, 723–724, 1311
Gion Matsuri, 294–295
Giorgi, Antonio Agostino, 871, 874–875, 879
Girimānanda, 252
Gishin, 2183, 2326–2327, 2344–2345
Gishō, 2046
Glan-dar-ma (king), 344
Glang ri thang pa, 1403
Glang ri thang pa Rdo rje seng ge, 1400–1401
Glass, Andrew, 639
Glassman, Bernie, 472, 911
Gleig, Ann, 198–199, 1118–1119, 1122–1123, 1955–1956, 2144, 2717
global Buddhism
  in colonialism, 1075–1077
  Hindu tantra and, 2285–2287
  Mahāyāna Buddhism and, 1080
  in modernity, 1083–1086
  from national Asian traditions, 1077–1080
  for non-Asians, 1080–1083
  post-global Buddhism, 198–199
  pre-global Buddhism, 194
  scholarship on, 195–196, 1072–1075, 1086–1089
  Tibetan Buddhism and, 1079–1080
global capitalism, 897
Global Citizens (Machacek and Wilson, B.), 2226
global culture, 159 n.56
global engaged Buddhism, 904–913
globalization. See *specific topics*
Global North, 1985–1986, 1990–1991
global Theravāda Buddhism
  bhikkhus and, 1101–1104
  colonialism and, 1096–1104
  full ordination in, 1102–1104
  heritage Buddhism and, 1115–1116
  in modernity, 1097–1100
  non-heritage Buddhism and, 1119–1121
  scholarship on, 1104–1106, 1121–1123
  Thailand and, 1100–1101
glocal Buddhism, 196–197
Gloria in Excelsis Deo, 812
glorification narratives, 1727–1731

Glorious Rangjung Dorjé's Liberation Story (Rangjung Dorjé), 2025
glossaries, 646, 674
GMD. *See* Guomindang
Gnanasara, Galangoda A., 1099
Gnoli, Raniero, 1466, 1801 n.5, 1837–1838
Gnyal zhig pa 'jam dpal rdo rje, 25
Goa, 865
Goble, Andrew Edmund, 279, 291–292
Goble, Geoffrey, 63
Godan Khan, 1503–1504
goddesses
  Dalai Lama and, 1750
  guardian/protector deities and, 1164–1167
  in *kālacakra-maṇḍala*, 1419–1420, 1421*t*, 1423–1429
  in Khmer Esoteric Buddhism, 1800 n.2, 1804 n.97, 1914–1918
  Palden Lhamo, 1159–1161, 1164–1167, 1171–1172
  Prajñāpāramitā and, 1914–1918
  in Tibet, 1160
"Goddess of Mercy." *See* Guanyin
Godem Ngodrup Gyaltsen, 838
gods, 692. See also *specific gods*
Goenka, S. N., 1117–1118
Gōhō, 2356
Gohonzon, 2218, 2220, 2224–2225
"Going from Hengyang to Shaozhou, I Visited Chan Master Neng" (Song), 1227
Gö Khugpa Lhetse, 2476–2478
Gokurakuji, 291–292
gold, 1544–1546
Gold, Jonathan, 11, 2088–2089
Goldberg, Michael, 710, 743–744
Golden Light Sūtra, 749–750
Golden Needle of the Great Perfection, 134
"Golden Rosaries of the Bka' brgyud Schools" (Smith, E.), 1553
Golden Rosary of Mahāmudrā, 1476–1477
Golden Urn. *See* Dalai Lama
Gold Refined from Ore, 833–834
Goldstein, Joseph, 1117–1118, 2142
Goldstein, Mervyn, 2025
Goldwater, Julius A., 39, 46–47
Gö Lotsawa Zhönu Pal (Gö Lotsawa Shönupel)
  compositions by, 2594
  Drokmi Lotsāwa and, 1552–1553
  history from, 858
  on Marpa Lotsawa, 1540, 1553
  reputation of, 1485, 2026
  scholarship from, 848, 1490
  tantra and, 2476–2478
Gombodorji, 1647–1648, 2019
Gombojab, 1657–1658
Gombrich, Richard
  influence of, 144 n.33, 575–576, 2257
  Obeyesekere and, 2127, 2145
  scholarship and, 1222, 1814–1815, 1890–1891
  on writing, 2560–2561, 2567
  Yu-shuang Yao and, 2294–2295
Gomchen Kunga Rinchen, 1440
Gómez, Luis O., 350–351, 1939–1940, 1946, 2088
Gonda, Jan, 969
Gonda Raifu, 2365
Gongga Laoren (Jagou), 2388
Goodall, Dominic, 1201, 2322 n.34
Goodell, Eric, 2294–2295
Goodman, Charles, 4, 171–172, 982, 2077–2079, 2088–2089
Gopacandra (king), 943–944
Gopāla I (king), 1788
Gopāla II (king), 1785, 1792
Gopāla III (king), 1786–1787
Gopāla IV (king), 1786–1787, 1792
Gorai Shigeru, 278
Gorakhnāth, 2309
Gorakṣa, 2309
Gorampa Sönam Senge, 1064–1065, 1463, 1966, 2748–2749
Gore, Al, 1013
Gorin kujimyō himitsu shaku, 2185–2186
Goshirakawa, 301–302
Goshōrai mokuroku, 2327, 2329
'Gos lo tsa ba Gzhon nu dpal, 1406–1407
Gospel of Buddha (Carus), 1308
The Gospel of Buddha (Carus), 702, 1941
Gotama, 506–508, 2255
Götsangpa, 2011–2012
Götshangpa Gönpo Dorje, 854, 855*f*, 857–858
Gough, Ellen, 1202
Goulah, Jason, 2226
Govinda Anagarika (lama), 2292–2293, 2479–2480
Govindacandra (king), 947
Gowans, Christopher, 983, 986
Gozu Tennō, 268, 294–296
Grags-pa bshad-sgrub, 26
Graham, Jack. L., 2128
Grammatica of Singaleesche Taal-kunst (Ruell), 1045–1046
The Grand Poem (Āryadeva the Brahmin), 686
"Grand Requiem for Praying," 2442–2443
Grant, Beata, 185
Grapard, Allan, 346, 356, 2357

Gray, David, 1490
Great American Songbook, 664–665
Great Buddha Land, 1011, 1013
The Great Bundle of Precepts, 690–691
Great Calming and Contemplation (Zhiyi), 210–211
Great Collection Sutra, 2219
Greater East Asian Buddhist Conference, 2281
Great Expanse of the Supreme Peak, 133
Great Exposition of Secret Mantra (Tsongkhapa), 1139
Great Exposition on Zhentong (Khenpo Lodrö Drakpa), 2747–2748
The Great Forty sutta, 1326–1327
Great Jewel Heap Sutra, 205
Great Leap Forward, 2021
The Great Liberation though Hearing in the Intermediate State (Kazi Dawa Samdup), 2469, 2471. See also *Tibetan Book of the Dead*
"Great Love Technology Company," 2618
Great Madhyamaka, 2753 n.2
Great Master Etō. *See* Rennyo
Great Matter, 120
Great Peahen, 271
Great Perfection, 131, 2546–2549, 2598–2600
The Great Perfection (Karmay), 840
Great Seal (mahāmudrā), 692, 2546–2548
"Great Simplicity" (Sargeant), 710, 725
Great Smallpox Epidemic (735-737), 293, 295–296, 306–307
Great Stages on the Path to Awakening (Tsongkhapa), 1062
The Great Stupa of Gyantse (Ricca and Bue), 443–444
Great Tang Records on the Western Regions, 101, 811
The Great Tibetan-Tibetan-Chinese Dictionary, 2514
The Great Treatise on the Stages of the Path to Enlightenment (Tsongkhapa), 1814–1815
Great Vehicle, 2460–2461
Greece, 866–867, 981
greed, 359
Green, Phillip, 1897, 1901, 1903, 1905–1906
Green, Ronald, 232, 400–403, 405–406
Greene, Eric, 2675–2677, 2696–2697
Green Tārā, 1377
Gregory, Henry, 1046–1047
Grether, Holly, 1200, 1212
Grieve, Gregory, 240, 2567
Griffith, D. W., 398
Griffiths, Arlo, 1528
Griswold, A. B., 73
Grönbold, Günter, 2566–2567
Groner, Paul
  on debate traditions, 752, 754, 759
  scholarship from, 2056, 2059 n.16, 2326–2327, 2358–2359, 2661, 2663–2664
Gross, Rita, 1982
Gross Domestic Product, 895–896
Gross National Happiness, 895–896
Groundhog Day (film), 237
group debates, 742
A Grove of Pearls from the Garden of Dharma (Daoshi), 210
Grünwedel, Albert, 113 n.20
guan, 2674–2677, 2687–2688, 2699 n.6, 2699 n.5, 2700 n.21
Guanding, 1003
Guangjiao Monastery, 2153–2155
guan jing. *See* visualization/contemplation sutras
Guanshyin, 1517
Guanyin, 83–93, 1873–1874, 2154, 2614–2615. *See also* bodhisattvas
Guanyin Sutra, 816
Guanzong Study Society, 2283
guardian/protector deities
  cosmology of, 1158–1160
  goddesses and, 1164–1167
  Mahākāla as, 1072 n.14, 1072 n.28, 1159–1160, 1162–1164
  mythology of, 1161–1162
  Nyingma trinity as, 1167–1170
  rituals for, 1160–1161
  scholarship on, 1173–1174
  Sinhala Buddhist guardian deities, 2245–2257, 2261 n.56
  in Tibetan Buddhism, 1072 n.16, 1158, 1170–1173
Guardians of the Buddha's Home (Starling), 778–779
Guarisco, Elio, 2469–2470
Guatamī Bālaśrī, 937
Guenther, Herbert, 840, 1446, 1489–1490, 1814–1815
Guhasena (king), 943
Gu Huan, 1001
Guhyagarbha Tantra, 831, 837, 1563, 2467, 2475–2478, 2639
Guhyasamāja tantra, 808, 1538, 1906–1907
Guhya Tantra, 2644–2647
Guifeng Zongmi, 667–669, 674–675
Guinness Book of World Records, 2555
Gulf War, 2617
Guṇabhadra, 1518–1519
Guṇamati, 9–10
Guṇānanda, Mohoṭṭivatte, 373–374, 1046–1047
Guṇaprabha, 2664
Gunaratna, Henepola, 1120
Gunasena, Amal, 967

Guṇavarman, 99–100, 1471 n.65, 1515–1516, 1518–1519, 1523, 2662
Gungaa Odser, 1651–1652
Guo Di, 1862
Guomindang (GMD), 1219–1220, 1440, 1445, 1449 n.11, 2154–2157, 2165–2166
Guo Moruo, 1444
Gupta dynasty, 494, 496–497, 2304
Gupta style, 2264
Gupta-Vākāṭaka period, 942–946
The Guru Drinks Bourbon? (Dzongsar Khyentse), 1143
Guruge, Ananda W. P., 895–896
Gurupañcāśikā, 2306
guruparaṃparā., 2302–2303
gurus, 838–839, 1143, 1437, 2306, 2314, 2323 n.67
Güshi Khan (Güshi Taishi), 1065–1066, 1603, 1648–1649, 1652–1655, 1745, 2015–2016
Gutenberg press, 326
Guthrie, Elizabeth, 1102
Güyüg Khan, 1624, 1626
Gya clan, 853, 858
Gyag-ston Sangs-rgyas-dpal, 25
Gyälpo Kyoppa, 850
Gyaltangpa, 852, 2612 n.34
Gyalthangpa Dechen Dorje, 858, 2594
Gyaltsen Norbu, 2023–2024
Gyalwa Chogyang, 1436–1437
Gyalwangje Kunga Penjor, 2595
Gyamo Öde, 1541–1542
Gyantse Monastery, 422–423, 428, 432–433, 442
Gyarawa Chökyi Gyatso, 2468
Gyatso, Janet, 185–186, 695, 1993, 2481
Gyayakpa, 856
Gyazurpo Tsape, 851, 2597
Gyeltsap Darma Rinchen, 1062–1063
Gyeltsap Je, 1062–1063
Gyergom Tsultrim Senggé, 2010–2011
Gyerpung Nangzher Löpo, 132
gyō (religious practice), 720–721
Gyōhō, 2325
Gyōki, 291, 2052, 2202–2203
Gyōnen, 1136, 2198
Gyōyū, 2187
Gyurme Dorje, 585–586, 695, 1446–1447, 2469–2470, 2480–2481, 2534
Gyurme Namgyel, 2017
Gyushi, 2528, 2530–2531, 2534
Gzhon nu dpal, 1657–1658

Haarh, Erik, 2586
Habito, Ruben, 1774, 2624–2625
Hackett, Paul, 12
Hagen, Stephen, 2142
hagiography
  autohagiography, 2367–2369
  of Drukpa Kagyü school, 845–847
  hagiographical compilations, 1222, 1397
  healing deities and, 208–210
  of Huineng, 1224–1227, 1235–1236
  of Jīvaka Kumārabhrta, 209
  of Padmasambhava, 2587
  philosophy of, 1231–1233
  scholarship and, 1230–1231
  thaumaturgy and, 209–210
  Xuanzang and, 291
Haichaoyin (magazine), 2281, 2283–2284, 2287–2288, 2296
Haimavatas. *See* Theravāda Buddhism
Haiyao bencao, 213
Haiyun, 1624–1625, 1627–1628
Hakamaya Noriaki, 101–102
Hakeda, Yoshito, 2336
Hakii Sanenaga, 1766–1767
Hakka settlers, 408–409
Hakuhō Buddhism, 2197
Hakuin, 716, 1701 n.3
Halbawchs, Maurice, 69
Halhed, Nathaniel Brassy, 873
Halifax, Joan, 472, 911
Halkias, Georgios, 1974
Hall, Kenneth, 1528
Hall, Robert, 564
hall caves, 781, 782*f*
Hallisey, Charles, 385–386, 576–578, 863 n.32, 983–984, 1104–1105, 1815
Halperin, David, 1981, 1997 n.38. *See also* Queer Theory
Hamayon, Roberte, 2499
Hamilton, Alexander, 875
Hamilton, James Russell, 820
Hammerstrom, Erik, 2294–2295
Hanasana, 1787–1788
Han Chinese Buddhism, 2163, 2165
Handbook of Contemporary Buddhism, 199–200
Handbook of Indian Art (Havell), 1670
Handbook of Propagation, 2212
Handing Down the Light (Fu Chi Ying), 1222
handwritten stage, of Buddhist media, 2557–2560
Han dynasty, 993–994, 996–997, 1184, 1861
Han ethnicity, 2152, 2168 n.1
Haney, Dawn, 910
Hanh, Thich Nhat
  activism by, 916
  biography of, 2435–2443, 2449 n.7
  D. T. Suzuki and, 195

engaged Buddhism and, 885 n.68, 905, 984, 2443–2446
on Humanistic Buddhism, 2435
influence of, 909, 914–915
mindfulness by, 906–907
pseudonyms for, 2450 n.20
reputation of, 359, 1570–1571, 2434
Sangharakshita and, 912
scholarship and, 986, 1022, 1081–1082, 1987, 1990–1991, 2446–2448
Taixu and, 2291
in U.S., 910, 2239
for Vietnam, 904
Vietnamese Buddhism and, 2451 n.58
in Zen Buddhism, 2445–2446
Hanrahan, Paschal, 469
Hansen, Anne, 577
Hansen, Armauer, 289
Hansen's disease, 266–267, 271–272, 289
Hanshan poems, 663–664
Han Yongun, 380
Hao, Chunwen, 821–823
Haoran, Hou, 2594
happiness, 982
Happy Science, 894
Harada Minoru, 2216
Harada Sogaku, 2160
Haraguchi Naoshi, 1705
Harbhajan Singh Khalsa (Yogi Bhajan), 2314
Hardacre, Helen, 346
Harding, John S., 417–418
Hardy, Robert Spence, 1032–1033, 2713
Hargett, James, 1867–1869
Haribhadra, 23–24, 26, 28–30
Harikela area, of Eastern India, 1795–1796
Harivarman, 2204
harmful intention, 2083
Harper, David, 233
Harrer, Heinrich, 1082
Harrington, Laura, 1148–1149
Harris, Elizabeth, 1032–1033
Harris, Ian, 360, 362, 1102
Harris, Sam, 2136
Harris, Stephen, 982–983, 2078, 2088–2089
Harrison, Paul, 1977 n.11, 2076–2077, 2088, 2566–2567
Harrison, Peter, 867–869
Harṣavardhana, 1784
Hart-Celler Act (1965), 1079
Härtel, Herbert, 1294
Hartl, Josef, 1708–1709
Hartman, Charles, 2641
Hartmann, Jens Uwe, 2566–2567
Haruko Wakabayashi, 2056
Harvey, Peter, 170–171, 1031, 1033, 1890, 1993
Hase, James, 1119, 1122
Hasra Kol stone inscription, 947, 947*f*
Hasshū-kōyō (Gyōnen), 1136
Hassler, Alfred, 2440
Hastings, Warren, 873
Haṭhayoga tradition, 2309
Hattori, Masaaki, 1801 n.4, 1838
Hattori Toshirō, 278, 311
Haunting the Buddha (DeCaroli), 1174
Havell, Ernest Binfield, 1670
Havnevik, Hanna, 1594
Hawaii. See also *specific topics*
D.T. Suzuki in, 707–709
Hawaiian Sugar Planters' Association, 1305
HHMH, 34–35, 1348–1349, 1357
Honpa Hongwanji Hawaii Betsuin, 1350*f*
Japan and, 1308, 1360 n.13
Japanese Americans in, 34, 39
Japanese Buddhisms in, 1348–1351, 1357, 1360 n.20
Nisei Buddhists in, 1309–1310
North America and, 1356, 1359 n.7
Olcott in, 1309
Shin Buddhism in, 1309
Taixu in, 1308
Hawkins, Jennifer, 2137–2138
Hayami Tasuku, 2355–2357
Hayashida Kumino, 708–709
Hayek, Matthias, 2208–2209
Hayes, Richard, 1465, 1698, 1837
Hayes, Steven, 1952
Haynes, Sarah, 1206
Hayward, Jeremy, 2533–2534
healing
bodies and, 112 n.9
in China, 203–205, 213–215
in Chinese medicine, 211–213
deities, 208–210
in embryology, 207
healers, 272–274
illness and, 159 n.56
in Indic medicine, 213
in monasteries, 207–208
in monastic hospitals, 212–213
in opthalmology, 211–212
pathogenesis and, 205–207
phlegm and, 212
physiology and, 205–213
rituals, 209–210, 298–304
to Sun Simiao, 211
syntheses of, 210–211

The Healing Buddha (Birnbaum), 213, 2696
heart (*hṛdaya*), 2–3
The Heart Drops of Dharmakaya (Shardza Tashi Gyeltsen), 138
The Heart of Buddhist Meditation (Nyanaponika), 1952–1953
The Heart of the Buddha's Teaching (Hanh), 2448
Heart Sūtra, 771–773, 777–778, 810, 1899–1900
Heartwood (Cadge), 2243
heaven, 2285–2287, 2291–2292, 2294
Heaven and Hell (Swedenborg), 704
Hegeler, Edward, 703
hegemony, 112 n.16, 198–199
Heian Buddhism, 2197, 2200, 2324–2325, 2330, 2335–2336, 2341, 2350. *See also* Nara schools
Heiler, Friedrich, 1942
Heim, Maria
  on action based ethics, 1329
  on Buddhaghosa, 1300 n.49
  on *cetanā*, 1344 n.155
  Devdas and, 1335–1336, 1343 n.120, 1344 n.152
  on the path, 1303 n.85, 1327
  scholarship from, 112 n.17, 153, 1335–1336
  on *Vibhaṅga*, 1342 n.104
Hei no Yoritsuna, 1766
Heissig, Walther, 2499
Heizei (emperor), 2327
Helderman, Ira, 2128, 2131, 2141, 2145
hell, 1996 n.24
Hellenism, 1200–1201
Hellenistic religions, 193
Heller, Amy, 1173–1174
Heller, Natasha, 183, 2559
H. E. Namkha Drimed Rinpoche, 1441–1442
Henjō, 2349
Henry VIII (king), 1647
Heo Kuen, 1709
heritage, 71, 75–76. *See also* World Heritage Sites
heritage Buddhism, 1115–1116
Hermanns, Matthais, 2500
hermeneutics, 913–916, 1991, 2457–2458, 2462–2465
Hermeneutics and Tradition in the Saṃdhinirmocana-sūtra (Powers), 2464
hermits, 69–70
heroic palimpsests, 2491–2494, 2502 n.23
Herrigel, Eugen, 234, 1947
heterosexuality, 1992
Hetucakraḍamaru, 1821
Hetuvālda. *See* Sarvāstivāda Abhidharma school
Hevajra images, 1897–1900, 1918–1919, 1923–1926
Hevajra Tantra, 691, 1474, 1489–1490, 1900
The Hevajra Tantra (Snellgrove), 1491
Hewavitarane, Don David. *See* Dharmapala, Anagarika
HHMH. *See* Honpa Hongwanji Mission of Hawaii
Hickey, Wakoh Shannon, 1122, 2141, 2145, 2717–2718
Hidalgo, Danielle, 2243
hidden lands, 1854, 1856
Hidehiro Okada, 1656–1657
Hidetada, 755
Higashi Honganji, 35, 705, 708, 720–721
Higgins, David, 2481
Higgins, Winton, 2132–2133, 2141
High, Mette, 1595
Higher Continuum, 1477, 1479, 1482, 1485, 1490
higher education, 160 n.59, 239–240, 463, 702–706, 1015
higher rites, 2643–2647
Higher Yoga tantric system, 2470
Hikari no Wa, 1708
Hikkaḍuvē Sumaṅgala, 383–384, 1046, 1097
Hill, Nathan, 2586
Hillis, Gregory, 1446–1447
Himalayan Buddhists. *See* Tibetan Buddhism
Himitsu bukkyō shi (Toganoo), 60
Himitsu mandara jūjushinron (Kūkai), 2179–2180
Hīnatịkumburē Sumaṅgala, 1046–1047
Hīnayāna, 2455–2456
Hinayana Buddhism, 1020, 1028
Hinduism
  Āyurveda in, 245, 260–261, 267, 305
  in Bali, 963
  Brahmanical Hindu literature, 1366
  Brahmanical philosophy and, 1515
  Buddhism and, 71–72, 84, 946, 1801 n.23, 2277–2279, 2301–2302, 2478–2479
  caste system in, 181, 907–908
  cosmology in, 481
  in culture, 566
  in Egypt, 870–871
  Goodall on, 1201
  Hindu Newars, 1043–1044
  Hindu Sanskrit literature, 875
  Islam and, 1669–1670, 2707–2708
  Jainism and, 260–261
  religious traditions and, 2313–2314
  Śaiva tradition in, 964–965, 1201, 1217 n.63, 2282–2283, 2304–2305
  scholarship on, 2318–2320
  siddhis in, 144 n.35, 586
  Tamil Hindus, 905–906, 919
  tantra and, 2280–2287, 2314–2317, 2321 n.18
Hino Noritsuna, 2036–2037

Hinüber, Oskar von, 154, 949–950, 2668
Hirakawa, Akira, 5, 2668
Hiranyagarbha, 1279, 2247
Hirata Atsutane, 338
Hiroaki Mori, 2480
Hirochika, Nakamaki, 1357–1358
Hirohashi Kanenobu, 2036–2037
Hirohito (emperor), 1306
Hirokazu Kore'ada, 404
Hiroko Kawanami, 1103, 1121
Hiroshima Prison, 1706
Hiroshi Sakemoto, 710
Hirschberg, Daniel, 2025
Hisamatsu Shin'ichi, 710
Hisatsune, Kimi, 226, 232
historical documents, 812–813, 1802 n.29, 1802 n.47
historic-ideological backgrounds, 2126–2131
historiography, 319–328, 796–798, 1036–1038, 2226–2227
The History of Abse (Kunga Migyur Dorje), 1162, 1172
History of Chinese Buddhism (Ch'en), 1192
A History of Early Chinese Buddhism (Zenryū), 1192
The History of Japan (Kaempfer), 870–871
History of the Meteoric Razor (bDud 'joms Rin po che), 2640–2641
History of the World Conqueror ("Ala"), 1657–1658
A History of Tibetan Painting (Jackson, D.), 443–444
Ho, Robert H. N., 416
Hōbōgirin, 213
Hodgson, Brian Houghton, 864–865, 876–879, 881, 1814, 2709–2710
Hofer, Theresia, 2534
Hoffman, Frank, 2566–2567
Hōgen, Yuijiri, 1351
Hōjō Hiroshi, 2215
Hōjō Masako, 2187
Hōjō Shigetoki, 1763
Hōjō Tokisuke, 1766
Hōjō Tokiyori, 1763
Holmes, Sandra Jishu, 911
Holt, John, 2257
holy people, 1854–1855
homa
  agnihotra and, 1196 n.14
  in Central Asia, 1202–1203
  in East Asia, 1203–1205
  functional categories of, 1205–1206, 1210–1211
  as Indo-European fire cult, 1199–1200, 1207
  in Indo-Iranian traditions, 1200–1201
  Jainism and, 1201–1202
  Northern Dipper, 1203–1204
  proto-homa, 1210
  rites, 1430–1431
  rituals in, 1198–1199
  as rituals syntax, 1206–1208
  Śaiva and, 1201, 1217 n.63
  scholarship on, 1211–1212
  symbolic meanings in, 1206, 1206*t*, 1210–1211
  in Tibet, 1202
  yogins and, 1209
Homage to Aparamitāyus Sutra, 808
home altars, 770–773, 772*f*
homogeneous causes (*sabhāga hetu*), 2116
homosexuality. *See* Queer Theory
Hōmyō, 2206
Hōnen, 268, 1761, 2037, 2039, 2055
Hong, De, 465
Honganji sahō no shidai, 2038
Honganji sect, 2036–2042
Hong Kong. *See* China
Hong Kong Mantra School for Lay Buddhists, 2365
Hongming Ji (Sengyou), 1001
Hongren, 1224–1229
Hongtaiji, 1652–1655
Hongwu, 2014
Hongyi, 1437, 2665–2666
Hongzan, 2284
Hongzhi guanglu (Hongzhi), 652
Hongzhi's Verses (Hongzhi Zhengjue), 666
Hongzhi Zhengjue, 652, 666, 672
Honigberger, Martin, 639
Honjō, Yoshifumi, 4–5
Honpa Hongwanji Mission of Hawaii (HHMH), 34–35, 1303–1313, 1348–1350, 1350*f*, 1357
Honpukuji yuraiki, 2038
honzon (object of worship), 1769–1770
Hoog, C., 1657–1658
Hoogervorst, 1468 n.4
Hookham, S. K., 2750
Hooykaas, Christian, 1212
Hopkins, Jeffrey, 628–629, 1466–1467, 1469 n.18, 1993–1994, 2464–2465, 2751
Hopkirk, Peter, 800, 825
Horé, 1549
Hori, Victor Sōgen, 417–418
Horikawa (emperor), 300
Horling Yülgyé, 2494
Horner, I. B., 184–185, 2072, 2256
Horner, Isaline Blew, 1814, 2667–2668
Horney, Karen, 1945, 1947
Hor ston Nam mkha' dpal, 1403
hospice, 450–451, 460, 462

hospitals, 212–213
Hossō. *See* Nara schools
hostility (*pratigha*), 7–8
"Household Altars in Contemporary Japan" (Nelson), 778–779
Houtman, Gustaaf, 604
Hou-Tu Gazetteer, 1869
"How Do We Study Buddhism in Canada?" (Hori), 417
"How Legends Developed About the First Jebtsundamba" (Miyawaki), 1386
How Zen Became Zen (Schlütter), 675–676
Hōzō, 2048
Hsayāgyī Pyi-loun-kyanthā Hsayā Kyaw-gyī, 596–597
Hsiao-Lan Hu, 1992–1994
Hsi Lai Temple, 1008, 1012–1015, 1102–1103
Hsin Bao, 1220
Hsing Yun. *See also* Fo Guang Shan
  Cheng Yen and, 2621
  innovation by, 2291
  scholarship and, 1008–1018, 1218–1222
  Shengyen and, 2170 n.36
Hsin Ping, 1219–1220
Hsu, Funie, 2718–2719
Hsuan Hua, 1987
Hsüan T'ung, 1605
Htin Aung, Maung, 586
Huaihai Yuanzhi, 2385–2386
Huan (emperor), 1182–1183
Huang, Julia, 2166–2167, 2615, 2625–2626
Huang, Zheng, 825
Huangbo Records (Pei Xiu), 649
Huangbo Xiyun, 649, 1235–1236
Huangjian Taishi, 821–823
Huang Kan, 813
Huang Xianian, 2296
Huan Xuan, 1000–1001
Huard, Pierre, 279
Huashan, 2279
Hua Tuo, 209, 213
Huayan jing, 1866–1867
Hu bencao, 213
Huber, Toni, 353
Huian, 1226
Huichang Persecutions, 321–322
Huichao, 1189–1190
Hui'e, 1867–1868
Huigo, 2178, 2328–2329, 2332, 2345–2346, 2353, 2364, 2384
Huijian, 998, 1230
Huijiao, 183
Huikong, 1227, 1239
Huilang, 58–59, 2384
Huineng
  appeal of, 1233–1234
  in China, 1230
  in Chinese Buddhism, 1231–1233
  in *Chuanxin fayao*, 1218 n.83
  Diamond Sutra and, 1234–1235
  in engravings, 1239
  hagiography of, 1224–1227, 1235–1236
  in Korea, 1230–1231
  in manuscripts, 1238–1239
  in modernity, 1230–1231
  in print, 324–325
  printing and, 1239–1240
  scholarship on, 1229–1230, 1236–1238, 2727
  Shenhui and, 1227–1230, 1232, 1235–1236
  to Song court, 1240
Huining, 1523
Huitong, 1867
Huiweng Wuming, 660
Huiyan Zhizhao, 669
Huiyuan, 999, 1187
Huizhao, 209–210
Huizong (emperor), 1862
Hülegü, 1624, 1636, 1642
human condition, 977
Humane Kings Scripture (Amoghavajra), 55–56
Human Genome Project, 169
humanism, 2613, 2621, 2623, 2632 n.34. *See also* Tzu Chi
Humanistic Buddhism, 1249–1250, 2735
  in Canada, 413–415
  Chan Buddhism and, 2290–2291
  in China, 1249–1253, 1258–1259, 1451 n.64
  Cihang for, 1250–1251, 1444
  Confucianism and, 2294–2295
  ethics of, 2735
  Fo Guang Shan and, 1219–1221
  Hanh on, 2435
  history of, 1247–1249
  to Lin Qiuwu, 1252–1253
  Mahāyāna Buddhism and, 1255–1256
  missionaries and, 1257–1258
  philosophy and, 1251–1252, 2289–2290
  Pure Land Buddhism and, 1259–1260, 2280
  renjian jingtu and, 1259–1260
  scholarship on, 1246–1247, 1260–1263, 1448 n.1
  in Southeast Asia, 1255–1256
  in Taiwan, 1253–1258, 1438, 2735
  Taixu for, 382–383, 2289–2291, 2294–2295
  transnational, 1256–1257
  Xuecheng on, 1259

Yinshun and, 1253–1255, 1438, 1452 n.86, 2735–2736
Zhao Puchu on, 1258
humanistic psychotherapists, 1949–1950
human-made sites, 1854–1855
Humans and Gods (Huiyan), 669
Hummel, Siegbert, 2500
humors, 2530–2531
Humphrey, Caroline, 1615
The Hundred Thousand Songs of Milarepa, 1485
Hundred Thousand Tantras of the Early Translation Period, 2641
Hungry Ghost Festival, 409
Hunt, Dorothy, 1308, 1349–1350
Hunt, Ernest, 39, 1308, 1349–1350
Huntington, John, 2641
Huntington, Susan L., 1294, 2263
Hunt-Perry, Patricia, 2443, 2447–2448, 2449 n.7
Huot That, 1052–1053
Hürelbaatar, Ujeed, 1615
Hu Shi, 675–676, 821, 1237–1238, 2735–2736
Hu Shih, 494, 724
Huxley, Aldous, 1949–1950, 2129
Hu Yinglin, 87–88
Huynh, Thuan, 2243
Hwa-om-kyung (film), 403–404
hybridity, 587–589, 593–595
The Hybridity of Buddhism (Jagou), 2388
Hyecho, 811, 1516, 1519
Hyegwan, 2204, 2207
hygiene, 207–208
hymns, 226, 1349–1350, 1966
hyperactive nationalism, 382
hypostatization, 1458, 1695–1697
hypotheses, in philosophy, 537

IABU. *See* International Association of Buddhist Universities
Ibn al-Kalbī, 1670
Ibn al-Muqaffa, 1674–1675
ibn al-Qāsim, Muḥammad, 1673–1674
ibn Anas, Mālik, 1674
Ibn Faḍlān, 1471 n.52
Ibrāhīm ibn Adham, 1678–1679
Ibuki Atsushi, 1234
Ichijō (emperor), 2053–2054
ICOMOS. *See* International Council of Monuments and Sites
iconography
aniconic, 1294
art and, 230, 788
iconographic rules, 1277
iconometry and, 112 n.8, 425, 428–433, 436*f*
in Pure Land Buddhism, 1971–1974
from Tibetan Buddhism, 788
in visual culture, 2264–2265
iconometry, 112 n.8, 425, 428–433, 436*f*
idealism, 1822–1823, 1828–1836
Idemitsu Sazō, 708–709
I Denounce Soka Gakkai (Fujiwara), 2226
ideology, 152–153, 379, 1576–1577, 2128–2129, 2288
idols, 1672–1674, 1677
Ifergan, Gidi, 1447
Ignatius of Loyola, 865
ignorance (*avidyā*), 7–8
ignorant person (*mūḍha*), 622
I Heart Huckabees (film), 232, 402
Ikeda Daisaku. *See also* Soka Gakkai
leadership of, 2215–2217, 2220
Lotus Sutra to, 2224
reputation of, 2213–2215, 2220–2222
scholarship and, 911–912, 1356
Toda and, 2212, 2220
Ikeda Mushim Patricia, 911
ikkeshū (family council), 2037–2038, 2041–2042
Ill Communication (album), 226
illegitimacy, 2143
illicit thoughts, 572
illness, 159 n.56, 204, 210, 250–254, 286–292, 310–311
Illouz, Eva, 2145
Illuminating the Path of Liberation (Lala Sonam Chödrup), 1968
Illumination of the Middle Way (Kamalaśīla), 1461
illusions, 1696, 2545
Illustrated Scroll on the Origins of the Crying Fudō, 301–302
illustrations, of Buddha, 1278
Imaeda, Yoshiro, 825
imagery, in *kālacakra-maṇḍala*, 1416–1422
Images of Tibet (Esposito), 2387–2388
imaging Buddha
in art, 1274–1278
in China, 1301 n.70
in literature, 1274, 1278–1281, 1300 n.43
Masset, D., on, 1298 n.18
metamorphosed bodies and, 1281–1282
philosophy of, 1290–1292, 1299 n.33, 1302 n.75
scholarship on, 1294, 1295 n.1, 1296 n.8, 1299 n.24
in South Asia, 1273–1274, 1282–1290, 1293, 1296 n.5
in Thailand, 1301 n.51, 2268–2269
in Tibet, 1297 n.10
veneration from, 1292–1293, 1301 n.63
Imamura families, 1303–1314. See also *specific people*

Immigrants to the Pure Land (Michihiro), 1313–1314
immigration
from Asia, 408
from Bangladesh, 1099
in Canada, 112 n.5
from China, 1012–1014, 1078
Chinese Exclusion Act and, 1078–1079
from Cuba, 1088
diaspora and, 1348–1351, 1359 n.7
Immigration Act, 1078–1079
Immigration and Naturalization Services, 14 n.18, 38–39, 49
from Japan, 1304, 1306–1307, 1309
language and, 415–416, 1112
reform, 410–412
refugees and, 1112
from Taiwan, 412, 1079
in U.S., 2715–2716
imperialism, 113 n.20, 190 n.74, 337, 383, 1117, 1132. *See also* colonialism
imprisonment camps
culture of, 42–45
history of, 34–35
Japanese American Buddhist clergy in, 35–39
Japanese Americans in, 45–48
scholarship on, 14 n.18
in U.S., 39–41
in World War II, 48, 2716
Inagaki, Hisao, 2525 n.51, 2696
inclusivity, 1119
Indāsabhavarañāna, Ambagahavattē, 2416
India. See also *specific topics*
activism in, 908, 923
Archaeological Survey of India, 70–71, 1914
astrology in, 1168
Avalokiteśvara in, 84
Bakula Rinpoche in, 908
Bhaiṣajyarāja in, 247–250
Buddhism in, 2456, 2744–2745
Buddhist media in, 2571 n.35
Buddhist texts from, 632
Candrakīrti in, 626–627
Central Asia and, 2312
China and, 9–10, 54, 225 n.98, 1181–1182, 1368, 2663
cosmological time in, 660
cosmology in, 480, 693
culture of, 1, 11, 585–586
East, 1280–1281
environmental justice in, 349–352
Esoteric Buddhism in, 63
Europe and, 429–430, 874
in globalization, 159 n.41
history of, 493–494, 889
illness etiology and, 253–254
illness in, 250–251
Indo-Tibetan tantra, 2174
influences from, 587–589
Japan and, 66–67, 179, 865, 1574–1575, 1864–1865
jātaka in, 1368–1369
Jīvaka in, 255–256
local deities from, 341–342
Mahabodhi temple in, 70–71, 76–77
mahāmudrā in, 1472, 1477–1478, 1490
Mahāyāna Pure Land Tradition in, 2285–2286
Mañjuśrī in, 1497–1500
Marpa Lotsawa in, 1542–1544, 1546–1548
medicine in, 245–247, 256–261
monasteries in, 208
Montagu-Chelmsford Reforms in, 1099
Nechung in, 1746–1748
Nehru in, 907–908
Nepal and, 424
ontology in, 1825
Pāla, 1923–1925
Prajñāpāramitā in, 1923–1925
pre-Islam in, 1469 n.18
reincarnation system in, 2008–2010
religion in, 1032–1033, 1601–1602
rituals in, 2522 n.11
Śākta tradition in, 2283–2284
scholarship from, 620
Shakyamuni Buddha in, 179–180
South, 1521–1522
Sri Lanka and, 54–55, 1521
stereotypes of, 182–183
Sukhāvatī in, 1978 n.35
Tang dynasty and, 55–56
teleology from, 11
Thailand and, 69–70
Theravāda Buddhism in, 2395–2396
three wheels of doctrine in, 2454
Tibetan Buddhism and, 17, 25–26, 684–685, 1378–1379
Tibet and, 1072 n.16, 1142, 1873, 2008–2010, 2470–2471
Vedic tradition in, 2471–2472
Vietnam and, 2233
vighna in, 2654 n.5
Vulture Peak in, 1439
Western, 1521
women in, 913, 1101, 1103
Xuanzang in, 2396

Yogācāra Buddhism in, 626
zhentong in, 2744–2745
India and Its Faiths (Pratt, J. B.), 1942
Indian Buddhism, 1253–1255
Indian Buddhist commentaries, 23–24
Indian Buddhist Theories of Persons (Duerlinger), 4
Indian Buddhist theory, 2541–2542
Indian Epigraphy (Salomon), 951
Indian Esoteric Buddhism (Davidson, Ronald), 969, 1212–1213
Indianization, 960
Indian Mahāmudrā Texts, 1485
Indian Mahāyāna Buddhist scholarly works, 1809–1814
Indian proto-Theriyas, 2397
Indian Tantric traditions, 969
Indicating the Aim for the Deaf and Blind (Kūkai), 2328
Indications of the Aims of the Three Teachings (Kūkai), 2328
Indic Buddhism, 829. *See also* Dzogchen
Indic medicine, 213
Indic tradition, 203–205
indigenous activism, 923
Individual Liberation Sutra, 1562–1563
Indo bukkyō himei mokuroku (Shizutani), 950
Indo bukkyō himei no kenkyū (Tsukamoto), 942, 950
Indo-European fire cults, 1199–1200, 1207
Indo-European languages, 885 n.56
Indo-Iranian tradition, 1199–1201
Indonesia, 54, 71–72, 1522–1525
Indo-Scythians, 938–943
Indo-Tibetan Buddhism (Snellgrove), 1407
Indo-Tibetan culture, 1990, 2654 n.2
Indo-Tibetica (Tucci), 443
Indra, 1283*f*
Indrabhūti, 2640–2641
Indradevī, 1914–1915
Indraji, Bhagwanlal, 948
Indra's Net, 1698–1699
Indravarma (prince), 939, 940*f*
inference, 536
inferential relations, 1824–1828
infirmaries, 256–257
informal education, 2138–2139
Ingen, 2051, 2054
Injustice and the care of Souls, 472
inner-Asian Buddhist exchanges, 1083–1086
inscriptions. See also *specific inscriptions*
Aśoka and, 932, 934, 2431 n.79, 2560, 2632 n.26
in Bharhut, 932, 934–936, 935*f*
Buddhist, 933–934, 946–948, 2560
in Buddhist media, 2560
donors in, 935, 938
epigraphy and, 886 n.101, 936–943
first Buddhist, 933–934
Iran in, 938
late Buddhist, 946–948
Mahāyāna Buddhist tantra in, 960–962
from Palola dynasty, 886 n.83
in sculptures, 1283
Senavrma in, 940, 941*f*
silence-and-illumination, 652–656
stūpas and, 934–936
Tsukamoto on, 860 n.1
Tulang Tuwo inscription, 960–961
types of, 932–933, 948–951
of Vipulaśrīmitra, 946–947, 946*f*
Inscriptions of Aśoka (Cunningham), 948–949
Insight Meditation, 1053, 1117–1118, 1950–1951
"Inspired by Dunhuang" (art exhibit), 796, 802
Institute of Oriental Manuscripts, 818
Instructional Tantra, 2528
instructions, 2543–2544
Instructions for the Mahāmudrā Joining the Coemergent, 1483–1484
The Instructions of the Eternal Victorious One, 132
Instructions on the Primordial A, 132, 134–135
Intan shipwreck, 1524
integration, 533–539, 1114–1115
The Intellectual Development of Venerable Sheng Yen (Shengyen), 2165–2166
intention (*cetanā*), 7
in Abhidharma theory, 1327–1335
action and, 452–454
Buddhaghosa on, 1333
cognitive, 1297 n.11, 1331–1333, 1335
conative, 1297 n.11, 1323, 1331–1333, 1335
deliberateness and, 1322–1324
Devdas on, 1299 n.31, 1301 n.62, 1344 n.146
functional, 1330–1331
harmful, 2083
karma and, 1321–1322, 1324–1326, 1328–1330
in Nikāyas, 1318–1320
the path and, 1303 n.85, 1326–1327
philosophy of, 1341 n.92
resultant, 1330–1331
saṅkappa/*saṅkalpa* and, 1299 n.31, 1317–1318, 1335–1336
scholarship on, 1335–1336
translations of, 1299 n.35, 1320, 1344 n.155
transmission and, 1333–1335
Vasubandhu on, 1331–1332
Intention sutta, 1322–1323, 1329, 1331

Interbeing (Hanh), 2448
intercultural mimesis, 385–386
interdependence, 159 n.47
interfaith dialogue, 1259
interfaith understanding, 456
interiorization, 1208–1210
intermediate state, 2471–2473
internal signs, 2544
International Academy of Naikan Therapy, 1709–1710
International Association of Buddhist Universities (IABU), 2070
International Buddhist Film Festival, 400
International Council of Monuments and Sites (ICOMOS), 77
International Dunhuang Project, 2566
international groups, 913
International Naikan Association, 1709–1710
International Women's Partnership for Peace and Justice, 906–907
interrelated self, 1953–1955
intersectionality, 922–923, 930 n.120
In the Buddha's Words (Bhikkhu Bodhi), 125
Into the Jaws of Yama (Karma Lekshe Tsomo), 170–171
Introduction a l'histoire du Buddhisme indien (Burnouf), 181, 875, 878–881, 1464, 1505–1506, 2412–2413, 2715. *See also* Burnouf
Introduction to Buddhist Ethics (Harvey), 170–171, 1993
An Introduction to Buddhist Ethics (Shields and Cozort), 986
Introduction to the Practices of Awakening. See *Bodhicaryāvatāra*
Introduction to the Practices of the Bodhisattva. See *Bodhicaryāvatāra*
Introduction to Zen Buddhism (D. T. Suzuki), 706, 714–715, 725, 1945–1946
introspection (*saṃprajanya*), 2082–2083. See also *Naikan*
Inventing Hui-neng (Jorgensen), 1238
Inventory of Medicines, 306–307
Ippolito Desideri, 733
Iran, 545–546, 938–939, 1199–1201
Iraq, 1668–1669
Iriya Yoshitaka, 675–676, 1237–1238
Irk Bitig, 810
Isaacson, Harunga, 1490
"Is a Buddhist Group Changing China? Or Is China Changing It?" (Wu and Johnson), 1222
Iśānavarman, 1788
Ishibashi, 1704
Ishida, Nitten, 47
Ishida Rokurō, 1705–1706
Ishihama Yumiko, 1387
Ishii Akira, 1708
Ishii Kōsei, 756–757
Ishimpō (Tanba Yasuyori), 211
Isidorji, 1647–1648
Islam
- in Abbasid empire, 1674–1679
- Arab-Muslim conquests, 1668, 1670–1672
- *al-budd*, 1469 n.30, 1676–1678
- Buddhism and, 1666–1671
- *al-budd* in, 1469 n.30, 1676
- in Burma/Myanmar, 907, 919, 922, 1099
- in China, 1860–1861, 1871–1873
- Christianity and, 236, 1104, 1650
- in colonialism, 159 n.55
- government and, 1636
- Hinduism and, 1669–1670, 2707–2708
- history and, 1471 n.52
- imperialism and, 383
- Islamic cosmopolis, 968–969
- knowledge in, 1678–1681
- in Malaysia, 1100
- monasteries with, 1469 n.21
- Persia and, 1515–1516
- pre-Islam, 1469 n.18
- religious practice in, 1672–1674
- scholarship on, 1469 n.26
- in South Asia, 1042–1043
- in Southeast Asia, 959
- to Tegüder, 1642
- in U.S., 48
- Zoroastrianism and, 1673–1674

Issei Buddhists, 36, 1304, 1309–1310
issei Japanese, 1351–1352
"Is There Really Esoteric Buddhism?" (McBride), 61–62
itipisogāthā, 1884
Itō Satoshi, 345–346
Iuchi, Maho, 1407
Ives, Christopher, 362, 986
Iwamura, Jane, 226, 234, 240, 398–399, 405–406
Iyanaga Nobumi, 303
Izumi Hōkei, 718

Jackman, Robert, 1950–1951
Jackson, David, 443–444, 1490
Jackson, Peter A., 1993
Jackson, Robert, 1311
Jackson, Roger, 1490–1491, 2024
Jacoby, Sarah, 185–186
Jacques, Claude, 1804 n.77
Jadamba, Lhavgademchig, 1595
Jaffe, Richard, 383–384, 709–710, 725, 2711–2712
Jagaddala Mahāvihāra, 1791, 1797–1798

Jagjivanpur Vihāra, 1791–1792
Jagou, Fabienne, 2388
al-Jāḥiẓ, 1673
Jaini, Padmanabh S., 11
Jainism
  Buddhism and, 2553
  Hinduism and, 260–261
  history of, 2301–2302
  Jains, 1321, 1323
  Pali Buddhism and, 1359 n.2
  philosophy of, 2305–2306
  rituals in, 1201–1202, 2313–2314
  worshiping in, 1498
Jalavāhana, 250–251, 275–276
Jalhanz Khutagt, 1608
Jambudvīpa, 479, 481–482
Jamchen Chöjé Shākya Yeshe, 1062–1063
'Jam-dbyangs bzhad-pa Ngag-dbang brston-'grus, 26
'Jam dpal rnam grol chos kyi rgyal mtshan, 1586
James, Simon P., 1698–1699
James, William, 703, 715, 721–722, 1774, 1942–1943
Jamgön Kongtrul Lodrö Tayé
  Chöd and, 685–687, 695–696
  Karmapa Mikyo Dorjé and, 2751
  scholarship and, 1142, 1487–1488, 2020, 2747, 2750
  typology of, 2512
Jamgön Mipam (Duckworth), 1567
Jamgön Mipham, 1463
Jampa Tenzin Trinley, 1067
Jampel Gyatso, 1380, 2017–2018
Jampel namdröl chökyi gyeltsen, 1383–1384
Jamsrano, 1609
Jamyang Chöje Tashi Palden, 1062–1063
Jamyang Chökyi Trakpa, 2595
Jamyang Gönpo, 691
Jamyang Khyentse Chökyi Lodrö, 1966
Jamyang Khyentsé Wangpo, 685, 1142, 2020, 2747, 2750
Jamyang Kunga Senge, 2610 n.7
Jamyang Zhepa Dorje Ngawang Tsondrü, 1066
Jaṅga Bāhadur Rāṇa, 1043–1044
Jangchub Dzuntrül, 2580–2581
Jangchub Gyaltsen, 1440–1441, 1484–1485
Jannidis, Fotis, 184
Jansen, Berthe, 892, 2671 n.37
Japan. See also *specific topics*
  activism in, 918
  Amoghavajra in, 58–59, 2177
  ancestry in, 776–777
  architecture in, 1308–1309
  Asia and, 1075, 1299 n.31
  Avalokiteśvara in, 93–94
  Buddhism in, 3–4, 1769–1770, 2058 n.5
  Buddhist chaplaincy in, 467–468
  Buddhist deity cults in, 144 n.31
  Buddhist ethics in, 171–172
  Buddhist literature from, 1802 n.35
  Buddho-Shinto relations in, 340–341
  Chan Buddhism in, 645
  China and, 4–5, 68, 83–84, 713 n.10, 751–752, 864–865, 1132, 1445–1446, 1768–1769, 2065, 2342–2343, 2728
  Christianity in, 35
  Code of Kami Law in, 2200–2201
  in Cold War, 2226
  colonialism and, 378–382, 1230–1231
  Confucianism in, 751–753, 759, 777, 1762, 2202–2203
  culture of, 753–756, 758–759, 766–768, 777–779, 1762–1764, 1946–1948, 2351–2358
  debates in, 747–751, 759
  dhāraṇī in, 320
  diagnosis in, 268–270
  domestic Dharma in, 764–766
  D. T. Suzuki in, 708–709
  education in, 701–702, 751–753, 2215
  elder care in, 773–776
  Enryakuji in, 2049–2050, 2053–2054
  Esoteric Buddhism in, 2332, 2363, 2696
  Eurocentrism and, 367
  exile from, 1764–1767
  family in, 764–765
  in Fifteen Year War, 381
  final age of, 296–298
  foreign relations with, 48, 2214
  geopolitics of, 2160
  Germany and, 101, 1708
  government in, 334, 2203
  Hawaii and, 1308, 1360 n.13
  history of, 1760–1767, 1773–1775, 2328–2329, 2335–2336, 2557–2558
  Immigration Act for, 1078–1079
  immigration from, 1304, 1306–1307, 1309
  imperialism by, 190 n.74
  India and, 66–67, 179, 865, 1574–1575, 1864–1865
  Jesuit missionaries in, 273–274, 865–870
  Jōdo Shū sect in, 1578
  Kami cults in, 332–341
  kōan collections in, 664–667
  Kōmei Party in, 2213, 2215–2217, 2227
  Korea and, 191 n.78, 378–382, 1578, 1731–1732
  Kūkai and, 272, 2351
  laymen in, 712 n.6
  LGBTIQ+ Buddhists in, 1987
  local cults in, 334–338, 342–345
  Lotus Sutra in, 271, 2047–2048, 2325–2326

Japan (*continued*)
Mahāyāna Buddhism in, 267–268
marriage in, 2069–2070
Marxism in, 1437
medical system in, 1705–1706
medicine in, 266–268, 278–280
medieval, 1297 n.13, 2632 n.26, 2633 n.44
meditation in, 277–278
military of, 2153
Ming Chan Masters in, 670
modernity in, 345–346, 1074, 1205–1206, 1206*t*
monastic doctors in, 272–274
Mongolia and, 1766–1767
Naikan in, 1702–1704, 1718 n.30
Nara schools for, 2198–2204, 2208–2209, 2342–2343
nationalism in, 724
Nichiren in, 909–910
Ōtani University in, 705–706, 716
Ox Festival in, 295–296
patient treatment in, 270–272
Patriarchal Courtyard in, 674
pharmacological knowledge in, 274–275
politics and, 1383, 2212–2213
popular Buddhism in, 2197
priests in, 2062
prisons in, 1704–1706
protection practices in, 769–770
Pure Land Buddhism in, 1761
reform in, 1136–1137
religion in, 765, 1305, 2196–2199
Religious Corporations Act in, 2212
Rennyo in, 2036–2043
research from, 675–676
ritsuryō codes in, 2208
rituals in, 275–277, 770–773, 2182
Saichō in, 2068
Sanskrit in, 29–30
scholarship and, 60, 2340–2341, 2350–2351
Seiryoji Temple in, 72–73
Shakyamuni Buddha in, 181–182
Shengyen in, 2171 n.40
Shin Buddhism in, 2063–2064
Shingon Buddhism in, 1198–1199, 1204–1208, 1211–1212, 2177–2179, 2182–2184, 2364
Shingon tradition in, 1198
Shinran on, 1297 n.13
Shinto in, 75
Shinto tradition in, 75, 2314
Singapore and, 2062–2063
Sino-Japanese War, 2152–2153, 2170 n.26
society in, 2212, 2217–2218, 2225–2226
Soka Gakkai in, 894
Sri Lanka and, 77
Taiwan and, 1576–1577, 2161–2162
Tang dynasty and, 1212
Tantric Buddhism in, 2324–2335, 2358–2359
tantric revival in, 2390 n.22, 2392 n.69
Tendai School in, 2663
Tenugi cleaning cloths in, 774, 775*f*
Thailand and, 75
Tibetan Buddhism and, 76
Tibet and, 1610
Tokyo, 704–705
Tokyo Imperial University in, 702, 704
tradition in, 756–758
U.S., and, 34–35, 48, 227–228, 707, 1079, 1133–1135, 1151, 1348–1349
vinaya texts in, 2663–2664
Waseda University in, 702
women in, 113 n.18, 774
in World War II, 35–39, 500–503, 703, 706–707, 1774, 2169 n.18
writing in, 2563–2564
Yokawa in, 2046–2047
Yoshida Shinto tradition in, 1203–1204
Zen Buddhism in, 867
Zen commentary from, 646
Japanese Americans
Alien Land Law for, 13 n.5
Buddhist clergy, 35–39
Christianity to, 15 n.25, 46
culture of, 48
in Hawaii, 34, 39
in imprisonment camps, 45–48
national identity of, 42–45
race to, 16 n.49
scholarship on, 48–49
in World War II, 34–35, 39–41
Japanese Buddhisms
Buddhism-based new religious movements from, 1355–1356
in diaspora, 1347–1348
in Hawaii, 1348–1351, 1357, 1360 n.20
in North America, 1351–1353, 1357
scholarship on, 1356–1358
in South America, 1353–1355, 1357–1358
in U.S., 1359 n.7
Zen Buddhism and, 1361 n.41
Japanese Religions at Home and Abroad (Nakamaki), 1357–1358
Japanese tantric paradigm, 2332–2333
Japan Naikan Association, 1707, 1714
Japan's New Buddhism (Murata), 2226
Jarin Korlo, 1549–1550

Jarme Longyang. *See* Longchenpa
jātaka
art and, 1368–1369
Avadānaśataka and, 1372
Buddhavaṃsa and, 1372
in Buddhist life, 1369–1370
Cariyāpiṭaka and, 1372
genre, 1363–1366
Jātakamālā, 1372
Jātakatthavaṇṇanā, 1371–1372
Mahāvastu and, 1372
in Mahāyāna Buddhism, 1367–1368
Paññāsa Jātaka, 1372
perfections in, 1806–1807
scholarship on, 1370–1371
in Southeast Asia, 1369
texts, 1366–1368
in Thailand, 1369–1370
Theravāda Buddhism and, 1364–1365, 1367
Xuanzang and, 1370
The Jātaka (Fausbøll), 1814
Jātakamālā (Āryaśūra), 944
Jātakastava, 809
Jātaka tales, 985
Jatiṃdhara, 250–251
Jatson Nyingpo, 838–839, 1164
Java, 962
Jayabhadra, 1521
Jayaccandradeva (king), 948
Jaya Indravarman (king), 1911
Jaya Indravarman II (king), 1901–1902
Jayānanda, 627
Jayanātha, 1794
Jayarājadevī (queen), 84, 1914–1916, 1916*f*
Jayavardhanapura, 2250
Jayavarman II, 1095–1096
Jayavarman V (king), 1519, 1902, 1904
Jayavarman VI (king), 962, 1907
Jayavarman VII (king), 84
in Khmer empire, 1914–1916, 1925–1927
Khmer Esoteric Buddhism and, 1897, 1907–1923
legacy of, 960, 962, 1519–1520, 1805 n.105, 1902–1903, 1919
scholarship on, 1897, 1925–1927
Jayülpa, 2010–2011
Jebtsundamba Khutugtus, 1387, 2019–2022. *See also* Mongolia
Je Khenpo, 2019
Je Naphuwa. *See* Ling Repa Pema Dorje
Jenkins, Stephen, 2078
Jennings, Ananda, 2728
Jennings, Pilar, 1955
Jepa Shönu Jangchub, 1444
Jerryson, Michael, 199–200
Jesuit missionaries, 273–274, 864–870, 878–881
"Jesus Loves Me," 226
Jetāri, Acārya, 1972–1973
Jé Tsongkhapa Lozang Drakpa. *See* Tsongkhapa
Jetsun Chökyi Gyaltsen, 1064–1065
Jewel Garland (Remdawa), 2748–2749
Jewel in the Ashes (Ruppert), 2209
Jewel Net of Indra, 358
Jewel Ornament of Liberation (Gampopa), 986, 1983–1984
Jewel Translucent Sūtra (Khan), 1750
Jewish art, 2262
Jewish Buddhists, 196
jhāna factors, 510–512, 514–520
Ji, Xianlin, 825
Jiang, Boqin, 821–823
Jiang Canteng, 1260
Jiang Tesheng, 1440
Jiang Wu, 183
Jiang Zemin, 1592
Jianming, 2382, 2384*f*
Jianying, 1443
Jianzhen, 1517, 2204
Jianzhong, 656, 660–661. *See also* flame-of-the-lamp records
Jiaojing, 5–6
Jiatai (Lei'an), 661
Jibik-Temür, 1635
Jichan, 2279
Jichen, 1443
Jichie, 2178–2179, 2181–2182, 2355
Jie. *See* Ryōgen
Jigme Lingpa, 830, 838–839, 1436, 1441–1442, 1966
Jigme Namkha Dorje, 137
Jigme Pema Wangchen, 1988, 2595
Jigme Puntsog, 839–840
Jigme Singye Wangchuck, 895–896
Jihen, 340
Jikaku Daishi. *See* Ennin
Jikten Sumgön, 1482
Jimon lineage, 2348, 2358–2359
Jinakālamālī, 1726–1727
Jinakālamālīpakaraṇaṃ, 1722
Jinamitra, 3
Jinapañjara-gāthā, 1884–1885
Jincheng Gongzhu (princess), 2574
Jin Dizang, 1868
Jin dynasty, 998
Jinfanwang banniepan jing, 998
Jing, Anning, 1656–1657

Jing'an Buddhist Seminary, 2154–2155
Jin'gang jing, 1224
Jin'gang jing zhengjie, 1234–1235
Jingde, 658–661, 664–665. *See also* flame-of-the-lamp records
Jingde chuandeng lu, 1224, 1226, 1233–1234
Jinggim, 1630
Jinghui, 2735
Jingjue, 1226–1227, 1232, 1237–1239
Jingsheng, Juqu, 2688–2689
Jing Si Dharma Lineage, 2621–2625, 2627
Jingtu yu Chan (Yinshun), 1452 n.86
Jinhua Weimian, 2662
Jinke Xuanlei, 2384–2385
jinlap, 2513–2515, 2525 n.58
Jinpa, Thupten, 1407
Jinul, 519
Jinyun, Wang. *See* Shih
Jinzen, 2047, 2051–2054, 2184
Jitō (empress), 2199
Jitsuhan, 2184
Jitsunyo, 2041–2042
Jiuhua Poetry Society, 1868
Jīvaka, 255–256, 279–280, 1518–1519
Jīvaka Kumārabhrta, 209
Jīvaka-Pustaka, 814
Jīvitagupta II (king), 1784–1785, 1788–1789
Jizang, 2207
"Jizoku in Sōtō Zen Buddhism" (Noriko), 778–779
Jñānagarbha, 1467, 1537–1538, 1543, 2464
Jñāna-prasthāna (*JPŚ*), 2, 2093–2098, 2101, 2115–2117. *See also* Sarvāstivāda Abhidharma school
Jñānaśrīmitra, 1828
Jñānasūtra, 837
Jo Bo. *See* Atiśa Dīpaṃkaraśrījñāna
Jōdokei shisōron (D. T. Suzuki), 719–720
Jōdo-shinshū, 164–165
Jōdo Shinshū Buddhism, 226, 232, 338–339, 912. *See also* Shin Buddhism
Jodo Shinshu Buddhist Temples of Canada (JSBTC), 1353
Jōdoshū Buddhism, 35, 1348, 1351
Jōdo Shū sect, 1578
Jōgen, 303–304
Jōgyō, 2355
John of Plano Carpini, 1625
John of the Cross (Saint), 508
John Paul II (pope), 1219–1220
Johnson, Charles, 237
Johnson, Ian, 1222, 1875
Johnston, E. H., 125
Jōjitsu. *See* Nara schools
Jōkei, 752–753
Jokhàng Temple, 434–435, 436*f*, 438
Jokpa Jangchup Penden, 1744–1745, 1748–1749
Jomo Zangngé, 1549
Jonang (Gyurme), 695
Jonang Dolpopa Sherab Gyaltsen, 1464
Jonang tradition, 2313
Jones, Charles B., 380–381, 1017, 2294–2295, 2625
Jones, Ken, 912, 917, 930 n.120
Jones, William, 872–875, 885 n.56, 1464
Jong, J. W. de, 1814
Jongeward, David, 941*f*
Jönggen (Lady), 1645, 1647, 1651–1652
Jorgensen, John, 1238
Josephson, Jason Ānanda, 865
Joshi, Khyati Y., 2716
Jōson, 2184
Journal of Buddhist Ethics, 2565
journals, 826
Jowo Rinpoche, 1731–1732
Jowo Śākyamuni statute, 2517
Jōyo, 2185
Jōyū, 1708
Jōyuishiki ron dōgakushō, 759–760
JPŚ. *See Jñāna-prasthāna*
JSBTC. *See* Jodo Shinshu Buddhist Temples of Canada
ju (lift up; raise), 665–667
Judaism, 159 n.45, 812, 916–917, 1672–1674
Judson, Adoniram, 1048
Judson, Ann Hasseltine, 1049–1050
Jueding pini jing, 2705 n.105
Juefan Huihong, 669–670
Juergensmeyer, Mark, 200, 1140, 2131
Ju Mipham Namgyel Gyatso (Mipham), 2476–2478, 2489, 2494–2497, 2747, 2750–2751
Jumo Horzang Chöling, 1559–1560
Junaysar (king), 1678
Jung, Carl, 1945–1948, 1953, 2469, 2479–2480
Junna (emperor), 2179
Junnin, 2199
Junnyo, 2037–2038
Jun Unchida, 191 n.78
Jurchen Jin dynasty, 1623–1624
Jushe lun ji (Puguang), 10
Jushe lun shu (Fabao and Shentai), 10
Juzan, 1262

Kabat-Zinn, Jon, 985, 1118, 1951–1953, 2131–2132, 2717–2718
Kabilsingh, Chatsumarn, 913
Kaccāyanagotta Sutta, 1453–1454
Kachem Kakölma, 2583
Kadam doctrine, 850

Kadam order, 1479
Kadampa
  Atiśa Dīpaṃkaraśrījñāna for, 1397–1399
  'Brom ston Rgyal ba'i 'byung gnas for, 1399–1400
  Buddhahood in, 1401–1402, 1405
  culture of, 1403–1405
  early teachers of, 1394–1401
  later lineages of, 1400–1401
  lineage, 1536
  mind training in, 1403, 1405–1406
  scholarship on, 1396–1397, 1406–1408
  in Tibetan Buddhism, 1393–1394, 1405–1406
Kadam tradition, 2313
Kaempfer, Engelbert, 870–871, 874–875
Kagami no Ookimi, 2205–2206
Kageyama Kyōshun, 278–279
Kagyü lineage. *See also* Drukpa Kagyü school
  hierarchies in, 1548
  identity of, 1547
  Kagyu tradition and, 10, 1482–1489, 1536, 1544, 1939–1940
  Marpa Lotsawa and, 1539, 1545
  Rangjung Dorjé for, 1483–1485
  religion to, 1472, 1481–1482
  tradition of, 1478, 2313
Kakkai, 2185–2187
Kakuban, 2184–2186, 2356, 2359, 2633 n.47
Kakuchō, 2051, 2055
Kakue, 2045–2046, 2350
Kakuhen, 752–753
Kakukei, 2048, 2051, 2054
Kakunyo, 2036
Kakuun, 2051, 2055
Kakuzo, Okakura, 75
Kālacakra, 484, 1416, 1418–1422
Kālacakra cosmology, 2745–2746
Kālacakra images, 429–430, 432*f*
Kālacakra literature, 2543, 2546–2548
kālacakra-maṇḍala
  bodhisattvas in, 1421*t*
  deities in, 1418–1422
  goddesses in, 1419–1420, 1421*t*, 1423–1429
  imagery in, 1416–1422
  powder and, 1426–1428
  purification of, 1428–1431
  in rituals, 1422–1431
  scholarship on, 1142, 1148–1149, 1416, 1431–1432
  structure in, 1416–1422
  symbolism in, 441–443
Kālacakratantra, 246, 258–259, 837, 1420–1422, 1501, 1566, 1679, 2546, 2749
Kālacakra tradition, 2548
"Kalachakra for World Peace" program, 1149
Kālayaśas, 2683, 2688
Kalila and Dimna, 1674–1675
Kalupahana, David J., 986
Kalyāṇavardhana, 1792, 2077
Kalzang Gyatso, 1066–1067, 2017
Kāmadeva, 1418–1419
Kamakura Buddhism, 2341
Kamalaśīla, 513, 685–686, 730–731, 1461, 1467, 1836, 2579–2580
Kāma Sūtra, 1561
Kamatari, Fujiwara no, 2205–2206
Kamhaeng (king), 1726
Kami cults, 332–341. *See also* Shinto
Kammatic Buddhism, 344–345
Kampo, 267, 278
Kan'ami, 757
Kanazawa, Shimeji, 912
Kandahjaya, Huydaya, 1471 n.65, 1528
Kanda Kumara-Skanda, 2249–2251. See also *satara varan devi*
Kandhapa, 1543
Fujiwara Kaneie, 2053–2054
Kangen, 2178–2179, 2355
Kang Senghui, 1518–1519
Kangxi (emperor), 325–326, 1377–1378, 1504, 1862–1863, 2017, 2499
Kang Youwei, 2279
Kāṅha, 1489–1490
kanhdas, 2102*t*
Kaniṣka (king), 543–545, 1733, 2562
Kanjōrekimyō, 2333–2334
Kanko, Kritee, 911
Kanmo Imamura, 1310–1311
Kanmu (emperor), 748–750, 755, 2203–2204, 2324–2328, 2343–2345
Kaṇṇakatthala Suttas, 250
Kannon, Shinran Kuse, 93
Kannon Bosatsu, 268
Kānphaṭa tradition, 2309
Kant, Immanuel, 717–718, 871, 1464–1465
Kapleau, Philip, 1947
Kaplonski, Christopher, 1386, 1613–1615
Kapoor, Shivani, 1927
Kapstein, Matthew
  Gyurme Dorje and, 1446
  Lopez to, 113 n.23
  on Marpa Lotsawa, 1551–1552
  on Mipam, 1567
  scholarship from, 4, 11, 695, 713 n.26, 821–823, 1068–1069, 1174, 1656–1657, 1974, 2750–2751
  on tantric revival, 2387–2388
  on Trisong Detsen, 2586

Kara, G., 1656–1658
Kāraṇḍavyūha Sūtra, 247, 1802 n.30, 1901–1902, 1918, 1972–1973, 1973*f*
Karaṇīyamettā Sutta, 1884–1886
Karate Kid (film), 233, 398–399
karchok (White Side), 2487–2488
karma
  benefits of, 2079
  bodies and, 114
  Buddhaghosa on, 1330, 1333–1334
  cetanā and, 1321–1322, 1324–1326, 1328–1330
  death and, 2102–2103
  diversity and, 1991–1992
  ethics and, 861 n.8, 975–976, 995, 1695–1696, 2103
  family, 777
  four noble truths and, 979
  intention and, 452–454, 1321–1322, 1324–1326, 1328–1330
  karmic connections, 1367
  karmic illness, 285–292, 310–311
  karmic recompense, 1772
  meditation and, 195
  to monks, 248
  psychology of, 861 n.11
  in Pure Land Buddhism, 327
  rebirth and, 2135–2136
  in secular Buddhism, 2134–2135
  theories of, 5
  translations of, 1299 n.25, 1319–1320
  Vasubandhu on, 1331–1332, 1334, 1344 n.162
Karma Chagme, 839, 1487–1488, 1966–1968, 1970–1972, 1974, 2502 n.9
Karma Kagyü, 2014, 2016, 2018, 2022
Karma Kagyü Buddhism, 1627, 2000 n.76
Karma Lekshe Tsomo, 170–171
Karma Lingpa, 2467–2470, 2475–2476
Karma Lodrö Chökyi Senge, 2022
Karma Pakshi, 1627, 2007, 2011–2013, 2024–2025
Karmapas. See *specific karmapas*
Karma Phuntsho, 845, 1567, 2025
Karmay, Samten, 840, 2481, 2488–2489, 2500, 2501 n.2, 2503 n.33
karmic merit (*puṇya*), 2088
Karpelès, Suzanne, 1052–1053
karuṇā (compassion), 167
Karunadas, 1634
Karunaratna, 1336
Karunatilake, H. N. S., 895–896
Kasato Maru (ship), 1353–1354
Kashima, Tetsuden, 35
kasiṇa, 515–516
Kasuya Makoto, 302
Katañ̃u Sutta, 993–994, 997, 1004–1005
Kathāvathu, 529–530
Kaṭhinakkhandhaka, 1052–1053
Kathmandu Valley, 1042–1045
Katja Triplett, 306
Kato, 2122 n.14
Katok Getsé Paṇḍita, 2747
Katok Situ, 1541, 1545
Katok Tsewang Norbu, 1540
Katsom Chenmo, 690–691
Katsunō Ryūshin, 2336
Katsura, Shōryū, 1466
Kātyāyanīputra, 2116–2117
Kaula tradition, 2308–2310, 2315
Kavīndrārimathana, 1902–1904
Kāvyādarśa (Daṇḍin), 1552
Kawahara Ryuzo, 1715
Kawamura, Leslie, 1815
kāyika-duḥkha (physical pain), 2084
Kaza, Stephanie, 362
Kazi Dawa Samdup, 1489–1490, 2469
Kazushi Iwao, 2586
Keenan, John P., 2464
Kegon. *See* Nara schools
Keiffer-Pülz, Petra, 1578–1579
Keiji, Nishitani, 1352–1353
Keikai, 287–288
Keiko Tosa, 571, 579–580, 604
Keimei, 2055
Keimyō, 2055
Keiō University, 1303–1304
Keira, Ryūsei, 29–30
Keizan Jōkin, 2187
Kekaya, 998
Kellner, Birgit, 1837–1838
Kelman, Harold, 1947, 1953
Kelsang Gyatso, 2077
Kelzang Tsültrim, 1751–1753
Kemper, Steven, 1098
kenmitsu ideology, 755
Kennedy, Hugh, 1469 n.26
Kensen, 300
Keown, Damien, 169–171, 885 n.68, 981
Kerouac, Jack, 723–724, 1311
Ketelaar, James, 182
Keüken Noyan, 1377
Khachö Wangpo, 2012
Khadro Crystal Chu Rinpoche, 1138
Khālid ibn Barmak, 1675–1676
Khalkha Jebtsundampa Zanabazar, 1376–1378

Khalkha Tüšiyetü Khan Ġombodorji, 1376
Khanchen Choijal, 1377
Khandro, Sera, 185–186
Khandro Nyingtig, 837–838
Khan family, 1639–1646. See also *specific people*
Kharbanda, 1642
Kharoṣṭhī Inscriptions with the Exception of Those of Aśoka (Konow), 948–949
Khedrub Je, 1441–1442
Khedrup Gelek Palsang, 1062–1063
Khedrup Jé, 1063, 2016
Khédrup sanggyé yéshé, 1376
Khema, Ayya, 913
Khenchen Palden Sherab, 2650–2651
Khenchen Thrangu Rinpoché, 695–696
Khenpo Jikme Phuntsok Jungné, 1505, 2495, 2497
Khenpo Lodrö Drakpa, 2747–2748, 2750
Khenpo Namdrol Rinpoche, 2650–2651
Khenpo Ngagchung, 1441–1442
Khenpo Sodargye, 1137–1138
Khenpo Tsewang Dongyal, 2650–2651
Khenpo Tsultrim Gyamtso Rinpoche, 2748, 2750
Khetsun Sangpo, 854
al-Khidr, 1681
Khitan Liao dynasty, 1623
Khmer art, 969
Khmer domains, 1526–1527
Khmer empire
  deities in, 1923, 1924*f*
  history of, 1095–1096, 1907, 1923, 1924*f*, 1927
  Jayavarman VII in, 1914–1916, 1925–1927
  monarchs in, 1907–1923
  Tantric Buddhism in, 1907
Khmer Esoteric Buddhism
  deities in, 1801 n.15
  epigraphy in, 1906–1907
  goddesses in, 1800 n.2, 1804 n.97, 1914–1918
  history of, 1907
  Jayavarman VII and, 1897, 1907–1923
  in Pāla India, 1923–1925
  Prajñāpāramitā and, 1897–1899, 1906–1907, 1925–1926
  Sab Bāk inscription in, 1906–1907
  scholarship on, 1926–1927
  Tibetan Buddhism and, 1938 n.123
  Wat Sithor inscription for, 1904–1906
Khmer Rouge regime, 906–907, 1052–1053, 1101, 2233, 2237
Khön family, 1479–1480
Không, Chân, 2436, 2439, 2441, 2447–2448
Không, Thích nữ Chân. *See* Phương
Khön Könchok Gyalpo, 688, 1479–1480
Khotan, 112 n.16, 113 n.19, 545–551
Khotanese-language materials, 808–809, 820–821
khri (mind), 113 n.21, 130
Khri-srong-Ide-btsan (king), 1503
Khro ru Klu grub rgya mtsho, 1491
Khuankaew, 914–915
Khubilai Khan, 1583
Khuddaka Nikāya, 1366
Khu ston, 1399
Khutughtai Sechen Khungtaiǰi, 1645
The Khutugtus of Urga (Pozdneev), 1386
Khyabdal Lhundrub, 1441
Khyabpa Lakring, 2545
Khyungpo Naljor, 688, 1480
Khyung Tsangpa Yeshe Lama, 850
Kibi no Makibi, 751–752
Kidder, Edward, 2209
Kiduk, Kim, 232–233, 404
Kieffer-Pülz, Petra, 153, 2067, 2660
Kielhorn, Franz, 950
Kieschnick, John, 183, 2518–2519
'l-Kifl, Dhū, 1670–1671
Kikkaduve Sumaṅgala, 1046–1047
Kikyō, 2049
Kīlaguhya Tantra, 2642
Kīlanirvāṇa Tantra, 2642, 2645, 2649–2650
kīlas
  dhāraṇī and, 2637
  nāga and, 2636
  in *Ṛgveda*, 2635–2636
  rites of, 2647
  in rituals, 2647
  sacred architecture with, 2636–2637
  symbolism of, 2641
  Vajrakīla tantras and, 2648–2650
  varieties of, 2648–2650
Kīla Tantra in Twelve Chapters, 2645
Kīla Vidyottama Tantra, 2641–2642
Kim, Jinah, 1926
Kim Chŏnghŭi, 1230–1231
Kim Ki-Duk, 405–406
Kim Kugyŏng, 1237
al-Kindī, 1676
King, Martin Luther, Jr., 905, 2439–2440
King, Sallie, 915–916, 986, 2444, 2447–2448, 2449 n.7
King Dohā Treasuries, 1475–1476
Kingdom of the Sick (Burns), 310–311
King Kao's Guanshiyin Sutra, 86–87
The King of Aspiration Prayers, 1967–1968
King of Concentrations, 1472–1473, 1477, 1482

Kinmei (emperor), 305–306, 334
Kinnard, Jacob, 1723–1724
Kinst, Daijaku, 455–456
Kirby, Thomas M., 1308
Kircher, Athanasius, 870–871, 875
Kirita Kiyohide, 710
al-Kirmānī, Abū ḤafṣʿUmar, 1670
Kīrtikalā (Ratnakīrti), 25–26
Kīrtipaṇḍita, 1519, 1526, 1902, 1904
Kīrtiśrī Rājasiṃha (king), 2245–2246, 2416
Kīrttivara, 1902
Kissinger, Henry, 2213
*Kitāb al-tanbīh wa'lishrāf*al-Masʿūdī, 1672–1673
Kitan Liao dynasty, 494
Kitano Yūrin, 273
Kitarō, Nishida, 1352–1353
The Kitchen God's Wife (Tan), 237
Kitiarsa, Pattana, 894–895
Kitsuse, John, 1714
Kittisaro, 913
Kiuchi Gyōō, 2334
Kizil, 112 n.5, 551–556
Kizō, 2046
Klaproth, Julius von, 876
Klimburg-Salter, Deborah, 443–444, 1669–1670, 1672, 1677
KMT. *See* Kuomintang
Knight Güyeng, 1655–1657
knowledge
  authority and, 622–623
  in Buddhaghosa, 1322–1323
  doctrinal, 2175–2176
  in Islam, 1678–1681
  knowing, 2539
  medical, 254–255, 2532–2533
  to Mipam, 1564
  pharmacological, 274–275
  of Sanskrit, 17
  science and, 499–500
  in Vedic tradition, 567–568
kōan collections, 664–667
Kōbō Daishi. *See* Kūkai
Köden Khan, 1625–1626, 1643
Kōdō Nishimura, 1987
Kōfukuji, 2037
Kōgi lineage, 2356
Kohn, Richard K., 1203
Kohomba Kankariya rite, 2260 n.46
Koji Sato, 1946–1947
Kōjō, 2330, 2345
Kokan Shiren, 289, 311
Kōkei, 2348
Kōken (empress), 2198–2199, 2202
Kokubungaku Kenkyū Shiryōkan, 759
Kōkūzō, 1760–1761
Kollmar-Paulenz, Karénina, 695, 1594, 1656–1658
Komatani, 1703
Kōmei Party, 2213, 2215–2217, 2227
Kōmyō (empress), 273, 275–276, 291–292, 306–307, 2198–2199
Kōmyō Shingon (Myōe), 2181
Konāgamana, 933–934
Kong, Chan, 905
Konggu Jinglong, 1234
Kongōkyō to Rokuso dankyō no kenkyu (Matsumoto), 1236
Kongtrul Lodro Taye, 422, 1553, 1970–1971
Kōnin (emperor), 2199
Kōnin ikai (Kūkai), 2331–2332
Konow, Sten, 639, 939, 948–949
Korea. *See also* colonialism
  Buddhism in, 169, 356–357
  Buddhist chaplaincy in, 176 n.69, 466–467
  Buddhist deity cults in, 144 n.31
  China and, 77, 645, 1348, 1709, 2667
  Christianity in, 466, 1709
  Huineng in, 1230–1231
  Japan and, 191 n.78, 378–382, 1578, 1731–1732
  monarchs in, 334
  monasteries in, 225 n.83
  movable type in, 2563–2564
  North America and, 1589–1590
  Taiwan and, 378–379, 1591
  Thailand and, 176 n.69
  Vietnam and, 83–84
  Zutang from, 658
Kornfield, Jack, 1081–1082, 1117–1118, 1956, 2142
Kőrös, Alexander Csoma de, 878–879, 2534
Korvin-Krasinski, Cyrill von, 2529–2530
Kōsetsu Rongishū (Kokubungaku), 759
Koshin Ogui, 1987
Kosofsky, Eve, 1981. *See also* Queer Theory
Kosygin, Aleksey, 2213
Kotte rulers, 2259 n.30
Kotwicz, Wladyslaw, 1606, 1614
Kōun, Kajiyoshi, 29–30
Koyama Satoko, 304
Kōyasan, 1136, 2181–2182, 2184–2185, 2374–2376
Koyasan Buddhist Temple, 1133
Kōyasan Jūkon-in, 2385–2386
Kozen, Shaku, 2711–2712
Kozlov, Petr, 1614

Kraft, Kenneth, 362
Kragh, Ulrich Timme, 105–106, 109–110, 1490
Krech, Gregg, 1709, 1715
Kripal, Jeffrey J., 1949
Kritzer, Robert, 11, 260–261
Kroraina, 545–551
Krotkov, N. N., 818
Kṛtajña Sūtra, 997
Kṣaṇikavādins, 2112
Kṣāntivādin, 115
Kṣāntivādin Jātaka, 1806–1807
Kṣitigarbha, 1518
Kṣitigarbha and the Ten Kings of Hell, 790–791, 792*f*
Kṣitigarbha Sutra, 807
Kṣudraka texts, 633–634, 636
Kubera, 2247–2249, 2253–2254
Kubilai Khan, 731, 1503–1504, 1519–1520, 2011, 2013–2015, 2563
Kubose Gyōmei, 45
Kubrawī Sufism, 1678–1679
Kucha, 113 n.20, 551–555
Kudara Kannon, 75
Kuda Rentarō, 1237
Kuiji, 533, 2207, 2284
Kuiming, 2392 n.52
Kuishans, 543–555
Kujaku Myōō, 301, 303
Kujip, Leonard van der, 1444, 1656–1657, 2024
Kūkai. *See also* Shingon Buddhism
  Abe Ryūchi on, 2359
  Amoghavajra to, 1524
  in China, 2187
  death of, 2347
  disciples of, 2345, 2349
  doctrinal views of, 2362 n.44
  Esoteric Buddhism and, 2333, 2364
  esotericism and, 299, 305–306
  esoteric scripture to, 2354
  Japan and, 272, 2351
  Kakuban on, 2362 n.47
  Kokan Shiren and, 311
  Kōyasan by, 2181–2182
  legacy of, 2352–2354, 2357, 2376
  major works of, 2180
  in maritime trade, 1519
  philosophy of, 2332–2333
  on power objects, 2525 n.51
  reputation of, 2344
  Saga and, 302, 306–307
  Saichō and, 2182–2183, 2324–2336, 2340–2343, 2346–2347, 2354–2355
  scholarship and, 749, 1137, 1351, 2324–2328, 2632 n.25
  Shingon Buddhism and, 2173, 2177–2180, 2333
  statues of, 2378–2380, 2381*f*
  studies, 2184–2185
  Taimitsu and, 2345
  Tantric Buddhism to, 2328–2329
  Tendai School and, 2182
  Vajrabuddhi to, 1524
Kūkai (Hakeda), 2336
Kukkuṭapāda, 100
Kukuripa, 1544
Kularatne, Tilak, 1045–1046
Kumagai, 858
Kumagai Naozane, 2185
Kumāra, 1518–1519
Kumārādza, 1438–1439, 1445–1446
Kumāragupta I (king), 1783–1784, 1788
Kumārajīva, 85–86, 497–498, 1187, 1461–1462, 1724–1725, 2218
Kundalini Yoga, 2314, 2321 n.15
Kündröl Drakpa, 132, 134, 136
Kündröl lineage, 137
Kundun (film), 233, 397–398
Kunga dondrub, 1063–1064
Kunga Migyur Dorje, 1162
Kunga Özer, 1437
Kung Fu (film series), 398–399
Kunsang, Erik Pema, 2587
Kunzang Pelden, 2077
Kuomintang (KMT), 2366
Kuroda Toshio, 311, 332, 346, 2633 n.44
Kuṣāṇas, 938–943
Kusha. *See* Nara schools
Kushan rulers, 1282–1283
Kushida Ryōkō, 2336
Kusunoki Junshō, 759–760
Kūṭadanta Sutta, 888
Kværne, Per., 1491
Kyabje Thinley Norbu Rinpoche, 1441–1442
Kyangmo Khapa, 856
Kyanzittha (king), 343, 1789–1790
Kyōgaku, 2037, 2040
Kyōgoku Itsuzō, 43–45
Kyōgyoshinshō (Shinran), 706, 708–709, 719–721, 725, 2037
Kyōjin, 2184
Kyo Sönam Lama, 687
Kyotön, 689
Kyōtsū Hori, 1774–1775
Kyungtsangpa, 1469 n.11, 1539–1540

labor politics, 1584
labrangs (estates), 2013, 2015, 2021
Lachs, Stuart, 183
LaFleur, William, 287–288
Lagpa Sonam Chodrub, 1442–1443
Lahaina Shingon Mission, 1351
LAHH. *See* Los Angeles Hompa Hongwanji
Lai, David Chuenyan, 417
Lai, Rongdao, 918, 921–922
Laiguo, 2733
Lai Rongdao, 2294–2295
laity, 212–213, 1113–1114, 1121
lakes, 1853
Lakṣagrantham Abhiprajñam, 1906
Lakṣaṇānusāriṇī (Purṇavardhana), 10
lakṣaṇas, 1279–1280
Lakṣmīṅkarā, 1901
Laliberté, André, 417, 1009, 1017, 2625–2626
Lalitavistara, 125, 184, 1043–1044, 1807–1808, 1814
Lalou, Marcelle, 820
The Lama Question (Kaplonski), 1614–1615
lamas, 1723–1724, 1727–1728, 1737. *See also* Dalai Lama
Lambakaṇṇa dynasty, 2433 n.109
Lamotte, Étienne
  on biography, 180, 184, 186
  scholarship from, 949, 1032–1033, 1506, 1815, 2264, 2464
Lamp for the Eyes of Contemplation (Nub Sangye Yeshe), 833–834, 840
Lamp for Wisdom (Bhāviveka), 623–624
Lamp That Illuminates the Expanse of Reality (Garungwa Lhai Gyaltsen), 2748–2749
lam rim (steps of the path), 1400–1403, 1406–1407, 1414 n.39
Lam-rimchen-mo (Tsongkhapa), 1815
Lancaster, Lewis, 1527, 2566–2567
Landresse, Ernest Augustin Xavier Clerc de, 876
landscape poetry, 355–356, 362
Lane, Beatrice. *See* Suzuki, Beatrice Lane
Lang, Karen, 627–629
Langdarma (king), 684–685
Lang Lhazik Repa, 1540
Lang Nyézik, 2574–2575
Lang Pelgi Senge, 2502 n.9
language
  Asian, 98–100, 151–153
  in Burma/Myanmar, 112 n.1, 567–574
  Chinese-language materials, 806–807, 819–820
  Chinese languages, 1963, 1978 n.31, 2208–2209, 2393 n.70
  of community, 2073 n.4
  connotations, 2265–2266
  debate, 735–737
  in Dunhuang texts, 806–810
  emic languages, 172
  European languages, 9–10
  foreign language schools, 1306
  genres and, 645–656
  grammatical inconsistencies, 1029
  ideology, 152–153
  immigration and, 415–416, 1112
  Indo-European languages, 885 n.56
  in Kusha, 112 n.6
  mantric words, 1424–1425, 1430–1431
  Old Turkic-language materials, 810
  of Pali Buddhism, 144 n.30, 2399–2400, 2427 n.29, 2711
  philosophy of, 2339 n.25
  Sanskrit-language materials, 810
  scripts and, 933
  semantics, 686–687, 2427 n.20
  Sogdian-language materials, 809–810
  in South Asia, 933
  syllables, 2647–2648
  Thai, 484–485, 965
  in Tibet, 740–741, 1378
  Tibetan Buddhism and, 686–687
  Tibetan language, 1603–1604, 2122 n.14, 2266
  Tibetan-language materials, 807–808, 820
  translations of, 1963–1964
  Uighur, 4
  Vasubandhu on, 1801 n.26
  vernacular, 1736–1737
  Western, 1212, 2696
  Zhang zhung, 128–129
Lanka, 656–657
Lankan monks, 2068–2069
Lankatilaka, 2250
Laṅkāvatāra Sūtra, 274–275, 706, 834
Laos. *See also* colonialism
  Cambodia and, 1096, 1100–1101, 1884, 2231–2232, 2235–2236, 2238–2239, 2242–2243, 2564
  Canada and, 1115–1116
  China and, 1574
  community and, 2235
  culture of, 2236–2237
  demographics of, 2232
  history of, 73–74
  Khmer Rouge regime and, 2233
  society in, 2232–2233
  Thailand and, 73, 1115, 1580, 1733–1734, 1890–1891
  Theravāda Buddhism in, 2417–2418
  U.S., and, 2238

Laozi, 1861, 1864
Laozi Xiang'er zhu, 812
Las chen Kun dga' rgyal mtshan, 1397
The Last King of Mongolia (Batsaikhan), 1386–1387
Latchford, Douglas, 1800 n.2, 1919, 1920*f*
late Buddhist inscriptions, 946–948
latent dispositions (*anuśaya-nirdeśa*), 5
Later Comments on the Spring and Autumn Annals, 813
Later Transmission period, 2313
Latin America, 1353–1355, 1357–1358
Latour, Bruno, 864, 880–882, 2142–2144
Lattimore, Owen, 1613
Lau, Arnold L., 2627
La Vallée Poussin, 1464–1465, 2088
lay Buddhism, 165, 168–169, 2418–2420
lay Buddhists, 317 n.103, 2289–2291, 2365
lay Christianity, 567
lay leadership, 2126–2127
Layman Mingyi, 1231
laymen, 712 n.6, 2061–2063, 2065–2068
laywomen, 2061–2063, 2067–2068
Lazarus, Ashton, 756–757
Lcang skya rol pa'i rdo rje, 1504–1505
Lce sgom Shes rab rdo rje, 1396–1397
leaders, in Buddhism, 2731–2733
Learman, Linda, 1131, 1150
Leary, Timothy, 2479–2480
Leclère, Adhémard, 1890
Ledi Sayadaw (Ledī Hsayādaw), 591–593, 605–606, 1097–1098
Lee, Chengpang, 2627
Lee, Jong Schoel, 3–4
Lee, Lois, 2128
Lee-Kalisch, Jeong-Hee, 443–444
Lefferts, Leedom, 2270
Lefmann, Salomon, 1814
legal documents, 812–813
Legend of Queen Cama, 499–500
Lei, Sylvian, 2711–2712
Lei'an Zhengshou, 661
Leibniz, Gottlieb Wilhelm Friedrich von, 872
Lele, Amod, 920, 986, 2088–2089
Lê Long Đĩnh (king), 1039–1040
Lelung Jedrung Zhepé Dorjé, 1746–1748, 2494–2495
Lelung Zhepe Dorje, 1161–1162, 1170
Lempert, Michael, 744
Lengqie shizi ji (Jingjue), 1226–1227, 1232, 1237–1239
Lengyan jing, 2282
Leng Yen texts, 2563
Lenin, Vladimir, 1609
Leninism, 1609, 1611–1612
Lennon, John, 2480
Leonard, Lou, 911
Leopold, Aldo, 357–358
leprosy, 271–272, 289–290
Lepsius, Karl Richard, 2468–2469
Letters. *See* Rennyo
letters, in Chan literature, 646, 671–672
Letters of Dahui (Dahui), 655, 666–667, 671–672
"Letter to a Friend" (Nāgārjuna), 1809–1810
Letter to My Disciples (Dölpopa), 2745–2746
Leuba, James Henry, 1942
Lévi, Sylvain, 29–30, 1527, 2283
Levinas, Emmanuel, 1982
Levine, Noah, 464, 1118–1119
Levine, Sarah, 1148
Levy-Rubin, Milka, 1671–1672
Lezun, 781
LGBTIQ+ Buddhists. *See also* Queer Theory
  anti-LGBTIQ+ sentiments, 1986–1987
  to Buddhist Churches of America, 1989
  Chao-Hwei for, 1987
  Chogyam Trungpa for, 1988
  feminism and, 1989
  in Global North, 1990
  identity of, 1988
  in Japan, 1987
  liberation to, 1990
  in Neo-Buddhism, 1989
  people of color and, 457
  philosophy and, 1988
  sexuality and, 1981
  in Thailand, 1990
  in Tibet, 1988–1989
  trans* people and, 1991–1993
  workshops and, 2002 n.113
Lha Belpo, 2574–2575
Lha bla ma Ye shes 'od (king), 1398–1399, 2313
Lhacham Pemasal, 1439
Lha gcig. *See* Atiśa Dīpaṃkaraśrījñāna
Lharik Dechen Yeshe Rölpatsel, 2495–2496
Lhazang Khan, 1066, 2017
Lhébon (prince), 2574–2575
Lhenkarma Catalogue, 2579
Lhorong Religious History (Lang Lhazik Repa), 1540–1541
Li, 1863
Li, Edward, 2376–2377, 2388
Lianchan, 1257–1258
Liandeng (Huiweng), 660
Liang Qichao, 2279, 2283

Lian Shen, 1138
Li Baoyu, 57–58
liberal Protestant thought, 2127–2128, 2130–2131
liberation, 1697
Liberation by Hearing in the Intermediate States, 1970
Liberation through Hearing, 2468
Liberation Through Hearing in the Bardo (Karma Lingpa), 839
Li Bo, 1869
Library Cave. *See* Dunhuang texts
Library of Congress, 637
Licheng Suanjing, 814
Lidai, 656–657
Lidai fabao ji, 1229–1230, 1237–1238
Li Fang-Kuei, 2586
"Life in the Womb" (Kritzer), 260–261
The Life of Marpa the Translator (Tsangnyön), 1485, 1538–1540
The Life of Milarepa, 1485, 1489–1490
The Life of My Teacher, 1068–1069
lift up; raise (*ju*), 665–667
Ligdan Khan, 1651–1655
Li Genyuan, 2727
The Light of Asia (Arnold, E.), 181
Light Rays of the Stainless Vajra Moon (Kongtrul), 2747
Li Ji, 1000
Li Jishen, 2732
Lili'uokalani (queen), 1309
Liljenberg, Karen, 840–841
Lin, Wushu, 823–824
Lin Chien-te, 2627
Lincoln, Abraham, 1304–1305
Lindblom, Sara, 1447
Lin Delin, 1262, 1443–1444
Lindtner, Christian, 1465–1467
Linehan, Marsha, 1952
ling (efficacy), 86–87
Ling Gesar (king). *See* Gesar
Ling Gesar Drupkor, 2495–2496
Lingre Kagyü school, 846–850, 858
Ling Repa Pema Dorje
  biography of, 848
  life of, 2600, 2612 n.35
  scholarship on, 848–849, 858, 1482
  statue of, 847*f*
  Tsangpa Gyare and, 846–850, 857–859, 861 n.5, 863 n.37, 2600, 2606–2607, 2612 n.34
Lingstang Xylograph, 2489, 2495
Lingtrul Rinpoche, 1441–1442
Lingwood, Dennis, 1989
Lingyou, 1234–1235
Lingyuan Hongmiao, 2157–2158, 2161–2162, 2170 n.31, 2172 n.48
Linji, 716
Linjilu (Linji Yixuan), 650–651
Linji Yixuan, 650
Linnaeus, Carolus, 2708
Lin Qiuwu, 1252–1253, 1260, 1262, 1443–1444
Lin Qixian, 2166
Linrothe, Rob, 1173–1174, 2641–2642
Lin Yun, 1138
Lin Ziqing, 2155–2156
Lion's Roar (Mipam), 1562
The Lion's Roar Affirming Zhentong (Mipham), 2747, 2750–2751
Li Shizhen, 212
listening, 454–456
Listening to a Frog (Mozong), 663
Listening to the Snow (Xutang), 663
A List of the Inscriptions of Northern India (Kielhorn), 950
Litalien, Manuel, 417
literature
  Brahmanic literature, 2248
  Buddhist, 428–429, 1802 n.35, 1809–1814
  on Buddhist chaplaincy, 112 n.9, 450
  Christian, 452, 458
  Confucian, 1039–1040
  Dunhuang, 796
  Dzogchen, 130–135
  extracanonical Buddhist, 324–326
  Hindu Sanskrit, 875
  imaging Buddha in, 1274, 1278–1281, 1300 n.43
  Kālacakra, 2543, 2546–2548
  literary ambitions, 615–616
  literary genres, 1722
  literary works, 813–814
  oral, 112 n.12
  Sanskrit, 245
  from Thailand, 499–500
  Vedic, 2247–2248
Little Buddha (film), 397–398
The Little Grains of Buddhagupta, 832, 841
Liu, Tannie, 417
Liu Benzun, 64
Liu Cheng, 1228
Liu Kuo-shen. *See* Hsing yun
Liu Meiling, 2614
Liu Renhang, 2286
Liu Xiang, 1864
Liu Xianhe, 57–58
Liu Xie, 1001–1002
Liu Xunning, 675–676
Liu Yuxi, 1230, 1232, 1240, 1866
Liu Zongyuan, 1226, 1230, 1240
Liuzu dashi Fabao tanjing jianzhu (Ding Fubao), 1236
"Liuzu Dashi fabao tanjing luexu," 1224

Liuzu Huineng zhuan (Layman Mingyi), 1231
lived religion, 564–574, 578–579
Lives of Eminent Monks (Huizhao), 209–210
Living Buddha Living Christ (Hanh), 2448
Living by Zen (D. T. Suzuki), 707
living traditions, 2267–2268
Li Wenhui, 1234–1235
Li Xuezhu, 627–628
Li Yuancong, 59
Li Zhichang, 1626–1627
Li Zhongzi, 212
Li Zhou, 1230
Lizong (emperor), 653
Li Zunxu, 660
Lo, James C. M., 798–799
Lo, Lucy, 798–799
Lo, Vivienne, 823–824
Lobel, Adam, 1447
Lobo, Wibke, 1897
Lobsang Lhalungpa, 1490
Lobsang Yongdan, 2025
Lobzang Chökdrub Gyatso, 2747–2748
Lobzang Chokyi Gyeltsen, 2015–2016
Lobzang Jikmé, 1751–1753
Lobzang Jivaka, 1989–1990
Lobzang Pelden Yeshe, 2017–2018
local cults, 334–338, 341–345
local deities, 341–344
local traditions, 1184–1185
Lochen Dharmasrī, 686, 2747
locus classicus, 2455
Loden Sherap Dagyab, 443–444
Lodrö nyingpo, 1652
logic, 733–735, 741, 1444, 1819–1824
Lohuizen-De Leeuw, Johanna van, 1294
Lokakṣema, 1497–1498, 1501–1502, 1961–1962
lokapala deities, 2247–2248
Lokesh Chandra, 443–444
lokottara (hypercosmic) deities, 1159, 1167
Lok To, 411
Lokya (Lo skya ston pa), 1542
Lokya José Jungyal, 1542
Lomi, Benedetta, 279, 302, 309
Loncke, Katie, 910, 922
Longchenpa (Longchen Rabjampa)
  biographies of, 1435–1436, 1449 n.26, 1450 n.30
  death of, 1448 n.1
  early life of, 1436–1439
  instructions from, 135
  instructors of, 1449 n.13
  later life of, 1439–1441
  legacy of, 1441–1442
  Mipam and, 1565–1566
  in Nepal, 1440
  Padmasambhava and, 1439
  philosophy of, 1445–1446
  protectresses and, 1437, 1439–1441, 1449 n.8
  reputation of, 830, 837–838, 841, 1143, 2549
  scholarship on, 1446–1447, 2476–2478
  in Tibet, 1441–1442
  title for, 1448 n.2
  Tsongkhapa and, 1445
  works of, 1442–1444
Long Reformation, 566
Lopez, Donald
  on Buddhist studies, 160 n.60
  colleagues of, 371, 871, 879, 2480
  on colonialism, 864
  on film, 397–398
  to Kapstein, 113 n.23
  scholarship from, 239, 1308, 1815, 1939, 1951–1952, 2025, 2480
  on Western scholarship, 181
Löpon Tenzin Namdak, 138
Lord, Albert, 2566–2567
Lorepa, 2593–2594
Lorepa Wangchug Tsöndru, 854, 855*f*, 856–858
Lorimer, D. L. R., 2499
Losang Chökyi Gyeltsen, 1065–1066, 1488
Los Angeles Hompa Hongwanji (LAHH), 46
Losol, D., 1608
Lost Horizon (film), 398
Lotsāwa Loden Sherab, 2744–2745
TheLotus Garland (Karma Chagme), 1967–1968
Lotus Light Charity Society, 415
Lotus-Nirvana Period, 2463
Lotus Sutra. See also *specific topics*
  authority of, 1762, 1765–1768, 1770–1772
  Burnouf on, 1464
  chanting and, 771–774, 1772–1773
  commentary on, 2347
  daimoku and, 1768–1769
  in debates, 754
  Diamond Sutra and, 815, 2562
  digital versions of, 229
  followers of, 890
  history of, 1761–1764
  to Ikeda Daisaku, 2224
  inspiration from, 2688
  interpretations of, 1772–1773, 2345–2347, 2352–2353
  in Japan, 271, 2047–2048, 2325–2326
  in Mahāyāna Buddhism, 1807, 2692–2693
  mutual inclusion of ten realms in, 1767–1768
  Nichiren and, 2212, 2216–2219, 2226
  origins of, 809, 811
  parables in, 276

Lotus Sutra (*continued*)
popularity of, 806–807
scholarship on, 84–89, 1774
scriptures and, 287
self-harm in, 115–116
shakubuku and, 1771
Sutra for the Golden Light and, 275–276
teachings in, 2050, 2053–2054, 2691–2692
translations of, 1768–1769
women and, 93
in Zen Buddhism, 2359
Zhiyan on, 2346
Louis IX (king), 1628
Loveday, Helen, 2696
Lowe, Brian, 2209
A Lower Ladakhi Version of the Kesar Saga, 2488–2489
lower rites, 2647–2648
Loy, David, 911, 930 n.120, 986
Lozang chö kyi gyel tsen, 1649
Lozang jamyang, 1381
Lozang norbu, 1380
Lozang penden yeshe, 1380
Lozang tenpé drönme, 1379
Lozang tenpe gyeltsen, 1376–1378, 1381
Lozang tsültrim jikme tenpe gyeltsen pelzangpo, 1381
Lozang tupten wangchuk jikme gyatso pelzangpo, 1380–1381
Lozang yeshe, 1379
Lü, Chao-Chow, 410–411
Lubsangdandzin, 1657–1658
Lubum Ge, 1643
Luczanits, Christian, 443–444, 1927
Lüders, Heinrich, 639, 937, 948–949
Lu Hwei-syin, 2625
Lu Jinchuan, 1231
luminosity, 2484 n.27
Luminous Bliss (Halkias), 1974
Lunyu, 1004–1005
Luo Shi, 1234–1235
Luo Tongbing, 2294–2295
Luo Zhenyu, 798
Lu Sheng-Yen, 1138
Lusthaus, Dan, 12
Lutz, Karl, 2529–2530
Lü Xiang, 1517
Lu Xingtao, 1224
Lu Zhiyi, 212
Lyon, David, 1122–1123
Lý Thái Tổ, 1039–1040

Ma Ba Tha movement, 922
Maborosi (film), 404
MacDonald, Anne, 627–628
Machacek, David, 2226–2227
Machick's Complete Explanation (Namkhai), 687–688, 691–695
Machig Labdrön and the Foundations of Chöd (Edou), 695
Machik Lapdrön, 631 n.13, 631 n.14, 686–691, 693, 695, 1480
MacLean, Derryl, 1671–1672
Macomber, Andrew, 279, 302
Macuch, Maria, 820
Macy, Joanna, 357–359, 363, 904, 910–911, 923
Madhyamāgama texts, 633–635, 1561
Madhyamaka Buddhism
BCA and, 2087
Candrakīrti on, 616–620, 1462–1463
in China, 1455–1456, 1470 n.33
in East Asia, 1461–1462
Great Madhyamaka, 2753 n.2
history of, 615–616, 1453–1454
Mādhyamika Śāntarakṣita and, 1460–1461
Mipam and, 1561–1562
Nāgārjuna and, 1456–1459, 1464, 1468 n.5
Nyingma school and, 1470 n.39
philosophy of, 1458–1459, 1687–1688, 1693–1694, 1698–1699
Prāsaṅgika-Madhyamaka and, 1564–1565
in Sanskrit, 1468 n.1
scholarship on, 1459–1460, 1464–1466
schools of, 623–626, 1454–1455, 2744
Sengzhao on, 1470 n.32
to Tāranātha, 1464
textual foundations of, 1455–1456
in Tibet, 1462–1464
to Tsongkhapa, 1470 n.34
Vajrayāna Buddhism and, 1462
Madhyamakāvatāra, 1810
Mādhyamika Śāntarakṣita, 621, 1459–1461
Madhyamika tradition, 2292
Madsen, Richard, 1017, 2166–2167, 2625
Mae Chee Kaew, 1887
Maeshiro Teruaki, 1709
Maggi, Mauro, 820
magic
illusions and, 1696
magical monks, 970
magical protection, 345
Magic Competition murals, 783–784, 796–797
monks and, 1891
scholarship on, 1210–1211
siddhis, 2304
Western magical practices, 2302
yogis and, 2063–2064
Magic and Mystery in Tibet, 694–695
The Magic Treasury of the Sky, 129–130
Magid, Barry, 1955
Magyal Pomra, 2491

Mahābhogāśrama, 1794
Mahābodhi Mahāmuni, 431*f*, 432–433, 442
Mahabodhi Society, 196, 1075–1077, 2127, 2279
Mahabodhi temple, 70–71, 76–77
Mahābodhivaṃsa, 1729
Mahachulalongkornrajavidyalaya University, 1578
Mahādibbamanta, 1884–1885
Mahā Gandhāri Weizzā, 568
Mahākāla
  as cult, 1631–1632
  Palden Lhamo and, 1165–1167
  scholarship and, 1072 n.14, 1159–1160, 1162–1164
  Yāma and, 1072 n.28
Mahākāśyapa (Mahā-Kassapa), 2175, 2410, 2691
Mahakeḷa (king), 1726
Mahamayuri, 2248
Mahā Moggallana, 249
mahāmudrā, 692, 1472, 1477–1478, 1487–1491
Mahāmudrā Attainment, 1475
Mahāmudrā Eliminating the Darkness of Ignorance, 1487
Mahan, Jeffrey, 229, 240
Mahānāma (king), 146
Mahānāman, 1789
Mahāparinibbāna Sutta, 2556
Mahāparinirvāṇa Sūtra, 1003
Mahāparitta, 1883
Mahaprajapati, 1101
Mahāprajāpatī, 2666–2667
Mahāprajñāpāramitāśāstra, 1810, 1815
Mahāprajñāpāramitāśastra (Nāgārjuna), 1498
Mahāprajñāparamitā Sūtra, 770
Mahā Praṇidhāna Kuta Mantrayāna (MPKM), 2377–2378
Mahārāja Bālaputradeva, 1786
Mahasammata (sage-king), 1630
Mahāsāṅ, 2396
Mahāsāṅghikas, 2396
Mahāsatipaṭṭhāna Sutta, 1883
Mahasena, 2251
Mahāsthāmaprāpta, 2685–2687
Mahasy, Sayadaw, 1081–1082
Mahāvairocana, 2175–2176, 2180–2181
Mahāvairocanābhisaṃbodhi Tantra, 1901
Mahāvairocana-sūtra, 1901–1902, 2174–2176
Maha-Vairocana Temple, 2382
Mahavamsa, 147–148, 1046–1047, 1098–1099, 1722, 1731–1732, 2249, 2251–2252, 2399–2401. *See also* Theravāda Buddhism
Mahāvastu, 1290, 1372, 1807, 1814
Mahāvhibhāṣā (commentary), 2
Māhavibhāṣa, 1807
Mahāvihāra lineage, 2428 n.35, 2428 n.38, 2429 n.49, 2433 n.111
Mahāyāna Buddhism
  Abhidharma Buddhism and, 617–618, 630 n.3
  Āryadeva and, 616
  bioethics in, 162–164, 170–171
  birth of, 2560–2562
  bodies in, 122–124
  Buddha in, 125, 619–620
  in China, 1078, 1445, 2174–2175
  Chinese Buddhism and, 2291
  cosmology in, 482–484, 1038–1039
  cultivation of, 22
  doctrine in, 2462
  domestic Dharma and, 766
  D. T. Suzuki and, 706, 716–718, 725
  East Asian, 1987–1988
  epics in, 2488–2489, 2491–2492
  ethics of, 838, 861 n.10, 979–980, 1403–1404
  global Buddhism and, 1080
  Hinayana Buddhism and, 1028
  history of, 84, 496–498, 634–635, 1687, 2076, 2265, 2661
  Humanistic Buddhism and, 1255–1256
  identity in, 2663
  Indian Buddhism and, 1446–1447
  Indian Mahāyāna Buddhist scholarly works, 1809–1814
  in Japan, 267–268
  jātaka in, 1367–1368
  Lotus Sutra in, 1807, 2692–2693
  Mahāprajñāparamitā Sūtra in, 770
  Mahāyāna Pure Land Tradition and, 2285–2286
  mainstream, 55–56
  mind training in, 1403
  monks in, 84
  Nāgārjuna and, 1454–1455
  Nichiren Buddhism and, 2217
  to non-Mahāyāna Buddhists, 616–617
  oral literature and, 112 n.12
  perfections in, 1807–1809
  philosophy of, 2076
  Pure Land Buddhism and, 2233
  reform in, 979–980
  repentance in, 2692
  scholarship on, 1497–1500, 2332–2333
  scriptures of, 247–250, 286–287, 2541
  Shingon Buddhism and, 2352
  spell culture in, 2177
  sutras in, 2506
  systems of, 17, 61–62
  in Taiwan, 915
  tantra and, 2403
  Theravāda Buddhism and, 72–73, 238–239, 703, 862 n.12, 982, 1103, 1442–1443, 2231, 2234, 2241, 2269, 2432 n.97
  in three wheels of doctrine, 2455–2456

Mahāyāna Buddhism (*continued*)
traditions in, 28–29, 2009
Two Truths Doctrine in, 915
Vajrayāna Buddhism and, 986
at Vulture Peak, 354
writing in, 2557–2558
Yogācārā Buddhism and, 1460–1461, 2332, 2462–2463
Mahāyāna Buddhist tantra
art historical evidence of, 961–962
in Bali, 963
in inscriptions, 960–962
Pali Buddhism and, 964–967
politico-historical contexts for, 959–960
in Sanskrit cosmopolises, 967–969
scholarship on, 963–970
in Southeast Asia, 958–963
Southeast Asian travelers and, 962–963
tradition in, 966–968
Mahāyānasūtra texts, 636–637
Mahāyañña Sutta, 994–995
mahāyoga tantras, 834, 1472–1477
Mahendrapāla (king), 1791–1792
Mahinda, 194, 2397, 2400–2402, 2410, 2427 n.28
Mahipāla I (king), 1785
Maḥmūd of Ghazna, 1672, 1679
Mai, Cuong, 2675, 2678, 2696
Main, Jessica, 918, 921–922
mainland Southeast Asia, 112 n.3, 375–378
mainstream Buddhism, 112 n.10, 496, 529
Mair, Victor Henry, 821–823
Maitreya Bodhisattva, 100–101, 551–552, 552*f*, 1499, 1562, 2181–2182
Maitreya Contemplation Sutra, 2675–2676, 2678–2679, 2688–2690
Maitreya cult, 1191
Maitreyanātha, 17, 2744. See also *Abhisamayālaṃkāra*
Maitreya Pure Land, 2284–2285
Maitreya School, 2278, 2281, 2284–2285, 2291–2292, 2294–2295
Maitrī, 1537, 2255
Maitrīpa, 1476–1477, 1537, 1544, 1548
Majer, Zsuzsa, 1585–1586, 1588, 1594–1595, 1615
Majjhantika, 2410–2411
Majjhima Nikāya, 357–358, 1326–1327
Major Rock Edicts, 633
Majumdar, N. G., 949
Mak, Bill, 2387–2388
Makara heads, 2654 n.11
Makiguchi Tsunesaburō, 2211–2212, 2219–2220, 2222–2223, 2226. *See also* Soka Gakkai
The Making of Buddhist Modernism (McMahan), 199–200
Makley, Charlene, 185
Makoto, Hayashi, 2208–2209
Makransky, John J., 28–29, 1147
Mālāda, 1784–1785
Malasri, Somya, 462, 465–466
Malay Peninsula, 1525–1526
Malaysia, 1077–1078, 1100
Mallmann, Marie-Therese de, 84
Malone, Kobutsu, 465
Malov, Efimovich, 818
Malunkyaputta (disciple), 400
al-Ma'mūn, 1672, 1677
managing sanghas, 2070–2071
Manase Dōsan, 273–274
Mancika, 1787
Maṇḍala Depiction of the 100 Peaceful and Wrathful Deities of the Bardo, 2477*f*, 2478
Maṇḍala of Eight Great Bodhisattvas, 788–790, 789*f*
maṇḍalas. See *specific topics*
màndalas, 436–437
Maṇḍalas in the Making (Wang, M. C.), 800–801
mandala system, 1094–1096, 2539
Mandāravā (princess), 1972–1973
Mandell, Jacqueline (née Schwartz), 1117–1118
Mandiar, Arvind-Pal, 1571–1572
Mandrasena, 1518–1519, 1526
Mandukhai secen khatun, 1641
Maṅgalasutta, 983–984
Manichaean Treatise on the Light-Nous, 812
Maṇicintana, 1519
Mani Kambum, 2583
Maṇi Rimdu rituals cycle, 1203
Mañjughoṣa, 1488
Manjushri Bodhisattva, 557
Mañjuśrī
Avalokiteśvara and, 1970
in China, 1501–1505
to Eison, 1469 n.19
emanations of, 1440
esoteric Indian Buddhism and, 1500–1501
incarnations of, 290, 1435–1436
in India, 1497–1500
philosophy of, 1497
scholarship and, 728 n.35, 792–795, 1505–1506, 1866–1868, 2681
Trisong Detsen and, 2584
Vajrapāṇi and, 1603
Mañjuśrībuddhaksẹtraguṇavyūha sūtra, 1499
Mañjuśrī-dharma-ratnagarbha-dhāranī sutra, 1502
Mañjuśrījñāna, 1792
Mañjuśrīmūlakalpa, 1500, 1506
Mañjuśrīnāmasaṃgīti, 1500–1501, 1501*f*, 1504, 1506
Mañjuśrī parinirvāna sūtra, 1499, 1502

Mañjuśrī Parinirvāṇa Sutra (Quinter), 2696–2697
Mañjuśrī Precious Treasury of the Law Dharani Sutra, 1866–1867
Mañjuśrīvikrīḍita sūtra, 1498
Mañjuśrımitra, 837
Manorathanandin, 1837–1838
Manson, Charles, 2024–2025
Mantegatius, Cajetanus, 1048
mantranaya. *See* Mahāyāna Buddhist tantra
Mantra School Bright Lineage (MSBL)
  in China, 2369
  MPKM and, 2377–2378
  scholarship on, 1137–1139, 1150
  Shingon Buddhism and, 1146
  in Taiwan, 1137–1139, 1146, 1150
  tantric revival and, 2369–2371
  Wuguang and, 2369–2370, 2391 n.39
mantric words
  daily chants and, 771–773, 1073
  mothering and, 767
  scholarship on, 1424–1425, 1430–1431
  syllables and, 967
  in tantra, 1203
  in Zen Buddhism, 766–767
A Manual of Buddhism in Its Modern Development (Hardy), 2713
Manual of Zen Buddhism (D. T. Suzuki), 714–715
Manuel, Earthyn, 910, 922, 1990
manuscripts. See also *specific topics*
  Dunhuang, 810–814, 831–833
  history of, 2558–2560
  Huineng in, 1238–1239
  Institute of Oriental Manuscripts, 818
  manuscript studies, 824
  publishing, 1036–1038, 1045–1047, 1053–1054
  Sanskrit, 98–99
  scholarship on, 1036–1038, 1045–1047, 1053–1054
  Tibetan Buddhist, 820
Many Petals of the Lotus (McLellan), 417
Maoism, 2731–2732, 2734–2735
Mao Zedong, 424, 1231, 1258–1259
māra (devil), 690–692, 1164, 2645
Māra (king), 309–310
Mara Serpochen, 687
Mara Tarki, 851
Marco Polo, 323–324, 1633
Margolin, Uri, 178
Margolis, Ramsey, 2138
Maritime Asia. See *specific topics*
Maritime Buddhism
  history of, 1512–1514
  maritime Asia and, 1513*f*, 1518–1521
  maritime mobility, 1516
  narratives of, 1517–1518
  scholarship on, 1527–1528
  in Sri Lanka, 1471 n.65
  tantra and, 1522–1525
  trade and, 1518–1521
  trans-Asian maritime networks in, 1521–1527
  in Western India, 1521
Marmapradīpa (Dignāga), 10
Marpa Chökyi Lodrö, 2470–2471
Marpa Dode, 1470 n.37, 1544, 1549–1550, 1553
Marpa Golek, 1539, 1545–1546
Marpa Goyak, 1541–1542
Marpa Kagyü lineage. *See* Kagyü lineage
Marpa Lotsawa Chökyi Lodrö
  biographical information on, 1470 n.46, 1540–1541
  disciples of, 1545–1546, 1550–1551
  family of, 1469 n.24
  history of, 1541–1551
  in India, 1542–1544, 1546–1548
  music of, 1469 n.16, 1551–1552
  Nāropā and, 1481, 1546, 1548–1549
  in Nepal, 1542, 1544–1545, 1548–1550
  reputation of, 847, 1481, 1485
  scholarship and, 688, 1538–1540, 1552–1553, 2010
  in Tibetan religious history, 1536–1538
Marquardt, Marie Friedmann, 200
marriage, 1987, 2037–2038, 2069–2070
Marshall, John, 949
martial law, 2164
Martin, Dan
  scholarship from, 631 n.14, 1553, 2481, 2519, 2606–2607
  on Tsangpa Gyare, 848, 858–859, 2606
Martön Tsultrim Jungne, 1539, 1541
Martun, 2593–2594
Marx, Karl, 383–384, 1609
Marxism
  Confucianism and, 1444
  in Japan, 1437
  Leninism and, 1609, 1611–1612
  philosophy of, 1101, 1260
  scholarship on, 383–384
  socialism and, 1251–1252
Marza Tarki, 2597–2598, 2599*f*
Masaharu Anesaki, 1774
Masahi Tamiya, 467–468
Masamichi Ichigō, 1467
Masatsugu, Michael, 45–46
masculinity, 180
Ma Shicheng, 1005
Maslow, Abraham, 1949–1950

Mason, Francis, 1048
Masset, D., 1298 n.18
mass media messages, 232–234
Masson, Charles, 639
Masson-Oursel, M. P., 29–30
Masuzawa, Tomoko, 864–865, 867–869, 881
al-Masʿūdī, 1672–1673
Matarajin, 295–296
material culture, 1188–1189
material forms, in Buddhism, 1318–1319
materialism, 1293
materiality, 230–231
materials, for art, 433–437
material wealth, 897
materia medica, 213, 271, 275, 304–310
Mathes, Klaus-Dieter, 1445, 1490, 2751
Mathurā
  Buddha in, 1274–1275, 1282, 1287, 1289, 1294
  scholarship and, 937–938, 1274–1275, 1283–1285, 1293
Mathurā Inscriptions (Lüders), 949
The Matrix (film), 233
Matrix of Gnosis, 1474
mātṛkā, 98
Mātṛṛceṭa, 1279–1281
Matsue, Regina, 1357–1358
Matsumoto Bunzaburō, 1236–1237
Matsunaga, Alicia, 1774
Matsuo Kōichi, 756, 758–759
Matsuura, Jane, 1310
Matsuura, Shinobu, 1310
Matthews, Bruce, 417, 1357, 2243
Mātuposaka Sutta, 995
Maull, Fleet, 465
Mauryan dynasty, 934
Māyājāla tantras, 831
Mayer, Robert, 821–823, 2481, 2641–2642, 2651
Mayer, Toby, 1678–1679
Mayskiy, I. M., 1607
Mazu Daoyi, 183, 1238
MCA, 226–227
McBride, Richard, 61–62
McCallum, David, 2209
McClintock, Sara, 1467
McCrae, Emily, 2719
McDaniel, Justin
  on categories, 970
  on colonialism, 377
  Dreyfus and, 1580
  scholarship from, 1579, 1887–1888, 1891–1892, 2270
  on tantra, 964–965
McDermott, Joseph P., 328
McHale, Shawn Frederick, 2447–2448
Mchims Nam mkha' grags, 1397, 1399
McLaughlin, Levi, 2226
McLellan, Janet, 417, 1115
McLuhan, Marshall, 228–229, 1036–1037
McMahan, David L.
  on modernity, 199–200
  scholarship from, 1118–1119, 1845, 1939, 1954–1955, 2716–2717
  on secular Buddhism, 2145–2146
  on writing, 2562, 2567
McMullen, James, 749, 759
McMullin, Neil, 294–295, 2056, 2350, 2358–2359
McNeill, William, 293
McNicholl, Andeana, 1122
McRae, John R., 675–676, 821–823, 1240
Meadows, Carol, 1814–1815
Meadows, James, 1119, 1122
Mean, Uang, 2237
The Meaning of Attaining Buddhahood in This Very Body (Kūkai), 2353–2354
The Meaning of the Syllable "Hum" (Kūkai), 2353–2354
The Meaning of Voice, Word and Reality (Kūkai), 2353–2354
Meares, John, 408
media. *See also* Buddhist media
  analog electronic mass, 2564–2565
  in archaeology, 2569 n.11
  authenticity in, 236–240
  Buddhism and, 226–228, 240–241
  commercialized Buddhisms, 234–235
  Diamond Sutra and, 2553
  digital, 2565–2566
  digital media technology, 2565–2566
  mass media messages, 232–234
  in monasteries, 2556
  news, 235–236
  as personal expression, 231–232
  studies, 227–230
  technology, 2553
  theory, 2553–2554, 2564–2565
  types, 230–236
medical knowledge, 254–255, 2532–2533
medical training, 254–255
medicine. See *specific topics*
Medicine Buddha, 208–209, 2180–2181
Medicine Buddha Hall,
"Medicine Congregation of the Buddha King," 596–597
medieval China, 208
medieval Christian nuns, 187

medieval history, 177, 180, 2324 n.98
medieval Japan, 1297 n.13, 2632 n.26, 2633 n.44.
See also premodern Japan
medieval Tibet, 1447
"Meditating the Power of Dharma" (Wallace), 1594
meditation
atiyoga and, 834–835
bodies and, 520–521
Buddhism and, 113, 1087
in Chan Buddhism, 1623–1624
chanding and, 2700 n.16
contemplation and, 506–508, 522–523
deities and, 1424
Dzogchen and, 829–839
for effort, 2085
focus in, 2085–2086
guan as, 2699 n.5
Insight Meditation, 1053, 1117–1118, 1950–1951
instructions, 108
in Japan, 277–278
karma and, 195
meditation stone, 356–357
mindfulness and, 459
in monasteries, 2741 n.52
in Nanbeicho period, 1187–1188
objects and, 514–522
philosophy and, 531
physical pleasure and, 124–125
practitioners of, 183, 517–518
psychotherapy and, 1702–1704
in Pure Land Buddhism, 144 n.37
ritual meditation manuals, 2650–2651
Sādhanamāla for, 1801 n.23
Śāntideva on, 2085–2087
scholarship on, 1117, 1354–1355
serenity, 1483–1484
sitting, 522, 1350–1351, 1354–1355, 1708–1709
Soper on, 2676–2677
in Sri Lanka, 967
tantra and, 124–125
theory, 2455
tradition of, 967–968
Tranquil Meditator stereotype, 234
in Vajrayāna Buddhism, 521
in Vipassna movement, 1117–1118
visualization/contemplation sutras and, 2674–2677
Zen, 1081, 2181
"Meditation, Repentance, and Visionary Experience" (Greene, E.), 2696–2697
meditative attainments (*samāpatti*), 9
mediums, 595, 597, 601–602, 1751–1753, 2542–2543
Medizingeschicte Japans (Rosner), 279
Meeks, Lori, 185
Meenakshi Rai, 1407
Meiji (emperor), 2036, 2041
Meiji Restoration, 75
Meisha yoin (Yabuki Keiki), 1237
Meizan, 2185
Mejor, Marek, 10
Melong Dorje, 1438
Memoirs of Eminent Monks (Yijing), 1865
memorials, 69–72
Memorials and Edicts (Amoghavajra), 53–55, 59–60, 63
Menander (king), 939
Mendelson, Michael, 579–580, 587–588, 594, 602–604
mental afflictions (*kleśa*), 7–8, 2080–2081
mental content theory, 1824–1828
mental pain (*daurmanasya*), 2083–2084
Men Yuanliao, 1005–1006
mercury, 1449 n.23
mercy killing, 171–172
merit, 286–292, 890–891, 894, 1290–1292, 2268–2269
Merton, Thomas, 708–709, 722
Mesick, Lillian Shrewsbury, 1309
metamorphosed bodies, 1281–1282
metaphysical nihilism, 1694–1695
metaphysics, 532–533, 538–539
Metön Tsönpo, 1539, 1550
Metteyya, 588–589, 591, 593, 600, 2255, 2413–2414, 2420–2421
Mettinger, Tryggve, 2262
Metzner, Ralph, 2479
Meyer, Fernand, 2534
Meyers, Karin, 11, 1335–1336, 1344 n.152
mgur, 1551–1552
Miao Kai, 1012
Miaolian (master), 2726
Miao-lo, 2218
Miaoshan, 91–92
Miaoxian, 1259
Miao Xiyong, 212
Michel-Zaitsu, Wolfgang, 279
Michigan, U.S., 2382
Michihiro, Ama, 1313–1314, 1357
Michinaga, Fujiwara no, 2181–2182, 2184–2185
Michon, Nathan Jishin, 471–472
Middle East, 1667–1672, 1674–1675, 1678. *See also* Islam
Middle Length Sayings collection, 1027
Middle Passage (Johnson, C.), 237
Middle Way, 1187
migration, 1351–1353
Mihoko Okamura, 707–709

Mijiao (secret teachings), 2174
Miki Yoshihiko, 1707, 1718 n.31
mikkyō. *See* Esoteric Buddhism; Tantric Buddhism
Mikkyō hattatsushi (Ōmura), 60
Mikmar Tsering, 1756
Mikyo Dorjé, 1064–1065, 1485–1486, 2746, 2751
Milarepa. *See also* Marpa Lotsawa Chökyi Lodrö
  biographical tradition of, 1550
  Gampopa and, 1536
  Marpa Golek and, 1539
  practice lineage to, 1550
  reputation of, 1551–1552
  scholarship and, 847, 1159–1160, 1481–1482, 1485
  songs of, 1552
Miles, Robert, 2708
Milindapañha, 253–254, 1336, 1721, 1881
Milindapañha-aṭṭhakathā (Ū Nārada Jetavana Sayadaw), 1048–1049
Milindapraśnaya, 1046–1047
militarism, 916
Military Chaplaincy in an Era of Religious Pluralism, 472
militia-priests, 2039
Millennium World Peace Summit of Religious and Spiritual Leaders, 2165
Miller, Willa Blythe, 450–451, 453–454, 471–472, 858–859, 2606–2607
Mills, Martin, 2025
Minami, Atsumi, 311
Minayeff, I. P., 2088
Mind and Life Institute, 1951–1952, 2533–2534
Mind Cure (Hickey), 2717–2718
The Mindful Nation (Ryan), 921
mindfulness
  in capitalism, 920–921
  concentration and, 509–514
  in culture, 920–921
  in engaged Buddhism, 920–921
  four mindfulnesses, 518–520
  by Hanh, 906–907
  hegemony and, 198–199
  Hickey on, 2145
  Kabat-Zinn on, 985
  meditation and, 459
  Mindfulness-Based Cognitive Therapy, 464, 1951–1953
  Mindfulness Based Stress Reduction Program, 1118
  repeated, 516–518
  Śāntideva on, 2082–2083
  scholarship on, 1117–1118, 1950–1953, 2717–2718
  secular, 931 n.136
  in Western Buddhism, 2717–2718
Mind-Life Institute, 1110 n.96
Mindon (king), 1048–1049, 2417, 2560
"Mind-Only" Buddhism, 617, 620–621, 668–669
mind training (*blo sbyong*), 1403, 1405–1406
Mind Treasury, 1475–1476
Ming Chan Masters (Yunqi), 670
Ming Zhengtong (emperor), 1182–1183, 1640–1641, 1731–1732
Minh, Phạm Văn, 2447–2448
Minh, Son Ngoc, 190 n.71
Minnan Buddhist Academy, 2283–2284
Minowa Kenryō, 753, 759
Mipam Chokyi Lodro, 1468 n.1, 1469 n.7, 1561–1567, 1968, 1988, 2022
Mipam Gönpo. *See* Dampa Sangyé
Mipam on Buddha Nature (Duckworth), 1567
Mipham. *See* Ju Mipham Namgyel Gyatso
Mipham's Beacon of Certainty (Pettit), 2750–2751
Mipham's Beacon of Uncertainty (Pettit), 1567
Mipham's Dialectics and the Debates on Emptiness (Karma Phuntsho), 1567
The Miracle of Mindfulness (Hanh), 2442, 2448
The Miracles of the Kasuga Deity, 298
miracle tales, 86–88, 91–92
The Mirror Illuminating the Royal Genealogies, 2580, 2587
Mirror of Poetry, 1566
miscellaneous texts, 639
mishirabe, 1702–1703
misogyny, 105
missionaries
  for Catholicism, 181, 2435
  in Central Asia, 85
  for Christianity, 370–371, 373–374, 376, 865–870, 919, 1075–1077, 1136–1137, 1589–1590
  Humanistic Buddhism and, 1257–1258
  Jesuit, 273–274, 864–870, 878–881
  Western Buddhism and, 2712–2713
"Missionaries of the Buddhist Faith" (*San Francisco Chronicle*), 1351–1352
Mitani Sokei, 2219
Mitchell, Donald W., 2061–2062
Mitchell, Scott, 234, 236, 240–241
Mitra, Rajendralal, 371
Mitra, Sailendranath, 639
Mitrayogin, 1970–1971
Miwang Pholhane Sonam Tobgye, 1171
mixed contemplation, 2687
Miyaji, Akira, 1294
Miyata Kōichi, 2226
Miyawaki, Junko, 1386

Mizuno (priest), 1707–1708
mKhas-sgrub bstan-pa dar-rgyas, 26
mobility, maritime, 1516
Mochizuki, Kaie, 1407
Modi, Narendra, 2385
Moerman, D. Max, 291
Mogao caves, 555–560, 781–784, 783*f*, 795–796, 801. *See also* Dunhuang art
Moggaliputta Tissa, 2410–2411
Mohe moye jing, 997–998
Moheyan, 2579–2580
Mohe Zhiguan (Zhiyi), 1186, 1702
Mohoṭṭivattē Guṇānanda, 1046
Mollier, Christine, 823–824
momentary mental events, 1820–1821
monarchs
  history of, 2574
  in Khmer empire, 1907–1923
  in Korea, 334
  model for, 1515–1516
  monks and, 1514–1516
  in Qing dynasty, 1862–1863
  scholarship on, 1781–1782, 1862–1863
  in Tantric Buddhism, 1913
  in Thailand, 1734
  Trisong Detsen and, 2580–2583
monasteries. See also *specific topics*
  agriculture and, 351–352
  artifacts from, 68
  of Avalokiteśvara, 943–944
  in Bhutan, 857
  in Bodhgaya, 1789–1790
  bodhisattvas in, 2640, 2661–2666, 2668
  Bön tradition in, 112 n.2
  bureaucracy in, 2071
  in caves, 1469 n.22
  chayik guidelines for, 2664–2665, 2671 n.37
  in China, 2064–2065, 2726, 2732
  communities in, 2202–2203, 2658, 2671 n.37
  Confucianism and, 2066
  criticism of, 1469 n.30
  culture of, 1113–1114
  dana in, 2130
  debates and, 730–733, 737–738
  diversity in, 1986–1987
  for Drukpa Kagyü school, 2612 n.38
  as economic epicenters, 891–893
  epigraphic mentions of, 1792
  epigraphy and, 1792
  Fo Guang Shan and, 1010–1012, 1015
  with Gelukpa, 1063–1065
  in Harikela area, 1795–1796
  healing in, 207–208
  image donations to, 1796–1797
  in India, 208
  with Islam, 1469 n.21
  in Korea, 225 n.83
  laymen in, 2065–2066
  little-known, 1792–1793
  media in, 2556
  medicine in, 144 n.37
  meditation in, 2741 n.52
  modernity in, 1579
  monastic doctors, 272–274
  monastic hospitals, 212–213
  monasticism, 1403–1405, 1415 n.62
  monastic settlements, 2395–2396
  in Mongolia, 1376–1385
  monks and, 351–352
  in Nanbeicho period, 1189–1190, 1195 n.5
  in North Bengal, 1791–1792
  nuns in, 896
  ordination processes in, 2069
  ordinations in, 890–891
  organization of, 2070–2071
  patronage to, 1781–1789, 1793–1800
  in Phempo, 1395*f*
  pilgrimage to, 1869–1871
  pravāraṇa ceremony in, 2672 n.57
  recitation in, 2705 n.103
  records from, 2575
  rules for, 2662–2663
  scholar monks, 750–753, 756–757
  scholarship on, 144 n.35, 1578–1580
  signatories in, 2576
  solitary retreats and, 2158–2160
  of South Bahir, 1788–1789
  in Sri Lanka, 2667
  in Taiwan, 1263–1264
  in Thailand, 74
  in Tibet, 730–731, 1754–1755, 2664
  in Tibetan Buddhism, 892
  vinaya texts for, 2656–2659
  in West Bengal, 1792–1793
  women in, 1085–1086, 1098
Monasteries and Temples of Bogdiin Khuree (Teleki and Majer), 1615
A Monastery in Time (Hürelbaatar and Humphrey), 1615
Möngke Khan, 1624–1629, 1637, 2011, 2013
Mongkut (king), 73–76, 376, 385–386, 1100, 1883–1884, 2127, 2417–2418

Mongolia. See also *specific topics*
Afghanistan and, 1624–1625
Autonomous Period of, 1606–1607
Buddhism to, 1593–1594
Buryat Buddhism in, 1469 n.8, 1600, 1603, 1608–1609, 1611
China and, 1141, 1379, 1383–1384, 1592–1593, 1645–1656, 2563
Christianity in, 1593
Confucianism in, 1631
culture of, 1385, 1612
Dalai Lama and, 1376, 1384
democracy in, 1582–1591
geopolitics of, 1591–1593
gers in, 1586
history of, 1468 n.1, 1469 n.6, 1503–1504, 1604–1607, 1614–1615
Jampel namdröl chökyi gyeltsen in, 1383–1384
Japan and, 1766–1767
Khalkha Jebtsundampa Zanabazar in, 1376–1378
Lozang tenpé drönmé in, 1379
Lozang tenpé gyeltsen in, 1381
Lozang tsültrim jikmé tenpé gyeltsen pelzangpo in, 1381
Lozang tupten wangchuk jikmé gyatso pelzangpo in, 1380–1381
manuscripts in, 2559
modernity and, 1601–1604, 1611–1613
monasteries in, 1376–1385
Ngakwang chökyi wangchuk trinlé gyatso in, 1381–1382
Ngakwang lozang chökyi nyima tendzin wangchuk in, 1382–1383
nuns in, 1588
Qing dynasty in, 1583, 1586, 1591–1592, 1629
rebirth in, 2013–2014
revolution in, 1606–1611
Russia and, 383–384, 1469 n.18
Sanskrit in, 1378
scholarship on, 694, 1385–1387, 1594–1595, 1613–1614, 1656–1657
socialism in, 1582–1583
Soviet Union and, 1610–1614
Tanguts in, 1631–1632
Tibetan Buddhism in, 1171
Tibet and, 1041, 1378–1379, 1382, 1385, 1387, 1599–1600, 1608
Tibeto-Mongol-Buryat medicine, 2529–2530
violence in, 1469 n.8
women in, 694
Yeke Shabi and, 1384–1385
Yéshé tenpé nyima in, 1380
Yuan dynasty in, 1622–1639
Mongolia (Bartholomew and Berger), 1656–1657
Mongolia (Berger, Patricia, and Rossabi), 1386
Mongolia and the Mongols (Pozdneev), 1386
Mongolian Buddhism
Altan Khan and, 1644–1656
Bogd Khaanate and, 1604–1607
Chinggis Khan and, 1469 n.15, 1622–1628
democracy and, 1591–1593
democratic revolution and, 1582–1584
history of, 1469 n.8
Khan family and, 1639–1646
in modernity, 1584–1587, 1599–1604
modernity in, 1613–1614
purges in, 1611–1613
with Qubilai Khan, 1628–1639
reform in, 1593–1594, 1606–1611
scholarship on, 1468 n.1, 1594–1595, 1614–1615
after socialism, 1588–1589
Tibetan Buddhism and, 1468 n.3, 1590
transnational Buddhism and, 1589–1591
Vajrayāna Buddhism and, 1592
vows in, 1588–1589
women in, 1587–1588
"yellow region" of, 1469 n.6, 1601–1604
during Yuan dynasty, 1656–1657
The Mongolia-Tibet Interface, 1594–1595
Monier-Williams, Monier, 1939–1940
monism, 149
monks
adaptability of, 1113–1114
aniyatas for, 2658
in asceticism, 2726–2727
bohisattvas and, 87–88
Bönpo, 2598–2600
Buddhist chaplaincy to, 176 n.69
in Cambodia, 1114
in Chan Buddhism, 1869–1871
in colonialism, 225 n.83
Dhammakaya, 895
donor, 936
in Dzogchen, 129–130
elderly, 2066
eminent, 209–210
environmental, 360–361
forest, 970
Gandhāran Buddhist, 639
karma to, 248
Lankan, 2068–2069
laymen and, 2061–2062

magical, 970
magic and, 1891
in modernity, 2725–2729
monarchs and, 1514–1516
monasteries and, 351–352
Namgyal, 2544
in Nara schools, 2354
nuns and, 712 n.6, 890, 1189–1190, 2063, 2656–2659, 2664–2666, 2672 n.57
offenses of, 249
ordainment of, 2067–2068
plants and, 308
prātimokṣa for, 2657–2660, 2668
Regulations for Monks and Nuns, 2202–2203
restoration activity for, 2727–2728
Rules and Regulations for Monks and Nuns, 2200
in Saffron Revolution, 1885
Śākyamuni and, 256–257
scholar, 750–753, 756–757, 1762, 2186–2187
scholarship on, 84
seafaring monks, 1518–1521
in Sri Lanka, 968
to Taixu, 2069
technology and, 1875
in Tendai School, 2063
in Thailand, 360–361, 895
vinaya texts and, 1879–1880, 2556
to Xuanzang, 2401–2402
Monks and Magic (Terwiel), 1891
Monkut Rama IV (king), 1049–1051
Mönlam Drup, 688. *See also* Machik Lapdrön
Monmu, 2199
Monnet, Mikel, 472
Monograph on Karma (Vasubandhu), 1332, 1334–1336
monographs, 821–824, 2144–2145, 2163, 2166–2167, 2227, 2269–2270
monotheism, 1594
Mon people, 2404–2407
Montagu-Chelmsford Reforms, 1099
Montsepa Kunga Palden, 1539, 1553
monuments, 960, 962
The Monuments of Sāñchī (Marshall and Foucher), 949
Moonbeans of Mahamudrā, 1486
Moonpaths (Cowherds), 986
Moore, G. E., 1465
morality. *See also* ethics
bioethics and, 162
Buddhist, 595
in Greece, 981
Harris, S., on, 982–983
moral life, 981
moral particularism, 983–984
moral psychology, 976–977
in Noble Eightfold Path, 978
scholarship on, 895
suffering and, 978
wealth and, 889
moral phenomenology, 982–983
Moral Theory in Śāntideva's Śikṣā samuccaya (Clayton), 986
moral virtue, 866
Moretti, Costantino, 824
Morita Therapy, 1705, 1709, 1947
Morosuke, 2350
Fujiwara Morosuke, 2047–2048
Morozova, Irina, 1613
Mortland, Carol, 1114, 2243
Moses, Larry, 1614–1615
motherhood, 19, 767, 773–776
Mountain Dharma (Dölpopa), 2745–2746, 2749
mountains. *See also* pilgrimage
in China, 1869–1871
in Confucianism, 1871
in Daoism, 1861–1864
Dharma Drum Mountain, 2163–2165, 2621, 2625, 2627–2628
Diamond Mountains, 498–499
mountain *nés*, 1801 n.23, 1852–1853
Sumanakuta mountain, 2253
Sumeru mountain, 478–479, 481–482, 487, 495
Mountains and Waters Sūtra (Dogen), 2565
Mount Emei Tourism Company, 1873–1874
Mount Meru, 1416–1417, 1428–1429
Mount Wutai, 728 n.35, 792–795
Mouzi, 993–994, 996, 999–1000
Mouzi Lihuolun (Mouzi), 993–994, 996–997, 999–1000
movable type, 2563–2564
moxibustion, 2532
Mozong Deben, 663
MPKM. *See* Mahā Praṇidhāna Kuta Mantrayāna
Mrozik, Susanne, 112 n.4, 120, 286–287, 1103–1104, 1120–1121
MSBL. *See* Mantra School Bright Lineage
Mu'an Shanqing, 674
Mucalinda (serpent king), 349–350, 1801 n.6
Mucalinda Sutta, 349–350
Muchimaro, Fujiwara, 2202
mudrās, 2266–2267
Muhammad (prophet), 1469 n.18, 1667–1668, 1670–1674, 1677. *See also* Islam
Muhon Kakushin, 666–667
Mujū Ichien, 2187

Mukai Akira, 101–102
Mukaveṭi, Alagiyavanna, 369
Mūlamadhyamakakārikah (Nāgārjuna), 1028, 1464–1465, 1498, 1688–1689, 1691, 1696–1697, 1701 n.10. See also *specific topics*
Mūlasarvāstivāda tradition, 2659
Mūlasarvāstivāda *Uttaragrantha*, 2659
Mūlasarvāstivāda Vinaya, 255–256
Mūlasāsana, 2555
Mullen, Eve, 233
Muller, Max, 1506
Müller-Saini, Gotelind, 2294–2295
multiculturalism, 416, 788–790
Multifaith Views of Spiritual Care, 472
Mumian jiasha (film), 1231
Munakata Shikō, 231–232
mundane rites, 1423*t*
Munétsen, 2576–2577
Muné Tsenpo (king), 1743–1744
Muñoz, José Esteban, 1992–1993
Murakami (emperor), 2047–2049, 2355–2356
Murakami Senshō, 182
Murakami Shigeyoshi, 2226
murals, 1862
Murasaki Shikubu, 304, 308–309
Murase Takao, 1705
Murata Kiyoaki, 2226
Murayama Shūichi, 346
Murphy, Michael, 1949–1950
Murray, Julia, 1871
Murti, Tirupattur, 1464–1465, 1698
Muruktsen, 2576–2577
Mus, Paul, 69–70
Mus chen Dkon mchog rgyal mtshan, 1403
museums
  Angkor National Museum, 1919–1923, 1922*f*
  Ashmolean Museum, 1908–1909, 1909*f*
  Bangkok National Museum, 74–75, 1805 n.108, 1908, 1919, 1920*f*, 1937 n.119
  Da Nang Museum, 1804 n.88
  Fo Guang Shan Buddha Museum, 1011–1012
  Nara Museum, 75, 77
  National Museum of Cambodia Phnom Penh, 1916, 1917*f*
  Sharf on, 72
  temples and, 72–75
  Wat Pô Veal Museum, 1897–1899, 1919–1923, 1926
music, 692, 694, 1469 n.16, 1551–1552
musk, 1673
Muslims. *See* Islam
Musō Soseki, 268
mutual inclusion, of ten realms, 1767–1768
Mutual Security Act (1951), 2156
MVŚ. See *Abhidharma-mahāvibhāṣā*
Myanmar. *See* Burma/Myanmar
My Master's Robe (Hanh), 2435–2436, 2448
Myōe, 1770, 2181
Myōgu, 2051, 2054
Myōhen, 2185
Myriad Relief Prescriptions (Kajiwara), 273
Mysticism (D. T. Suzuki), 707–708, 722
mythology, 1161–1164, 1746–1750, 2247, 2489–2490, 2497, 2500

al-Nadīm, 1676–1678
nāga, 2636
Nāgābhodi, 2176
Nāgabodhi, 1519
Nāgabuddhi, 1522
Naganuma Myoko, 909–910
Nagao, Gadjin, 2457–2458
Nagaraju, S., 936–937
Nāgārjuna, 211. *See also* Candrakīrti
  Abhidharma Buddhism and, 1454, 1689–1690
  Āryadeva and, 748–749, 1498
  Candrakīrti and, 1467, 1488
  concepts of, 615–617, 623–627, 1028, 1062, 1403, 1809–1810, 1815
  on emptiness, 623–624, 1688–1689, 1691–1697
  Madhyamaka Buddhism and, 1456–1459, 1464, 1468 n.5
  Mādhyamika Śāntarakṣita and, 1459–1460
  Mahāyāna Buddhism and, 1454–1455
  Nāgabodhi and, 2176
  philosophy of, 985–986, 1820, 2207
  Sanskrit to, 1468 n.2
  scholarship and, 1461–1462, 1464–1467, 1469 n.12, 1687–1689, 1697–1700
  tantra to, 1474
  translations of, 1466
  Tsongkhapa and, 1463
  zhentong and, 2744
Nāgārjuna II (king), 1785
"Nāgārjuna's Appeal" (Hayes, R.), 1465
Nāgasena, 246, 253–254, 1526
Nagatomi Shinjō, 40–41
Nagoe-no-ama, 1762
Nag tsho lo tsa ba, 1401
Nag tsho lo tsa ba Tshul khrims rgyal ba, 1394, 1397–1399
Nagtso Lotsāwa, 1538, 1548
Nahapāna, 937
Naikan
  globalization of, 1708–1710

history of, 1702–1704
institutionalism of, 1707–1708
in Japan, 1702–1704, 1718 n.30
medicalization of, 1705–1706
methods, 1710–1713
in prisons, 1704–1705
Pure Land Buddhism and, 1715
scholarship on, 278, 1714–1715
for self-reflection, 1713–1714
in Shin Buddhism, 1708
temples for, 1707–1708
in U.S., 1709
Naikanhō no tsutaekata (Yoshimoto), 1704
Naikan no yonjū nen (Takeuchi), 1705
Nair, Urmila, 1755
Nakamaro, 2202–2203
Nakamaro, Fujiwara no, 2202, 2206
Nakamura, Rose, 912
Nakamura Hajime, 1974
Naka no Ōe, 2199–2200
Nakatomi no Kamatari, 2199–2200
nakchok (Dark Side), 2487–2488
Naktso Lotsawa Tsül trim Gyelwa, 627
Nalanda inscription of Vipulaśrīmitra, 946–947, 946*f*
Nalanda Mahāvihāra, 1783–1786, 1798–1800
Namchö Mingyur Dorje, 1145–1146, 1966, 1970–1972
Namdru Remati, 1437
Namgyal monks, 2544
Namkha Drimed, 2497
Namkhai Gyaltsen, 687–688
Namkhai Norbu, 1144–1145
Namkha sönam drakpa, 1376
Nam-lin Hur, 35
Namo, 1627
Namtso Dopa Mikyö Dorjé, 692
Nanak (guru), 2314
Ñānavimalatissa, Ambagahapitiyē, 2416
Nanbeicho period
Buddhism in, 1182–1183, 1185–1186
Buddhist literature from, 1185
Buddhist persecution in, 1190
importance of, 1181–1182, 1191
local tradition in, 1184–1185
material culture of, 1188–1189
meditation in, 1187–1188
monasteries in, 1189–1190, 1195 n.5
philosophy in, 1186–1188
popular Buddhism in, 1191
scholarship on, 1192
translations in, 1183–1184
Nandin, 1516
Nangklao Rama III (king), 1049–1050
Nang Nak (film), 404
Nangzher Löpo, 113 n.25, 136
Nanjing massacre, 1219
Nanjō Bunyū, 1136
Ñāṇodaya (Buddhaghosa), 145
Nan Shan Temple, 411
Nanyang Heshang dunjiao jietuo chanmen zhiliaoxing tanyu, 1227–1228
Nanyang Huizhong, 1233–1234, 1237–1238
Nanyue Huairang, 1232
Naphu monastery, 847–850, 857–858
Napoleon III, 375
Naquin, 1874–1875
Nara Museum, 75, 77
Nara schools
history of, 2207–2208, 2324–2325
for Japan, 2198–2204, 2208–2209, 2342–2343
Kanmu and, 2343
monks in, 2354
ordination at, 2325
religion at, 2196–2199
Six, 2198, 2203–2209
Tokuitsu and, 2352–2353
Nara Youth Prison, 1704
Nāro, 1537
Nāropā
as Bhadrapā, 1551
death of, 1547
disciples of, 1542–1544
doctrine, 850
Maitrīpa and, 1537, 1548
Marpa Lotsawa and, 1481, 1546, 1548–1549
Ngok Dodé and, 1551
reputation of, 1538
scholarship on, 1397, 1968–1969
Six Doctrines of, 1552–1553
tantric, 1474
Tilopa and, 1476–1477, 1536
narratives
affinity, 1722–1725
of authority, 1731–1734
Buddhist, 1719–1721, 1734–1736
of Buddhist images, 1720
of glorification, 1727–1731
of Maritime Buddhism, 1517–1518
narrative theology, 144 n.37
of Padmasambhava, 2491–2492
of prediction, 1725–1727
psychology of, 177–179
standard secularization narrative, 2131
in Thailand, 1729
Nash, Manning, 575

Nath, Chuon, 377
Natha, 2245–2246, 2255–2257, 2314. See also *satara varan devi*
Nāth tradition, 2309
national Asian traditions, 1077–1080
National Health Service, 469
national identity, 42–45
nationalism
in Cambodia, 378
in China, 2168 n.13, 2169 n.18
Chinggis Khan and, 1584
colonialism and, 916
cultural, 1116
hyperactive, 382
in Japan, 724
national Buddhisms, 494, 500–501
resistance to, 1097–1100
socialism and, 1442–1444
in Sri Lanka, 71–72, 2432 n.93
in Taiwan, 2169 n.18
transnationalism, 1259
National Library of China, 815, 818–820
national memory-making
Buddha images and, 72–75
with Buddhist sites, 69–72
cultural memory and, 73
scholarship and, 66–68, 77–78
National Museum of Cambodia Phnom Penh, 1916, 1917*f*
Native American Bearing Witness, 923
Native Tibetans, 2650–2651
nats cults, 343–344
Natural Arising of the Three Bodies, 134–135
The Natural Arising of the Three Bodies (Shardza Tashi Gyeltsen), 132
natural sites, 1854
The Nature of Buddhist Ethics (Keown), 981
Naughton, Alexander T., 29–30
Navayāna movement, 984
Nazi Germany, 36
Neal, Alexandra David, 2709
Nebesky-Wojkowitz, René de, 1173–1174, 1744, 1755, 2498–2499, 2641, 2651
Nechung monastery
Dalai Lama and, 1754–1755
mythology at, 1746–1750
scholarship on, 1718 n.30, 1718 n.32, 1755–1757
Tibetan Buddhism at, 1742–1746
Tibet and, 1750–1754
U.S., and, 1718 n.33
Nechung Monastery (Mikmar Tsering), 1756
Nechung Record (Sangyé Gyatso), 1744–1745, 1748, 1750–1751
Necklace of Gems (Dudjom), 2640
Neelis, Jason, 892–893, 1512–1514
"Negotiating Self and Other" (Jadamba and Schnittich), 1595
Nehru, Jawaharlal, 70–71, 384–385, 907–908, 2292–2293
Neichi toyin, 1648
Nelson, John, 778–779, 1357
neo-Buddhism, 984, 1944–1945, 1989–1990
neo-Confucianism, 92–93, 267, 675–676, 2055
Neo-Daoism, 1184
Neo-Kadam order, 1484–1485
neoliberalism, 192, 2129–2131
neo-Orientalism, 113 n.23
neo-orthodox Mahāvihāra Sangha, 2404–2405
neo-Zhenyan movements, 2385–2387
Nepal. *See also* Tibet
BCA in, 2077
India and, 424
Longchenpa in, 1440
Marpa Lotsawa in, 1542, 1544–1545, 1548–1550
scholarship on, 1145, 1148, 1150
Thailand and, 1574–1575
nés, 1801 n.23, 1850–1853
neuropsychology, 1950–1953
neuroscience, 172
new-age spirituality, 2479
New Age Tantra, 2314
Newar Buddhism, 1148, 2077
New Bahār, 1669
new Buddhism, 2132–2134
Ne Win, 570–571, 597, 601, 2417
New Kadam school, 1061–1062. *See also* Gelukpa
Newland, Guy, 1815
Newly Compiled Record of Surnames (Kinmei), 305–306
new religious movements, 1708, 1988
news media, 235–236
New-Style Mañjuśrī, 793–794, 794*f*
New Zealand, 112 n.9, 469–470, 2137–2138
Neyapāla (king), 1398–1399
Ng, Edwin, 915–916, 1982
Ngag dbang blo bzang rgya mtsho, 1657–1658
Ngag-dbang dpal-ldan, 26
Ngakwang chökyi wangchuk trinlé gyatso, 1381–1382
Ngakwang lozang chökyi nyima tendzin wangchuk, 1382–1383
Ngakwang trinlé, 1380
Ngamdzong Tönpa, 1537–1539, 1542–1543, 1551
Ngari Panchen Pema Wangyal, 1171–1172
Ngawang Chöpel, 2747
Ngawang Lozang (Losang) Gyatso, 1065–1066, 1653–1654, 2015–2017, 2025, 2517, 2529, 2585, 2746–2747

Ngawang Namgyel, 2019
Ngawang Trashi Drakpa, 2014
Ngawang Tsoknyi Gyatso, 2747–2748
Ngawang Yeshe Gyatso, 2017
NGB. *See Nyingma'i rgyud 'bum*
Ngok Chödor, 1539, 1541, 1545–1546, 1550
Ngok Dode, 1539–1542, 1545, 1547, 1551
Ngok Lekpe sherap, 731
Ngok Loden sherap, 731
Ngok Lotsāwa, 2744–2745
Ngorchen Kunga Sangpo, 2303
Nguyen, Cuong Tu, 2434, 2445
Nichidatsu Fujii, 909–910
Nichikan, 2224
Nichiren
  Ashoka and, 917
  career of, 1760–1767, 2325, 2624–2625
  exile of, 1764–1767
  first remonstration of, 1762–1764
  in Japan, 909–910
  Lotus Sutra and, 2212, 2216–2219, 2226
  propagation by, 1772–1773
  Pure Land Buddhism and, 866
  reputation of, 2219
  Śākyamuni and, 2624–2625
  scholarship on, 1719 n.50, 1773–1776, 2055, 2341
  teachings of, 271–272, 1770–1771, 2217–2219
  in Tendai School, 2335
  Zhiyi and, 1764–1766
Nichiren (Rodd), 1774
Nichiren, the Buddhist Prophet (Masaharu), 1774
Nichiren Buddhism
  daily chants in, 771–773
  Mahāyāna Buddhism and, 2217
  scholarship on, 766–767, 1348, 1353–1354, 1356–1357
  sects of, 2211
  to Toda, 2221
Nichiren Shōshū, 2211–2212, 2215–2219, 2222–2226
Nichiren Shoshu Soka Gakkai of America (NSA), 1356
Nichirenshū, 1718 n.31
Nidāna-kathā, 1280–1281, 1366–1367
Niepan jing, 1224–1225
Nietzsche, Friedrich, 2140
night yoga, 2546
nihilism, 1464–1465, 1694–1695, 1697–1699, 1992–1993, 2458–2460
Nihom, Max, 969
Nihon Chūsei shakai no keisei to ōken (Uejima), 759
Nihon teki reisei (D. T. Suzuki), 706, 719–720
Nihonyanagi Kenji, 213, 278, 307
Nikāyas. See also *specific topics*
  debates on, 1325–1326
  divisions of, 2408–2410
  heresy to, 2427 n.23
  history of, 2406–2407
  Sanskrit and, 2426 n.13
  scholarship on, 1318–1320
  Theravāda Buddhism and, 2412–2414, 2430 n.69
  Theriya lineage to, 2397, 2410–2411, 2432 n.97
  Theriya sub-Nikāyas, 2397, 2401, 2417–2418, 2432 n.99
  vinayas of, 2430 n.68
Nikkei Buddhists, 35, 45–48, 1298 n.17, 1303–1307
Nikolai (tsar), 1609
Nikolay II (tsar), 2529
Nimibutr, Nonzee, 404
the nine grades of rebirth, 2687–2688
Nine Stages of Bodily Decay, 279–280
The Nine Ways of Bon (Snellgrove), 112 n.1
Ningai, 2185, 2356
Ninmyō (emperor), 294
Ninshō, 290
Nipponzan Myohoji, 906–907, 909–910
Ni Qing, 213
nirodho (ending), 1026–1027
nirvāṇa. See *specific topics*
Nirvāna and Other Buddhist Felicities (Collins, S.), 577
Nirvana Sutra, 1228–1230, 1232–1233, 1235
Nisei Buddhists
  in Hawaii, 1309–1310
  scholarship and, 16 n.38, 41–46, 48
  tradition and, 35–36, 38–39
Nishida Kitarō, 701–702, 705, 719, 724
Nishi Honganji, 34–36, 38–39, 1303–1304, 1307, 1987
Nishijima, Kakuryo, 2715
Nishio Masahito, 294
Nishitani Keiji, 710, 720, 724
Niṣpanayogāvalī, 1912
Nittō, 2045–2046
Niwano Nikkyo, 909–910
noble beings (*ārya*), 27–28
Noble Eightfold Path, 112 n.16, 452–453, 975–976, 978
Nobles (*āryas*), 531–532
Nobunaga, 2041
Noé, Gaspar, 2480
No Intention Needed sutta, 1327
Nomads on Pilgrimage (Charleux), 1615
Nomon Khan, 1376
nonabiding practice, 2159–2160
nonanthropocentrism, 358
non-Asians, 1080–1083
non-attachment, 1364
nonconceptual perception, 1828–1836
non-dual *mahāmudra*, 1477–1478

Nondual School of Kashmir Śaivism, 2308–2309
Nongchan Monastery, 2162*f*
nongovernmental organizations, 1073, 2613, 2619, 2623
non-heritage Buddhism, 1119–1122
nonhuman agents, of disease, 254
non-injury, 166–167
non-materiality (*arūpya-dhātu*), 6–7
No-Nonsense Buddhism for Beginners (Rasheta), 2139
non-religions, 2128–2129
nonself, 1953–1955
  no-self (*anātmavāda*) and, 113, 1836–1837
  no-self doctrine and, 977
non-Sīhaḷa lineages, 2406–2407
non-violence, 1584
Nora, Pierre, 70–71
Norbu, Khytense, 401
Norbu, Namkhai, 839–840, 2469–2470
Norihira, 2047
Norihisa Baba, 154
Noriko Kawahashi, 778–779
Noritoshi Aramaki, 101–102
Norman, K. R., 151, 1028–1033
normative texts, 886 n.101
Norodom (king), 376, 1095–1096
Norow (mistress), 1382
North America. See also *specific countries*
  Buddhist chaplaincy in, 159 n.45, 449–450, 460–465
  Chinese Pacific Railway, 409–410
  Cold War in, 2071–2072
  Europe and, 72, 897, 981, 1802 n.35, 2277–2278
  Fo Guang Shan in, 1010, 1013
  Hawaii and, 1356, 1359 n.7
  Japanese Buddhisms in, 1351–1353, 1357
  Korea and, 1589–1590
  refugees in, 1101
  scholarship in, 1071 n.3
  Shingon Buddhism in, 1351, 1357
  society in, 2242–2243
  South America and, 1354–1356
  Southeast Asian refugees in, 2231–2239
  Vietnamese Buddhism in, 2239–2242
  White privilege in, 2718–2719
North Bengal, 1791–1792
Northern Dipper homa, 1203–1204
The Northern School and the Formation of Early Ch'an Buddhism (McRae, J. R.), 675–676
Northern Treasures (Godem Ngodrup Gyaltsen), 838
North Korea. *See* Korea
Norway, 633
no-self. *See* nonself
"Not a Day but a Vu Lan Festival" (Truitt), 2243
Notes of a Simple Physician (Kajiwara), 291–292
novice ordination, 2068
NSA. *See* Nichiren Shoshu Soka Gakkai of America
Nub Sangye Yeshe, 833–834
nuclear weapons, 2225
Nukariya Kaiten, 1444
Numrich, Paul, 1114, 1122, 2718–2719
nuns
  in Australia, 907–908
  in Cambodia, 1102
  in China, 1102–1103, 1436–1437
  laywomen and, 2061–2062
  medieval Christian, 187
  in monasteries, 896
  in Mongolia, 1588
  monks and, 712 n.6, 890, 1189–1190, 2063, 2656–2659, 2664–2666, 2672 n.57
  ordainment of, 2067–2068
  Regulations for Monks and Nuns, 2202–2203
  Rules and Regulations for Monks and Nuns, 2200
  sexism against, 1119–1121
  Soto Zen, 185
  in Southeast Asia, 1103
  in Taiwan, 909, 1257–1258
  in Taiwanese Luminary Nunnery, 2666
  in Theravāda Buddhism, 2073
  vinaya texts and, 2666–2667
Nup Sanggye, 2011–2012
Nurhaci, 1652–1654
nursing, 207–208
Nya dbon kun dga' dpal, 25
Nyagt Bilegt Beile Lama Puntsagdorj, 1606–1607
Nyamme Sherab Gyeltsen, 136–137
Nyanaponika Thera, 1952–1953
Nyangrel Nyima Özer
  scholarship on, 834–835, 1503, 1746–1748, 1972–1973, 2011, 2024–2025
  Trisong Detsen and, 2583–2585, 2587
Nyang Tingedzin, 2578
Nyawon Kunga Pel, 2745–2746
Nyāyānusāra, 3
Nyāya school, 1687–1689
Nyen Palyang, 832
nyepas, 2530–2532
Nyida Chöje, 2468
Nyida Sangye, 2468
Nyima Özer, 1437
Nyima Tenzin, 134
Nyingma Gyubum, 1169
Nyingma'i rgyud 'bum (NGB), 2651
Nyingmapa, 112 n.7, 112 n.9, 2010

Nyingmapa tantric traditions, 2490
Nyingma school. *See also* Dzogchen
  Bönpo school and, 133
  Dzogchen to, 134
  objects in, 2512–2513
  Sakya school and, 2513
  scholarship on, 808, 829–831, 833, 835, 838–840, 1470 n.39
  tantra in, 2523 n.33
Nyingma tantras, 2641
Nyingma tantric canon, 2317
Nyingma tradition
  Dzogchen and, 128
  epistemology of, 1564
  funeral rites in, 2481
  Gesar in, 2495
  Mipam on, 1560–1561, 1563
  Padmasambhava and, 2475–2476
  reform in, 1602–1603
  scholarship on, 1478–1479
  visionary Buddhism and, 2545–2546
Nyingma trinity, 1167–1170
Nyingtik Yabshi, 1445
Nyoenni, 2036
Nyogen Senzaki, 42, 46–47
Nyojō, 2038
Nyö Lotsawa Yonten Drak, 1542–1545
Nyoryō, 2037–2038
Nyoshul Khenpo, 1446
Nyoshul Khen Rinpoche, 1442–1443

oath substance, 2510–2511
Obadia, Lionel, 896–897
Obermiller, Eugene, 27, 29–30
Obeyesekere, Gananath, 575, 2127, 2145, 2257
Obinata Daijiō, 213
object of worship (*honzon*), 1769–1770
objects, 514–522
OBOR initiative. *See* One Belt, One Road initiative
obstructers, 2647–2648, 2653 n.1
Occupy Wall Street, 921
Ocean of Definitive Meaning, 1487
The Ocean of Kagyü Songs, 1485–1486, 1552
Ocean of Oath-Bound Guardians of the Teachings (Lelung Jedrung Zhepé Dorjé), 1746–1748
The Ocean of Reasoning (Tsongkhapa), 1062
The Ocean of Texts on Valid Cognition, 1485
O Daishi kyokai, 1133
Odani, Nobuchiyo, 4–5
Oda Nobunaga, 2040, 2187
Odantapuri Mahāvihāra, 1788–1789
offenses, 249
ofudas, 770, 772*f*
Ögedei Khan, 1624–1626, 1628–1629
Ōgen, 2038
Ogui, Koshin, 912
Ogyan Lingpa, 1746–1748
Ogyen Tinley Dorje, 1988, 2000 n.76
Ohnuma, Reiko, 180
Oidtman, Max, 2024
Oidtmann, Both, 2032 n.88
Oirat Galdan Bośugtu, 1377–1378
Oirats. *See* Mongolia
Ōjōraisan (Shandao), 2039
Okakura Kakuzo, 384–385
Okihiro, Gary, 1306
Ōkubo Ryōshun, 2336
Okumura Takie, 1306
Olcott, Henry Steel, 373–374, 916, 1308–1309, 1941–1942, 2256
Old Bön. *See* Bön tradition
old Buddhism, 2134–2137
Oldenberg, Hermann, 181, 1939, 1944–1945, 2554–2555, 2667–2668
Ol'denburg, Sergeĭ Fedorovich, 639, 818
Oldmeadow, Peter, 2088
Old Tang Annals, 2574–2575
Old Tibetan Annals, 808, 813, 2574–2575
Old Tibetan Chronicle, 2575, 2580–2581
Old Turkic-language materials, 810
Ole Nydahl, 1087
Öljeitü (sultan), 1642
Olson, Carl, 1982
omamoris (protective amulets), 767, 769, 769*f*
Omi, Michael, 2632 n.30, 2714–2715
Ōmiwa, 292–293
omniscience, 18–23
Omniscient One. *See* Longchenpa
Omthangpa, 850
Ōmura Seiga, 60
o'Naghten, Hedwige Multzer, 1897
Öndör gegen Zanabazar, 1647–1648
Ondür Gegen, 1376–1378
One Belt, One Road (OBOR) initiative, 795
100 peaceful and wrathful deities, 2476–2478
"One Plus One Makes Three" (Gyatso), 1993
"On Esoteric Buddhism" (Sharf), 61
Ong, Walter, 2567
Onjōji, 303–304
Onkun, 2045–2046
online Buddhist communities, 501
Onoda Shunzo, 743–744, 1974

"On the Establishment of a Pure Land in the Human Realm" (Taixu), 2285–2287, 2294–2295
ontology, 1071 n.7, 1431–1432, 1825
Ookhnoi, Batsaikhan, 1386–1387
Ooms, Herman, 2208–2209
Opening an Unlimited Door (Ratna Lingpa), 1966
Opening Printing Blocks for an Edition of the Canon (Zhitang), 663
Opium Wars, 408, 1135–1136
opthalmology, 211–212
oracles, 1717 n.22, 1718 n.32, 1743, 1746–1748, 1750–1756. *See also* Nechung monastery
Oracles and Demons of Tibet (Nebesky-Wojkowitz), 1173–1174, 1755, 2641
oral canons, 634–637
oral communication, 2553–2557, 2559–2560
oral literature, 112 n.12
oral tradition, 2570 n.20
Oral Tradition from Zhang Zhung, 2549
Oral Transmission known as the Naked Vision of Awareness (Bönzhik Khyung-nak), 134
Oral Transmission of Zhangzhung, 132, 134–136
Ordinary Mind (Magid), 1955
ordination
  bhikkhunī, 1085–1086, 1577
  hierarchies, 2068–2069
  methods of, 1575–1576
  in monasteries, 890–891
  at Nara schools, 2325
  ordained women, 2066
  platform, 1770–1771
  processes, 2067–2069
  reordination, 2158
organ donation, 171
Orgyan Pema, 2493
Orgyen Choje, 1441
Orgyen Chowang, 1144
Orgyen Lingpa, 2585
Orgyenpa Rinchen Pel, 2007–2008
Orgyen Terdak Lingpa, 1441–1442
Orgyen Trinlé Dorjé, 2021–2022
Orientalism, 370–371, 377, 2707–2712, 2715–2716. *See also* colonialism
Orientalism (Said), 1679, 2707–2708
original authority, 2140
original enlightenment, 340
Original Enlightenment (Stone), 2227
Orlovsky, Peter, 723–724
Ornament for Clear Realization. *See Abhisamayālaṃkāra*
Ornament of the Mahāyāna Sūtras, 1809–1810
Ornament of the Middle Way (Śāntarakṣita), 1461, 1467
Ornament of Zhentong (Tāranātha), 2746–2747
Orsi, Robert, 564, 573–574
orthodoxy, 1687–1688, 1691, 1701 n.10, 1772
Orzech, Charles, 62–63
Ösal Rangdrol, 1441
Ösel Tendzin, 2022–2023
Ōshita Daien, 467
Ösrung, 1964–1965
ossuaries, 2379–2380
Osterhammel, Jürgen, 112 n.7
Ōtani Honganji, 2039
Ōtani Kōshō, 1306
Ōtani Kozui, 818–819
Ōtani University, 705–706, 716
other-emptiness. *See* zhentong
The Other Emptiness (Sheehy and Mathes), 2751
Ötrul Rinpoche, 1590–1591
Ottoman Empire, 367
Ōuchi Fumi, 758
Our Great Qing (Elverskog), 1615
The Outline of Esoteric Buddhism (Gonda Raifu), 2365
Outlines of Mahayana Buddhism (D. T. Suzuki), 703, 725
Ouyang Jingwu, 2294–2295
Overseas Materia Medica (Haiyao bencao), 213
Ōwa debate, 754, 2047–2049
Owens, Rod, 911, 915–916, 1990, 2719
Ox Festival, 295–296
The Oxford Handbook of Secularism (Shook and Zuckerman), 2145
Ōyama Kōjun, 2334
Özbeg Khan, 1642
Ozeray, Michel-Jean-François, 864–865, 870, 875–876, 878, 880–881
Özer Gocha, 1439

Pabongkha Dechen Nyingpo, 1146, 2020–2021
Packer, Toni, 1118
Padampa Sangye, 1480, 1489–1490
Paddhati (Vasubandhu), 23–24
Padma, Sree, 2257
Padma AG, 2529–2530
Padma Katang, 1163–1164
Padmasambhava
  Avalokiteśvara and, 2491–2492
  biographies of, 1444, 1972–1973
  deities and, 1159–1160, 1163
  depictions of, 1973–1974
  disciples of, 1436–1437
  Gesar and, 2492–2494, 2498
  Gesar epic and, 2489
  hagiography of, 2587

Karma Lingpa and, 2475
Lhacham Pemasal and, 1439
Longchenpa and, 1439
narratives of, 2491–2492
Nyingma tradition and, 2475–2476
on oracles, 1743
prophecies of, 1440
scholarship and, 808, 830, 835, 837, 1960–1961, 2641–2642
stories from, 1169–1170, 1563, 1970–1971
supplication to, 1566
teachings of, 2475
in Tibet, 2641
Trisong Detsen and, 2580, 2583–2586
Yeshe Tsogyal and, 134, 2511
Padoux, André, 2302–2304
Pagan dynasty, 1095–1096
Page Daiching, 1655–1657
Pagoda, Từ Hiếu, 2435–2436
pain (*dukkhaṃ*), 1024–1025
Paiṇḍapa, 1542–1543
Pajjota (king), 255–256
Pakistan, 632–633, 1200–1201
Pakmodru, 1484–1485
Pakmo Drupa, 1482
Paksam Wangpo, 2595
Pal, Pratapaditya, 2269–2270
Pala dynasty, 70, 1783–1789, 1798
Pāla India, 1923–1925
Pāla style, 2264
Palden Lhamo (Śri Devī), 1159–1161, 1164–1167, 1171–1172, 2544
Pali Buddhism. *See also* four noble truths; Theravāda Buddhism
in Asia, 2658, 2660
authority in, 2403
Buddhaghosa and, 150–151
Buddha's body in, 116–117
canon, 985, 1020, 1023–1028, 1031–1032, 1046–1047, 2139–2141
China and, 637
culture of, 1888
on disease, 254
dominance of, 960–962
ethics of, 861 n.2
history of, 1522
influence of, 2412–2413
Jainism and, 1359 n.2
Kataññu Sutta in, 993–994
language of, 144 n.30, 2399–2400, 2427 n.29, 2711
Mahāyāna Buddhist tantra and, 964–967
medical training in, 254–255
medicine in, 248–250
Pali Abhidhamma tradition, 1330–1331
Pali cosmopolises, 967–969
Pali suttas, 1327–1328
Pali Text Society, 153, 370, 996, 1032–1033, 1117, 1736–1737, 1939, 2256, 2564
Pali University, 1578
Penetrative sutta in, 1299 n.34
records of, 2566
reform in, 2140
Rhys Davids, T. W., on, 119
for sacred objects, 14 n.9
Śākyamuni in, 2134–2135
Sanskrit and, 637–639, 1364–1365, 2541, 2714–2715
Sanskrit sources for, 250, 252–254
scholarship on, 863 n.37, 2427 n.21
surgery in, 251–252
Suttas of, 2555
Theravāda Buddhism and, 113 n.25, 1335–1336, 1521, 2068–2069, 2408–2411
translations of, 1345 n.183, 2411, 2425 n.9
treatments in, 250
vinayas in, 2067, 2138–2139
Paljor Gyaltsen, 1441
Palmer, James T., 177, 180
Palola dynasty, 886 n.83
Palumbo, Lorraine Reiko Minatoshi, 1308–1309
Pāñcarātra tradition, 2306, 2309–2311
Pañcatantra, 1674–1675
Pañcaviṃśatisāhasrikā Prajñāpāramitā, 1810–1812
Paṇ chen bla ma Blo bzang ye shes, 1397
Paṇ-chen bSod-nams grags-pa, 26
Paṇ chen Bsod nams grags pa, 1397
Panchen Lama, 1376–1377, 1379–1382. See also *specific Lamas*
Panchen Lobsang Chökyi Gyaltsen, 1966
Paṇchen Sönam Drakpa, 1064–1065
paṇḍaka (gender category), 271, 1984–1986
Paṇḍit Nisṭ ḥ ānanda Vajrācārya, 1043–1044
Pangtangma, 2579
Pāṇini, 159 n.43
Paññāsa Jātaka, 1372
Panorama of Mount Wutai, 793, 793*f*
Pan Xuan, 2625
Paper, Jordan, 417
Paper, Li Chuang, 417
Parābhava Sutta, 995
"Parable of the White Path" (Shandao), 483
parables, 993–994, 1005–1006
pārājika offenses, 2658

Parākramabāhu I (king), 153, 1095, 2403–2404, 2416, 2420
Paramārtha, 3–4, 12, 618, 1518–1519, 1526, 2204
Paramārthasamudgata, 2457, 2460–2461. *See also* three wheels of doctrine
pāramitās. *See* perfections
Paranvitana, S., 2257
paritta chanting, 1881, 1883
paritta manuscript, 2559–2560
Paritta texts, 1883–1884
Parittaṭṭhakathā (Buddhaghosa), 145
Pariwa Yeshe Gönpo, 856
Park, Changhwan, 11
Park, Jin Y., 1982
Parker, Anne O., 1447
Parsons, William, 1943–1944
particularism, 983–984
Pas, Julian, 2688, 2696
Pasenadi (king), 250, 2268
the path, 1303 n.85, 1326–1327
Pathet Lao, 1101
"The Path of Mystic Sacrifice" (Evans-Wenz), 694–695
Path of Purification (Buddhaghosa), 978–979, 1027
pathogenesis, 205–207
Path Omniscience, 20
paths and persons (*mārgapudgala-nirdeśa*), 5
Paths to Liberation (Buswell Jr. and Gimello), 1027–1028
patience (*kṣānti*), 2083–2085
patients, 256–257, 270–272
Pātimokkha, 1052–1053
paṭipadā (way), 1027–1028
Patriarchal Courtyard (Mu'an Shanqing), 674
patriarchy, 1120
patriotism, 1304–1305
patronage
  at Bodhgaya, 1789–1790
  epigraphic mentions of, 1792
  in Harikela area, 1795–1796
  with image donations, 1796–1797
  at Jagaddala Mahāvihāra, 1791, 1797–1798
  at Jagjivanpur Vihāra, 1791–1792
  to little-known monasteries, 1792–1793
  to monasteries, 1781–1789, 1793–1800
  to Nalanda Mahāvihāra, 1783–1786, 1798–1800
  to Odantapuri Mahāvihāra, 1788–1789
  royal, 1781–1782
  in Samataṭa area, 1794–1795
  at Somapura Mahāvihāra, 1790–1791
  to Vikramaśila Mahāvihāra, 1786–1788, 1797–1798
Patrul Orgyen Jigme Chökyi Wangmo, 1968
Patrul Rinpoche, 986
Patsap Nyimadrak, 627, 1964
Paṭṭhāna, 1882, 1884–1885
Patton, Thomas, 579–580, 603–604
Paul, Diana, 184–185
Paul III (pope), 865
Payne, Richard, 1151, 1212, 1357, 2144–2145, 2363
Payutto, Venerable, 895–896
peace activities, 2214–2215, 2220–2222
Peaceful and Wrathful Aspects of the Guru, 1437
Peaceful and Wrathful Deities (Karma Lingpa), 2468–2470
Peacock Sutra, 301
Pehar, 1742, 1744–1750, 1755–1756
Pei Xiu, 649, 1235–1236
Pelliot, Paul, 798, 817–819, 823–824, 826
Pelliot Tibétain, 1964–1965
Pema Chödrön, 2077
Pema Jungné, 2492–2493
Pema Karpo, 857, 1486–1487, 1489–1490, 2019, 2594–2595
Pema Karpo Ngawang Norbu, 853
Pema Ledrel Tsal, 1439, 1441–1442
Pema Lingpa, 1441–1442
Pema Rigzin, 2502 n.9
Pema Tönyö Nyinje, 2022
Penetration sutta, 1322
Penetrative sutta, 1299 n.34, 1321, 1328
Pennsylvania, U.S., 2384–2387
People Dohā Treasuries, 1475–1476
people of color, 457
People's Republic of China. *See* China
perception, 1824–1836
"Percept-Only" Buddhism, 620–621
perceptual awareness, 1832
Percotius, Johannes, 1048
Perdue, Daniel, 743–744
perennialism, 2129
Perera, G. A., 1891
Perera, L. P. N., 1993
Perfect Eon concept, 2745–2746
Perfection of Wisdom discourses, 2454–2455
Perfection of Wisdom in 100,000 Sections, 810
Perfection of Wisdom Scripture for Humane Kings to Protect Their States, 497–498
Perfection of Wisdom Sutras, 808, 811, 1454–1455, 2330, 2541, 2579
perfections
  in Buddhist literature, 1805–1814
  in Indian Mahāyāna Buddhist scholarly works, 1809–1814
  in *Jātakas*, 1806–1807

in Mahāyāna Buddhism, 1807–1809
in Sanskrit, 1805–1806
Śāntideva on, 2080–2081
scholarship on, 1814–1815, 2690
translations of, 1805–1806
virtue of, 2081
performativity, 1992
performing arts, 757
Performing the Visual (Fraser), 800–801
Perls, Fritz, 1949
permanence, 2114–2115
Perrière, Brac de la, 579–580, 604
persecution, 1190, 1771–1772
Persia, 1515–1516
personal expression, 231–232
persons of color, 1119, 1982, 2137–2138
Petech, Luciano, 1656–1657, 2024
Pettit, John W., 1468 n.1, 1567, 2750–2751
Petzold, Bruno, 1774
Phabongkhapa Dechen Nyingpo, 1067. *See also* Jampa Tenzin Trinley
Pha Dampa. *See* Dampa Sangyé
Phagpa Pandita, 1626
'Phags pa lama, 1626, 1629–1635, 1645–1646, 1657–1658
Pha Gyagar. *See* Dampa Sangyé
Phajo Drugom Zhigpo, 845, 854
Phakmo Drupa Dorje Gyälpo, 847, 849–851
Pham-Quang-Hao, 466
Pha Nakpo. *See* Dampa Sangyé
Phangthangma Catalogue, 1963
Pháp Loa, 1039–1040
pharmaceutical treatments, 250
pharmacological knowledge, 274–275
Phempo, 1395*f*
phenomenology, 112 n.5, 567–574, 982–983, 1320
Philippines, 1527, 2627
philology, 1045–1047, 2265
Philosophical Investigations (Wittgenstein), 1465, 1470 n.46
"The Philosophical Works and Influence of Dignāga and Dharmakīrti" (Arnold, D.), 1838
philosophy. See also *specific topics*
of Abhidharma Buddhism, 529–530, 1819–1824, 1833
of Abhidharma theory, 1690
Advaita Vedānta, 1464–1465, 1698
of amulets, 966
in Anglo-American society, 2141
in *apoha* doctrine, 1824–1828
of Aristotle, 981
Brahmanical, 1822, 1836–1837, 2252
of *cetanā*, 1341 n.92
in China, 1195 n.2
clear comprehension, 1300 n.48
of Confucianism, 701, 1260
of demons, 1158–1159
deviant logic in, 536–537
of dharma, 1321
of Dharmakīrti, 537–538
of Dignāga, 533, 625–626
of Dzogchen, 836
of emptiness, 1694–1696
epistemology and, 535–536, 739–740
of filial piety, 999–1004
fusion, 534–535
of Gelukpa, 1061–1068
of GMD, 1440, 1449 n.11
of hagiography, 1231–1233
of Han dynasty, 996
of happiness, 982
of heaven, 2285–2287, 2291–2292, 2294
Humanistic Buddhism and, 1251–1252, 2289–2290
of humanity, 2086–2087
hypotheses in, 537
of illegitimacy, 2143
of imaging Buddha, 1290–1292, 1299 n.33, 1302 n.75
of institutions, 2071–2073
of Jainism, 2305–2306
kenmitsu ideology, 755
of Kūkai, 2332–2333
of language, 2339 n.25
LGBTIQ+ Buddhists and, 1988
liberal Protestant thought, 2127–2128
literary ambitions and, 615–616
of Longchenpa, 1445–1446
of Madhyamaka Buddhism, 1458–1459, 1687–1688, 1693–1694, 1698–1699
of Mahāyāna Buddhism, 2076
of Mañjuśrī, 1497
of Marxism, 1101, 1260
mediation and, 531
of meditation theory, 2455
metaphysics and, 532–533
of Nāgārjuna, 985–986, 1820, 2207
in Nanbeicho period, 1186–1188
of nihilism, 1694–1695, 1697–1699
of nonconceptual perception, 1828–1836
philology and, 539
philosophical queering, 1991
philosophical works, 813–814
of pilgrimage, 1851–1852
of *Platform Sutra*, 1234–1236

philosophy (*continued*)
of possible worlds, 112 n.4
of Pure Land Buddhism, 2279
of reality, 1691–1694
of rebirth, 2009
religion and, 703
resistance, 2126–2127
of Saichō, 2333
of *saṅkappa/saṅkalpa*, 1317–1318
Sanskrit and, 973–974
of Śāntarakṣita, 538
of Sarvāstivāda Abhidharma school, 2100–2101
of *sautrāntikas*, 1819–1820
scholarship and, 628–629, 1053–1054, 1837–1838
sexuality and, 1983
shakubuku as, 1771
Shinto and, 340–341
of space, 2105
of suffering, 1312
of *summum bonum*, 981–982
of Taixu, 1249–1250
Tiantai, 268, 1257
of Tibetan Buddhism, 735–737, 2547–2548
of translations, 12
of unpleasant situations, 2084–2085
of Vajrakīla tantras, 2640–2643
of Vasubandhu, 1
of Vedic tradition, 2256
of visual culture, 2268–2269
Western, 4, 527–529, 534, 702, 2140
of Yogācāra, 620–621
of Yogācārā Buddhism, 535, 620–621, 1565, 1809–1810, 1819–1822, 1833, 1836, 2282, 2285, 2464
of Yoshimoto, 1701 n.7, 1702–1709
of Zen Buddhism, 718
of Zhiyi, 1768, 2343–2344
Phimeanakas inscription, 1914–1915, 1916*f*
phlegm, 206, 212
Phra Kaeo Morakot, 73–74
Phra Phothirak, 895
phrasebooks, 814
Phra Wontham, 1990
Phu chung ba Gzhon nu rgyal mtshan, 1400–1401
Phüntsok Lodrö, 137–138
Phương, Cao Ngọc, 2439
Phur pa khrag 'thung rtsa ba'i rgyud, 2648
physical pain (*kāyika-duḥkha*), 2084
physical pleasure, 124–125
physiology, 205–213, 2530–2532
physiomoral discourse, 112 n.4
Picart, Bernard, 868–869, 871, 873, 875
Pierce, Lori, 1314
pilgrimage
art and, 1869
bodhisattvas and, 1866–1868
in China, 792–795, 876, 1860–1864, 1873–1875
in Chinese Buddhism, 1869–1871
in Confucianism, 1871
for Daoism, 1861–1864
history of, 1849–1850
holy people and, 1854–1855
to monasteries, 1869–1871
to *the né*, 1850–1851
philosophy of, 1851–1852
scholarship on, 792–795, 1855–1857, 1875–1876
in Tibet, 1844–1854
in Tibetan Buddhism, 1871–1873
The Pilgrimage of Buddhism and a Buddhist Pilgrimage (Pratt, J. B.), 1942
Pilindavaccha, 248–249
The Pillow Book (Sei no Shōnagon), 304
Pinault, Georges-Jean, 951–952
Pind, Ole Holten, 1838
Piṇḍola, 100
pious care, 75–77
"The pious gift of Devasiṅga," 941–942, 943*f*
Pittman, Don, 2294–2295
The Place of Provenance, 443
plague deities, 292–298
Plagues and Peoples (McNeill), 293
plantations, 1305
Platform Sutra
Chuanxin fayao and, 1218 n.83
in culture, 648–649, 1226, 1229–1230, 1232, 1236–1238
Diamond Sutra and, 1234–1235
from Library Cave, 807
to Mao Zedong, 1231
philosophy of, 1234–1236
pre-*Platform Sutra* texts, 1232
printing of, 324–325
in Tang dynasty, 1233–1236
The Platform Sutra of the Sixth Patriarch (Yampolsky), 675–676
Pledge Wheel, 1474
Pliny, 1516
Poceski, Mario, 183
Poe, Marshall, 2567
poetry, 355–356, 362, 645, 654, 661–664, 674–675, 1868, 2056
Pointing at the Essentials (Kündröl Drakpa), 132, 134
Pokorny, Charlie, 12
Pökyapa Senge Rinchen, 2594
Polhané, 2017

The Political Role of Mongolian Buddhism (Kaplonski), 1614–1615
politics
  of Amoghavajra, 1502–1503
  in Burma/Myanmar, 571–572, 907
  in Cambodia, 2237
  in China, 2731–2733
  of Cihang, 1260
  of communism, 1873–1874, 2729
  Confucianism and, 753–756
  of democracy, 1593–1594
  of D. T. Suzuki, 706–707
  geopolitics, 2160
  Japan and, 1383, 2212–2213
  labor, 1584
  neoliberalism, 2129–2131
  of Nichiren Shōshū, 2211–2212
  patriotism, 1304–1305
  political imaginary, 598–600
  politico-historical context, 959–960
  radical, 2294–2295
  reform in, 2279
  religion and, 1385, 2234–2236
  socio-politics, 2517–2518
  of Soka Gakkai, 2216–2217
  of Southeast Asia, 2072–2073
  of Theravāda Buddhism, 1889–1890, 2231–2232
  of Tibet, 1592–1593
  of Tzu Chi, 2625–2626
Politics and Transcendent Wisdom (Orzech), 62
Pollock, Sheldon, 150
Pol Pot, 1101
Pomdrakpa, 2011
pool of tradition, 2501 n.2
Poppe, N., 1656–1658
pop-psychology, 2145
popular Buddhism, 1191, 2197
popular religion, 565–566
Porcu, Elisabetta, 232–233
Portland, Oregon, 1134–1135, 1151
portraits, 431–432, 434, 434*f*
poṣadha ceremony, 2659
positivist taxonomies, 77–78
possible worlds, 112 n.4
postcolonial studies, 864
post-death experiences, 2544–2545
post-global Buddhism, 198–199
post-Heideggerian scholarship, 1447
post-modal metaphysics, 538–539
post-modernism, 195
postmodernity, 1122–1123
postmodern queer Buddhists, 1991–1993
Po to ba Rin chen gsal, 1400, 1402, 1406–1407
Potter, Karl, 628–629, 1837
pounces, 784, 785*f*
powder, 1426–1428
power objects
  abodes and, 2509, 2513
  efficacy of, 2513–2515
  key terms for, 2508–2513
  Kūkai on, 2525 n.51
  oath substance and, 2510–2511
  origins of, 2505–2508
  as receptacles, 2508–2509, 2513
  substance and, 2511–2513, 2633 n.38
  in Tibet, 2517–2518
  in Tibetan Buddhism, 2503–2505, 2518–2520
  translations and, 2525 n.58
  treasure concealers and, 2524 n.39
  treasure substance and, 2511–2513, 2515–2516, 2524 n.38
  typology of, 2515–2517
Powers, John, 125, 180, 1068–1069, 1137–1138, 1150, 1993, 2464
Pozdneev, Aleksei Matveevich, 1386, 1614
Prabhahasti, 2640–2642, 2655 n.23
Prabhūtaratna, 1770
Practically Religious (Tanabe and Reader), 778–779
Pradhan, Prahlad, 3–4
Prajña, 1517, 1519, 1522, 2328–2329
prajñā (wisdom), 2087. *See also* wisdom
Prajñādeva, 1788
Prajñākaramati, 626–627, 2077, 2088
Prajñāpāramitā
  in Bat Cum inscription, 1804 n.79
  caitya pillars and, 1897–1899, 1919–1923
  four classes and, 27
  goddesses and, 1914–1918
  hearing, 27
  history of, 1899–1901
  homage to, 18–19
  in India, 1923–1925
  influence of, 17, 2561
  Khmer Esoteric Buddhism and, 1897–1899, 1907–1923, 1925–1926
  Khmer Esoteric Buddhism epigraphy and, 1906–1907
  Prajñāpāramitā, 1184, 1809
  scholarship and, 17, 23–26, 1804 n.85, 1926–1927
  Tantric Buddhism and, 1803 n.58
  on votive tablets, 1918–1923
  Wisdom Sutras and, 1803 n.60
The Prajñāpāramitā Literature (Conze), 1814–1815, 1926
Prajñāpāramitā Sutra, 1906
Prajñaptivādins, 2112

Prajñavarma, 99–100
Prakaraṇa-pāda (PrP), 2094. *See also* Sarvāstivāda Abhidharma school
Prakrit, 495
Pramāṇasamuccaya (Dignāga), 1801 n.4, 1822, 1830, 1838
Pramāṇavārttika, 1801 n.6, 1835–1838, 2307–2308
Pramāṇaviniścaya (Dharmakīrti), 1801 n.6, 1822–1823, 1831–1832
Pranke, Patrick, 579–580, 588, 592–593, 604
prapañca. *See* hypostatization
Prāsaṅgika (consequentialism), 623–626
Prāsaṅgika-Madhyamaka, 1564–1565
Prasannaśīla, 100
Prasat Beng inscription, 1904
Prasat Chikreng inscription, 1901–1902, 1916
Prasat Phimai, 962, 969
Prasat Ta An inscription, 1901–1902
prasenā, 2542–2543
Prasenajit (king), 1292
Prathamaśiva (king), 1783–1784
prātimokṣa, 2657–2660, 2668
pratītyasamutpāda, 164–165
Pratt, James Bissett, 1942–1943
Pratt, Sunya, 39
pravāraṇa ceremony, 2672 n.57
prayer, 456
Prayer for Rebirth in Sukhāvatī (Tsongkhapa), 1966
Prayer of the Mahāmudrā of Definitive Meaning, 1483–1484
Prebish, Charles, 2237, 2718
Precept and Practice (Gombrich), 575
Preceptor Sizhou Puzhao's Verses on Old Standards, 666
Preceptor Tianmu Zhongfeng's Extended Record (Mingben), 673
Precious Garland (Nāgārjuna), 1455–1456
Precious Key to the Secret Treasury (Kūkai), 2354
Precious Lamp (Remdawa), 2748–2749
prediction narratives, 1725–1727
Preface to the Dhyāna Sūtra, 657
pre-global Buddhism, 194
pre-iconism, 1302 n.79
pre-Islam, 1469 n.18
"A Preliminary Study of Mongolian Buddhism in Present Day" (Havnevik), 1594
Premasiri, P. D., 163–164
premodern Japan
  exogenous disease agents in, 296–298
  healing rituals in, 298–304
  karmic illness in, 286–292
  materia medica in, 304–310
  medicine in, 284–286, 310–311
  treatment in, 289–292
pre-*Platform Sutra* texts, 1232
prestige, 593–595
pretend dialogues, 646, 672–673
Price, Richard, 1949–1950
Priest, Graham, 1466, 1699
Primiano, Leonard, 566–567
Primordial Buddha Tantra, 1423, 1425, 1428
Primordial Mind Dispelling Limitations, 133
Princes et Princesses (film), 1696
Princeton Dictionary of Buddhism (Lopez and Buswell), 1815
Principles for the Conservation of Heritage Sites in China, 795–796
Principles of Biomedical Ethics (Childress and Beauchamp), 165–166
Prinsep, Henry Thoby, 876–877
Prinsep, James, 948
printing. *See also* publishing
  blockprinting, 2562–2563
  comparison in, 326–328
  Daoism and, 319–320
  history of, 144 n.39, 319–320
  Huineng and, 1239–1240
  for lay Buddhists, 317 n.103
  of *Platform Sutra*, 324–325
  print culture, 144 n.37, 144 n.39, 319–328
  religious, 2169 n.24
  scholarship and, 1036–1039, 1041–1047, 1053–1054
  woodblock, 320–324
Prisoners of Shangri La (Lopez), 397–398, 2025
prisons, 1704–1706
privatization, 2362 n.26
problematization, of suffering, 977–978
proclivity (*śākti*), 7–8
professional chaplains, 459–470
professional conservation, 75–76
Profound Inner Meaning (Rangjung Dorjé), 2026
Profound Meaning of the Lotus Sūtra (Nichiren), 1768–1769
The Profound Teaching of the Peaceful and Wrathful Deities (Karma Lingpa), 2467, 2476
Progressive Stages of Meditation on Emptiness (Khenpo Tsultrim Gyamtso Rinpoche), 2748, 2750
Proof of Conventions (Nāgārjuna), 1455
propagation, 1772–1773
prophecies, 2543–2544
Prophecy of Gośṛṅga, 1503
The Prophecy of the Khotanese Arhat, 2581
Prophecy of the Li Region, 1503
A Proposal for Institutional Reform in the Sangha (Taixu), 2282–2283

prose biographies, 1396
proselytizing, 1046
prosperity Buddhism, 601–602, 894, 1104–1105
protection practices
  abhayamudrā as, 1286–1287
  criticism of, 1889–1890
  economy of, 1887–1888
  history of, 1888
  multifaceted protection, 1885–1886
  for Pali Buddhism, 1879–1885
  with Pehar, 1746–1750
  power dynamics in, 1886–1887
  protective texts, 1884–1885
  for *sāsana*, 1888–1889
  scholarship on, 769–770, 1890–1892
  for Theravāda Buddhism, 1879–1885
protective amulets (*omamoris*), 767, 769, 769*f*
protectors. *See* guardian/protector deities
Protestant Christianity
  in Europe, 2564
  liberal Protestant thought, 2127–2128
  Protestant Buddhism and, 2145
  Protestant religious culture, 2137–2138
  religion to, 186, 194, 499–500
  scholarship on, 1086–1087, 1890, 2710–2711
  Western scholarship and, 966–967
The Protestant Ethic and the Spirit of Capitalism (Weber), 888
Prothero, Stephen, 40, 1098
proto-homa, 1210
PrP. See *Prakaraṇa-pāda*
Pruden, Leo, 4
Psalm of the Great, 809–810
psychedelic drugs, 2479
Psychedelic Experience (Metzner and Alpert), 2479
psychoanalysis, 1714, 1943–1946, 1953–1955
psychological Buddhism
  history of, 1939–1941
  to humanistic psychotherapists, 1949–1950
  in modernity, 1955–1956
  in neuropsychology, 1950–1953
  psychoanalysis and, 1943–1946, 1953–1955
  religion in, 1942–1943
  scholarship on, 1956
  after World War II, 1946–1948
"Psychological Commentary" (Jung), 2479
psychology
  Buddhist, 358–359
  of colonialism, 113 n.21
  evolutionary, 2141–2142
  of karma, 861 n.11
  moral, 976–977
  of narratives, 177–179
  neuropsychology, 1950–1953
  pop-psychology, 2145
  in Shin Buddhism, 1703
  Western, 694
"Psychology in Primitive Buddhism" (Thompson), 1944
psychotherapy, 1117–1118, 1702–1705, 1710
Psychotherapy and Buddhism (Rubin), 1953–1954
Psychotherapy East and West (Watts), 1949–1950
Pu (master), 1867
publishing
  book collecting and, 144 n.37, 326–327
  book formats, 814–815
  Burmese vicissitudes and, 1048–1049
  curatorship in, 1051–1053
  extracanonical Buddhist literature, 324–326
  historiography and, 1036–1038
  manuscripts, 1036–1038, 1045–1047, 1053–1054
  printing, 1036–1039, 1041–1047, 1053–1054
  in South Asia, 1036–1038
  Thai scriptural nation-building and, 1049–1051
  translations and, 14 n.11
  in Vietnam, 1039–1041
  woodblock printing, 320–324
Pudgalavādins, 2112
Püdon, 2460
Puguang, 5–6, 10, 2097, 2098*t*
Puji, 1228
Puṇḍarīka, 1428, 1474
puṇya (karmic merit), 2088
Puṇyasambhava, 1964
Puṇyodaya, 1519, 1522, 1526
Puranic religious orientation, 2256
pure esotericism, 299
Pure Gold of the Glorious Black Goddess, 1165–1166
Pure Land Buddhism
  Amitābha in, 557–560, 558*f*
  Avalokiteśvara and, 356
  Chan Buddhism and, 2733–2734
  Christianity and, 719
  domestic Dharma in, 777
  D. T. Suzuki on, 704–706, 719–721, 725
  esoteric scriptures and, 1970–1971
  Esoteric Tendai Pure Land practices, 2183
  exoteric scriptures in, 1965–1968
  faith in, 231
  history of, 909
  Humanistic Buddhism and, 1259–1260, 2280
  iconography in, 1971–1974
  in Japan, 1761
  karma in, 327
  Mahāyāna Buddhism and, 2233
  Maitreya, 2284–2285

Pure Land Buddhism (*continued*)
  meditation in, 144 n.37
  Naikan and, 1715
  Nichiren and, 866
  Nichiren Buddhism and, 766–767
  philosophy of, 2279
  Pure Land Sutras, 1962–1965
  reconstruction of, 1312
  Rennyo for, 2036–2043
  rituals in, 2682–2688, 2690
  scholarship on, 1348–1350, 1354, 1357, 1974–1975
  Shin Buddhism and, 706, 719–720, 1702
  Shingon Buddhism and, 2180–2181
  Sukhāvatī in, 1977 n.11
  sutras for, 1962–1965, 2683–2684
  Taixu on, 2285–2287
  in Tibet, 1960–1968, 1971–1974
  Yogācārā Buddhism and, 2282
  Zen Buddhism and, 2341, 2441
"Pure Land Buddhism in Tibet?" (Kapstein), 1974
Pure Land Cave, 1013
The Pure Rules for the Chan Monastery (Changlu), 2662
pure vision, 2545
purity, 1027, 1206–1207, 1421*t*, 1428–1431, 2662
Purṇavardhana, 10
Pūrṇavarman (king), 1783–1784
Purser, Ronald, 2717–2718
Pusa dichi jing, 2662
Pusa shanjie jing, 2662
Pusa Shanzi Jing, 993–994, 1005
Putidamo Nanzong ding shifei lun (Dugu Pei), 1227–1228
Put Your Hands Together and Pray for the White Dove (Hanh), 2440
Pyi Phyo Kyaw, 1891
Pyu people, 2403–2407

Qasar Khan, 1648
qi, 204
Qianfeng Ruwan, 663
Qian Hongshu, 320–322
Qianlong (emperor), 85, 1504, 1862–1863
Qi dynasty, 1189
qigong, 1231
Qing dynasty
  Bogd Khaanate and, 1614
  in China, 2280
  collapse of, 1605
  culture of, 1379
  Dalai Lama and, 2017–2018
  Geluk tradition and, 1603, 1608
  history of, 2016
  monarchs in, 1862–1863
  in Mongolia, 1583, 1586, 1591–1592, 1629
  power of, 1599–1600
  reform in, 2281
  Russia and, 1600–1601
  Tang dynasty and, 92
  Tibet and, 1135
  Yuan dynasty and, 1639
Qing Guanyin jing, 89–90
qing gui, 2662
Qingyuan Xingsi, 1232
Qinshi Huangdi, 1641
Qin Shihuangdi (emperor), 1862–1863
Qiqian fo shenfu jing, 1185
Qisong, 993–994, 996, 1002–1003
Qiyun, 2280
Qongghor Ejei, 1655
Qoshila, 1638
QT. *See* Queer Theory
qualitative research, 454–455
Quán, Tâm. *See* Hanh
Quan Deyu, 53–54
Quang, Thích Huệ, 2436
Quang, Thích Huyen, 2240
Quang, Thích Trí, 2438
Quanmiao. *See* Wuguang
Qubilai Khan
  Chinggis Khan and, 1640
  incarnations of, 1646–1647
  leadership of, 1626–1627
  legacy of, 1645–1646
  Mongolian Buddhism with, 1628–1639
  'Phags pa and, 1646
  relatives of, 1626
  Tanguts to, 1623
  translations and, 1635
Queen, Christopher, 916
Queen Dohā Treasuries, 1475–1476
Queer Theory (QT)
  Buddhism and, 1981–1982
  in modernity, 1986–1989
  for postmodern queer Buddhists, 1991–1993
  scholarship on, 1993–1994
  sexuality in, 1983–1989
  Theravāda Buddhism and, 1986–1987
  Tibetan Buddhism and, 1988–1989
  Western Buddhism and, 1989
The Questions and Answers on Vajrasattva (Nyen Palyang), 832, 841
Questions of King Milinda, 246, 509–510
Questions of Subāhu Tantra, 2542

Question Your Life (Krech), 1715
Qufu, 1871
Quinter, David, 2695–2697
Quintman, Andrew, 846
Quli, Natalie, 239–240, 1104–1105, 1113–1114, 1119–1120, 1122
Qu Ruji, 2290–2291
Qutuγtu, 1605

RAC. *See* Religious Affairs Committee
race
  to Japanese Americans, 16 n.49
  racial justice, 912, 915–916
  racial projects, 2722 n.30
  refugees and, 1115–1116
  religion and, 48
  scientific racism, 2708
  in U.S., 2715–2716
  Western Buddhism and, 2707–2708
  White privilege, 2718–2719
Racism (Miles), 2708
Radhakanta Tarkavagisha, 873–875
Radhakrishnan, Sarvepalli, 708–709
radiating Lokeśvara, 1916–1918, 1918*f*, 1937 n.113
radical Buddhism, 2280–2281
Radical Dharma, 911, 1990
Radical Dharma (Williams, A. K., Owens, and Syedullah), 2719
radical politics, 2294–2295
Radich, Michael, 125
radio, 2564–2565
Radreng rinpoché, 1383–1384
Rāhula, 1167–1170, 1173
Rāhulabhadra, 1785
rai, 289–292. *See also* karma
Raiyu, 2186, 2356
Rājabhaṭa (king), 1794
Rājadvāra, 1526–1527
Rajapakse, Mahinda, 1099
Rājarāja, 1794
Rājendravarman (king), 1902–1903
rākṣasas, 258–259, 2247–2248, 2631 n.11
Ra Lotsawa, 850, 1470 n.37, 1549–1550, 1553
Ralpacan (king), 1066, 2414
Ralung monastery
  Drukpa Kagyü school and, 2600–2602, 2606
  leadership at, 858, 2592, 2595–2597, 2596*f*
  scholarship on, 846, 852, 852*f*, 854, 857–858, 2606–2607
Rama, 2252–2253
Rāmacaritam (Sandhyākaranandī), 1791
Rama I (king), 376, 385–386
Rama IV (king). *See* Mongkut
Rama IX (king), 2067–2068
Rāma Khamhaeng (king), 2406
Ramalocana Kanthavarna, 873–875
Ramapāla, 1791
Rama V (king), 465, 1579
Rama VI (king), 465
Rāmāyaṇa, 809, 814, 1167, 2245–2249, 2251, 2253–2254, 2258
Ramayana (Valmiki), 2247, 2254
Rambelli, Fabio, 67, 230, 240, 887, 895, 2358, 2518–2519
Ramses the Great, 1637
Ramstedt, Gustaf John, 1606, 1614
Rangjung Dorje
  in culture, 691–692, 1437–1438
  for Kagyü lineage, 1483–1485
  scholarship and, 2007–2008, 2012–2014, 2024–2026
Rangjung Rigpe Dorje, 2021
Rangtong Madhyamaka, 2745, 2748–2749
Rappo, Gaétan, 755–756
Raschmann, Simone, 821–823
Rasheta, Noah, 2139
Rashomon (film), 404
Rāṣṭrapālaparipṛcchā-sūtra, 1807
Ratanakul, Pinit, 113 n.24, 161, 164–171
Ratanasara, Havanpola, 1120
Ratana Sutta, 1885–1886
Ratnabuddhi, 1516, 1522
Ratnākaraśānti, 25–26, 29–30, 626–627, 1398–1399
Ratnaketu, 55–56
Ratnakīrti, 23–26, 1828
Ratna Lingpa, 1966
Ratnāvalī, 985–986, 1466–1467, 1688–1689
Ratön Tenzin Wangyel, 136–137
Raudrākṣa, 783–784
Rauschenberg, Robert, 723–724
Ray, Himanshu Prabha, 70, 1527
Ray, Reginald, 184
Reader, Ian, 778–779, 896–897
Readings of the Platform Sūtra (Schlütter and Teiser), 1238
Reagan, Ronald, 2129–2130
reality, philosophy of, 1691–1694
realized beings, 619
Realizing Principles through Propriety (Shih), 2628–2629
realms of desire (*kāma-dhātu*), 6–7, 2149 n.59
Reason's Traces (Kapstein), 4
rebellion, in Burma/Myanmar, 225 n.90, 225 n.97

rebirth. *See also* reincarnation system
agnosticism and, 2135
death and, 2080
Dharmakīrti on, 1801 n.19
doctrine of, 861 n.8
emanations and, 2010–2011
ethics of, 2135
karma and, 2135–2136
Karmapas and, 2011–2012
in Mongolia, 2013–2014
motivation from, 1695–1696
the nine grades of, 2687–2688
philosophy of, 2009
process of, 114
suffering and, 115–116, 1719–1720
in Vajrayāna Buddhism, 2019
receptacles, 2508–2509, 2513
Recherches sur l'Épopée et le Barde au Tibet (Stein, R. A.), 2499–2500
Rechungpa Dorje Drak, 1539, 1553, 1972–1973, 2011–2012
recidivism, 1704–1705
recitation, 2677–2678, 2705 n.103
Recognizing Reality (Dreyfus), 1837
Record of Miraculous Events in Japan, 287–288
Record of Nourishing Life by Drinking Tea (Yōsai), 296, 309–312
A Record of the Buddhist Kingdoms (Faxian), 1865
Record of the Doctrinal Points of the Yogācārabhūmi-Śāstra, 807
A Record of the Inner Law Sent Home from the South Seas (Yijing), 208
The Record on Drinking Tea for Nourishing Life, 274
Records of Miraculous Events in Japan, 287–288
Records of Pointing at the Moon (Qu Ruji), 2290–2291
Records of the Grand Historian, 813
Red Hot Chili Peppers, 226
The Red Thread (Faure), 1982, 1993
Reed, Catriona, 1990
Reed, Marcia, 825
reference works, 821–824
Refined Gold of the Great Perfection, 134
reflection, 457–458
Reflections on Reality (Hopkins), 2464–2465
reflexive awareness (*svasaṃvitti*), 1823, 1831–1832
The Reflexive Nature of Awareness (Williams, Paul), 1567, 2750–2751
reflexivity, 1991
reform
in Bangladesh, 1889–1890
at Bodhi College, 2140
in China, 1079–1080, 2284, 2294–2295
immigration, 410–412
in Japan, 1136–1137
Long Reformation, 566
in Mahāyāna Buddhism, 979–980
in Mongolian Buddhism, 1593–1594, 1606–1611
Montagu-Chelmsford Reforms, 1099
in Nyingma tradition, 1602–1603
in Pali Buddhism, 2140
by Parākramabāhu I, 2403–2404
in politics, 2279
in Qing dynasty, 2281
in Sangha, 2282–2283
sanghas and, 1096
schools, 2335
social, 919–920
socialism and, 906
Speranski Reforms, 1609
in Sri Lanka, 2402–2403
Taika reforms, 2199–2200
from Taixu, 1076–1077, 1579
in Theravāda Buddhism, 2399–2402
transparency and, 1583–1584
by Tzu Chi, 2616–2617
refugees. See also *specific topics*
in Canada, 2235–2236
immigration and, 1112
race and, 1115–1116
Refuge Act, 2235
scholarship on, 1101
to Tzu Chi, 2619–2620
UN and, 2619–2620
UN High Commission for Refugees, 2235–2236
in U.S., 1115–1116, 2234–2236
Refuge Recovery (Levine), 464
regionalism
borderland complex, 498–499
geography and, 493–494, 496–498, 503
modernity and, 499–503
national Buddhisms, 500–501
Western colonialism and, 501–503
Regional Styles in Tibetan Painting (Jackson, D.), 443
Regulating Act, 873
Regulations for Monks and Nuns, 2202–2203
reincarnation system
bodies in, 114–116
in Central Asia, 2007–2008
colonialism and, 2022–2023
evolution of, 2012–2013
in India, 2008–2010
lineages in, 2593–2594

in modernity, 2023–2024
scholarship on, 2024–2025
in Tibet, 2010, 2018–2020
Reinders, Eric, 887, 895
Reinke, Jens, 1017
Reiyūkai Buddhism, 1355–1356
Reizei (emperor), 2047
relativism, 1824–1825
relics. *See also* Buddhist relics
antiquities and, 2267–2268
in Asia, 1720
in Christianity, 67
ethics and, 1720–1721
of Indravarma, 939, 940*f*
relic shrines, 1725
of Śākyamuni, 939–940, 962
scholarship on, 57–58, 1737
in South Asia, 1736–1737
from Southeast Asia, 963
in Thailand, 1525–1526
in Tibet, 2583
Xuanzang on, 1733
religion. See also *specific religions*
AAR, 1982
acculturation of, 1357–1358
active, 2137
in anthropology, 112 n.12
in Asia, 1622
authority in, 2223–2224
bioethics and, 161
of Bonpo people, 2497–2498
Buddhism and, 2128–2129
in Burma/Myanmar, 890–891
Burnouf on, 864–865
celibacy in, 1588–1589
in China, 1261–1262, 1861, 2369–2382
Chinese, 408–410, 417–418
to Christianity, 194
culture religiosity, 191
democracy and, 1593
in diaspora, 1347–1348
ethics and, 888
ethnicity and, 71–72
to *European Buddhist Union*, 1986–1987
globalization and, 193
in Han dynasty, 1861
hegemony of, 112 n.16
Hellenistic religions, 193
heterosexuality and, 1992
history of, 371
identity and, 729
in India, 1032–1033, 1601–1602
in Japan, 765, 1305, 2196–2199
to Kagyü lineage, 1472, 1481–1482
legitimacy in, 919–920
liberal Protestant thought, 2127–2128
Library Cave and, 812
lived, 564–574, 578–579
with monotheism, 1594
at Nara schools, 2196–2199
new religious movements, 1355–1356, 1708, 1988
of Nikkei Buddhists, 35
Orientalism and, 2710
philosophy and, 703
politics and, 1385, 2234–2236
popular, 565–566
to Protestant Christianity, 186, 194, 499–500
Protestant religious culture, 2137–2138
in psychological Buddhism, 1942–1943
Puranic religious orientation, 2256
race and, 48
secularism and, 1571–1572
semiotics of, 2131–2132
spirituality and, 2128
state religions, 2202
in Taiwan, 909, 2163
Tantric Buddhism as, 1140–1146
in Thailand, 2236–2237
theism, 2140–2141
theory of, 721–722, 1946–1948
Theravāda Buddhism as, 863 n.35
in Tibet, 1376
tourism and, 1014
Tzu Chi as, 2627
UN Millennium World Peace Summit of Religious and Spirituals Leaders, 2165
in U.S., 45–46, 2715–2716
in Vietnam, 2234
violence and, 2136
Western, 2137
World Parliament of Religions, 1941, 1943
in World War II, 462
"Yellow Religion," 1601–1604
in Yoshizaki, 2040
Religion and Ethnicity in Canada (Seljak), 417
Religion and Globalization (Beyer, P.), 1087
"Religion and Media" (Mahan), 240
Religion and Politics in Contemporary Japan (Fisker-Nielsen), 2227
Religion and Popular Culture in America (Forbes and Mahan), 240
Religion of Tibet (Bell, Charles), 1406–1407

The Religions of Tibet (Tucci), 694–695
religious activity, 765–766
Religious Affairs Committee (RAC), 1009
religious art, 66
religious authority, 1385
Religious Corporations Act (Japan), 2212
religious culture, 1875, 2126
religious history, 1536–1538
religious imagery, 113 n.19
religious merit, 890
religious practice, 720–721, 1672–1674
religious printing, 2169 n.24
religious texts, 823–824
religious traditions, 2313–2314
The Religious Traditions of Japan (Bowring), 2056, 2336
religious wars, 867–868
Relpachen, 2576–2577
The Remaining Signs of the Past Ages (al-Bīrūnī), 1679
Remdawa Zhonnu Lodrö, 2748–2749
remonstration, 1762–1764
renjian Buddhism, 2287–2288
renjian fojiao (Yinshun), 1247–1248, 1258, 1439–1441, 1446–1447, 2621–2622, 2626–2627. *See also* Humanistic Buddhism
renjian jingtu, 1259–1260
Renki, 311–312
Rennyo, 1307, 2036–2043
Rennyo (Rogers, A. T., and Rogers M. L.), 2042–2043
Rennyo and the Roots of Modern Japanese Buddhism (Shin'ya and Blum), 2042–2043
Rennyo Shōnin itokuki, 2036
Renondeau, Gaston, 1774
Renou, Louis, 1032–1033
Renshan, 2280
rensheng Buddhism, 2287–2288
rensheng fojiao (Taixu), 1439–1441. *See also* Humanistic Buddhism
Renwang Bore Boluomi Jing, 1003
reordination, 2158
repeated mindfulness, 516–518
repentance, 2679–2681, 2692, 2701 n.33
representationalist epistemology, 1831
Research on Buddou (Ozeray), 870, 880
resettlement, 1112–1113
resistance, 2126–2127
Resources for Hearers, 98
Resources for Solitary Realizers, 98
responding, 454–456
restoration activity, 2727–2728
resultant intention, 1330–1331
Reting Rinpoche, 1383–1384, 2543
retribution, 2117
The Return Home (Shengyen), 2165–2166
Revisiting Nichiren, 1774
The Revival of Chinese Buddhism (Welch), 1579
revolution, 1582–1584, 1606–1611, 1885. See also *specific revolutions*
Reynolds, David, 1709, 1715
Reynolds, Frank, 181, 578–579
Reyonds, John Myrdhin, 841
Rey-sheng, Her, 2627
Ṛgveda, 247, 481, 2635–2636
Ṛg Veda, 480
rGyal tshab rje dar ma rin chen, 25–26, 2077
Rhi, Juhyung, 1294
Rhys Davids, Caroline
  gender to, 184–185
  Metteyya and, 2413–2414
  Pratt, J. B., and, 1943
  reputation of, 371
  scholarship from, 1076, 1080–1081, 1939–1941, 2256, 2709, 2711
  on thinking, 1297 n.9
  translations by, 1941
Rhys Davids, T. W. *See also* Western Buddhism
  contributions from, 2709–2711
  Metteyya and, 2413–2414
  Oldenberg and, 1939, 2554–2555
  Pali Text Society and, 1939
  reputation of, 371, 1117
  scholarship from, 119, 125, 1371, 1939–1940, 2256, 2667–2668
  in Sri Lanka, 1032–1033
  translations by, 1105, 1941
Ricca, Franco, 443–444, 1755
Ricci, Matteo, 870, 1080–1081
Rich, Thomas Frederick, 2022–2023
Richardson, Hugh Edward, 1068–1069
Richthofen, Ferdinand von, 1468 n.3
Rietberg tablet, 1923
Rifkin, Jeremy, 2553–2554
Rigdzin Draktsel Dorje, 2495
Rigdzin Nyima Dragpa, 2467–2470. See also *Tibetan Book of the Dead*
Right Action, 452–454
right speech, 508
Rig pa rang shar chen po'i rgyud, 1727
Rigveda, 2247
Rigzin Gödem, 1970–1971
Rikzin Tsewang Norbu, 2747
Rimé movement, 1142–1143, 2747
Rin chen bzang po, 1398–1399, 1403–1404, 2313

Rinpoché Thubten Jampel Yeshé Gyaltshan, 1067
Rinzai Zen Buddhism, 1350, 1352, 2187
Ripley, Philip H., 1048–1049
Risen, 2045–2046
Risshō ankokuron, 2218
Rissho Kosei-kai, 468, 909–910
Risshō Kōseikai Buddhism, 1355–1356
rites, 1423, 1423*t*, 1430–1431, 2643–2648
Ritsu. *See* Nara schools
ritsuryō codes, 2208
Ritter, Franz, 1708
ritual efficacy, 1206, 1210–1211
ritualized activities, 770–773
Ritualized Writing (Lowe), 2209
rituals
  architecture and, 2526 n.69, 2526 n.71
  in Bön tradition, 112 n.6
  with Buddha,
  chanting and, 776
  of Chöd, 691–694
  in Daoism, 2164
  domestic Dharma and, 766–767
  esoteric, 318 n.113
  fire, 1198–1199
  for guardian/protector deities, 1160–1161
  healing, 209–210, 298–304
  in homa, 1198–1199
  in India, 2522 n.11
  in Jainism, 1201–1202, 2313–2314
  in Japan, 275–277, 770–773, 2182
  kālacakra-maṇḍala in, 1422–1431
  kīlas in, 2647
  Kohomba Kankariya rite, 2260 n.46
  materiality and, 230–231
  meditation manuals, 2650–2651
  nirvāṇa and, 2637
  paraphernalia, 2516
  prayer and, 456
  protector, 1160–1161
  in Pure Land Buddhism, 2682–2688, 2690
  ritual poses, 2266–2267
  Rokuji raisan, 2039
  Sekitan, 748–749, 751–752, 759
  sexual, 964–965
  in Shingon Buddhism, 2180–2181
  smoke purification in, 2494
  soils in, 1423*t*
  of supreme worship, 2080
  Swearer on, 970
  syntax, 1206–1208
  of tantra, 1195 n.1
  in Tantric Buddhism, 1904
  in *Tibetan Book of the Dead*, 2544–2545
  in Tibetan Buddhism, 1755–1756, 2495–2497, 2504
  with Vajrakīla tantras, 2643–2647
  vajra masters in, 1422–1431
  Zen Buddhism, 361
Ritzinger, Justin, 2294–2295
Rnam thar rgyas pa (biography), 1399
Rngog Blo ldan shes rab, 1394
Rngog Legs pa'i shes rab, 1397, 1401
Rngog lo-tsā-ba blo-ldan shes-rab, 24–25
"Roads Taken and Not Taken in the Study of Theravāda Buddhism" (Hallisey), 577
Robb, Christina, 1954–1955
Rōben, 293–294
Roberts, Michael, 1098
Roberts, Peter, 1490, 1553, 2028 n.19
Robertson, Roland, 192–193, 200, 1087
Robinson, Richard, 1465, 1698
Robson, James, 354–355, 2208–2209
Rocha, Cristina, 194, 234, 1357–1358
Rocher, Ludo, 2566–2567
Rodd, Laurel Rasplica, 1774
Rodrigues, João, 870, 875
Roerich, George N., 694–695, 1406–1407, 1489–1490, 1553, 1657–1658, 2498–2499
Rogers, Ann T., 2042–2043
Rogers, Carl, 451, 1949, 1953
Rogers, Joseph, 464
Rogers, Minor L., 2042–2043
Rok Bendhe Sherap Ö, 631 n.13
Rōko shiiki (Kūkai), 2328
Rokuji raisan, 2039
Rokujō (lady), 308–309
The Role of Religion in Ethnic Self-Identity (Rutledge), 2242–2243
Rolland, Romain, 1943–1944
Rölpe Dorje, 1637, 1643, 2013–2014
Roman Empire, 1669
Romanticism, 721–722
Rome, 866–867
Rongdao Lai, 381
Rongi no kenkyū (Chisan), 758
Rong ston shes bya kun rig, 25
Rong Xinjiang, 798, 800, 819, 823–825
Rongyong, 2374–2376
Rongzom Chokyi Zangpo, 834–835
Rongzom Paṇḍita, 1437
Roosevelt, Franklin D., 1079, 2716
Root Tantra, 2528

Root Verses of the Middle Way (Nāgārjuna). *See also* Madhyamaka Buddhism
Buddhapālita on, 1459–1460
Candrakīrti on, 1460
Delhey on, 1469 n.13
methodology of, 1466–1467
scholarship and, 1454–1459
translations of, 1466
Rosary Views on the Instructions, 831
Rosen, Friedrich August, 878
Rosenberg, Charles E., 286
Rōshi, Maezumi, 1352–1353
Roshi, Robert Aitkin, 910
Rōshi, Shunryu Suzuki, 1352–1353
Rōshi, Soyu Matsuoka, 1352–1353
Rosner, Erhard, 279
Rospatt, Alexander von, 11
Rossabi, Morris, 1386
Rotạsiddhavr̥ddhi, 944
Rothberg, Donald, 910
Rotraut Jampa Wurst, 2002 n.113
Rottạjayavr̥ddhi, 944
Roudometof, Victor, 200
Rowe, Mark, 778–779
The Royal Chanting Book, 1883–1884
Royal Genealogy, 813
royal patronage, 1781–1782
Rozenberg, Guillaume, 579–580, 602–603
Rubin, Jeffrey, 1953–1955
rubrics, for Tibetan Buddhism, 2511–2513
Ruch, Barbara, 2209
Rudra, 1163–1164, 1173–1174
Ruegg, D. S., 23–24, 28, 1465, 2750
Ruell, Joannes, 1045–1046
Rufa, 1259
Rules and Regulations for Monks and Nuns, 2200
Rupen, Robert, 1608
Ruppert, Brian, 2209
Russell, Bertrand, 1465
Russell-Smith, Lilla, 800–801
Russia
China and, 1383, 1605–1607
England and, 1604
Europe and, 1600, 2534
in geopolitics, 1599–1601
Mongolia and, 383–384, 1469 n.18
Qing dynasty and, 1600–1601
scholarship from, 29–30
Siberia and, 1603
as Soviet Union, 1384, 1583–1584, 1610–1614, 2213
Tibet and, 1382
Tibeto-Mongol-Buryat medicine in, 2529–2530
U.S., and, 1079
Rutledge, Paul, 2242–2243
Ruyou, 661
Rwa Lotsāwa, 1159–1160
Ryan, Tim, 921
Ryōben, 2201, 2207–2208
Ryobu Shinto, 339–340, 344
Ryōgen
in debates, 754, 2046–2049
early years of, 2045–2046
leadership of, 2184
legacy of, 300–301, 2055–2056, 2357
power of, 2046–2050
promotions of, 2049–2050
Saichō and, 2350, 2358–2359
scholarship on, 2045, 2053–2054, 2056, 2058 nn.1–2, 2059 n.12
Taimitsu and, 2350
Tendai school and, 2045–2046, 2051–2052
unity to, 2348
Ryōgen and Mount Hei (Groner), 2056
Ryōshun Kajihama, 1974
Ryūkoku University, 1310
Ryūsaku, Tsunoda, 1309
Ryusei Keira, 1467

Sabbadisabuddhamaṅgala Paritta, 1884–1885
Sab Bāk inscription, 1906–1907
Sabrahma Sutta, 994–995
Sachen Künga Nyingpo, 2011
sacred architecture, 2636–2637
sacred landscapes, 69–72
sacred objects, 14 n.9, 67–68, 76
sacred places, 1846–1848, 1854, 1866–1868. See also *specific places*
"Sacred Secularities" (Reinke), 1017
sacred texts, 1884–1885, 1890–1892
Saddharmapuṇḍarīka, 1814
Saddharmapuṇḍarīka-sūtra. See *Lotus Sutra*
Saddharmapuṇḍarīka Sūtra, 482–483
Saddharmasmr̥tyupasthāna sūtra, 1811–1812
Saddhasena, D., 1815
sādhana. *See* meditation
Sādhanamāla, 1801 n.23, 1804 n.93, 1900–1901, 1912
Saeki, Kyokuga, 3–4
Saffron Revolution, 1885
Saga (emperor), 302, 306–307, 2178, 2327, 2329
Saghang Sechen, 1657–1658
sahabhū causality, 2115–2118
sahopalambhaniyama argument, 1831–1832

Sahura/Sahvara (king), 1787–1788
Sahvara (king), 1787–1788
Sai, 292–293
Saichō. *See also* Tendai School
  China and, 2343–2345
  death of, 2345–2346
  disciples of, 2338 n.4, 2345–2350
  esoteric scripture to, 2354
  Kūkai and, 2182–2183, 2324–2336, 2340–2343, 2346–2347, 2354–2355
  leadership of, 2182–2184
  legacy of, 2352–2353
  philosophy of, 2333
  Ryōgen and, 2350, 2358–2359
  scholarship on, 749, 1762–1763, 2045, 2050, 2068
  Tendai School and, 2361 n.6
Saichō (Groner), 2056
Said, Edward, 1679, 2707–2708
Sa'id, Abu, 1642
Saigyō, 2185
Saikainō Kōyō, 1236
saint-making, 2729–2731
Saisen, 2184
Saito, Akira, 12, 2076–2077
Saitō, Shōji, 2226
Saitō Tokiyori, 2185
"The Śaiva Age" (Sanderson), 2318
Śaiva tradition, 964–965, 1201, 1217 n.63, 2282–2283, 2304–2305
Śaivite complex, 1162–1164
Sakade, Yoshinobu, 176 n.67
Sakai Shizu, 278
Sakka, 2251–2252
Sakō Nobuyuki, 303–304
Śakrāditya (king), 1783–1784
Śākta tradition, 2283–2284
Sakurabe, Hajime, 4–5
Sakyadhita International, 913, 1083–1084, 1102–1103, 1120–1121
Śākyakīrti, 1524
Śākyamuni
  Aśoka and, 933–934
  Batchelor and, 2136
  in China, 483
  cosmology and, 112 n.4
  on enlightenment, 974–975
  inspiration for, 120, 1498
  monks and, 256–257
  Nichiren and, 2624–2625
  in Pali Buddhism, 2134–2135
  as physician, 245–247, 284–285, 305–306
  relics of, 939–940, 962
  scholarship on, 494–495, 1765–1766, 1770, 1801 n.6, 1923, 1923*f*
  teachings of, 2129, 2131–2132, 2140, 2180–2181, 2305, 2505–2506
Sakya Paṇḍita Künga Gyeltsen
  criticism from, 1490
  leadership of, 1625–1626
  reputation of, 1629, 1635, 1643
  scholarship and, 835, 1482–1483, 1486–1487, 1970
Sakya school, 2513
Sakya tradition, 1566, 2313
Śakya Yarpel, 1751–1753, 1753*f*
Śākya Zangpo, 1440–1441
Sakyong Mipham, 1144, 1988, 1999 n.75
Salgado, Nirmala, 1103–1104, 1120–1121
Salguero, C. Pierce, 176 n.67, 213–215, 279, 310–311
Salomon, Richard, 639, 941*f*, 949–951, 2567
Salzberg, Sharon, 1117–1118, 2142
samādhi, 9, 2690–2693. See also *specific topics*
Samādhi of Direct Encounter, 2542
Samādhi Sea Sutra, 2675–2678, 2681–2683
Sāma Jātaka, 998
Saman. See *satara varan devi*
Samantabhadra, 1522, 2676, 2680–2681, 2690–2693
"Samantabhadra and Rudra" (Kapstein), 1174
Samantabhadra Contemplation Sutra, 2676, 2678, 2680–2681, 2690–2693, 2701 n.39
Samantapāsādikā, 152, 257, 2660
Saman-Yama-Lakshmana, 2252–2253
Samataṭa area, of Eastern India, 1794–1795
samatha (calm), 509–514, 518–520
samayas, 2510, 2632 n.33
Sambor Prei Kuk inscription, 1901
Sambuddhe-gāthā, 1885
Saṃdhinirmocana Sutra, 1021–1022, 1499, 2744
Samding Dorjé Pakmo, 2021
Samding Dorjé Pakmo lineage, 2019
Samdong Rinpoche, 1491
same-sex marriage, 912, 1086, 1987
Saṃghabhadra
  on *apratisaṃkhyā-nirodha*, 2105
  epistemology from, 2110–2111
  on permanence, 2114–2115
  scholarship from, 3, 2100, 2108
  on Vaibhāṣika theory, 2111–2112
Saṃghātasūtra Dharmaparyāya, 247
saṃjñā (cognition), 6, 1831–1832, 1834
Sammohavinodanī, 152
Samouth, Tou, 190 n.71
saṃsāra. See *specific topics*

Samten Gyaltsen Karmay, 2025
samudayo (arising), 1025–1026
Samuel, Geoffrey, 2500
Samuels, Jonathan, 744–745
Saṁvarodaya tantra, 1206, 1210
Samyé, 1742
Samyé debate, 730
Sàmye Monastery, 421, 424, 429, 441
Saṃyuktāgama sutras, 633–636
Saṃyutta Nikāya, 246–247, 253–254, 1324–1325
San, Aung, 907
Sanbōkyōdan, 2161
Sāñcī, 2264
Sandai hihō honjōji (Nichiren), 1770–1771, 1775
Sandalwood Image, 72–73
Sanderson, Alexis, 1201–1202, 2307, 2318
Sandhyākaranandī, 1791
San Francisco Chronicle, 1351–1352
San Francisco Zen Center, 1352–1353
Sanggyebum, 2593–2594
Sanggye Gyatso, 1066, 1744–1745
Sanggye Lingpa, 2585
Sanggye Tenpa, 2502 n.9
Sangha Act (1902), 1100
Sangha Act (2017), 2417–2418
Sangha Education Association, 2280
Saṅghapāla, 1518–1519, 1526
Sangharakshita, 907–908, 912
sanghas
  constituting, 2066–2070
  as institution, 2061–2066
  managing, 2070–2071
  recommendations in, 2203
  scholarship on, 1095–1097, 1099–1104, 2071–2073
Saṅghavarman, 1516, 1518–1519
Saṅgīti Sutta, 2556–2557
Sangke, 1631
Sang-ngak Lingpa, 134–135
Sango, Asuka, 2209
Sangpo, 1301 n.58
Saṅgrāmadhanañjaya (king), 1524
Sangsō shiki (Kūkai), 2177–2178
Sangs rgyas Rgya mthso, 1657–1658
Sangye Gyatso, Desi, 1744–1745, 1750, 2016–2017, 2529, 2534
Sangye Lingpa, 137, 838
saṅkappa/saṅkalpa. *See* intention
saṅkhāra, 1324–1326
Sankrityayan, Rahul, 383–384
Sanlun School, 1461–1462, 1470 n.33
Sanmon-Jimon schism, 2053–2054, 2358–2359
"The Sanmon-Jimon Schism in the Tendai School of Buddhism" (McMullin), 2358–2359
Sanron. *See* Nara schools
Sanskrit
  Buddhaghosa in, 151–153
  Buddhist texts in, 1028, 2660
  Chinese and, 1963, 1978 n.31
  Clear Words in, 627–628
  cosmopolises, 967–969
  dathu in, 14 n.8
  for hands, 2267
  Hindu, 875
  in Japan, 29–30
  knowledge of, 17
  literature, 245
  Madhyamaka Buddhism in, 1468 n.1
  mantras in, 2173
  manuscripts, 98–99
  in modernity, 3–4
  in Mongolia, 1378
  to Nāgārjuna, 1468 n.2
  Nikāyas and, 2426 n.13
  Pali Buddhism and, 637–639, 1364–1365, 2541, 2714–2715
  perfections in, 1805–1806
  philosophy and, 973–974
  by Prajña, 2328–2329
  Sanskrit-language materials, 810
  sources, 250, 252–255
  Tibetan and, 1964, 2122 n.14, 2266
  translations of, 1701 n.1, 1801 n.10, 1836–1837, 2474
  utterances in, 693
  Vasubandhu and, 15 n.34
  vinayas and, 151–152
  Yaśomitra and, 3–5, 9–10
Sanskritic Buddhisms, 1521–1527
Sanskrit Texts from the Tibetan Autonomous Region (Franco), 1837–1838
Sanskrityayan, Rahul, 4
Santacitta, Ayya, 1117
Śāntarakṣita
  Candrakīrti and, 1463
  Kamalaśīla and, 1467
  leadership of, 2578
  philosophy of, 538
  scholarship and, 730–731, 1436–1437, 1461, 1828, 1836
Santi Ashok, 895
Śāntibhadra, 1537–1538, 1544
Śāntideva
  on awakening, 2076
  on BCA, 2079–2080

on effort, 2085
ethics of, 863 n.32
on generosity, 2081–2082
influence of, 2077–2079
on meditation, 2085–2087
on mindfulness, 2082–2083
in modernity, 2077–2079
on patience, 2083–2085
on perfections, 2080–2081
scholarship on, 982, 1810–1811, 2076–2077, 2088–2089
on wisdom, 2087
Sapan. *See* Sakya Paṇḍita Künga Gyeltsen
Sa Pang. *See* Sakya Paṇḍita Künga Gyeltsen
Sā Phussadeva, Saṅgharāja, 1883–1884
Saptaśatikā-prajñāparāmitā sūtra, 1499
Saraha, 1475–1476, 1482, 1489–1490, 1542, 1551–1552, 1566
Sarama, 2247
Saranankara, Välivitiyē, 1097, 2416
Sarat Chandra Das, 1406–1407
Sargeant, Winthrop, 710, 725
Śāriputra, 783–784
Sāriputta, 249
Sarma tradition, 1566
Sārnāth, 1293
Sartaq, 1628
Sarvabuddhasamāyoga, 835
Sarvadurgatipariśodhana tantra, 1212
Sarvāstivāda Abhidharma school
Abhidharma-mahāvibhāṣā and, 2121 n.1
central doctrine of, 2110–2115
dharmas in, 2101–2106
doctrinal perspectives of, 2106–2107
doctrine of causality and, 2115–2118
fundamental treatises of, 2093–2098
history of, 2098–2100
methodology of, 2106
MVŚ and, 2093–2094, 2106, 2112–2113, 2121 n.1
philosophy of, 2100–2101
sūtras in, 2107–2110
Sarvāstivāda Vaibhāsika school, 1328–1329, 2110–2115
Sārvāstivādins. *See* Theravāda Buddhism
Sarvatathāgatatattvasaṃgraha Tantra, 484, 1906, 2636
Sasaki, Ruth Fuller, 675–676, 724, 1237–1238
Sasaki Gesshō, 704–705, 719
sāsana, 1888–1889
Sāsanavaṃsa, 1722, 1728–1729
Sa skya Paṇḍita Kun dga' rgyal mtshan, 1041, 1503–1504
Sa skya school, 2655 n.19
Saso, Michael, 1212
Śāstrī, Dwārikādās, 2088
Śatapañcāśatka (Mātṛceta), 1279–1281
satara varan devi, 2245–2257
Satipaṭṭhāna-sutta, 520–521
Satō Hiroo, 345–346
Satō Kōji, 1705
Satomi Hōji, 1360 n.13
Satomi Hōni, 1303–1304
satori. *See* enlightenment
Sattva (prince), 114–115
Satya Narayan Goenka, 1081–1082
Saussure, Ferdinand de, 237
sautrāntikas, 1800 n.1, 1819–1820, 2112. See also *specific sautrāntikas*
Śavaripa, 1476–1477
savior cults, 1514–1515
Sayadaw, Ledi, 372, 1048–1049, 2716–2717
Saya San, 225 n.90, 225 n.98
"Sayings of a Modern Tariki Mystic" (D. T. Suzuki), 722
Sazang Mati Paṇchen, 2745–2746
Schade, Gabriel, 1045–1046
Schaeffer, Kurtis R., 1068–1069, 1656–1657
Schaik, Sam van, 820–824, 840, 2481
Scharf, Robert, 396
Schayer, Stanislaw, 1465
Scherer, Bee, 1993–1994
Scherer, Burkhard, 1132–1133
Schlegel, August Wilhelm von, 878
Schlegel, Friedrich, 1080–1081
Schlingloff, Dieter, 1527–1528
Schlütter, Morten, 675–676, 1238
Schmalkaldic League, 867
Schmidt, Isaac Jacob, 878–879, 2499
Schmithausen, Lambert, 102–103
Schneider, Ralf, 184
Schnittich, Bernard, 1595
Schober, Juliane, 177–178, 579–580, 1579, 1722–1723, 2567
Schoening, Jeffrey D., 24
scholar monks, 750–753, 756–757, 1762, 2186–2187
scholars, 1116–1117
The Scholar's Feast, 1965
scholastic debates, 738–740
School of Youth for Social Service (SYSS), 2439–2440
Schopen, Gregory
archaeology from, 889–890
on cults, 2506
epigraphy and, 949–950
interpretations from, 186, 951
Lüders and, 949
scholarship and, 84, 993–994, 1784–1785, 1790–1791, 2270, 2668, 2714
on *vinayas*, 1578–1579
on *vinaya* texts, 2072

Schopenhauer, Arthur, 1077, 1080–1081
Schøyen, Martin, 633, 639
Schuh, Johanna, 1708–1709
Schuman, Michael D., 1407
Schwartz, Jacqueline, 1117–1118
Schwieger, Peter, 1068–1069, 1974, 2016–2017, 2024, 2028 n.19
science
  authority of, 2141–2142
  of bodies, 205–207
  Christianity and, 485
  contemplative, 984–985
  Kabat-Zinn and, 2131–2132
  knowledge and, 499–500
  to secular Buddhism, 2141–2142
  social, 2144
  Theory of Relativity, 1609
  Tzu Chi University of Science and Technology, 2618
  Western, 485–486
Science of Medicine in Surgery in Buddhist Tantra (Talim), 260–261
scientific conservation, 75–77
scientific texts, 814
Scott, Gregory, 2567
Scott, Rachel, 889
scripts, 933
Scripture of Dizang's Original Vow (Dizang), 89–90
Scripture of Past Vows, 89–90
The Scripture on Explanation of the Underlying Meaning (Keenan), 2464
The Scripture on the Ten Kings, 90–91, 324–325
Scripture on the Ten Wheels (Dizang), 89
sculptural ensembles, 781, 783*f*
sculptures, 112 n.5, 112 n.13, 112 n.15, 433–437
seafaring monks, 1518–1521
Seager, Richard Hughes, 229, 1357
sealed retreat, 2282–2283
seasonal diets, 250–251
Seated Buddha statue, 1285*f*
Se btsun Dbang phyug gzhon nu, 1399–1400
Sečen Khan Ardasida, 1381–1382
Second Life (video game), 2565–2566
Secret Assembly, 1478–1479
The Secret Assembly, 1474
The Secret Doctrine (Blavatsky), 2478–2479
The Secret History of the Mongols, 1623
Secret Key to the Heart Sutra (Kūkai), 2353–2354
Secret Matrix, 1478–1479
Secret Potency, 2505, 2507–2508, 2518
secret teachings (*Mijiao*), 2174
secret yoga, 54–55
secular Buddhism
  authority in, 2139–2142
  in China, 2280–2281
  cosmology and, 2149 n.59
  discourse of, 2132–2137
  education in, 2138–2139, 2150 n.80
  experiential authority in, 2139–2142
  Font on, 2150 n.74
  historic-ideological background for, 2126–2131
  institutions for, 2137–2142
  Latour on, 2142–2144
  liberal Protestant thought and, 2127–2128
  modernity in, 2126–2127
  to neoliberalism, 2129–2131
  as new Buddhism, 2132–2134
  old Buddhism and, 2134–2137
  original authority in, 2140
  perennialism in, 2129
  scholarship on, 1118–1119, 2125–2126, 2144–2146
  science to, 2141–2142
  Secular Buddhist Association, 2138, 2143–2144, 2150 n.71
  Secular Buddhist Network, 2133–2134, 2138, 2143–2144
  semiotics of, 2131–2132
  Soka Gakkai and, 2127
  in Sri Lanka, 2145
  technology and, 1118–1119
  textual selectivity with, 2140–2141
  in U.S., 2127–2128
  Victorian Buddhism and, 2128–2129
  virtual communities for, 2137–2138, 2150 n.71
  websites for, 2136
  Western Buddhism and, 2125–2126
  on YouTube, 2137
secular documents, 812–814
secularism, 1571–1572, 1611–1613, 1704–1705
secularized tantra, 1144
Secularizing Buddhism (Payne), 2144–2145
secular mindfulness, 931 n.136
secular texts, 823–824
sedimentation, 1992
seeds (bīja), 7–8, 1834–1835
Seeing Like the Buddha (Cho), 233–234, 240, 400–401, 404–406
"Seeking Sakyamuni" (Jaffe), 2711–2712
Segal, Zindel V., 1951
Seiji Kumagai, 859, 2607
Sei no Shōnagon, 304
Seiryoji Temple, 72–73
Sekarma, 1553

Sekitan rituals, 748–749, 751–752, 759
Sekyā Min, 225 n.98, 599–600, 602–603
Seldeslachts, Erik, 1669
Selected Works of D. T. Suzuki (Jaffe), 709–710, 725
Select Inscriptions Bearing on Indian History and Civilization (Sircar), 951
self. *See ātman*
"Self Discovery Society," 1707
self-harm, 115–116
self-help, 2145
self-identification, 1764
selflessness, 169–170. See also *anātmavāda*; nonself
self-reflection, 1705, 1713–1714
Self-Reflection Will Guide You to the Right Way (Yoshimoto), 1704
self-transformation, 976–977
Seljak, David, 417
semantics, in Chöd, 686–687
Seminal Heart of the Vast Expanse (Jigme Lingpa), 838–839
Seminal Heart texts, 837–838
semiotics, 340, 2131–2132
Sems dpa' chen po Gzhon nu rgyal mtshan, 1403
Sen, Tansen, 1527–1528
Sena I (king), 2433 n.109
Senart, Émile, 639, 1814
Senauke, Alan, 910
Senavrma, 940, 941*f*
Senga, 2051, 2054
Sengai, 708, 714–715
Sengcan, 661–662
Seng Chao, 533, 1187
Sengchen Norbu Drandul, 2492
Sengge Dügüreng Khungtaiji, 1647, 1651, 1653
Sengoku Mari, 1709
Sengyou, 1001, 2688–2689, 2697
Sengzhao, 1461–1462, 1470 n.32
Senior, Robert, 632–633, 636–637, 639
sensory objects. *See* power objects
sentience, 2079
Sequence of the Four Seals, 1476–1477
Se-ra rje-btsun chos-kyi rgyal-mtshan, 26
serenity meditation, 1483–1484
serfs, 2064–2065
sermons, 2064–2065
Sermons of a Buddhist Abbot (D. T. Suzuki), 704
Serruys, H., 1656–1657
services, 895
Seshadri, Gokul, 1528
Setsubun ceremonies, 770
"Seven Attainment Texts," 1475
Seventeen Tantras, 2549
The Seventeen Tantras, 837–838
Seven Tengu Scrolls (Haruko), 2056
Seven Treasuries, 1443–1444
Seven Treatises on Valid Cognition, 1437–1438
Seventy Stanzas on Emptiness (Nāgārjuna), 615–616, 1455–1456. *See also* Candrakīrti
Seven Years in Tibet (film), 226, 233, 397–398
Seven Years in Tibet (Harrer), 1082
Seven Year's War, 872
sex, 1210. *See also* tantra
sexism, 105, 1119–1121
sexual abuse, 1988, 1999 n.75, 2022–2023
sexual ethics, 980, 1983–1984, 1996 n.24
sexuality
  bodies and, 120–122
  Foucault on, 2002 n.119
  gender and, 1997 n.38
  LGBTIQ+ Buddhists and, 1981
  philosophy and, 1983
  in QT, 1983–1989
  in *vinaya* texts, 1986
Sexuality in Classical South Asian Buddhism (Cabezón), 1993
sexual minorities, 2002 n.114
sexual misconduct, 1989
sexual rituals, 964–965
sexual yoga, 1474
Sferra, Francesco, 1490
Shabdrung Ngawang Namgyel, 853–854, 858, 2592, 2595
Shabdrung Ngawang Nyamgyal, 845
shabi. *See* disciples
Shahidullah, M., 1489–1490
al-Shahrastānī, 1679–1681
Shakabpa, W. D., 1068–1069
Shaka Buddha, 2197–2198
Shaku, Soyen, 1081
shakubuku, 1771, 2216
Shakubuku kyōten (Handbook of Propagation), 2212
Shaku Kōzen, 383–384
Shaku Sōen, 383–384
Shakya Chokden, 1464
Shākya Chokden, 1064–1065, 2746, 2749, 2751
Shakyamuni Buddha, 177, 179–182, 185, 1309, 1311–1312, 2218
shamanism, 1469 n.18
"Shambala" (song), 226
Shambhala mythology, 2497
Shambhala organization, 1144
Shandao, 483, 2039

Shang Rinpoché, 1482–1483
Shaping the Lotus Sutra (Wang, E. Y.), 800–801
Shapkar Tsokdruk Rangdrol, 1487–1488
Sha ra ba Yon tan grags, 1400–1401, 1403
Shardza Rinpoche, 133, 135, 137–138
Shardza Tashi Gyeltsen, 112 n.15, 132, 136–138, 836, 2545
shared sovereignty, 2208
Sharf, Elizabeth Horton, 301–302
Sharf, Robert
  on cave shrines, 713 n.27
  Faure and, 301–302
  on museums, 72
  scholarship from, 61–63, 724
  on visualization/contemplation sutras, 2675–2676, 2678, 2699 n.11
Sharmapa, 2021
Sharrock, Peter, 1801 n.6, 1897, 1927, 1937 n.117
Shastri, Dwarakidas, 3–4, 9–10
Shastri, Haraprasad, 371, 1491
Shaw, Graham, 1042–1043
Shaw, Julia, 351, 362
Shaw, Rosalind, 1593–1594
Shaw, Sarah, 2132
Shazhou Dunhuang ershi yong, 812
Shazhou tujing, 813
Shcherbatskoi, Fedore Ippolitorich. *See* Stcherbatsky, Theodore
Sheehy, Michael, 2751
Shen, C. T., 2160–2161, 2171 n.42
Shenchen Luga, 835–836
Sheng-chi, 1794
Shengjian, 998
Shengyan, 1260, 1438, 2735
Shengyen (Sheng Yen)
  academic education of, 2158–2160
  in army, 2155–2157
  autobiography of, 2172 n.55
  for Chan Buddhism, 2160–2163, 2171 n.44
  in China, 2169 n.21
  Deguchi Tetsujyo and, 2171 n.41
  Dharma Drum Mountain and, 2163–2165, 2627–2628
  Dongchu and, 2158, 2170 n.35, 2171 n.40, 2171 n.46
  early years of, 2152–2153
  Han ethnicity and, 2152, 2168 n.1
  Hsing Yun and, 2170 n.36
  influences of, 413
  innovation by, 2291
  in interviews, 2170 n.38
  in Japan, 2171 n.40
  at Jing'an Buddhist Seminary, 2154–2155
  legacy of, 183
  Lingyuan and, 2157–2158, 2162, 2172 n.48
  at Nongchan Monastery, 2162*f*
  novice years of, 2153–2154
  published essays by, 2170 n.25
  reordination of, 2158
  scholarship on, 414–415, 909, 2165–2167
  on Shen, 2171 n.42
  in solitary retreat, 2159*f*
  spiritual awakening of, 2157–2158
  Sun Yat-sen and, 2169 n.18
  in Taiwan, 2169 n.24
  Taixu and, 2160, 2627–2628
  in telegraph squad, 2157*f*
  Xingyun and, 413
Shenhui
  Huineng and, 1227–1230, 1232, 1235–1236
  reputation of, 1232–1234
  scholarship and, 648–649, 1226, 1229
  texts from, 1237–1238
Shenpa Sok Drubma, 1439
Shentai, 10
Shenxiu, 1225–1226, 1228–1230
Sherab Dutsi Korlo. *See* Tsangpa Gyare
Sherab Gönpo, 1441
Sherab Gyeltsen, 136
Sherab Sengge, 1635
Sherap Özer, 685
Sherap Sengé, 1062–1064
Shi, Xiaoying, 821–823
Shichiri Gōjun, 722
Shicketanz, Erik, 2387–2388
Shields, James Mark, 986
Shiga Takayoshi, 1239–1240
Shigeo Kamata, 1192
Shih, Cheng Yen (Cheng Yen)
  scholarship and, 909, 2166–2167, 2613–2616, 2622–2629
  Tzu Chi and, 413–414, 2616–2619, 2621, 2625–2626
Shihu, 1524
Shiji (Sima Qian), 656, 659
Shijialuoyue liufangli jing, 997
Shiji jing, 482
Shimazono, Susumu, 1715
Shin, Jeanette, 462
Shin Buddhism
  acculturation of, 1357
  to Beat Generation, 1313
  Caucasian Buddhists and, 1311
  clergy in, 1307
  clerical training in, 2037

communities with, 1351–1355
in Hawaii, 1309
history of, 1348–1350, 1350*f*
Honganji sect of, 2036–2042
in Japan, 2063–2064
Naikan in, 1708
Nishi Honganji for, 1303–1304
priests in, 1704
psychology in, 1703
Pure Land Buddhism and, 706, 719–720, 1702
Rennyo and, 2036–2043
scholarship on, 34–35, 40–42, 46, 863 n.36, 1357
in U.S., 1079
Zen Buddhism and, 705, 1357–1358
Shinchi Kakushin, 2187
Shine Wontham, 1992
Shinga, 2184, 2355–2356
Shing Cheung, 411
Shingi Shingon School, 2186, 2356
Shingon Buddhism
in China, 2177
Esoteric Buddhism and, 2173–2175, 2177–2179
in Japan, 1198–1199, 1204–1208, 1211–1212, 2177–2179, 2182–2184, 2364
to Kakuban, 2185–2186
at Kōyasan, 2181–2182
Kōyasan revival for, 2184–2185
Kūkai and, 2173, 2177–2180, 2333
Mahāyāna Buddhism and, 2352
major works of, 2180
in modernity, 2185–2187, 2194 n.1
MSBL and, 1146
in North America, 1351, 1357
rituals in, 2180–2181
scholarship on, 2174–2177, 2187–2188, 2351–2358
Shingon Esoteric Buddhism, 2355–2356
Shingon Risshu, 2186
Shingon Shinto, 339
tantra in, 1198–1199, 1204–1208, 1211–1212
Tantric Buddhism and, 1136–1137
Tendai School in, 2181–2184, 2333–2334, 2350–2351, 2358–2359
tenets of, 2332
Tibetan Buddhism and, 1132–1133
tradition, 2180–2181
Zen Buddhism and, 2186–2187
Zhenyan Samantabhadra lineage and, 2369
Shingon Mission, 1133–1135
Shin'ichi Hisamatsu, 1946–1947
Shinichi Tsuda, 1206
Shinji Kakushin, 2187
Shinmura Taku, 278, 308–309, 311
Shinnen, 2355
Shinra Myōjin, 268, 295–296
Shinran. *See also* Pure Land Buddhism; Shin Buddhism
Dōgen and, 2325, 2335, 2341
D. T. Suzuki and, 706, 719–721
to Fujikawa, 277–278
history of, 93, 1349–1350, 1770, 1774, 2055
on Japan, 1297 n.13
legacy of, 277
scholarship on, 2036–2039, 2041–2042, 2341
Shinsan Zenseki mokuroku, 675–676
Shin sarugaku ki (Akihira), 756–757
"The Shin Sect of Buddhism" (D. T. Suzuki), 706, 719–720
Shin shūkyō ron (D. T. Suzuki), 721
Shinto
Bön tradition and, 342–344
Buddhism and, 332–333, 344–346
Daoism and, 2313, 2340
deities in, 336–337
Esoteric Buddhism and, 338–340
history of, 333–334
local cults and, 334–338, 341–344
local deities with, 341–344
philosophy and, 340–341
Shugendō practice in, 1203–1205
tradition, 75, 2314
Yoshida Shinto tradition, 1203–1204
Shin'ya Yasutomi, 2042–2043
Shin-Yi Chao, 1863–1864
Shinzei, 2181–2182, 2355
Shinzen, 2181–2182, 2184
Shirakawa (emperor), 2185
Shiregetü Güüshi Chorjiwa, 1647–1648, 1651–1652
Shirīzu Nichiren, 1773–1774
Shi Shuqing, 2166
Shisier zhang jing, 1182–1183
Shixi Xinyue, 653
Shixi yulu (Shixi Xinyue), 653
Shizi xiemo zhuan (Shenhui), 1228–1229
Shizutani Masao, 950
Shōbō, 2184, 2355–2356
Shōgaito, Masahiro, 4
Shōhondō temple, 2223–2224
Shoji, Rafael, 1134–1135, 1151, 1357–1358
Shoji jissō gi (Kūkai), 2180
Shôji Yamada, 234
Shōken, 303–304
Shoki no Zenshi I (Yanagida), 1238–1239
Shoki Zenshūshisho no kenkyu (Yanagida), 1237–1238

Shōku, 2048, 2054
Shoma, Morita, 1947
Shōmen Kongō, 302
Shōmu (emperor), 273, 293–294, 306, 2199, 2201
Shook, John R., 2145
Shōrai mokuroku, 2333–2334
Shore-Goss, Robert, 1993–1994
Shōrin, 2037
Shōsan, 2053
Shōshin, 2184
Shōshinge (Shinran), 2039–2040
Shōshinge-tai'i (Rennyo), 2039
Shōtoku (prince), 497
Shōtoku Taishi, 272–273, 2199, 2206
Shōwa teihon (Nichiren), 1774–1775
Shōzen, Kajiwara, 269, 273, 275, 291–292, 310–311
Shramadana, Sarvodaya, 905–906
shrines, 336–338, 1871–1873. *See also* Buddhist wall paintings
Shtcherbatsky, Fyodor Ippolitovich, 1464–1465
Shūei, 2355
Shugendō practice, 1203–1205
Shulman, Eviatar, 1890
Shunpan, 1762
Shunryu Suzuki, 1947
Shunxiao, 2326–2327
Shun Zi (emperor), 93, 1000, 1066, 2016
Shu Qi, 999–1000
Shutai Aoyama, 1133
Shuyi, 1443
Siam, 871–872, 967, 1095–1096, 1100, 2063–2064. *See also specific countries*
Siamese Archaeological Service, 74
Siberia, 1603, 2487–2488
Siddhartha (biography), 1016
Siddhārtha (prince), 121–122, 2265
Siddhārtha Gautama, 2262
siddhis, 144 n.35, 586, 2304
Siderits, Mark, 11, 1465–1466, 1699, 1838
Siegal, Ron, 1952–1953
Siegel, Dan, 1952
Sierksma, Fokke, 744
Sīgālovāda Sutta, 1879–1880, 1883
signatories, in monasteries, 2576
signification, 1991
Sīhaḷa lineages, 2406–2407
Sihingkhanithan, 1729–1730
Sihlé, Nicolas, 890
Sikhism, 2314
Śikṣananda, 999
Śikṣāsamuccaya, 1810
śīla (ethical discipline), 2082–2083
Silence-and-Illumination Inscriptions (Hongzhi), 652–656, 672
silent mentors, 2618, 2627
Silk, Jonathan, 1528, 2696
Silk Road, 496, 632, 806, 1468 n.3, 1514, 1522–1523, 1623. See also *specific Dunhuang topics*
The Silk Road (Whitfield, S., and Sims-Williams, U.), 802, 825
The Silk Route and the Diamond Path (Frederick S. Wight Art Gallery), 802
Silla Buddhism, 2201
Silla Kingdom, 497
Silva, David de, 1046–1047
Silva, Lily de, 1891, 2636
Silva, Ozawa-de, 1714–1715
Silva, Ranjani de, 1103–1104
Silver Screen Buddha (Suh), 240, 400–401, 403–406
Sima Qian, 656, 659
Sims-Williams, Nicholas, 820
Sims-Williams, Ursula, 825
sin, 2129
Singapore, 1256, 1578, 2062–2063
Singh, Upinder, 1528, 1786
Singhalese, 2711
Sing Hung, 411
Singu (king), 1048
Sinhala Bōdhivaṁśaya, 1729
Sinhala Buddhism, 144 n.33, 905–906, 2428 n.35
Sinhala Buddhist guardian deities
  in *satara varan devi*, 2245–2255
  in Sri Lanka, 2256–2257, 2261 n.56
Sinhala ethnic identity, 71–72
Sinhala Thūpavaṃsa, 1728
Sino Esoteric Buddhism Association, 2384
Sino-Japanese War, 2152–2153, 2170 n.26, 2292–2293
Sino-Tibetan Doctrinal Institute, 2283, 2292–2293
Sircar, Dines Chandra, 951–952
Sīrimaṅgala Sutta, 1883
Sirinivāsa (king), 146
Siripāla (king), 146
Siriphon, Aranya, 2627
sitting meditation, 522, 1350–1351, 1354–1355, 1708–1709
Situ Paṇchen Chökyi Jungné, 1487–1488, 2025, 2747
Śiva (god), 1163–1164
Sīvaka, 251
Sivaraksa, Sulak, 895–896, 904, 906
Sivikumāra, 251
Six Dharmas of Nāropā (Nāropā), 1968–1969
sixfold yoga, 2749
Six Pieces of Instruction, 631 n.13, 687
six sense organs, 2674–2675, 2679–2680, 2691, 2693, 2704 n.93
Six Nara Schools, 2198, 2203–2209. *See also* Nara schools

Sixty Stanzas on Reasoning (Nāgārjuna), 615–616, 1455–1456. *See also* Candrakīrti
six yogas, 2546
Six Yogas of Nāropa, 2470–2473
Siyam Nikaya, 577
Ska ba dPal brtegs, 3
Skanda. *See* Kanda Kumara-Skanda
skandhas, 2102*t*
Skandhila, 2098
Skeen, George J. A., 1046–1047
"Sketch of Buddhism" (Hodgson), 877
Skilling, Peter, 2266, 2268, 2270, 2419, 2557, 2567
Skilton, Andrew Trevor, 963–964, 967
Skjærvø, Prods Oktor, 820
Skorupski, Tadeusz, 1202, 1205, 1212, 1815, 1974, 2481
sKyabspa, 112 n.13
Sky Dharma, 1145–1146
Sluyter, Dan, 400–401, 405–406
smallpox, 293, 295–296, 306–307, 2202
Small Pure Land Scripture, 1187
Smith, E. Gene, 1068–1069, 1443, 1446, 1491, 1553, 2750
Smith, Huston, 2129
Smith, Jonathan Z., 587
Smith, Sharon, 861 n.8
Smith, Simon Gareth, 1982
Smith, Wilfred Cantwell, 397
smoke purification, 2494
smṛti (mindfulness), 2082–2083. *See also* mindfulness
Smyug rum pa Brtson grus 'bar, 1401
Sna nam Rdo rje dbang phyug, 1400
Snediker, Michael, 1992–1993
Snellgrove, David, 112 n.1, 858, 1068–1069, 1407, 1415 n.62, 1489–1491, 2606
Snodgrass, Judith, 1104–1105
Snow White (film), 405–406
Snyder, Gary, 361, 363, 723–724, 910, 1081, 1311
socialism
  democracy and, 1583–1584
  education in, 1612–1613
  Marxism and, 1251–1252
  in Mongolia, 1582–1583
  Mongolian Buddhism after, 1588–1589
  nationalism and, 1442–1444
  non-violence and, 1584
  reform and, 906
  to tsars, 1608
  violence and, 1583, 1585
socialization, 1120
social reform, 919–920
social science, 2144
social status, 593–595
Société Asiatique, 1814
society
  Anglo-American, 2129–2131, 2141
  Buddhist, 1593–1594, 2071
  hierarchies in, 2065
  in Japan, 2212, 2217–2218, 2225–2226
  in Laos, 2232–2233
  liberal Protestant thought in, 2130–2131
  Lotus Light Charity Society, 415
  Mahabodhi, 2127
  Mahabodhi Society, 196, 1075–1077, 2127, 2279
  in North America, 2242–2243
  Pali Text Society, 153, 370, 996, 1032–1033, 1117, 1736–1737, 1939, 2256, 2564
  Swedenborg Society, 704–705
  of Taiwan, 2620–2621
  iXiu Ming Society, 2376–2377
Society of Jesus, 865
sociology, 567, 1983
socio-politics, 2517–2518
Sodō Mori, 153
Sōen, Shaku, 702–705, 714, 716, 722, 1352, 1941, 2435, 2711–2712
soft power, 1259
Soga clan, 2206–2207
Soga no Iruka, 2199–2200
Soga no Umako, 2206–2207
Sogdian-language materials, 809–810
Sōgō bunin records, 753
Sögyal Rinpoche, 2023
soils, in rituals, 1423*t*
Soka Gakkai
  Buddhism, 1088–1089, 1355–1357, 1774
  in China, 2213
  globalization of, 2214
  historiography of, 2226–2227
  history of, 2211–2217
  internationalization of, 2214
  leadership of, 2213–2214
  in modernity, 2219
  Nichiren Shōshū and, 2215–2219, 2222–2226
  peace activities by, 2214–2215, 2220–2222
  politics of, 2216–2217
  Rissho Kosei-kai and, 909–910
  scholarship on, 861 n.8, 894, 2227
  secular Buddhism and, 2127
  Soka Gakkai International, 196, 911–912, 1355–1356, 1774–1775, 2214–2215, 2222, 2225
  in Soviet Union, 2213
  Toda and, 2219–2220
  UN and, 2214–2215
  in U.S., 2214

Sōka Gakkai–Kōmeitō (Murakami Shigeyoshi), 2226
Sōka kyōikugaku taikei (Makiguchi), 2211
Sokushin jōbutsugi (Kūkai), 2180
solitary retreats, 2158–2160
Soma, 938
Somapura Mahāvihāra, 1790–1791
Somaśambhupaddhati, 1201, 1212
Somdet To, 965, 970
"Some Logical Aspects of Nāgārjuna's System" (Robinson), 1465
Sönam Chöpel, 1065–1066, 2015–2016
Sönam Drakpa, 1064–1065, 1602
Sönam Gyatso, 1065, 1645–1649, 1651–1652, 2014–2015
Sönam Gyen, 1437
Song dynasty
  Chan Buddhism in, 664–665
  Chan compendia in, 667–670
  culture of, 2364
  legacy of, 1634
  Lizong for, 653
  scholarship on, 59–62, 494, 2077 (*See also* Chan Buddhism)
  Song court, 1240
  sutras in, 2683
  Tang dynasty and, 675–676
  yulu genre in, 647–656
Song Dynasty Biographies of Eminent Monks (Zanning), 59–60
Song gaoseng zhuan (Zanning), 1230
Song of Realizing the Way, 662, 674
Song of the Queen of Spring, 2016
Songpo Zongqi, 663–664
Songtsen Gampo (king)
  scholarship on, 352, 1066, 1731–1732, 1965, 1973–1974, 1973*f*, 2474, 2544, 2584
  Trisong Detsen and, 2581–2583
Songyun, 1370
Song Zhiwen, 1227–1228
Son'i, 2045–2046
Sonnen (prince), 754–755
Sonoda, Shuya, 2715
A Son's Flesh sutta, 1319
Sonshun, 340
Soper, Alexander, 2674–2677, 2690, 2696
Sørensen, Henrik H., 825
Sørensen, Per, 2587, 2594
Soshin, 269–270
Sōshō, 750–753
soteriological aims, 2547–2548
soteriological analysis, 918, 1696–1697, 1771–1772, 2109–2110
soteriological optimism, 599–600
soteriology, 344–345, 584–585, 589–591, 2540
Sōtō Zen Buddhism, 751, 1348, 1352–1353
Sōtō Zen Buddhist Association, 911
Sōtō Zen nuns, 185
Soucy, Alexander, 417–418
soul boys, 2021
"The Soul Theory of the Buddhists" (Stcherbatsky), 4
Soundings in Tibetan Civilization (Aziz and Kapstein), 695
South Africa, 913, 1014
South America, 1353–1358
South Asia. See also *specific countries*
  Avalokiteśvara in, 84–85
  Buddhism in, 11, 1038–1039
  chronology of, 946–948
  culture of, 1984
  diaspora, 2311
  engaged Buddhism in, 905–910
  epigraphy in, 932
  history of, 151–153
  imaging Buddha in, 1273–1274, 1282–1290, 1293, 1296 n.5
  inscription types in, 932–933, 948–951
  Islam in, 1042–1043
  language in, 933
  publishing in, 1036–1038
  relics in, 1736–1737
  Southeast Asia and, 369–375, 2262–2270
  technology in, 1042–1045
  temples in, 1112–1113
  Tibetan Buddhism in, 1140
  vinaya texts in, 2660
South Bihar, 1788–1789
Southeast Asia. See also *specific countries*
  art historical evidence from, 961–962
  Avalokiteśvara in, 84–85
  Bhutan and, 2062–2063
  Buddhism in, 2231–2234
  Buddhism schools in, 2231
  China and, 1299 n.31
  communism in, 2233
  cosmology in, 484–485
  disciplinary codes in, 2063
  East India and, 1284–1285
  engaged Buddhism in, 905–907
  England in, 225 n.98
  Esoteric Buddhism in, 959, 967–969
  footprints in, 69
  history of, 151–153
  Humanistic Buddhism in, 1255–1256
  Islam in, 959
  jātaka in, 1369
  Mahāyāna Buddhist tantra in, 958–963
  mainland, 112 n.3, 375–378

nuns in, 1103
Pagan dynasty in, 1095–1096
politico-historical context in, 959–960
politics of, 2072–2073
publishing in, 1036–1038
relics from, 963
South Asia and, 369–375, 2262–2270
Sri Lanka and, 1094–1095
temples in, 1112–1113
texts from, 960–962
Thailand and, 1730
Theravāda Buddhism in, 2406–2407
Theriya zones in, 2414–2418
travelers to, 962–963
vinaya texts in, 2660
Western art and, 66–67
Southeast Asian refugees
in North America, 2231–2239
scholarship on, 2242–2243
Vietnamese Buddhism and, 2239–2242
Southeastern Bengal, 1793–1796. *See also* Bangladesh
South India, 1521–1522
South Korea, 176 n.69, 466–467. *See also* Korea
sovereignty, 73–74, 2208
Soviet Union, 1384, 1583–1584, 1610–1614, 2213. *See also* Russia
Sowa Rigpa, 2530, 2532–2535
Soygal Rinpoche, 1143
space, 2105
Spain, 913, 1650
Sparham, Gareth, 29–30, 986
Special Issue (Nishitani and Hiroshi), 710
"Speculative Non-Buddhism" (website), 2131–2132
Speech Treasury, 1475–1476
spell culture, 2177
Speranski Reforms, 1609
Sperling, Elliot, 1656–1657, 2024, 2028 n.88
Sphutārthābhidharmakośavyākhyā (Yaśomitra), 9–10
The Spirit of the United States and Freedom of Religion (Emyō), 1305
spirituality, 197, 2128, 2157–2158, 2165, 2479
Spiritual Mapping movement, 1149
spiritual power, 1290
spiritual progress, 619
Spiritual Warfare movement, 1149–1150
Spiro, Melford, 344–345, 575, 579–580, 602–604, 1890–1891
"Split-Ear" tradition, 2309
Spring, Summer, Fall, Winter… and Spring (film), 232–233, 403–406
Spyan snga ba Tshul khrims 'bar, 1400–1401
Śri Devī. *See* Palden Lhamo
Śrīdhāraṇarāta, 1794
Śrīgupta, 1445–1446
Sri Lanka. *See also* Theravāda Buddhism
Amoghavajra in, 2176–2177
Buddha images in, 67
Buddhism in, 1076, 1084–1085, 1729–1730
Burma/Myanmar and, 76–77, 1100, 2236, 2292–2293
China and, 2277–2278
colonialism in, 1045–1047
culture of, 1576–1577, 1722, 2399–2402, 2426 n.13
demons in, 1167
engaged Buddhism in, 905–906, 921
England and, 1075–1076
Gampola period, 2245–2246
history of, 152–153, 916, 1731–1732, 2394–2395, 2426 n.14
independence of, 500
India and, 54–55, 1521
Japan and, 77
Kanda Kumara-Skanda in, 2251
Kohomba Kankariya rite in, 2260 n.46
Kotte rulers in, 2259 n.30
Lambakaṇṇa dynasty of, 2433 n.109
Maritime Buddhism in, 1471 n.65
meditation in, 967
monasteries in, 2667
monks in, 968
Natha in, 2255–2256
nationalism in, 71–72, 2432 n.93
Pali University of, 1578
philology in, 1045–1047
proto-Theriyas in, 2397
Pyu people in, 2406
reform in, 2402–2403
relic shrines in, 1725
Rhys Davids, T. W., in, 1032–1033
Saman-Yama-Lakshmana in, 2252–2253
scholarship and, 54–55, 2245–2251, 2667–2668
secular Buddhism in, 2145
Sinhala Buddhist guardian deities in, 2256–2257, 2261 n.56
Southeast Asia and, 1094–1095
South India and, 1521–1522
Sthaviras in, 2425 n.10
Tamil Hindus in, 919
Thailand and, 906–907, 1572–1574, 1578, 1726, 2243
Theravāda Buddhism in, 2245–2246, 2396–2399, 2403–2404, 2416, 2427 n.30, 2429 n.49
Tibetan Buddhism and, 83–84
Upulvan-Rama-Vishnu in, 2251–2253
U.S., and, 1114–1115
Vibhishana in, 2253–2254
Vishnu in, 2260 n.49
Śrīmitra, 948, 1186

Śrīsiṃha, 2640–2641
Śrī Siṃha, 837, 2475
Śrī Vijaya, 960–961, 963
Srong btsan sgam po (king), 85, 1399
Stainless Light Commentary, 1418, 1420–1422, 1474, 2548
Stalin, Joseph, 1613
standard secularization narrative, 2131
standards-with-comments collections, 664–667
Standing Buddha statue, 1288
Stanford University, 985
Stark, Rodney, 2627
Starling, Jessica, 113 n.18, 778–779
state religions, 2202
statues, 112 n.7. See also *specific statutes*
Stcherbatsky, Theodore (Shcherbatskoi, Fedore Ippolitorich), 4, 29–30, 628–629, 1698
Stearns, Cyrus, 2750
Stein, Aurel, 112 n.7, 798, 807, 816–817, 826
Stein, Marc Aurel, 2637
Stein, R. A., 2028 n.17, 2488–2489, 2498–2500
Steinbeck, John, 2022
Steinbeck, Nancy, 2022
Steinhardt, N., 1656–1657
Steinke, Gerald, 1709
"Stele for a Buddhist Shrine at the Mogao Caves by Mr. Li" (Lezun), 781
steps of the path (*lam rim*), 1400–1403, 1406–1407, 1414 n.39
Sternberg, Ungern von, 1601
Stevens, John, 1993
Stevenson, Daniel, 2680–2681
Stewart, Charles, 1593–1594
Sthaviras, 2395–2397, 2425 n.10, 2430 n.69. *See also* Theravāda Buddhism
Sthiramati, 1318–1319, 1331, 2204
Stoddard, Heather Karmay, 443–444
Stoeber, Michael, 2314
Stoltz, Jonathan, 1444
Stone, Jacqueline, 758, 1774, 2227, 2358
Storehouse of Mahāmudrā, 1486–1487
Storhoff, Gary, 240, 400–403, 405–406
Straw Hat Jizō, 768
"Stream in the Sea" (Kanmo), 1312
Streng, Frederick, 1465
Strickmann, Michel
  on East Asia, 1212
  on proto-homa, 1210
  scholarship from, 60–61, 213, 278, 296–297, 1205, 2056
  on shaman superstition, 304, 310
  on Yixing, 1209
Strong, John, 179–180, 993–994, 1371, 2270
structure, in *kālacakra-maṇḍala*, 1416–1422
STTS. See *yogatantra Sarvatathāgatatattvasaṃgraha Tantra*
Studies in the Lankavatara Sutra (D. T. Suzuki), 718, 725
Studies in the Minor Rock Edicts (Andersen), 951
A Study into the Thought of Kougyoudaishi Kakuban (Veere), 2359
The Stupa of Bharut (Cunningham), 948
"Stupa of the 6th Patriarch's Uṣṇīṣa" (Kim Chŏnghŭi), 1230–1231
stupas, 57–58, 68–73, 75–76, 934–936
Sübe'etei Ba'atur, 1625
Śubhakarasiṃha, 55–56, 60–63, 2175–2176, 2363–2364
Subhuti, Ven Waskaduve, 2710–2711
subjectivity, 1831, 2130
Subsequent Tantra, 2528
substance, 2511–2513, 2633 n.38
"Succinct Biography of Master Xuyun of Zhusheng Monastery of Mount Jizu in Yunnan" (Ye Qingyan), 2736
Śuddhamatī (Ratnākaraśānti), 25–26
Śuddhodana, 121
Sudhanāvadāna, 809
Sueki, Yasuhiro, 821–823, 2332
Sueki Fumihiko, 345–346, 2358
suffering
  ethics in, 861 n.7, 974–976
  from mental afflictions, 2081
  morality and, 978
  philosophy of, 1312
  problematization of, 977–978
  rebirth and, 115–116, 1719–1720
  scholarship on, 1024–1025
Sufism, 1678–1679, 1871–1873
Sugata Assembly of the Eight Teachings, 1437
Suh, Sharon A., 144 n.31, 232–233, 240, 400–401, 403–406
Suharto, 71–72
Sui dynasty, 211, 1181–1182, 2683
Suiko (empress), 2199, 2206
Sujung Kim, 295–296
Sukhāvatī, 1960–1971, 1977 n.11, 1978 n.35. *See also* Pure Land Buddhism
A Sukhāvatī Prayer (Padma Karpo), 1966
Sukhāvatīvyūha Sūtra, 482–483, 1187, 1291, 1807, 1961–1962, 1974. *See also* Pure Land Buddhism
Sulak Sivaraksa, 359
Sullivan, Brenton, 1068–1069
Sumanakuta mountain, 2253
Sumaṅgala, Hikkaḍuvē, 372–373

Sumangala, Inamaluwe, 1104
Sumangalavilāsinī, 250, 257
Sumatiśīla, 1343 n.142, 1345 n.182
Sumedho, Ajahn, 1950–1951
Sumeru mountain, 478–479, 481–482, 487, 495
Sumidera, 2201
Summary of Errors (Torres), 866, 869
summum bonum, 981–982
Sümo Darchung, 850
Sumpa Khenpo Yeshé Paljor, 1066–1067, 2499
Sum pa mkhan po, 1406–1407
Sun Chuo, 1000
Sundberg, Jeffrey, 1527–1528
Sun Dianqi, 326
Śuṅga period, 934–936
Sun Jingde, 87
Sunlun Sayadaw U Kavi, 1887
Sun Simiao, 211, 305
Sun Yat-sen, 413, 1440, 2168 n.13, 2169 n.18, 2281, 2727
Sunzi Suanjing, 814
supernatural aspects, 112 n.15
supernatural powers, 1417–1418
superstitions, 2164
Suppiyā, 249–250
Supplement to the Materia Medica (Bencao shiyi), 213
Supreme Primordial Buddha Tantra, 1417–1418
Supreme Vehicle of Madhyamaka (Tāranātha), 2746–2747
Śuraṅgamasamādhi sūtra, 1498–1499
surgery, 251–252
Surinyavongsa (king), 1096
Surrey, Jan, 1954
Suryāprabhāsiṃha, 1437
Su Shi, 355–356
Susiddhikara sūtra/tantra, 1208, 2175
sustainability, 2616, 2619, 2621–2625
Su Tianjue, 1657–1658
Sutra for the Children, 270
Sutra for the Golden Light, 275–276
sutra lectures, 729 n.49
Sutra of Golden Light, 809, 811, 816
Sutra of Infinite Life, 807
Sutra of Maitreya's Ascent, 2284–2285
The Sūtra of the All-Creating King, 833–834
Sutra of the Buddha of Infinite Life, 816
Sutra of the Buddha's Names, 816
Sutra of the Condemnation of Intoxicating Drink, 809
Sutra of the Divine Dhāraṇī on the Eleven-Headed Guanyin Spoken by the Buddha, 89–90
Sūtra of the Gathered Intention, 2637–2638
Sutra of the Meditation on the Buddha of Immeasurable Life, 557–559
Sutra of the Meditation on the True Law, 288
Sūtra of the Samādhi of Direct Encounter with the Buddhas of the Present, 2541
Sutra of the Ten Kings, 807, 816
Sutra of Ultimate and Mysterious Happiness, 812
Sutra on Causes and Effects, 809
Sutra on Maitreya's Descent to Rebirth, 2689
Sutra on Profound Merits, 2694
Sutra on the Base of Mindfulness, 205
Sutra on the Great Kindness of Parents, 807
Sūtra on the Major and Minor Bodily Marks, 2678
Sūtra on the Names of the Buddha, 784, 786*f*
Sutra on the Origin of Origins, 812
Sutra on the Wise and the Foolish (Xianyu jing), 1636
sutras. See *specific sutras*
Sutra Spoken by the Sixth Patriarch Wei Lang (Wong Mou-lam), 1236
sutra zhentong, 2749–2750
Sutta Nipāta, 2556
Sutta on the Noble Quest, 1030
Sutta on the Turning of the Dhamma Wheel, 1022, 1024–1033. *See also* four noble truths
Sutta Piṭaka, 2408
suttas. See *specific suttas*
Suu Kyi, Aung San, 907
Suvarṇaprabhāsottama Sūtra, 250–251
Suwaki Hiroshi, 1705–1706
Suzong (emperor), 54–55, 57–58, 1230, 1517
Suzuki, Alan Masaru, 705–706
Suzuki, Beatrice Lane, 704–706
Suzuki, Lester, 39
Suzuki Daisetsu (Hisamatsu), 710
Suzuki Daisetsu kenkyū kiso shiryō (Kirita), 710, 725
Suzuki Daisetsu Teitarō (D. T. Suzuki)
  biography of, 701–702, 709–710, 725
  in culture, 723–725, 1081
  Fromm and, 707–708, 723–724, 1947–1948, 1952
  Hanh and, 195
  influence of, 384, 398–399, 500–501
  in Japan, 708–709
  Mahāyāna Buddhism and, 716–718, 725
  at Ōtani University, 705–706
  politics of, 706–707
  on Pure Land Buddhism, 704–706, 719–721, 725
  religious theory of, 721–722, 1946–1948
  scholarship and, 234, 1237, 1352–1353, 1941, 1945–1946
  Sōen and, 2435
  in Tokyo, 704–705
  in U.S., 703–704, 707–708, 723–724
  Zen Buddhism and, 502, 702–703, 706, 714–716, 725

Suzuki Daisetsu zenshū, 709–710, 725
svasaṃvitti (reflexive awareness), 1823, 1831–1832
Svātantrikas, 1462–1463, 1467
Śveḍavarma, 945
Svetambara tradition, 1202
Swearer, Donald, 359–362, 578, 966, 970, 1891, 2270
Swedenborg, Emanuel, 704–705, 722
Swedenborg Society, 704–705
Sweet, Michael, 1993, 2088
Swidler, Amy, 182–183
The Swift and Unobstructed Path to Sukhāvatī (Panchen Lobsang Chökyi Gyaltsen), 1966
Switzerland, 2529–2530
Syedullah, Jasmine, 911, 1990, 2719
syllables, 2647–2648
symbolic meanings
  of animals, 1281–1282
  in homa, 1206, 1206*t*, 1210–1211
  of Kālacakra's body, 1416, 1418–1422
  of light, 1301 n.58
  structure and, 1416–1422
The Symbolic Secret Jewel (Mipham), 2495
symbolism, in *kālacakra maṇḍala*, 441–443
The Symbolism of Buddhism (HHMH), 1308
syncretism, 112 n.14, 575–576
Syria, 1675–1676
SYSS. *See* School of Youth for Social Service
systematic interpretations, of Buddhist ethics, 983–984

Tabo, a Lamp for the Kingdom (Klimburg-Salter), 443–444
Tachibana no Moroe, 2202
Tachibana Zuichō, 798, 818–819
Tachikawa Musashi, 2359
Tagore, Abandrinath, 384–385
Tagore, Rabindranath, 384–385, 2292–2293
Tagsham Nuden Dorje, 1966
Taihan, 2330–2331, 2345, 2355
Taika reforms, 2199–2200
Taimitsu
  Annen and, 2348–2349
  contributions, 2350–2351
  Enchin and, 2347–2348
  Ennin and, 2345–2347
  Kūkai and, 2345
  Ryōgen and, 2350
  scholarship on, 2343–2351
  Tōmitsu and, 2340–2341, 2357–2359
"Taimitsu" (Dolce), 2358–2359
Taiping Rebellion, 326–328
Taira Masayuki, 307, 345–346
Taira no Kiyomori, 301–302, 2055, 2185
Taira Sadafusa, 2037–2038
Taisen Miyata, 1133, 1206
Taisho Canon, 1630
Taishō canon, 1517, 2674, 2687–2688, 2695
Taishō shinshū daizōkyō, 759–760
Taishō Tripiṭaka, 2317
Tai Situpa, 2000 n.76
Taiwan
  army, 2155–2157
  art in, 1633–1634
  BLIA and, 1010
  Buddhism in, 2171 n.40
  Buddhist chaplaincy in, 468
  Chiang Kai-shek for, 2169 n.18
  China and, 64, 1013–1014, 1219–1220, 1260, 1438–1439, 1443–1444, 2155–2157
  Chinese Buddhism in, 2160, 2164–2165
  Chinese Buddhist Electronic Text Association in, 328
  Cihang and, 1438
  colonialism in, 1252–1253, 1437
  culture of, 1011, 1015–1017, 1231
  Daoism in, 2166–2167
  Fo Guang Shan in, 1009, 1011
  government, 2163–2164, 2615
  health care in, 2620
  Humanistic Buddhism in, 1253–1258, 1438, 2735
  identity in, 1262
  immigration from, 412, 1079
  Japan and, 1576–1577, 2161–2162
  Korea and, 378–379, 1591
  Mahāyāna Buddhism in, 915
  martial law in, 2164
  in modernity, 2665–2666
  monasteries in, 1263–1264
  MSBL in, 1137–1139, 1146, 1150
  Mutual Security Act, 2156
  nationalism in, 2169 n.18
  Nongchan Monastery, 2162*f*
  nuns in, 909, 1257–1258
  religion in, 909, 2163
  scholarship on, 1017, 2625
  Shengyen in, 2169 n.24
  society of, 2620–2621
  Taiwanese Luminary Nunnery, 2666
  tantra in, 1136
  tantric revival in, 2382
  Tibetan Buddhism in, 2365, 2388
  tourism to, 1011–1012
  tradition in, 2170 n.26
  Tzu Chi for, 413

Tzu Chi Stem Cell Center in, 2618
U.S., and, 2160, 2734–2735
Vietnam and, 1084, 2667
Wang Jinyun in, 2613–2614
World War II in, 2072–2073
Tai Wudi (emperor), 1001
Taixu (Tai Xu). *See also* Humanistic Buddhism
on Chan Buddhism, 2290–2291, 2298 n.9
in China, 2127, 2154–2155
Cihang and, 1256, 1437, 1441–1443, 1445
death of, 1437–1438
Dharmapāla and, 1075–1077, 1086–1087
disciples of, 1136
doctrinal classification of, 2291–2292
Dongchu and, 2154–2155, 2158
early life of, 2278–2279
final ten years of, 2292–2293
Hanh and, 909
in Hawaii, 1308
for Humanistic Buddhism, 382–383, 2289–2291, 2294–2295
influence of, 381, 413–415
leadership of, 377–378
legacy of, 1253–1255, 1262, 1438, 1443–1447, 2365
Maitreya School and, 2284–2285
methodology of, 2277–2278
in modernity, 2294
in monastic education, 2283–2284
monks to, 2069
motivations of, 2387–2388
philosophy of, 1249–1250
on Pure Land Buddhism, 2285–2287
radical Buddhism and, 2280–2281
reform from, 1076–1077, 1579
rensheng fojiao, 1439–1441
scholarship on, 413, 918, 1217 n.63, 1219, 1222, 1258, 1271 n.89, 2294–2295, 2733, 2735
in sealed retreat, 2282–2283
Shengyen and, 2160, 2627–2628
tantra and, 1139, 2365
Xingyun and, 1437
Yinshun and, 413, 2621–2622
Taixu dashi quanshu (Yinshun), 2295–2296
Taizong (emperor), 1868–1869
Taizu (emperor), 322, 1868–1869
Takagi Shingen, 2336, 2632 n.25
Takahashi Shinji, 1708
Takata, Tokio, 825
Takeda Ryōji, 1705
Takemoto Takahiro, 1707
Takeuchi Katashi, 1705
Takeuchi Ryo'on, 918
Takie Sugiyama Lebra, 1714
Taktra Rinpoché Ngawang Sungrab, 1067
Takzik, 2492–2493
Takzik Norgyé, 2492–2493
Tale of Genji (Murasaki), 304, 308–309
The Tale of Genji, 757
Tales of an Old Lama (Bawden), 1386
Taliban, 66
Talim, Meena, 260–261
"Talk on Fear and Terror" (Norman), 1029
Tamanaha family, 38
Tambiah, Stanley, 576, 603–604, 970, 1890–1891, 2072–2073, 2257, 2518–2519
Tamil Hindus, 905–906, 919
Tamil Tigers, 71–72
Tam Kung Temple, 408–409
Tamura Yoshirō, 2358
Tan, Amy, 237
Tanabe, George, 778–779, 896–897, 1309, 1357
Tana Daishō, 41, 43, 46–47
Tanaka, Kenneth, 821, 2683, 2696
Tanaka, Ryōshō, 821–823
Tanaka Chigaku, 2219
Tanba Yasuyori, 211
Tang, Li, 823–824
Tang Dayuan, 1440
Tang dynasty. *See also* Chan Buddhism; China
Amitābha Buddha in the Western Pure Land from, 796, 797*f*
art from, 555–560
culture of, 54–60, 63, 1865, 2363–2364
Han dynasty and, 996–997, 1184
history of, 53–54
India and, 55–56
Japan and, 1212
Mogao caves during, 555–560, 795–796
Platform Sutra in, 1233–1236
scholarship on, 57–58, 92, 1624, 2096
sculptural ensemble from, 781, 783*f*
Song dynasty and, 675–676
Sui dynasty and, 211, 1181
translations from, 2293
Xin Tang shu in, 1234
"Zhai family cave" from, 787
Zhenyan Samantabhadra lineage in, 2366
Tang Jiyao, 2727
Tanguts, 1623, 1631–1632
Tang Yongtong, 1001
Taniguchi, Shōyō, 164–170
Tanjing, 997–998

Tan-Kwong, 1795–1796
Tannishō (Shinran), 706, 719–720, 2037
Tan Sitong, 2279
tantra. See also *specific topics*
 Black Razor Tantra, 2638–2639
 Buddhist tantras, 1473–1474
 Buddhist tantra traditions, 2311–2313
 contestation of, 1148–1149
 deities in, 1207
 doctrinal themes in, 2642–2643
 in East Asia, 2194 n.1
 fire rituals, 1198–1199
 Four Tantras, 2528
 Geluk tradition and, 2313
 gold and, 1544–1545
 Gö Lotsawa Zhönu Pal and, 2476–2478
 Guhyagarbha Tantra, 2639
 Guhya Tantra, 2644–2647
 higher tantras, 131
 Higher Yoga tantric system, 2470
 Hinduism and, 2280–2287, 2314–2317, 2321 n.18
 Hundred Thousand Tantras of the Early Translation Period, 2641
 Indian Tantric traditions, 969
 in Indo-European fire cults, 1199–1200, 1207
 Indo-Tibetan, 2174
 interiorization and, 1208–1210
 Kālacakra and, 484
 Kīlaguhya Tantra, 2642
 Kīlanirvāṇa Tantra, 2642, 2645, 2649–2650
 Kīla Tantra in Twelve Chapters, 2645
 Kīla Vidyottama Tantra, 2641–2642
 lamas and, 1737
 Mahāyāna Buddhism and, 2403
 Mahāyoga, 1472
 mahāyoga tantras, 1472–1477
 Maitreya School and, 2291–2292
 mantric words in, 1203
 Maritime Buddhism and, 1522–1525
 McDaniel on, 964–965
 medical mantras, 259–260
 meditation and, 124–125
 monasticism and, 1403–1405
 to Nāgārjuna, 1474
 neo-Zhenyan movements and, 2385–2387
 Nyingmapa tantric traditions, 2490
 in Nyingma school, 2523 n.33
 Nyingma tantras, 2641
 Nyingma tantric canon, 2317
 practitioners, 478
 Primordial Buddha Tantra, 1423, 1425, 1428
 research on, 1110 n.96
 Rimé movement and, 1142–1143
 rituals of, 1195 n.1
 Śaiva Tantra, 964–965
 Samvarodaya, 1206
 Sarvatathāgatatattvasaṃgraha Tantra, 2636
 scholarship on, 2318–2320
 secularized, 1144
 in Shingon Buddhism, 1198–1199, 1204–1208, 1211–1212
 stereotypes of, 307
 STTS, 2637
 Supreme Primordial Buddha Tantra, 1417–1418
 in Taiwan, 1136
 Taixu and, 1139, 2365
 tantric lineages, 1217 n.71
 tantric manifestations, 426–427, 427*f*
 tantric Nāropā, 1474
 tantric Theravāda, 967–969
 tantric vows, 1430
 in *terma* collections, 1161–1162
 in Tibet, 1135–1140, 1158, 2312–2313, 2516
 Tibetan Tantric Buddhism, 1537
 Tongue of Flames Tantra, 2643–2644
 tradition of, 2277–2279, 2301–2302
 translations of, 2315
 Unexcelled Yoga, 1416
 Vajrayāna Buddhism and, 521–522, 977–978, 1813–1814, 2432 n.97
 in Vedic tradition, 1200–1201, 1217 n.66
 Vidyottama Tantra, 2642
 yoga and, 2321 n.15
 Yoga Tantras, 967–968, 1416
 Yoginī, 1472
 yoginī tantras, 1472–1477
 in Yuan dynasty, 1135
 zhentong, 2749–2750
Tantra (Urban), 2318
Tantra Mantra (film), 2302
The Tantra of the Principles of the Three Bodies (Sang-ngak Lingpa), 134–135
The Tantra on the Elimination of All Evil Rebirths, 2474
The Tantric Body (Flood, G.), 2318
Tantric Buddhism. See also *specific topics*
 in Black Sect Esoteric Buddhism, 1138
 in China, 1135–1140
 Chogyam Trungpa for, 1144
 deities in, 1911, 1913*f*
 Dorje Shugden and, 1146–1148
 Dzongsar Khyentse for, 1142–1143
 Esoteric Buddhism and, 2340–2351

FPMT for, 1140–1146
globalization of, 1131–1132, 1146–1150
history of, 1132–1133
in Japan, 2324–2335, 2358–2359
Japanese tantric paradigm in, 2332–2333
kālacakra-maṇḍala and, 1148–1149
Kami cults and, 338–340
in Khmer empire, 1907
to Kūkai, 2328–2329
monarchs in, 1913
Newar Buddhism and, 1148
Prajñāpāramitā and, 1803 n.58
as religion, 1140–1146
rituals in, 1904
scholarship on, 1110 n.96, 1150–1151, 2335–2336
Shingon Buddhism and, 1136–1137
Shingon Mission and, 1133–1135
Tenzin Gyatso for, 1141–1142
in Tibet, 1137–1140, 1160
Tibetan yoga and, 1144–1146
in True Buddha School, 1138
wisdom in, 1900
Yogi Chen for, 1138–1139
in Zhenyan Samantabhadra lineage, 1137–1140
"Tantric Ethics" (Sparham), 986
tantric revival
ceremonies in, 2391 n.39
in China, 2363–2369, 2384–2388
at Fu Dong Ji, 2378–2382
in Japan, 2390 n.22, 2392 n.69
at Kōyasan Muryōkō-in Branch Temple, 2374–2376
to Mahā Praṇidhāna Kuta Mantrayāna, 2377–2378
Mantra School Bright Lineagea nd, 2369–2371
in Taiwan, 2382
in Xiu Ming Society, 2376–2377
to Zhenyan Samantabhadra lineage, 2371–2374
"Tantric Theravāda" (Crosby), 959
Tantric Treasures (Jackson, Roger), 1491
"Tantrism in China" (Zanning), 60
Tanwuchen, 2662
Tanxu, 1437, 2665–2666
Tan Xu, 411
Tanyao, 998
Tao Hongjing, 211, 213
Taoism, 870, 1077–1078, 2278–2279
Tao Zongyi, 1657–1658
Tapihritsa, 136
Tārā, 689–690, 1911–1912, 1913*f*
Tārā cult, 1203
Tāranātha
Madhyamaka Buddhism to, 1464
in maritime trade, 1519, 1526
Mathes on, 2751
scholarship and, 100, 1376–1378, 1386, 1788, 1796, 1966, 2746–2747
zhentong to, 2746, 2750
Tarkapañcanana, Jagannatha, 873
Tarmashirin, 1637
Tarthang Tulku, 1446, 2497
Tashi Gomang Stupa, 856*f*
Tashi Namgyel, Dakpo, 1486–1487, 1490
Tath, Huot, 377
Tathāgata, 1456
Tathāgatagarbha tradition, 2292
Tatsag Tsewanggyal, 848, 853, 2594
tattoos, 113 n.24, 232, 238
Tattvasaṃgraha tantra, 1208
Tattvaviniścaya (Asaṅga), 23–24
Tatz, Mark, 213
Taube, Manfred, 1657–1658
taxonomies, 591–593, 2350–2351, 2718–2719
teachers, 1116–1117
Teaching on Empowerment, 1476–1477
teachings. *See* education
tea drinking, 646–647
Teasdale, John, 1950–1951
technology
apps, 1016
digital media, 2565–2566
education and, 1014–1016
entertainment and, 1015–1016
"Great Love Technology Company," 2618
media, 2553
in modernity, 387
monks and, 1875
for online Buddhist communities, 501
secular Buddhism and, 1118–1119
in South Asia, 1042–1045
Tzu Chi University of Science and Technology, 2618
Teeuwen, Mark, 346
Tegüder, 1642
Teiser, Stephen F., 821–823, 1238
Teja, Jaya, 112 n.13
telegraph squad, 2157*f*
Teleki, Krisztina, 1585–1586, 1588, 1594–1595, 1615
Il Tempio Oracolare di gNas-chuṇ (Ricca), 1755
"Temple and Society in the New World" (Bankston and Hidalgo), 2243
Temple of Universal Brightness (TOUB), 2370, 2372–2373

temples. See also *specific topics*
in Cambodia, 1887
in Canada, 1115–1116
in China, 1869–1871
museums and, 72–75
for *Naikan*, 1707–1708
resettlement and, 1112–1113
Tendai School. See also *specific topics*
Annen on, 2336
exoteric thought in, 2333
history of, 750, 2036–2039, 2045–2046, 2051–2052, 2330, 2663 (See also *specific topics*)
Kūkai and, 2182
monks in, 2063
Nichiren in, 2335
Saichō and, 2361 n.6
scholarship on, 2351–2358
in Shingon Buddhism, 2181–2184, 2333–2334, 2350–2351, 2358–2359
taxonomies in, 2350–2351
to Tokuitsu, 2331–2332
Tendai zasu Ryōgen kishō (Ryōgen), 2051–2052
Tendzin Drakpa, 2495
Tenga Rinpoche, 695–696
Tenji (emperor), 2196, 2199–2200, 2202–2203
Ten Kings of Hell, 790–791, 792*f*
Tenmu (emperor), 2199–2200
Tennent, Emerson, 1045–1046
Tennyi Lingpa, 134
Tennyson, Alfred Lord, 717–718
Tenpé nyima, 1381
Ten Point Sādhana (Nyangrel Nyima Özer), 1746–1748
ten realms, 1767–1768
Ten Stanzas on Reality, 1476–1477
Tensung, 1436–1437
Ten Troublemakers, 271
Tenugi cleaning cloths, 774, 775*f*
Tenzin Dalai Khan, 2016–2017
Tenzin Gyatso
Kelsang Gyatso and, 2077
leadership of, 908, 1586
in lectures, 2077
in modernity, 2533–2534
scholarship on, 433–437, 1067–1068, 1141–1142, 1951–1952, 2021
Tenzin Mariko, 1989
Terbish, L., 1386–1387
Terdak Lingpa, 1442
Teresa of Avila, 508
terma collections, 838–839, 1140, 1161–1162. See also *specific texts*
Termas, 112 n.4
terminal abbreviation, 1208
territorial rulers, 1800*t*
Terwiel, B. J., 575–576, 970, 1891
Testament of Ba, 808, 2582
Testament of Wa, 2542–2543
tetralemma (*catuṣkoṭi*), 536–537
Tetsugen, 2563
Teun Goudriaan, 2303–2304
Texas Christian University, 2382
Text of a Prayer Made by the Great Master Zizhe of Tiantai, 807
texts. See *specific texts*
textual revelation, 2545
textual selectivity, 2140–2141
Thailand
activism in, 904, 913
artifacts in, 75–76
authority in, 2067–2068
Bangkok National Museum in, 74–75, 1805 n.108, 1908, 1919, 1920*f*, 1937 n.119
Buddha images in, 66–67
Buddhism in, 1573–1574, 2277–2278
Buddhist chaplaincy in, 176 n.69, 465–466
Buddhist media in, 2571 n.36
Burma/Myanmar and, 70, 1579, 1729–1730, 2068–2070, 2265–2266, 2404–2407, 2560
Cambodia and, 2214, 2406
Chakri dynasty in, 2063–2064
China and, 1576, 2069
cosmology in, 486
culture of, 906, 1576, 1884
Dalai Lama in, 1073
education in, 1573
ethnicity in, 1891
Fine Arts Department in, 76–77
global Theravāda Buddhism and, 1100–1101
government of, 1579
higher education in, 1578
history of, 68, 375–378, 1095–1096, 1100
imaging Buddha in, 1301 n.51, 2268–2269
India and, 69–70
interdependence in, 159 n.47
International Council of Monuments and Sites to, 77
Japan and, 75
jātaka in, 1369–1370
Laos and, 73, 1115, 1580, 1733–1734, 1890–1891
lay Buddhism in, 165, 168–169
LGBTIQ+ Buddhists in, 1990
lineages in, 963–964
literature from, 499–500

Luang Phor Khoon in, 894
Mahachulalongkornrajavidyalaya University in, 1578
in modernity, 2432 n.94
monarchs in, 1734
monasteries in, 74
Mongkut in, 2127
monks in, 360–361, 895
Mūlasāsana in, 2555
narratives in, 1729
Nepal and, 1574–1575
paritta manuscript in, 2559–2560
relics in, 1525–1526
religion in, 2236–2237
The Royal Chanting Book in, 1883–1884
royalty in, 1046
Sangha Act in, 2417–2418
scholarship on, 1891–1892
Somdet To in, 965, 970
Southeast Asia and, 1730
South Korea and, 176 n.69
sovereignty in, 73–74
Sri Lanka and, 906–907, 1572–1574, 1578, 1726, 2243
Thai Forest Tradition, 1081–1082, 1085–1086, 1117, 1950–1951
Thai language, 484–485, 965
Thai scriptural nation-building, 1049–1051
Theravāda Buddhism in, 499, 2236, 2417–2418, 2665
Tibet and, 2518–2519
tourism in, 1081–1082, 1085
tradition in, 1103
translations of, 2061–2062
Tzu Chi in, 2627
U.S., and, 2235
Vietnam and, 466
women in, 1102, 1117, 1119–1120, 2665
YBA in, 2127
Zen Buddhism in, 176 n.68
Thammayut sect, 967
Thăng Long, 1039–1040
Thangthong Gyalpo, 2489
Thanh, Son Ngoc, 190 n.71
Ṭhānissaro, 913, 1815
al-Thaqafī, Muhammad ibn al-Qāsim, 1671–1672
Thatcher, Margaret, 2129–2130
thaumaturgy, 209–210
Theg chen po la 'jug pa (Gnyal), 25
theism, 2140–2141
Theodotos, 939–940
theology, 144 n.37, 708–709, 1211, 1672–1674, 1681, 2627
Theory of Relativity, 1609
therapy rooms, 1706, 1711
Theravāda Buddhism. See also *specific topics*
Abhayagiri branch of, 2429 n.45, 2433 n.109
bioethics in, 162–163, 170–171
Buddha in, 1888–1889
in Burma/Myanmar, 2417
in Cambodia, 2417–2418
Chinese Buddhism and, 998
culture of, 1885–1888, 2658
education with, 2433 n.114
ethics in, 997
history of, 2394–2399, 2420–2421
in India, 2395–2396
international relations and, 2402–2403
jātaka and, 1364–1365, 1367
Khuddaka Nikāya in, 1366
in Laos, 2417–2418
lay Buddhism and, 2418–2420
Mahāyāna Buddhism and, 72–73, 238–239, 703, 862 n.12, 982, 1103, 1442–1443, 2231, 2234, 2241, 2269, 2432 n.97
mercy killing in, 171–172
modernity and, 1148, 2412, 2414–2418
Nidāna-kathā in, 1366–1367
Nikāyas and, 2412–2414, 2430 n.69
nuns in, 2073
origins of, 2235–2239
Pali Buddhism and, 113 n.25, 1335–1336, 1521, 2068–2069, 2408–2411
politics of, 1889–1890, 2231–2232
protection practices for, 1879–1885
Queer Theory and, 1986–1987
reform in, 2399–2402
as religion, 863 n.35
sacred texts of, 1884–1885, 1890–1892
scholarship on, 144 n.33, 2429 n.42
Shakyamuni Buddha and, 1309
in Southeast Asia, 2406–2407
in Sri Lanka, 2245–2246, 2396–2399, 2403–2404, 2416, 2427 n.30, 2429 n.49
in Thailand, 499, 2236, 2417–2418, 2665
Theriya lineage and, 2407–2411
tradition of, 1053
in Vietnam, 2233
women in, 2666
Thibaw (king), 370, 1049
Thihathu (king), 1732
thinking, 1297 n.9, 1317–1318. *See also* intention
Thin Red Line (film), 404–405
Thomas, Edward, 948
Thomas, Frederick William, 820, 1814

Thompson, Joseph, 1944
Thoreau, Henry David, 2710
thought. See *specific topics*
thought concomitants (*caitasika*), 6
Thousand Buddhas, 547–548, 548*f*
A Thousand Hands (Fisher and Michon), 454, 471–472
Three Essentials of the Maitreya School (Taixu), 2284–2285
Threefold Lotus Sutra, 2624
three Nyepas (humors), 2530–2531
three-pagoda system, 2051–2052
Three Principal Aspects of the Path (Tsongkhapa), 1566
"Three Principles of the People" (Sun Yat-sen), 2281
"Three Turnings of the Wheel of Dharma" (Blumenthal), 2464
three wheels of doctrine
  awakening in, 116–117
  Gautama Buddha and, 2453–2454
  hermeneutics and, 2457–2458, 2462–2464
  Mahāyāna Buddhism in, 2455–2456
  nihilism in, 2458–2460
  outline of, 2460–2462
  scholarship on, 2464–2465
Throthung, 2490
Thủ, Thích Trí, 2438
Thub bstan rgya tsho, 1504
Thubten Chokyi Nyima, 2020–2021
Thubten Gyatso, 1067, 2020–2021
Thubten Yeshe, 1140
Thubten Zopa, 1140–1141
thukdam, 2507
Thūpavaṃsa, 1722, 1724, 1726, 1729
Thupten Gyatso, 2530
Thupten Lungtok Namgyal Trinlé, 1068–1069
Thurman, Robert A. F., 628–629, 1142, 2455–2456, 2464–2465, 2469–2470
Tianbao shidao lu, 813
Tiansheng (Li Zunxu), 660–661. *See also* flame-of-the-lamp records
Tiantai, 2218, 2224
  doctrine, 2325–2326
  philosophy, 268, 1257
  school, 288, 336, 2463–2464
  studies, 2182
Tiantai Deshao, 658
Tibet. See also *specific topics*
  Advayasamatāvijayamahākalparāja in, 1469 n.19
  Afghanistan and, 1604
  Amitābha in, 1970–1971
  aspiration prayers in, 1965–1968
  Atiśa in, 1405–1406, 1546–1547
  authority in, 1384
  autobiography in, 185–186
  Avalokiteśvara in, 1979 n.45
  Bön tradition in, 127–130, 2314
  Buddhist teachers in, 1394–1401
  caves in, 1853–1854
  Central Asia and, 1501–1505
  China and, 112 n.5, 138, 1067–1068, 1092 n.53, 1132–1133, 1461–1462, 1591–1592, 1610
  cosmology in, 486–487
  culture of, 743, 2023, 2631 n.10
  Dalai Lama in, 94, 1132
  Dhāraṇī of the Heart of Ārya-Aparimitāyurjñāna in, 1964
  diaspora in, 501
  Drukpa Kagyü school in, 862 n.17
  Dunhuang and, 807–808
  Dunhuang texts in, 1964–1965
  Dzogchen in, 835–836, 1141
  education in, 1063–1064
  emperors in, 2575–2576
  environmental justice in, 352–354
  exile from, 2021–2022
  Free Tibet movement, 908
  funeral rites in, 2473–2475
  Ganden Potrang government in, 2504, 2517
  geo-cultural, 421–424
  in globalization, 1144–1146
  goddesses in, 1160
  gold in, 1545–1546
  government of, 2544
  hidden lands in, 1854, 1856
  homa in, 1202
  imaging Buddha in, 1297 n.10
  India and, 1072 n.16, 1142, 1873, 2008–2010, 2470–2471
  Indo-Tibetan tantra, 2174
  Japan and, 1610
  lakes in, 1853
  lamas in, 1727
  language in, 740–741, 1378
  LGBTIQ+ Buddhists in, 1988–1989
  Longchenpa in, 1441–1442
  Madhyamaka Buddhism in, 1462–1464
  mahāmudrā in, 1472, 1487–1489
  medieval, 1447
  mediums in, 1751–1753
  Mipam in, 1560
  modernity in, 2642
  monasteries in, 730–731, 1754–1755, 2664
  monasticism in, 1415 n.62

Mongolia and, 1041, 1378–1379, 1382, 1385, 1387, 1599–1600, 1608
mountain *nés*, 1801 n.23, 1852–1853
Naphu monastery in, 847–850
Native Tibetans, 2650–2651
natural sites in, 1854
Nechung monastery and, 1750–1754
nés in, 1850–1851
ontology in, 1071 n.7
oracles in, 1755–1756
Padmasambhava in, 2641
pilgrimage in, 1844–1854
politics of, 1592–1593
power objects in, 2517–2518
Pure Land Buddhism in, 1960–1968, 1971–1974
Qing dynasty and, 1135
reincarnation system in, 2010, 2018–2020
relics in, 2583
religion in, 1376
religious history of, 1536–1538
Rimé movement in, 2747
Russia and, 1382
sacred places in, 1846–1848
Śrī Vijaya in, 963
Sukhāvatī in, 1977 n.11
tantra in, 1135–1140, 1158, 2312–2313, 2516
Tantric Buddhism in, 1137–1140, 1160
teachings from, 2744–2745
Thailand and, 2518–2519
tradition in, 1731
translations from, 1962–1965, 2027 n.1, 2076–2077, 2323 n.79
Tsongkhapa in, 1469 n.8
Tucci on, 2469
Uyghurs and, 787–788
Vajrayāna Buddhism and, 969, 2487
vinaya texts in, 2664
visionary Buddhism in, 2542–2545
visionary yogas in, 2547–2548
Western appropriation of, 1092 n.53
women in, 2668
Yoga Tantras in, 967–968
zhentong in, 2745–2748
Tibet (Shakabpa), 1068–1069
Tibetan Academy of Social Sciences, 1755–1756
Tibetan art, 112 n.8
Tibetan Autonomous Region, 1801 n.6, 1837–1838
Tibetan Book of the Dead
in anthropology, 2484 n.32
death in, 2470–2471
funeral rites in, 2473–2475
history of, 2467–2468
intermediate state in, 2471–2473
luminosity in, 2484 n.27
100 peaceful and wrathful deities in, 2476–2478
rituals in, 2544–2545
scholarship on, 839, 1945, 1970, 2480–2481
teachings in, 2475–2476
translations of, 2468–2470
in Western scholarship, 2478–2480
Tibetan Buddhism. See also *specific topics*
Abhisamayālaṃkāra in, 24–25
Atiśa in, 1409
authority in, 2526 n.69
Avalokiteśvara to, 93–94
Buddhist wizards in, 585–586
Candrakīrti in, 627
in Central Asia, 1038
in China, 5, 12, 61, 63, 1084, 1143
Chöd in, 692
consequentialism in, 623
culture, 2008–2009
debates in, 729–730, 733–735
deities in, 1072 n.10, 1158–1160
direct experience in, 2541–2542
divination in, 2542–2543
in East Asia, 2
education in, 1376–1377
environment to, 352–354
evolution of, 1849–1850
eyes in, 2540
Geluk tradition in, 1754–1755
Gesar epic and, 2487–2490, 2499–2500
Gesar in, 2494–2495, 2497–2499
global Buddhism and, 1079–1080
Great Perfection in, 2546–2549
guardian/protector deities in, 1072 n.16, 1158, 1170–1173
heroic palimpsests in, 2491–2494, 2502 n.23
history of, 730–733, 1062–1063, 2505–2508
iconography from, 788
illusions in, 2545
India and, 17, 25–26, 684–685, 1378–1379
Japan and, 76
jinlap in, 2513–2515, 2525 n.58
Kadampa in, 1393–1394, 1405–1406
Kagyü school of, 1536, 1551–1552
Kālacakratantra in, 2546
Karma Kagyu in, 2000 n.76
Khmer Esoteric Buddhism and, 1938 n.123
language and, 686–687
later lineages of, 1400–1401

Tibetan Buddhism (*continued*)
LGBT workshops and, 2002 n.113
in modernity, 737–745
monasteries in, 892
in Mongolia, 1171
Mongolian Buddhism and, 1468 n.3, 1590
mythology in, 1161–1162
at Nechung monastery, 1742–1746
Pehar in, 1746–1750
philosophy of, 735–737, 2547–2548
pilgrimage in, 1871–1873
post-death experiences in, 2544–2545
power objects in, 2503–2505, 2518–2520
practitioners of, 2546–2548
prophecies in, 2543–2544
protector rituals in, 1160–1161
QT and, 1988–1989
rituals in, 1755–1756, 2495–2497, 2504
rubrics for, 2511–2513
Śaivite complex in, 1162–1164
scholarship on, 9–10, 694–695, 1394–1401, 2524 n.36
schools of, 10
Sherap Özer and, 685
Shingon Buddhism and, 1132–1133
socio-politics in, 2517–2518
source materials for, 696
in South Asia, 1140
Sri Lanka and, 83–84
in Taiwan, 2365, 2388
textual revelation in, 2545
theories in, 2513–2515
Tibetan Buddhist manuscripts, 820
Tibetan Tantric Buddhism, 1537
tradition in, 1415 n.62, 2540–2542
transcendent eyes in, 2540–2541
Tsadra Foundation for, 695
tu in, 2513–2515, 2526 n.59
Vinayasūtra in, 2664
visionary Buddhism and, 2539, 2548
Western scholarship on, 1072 n.14
worldly aims of, 2542–2545
Tibetan Freedom Concert, 226
Tibetan language, 1603–1604, 2122 n.14, 2266
Tibetan-language materials, 807–808, 820
Tibetan mediatic mimesis, 1041–1042
Tibetan medicine, 1449 n.23, 2519–2520, 2527–2535
Tibetan Painted Scrolls (Tucci), 443, 1068–1069
Tibetan Religious Art (Loden Sherap Dagyab), 443–444
Tibetan Renaissance, 1472, 1478–1480
Tibetan Renaissance (Davidson, Ronald), 2024
Tibetan Tantric Buddhism, 1537
Tibetan writing system, 1612
Tibetan yoga, 1144–1146
Tibetan Yoga and Secret Doctrines, 694–695
Tibetology, 846
Tibeto-Mongol-Buryat medicine, 2529–2530
Ṭīk chung (Rngog), 24–25
Tillemans, Tom, 627–629, 1465, 1838
Tilopa, 1476–1477, 1536
timira, 630 n.2
Tinabotuo, 1786
Tinsley, Elizabeth, 758–759
Tintai tradition, 2325
Tipiṭaka, 145, 150, 2408, 2555, 2560, 2564, 2570 n.28. *See also* Pali Buddhism
Titmuss, Christopher, 912
Toba (emperor), 2185
Tōdaiji, 2184, 2201–2202, 2207–2208
Toda Jōsei. *See also* Soka Gakkai
biography of, 2221
death of, 2213
Ikeda Daisaku and, 2212, 2220
leadership of, 2211–2213
Nichiren Buddhism to, 2221
reputation of, 2212, 2219–2220, 2222
Toganoo Shoun, 60
Togashi Masachika, 2041
Toghan-Temür, 1638–1639
Togtoo-Bukha (emperor), 1640–1641
Tōin, Vincente, 866
Tōji Temple, 2178–2179, 2181–2182
Tōjō Kagenobu, 1762
Tokden Jampal gyatso, 1062–1063
Tokī, Hōriou, 1212
Toki Jōnin, 1762
Tokugawa Ieyasu, 755
Tokuitsu, 2331–2332, 2352–2353
Tokunaga Seiko, 303–304
Tokyo, Japan, 704–705
Tokyo Imperial University, 702, 704
Tola, Fernando, 1466–1467
Tomabechi Seiichi, 747, 755, 759
Tomatsu, Yoshiharu, 472
Tominaga Nakamoto, 182
Tōmitsu, 2340–2341, 2349, 2355–2359. *See also* specific topics
Tomoe, Moriya, 1357
"Tomorrow Never Knows" (song), 2480
Tongue of Flames Tantra, 2643–2644
Tōnomine, 2054
Tōnomine ennen shishō, 757
Tönpa Shenrab, 112 n.8, 2545
Tönyön Samdrup, 689
Tooth Relic Temple, 71–72
Töpa Bhadra, 689
Topmiller, Robert J., 2440, 2447–2448

Toqto'a, 1636, 1642
Toramāṅa (king), 944–945
Töregene (empress), 1624
Törö Baikhu, 1648
Torres, Cosme de, 866, 875
Toshiichi Endō, 153
Total Omniscience, 19–20
To the Wonder (film), 404–405
TOUB. *See* Temple of Universal Brightness
To Understand Buddhism (Hanh), 2437
tourism
  during COVID-19, 192
  from Europe, 232
  at Great Buddha Land, 1011
  to Hsi Lai Temple, 1013
  human-made sites and, 1854–1855
  Mount Emei Tourism Company, 1873–1874
  religion and, 1014
  to Taiwan, 1011–1012
  in Thailand, 1081–1082, 1085
  at Tooth Relic Temple, 71–72
  at World Heritage Sites, 68
"Toward a Modern Buddhist Hagiography" (Chia), 1222
Toward a Modern Chinese Buddhism (Pittman), 2294–2295
Toyotomi Hideyoshi, 2356
trade, Maritime Buddhism and, 1518–1521
tradition. *See also* specific traditions
  in art, 425
  of Buddhist philosophy, 529–533, 539–540
  in China, 2294, 2312
  in Christianity, 453
  in Confucianism, 2290
  Cousins on, 969–970
  Crosby on, 964, 967, 969–970
  in Daoism, 269
  in East Asia, 2313
  education and, 2131–2132
  engaged Buddhism and, 919–920
  of four noble truths, 974–976
  Indic, 203–205
  of Kagyü lineage, 1478, 2313
  living traditions, 2267–2268
  in Mahāyāna Buddhist tantra, 966–968
  of meditation, 967–968
  religious, 2313–2314
  in Taiwan, 2170 n.26
  of tantra, 2277–2279, 2301–2302
  in Tibetan Buddhism, 1415 n.62, 2540–2542
  in Vajrayāna Buddhism, 980
  in Yogācārā Buddhism, 1464, 2292
  Yoshida Shinto, 1203–1204
Tragthung Dudjom Dorje, 1970–1971
Trailokyavijaya, 961
Training Manual (Śāntideva), 2088
The Training of the Zen Buddhist Monk (D. T. Suzuki), 714–715
Trần Nhân Tông, 1039–1040
Tranquil Meditator stereotype, 234
trans-Asian maritime networks, 1521–1527
Transcendentalism, 702, 721–722, 1080–1081
transcendent eyes, 2540–2541
transformation, 1333–1335
transimperial networks, 113 n.20
Translating Buddhist Medicine in Medieval China (Salguero), 213–214
translations. See also *specific topics*
  ancient, 684–685
  by Bodhiruci, 1205
  of Buddhist sutras, 996–999
  by Burnouf, 872–873, 1464, 1814
  of Candrakīrti, 1462
  of Cantonese, 2392 n.52
  of *cetanā*, 1320
  of Chan literature, 683 n.88
  from China, 3–4, 10
  of Chinese, 2393 n.70
  in colonialism, 873–875
  of *Dhāraṇī of the Heart of Ārya-Aparimitāyurjñāna*, 1964
  in digital materials, 12
  of Dunhuang texts, 1964–1965
  by Dzongsar Khyentse, 1142
  into European languages, 9–10
  of filial piety, 1004–1005
  of four noble truths, 1031–1032
  from France, 33 n.60
  of Gesar epic, 2503 n.29
  with *The Great Tibetan-Tibetan-Chinese Dictionary*, 2514
  by Green, P., 1903, 1905–1906
  by Halhed, 873
  from Hattori, 1801 n.4
  by Hopkins, 1469 n.18
  in Kagyu tradition, 10
  by Kumārajīva, 85–86
  of language, 1963–1964
  of *Lotus Sutra*, 1768–1769
  of Nāgārjuna, 1466
  in Nanbeicho period, 1183–1184
  of Pali Buddhism, 1345 n.183, 2411, 2425 n.9
  of perfections, 1805–1806
  philosophy of, 12
  power objects and, 2525 n.58
  publishing and, 14 n.11
  of Pure Land Scriptures, 1962–1965
  Qubilai Khan and, 1635
  by Rhys Davids, C., 1941
  by Rhys Davids, T. W., 1105, 1941

translations (*continued*)
by Rin chen bzang po, 1398–1399, 1403–1404
of Sanskrit, 1701 n.1, 1801 n.10, 1836–1837, 2474
scholarship and, 2–5, 2322 n.34
by Skorupski, 1212
of *Somaśambhupaddhati*, 1212
of suttas, 994–995, 1114
from Tang dynasty, 2293
of tantra, 2315
from Tibet, 1962–1965, 2027 n.1, 2077, 2323 n.79
of *Tibetan Book of the Dead*, 2468–2470
by Xuanzang, 85, 99–100, 1801 n.11, 2096–2097, 2662
trans men, 1989
transmission, 1333–1335
Transmission of Experiences, 132
"Transmission Problems?" (Gardiner), 2336
transnational Buddhism, 1589–1591
transnational Humanistic Buddhism, 1256–1257
transnationalism, 1259
trans-Pacific Buddhist network, 229–230
transparency, 1583–1584
trans* people, 1990–1993
trans women, 1989
Trashi Gomang, 854
Travellers and Magicians (film), 401
treason, 1545
treasure concealers, 2524 C127.P75 p.39
Treasure of Songs (Saraha), 1566
treasure substance, 2511–2513, 2515–2516, 2524 n.38
Treasure-Trove of Material Arts (Mipam), 1566
Treasury (Vasubandhu), 1331–1332, 1334–1336
Treasury of Abhidharma, 2540–2541
Treasury of Blessings (Mipam), 1566
Treasury of Good Sayings (Shardza Rinpoche), 133
Treasury of Higher Dharma and Commentary, 1328
Treasury of Higher Knowledge with Self-Commentary. See *Abhidharmakośabhāṣya*
Treasury of Jewels, 1563
Treasury of Kagyü Masters (Ducher), 1553
Treasury of Knowledge (Kongtrul), 1553, 2747, 2750
The Treasury of Knowledge (Kongtrul), 695
Treasury of Precious Instructions (Kongtrul), 695
Treasury of Space and Awareness (Shardza Rinpoche), 112 n.15, 135
Treasury of the Supreme Vehicle (Longchenpa), 838
Treasury of Topics (Longchenpa), 135, 838
Treatise Distinguishing the Two Teachings, Exoteric and Esoteric (Kūkai), 2353–2354
Treatise of Resources for Yoga Practitioners. See *Yogācārabhūmi-śāstra*
Treatise on Filial Piety (Qisong), 1003
Treatise on Pulverization (Nāgārjuna), 1455–1456
Treatise on the Great Perfection of Wisdom, 289–290
Treatise on the Ten Stages of Mind of the Secret Mandala (Kūkai), 2354
treatments, in Tibetan medicine, 2532
Treaty of Wesphalia, 1649–1650
"treaty temple," 713 n.26
Tree of Awakening, 118–119
The Tree of Life (film), 404–405
Tricycle (magazine), 2132–2133, 2139
Tri Desongtsen, 2576–2578
Tri Detsuktsen, 2574–2575
Tri Düsong, 2574–2575
Triết, Nguyễn Minh, 2443
Trigault, Nicolas, 870
Trika tradition, 2308
Trilogy of Dispelling Darkness, 1444
Trinkler, Emil, 112 n.16
Trinlé Thayé Dorjé, 2022
Trinley Thaye Dorje, 908, 2000 n.76
Tripitaka, 811, 2558
Triplett, Katja, 279, 310
Trisong Detsen (emperor/king)
Buddhism of, 2577–2580
legacy of, 127–128, 421, 1066, 1742–1743, 1748, 2475, 2494, 2545
life of, 2574–2577
monarchs and, 2580–2583
scholarship on, 2585–2586
yogins and, 2583–2585
Trisvabhāva (Boquist), 2464
Tri Tsukdétsen, 2576–2577, 2583
Trogawa Rinpoche, 2530
Trudeau, Pierre Elliot, 410
True Buddha School, 414–415, 1138
True Realism (Taixu), 2289–2291
"A True Way to Save the World" (Yoshimoto), 1703
Truitt, Allison, 2243
Trungpa, Chogyam, 1988–1989
Truschke, Audrey, 2316
Trust-in-Mind Inscription (Sengcan), 661–662
truth, 1564–1565
Truth, History and Politics in Mongolia (Kaplonski), 1386
Tsadra Foundation, 695
Tsai Ing-wen, 1009
Tsam dance, 1585
Tsangnyön Heruka, 1485, 1538–1541, 1544–1547, 1549–1550, 1552–1553. *See also* Marpa Lotsawa Chökyi Lodrö
Tsangpa Gyare
biographies of, 2593–2594, 2611 n.25, 2611 n.14
birthplace of, 851*f*

collected works of, 2605–2606
Darma Senge and, 854
death of, 2595, 2612 n.39
depictions of, 846*f*
Drukpa Kagyü school and, 851–853, 856–857, 861 n.5, 863 n.37, 2592–2593, 2606–2607
historical map of, 2594–2597
images of, 2593*f*
Jamyang Kunga Senge and, 2610 n.7
leadership of, 850
life of, 2597–2605, 2612 n.35
Ling Repa and, 846–850, 857–859, 861 n.5, 863 n.37, 2606–2607, 2612 n.34
Martin on, 848, 858–859
scholarship on, 846, 851–857, 2610 n.2
Vajrayāna Buddhism to, 2598, 2605
Tsangyang Gyatso, 1066–1067, 2017
tsars, 1599–1601, 1604–1605, 1608, 2529–2530
Tsay Ching, 408–409
Tsele Matsok Rangdrol, 1487–1488
Tselpa Kagyü, 1744
Tsen Kawoché, 2744–2745, 2750
Tserendorji Gung, 1382
Tsering Wangdu Rinpoche, 695–696
Tsewang Chökdrup, 2747
Tshad ma ris pa'i gter, 1041
Tshal pa Kun dg' rdo rje, 1657–1658
Tshe mchog gling yongs 'dzin Ye shes rgyal mtshan, 1397
Tsiu Marpo, 1170–1173
Tsoght Taij, 1655
Tsoghtu taiji, 1652
Tsomo, Karma Lekshe, 913, 1102–1104, 1120–1121
Tso Nam Lee, 1231
Tsong-kha-pa blo-bzang grag-pa, 25–26, 29–30, 627–629, 1041
Tsong kha pa Blo bzang grags pa, 1401–1402
Tsongkhapa Lobzang Drakpa
distinctions from, 1462–1463
Gorampa Sönam Senge and, 1463
in hierarchies, 136
leadership of, 1601–1602, 1643
Longchenpa and, 1445
Madhyamaka Buddhism to, 1470 n.34
to Mipam, 1566
Nāgārjuna and, 1463
scholarship and, 1061–1064, 1139, 1814–1815, 1966, 2014, 2303, 2748–2749 (*See also* Gelukpa)
on three wheels of doctrine, 2460–2462, 2464–2465
in Tibet, 1469 n.8
Tsong Khapa's Speech of Gold in the Essence of True Eloquence (Thurman), 2464–2465
Tsuda Naoshige, 297–298
Tsuen Hsuin Tsien, 2567
Tsuguhito Takeuchi, 2586
Tsuji Zen'nosuke, 2335
Tsukamoto Keisho, 860 n.1, 861 n.5, 942, 950–951
Tsunehiko Sugiki, 1210
Tsunesaburo Makiguchi (Goulah and Gebert), 2226
Tsurtön Wangngé, 1539, 1550
Tsushima Mamoru, 1705
Tsydenov, Samdan, 1601
tu, 2513–2515, 2526 n.59
Từ, Thích Thanh, 2437
Tubten Gyatso, 1604
Tucci, Giuseppe
on Buddhas, 1961
Namkhai Norbu and, 1144–1145
scholarship from, 29–30, 443, 694–695, 1068–1069, 1656–1657, 2641
on Tibet, 2469
on Trisong Detsen, 2586
Tuck, Andrew, 628–629, 1464–1465, 1698
Tucker, Mary Evelyn, 362
Tughlugh-temür, 1637
Tukwan Lobzang Chökyi Nyima, 2594, 2749–2750
Tulang Tuwo inscription, 960–961
Tulku Thondrup, 1446
Tulku Töndup, 1551–1552
Tümen Jasagtu Khan, 1645, 1649–1650, 1653
Tümenkin, 1649
Tümenkin Tsoghtu Khongtayiji, 1655
Tumurtogoo, D., 1657–1658
Tung Lin Kok Yuen, 416
Tứ Phần Luật, 1039–1040
Tupten Ngödrup, 1751–1753
Tupten Püntsok, 1756
Tuq-Temür, 1638
Turkey, 367, 810, 2487–2488
Turner, Alicia, 1097–1098, 1579, 1892
Turner, James, 872, 874
"The Turning of the Dhamma Wheel" (lecture), 1020–1023
Turnour, George, 878–879, 1046–1047
Tüsheet Khan (Tüsiyetü), 2019
Tuttle, Gray, 1068–1069, 1151, 1656–1657, 2025
Tuyuhun Annals, 808
Tweed, Thomas, 240–241, 1088, 1131
Twelve Deeds of Buddha (Poppe and Cleaves), 1656–1658
Twelve Gate Treatise (Nāgārjuna), 1461–1462
twelve sense spheres (*āyatana*), 6
"Twenty-five Works on Inattention" (Maitrīpa), 1475–1477
Twenty-One Profound Points (Tāranātha), 2746
twenty-two controlling faculties (*indriya*), 6

"Two Buddhisms, Three Buddhisms, and Racism" (Hickey), 2718
Two Guardian Kings, 433, 433*f*
Tworkov, Helen, 2132–2133, 2718–2719
Two Truths Doctrine, 915
typological surveys, 933–948
typology, 519, 2515–2517
Tzu Cheng Faith Corps, 2615–2616
Tzu Chi
  abroad, 412
  in Canada, 413–414
  Cheng Yen and, 2613–2616
  during COVID-19, 2620, 2628
  disaster relief to, 2617–2620
  environmental justice to, 2618–2619
  legacy of, 2613, 2625–2628
  reform by, 2616–2617
  refugees to, 2619–2620
  scholarship on, 909, 915, 1254, 1256, 1259–1260, 2628
  schools to, 2620
  Shih, 413–414
  sustainability to, 2620–2625
  for Taiwan, 413
  Tzu Chi Foundation, 196, 2613, 2616–2617, 2617*t*, 2619, 2624, 2626, 2632 n.20
  Tzu Chi Medical Foundation, 2618
  Tzu Chi School of Buddhism, 2621–2625
  vegetarianism to, 2619, 2628
Tzu Chi Culture and Communication Foundation, 2618
Tzu Chi Educational Foundation, 2618

Uccaganāga, 1790–1791
Uda (emperor), 2181–2182, 2184
Udale, Frank B., 39
Udayana (king), 1292, 1724–1725, 1727, 2268
Ueda, Noboru, 29–30
Uejima Susumu, 759
Ueno Katsuyuki, 303–304
Ugraparipṛcchā, 1807–1808
Uighur language, 4
U Kalā, 586
U Kyaw, 566
Ullambana Sūtra, 996, 1002–1005
ultimate truth, 618, 2087
Umayyad dynasty, 1674–1676
Umbrella War, 378
UN. *See* United Nations
Ū Nārada Jetavana Sayadaw, 1048–1049
unborn Zen, 706
unconditioned factors (*asaṃskṛta*), 6
UNESCO. *See* United Nations Educational, Scientific and Cultural Organization
Unexcelled Yoga Tantras, 1416
unfilial practices, 993–994. *See also* filial piety
Unhissavijayagāthā, 1880, 1884–1885, 1888
Unified Buddhist Church of Vietnam, 2234, 2239–2240, 2438–2439, 2442–2443
Union of the Three Jewels (Jatson Nyingpo), 838–839
United Kingdom, 468–469, 2137. *See also* England
United Nations (UN)
  Buddha's Light International Association to, 1009–1010
  Economic and Social Council, 2613
  High Commission for Refugees, 2235–2236
  Millennium World Peace Summit of Religious and Spirituals Leaders, 2165
  refugees to, 2619–2620
  Soka Gakkai and, 2214–2215
  Sustainable Development Goals, 2616, 2619
  Tzu Chi Foundation and, 2619, 2626
United Nations Educational, Scientific and Cultural Organization (UNESCO)
  art to, 795
  Buddhist architecture to, 33 n.55
  contemporary art to, 795–796
  ICOMOS and, 77
  policy, 68
  Ratanakul on, 113 n.24, 165, 167
United States (U.S.)
  activism in, 904–905, 923
  AIBS, 1142
  Alien Land Law, 13 n.5
  Amida Buddha in, 1312
  Anglo-American society, 2129–2131
  Asian Americans, 457
  Australia and, 2137
  Brazil and, 1133–1135
  Buddhist communities in, 2718–2719
  California, 802, 1008, 1012–1014, 1351–1353
  Cambodia and, 2239
  Canada and, 36, 112 n.6, 112 n.8
  Chan Buddhism in, 2160–2163, 2170 n.38
  China and, 1013
  Chinese Exclusion Act in, 1078–1079
  Christianity in, 1311–1312, 1349, 1351–1352
  citizenship, 176 n.69, 462–463
  City of Ten Thousand Buddhas in, 2735
  Constitution, 1648–1649
  culture, 235–236, 922
  decillion in, 1468 n.4
  D. T. Suzuki in, 703–704, 707–708, 723–724
  Emyō in, 1349–1350, 1357

engaged Buddhism in, 910–912
Europe and, 1121, 1361 n.41, 1940, 1945, 2143, 2311
Great American Songbook in, 664–665
Hanh in, 910, 2239
Hart-Celler Act in, 1079
HHMH in, 34–35, 1348–1349, 1357
hunger strikes in, 2438
Imamura families in, 1303–1314
immigration in, 2715–2716
imprisonment camps in, 39–41
Islam in, 48
Japan and, 34–35, 48, 227–228, 707, 1079, 1133–1135, 1151, 1348–1349
Japanese Buddhisms in, 1359 n.7
Kanmo Imamura in, 1310–1311
Kundalini Yoga in, 2314
Laos and, 2238
Library of Congress in, 637
Michigan, 2382
Mutual Security Act, 2156
Naikan in, 1709
Nechung monastery and, 1718 n.33
new-age spirituality in, 2479
Nikkei Buddhists in, 45–48, 1298 n.17
Nisei in, 35–36, 38–39, 41–46, 48
Pennsylvania, 2384–2387
race in, 2715–2716
Refuge Act in, 2235
refugees in, 1115–1116, 2234–2236
religion in, 45–46, 2715–2716
Russia and, 1079
secular Buddhism in, 2127–2128
Shin Buddhism in, 1079
Soka Gakkai in, 2214
Soka Gakkai International in, 911–912
Sri Lanka and, 1114–1115
Taiwan and, 2160, 2734–2735
Texas Christian University in, 2382
Thailand and, 2235
Vietnam and, 2435–2443
violence in, 2225
Western Europe and, 1577
White privilege in, 2718
World War II and, 45–49, 574–575
universal Buddhism, 1308–1313
Universal Buddhist Temple, 410–412
universal causation, 2078–2079
universal causes (*sarvatraga hetu*), 2116
Universalist bioethics, 169
universal ruler (*cakravartin*), 1279
University of California Berkeley, 1310–1311
University of Leipzig, 2145–2146
unmanifest forms, 1344 n.159
Unnanse, Yataramulle, 2710–2711
unpleasant situations, 2084–2085
Unschuld, Paul U., 213–214
U Nu, 375, 599–600, 1883
U Ottama, 375
Upajjhatthana Sutta, 976
Upāli, 2410, 2689–2690, 2693–2695
Upāli's Questions Sutra, 2705 n.105
Upāli sutta, 1322–1323
Upaniṣads, 2306
Upāsakaśīla Sūtra, 1003
Upāyapāśatantra, 808
Upulvan-Rama-Vishnu, 2251–2253
Urban, Hugh, 1141, 2318
urbanization, 778
Urgyen Wangchuk, 2019
U.S. *See* United States
Usami Shue, 1708–1709
Usarski, Frank, 1357–1358
Uṣṇīṣavijayadhāraṇī, 1888
Utah, 1351–1352
ʿUthmān, 1675–1676
Uttarādhyayana sūtra, 1209–1210
Uttarakuru, 2127, 2286–2287
Uttaratantra, 2750
U Wāyāmā Bhiwuntha, 144 n.36
U Wirathu, 1099
Uyghur Patronage in Dunhuang (Russell-Smith), 800–801
Uyghurs, 787–788, 1871–1872
Uygur Buddhism, 1623, 1631, 1634–1637
Uzbekistan, 632–633

Vade Mecum (HHMH), 1308
Vāgīśvarakīrti, 1519, 1526
Vaibhāṣika theory, 1344 n.164, 2110–2115
Vaidalyaprakaraṇa, 1688–1689
Vaidehī (queen), 2679, 2683–2688
Vaidya, P. L., 125, 1044–1045, 2088
Vaināśikas, 2112
Vainyagupta (king), 1794
Vairocana, 293, 306–307, 1503, 1527, 2578, 2584
Vairocanābhisaṃbodhi, 1521
Vairocanābhisaṃbodhi tantra, 1208–1209, 1212
Vairocana Buddha, 2201
Vairocanarakṣita, 2077
Vaiṣṇava Pāñcarātra tradition, 2306, 2309–2311
Vajrabodhi
legacy of, 963, 2175–2176, 2363–2364
scholarship and, 53–55, 60–63

Vajrabuddhi, 1517, 1519, 1522, 1524
Vajracchedikā-prajñāpāramitāsūtra, 1038–1039
Vajradeva, 1791–1792
Vajrakīla-mūlatantrakhaṇḍa (VKMK), 2642
Vajrakīla tantras
  birth of, 2637–2638
  as conqueror, 2638–2639
  destruction with, 2647–2648
  kīlas and, 2648–2650
  philosophy of, 2640–2643
  rituals with, 2643–2647
  in Sa skya school, 2655 n.19
  scholarship on, 2641–2642, 2650–2651
  as vedic antecedents, 2635–2636
Vajrakilaya, 2650–2651
vajra masters, 1422–1431
Vajrapāṇi, 549–551, 549*f*, 555–557, 1603, 2583
Vajrapañjaratantra, 1553
Vajra Realm Mandala, 2176, 2181, 2185
Vajrasadhu, 1444
Vajrasattva, 1419–1420, 1423–1425, 1428, 1527
Vajravarman, 1205
Vajrayāna Buddhism
  cosmology in, 484, 486
  demons in, 2492
  Madhyamaka Buddhism and, 1462
  Mahāyāna Buddhism and, 986
  medicine in, 257–260
  meditation in, 521
  Mongolian Buddhism and, 1592
  organizations, 1591
  rebirth in, 2019
  scholarship on, 62, 2009–2010
  tantra and, 521–522, 977–978, 1813–1814, 2432 n.97
  texts from, 2353
  three wheels doctrine and, 2463
  Tibet and, 969, 2487
  tradition in, 980
  to Tsangpa Gyare, 2598, 2605
  weikzas in, 2063–2064
  Yogācārā Buddhism and, 1463
Vakkali (monk), 116
valid cognition, 630 n.5
Valignano, Alessandro, 866, 870, 875
Valmiki, 2247, 2254
Vaṃsadīpanī, 1722, 1728–1729
vaṃsa texts, 1722–1723, 1731
varadamudrā, 1292–1293
Varāhadeva, 944
Varela, Francisco, 1951–1952, 2533–2534
"Variant Dharma" (Scherer), 1993
The Varieties of Religious Experience (James, W.), 703, 715, 721–722
Varṇarītiya, 1046–1047
Vásquez, Manuel A., 200
The Vast Expanse of the View, 134
vastus, 2657
Vasubandhu
  on Abhidharma Buddhism, 1–2, 1833, 2097
  on accumulation, 1330
  AKB and, 2111, 2113–2114
  Asaṅga and, 23–24
  Atiśa and, 1401–1402
  on *ātman*, 9
  Buddhaghosa and, 117, 1327–1328, 1331–1332, 1334–1335, 1343 n.139
  on cosmology, 6–7, 481–482, 484
  Dignāga and, 529–530
  epistemology of, 1802 n.29
  on existence, 2471–2472
  on five effects, 6
  Ganeri and, 11
  on *Hṛdaya*, 2
  influence of, 2204
  on intention, 1331–1332
  on karma, 1331–1332, 1334, 1344 n.162
  Kritzer and, 11
  on language, 1801 n.26
  philosophy of, 1
  Puguang and, 2097, 2098*t*
  on *samādhi*, 9
  on *saṃsāra*, 8
  Sanskrit and, 15 n.34
  as *sautrāntika*, 1800 n.1
  scholarship and, 2, 11–12, 15 n.32, 1335–1336, 1819–1820, 1833
  on sentient beings, 7
  on thought, 1343 n.144
  Treasury of Abhidharma, 2540–2541
Vasumitra, 9–10, 2122 n.3, 2395–2396, 2398–2399
Vātsīputrīya. *See* Theravāda Buddhism
Vedic tradition. *See also* Hinduism
  chandasi and, 159 n.43
  fire in, 1217 n.66
  in India, 2471–2472
  Indo-Iranian tradition and, 1199–1200
  knowledge in, 567–568
  philosophy of, 2256
  scholarship on, 1200–1201
  Vedas, 144–145, 2305
  vedic antecedents, 2635–2636
  Vedic literature, 2247–2248
  Zoroastrianism and, 2487–2488
Veere, Hendrik van der, 2359
vegetarianism, 915, 2619, 2628
Veidlinger, Daniel, 240, 2567

Veith, Ilza, 311
Ven, Deibbasek, 1732
veracity, 166
Verchery, Lina, 396, 399–400, 417
Vergara, Paola Mortari, 443–444
Vermeulen, Michael, 2002 n.114
vernacular language, 1736–1737
Verses of the Chan School, 661–662
Verses of the Elder Monks, 116
Vertovec, Steven, 1347–1348, 1359 n.2
Vesely-Flad, Rima, 922
Vessantara (prince), 1364–1365, 1370
Vetter, Tillman, 1838
Vetturinim, Gianpaolo, 1407
Vibhajjavāda, 2398
Vibhajjavādins, 2112, 2426 n.16, 2431 n.79
Vibhaṅga, 1342 n.104
Vibhanga Aṭṭhakathā, 257
vibhangas, 2657
Vibhishana, 2247, 2249–2251, 2253–2254. See also *satara varan devi*
Vichy France, 378–379
Victoria, Brian, 724
Victorian Buddhism, 2128–2129, 2708–2709
vidhyadhāra. *See* Buddhist wizards
Vidya Dehejia, 1294
Vidyādhara, 948
Vidyalankara, Baneshvara, 873
Vidyārāja, 271
Vidyodaya Buddhist College, 372–373
Vidyottama Tantra, 2642
Vietnam. *See also* colonialism
  Buddhist chaplaincy in, 466
  Cambodia and, 2235, 2311
  Canada and, 2239–2241
  Chan Buddhism in, 1987
  communism in, 190 n.71, 906–907
  culture of, 1039–1041, 2002 n.113, 2233, 2242, 2451 n.58
  Hanh for, 904
  India and, 2233
  Korea and, 83–84
  publishing in, 1039–1041
  religion in, 2234
  Siam and, 1095–1096
  Taiwan and, 1084, 2667
  Thailand and, 466
  Theravāda Buddhism in, 2233
  Unified Buddhist Church of Vietnam, 2234, 2239–2240, 2438
  U.S., and, 2435–2443
  Vietnamese Buddhism, 2239–2242, 2434–2448, 2449 n.7, 2451 n.58
  War, 466, 904–905
Vietnam (Hanh), 2439–2441, 2448
vighna, 2654 n.5
Viīrendravikhyāta, 1902
Vijayabāhu (king), 1520, 2404
vijñāna (consciousness), 6, 2028 n.19
Vikings, 1471 n.52
Vikramaśila Mahāvihāra, 1786–1788, 1797–1798
Vimalakīrti, 289, 556*f*, 557
Vimalakīrti Nirdeśa Sūtra, 483, 1437, 1501–1502, 1807, 1809
Vimalakīrti Nirdeśa Sūtra (Lokakṣema), 1498
Vimalakirti Sutra, 557
Vimalamitra, 835, 837, 1438–1439, 1445–1446, 2584
Vimalaratnalekha (Atiśa), 1398–1399
Vimalaśaṅkha, 1517
Vimānavatthu, 1889–1890
Vima Nyingtik, 1438
Viṃśatikā (Vasubandhu), 1802 n.29
Vimuktisena, Ārya, 25–26, 28–29
Vimuttimagga, 113 n.24, 113 n.26, 149–150
vinayas
  balance in, 2158–2159
  doctrine and, 601
  eyes and, 2540
  of Nikāyas, 2430 n.68
  in Pali Buddhism, 2067, 2138–2139
  rules from, 207–208
  Sanskrit and, 151–152
  scholarship on, 144 n.34, 208, 1578–1579, 2066–2067
  sūtras and, 2098–2099
  women in, 2666–2667
Vinayasūtra, 2664
vinaya texts
  in China, 1865
  codes in, 1185–1186
  cooking in, 113 n.24
  in East Asia, 2660–2663
  in Japan, 2663–2664
  in modernity, 2664–2666
  for monasteries, 2656–2659
  monks and, 1879–1880, 2556
  nuns and, 2666–2667
  origins of, 810
  rules of, 2070
  scholarship on, 637, 2554–2555, 2667–2668
  Schopen on, 2072
  sexuality in, 1986
  in South Asia, 2660
  in Southeast Asia, 2660
  in Tibet, 2664
  Vinaya Piṭaka, 150–151, 248–252, 255–256, 2408–2409

Vincent, Brice, 1897
violence, 1469 n.8, 1583, 1585, 1611–1613, 2136, 2225
Viollet-le-Duc, E. E., 76–77
Vipassana movement, 509–514, 1053, 1104–1105, 1117–1118, 2566
Vipulaśrīmitra, 946–947, 946*f*, 1785–1786, 1791
Vīradeva, 947
virtual communities, 2137–2138, 2150 n.71
Virtual Orientalism (Iwamura), 233, 240, 398–399, 405–406
virtue, 1065–1068, 1805
virtue ethics, 981–982
Viśa Śūra (king), 808
Vishnu, 554*f*, 555–556, 2249, 2252–2253, 2257, 2260 n.49. See also *satara varan devi*
Vishnudharmmottara Purana, 2247
visionary Buddhism
  awareness in, 2551 n.31
  Indian Buddhist theory and, 2541–2542
  soteriological aims, 2547–2548
  in Tibet, 2542–2545
  Tibetan Buddhism and, 2539, 2548
visionary yogas, 2547–2548
Visions and their Significance, 2543
visual culture
  art history and, 2265–2266, 2272 n.18
  iconography in, 2264–2265
  images in, 2263–2264
  living icons in, 2267–2268
  philosophy of, 2268–2269
  ritual poses in, 2266–2267
  scholarship on, 2262–2263, 2269–2270
"Visualization and Mandala in Shingon Buddhism" (Sharf), 2675, 2678
visualization/contemplation sutras
  with *Ākāśagarbha Contemplation Sutra*, 2677, 2679–2681, 2693–2695
  with *Amitāyus Contemplation Sutra*, 2675, 2679, 2683–2688
  with *Bhaisajyarāja Contemplation Sutra*, 2676–2677, 2679–2680, 2688
  in caves, 2699 n.4
  instructions for, 2684–2688
  with *Maitreya Contemplation Sutra*, 2675–2676, 2678–2679, 2688–2690
  meditation and, 2674–2677
  recitation of, 2677–2678
  repentance with, 2679–2681
  with *Samādhi Sea Sutra*, 2675–2678, 2681–2683
  with *Samantabhadra Contemplation Sutra*, 2676, 2678, 2680–2681, 2690–2693, 2701 n.39
  scholarship on, 2674, 2681–2697
  Sharf on, 2675–2676, 2678, 2699 n.11
  six sense organs and, 2704 n.93
  Visualization Sutras, 517
  Yamabe on, 2700 n.12
Visuddhimagga, 113 n.24, 145–150, 153, 1046–1047, 1336
Viśvamātā, 1419
Vitali, Roberto, 443–444, 1068–1069
VKMK. See *Vajrakīla-mūlatantrakhaṇḍa*
volition, 1299 n.31
Voltaire, 872–873
Vorob'eva-Desiatovskaia, Margarita I., 819
votive tablets, 1918–1923
vows, in Mongolian Buddhism, 1588–1589
Vraḥ Dhanus, 1906–1907
Vrajvallabh Dwivedi, 1491
Vṛtra, 2635, 2653 n.1
Vulture Peak, 354, 356–357, 1439
Vyākhyā (Yaśomitra), 3–4

Wachirayan, 1049–1050
Waddell, Laurence A., 1406–1407
Waipahu Honganji Buddhist Temple, 1310
Wakaki Makiguchi Tsunesaburō (Saitō, S.), 2226
Wake no Hiroyo, 2326–2327
Waking Life (film), 402
Waldheim, Kurt, 2214
Wallace, Vesna, 260–261, 1594–1595, 1615
Wallis, Glenn, 2131–2132, 2144–2145
Walsh, Michael, 891
Walters, Jonathan, 968, 1150, 2427 n.17
Walther, Marco, 850
Wang, Eugene Y., 800–801
Wang, Michelle C., 800–801, 821–823
Wang, Shuqin, 821–823
Wangchen Nyima, 2497–2498, 2502 n.23
Wang Chieh, 2553
Wangchuk Dorjé, 1487
Wangchuk Özer, 1541–1542
Wang Hongyuan, 2365
Wang Jianchuan, 2735–2736
Wang Jie, 321–323
Wang Kentang, 212
Wang Mi, 1000–1001
Wang Tao, 211
Wang Wei, 1228–1229, 1240
Wang Xizhi, 815–816
Wang Yuanlu, 816
Wang Zucheng, 1709
Wan Li texts, 2563
Wannapok, Sathienpong, 2061–2062

Wansong Xingxiu, 666, 1234
war. See *specific wars*
Ward, William, 2252
Warner, Langdon, 798–799
warnings, 2543–2544
War Relocation Authority (WRA), 14 n.18, 16 n.40, 38–41, 45, 49
Waseda University, 702
Watanabe Mariko, 755
Wat Pô Veal Museum, 1897–1899, 1919–1923, 1926
Wat Sithor inscription, 1904–1906
Watson, Burton, 1774–1775
Watts, Alan, 723–724, 1081, 1949–1950
Watts, Jonathan, 472
Waugh, Daniel C., 800
way (*paṭipadā*), 1027–1028
The Way Into the Study of Zen (Hanh), 2442
Wayman, Alex, 101–102, 969, 1311, 1814–1815, 2321 n.18
The Way to Heaven (Judson, A.), 1048
Wazargān āfrīwan, 809–810
"We Are All Gzhan stongpas" (Kapstein), 2750–2751
The Weaving of Mantra (Abe Ryūchi), 2336, 2359
Weber, Max, 888, 892–893, 1017, 2256
Wedemeyer, Christian K., 628–629, 2524 n.36
Wei Chuhou, 1233–1234
weikzas, 2063–2064
Weili, 2378–2382, 2384*f*, 2388
Weinberger, Steven Neal, 1205
Weixiang (Wei Xiang), 2326–2327, 2344–2345
Wei Yuansong, 1233
weizzā. *See* Buddhist wizards
Welch, Holmes, 1579, 2294–2295, 2736
Weller, Robert P., 2625
Welter, Albert, 675–676
Wencheng (emperor), 85
Wensa trūlku, 1376
Wentz, W. Y. Evans, 1489–1490
"We're Not Who You Think We Are" (Chenxing), 1122
West Bengal, 1783, 1792–1793
Westerhoff, Jan, 538, 1465, 1699
Western appropriation, 1092 n.53
Western art, 66–67
Western bioethics, 164–166, 168
Western Buddhism
  Buddhist taxonomies and, 2718–2719
  Christian normativity in, 2713–2715
  culture of, 2715–2716
  elitism in, 1074–1075
  mindfulness in, 2717–2718
  missionaries and, 2712–2713
  in modernity, 185–186, 2716–2717
  Orientalism and, 2707–2712
  QT and, 1989
  race and, 2707–2708
  scholarship on, 2131–2132, 2719
  scientific racism and, 2708
  secular Buddhism and, 2125–2126
Western Cave complexes, 936–937
Western colonialism, 501–503
Western consequentialism, 2077–2078
Western epistemology, 538–539
Western esotericism, 1211
Western Europe, 367, 1577
Western imperialism, 192
Western India, 1521
Western Indonesian Archipelago, 1522–1525
Western Kṣatrapas, 938–943
Western language, 1212, 2696
Western magical practices, 2302
Western modernity, 369, 913–914
Western Orientalists, 113 n.24
Western philosophy, 4, 527–529, 534, 702, 2140
Western psychology, 694
Western religion, 2137
Western scholarship
  ethics in, 172
  gong'an collections in, 664–667
  Lopez on, 181
  perceptions of, 60–61, 1103
  Protestant Christianity and, 966–967
  Tibetan Book of the Dead in, 2478–2480
  on Tibetan Buddhism, 1072 n.14
  Tibetan medicine in, 2533–2534
Western science, 485–486
"We've Been Here All Along" (Hsu), 2718–2719
Whalen, Philip, 361, 1311
Whalen-Bridge, John, 232, 237, 240, 397–403, 405–406
Wheel of Time (Puṇḍarīka), 1474
When the Clouds Part (Brunnhölzl), 2751
While, Alex S., 39
White, David, 144 n.38, 964–965, 2318
White, Marybeth, 1115–1116, 2243
White Crystal Rosary (Nyangrel Nyima Özer), 1746–1748
white leprosy, 289–290
White Lotus (Mipam), 1566
"White Lotus of the Good Law" (Thoreau), 2710
White privilege, 1122, 2718–2719
White Side (*karchok*), 2487–2490
White supremacy, 2719
"White Tantric Kundalini Yoga" (Wild), 1110 n.96
White Tārā, 1377, 1382
Whitfield, Roderick, 800

Whitfield, Susan, 799–800, 824–825
Whitman, Walt, 2710
Why Buddhism Is True (Wright, R.), 2141–2142
Why Has Bodhidharma Left for the East? (film), 402–406
Wichai, Khrūbā, 376
Wickramasinghe, Nira, 1098
Wilber, Ken, 1949–1950
Wild, Heather Jaskirat, 1110 n.96
Wild Geese (Harding and Soucy), 417–418
Wilkens, Jens, 821–823
Wilkins, Charles, 873, 875
Willemen, Charles, 3, 5–6
William, Thomas, 1076, 1080–1081
William of Rubruck, 1628, 1636–1637, 1656–1658
Williams, Angel Kyodo, 911, 1990, 2719
Williams, Duncan Ryūken
  on Japanese American Buddhism, 15 n.25, 40–41, 46, 48–49
  scholarship from, 279, 362, 2716, 2719
Williams, J. Mark G., 1951
Williams, Paul, 17–18, 986, 1567, 2088, 2750–2751
Willis, Jan, 2719
Willock, Nicole, 2025
Wilson, Bryan, 2226–2227
Wilson, H. H., 1814
Wilson, Jeff, 1118, 2145
Wilson, Liz, 184–185
Wilson, Woodrow, 1304–1305
Wimalajothi, Kirama, 1104
Winant, Howard, 2259 n.30, 2714–2715
Wind and Moon (Songpo), 663–664
Winslow, Deborah, 2250
Winternitz, Moriz, 2315
Wirathu, Ashin, 919, 922
wisdom, 19–20, 508, 687, 2087
Wisdom of Buddha (Powers), 125
Wisdom Period, 2463
Wisdom Sutras, 621, 1803 n.60, 1805 n.109
Wittgenstein, Ludwig, 1465, 1470 n.46
Witzel, Michael, 1212
wizards. *See* Buddhist wizards
Wogihara, Unrai, 29–30, 98–99
Wolf, Wade Clark, 200
Wolters, Oliver William, 587
Womb Realm Mandala, 2181–2182, 2185
women. See also *specific topics*
  in Asia, 1119–1121
  biography and, 184–185
  in Buddhism, 93, 1574–1575
  donations from, 1796–1797
  elder care by, 774
  female lamas, 1591
  feminism, 1982, 1989
  in film studies, 144 n.31
  in Hsi Lai Temple, 1102–1103
  illicit thoughts and, 572
  in India, 913, 1101, 1103
  in Japan, 113 n.18, 774
  Kannon and, 93
  laywomen, 2061–2063, 2067–2068
  misogyny, 105
  in monasteries, 1085–1086, 1098
  in Mongolia, 694
  in Mongolian Buddhism, 1587–1588
  ordained, 2066
  in Thailand, 1102, 1117, 1119–1120, 2665
  in Theravāda Buddhism, 2666
  in Tibet, 2668
  trans women, 1989
  in *vinayas*, 2666–2667
  Women's Buddhist Association, 1304, 1306
  women's rights, 918
"Women Challenging the 'Celibate' Buddhist Order" (Noriko), 778–779
Women of Wisdom (Allione), 694–695
Woncheuk, 2454, 2457, 2464
Wong Mou-lam, 1236, 1238
Wood, Thomas E., 1698
woodblock printing, 320–324
Woodroffe, John, 2478–2479
Woods, Tiger, 235–236, 239
Woodside, Alexander B., 2447–2448
Woodward, Hiram
  on Esoteric Buddhism, 959, 961–962, 969
  scholarship from, 1515–1516, 1897, 1904, 1908–1909
Words of My Perfect Teacher (Patrul Rinpoche), 986
world (*loka-nirdeśa*), 5
The World as Will and Representation (Schopenhauer), 1077
World Buddhist Institute, 2283
World Fellowship of Buddhists, 2070
World Health Organization, 1709
World Heritage Sites, 33 n.56, 68, 71–72, 77. *See also* United Nations Educational, Scientific and Cultural Organization
World Parliament of Religions, 1941, 1943
World War I, 465, 2282
World War II
  American Buddhism during, 34–35, 39–41, 1313
  Asia after, 2164
  atomic weapons in, 380–381
  BMNA during, 37–38
  Brazil in, 1134–1135
  Dalai Lama in, 1079–1080
  history of, 48–49
  imprisonment camps in, 48, 2716

Japanese American Buddhist clergy in, 35–39
Japanese Americans in, 34–35, 39–41
Japan in, 35–39, 500–503, 703, 706–707, 1774, 2169 n.18
Nanjing massacre in, 1219
Nazi Germany in, 36
psychological Buddhism after, 1946–1948
religion in, 462
in Taiwan, 2072–2073
U.S., and, 45–49, 574–575
The Worship of Confucius in Japan (McMullen), 759
Wo-suk Hwang, 169
WRA. *See* War Relocation Authority
Wright, Dale Stuart, 1815
Wright, Robert, 2141–2142
writing, 2557–2562, 2570 n.28, 2570 n.20
Writings of Nichiren Shōnin (Kyōtsū), 1774–1775
written canons, 634–637
Wu (emperor), 498
Wu (empress), 320–321, 1190, 1228–1229, 1231–1232, 2201
Wu, Adam, 1222
Wuchang Buddhist Academy, 2283–2285
Wuguang
autohagiography of, 2367–2369
biographical information about, 2391 n.33
to Li, 2376–2377
MSBL and, 2369–2370, 2391 n.39
scholarship and, 1137, 1139–1140, 2367–2369, 2388
to Weili, 2380
Zhuxi Temple and, 2367
Wu-hing, 1795–1796
Wu Hung, 729 n.49
Wujastyk, Dominik, 2316
Wujinzang, 1224–1225
Wumen (Wumen), 666–667
Wumen Huikai, 666–667
Wu of Liang (emperor), 90–91
Wutaishan, 1501–1506, 1632
Wu-xing, 2311
Wu Zetian (emperor), 85, 212, 1038–1039
Wuzhen, 1237–1238
Wuzhun Shifan, 653
Wuzhun yulu, 653
Wuzong (emperor), 2183, 2312
Wylie, Turrell, 1553, 1656–1657, 2024
Wynne, Alexander, 2566–2567

Xavier, Francis, 865–867
Xiandai foxue (periodical), 2730–2731
Xian'er (robotic monk), 1875
Xiang Kai, 1182–1183
xiangke. *See* pilgrimage
Xianyu jing, 1636
Xiaojing, 999–1000, 1002
Xiaolun (Qisong), 993–994, 996
Xiao Lun (Qisong), 1002
Xiaoshan, 212
Xiaowu (emperor), 659
Xiaoyun, 1257
Xiao Yutang, 2726
Xie Jan, 1226
Xie Lingyun, 1232–1233
Xi Jinping, 1231, 1259, 1451 n.64, 2385
"Xin fohua zhi biaozhun" (Tang Dayuan), 1440
Xingci, 2665–2666
Xingxiu, 1234
Xingyun, 413, 1437–1438, 1446–1448, 2166–2167, 2170 n.36
Xingzhanshu, 814
Xinjiang Uyghur Autonomous Region, 1871–1872
Xinjiapo cijishi, 2627
Xinji tianxia xingwang shizu pu, 812–813
Xin Tang shu, 1234
Xinyang yu duihua (Xuecheng), 1259
Xiong, 2392 n.65
Xiongyu, 2377–2378
Xiudao, 2613–2614
Xiu Ming Society, 2376–2377
Xi Xia dynasty, 1623
Xiyuolu (Yelü Chucai), 1657–1658
Xi Zhongun, 1231
Xuanhua, 2735
Xuantong (emperor), 2020
Xuanyan, 1227–1228
Xuanzang
on architecture, 1672
on Buddha images, 1292
in Central Asia, 1291
documents from, 811, 1072–1073
family of, 2176
Faxiang school and, 1187
foundations of, 2204
hagiography and, 291
history from, 101, 1781–1784, 1788, 1792–1793
in India, 2396
jātaka and, 1370
legacy of, 184
monks to, 2401–2402
on relics, 1733
scholarship and, 3–4, 10, 12, 84, 1865, 2284
on three wheels of doctrine, 2464
translations by, 85, 99–100, 1801 n.11, 2096–2097, 2662
on Yogācāra Buddhism, 2069
Xuanzong (emperor), 54–55, 212, 1227–1228

Xuāstvānīft, 810, 812
Xu Dai, 1230
Xuecheng, 1259
Xuedou Chongxian, 665
Xuedou Verses (Xuedou), 665
Xuefeng Icun, 658
Xueyan Zuqin, 664–665
Xue Yu, 382
Xutang yulu (Xutang), 654
Xutang Zhiyu, 654, 663
Xu Xiaoming, 1231
Xu You, 999–1000
Xuyun
  authority of, 2727–2728
  awakening of, 2726–2727
  biography of, 2725–2731, 2735–2737
  as Buddhist leader, 2731–2733
  in Chan Buddhism, 2733–2735
  as Empty Cloud, 2157
  Hongyi and, 1437
  Lingyuan and, 2170 n.31
  scholarship on, 2665–2666, 2735–2736
  in Yunmen incident, 2728–2729
Xuyun heshang nianpu chang-bian (Ye Bing), 2736
Xuzangjing, 1234
xylography, 2563–2564

Yabuki Keiki, 1237
Yagde Panchen, 1441
Yag gzher sku gshen, 1399
Yaḥyā al-Barmakī, 1679–1680
Yaḥyā ibn Khālid, 1675–1676
Yajñavarman, 1794
Yakazu Dōmei, 278
yakṣas, 258–259, 2247, 2249, 2253–2254, 2258 n.11
Yakushi Nyorai, 268, 294, 2350
Yama, 2253. *See also* Saman-Yama-Lakshmana
Yāma, 1072 n.28
Yamabe, Nobuyoshi, 2675, 2678, 2681–2683, 2688, 2696, 2700 n.12, 2705 n.105
Yamada Yūji, 297–298
Yamaguchi, Susumu, 4–5
Yamamoto Hiroko, 295–296
Yamamoto Satomi, 288, 302
Yamāntaka, 1500
Yamaoka, Haruo, 462
Yamashina Honganji, 2040–2041
Yampolsky, Philip B., 675–676, 1237–1238, 1774–1775
Yamthap, Sunanta, 2627
Yanagida Seizan, 675–676, 1237–1240
Yanagi Sōetsu, 724
Yanagita Kakusei, 1712
Yancy, George, 2719
Yandabo Treaty, 599
Yang, Larry, 911, 1990
Yang Fuxue, 821–823
Yang Huinan, 2294–2295
Yangpachen, 2018
Yang Wenhui, 326, 1136, 2283
Yang Yi, 658–660, 1240
Yan Naing Lin, 1048–1049
Yanpei, 1255–1256, 1262
Yanshou ming jing, 1185
Yanxi Guangwen, 653–654
Yanxi yulu (Yanxi Guangwen), 653–654, 663
Yan Ying, 53–54
Yao (emperor), 93, 1000
Yar lung jo bo Shākya rin chen sde, 1406
Yaśodharā, 121
Yaśomitra, 3–5, 9–10, 1301 n.58, 1342 n.114
Yaśovarmadeva (king), 1784–1785
Yaśovarman (king), 1788–1789
Yasutani Haku'un, 2160
Yatkansin Taung Sayadaw, 568, 570*f*
Yauch, Adam, 112 n.4, 226, 238–239
YBA. *See* Young Buddhist Associations
Ye Bing, 2735–2736
Yeke Shabi, 1384–1385
Yekkansin Taung Hsayādaw, 601–602
The Yellow Book, 1146, 2022
Yelü Chucai, 666, 1624–1627, 1656–1658
Yemyo Imamura, 40
Yemyo Imamura (Moriya), 1314
Yen Pei, 1078
Ye Qingyan, 2736
Yeshe, Ayya, 907–908
Yeshe Dé (Ye shes sde), 99–100, 1963
Ye shes rtse mo, 1397
Yéshé tenpé nyima, 1380
Yeshe Tsogyal, 134, 1439, 1966, 1970–1971, 2467, 2476, 2511
Yeshe Wangpo, 1436–1437
Yesün-Temür, 1632
Yicheng, 2734–2735
Yiengpruksawan, 301–302
Yijing
  legacy of, 208, 320, 1519, 1524
  scholarship and, 55–56, 1292–1293, 1518, 1788, 1794–1796, 1865, 2658
yijing (suspicious scriptures), 86
Ying (prince), 1183, 1195 n.5
Yinguang, 1437, 2665–2666
Yin Jiazheng, 787
Yinshun (Yin Shun)

as editor, 2295, 2613–2614
Humanistic Buddhism and, 1253–1255, 1438, 1452 n.86, 2735–2736
Kato and, 2122 n.14
legacy of, 415, 1255–1257, 1260–1262
renjian fojiao, 1247–1248, 1252–1253, 1258
scholarship and, 2122 n.3
on supernatural aspects, 112 n.15
Taixu and, 413, 2621–2622
Yinyuan Longqi, 183, 185, 670
Yinzong, 1226, 1230
Yisün-temür, 1637
Yixia Lun (Gu Huan), 1001
Yixing, 1209, 2175, 2325–2327, 2344–2345
YMBA. *See* Young Men's Buddhist Association
YMCA. *See* Young Men's Christian Association
yoga. See *specific topics*
Yoga (Diamond), 2317
Yogācārā-Bhūmi, 97, 99–103, 109–110
Yogācārā-Bhūmi-śāstra, 97. See also *Bodhisattva-bhūmi*
Yogācārā Buddhism
on causality, 2118
cognition in, 2111
doctrine of, 2290
hermeneutics, 2464–2465
humans in, 2457–2458
in India, 626
Mahāyāna Buddhism and, 1460–1461, 2332, 2462–2463
philosophy of, 535, 620–621, 1565, 1809–1810, 1819–1822, 1833, 1836, 2282, 2285, 2464
Pure Land Buddhism and, 2282
scholarship on, 716–717, 1187, 1336, 2746
Soshin in, 270
three wheels of doctrine in, 2462
tradition in, 1464, 2292
treatises in, 2288
Vajrayāna Buddhism and, 1463
Xuanzang on, 2069
Yoga Tantras, 967–968, 1416
yogatantra Sarvatathāgatatattvasaṃgraha Tantra (STTS), 2637
Yogi Bhajan (Harbhajan Singh Khalsa), 2314
Yogi Chen, 1138–1139
yogic practices, 21–22, 54–55
yoginī tantras, 1472–1477
yogins, 1209, 2583–2585, 2643–2647
yogis, 2063–2064
yojanas, 144 n.36
Yokawa, 2046–2047
Yokei, 2053–2054
Yokoyama Shigeo, 1705–1706
Yongdin Lopön Tenzin Namdak, 1145
Yongdzin Sangye Tenzin, 138
Yongdzin Tenzin Namdak Rinpoche, 113 n.24
Yongle (emperor), 2014
Yongming Yanshou, 669
Yongming Yanshou's Conception of Chan (Welter), 675–676
Yönten Gyatso, 1065, 1653, 2015
Yoo, David, 39
Yorimichi, Fujiwara, 2185
Yoritomi Motohiro, 2359
Yōsai, 296, 309–312
Yoshida, Yutaka, 820
Yoshida Kanetomo, 333–334, 340
Yoshida Shinto tradition, 1203–1204
Yoshikawa Koichirō, 798, 818–819
Yoshimoto Ishin. See also *Naikan*
legacy of, 278, 1710, 1712–1713
philosophy of, 1701 n.7, 1702–1709
scholarship on, 1715, 1947
Yoshiro Imaeda, 845
Yoshito Fujii, 38
Yoshizaki, 2040
Young Buddhist Associations (YBA), 39, 1309–1310, 2127
Young Men's Buddhist Association (YMBA), 374–375, 595, 1304, 1309–1310
Young Men's Christian Association (YMCA), 1075–1076
Young Women's Buddhist Association (YWBA), 1304
YouTube, 2137
Yōzei (emperor), 2181–2182
Yozo Taniyama, 467
Yü, 1874–1875
Yü, Dan Smyer, 1137–1138
Yu, Jimmy, 1136–1137, 2627–2628
Yuance, 2207
Yuanchao mingchen shilue (Su Tianjue), 1657–1658
Yuan dynasty
China and, 1639–1646
end of, 1645–1656
in Mongolia, 1622–1639
Mongolian Buddhism during, 1656–1657
scholarship on, 63, 891, 1135, 1639
Yuanjue Zongyan, 650–651
Yuan Shikai, 2727
Yuanwu Keqin, 665
Yuan Zai, 57–58
Yuanzhao, 53–54, 1519, 1524
Yu Chang, 212
"Yu Dao Lun" (Sun Chuo), 1000
Yudrönma, 1439
Yueji (master), 2157

Yuexia, 2283
Yuezun, 555–556
Yuiitsu Shinto. *See* Shinto
Yuishikiron dōgakushō, 753
Yui Suzuki, 294
Yūkai, 2186–2187, 2356
Yukari Hayashi, 2480
Yuktiṣaṣṭikā, 1688–1689
Yulanpen Jing, 993–994, 1005
yulu genre, 631 n.7, 645, 647–656, 664–665
Yumo Mikyö Dorjé, 2548, 2750
Yunfeng Yue, 669–670
Yungdrung Ling authorities, 137–138
Yungdrungpel. *See* Tsangpa Gyare
Yungdrung Tenzin Tsukphü, 134
Yunmen guanglu, 650–651
Yunmen incident, 2728–2729
Yunmen Wenyan, 650–651
Yunqi, 1523
Yunqi Zhuhong, 654–655, 670
Yu-Shuang Yao, 1222, 2294–2295, 2627
Yu Udomslip, 465
Yu Zezhen, 819
YWBA. *See* Young Women's Buddhist Association

Zabaozang jing, 998
Zablocki, Abraham, 2366
Zahler, Leah, 28
Zanabazar, 1587
Zanglingma, 2580, 2584–2585, 2587
Zangnian, 2279
Zanning, 53–54, 59–62, 1230, 1240
Zanzabar, 2019
Zava Damdin Lubsangdamdin, 1610
Zaya Bandida Namkhaijamtsu, 1651–1652
Zaya Pandita, 1377, 1386, 1603, 1652, 1657–1658
zazen (sitting meditation), 522, 1350–1351, 1354–1355, 1708–1709
Zeami, 757
Zen and Its Influence on Japanese Culture (D. T. Suzuki), 707–708, 714–715
Zen and the Art of Archery (Herrigel), 1947
Zen Buddhism. See also *specific topics*
  aesthetics in, 1488–1489
  Chan Buddhism and, 1027–1028, 2161
  China and, 716–717, 724
  commercialization of, 144 n.39, 226, 238
  D. T. Suzuki and, 502, 702–703, 706, 714–716, 725
  in Europe, 707
  Hanh in, 2445–2446
  in Japan, 867
  Japanese Buddhisms and, 1361 n.41
  leadership in, 2435
  Lotus Sutra in, 2359
  mantric words in, 766–767
  philosophy of, 718
  Pure Land Buddhism and, 2341, 2441
  reflection in, 458
  Rinzai, 1350, 1352, 2187
  rituals, 361
  schools, 509
  Shin Buddhism and, 705, 1357–1358
  Shingon Buddhism and, 2186–2187
  Sōtō, 751, 1348, 1352–1353
  in South America, 1355
  in Thailand, 176 n.68
  unborn Zen, 706
Zen Buddhism and Psychoanalysis (D. T. Suzuki, Fromm, and DeMartino), 707–708, 723–724
Zen commentary, 646
Zengaku daijiten, 675–676
Zengje, 88
Zengyi ahan jing, 997
Zen Hospice project, 450–451, 462
Zen in the Art of Archery (Herrigel), 234
Zen Keys (Hanh), 2448
A Zen Life (Masao), 710
Zen meditation, 1081, 2181
Zen Mind, Beginner's Mind (D. T. Suzuki), 1081
Zen no goroku, 675–676
Zen Noir (film), 403–404
Zenryū Tsukamoto, 1192
Zenshu, 2205
Zepa (Bzad pa), 852
Zeshan Yixian, 2662
Zeshō-bō Renchō, 1760–1761
Zhabtrung Ngawang Namgyel, 2518
"Zhai family cave," 787
Zhamsaran, 2529
Zhang (lady), 57–58
Zhang (lama), 1539–1540, 1545, 1744, 2600
Zhang Daqian, 798–799
Zhang family, 2152
Zhang Gyu brag pa Brtson, 852
Zhang Jingman, 1230
Zhang Mantao, 1261
Zhang Nyima Bum, 133
Zhang Rong, 1001–1002
Zhang Sna nam Rdo rje dbang phyug, 1399–1400
Zhang Taiyan, 2279
Zhang Xingchang, 1228
Zhang Yue, 1227
Zhang zhung language, 128–129
Zhanran (Tiantai patriarch), 358

Zhao Erfeng, 2020–2021
Zhaohui, 1258
Zhao Puchu, 1258, 1438, 1441, 2291
Zhaoqian, 54, 57
Zhao Xianke, 212
Zharmapa Kachö Wangpo, 2746
Zhengfa Nianchu Jing, 1003–1004
Zhengfeng. *See* Lin Qiuwu
Zheng Jinbao. *See* Wuguang
Zhengyan, 1254, 1256–1257, 1259
Zhengyan fashi de Ciji shijie (Chen Huijian), 2625
Zhenshu, 1238
zhentong
  emptiness in, 2743–2744
  Great Madhyamaka and, 2753 n.2
  in India, 2744–2745
  Rangtong and, 2748–2749
  scholarship, 2745–2748, 2750–2751
  sutra, 2749–2750
  tantra, 2749–2750
  in Tibet, 2745–2748
Zhenwu cult, 1863–1864
Zhenyan Samantabhadra lineage. *See also* Esoteric Buddhism
  communities with, 2388
  history of, 2364
  neo-Zhenyan movements, 2385–2387
  scholarship on, 1137–1140
  Shingon Buddhism and, 2369
  in Tang dynasty, 2366
  tantric revival to, 2371–2374
  Zhenyan school and, 963, 969
Zhenyuan Era (Yuanzhao), 53–54
Zhenyuan shidao lu, 813
Zhenzong (emperor), 658
Zhiding, 2735
Zhi Qian, 999
Zhishen, 1229
Zhitang Biao, 643 n.62, 663
Zhiyan, 2207–2208, 2346
Zhiyi
  on bodies, 277
  on diagnosis, 268–269
  on disease, 204–205, 210–211, 270
  inspiration to, 2325
  Nichiren and, 1764–1766
  philosophy of, 1768, 2343–2344
  scholarship and, 1003, 1186, 1702, 2680–2681
  Shōzen and, 291–292
  teachings of, 278, 288, 2217
  for Tiantai school, 288, 336, 2463–2464
  writings of, 2346
Zhongben, 185
Zhongdao (Middle Way), 1187
Zhongfeng Mingben, 183, 664, 673
Zhongguo shiku, 802
Zhongmi, 1003
Zhongzong (emperor), 1226, 1228–1229, 1232
Zhötön Ngödrup, 133
Zhou (emperor), 1000–1001
Zhou Anshi, 326
Zhou dynasty, 85, 2156
Zhou Enlai, 2213
Zhou Gazetteer, 1869
Zhuangzi, 1861
Zhuangzong (emperor), 59
Zhu Fotudeng, 209–210
Zhu Qeiqun, 2008
Zhuqu Jingsheng, 998
Zhuxi Temple, 2367–2369
Zhuying ji, 813
Zhu Yuanzhang, 1638–1639
Zhu Zhen, 59
Ziegler, Leopold, 1942, 1944–1945
Zieme, Peter, 821–823, 1656–1657
Zimmer, Heinrich, 2247
zinc, 112 n.15
Zisheng, 661
Zivkovic, Tanya, 2025
Zōga, 2054–2055
Zongbao, 1237
Zongmi, 1002, 1004–1005, 1227–1228, 1232, 1235–1236, 2291
Zongti lun, 2290
Zongyi lun, 2289–2290
Zonkaku, 1307
Zonnyo, 2036–2038, 2042
Zoom, 2138
Zopa Rinpoche, 1590
Zorastrianism, 1672–1673
Zoroastrianism, 1200–1201, 1212, 1669–1670, 1673–1674, 2487–2488
Zoysa, Asoka de, 2260 n.49
Zuckerman, Phil, 2145
Zürcher, Erik, 1192, 1203–1204
Zutang, 657–658
Zwilling, Leonard, 1993
Zysk, Kenneth, 260–261, 305, 1023–1024